SOLARIS™ 8

Barrie Sosinsky
and Carol Tanielu

San Francisco • Paris • Düsseldorf • Soest • London

Associate Publisher: Richard J. Staron
Acquisitions & Developmental Editors: Maureen Adams, Diane Lowery
Editor: Judy Flynn
Production Editor: Mae Lum
Technical Editor: Sean Schluntz
Book Designers: Patrick Dintino, Catalin Dulfu, Franz Baumhackl
Graphic Illustrator: Tony Jonick
Electronic Publishing Specialists: Jill Niles, Maureen Forys, Happenstance Type-O-Rama
Proofreaders: Nancy Riddiough, Laurie O'Connell, Yariv Rabinovitch, David Nash, Nelson Kim
Indexer: Jerilyn Sproston
Cover Designer: Design Site
Cover Illustrator/Photographer: Sergie Loobkoff

Library of Congress Card Number: 2001089830

ISBN: 0-7821-2816-5

Manufactured in the United States of America

10 9 8 7 6 5 4 3 2 1

I dedicate this book to my aunt and uncle, Katie and Harry Reif, whose presence will sorely be missed. They left the world a better place than they found it. Their kindness and devotion to their family is a testament to the importance they had in so many lives.

–Barrie Sosinsky

I dedicate this book to Shililo Tipa Tanielu. Alofa ote oe!

–Carol Tanielu

ACKNOWLEDGMENTS

We would to thank the various people who made this book possible, including the folks at Sybex who were involved in commissioning the title and in its production. We would like to thank Diane Lowery, who acquired the title, and Maureen Adams, who took over the project after Diane left to deliver her baby. Mae Lum and Judy Flynn were the production and copy editors on the project and were very attentive to detail and to making the book better.

We owe a special debt of gratitude to Sean Schluntz, who served as the technical editor on the project. Sean lent his considerable technical expertise and experience administering Solaris systems and networks to this book, and as a result, many useful suggestions on additional content were added in the editing process and many errors and inaccuracies were eliminated.

We wish to thank Doris Hoffman and AutoGraph International, Inc. of San Jose, California (`www.augrin.com`; 408-282-7880), the publishers of EasyCopy and EasyCapture. The company provided its screen capture utility to us at a reduced price. This fine tool was used for nearly all of the screen captures in this book.

Jay Daliparthy and his group at Sun provided several of the screen captures you see in the chapter on installation, for which we are grateful.

We also wish to thank our literary agent, Chris Van Buren of Waterside Productions, for his help in arranging for the publication of this title, as well as for his ongoing support and good advice.

It is clear from our work on this book that Sybex is a superior publishing house, one that really cares about the quality of its products. The care taken with its projects and the manner in which its authors are treated were evident. It was a pleasure working with Sybex on this book.

Sybex would also like to thank graphic illustrator Tony Jonick; electronic publishing specialists Jill Niles and Maureen Forys; proofreaders Nancy Riddiough, Laurie O'Connell, Yariv Rabinovitch, David Nash, and Nelson Kim; and indexer Jerilyn Sproston for their valuable contributions to this book.

CONTENTS AT A GLANCE

Introduction .... *xvii*

PART I	**INTRODUCTION TO SOLARIS**	**1**
1	The Solaris 8 Operating System	3
2	About Solaris	23
3	Installing Solaris 8	61
4	Basic Operations	91
5	The File System	121
6	Devices	181
7	The Solaris Desktop	223
8	Security	291
PART II	**SOLARIS AND THE NETWORK**	**323**
9	Network Services	325
10	Printing	389
11	User Accounts and Groups	421
12	Working with File Utilities	479
13	Mailer and Calendar	511
14	Networking and the Internet	559
15	Memory and Process Management	601
PART III	**WORKING WITH SHELLS IN SOLARIS**	**637**
16	Using the vi and Text Editor	639
17	Understanding Shells	671
18	The Bourne Shell	693
19	The Korn Shell	723
20	The C Shell	761
PART IV	**TROUBLESHOOTING**	**789**
21	Troubleshooting	791

Index .... *.830*

CONTENTS

Introduction ..... *xvii*

PART I • INTRODUCTION TO SOLARIS

1 The Solaris 8 Operating System **3**

Introducing Solaris 4
- Solaris and Unix 4
- The Advantages of Solaris 6

What's New in Solaris 8? 9
Additional Resources 10
- man and xman Pages 10
- Sun Resources 14
- AnswerBook2 15
- Third-Party Web Sites 18
- Newsgroups, Mailing Lists, and FAQs 18
- Web Searches 21

Summary 21

2 About Solaris **23**

A History of Unix 24
- The Development of Solaris 25

Kernel Architecture 27
- Threads 31
- Virtual Memory 33
- Interprocess Communication 34
- Signals 35

The Hierarchical File System 35
I/O Architecture 41
- The Solaris Kernel 42
- System Clock 44
- Synchronization 45
- Directory Hierarchy 48
- Linking 49

Memory Architecture 50
- Anonymous Memory 54
- Pages 58

POSIX 59
Summary 60

3 Installing Solaris 8 61

The Solaris Distributions 62
Installing Solaris 65
  Installation Types 65
  Partitioning Schemes 66
  Network Addressing 69
  Intel Hardware Compatibility 70
Installation Procedure 71
  SPARC Installation 71
  Intel Installation 83
  StarOffice Installation 85
Patches 87
Summary 89

4 Basic Operations 91

Startup 92
  The Console Port and OK Prompt 93
  Boot Options 95
  Halting or Freezing the Operating System 97
  Run Levels 97
  Control Scripts 98
The GUI Login Screen 102
The dtlogin GUI 103
  Customize the CDE Desktop 105
  Customize OpenWindows 106
Terminal and Console Windows 107
  Opening a Terminal Window or a Console Window in CDE 108
  Opening the Command Tool or Shell Tool in OpenWindows 109
  Basic Command-Line File and Directory Manipulation 110
  The find Command 111
  Finding Basic System Information 114
  The file Command 115
Exiting the CDE and OpenWindows 117
  Exiting the CDE 117
  Exiting OpenWindows 118
Summary 118

5 The File System 121

File System Structure 122
Working with Files 124
  Filenames 125
  File Attributes and Properties 127
Directories 137
  Creating Directories and Files 152
  Navigating Directories 154
  Deleting Directories and Files 156
  Copying and Moving Directories and Files 157
  Links 158

Disk Storage 160
File Systems 161
Virtual File Systems 162
Disk Structures 165
Superblocks and Inode Tables 166
Adding New File Systems 168
Mounting File Systems 169
Unmounting File Systems 171
Disk Utilization 172
Summary 179

6 Devices 181

About Devices 182
Device Mappings 183
Device Types 184
Addresses 186
Installing and Removing Devices 187
Device Drivers 189
Volume Management 193
Mount Points and Symbolic Links 194
Mounting Removable Media 195
CD-ROMs 197
Mounting CD-ROMs 197
Working with Files and Directories on CDs 200
Ejecting CD-ROMs 202
Diskettes 204
Mounting Diskettes 205
Formatting Diskettes 205
Working with Files and Directories on Diskettes 207
Ejecting a Diskette 210
Zip and Jaz Drives 211
Hard Drives 212
Slices or Partitions 213
Disk Management 216
Adding a Disk 219
Tape Drives 221
Remote MagTape Protocol 221
Summary 222

7 The Solaris Desktop 223

Solaris and GUIs 224
Window Managers 225
The CDE Desktop 226
Log On 227
Menus 230
Windows 232
The File Manager 244

The Front Panel .253
Actions .267
Workspaces .271
Customizing the Desktop .272
Desktop Controls .273
The Hotkey Editor .277
OpenLook Desktop .280
The X Window System .283
X Clients and Servers .284
X Sessions .286
X Applications .287
Summary .289

8 Security 291

Permissions and Passwords .292
File Permissions .293
Link Permissions .297
More About Symbolic Links .300
Encryption .303
E-Mail Security .305
Firewalls .311
Security and the Superuser .312
Remote Access Security .315
Encrypted Authentication Clients .317
Kerberos .318
Login Security .320
Viruses .320
Physical Security .321
Summary .322

PART II • SOLARIS AND THE NETWORK

9 Network Services 325

Overview of Network Services .326
The ISO/OSI Model .327
Network Topologies .337
The SNIA Shared Storage Model .340
TCP/IP .343
Addressing .344
Adding Networks .346
User Datagram Protocol (UDP) .348
Hosts and Routers .349
Name Services .350
Domain Name Service .350
NIS and NIS+ .356
TCP/IP Administration .357
The Seven Critical Network Files .359

Dynamic Host Configuration Protocol (DHCP) 360
The Network File System 362
Network Utilities 370
Remote Login Utilities 371
The ping Utility 373
The arp Utility 375
The snoop Utility 377
The netstat and ifconfig Utilities 382
The nslookup Utility 382
The whois utility 383
File Transfer Utilities 384
Daemons and the Network 385
Remote User Mail 386
Summary 387

10 Printing 389

The Solaris Print Subsystem 390
Print Tools 395
Print Schedulers 401
Print Filters 405
Finding Printers on the Network 406
Adding Printers 407
Printer Status 410
Local Printers 411
Networked Printers 413
Printing a File 418
Summary 420

11 User Accounts and Groups 421

User and Groups 422
The User Database 423
The passwd File 423
The shadow File 426
Working with User Accounts 428
User Account Commands 428
Managing User Accounts with Admintool 431
Creating User Environments 435
Password Commands 443
The Root Account 445
Changing User Status 449
Working with Group Accounts 449
Group Account Commands 451
Managing Groups Using Admintool 452
Group Identification Numbers 454
Changing Group Status 456
Using AdminSuite 3 for Account Management 456
Managing Network Users with AdminSuite 459
Add a User Account 460

Managing Network Groups with AdminSuite .464
The Role Databases .468
Creating Roles .474
AdminSuite and Access Rights .476
Summary .478

12 Working with File Utilities 479

Archives .480
Compression .486
Encryption .488
Packages .490
Backup and Restore .495
Backup Strategies .498
Backup Utilities .502
Backup and Restore Commands .504
Local vs. Network Backup .507
Third-Party Backup Programs .507
Summary .509

13 Mailer and Calendar 511

Mailer .512
Starting Mailer .513
Creating a Mail Message .516
Viewing Mail Messages .518
Customizing Mailer .521
Attachments .529
Mailer and the File Manager .530
Creating a Custom View .531
Creating a New Mailbox .534
Calendar .535
Starting Calendar .535
Changing Views .537
Appointments .539
To Do Items .540
Replicating Meetings .541
Searching the Calendar .543
Customizing the Calendar .544
Group Meetings .549
Combining Calendar and Mail .550
Command-Line Utilities .552
Calendar and the Federated Naming Service .556
Summary .557

14 Networking and the Internet 559

Internetworking Overview .560
Network Communications .561
DNS and the Internet .565
Host Addresses .566

The Internet and the World Wide Web 567
HTTP 568
The Common Gateway Interface 571
Browsers 573
Netscape 575
Electronic Mail 579
Using pine for Electronic Mail 581
The pine Newsreader 584
Sharing Information 585
Apache 587
Configuring Apache 590
Summary 600

15 Memory and Process Management 601

System Process Overview 602
Viewing Processes 606
The Process File System 618
Controlling Processes 622
Performance Meter 625
Managing Jobs 627
Memory 630
Physical Memory 631
Virtual Memory 632
Summary 635

PART III • WORKING WITH SHELLS IN SOLARIS

16 Using the vi and Text Editor 639

About the vi Editor 640
An Overview of the vi Editor 641
vi Modes 645
Invoking vi 647
Working with Files 648
Navigating in the vi Editor 650
Editing in the vi Editor 653
Deleting and Undoing 654
Copying and Pasting 657
Searching and Replacing 657
Working with Buffers 659
Setting Parameters 660
Spawning a Shell 662
Other Editors 663
Unix Editors 664
Using Text Editor 665
Text and the StarOffice Word Processor 668
Summary 670

17 Understanding Shells 671

The Background of the Shell .672
Creating Scripts .674
Job Control .675
Separate and Group Commands .676
Parameters and Variables .679
Built-Ins .686
Shell Compatibilities .690
Summary .691

18 The Bourne Shell 693

About the Bourne Shell .694
Control Structures .695
The if...then structure .695
The if...then...elif structure .703
The for...in structure .704
The for structure .706
The while Structure .706
The until Structure .707
The case Structure .709
The here Script .714
Variables .715
Bourne Built-Ins .716
Functions .717
Summary .720

19 The Korn Shell 723

Korn Shell Basics .724
Start Files .725
Korn Shell Variables .727
Keyword Variables .729
Built-In Variables .730
Shell Variable Expansion .733
Array Variables .734
Korn Shell Control Structures .735
The Select Control Structure .735
Processing Options .737
Parse Option getopts .737
Korn Shell Special Characters .738
Generating Filenames .738
Korn Shell Arithmetic .741
Input and Output .743
Redirecting I/O and the Coprocess .744
Functions .748
Command-Line Editing .751
Using vi in the Korn Shell .751
Using emacs in the Korn Shell .754

History Files 755
Processing Commands 757
Summary 759

20 The C Shell **761**

Starting in the C Shell 762
The history Built-In in the C Shell 764
The C Shell alias Built-In 766
The C Shell and Command-Line Expansion 767
Directory Stacks 768
C Shell Variables 771
Environmental Variables, Variables and Substitution 773
Creating Scripts 777
C Shell Built-Ins 780
Summary 788

PART IV • TROUBLESHOOTING

21 Troubleshooting **791**

The Three Layers of Failure 792
Planning Ahead 793
Documentation 794
Backups 794
The Psychology of Troubleshooting 796
Resources 797
Web Sites 797
Searchable Collections 799
Support Accounts 801
Educational Resources 803
Troubleshooting Hardware 805
The OpenBoot Prompt 806
Hardware Troubleshooting within the Operating System 814
File System Problems 816
Operating System Problems 818
Working with Patches 820
Useful Diagnostics Commands 821
System Communication 822
Applications and Scripts 824
Summary 828

Index 830

INTRODUCTION

The book you are holding in your hand, Sybex's *Mastering Solaris 8*, is a beginning-to-intermediate introduction to Sun's Solaris operating system and its operation and administration. You don't need to know Solaris to read and understand the material in this book, but it is helpful to have some experience working with computers and networks. In writing this book, we have tried to present common operations that you will perform on Sun workstations and servers in your day-to-day practice. This book contains reference material that you can use in your work going forward. Therefore, we hope that this book will find a place on your desk next to your Sun system.

Although this book was written to be read sequentially, you don't need to do so to get value out of it. Many of the chapters are written as individual units; for example, Chapter 13, which describes the Solaris Mailer and Calendar utilities, can stand on its own.

What We Cover in This Book

Three different authors contributed to this book, which is divided into four different parts.

Part I: Introduction to Solaris

Barrie Sosinsky starts the book in Chapter 1 by giving a general description of the Solaris 8 operating system. Carol Tanielu continues in Chapter 2 by giving you a detailed overview of the Solaris system architecture. With those two chapters in hand, you should be ready to tackle some of the operational features of the Solaris OS.

If you obtained a Solaris workstation or server directly from Sun, then chances are that you didn't get the full documentation that describes in detail how to install the operating system. You can also download both the SPARC and Intel x86 versions of Solaris 8, and they don't come with documentation either. In Chapter 3, Barrie

Sosinsky takes you through an OS installation and highlights the important choices you should be aware of. Chapter 4, "Basic Operations," was written by Steven Beebe and should prove useful to beginning users.

The introduction of Solaris continues with some detailed technical chapters on the file system (Chapter 5), devices (Chapter 6), and the Solaris desktop (Chapter 7), all of which were contributed by Barrie Sosinsky. The introduction ends with a chapter by Carol Tanielu on security (Chapter 8), which includes a further discussion of file attributes described in Chapter 5.

Part II: Solaris and the Network

Solaris is first and foremost a network operating system. That's why a substantial portion of this book is dedicated to networking and network services. In Chapter 9, Barrie Sosinsky and Carol Tanielu describe some of the networking concepts that you need to know in order to work with servers and other computers on your network. Although printing is sometimes done locally, most often Solaris users print to network printers. That is why in Chapter 10, Barrie Sosinsky provides a description of the Solaris print services and how to configure and use printers. Continuing on in Chapters 11 and 12, Barrie Sosinsky explains how to manage users on a network and how to work with files that are transferred over a network. Chapter 12 also includes descriptions of common utilities, such as those used for compression, encryption, archiving, and backup.

The networking part continues in Chapter 13 with Steven Beebe describing the mail and calendar utilities that are built into Solaris. In Chapter 14, Carol Tanielu describes the networking aspects associated with using the Internet, including protocols, addressing, and browsers and other utilities. Chapter 15 concludes the networking section with Barrie Sosinsky describing memory and process management, both locally and on remote systems.

Part III: Working with Shells in Solaris

The third part of this book explains how to manipulate Solaris using commands entered at the command line. Many of the command, preference, and script files in Solaris are text files that can be modified using text editors. Solaris contains a very powerful command structure, and many of the commands and their most powerful options are accessible only through the command line or the prompt. In Chapter 16, Barrie Sosinsky explains how to use the `vi` editor and other text editors to work with text files. Carol Tanielu continues in Chapter 17 to explain how shells work, and then in Chapters 18, 19, and 20, she describes the three most important shells that come with Solaris, the Bourne, Korn, and C shells, respectively.

Part IV: Troubleshooting

The book ends with Chapter 21 from Steven Beebe describing some of the more common problems that you might encounter working with Solaris, from both a software and a hardware perspective. The chapter also describes an approach to diagnosing system problems that you should find useful, in addition to pointing you to some troubleshooting resources.

Conventions Used in This Book

Some of the material is presented as a set of procedures that you can execute. Care was taken to describe the features not only by name but by feature type. Thus, you will see instances where we say things such as "Select the Open command from the File menu." Although somewhat pedantic, at least the meaning will be clear.

Commands that you can enter from the command line and paths to files or directories are presented in a different font to distinguish them from the rest of the text. Thus you might see `vi` editor or the `/opt/program1/file1` in the text.

Sections that require lines of code are set apart from the text by a special set of styles. Thus a short script might look something like this:

```
Initiate script
Script step 1
Script step 2
End script
```

Throughout the book you will encounter tips, notes, and warnings. The purpose of these features is common to their purpose in other computer documentation you might read. A tip is something that will help you in your work. A note contains information that is valuable but supplementary to the topic being discussed. And finally, a warning is just that: it warns you of some operation or setting that can get you into trouble if you don't pay attention.

In all other aspects of writing this book, we endeavored to conform to the conventions used by Sun in its standard documentation.

About the Authors

Three authors contributed chapters to this book:

Barrie Sosinsky, Ph.D. Barrie is the chief analyst and founder of the Sosinsky Group (www.sosinsky-group.com). He has written or contributed to over 35 technical books and 400 articles and is a contributing editor for *Windows 2000 Magazine* and the founding editor of the Storage Update e-mail newsletter. His research follows the network operating system, storage, server, and enterprise application fields. Barrie can be contacted at barries@sosinsky-group.com.

Carol Tanielu Carol is a senior project manager with more than 25 years experience in programming, design implementation, and relational databases for a major pharmaceutical company. She has served as a system administrator for a government in the South Pacific and specializes in system troubleshooting and technical writing. Carol may be contacted at kayt@sosinsky-group.com.

Steven Beebe Steve is a Sun certified system administrator who works at Avontra (www.teachmesun.com), a Sun training company in Colorado Springs, Colorado. He can be contacted at contact@teachmesun.com.

PART I

Introduction to Solaris

LEARN TO:

- ***Understand how Solaris relates to Unix***
- ***Install and use your system***
- ***Use the Solaris desktop***
- ***Work with devices and files***
- ***Customize security features to protect your data***

CHAPTER 1

The Solaris 8 Operating System

FEATURING:

Solaris and Unix 4

Advantages of Solaris 6

What's new in Solaris 8 9

Man and xman pages 10

Sun resources 14

AnswerBook2 15

Sun Microsystems (www.sun.com) has been a hot act in the computer business for quite some time now. Sun is one of the few companies that has been able to successfully compete with today's dominant desktop operating system, Windows, and many of its applications are considered best-of-breed. Unlike Microsoft, Sun is both a hardware company and a software company. Sun sells everything from terminals and workstations to servers, and it sells an operating system and applications that operate on its hardware. This chapter describes one of the most important products Sun distributes, which is the basis for all of the other products, the Solaris operating system.

Introducing Solaris

Solaris 8 is the latest edition of Sun's operating environment. It offers advanced multitasking, symmetric multiprocessing, and 64-bit data processing that runs on systems as small as a Sun Blade 100 (Sun's sub-$1,000 entry desktop system), on Ultra 5 workstations, or on the 64-processor Sun Ultra Enterprise (UE) 10000, a near mainframe-class system. We say "operating environment" because, strictly speaking, Solaris runs on top of the SunOS, which provides kernel-level services. As this book is being written, SunOS is at version 5.8. Sun released its SunOS 4.1.2 operating system bundled with the OpenWindows graphical user interface (GUI) as the Solaris 1.0 package.

On a computer, an operating system is the program that controls the input and output, assigns and manages resources, and schedules tasks. Therefore, any device—be it internal to the computer (such as the CPU, hard drive, memory, and so on) or external (such as your monitor, keyboard, printer, and so on)—is managed by the operating system. Giving commands to the Solaris operating system is as close as you can get to actually controlling the hardware that you work with. Solaris offers the capability to manage your workstation locally as well as the capability to manage remote computers over the network.

Solaris and Unix

Solaris/SunOS is Sun's version of the Unix operating system, based—as you shall see in the next chapter—on the Berkeley Software Distribution (BSD) and AT&T System V. Solaris is specially tweaked for the computers that Sun sells, offering many special features. Solaris is largely compatible with most versions of Unix. It supports the industry standard for Unix, POSIX (Portable Operating System Interface for Computer Environments), which is based on the Unix System V Interface Definition (SVID).

Solaris supports both POSIX.1 and POSIX.2, as well as the X/Open Common Application Environment (CAE), Networking Services Issue 4 (XNET4), and the Portability Guide Issue 4 Version 2 (XPG4v2). Many of these standards, which led to the development of Unix, were the result of efforts initiated by the United States government and military to reduce the cost of supporting multiple computer operating systems with duplicative software and hardware.

Therefore, although there may be some differences—the command syntax, the location of the configuration files, the structure of the file system, the shell or graphical user interface—a person with some Unix experience will likely feel right at home working on the Solaris platform. Often the similarities vastly outweigh the differences, so that the experience that you gain using the Common Desktop Environment (CDE) GUI on Solaris will directly translate to using that GUI on another platform.

Many Solaris shops interoperate with the other vendors' versions of Unix, some of which (HP-UX, IBM AIX, the open source version Linux, and several other flavors) have significant installed user bases. For this reason, Sun describes its platform as "open" architecture or as based on an "open" standard. This notion of openness relates to Solaris having a level of interoperability that bestows upon Sun's customers the ability to buy software from many vendors that serve the Unix community and the ability to connect to peripherals designed and built first to work and run on other platforms, such as a Silicon Graphics workstation. For many enterprises, the ability to buy from multiple vendors computer software and hardware that will work with the software and hardware you already have is seen as a form of investment protection that is very desirable.

Unix and Solaris have both had a very long development cycle and are considered by the IT community to be mature operating systems. Unix was first developed in the 1970s, and the first versions of Solaris appeared in the mid-1980s. Sun released several versions of the Solaris operating system as first 1.*x* (then referred to as the SunOS 4.*x* version) and then 2.*x* (the SunOS 5.*x* version) before adopting the use of integers instead of fractions to describe releases. Thus, Solaris releases 2.5.1 and 2.6 were followed by version 7, and now by version 8 (which, depending on how you check the version information, will be called Solaris 7/8, Solaris 2.7/2.8, or SunOS 5.7/5.8).

Although in many cases it ran and continues to run reliably, the hardware for many applications (such as Internet firewalls, mail and news servers, and other applications that ran on Sun SPARC systems) became obsolete with the upgrade from SunOS 4.*x* to the System V version of the Sun operating system, Sun 5.*x*. For this reason, the decision to upgrade to later versions of the Solaris operating system was often a difficult one. There are many shops still running Solaris 2.6; even some large enterprise applications run on this version. Typically, it is the desire to run 64-bit applications or the need to use UltraSPARC systems that have spurred companies to upgrade or install Solaris 7 and 8 in their shops.

In fact, there is a high degree of compatibility between Solaris 8 and Solaris 7, as there is between all versions of the SunOS 5.*x* family of operating systems. On a regular basis (typically quarterly), Sun posts to its Web site what it calls jumbo patches, which allows administrators running versions of Solaris that aren't the most current version of that release to fix bugs and security holes and maintain compatibility between different versions of the operating system.

The Advantages of Solaris

The reliability of Sun servers running Solaris is one of the reasons that Sun has been able to establish its hardware as the platform of choice on many of the world's largest Web sites, and particularly on those running database systems that are extremely transaction intensive. Perhaps eight or nine of the world's ten highest-volume Web sites run on Sun systems. So even desktop users who may not be familiar with Sun or Solaris are using the services of a Sun server every time they log on and work on the Internet. A very significant percentage of the world's Internet e-mail passes through or originates on Sun servers running sendmail or the Sun Network File System (NFS). As Sun likes to say in its advertisements, "We're the dot in .com."

Unlike Microsoft, whose development of Windows started on PCs and was extended through peer-to-peer networking into server-class systems (with the advent of Windows NT), Sun's intent had always been for the Solaris operating system to be at its heart a network operating system. Until quite recently, it was fair to say that Sun was predominantly a server company, with a strong workstation component in a supporting role. Several things have happened in the recent past to modify this view of Sun's focus.

First, the development of the browser as a portal on any type of computer system (client) to view information processed on a Web server has led to Sun's development of the Java programming language (see `www.sun.com/java`), which is currently distributed under a Sun Community Source License (SPSL, see `www.sun.com/981208/scsl`). Very significant program development for Java has been done by other companies such as IBM and by the open source community as a whole, all of whom are quite devoted to the use and promulgation of Java as a development platform. Java is now widely used and supported throughout the industry; anything created with the Java programming language can be viewed on any client that has a Java Virtual Machine (JVM) installed. This includes a PC, a Macintosh computer, a network computer, and even new technologies such as Internet screen phones. Sun will apply the Java platform to next-generation telephones, household appliances, TV set-top boxes, smart cards, and so on. With Java, the appeal is that you can develop "write once, run anywhere" applications.

Java runs in a browser on the client side as a Java applet, which is a small, encapsulated, self-running application that is typically downloaded to a client and run when needed, or as JavaScript, which is an offshoot of Java developed by Netscape for use on the Web without a Java compiler. When you visit a Web page that requires the services of that Java applet, the appropriate calls are issued and the applet is invoked. Although Java applets are most typically used in Internet applications through a browser, they can and often do run by themselves. Many companies are programming their utilities as Java applets because of the cross-platform capabilities that they offer. When the information generated by a Java program is required by many computers at once or requires a more powerful processing environment, it is often deployed as a servlet running on a back-end server. Many complex databases, messaging, and other multitiered applications run as servlets.

The second interesting recent development has come to pass as a result of the rising popularity of Linux. The Linux platform is an open source development version of Unix, and Linux has established itself as a widely used desktop, workstation, and low-end server environment that competes with Sun Solaris and products offered by other Unix vendors. To counteract Linux's popularity, in part, Sun decided to offer a free version of Solaris 8 for both the SPARC and Intel x86 computer platforms. You can download these applications from the Sun Web site by going to the Solaris home page and clicking the Solaris button near the title bar. That button takes you to a page where you can begin the registration process to download the operating system. It's faster to start, though, to obtain the software at the following pages:

- `www.sun.com/solaris/binaries/` (for the SPARC version of Solaris)
- `www.sun.com/software/intel/get.html` (for the Intel version of Solaris)

If you have a slow Internet connection, you can order the CD and documentation set from Sun directly for $75, but all of the software you need to get a Sun workstation up and running on an unlimited number of computers with a capacity of eight or fewer CPUs is available to you on the Sun Web site. Therefore, if you have a Windows server or SCO OpenServer deployed in your enterprise, you can switch these Intel servers over to Solaris for free.

The popularity of Linux as a desktop alternative to Microsoft Windows and to the Apple Macintosh has caught many in the industry by surprise. Linux had already achieved a following as a small Web server platform and as a desktop environment through the deployment of programs like GNOME, and it even has productivity applications like StarOffice that run on it. There are rumors in the industry that Sun may one day offer a version of GNOME as a regular part of Solaris should that environment become standardized, but it's unclear at the moment when that might happen. The push for Unix on the desktop has been enhanced by Apple Computer's new

OS X, which is based on the BSD distribution of Unix (like Solaris 1.*x* is) with a new graphical interface developed by Apple. Work by Sun, Apple, and many other developers is showing that you don't have to use Windows; there are alternatives.

The StarOffice suite is an alternative to and compatible with the widely used Microsoft Office, and its developing popularity had suggested to many that desktop Unix might have a future. StarOffice contains the following components:

- StarOffice Write, a word processor
- StarOffice Calc, a spreadsheet
- StarOffice Impress, a presentation package
- StarOffice Base, a database
- StarOffice Schedule, an organizer
- StarOffice Mail, a mailing program
- StarOffice Discussion, a newsreader for Internet newsgroups

StarOffice successfully re-creates much of Microsoft Office's more commonly used functionality, and it can read and write to native Microsoft Office files. In 1999, a year before Sun released Solaris 8, Sun purchased StarOffice and released it as free software to run on the Solaris platform as well as the other platforms that StarOffice runs on. Today, Sun develops StarOffice in concert with the open source community, making its source code freely available under the GNU General Public License (GPL), the GNU Limited General Public License (GLPL), and the Sun Industry Standards Source License (SISSL) under the name OpenOffice, which can be seen at `www.openoffice.org`. Developing StarOffice with the open source community also expands the platform support for StarOffice.

Version 5.2 of StarOffice may be downloaded from the Sun Web site at `www.sun.com/staroffice/` in any one of the following languages: Danish, Dutch, English, French, German, Italian, Polish, Portuguese, Russian, Spanish, and Swedish. It is offered for the following four platforms:

- Solaris on SPARC
- Solaris on Intel (x86)
- Linux (x86)
- Windows (NT/9*x*)

The fact that you can download and install these different versions of StarOffice means that you can seamlessly share StarOffice files created on any one of those platforms with the version of StarOffice running on any of the others. Today, StarOffice is loaded on all Sun workstations and is part of the Solaris standard distribution. Many examples in this book of Solaris functionality are shown using one component or another of StarOffice.

What's New in Solaris 8?

There are many new networking and administration features included with Solaris 8 that weren't in the previous version of Solaris, version 7. Additions have been made to both the client and server versions of Solaris, and only some of the larger additions and modifications can be noted here in this short section. The following system functions were added to Solaris 8:

- Automated Dynamic Reconfiguration and the Reconfiguration Coordination Manager
- Better crash dump analysis
- Enhanced DHCP
- IEEE 1394 support
- IPSec for IPv4 and IPv6
- Ipv6 support
- Java 2 SDK
- LDAP
- Network installs using DHCP
- Perl version 5.005_03
- Role-based access control
- Sendmail 8.9.3

On the client side, the biggest addition to the standard distribution of Solaris 8 (as noted in the preceding section) was StarOffice. Additionally, Solaris 8 added better multimedia support, musical instrument digital interface (MIDI) audio, and streaming media support for several formats. Out of the box there is some support for data communication with mobile devices like the Palm Pilot Personal Data Assistant (PDA).

Sun added many more components to the Solaris 8 distribution as additional CDs in the box. In addition to the StarOffice disc, you will find an administration software disc that installs the components found on the BigAdmin Web site, as well as the Solaris Software Companion CD. There are many GNU utilities found on the Software Companion and a wide array of third-party software that you would typically tend to download from an Internet site.

TIP Before downloading additional software from the Web, check the Solaris Software Companion CD to see if there is a version of that software on it. The software found on the Software Companion CD is specially recompiled and works with Solaris 8. The version on the CD, however, may not be as current as the version you download from Sun's Web site.

On the server side for Solaris, the server software now comes with the very popular and open source Apache Web server software installed on it. Another notable inclusion is that Solaris ships with `lxrun`, an emulator that allows you to run Linux software on Solaris on Intel. (There is no SPARC counterpart at the moment for `lxrun`, although one will probably be made available at some point.) Server-side security has been enhanced with the addition of Kerberos v5 security to the operating system.

Additional Resources

There are many types of resource materials on the Solaris operating system. There are sources that exist on your local system, some that may exist on your network, and many others that exist on the Web.

man and xman Pages

Solaris, as well as other versions of Unix, come with an online documentation system called the man (short for manual) pages. On the X Window System, this online documentation system is referred to as the xman pages, but in both cases the content is similar. You will find documentation for nearly all Solaris commands in the man pages, along with documentation for the various options and arguments that these commands take. When there is a variation of the usage of a particular command from the standard Unix version, that difference is generally noted in the command's man page. Additionally, man pages display several examples of the usage of the command in question as well as the development history or versioning of the command.

To access a command's man page in the CDE, open a terminal window and enter the following command:

```
$ man <commandname>
```

Figure 1.1 shows a sample man page.

FIGURE 1.1

An example of a command from the Solaris man pages

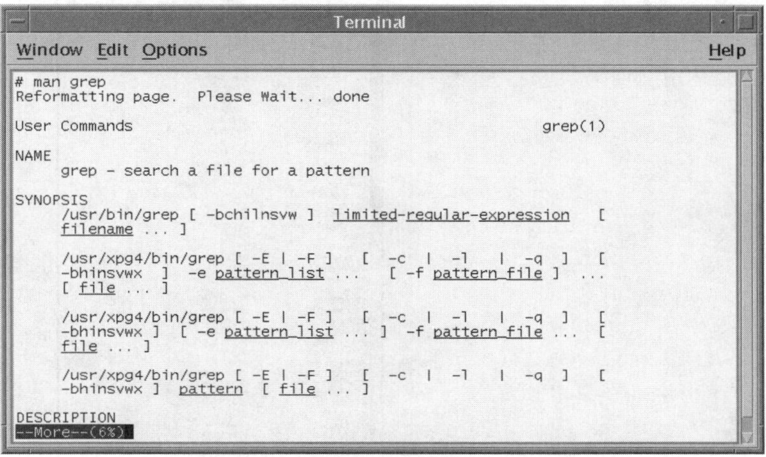

Unlike the man pages, the xman system is a point-and-click help system.

Follow these steps to access a command's xman page (or man page equivalent) in OpenWindows and get an in-depth explanation of that command's functions:

1. Open a terminal window and enter the following:

   ```
   $ xman&
   ```

   The & after the command runs the xman system in the background. The xman window (shown in Figure 1.2) appears.

FIGURE 1.2

The xman window

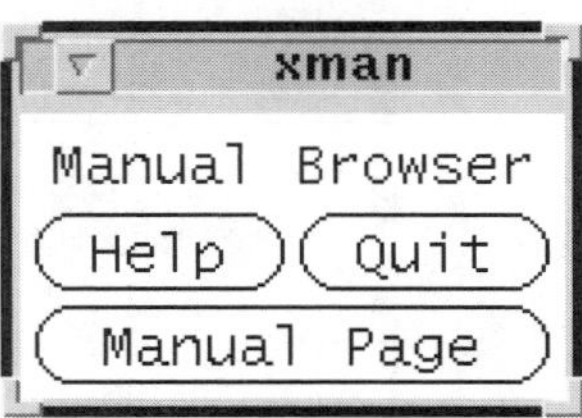

2. Click on the Manual Page button to view the help screen.
3. Then select the Directory command from the Option menu to view a list of commands that you can access, shown in Figure 1.3.
4. Click on the command of interest to view the manual page of a particular command in the xman system, an example of which is shown in Figure 1.4.

FIGURE 1.3

The list of commands in the Manual Page window of the xman system

FIGURE 1.4

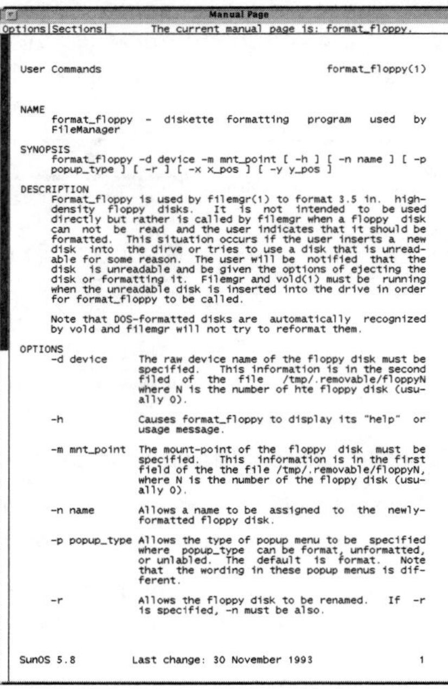

A sample xman command page

When the display of a man page exceeds your screen's capacity, the text stops until you press the Spacebar key to see an additional screen. The command is parsed by the `more` pager, which offers several commands that you can see by pressing the h (help) key. The q (quit) key returns you to the shell prompt, ending the man page's display. Figure 1.5 shows you the various commands associated with the `more` pager.

FIGURE 1.5

The `more` pager offers a number of commands that affect the display of the pages in a terminal window.

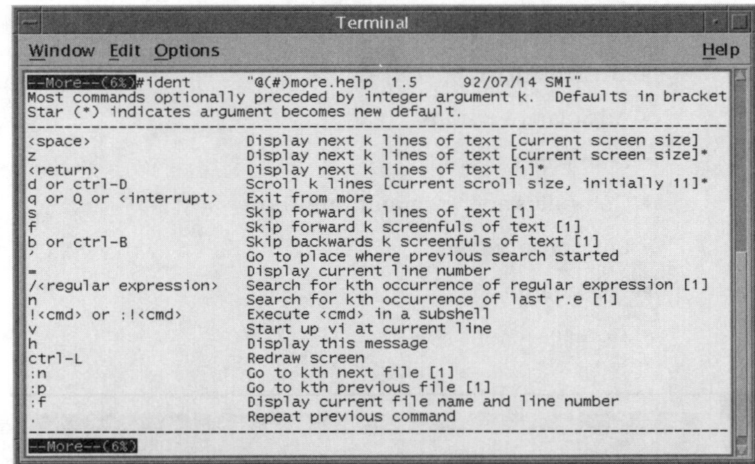

The man pages offer a very detailed but highly stylized and terse description of a command. You will find the following sections in most man pages (only some of these sections are listed for some commands):

- User commands, described in alphabetical order.
- System calls are commands you can use to modify your system.
- Library functions are commands that invoke Unix system primitives.
- File formats are descriptions of how data is stored or passed.
- Headers, tables, and macros describe how character sets and tables are described in data.
- Demos describe any games or demos available for this command.
- Device and network interfaces describe files that command hardware, peripherals, and device drivers.
- (None)
- DDI and DKI offers a description of reference information needed to write device drivers in the kernel operating system.

Sun Resources

One of the best places to start is on Sun's Web site itself in the section docs.sun.com (the URL is `http://docs.sun.com`). The home page for docs.sun.com, shown in Figure 1.6, lists multiple documentation sets for a wide variety of hardware and software that Sun has released. Much of the material is both operational and referential, and better yet, searchable across editions. Categories covered include the following:

- Solaris 8
- Trusted Solaris 8
- All Solaris Versions
- Man pages
- Compilers and Programming Tools
- Enterprise Servers
- Workstations
- Storage

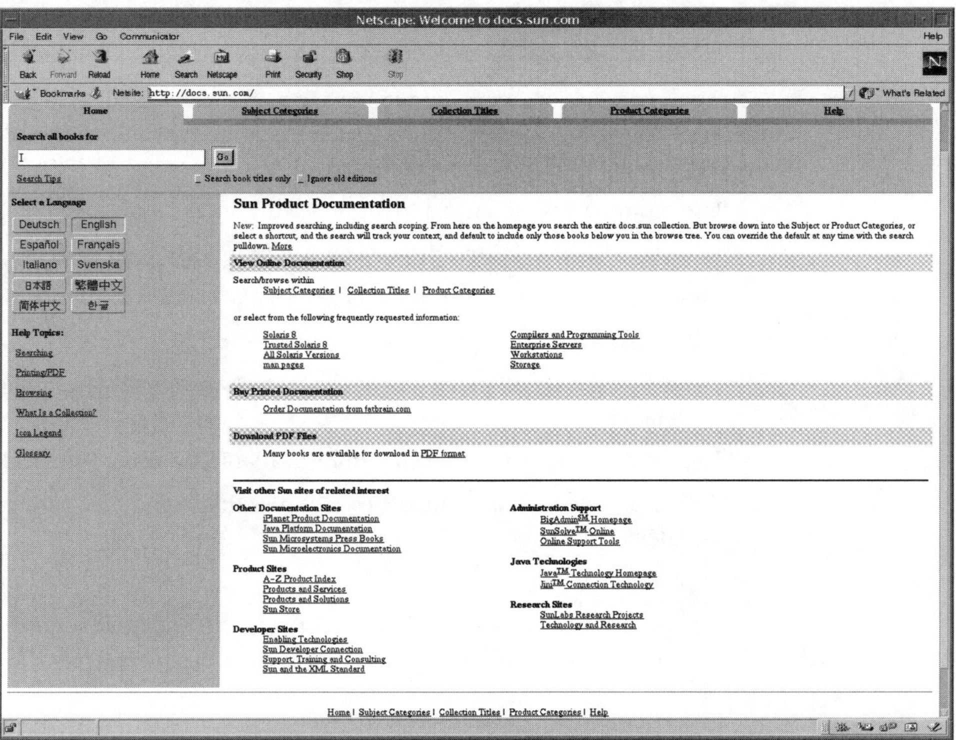

FIGURE 1.6

The home page for docs.sun.com

Many of the books contained on docs.sun.com can be downloaded in the Adobe Portable Document Format (PDF) and read with the free reader software that Adobe offers from its Web site at `www.acrobat.com`. You can also purchase from Fatbrain.com (`www.fatbrain.com`) printed copies of the Sun documentation sets.

From docs.sun.com's home page, you can also find links to many of the Sun sites that offer additional software that is described in detail in this book:

- iPlanet
- Java Platform
- Sun Microsystems Press
- Sun Microelectronics Documentation
- BigAdmin Homepage
- SunSolve Online
- Online Support Tools

You can also find links to sites on Java technology and to product, developer, and research sites. If you work regularly with Solaris, you will probably want to bookmark the docs.sun.com home page in your browser.

AnswerBook2

If your working environment is large enough to support it, you may find that your system administrator has installed the Sun Solaris AnswerBook2 on your workstation or on a server. If not, you can access this online help system with your browser over the network on an AnswerBook server using your company's intranet. You will also find that the AnswerBook2 is on the Sun Web site at docs.sun.com. The AnswerBook is one of the optional installation packages that comes on its own compact disc as part of every Solaris distribution. It's a collection of PDF files that includes the following:

- 64-bit developer's guide
- Binary compatibility guide
- CDE transition guide
- CDE user's guide
- Device driver developer's guide
- Internationalization developer's guide
- Jumpstart guide
- Mail server guide

- Naming services guide
- NFS administration guide
- NIS+ guide
- OpenWindows user's guide
- Power management user's guide
- Source compatibility developer's guide
- SPARC assembly language developer's guide
- STREAMS developer's guide
- SunShield security guide
- WebNFS developer's guide

To access the AnswerBook2 locally on your system, click the Help subpanel of the front panel and select the AnswerBook2 command, as shown in Figure 1.7. Or you can open a terminal window and enter the following command:

```
/usr/dt/bin/answerbook2
```

In either case, the AnswerBook will open inside your browser, which for Solaris 8 defaults to Netscape Navigator 4.7. If your browser isn't working, or when you are working inside StarOffice, you should note that you can also access the AnswerBook using StarOffice's browsing function.

FIGURE 1.7

The AnswerBook2 command on the Help subpanel of the CDE front panel

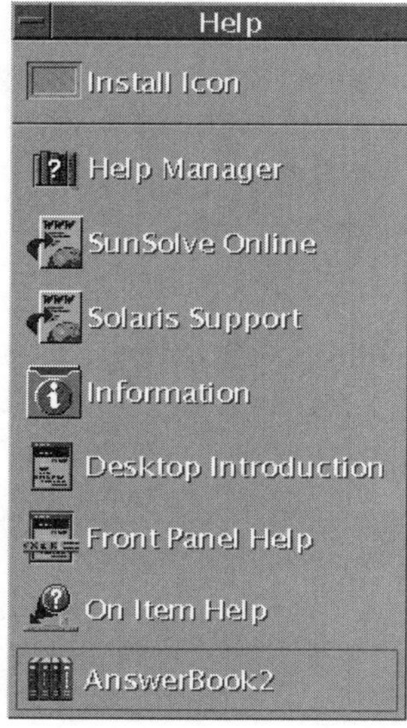

The AnswerBook may also be viewed online at `docs.sun.com/ab2/`, and from that location you can select the language as well as specify the particular AnswerBook subject you require. You can also view the AnswerBook for previous OS versions. When you click the Solaris 8 link, you are taken to the screen shown in Figure 1.8. Sun's Web site has a searchable function that is particularly invaluable, whereas the version you can access locally on your network does not.

For information that is about Solaris on either SPARC or Intel but isn't official Sun documentation, you will want to start with the home pages for both of these platforms: `www.sun.com/solaris` (for SPARC) and `www.sun.com/intel` (for Intel).

Links off these pages take you to overviews, in-depth views, resources, FAQs, solutions, and downloads for various software packages designed to work with each of these platforms. The Solaris Developer Connection at `http://solaris.java.sun.com` is another resource with in-depth technical material and access to developer programs that will be of interest to programmers. Users joining the developer program can also have special access to many software packages and obtain reduced pricing or free downloads depending upon their developer status.

FIGURE 1.8

The complete Sun and Solaris AnswerBook2 system

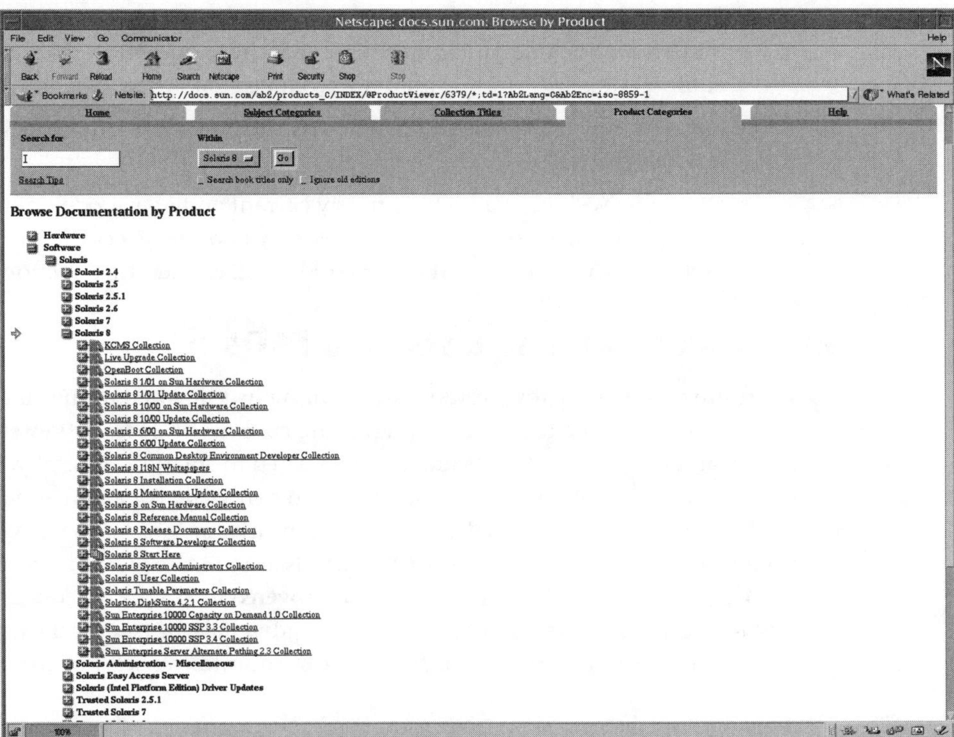

Third-Party Web Sites

You can find many resources for Solaris users and administrators on third-party Web sites. The following list includes some of the more well known:

- The Sun Freeware site at `www.sunfreeware.com`. This site offers free precompiled software for various versions of SPARC Solaris (including version 8) that you can download and install directly onto your system.
- The Solaris 8 for Intel site at `ftp://x86.cs.duke.edu/pub/solaris-x86/bins/`. This site contains precompiled versions of Intel Solaris programs that you can download and install directly onto your system.
- Precompiled packages for many versions of Solaris can be found at `www.ibiblio.org/pub/solaris/sparc` in an easy-to-follow graph. This site is maintained by the University of North Carolina.
- The SunHELP site at `www.sunhelp.org`. This site contains a Solaris 8 FAQ as well as links to various topics on the Sun site.

For hardware, consider the following:

- The SunSunSun hardware, site at `www.sunsunsun.net`, a clearinghouse of used and reconditioned Sun computers. Another good and reliable source of used equipment is the MiniComputer Exchange at `www.mce.com`.
- For new Sun hardware you can access the Sun store from the Sun Web site at `www.sun.com`.
- Often you will find Sun selling nearly current and new models of its workstations and servers on an auction site such as eBay (`www.ebay.com`). This is in addition to used Sun workstations and servers sold on eBay and other auction sites.

Newsgroups, Mailing Lists, and FAQs

There are many newsgroup forums and mailing lists devoted to the Solaris operating system. One widely cited Usenet group is the `comp.unix.solaris` newsgroup, which maintains an extensive discussion of issues related to Solaris 8. Typically, the discussion in this newsgroup centers around SPARC-based hardware. For a newsgroup focusing on Intel issues, you should consider frequenting the `alt.solaris.x86` newsgroup. Administrative issues for both Solaris platforms are discussed in `comp.sys.sun.admin` forum.

Many specific questions about Solaris are covered in FAQs, or Frequently Asked Question lists, that are posted on the Internet. The advantage of reading a FAQ over asking a question in a newsgroup forum is that you can educate yourself in anonymity. One FAQ that covers both the SPARC and Intel platform may be found at www.cs.uu.nl/wais/html/na-dir/comp-sys-sun-faq.html; it is run by the comp.sys.sun.admin group. Another FAQ that focuses on the Intel platform alone is found at www.sun.drydog.com/faq/. One frequently cited Solaris 8 FAQ is the one that is posted by Casper Dik at www.wins.uva.nl/pub/solaris/solaris2/. Table 1.1 lists common Solaris sites, resources, and FAQs.

TABLE 1.1: SOLARIS SITES AND FAQS

Topic	URL
Access1 Sun Software Support	http://access1.sun.com/
CDE FAQ	www.laxmi.net/cde.htm
CD-ROM FAQ	http://Saturn.tlug.org/suncdfaq/
Celeste's Tutorials on Solaris/SunOS Modems and Terminals	www.stokely.com/unix.serial.port.resources/tutorials.html
CERT Coordination Center	www.cert.org
Colormap FAQ	http://bul.eecs.umich.edu/~crowej/sunfaq/ColormapFAQ.html
Computer Incident Advisory Capability (CIAC) security	http://ciac.llnl.gov/ciac/
Frame Buffer FAQ	http://bul.eecs.umich.edu/~crowej/sunfaq/FrameBuffer.html
Inside Solaris	www.zdjournals.com/sun/
Intel Hardware Compatibility List	http://soldc.sun.com/support/drivers/hcl/
Intel x86 FAQ	http://sun.drydog.com/faq/
IP Filter (firewall/NAT software)	http://playground.sun.com/pub/ipng/html/ipng-main.html
Ipfilter/NAT Configs	www.riddleware.com/solx86/nat-config.html
ISP Connections	www.kempston.net/solaris/connectanyisp.html
NIS+ FAQ	www.eng.auburn.edu/users/rayh/solaris/NIS+_FAQ.html
NVRAM/hosted FAQ	www.squirrel.com/squirrel/sun-nvram-hostid.faq.html
Open Look FAQ	www.faqs.org/faqs/open-look/03-xview/
Passwd+ security	ftp://ftp.Dartmouth.edu/pub/security/

Continued

TABLE 1.1: SOLARIS SITES AND FAQS (CONTINUED)

Topic	URL
PPP dial-in/out	www.kempston.net/solaris/pppserver.html
PPP FAQ	www.sunhelp.org/faq/sunppp.html
Printing FAQ	www.ebsinc.com/solaris/printfaq.html
RTFM documentation site	www.solarisguide.com/
Securing Solaris	www.securityfocus.com/focus/sun/articles/securing.html
Solaris Central	www.solariscentral.org
Solaris FAQ (x86)	www.sun.drydog.com/faq/
Solaris FAQ (Casper Dik)	www.wins.uva.nl/pub/solaris/solaris2/
Solaris Helpers Page	http://home1.swipnet.se/%7Ew-10694/helpers.html
Solaris WWW Resources	oak.ece.ul.ie/~griffini/solaris.html
SparcBook FAQ	http://home.kabelfoon.nl/~hvdkooij/SparcBook-FAQ/sparcbook-faq.html
Sun Administration FAQ	http://sunhelp.org/faq/sunadm.html
Sun documentation site	http://docs.sun.com
Sun Managers Archive	http://latech.edu/sunman.html
SunExpert	www.hillside.co.uk/articles/sunexpert.html
SunHELP	www.sunhelp.org
Suns at Home Page	www.net-kitchen.com/~sah/
SunSolve Online Public Patch Access	http://access1.sun.com
TAMU Tiger Security Scripts	ftp://coast.cs.purdue.edu/pub/tools/unix/crypto/
Tools for workstations	www.squirrel.com/squirrel/sun-stuff.html
ZD Tip of the Week	www.elementkjournals.com/zdtips/sun/zdt-f.htm

A mailing list is a forum discussion held in a sequenced or threaded conversation instead of the rough-and-tumble environment of a newsgroup discussion. Because participants have a little time to think about things, and there is usually an editor (as is often the case with many mailing lists—especially when things get out of hand), a mailing list often provides thoughtful analysis of past and current system issues. Many important business and technical relationships start as threads on a mailing list. The Sun Managers List is perhaps the best known example of this format for Solaris information. You can access the Sun Managers List at www.sunmanagers.org/. For an Intel mailing list, go to www.egroups.com/group/solarisonintel/.

Newsgroups, FAQs, and mailing lists are often loaded with general advice, tips, tricks, and traps, as well as very specific hardware and software information.

Web Searches

The Sun Web site, its AnswerBook pages, and many other Solaris sites on the Internet are among the most frequently visited Web pages that exist. As such, they rate highly on any Web search engine that sorts pages by the number of links to that page from other sites (as Google does), or they may show up if you search with any search engine that indexes content using bots or other informational gathering tools, as do sites like Lycos, Northern Light, and AltaVista. If you have a specific topic about Solaris that you wish to search for, don't hesitate to use one of these search engines to locate a potential match. Often they work better and faster than the search engines on any of the sites mentioned in the previous sections do.

Summary

In this chapter, you were introduced to the Solaris operating system. Solaris is a variant of Unix, based on the BSD Unix distribution and AT&T System V. Many of the advantages Solaris has over other versions of Unix relate to Sun's role as a hardware vendor as well as a software vendor. Solaris is a mature network operating system that has a reputation for reliable and scalable service that has made it a favorite in many industries, particularly in Internet applications. You learned in this chapter that Solaris 8 adds StarOffice, the Apache Web server, and numerous system and network utilities to previous versions of the operating system.

You were introduced to several of the help features in the operating system. Commands are documented in the man and xman pages, which can be accessed online from a terminal window. The AnswerBook2 is a complete documentation set that can be viewed in your browser. AnswerBook2 may be found locally or on a network server and is posted on Sun's docs.sun.com site. Finally, this chapter included information on how you can find numerous Solaris resources such as Web sites, newsgroups, mailing lists, and FAQs.

CHAPTER 2

About Solaris

FEATURING:

A history of Unix 24

Kernel architecture 27

The hierarchical file system 35

I/O architecture 41

Memory architecture 50

POSIX 59

This chapter includes a brief overview of the history of Unix, a description of the architectural structure of the Solaris operating system, and a discussion of the relationship between Unix and Solaris 8. You will learn how the main features and functions of Solaris interface with the kernel, or core, of the operating system. You'll also learn about the hierarchical file system, file security, and compatibility issues. Processes and mechanisms to access operating services will be discussed so that you can gain a comfortable level of knowledge of how Solaris operates in the workplace. Although it is not within the scope of this book to discuss the highly technical aspects of the operating system, a general description of the basic functions of the Solaris 8 operating system should provide you with a clear view of how the operating system performs and how the different levels interact with each other.

A History of Unix

In the latter half of the 1960s, AT&T Bell Laboratories produced an operating system call Multics, designed for an in-house, multiuser, interactive system housed in a GE mainframe computer. Although AT&T withdrew from the project in 1969, what was to become Unix was well under way. Bell's Ken Thompson experimented with the early Unix version using a PDP-11/20, and his operating system was patented in 1971. His efforts produced several assembler language utility programs. Dennis Ritchie, also of Bell Labs, rewrote the Unix system utilizing his own creative language, the C programming language. Written specifically for use with the Unix system, the C programming language proved to be an excellent all-purpose language and highly adaptable to other types of systems. Unix thus became portable to other platforms with very good results. Unix quickly became a favorite with the University of California, Berkeley; the Massachusetts Institute of Technology; and other academic institutions. Because they could obtain the source code for a small fee, it was widely used and developed further in university environments, particularly at UC Berkeley.

In the late 1970s, businesses began to take notice of Unix even though it had not been initially designed to be a commercial operating system. Several companies purchased the source code, made enhancements, and tailored the code to fit their own hardware, making it less portable. Competition developed, but in 1978, Bell Labs released System III, version 7, which is the precursor to today's systems. It came with the first Bourne shell command interpreter and offered a combination of powerful language capabilities and interactive command-line programming. It grew and developed until the late 1980s when AT&T formed a company called UNIX Systems Laboratories, or USL. This company produced all of the source code for Unix System V and its derivatives. Soon thereafter, the Unix Desktop was introduced, as well as PC hardware support such as CD-ROM drives, SCSI devices, video cards, and so on. USL was purchased by Novell in 1993 and then again by the Santa Cruz Operation (SCO) in 1996. Over the years, several offshoots of Unix—such as BSD v4, Free BSD, BSDI, and Sun Microsystem's SunOS and Solaris, among others—sprang up to add to the mix (Linux, however, is a new creation modeled after Unix). Today, after many twists and turns in development, The Open Group owns the actual UNIX trademark, as well as the specification that determines what the Unix system is. SCO now owns the source code for Unix.

The Unix operating system, like many others, is layered (or modular) in design. The top level is the user on a workstation. The second level comprises applications, e-mail, editors, and compilers. The third level is where the shells and utilities live. The fourth level is the kernel (core), where complex processes occur and switching from one process to another happens at high levels of speed. The fifth level encompasses the hardware and devices necessary to accomplish the desired tasks. These operations will be expanded upon further into the chapter. Figure 2.1 illustrates loosely what the different levels represent.

FIGURE 2.1
Top-level overview of the Unix operating system

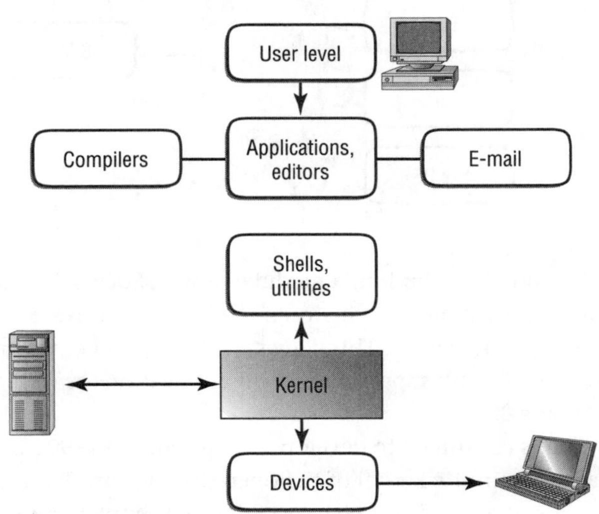

The Development of Solaris

During the early 1980s when Unix systems were becoming popular, SunOS 1.0 was developed based on a port of BSD 4.1 from UC Berkeley labs. At that time, it was used on the Motorola 68000 workstations. By 1984, SunOS 2.0 premiered with virtual file system framework, which supported the Network File System (NFS), now in almost every operating system in today's technology. Sun has developed new applications and new virtual memory systems. The input/output infrastructure required further system changes. Sun and AT&T participated in a joint project producing a new core Unix that incorporated the best features of SunOS, BSD, SVR3, and Xenix. The finished product, System V Release 4 (SVR4), was ported to the SPARC processor. Sensing the impending growth in multiprocessor systems, Sun developed a new operating system kernel that focused on multiprocessor scalability while allowing multiple threads of execution and facilities for threading at the application level. This new kernel and the SVR4 operating environment are the foundation of the present-day version of Solaris. Figure 2.2 details the evolution of Solaris 2.0.

FIGURE 2.2

The development of Solaris 2.2 from previous versions of Unix

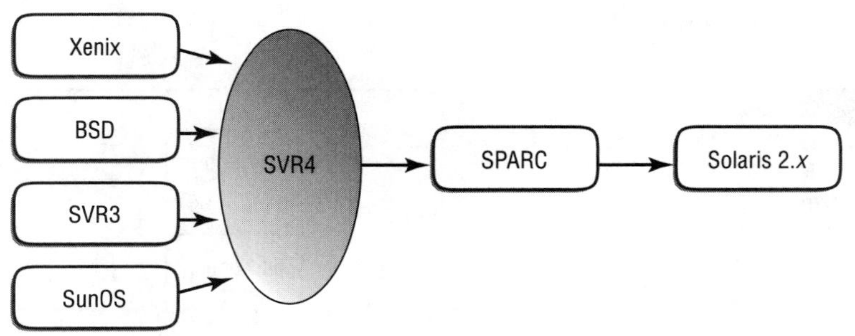

Because it was built in a modular design, Solaris 2 could be implemented on multiple platforms with different instruction set architectures. Solaris 7 introduced a 64-bit data type implementation. This allows the kernel and other processes to access large address spaces while still supporting 32-bit applications as well. These innovations continue in Solaris 8.

Solaris continued to develop throughout the 1990s and produced innovative features that reside in the kernel of the operating system. These features will be explained in more detail later in this chapter. Solaris has implemented new features that enhance the original Unix implementations. The new features include a fully preempted kernel, which does not require manipulation of hardware interrupt levels for the protection of critical data. Data locks synchronize access to kernel data. Threads can interrupt one another if they need to run. A low-priority thread will give way to a higher-priority thread rather than wait for the scheduler to run. Systems can load applications on demand rather than load them into memory. Called *demand paging*, it can speed up application startup and reduce memory usage, or footprint. Processors can be configured into scheduling groups in order to partition system resources, which includes binding processes to processors.

The hierarchy of buses and devices can be installed and configured by means of dynamically loadable device and bus drivers. Device drivers have maximum portability and are shielded by a device driver interface. Multiple schedulers can operate concurrently. Each scheduler has its own algorithms and priority levels. Supplied as kernel modules, they are dynamically loaded to the operating system. Solaris offers a time-sharing user scheduler, a window system time-share scheduler, and a real-time fixed-priority scheduler. A fair-share scheduler is offered as an option with Resource Manager. Multiple-platform support is presented with SPARC and Intel x86 microprocessor-based architectures. Solaris provides linear scalability for up to a maximum of 64 processors.

Dynamic linking and dynamic modules are used to divide the kernel into modular binaries. A core binary contains schedulers, file systems, device drivers, and some system calls. Kernel compiles are not necessary with a binary if and when parameters change. As mentioned earlier, a process can run multiple threads concurrently on one or more processors. Solaris uses threads for scheduling and execution. The kernel schedules interrupts and services as regular kernel threads. Unlike the Unix implementations, Solaris provides exclusive access to data structures by scheduling interrupts as threads that use regular kernel locks. The Solaris kernel provides real-time capabilities. The previously mentioned features create a perfect environment for real-time applications. The integrated Internet protocol TCP/IP is implemented by Solaris by use of the Data Link Provider Interfaces (DLPIs). These interfaces can link data with multiple concurrent network interfaces and can be configured with a variety of different protocols, including Ethernet, Fiber Distributed Data Interface (FDDI), token bus, bi-sync, Synchronous Data Link Control (SDLC), Integrated Services Digital Network (ISDN), X.25, and so on. A configurable scheduler environment is an important feature of Solaris 8. The Virtual File System (VFS) allows multiple file systems to be configured in the system. MS-DOS, the Unix file system (USF), the High Sierra file system (HSFS), the Network file system (NFS) can all be implemented on Solaris. Pseudo file systems such as the process file system (PROCFS) and others can be integrated with the virtual memory system to provide file system caching that uses available free memory.

Kernel Architecture

The *kernel* is the core of the operating system, whether it is Solaris 8 or another operating system. The kernel manages all of the hardware while providing the means to execute processes and programs. It allocates its resources and supplies services for programs and processes to use, sometimes simultaneously. Operating systems in general provide a machine environment that integrates and executes multiple processes and programs concurrently. Although that sounds fairly simplistic, the kernel of an operating system routinely executes complex instructions from several sources at the same time. These sets of instructions are called *processes*. Each process is separate from other processes on the system and can have one or more threads of execution, which share virtual memory with the process. Each thread executes concurrently within the environment of the owner process. The execution of the threads is managed by the kernel scheduler. The scheduler passes them in and out of processors after assigning a unique process identification number (PID). The kernel creates a systemwide process table that keeps track of each process by PID, process name, and other relevant data.

Although similar to the Unix kernel, Solaris differs in that it provides support for multiple threads of execution within each process. When implemented on multiprocessor hardware, it provides efficient use of operating system overhead. Whereas the original Unix operating system used a time-sharing schedule policy that distributed CPU time evenly for all processes, the Solaris kernel implements scheduling classes that use a dispatch table of values and parameters guaranteed to produce more efficient thread processing.

Process management and monitoring has evolved into a fast, sophisticated, timesaving method of computing. The results can be viewed by accessing the process file system (PROCFS). PROCFS details the kernel's process model, which provides an interface for abstracting process data along with facilities for process control and debugging. Each process has an address, which is a kernel abstract used to manage memory allocated to the process. The instructions, data, temporary processing space, and stack information are stored in the address space. Hardware-specific definitions for the execution of the process, such as general registers, stack pointer, frame pointer, and so on, are also stored in the address. The address space maps the memory pages for a process's address space. Figure 2.3 illustrates the various segments of a process and how it is executed.

The PID, the parent process ID, and the ID of the process group are all maintained in the address space. Each process will usually have three opened files. These are the standard input file, the standard output file, and the standard error file. They define the source and destination of input and output for the process. They may link to device information for the terminal used or to a file. Signals and signal handling, execution priority, and scheduling class are all handled at this level. Threads of execution move on and off the processors. When a thread moves off a processor, its execution environment is saved for later rescheduling. The environment is restored and execution resumes as scheduled.

FIGURE 2.3
A sequence of process execution

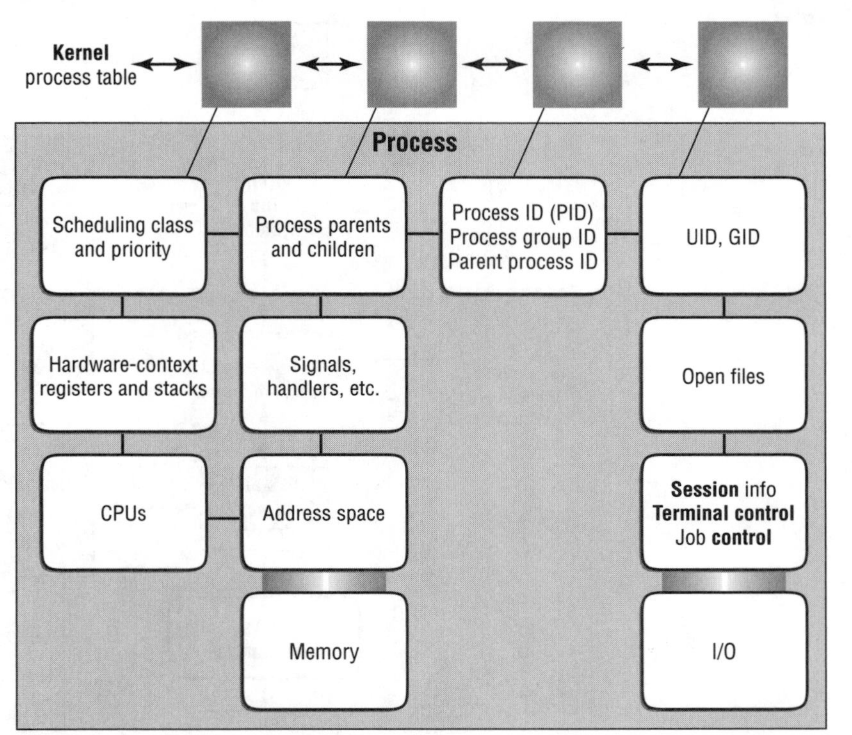

The kernel permits the access of file I/O, process and thread creation, networking, process control, process signaling, memory management, and interprocess communication by means of system calls. These are programming interfaces for types of devices such as CD-ROM storage, printers, tape drives, and disks, through which the operating system is entered so that the kernel can perform tasks outlined by the calling thread. Being modular in design, the Solaris 8 kernel comprises several major components. Figure 2.4 illustrates these components and their basic functions within the kernel. Each will be discussed in this chapter.

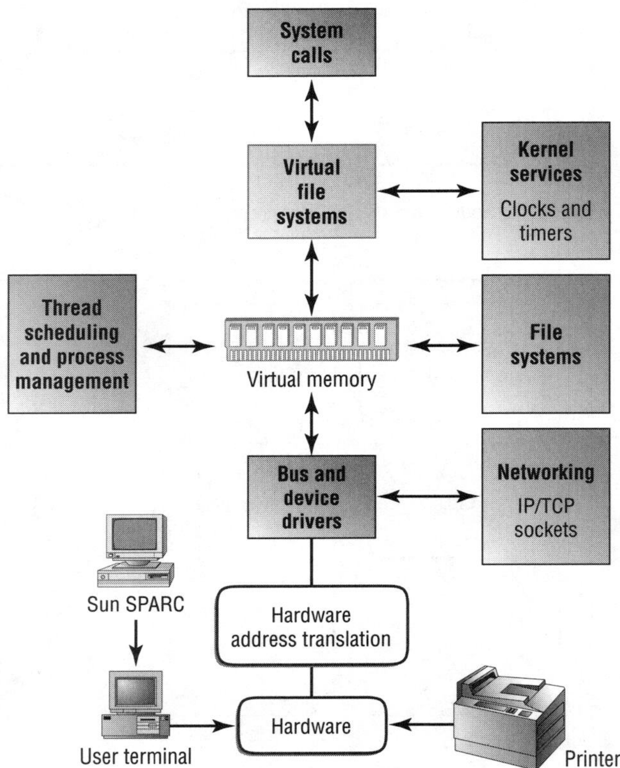

FIGURE 2.4

The Solaris 8 kernel architecture

Because it is a multitasking operating system, Solaris 8 allows processes to communicate with each other while being fully protected from all other processes. Additional jobs can be run in the background while you are working on a job on the terminal screen. You can run different jobs on different screens and keep track of them simultaneously. Many other users can be doing the same thing at the same time. The kernel is a very busy entity indeed.

The mechanisms used to access the operating system—such as file I/O, process and thread creation and termination, process control, signaling, networking, memory management, and interprocess communication—are all system services. You can access these services through the use of system calls. A user can use a system call to interact with many services at a time as shown in Figure 2.4. The kernel will then perform the work required by the calling thread.

Threads

The Solaris kernel is implemented with threads of execution, which are organized streams of instructions sent to the processor for processing. Threads can execute concurrently across multiple processors. Threads allow multiple streams of execution within a single virtual memory environment. Switching execution between threads is inexpensive simply because no virtual memory context switch is required. Threads are used for kernel-related tasks. They are used for process execution and for interrupt handling as well. Figure 2.5 illustrates how kernel threads, processes, and lightweight processes (LWPs) interact.

FIGURE 2.5
Kernel threads and processes

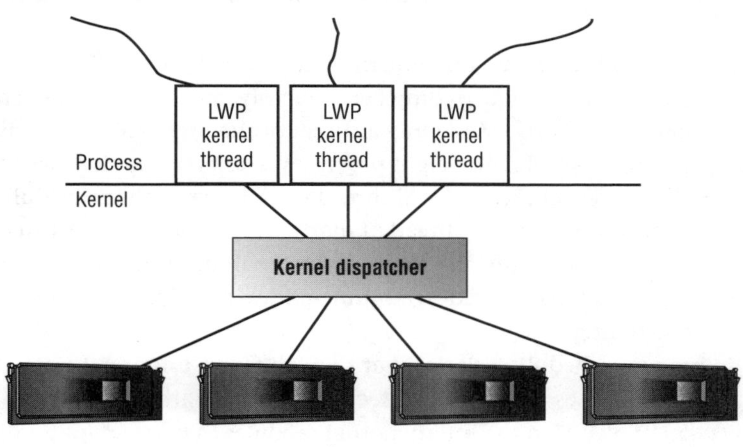

Processes can contain one or more threads, which share the virtual memory environment as well. Each process has a lightweight process or a virtual execution environment for each kernel thread within it. The lightweight process allows each kernel thread to make system calls independently of other threads within the same process. Without the lightweight process, only one system call could be made at a time. Each time there is a system call, its registers are placed on a stack within the lightweight process. System call return codes are placed in the lightweight process. The kernel dispatcher manages run queues of kernel threads and schedules kernel threads onto available processors according to priority and class. In a two-level thread model, a layer called user threads is managed by the kernel. It is a more-efficient, less-expensive means of thread management. Figure 2.6 demonstrates how this operates.

FIGURE 2.6

The two-level thread model

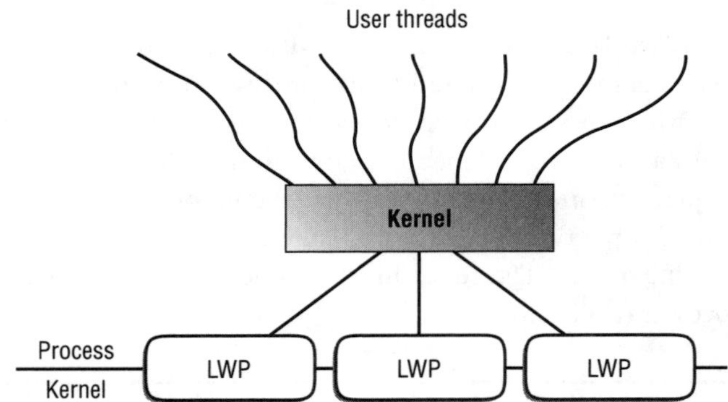

User threads are implemented in a thread library. They can be created and destroyed without needing kernel involvement and can be scheduled on and off the lightweight processes. Only a subset of the user threads is active at any given time. The number of lightweight processes is adjusted by the user thread library.

The kernel uses a global thread priority system for scheduling. The dispatcher selects which kernel thread of many will execute next. A thread with a higher priority can preempt a running thread, which will be executed at a later time. The kernel itself is preemptable, providing for time-critical scheduling of high-priority threads. Different scheduling policies can be applied to threads by the Solaris dispatcher. The dispatcher assigns scheduling classes that allow different priorities to run at different times. Scheduling classes are a modular technology in Solaris. You can download from Sun and other places on the Internet other modules that are useful for different situations. The following list describes the primary scheduling classes:

TS Time-share scheduling class is the default class for processes and all kernel threads. It changes priorities according to recent processor usage. TS tries to allocate processor resources evenly. It uses a priority range of 0 to 59.

IA Interactive class is an enhanced version of the TS class used by desktop windows to boost priority of threads. Uses the same priority numeric range of 0 to 59.

SYS System class is used by the kernel for kernel threads. These are bound threads with no time quantum. They will run until they block. Uses the priority numeric range of 60 to 99.

RT Real-time class uses fixed-priority, fixed-time-quantum scheduling. Uses priority numeric range of 100 to 159.

TIP Real-time class has a higher priority over kernel threads than the SYS class.

Virtual Memory

Virtual memory (VM) manages the system's memory. Its main task is to manage the efficient allocation of the system's physical memory to the processes and kernel subsystems running within the operating system. To accommodate large programs, it will store data that does not fit within the physical memory of the system into slower storage media. It will keep the most frequently used portions within physical memory for easy access.

The VM system presents an address space for processes. Each address space has several segments that are mappings of the executable, heap space, shared libraries, and a program stack. Each segment or page is of equal size and is managed by the memory management unit (MMU), which delivers it to physical memory. Figure 2.7 demonstrates the virtual memory address space, segments, and pages.

FIGURE 2.7

The virtual memory address space, segments, and pages

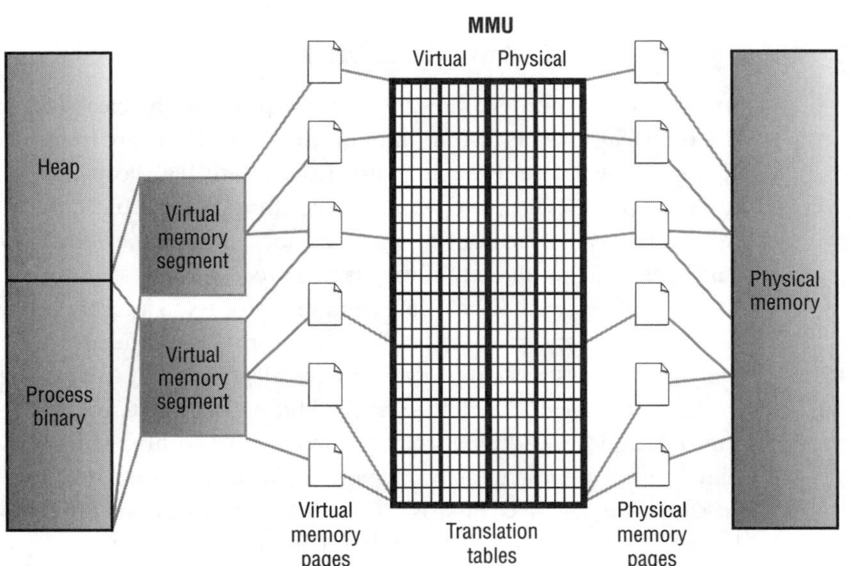

The virtual memory system is also modular in design. The components are mostly hardware platform specific and are implemented in the hardware address translation

(HAT) layer. The VM system implements demand paging, causing pages of memory to be allocated on demand, as they are referenced. This lowers the memory footprint and the startup time of a process. When virtual memory is accessed, the MMU tells the kernel that an access has occurred. If that area of memory does not have physical memory mapped to it, a page fault will occur. The same thing happens to the heap of a process because, initially, only VM space is allocated. A page fault occurs and memory is then allocated one page at a time. The VM system uses a global paging model that manages the allocation of memory between processes. The least-used portion of physical memory is calculated by a scanning algorithm. A kernel thread scans memory in physical page order. Pages not used recently are stolen and placed onto a free list for use by other processes.

Memory is needed for kernel instructions, data structures, and caches. Because most of the kernel's memory is not pageable but is allocated from physical memory, it cannot be stolen by the page scanner. This avoids deadlocks, which might occur if a kernel memory management function created a page fault while holding a lock for another resource. The kernel implements its own memory allocation systems. It uses the slab allocator for kernel data structures. The allocator subdivides large contiguous slabs of memory into smaller chunks for data structures. It manages the slabs efficiently and, by doing so, avoids fragmentation.

Interprocess Communication

Interprocess communication (IPC) allows processes to speak to each other through the transfer or synchronization of information. There are four distinct groups of IPC supported by Solaris: basic IPC, advanced Solaris IPC, Portable Operating System Interface (POSIX) IPC, and System V IPC. Interprocess communication is implemented by traditional IPC facilities such as local sockets and pipes. A local socket is a system call (socket 2) that directly connects two processes.

A pipe directly channels data from one process to another. Data flows through the pipe from one end to the other in a first-in-first-out order. Data is read and written on a pipe with the standard file I/O system calls (`pipe2`). It can also be created in the file system with `mknod(1)` and the standard file `open(2)` system call. The default file descriptors 0, 1, and 2 are automatically opened by the C runtime library. O represents standard input, 1 represents standard output, and 2 represents standard error in a process.

Doors are advanced Solaris IPC calling procedures that are fast and have low latency when invoked. A door server contains a thread that sleeps while it waits for a call from the door client. Once the client makes a call to the server through the door, scheduling control is passed to the thread in the door server. When the door server has handled the request, it passes control and response back to the calling thread.

There is low-latency turnaround because the client does not need to wait for the thread to be scheduled to complete the request.

The POSIX IPC facilities are abstracted on top of memory-mapped files. The POSIX library routines are called by a program to create a shared memory segment, a new semaphore, or a message queue by using the file I/O system calls: `open(2)`, `read(2)`, `mmap(2)`. The IPC objects exist as files in the POSIX library and are exported to the program through the POSIX interfaces.

System V IPC facilities were originally developed for Unix and are now standard across all Unix implementations. The common IPC mechanisms are shared memory, message passing, and semaphores.

A process creates a segment of shared memory that tells the CPU what changes have occurred. Messages are queued with a head and a tail. That is, a message is packed on the tail of the queue and is received on the head. Each message contains a 32-bit type value followed by a data payload. Semaphores are integer-valued objects that support an increment or decrement of the value of the integer. Processes can sleep on semaphores greater than zero, then awaken when the value reaches zero.

Signals

The signal facilities provide the means to interrupt a process or a thread within a process as a result of a specific event. Synchronous signals, or those directly related to the current instruction stream, actually originate as hardware trap conditions arising from illegal address references or illegal math operations and similar events.

Asynchronous signals (such as kill signals or job control signals) that result from external events not related to the current instruction stream are also implemented in Solaris 8. These mechanisms have been handed down from the first Unix systems and remain an important feature today. Most signals will be ignored, or a signal can be caught and a handler will be invoked, or a process can permit the default action to occur. Every signal has a predefined default action. It is possible to mask a signal or to assign a specific signal handler to the signal. The original concept of signals was based on the assumption that a process would have a single execution stream. Because Solaris allows multithreaded process architecture, signals can be directed to a specific thread in the process. Masking (blocking signals) at the thread level is an added feature.

The Hierarchical File System

The Solaris 8 file system has a hierarchical format. In the file system, data is contained first in a file, second in a directory, and third in a storage medium. Figure 2.8 demonstrates the hierarchical structure of a typical Solaris file system.

FIGURE 2.8

The file system hierarchy

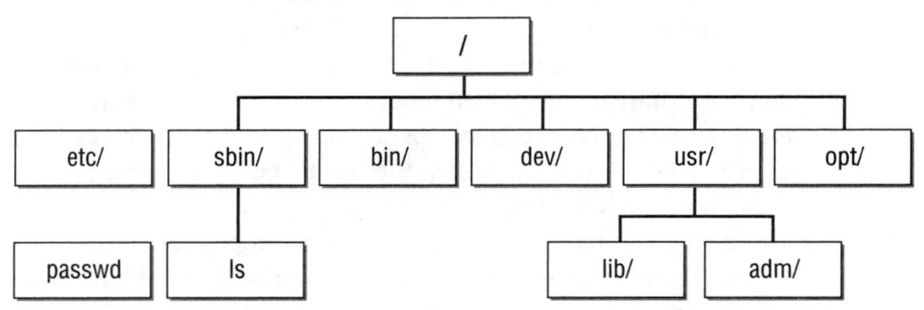

Processes use file-related system calls to access the data in files. The files can be identified by their path name in the file system and a file descriptor (an integer number that identifies an open file within a process). Each process has a table of open files that start with file descriptor 0 and progress upward as more files are opened. The system call `open()` is used to open a file named by a path name and to return a file descriptor identifying the open file. Once a file is open, a file descriptor can be used for further operations on the file. A file descriptor is eventually closed by the `close()` system call or by the process's `exit` command.

The Virtual File System (VFS) framework implements multiple file system types. There are three types of file systems in the Virtual File System group. The storage-based files such as those in the Unix file system (UFS) and PC/DOS file systems are regular files that manage data. Network File Systems (NFSs) appear to be in a local directory but are actually stored on a remote network server. Pseudo file systems present various abstracts as files in a system. The `/proc` pseudo file system represents the address space of a process as a series of files. This file system was developed so that the NFS could coexist with UFS. It is now a standard in Solaris 8. The addition of a new type of file system would require extensive modification to the kernel and system utilities. VFS simplified this process by implementing vnode, which abstracts the operations that can be performed by the kernel on an inode. Every time a file is opened, closed, read, or written to, the vnode for the file is accessed instead of its inode. This method allows for different file systems to be written as modules that the kernel can access without having to know any details about the file system. Solaris also implements the High Sierra file system (HSFS), the PC file system (PCFS), the Portable CD-ROM File System (iso9660), the process file system (PROCFS), and the temporary, or tmp, file system (TMPFS). The HSFS is the standard file system used for accessing CD-ROMs under Solaris. Rock-Ridge is a set of extensions to the High Sierra that allow CD-ROMs to support the full range of Unix file information. CD-ROMs formatted with Rock-Ridge extensions have file and directory names that contain characters supported under UFS.

The PCFS allows for read and write access to DOS-formatted file systems. You can access a DOS file system under Solaris and manipulate it using standard Unix commands such as `ls`, `touch`, `mkdir`, and so on.

The proc file system was borrowed from an experimental operating system developed by AT&T. The proc file system provides all programs with a uniform interface into the kernel via a special file system mounted on the directory `/proc`. Each name of a directory in `/proc` corresponds to an active process ID. The owner or user of the directory is the UID of the process, and the group directory is the GID of the process. This allows the owner of a process to have access to its information.

The TMPFS is a memory-based file system that combines all of the available physical and virtual memory into a single file system. It is mounted on `/tmp`. The files and directories located in a TMPFS are lost if the system is rebooted because the files are contained partially in system memory that does not maintain data upon reboot. This file system provides high performance for processes that create a large number of temporary files with large compilations. Because the memory used to store files in TMPFS is the same memory that is used when commands are executed, storing large files in the temporary file system can affect the amount of memory that is available for programs. By the same token, programs that require large amounts of memory will reduce the amount of space available in a temporary file system. The number of files that can be present in a temporary file system is determined from the amount of physical memory on the system but is not affected by the amount of virtual memory (swap space) that is configured. A PROCFS is added and deleted using the `swap` command. Table 2.1 describes the files contained in the PROCFS.

TABLE 2.1: PROCESS FILES AND DIRECTORIES IN PROCFS

File/Directory	Description
`as`	Contains the address space image of a process
`cred`	Contains permissions associated with the process
`cwd`	Acts as symbolic link to the process's current working directory
`fd`	Contains a directory of references to open files of the process
`psinfo`	Contains information about the process needed by the `ps` command
`root`	Acts as symbolic link to the root directory
`sigact`	Contains array that describes the signal handlers for the process

File System Layout

There are four major areas of the directory tree in Solaris 8:

- Configuration directories
- Device directories
- Program directories
- Temporary or variable file directories

Solaris 8 stores configuration files in the /etc directory. The boot and shutdown scripts used to start processes and stop them are also stored in /etc. Table 2.2 shows some of the most important configuration files in /etc. It is wise to get familiar with these files when time allows. If you will be writing scripts, you will find them useful when running a process.

TABLE 2.2: CONFIGURATION FILES IN /etc

File	Contents
/etc/auto_*	Directory used by the automounter to allow you to access NFS volumes
/etc/format.dat	Device descriptions for all hard drives and removable media types
/etc/group	List of valid groups on the system
/etc/hostname.*	Files that define the host name for your system (for example, /etc/hostname.le0) or the IP address of the interface listed after the dot
/etc/inetd.conf	List of network services with associated applications that the inetd service listens to
/etc/issue	Login banner displayed by the system before login
/etc/motd	Message of the day file displayed on login
/etc/mnttab	List of currently mounted file systems
/etc/nodename	Name of your system displayed with uname-*n*
/etc/nsswitch.conf	Nameservice and NIS/NIS+ configuration information
/etc/pam.conf	Pluggable Authentication Modules (PAM) framework configuration information
/etc/passwd	Local user password database for your systems
/etc/profile	Default configuration file for Bourne shell (/bin/sh) and Korn shell (/bin/ksh)
/etc/resolv.conf	Information used by system to translate host names into IP addresses if DNS is listed in the /etc/nsswithc.conf file under the hosts: category
/etc/services	List of well-known ports for network applications

Continued

TABLE 2.2: CONFIGURATION FILES IN /etc (CONTINUED)

File	Contents
/etc/shadow	Passwords for all local users of system, read only by root
/etc/shells	List of approved shells on system
/etc/syslog.conf	The syslogd daemon's configuration file of significant events
/etc/system	Configuration parameters for the kernel
/etc/termcap	Parameters describing the different types of supported terminals
/etc/vfstab	Default definitions for each file system to be mounted, what file system types they are, when they should be checked, and if they are mounted at boot
Directory	**Contents**
/etc/cron.d	Configuration files for the cron command, stored cron scripts
/etc/default	Files that control default behaviors of the system
/etc/dfs	Configuration files used by the NFS server
/etc/inet	Configuration files related to the network
/etc/init.d	Startup and shutdown scripts for the system
/etc/rc*.d	The /etc/rc0.d through /etc0rc3.d and /etc/rcS.d directories containing hard and soft links to the /etc/init.d directory
/etc/lp	Printer configuration files

Device directories contain files related to devices on the system. They are stored in /dev and /devices. The /dev directory in Solaris 8 contains a set of links from the files in /devices, which was an older version of the directory used by Unix. Your directory tree will also contain directories for a CD-ROM drive or a floppy drive. These are automatically mounted when you insert a CD or disk into the appropriate drive. Most removable media comes with software that allows this automatic mount. Table 2.3 lists some important directories in /dev.

TABLE 2.3: DIRECTORIES IN /dev

Directory	Purpose
/dev/cua	Accesses devices connected to serial ports of workstation
/dev/dsk	Accesses file systems on hard drives, used with mount
/dev/fd	Accesses particular file descriptors such as STDIN, standard input
/dev/pts	Allows logins on pseudo-terminals via telnet, remote shell, and so on
/dev/rdsk	Accesses the raw media of hard drives, used with fsck command

Program directories are stored in /usr or /opt. The programs stored in /usr are required by most users and may be needed to boot and run. Programs in /opt are usually optional software packages needed by some, but not all, users on a system. Prepackaged freeware is usually also stored in /opt. Some of the most important directories stored in /usr are listed in Table 2.4.

TABLE 2.4: DIRECTORIES IN /usr

Directory	Contents
/usr/ccs	Programs and libraries used for compiling and building programs
/usr/dt	CDE configuration files, binaries, and libraries
/usr/include	Language header C files for libraries
/usr/java	Java Development Kit and Java Runtime
/usr/lib	Libraries used by programs on system
/usr/openwin	Libraries and programs for X Window System and OpenLook
/usr/platform	Libraries and programs intended for particular hardware
/usr/sbin/static	Statically linked version for critical commands
/usr/share/man	Manual pages of system
/usr/ucb	SunOS and BSD compatibility commands
/usr/xpg4	Standard set of programs that adhere to the X/Open XPG4 standards

The main directories for temporary and variable files are /tmp and /var. The /tmp directory usually contains files that are required by the system. It is stored partly in system memory and partly on disk using a special type of file system called tmpfs. Compiling and executing programs from a tmpfs-based directory like /tmp is extremely fast, simply because the files are already in memory. Pipes and special device files used by database engines would be included in this directory. The /var directory contains files whose contents are variable and change fairly often but need to be kept intact after reboot. The most important directories stored in /var are listed in Table 2.5.

TABLE 2.5: DIRECTORIES IN /var

Directory	Contents
/var/adm	System logging and accounting files, message files
/var/cron	Log files for cron
/var/mail	Directory where users' mail is kept

Continued

TABLE 2.5: DIRECTORIES IN /var (CONTINUED)

Directory	Contents
/var/nis	NIS+ databases
/var/preserv	Backup files for vi and ex
/var/sadm	Databases maintained by the software utilities
/var/sadm/pkgs	Removal/backup information for software packages on system
/var/spool	Root directory for printer spooled files, mail delivery, cron, and at

I/O Architecture

Unix employed kernel resident device drivers to interface with hardware. A device driver manages the transfer of data and register input and output as well as device hardware interrupts. The driver knows all the details of the device as well as the layout of buses to which the device is connected. Solaris takes this a step further by using separate drivers for devices and a bus nexus driver for different buses. Figure 2.9 illustrates a typical Solaris device tree. Each bus connects to another bus through a bus nexus.

FIGURE 2.9

The Solaris device tree

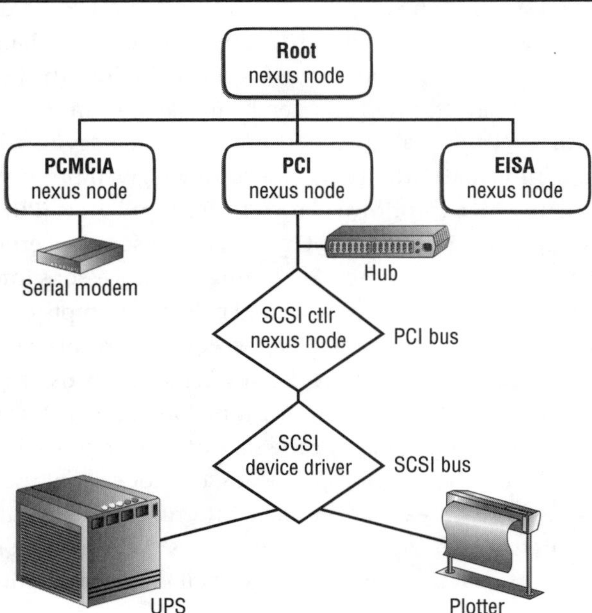

The Solaris device driver interface (DDI) hides the specifics of the platform and bus hierarchy from the device drivers. It does provide interfaces for registering interrupts, mapping registers, and accessing DMA memory. The device drivers are loaded automatically the first time you access a device. They are loadable modules containing driver code.

The Solaris Kernel

The Solaris kernel, or core of the operating system, manages resources and provides services to the user's processes. Solaris recognizes two distinct processor execution modes: a privileged mode called kernel mode and a nonprivileged mode called user mode. The difference between the two is simple. In the kernel mode, a process has access to all of the kernel's data structures and underlying hardware. In the user mode, a process has access to only its own memory. The kernel will execute a process in user mode to prevent the process from accessing data structures or hardware registers that may affect other processes. Because only Solaris kernel instructions can execute in kernel mode, the kernel can mediate access to kernel data structures and hardware devices. If a user process needs to access kernel services, a thread will access those services through a system call, `read()`. The system call will execute special machine code instructions that change the processor into kernel mode. Once the kernel performs the `read()`, then the I/O on behalf of the calling thread, it then returns to user mode status.

The system can enter kernel mode in response to a device interrupt or a processor trap or to take care of any situations that cannot be handled in user mode. To clarify, an interrupt is a vectored transfer of control into the kernel, usually initiated by a hardware device. Interrupts can be initiated from software as well.

An interrupt is a signal to the kernel that a device sends to indicate that it needs some immediate attention. Interrupts are given priority levels 1 through 15, with 15 being the highest priority. Process Interrupt Levels (PILs) or serial interrupts hold the five highest priority levels. On each processor, the kernel can mask interrupts below a given priority level simply by setting the processor's interrupt level, which blocks all interrupts at the specified level and below. Interrupts that occur below that priority level are temporarily ignored. The higher-level interrupts will be serviced faster than lower-priority interrupts. They are, however, more expensive to run because they block other interrupt handlers from running for a long time. Below a priority level of 10, interrupts are handled by threads. For the sake of efficiency, each processor maintains a pool of partially initialized interrupt threads, one for each of the lower nine priority levels, plus a systemwide thread for the clock interrupt. When an interrupt occurs, the kernel uses the interrupt thread stack and initializes it if it blocks on a synchronization object. Interrupts above the level of 10 block all lower-priority interrupts until they complete.

The kernel can send an interrupt or trap (as described in the next paragraph) to another processor when it is required. Interprocessor interrupts are delivered via the `poke-cpu()` function. This function may be used to preempt the dispatcher if a thread needs to signal a thread running on another process to enter kernel mode. The delivery of a signal may require interrupting a thread on another processor. The kernel can send an interrupt or trap to start or stop `/proc` threads on different processors. The kernel also employs a cross-call. Cross-calls are part of the processor-dependent implementation and are used to execute a specific low-level function processor to processor. Besides implementing interprocessor interrupts, cross-calls can maintain virtual memory translation consistency by issuing an `unmap` operation via the CPU on which the thread has run. Address space `unmap` operations within the kernel address space make a cross-call to all processors for each `unmap` operation.

A trap is a vectored transfer of control into the kernel, initiated by the processor. They usually occur as a result of the current executing thread. With SPARC processors, a trap is also the mechanism used to initiate interrupt handlers, so the distinction can be blurry. Traps are used to handle system calls, processor exceptions, and interrupts. UltraSPARC I and II employ a resident trap table that contains the first eight instructions for each type of trap. The trap table resides in memory in the address register, Table Base Address (TBA), which initializes during boot. The trap table contains one entry for each type of trap and also provides a handler for each trap type. There are several different types of traps. The following list outlines the types of traps recognized by Solaris 8:

Floating point Floating point exceptions, floating point mode instruction attempted when floating point unit is disabled

Instructions Attempts to execute privileged instructions from nonprivileged mode or illegal instructions

Memory management MMU page faults, memory errors, page protection violations, and so on

Processor resets Power on reset, machine reset, software resets

Software traps SPARC-initiated trap instruction used for system call entry

Each trap is assigned a priority level. The processor will decide which trap will take precedence if more than one trap occurs on a processor at the same time. The highest-priority trap will always be handled first. Zero is the highest-priority rating. Interrupt traps are compared against the processor interrupt level (PIL), and only those interrupt traps that have an interrupt request level greater than that stored in the processor's PIL register will be handled by the processor. With UltraSPARC, a trap can be received while another trap is being handled. These are called nested traps. When a trap occurs, the central processing unit (CPU) adds increments to the trap level. The most recent processor state is saved on the trap stack, and the trap handler goes into action. When it exits from the handler, the trap level is decremented.

Software traps are initiated by the trap instruction, `tcc`. Software traps are used primarily for system calls in the Solaris kernel. There are also several fast system calls that act as their own trap. These system calls pass their arguments back and forth via the registers. Because their arguments are not passed on the stack, less of the process state needs to be saved during the transition into kernel mode, thus resulting in a faster system call implementation.

System calls are interfaces that have the kernel perform a specific function on behalf of the calling thread. System calls arrive as part of the application programming interfaces (APIs) that ship with the operating system. When you invoke a system call, the processor changes from user mode to kernel mode. This change happens as a result of the trap mechanism. The kernel is equipped with a `sysent` table, which contains an entry for every system call the system supports. The `sysent` table is an array filled with `sysent` structures that represent each system call. The array is indexed by the system call number. If you use an editable system file, you can add system calls to Solaris without requiring kernel source. Some system calls are dynamically loadable modules that can be loaded into the system when it is called for the first time. You can store loadable system calls in the `/kernel/sys` and `/usr/kernel/sys` directories.

When a system call is sent, the software issues a trap instruction, which then enters the kernel to process the system call. The trap handler is entered and any preprocessing needed is done. The system call is then executed on behalf of the calling thread.

Once the trap handler is entered, the trap codes saves a pointer to the CPU on which the system call will execute. It saves the return address and adds increments to a system call counter. Two flags in the kernel thread indicate that pre–system call or post–system call processing is required. Once that is accomplished, the system call is executed.

System Clock

The kernel performs housekeeping chores at regular intervals. Hardware timer interrupts are an integral part of this process. The system clock tells the dispatcher when to recalculate process priorities at regular intervals and also initiates callout queue processing. The kernel's software sets up the interrupt generator, which in turn generates a clock interrupt. Each time the clock interrupt occurs, a handler is entered. The kernel performs several functions as a result of this interrupt:

- Sets available kernel space for tracking and reporting
- Sets free memory value for tracking and reporting

- Adjusts the time-of-day clock
- Calculates CPU usage for the user, the system, the wait I/O, and system dispatch
- Performs clock-tick processing for the thread running on the CPU and the threads that are exiting
- Processes the kernel callout table
- Updates the 1bolt counter, which counts the number of clock ticks since boot-up
- Calculates kernel swap parameters and adjusts run queue size and swap queue size

When the clock interrupt handling has completed, the thread is switched off the processor and the thread that was executing when the interrupt occurred resumes execution.

Synchronization

Solaris 8 is a multiplatform operating system. Its architecture lends itself well to the SPARC and Intel processors as well as to other symmetric multiprocessors. Solaris's shared memory architecture—which implements a single kernel shared by all the processors and a single, uniform memory address space—requires that the kernel synchronize access to critical data. To maintain data integrity, the kernel synchronizes access by defining a lock for kernel data structures or variables. It requires that code reading or writing the data must first acquire the appropriate lock. The lock holder must release the lock once the data operation is complete. Figure 2.10, a block diagram of the Solaris 8 operating system, illustrates a top-down view of the platforms.

FIGURE 2.10

A block diagram of the Solaris 8 operating system

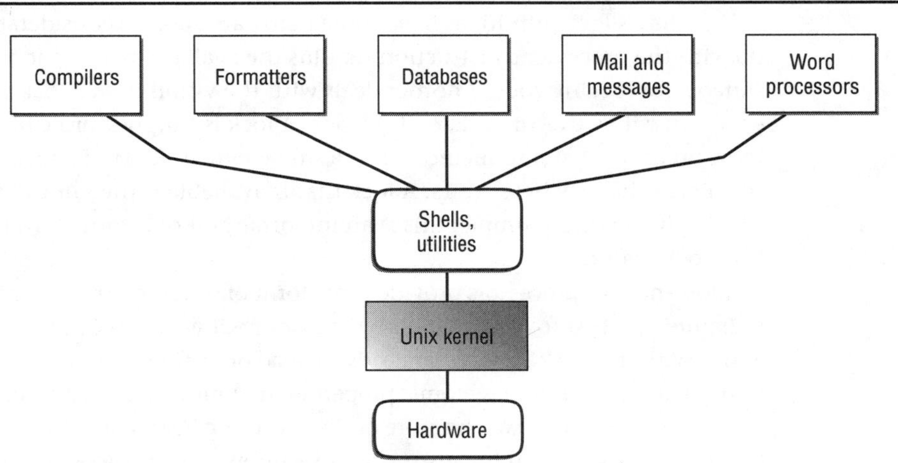

One of the major strengths of the Solaris kernel is its scalable performance on multiprocessor systems. All kernel subsystems—such as device drivers, the dispatcher, file systems, and process and thread support code—use the synchronization primitives. One of the engineering goals of late has been to reduce the need for locks without compromising the integrity of data.

Solaris 8 is designed to run on multiprocessor systems, whether it be SPARC from Sun Microsystems or Intel-based x86 platforms. Both architectures are considered to be symmetric multiprocessor (SMP) systems. This means that a peer-to-peer relationship exists among all the processors. They are all equal. There are other types of models that do not achieve the parallelism needed for optimal computing, such as the shared memory model and the massively parallel processor (MPP) model, which are built on nodes and contain a small number of processors. To achieve scalable performance, the operating system must support multiple processors that execute operating system code concurrently. Concurrency is the key to scalability, and Solaris 8 fits the bill easily.

Data integrity is difficult to maintain. The system cannot allow threads running on multiple processors to manipulate pointers to the same data structure at the same time. If one processor is reading a bit of critical information while a thread executing on another processor is changing the same data, chaos will result. The kernel implements locking mechanisms to prevent this from happening. It requires that all operating system code be aware of the number and type of locks that exist in the kernel and comply with the locking hierarchy. It must obey the rules for acquiring locks before reading or writing data to the kernel. What's more, multithreaded applications must also synchronize access to shared data. They use the same locking primitives and techniques that are used in the kernel. These complex issues make operating system development a universal challenge.

A system's lock primitives have some hardware-specific considerations. One has to do with the processor's instruction set plus the availability for machine instructions suitable for locking code. Another deals with the visibility of a lock's state when it is encountered by executing kernel threads. A lock is simply a piece of data at a specific location in the system's memory. It is a single byte in RAM. If a lock is set, or held, all the bits in the lock byte are 1s. A lock that is available is the same byte with all 0s. Although seemingly simple, this is an important bit of information in understanding how locks work.

Most modern processors provide some form of test-and-set instruction that is atomic in nature. It is best to remember that the read-modify-write sequence is one atomic operation. With the SPARC processor, reads are load operations and writes are store operations. If an instruction has atomic properties, that means that no other store operation is allowed between the load and store of the executing instruction. Lock operations must be atomic in that, when the instruction execution to get the lock is complete, either the lock is available or the lock is being held. If that process is not foolproof, a thread executing on one processor could issue a load on the lock, and while it is doing a test operation, another thread executing on another processor issues a lock call to get the same lock at the same time. If the lock is not held, both threads would assume that the lock is available and would issue a store to hold the lock. The atomic instructions prevent such a disaster from happening.

Another important consideration involves the visibility of the lock state to the processors when the lock value is changed. It is mandatory that all processors have a consistent view of data in memory. The most recent state of the lock must be visible to all processors on the system at all times.

The Solaris kernel employs several types of synchronization objects. Locks come in different forms. The most commonly used lock in the Solaris kernel is the mutex lock, which provides exclusive read and write access to data. RW locks are read/write for situations where multiple readers are allowed but only one writer is allowed at a time. Kernel semaphores are used in some areas of the kernel where a finite number of resources must be managed. Another type of mutex lock called a dispatcher lock is used by the kernel when access protection is required as well as protection from interrupts. Several hundred locks are defined in the kernel source code, but that number is not accurate. Because the actual number of locks that exist in a running system is dynamic and grows with the size of the system, it is impossible to guess how many are available at one time. Again, this feature is one of the primary attractions of Solaris 8. It is able to provide the scalability and scaling synchronization primitives dynamically according to the size of the kernel. It is quite possible to have thousands of locks on a large system. Much more can be written about locks, but it is not the intent of this book to present more than an overview.

A semaphore provides a method of synchronizing access to a shared resource by multiple process or threads. It can be used as a binary lock for exclusive access. For concurrent access by multiple threads, it is used as a counter. Semaphores are used in very few areas of the operating system. When the semaphore is used as a counter, its value is initialized to the number of shared resources. Whenever a resource is used, the semaphore value is decreased to indicate that there is one less resource available. When the process completes, the semaphore value is incremented. When zero (0) is reached, the calling process knows that no resources are available. These functions are called P and V operations; the P operation attempts to access the semaphore and the V operation releases it. The Solaris kernel uses semaphores only when appropriate. The counting functions they provide make them compatible with the allocation of fixed amounts of resource.

Directory Hierarchy

The Solaris kernel, being modular in design, does not originate on disk as a single binary object but is constructed in memory and loads during bootstrap operations. The object modules are well defined and live in a name space in the `root` and `usr` file directories. Core modules are split across multiple directories in one of three categories. These categories determine where the modules are placed in the directory hierarchy. The first category is platform and hardware independent, the second is platform dependent, and the third is hardware class dependent. The `/directory` tree contains operating system modules that load at boot time. Hardware class–dependent modules are derived from the processor type. You can determine the hardware class of a system by using the `uname(1)` command with the `-m` option. The platform-dependent category includes the type of system. The `-i` option will show hardware implementation. Solaris will usually be housed on Sun-based platforms such as SUNW, Ultra-5, and SUNW, and Enterprise. The kernel modules that deal with machine dependencies, reside in the directory tree that begins with `/platform/`*`<platform-name>`*.

Other kernel modules are located under the `/usr` directory. This tree also contains kernel (`/usr/kernel`) and platform (`usr/platform`) subdirectories. These modules are loaded on an as-needed basis.

TIP You can request that the system load optional modules at boot by using the `forceload` directive in the `/etc/system` configuration file.

Only one `genunix` binary gets loaded when you boot the system; usually the SPARC version or the `/kernel/genunix` on all other systems. These include callback and callout facilities, clock and timer, kernel memory allocator, management routines, runtime linker, synchronization primitives, device driver interfaces, and kernel thread and lightweight process code.

These binary kernel modules, resident in memory, construct the kernel upon bootup. The following sequence is based on a local disk boot; networks use different boot programs:

1. The boot block is loaded into memory.
2. The secondary boot program is located and loaded into memory.
3. The `ufsboot` locates and loads the core kernel images and the runtime linker.
4. Mandatory modules are loaded from the root directory tree and execute startup code.

5. Kernel startup code creates and initializes structures, resources, and software.
6. System executes shell scripts from system directories.

Although the SPARC systems have been discussed, much of the initialization process is hardware independent once the boot phase is complete and the kernel is loaded. Control then passes to Unix, which is loaded near the top of physical memory space and takes over execution. The Memory Management Unit (MMU) is enabled and the first 16 megabytes of memory are mapped. Devices are then mapped. One of the first devices to be mapped is the Electrically Erasable Programmable Read Only Memory (EEPROM on SPARC), which holds the Open Boot Prom (OBP) code. It occupies a part of the physical address space. Calls into the PROM are required during the boot-up. PROM aids in the retrieval of hardware and version information. Once `mlsetup()work` is finished, the kernel begins the function calls into the higher-level areas of the kernel. The `main()` function is entered. It calls into hardware routines for initialization steps and then returns to the common code to complete the boot process. Although there are innumerable processes going on behind the scenes, you need only know that kernel module loading occurs at various points in the boot process. During the platform-specific startup, the `swap`, `spects`, and `procfs` are loaded. Scheduling classes are loaded during the `dispinit()` function, which initializes the kernel dispatcher subsystem. Once the virtual memory support is initialized, the `specfs` and `swapfs` file system support modules are loaded and initialized. Kernel modules set for `forceload` are loaded with the ``forceload: drv/foo`` command in `/etc/system` and the kernel trap table is set. Housekeeping is performed, interrupt threads are created, initialization functions for subsystems are started, and the first `init` process for the user is created by the system. All further processes are forked by `init`.

Linking

Kernel architecture is layered. Many of the kernel subsystems access a common set of lower-level services. The interfaces are not public for use with application software development but are private to the kernel itself. Device drivers and STREAMS modules are exceptions to this generalization. The dynamic loading process follows a prescribed path:

1. Loads the module into memory
2. Establishes kernel address mappings for segments
3. Links the module segments into the kernel
4. Perform the module's install function

Loadable module types are defined in `/usr/include/sys/modctl.h`. Included are file systems, device drivers, exec modules, systems calls, miscellaneous modules, and

STREAMS modules. Each module has its own installation procedure to follow before the loading process is complete. The steps are similar to those of the dynamically linked programs. Shared objects to which a binary is linked are dynamically loaded into memory and linked into the process's address space. Loading a kernel module involves reading a target module into memory and creating an address space mapping. Any kernel module may be dependent on the existence of other kernel modules in order to function. Such dependencies are defined in the module code and maintained in the `modctl` structure. The kernel module loading facility is threaded to perform the module load function. Concurrent module loads are possible on multiprocessor systems and so provide faster system boot and initialization. Once the thread is created, the kernel follows a sequence of events to complete loading and linking the module. The following steps are an example of how linking is accomplished:

1. Creates and allocates a `modctl` structure after searching the linked list.
2. Enters the runtime linker to create address space segments and then loads the object into memory.
3. Sets the mod-loaded bit in the module's `modctl` structure, and adds increments to the `mod-loadcnt`.
4. Creates a link to the module's `mod-linkage` structure.
5. Executes the module's `mod-install` function by calling the `-init()` routine.

The major kernel subsystems involved in module loading are the module facility and the runtime linker (`krtld`), which is loaded early in the boot process. Because the Solaris 8 kernel is dynamic, and because objects can be loaded and unloaded during the life of a running system, the kernel maintains a symbol table that holds information required to resolve an object's symbolic references. The symbol table is updated by a kernel thread created for that purpose. The runtime linker issues a wake-up to the thread when a module is loaded, and the symbol table is updated to reflect the current loaded kernel objects.

These kernel components also make use of other kernel services. The memory allocator, locking primitives, and the kernel `ksyms` driver can also be pressed into service, which is one of the primary advantages of a modular design kernel.

Memory Architecture

The Solaris 8 virtual memory system offers several distinct benefits. It provides a programming model with a larger memory size than the available physical storage like RAM. It also provides a secondary place to store pieces of memory that do not fit in physical memory. It provides a simple programming model to applications. It provides processes with a linear range of bytes in address space, no matter what fragmentation has occurred. Address space is managed by the VM system by keeping the most frequently referenced portions of memory in the faster primary storage. If a shortage of RAM occurs, the VM system is required to free RAM by transferring infrequently used memory to the backing store. With this action, the VM system guarantees an optimal performance and removes the need for users to manage the allocation of memory. Figure 2.7, earlier in this chapter, depicts the address space, segments, and pages.

One highlight is that multiple users' processes can share memory within the VM system. Multiple processes can be running the same process executable binaries. Sharing the program binaries and application data optimizes memory. Memory is not wasted. The VM system also provides memory protection by preventing a process from accessing memory outside of its legal address space unless it is explicitly shared between processes. Pages are fixed-sized pieces of physical memory (RAM). The average page is 8KB. Each page is associated with a file and offset that identify the backing store for the page. This is the location to which the physical page contents will be migrated (also known as page-out) if needed for another use. Use page-in to read back in from the backing store if the physical page contents have migrated.

Pages used for process heap and stack have the swap file as their backing store. This is called anonymous memory. A page can also be a cache of a page-sized piece of a regular file. Its backing store is the file it's caching. If a page has had its contents modified, it is considered a "dirty" page. Anonymous memory is paged out to the swap device when the page is freed. If a file page needs to be freed and hasn't been modified, then it is simply freed. Once it has been modified, it is first written back out to the backing store and then freed.

Page-sized pieces of memory are managed rather than bytes of memory. Solaris breaks up the linear virtual address space into segments that represent each type of memory in the address space. Each segment manages the mapping for a virtual address range and converts that mapping into MMU pages. The MMU maps those pages into physical memory by using a platform-specific set of translation tables. Each table entry has the physical address of the page in RAM so that memory access can be converted quickly in hardware. The operating system can overflow memory onto a slower medium like a disk or swap space. When there is a shortage of memory, all of the pages of the least-active process are swapped to the swap device, freeing memory for other processes. The advantage to this system is that a page at a time is swapped out, allowing processes to continue. Another advantage is that the VM system manages file system buffering.

As with other aspects of Solaris 8, the virtual memory system is modular in design. It provides scalable performance on multiprocessor platforms and has been ported to many different platforms. The MMU manages the physical memory with a hardware-specific address translation layer known as the Hardware Address Translation (HAT) layer. Each memory management type has its own specific HAT to wear. The common machine-independent memory management layers can be separated from the hardware-specific components to minimize the amount of platform-specific code that must be written.

Address spaces are mappings of segments that are created by segment device drivers. Each segment driver manages the mapping of a linear virtual address space into memory pages for different devices. The segment drivers access the HAT layer to create the translations between the address space and the physical pages. The kernel also supports sharing of memory, files libraries, and executable scripts. They can be mapped into the address space during program startup. When a file is mapped into a process's address space, it can be mapped and shared so that all processes have access to the same physical memory pages.

Memory segments manage the mapping of a linear range of virtual memory into an address space. The mapping is between the address space and a device. Because object architecture allows different behaviors for different segments, there is no longer any need for hard-coding memory and device information into the address space. A segment driver is required to implement an address space and create a mapping for a linear address range. It is also needed to provide page fault handling routines to deal with machine exceptions within a linear address range. The segment driver implements a subset of methods and a constructor function that creates the first instance of the object. The segment's create routine is passed as an argument to `as-map()`, the segment object is created, and a segment object pointer is returned. Other parts of the virtual memory system can call into the segment for different address space without hindrance.

The Solaris 8 kernel supports several segment drivers for various functions. The vnode segment driver manages process address space mapping, including data-, heap-, stack-, and memory-mapped files. Table 2.6 lists the segment drivers that are associated with kernel memory mappings or hardware devices.

TABLE 2.6: SEGMENT DRIVERS

Segment	Function
`seg_dev`	Supports mapped hardware devices
`seg_drv`	Provides mapping support for hardware graphics devices
`seg_kmem`	Allocates nonpageable kernel memory
`seg_kp`	Allocates pageable kernel memory
`seg_lock`	Supports mapping for hardware graphics between user and kernel
`seg_map`	Maps files (vnodes) into the kernel's address space
`seg_mapdev`	Provides support for mapped hardware devices
`seg_mdi`	Provides mapping support for the `cgfourteen` graphic frame buffer

Continued

TABLE 2.6: SEGMENT DRIVERS (CONTINUED)

Segment	Function
`seg_nf`	Nonfaulting memory driver
`seg_spt`	Shared page table segment driver
`seg_sx`	Provides mapping support for the SPARCstation 20 SX graphics

The most commonly used segment driver is the `seg_vn` (vnode) driver. It maps a file into an address space using physical memory as a cache. The `seg-vn` segment driver also creates anonymous memory with the process address space for the heap and stack. In addition, it provides support for System V shared memory.

A vnode segment handles memory address translation and page faults for the memory range requested in the `mmap` system call and the new segment is added to the list in the processes address space. Once the segment is created, the `seg_vn` driver initializes the structure with the address and length of the mapping, then creates a `seg_vn`-specific data structure.

A file can be mapped into a process's address space with the `mmap` system call. When we call into the address space routines to create a new vnode segment, the vnode segment handles memory address translation. It also handles the page faults for the memory range requested in the `mmap` system call. The new segment is then added to the list in the process's address space.

The hat map function is the central function for the creation of address space mappings. It talks to the hardware's memory and calls for the platform to program the MMU. The memory address references will trigger the page fault handler in the segment driver until a valid physical memory page has been placed. When the MMU mapping is complete, the `seg_vn` driver begins handling page faults within the segment.

System calls write to a mapped file by updating the contents of memory within the segment. Because there is no software or hardware event, updates occur periodically after the system flush daemon sees a modification in the memory page.

When two or more processes are mapped, the `seg_vn` segments point to the same vnode. The processes share the same physical memory pages for the files. The first segment to cause a page fault reads a page into physical memory. Any segments after the first create a reference to the existing physical memory page.

Each process creates its own segment object. Both segments point to the same file and are mapped to the same physical pages. Several options determine how a file is shared when it is mapped for more than one process. Figure 2.11 demonstrates how two processes map to the same file.

FIGURE 2.11

Two processes mapped to the same file

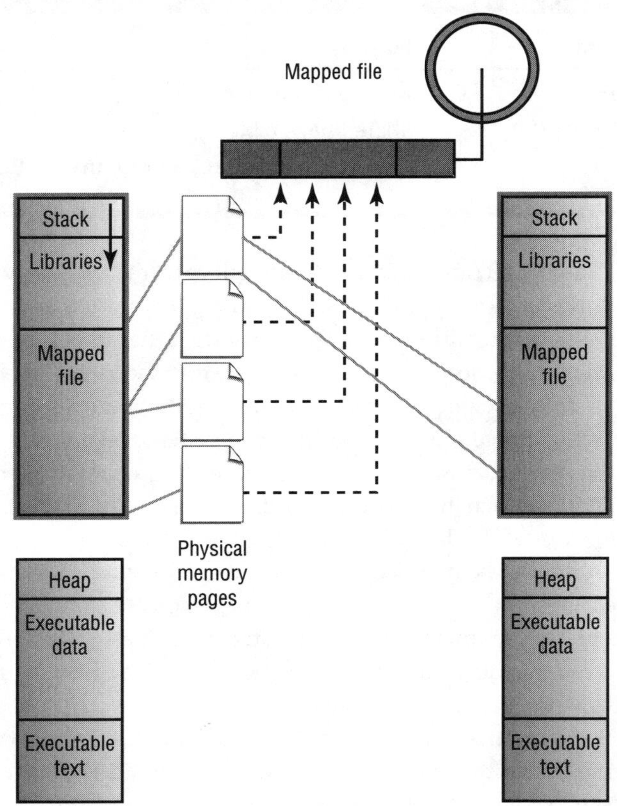

Anonymous Memory

Anonymous memory pertains to pages that are not associated with a vnode. These pages are used for heap space, a stack, and copy-on-write pages. Two subsystems are dedicated to managing anonymous memory. The first is the anon layer, the second is the `swapfs` file system. When a segment receives a page fault, it allocates an `anon` map structure and points to the anon header in the amp field on the anonymous map. A slot array is then allocated. It is big enough to hold the number of pages in the segment. Depending upon how many slots are required, the slot array may be a single or double indirection list.

Double indirection is indicated when segments are larger than 16MB; 32-bit systems fall into this category, as do 64-bit systems for segments larger than 8MB. For single indirection, the anon header `array-chunk` directly references the anon slot array. For double indirection, the array is broken up into sizeable chunks. The allocation is handled by the anon layer interface `anonmap_create`.

The `swapfs` layer implements space-efficient swap allocation. It is a pseudo file system between the anon layer and physical swap devices. Figure 2.12 demonstrates how data is swapped from memory to disk.

FIGURE 2.12

How data is physically swapped from memory to disk

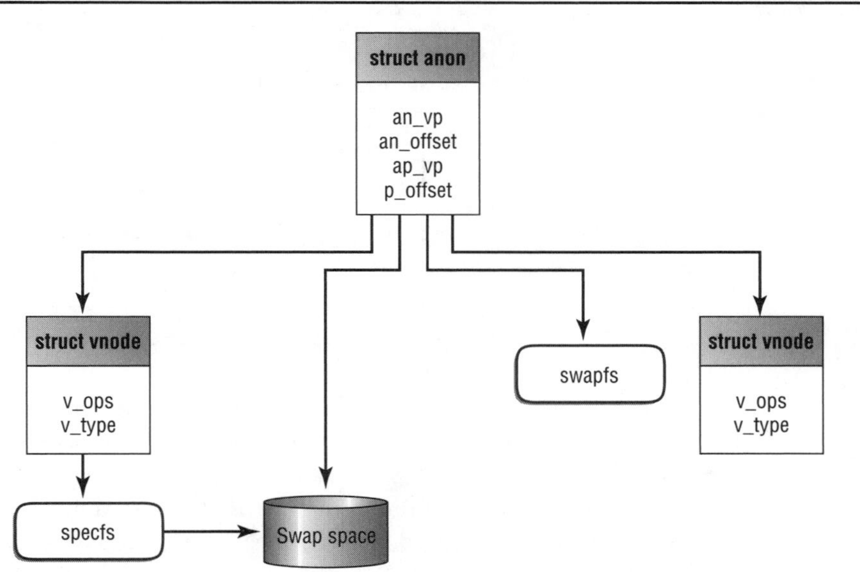

Each physical page of memory has a vnode and offset, which identify a backing store that tells where to find the page when it is not in physical memory. With a regular file, the physical page that caches the file has a vnode and offset. Swap space is used so that if memory becomes full, a page can be copied out to disk, thereby freeing up a page of memory. Space is reserved up front to ensure that enough swap space is available for required uses. Solaris 8 allows the allocation of anonymous memory without the reservation of physical swap space when sufficient memory is available. Swapping is not always necessary, but it usually consumes one page of swap space for one page of writeable virtual memory. There are three stages of swap space allocation: reserve, allocate, and swap. Reserved swap space is allocated when a segment is created with `private/read/write` access and represents the virtual size of the area being created. Virtual swap space is allocated when the first physical page is assigned. A `swapfs` vnode and offset are assigned against the anon slot at that time. If a memory shortage occurs, a page may be swapped out. If the scanner calls `swapfs_putpage()`

for the page, the page is migrated to physical disk or file swap. Swap space is also reserved whenever a heap segment is created. An equal amount of space is reserved. Figure 2.13 demonstrates virtual swap.

FIGURE 2.13
How data is swapped from memory to disk

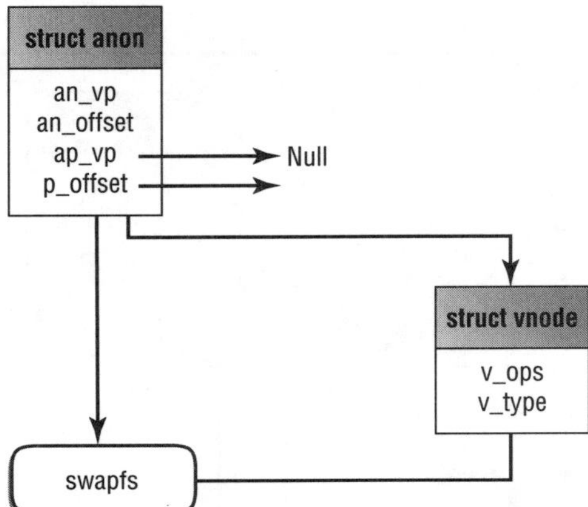

To avoid running out of swap space during execution (and without means of detection), virtual swap space is reserved up front so that swap space allocation can be performed at the time of request. Solaris allows you to fail a request for memory prior to when it is needed to prevent the possibility of processes failing during normal execution. Most operating systems do exactly the opposite, and when the resource is exhausted, the process is sent a `SIGDANGER` signal. If you run a `malloc()` request, it will help you to keep processes from failing while executing. The `swapfs` file system includes pageable memory. It is used as virtual swap space. You can actually reserve and allocate virtual swap space when a first page is touched. When swap rather than disk space is reserved, virtual swap space from the `swapfs` file system is reserved. The disk swap pages are allocated once a page is actually paged out.

A system global variable, `availrmem`, keeps track of the pageable physical memory available in the system and adds it to the total amount of swap space. If virtual swap is reserved, the amount of virtual memory is decremented. The swap allocations will succeed as long as there is enough available memory and physical swap space. In Solaris 8, anonymous pages are assigned `swapfs` vnode and offsets when the segment driver calls `anon_alloc()` to get a new anonymous page. That function calls into `swapfs` through `swapfs_getvp()` and in turn calls `swapfs_getpage()` to create a new page with

swapfs vnod/offset. This triggers the anon structure members an_vp and an_offset to reference the vnode and offset within the swapfs virtual swap device.

When physical swap space is exhausted, memory performance problems result. A failure does not occur when physical swap space fills. Because sufficient available virtual swap space made up of both physical memory and physical swap space was allocated during reservation, the swapfs_putpage() leaves the page in memory and does not push a page to physical swap. Once the physical swap is fully allocated, the remaining pages get locked down in physical memory.

The amount of anonymous memory in the system is recorded by the anon accounting structures. This layer tracks how many anonymous pages have been allocated to the kanon_info structure. Figure 2.14 demonstrates a typical pattern of swap allocation.

FIGURE 2.14
How Solaris assigns swap allocations in memory

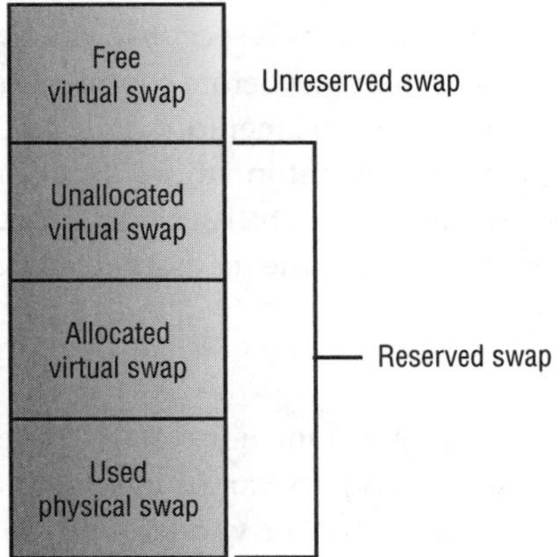

Virtual memory watchpoints are Solaris features that mimic breakpoints. A watchpoint stops execution when an address location is read or modified. They also provide the ability to implement breakpoints through the watchpoint interface. You can set or clear watchpoints through the /proc file system interface. Open the control file for a process and send a pcwatch command; the pcwatch command is accompanied by a prwatch structure, which contains the address, the length of the area to be affected, and the type of watchpoint. Table 2.7 lists the watchpoint flags and what they are used for.

TABLE 2.7: WATCHPOINT FLAGS

Flag	Description
WA_READ	Read access
WA_WRITE	Write access
WA_EXEC	Execution access
WA_TRAPAFTER	Trap after the instruction completes

When a watchpoint is triggered, a traced process makes a memory reference that covers at least one byte of a watched area and the memory reference that covers a bit mask is as specified in `pr_wflags`. When a watchpoint is triggered, it triggers a watchpoint trap. The trap occurs before the instruction completes unless `WA_trapafter` was specified. If `WA_trapafter` was specified, the trap will occur after the instruction completes. When the trap occurs before completion, the memory is not modified. If it occurs after completion, the memory is modified if the access permission is a write access. The `/proc` process information file, `prinfo`, contains information pertinent to the watchpoint trap and can be read into a `struct pr_info`. The `si_addr` field contains the virtual address of the memory reference that triggers the watchpoint.

Pages

Pages are units of physical memory. Active pages in the kernel are mappings between a vnode and memory. A page can be identified with a vnode pointer and the page size offset within the vnode, or the vnode/offset pair, which is the backing store for the page and represents the file and offset that the page is mapping. The HAT and address space layers manage the mapping between the physical page and its virtual address space. The vnode/offset pair is reusable by other tasks because it synchronizes its contents in RAM with its backing store before reuse. A global hash list is an array of pointers to linked lists of pages. The virtual memory system hashes pages with a valid vnode/offset pair onto a global hash list so that they can be located by vnode and offset. There are three functions that search the global hash list: `page_find()`, `page_lookup()`, and `page_lookup_nowait()`. These functions use vnode and offset as arguments and return a pointer to a page structure if it finds one.

The Solaris kernel also uses a segmented global physical page list. This is made up of segments in contiguous physical memory. These segments are added during the system boot. They are also added and deleted dynamically when physical memory is added or removed while the system is running. A free list and cache list hold pages that are not mapped into any address space and have been freed by `page_free()`. Although they may be reported as free pages by `vmstat`, they can still contain a valid page from a vnode/offset and are still part of the global page cache. Caching pages can appear on the free list. Memory on the cache list is not really free either, but it is a valid cache of a page from a file. The cache list demonstrates how the file systems use memory as a file system cache.

If a page has been destroyed and removed from a vnode's hash list, it will appear on the free list. The free list is usually small because most pages used by a process still keep their vnode/offset information intact. When a process exits, pages are put on the free list. This frees anonymous memory pages such as heap, stack, and copy-on-write pages.

Page sizes may vary depending upon the hardware. The Solaris kernel uses a page size that is usually 8KB. The MMU page size causes somewhat of a trade-off of performance and memory size efficiency. A larger page gives better performance because of less memory management overhead, but a smaller page size wastes less memory.

Solaris 8 controls many page-related activities with the use of algorithms. Although there are too many to delve into, suffice it to say that algorithms to fine-tune the page coloring, page scanner page-out, and scan rate operations are all as efficient as any operating system can make them. Shared libraries have been optimized to prevent stolen pages. Demand paging allows the file system cache to grow and shrink as required by "stealing pages" not recently used by other subsystems. Solaris 8 is capable of sustaining much higher I/O rates because of this. Memory is conserved through various means. The CPU scheduler/dispatcher can swap out entire processes to conserve memory.

POSIX

Portable Operating System Interface (POSIX) standards are used with Solaris 8. They were implemented with the System V IPC (Interprocess Communication) set: shared memory, semaphores, and message queues. The implementation in Solaris 8 is different from that in System V. The POSIX name convention provides abstraction, as well as a file descriptor to enable the use of the file memory mapping interface, `mmap(2)`, on which all the POSIX IPC mechanisms are built. The IPC facilities need not be files in a file system, but they must look like they are. The old key values used by System V have been done away with in Solaris 8. With POSIX, the processes acquire the desired resource by using filename conventions. The POSIX interfaces require linking with the `libposix4.20` shared object library when running code that uses any POSIX IPC facilities on Solaris.

All of the POSIX IPC functions are directly or indirectly based on memory-mapped files. The message queue and semaphore functions make direct calls to the `mmap(2)`. This creates a memory-mapped file based on the file descriptor returned from the `xsx_open(3R)` call. If you use the POSIX shared memory, you must make the `mmap(2)` call from the application code. The `mmap(2)` system call maps a file directly from the code.

Summary

In this chapter, you learned how Solaris 8 was developed. Multics, which was developed by AT&T and designed for an in-house system, was the grandparent of Solaris 8. Solaris 8 has been refined and the operating environment includes all of the tools, applications, and services that make use of SunOS, the Sun Operating System. The C programming language, which was written specifically for the Unix system, is used by Solaris 8.

Solaris 8 employs the modular or layered design made popular by Unix. Sun developed a new operating system kernel, which is used by Solaris today. Solaris 8 uses multiple threads of execution. The hierarchical structure of Solaris 8 is followed through each module of the operating system, making for a uniform structure. Buses and devices can be installed and configured by dynamically loadable devices and bus drivers.

This chapter also covered schedulers. You learned that each scheduler has its own algorithms and priority levels to optimize operations and that the virtual file system framework implements multiple file system types. The proc file system provides all programs with a uniform interface into the kernel. Solaris recognizes two distinct processor execution modes: a privileged mode called kernel mode and a nonprivileged mode called user mode.

In addition to schedulers, this chapter covered interrupts and traps. An interrupt is a signal that a device sends to the kernel indicating that something needs immediate attention. The kernel can send an interrupt to another processor when required. A trap is a vectored transfer of control into the kernel initiated by the processor. Software traps are used for system calls in the Solaris kernel.

This chapter also showed how Solaris employs shared memory architecture, which implements a single kernel shared by all processors and a single memory address space. You read how data threads are prioritized and high-priority threads can interrupt lower-priority threads upon execution and how the virtual memory system provides a programming model with larger size.

Finally, you learned that memory is managed by page size rather than by bytes.

CHAPTER 3

Installing Solaris 8

FEATURING:

The different Solaris distributions 62

The SPARC installation 71

Solaris on Intel installation 83

StarOffice and additional component installations 85

Patches 87

The amount of "installation" that you have to do with Solaris is dependent upon the state of the system you will be working on. Chances are that most people won't be installing Solaris on a server by themselves. If you have purchased a workstation from Sun, you will be asked a few questions (mainly about your system's name and addressing scheme) during the initial boot process and the system will be configured. Seemingly there is little to go wrong in a preinstalled workstation setup, but there are issues that can cause you problems even with a simple setup.

For a complete installation starting from scratch, there are many more choices that you must make. This chapter leads you through some of the thought processes involved in installing Solaris on either a SPARC system or an Intel x86 system. At some point in your system's lifetime, either through operator error or through the need to upgrade and modify your system, you may be forced to reinstall the operating system. Also, given that Solaris is now available free for download from Sun's Web site, many more people are confronted with the task of installing their system's operating system.

The Solaris Distributions

Sun makes Solaris available under either a noncommercial license or a commercial license. If you are using Solaris at home or if you are a student, you are free to download and install a copy of Solaris on your workstation or personal computer. You can buy the noncommercial version of Solaris directly from Sun for the nominal cost of the disks plus postage, and at the moment, this version is priced at $20.00. Both the SPARC and Intel versions of Solaris are available under the noncommercial license. When you purchase Solaris under this program, you get only the discs: the CD-ROMs for SPARC or the CD-ROMs and the floppy boot diskette for the Intel environment. You do not get the installation guide or any of the printed documentation that comes with the other license programs.

The noncommercial version of Solaris is also available to developers under a program that Sun calls the "Free Solaris Binary License Program." Actually, this version is not free, but it is delivered at a cost that most people would find competitive with the cost of other desktop operating systems, such as Microsoft Windows or the Apple Macintosh. For $75.00 plus shipping, this version lets you install Solaris on any system with eight processors or less. The program is described at `www.sun.com/developers/solarispromo.html`, and the same page can be accessed from the URL `www.sun.com/solaris/how-to-buy.html` (see Figure 3.1).

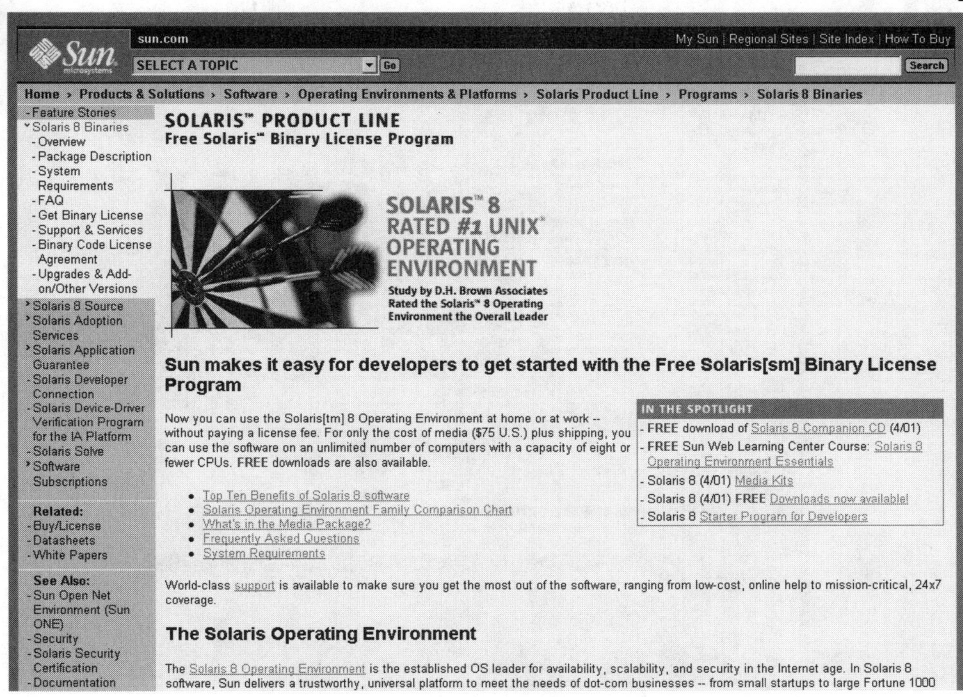

FIGURE 3.1 *The Solaris How to Buy page is a jumping-off point for obtaining the various Sun Solaris distributions.*

Sun requires that businesses using the Solaris operating system purchase a commercial license. This license applies to either a departmental or corporate server and to a developer's workstation. When you purchase a new system from Sun, the cost of the commercial license is part of the package. However, you may find that in many instances, particularly when you purchase a workstation, the documentation set is not included with your system. The documentation may be purchased from Sun as part of the distribution described in the preceding paragraph, in that case. For instances in which you wish to upgrade your system from a previous version of Solaris to Solaris 8, be aware that Sun also sells an upgrade version of the operating system.

All of the different versions of the Solaris operating system may be purchased directly from Sun through the Sun store on the Sun Web site (see Figure 3.2). Access to the Sun store may be found through a button on the Sun home page labeled Sun Store or by clicking the button labeled How to Buy in the title bar on many pages of Sun's site. The direct URL to the Sun store is `http://store.sun.com`.

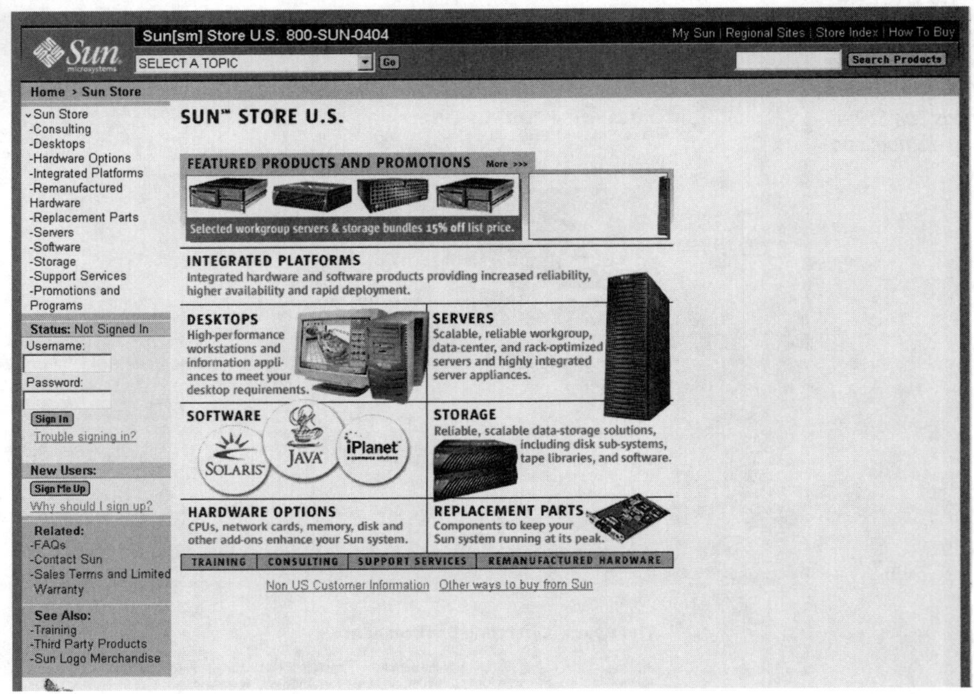

FIGURE 3.2

The Sun Store sells both Sun systems and Sun hardware as well as Sun software.

TIP Sometimes you will not be allowed to install on a disk that has not already been partitioned. If you have a brand-new hard disk for your SPARC system, it is a good idea to label and partition it on a working Solaris system before trying to install an OS on it.

Sun also offers free for download both versions of the Sun operating system that you can access using your browser. The downloaded version of the operating system is fully enabled and may in fact be even more current than the version that you purchased from Sun or that was loaded on a server or workstation you purchased recently. The How To Buy page has links on it to both versions of the Solaris OS. When you download either version, you are asked to register with the site, but no other requirement is made of you. You can return at any time to download Solaris, and after you log in, you may download Solaris any number of times. Related Sun sites such as BigAdmin (`www.sun.com/bigadmin`), which offer Solaris utilities free for download, have a similar login scheme. You will see BigAdmin appear during the Web Start portion of the installation described later on in this chapter.

Sun's low prices for its Solaris operating system are driven by the company's need to encourage developers to develop applications for Solaris and for users to adopt the operating system. With the relative success of Linux on the desktop and in the low-end server market, Sun hopes that its pricing strategy will entice users to learn Solaris and will keep experienced users in the Solaris fold.

Installing Solaris

Your installation of Solaris will proceed more smoothly if you have in hand at the time of the installation documentation of the network characteristics you desire for your system as well as a partitioning scheme for your hard drives.

You can rest assured that the equipment for a SPARC system purchased from Sun is likely compatible with Solaris, provided that the system is sufficiently new. However, you will need to check the system components for an Intel x86 system to make sure the system conforms to Sun's hardware compatibility requirements. The Intel Hardware Compatibility List, or HCL, may be viewed at `www.sun.com/software/intel/hcl/index.html`, and the list may be downloaded in any one of several formats for later use from `http://soldc.sun.com/support/drivers/hcl/index.html`. Developers wishing to get their systems certified for Solaris may go to the Solaris software certification site at `http://soldc.sun.com/support/certify/HCTS/`.

Assuming that your Intel hardware is compatible with Solaris 8 and that you have in your possession a complete Solaris 8 distribution, you will need to also have a boot diskette in order to install Solaris on Intel. Should the boot diskette that came with your distribution not function properly, or if you're working with a downloaded copy of Solaris on Intel, you can download the disk from `http://soldc.sun.com/support/drivers/dca_diskettes/` and download the necessary files to prepare a 1.44MB floppy disk that you can use as your Intel boot diskette. If you download the file `boot.3` on a DOS/Windows or Linux system, you should use the `rawrite.exe` command to make an image copy of this file on your floppy disk. If you download the file on a Solaris system, use the following command to prepare the boot floppy:

```
$ dd if=boot.3 0f=/dev/fd0 bs=1440K
```

For additional help with creating the boot floppy, go to `http://soldc.sun.com/support/drivers/copytodisk.html`.

Installation Types

There are four general methods used to install Solaris on a system:

Web Start installation This method is used for an Initial Install and is not used for an Upgrade Install. Web Start uses a Java program to present to the person installing Solaris a graphical interface in which the installation can be conducted using a mouse and keystrokes.

Interactive installation An interactive installation is used by an administrator when installing Solaris on a single system. During the interactive installation, you can preserve file systems so that they are not overwritten. You can also specify which file systems are to be preserved. An interactive installation is typically much faster than a full installation conducted using Web Start.

Network installation In a network installation, the Solaris OS is installed over a network to a system. Administrators use a network to install Solaris on equipment that doesn't have a CD-ROM drive. The necessary files are copied over to the hard drive of the machine.

JumpStart installation This is an automated installation of the Solaris operating system from a JumpStart server. The JumpStart method can be applied to multiple systems and be used to "roll out" Solaris. Typically, companies specify a standard build for a Solaris system and create a system image for each particular system type. The JumpStart server then copies this image to each system using a set of scripts.

In this chapter, the Web Start installation is fully described. To learn about the network installation or the JumpStart installation, consult the Solaris "Advanced Installation Guide" (see `http://docs.sun.com/ab2/coll.214.7/SPARCINSTALL/@Ab2TocView?Ab2Lang=C&Ab2Enc=iso-8859-1`).

Partitioning Schemes

If you accept Solaris's default installation, the installer will create a partitioning scheme for you. That partitioning scheme may not be what you will need or desire over time. For example, on the 8GB hard drive that came with the Ultra 5 that the authors wrote this book with, Solaris puts most of the space on the hard drive into an `/export` partition. As a result, little space is left in the root partition for program installation. Although that scheme is useful to a network or system administrator servicing many users with limited program requirements, it is hardly useful to someone using that workstation for serious testing, development, or administration purposes. Partitioning your system after the fact, although possible, is more difficult and may require the use of a third-party application such as Veritas's Volume Manager. Thus, you are encouraged to consider your choice of partitioning scheme carefully prior to installation.

The Solaris operating system installs in five different forms, with five different base sizes:

- The core Solaris system is 205MB.
- The end user system (64 bit) is 562MB.
- The developer system (64 bit) is 922MB.
- The entire system (64 bit) is 980MB.
- The entire system with additional original equipment manufacturer (OEM) support is 988MB.

Most systems these days have disks greater than 2GB, and so you are encouraged to install the complete Solaris distribution on your system whenever possible. If you plan on using additional hardware such as add-in cards, you may need to also install OEM support.

In deciding to partition your system, you need to consider how many users are going to be working on it. For a single-user system, you may want to create a large partition on your disk for the root partition; for a multiuser system, you may want to create additional partitions to protect the system from problems that might arise. One of the two most troublesome problems you'll encounter is that a user can fill up a partition and, if it is a single partition, the system will slow down considerably. Unlike other operating systems, Solaris will not crash when the disk is full. Solaris reserves about 5 percent of the space on the root partition for the system administrators' use, which allows system maintenance to restore the system to good working order. In a multiuser situation, you can set on users' disk quotas that allow you to control how much disk space any user can consume.

The second problem you'll encounter related to Solaris, one that is generally true of all Unix systems, is that you may over time have a rogue daemon fill up a partition by creating a large log file. A rogue daemon is not necessarily a virus, although it is entirely possible that it could be. In the Unix world, due to strict system security, it is hard for a process to obtain root privileges from the outside and make a system unusable. Much more common is the process by which a system utility is given root privileges by an administrator to track events or processes and then writes to a log file. When that rogue daemon runs as root and consumes all available disk space, the system can either become inaccessible or perform too slowly to be useful. In some instances, you may find that you will need to use the Solaris installation CD-ROM to restore the system to use.

To some extent, you can use partitioning to help you with these two problems. Partitioning segments your hard drive into different areas that are used by different directories. You can use the Solaris security scheme to restrict users and processes like daemons so that they can access only certain partitions. Thus, if a partition is either filled or corrupted, your main or root partition continues to function unaffected.

The following Solaris partitions are commonly created:

/ (root) partition Solaris stores the kernel in the root partition. During operation, log files and core files are stored in root. You want to be certain that root is large enough to store several large log files. The root partition should be greater than 64MB, but you should keep it at a moderate size. Typical larger root partition sizes are in the range of 128MB to 256MB, depending upon the amount of disk space you have available. If you decide not to make a `/var`, `/usr`, or `/opt` directory, you must leave enough room in the root partition for that content as well.

/home partition Many administrators create a `/home` partition to store user home directories. For a system that has only a single user, you may not want or need to create this partition. In a multiuser situation, the number of users you wish to accommodate will determine how large you may want to make this partition, and you should take into account the kind of work you do in your organization in determining how much disk space you'll allocate for each user's directory in the `/home` partition. If possible, determine an average `/home` usage per person before setting the size of this partition because the range can vary dramatically.

/opt partition The `/opt` partition stores optional applications that users may install on their system. If several large applications are going to be added to your system, the `/opt` directory should be made large.

swap partition The `swap` partition stores recently used application, data, and system code, serving as an extension of your system's physical memory or RAM. You set up the `swap` partition during the initial phases of your installation. If you have less than 512MB of RAM, a good rule of thumb is that the amount of swap space you'll need is two times the amount of RAM you have.

/usr partition Many people use the `/usr` partition to store the Solaris utilities that are installed into the `bin` and `sbin` subdirectories instead of installing them in the `/opt` partition. If you will be installing several large and optional applications on the `/usr` partition, you should make it large.

/var partition Solaris administrators sometimes create the `/var` partition to store volatile or temporary files such as print, log, or mail files. The `/var` partition is particularly valuable on a server, less so on a workstation. For server applications, `/var` is often a large partition.

The only partition that is actually required is the root partition, but these other partitions offer conveniences that make their addition useful. A reasonable partition scheme is particularly useful in server deployments.

When you are installing Solaris on an Intel x86 system that contains another operating system such as Microsoft Windows or Linux, you will need to use a utility such as `fdisk` or Partition Magic within the other operating system to create additional partitions. If possible, use a separate disk on which to install Solaris when you are installing Solaris on a system that has another operating system on it.

Network Addressing

Solaris is a network operating system. To obtain essential network services and successfully install Solaris, you will need to supply various network parameters. It's a good idea to have this information available prior to installation. You need to know the following parameters (if you are unfamiliar with any of them, you should consult your system administrator for details):

Host name The name of your system. The name you enter is case sensitive.

IP address The unique address, either public or private, that identifies you on the network or on the Internet. It's entered in the form ###.###.###.###.

Subnet mask The number that defines which subnet your system will belong to.

Domain name The name of the domain that allows people on the Internet to access your system. An example of a fully qualified domain name (FQDN) would be www.sosinsky-group.com; the domain name would be more simply sosinsky-group.com.

Name service The type of name service used to find other systems on your network. Choices include NIS, NIS+, DNS, and no name service.

Address service Your network may uses DHCP to assign an IP address to your system, thus obviating the need to assign a static IP address.

Date and time You will need to supply the current date and time to the system.

Root password The root password used by the administrator or owner of the system is required during installation.

Proxy server information If your access to the Internet is through a proxy server, you will need to supply the IP address of the server as well as the port number of the service.

Power management Solaris supports power management features such as power-down after a period of inactivity. If your enterprise has a policy, you should conform to it. Otherwise, at installation time you can make decisions about the type of power management, if any, you desire.

Intel Hardware Compatibility

Solaris 8 supports a wide variety of PC hardware, but not as wide a variety as Microsoft Windows does. That makes it much more important to check to see whether your PC hardware is supported on the Solaris Hardware Compatibility List (HCL) at `www.sun.com/software/intel/hcl/index.html`. A specific system list by system name and model is contained in the HCL.

In brief, Solaris 8 supports the following Intel system hardware:

Intel, AMD, and Cyrix processors Support includes Intel Pentium, Pentium Pro, Pentium II, and Celeron; AMD K5, K6, and K6-2; and Cyrix 5x86 and 6x86 processors.

Memory Solaris 8 requires a minimum of 64MB for light workstation system use. For production use, memory allocations of from 256MB to 512MB are recommended.

Bus architectures Solaris supports the ISA (Industry Standard Architecture), EISA (Extended Industry Standard Architecture), PCI (Peripheral Component Interconnect) bus, and VLB (Video Electronics Standards Association's Local Bus) standards. Sun is also committed to supporting versions of the Infiniband standard architecture when they become available in 2002–2004. Solaris does not support the IBM Micro-Channel bus or the AGP (Accelerated Graphics Port) standards.

Hard drives Nearly all IDE (Intelligent Drive Electronics), EIDE (Enhanced Intelligent Drive Electronics), and SCSI (Small Computer System Interface) drives, both permanent and removable, are supported. Solaris supports and recognizes the drives from most major manufacturers automatically.

CD-ROM drives Solaris supports most CD-ROM drives with speeds of 2X or greater. The latest high-speed drives of 40X and 44X can prove troublesome, and the BIOS on some PCs will not support booting from CD-ROM drives. If the latter is the case, you will need to have a floppy drive in order to perform a Solaris installation.

PC Cards A common area of incompatibility is with add-in cards. Although popular industry standards such as Adaptec SCSI boards; Sound Blaster 16 and Pro audio boards; and 3COM, Intel, and Netgear NIC cards are supported, it is a good idea to check the specific cards that are installed in your system with the HCL, particularly for an Intel x86 installation.

Video cards The second most troublesome area for Solaris installations, particularly with Intel, is video cards. Solaris's support for video cards is based on the particular chip set installed in the card. Among the popular series supported are ATI Rage and Mach boards; Chips and Technologies F655xx series; Cirrus Logic's GD54xx series; Matrox MGA series; and the S3 Trio, Vision, and Virge series.

TIP The major problem with video board selection is that Solaris's inability to support AGP video cards significantly limits your choice of cards and vendors. AGP is now the most commonly purchased video board and is supported by all current PC vendors. You may have better luck locating a particular PCI board for your Solaris system by buying online instead of at a video store.

Installation Procedure

The following sections illustrate a complete install (Initial Install) using the Solaris Web Start program. The routine is described for the SPARC distribution, and the steps required to prepare an Intel x86 system are also described. To install Solaris on your Intel system, you'll find that, once the preliminary steps are performed, you'll follow the same steps and use the same dialog boxes you would use for a SPARC installation.

Depending upon the version of Solaris 8 that you install, you may find that the sequence of steps you see is somewhat different. A preinstalled version of Solaris on a workstation requires fewer steps because the mini-kernel is already installed (that is, the installation files are copied onto disk, but the installation sequence itself hasn't been initiated). An Upgrade Install will also require fewer steps because it leaves your partitions and file system intact. Therefore, use the installation sequence described in the next section as a general guide for what is necessary for you to do during an install.

The installation shown in this chapter is for workstations. Server installations, although similar, involve additional matters that are beyond the scope of this chapter.

SPARC Installation

You have a choice of performing a full or initial installation or an upgrade installation. An initial installation will overwrite all files, create new partitions, and erase all settings. An upgrade installation will merge your previous version of Solaris with the new version. Many system parameters and settings are saved in an upgrade. The upgrade saves you time and may be appropriate when installing a newer version of the OS over a healthy system.

NOTE Note that the Solaris Installation Guide separates the full installation and the upgrade installation into two separate procedures. Additionally, tables at the back of the guide list the packages that are installed as part of the Solaris 8 installation procedure.

TIP Before upgrading a system, it is advisable to back it up.

What follows is the description of a full or initial installation on a SPARC system. Should your system become corrupted, you can perform this full installation to restore it if the Solaris installer does not give you the option of allowing an upgrade installation. To launch the installer, follow these steps:

1. Put the Solaris Install CD into the CD-ROM drive.
2. Reboot.
3. During startup, press the Stop+A keystroke.
4. At the OK prompt, enter **`boot cdrom`**.
5. Press the Return key.

When you purchase a new Solaris workstation, the initial mini-kernel installation is already on the disk for you. When you power up the system, you will find yourself in the graphical part of the installation after the preboot process answering questions about your network configuration.

Preboot Process

For a fresh installation of Solaris, during which the operating system is completely installed, new partitions are established, and all of your previous system information, settings, and data are destroyed, you will be taken through the following sequence:

```
Your system appears to be upgradeable.
Do you want to do an Initial Install or Upgrade?

    1) Initial install
    2) Upgrade
    Please Enter 1 or 2> 1
```

You'll come across questions that require a yes or no answer. You must supply it. Pressing the Return key establishes a default condition such as swap partition size.

The main difference between the Initial Install and the Upgrade is that the Initial Install reformats your disk and lets you establish a new partition scheme. It also allows you to set a new swap partition size. If you choose to upgrade your system, the installation reboots into the graphical part of the installation process. Continuing on with the Initial Install, you'll see Solaris post the following information in an interactive mode:

```
The default root disk is /dev/dsk/c0t0d0.
The Solaris installer needs to format
/dev/dsk/c0t0/d0

WARNING: ALL INFORMATION ON THE DISK WILL BE ERASED!

Do you want to format /dev/dsk/c0t0d0 [y,n,?,q] y
```

The installer will also seek to establish a swap partition for a fresh installation. Solaris determines the swap size by considering the amount of memory you have installed in your system as well as the size of your hard drive. Unless you have specific performance requirements that would require a larger swap file, you should accept Solaris's recommendation. You should also not make your swap file smaller than is recommended. The Solaris install process copies the install image into the swap space and then boots off of the swap space. The install process will not let you select a swap space that is smaller than the amount of space needed for that image. Here is the output you'll see on the screen:

```
NOTE: The swap size cannot be changed during the filesystem
    layout.

Enter a swap size between 384MB and 8691MB, default = 512MB [?]

The installer prefers that the swap slice is at the beginning
   of the disk. This will allow the most flexible filesystem
   partitioning later in the installation.

Can the swap slice start at the beginning
    [y,n,?q] y

You have selected the following to be used by the Solaris
    installer:

        Disk Slice : /dev/dsk/c0t0d0
```

```
        Size       : 512MB
        Start cyl. : 0

WARNING: ALL INFORMATION ON THE DISK WILL BE ERASED!

Is this OK [y,n,?q] y

The Solaris installer will use disk slice, /dev/dsk/c0t0d0s1.
After files are copied, the system will automatically reboot
   and Installation will continue.
Please Wait...

Copying mini-root to local disk….done.
Copying platform specific files....done.

Preparing to reboot and continue installation.
```

System Configuration

Once the system reboots, you will see the Welcome screen shown in Figure 3.3, which is the official beginning of the graphical part of the installation process. The Welcome screen lists the system and network configuration information you'll need to supply. This screen will appear for both an initial installation and an upgrade, but the steps that follow are different for each.

FIGURE 3.3
The installer Welcome screen

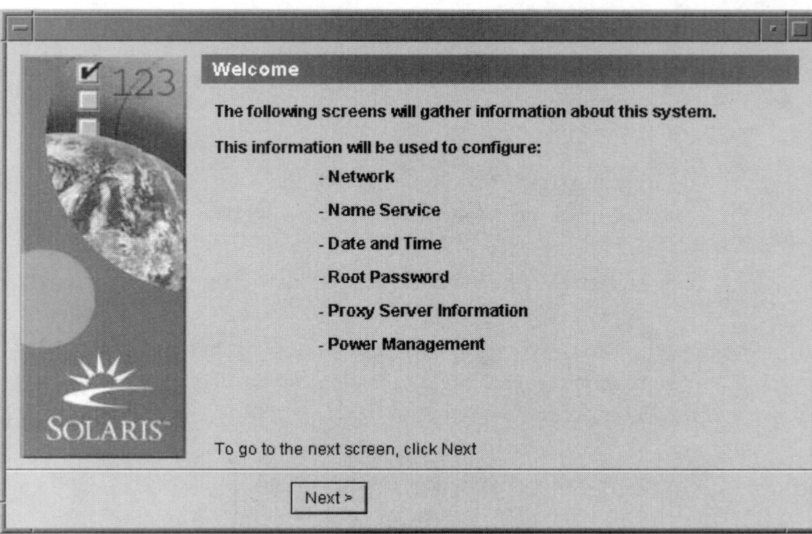

The second screen is called Network Connectivity and is shown in Figure 3.4. This dialog box alters your installation path. It offers you the choice of two different radio button options: Networked and Non-networked. Although Non-networked is the default installation, in most instances you will select the Networked radio button to allow Solaris to participate in networked services. The next screens will prompt you for the time zone, date and time, and root password.

FIGURE 3.4

The Network Connectivity dialog box

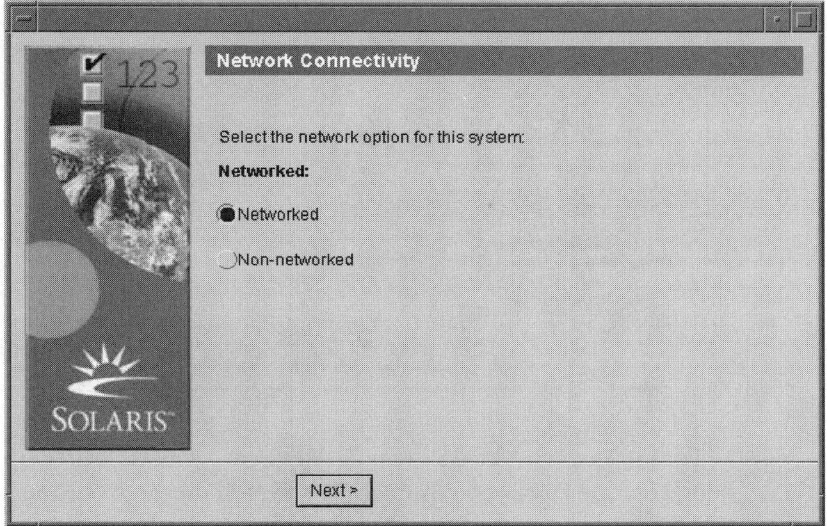

For a networked installation, the third screen is the DHCP screen. It allows you to determine whether your system will accept an IP address generated by a Dynamic Host Configuration Protocol (DHCP) server or whether you will have to enter a static IP address manually. This screen also sends you down two different installation paths. If you select No, you must enter the host name and IP address manually in the next screen.

If you enable DHCP, in the next set of screens you'll be asked to enable IPv6, provide the active name service, and enter the time zone, date and time, and root password.

When DHCP is not enabled, you will be asked to provide the host name, the IP address, and the netmask (subnet). You'll also be asked whether to enable IPv6 and to enter the name service in use. Figure 3.5 shows the Name Service screen, which prompts you to provide the type of database listing of network systems and resources that maps IP addresses to friendly names. When you enter a name service like NIS/NIS+ or DNS, the Domain Name screen appears asking you to enter the name of the domain that you wish this system to participate in. You might enter something like sosinsky-group.com as a domain name.

FIGURE 3.5
The Name Service screen

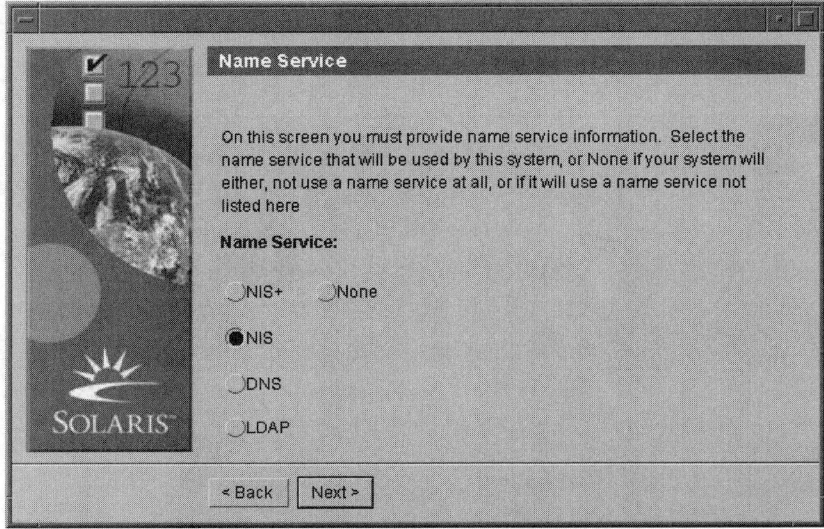

For the Domain Name System (DNS) service, you will be required to enter the IP address of the DNS server in the DNS Server Address screen. You must enter at least one DNS name server address. The DNS service may be provided internally on your network through a DNS server or by using one of the name servers available on the Internet at your ISP or on major sites. When possible, use an internal service because it will be faster and provide caching. In the next screen, DNS Name Server Address, you will be asked to enter in the DNS Search List box a list of domains to be searched when a DNS query is made. You should list your local domain first and then list additional domains in your enterprise; you can list any domain that you visit frequently as well. If you don't enter any domains in the list, Solaris searches your local domain only.

NOTE The sequence of steps that the Solaris 8 installer takes to configure name services and addressing is slightly different from one version of the installation to another.

For the other name services, you may be prompted to either automatically find a name server or to specify one in the Name Server screen. If you specify a name server, you will be prompted in the Name Server Information screen to enter the server's host name and IP address. Once the domain name is entered and the name services are specified, the next screens ask you to set the time zone, date and time, and root password for the system.

The next screen in the installation sequence is the Power Management screen shown in Figure 3.6. This screen lets you turn power management either on or off, and it also gives you the option of setting the power management characteristics of your system each time you reboot. The power management feature, which powers down your system after it is idle for 30 minutes, is automatically turned on by default.

WARNING Do not turn on the power management features for any system that needs to be reached across a network (like a server) because if that system is inactive for a while, it will go in to power-saving mode and will become unavailable to network users.

FIGURE 3.6
The Power Management screen

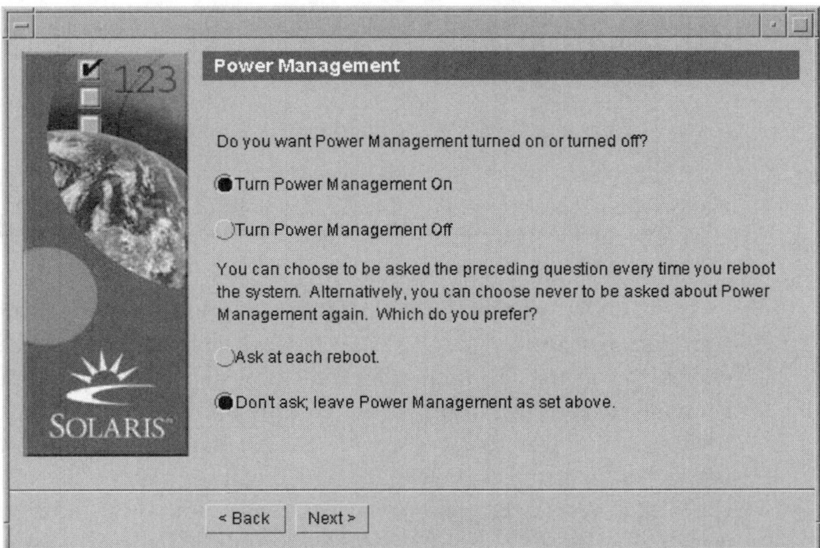

After you set the Power Management feature, you are prompted by the Proxy Server Configuration screen shown in Figure 3.7 to indicate whether you use a proxy server or not. If you have a workstation with a firewall between you and the Internet, leave the default choice, Direct Connection to the Internet, selected. For a network that contains a proxy service between you and the Internet (whether a firewall is used or not), you should enter the IP address of the proxy server in the Host text box and the number of the port used by the proxy service in the Port text box. Each proxy service uses a specific port number, and you should obtain this information from your system administrator if needed.

FIGURE 3.7
The Proxy Server Configuration screen

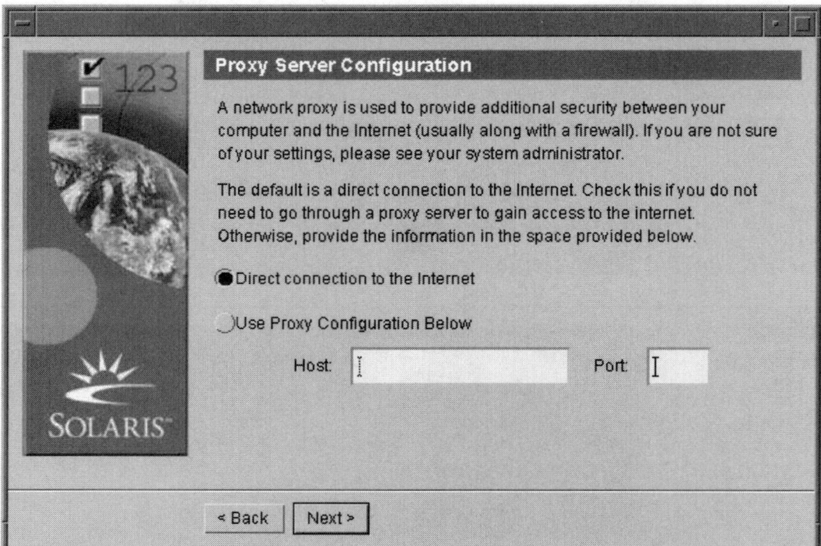

The last screen in the system configuration portion of the installation is the Confirm Information screen. It lists the choices you made and provides you with a final chance to backtrack through the installation steps and change your settings. It's a good idea to read this information carefully prior to confirming your selections. Click the Confirm button to proceed with the installation, and after a reboot, the Web Start portion of the installation will begin. You will see a system message, `Please wait while the system is configured with your settings...`, after which, if an error wasn't discovered, the Solaris Web Start Installation Kiosk is displayed.

Web Start

The Solaris Web Start Installation Kiosk, shown in Figure 3.8 with the Welcome screen, is a limited version of a browser running in the kiosk mode. You can't minimize the kiosk window, but all of the browser buttons are active and you can use them to obtain information and navigate the Web. The Sun BigAdmin page (`www.sun.com/sysadmin`) is the display's background at this stage in the installation. Should you use the browser and cover the installation screen, click the Send Kiosk to Background button in the left frame to display the screen again.

TIP The Kiosk allows you to search the Internet for information of interest. You can use this interface to search Sun's site for specific information that will help you figure out what configurations to specify in your installation.

Once you click the Next button on the Web Start Welcome screen, you will be prompted to insert the Solaris 8 Software CD and then Solaris will initialize your system. You will be taken to the Select Type of Install screen shown in Figure 3.9. There are two radio buttons on this screen: Default Install and Custom Install. The default installation sets up a set of partitions and selects a default set of software to install along with Solaris 8. Use the custom installation to set up your own partitions and determine which software packages you wish to install on your system.

FIGURE 3.8

The Web Start portion of the installation lets you configure Solaris while having an active working browser window (in kiosk mode) running in the background.

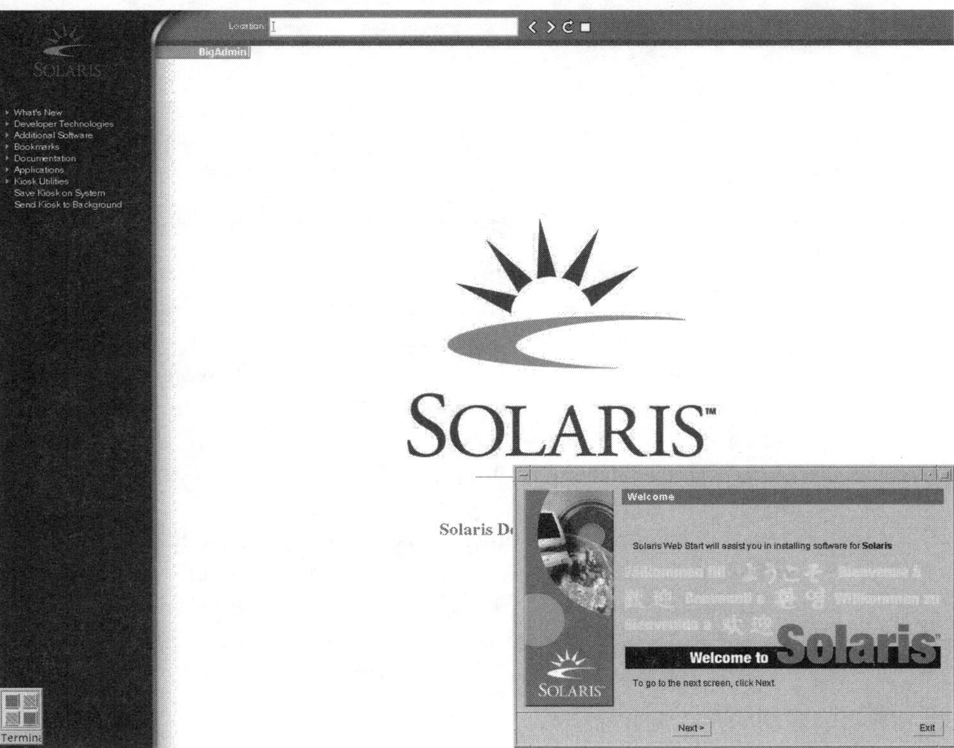

WARNING The choice you make in the Select Type of Install screen is critical to the installation process. If you accept the default installation, you won't be able to choose the size of your partitions and which software package to install or not install. It is recommended that you perform a custom installation, even if you accept the default choices that Solaris offers you.

FIGURE 3.9

In the Select Type of Install screen, you can choose the installation method.

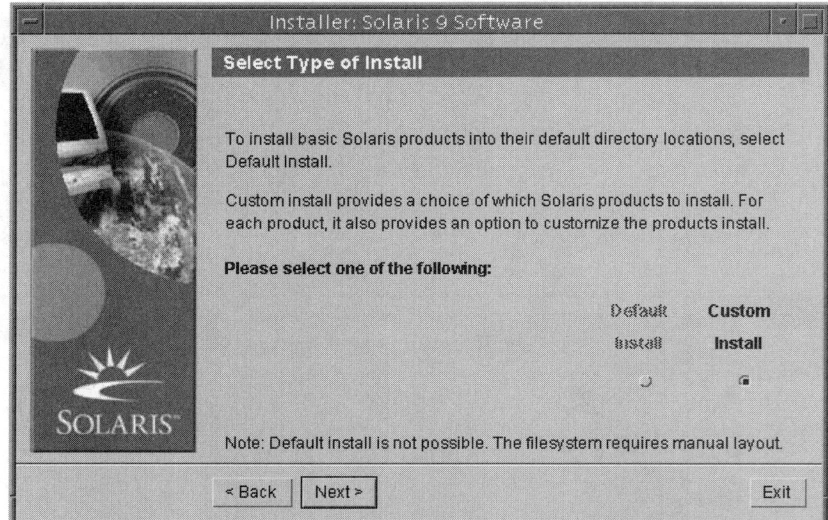

If you select a Custom Install, you will be prompted to select the software localizations you require, the system locale, which CDs and products you wish to install, and where Web Start should scan for additional products. You will also be asked if you wish to install 64-bit software along with the 32-bit version or just the 32-bit version of the operating system. In the next screen in the custom installation, you're asked which version of Solaris you wish to install: Core, End User, Developer, Entire, or Entire Solaris Software Group plus OEM. These selections were described earlier in this chapter in the section "Partitioning Schemes."

After you select your software install, you will be in the disk partitioning portion of Web Start. In this portion of the installation, you set up one or more disks to use with the partitions you desire. You use the Disk Selection screen (shown in Figure 3.10) to add the disks that your system has discovered to the file systems you will create. Click a disk in the Available Disks list box, then click the Add button to add it to the list of disks that can be partitioned. To remove a disk from use, click the disk name in the Selected Disks list box and click the Remove button. Click Next to proceed with the partitioning sequence.

FIGURE 3.10

The Disk Selection screen

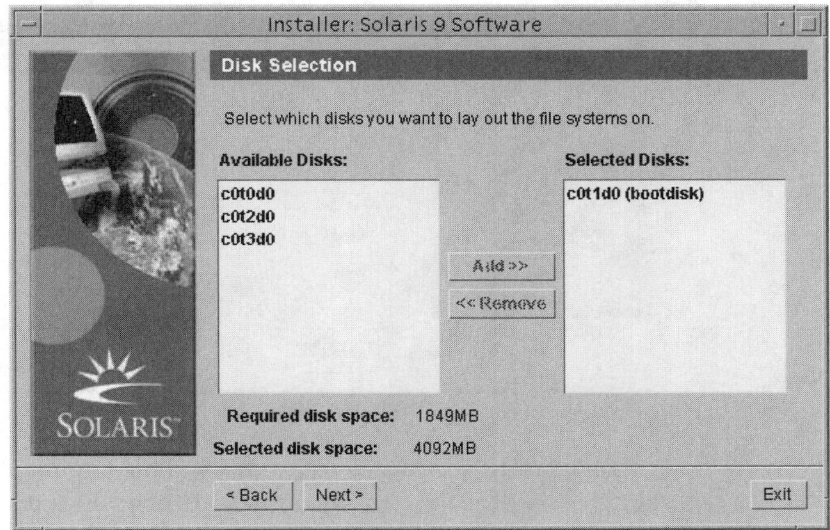

After the information about the amount of space the installer requires is collected, the Lay Out File Systems screen (shown in Figure 3.11) is posted. This screen shows you the minimum space requirements for your system software and allows you to create and modify your partition scheme.

WARNING Unless you click the Modify button and set up your desired partition scheme, you are accepting Solaris's default partitions. See "Partitioning Schemes" earlier in this chapter for advice on setting partition sizes.

Follow these steps to modify a disk's partitioning scheme:

1. Click the disk's name in the Lay Out File Systems screen.
2. Click the Modify button.
3. In the Disk Partitioning dialog box, enter the name of the file system you wish to create and the size of the partition, and click OK.

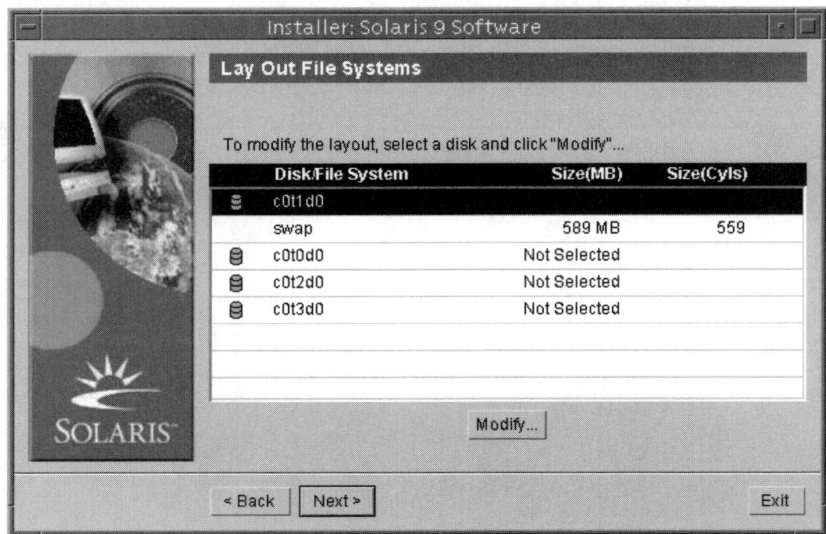

FIGURE 3.11 *The Lay Out File Systems screen*

The Disk Partitioning dialog box shows you the minimum size each partition must be as well as the capacity of the disk, how much disk space is allocated, and how much disk space is free.

4. Click the Next button when finished.

Solaris posts a confirmation screen and then displays the Installing screen as software is copied from the CDs to your drive(s). You will be prompted to insert the Solaris 8 (SPARC) Software 2 of 2 CD, and after a reboot, the installation will continue. After the software is copied, an Installation Summary screen is posted, showing which software was installed. You can click the Details button to view specific information or click the Next button to proceed with the rest of the installation routine.

NOTE You can also do a network installation from an install server or JumpStart server. The system software images are transferred over the network to your local machine. This installation is covered in the "Advanced Installation Guide," which should come with your distribution. It's also available from Sun at `http://docs.sun.com/ab2/coll.214.7/@Ab2CollView?Ab2Lang=C&Ab2Enc=iso-8859-1`.

Depending upon what components you indicated that you wish to install, the Solaris installer will request additional CD-ROM discs, such as the Documentation CD-ROM (for the Solaris AnswerBook2). It will then post progress screens and completion screens during the later stages of the installation, after which the installation will be complete.

Intel Installation

In most ways, the Solaris installation on Intel systems is identical to the installation on SPARC systems, which you have just read about. This section highlights the differences and explains what you must do to address these platform-specific issues. The main differences in the Intel installation is in the manner in which you format and partition your disk(s), the type of hardware detection that the installer does, and the way driver installation is handled.

Prior to beginning your installation of Solaris on Intel, you should prepare the partitions Solaris needs. If Solaris is the only operating system on your PC, you can use the Solaris installer to create the necessary partitions. If there is another operating system that shares this system with Solaris 8, use the partitioning software that is compatible with that operating system. For Windows, that software is `fdisk` or the commercial software package Partition Magic. Partition Magic is a worthwhile package to own because it supports multiple operating system launches such as Linux, NetWare, OS/2 Warp, and others.

You begin an Intel installation by inserting the Solaris 8 CD-ROM into your PC's CD-ROM drive. Some systems require that the computer be powered on prior to the insertion of the CD-ROM and others don't, so you may need to experiment. Also, many Intel-based PCs will not boot from the CD-ROM and will require that you insert the boot floppy for the Solaris on Intel installation into the floppy disk drive and reboot. You may find that the system's BIOS can be modified to boot from either the CD-ROM or floppy disk drive, and so you should check to see whether this setting exists first.

Once your system reboots, the Solaris Device Configuration Assistant (DCA) launches and offers you the following services:

Hardware identification You can use the F2 key to launch this detection sequence.

Diagnose scan failures You can use the F3 key to launch the diagnosis.

Add new drivers You can use the F4 key to add new hardware drivers to your system.

The scan portion of the DCA returns a list of all of the devices that the routine finds on your system. You will see something like the following appear:

```
The following devices have been identified on this system. To
Identify devices not on this list or to modify device
Characteristics, choose Device Task. Platform types may be
included in this list.
```

```
ISA: Floppy disk controller
ISA: IDE controller
ISA: Motherboard
ISA: PS/2 Mouse
 - more listed here --
ISA: PnP bios: ECP 1.x compatible parallel port
ISA: System keyboard (US-English)
```

When you press the F4 key, you display the Device Tasks screen, which lets you view and alter the following device characteristics:

- View/Edit Devices
- Set Keyboard Configuration
- Save Configuration
- Delete Saved Configuration
- Set Console Device

The default settings are generally best. When you press the F2 key in the Identified Devices screen, the Solaris installer begins to load the device drivers that are appropriate for each specific device that was discovered by the DCA. The process of installing drivers can take up to a few minutes, depending upon the complexity of the system, but once the drivers are loaded, you will see a list of the devices the Solaris installer has prepared that can boot the Solaris 8 operating system. Typically, that list contains a hard drive and a CD-ROM drive in the following format:

```
[] DISK: Target 0, (Manufacturer and Model are listed) on ISA
   bus at (location listed)
[] CD  : Target 0, Manufacturer and Model are listed) on ISA
   bus at (location listed)
```

To set the boot device, do the following:

1. Press the F4 key at the Boot Solaris screen.
2. In the Boot Tasks screen, select View/Edit Autoboot Settings and press the F2 key to view any devices from which you can boot Solaris.
3. Select the boot device desired and press the F2 key again to return to the View/Edit Autoboot Settings screen.
4. Select the Set Autoboot (ON/OFF) command, press the F2 key, and select the ON setting.
5. Press the F2 key to return to the View/Edit Autoboot Settings screen.
6. Select Accept Settings and press the F2 key.

7. After you are returned to the Boot Task screen, press the F3 key to save the setting. The device you selected as the boot device should be marked with an asterisk, as shown here:

```
[] DISK: (*) Target 0, (Manufacturer and Model are
  listed) on ISA bus at (location listed)
```

At this point in the installation, you should reboot your system. The boot device you selected will boot your system and guide the installation process. The screens posted by the installer and the procedure for installing Solaris on Intel are nearly identical to the procedure outlined in the section on installing SPARC earlier in this chapter. Refer to those instructions for further details.

StarOffice Installation

StarOffice is Sun's free office suite. Many people who use Solaris also install this program on their systems. StarOffice 5.2 ships with the Solaris 8 distribution. You can also download the software for free from Sun's Web site at `www.sun.com/software/star/staroffice/get/get.html`. If you purchase a new workstation from Sun, you'll find that StarOffice is preloaded.

Follow these steps to install StarOffice 5.2:

1. Insert the StarOffice 5.2 CD-ROM into your CD-ROM drive.
2. Open `/cdrom/english/solaris/office52` and double-click the `setup` script file.
3. The StarOffice installer launches and displays the Welcome screen shown in Figure 3.12.

FIGURE 3.12

The Welcome screen begins the StarOffice installation process.

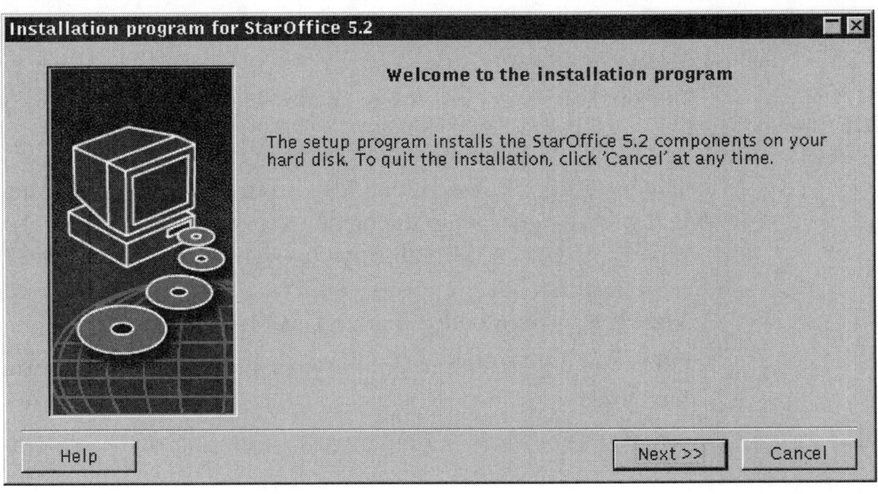

4. Click Next, accept the license, and fill in the registration screen. When you next click the Next button, you will see the Select Installation Type screen shown in Figure 3.13.

TIP If you need to install all of the filters, you may be better served doing a custom installation rather than the default installation.

FIGURE 3.13

Choose whether to install all or part of the StarOffice Suite in the Select Installation Type screen.

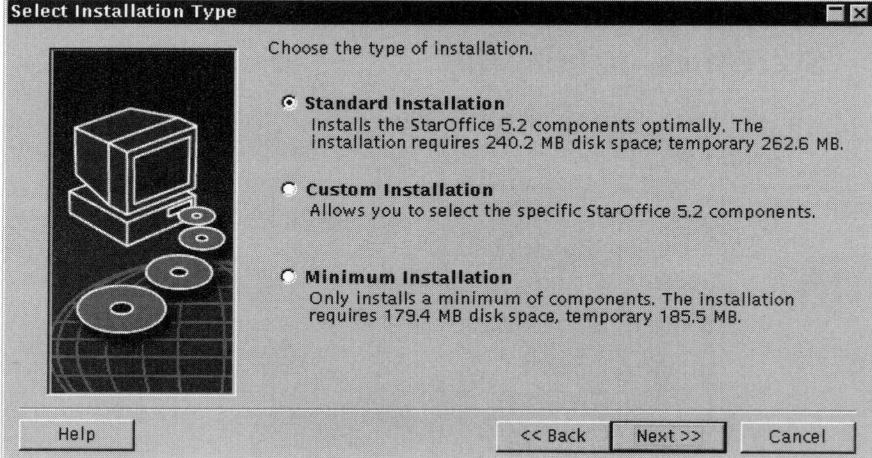

5. Click the Next button, and in the Select Installation Directory screen, either accept the default directory (`/office52`) or enter another. Then click the Next button. Solaris will ask you to create the directory, if necessary.
6. In the Start Copying screen, click the Complete button to initiate the installation.

   The installer will search for a Java Runtime Environment, and if it finds one, it will post the Java Setup dialog box shown in Figure 3.14. The Java Setup dialog box displays each Java Runtime Environment found by the StarOffice installer. Enabling this option allows you to use StarOffice components to browse the Web. It is recommended that you enable this option.
7. Click the OK button to enable Java support and to continue installing the StarOffice suite.

FIGURE 3.14

Set up the Java Runtime Environment in the Java Setup dialog box.

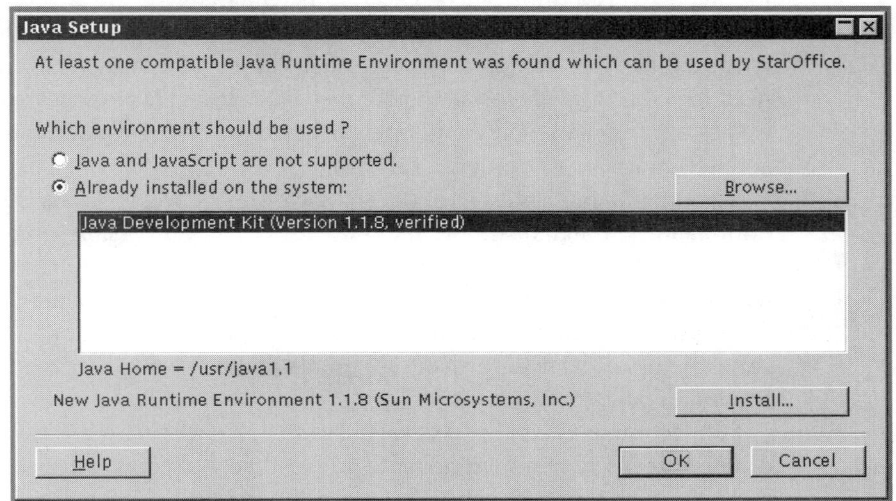

The installer displays some informational screens in the main window and a clock with a progress bar in the left frame. When the installation is complete, the installer posts a dialog box that indicates that an icon was added to the front panel, as shown in the following graphic. Finally when you click the OK button, an Installation Complete dialog box appears.

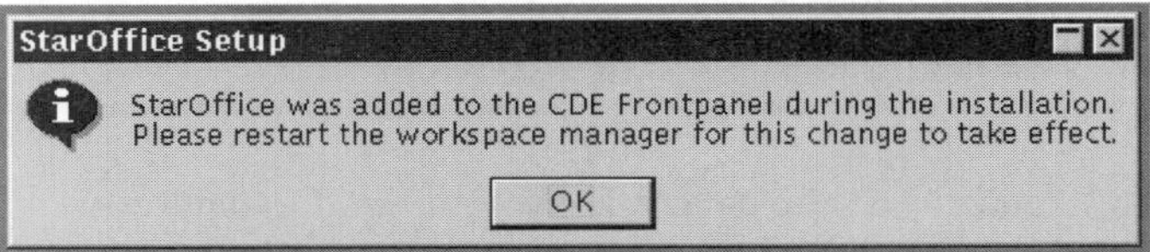

8. Click the Complete button to end the installation.

After you complete the StarOffice installation, the Adabas D installation launches. This installer installs components necessary for StarOffice Base (the StarOffice database program) in the /adabas directory unless you change its location during the installation. If you don't want this feature, you can skip this part of the installation.

Patches

A patch is a software upgrade of your operating system. Many large software programs such as StarOffice, the Apache Web server, and others also may have patches released for them. You can think of a patch as an incremental upgrade of your software. Indeed, Sun has a policy of releasing new versions of the Solaris operating system every quarter, and thus the company provides a patch for previous versions that eliminates the need to do an Upgrade Install to your system. Patches are also released for hardware as well as software and typically to upgrade device drivers. A patch can either fix bugs or add new functionality, or it can do both.

You can obtain patches from the SunSolve Online Web site (`www.sunsolve.sun.com`) or from Sun through distribution CD-ROMs. Whenever possible, especially if you have a fast pipe to the Internet, downloading patches from the SunSolve Web site is the preferred method. If you have a SunSolve subscription or support agreement, you may have access to additional patches, a database of patch information, a troubleshoot and issue resolution database, and other resources such as white papers and an e-mail notification of patch releases.

Sun recommends that you install all of the patches that it releases for Solaris. This certainly keeps your system current and is unlikely to get you into serious trouble, but there are some things to consider. Each patch is a little different, and although each patch solves many more problems than it creates, you may find an additional incompatibility that didn't exist before you installed the last patch. Therefore, many companies either install only the necessary patches or avoid patch installation on production equipment as much as possible.

TIP It is always a good idea to install patches on a test system before applying them to production systems.

You can use the `patchadd -p` command to determine which patches have already been applied to your system. Once you have downloaded the patches you have decided to install, use the `patchadd` command to apply them your system. Each patch contains installation information that describes the fixes the patch applies and any new features it adds. You should read the patch information prior to installing the patch. It's not a bad idea to test a patch prior to widespread use, if that is possible.

Sun supplies patches for applications that run on Solaris. However, the software upgrades that you obtain from third-party sources, for either hardware or software, may or may not use the patch system and may or may not be supplied as a package format. A patch or a package installation is something you should install only after you have considered its source and its purpose. A patch from another vendor can introduce instability into your system, or even be a source of viruses. Thus some commonsense caution needs to be observed in their use.

Summary

There are several different Solaris 8 distributions that you can employ to install Solaris on your system. The Sun Web site offers a free download of the software, a developer distribution, and versions for noncommercial (home and educational) and commercial use. Sun prices its commercial distributions based on the number of processors in your system, with the basic OS version good for up to eight CPUs.

In this chapter, you learned about the different types of Solaris installations: Web Start, Interactive, Network, and JumpStart. The installation described in detail in this chapter is the Web Start installation. You use a different initial setup routine for other installations but many of the same steps once the Solaris installer is launched.

Prior to installing Solaris, you should collect the important network information that the installer requires. You should also determine the partition and file system scheme that you will employ. This chapter gave you specific recommendations about the different partitions and file systems that people use. When you create partitions on an Intel x86 system with another operating system, you must use a different partitioning program.

This chapter described Solaris installation on a SPARC workstation in detail. The installation can take a couple of hours and requires you to enter the information necessary to identify the system over the network and to provide access to network services such as DHCP and to name services such as NIS, NIS+, DNS, and others. Additionally, the StarOffice installation was covered in this chapter.

Over time, Sun makes available bug fixes and upgrades through a series of patches that you can apply to Solaris, your hardware, and application programs. Other vendors may also release upgrades of this type. Your needs to stay current and eliminate particular problems should be weighed against introducing incompatibilities in determining whether to apply these patches.

CHAPTER 4

Basic Operations

FEATURING:

Startup options 92

Logging in 102

The common desktop environment 105

Terminal and console windows 107

Exiting the CDE and OpenWindows 117

This chapter presents some basic information about starting up, operating in, and exiting from Solaris 8. It covers both the Intel version of Solaris and the Scalable Processor ARChitecture (SPARC) version. I'll cover a variety of fundamental issues pertaining to the two main desktop environments—the Common Desktop Environment (CDE) and OpenWindows—and to the Command Line Interface (CLI), including what you see on your screen as your computer boots up and what options you can set.

After a quick tour of the SPARC hardware, you'll learn different ways to log in to the operating system, such as the GUI login (`dtmanager`), X terminal and X terminal emulator programs, and the command-line login. The chapter will cover some basic configuration options for both desktops, such as opening a terminal and console window. You will also find an introduction to using the Solaris file system, as well as a discussion of how to properly exit your system and shut down gracefully. There are numerous command-line utilities that can help a user and system administrator find and manipulate files and directories. This chapter touches on these utilities, providing a basic reference. They are covered in greater detail in subsequent chapters.

After the session is through, you must perform an `exit` command from the CDE and OpenWindows desktops to return to the logon screen. The user then has the option of starting another CDE or OpenWindows session, going to the command line, or shutting down the server gracefully. If the desktop session and operating system are not shut down gracefully, the file system and system configuration files may be inconsistent and possibly damaged. Cases where a more forceful method for closing your session, such as using the `shutdown` command, are also covered in this chapter.

Startup

The Intel version of Solaris runs on a wide variety of systems, from small home computers to large-scale Compaq servers. The home personal computers (IBM PC compatible) can boot from different devices, such as a floppy disk, CD-ROM (on newer hardware), and the primary hard drive. Most likely, you will not have to change your Intel system's BIOS to accommodate the Solaris 8 operating system. When your computer starts, there is usually a BIOS breakout option like F1 or Ctl+Alt+Esc you can use to enter the system BIOS. The BIOS on personal computers varies a great deal due to the large number of manufacturers of system boards and the BIOS chips manufacturers can select from. Once you have entered the BIOS interface, there will be an option to select the boot device from a menu of choices.

You can select other devices to boot before the hard drive. The only catch is that any device you specify cannot have bootable material in it during the boot phase. Suppose, for example, that your BIOS has this boot option:

```
CDROM A: C:
```

The CD-ROM drive is checked to see if there is a disc in it. If there is, then the BIOS tries to read a boot section on the device. If the BIOS doesn't find a boot section, it displays the error message `Non-bootable device in the CDROM drive, press any key to continue`. This message can vary depending on the BIOS chips installed on the motherboard and the firmware version of those chips. The exact same process occurs for the floppy disk.

Higher-end Intel-based servers tend to have some special BIOS features that are similar to what you might see on a desktop PC. The setup of these servers is beyond the scope of this book. Consult your owner's or system administrator's manual for the steps necessary for system startup.

WARNING Some high-end servers, such as Compaq's Storage Array servers, have special utilities on the first sector. Do not delete this partition. This partition contains the boot (F10) utilities that are used to diagnose and change hardware settings.

On the SPARC hardware platform, there are some basic OK PROM (programmable read-only memory) options that must be set on the system before the operating system will start automatically during a server power-on. These options specify the default boot device and determine if the server should boot automatically when powered on.

The Console Port and OK Prompt

Almost all Sun servers and desktops have a hardware direct interface known as the console port. The *console port* is typically a standard serial port (DB-25 female connector) or an RJ-45 connector. This port gives the system administrator direct access to the system board's chips and some hardware-connected devices. The console port is active whenever the system is powered on. It does not rely on the operating system. You can access the console port even on a server or workstation that does not have a hard disk installed.

To work with the console port, you will need to purchase a null modem cable. The null modem cable is designed to connect 9-pin and 25-pin COM ports together with a pin 2 and 3 wired crossover. A null modem cable is best purchased from most major electronics stores or computer stores rather than jerry-rigged together because an improperly wired modem cable can damage your computer. When you install a Sun server for the first time, you may want to connect a laptop computer to the server by connecting the null modem cable to the back of the laptop's 9-pin COM1 port and the Sun server's console port. In cases where the console port is an RJ-45 connector, such as on some Netra servers, special cables need to be purchased from Sun.

TIP Once the null modem cable is attached between a standard PC COM port and the console port on the Sun server or desktop, you can use the HyperTerminal software that is supplied with Microsoft's Windows operating system (Windows 9*x*, ME, NT, or 2000 all have HyperTerminal) to access the OK prompt. You need to set up HyperTerminal to match your server's or desktop's requirements.

TIP As a general rule of thumb, set up HyperTerminal as a VT100 terminal with the following settings: 9600 baud, no parity, 8 data bits, 1 stop bit, hardware flow control, and 500 lines scroll back. You can set this up using the Properties dialog box, opened using the Properties command on the File menu.

With a null modem cable attached to a laptop's COM port and the server's or desktop's console port, you should start HyperTerminal and power on the Sun Solaris computer. An OK prompt appears within the HyperTerminal screen. So what is this OK prompt? If you ever watch an Intel-based computer start up, you will notice that there is a brief moment where you can press F1 (or some other key combination) and then you can make changes to the system's BIOS. Sun servers and desktops have something equivalent to your PC's BIOS. It's called the PROM (programmable read-only memory). It's commonly referred to as the OK prompt.

The console port has two uses. Before the operating system is running, the console port displays the OK prompt. The OK prompt interface is burned directly into the programming logic on the motherboard and will operate even without a hard drive or operating system installed. This interface gives a system administrator direct access to the main system board chips. After the operating system starts, the console port is used for a console session.

Here is an easy way to understand this concept:

- The console port is the hardware interface to the main system board.
- The OK prompt is the communication with the system board before the operating system starts.

- The console session is the communication with the operating system after the operating system has started.

The OK prompt is based on the Forth programming language and, as mentioned earlier, is burned directly into one of the system board's chips. After the operating system starts, the console port can be used for a console session or term session. *Term session* refers to the fact that you can attach a terminal server to the console port.

TIP A terminal server is basically a device that makes a connection from the network to the console port. On one end of the device is a standard Ethernet port. On the other end is a cable that connects directly to the back end of a Sun server's console port. If the server goes down for some reason, a terminal server gives you direct access over the network to the console port and hence the system board of your server. If a server is local, you might not need a terminal server, but if a server is located in a remote location or another state, it is extremely handy to have a direct connection to the back of your box.

A console session works just like a Telnet session. It is a command-line interface directly to the operating system. No GUI applications can run through a console port.

Boot Options

For a Sun server or workstation to boot automatically on power-up, the OK prompt value `auto-boot?` must be set to `TRUE`. To see the current OK prompt values, type this command:

```
printenv
```

The results should look something like Figure 4.1. The actual output varies depending on the type of server and the firmware version of the chips on the system board.

The last piece of information that is needed to specify the boot-up is the actual boot device itself. The OK prompt variable *<boot-device>* must be specified. This variable is set by default to the hardware device aliases `disk` and `net`. Most of the time, the alias `disk` refers to the first boot device, `c0t0`. The device alias `net` indicates that Solaris will boot off of the network card. If the first boot device specified is `disk` and that device is not available, the second device can be tried (depending on some other OK prompt values, such as `watchdog-reset`). During the installation of Solaris 8, the install program will prompt you to change the boot device to match the install options. This install option is manually changing the *<boot-device>* variable during installation. Chapter 3, "Getting Started," goes into greater detail on installation and troubleshooting install problems.

FIGURE 4.1

The `printenv` command at the OK prompt

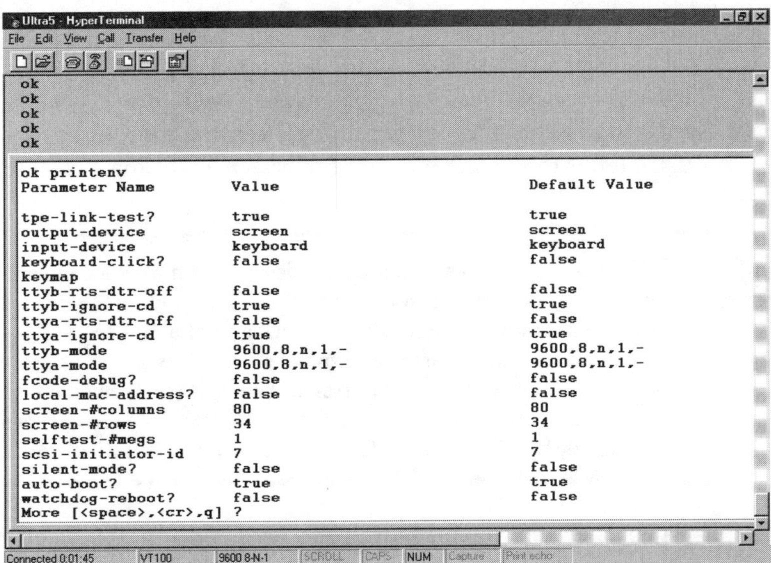

You might have to change the boot device after you install Solaris 8. For example, a Sunstation 5 workstation boots to the device `c0t3` by default, but it can also be set up to boot to `c0t0` if a second hard drive is installed in the workstation.

The `boot` command has several boot options:

`boot -s` The command `boot -s` starts the server or desktop in the single-user mode. Single-user mode allows the system administrator to enter run level 1 (the default run level is 3).

`boot cdrom -s` One of the most useful commands is `boot cdrom -s`, entered at the OK prompt with a bootable Solaris disk in your CD-ROM drive. This command runs a memory-based operating system from which you can mount the hard drives and perform system administration.

`boot -a` The command `boot -a` starts the operating system in interactive mode. This presents the system administrator with several questions regarding the boot process.

`boot -r` The command `boot -r` checks for new devices and rebuilds the `/dev` and `/devices` directories.

`boot -d` The command `boot -d` runs a very extensive series of diagnostic tests. This topic is covered in Chapter 21, "Troubleshooting."

To start the operating system, just type the following command:

```
boot disk
```

If the *<boot-device>* alias is set up correctly, you can type just this:

```
boot
```

Halting or Freezing the Operating System

For a SPARC system, when the operating system is running, the user can press the Stop and A keys simultaneously on a Sun keyboard to break out of the operating system and go directly to the OK prompt. If the user has an Intel keyboard or is working from a terminal, the keystrokes Ctrl+Pause or Ctrl+Break will usually send the same signal to a server. Either way of invoking the OK prompt from the operating system causes the operating system to essentially "freeze." Changes can be made at the OK prompt (in some very limited instances) and then the user can type **go** at the prompt to return to the operating system.

WARNING The Stop+A keystroke is considered to be very dangerous to use on production-level and mission-critical servers because the operating system might not start up again properly. When the operating system is frozen, time-stamped critical databases and other running programs might become confused and can crash.

The Intel version of Solaris 8 does not have any type of Stop+A or Ctl+Break option that will work on desktop or home PCs. The BIOS on these machines is not set up to take commands from `eeprom` either.

Run Levels

Solaris 8 has eight different run levels. Each run level gives the user access to certain resources and access levels. Server resources are basically turned on or shut off depending on the current run level. For example, certain network services may be shut off if the system is multiuser, and different network services will be shut off if the system is single user. The operating system can run at only one run level at a time; it would be impossible to run at level 0 and level 3 at the same time. Table 4.1 gives a brief description of the Solaris run levels.

TABLE 4.1: THE SOLARIS RUN LEVELS

Run Level	Description
0	Power Down state. This brings the operating system down from any run level to the OK prompt. With Intel-based architecture machines, it is safe to shut down the machine at this run level.
S or s	Single User state. This is the state where only the root user can access the server. This state is typically used when maintenance is needed.
1	Administrative state. This is very similar to run level S except that the only file systems that are mounted are the root (/) and the `/usr` file systems. If `/usr` is not a separate file system, it is still accessible.
2	Multiuser state. In this state, multiple users can telnet or have other types of sessions on the server. Resources such as file and print services are not exported.
3	Multiuser state with Resources Exported. In this state, file and print resources can be exported (provided the root user wants to export these resources). Multiple users can access the system at the same time.
4	Undefined.
5	Power Down state. There are some workstations that support this mode of operation. Most system administrators do not use or like this setting when it comes to production-level servers.
6	Reboot. This cycles the server from its current run level to run level 0 and then back to the default run level (run level 3).

Control Scripts

For each run level, there is a series of run level control scripts that execute. These scripts are called on from the `init` process after it reads the `/etc/inittab` file. They take care of some basic "housecleaning" chores such as starting the FTP service, starting the DNS service, and other tasks.

The following subdirectories contain the run level control scripts:

```
/etc/rc0.d
/etc/rc1.d
/etc/rc2.d
/etc/rc3.d
/etc/rcS.d
```

Each of these subdirectories has a series of shell scripts that have the following naming convention: `[K , S] [0-9] [0-9] [ASCII name]`. The script's name can start with a *K* or an *S*. The next two characters are the numbers 0 through 9, and finally, an ASCII name follows. For example, in the `/etc/rc2.d` directory, you may find the files shown in Figure 4.2 on a Sun Ultra 5 workstation.

FIGURE 4.2

The `/etc/rc2.d` directory, containing scripts associated with run level 2

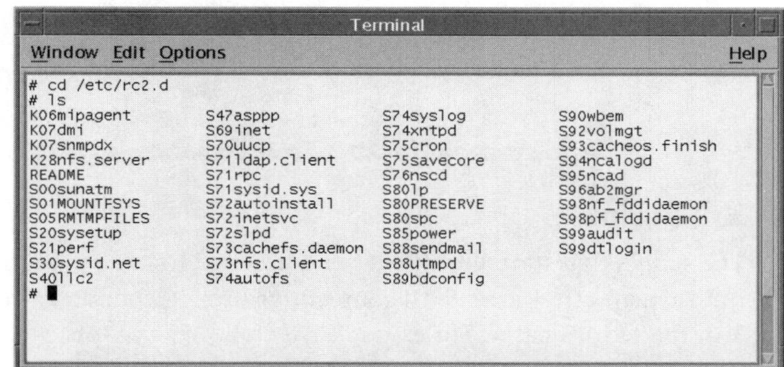

These scripts in the run level subdirectories are all Bourne shell scripts. Almost all of the scripts in the `rc?.d` directories are hard links to `/etc/init.d`, although there are a couple of exceptions, as well as a few soft links from the scripts in the `rc?.d` directories to the scripts in the `/etc/init.d` directory. You can edit them, create additional scripts, or disable them to completely customize your server or workstation. There are also some scripts that are symbolically linked back to the `/etc/init.d` directory. To become more familiar with scripts, take a close look at one startup script in particular, `S89bdconfig`, which is a soft link to the file `/etc/init.d/buttons_n_dials-setup`. This script contains only one functional line (other than comments), as you can see in Figure 4.3. Be aware that if you change these scripts, in most cases you will not be able to revert back to the original script unless you first save the file as a backup copy (always a good idea).

Any line that starts with a # symbol is just a comment and any text behind the # is completely ignored. The only functional line in this script is `/usr/sbin/bdconfig` with the argument `startup`. The Sun Microsystems engineers decided to put in a line `/usr/sbin/bdconfig status` as a commented line. If `bdconfig`'s operation is of particular importance to your server, you can uncomment the line for verbose output when `bdconfig` runs.

FIGURE 4.3

Some scripts contain very simple instructions calling other programs or routines.

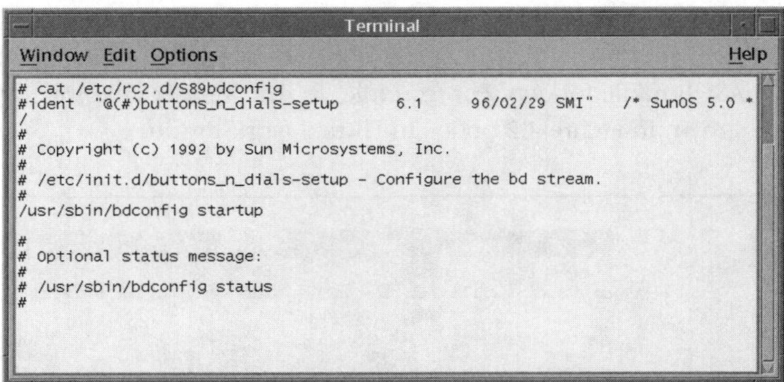
Terminal
Window Edit Options Help
cat /etc/rc2.d/S89bdconfig
#ident "@(#)buttons_n_dials-setup 6.1 96/02/29 SMI" /* SunOS 5.0 *
/
#
Copyright (c) 1992 by Sun Microsystems, Inc.
#
/etc/init.d/buttons_n_dials-setup - Configure the bd stream.
#
/usr/sbin/bdconfig startup
#
Optional status message:
#
/usr/sbin/bdconfig status
#

Kill Scripts

The scripts that start with the letter *K* are used to kill a process. All of the K scripts are run first, and they are run in consecutive order, depending on the number behind the *K* in the script's name. For example, the following scripts, which are only examples, would run in this order:

```
K01cde
K21netproc
K35bpsdaff
```

The `K01cde` script would be executed first because it has the number 01 directly behind the letter *K*. The `K21netproc` script would be executed next because 21 follows 01 in numeric order. The `K35bpsdaff` script would be executed last because of the numeric order of 35. It is possible to have the two scripts `K01cde` and `K01zzz` in the same directory. The first script to run would be `K01cde`, followed by `K01zzz`. The `cde` script would run first because the c in *cde* comes before the *z* in *zzz*.

After all the K run control scripts have been run, all the S run control scripts execute. The same rules of numeric order apply to the execution of these scripts as well.

TIP A simple way to disable a script is to change the letter *K* or *S* to *disabledK* or *disabledS*. The script `S72mscdf` will execute, but the script `disabledS72mscdf` will not. Any script that does not start with a *K* or an *S* is simply ignored without any negative consequences.

Init Process

In addition to the execution of the run control scripts, the `init` process checks the `/etc/inittab` file during the boot process. Each entry in the `inittab` file has the following format:

```
id:runlevel:action:process
```

There is one special line in the `/etc/inittab` file that tells the system which default run level it should start up in. The line is similar to this:

```
is:3:initdefault:
```

It can be used to tell Solaris to boot to a different run level than 3. For example, 2 would be used if you want to make sure the system comes up without exporting any file systems. The `init` process starts the other processes when the indicated run level is reached. To determine the current run level, type the following command at the command prompt:

```
who -r
```

Here is a typical output for this command:

```
run-level 3 Feb 6 15:25 3  0  S
```

Shutdown Commands

To shut the server down gracefully from the console port, there are several commands you can type. This command will bring the server back down to the OK prompt:

```
init 0
```

Another way to shut down the server is to use the following command:

```
shutdown -y -g60 -i0 "server is coming down"
```

This command will send the message `Server is coming down` to all the users and designate a 60-second (g60) delay before the shutdown process starts. When the server is at the OK prompt, it is safe to turn off the power. No file system or configuration file damage will occur.

WARNING Never power off a server if it is not at run level 0 (the OK prompt). The file system can become badly damaged and need repair if the server "crashes" or has sudden power loss. Also, the configuration files could contain errors. If the file system is damaged beyond repair or the configuration files are badly damaged, a server tape restore or a server partial rebuild may be your only option.

The GUI Login Screen

The console port is a useful tool for system administrators to gain access to the server's hardware and operating system. The only problem with the console port is that only one user can use it at a time. To have a true multiuser system, users need to have access to the server through a Telnet session, terminals, or some other multiuser connections.

TIP A security feature in Solaris 8 prevents the root user from telneting into the server. The root user needs to have direct console access or direct monitor/keyboard/mouse access to a system to use the system. This makes it harder for hackers to attack the system from the network because it denies them the opportunity to log in as root through a Telnet connection and work on the system with superuser privileges. This security feature can be disabled, but it is not recommended. You can log in as a regular user and then use the `su` command to gain root access.

If you want to log in remotely, you will need to use a utility like Telnet to do so. To create a Telnet session, you need to create a generic user account. Type the following command in at the console port with root privileges:

```
useradd -m -d /usr/user12 user12
```

This creates a user named user12 with a home directory of `/usr/user12`. To set the user's password, type the following command:

```
passwd user12
New password :
Re-enter new password:
(Selected CodeList)
```

Select a password that you can easily remember. If for some reason you forget the user's password, just retype the command **`passwd user12`**. This will reset a new password for user12. For security reasons, only the root user can reset a password. There is no file or other location that will let you see a user's password. If a password is forgotten, the only option available is to create a new one. The reason for this is security. You don't want to give a hacker a chance at reading a password file.

WARNING If you type the command **passwd** by itself, you will change the root user's password.

Now that a generic user account has been created, a Telnet session is possible. To perform a Telnet session, you need another operating system that has a Telnet window available. All standard Unix operating systems have a Telnet window, and Microsoft Windows 9*x*, ME, NT, and 2000 all come with Telnet windows. To initiate a Telnet session, type one of the following commands, where 136.14.32.18 is an IP address and `goose` is a recognized hostname of a machine hosting a Telnet session:

```
telnet 136.14.32.18
telnet goose
```

Within the Microsoft Windows 9*x* family, a Telnet window will pop up and then you can start a Telnet session. The Telnet screen is just a text-based interface to the operating system. It is not possible to "see" graphics through a Telnet session.

To "see" a GUI through Microsoft Windows, you need an X Windows terminal emulator. Exceed software produced by Hummingbird Ltd. (`www.hummingbird.com`) makes a high-quality X-terminal emulator. It allows you to access Unix-based applications (X clients) from within the Microsoft Windows environment. Linux also has a built in X-terminal emulator that brings GUI applications to your desktop.

The *dtlogin* GUI

The Solaris operating system has a GUI login manager called `dtlogin`. (The exact details of `dtlogin` are covered in Chapter 7, "The Solaris Desktop.") When you log in to a Solaris server, from either an X-terminal emulator or from a screen and keyboard directly attached to the workstation itself, you'll see the screen shown in Figure 4.4.

This screen is the GUI interface to the `dtlogin` manager. It includes a text field in which you can enter your username and password. There are four buttons at the bottom of the screen:

OK Works the same as pressing the Enter key

Start Over Resets the `dtlogin` manager and restarts the session

Options Opens a drop-down menu with four selections:

- Change the session language used (such as English, French, German, etc.).
- Choose how to start the session. The options are CDE Desktop Environment, OpenWindows Desktop Environment, User's Last Desktop, or Failsafe Session. The CDE desktop and OpenWindows desktop are graphical user interfaces. Normally the User's Last Desktop option is selected. If you are having a problem logging in, the Failsafe Session option lets you log in with a minimal desktop environment (limited driver support) so that you can fix whatever problem has arisen with your login procedure.

- Start a text session (Command Line Login).
- Quit the program (Return to Local Host).

Help Gives further advice on the use of GUI login

FIGURE 4.4

The desktop login screen

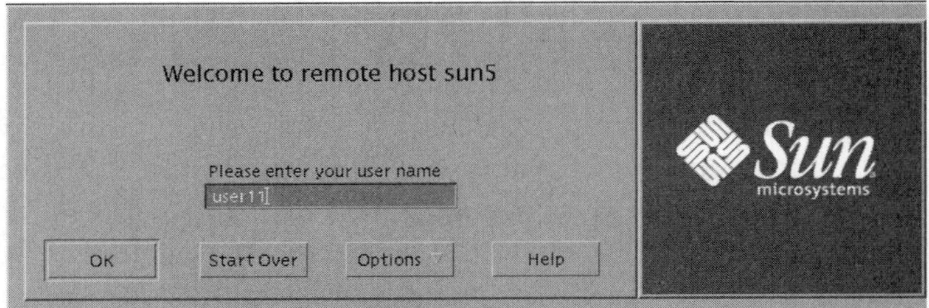

The first time a user logs in to the desktop, they are given the option of choosing a CDE desktop or an OpenWindows desktop. The `dtlogin` manager will ask for this selection only the first time. Any further logins to the system will take the user to the desktop they used in their last login session. If you select the CDE, you'll see a screen that looks like the screen in Figure 4.5.

FIGURE 4.5

The CDE desktop

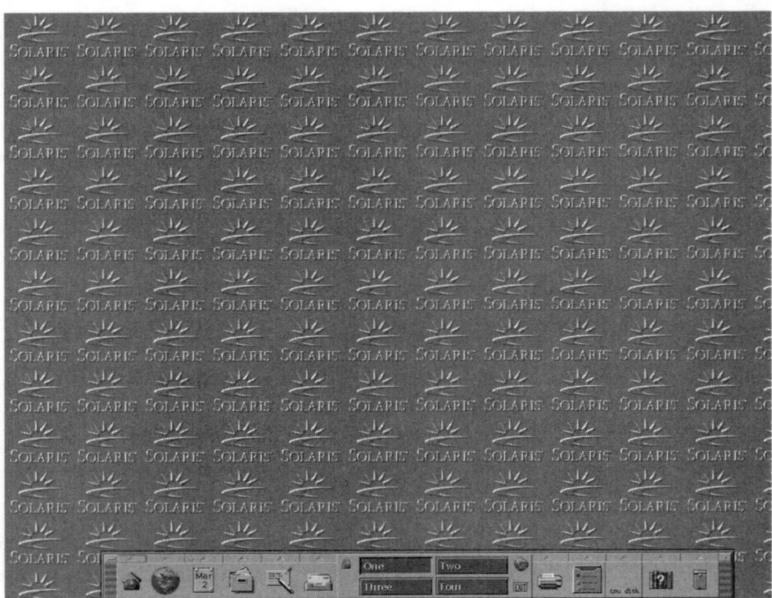

NOTE Sun is planning on removing OpenWindows from its distribution of Solaris, and therefore your time is best spent learning and becoming familiar with the CDE instead.

Customize the CDE Desktop

There are two desktop environments that come by default with Sun Solaris 8: the Common Desktop Environment (CDE) and the OpenWindows desktop. The CDE desktop has two main features: the front panel and a Workspace menu.

The front panel is shown in Figure 4.5, at the bottom of the CDE desktop. The front panel has several drawers, each with a prominent icon on the front. You can select the icon (for `dtmailtool`, Internet browser, Calendar, etc.) or select a subpanel icon by clicking the tiny arrow above the drawer. There are also four desktop buttons labeled One, Two, Three, and Four. These buttons allow you to switch between four different desktops. As you will see in Chapter 7, the desktop button feature is customizable, and you can add or remove buttons or rename them as you desire.

In addition to the front panel, there is a Workspace menu. It pops up when you right-click (button 3) anywhere in the unoccupied desktop environment. The front panel also features the Exit button.

OpenWindows, the other desktop that comes with Sun Solaris, does not feature the front panel. It features only a Workspace menu and some miscellaneous icons (such as Trash). The Workspace menu pops up when you right-click anywhere in the unoccupied desktop. (Chapter 7 covers the CDE and OpenWindows in greater detail.)

When you log in to the CDE for the first time, a series of windows will open automatically by default: the Solaris User Registration window, the File Manager window (*hostname : username*), and the Help viewer (showing the "Introducing the Desktop" topic).

TIP One of the default applications that keeps appearing is the User Registration package. There are two buttons at the bottom of the Window: Register and More Information. You can choose to register the software or select More Information. If you select More Information, a new page is displayed with three new buttons at the bottom. You can select Never Register. As a system administrator, you can customize the software installation during the system installation. One of the software packages you can choose not to select is the User Registration package. That would be an appropriate choice if the workstation or server has been properly purchased in a corporate environment.

After you log out of the CDE, only the windows you choose to keep open when you leave will reappear (with the exception of the Solaris User Registration window) when you open the CDE desktop again. The CDE desktop "remembers" your last desktop and saves the configurations. You can change the behavior of CDE in this regard.

Chapter 7 discusses how to manipulate windows in great detail. You should be aware, though, that there is a small button with a dash (–) on it in the upper-left corner of the window border. This is known as the Window menu button. If you left-click it, a pop-up menu called the Window menu is displayed. From here, you can choose various options to manipulate the window, such as Maximize, Minimize, Close, and so on.

You can use the Application Manager to customize the CDE. Open the Application Manager by clicking the Applications drawer on the front panel and selecting the Applications command. On the Application Manager window (shown in Figure 4.6) are icons that open applications you can use to customize your desktop. These applications interact with the Session Manager. (The Session Manager is covered in greater detail in Chapter 7. Basically, it is responsible for starting the desktop and saving the state of the desktop when you log out.)

FIGURE 4.6
The Application Manager's desktop controls

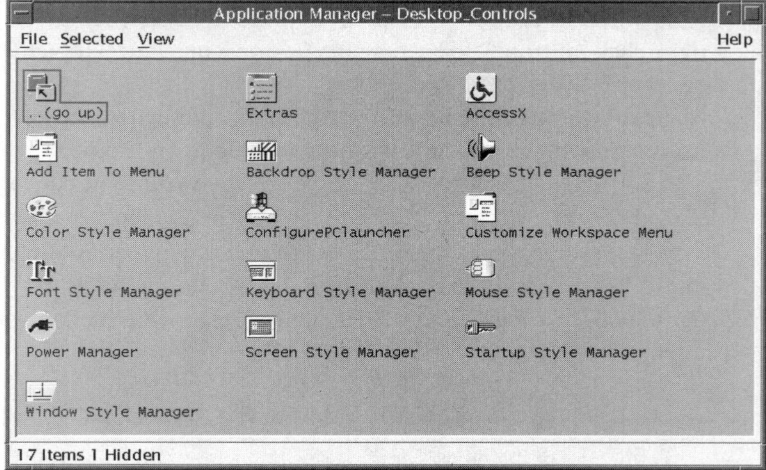

Customize OpenWindows

To customize the OpenWindows environment, right-click (button 3) anywhere in unoccupied desktop space to access the Workspace menu. At the bottom of the Workspace menu is an item called Properties. The menu selections offer you the following choices:

Color Change the foreground color, background color, and so on.

Keyboard Turn off/on keyboard clicks, repetition of characters, and keyboard strokes that emulate the mouse.

Font Change the size and type of default system font.

Mouse Choose mouse settings, such as speed, right or left hand, click speed, and so on.

Menu Change how the menu reacts to mouse movements and clicks.

Programs Menu Add, delete, and rearrange menu items.

Miscellaneous Change miscellaneous settings, including Screen Saver, Beep Alert, Set Active Windows (select mode, click, or select by mouse cursor position), and Icon and Scrollbars (select where to place icons and scroll bars).

Locale Select your local language.

Terminal and Console Windows

Within the CDE and OpenWindows environments, you can open up different shell interpreters. The shell interpreters have one basic function: to give the desktop or terminal user a text interface to a shell (`sh`, `ksh`, `csh`). The windows opened are somewhat similar to an MS-DOS prompt in Microsoft Windows.

The CDE has two shell interpreters: the console window and the terminal window. Both are very basic text panes that present users with a default shell and shell prompt. The main difference between the two windows is that the terminal window does not display system and error messages and the console window does. In a situation where you use the console to open an application, the last console window you open would show the latest system and error messages. The console window displays messages like `Sendmail, can not resolve domain name`, which can easily by cleared by keystrokes or through a menu selection. They have no effect on the text currently displayed in the window, but they sometimes are repetitive and annoying! This is particularly true when you are using the `vi` editor (which is the topic of Chapter 16, "Using the `vi` and Text Editor").

OpenWindows has three different shell interpreters: the Command tool, the Shell tool, and the console window. There is no terminal window in the OpenWindows environment; the Command tool and the Shell tool take the place of the terminal window. All of these applications are shell tools that interpret typed commands but with slightly different menus and characteristics.

The three OpenWindows tools have the following purposes:

Command tool The OpenWindows Command tool has a built-in editor. For users who are not familiar or comfortable with the `vi` editor, the Command tool window is the best bet. The Command tool gives the user the option to edit the command line as if they were using a standard text editor. You can click a mouse pointer over the text and then use the Backspace or Delete keys.

Shell tool The OpenWindows Shell tool is similar to the Command tool except it doesn't have a built-in text editor. Also, it does not have a scrolling window by default, but this feature can be enabled if needed.

Console window The OpenWindows console window displays system and error messages. The Command tool and the Shell tool do not have this feature. Just like the Shell tool, there is no built-in text editor within the console window. Users need to use `vi` or another command-line editor to edit text within the console window.

Opening a Terminal Window or a Console Window in CDE

To open a terminal window within the CDE, right-click anywhere within the unoccupied desktop area to display the Workspace menu. Then, from the Tools menu, select the Terminal command. The terminal window gives you a direct text interface to the operating system. The following graphic shows the Workspace menu and the Tools submenu.

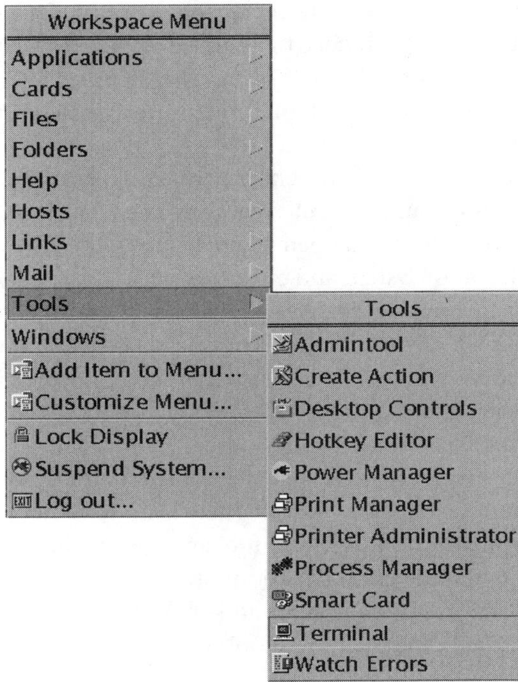

You can also find the terminal window icon scattered all around the Application Manager's submenus. Just double-click (the left button, or mouse button 1) on the terminal window icon to open a terminal window.

NOTE Solaris uses a three-button mouse. When you left-click, you use mouse button 1; when you right-click, you use mouse button 3. The middle button, mouse button 2, is used for copy and edit functions.

The console window is buried away in the CDE. On the front panel display there is an icon labeled CPU Disk The Hosts subpanel that opens above it includes the Console icon as a menu selection. To reach this icon, click the small arrow above the CPU Disk label. When you do so, a pop-up menu labeled Hosts appears. The Console icon is one of the choices. Click (button 1) on this icon to open the console window. The following graphic shows this pop-up menu, which is also a tear-off menu. A *tear-off menu* is a convenient interface device that allows you to click and drag a menu from a window or panel. That menu then becomes its own floating window on your desktop.

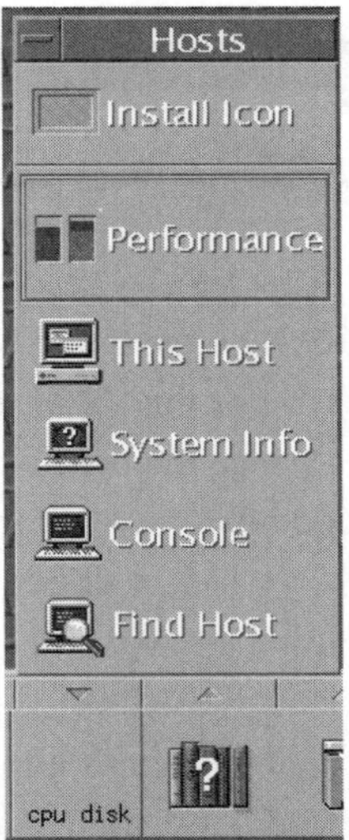

Opening the Command Tool or Shell Tool in OpenWindows

To open the Command tool in OpenWindows, follow these steps:

1. Right-click anywhere on the unoccupied desktop space. The OpenWindows Workspace menu appears.
2. Select Programs, then the Command tool command.

Here's how to open the Shell tool:

1. Open the Workspace menu by right-clicking the desktop.
2. Choose Programs, then select the Shell tool command. The Console window appears on the desktop.

Basic Command-Line File and Directory Manipulation

The sections that follow cover the basics of file and directory manipulation using the command line, including how to create simple text files and directories. You'll also learn how to move files and directories and view file permissions. The most important commands you will need to learn to work from the command line are described briefly in Table 4.2. (These commands are described elsewhere in this book in more detail.)

TABLE 4.2: BASIC COMMAND-LINE COMMANDS

Command	Purpose
awk	Sophisticated pattern-scanning and processing language.
cat	View a file.
chgrp	Change the group owner of the file.
chmod	Change the file's read, write, execute permissions.
chown	Change the owner of the file.
comm	Compare two sorted files.
cp	Copy files or directories.
diff	Compare two files.
file	Describe a file.
find	Find a file or directory, device or line. Acts as a file system search tool.
grep	Find a text string in a file.
head	Look at top 10 lines of a file, or more.
ln	Create links to files and directories.
lp	Print a text file to a printer.
ls	View the files and directories.
mkdir	Make a directory.
more	Display a text file one screen at a time.
mv	Move files and directories, change the name of a file.
od	Display text and binary files contents, including hidden characters.
pg	Display a file one screen at a time.
pwd	Show the present working directory.

Continued

TABLE 4.2: BASIC COMMAND-LINE COMMANDS (CONTINUED)

Command	Purpose
`rm`	Remove files and directories.
`rmdir`	Remove directories.
`sed`	Sophisticated streamlined batch editor.
`sort`	Sort text in a file alphabetically or numerically.
`spell`	Check the spelling in a text file.
`stty`	Set the terminal settings.
`tail`	Look at bottom 10 (or more) lines of a file.
`tee`	Copy standard input to standard output and to one or more files you specify.
`touch`	Create or modify a file's access date and time.
`uniq`	Display a text file and remove any repetitive text lines.
`vi`	Text editor.
`wc`	Summarize the total number of words, lines, and characters in a file.

The *find* Command

With the `find` command, you can search a directory tree for a file that matches various search criteria, such as the date modified, the name of the file, and so on. If a match is found, the `find` command can report the location of the file or trigger the execution of a command. This utility can be integrated into shell scripts or can be used in the command line in conjunction with other utilities. There are three basic parts to the `find` command:

- The path describes where to start the search. Unless you specify a path, you start at the root (/), which is the start of the directory tree. An example of the path is `/usr`, and if you specify that directory, you search for a match(s) only in that directory and its subdirectories. You can use more than one path (also called a path name) to a search.
- The expression describes what to search.
- The command describes what to do when a match is found.

The `find` command has the following syntax:

```
find <pathname> <expression> <execute command>
```

The path argument is always required. This is the jump-off point for a search. If a user knows a file is in the `/etc` directory, it makes no sense to search the entire directory tree for the file. If you are in the directory where you want to start the search, you can use a dot (.) as the path. That dot represents the current working directory.

WARNING On large-scale enterprise servers with extremely large partitions (2 to 4 terabytes), use of the `find` command can cause disk performance issues. Also, try not to use the `find` command on databases or other potentially sensitive files. Try not to use `find` across NFS mounted partitions; try to log in locally to that system to run `find` because it uses less system resources and is faster.

For the <*expression*> parameter, you can use any of the following search string expressions (all of which need to be preceded with a hyphen, or - character):

`ctime` ***`n`*** Search by when a file was last accessed.

`depth` Opposite of `prune`, search to a specific depth. The `depth` expression cancels out the `prune` expression if both are on the command line.

`follow` Follow a symbolic link to open the original file. This option will track an infinite loop symbolic directory.

`fstype` Search for a file on a certain type of file system (UFS, NFS, etc.).

`inum` ***`n`*** Search for a file that has inode number *n*.

`links` ***`n`*** Search for a file that has *n* links to it.

`mount` ***`<mount point>`*** Search only the specified mount point.

`mtime` ***`n`*** Search for a file by when it was last modified.

`n` **`= days old`** Search for a file a specific number of days old. Can be *n* (exactly *n* days ago, +*n* (more than *n* days ago) or -*n* (less than *n* days ago).

`name` Search for a file that matches a particular name.

`newer` Search for a file that has been modified before a certain date.

`nogroup` Search for a file with a group owner that is not in the `/etc/group` file or in an NIS or NIS+ database.

`nouser` Search for a file with a user that is not in the `/etc/passwd` file or an NIS/NIS+ database.

`perm` Search for a file with permissions that match the given permissions.

`prune` Do not search below a certain directory depth.

`size` Search for a file that is larger than a specified size in blocks. When the size expression is followed by a `c` argument, any file larger than a specified size in bytes is a match.

type c Search for a file of the specified type *c*. (See Table 4.3.)

user Search for a file with a user in the `/etc/passwd` file or a NIS/NIS+ database.

NOTE An infinite loop symbolic directory exists when a symbolic link to a directory points to one of its higher-level directories. In the example `ln -s /usr/home/me /usr/home`, the `me` directory points to `/usr/home`. When you run a `find` against an infinite loop, it might try to look in the `/usr/home/me` (for example) and see that it is a symbolic link to `/usr/home`. It would then look in `/usr/home` and see the directory me and try to look in it again. This loop would give the appearance that find was hung and it would have to be killed.

Table 4.3 shows the values that can be substituted for `c` in the search string expression `type c`.

TABLE 4.3: TYPE ARGUMENTS

`c` Value	Type of File
b	Block-special file
c	Character-special file
d	Directory
D	Door
f	Plain file
l	Symbolic link
p	FIFO named pipe
s	Socket

The <*execute command*> portion of the `find` command is used to execute a command when a file matches the criteria specified in the search string expressions listed earlier. Among the various commands you can execute are the following (again, preceded by a hyphen):

exec <*command*> `{} \;` Run the command.

cpio <*devicename*> An executable command. Means that, if a file matches the search criteria, write the current file on the specified device in copy in/out (cpio) format.

print Cause the current path to be printed. This is the default execution if nothing else is specified.

ls Print the current path and all the file information found with the `ls -l` command.

ok Use the `OK` command to prompt the user for a `y` response before executing a command.

In addition, you can perform complex expressions on the preceding criteria, as in the following:

(expression) The `find` command runs when the entire expression is true.

! expression The `find` command runs when the expression is false.

expression -a expression The `find` command runs when the logical `AND` operation is true.

expression -o expression The `find` command runs when the logical `OR` operation is true.

Finding Basic System Information

One common task for a system administrator is to document the current setup of the servers. If a system crashes or day-to-day maintenance is needed on the servers, a good set of documents can help. Take a case in which a junior system administrator accidentally deletes the `/etc/hosts` file and damages the network interface. What if your backup solution is a network backup? There will be times when having system information is crucial to bringing a server back to good health. There are numerous command-line utilities that can help in this process.

One important tool is the `uname` command. The `uname` command was designed to give a wide variety of system information and can be used with any of the following parameters:

-a option Print all the information about the system.

-i option Show the platform hardware.

-p option Print the node name.

-s option Print the name of the operating system.

-v option Print the operating system version.

-X option Print all the system information one element per line.

Six other commands are particularly useful in ascertaining your system's configuration: `hostid`, `env`, `release`, `ifconfig`, `arp`, and `prtconfig`. They have the following uses:

hostid Print the alphanumeric identifier of the system. This is commonly used with software licenses.

env Print the environmental variables such as `SHELL`, `TERM`, `TZ`, and others.

cat /etc/release The cat command, when applied to the release file, prints very detailed information on the current version of the operating system.

ifconfig -a Use this command to display the network configuration information about all the network interfaces that are configured and that the operating system is aware of. Installed devices that aren't properly configured appear when you use the dmesg command. The ifconfig command also displays the status of the network card (UP, BROADCASTING, etc.), the Maximum Transmission Unit (MTU), the IP address, the subnet mask in hexadecimal, the broadcast address, and the Ethernet address.

arp -a Display the current arp table (Ethernet to IP).

prtconf List all peripherals and device drivers used to manage the peripherals. Included in the output of the prtconf command are the device path of the console frame buffer, firmware device derived from the PROM, information on pseudo devices, platform-dependent PROM information, PROM firmware version on the system, the actual hardware memory, and the machine architecture.

There are several files in the /etc directory that contain important network configuration information that you should examine in detail and keep records of. You might want to keep a printout of these files so that you can reestablish their values should something go wrong with your system. Although these files are described more fully in Chapters 9 and 14, they are briefly presented to you here:

hosts IP address to hostname table, which is a symbolic link to the /etc/inet/hosts file.

netmasks The netmask applied to the system, which is a symbolic link to the /etc/inet/netmasks file.

defaultgateway The default router.

nsswitch.conf Where the system gathers information.

resolv.conf The IP addresses of the DNS servers.

nodename The node name of the system.

hostname (Ethernet name) The hostname attached to an interface. Two examples of interfaces names are hostname.hme0 and hostname.lo0.

dhcp (Ethernet name) Present if the client is controlled by Dynamic Host Configuration Protocol (DHCP).

The *file* Command

There are situations in which a system administrator will come across a mystery file. One of the most useful commands with Solaris is the file command. This command performs a series of tests on a file to determine what type of file it is. The file command uses a series of basic tests and a "magic" file that is located under the /usr directory or the /etc directory. These magic files provide a series of instructions for the file command to use when you're trying to determine a mystery file's type.

One of the concepts that must be known to understand the file command is that the highest-level object in Unix is a file. A directory, for example, is a file that contains other files. A raw device is a character file.

The first thing the file command does is to try to make a general classification of the unknown file. This command can recognize if the file is a directory, a first-in-first-out (FIFO) file, a block-special file, or a character-special file or if the file is an empty file (zero byte length). If the file is a text file, the first 512 bytes are scanned for typical characters of known programming languages.

If none of these tests produces results, the file command tries to find a "magic" file that corresponds to the local language. Obviously, the characters and symbols used in Germany would not be the same as the characters used in Taiwan. The file command matches the local language with a directory under /usr/lib/locale. The magic file for Japan is /usr/lib/locale/ja/LC_MESSAGES/magic.

If a locale file is not present or cannot be used, the default magic file used is the /etc/magic file. The file command uses the best magic file it can find. The magic file has a series of numbers and letters the file command uses for testing. The first column, Byte Offset, tells the file command where to start the comparison test—how many bytes into the mystery file the file command should start testing: the 1st byte, the 2nd byte, or the 10th byte. Next comes the Value Type column. The value type specifies how many bytes to test for: 1 byte, 2 bytes, 4 bytes, or a string of bytes.

So now the file command has the offset and number of bytes to test for. The last key piece of information needed is the results of the test, or the "value to match." These work in principle just like a cyclic redundancy check (CRC). The find command will perform a test on the mystery file. If the test produces the same results as specified in the Value to Match column, then a match has been found. The String to Print column is used by the find command to print out the results to the system administrator.

The magic file also has a corresponding message that will accompany the known message files. It looks like the following text:

```
Byte offset  value type  value to match  string to print

0  short    070701      cpio archive
0  string   070701      ASCII cpio archive
0  short    070702      cpio archive - CRC
0  string   070702      ASCII cpio archive - CRC
0  short    070707      cpio archive - CHR (-c)
```

There are a couple of arguments and flags that can be used with the `file` command:

`-c` option Check the magic file for errors (rarely used or needed).

`-h` option Do not follow symbolic links.

`-f` *<ffile>* option Use a file *<ffile>* that contains a list of files to examine.

`-m` *<mfile>* option Use an alternate magic file.

As an example, this is the output of a `file` command analysis of a file named `mc68040`:

```
# file mc68040
mc68040: ELF 32-bit MSB executable SPARC
Version 1, dynamically linked, d
#
```

Exiting the CDE and OpenWindows

There are two ways to exit the CDE:

- Click the CDE Exit icon located on the front panel.
- Choose the Log Out option from the Workspace menu.

There are two ways to leave an OpenWindows desktop session:

- Select the Exit option from the Workspace menu, then click the Log Out button on the confirmation dialog box that appears.
- You can also type **`exit`** or **`logout`** at the command line and OpenWindows will exit the desktop.

Exiting the CDE

The way in which CDE shuts down is determined by the shutdown options chosen with the Style Manager Startup dialog box. If you selected Resume Current Session, the contents of the workspace will remain the way you leave them during your current session. This includes any client modifications or resource modifications. The Session Manager will remember the contents of your desktop at the time you exited it.

If you selected Return to Home Session, the contents of your current workspace will not be saved. A default workspace will be used the next time the CDE is started.

There is also an option to have a logout confirmation dialog box pop up just before you exit CDE. This dialog box is a safety net just in case you accidentally click the Exit icon. Otherwise, any open applications could become corrupted and lose data.

The Session Manager saves the state of the desktop, including the condition of applications open on the desktop, the settings for desktop components, and some environmental settings such as backdrop color, fonts, mouse and keyboard settings, and so on.

In each user's home directory, there is a file and a directory associated with the Common Desktop Environment: the `.dtprofile` and `.dt` directory. The Session Manager saves the user's information in the `.dtprofile` file, which is kept in the `.dt` directory. Each time you log in to the CDE, your `$HOME/.dtprofile` is read. This file contains environmental variables for your session's applications. If you use an application that changes an environmental variable, this setting is saved in the `$HOME/.dtprofile` file.

The Session Manager also saves information in the `$HOME/.dt` directory. There are two subdirectories under `$HOME/.dt`: `$HOME/.dt/session` and `$HOME/.dt/Desktop`. When the user exits the CDE, these directories are updated with the user's last changes. Session Manager makes a directory under the `$HOME/.dt/session` directory named `home` or `current`. Which directory is created depends on if the user wants to go back to a default home desktop or the last desktop used (current). Before the Session Manager exits the session, it saves the home or current information in another directory called `current.old` or `home.old`. Again, this depends on whether the user has chosen the default home desktop or the last desktop. The Session Manager also updates the `$HOME/.dt/display/current` or the `$HOME/.dt/display/home` directory with some display information when it exits.

Exiting OpenWindows

With OpenWindows, just right-click anywhere in the unoccupied desktop area. A Workspace menu will pop up. One of the options is Exit. If you select this option, a confirmation dialog box appears, asking you if you really do want to leave the session.

You can also leave an OpenWindows session by typing **`exit`** or **`logout`** in the console window, Command tool or Shell tool. When OpenWindows exits, it saves information to a file called `$HOME/.xinitrc`. This file saves the user's last desktop.

Summary

This chapter described some of the basic operations that you need to perform in order to use Solaris 8. The Solaris 8 software comes in two version, an Intel version and a SPARC version. Although the operating system is nearly identical in software, hardware differences between the two platforms introduce important differences in the way the two versions start up and are modified. Some of these differences were highlighted in this chapter.

To access the OK prompt, a system administrator needs to use a null modem cable through the console port. The SPARC platform version of Solaris 8 features a command, `eeprom`, that can interact with the OK prompt in a limited manner. The user requires access to a video display and keyboard connected directly to the system to use the `eeprom` command.

When Solaris is running, the operating system uses run levels to designate the resources that can be shared and whether the system is in single-user mode or multi-user mode. You have control over these run levels and can alter them to change security features, get more powerful access to hardware features, shut down a system, and perform many other functions.

Solaris features a GUI login manager named `dtlogin` that presents for user logins a GUI interface from which the user can select the CDE or OpenWindows desktop. The CDE and OpenWindows desktops both feature various shell windows that give a user the option of typing directly to their default shells. The CDE has the Telnet window and console window. OpenWindows has the Command tool, the Shell tool and the console window. The console window in both systems displays system messages and warning messages not found in other shell interpreter windows.

Several important commands were introduced in this chapter. The `find` command is used to find various files and directories. After a file or directory is found, an executable command can be started to manipulate the file and perform other functions. The `file` command is very useful in figuring out what a mystery file is by performing a series of basic tests on the file. If the file is not a common file, the `file` command will perform a byte check using a local magic file. System commands like `ifconfig` and several system files found in the `/etc` directory were also briefly presented in this chapter.

This chapter also covered closing the various Solaris GUIs and shutting down your system. To exit the CDE or OpenWindows desktop, right-click anywhere in unoccupied desktop space and select the Exit command. This will save your current desktop settings or revert to a default home session, depending on your preference. You can use the shutdown command to bring your system into a state that is consistent and can be powered off.

CHAPTER 5

The File System

FEATURING:

The file system structure 122

Filenames, file types, path names, and attributes 124

Access rights and permissions 131

Working with directories, files, and links 137

Disk storage structures, inodes, and blocks 160

Mounting and unmounting files 169

Disk utilization and disk quotas 172

In this chapter, I'll describe the files and directory structures used by Solaris. Solaris uses both real and virtual file systems to provide support for the many devices described in Chapter 6. Among the topics described in this chapter are how to name files, what types of files Solaris creates, and how to recognize and work with files and directories. The important directories and system files are documented in this chapter, as are the many different file systems and their usage. You will also find information about how data is written to disk and how file systems are related to data on disk. This chapter also describes how to determine disk utilization, both at a partition and directory level, as well as for individual files. Finally, you'll learn how you can use disk quotas to limit the amount of disk space individual users have access to.

File System Structure

File systems allow the operating system interface to interact with data stored on devices. Solaris uses the Unix file system, or UFS, as its primary file system. The UFS was developed as part of the Berkeley Software Distribution (BSD) in the 1980s. Solaris also uses some other file systems to manage storage on CD-ROMs and other devices, which is described in the section "File Systems" later in this chapter. All of these devices store data on partitions logically defined on disks. Solaris also uses a virtual file system to abstract file system objects so that file system data can be accessed from remote systems, which is also described later in this chapter.

The Solaris and Unix file systems are organized in a hierarchical tree structure with a single directory called the root directory (/) at the top and additional files and directories branching off from that top directory. Viewed topologically, the directory tree is upside down compared to a real tree in the sense that the root directory is at the top. In Unix, the root directory contains all devices that you mount, so that floppy disks, hard drives, CD-ROMs, and other devices appear as subdirectories or folders of the root directory. You may be familiar with Windows or the Macintosh, but the Solaris arrangement is a little different. The Windows and Macintosh operating systems have device directories that are mounted at the same level as the root (/) directory.

All directories, including the root directory, can have files and other directories contained in them. A directory that appears above another directory in the file system hierarchy is called the parent directory; the subdirectory of that file is often referred to as the child directory. Although you can certainly have two or more files with the same name, say `memo1`, those two files cannot be placed in the same directory. Similarly, no two subdirectories in the same directory may have the same names, nor can there be a file and a subdirectory with the same name in the same directory. Figure 5.1 shows a directory tree with some of the elements labeled.

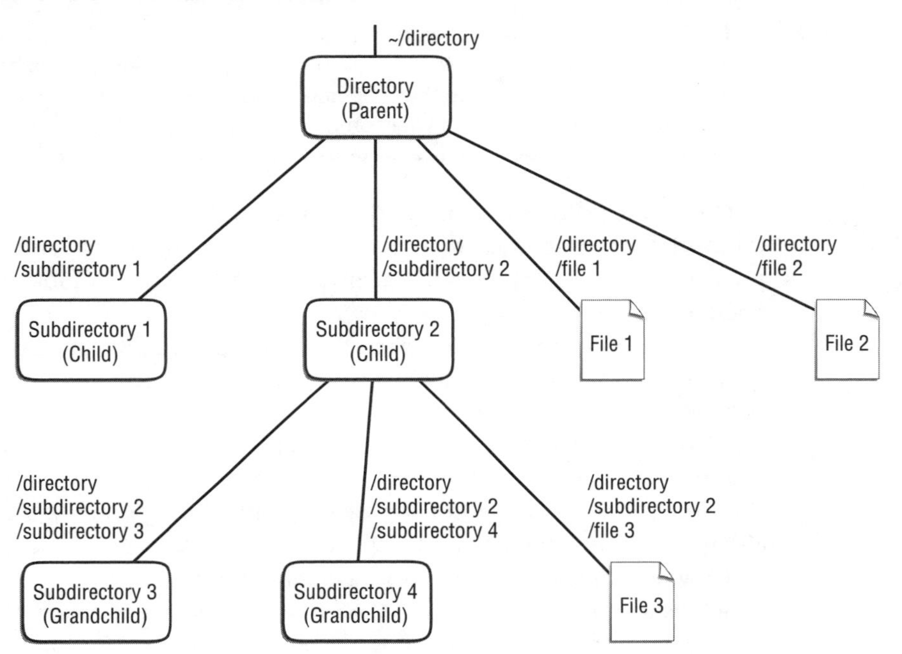

FIGURE 5.1

A directory tree contains a hierarchy of directories and files in top-down order.

Every file or directory in the Solaris file system (and any file system, for that matter) must contain a unique /*<pathname>*/*<filename>* combination. A path name is the address for a directory in the file system. For example, `/usr/bin/sparcV9/cputrack` is the path to the `cputract` file, and `/usr/bin/sparV9/` represents the four directories you have to traverse down from the root to get to that file. Each forward slash represents yet another directory or level that you have to descend from the root directory, indicated by the first / in the path name. As you will see later in this chapter, and in other chapters that describe networking and the Internet, there are several addressing schemes that are used to provide the path name to other computers on a network or to remote computers over the Internet.

There is no theoretical limit to the number of subdirectories a directory can have, but there is a practical limit. The more directories you place in a single directory, the longer certain system commands and operations take to complete themselves. That same consideration applies to the number of files in a directory. The Unix file system imposes a limit of 2^{10} (or 1,024) characters in a directory path name. Unless you insist on using very long directory names, the limit isn't usually a practical problem. Most people use the shortest directory names they can because it cuts down on errors when they're entering those names in at the command line.

NOTE In this chapter, I often refer to being in the command line or working at the command line when you enter commands into the terminal window. It is better terminology, and more explicit, to refer to these operations as being in the shell or at the shell prompt when the shell is interpreting your commands.

One of the features that makes the Unix file system different from others is that directories with important files such as system files are locked. Only users with root privileges can modify locked files, which tends to make Unix more stable than other operating systems.

The organizational structure of the file system is such that directories can be reserved for your local system or shared by several systems in a networked environment with common settings and users can have home directories with user-specific information. With this scheme, files that are stored locally on a server or workstation can be shared over a network with other systems by using a remote file access protocol like the NFS (Network File System) protocol. Segregating content in this manner on your file system also makes it easier for Solaris to upgrade the operating system as new software packages and upgrades or new versions of the operating system appear.

Solaris requires that the root (/) and `/usr` file systems be mounted during boot-up. Certain directories are specified as the approved locations for Foundation Solaris software installed in the Solaris distribution. Notably, the `/etc` directory is where platform-dependent configuration files are stored, and `/etc/opt/packagename` is the directory in which files for add-on applications are stored.

NOTE The section "Directories" contains a detailed list of important Solaris directories and their purposes.

Working with Files

In the sections that follow, I'll describe the types of files Solaris uses as well as how to name them. Files are the primary objects you use to manipulate data in an operating system; therefore, they can contain simple data, complex programs, or anything in between. Some files are required by your operating system to function, and so Solaris keeps them hidden from view unless you specify otherwise. Files also have attributes that describe what they are, who can use them, and in what ways they can be used.

Filenames

A *filename* is the specification of an object in the file system. The name refers to data stored on a disk or other storage medium that can be manipulated in some way. Filenames can contain either one or two parts: a specific name and possibly an extension. A filename can be up to 255 characters long (2^8–1) and can contain alphanumeric characters (a–z, A–Z, 0–9) in any combination. Certain other characters are allowed in filenames, namely hyphens, commas, periods, and underscores. For example, you can name a file `memo_1.12.20.00`, should you have a mind to. Solaris doesn't enforce strict rules on the use of punctuation as Windows does.

Solaris, as are other flavors of Unix, is case sensitive. Although you can't have two files named `memo1` in the same directory, you can have one file named `memo1` and another named `Memo1`. This is certainly not the case for Windows or DOS where, although password logons are case sensitive, full path specifications are not.

NOTE If you use special characters such as underscores in a filename, you must use those characters when you perform an action on that file. For example, if you create a file named `_myfile` and you then want to remove it, you would have to use the command `rm _myfile`. If you leave out the underscore, Solaris will not find the file and will post an error message.

Filename Extensions

Solaris doesn't enforce a system of filename extensions that are registered to specific programs, as Microsoft Windows and the Macintosh operating system do. If you choose to do so, you can use filename extensions as optional designations that help you remember what the file contains. However, some programs require filename extensions in order to open and view a file. For example, the C programming language looks for files with the extension `.c`, Adobe Acrobat reads files with the `.pdf` extension, and StarOffice creates word processor files with the extension `.sdw` (if you select the Automatic filename extension option in the Save or Save As dialog box). These extensions designate what are called native file formats, which these specific applications create and require.

Many file extensions indicate an industry-standard file format, such as `.tif` (called TIFF, which stands for Tagged Image File Format), `.jpg` (called JPEG, which stands for Joint Photographic Experts Group), or `.html` (called HTML, which stands for Hypertext Markup Language). You can use many different programs to open and save industry-standard file formats and work with the data they contain. Most typically, programs that work with standard file types will create the file extension for you. In many instances, industry-standard file formats are created as interchange formats. An interchange format is a special format that converts not only data but formatting information into a text-only format that can be more easily transported between programs and between platforms (operating systems). Rich Text Format (RTF), which is supported by StarOffice's word processor on Solaris and Word on Windows, is one example of an interchange format; two more are SYLK (symbolic link), supported by StarOffice's spreadsheet module and Microsoft Excel, and PS (or PostScript), created and used by many vector graphics programs such as Adobe Illustrator. If you create a standard file type and the creator program doesn't automatically place the extension on the filename, you should certainly do so.

Invisible Filenames

Files that start with a period character are called *invisible files* or *hidden files*. These files don't appear when you use the list (`ls`) command unless you use the `-a` (all) option. In the Common Desktop Environment (CDE), files of this type are hidden from view; you must choose the Show Hidden Objects command (Ctrl+S) from the View menu in the File Manager to view them. When you select that command, every directory or folder shows two additional entries (at least): the single period (`.`) folder points to the current folder itself, and the double period (`..`) folder points to the parent folder or to the next folder up in the file system hierarchy (toward the root).

Path Names

A *path name* consists of the filename preceded by its parent directory and all the directory names of the parent directories up to and including the root directory. Many commands in Solaris require a full path specification, but many commands require that you enter the path only when it is different from the current directory. A full path specification is called an *absolute path name*, and although it may be tedious to type, it will always point to the correct location of a file in the file system.

You can also specify the relative path name for many commands. A relative path name points from the directory you are in at the moment to another directory or file. To create a relative path, you replace some portion of the path starting at the root directory with the double period symbol (`..`). For example, if you are in the `/usr/dt/lib/security` directory and you want to access `/usr/dt/lib/dtksch/DtFuncs.dtsch`, you can use the relative path `../dtksch/DtFuncs.dtsh` in place of the full path.

This relative path points to a directory one level up from the parent directory of the `DtFuncs.dtsh` file. Obviously, you need to know what your current directory is to make sense of a relative path name. Should you ever have to move this directory and then use this relative address in a script, the relative path would still point to a directory one level up. In many instances, this addressing scheme will still work, and it will save you the trouble of having to go back and change the path names in that script. For users who have worked with spreadsheets, the concept of absolute versus relative path names is completely analogous to absolute versus relative addresses for cells.

Nearly all important Solaris commands that take path name arguments will accept a relative path name in place of a full path specification or absolute path name.

TIP Although Solaris supports filenames of up to 255 characters, other forms of Unix do not. To be compatible with all forms of Unix, use 14-character names; to be compatible with MS-DOS, use 8-character names and 3-character file extensions (the eight dot three nomenclature).

All of the important Solaris shells—the Korn, Bourne, and C shells—support a reference to the home directory using the tilde character (~). You can use the tilde character in place of the path name for the home directory path. In a default Solaris installation, your home directory is the root directory when you log in under the root account, and the tilde character doesn't save you much data entry. Still, should you change the location of your home directory, if you have used the tilde character to specify the home directory, that path name would still be correct. If you add a username after the tilde character in a path, these shells substitute the home directory for that particular user. Therefore, `~barries` would move me to my home directory, `/barries`.

Most people don't log in to the root account unless they are doing administrative work on their system and have root privileges. It's generally a good idea to set your home directory to something other than root (/). Typically, your home directory might be something like `/users/barries`.

File Attributes and Properties

Among the file attributes and properties discussed in the following sections are those that describe the type of file you are looking at or working with. Many times you will need to understand and modify access rights in order to perform specific operations with files, so in the sections that follow, you'll also learn how to recognize access rights and modify them.

File Types

Unix uses several different types of files to store data, to provide address locations, and to point to other addresses and files in the file system. Files store all sorts of information, including simple text, extended characters and symbols, and instructions on how a graphics engine like PostScript can create a drawing.

Use the list command to determine the specific file type of any file in a directory that you are interested in. When you specify the long output form of the list command, the very first letter, shown here by the placeholder <?>, tells you the file type:

```
ls -l <pathname>/<filename>
<?>rwr-xr   1  <foldername>   <groupname>   3268 Dec 18 2000
   <filename>
```

In the following sections, I'll describe the different types of files you'll work with.

Regular File

A *regular file* (the first letter designation of the list command is -), or as it is sometimes called, an ordinary file, is the most prevalent file type used by Solaris. Regular files can be text files, extended text files used by applications, and binary format executable or program files. Regular files can be any size, from very small to very large. The data in a regular file is in a format that Solaris can write and read, but it isn't a requirement that Solaris be able to actually use the data in any way. For example, the data can be application specific or it can describe a program that Solaris can't actually execute.

Even if you determine that a file is of the regular file type, you know very little that is useful about the file. You might want to know if it is a program file, a data file, or something else. The `file` command offers more information about the purpose that regular file types serve.

One example of a regular file is the core file that you may see appear in any of Solaris's directories. This file is a dump file. Solaris writes into a core file information that describes an error condition that occurred. You can delete any of these files without concern, particularly after they haven't been accessed for a while.

Block-Special File

A *block-special file* (the first letter designation of the list command is b) is one of the two device files that Solaris maintains. This file format provides a method for transferring large amounts (blocks) of data to and from device drivers in the Solaris file system. Block file transfer is used by parallel ports and SCSI buses. Most block-special files are used to describe removable media and hard drives. Consider the `ls -l` command run against the `/dev/sda` file. It returns the following:

```
brw-rw--    1 root    disk    8, 0 Dec 18 20:32 /dev/sda
```

Note that the b character indicates a block-special file and that files of this type have both major and minor device numbers (8 and 0, respectively) that Solaris uses to determine what class of device driver (and what specific device driver within that category of device drivers) this data can communicate with. Chapter 6 discusses this concept in more detail.

Character-Special File

A *character-special file* (the first letter designation of the list command is c) is the second of the two device files that Solaris (and Unix) maintain. A character-special file communicates serially, one character at a time. Serial devices use these types of files: displays or terminals, mice, and keyboards, for example. When you apply the `ls -l` command to a file like /dev/tty0, you'll see the following output returned:

```
crw-rw--    1 barries    users    4, 0 Dec 18 22:32 /dev/tty0
```

Notice again that you see a major and minor device number (4 and 0) returned that specifies the device driver class and particular device driver.

Directory File

A *directory file* (the first letter designation of the list command is d) is a container file for files and other directories. A directory file is typically quite small, often only 300 to 400 bytes in size. A directory file stores the information and permissions relating to the files and directories within it. An assigned reference number called an inode number tracks each file and folder described in a directory file. The Solaris kernel assigns the inode number upon creation of each file, and the file system uses the inode number to find the corresponding object quickly during searches. You can think of a directory file as serving the purpose of a table of contents. The directory file for a directory containing hundreds of files can swell considerably, but it's nevertheless a small file.

Symbolic Link File

A *symbolic link file* (the first letter designation of the list command is l) is a small file that serves as a pointer to another file or folder in the file system. Symbolic links store the full path specification for the object that they are connected to. When you act on a symbolic link file, it opens a directory or launches the file that it is linked to. Because you can have any number of symbolic links, you can provide access to the reference object in many different locations. Symbolic link files are entirely analogous in their action on the desktop to shortcuts in Microsoft Windows and aliases in the Macintosh operating system. The section "Moving, Copying, and Renaming Files and Folders on the Desktop" in Chapter 7 describes working with symbolic links on the CDE desktop.

It is probably more convenient to create symbolic links using the graphical interface, either through clicks and drags or by using the Link To command on the Selected menu in the File Manager. Working from the command line, you can create symbolic links using the link command with the -s option; the command has the following syntax: `ln -s` *<source_pathname>/<filename> <target_pathname>/<symbolic_linkname>*. In the source specification, you can substitute a directory name in place of the filename for a symbolic link to that directory. If you don't specify a target path name for the symbolic link file you are creating, the symbolic link file is created in your current working directory.

Should you move the original object that the symbolic link points to, the symbolic link will no longer work properly; Solaris posts an error message when you try to act on the symbolic link. Symbolic links are used heavily in the Solaris interface. All of the controls in the front panel are symbolic links, as are any files or directories moved to the Solaris workspace.

Named Pipe File

A pipe specifies that an output from one program or command is used or piped as the input of another program or command. The action of a pipe is often referred to as redirection, particularly in other operating systems like MS-DOS. For example, the command `ps -l | print` entered at the command line takes (pipes) the process command's long output format and sends it to the print command so that you see a list of the processes currently running on your system. This command is commonly used to diagnose system problems. When entered from the command line, a pipe of this sort is referred to as an anonymous pipe. The vertical bar is the symbol used to create redirection and provide the pipe command. There is no restriction on the number of pipes used in a command line.

Solaris (and Unix in general) provides what is called a *named pipe*, using an intermediary file as the target of one command or program and the source of the data for the second command or program. (The p in the first line below specifies the creation of a named pipe.) Named pipes provide a method for interprocess communication (IPC) between two applications, commonly through the use of a temporary file.

To create a named pipe, use the make node command (`mknod`), as follows:

```
mknod /tmp/<tmpfilename> p
lp > /tmp/<tmpfilename>
rm tmp/<tmpfilename>
```

This creates the *<tmpfilename>* file as a pipe file and makes the process that writes the file a background process so that you can specify the next command to run. The second command sends the *<tmpfilename>* to the line printer, which prints the file's data as soon as it is available. The last command removes the temporary file. Many installation routines use named pipes, and most often these installers clean up after themselves—but not always. You are most likely to find named pipe files in the various `/tmp` directories that Solaris maintains.

Socket File

Socket files (the first letter designation of the list command is `s`) store data used when the local and a remote computer use a named connection to communicate. You use sockets when you use e-mail programs or when you open a browser such as Netscape

Navigator. Some sockets, called secure sockets, offer encrypted transmission between client and server. In any case, socket files give you a means of storing data when working with the transient connections that wide area network (WAN) connections like the Internet offer you.

Access Permissions

Solaris uses a set of file and directory permissions to determine who can do what to the contents of your file system. Each object in the file system comes with three sets of access permissions or rights:

- Owner permissions
- Group permissions
- Other permissions

Typically, the owner of a file or directory is the person who created it. That person has full privileges to modify or delete that object. Other people can be given an owner's rights, and it is also possible for the owner or an administrator to remove certain rights. For example, when someone installs a program file, the binary file is often specified as readable and executable but it cannot be modified or written to. To simplify the levels of permissions for an object, you can put users into groups and give each group the same access rights. Last, the Other permissions (sometimes called World permissions, also known as World readable) are granted to anyone who is not the owner or a member of any group. Each of these three access levels is assigned permissions for the following actions:

Read access (`r`) The read access allows you to view a file or folder on your screen or a file or directory in the file system. Without this attribute set on, users will not be able to use the list command to view an object's permissions.

Write access (`w`) The write access allows you to modify the contents of a file or directory. This privilege also allows you to add and remove files from a directory.

Execute access (`x`) The execute access permission allows you to run a program. The execute access permission must also be specified to view or write to a directory.

Each of these privileges comes with an access bit that is turned on and off. Thus, for read, the `r` bit (or read bit) is either allowed or disallowed for a particular user or group. In a long listing of files, these bits appear at the left side of a file's listing when the list command is used. You can also see the read, write, and execute bit settings in the Properties dialog box for files and folders in the CDE.

The access privileges set on a parent directory affect what a user can do to the files and subdirectories it contains. If only the execute privilege is set on a directory, a user with that privilege cannot view the contents of the directory, nor can they modify or delete any files that are contained in it. A user can run an executable program file in a directory with execute-only privileges.

Viewing Access Rights

The list command's long listing (`ls -l`), which you have seen several times in this chapter, lists 10 different file or directory attributes: the file type and three sets of three read, write, and execute permissions. The first set of three attributes describes what the owner of the file can do; the second set of three attributes describes what the group listed in the output can do; and the third set lists what a user who is neither the creator or a member of the specified group can do. For example, the string `-rwxr-xr--` gives you the following information:

- The file is a regular (or ordinary) file.
- The owner has full read, write, and execute privileges.
- The current group can read and execute but not write to the file or directory.
- Anyone other than the owner and that group member can read but cannot write to or execute the file or directory.

When you want to secure a file, make sure that the write permission is denied for both the file and the directory that contains that file; the permission needs to be denied for the owner and any groups and all others who could access the file.

Figure 5.2 shows you the output of the `ls -l` command for some sample files.

Solaris offers a permissions scheme based on access control lists (ACLs) that overlays the permissions that you can assign to a file. When an ACL has been applied to a file, you will see a plus sign appear to the right of the list of nine file permission status flags when you give the `ls -l` command, as in `rwxr-xr-+`. The purpose of ACLs is to allow group access to a file in a more controlled fashion than the simple User/Group/Owner attributes would allow you to have.

FIGURE 5.2

Shown here is the list command for the root directory.

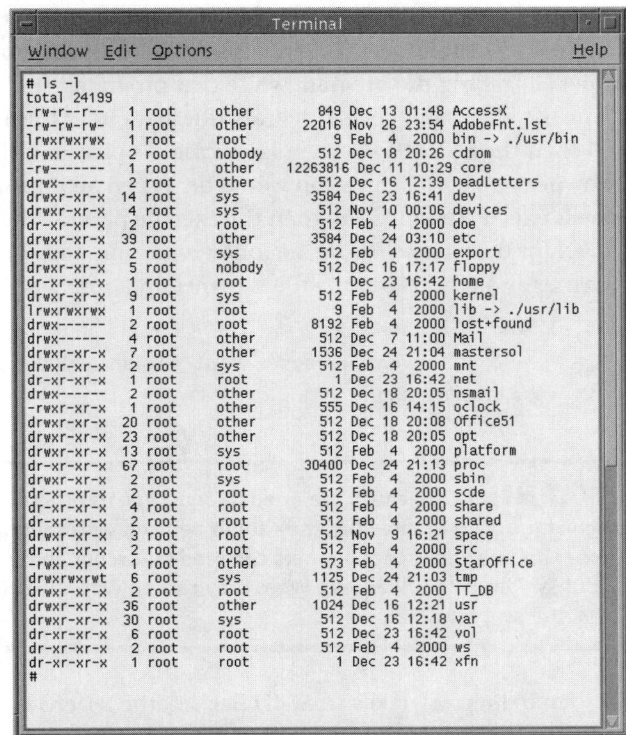

Terminal
Window Edit Options Help
ls -l
total 24199
-rw-r--r--   1 root   other   849 Dec 13 01:48 AccessX
-rw-rw-rw-   1 root   other   22016 Nov 26 23:54 AdobeFnt.lst
lrwxrwxrwx   1 root   root   9 Feb 4 2000 bin -> ./usr/bin
drwxr-xr-x   2 root   nobody   512 Dec 18 20:26 cdrom
-rw-------   1 root   other   12263816 Dec 11 10:29 core
drwx------   2 root   other   512 Dec 16 12:39 DeadLetters
drwxr-xr-x 14 root   sys   3584 Dec 23 16:41 dev
drwxr-xr-x   4 root   sys   512 Nov 10 00:06 devices
dr-xr-xr-x   2 root   root   512 Feb 4 2000 doe
drwxr-xr-x 39 root   other   3584 Dec 24 03:10 etc
drwxr-xr-x   2 root   sys   512 Feb 4 2000 export
drwxr-xr-x   5 root   nobody   512 Dec 16 17:17 floppy
dr-xr-xr-x   1 root   root   1 Dec 23 16:42 home
drwxr-xr-x   9 root   sys   512 Feb 4 2000 kernel
lrwxrwxrwx   1 root   root   9 Feb 4 2000 lib -> ./usr/lib
drwx------   2 root   root   8192 Feb 4 2000 lost+found
drwx------   4 root   other   512 Dec 7 11:00 Mail
drwxr-xr-x   7 root   other   1536 Dec 24 21:04 mastersol
drwxr-xr-x   2 root   sys   512 Feb 4 2000 mnt
dr-xr-xr-x   1 root   root   1 Dec 23 16:42 net
drwx------   2 root   other   512 Dec 18 20:05 nsmail
-rwxr-xr-x   1 root   other   555 Dec 16 14:15 oclock
drwxr-xr-x 20 root   other   512 Dec 18 20:08 Office51
drwxr-xr-x 23 root   other   512 Dec 18 20:05 opt
drwxr-xr-x 13 root   sys   512 Feb 4 2000 platform
dr-xr-xr-x 67 root   root   30400 Dec 24 21:13 proc
drwxr-xr-x   2 root   sys   512 Feb 4 2000 sbin
dr-xr-xr-x   2 root   root   512 Feb 4 2000 scde
dr-xr-xr-x   4 root   root   512 Feb 4 2000 share
dr-xr-xr-x   2 root   root   512 Feb 4 2000 shared
drwxr-xr-x   3 root   root   512 Nov 9 16:21 space
dr-xr-xr-x   2 root   root   512 Feb 4 2000 src
-rwxr-xr-x   1 root   other   573 Feb 4 2000 StarOffice
drwxrwxrwt   6 root   sys   1125 Dec 24 21:03 tmp
drwxr-xr-x   2 root   root   512 Feb 4 2000 TT_DB
drwxr-xr-x 36 root   other   1024 Dec 16 12:21 usr
drwxr-xr-x 30 root   sys   512 Dec 16 12:18 var
dr-xr-xr-x   6 root   root   512 Dec 23 16:42 vol
dr-xr-xr-x   2 root   root   512 Feb 4 2000 ws
dr-xr-xr-x   1 root   root   1 Dec 23 16:42 xfn
#

SUID and SGID Permissions

Executable files can have additional permissions called the Set User ID (SUID) and Set Group ID (SGID) applied to them. When there is no SUID or SGID permission set, the permissions that are applied to a program file are the permissions of the person who calls the file. When you execute an application that has the SUID bit set, the program runs as if it were started by the person who owns it, with their access privileges applied to the executable file instead of yours. In other words, the user inherits the owner's permissions. The use of an SUID flag is best illustrated when you change a password with the passwd command. That command is owned by root and the SUID flag is enabled. When you issue the passwd command, you assume the root's permissions to it while the passwd process runs.

The SGID has a similar function. Programs are usually executed with the group permissions of the person calling the program. When you set the SGID flag to on, the group owner of the executable file is applied to the program's execution in place of the person calling the program while that program runs.

The list command (`ls -l`) reveals whether either the SUID or SGID flag has been set. When the SUID flag is set, a lowercase *s* is placed in the permissions list where the owner's execute permission would be. When an uppercase *S* appears in place of the owner's execute permission, then the execute permission is not set. You can see this applied for the `passwd` file in the following command. Here the SUID flag was set for both user and group, and the file is owned by root:

```
ls -l /usr/bin/passwd
-r-sr-sr-x    3 root    sys    101744 Jan 5 2000
    /usr/bin/passwd
```

WARNING Because the `setuid` and `setgid` programs allow anyone to use a particular program or directory, they are to be used with caution. When you add the `setuid` program to a shell script, hackers can read that script and in some cases use it to get into your system with full access. What they can do with the script depends upon the action that the script has.

When a directory takes an SGID flag set, the letter *s* is placed in the executable flag (the execute permission) of the group permissions. Files added to a directory on which the SGID flag is set automatically belong to the group the directory belongs to and not the group the person writing the file to the directory belongs to. For example, if an upload directory is given the SGID flag, any files uploaded to it automatically belong to the group that owns the upload directory (applying the `chgrp` command would have the same effect).

The SGID flag is sometimes referred to in Unix as the *sticky bit* because it offers additional permissions to users working with files inside a directory on which it is set. If a user has write permissions to a directory, the user can add or delete files from the directory. A user can delete files from the directory even if their privileges match only one of the permissions of the file. With the sticky bit on, a user can delete a file if they are the owner of the sticky directory, the owner of the file, or a superuser or root. Therefore, enabling the sticky bit is useful when you have a directory used by non-privileged users, such as a temporary directory or any directories that are used as public file upload repositories. Note that you do not need to use the sticky bit to let root access files; root can always access all files unless you are running Trusted Solaris.

Modifying Access Rights

If you have read privileges, you can view a file or directory and its permissions. With write privileges, you can also modify those permissions or access rights. There may be instances in which you need to either add or remove permissions from an owner, group, or others. The change mode command provides this capability at the command line. Its syntax is as follows:

```
chmod <expression> <filename(s)>
```

The *<expression>* portion of the command describes in either symbolic or octal form how the permissions should be altered. In the symbolic method you specify the expression as follows:

```
chmod <options> who operator <permissions> <filename(s)>
```

The `who` portion is `u` for owner, `g` for group, `o` for other, or a for all. This designation of `u` for owner and `o` for other is a little counterintuitive. Another way to think about this is that `u` is the user listed for the file. You might assume that `o` would stand for owner, but with the `chmod` command, it doesn't. The actions are + (add the permission), - (remove the permission), or = (set the file or directory permission according to a statement that follows). Finally, the `permissions` portion specifies the `r` (read), `w` (write), `x` (execute), or `s` (SUID or SGID) permissions. Therefore, the command `chmod a=w *` would give all the files in the current working directory write permission, as would the equivalent statement `chmod guo=w *`. To add or delete attributes, you could use the statement `chmod ug+x,o-x` *<filename>*, which would add execute privileges for users and groups and remove that permission for others.

The octal method, on the other hand, uses a numbering scheme to set the permissions for a file or directory. In the octal scheme, the execute permission is assigned the value of 1, the write permission is assigned the value of 2, and the read permission is assigned the value of 4. To get the total permissions, you would add these values to get a number from 0 (no permissions allowed) to 7 (all permissions allowed). Full specification requires that you list the four different groups of access in this order: special group (SUID or SGID), owner, group, and others. Thus, the command `chmod 0666 *` sets all files in the current directory to read and write but not to execute for all access groups except the special group. You use the octal method to set permissions but not to modify them; the symbolic method is more convenient for that purpose, although some people find it otherwise.

To change ownership or groups, you use the change owner (`chown`) and change group (`chgrp`) commands. All of these commands—`chmod`, `chown`, and `chgrp`—are fully documented in the Solaris man pages.

Here is the syntax for the chown command:

```
chown <options> <username>:<groupname> <filename(s)>
```

The *<username>* can be either the logon name or the user identification number (UID) of a user, and similarly, *<groupname>* can be either the group or its group identification number (GID). If you want to change the owner and not the group, you omit *<groupname>* from the command. You must be the root to change the ownership of a file or directory to someone else. Once you have changed the ownership, only the new owner of the object or the system superuser or root can change the ownership attribute. The three options offered by Solaris for chown are -f (don't report errors), -R (recursively move through a directory and subdirectory to change ownership), and -h (change the ownership of a symbolic link without changing the ownership of the file to which the link originally points). Of these three options, -R is particularly important and widely used. Therefore, the command `chown -R barries *` gives ownership of all files in the current directory and all files in any subdirectories to barries. The chown command may be limited in operation when disk quotas are in place; otherwise, this command can be used to defeat disk quotas by reassigning ownership.

The syntax for the chgrp command is as follows:

```
chgrp <options> <groupname> <filename(s)>
```

The chgrp command is very similar in operation to the chown command. The same three options described previously also apply to the chgrp command: -f, -R, and -h. The chown command is somewhat limited in what it allows standard users to do. However, the chgrp command allows any user to change the group of a file to any group that that user is a member of, which is quite useful.

The command line is not the only place that you can go to view a file or directory's permissions; you can also view and change permissions in the File Manager. For each object in the File Manager, there is a Properties dialog box that displays this information in an easy-to-understand format. In addition to the various permissions, you can also view the current owner and group names and modify the permissions (see Figure 5.3).

To view and modify the permissions for a file or folder, follow these steps:

1. Click a file or folder to select it. (You can also press the Tab or arrow keys to move to an object and then press the Spacebar key to select it.)
2. Choose the Properties command from the Selected menu. (You can also press Ctrl+Backspace.) The Properties dialog box appears.
3. Click the permission you want to change. (You can also press the Tab key to move to the permission and then press the Spacebar key to select it.)

4. Click the Apply Changes To drop-down list and select either All Files in Parent Folder or All Files and Their Subfolders (choose the latter if you want your changes inherited and not just applied to the currently selected file or folder).
5. Tab to the Owner and Group text boxes and edit the values as desired.
6. Click the Apply button to post your changes or the OK button to post your changes and close the Properties dialog box.

FIGURE 5.3

The Properties dialog box for a file in the File Manager

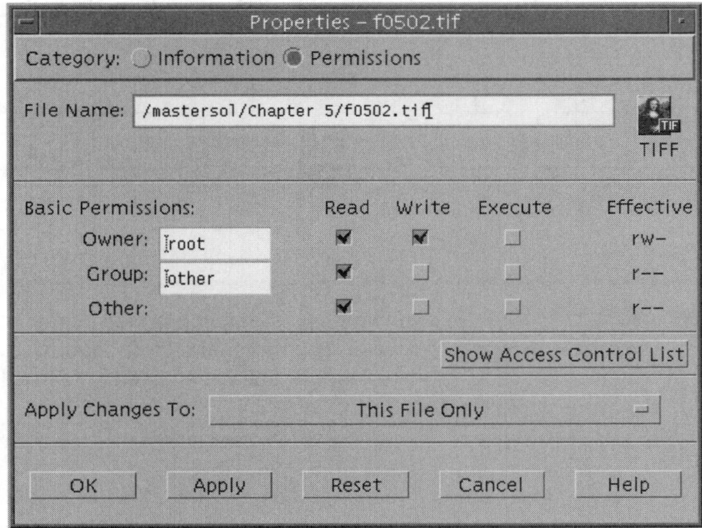

Directories

Solaris's file system contains a number of directories that store important files and programs in locations where the operating system expects them to be in order for your system to run correctly. There are also many directories that are optional and can be renamed and moved as desired, but many cannot. As you work with the file system and add programs and data files, you will continue to modify many of the directories. Understanding the directory structure, what components are required and what are optional, and where Solaris stores important system files and data structures will help you understand how Solaris operates and aid you when you need to debug problems that relate to files. In this section, I'll introduce you to directories and highlight some of the more important ones. Figure 5.4 shows you an overview of the first three levels of the Solaris directory hierarchy.

FIGURE 5.4

The first few levels of important Solaris directories

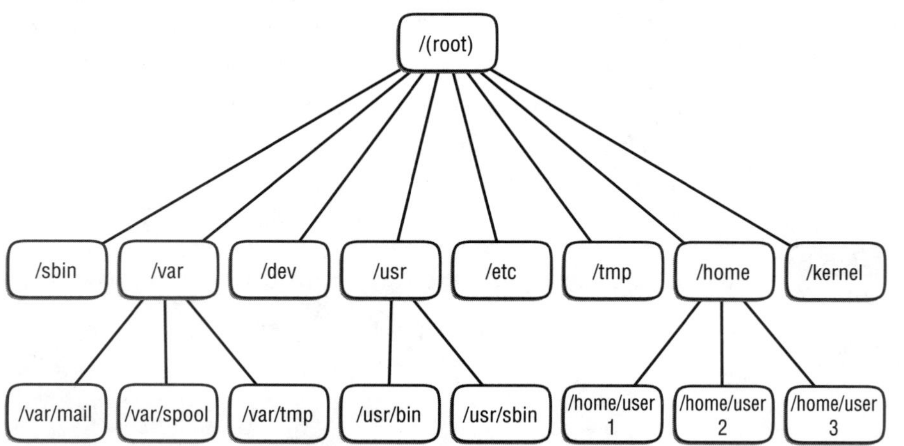

WARNING It is very important that you understand what directories are used for because when you remove or rename certain system directories, it can cause your system to stop operating. In some cases, you may be forced to reinstall your operating system to get your system running again.

NOTE One very important note about terminology: Throughout this book, the terms *directory* and *folder* are seemingly used interchangeably. A directory describes an address or location in the Solaris file system. A folder represents the icon representation of a directory in a graphical user interface such as the Common Desktop Environment (CDE) or the OpenWindows GUI. It's a minor point, but one that aficionados tend to stress. When describing operations at the command line, use the term *directory* exclusively.

The following is a list of important directories that you find in the Solaris 8 root file system:

/ or root directory The root directory (/) is the top directory in a Unix file system. Figure 5.5 shows the File Manager's view of the root directory of a Sun Ultra 5 workstation as it normally appears. Figure 5.6 shows that same directory when the Show Hidden Files option (Ctrl+S) in the View menu is selected.

FIGURE 5.5

The File Manager window of the root directory of a Sun Ultra 5 workstation

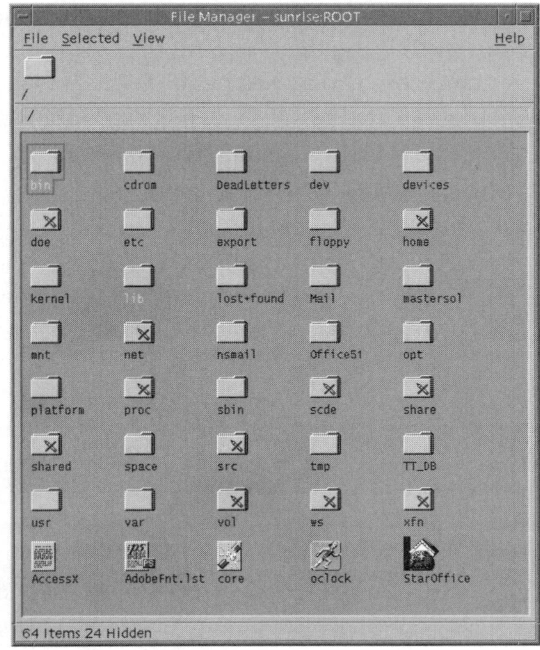

FIGURE 5.6

The same root directory window shown in Figure 5.5 with the Show Hidden Files option turned on

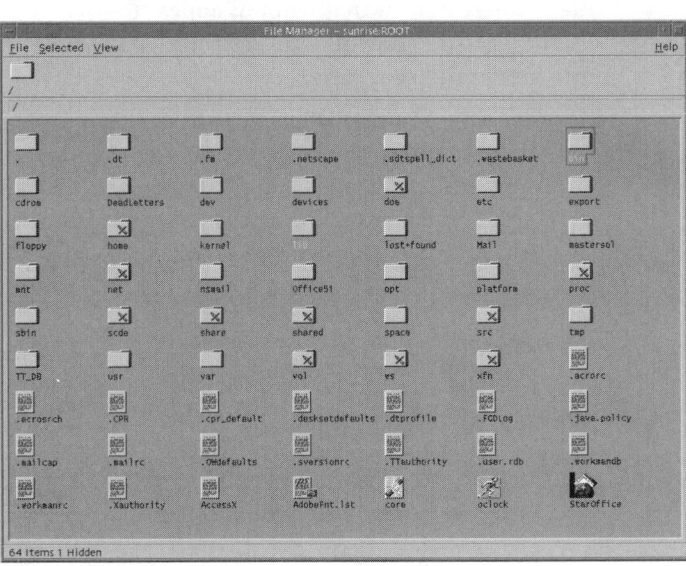

Many of the important files found in the root directory are hidden files, including the `.profile` file, which contains commands executed by the Bourne and Korn shells when they establish the environment, and the `.cshrc` file, which contains commands used by the C shell to establish the environment. The `.login` file, used by the C shell at boot-up for the same purpose the `.cshrc` is used, appears in the `/home` directory for a user.

`/bin` directory The `/bin`, or binary, directory stores programs such as editors (`vi` and `ed`), file system (`dd`, `df`, `sync`, and many others) and manipulation (`cp`, `mv`, `rm`, `ln`, `tar`) utilities, the Solaris shells (`ksh`, `sh`, and `csh`), system utilities (`arch`, `hostname`, and `uname`), and the login program. The `/bin` directory is actually a symbolic link (or soft link) to the `/usr/bin` directory where the actual programs are stored.

NOTE Not every directory installed as part of a default Solaris installation is described in this section, although most of the important ones are.

`/dev` directory This directory stores device files used by the kernel and hardware to communicate and function. Files in this directory represent peripheral devices that are part of or attached to your system. Solaris creates device files to correspond to the hardware and kernel of your computer system. The `/dev/null` file is where output that will not appear to users is sent; it is also called the *bit bucket*. The following subdirectories are some of the more important subdirectories in the `/dev` directory:

`/dev/cfg` Symbolic links to physical ap_ids. An ap_id is an attachment point identifier. There are two different kinds of ap_ids: logical and physical. A physical ap_id refers to a path reference, and a logical ap_id uses a friendly name. When describing a SCSI controller, the logical ap_id would be the disk controller number, such as c0.

`/dev/cua` Device files for uucp.

`/dev/dsk` Block disk device files.

`/dev/fbs` Frame buffer device files.

`/dev/fd` File descriptors.

`/dev/md` Files for volume management of logical or metadisk devices.

`/dev/pts` Pseudo-terminal devices.

/dev/rdsk Raw disk device files.

/dev/rmt Remote tape management files.

/dev/sad Links to the STREAMS Administrative Driver (SAD).

/dev/sound Audio device files.

/dev/swap Default swap device.

/dev/term Terminal devices.

/devices directory Contains device files subtrees. There are links in /dev that point to the files in this directory.

/etc directory The /etc directory (pronounced "e-t-c" or "et-cee," but never "etcetera") stores platform-dependent local administrative and configuration files that define a system's local identity. In this directory, you will find files such as passwd, a system user database; vstab, a list of devices that the file system can mount; hosts, a correlation file for system names and their related IP addresses and the location of the IP address provider; and profile, the system shell configuration file. Some of the important files found in the /etc directory, albeit not all of them, are listed here:

/etc/aliases Here the mail system sendmail creates aliases for users. The /etc/aliases directory is a symbolic link to the /etc/mail/aliases directory.

/etc/dumpdates Contains information about the use of ufsdump backups.

/etc/group This file contains group information.

/etc/inittab This file contains an initialization table that specifies processes to run at boot-up, as well as the run level the system boots up into.

/etc/magic This file lists file types and assignments.

/etc/mnttab The mount table lists all mounted devices.

/etc/passwd This file that stores the list of users for a system and the location of the users' home directories and the shells that they use. Passwords are now kept in a shadow directory.

/etc/power.conf This file is used for power management.

/etc/printers.conf This file is used to control the printer subsystem.

/etc/profile The profile file used by the system login shell initialization script (Bourne and Korn shells).

/etc/.login The .login file is used by the system login shell initialization script (C shells).

/etc/shadow This file contains encrypted user passwords and password aging information.

/etc/vfstab The virtual file system table lists devices used by `fsck` and at boot-up to mount file systems and the swap space.

Solaris and other System V Unix distributions differ from other versions of Unix in that the `/etc` folder contains subfolders named `rcx.d`, where *x* is a number from 1 to 6. These folders, `rc1.d` through `rc6.d`, represent the different run levels that are supported by the init program in its initialization file at `/etc/inittab`.

The `/etc` directory contains numerous important subdirectories, the most important of which are listed here:

/etc/acct Accounting or system logging of configuration status.

/etc/cron.d Configuration for the scheduling utility `cron`.

/etc/defaults Default information for a variety of programs.

/etc/dfs Configuration information for the distributed file system.

/etc/dhcp Configuration information for the Dynamic Host Configuration Protocol (DHCP) service that assigns IP address over a network from a pool of addresses.

/etc/dmi Solstice Enterprise Agents (SEAs) configuration file.

/etc/fn Federated Naming Server and X.500 directory support files.

/etc/fs Binaries used by file system types for startup before the /usr file system is mounted.

/etc/gss Generic Security Service (GSS) application programming interface configuration file.

/etc/inet Internet services configuration files.

/etc/init.d The shell scripts used when changing run levels.

/etc/lib Shared library files used during boot-up.

/etc/lp Line printer configuration files.

/etc/llc2 Logical link control (llc2) driver configuration files.

/etc/lp Printer subsystem configuration files.

/etc/mail Mail system configuration files.

/etc/net Transport-independent network service configuration information.

/etc/nfs NFS server logging configuration files.

/etc/opt Configuration data for any optional packages that were installed.

/etc/openwin OpenWindows configuration files.

/etc/rcn.d These directories contain the scripts used to enter or leave a run level (*n*=0 to 3). A main script specifies which scripts in a particular directory run and in what order they should be run at each run level.

/etc/rcS.d Scripts for single-user mode operation.

/etc/rpcsec Used to store an NIS+ authentication configuration file.

/etc/saf Service Access Facility (SAF) files.

/etc/security Basic Security Module (BSM) configuration files.

/etc/skel Default profile scripts that are used by the `adduser` command to create new user accounts.

/etc/tm Trademark files whose content is displayed at boot-up.

/etc/uucp UUCP configuration data.

/etc/volatile Temporary system files used for installation of Solaris distribution software. Unless an active installation is in progress, you may not find this directory listed.

TIP The command `man filesystem` provides a rather detailed online description of the Solaris file system.

/export directory The `/export` directory is the location used to export file systems stored on a local machine (a server, for instance) to other systems. Network terminals without hard drives make use of this directory on a remote system. Note that `/export` is one of the directories not required by Solaris, and many systems are used without it.

/home directory The `/home` directory stores the home directories for any and all users of the system. In addition to actual `/home/`*`<username>`* folders, the `/home` directory contains directories for the FTPD (FTP daemon) and the HTTPD (HTTP daemon). The `/home` directory is a read and execute directory. You can't write to this directory without superuser login status. Some systems store user-specific `/home` directories under the `/inhouse` or `/clients` directory. The automount program (automounter) is used to mount and unmount the `/home` directory.

/kernel directory The /kernel directory stores platform-specific kernel modules that are loaded in the boot-up sequence. This directory, along with /usr/kernel and /platform, contain the bulk of the Solaris kernel's device drivers and loadable modules.

Other important subdirectories and files found in /kernel are /kernel/drv, which stores 32-bit device driver files; /kernel/dr/sparcv9, which stores 64-bit SPARC device driver files; the /kernel/genunix file, which contains the generic part of the Unix kernel; and /kernel/subsystem/ia64, the 64-bit Intel platform modules loaded in the boot-up sequence.

/lib directory This directory contains a symbolic link to the /usr/lib directory.

/mnt directory The mount directory is where you'll find files describing any removable devices like CD-ROMs, floppy disks, and Zip or Jaz drives in Unix. Solaris makes mount directories (/floppy, /cdrom, and others) subdirectories of the Solaris root directory. The /mnt directory is an empty directory that is used to temporarily mount file systems.

/opt directory Solaris stores optional or add-on packages in the /opt directory. Among the programs that use this directory are Netscape Communicator, the GNU C compiler (gcc), and the Sun Workshop C compiler (cc). Note that when you get GNUgcc as part of a Solaris install, this is the location it is stored in. If you install GNUgcc from a downloaded version, you will find that newer versions install into the /usr/local directory.

/platform directory This directory and its subdirectories store platform-specific objects that are used to support the root directories of the supported platforms. Among the subdirectories you will find in the /platform directory are those found listed here (files in these directories are best left untouched except by standard installation routines because their manual modifications can cause serious system malfunctions):

/platform/'uname -i'/kernel Platform-dependent modules required to boot your system

/platform/'uname -m'/kernel Hardware boot modules

/platform/'uname -i'/kernelsubsystem/1a64 Intel 64-bit boot modules

/platform/'uname -i'/kernel/subsystem/sparcv9 SPARC 64-bit boot modules

/platform/'uname -i'/kernel/sparcv9/unix 64-bit platform-dependent kernel

/platform/'uname -i'/kernel/unix 32-bit platform-specific kernel

/platform/'uname -i'/lib Platform-specific shared objects required for the boot-up sequence

/proc directory The /proc directory stores the process file system (PROCFS) used to reference objects in memory identified by the process ID. The /proc directory contains a number of important files: as, which stores the address-space image of a process; psinfo, which contains the information about a process used by the ps command; cred, which stores information about permissions associated with a process; sigact, which has the array that contains signal handlers for a process; cwd, which is a symbolic link to the current working directory; fd, which is a reference to open files that are used by the process; and root, which is a symbolic link to a processes root directory. Unless you use the chroot command for a process or the process(es) that spawned that process, the root referred to is the same root as the system.

/sbin directory This directory (and /usr/sbin) stores binary files (programs) that relate to system functions. Among the common programs you find are utilities like fsck, fdisk, mkfs, and shutdown. The *sbin* stands for "statically linked binary files." To be used, these files do not require that any other file systems are mounted (although many of the programs in /bin do). You'll also find files like mount, umount, sync, and ifconfig in /sbin.

/tmp directory The temporary directory contains files that are used briefly and then deleted. The default Solaris install mounts the system's swap file space in /tmp to save space on the root file system. If you find you are running out of swap space, you can turn this feature off. Many installations and program builds use the /tmp directory to store files that are used during a program's installation. On a multiuser system, you will find that /tmp contains subdirectories with each of the usernames for people who have logged in to the system. Files in the /tmp directory are deleted as part of the boot-up process.

If you want to monitor the swap space usage, use the df -k /tmp command. You can also get a look at the condition of your swap file by clicking the System Info control in the Hosts subpanel of the front panel in the CDE. That control opens the Workspace Information dialog box with virtual memory statistics.

/usr directory The user directory is where most programs, as well as files that are user related, are stored. Many of the folders you see in the /usr directory are duplicates of folder names you see in the root directory. For example, you see folders like /bin, /etc, /opt, and /sbin in the /usr directory. Those folders store user-specific information that programs need. The /usr directory forms a second major file system hierarchy, containing many of the same subdirectories you find on the /root itself. Figure 5.7 shows the /usr directory.

FIGURE 5.7

The /usr directory contains optional program installations and related files.

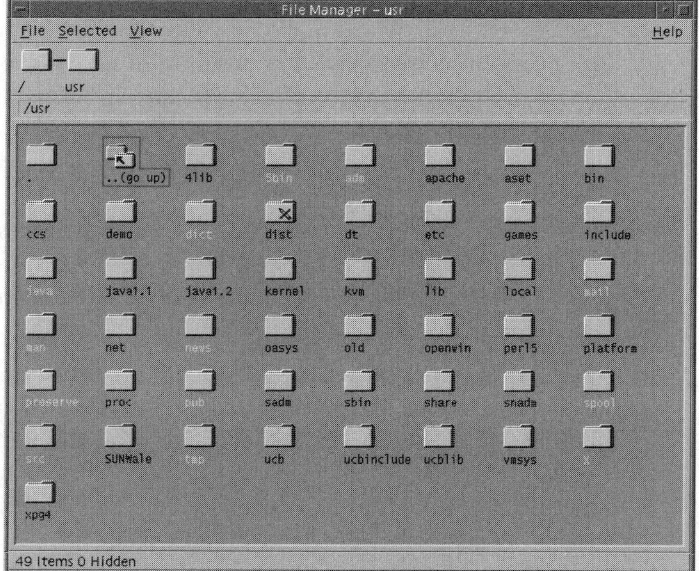

The various /usr directories that start with the letter *X* refer to different settings and aspects of the X Window system. The X and the xpg4 directories are two examples. Inside the X directory, for example, are folders that store documents (/docs), programs (/bin), libraries (/lib), man pages (/man), and so forth. (Keep in mind that the X directory is a symbolic link to the openwin directory described later in this chapter.) One important directory is the /usr/local directory and its subdirectories. Any files specific to the type of workstation or server that is in use locally are stored in this directory tree.

Many people use the /usr/local directory to install applications that they have compiled for the system. It's taken from the BSD method of using / and /usr for system installed files and using /usr/local for software additions the user makes. Most software downloaded from SunSites (like sunsite.unc.edu) install to the /usr/local directory even through they are Solaris packages.

The following list includes descriptions of the important /usr subdirectories:

/usr/adm Symbolic link to /usr/bin.

/usr/aset Automated Security Enhancement Tools (ASET) program and files directory.

/usr/bin Platform-specific command programs executed as part of your environment (e.g., $PATH); a wrapper points to the appropriate version. Subdirectories in this directory contain the specific binary files. The /usr/bin stores files that are used in shared or network mode and not in single-user mode (those are stored in the /sbin directory).

/usr/ccs C compilation system and the files used by make, sccs, and yacc.

/usr/demo Demo programs and data.

/usr/dict Symbolic link to the /usr/share/lib/dict dictionary file used by the Unix spell program.

/usr/dt The root directory for CDE programs. This directory contains the subdirectories /usr/dt/bin, binary files for CDD system utilities; /usr/dt/include, header files for CDE software; /usr/dt/lib, library files for CDE software; and /usr/dt/man, CDE manual pages.

/usr/include The include headers for C programs.

/usr/java Java programs and libraries.

/usr/kernel Platform-specific loadable kernel modules that are not an essential part of the root file system.

/usr/kvm Mount point for binaries and libraries, provided for backward compatibility and no longer used.

/usr/lib Platform-specific libraries, databases, commands, and daemons used by your system. This directory contains both shared and static libraries, profile libraries, and locale information.

/usr/local Files and directories that are added to Solaris and are locally important.

/usr/mail Symbolic link to the /var/mail directory.

/usr/man Symbolic link to the /usr/share/man directory.

/usr/news Symbolic link to the /var/news directory.

/usr/oasys The commands and program files used in the Form and Menu Language Interpreter (FMLI) execution environment.

/usr/old Programs being discontinued. This directory is usually empty.

/usr/openwin Installation or mount point for OpenWindows software. The files in this directory are used by the X System, OpenLook, and the CDE. This directory contains the subdirectory /usr/openwin/lib/X11, which has in it X Window System libraries.

/usr/perl5 Perl 5 documentation and program files.

/usr/platform Platform-specific objects not required by the root file system. This is a shadow directory of the /platform directory.

/usr/preserve Symbolic link to the /var/preserve directory.

/usr/proc The process tools.

/usr/pub Contains the files that run the online man pages and character processing system. This directory is a symbolic link to the /usr/share/lib/pub directory.

/usr/sadm System administration files and directories, system upgrade scripts, package maintenance executables, and other files.

/usr/sbin Platform-dependent programs that are used by system administrators but are not vital to everyday administration. The location for third-party system software that mirrors this directory is /opt/packagename/sbin.

/usr/share Platform-independent shareable files such as manual pages, dictionaries, terminal data, and time zone information.

/usr/snadm System and network administration files.

/usr/spool Symbolic link to the /var/spool directory.

/usr/src Symbolic link to the /usr/share/src directory.

/usr/tmp Symbolic link to the /var/tmp directory.

/usr/ucb Berkeley compatibility package binary files.

/usr/ucbinclude Berkeley compatibility package headers.

/usr/vmsys Commands and files used by the Framed Access Command Environment (FACE) programs.

/usr/X This directory is a symbolic link to the X Window System's files installed at /usr/openwin.

/usr/xpg4 The directories used by utilities that are compliant with Portable Operating System Interface (POSIX) and XPG4. Refer to man xpg4 for more information.

/var directory The /var directory is used to contain files with a longer lifetime than the files stored in the /tmp directory, and they are unique to a specific system. Many of the /var files are log files, some are spool files, some are user mailbox files, and some are system databases like the packages database.

Figure 5.8 shows the contents of the /var directory, but what you see in your /var directory depends upon what programs and services you install on your system.

FIGURE 5.8

The /var directory contains many subdirectories used to store settings, states, and messages for different programs and system functions.

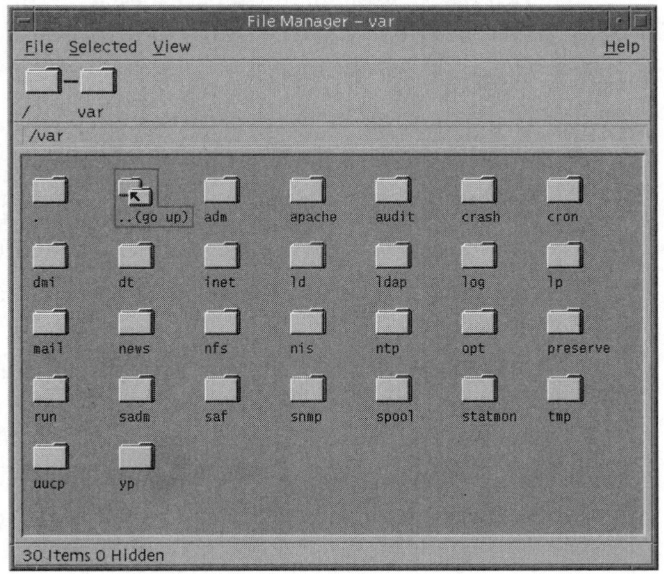

Familiarity with the various subdirectories contained in the /var directory is important; they all serve rather critical system functions. The following list includes some of the important /var subdirectories:

/var/adm System logging and accounting files.

/var/audit Basic Security Module (BSM) audit files.

/var/crash Kernel crash dump files.

/var/cron Log files for cron processes.

/var/dmi Solstice Enterprise Agents (SEA) Desktop Management Interface (DMI) runtime components. DMI is used to manage systems remotely on a network.

/var/dt The `dtlogin` configuration files.

/var/ftp The default FTP (File Transfer Protocol) server directory.

/var/inet IPv6 router table files.

/var/log System log files.

/var/lp Line printer logs.

/var/mail User mail.

/var/news Community service message. (This is not the Internet's Usenet news service.)

/var/nfs NFS server logs.

/var/nis NIS+ network databases.

/var/ntp NTP (Network Time Protocol) server state directory.

/var/opt The location used to install software packages.

/var/preserve Backup files for the `vi` and `ex` text editors.

/var/run Temporary files related to the run state. Not used in the boot process.

/var/sadm Software administration database used to manage installed packages. This directory also stores patches to the operating system, install information, and documents for the current operating system version.

/var/sadm/system/logs The status logs for the `sadm` function. You will find installation logs in this directory.

/var/saf Service access facility logging and account files.

/var/spool Spooled files for printing (`/var/spool/lp`) and output as well as `cron` files (`/var/spool/cron`) and mail delivery files (`/var/spool/mqueue`) are stored in the subdirectories here.

/var/statmon Network status monitor files.

/var/tmp Temporary files created for use with application installations and other nontransient operations.

/var/uucp The `uucp` log and status files.

/var/yp Files that provide backward compatibility between NIS and `ypbind`. NIS+ makes this translation unnecessary.

The Working and Home Directories

Your *working directory* is also your current directory. This designation refers to the fact that you can view, modify, and execute files and directories in the working directory without having to specify a path name. In a graphical user interface, or GUI, such as the CDE or OpenWindows, the current directory is not necessarily the window that has the focus on your screen. (To determine that this is true, open a terminal window and give the `pwd` command after you boot up.) You have to specifically use the `cd` (change directory) command to be working in another directory.

When you log in to Solaris, the system boots up to the login screen. You then log in to the graphical or text interface and are placed into your home directory by the login process. To begin a session, therefore, your current or working directory is the same as your home directory. In a window manager like the CDE or the OpenWindows desktop, you will see any previously opened File Manager windows, and one of those windows may have the focus.

To change directories to the home directory, do either one of the following:

- Enter the `cd` command without any other options or arguments.
- Click the Home Folder icon (shown in the following graphic) in the front panel of the CDE.

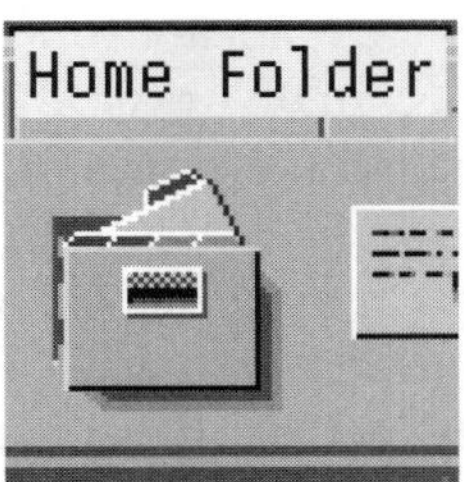

You open your home folder and any terminal window session from the window that has as its current directory your home directory. You can verify your home directory by using the `pwd` (print working directory) command after you log on to your system.

Startup Resource Files

Your system contains a set of startup files that provide whatever shell you are using with the necessary information to configure your system for you as a user. The important information those startup files contain includes display configuration commands using the `set terminal` or `stty` command and `set prompt` and `set home` statements to change the prompt and home directory. Each shell contains one or more startup files, and those files are read anytime the shell initializes. In multiuser environments, a system will store specific startup files for each username that logs in to the system.

Solaris shells use a template system for creating startup resource files. There is usually a systemwide shell resource file for each of the shells that are copied into the home directory. An administrator can modify the template resource file as well as any user's resource file. A user can modify the resource files in their own home directories by adding shell commands to the files. Thus, a user has control over the nature of their environment. The standard Solaris distribution comes with three shells—Bourne, Korn, and C shells—although you can add other shells to the system if you like. By default, the standard shell is the Bourne shell. The Bourne and Korn shells use the `/etc/.profile` file as a startup file, and the C shell uses the `.cshrc` and `.login` files. The first time you log in to the C shell, it reads the `.login` file, and any subsequent times you start up a new C shell, it reads the `.cshrc` file.

NOTE The Bourne shell is described in Chapter 18, the Korn shell in Chapter 19, and the C shell in Chapter 20.

The graphical user interfaces such as the Common Desktop Environment (CDE) and OpenWindows are full-featured window managers that offer desktop features. Those environments run on top of X Window sessions. There are many configuration and startup files that set up your environment for these different systems, and those files are described at the beginning of Chapter 7, "The Solaris Desktop." Typically, you use desktop controls in the form of icons that call configuration programs or utilities to change the resource file settings in a window manager. It is possible to modify X Window resource file settings directly, as is described in "Customizing the Desktop" and the sections on the X Window System toward the end of Chapter 7.

Creating Directories and Files

You can create a directory from the command line using the `mkdir` (make directory) command or in the File Manager by using the New Folder command on the File menu. The command-line option is somewhat more powerful, allowing you to create a directory anywhere in the file system with options that even help create a path or set the access privileges for that directory.

The syntax for the `mkdir` command is as follows:

```
mkdir options (<pathname>/<directoryname list>)
```

There are really only two significant options that you might want to use with the mkdir command:

- The -m, or mode, option sets the access privileges of the directory using either symbolic or octal nomenclature (these two systems are described in the section "Modifying Access Rights" earlier in this chapter).
- The -p, or parent, option will create any directory name in the path you specified if it doesn't already exist.

For example, if you specify a list of directory names without paths, then mkdir creates those directories in your current directory. If you give the command `mkdir -p /usr/docs/letters/1200letters` from within the docs directory and the docs directory doesn't already have a /usr/docs/letter subdirectory, then this command creates the /usr/docs/letters subdirectory and places the 1200letters directory into that new subdirectory. This is a pretty convenient option to use if you can remember it.

The second option (-m) that allows you to set the access privileges of a new directory is illustrated by the command `mkdir -m ugo=rx-w 1200letters`, which creates the new directory and gives the user, group, and others access rights to read and execute but not to write. In octal format, a similar command, `mkdir -m 600 1200letters`, creates the directory and sets the user's access permissions to read (4) plus write (2).

In the CDE, to use the File Manager window to create a new folder, follow these steps:

1. Select the New Folder command from the File menu. The New Folder dialog box, shown in the following graphic, appears.

2. To have Solaris create the new folder at the location you specify, enter the path name and folder name (in the format *<pathname>/<foldername>*) into the New Folder Name text box.
3. Click the Apply button to create the folder or the OK button to create the folder and close the dialog box.

The New Folder dialog box is not a command-line processor; it doesn't support the -p or -m options, nor will it accept a folder name list.

The File Manager window offers you an opportunity to create new data files by selecting the New File command from the File menu. The following graphic shows you the New File dialog box. If you enter a name without a suffix in the New File Name text box, you create a data file. If you add a suffix, like `.tif`, to the filename, Solaris creates a file of that type.

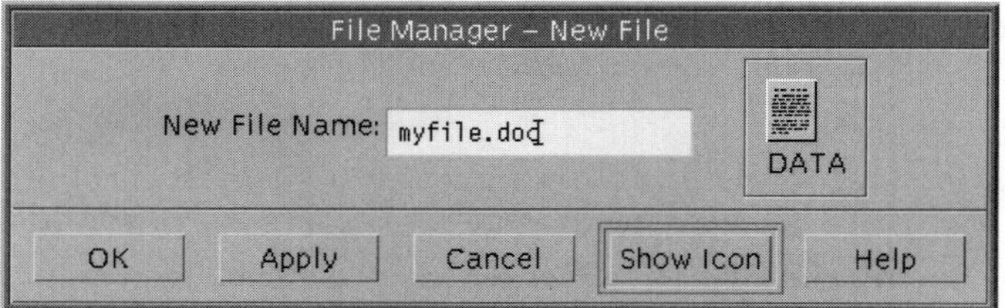

The copy command (see "Copying and Moving Directories and Files") is yet another way of creating new directories (as duplicates) from old ones. Solaris supports both the `cp` (copy) command-line expression and a Copy command in the CDE File Manager. The `cp` command creates a duplicate of any directory that you have write privileges to and copies all of the contents of that directory as well. The `cp` command works with both files and directories (or folders).

Here is the syntax for the `cp` (copy) command appropriate to creating directories:

```
cp <options> <source_directoryname list> <pathname>/<target_directoryname>
```

It can take a list of directories and copy them and their contents to another location. Use the `-r` flag for a recursive copy or the `cp` command will respond `cp xx is a directory` and will not perform the copy.

From a File Manager window, you can copy selected folders using the Copy To command (Ctrl+C) on the Selected menu. In the resulting Copy To dialog box, enter the name of the copied folder into the Name for Copy text box and the path into the Destination text box. The Copy To dialog box creates a folder in the location you specify. Chapter 7 describes using the File Manager to copy, move, and rename files and folders in more detail.

Navigating Directories

You often need to move the focus of your actions to a directory to act on it and the files it contains. The command that changes your focus to a new working directory without modifying the directory is the `cd` (change directory) command. The `cd` command is a Solaris utility, but it is also one of the built-in shell commands for each of the three main Solaris shells (Korn, Borne, and C shells). The syntax for this very simple but important command is as follows:

```
cd <pathname>/<directoryname>
```

Once you use this command, your actions affect files and subdirectories in your new working directory. If you have forgotten or don't know where in the file system you are, then use the pwd (print working directory) command to have Solaris return the path name and directory name `<pathname>/<directoryname>` of the current directory.

You can use the parent pointer to move up one directory in the file system, as follows:

```
# pwd
/usr/docs/letters/12letters
# cd ..
# pwd
/usr/docs/letters
```

The following command moves you to the root folder:

```
# cd /
# pwd
/
```

If you are familiar with MS-DOS, then you know that it sets as a default a prompt that shows the path of the current working directory. If you want to see this kind of prompt in any of the Solaris shells, you can modify your shell prompt by including the following `set` command (shown for the Korn shell, the first is for root and the second is for users):

```
'PS1="'pwd' #"'
'PS1="'pwd' $"'
```

For the C shell, that `set` command would be as follows:

```
% set prompt="'pwd' %"
```

Now if you log in to the `/usr/home/barries` directory at startup, as you might if your username were `barries`, then what you see for a prompt is the following:

```
/usr/home/barries #
```

For the Korn shell, the environmental variables are set in the `/etc/.profile` or the `~/.profile` files, and the C shell uses the `~/.cshrc` and `~/.login` files. You can also use the home environmental variable command in those files to set (`set`) the location of the home directory.

Deleting Directories and Files

To delete a directory or file (or multiple directories or files), do any of the following:

- Issue the `rmdir` (remove directory) command or the `rm` (remove files) command at the command line to remove any empty directories. Any directories that are not empty will not be deleted.
- Drag the directory or files to the Trash icon at the far right of the front panel.
- Select the directory's folder or the file's icon in a File Manager window on your desktop and press the Del key.

The second and third methods for deleting directories and folders in the CDE are described in some detail in Chapter 7 in the section "The Front Panel."

Solaris provides the standard Unix commands `rm` (remove files or links) to delete files and symbolic links and `rmdir` to delete any empty directories other than the working or current directory. When you give the `rmdir` command, it cannot delete any subdirectories that aren't already empty. The directory entries of the link to the parent directory (`..`) and the representation of the directory itself (`.`) are automatically removed when you use the `rmdir` command on a directory. The `rmdir` command has as its close cousin the `rm` command that removes files.

Use the following syntax for the remove files command:

```
rm <options> <filename list>
```

This is the syntax for the remove directories command (for empty directories only):

```
rmdir <directoryname list>
```

There are no significant options for the `rmdir` command, but the `rm` command has the powerful `-r` (recursive) option that you can use. When you specify `rm -r`, Solaris deletes files, including subdirectories within any directory contained in the specified directory, and also deletes the directory itself. The `-f` option for the `rm` command will forcibly remove files for which you do not have write permissions without asking you to approve the action. The force option only works if you are logged in as root or if you own the directory that you are in. The `rm` command also has the `-i` (interactive) command that asks you to approve before it deletes any file.

WARNING The `rm -r` command is a powerful and dangerous command. If you use this command without carefully specifying a file reference, it may delete your home directory and everything that it contains, as well as your entire file system tree. Ouch! Pay particular attention when you use this command.

Remember that you need to have write and execute permissions for the parent directory to delete a file or directory inside the parent directory, although you do not have to have those permissions for the specific file you are deleting. When you use the `rm` command from the keyboard and you do not have write permission for the file, Solaris will ask you before it deletes the file. You cannot use the `rm -r` command to delete a subdirectory that you don't own, even if you own the parent directory.

Copying and Moving Directories and Files

You can copy files from the command line using the `cp` (copy) command or through actions in the CDE. A move operation is functionally equivalent to a copy operation followed by a deletion of the original object or objects. The `mv` (move command) offers the additional option of allowing you to change both the path of a file and its name. If you own a folder, you can use the move command to move that folder whether it has files or directories in it or not.

To copy a directory or file (or multiple directories or files), do any of the following:

- Issue the `cp` (copy) command at the command line.
- Select the directory's folder or the file's icon in a File Manager window and drag that object to another File Manager window showing the target directory.
- Select the directory's folder or file's icon in a File Manager window and then use the Copy To command (Ctrl+C) on the Selected menu to copy the file or directory to another location.

In Chapter 7, the second and third methods of copying files and folders are described. Here I'll describe how the operation is done from the command line.

The syntax for the copy file command is as follows:

```
cp <options> <pathname>/<source_filename pathname> /<target_filename>
cp <options> <pathname>/<source_filename list> \
    <pathname>/<target_directoryname>
cp <options> <pathname>/<source_directoryname list> \
    <pathname>/<target_directoryname>
```

You can use the copy command to copy either one or more than one regular file. Files can be static data files (text, graphics, etc.), or they can be binary files. In the preceding examples, the first version of the command copies one file to a directory, and the second version copies one or more files to a directory. The third version, when used with the `-r` (or recursive) option, takes an entire directory(or directories) and copies it to another directory.

There are three options that you might want to use for the copy command: `-i` (interactive) seeks your permission before each copy operation; `-p` (preserve) preserves the owner, group, permissions, and modification dates of the source file in the target file; and `-r` (recursive) copies all subdirectories and any files contained therein into the target directory and is required to copy a directory. The preserve option requires you to be the owner of either the file or the root, and if you copy files owned by another person and you are not root, the copy is owned by you and not the original owner.

The following examples should help clarify the copy command's usage:

```
cp memo1 memo2 /archive/mystuff
```

This command copies the two files in the current directory to the `/mystuff` directory. Notice that the source list requires only spaces between each item. To copy a file from a location other than your working directory, try this:

```
cp /test/myfile1
```

This command copies the `myfile1` file from the `/test` directory into the current or working directory.

The `mv` (move) command has the following syntax:

```
mv <options> <pathname>/<source_filename> <pathname>/<new_filename>
mv <options> <pathname>/<source_filename list> <pathname>/<new_directory>
```

In the first instance, you move a file from one directory to another, renaming that file if you specify a different name for *<new_filename>*. In the second instance, you can move one or more files to a preexisting directory. If the `mv` command specifies as a target another file system and cannot rename the file, the file is moved bearing the same name. The move command takes the `-f` (force) and `-i` (interactive) options described for the copy command.

As an example, the following command moves the contents of the current directory to the `/archive` directory:

```
mv * /archive
```

Links

A link is a pointer to a file or directory. A *hard link* is a directory entry that points to a file, whereas a *symbolic link* (or soft link) can be applied to both files and directories and has the same contents as the file or directory to which it points. Links, particularly symbolic links, are widely used in Solaris in many places that you might not expect. For example, the front panel of the CDE desktop is a container for symbolic links to programs, files, and actions.

When you create a file, you create a hard link in a directory to a data file elsewhere on disk. That's the purpose of the duplication in Solaris's file system directory tree. It doesn't matter how you create the file; whether you use the copy command, the `vi` editor, or the New File command in the File Manager, you still create a link. Because the copy command also creates links, you might wonder what the difference between the link command and the copy command is. The link command does not create a copy of a file as the copy command does. Any command that includes a filename starts a program that passes the filename as a pointer to the location on disk where the data for that file is found. Symbolic links, therefore, offer a convenient method for allowing multiple points of access to data; in other words, they allow users to share files.

NOTE If you create a link to allow other people to share a file, don't forget that you have to provide appropriate access permissions to the parent directory of that file.

The `ln` (link) command creates a hard link to an existing file. The syntax for the link command is as follows:

```
ln <options> <pathname>/<filename pathname>/<linkname>
```

Use of the link command without the `-s` option creates another pointer (a hard link) to a preexisting file, not a copy of that file.

When you use the `-s` option, you create a symbolic link. In the following example, a symbolic link is created and the list command is used to display information about the link file. You can substitute a directory name (*<directoryname>*) for the filename (*<filename>*) and create a symbolic link to that directory. Notice that there is an `l` before the permission list for a link file, a pointer appears after the filename, and the original filename is displayed, as shown:

```
# ln -s /test/myfile
# ls -l myfile /test/myfile
-rw-r-r-     1 root     other    1054    Dec 22 01:12 /test/myfile
lrwxrwxrwx     1 root     other    12    Dec 22 01:14 myfile -> /test/myfile
```

All of the links to the same file show the same file information—including access permissions, owner, group—and are stamped with the date and time the link was created. Two or more links to the same file look the same in all respects but the following: The inode number for each is different, the date and time stamp are different, and the links are owned by different owners/groups than the person who created them. If you delete a link from a set of links, you can still access the original file from any of the other links. However, if you delete the original file, all of the links stop working but the link files do not also get deleted.

You can also create a link in the CDE by using the Copy as Link command on the Select menu for files and folders. Links created with this command are symbolic links (see Chapter 7 for a description of the Copy as Link command). When you right-click a link in the File Manager window, the pop-up menu includes a Properties command, but the Properties command is not included on the pop-up menu of a link placed on the workspace.

Symbolic links work around one of the limitations of hard links: A hard link can't be a pointer to a directory. Symbolic links also allow you to link to a file that is located anywhere in the file system, or even on other file systems. You can even point a symbolic link to a nonexistent file, which is helpful when a file is removed from the file system and then restored. When you restore the file, you don't have to re-create the link. Hard links can only be applied to files on the same file system. Because Solaris uses multiple file systems, each with its own inode tables and its own file system hierarchy, hard links severely limit your flexibility.

The `rm` (remove file) command may be used to delete a hard link. If you remove the last hard link to the original file, Solaris deletes the data file as well. The data is no longer available on your system as a file, and Solaris releases the space on disk that the file occupies. If you delete that last hard link, even if there are any symbolic links to the original file, Solaris still deletes the data file. In the CDE, Solaris will show a broken link icon for that symbolic link, as shown in the following graphic. If you're working in the CDE and you try to delete the last hard link to a file, Solaris will warn you that it will delete the original file and ask you for a confirmation before it does so.

Disk Storage

In the sections that follow, I'll describe how Solaris stores data on disk in file systems. After describing the various types of file systems available, I'll show you how these file systems are written to disk and the various ways you can manage files in file systems.

File Systems

Solaris uses several different file system formats for storage and for data processing. On your hard drives and diskettes, Solaris uses the Unix file system (UFS), which is a standard for Berkeley System Distribution. When Sun moved Solaris from the BSD version of Unix (SunOS 1–4*x* or Solaris 1.*x*) to the AT&T System V Unix-based distribution, they decided to keep the UFS file system. The USF can be read from and written to by all versions of Unix, and Linux recently added full support for it. The UFS is sometimes referred to as the 4.2 file system, or the Berkeley Fast File System. On IA x86 systems, Solaris uses the S5FS file system, based on the BSD Fat Fast File System that was part of the Tahoe 4.3 release.

NOTE Chapter 6 describes both disk formatting and device addressing.

Solaris uses the High Sierra file system (HSFS) for CD-ROM storage. The HSFS uses the ISO 9660 industry standard for CD-ROMs, a cross-platform industry standard. Given that ISO 9660 supports the MS-DOS file system, for cross-platform support, you must use the 8.3 file-naming scheme—eight letters for the filename and three letters for the file extension—for all CD-ROM filenames. The format itself allows a filename of up to 28 characters and a three-character extension and adds a version using the following syntax: `<filename>.<ext>;<version>`. High Sierra is an industry standard that is used on all Unix platforms, Windows, DOS, and the Macintosh. There are two Unix extensions to High Sierra: One is part of High Sierra itself and the other is called Rock-Ridge (the latter is used on all versions of Unix).

New to Solaris 8 is support for the Universal Disk Format (UDF) file system, an industry-standard format for Digital Versatile Disk (DVD). The support for the UDF file system is found in the packages SUNWudfr, the 32-bit kernel module; SUNWudfrx, the 64-bit kernel module; and SUNWudf, the `/usr` module. The Solaris UDF file system is a cross-platform file system and supports standard CD-ROM and DVD-ROM and enhanced playback and record modes. UDF does not support write-once media, CD-RW, or DVD-RAM with either sequential one-disk writes or incremental writes. UDF also does not support quotas, ACLs, transaction logging, file system locking, or file system threads.

Solaris also supports the MS-DOS file system for floppy disks or diskettes. That file system is more commonly called the PC file system (PCFS). Solaris refers to the floppy disk in this format as `fd` in the `/etc/vstab` file listing. PCFS is used to transfer files between Solaris and Windows systems, mostly. You can use standard Unix commands like `mkdir`, `del`, `ls`, `mv`, `touch`, and so forth to alter the contents of a PC file system.

To summarize, these real file systems are associated with the following devices:

- UFS (Unix file system) and S5FS are associated with hard drives, tapes, CD-ROM, and diskettes.
- HSFS (High Sierra file system) is associated with CD-ROM.
- PCFS (PC file system) is associated with diskettes.
- UDF (Universal Disk Format) is associated with DVD.

Virtual File Systems

In addition to the file systems discussed in the preceding section, Solaris uses virtual file systems, or pseudo file systems, to provide memory-based file systems meant to speed up access to kernel information. With the exception of the SWAP file system (SWAPFS), most virtual file systems do not consume disk space (only their pointers are stored on disk). The Cache File System (CacheFS) is another example of a file system stored on disk that is sometimes used to speed up the performance of slow devices such as CD-ROM drives.

In order to manage files used in memory by the SunOS kernel, Solaris uses the `/proc`, or process file system (PROCFS). This file system, which is mounted in the root directory, stores references to files being used by each process running on Solaris in a set of read- and execute-only folders. Figure 5.9 shows the `/proc` folder in the CDE as well as one of the process folders. The icons you see don't represent real data files; they represent references to the data that the kernel creates and uses. A user or system administrator doesn't manipulate the `/proc` directory in any way; the kernel modifies the references as needed and uses these references to correct system malfunctions.

The `proc` file system solves several problems on Solaris. When it's installed, programs like `ps` or `top`, which must access the kernel to get information about its state and the processes running on it, had to be recompiled for each version of the operating system. The `proc` file system provides a uniform interface from the file system to the kernel so that each OS version of the commands that access the system kernel can do so through the file system. To view information about the `proc` file system, use the `man proc` command.

Another virtual file system that is managed by the Solaris operating system for system functions is the SWAP file system (SWAPFS), also referred to as the memory-based file system or temporary file system (TMPFS). The TMPFS describes the locations on disk that are used to access real memory and the space on disk used for virtual memory. Swap files are files that are on disk and used as an extension of physical system RAM, or virtual memory. Solaris puts all of the TMPFS entries into the `/tmp` directory, something that isn't done in other versions of Unix (they don't mount SWAP file systems into a directory). The Solaris `/tmp` directory is a function of the amount of available

RAM plus the SWAP file system, so large amounts of RAM manage large /tmp directories on disk. Because some of the /tmp directories in Solaris consist of programs already compiled in memory, there is a performance boost over systems on which programs must be retrieved from disk and compiled.

FIGURE 5.9

The /proc folder stores references to files being used in memory for each of the processes Solaris is running.

TIP Storing programs in the /tmp directory can also be a detriment for applications that need a lot of memory and work with large amounts of temp data. In these cases, the program will fight itself for temp space and RAM and will eventually error out with a `file system full` error in the /tmp directory. With applications such as these, you get better performance by turning off TMPFS in /etc/vfstab and not using it.

The TMPFS used in memory to store files that are swapped to the TMPFS on disk must compete with the same physical memory that is used for executed commands. When storing large files in the TMPFS, you lower the amount of memory that programs have available for execution. Programs that make large memory demands can also have an impact on the amount of memory available to the virtual memory file system. Also, the maximum number of files that can be stored in the TMPFS is determined by the amount of RAM plus the SWAP file system in your system and is altered by assigning more space on disk to the swap space. When you format a disk and partition it, you can assign a partition to the TMPFS. Unlike other file systems, you can use the swap command to add and delete this temporary file system from disk.

The loopback file system, or LOFS, is a new virtual file system that allows you to access files using a loopback mount of root (/) as well as any mounted file system mapped onto a directory such as `/tmp/`*`<newrootname>`*. This system re-creates the entire file system hierarchy under the `/tmp/`*`<newrootname>`* directory as well as any file systems that were mounted on your system by NFS servers. This system provides an additional access point to files on your system.

Another addition to Solaris 8 was the mount table file system (MNTFS). This system stores a file system reference table at `/etc/mnttab`, and the reference table is modified whenever a file system is mounted or unmounted. The `mnttab` mount table file used to be a text file that grows out-of-date due to synchronization problems. Now `/etc/mnttab` is a file system that offers read-only kernel information about mounted local file systems. You cannot write to `mnttab` as you could in the past, nor can you use the `mount -m` option to fake `mnttab` entries or even edit the file. Use the `man mnttab` command to view information about this new file system.

Solaris also offers the following virtual file systems, none of which require any user intervention to operate or run:

FIFOS The first-in-first-out file system supports named pipe files to provide process access to data.

FDFS The file descriptor file system offers explicit names to use file descriptors to open files.

NAMEFS The name file system is used by STREAMS to dynamically mount file descriptors on top of files.

SPECFS The special file system offers access to special characters and block devices.

Table 5.1 lists the default mount points of the hierarchical file system for Solaris 8.

TABLE 5.7. DEFAULT MOUNT POINTS OF THE HIERARCHICAL FILE SYSTEM

Mount Point	File System	Notes
/	UFS	The root directory is the top of the tree. It contains mount points for local and remote file systems that attach to the file tree.
`/etc/mnttab`	MNTFS	The mount table file system provides read-only access to mounted file systems.
`/export/home`	UFS, NFS	This is the mount point for home directories.

Continued

TABLE 5.7. DEFAULT MOUNT POINTS OF THE HIERARCHICAL FILE SYSTEM (CONTINUED)

Mount Point	File System	Notes
`/opt`	UFS, NFS	This is the mount point for an optional file system, or a UFS file system on a slice (but not on all systems; sometimes it is part of the root file system).
`/proc`	PROCFS	This file system contains symbolic links to process objects.
`/tmp`	TMPFS	The SWAP file system can be part of `/tmp` unless it is disabled; when disabled, it is part of the root or its own partition.
`/usr`	UFS	This contains the system files that are shared by others. It is not used on all systems and can be part of the root.
`/var`	UFS	This contains the variable files. It is not used on all systems and can be part of the root.

Disk Structures

Modern hard drives use rigid disks or spinning platters that have magnetic particles on them. The disk head spins over these platters and applies a minute focused magnetic field to the disk, which creates magnetized domains on the disk. Those domains are read as an "on" or 1. The write head can also demagnetize a domain, changing its state back to a form that the read head recognizes as "off" or 0. Optical disks work similarly, except that light is used to change the underlying structure of an optical disk in some way. For WORM disks (Write Once Read Many optical disks), a laser creates a small pit in a surface that is read as a 1. However it's done, the bits on a recording media are organized into further structures that can be referenced by a file system.

In formatting a hard drive, the process writes a set of cylinders, which are called tracks, on the disks and then subdivides each track into blocks. Blocks are the fundamental storage unit used by a file system to locate data written to or read from disk. When you're creating a file system and formatting a disk, you specify the size of the file system as a partition on the disk and the formatting utility enters the start and end block for that partition into an address table that it creates. A file system's address tables serves as a lookup for locating files on blocks, with all of the blocks on disks addressed as if they were in a linear sequence. The file system table that is created is a rich object relational database that matches addresses on disk to logical structures in the file system.

Some blocks are used for special purposes. One block located at the beginning of a disk is the boot block. When you mark a file system as bootable, information that allows Unix to boot is written to the boot block. If the file system isn't bootable, then the boot block is left untouched. UFS uses a set of repeating blocks throughout the partition that the file system is loaded on. Another important block on disk is a cylinder group summary block. That block maintains summary information on the size of the file system, inodes, data contained in blocks on disk, pointers to the last block and inode that was assigned, the used inode map, and the free inode map.

Superblocks and Inode Tables

There is a secondary structure used in Unix called a superblock, which stores information about a disk's geometry, free space, and inodes (file pointers). Superblocks maintain critical system information that doesn't change, and they are replicated in several places as secondary superblocks on a disk to ensure file system integrity should there be disk corruption of the primary superblock. The secondary superblocks are stored on each cylinder group, offset by one track from each preceding cylinder group.

A superblock stores information about a file system's state, including the size of the file system, the number and location of free blocks, and the location for the next free block that is to be assigned. As much as possible, the UFS attempts to write files to the same block to cut down on fragmentation and improve on disk access. The UFS uses a 1-bit bitmap, an array of 1s or 0s, to locate free blocks. In assigning a file to a block or set of blocks, UFS uses the bitmaps to find a set of contiguous free blocks that has the appropriate size to write the file to.

When you format a disk with USF, you create an inode (information node) table that stores directory listings, filenames, and file attributes as well as references to (pointers to) the location of a file on disk in blocks. Every time a directory or file is created, the kernel assigns it an inode number. This system allows the file system to quickly locate pieces of data on the hard drive in one or more locations so that a file can be read and manipulated.

An inode is 128 bytes in length and stores all of the file attributes. In addition to the filename, inodes store the following information:

- File type
- Permissions (`mode`)
- Ownership, both the user identification (`UID`) and the group identification (`GID`)
- The file size in bytes (`size`)

- The time the file was created (`ctime`) and last time the file was accessed (`atime`) and modified (`mtime`)
- 12 address pointers

With the exception of the pointers, this is information that you see as output returned from the list command (`ls -l` for modification time and `ls -lu` for last access time) or in the Permissions dialog box for a file in the File Manager. Pointers point to data blocks that are typically 8,192 bytes in size for a total access of 96KB. The sizes of the blocks used are determined by your disk's format and the requirement of the operating system. A couple of additional inode entries contain pointers to additional data blocks that contain 2,048 addresses so that larger file sizes may be accommodated, up to a size of 2GB at an 8KB block size. Note that inode pointers point to direct blocks, which contain the primary data on disk, or to indirect blocks, which contain additional pointers. To support large file sizes, UFS supports triple indirect blocks. Smaller sizes use double indirect blocks. Figure 5.10 shows a schematic of an inode table.

FIGURE 5.10

Solaris uses inode tables to store file attributes and locations on disk.

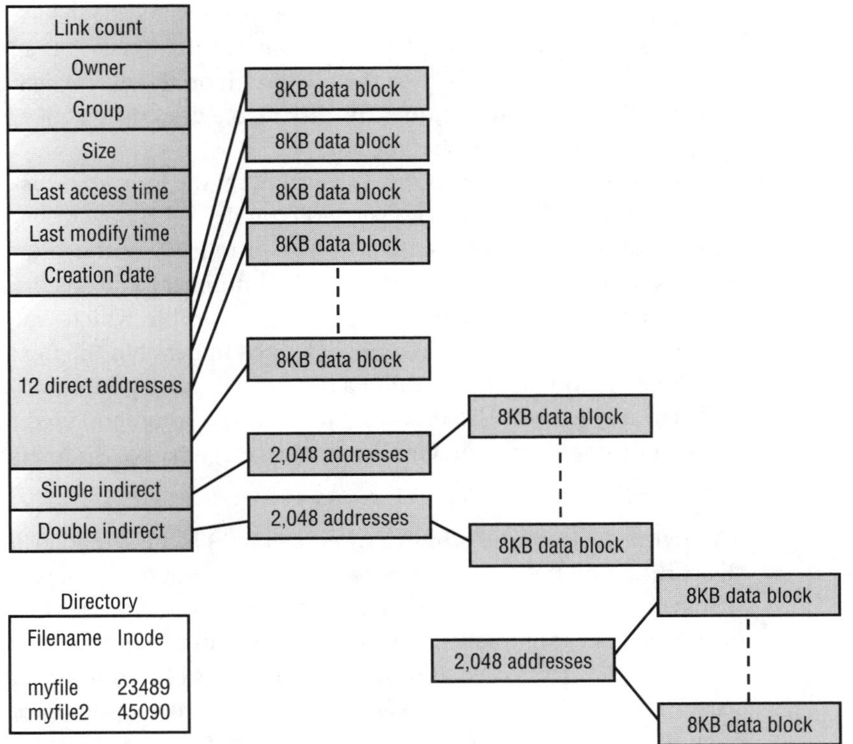

Originally, the SunOS supported just UFS and the Network File System (NFS), as well as the floppy disk format for DOS disks. To support the more facile addition of other file systems to Solaris to allow for system extension, the Virtual File System (VFS) interface was created. VFS introduces virtual nodes (vnodes), which are pointers to the inodes. By abstracting inodes to vnodes, other file systems can use vnodes to perform all of the operations on a kernel that the inodes perform, such as opening, closing, reading, and writing files. That allows other file systems to be added to Solaris as modules without needing to know anything about the file system's implementation scheme. Among the common file systems using the VFS interface are UFS, NFS, HFSF, PROCFS, TMPFS or SWAPFS, and others.

Adding New File Systems

When you add a disk to Solaris, or when you are reconfiguring a disk, you use the `format` command on SPARC systems; on Intel x86 systems, the `fdisk` command to create a partition followed by the `format` command to format a drive. (The procedures for adding a drive and formatting a disk are described in the next chapter.) Devices have both physical device names and logical device names. The device files in the `/devices` directory correspond to the physical device path names, and the files in `/dev/dsk` and `/dev/rdsk` are symbolic links to the file system on the disk. The `r` in `rdsk` corresponds to a raw device, which identifies the disk media used instead of pointing to the file system that is located on that media.

The list command returns multiple listings of the form `/dev/dsk/c[C]t[T]d[D]s[S]`. The listings describe the various partitions on devices that your system recognizes. The representation is as follows: `C` for the disk controller, `T` for the disk target number, `D` for the disk number (or for SCSI disks, the SCSI number), and `S` is the slice or partition number (from 0 to 7). A partition is the logical unit in which you install a file system. (Partitions and formatting disks are described in detail in the next chapter.)

When you format and partition a disk or add a new partition to your drive, the next step is to create a new UFS on each partition. The command used to add a file system is the `newfs` (new file system) command, and its syntax is as follows:

```
# newfs <options> <logical devicename>
```

The logical device name (`<logical devicename>`) is the symbolic link to the location of the partition on the media. The `newsf` takes as its argument a regular device name; only commands that operate on the actual media itself, such as `fsck`, take the raw logical device names as arguments. The `newfs` command will output the number of sectors, cylinders, and tracks used as well as the superblock locations for both primary and secondary superblocks. The `newfs` command takes two options: `-m`, which controls the amount of reserved space on the file system on disk, and `-o`, which specifies whether the system will optimize the file system for space or for the allocation time. For example, the following command reserves 10 percent of the file system on slice 5:

```
# newfs -m 10 /dev/dsk/c0t3d0s5
```

The UFS is tuned for reducing the fragmentation on the disk as much as possible. In doing so, time is spent moving data on disk to create the most contiguous free space possible. However, there are many instances where higher disk performance is preferred over minimizing fragmentation. Multiuser server applications create disk hits all over the disk (there are hot spots for commonly used files) that limit defragmentation's performance benefit. Also, Web servers or FTP servers are better served by increasing the speed of disk reads for files over the defragmentation process. In any case, you can use the `-o` option of `newfs` to tune the disk to optimize either time or space. To optimize for time, enter the following command:

```
# newfs -o time /dev/dsk/c0t3d0s5
```

WARNING Running `newfs` on a partition will erase all of the data that was there before. If you want to switch from a time-based optimization to a space-based optimization, the partition has to be erased.

Mounting File Systems

To use a file system, you must mount it first. When you boot up a Solaris system, several of the file systems are mounted automatically, depending upon your specific system configuration. The boot process will usually mount your hard drive's file system and the `/proc` and `/tmp` file systems as well. As you work with an additional device, like a CD-ROM or tape drive, you will need to mount the device's file system in order to work with its contents. Two file systems need to be mounted on Solaris to have a functioning system: the root (/) and `/usr`, and only if `/usr` is not part of the / file system. The root file system gets mounted automatically by the kernel at boot-up, whereas the `/usr` file system is mounted as part of a system's startup script, which runs after the operating system has loaded in the boot-up.

You mount a file system using the `mount` command:

```
mount <options> <devicename> <directoryname>
```

The device name (<*devicename*>) refers to a block-level device such as a disk. The directory name (<*directoryname*>) you specify is the directory that was created as the root of the file system, also known as the mount point. Thus, when you mount a

CD-ROM disk using the mount command, it mounts into the preexisting `/cdrom` directory that was created for the device when you installed the drive. In the CDE, you use the Open CD-ROM action to mount the CD-ROM. For a new partition you might create, you will need to use the `mkdir` command to create the mount point prior to using the mount command to mount the file system for the partition or Solaris posts an error message that the mount point does not exist.

Another important point to keep in mind is that, when you mount a file system into a directory, the content of that directory disappears and is replaced by the content of the file system. In other words, the file system overlays the directory and any references to the directory returns the content of the mounted file system. In Solaris, you can use the `-O` option to overlay an existing mount point containing a file system, replacing that file system with the one you are mounting.

The mount command takes several options listed in the man pages. Among the more commonly used options are `-a`, which performs mount operations in parallel; `-p`, which prints a list of mounted file systems; `-r`, which opens the file system as read-only (not required for a CD-ROM); `-o`, which specifies the file system type; `-O`, which means to use an overlay mount; and `-v`, which prints a list of file systems in verbose format.

Solaris stores a list of all automatically defined partitions and file systems mounted on your drive in the `/etc/vfstab` configuration file shown in Figure 5.11. Any manually mounted file system will not be listed in `/ect/vfstab`. The `/etc/vfstab` is a user-maintained file and is not updated by Solaris itself. On other Unix systems, this information is stored in the `/etc/fstab` file. The `vfstab` file lists any partitions that are mountable and specifies which partitions are to be mounted when your system boots up, as well as any options that need to be set for the file system when it is mounted. Administrators can modify the `vstab` file to control various aspects of the mounting process. The heading line is commented out using the # symbol.

FIGURE 5.11

The `/etc/vfstab` file stores information about all of the partitions and file systems mounted on a Solaris system.

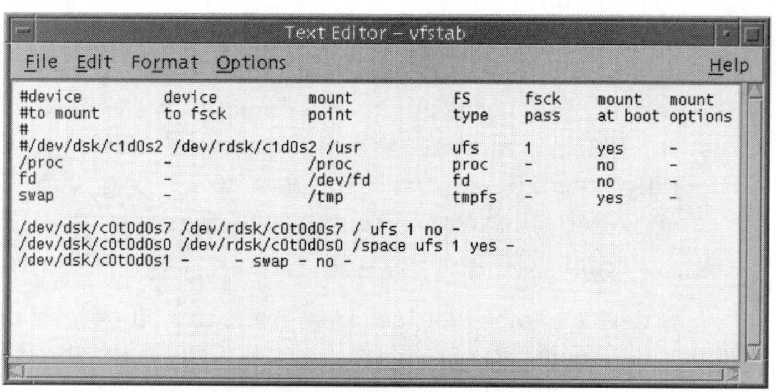


```
#device         device          mount           FS      fsck    mount   mount
#to mount       to fsck         point           type    pass    at boot options
#
#/dev/dsk/c1d0s2 /dev/rdsk/c1d0s2 /usr          ufs     1       yes     -
/proc           -               /proc           proc    -       no      -
fd              -               /dev/fd         fd      -       no      -
swap            -               /tmp            tmpfs   -       yes     -

/dev/dsk/c0t0d0s7 /dev/rdsk/c0t0d0s7 / ufs 1 no -
/dev/dsk/c0t0d0s0 /dev/rdsk/c0t0d0s0 /space ufs 1 yes -
/dev/dsk/c0t0d0s1 -     - swap - no -
```

As you can see in Figure 5.11, the vfstab file for a Solaris 8 system shows the following (from left to right):

- Logical <*devicename*>.
- The raw logical <*devicename*> to run the fsck program against (/rdsk in place of /dsk, for example).
- Mount point (directory) for the file system.
- File system type (most often UFS or PCFS).
- A description of how the fsck command runs against the file system. A 1 indicates that the system will not boot until fsck has run successfully. When you see -, fsck is not run against the file system at boot-up.
- If a yes appears, an indication that the file system is mounted at boot-up.
- Any mount options.

Although you can certainly remove any of the device files relating to physical disks (such as diskettes) and Solaris will still start up, if you remove the SWAP or process file systems, Solaris will cease to function. If you wish to add additional SWAP file systems, you can use the swap -a command as part of a script that runs at boot-up to do so.

In the vfstab file, fd (file descriptor) is used by all programs for Standard Input (STDIN), Standard Output (STDOUT), and Standard Error (STDERR). /SWAP and /proc always mount automatically because they are required for your system to operate correctly.

Unmounting File Systems

The umount command prevents users from viewing or manipulating the mounted file system. The syntax of the umount command parallels that of the mount command:

```
umount <options> <devicename> <directoryname>
```

Typically, the command is given as either umount <*devicename*> or umount <*directoryname*>, with the appropriate options specified. The major new option of interest in the umount command is the -f option, which forcibly unmounts a file system. You want to use the -f option with some caution. It is best used after you try to find and kill the offending process or you can end up with running processes that can no longer access needed system resources. Those processes will be hung and may cause system malfunctions and file system errors. You can use the -all option to unmount all file systems that are not in use. The system uses the -all option near the end of the shutdown process.

After you unmount a file system, the original directory structure reappears in view, replacing the file system that you unmounted.

There are instances when you will attempt to unmount a file system and either the mount point directory or one of the subdirectories contained therein is involved in a process. To prevent you from corrupting the data on the file system, the `umount` command will not permit you to unmount a busy directory. When you try to use the `umount` command in this situation, you will see the following message returned:

```
umount: /dev/dsk/c0t3d0s5: device busy
```

To unmount a file system from a busy device, use the `lsof` command to identify the process ID running on the device, then use the `kill` command to terminate that process. Then you should be able to unmount the file system successfully. Note that `lsof` isn't part of a default installation. You need to install that package separately.

Disk Utilization

In Solaris, when you format a disk (`format` on SPARC or `fdisk` to create a partition followed by `format` to format it on Intel x86, described in the next chapter), you create partitions and file systems as part of the formatting process. As you add applications and create documents, you tend to fill up partitions. It is good administrative practice to keep track of how much free space is available on your partitions so that you can buy additional disks when needed or archive data and clean off unnecessary files. Solaris provides some utilities that let you monitor your overall disk usage.

WARNING Solaris's disk performance degrades significantly when you get close to filling up the total amount of space on a partition. It is recommended that you keep at least 15 percent of the space on each partition free to allow for the growth of `swap`, `proc`, and other temp files used by the system. File systems running close to full also are much more prone to fragmentation than partitions with adequate free space.

The first command to use is the `df` (disk free space) command, whose syntax is as follows:

```
df <options> <pathname>/<directoryname list>
```

When you don't use any options or specify a directory name (*<directoryname>*), the output shows the free space remaining on every mounted device. Figure 5.12 shows the output of the `df` command on a new Solaris Ultra 5 with an 8GB hard drive (without options and with the `-k` option).

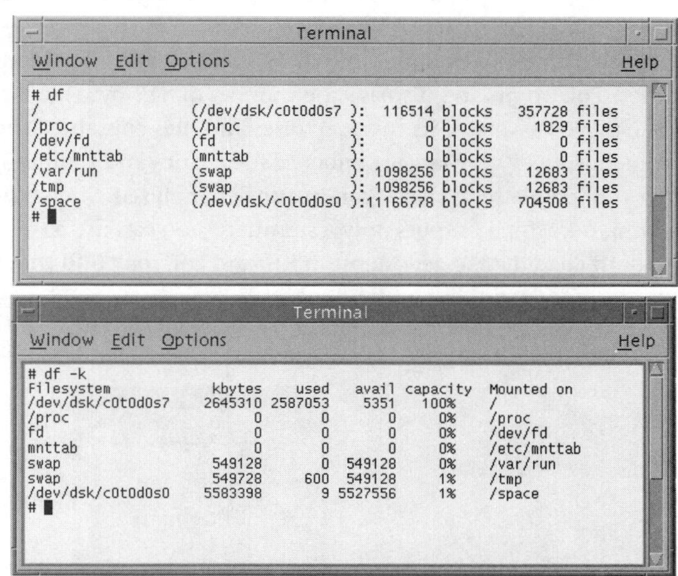

FIGURE 5.12

The df command reports on disk utilization at the file-system level.

The df command takes numerous options, the most important of which are listed here:

-a option Reports on all file systems.

-k option Gives the file system name, the size in KB, the amount of used and available space, and the percentage of space that has been filled. The -k option gives output very similar to the df command issued on other types of Unix systems, such as AIX, Linux, and FreeBSD. Because the first line in this output is a header, the -k report is the easiest to read. You can see the difference by examining the second output list in Figure 5.12.

-l option Reports on only local file systems.

-oi option Reports on the number of inodes used and free.

NOTE If you use a lot of small files and run out of inodes, you won't be able to add more files to the file system. Change the partition size and create a new file system or move or delete some of the files to free up inodes.

The second useful Solaris command is the `du` (disk utilization) command. Whereas the `df` command reports on the file utilization of an entire file system, the `du` command lets you drill down and measure the disk utilization of components like files and directories. This command displays the number of 512-byte blocks that a file or directory uses, as well as any of its subdirectories and files contained therein. The `du` command alone outputs a very large number of file entries and is more suitable for output to a report or database so that it can be further analyzed. Shown in Figure 5.13 is the `du -s` command, which outputs only a summary. You can use `du -sk` and you can also use `-k` on both `du` and `df` to get output in KB, and you may find that the output is easier for you to understand than output in blocks.

FIGURE 5.13

The `du -s` *command shown here for the* `/opt` *directory*

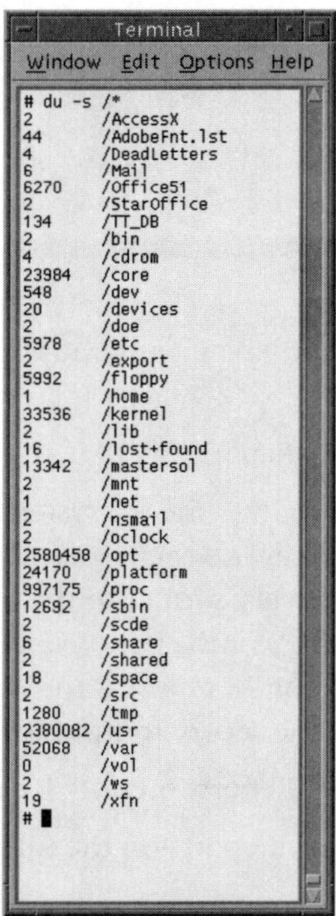

The syntax for the `du` command is entirely analogous to the syntax for the `df` command, as follows:

```
du <options> <pathname>/<directoryname list>
```

Here are the important options for the du command:

-a option Report on the space occupied by all regular files.

-d option Report on the files and directories on the same file system as the directory or directories specified.

-k option Display sizes in 1,024-byte blocks.

-r option Issue error messages for any directory or files that can't be read. Normally the du command suppresses these error messages.

-s option Displays only the summary or total usage of each directory, without listing the usage of the components.

TIP If you are running out of disk space quickly, you may have a runaway process. Use the `ps -ef` command to determine what process might be responsible for writing a large disk file or multiple disk files, then either contact the user responsible for that process to terminate it or use the `kill` command to terminate the process yourself manually.

System Accounting

Solaris has a service that audits processes and tasks that a system is running and writes them to a log. The service, known as system accounting, is used to troubleshoot system failures, monitor resource usage, identify network or system bottlenecks, and check for system security. Many programs use the system accounting service to provide the basis for real accounting, billing for system usage based on the parameters in the log file. To collect data, you create a startup script when the system goes into multiuser mode. Optionally, you can create a kill script to end data collection prior to the system shutting down.

With accounting is done, information about processes, storage access, and user activity is put into log files, which are processed every day by the `/usr/lib/acct/runacct` program. Output from the `runacct` program is processed by the `/usr/lib/acct/prdaily` program, which generates usage reports. A monthly billing program, `/usr/lib/acct/monacct`, creates monthly reports and accounts for each user. You can find documentation for the accounting system, as well as some sample startup scripts, by using the `man runacct` command. The `monacct` and `prdaily` programs are also documented in the man pages. With accounting enabled, reports are typically generated by running a `cron` job.

Disk Quotas

Solaris offers a disk quota system, as do other forms of Unix, which allows an administrator to set the amount of disk space that a user can store on a partition. The feature isn't often set up on a stand-alone workstation or even on a workstation on a network; it is applied in multiuser environments such as captive disks inside a server, on server-attached RAID systems, or on large storage arrays with Solaris server support. Using disk quotas is a very important tool in managing storage as a network asset because they can save a company money as well as prevent a rogue process such as a virus from completely filling up a partition and bringing a system to a halt or slowing a system down enough so that it is unusable.

In setting disk quotas, an administrator needs to know how much disk space is available for use, the number of users that space will support, and which volumes should have quotas applied to them. The specification uses a soft limit and a hard limit. With the soft limit, a warning is issued to a user when the user is close to exceeding the limit; with a hard limit, additional files may not be created until the user frees up disk space already consumed. In Solaris, when a user exceeds their soft limit, the system sends a specified number of error messages (as set by the system administrator) and then behaves as if the hard limit was reached.

The `edquota` command is used to define quotas inside the `vi` editor (unless you have another editor specified in your `EDITOR` environmental variable) and has the following syntax:

```
edquota <username>
```

As an example of setting a disk quota, do the following:

1. Log in as root. (Only a superuser can edit disk quotas, but any user can determine their quota settings and usage with the `quota` command for their particular username. A superuser can pass a list of usernames as the argument to the `quota` command to review settings and usage for two or more users.)
2. Enter **`vi /etc/vfstab`** at the command line, then add the `rq` flag to the mount options for the file system you wish to set the quota on.
3. Enter **`cd`** ***`<directoryname>`*** (change directory), where *`<directoryname>`* is the directory that serves as the mount point for the file system that will have the quota.
4. Create a file called `quotas` in that directory by entering the `touch quotas` command at the command line.
5. Enter **`chmod u+rw,go-rwx quotas`** to allow quotas to be read and written for the root user only.

6. Enter **edquota <*username*>**, then enter the number of inodes and 1KB blocks available, as follows:

```
fs /<filesystemname> blocks (soft=20000, hard=22000)\
     inodes (soft=0, hard=0)
```

   This command sets a 20MB soft quota on disk and a 22MB hard quota for user *username*.

7. Enter **quota -v <*username*>** to see if your desired settings were applied.
8. Turn the quota on by entering **quotaon /<*filesystemname*>**.

Use the edquota command to add or subtract from a disk quota. To see all of the user quotas in effect, use the repquota /<*filesystemname*> command. Disk quotas are usually set only on the specific directories that users can access and store personal files on, such as the /home directory. You issue the quotaon <*filesystemname*> (for example, quotaon /home) command to turn on quotas, typically as part of a startup script or a script that mounts a file system. The quotaon command turns on accounting, which is a logging system that reports on disk utilization for disk quotas on a per-user basis. When a file system is unmounted, the disk quotas are turned off. You can also turn quotas off by using the quotaoff <*filesystemname*> command. The vfstab file lists userquota or groupquota for any file system for which the repquota option is set.

NOTE If you establish disk quotas, you should inform users what those quotas are. Otherwise, when a user exceeds their quota and sees a message like file system full or write failed for operations such as saving edited files or trying to retrieve e-mail, they won't be able to diagnose the problem from standard commands that show the amount of disk free space, such as df and du (described earlier).

Disk Repair

For any number of reasons, file systems get corrupted. This can occur when your system crashes and a file isn't properly written back to disk from memory, when power is lost, or when a disk gets a physical error (damaged sector). Solaris provides the fsck (file system check) command to maintain and repair disk partitions, and when you give this command, a file system–specific fsck program is called and runs.

The fsck command goes through the following sequence of steps:

1. *Check blocks and sizes.* Inodes are checked for valid entries. When an error is detected, fsck posts the error PARTIALLY TRUNCATED INODE I=n (Salvage)? Answering Y (yes) repairs this error.

2. *Check path names.* Any bad directory entries are removed during the path name check. Should you see a message ROOT INODE NOT A DIRECTORY (FIX)?, your file system has sustained substantial damage. After you repair the file system, you should take measures to back up important data and reestablish a fresh file system. Other messages are of minor consequence.
3. *Check connectivity.* This part of fsck checks to see if there are any directories on your file system that aren't referenced by other directories and are thus orphans. Any directory of this type is placed into the /lost+found folder.
4. *Check reference counts.* Here fsck checks for files that aren't correctly referenced in the file system. These errors are most often corrected automatically, although you may see a message that asks you to clear a file.
5. *Check cylinder groups.* In this last phase of the fsck operation, the program verifies that the free block and unused inode counts are correct.
6. *Salvage free list.* This step corrects the problems found in step 5.

Each step is posted as output of the fsck command, with a final line shown that gives you the number of files, the blocks used and free, and how much fragmentation there is. After the sequence of steps for the fsck command are complete and when all problems have been corrected, you should see the message /home: clean appear.

Fragmentation isn't a major problem on Solaris as it can be on Microsoft Windows. If you have a badly fragmented file system, you can back it up, create a new one, and restore it to defragment it.

You can run fsck only on unmounted file systems. On workstations with a single file system or to check all file systems, you should log out of your session and log back into Solaris's command-line prompt in single-user mode as a superuser. Then enter the fsck command with any of the options you desire. The syntax for the fsck command is as follows:

```
fsck <options> (<filesystem list>)
```

When you omit <*filesystem* list>, Solaris uses the /etc/vfstab file as the source of the file systems to check. Although you can unmount file systems other than the root file system and run the fsck command on them, if you want to check and repair the root file system, which cannot be unmounted, you need to be in single-user mode and have the root file system quiescent (in other words, you can't be reading and writing files to root while you are running fsck). Many startup scripts specify that fsck is run against all file systems before the system is switched into multiuser mode.

WARNING If you run `fsck` on a mounted file system, you can damage that file system so that it is unusable. Press Ctrl+C to terminate the `fsck` command as quickly as you can to prevent any damage.

There are numerous options and suboptions for the `fsck` command. Among the most important are those listed here:

`-F` *`<filesystemtype>`* option Check for only this type of file system.

`-m` option Check that the file system can be mounted.

`-n` option Answer no to any question posed by `fsck`.

`-of` option Force `fsck` to skip clean or checked file systems.

`-op (or preen)` option Run `fsck` so that it automatically repairs any errors it finds. If there is an error that can't be fixed and requires user intervention, this option forces `fsck` to quit or exit.

Summary

This chapter described the various file systems in use by Solaris 8 and how they're used. Solaris uses many different file system types, both real and virtual. Some file systems mount automatically, and others require manual mounting and unmounting. The file system hierarchy is a tree structure with the root directory at the top of the tree. Filenames, file types, path names, and file attributes provide ways to describe files that allow them to be stored in the file system, retrieved, and recognized for the data they contain.

Directories are containers that store files and other directories. This chapter listed the important directories and files that Solaris contains. I discussed working with directories, files, and links and showed you how to create, copy, move, and delete them both in Command Line Interface (CLI) operations and through the CDE.

I also discussed access rights and permissions, which provide a scheme for protecting files and directories by setting security as well as determining what operations may be performed on an object.

Finally, this chapter include a discussion of disk storage structures, inodes, and blocks, which provide a means to store data on disk and relate the data to a file system so that the data may be used when needed. You learned about several commands you can use to determine your disk and file utilizations as well as set disk quotas to limit disk usage by specific users.

CHAPTER 6

Devices

FEATURING:

Device mapping 183

Device types 184

CD-ROMs 197

Diskettes 204

Zip and Jaz drives 211

Hard drives 212

Tape drives 221

Devices are physical subsystems that you install on your computer (such as hard drives, CD-ROM drives, diskette drives, tape drives, and so forth), other systems that you attach to your system (like external RAID), or even nonmedia-related hardware like a network card or a SCSI card. From the standpoint of the operating system, Solaris allows you to define logical devices, which use some or all of a physical device's resources. Logical device definition provides a means for making physical devices do the work of several devices and support multiple applications and configurations. After reading this chapter, you'll have a better understanding of what a device is, how to name and address devices, and how to work with some important device types.

It isn't possible to cover all of the device types that can potentially work with Sun workstations and servers. Mice, trackballs, input pens and tablets, and many, many other devices are available to Solaris users. A discussion of all of the device types that can be used with Solaris is more appropriately handled in a book on hardware. The important thing to understand about devices is that, although they use a particular addressing scheme and are supported by different system commands and device utilities, they all require device drivers that must be installed to provide I/O to work with the Solaris kernel. The skills you'll learn in this chapter will help you work with the devices you buy as well as install and manage them properly.

This chapter covers some basic devices, mainly storage devices that require OS support. You will learn how to format diskettes and hard drives, how to open or mount CD-ROM disks, how to manage tape drives, and in some instances, how to do basic work with the contents of storage devices. There is information in this chapter on how to create file systems and on partitions, slices, and other device-specific concepts.

You'll find basic information about working with content in many other chapters, and there is a much more in-depth discussion about the file system in Chapter 5, "The File System." You'll also find additional device information in the chapters relating to the task that a specific device performs (for example, Chapter 10 covers printing). This chapter is yet another building block to help you understand how to work with Solaris from a conceptual level and to offer you some practical system administration skills.

About Devices

The Solaris operating system supports a wide range of system devices that users and system administrators need to know about. Solaris refers to devices in one of three different ways:

- As a physical device name, often displayed at boot-up on your screen
- As a physical device file with a file that is stored in the `/devices` directory and that defines the device and how to access it

- As a logical device name, as in the example of disk slices or partitions, which are sections of a disk that act as if they were independent disks themselves with their own file systems

Device Mappings

The mapping of a physical device name to a physical device file in the `/devices` directory is kept in the `/etc/path_to_inst` file and is there for you to review. That mapping isn't constant, but it can be altered and reassigned as needed. In the `path_to_inst` file, the assigned addresses for devices appears as a string of letters and/or numbers, as shown in Figure 6.1.

FIGURE 6.1

To show the mapping of physical devices to their physical device files, Solaris uses the `path_to_inst` *file shown here in the text editor.*

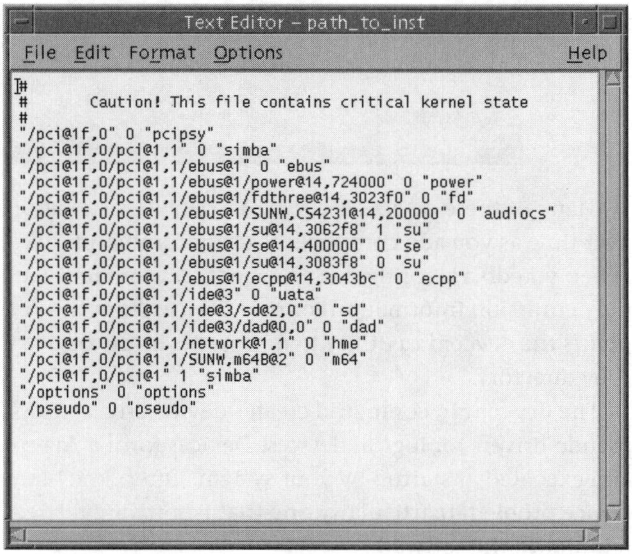

Text Editor – path_to_inst

File Edit Format Options Help

```
#
#       Caution! This file contains critical kernel state
#
"/pci@1f,0" 0 "pcipsy"
"/pci@1f,0/pci@1,1" 0 "simba"
"/pci@1f,0/pci@1,1/ebus@1" 0 "ebus"
"/pci@1f,0/pci@1,1/ebus@1/power@14,724000" 0 "power"
"/pci@1f,0/pci@1,1/ebus@1/fdthree@14,3023f0" 0 "fd"
"/pci@1f,0/pci@1,1/ebus@1/SUNW,CS4231@14,200000" 0 "audiocs"
"/pci@1f,0/pci@1,1/ebus@1/su@14,3062f8" 1 "su"
"/pci@1f,0/pci@1,1/ebus@1/se@14,400000" 0 "se"
"/pci@1f,0/pci@1,1/ebus@1/su@14,3083f8" 0 "su"
"/pci@1f,0/pci@1,1/ebus@1/ecpp@14,3043bc" 0 "ecpp"
"/pci@1f,0/pci@1,1/ide@3" 0 "uata"
"/pci@1f,0/pci@1,1/ide@3/sd@2,0" 0 "sd"
"/pci@1f,0/pci@1,1/ide@3/dad@0,0" 0 "dad"
"/pci@1f,0/pci@1,1/network@1,1" 0 "hme"
"/pci@1f,0/pci@1,1/SUNW,m64B@2" 0 "m64"
"/pci@1f,0/pci@1" 1 "simba"
"/options" 0 "options"
"/pseudo" 0 "pseudo"
```

You can find a listing of device names in the `/dev` directory, primarily as alphanumeric codes, as shown in Figure 6.2. Solaris, and Unix in general, attempts to use device names that are descriptive so you will recognize them. For example, `console` is the file for your display (actually, it is terminal output in character mode except in graphical interfaces), `dsk` is disk or hard drive, `kbd` is the keyboard, `mem` is memory, `/swap` is the swap file, `/pcmcia` is a PC Card, `tty` is your terminal device, and so on. The purpose of the `/dev` directory is similar to the purpose of DNS. It shields the user from having to remember the actual device name as an alphanumeric string, substituting instead a "friendly name" such as `/dev/diskette` in its place.

FIGURE 6.2

The /dev directory stores device files for all physical and logical devices.

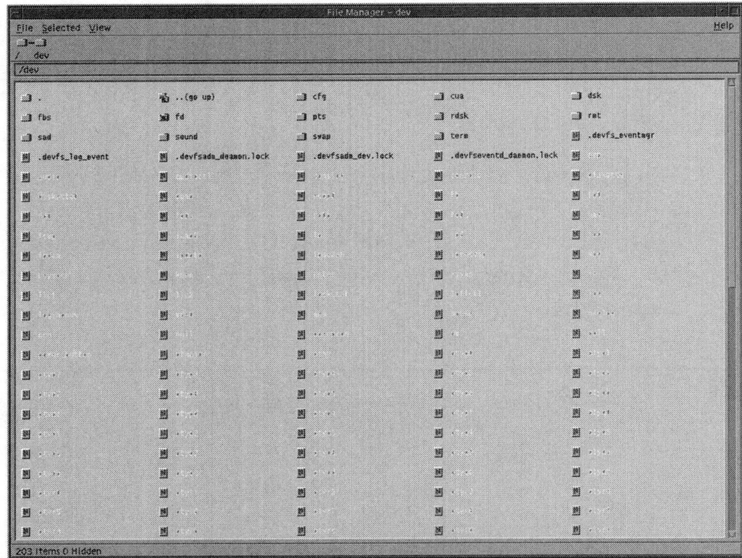

Many of these devices are part of a default installation, others you add to the system over time as you add components using commands like the `drvconfig` command. When you do a reconfiguration reboot, `drvconfig` is automatically run and reads the file permission information for new devices from the `/etc/minor_perm` file, which points the `drvconfig` utility to new nodes in the device tree and then adds a file to the `/dev` directory.

The `drvconfig` command creates device drivers for physical devices and logical or pseudo drivers for logical devices. Devices form a `/devices` directory tree that is read and executed at startup by your system. Often, the best way to solve a recalcitrant device problem (particularly one that is software related) is to reboot your system and reinitialize the software.

Device Types

To see the contents of the `/dev` directory, use the `ls -lL` command. The `-L` option displays the contents of the `/dev` directory by names rather than as symbolic links to the `/devices` directory. In a typical entry returned from the command, you would see the following:

```
crw-rw-rw-  1 root     sys    13, 12 Mar 12 08:05 zero
```

Here, the initial character tells you what the link type is: *b* for block, *c* for character, *d* for directory, *D* for door, *l* for symbolic link (or named pipe), and *s* for AF-Unix sockets.

Doors are interprocesss communications mechanisms, and sockets are named communication connections. After the initial letter are the permissions, which are followed by the number of hard links and the names of the owner and group.

In the preceding entry, you see the major and minor numbers (13 and 12) listed; they are listed together separated by a comma. A major device number defines the class of hardware device to which the listing belongs: terminal, disk, printer, and so on. The major device number specifies the device driver that the kernel uses to talk with that device. A minor device number defines the kind of hardware within a class of device, such as ttyq0, ttyq1, and so on for a terminal type. The minor device number references the location of the device in the system, and it can be used to activate and deactivate features of a device. This system of nomenclature is meant to allow a piece of software to service a device class while still being able to discriminate between two different pieces of equipment of that type.

Solaris defines several different device types, most notably block, character, and raw devices. Each of these device types has different characteristics that require a particular type of device driver.

A *block device* has the following features:

- Can do random access reads
- Reads a chunk of data as a block size and as a single transaction
- Works with blocks of data sequentially
- Is addressed by the operating system as a set of *n* blocks numerically from 0 to *n*-1
- Can be initialized with a file system and have that file system mounted
- Has data input to the device and output from the device buffered by the kernel in cache

The prototypical examples of a block-oriented device is a partition or slice on a disk, a CD-ROM, and a diskette.

The device drivers used for block devices can typically be used in one of two ways: either as block device or as character devices. Many devices access data by both block and character means.

When a block device uses the character device access method, it is referred to as a *raw device*. A raw device offers the following:

- Direct I/O without kernel buffering
- Device restrictions on the I/O type
- Direct correlation between system calls and hardware requests

By comparison, there are many devices that are *character devices*. Character devices read data as a stream of characters; they read one character after another or, in some instances, a line at a time, depending upon how the device driver was written. When a program reads single characters, it typically does that in raw mode without any interpretation of the data. (Raw mode has no association with raw devices.) When a program reads data a line at a time, the driver will manage the data stream so that input such as deletions or kill characters aren't part of the data stream that the program sees. When reading lines, a program reads from the beginning of a line up to the Return character. Examples of character devices are printers, modems, terminals, and tape drives.

Data stored on a device can either be stored in block form or as character data. Character data is also referred to as raw data. Working with these two different kinds of data requires two different interfaces. Solaris separates these two types of data out into different interfaces and uses different addresses. Block-accessed data is buffered and read and written in chunks; raw data is read and written in small amounts without a buffer. Therefore, block transfer is much faster than raw data transfer. In using data access commands, check to see whether they are meant for block or raw data devices. For example, `mount` and `df` are block commands; `fsck`, `newfs`, and `prtvtoc` are raw data commands.

Addresses

Devices refer to both physical and logical entities in Solaris, and in order to work with devices, you need to know how to name and address them. Each type of device has a system device file that is part of the device hierarchy of the system. At boot time, your system uses the device hierarchy to load drivers, associate them with the appropriate devices, and create a set of pointers to the drivers. Physical devices may be found in the `/devices` directory, whereas logical devices are found in the `/dev` directory and are symbolically linked to physical device files in the `/devices` directory.

A hard drive, CD, or diskette represents a physical device. Solaris differs from other Unix systems in the addressing for physical devices. On a BSD or Linux system with two IDE drives and two SCSI drives, you would see the following defined devices in the `/dev` directory: `/dev/hda` and `/dev/hdb` for the IDE drives and `/dev/sda` and `/dev/sdb` for the SCSI drives. When you create partitions on those drives for BSD or Linux, you see them appear as follows in the `/dev` directory: `/dev/hda1` and `/dev/hda2`. On Solaris, however, devices are contained in the `/dev/dsk/` subdirectory with a four-part identifier, described in the next paragraph.

Often, these devices are subdivided or partitioned into what Solaris calls slices. A slice is an example of a logical device. That logical device must be named and addressed so that, when you work with that resource or it becomes available, it can be recognized and accessed. An example of a logical address for a CD-ROM would be `/dev/dsk/c0t2d0s2`, where `/dev/dsk` is the disk subdirectory and `c2t2d0` is the slice.

Controller (c), target (t), drive (d), and slice (s) identifiers are addressed using this scheme.

Controller numbers are logical assignments made at startup, but the exact slice specification depends upon the kind of system or disk you use. Disks with direct controllers, those with bus-oriented controllers, and those with SCSI controllers have different addresses that also vary by platform.

For example, a logical tape device is stored in the `/dev/rmt/*` directory with symbolic links from the `/devices` directory. The first tape is assigned the logical unit number, or LUN, of 0, and the logical address of a tape drive would be `/dev/rmt/`*xy*, where *x* is the LUN and *y* is the tape density. Solaris supports a variety of tape drives, such as QIC-11, QIC-24, QIC-150, Exabyte, AIT, and many, many more. Tape density values are given letter assignments like `l`, `m`, `h`, `c`, and `u`. You will find the addressing scheme for CD-ROM devices covered in the section describing those devices.

Installing and Removing Devices

It is recommended that you turn your system off whenever you add a new peripheral device and remove the power cord. This is particularly true for SCSI devices because devices on a SCSI bus can be very sensitive to power variances. However, it is a good idea for nearly any device. You should also wear an antistatic strap when you install devices inside a computer's case. An antistatic strap is included with new Sun workstations and servers as a matter of course.

To add a peripheral to your system, follow these steps:

1. Log in as superuser, **su**, and enter your password.
2. Install the driver using the following command (if necessary):

   ```
   # pkgadd -d <devicepath packagename>
   ```

   <packagename> identifies the package that contains the device driver. If you are installing the device driver after you have attached the device, put the media (tape, diskette, or CD) into the drive. You can verify that the `pkgadd` command is worked using the `pkgchk` *<packagename>* command. When the package is installed, your system will return a prompt with no response.
3. Enter the `touch /reconfigure` command to create the `/reconfigure` file. (If you use the `boot -r` command from the OK prompt, you can accomplish the same thing.)
4. Use the `shutdown i0 -g30 -y` command to shut down the system.

   The parameter `-i0` refers to the 0 init state, `-g30` shuts the system down in 30 seconds, and `-y` forces an automatic system shutdown.

5. When you see an OK or > prompt on a SPARC system or the message `Type any key to continue` on an Intel x86 system, turn the power switch to off.
6. With the power off to all attached devices, connect the peripheral device.
7. For devices like SCSI devices that require an address to be set, make sure you set the hardware switch or jumper settings so that the address chosen does not conflict with other devices already attached to your system. Refer to your peripheral device's manual to see how this procedure is done.
8. Turn power to peripheral devices back on, then turn your computer system on.
9. After the system boots, log in and verify that the device works by trying to use it.

Not all computers require this manual shutdown and restart. Newer equipment supports *hot-plugging*, which means you can add and remove components while the computer is running. Solaris 8 adds to this support so that you can use the `cfgadm` command to hot-plug SCSI devices on both SPARC and IA systems. On x86 systems, you cannot remove PCI adapter cards that have critical system resources attached to them. Additionally, a card's device driver must support hot-plugging.

WARNING When you're adding or upgrading a driver, it is possible to crash a system if a device is malfunctioning. This is known as *system panic*, because the driver has low-level kernel access that can bring a system down. If a device driver contains a bug, that too can disable a system by performing an illegal operation such as writing to a portion of memory reserved for another process. The best way to deal with this problem is to remove the offending device and/or device driver.

Solaris performs dynamic configuration to move or disable system resources, both hardware and software, as needed. You can use the `cfgadm` command to determine the status of, test, and configure components and obtain configuration help for both SCSI and PCI controllers as well as for the Sun S-Bus. The `cfgadm` command displays attachment points where dynamic reconfiguration can be done. For a list of SCSI and PCI controllers that support hot-plugging, check the Intel Hardware Compatibility List (HCL). Cards on SPARC systems support this feature. Future OS features like multipathing and failover software will add to this capability.

Just as you must perform a reconfiguration reboot when you install a device, you must perform a reconfiguration reboot when you remove a device. In many instances, your system may continue to operate correctly without the device, but you can run into trouble in situations where multiple people administer your system if there are spurious device entries for devices that are no longer attached to the system. For example, you should remove the /etc/vstab entry for a hard drive after you remove that disk and then do a reconfiguration reboot to reestablish your system.

Device Drivers

A device driver is a program with low-level access to the Unix kernel that provides input/output to peripheral devices and storage. Your Solaris workstation or server contains drivers for your mouse and keyboard and for SCSI devices. You must install a device driver for any additional devices you might add, such as printers, plotters, scanners, digitizers, cameras, and so forth. The device driver takes commands from the Solaris kernel and translates or interprets them into a data format and transmission protocol that the device can understand. Modems, for example, require modem drivers, and one of the important functions of that driver is to auto-negotiate transmission speed with another modem. Similarly, the driver takes data from the device and translates it back into a form that can be passed back to the Solaris kernel.

Solaris 2.*x* (SunOS 5.*x*) is based on Berkeley Software Distribution (BSD) Unix and contains a small standard Unix kernel at /kernel/genunix. The Solaris OS is supplemented by additional kernel modules that are platform specific. Platform-specific kernel components needed to boot a particular system are found in the directories at /platform/<*systemname*>/kernel files, where <*systemname*> is the specific kind of computer. A Sun Ultra 5, for example, would be found in the folder SUNW/Ultra-5_10. Finally, any kernel components that are used by all systems with a certain instruction set are found in the /usr/kernel folder.

NOTE SunOS v1-4.*x* (aka Solaris 1.*x*) was based on BSD Unix. With Solaris 2.*x* (aka SunOS 5.*x*), Sun switched to the AT&T System V Unix and the BSD Unix became the "compatibility mode" (the emulations software necessary to run the compatibility mode is loaded in /usr/ucb, as in University of California, Berkeley) and run only when needed. The BSD kernel is available with the OS, but you do not have to install it. The development of Solaris internals was covered in Chapter 2, "About Solaris."

When your system boots, it loads the modules it needs based on the devices it finds, a process called *autoconfiguration*. The settings for loading kernel modules are contained in the /etc/system file. Only the modules that are required are loaded, and when you add a device, Solaris loads the required supporting module. This means that drivers are loaded without your having to reboot the system or having to rebuild the kernel and that memory is more efficiently used because drivers are not loaded unless they are needed. When you add a new device and driver to Solaris, you have to perform a reconfiguration reboot so that your system will, through autoconfiguration, recognize the new device.

Device drivers are stored in the following directories:

- `kernel/drv`
- `/platform/<systemname>.kernel/drv`

Solaris comes with support for many devices right out of the box. However, when you purchase a device that is either unsupported or has come out soon after the most-recent version of Solaris was released, you should get from the device manufacturer the software and drivers required for Solaris 8. Device software typically comes with a device driver and configuration (`.conf`) file. One resource for Solaris x86 drivers is on the Sun site at `www.sold.sun.com/support/drivers/boot.html`.

Device Diagnostic Utilities

To identify the peripheral devices attached to your computer, use the `prtconf` and `sysdef` commands. The `prtconf` command lists the system configuration, amount of memory, and device configuration in the form of a device tree. You'll see defined any physical and logical devices, their addresses, and their condition. Figure 6.3 shows the output of `prtconf` for a standalone Sun Ultra 5 computer. You see a number of instances where the device is identified with the this message:

```
<devicename>, instance #number (driver not attached)
```

This message doesn't mean that there is no driver installed, simply that the driver isn't currently attached because there is no device in use. You only load the drivers when the device is being accessed. Drivers are unloaded when the device isn't in use, so this message really means that there is no device in use at the node specified. Solaris loads drivers when you access a device and will unload device drivers when the device isn't active. Unloading drivers saves memory and makes a Solaris system more stable than other operating systems that don't perform this function.

The `sysdef` utility will output the current system definition to your display. The command lists all hardware devices, pseudo devices, loadable modules, and the value of kernel tunable parameters for a bootable operating system. You can specify the bootable OS as a parameter to the `sysdef` command by using the `-n` flag. The `sysdef` command derives its information from the `/dev/kmem` file, so you can also list bootable disks in that file as well have their definition appear. Much of the information about devices that you find in the `prtconf` command's response is also found in the `sysdef` command's response. You can also use the `sysdef` command to find out what kind of system you are accessing remotely from a server after you log in; using the `uname -a` command will only give you basic information such as version, name, and platform.

FIGURE 6.3

Use the `prtconf` *command to list your system configuration, including attached devices. This figure shows the output from a Sun Ultra 5 workstation.*

```
Terminal
Window Edit Options                                    Help
# prtconf
System Configuration:  Sun Microsystems  sun4u
Memory size: 128 Megabytes
System Peripherals (Software Nodes):

SUNW,Ultra-5_10
    packages (driver not attached)
        terminal-emulator (driver not attached)
        deblocker (driver not attached)
        obp-tftp (driver not attached)
        disk-label (driver not attached)
        SUNW,builtin-drivers (driver not attached)
        sun-keyboard (driver not attached)
        ufs-file-system (driver not attached)
    chosen (driver not attached)
    openprom (driver not attached)
        client-services (driver not attached)
    options, instance #0
    aliases (driver not attached)
    memory (driver not attached)
    virtual-memory (driver not attached)
    pci, instance #0
        pci, instance #0
            ebus, instance #0
                auxio (driver not attached)
                power, instance #0
                SUNW,pll (driver not attached)
                se, instance #0
                su, instance #0
                su, instance #1
                ecpp (driver not attached)
                fdthree, instance #0
                eeprom (driver not attached)
                flashprom (driver not attached)
                SUNW,CS4231 (driver not attached)
            network, instance #0
            SUNW,m64B, instance #0
            ide, instance #0
                disk (driver not attached)
                cdrom (driver not attached)
                dad, instance #0
                sd, instance #0
        pci, instance #1
    SUNW,UltraSPARC-IIi (driver not attached)
    pseudo, instance #0
#
```

If you wish to generate a listing of the devices that are connected to your system after your last reboot, use the `dmesg` command. Figure 6.4 shows the output of the `dmesg` command on a Sun Ultra 5 workstation. This command can also be used by the OpenBoot monitor to detect hardware errors before the kernel is loaded and identify bus issues such as SCSI problems and whether devices are responding or not. To see a list of devices at boot time, force a reboot using the `ok reset` command. Just after your system boots, run the `dmesg` command. On a Sun workstation, `dmesg` shows the boot sequence: a memory test, establishment of the Ethernet address and network interface, PCI and S-Bus bus initialization, hard drive recognition and mapping, and activation of keyboard and mouse. You will see a different sequence for an IA x86 box.

FIGURE 6.4

Use the `dmesg` *command to list devices that have been connected to your system since your last reboot.*

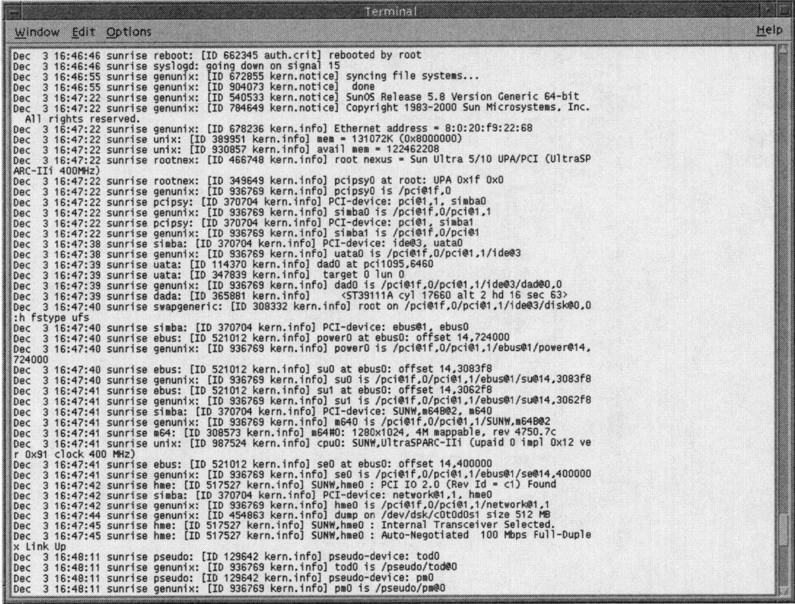

Serial Ports

Solaris supports RS-232-C and RS-423 serial ports as well as parallel (or printer) ports. Serial ports are used to connect modem and terminals to a system. Using a terminal allows you to avoid the cost of a computer monitor and graphics card and still be able to control the boot-up of a system.

You can use the `admintool` program to graphically manage serial port and parallel port devices such as modems and printers, respectively. Solaris uses the `ttymon` port monitor to communicate between devices and the operating system. Serial devices issue `getty` requests, often concurrently, which are passed through the port monitor. These commands may be found on the Sun site (`www.sun.com`) by searching for "managing terminals and modems".

Follow these steps to configure a port for a terminal:

1. Open `admintool`, found in the `system_admin` folder, by clicking the Applications drawer of the front panel and then clicking the Applications control.
2. Enter one of the user modes.
3. Enter the default terminal type, the transfer rate in baud, and any flow control or carrier detection.

4. Save your settings.
5. Test your settings by entering the following command:

```
# pmadm -l -s ttyb
```

Similarly, you can use admintool to set up a modem for incoming, outgoing, or bidirectional communication using the same procedure. When you are done, test for the successful installation using the tip *<devicename>* command to connect to a remote system, where *<devicename>* points to the /etc/remote file. This command is documented using man tip, which displays connected on a terminal when it detects the port. If you want to test for a Hayes command set, enter the command string ATE1V1. That command should return OK on your terminal. You can also enter AT, at which the modem will reply with an OK.

In the past, Unix servers that were servicing terminals used a system of serial port addresses called pseudo ports to provide a means for each terminal to reference a serial port. This system is still used for programs like X-terminals, where each program like xterm emulates an old-style character terminal. When you log in to a server over the network using Telnet or rlogin rather than using a modem or terminal to directly connect to a serial port, you use a pseudo port or pseudo tty. Solaris, as with other Unix implementations, establishes a certain number of pseudo ports. The main thing to know about pseudo ports, particularly in a server environment, is that, if you run out of the default number of pseudo ports, you can always increase the number.

Volume Management

In Solaris, working with CDs and diskettes is referred to as volume management. Volume Management services for removable media are provided from the /vol/dev directory. For floppy disks, the subdirectories are named diskette0 and rdiskette0. When a system has a second and third disk drive, Volume Management creates the following pairs of subdirectories: diskette1 and rdiskette1, and diskette2 and rdiskette2, respectively. The diskette directories provide file access, and the rdiskette directories provide access to raw data like tar or cpio. When you insert a diskette into a drive, that diskette's contents appear in a subdirectory of these other directories, and which one is used depends on the format of the diskette. UFS diskettes that don't have UFS file systems mount under the rdiskette directories; DOS diskettes mount under the diskette directories. CD-ROMs that use the ISO 9660 High Sierra File System (HSFS) are the only type of media that is platform independent.

Support for CD-ROMs are provided from the /vol/dev directory using the /dsk and /rdsk subdirectories for blocks and raw directories, respectively. A CD's contents will appear under the dsk subdirectory using a directory name like c0t2d0 (yours will be different). For a system with a single diskette and CD-ROM, you would see the following if you used the `ls` command:

```
ls -L -l /vol/dev
total 0
dr-xr-xr-x  4 root      root  512 Nov 30 14:21  aliases
dr-xr-xr-x  3 root      root  512 Nov 30 11:47  diskette0
dr-xr-xr-x  3 root      root  512 Nov 29 17:03  dsk
dr-xr-xr-x  3 root      root  512 Nov 30 11:47  rdiskette0
dr-xr-xr-x  3 root      root  512 Nov 29 17:03  rdsk
```

You can use the `ls` command again on each of these four device subdirectories to return the diskette name or the CD-ROM name.

Mount Points and Symbolic Links

Unix uses the `/floppy` and `/cdrom` mount points to provide access to floppy and CD-ROM devices, and the `/vol/dev/diskette0` and `/vol/dev/dsk/c0t2d0` subdirectories are mapped to these mount points. When you use these mount points under `rmmount`, you can then access a diskette or CD using the `/floppy/`*<diskettename>* or `/cdrom/`*<cdname>* mount point. Because the mount points can be used from any location if the disk is formatted, even remote systems if you make these devices available to other users over the network, this simplifies your naming convention. Unformatted disks are only available locally and not from the mount points.

In addition to mount points, you can create symbolic links to removable media. The symbolic links for file system access are as follows:

`/floppy/floppy0` → `/floppy/`*<diskettename>* → `/vol/dev/diskette0/`*<diskettename>*

`/cdrom/cdrom0` → `/cdrom/`*<diskname>* → `/vol/dev/dsk/c0t2d0/`*<diskname>*

Here are the symbolic link for raw device access:

`/floppy/rfloppy0` → `/floppy/`*<diskettename>* → `/vol/dev/rdiskette0/`*<diskettename>*

`/cdrom/rcdrom0` → `/cdrom/`*<diskname>* → `/vol/dev/rdsk/c0t2d0/`*<diskname>*

Therefore, you can use the name `cdrom/cdrom0` to access a CD's file system without having to know the name or location of the disk.

Not all CD-ROMs are formatted using only the HSFS format. Some disks contain two or more partitions, or slices, and those slices can contain a UFS_SPARC or UFS_x86 slice. This scenario of having multiple disks slices often happens when a disk is set up to install applications for which there will be three slices: Slice0, UFS_SPARC for raw SPARC data; Slice1, UFS_x86 raw data; and Slice2, ISO 9660. On a SPARC system, you would see s0 and s2 appear under both the `/cdrom/cdrom0` and `/vol/dev/dsk/c0t2d0` subdirectories. On an Intel x86, box you will see s1 and s2 appear under those two subdirectories.

Mounting Removable Media

You can either automatically mount CDs and floppy disks, or you can manually mount them. Automatic mounting is much easier than manual mounting and doesn't require you to be a superuser and have root privileges. When they're automatically mounted, the CDs and diskettes you insert into your local computer can be accessed by users at other computers on the network.

NOTE If you want to work with diskettes or CDs manually, without the Volume Manager running, then as superuser, enter the following command to stop Volume Manager: **`/etc/init.d/volmgt stop`**. Use **`/etc/init.d/volmgt start`** to restart Volume Manager.

To automatically mount CDs or floppy disks, follow these steps:

1. Insert the disk.
2. For a floppy disk, at the command line enter the `volcheck` command.

   Solaris's Volume Management then mounts the disk. A CD mounts automatically, and a window opens on your desktop. A floppy disk mounts without a window opening. The `volcheck` utility checks for floppy disks every minute for up to an hour after the command is issued last.
3. Give the `vold` command at the command line to open the floppy disk.

   `vold` is the Solaris volume management daemon; it runs in the background in multiuser mode. `vold` can access both the Unix file system (UFS) and the High Sierra file system (HSFS), and it can work with both diskettes and CDs.
4. Use the files on your disk.
5. Eject the media.

When you automatically mount CDs and diskettes, they are mounted in standard locations. Check for files and raw data on a floppy disk using the `volcheck` utility at `/vol/dev/aliases/floppy0`.

When the CD mounts, you will find files at /cdrom/cdrom0. If you are working with a system that has two CD-ROM drives or two floppy disk drives, you will find the file system and raw data for the first floppy drive at /floppy/floppy0 and for the second floppy drive at /floppy/floppy1. To access the file system on the first CD-ROM drive, you will find the mount point at /cdrom/cdrom0; the mount point for the second drive will be at /cdrom/cdrom1. If you want to access raw data on two CD-ROM drives, the mount point locations are /vol/dev/aliases/cdrom0 and /vol/dev/aliases/cdrom1 for drive 1 and 2, respectively. For a system with three CD-ROM drives, the alternate names of each drive would be cdrom0, cdrom1, and cdrom2.

Compare the simple automatic mounting procedure to what you must do to manually mount a CD or floppy disk. To manually mount a disk, do the following:

1. Insert the disk.
2. Log in as superuser, entering **su**, then the password.
3. Determine the location of the disk.
4. Create a mount point.
5. Mount the device using the mount command, with the correct options from a directory that is *not* the mount point (an example would be mount -t <*xxx*> dev/disk/cdrom).
6. Log out as superuser by typing **exit**.
7. Use the files on the disk.
8. Log back in as superuser.
9. Unmount the disk.
10. Eject the disk.
11. Log out as the superuser.

In the sections that follow, you will see how to format, mount, work with content, and eject CD-ROM and floppy diskettes. If you are using a Solaris laptop or a computer that uses a PCMCIA Memory Card (also now called a *PC Card*), then you will need to perform all of these same steps for your PCMCIA Memory Card. The steps are quite similar to those described in the sections on diskettes. For example, you can format a PCMCIA Memory Card to be a DOS or UFS disk, and you can use the Volume Manager (volcheck -v command) to load the card and view its contents within a window. To view the contents of the card, use the ls -L -l command. The location of the PCMCIA card is /pcmem/pcmem0, and files can be copied to or moved from there using the cp or mv commands. To eject a card, to access a remote card, or to make a card available to other users, follow the instructions given for diskettes, substituting the name pcmem for floppy and pcmem0 for floppy0.

CD-ROMs

Nearly every Solaris workstation and server comes with a CD-ROM drive. Currently, the CD-ROM is the most common method for locally installing applications and for viewing reference material. That may change over time as the DVD format slowly replaces CD-ROM over the next couple of years, but ultimately, broadband access will probably become the dominant information and application distribution method. Still, today the CD-ROM is one of the most important devices you will need to work with on your system.

Solaris typically uses SCSI-2 CD-ROM drives set to a SCSI target ID of 6; although it is possible to use other addresses, this is the default one. Many applications expect to use ID 6, so it isn't recommended that you change this assignment. Sun systems ship with Sun-branded CD-ROM drives, but as of Solaris release 2.6, support for third-party CD-ROMs was added, provided that the drives supported 512-byte sectors.

TIP One problem that crops up with CD-ROM drives for Solaris IA x86 users is that not many drives are fully supported. Some SCSI cards are not supported by Solaris, so it is best to check to see if your CD-ROM and any accompanying SCSI cards are on the Hardware Compatibility List.

You can attach both CD-R (Readable) and CD-RW (ReWriteable) drives to Solaris systems. If you set the SCSI ID to 6, a SPARC system will recognize the device just as it would a CD-ROM. To record to a CD-RW drive, consider either cdrecord by Jorg Schilling (`ftp://ftp.focus.gmd.de/pub/unix/cdrecord/`) or the commercial software packages such as GEAR for Unix (`www.gearcd.com/html/products/gear/unix/index.html`) or CDR Publisher from Creative Digital Research (`www.cdr1.com`).

Mounting CD-ROMs

It is particularly easy to work with CD-ROM drives in the Solaris 8 OS because they automount and the content shows up on your desktop in a window. The mount point is `/cdrom` unless you specify something different using the `mount` command from the command line.

Solaris will work with any ISO 9660 standard CD-ROM. You can view the contents of a CD-ROM in iconic form in the Volume Manager window, as shown in Figure 6.5 for the installation disk of the Easy Capture screenshot and image editing utility.

FIGURE 6.5

A CD-ROM's contents as they appear in a CDE window

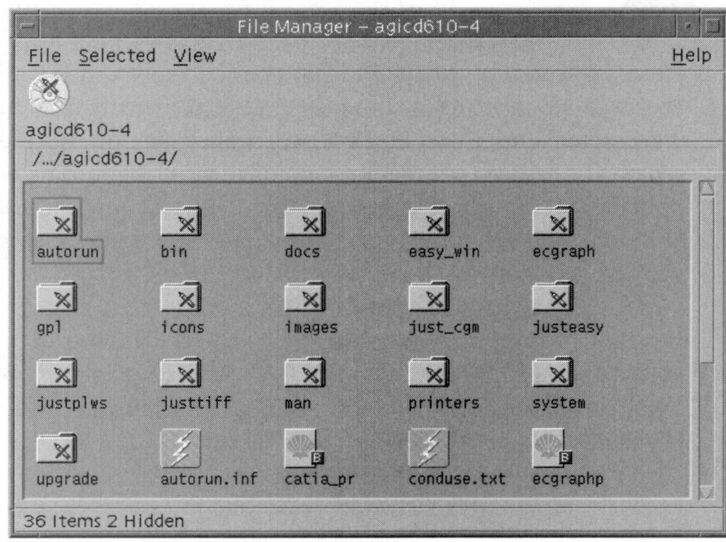

Alternatively, you can use the list (`ls`) command to obtain a directory listing of a CD-ROM's contents from the command line. The syntax for this command for CD-ROM1 is as follows:

```
ls -L [-l] /cdrom/cdrom0
```

The `-L` tells the list command to list the symbolic links, and `-l` specifies the long format listing that includes both permissions and owners. Figure 6.6 shows the list command's output for the CD-ROM whose contents were shown in Figure 6.5.

To access a CD over the network, you must first create a directory and then mount it. Do the following:

1. Enter the `mkdir` *<directory>* command at the command line to create a directory name that will be the mount point for the CD.
2. Find the name of the CD you want to mount by entering the first line of the following:

   ```
   showmount -e system-name
   export list for system-name
   /cdrom/sol_8_sparc
   ```

3. Log in as superuser (if needed) by entering first **su**, then the su's password.
4. Then mount the CD-ROM using the following command:

   ```
   # mount -F nfs -o ro <system-name>:/cdrom/<cd-name>\
       <local-mount-point>
   ```

The <*system-name*> is the name of the computer whose CD you wish to mount, <*cd-name*> is the name of the CD that will be mounted, and <*local-mount-point*> is the local directory that will mount the remote CD.

5. Log out as the superuser with the `exit` command.
6. Then use the `ls /cdrom` command to see if your CD is mounted.

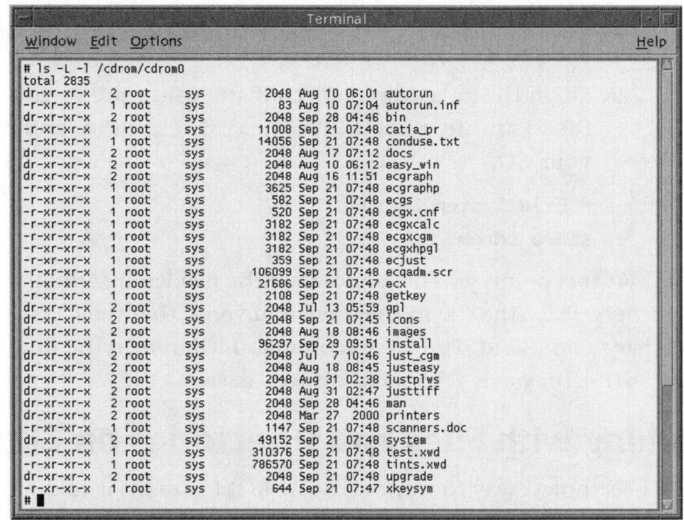

Terminal
Window Edit Options Help
ls -L -l /cdrom/cdrom0
total 2835
dr-xr-xr-x 2 root sys 2048 Aug 10 06:01 autorun
-r-xr-xr-x 1 root sys 83 Aug 10 07:04 autorun.inf
dr-xr-xr-x 2 root sys 2048 Sep 28 04:46 bin
-r-xr-xr-x 1 root sys 11008 Sep 21 07:48 catia_pr
-r-xr-xr-x 1 root sys 14056 Sep 21 07:48 conduse.txt
dr-xr-xr-x 2 root sys 2048 Aug 17 07:12 docs
dr-xr-xr-x 2 root sys 2048 Aug 10 06:12 easy_win
dr-xr-xr-x 2 root sys 2048 Aug 16 11:51 ecgraph
-r-xr-xr-x 1 root sys 3625 Sep 21 07:48 ecgraphp
-r-xr-xr-x 1 root sys 582 Sep 21 07:48 ecgs
-r-xr-xr-x 1 root sys 520 Sep 21 07:48 ecgx.cnf
-r-xr-xr-x 1 root sys 3182 Sep 21 07:48 ecgxcalc
-r-xr-xr-x 1 root sys 3182 Sep 21 07:48 ecgxcgm
-r-xr-xr-x 1 root sys 3182 Sep 21 07:48 ecgxhpgl
-r-xr-xr-x 1 root sys 359 Sep 21 07:48 ecjust
-r-xr-xr-x 1 root sys 106099 Sep 21 07:48 ecqadm.scr
-r-xr-xr-x 1 root sys 21686 Sep 21 07:47 ecx
-r-xr-xr-x 1 root sys 2108 Sep 21 07:48 getkey
dr-xr-xr-x 2 root sys 2048 Jul 13 05:59 gpl
dr-xr-xr-x 2 root sys 2048 Sep 21 07:45 icons
dr-xr-xr-x 2 root sys 2048 Aug 18 08:46 images
-r-xr-xr-x 1 root sys 96297 Sep 29 09:51 install
dr-xr-xr-x 2 root sys 2048 Jul 7 10:46 just_cgm
dr-xr-xr-x 2 root sys 2048 Aug 18 08:45 justeasy
dr-xr-xr-x 2 root sys 2048 Aug 31 02:38 justplws
dr-xr-xr-x 2 root sys 2048 Aug 31 02:47 justtiff
dr-xr-xr-x 2 root sys 2048 Sep 28 04:46 man
dr-xr-xr-x 2 root sys 2048 Mar 27 2000 printers
-r-xr-xr-x 1 root sys 1147 Sep 21 07:48 scanners.doc
dr-xr-xr-x 2 root sys 49152 Sep 21 07:48 system
-r-xr-xr-x 1 root sys 310376 Sep 21 07:48 test.xwd
-r-xr-xr-x 1 root sys 786570 Sep 21 07:48 tints.xwd
dr-xr-xr-x 2 root sys 2048 Sep 21 07:48 upgrade
-r-xr-xr-x 1 root sys 644 Sep 21 07:47 xkeysym
#

FIGURE 6.6

The list (`ls`) command offers a command-line view of a CD-ROM's contents.

If you wish to make a local CD available to other computers over the network, do the following:

1. Log in as superuser.
2. Use the `ps` command to determine if the NFS daemon (`nfsd`) is running:

   `# ps -ef | grep nfsd`

   If this daemon is running, you will see a process line returned that includes the `/usr/lib/nfs/nfsd` attribute.
3. If you do not see this daemon, perform steps 4 through 6; otherwise go directly to step 7.
4. Use the `mkdir /`<*directoryname*> command to create a directory that will be used by `nfsd` as the share.
5. Add the line **`share -F nfs -o ro [-d comment] /`<*directoryname*>** to the `/etc/dfs/dfstab` file.

6. Create the NFS daemon by entering the following:

   ```
   # /etc/int.d/nfs.server start
   ```

   To verify that this daemon is running, reenter the command in step 2, looking for the `/usr/lib/nfs/nfsd` attribute to be returned.

7. Eject the CD-ROM by entering the **`eject cdrom0`** command.

8. Enter the `chmod` command below to allow write permission to the `/ect/rmmount.conf` file:

   ```
   # chmod 644 /etc/rmmount.conf
   ```

9. Open the `/etc/rmmount.conf` file using the `vi` editor (see Chapter 16, "Using the `vi` and Text Editor") or the CDE text editor and enter the statement to share your CD:

   ```
   # File System Sharing
   share cdrom*
   ```

At this point, you have provided the needed information to share your CD with others. Place the CD in the drive and verify that the CD is available by using the `share` command. The `share` command will return the line `/<directoryname> ro "<directoryname> to wake up NFS daemon"`.

Working with Files and Directories on CDs

The simplest way to work with CD-ROM content is to double-click the icon in the File Manager window when the window appears. In some instances, for example, when you have an installable program file or multimedia content on CD-ROM, the manufacturer will include an autostart script that will launch the installer program. That kind of CD-ROM starts up by itself.

To copy files and directories from a CD-ROM on the desktop, click and drag them to the location in which you wish to make the copies. A CD-ROM being read-only, those files are copied to a new location and are not moved (deleted) from the CD-ROM. To copy the files or directories from the command line, use the copy command for files:

```
# cp /cdrom/<destination path>/<filename>
```

Use the copy command with the `-r` option for directories:

```
# cp -r /cdrom/<destination path>/<directoryname>
```

When you copy a file or directory, you become the owner but it still has the same permissions it has on the disk, which is –r–r–r–. To change the permissions so that you can write to the file or directory, do one of the following:

- Right-click the file or directory, select the Properties command, and set the file attributes in the Properties dialog box by clicking the appropriate check boxes.
- From the command line, use the `chmod` command.

Playing Audio CDs with WorkMan

Solaris doesn't come with a utility to play audio CDs, as do the Windows and Macintosh operating systems. However, you can add that capability by installing WorkMan, a third-party freeware utility. You can download a package for WorkMan or an archive for the files you compile from WorkMan's home page at `www.midwinter.com/workman/`. To install WorkMan, see the section "Packages" in Chapter 12, "Working with File Utilities."

Once the WorkMan package is properly installed, it will work with Volume Management to mount audio CDs and put on your screen a graphical CD player. You will first need to attach either external speakers or headphones to your CD-ROM drive to hear the sound.

To attach external speakers or headphones to WorkMan, follow these steps:

1. Log in as a superuser at the command line (enter **su**).
2. Install the WorkMan package as described in Chapter 12.
3. Edit the `/etc/rmmount.conf` file to add the line **`action cdrom action_workman.so`** ***`<path>`*** **`/workman`** ***`<options>`***.
4. Insert an audio CD into your CD-ROM drive.
5. Open a Terminal window and enter **`workman`** at the command line.

The WorkMan utility shown in the following graphic offers you volume and audio controls. You can also create and manage play lists using this program. If you close WorkMan, the audio CD will continue to play, but you can also use this utility to eject audio CDs.

Ejecting CD-ROMs

You can use one of the following three methods to eject a CD-ROM:

- The Eject CD-ROM system utility
- The Eject command in the File Manager window for the CD-ROM
- The eject command at the command line

However, if there are other users accessing the CD-ROM from other systems, you will need to inform them verbally or by e-mail to close their session. If you can't get another person to close their session on your CD-ROM by their own volition, you can kill the process manually before you eject the CD-ROM. If you are using a shell, before you eject the disk you also need to make sure that you aren't one of the users who is using the CD simply by having your working directory on that CD-ROM.

To identify sessions accessing a CD-ROM, give the following command at the command line:

```
# fuser -u [-k] /cdrom/cdrom0
```

The `fuser` command takes `-u` as the option that identifies the user of the CD and `-k` as the option that kills their process. If two processes are running—for example, number 6400 by root and 6399 by jones—they are returned in the usage response:

```
/cdrom/cdrom: 6400c(root) 6399c(jones)
```

When you use the `-k` option to kill all processes, the system returns the following:

```
/cdrom/cdrom0: 6400c(root)Killed 6399c(jones)Killed
```

If you are the only user accessing the CD-ROM drive, you can use the Eject command on the File menu of the File Manager window to eject the CD-ROM, as shown in Figure 6.7. If your working directory is on the CD, you will get a `device busy` message should you try to eject the disc.

CD-ROMs that come with an autostart script are often used to do program installation. You may find that an installation program starts up and runs you through a wizard that asks for input, and when the installer is finished, the program quits. You never see a File Manager window appear. Now you are faced with the task of ejecting the CD. You can use the `eject` command at the command line, but if you want to perform this operation in the CDE graphical user interface with a point and a click, here's how.

To eject a CD-ROM using the system utility, follow these steps:

1. Click the Applications drawer on the front panel, then click the Applications icon.
2. Click the `System_Admin` folder in the Application Manager window. The System_Admin window appears (shown in Figure 6.8).
3. Click the Eject CD-ROM icon to perform that action.

FIGURE 6.7

Using the Eject command from the File menu of a CD-ROM File Manager window is one way to eject a disk.

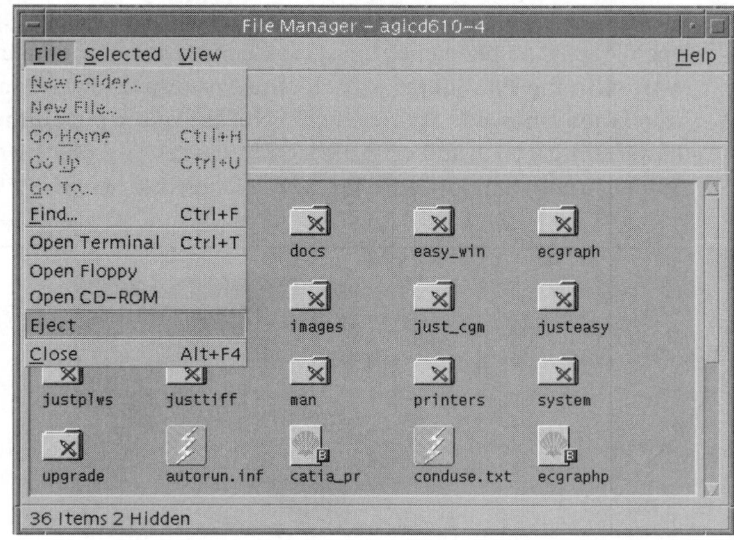

FIGURE 6.8

The System_Admin window contains a number of useful device management tools.

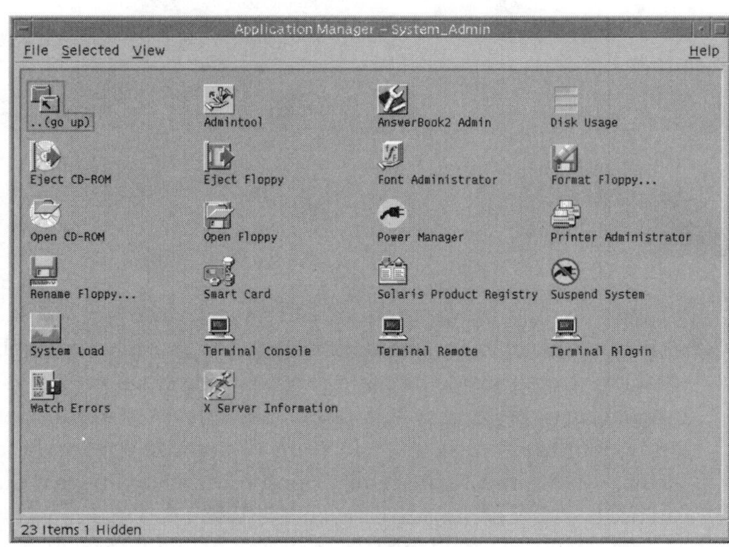

You will note that there are several disk management tools in the System_Admin window, including Eject CD-ROM, Eject Floppy, Format Floppy, Open CD-ROM, Open Floppy, and Rename Floppy. Some of these actions are installed by default as controls in the Files subpanel of the front panel as part of a standard workstation installation (shown in Figure 6.9). To add any of the remaining actions to the Files drawer, simply click and drag the icon of the action from the Application Manager's System_Admin window onto the Install Icon control of the Files subpanel

FIGURE 6.9

The Files subpanel of the front panel is a good place to put device actions.

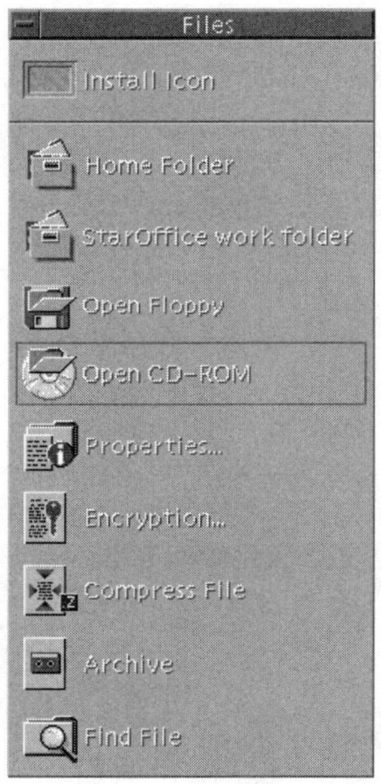

Diskettes

Most SPARC and IA workstations and servers come with a diskette drive. Even though diskettes can't hold enough data to contain most modern applications, they are still useful for holding data files and for providing small programs that can start up an installation or perform system tasks. Therefore, IA platforms perform their initial installation boot from a diskette, and you will find diskettes useful as a secondary storage media. Solaris provides diskette support using standard daemons such as `volcheck`. You can use the `vold` command to open a diskette, and you can format diskettes and install file systems on them. Many terminals and network computers that are found on Sun networks do not come with or support diskette drives.

Mounting Diskettes

If your diskette is formatted, you can simply notify the Volume Manager and the diskette will mount and open a File Manager window on the CDE. If not, you will have to format the diskette and, for UFS diskettes, add a file system (see the next section, "Formatting Diskettes").

Do the following to load a diskette:

1. Insert the diskette.
2. At the command line, enter **`volcheck -v`** and press the Return key.

   The Volume Manager will post the message `media was found` if the diskette was detected, and it will mount it into the `/floppy` directory. If you get the message `no media was found`, most likely the diskette is either unformatted or damaged.
3. Use `ls /floppy` to check that the diskette was mounted and to view the contents.

   Solaris should return either `floppyname` *<filenames>* (if you assigned a name) or `unnamed_floppy` *<filenames>* (if you didn't assign a name).
4. Use the Open Floppy action on the Files drawer of the front panel (see Figure 6.9) of the CDE to open a window with the diskette's contents showing.

   The Open Floppy action initiates an applet in the `System_Admin` folder, which is in turn found in the `Application Manager` folder, accessed from the Applications drawer on the front panel.

Formatting Diskettes

If you insert an unformatted floppy disk, or a disk with formatting that Solaris 8 doesn't recognize, and then use the Open Floppy control on the File drawer in the front panel, Solaris will open the Format Floppy dialog box shown in Figure 6.10.

FIGURE 6.10

An unformatted diskette will cause the Format Floppy dialog box to open when the Open Floppy action is used.

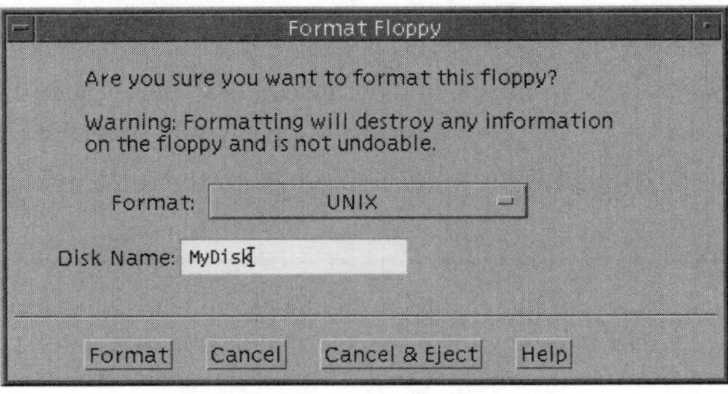

You can select any one of the three options from the Format drop-down menu:

UNIX Opens a UFS disk, which can be read only on the platform (SPARC or Intel) on which it was formatted

DOS High Density Creates a diskette (1.44MB) that a standard PC can read

NEC-DOS Medium Density Creates a diskette that can be read on NEC computers.

Once you've selected an option from the Format menu, click the Format button to initiate the format sequence.

The procedure for formatting diskettes from the command line offers more options; it is as follows:

1. Put the diskette into the disk drive.
2. If the disk is unformatted, format it for UFS or DOS using the `fdformat` command.

   Depending upon your drive type, Solaris can format any of the following: 3.5-inch Extended Density (2.88MB), High Density (1.44MB), Medium or Double Density (1.2MB), Low Density (720KB); 5.25-inch High Density (1.2MB), Medium Density (720KB), or Low Density (360KB).

NOTE Use the `man fdformat` command to view the options that are required to create different formats in drives with different densities. No option is required for the `fdformat` command if you're formatting a 1.44MB diskette for a standard 1.44MB drive, a 1.2MB diskette for a 1.2MB drive, or a 720KB diskette for a 720KB drive.

3. If the disk was formatted for UFS, add a UFS file system if you intend to store files. DOS diskettes work on both SPARC and IA platforms; however, a UFS disk works on only the platform it was formatted on. To store characters on a UFS diskette, you do not need to add a UFS file system.
4. Eject the diskette.

UFS is platform specific because SPARC is a little-endian processor and IA is big-endian. The UFS codes for this difference. To format a UFS diskette, do the following:

1. Close the File Manager and insert the unformatted diskette.

TIP Make sure that the write-protection tab is closed so that the disk can be written to. The File Manager will open a formatting window when you insert an unformatted disk.

2. At the command line, enter **fdformat -v -U** ***<density> <options>***, then press the Return key.
3. Unless you use the -f option, you will see the following message:

```
Formatting 1.44 M in /vol/dev/rdiskette0/unformatted
Press return to start formatting floppy.
```

4. Press the Return key to format or Ctrl+C to continue.

In step 2, the -v parameter verifies formatting, and the -U option unmounts the diskette if it was mounted. For a 1.44MB diskette, use no density parameter for UFS, -d for MS-DOS, or -D for 720KB. If you leave the density option parameter blank, the command returns a list of all options but does not format the diskette. The other options are -e, which ejects the diskette when formatting is complete; -f, which formats without confirmation; -b *<labelname>*, which names the diskette (up to eight characters either case); and -z, which lists all options of the fdformat command without formatting the diskette. If you do not apply a label using the -b option, then the diskette is referred to as noname. The diskette drive itself is labeled floppy0 for the first floppy drive.

After formatting, you can store data such as tar or cpio on the diskette. To store files, you must install the UFS, as follows:

1. At the command line, enter **$ /user/sbin/newfs -v /vol/dev/aliases /floppy0**, then press the Return key.

   The following message appears:

   ```
   Newfs: construct a new file system
           /vol/dev/alias/floppy0 (y/n)? y
   ```

2. Press the Return key, and the diskette's file system is created.
3. Enter the following command to notify the Volume Manager of the diskette: **volrmount -i floppy0**.
4. Use the ls /floppy command to see if the diskette and its UFS was mounted. The ls /floppy command returns the name of the floppy: floppy0.

Working with Files and Directories on Diskettes

With a mounted diskette viewable from a File Manager window in the CDE, the easiest way to copy files and directories is to select them and drag them to the location you wish to copy them to.

You can also use the copy command at the command line to perform the copy function. Here is the syntax:

```
cp /floppy/floppy0/<filename> /<targetpath>/<targetfilename>
```

This command copies the file on the floppy to the new location and changes the filename of the new copy. If you do not specify a target filename, the original name of the file on the floppy disk is used. If you substitute the period (.) symbol for the target, the file is copied to the current directory.

Use the `cp -r` parameter to copy directories and their contents to a target directory. The syntax is as follows:

```
cp -r /floppy/floppy0/<directoryname> \
    /<targetpath>/<targetdirectoryname>
```

Similarly, if the floppy disk is write-enabled and you have the permission to delete files, you can use the move command to copy files or directories to a new location and delete them on the diskette. Here is the syntax:

```
mv /floppy/floppy0/<filename list> \
    /<targetpath>/<targetdirectoryname>
```

When you copy a file, you become the owner, but if you were not the owner of the file on the diskette, you may be restricted from writing to or modifying it. You will need to reset the permissions, either by right-clicking the file icon in the CDE and selecting the Properties command or by changing the attributes from the command line.

The File Manager window of a floppy offers you several commands that allow you to work with diskettes. You can format the diskette, rename it, eject it, and so on, as shown in Figure 6.11.

FIGURE 6.11

The diskette CDE File Manager window offers you several disk management features.

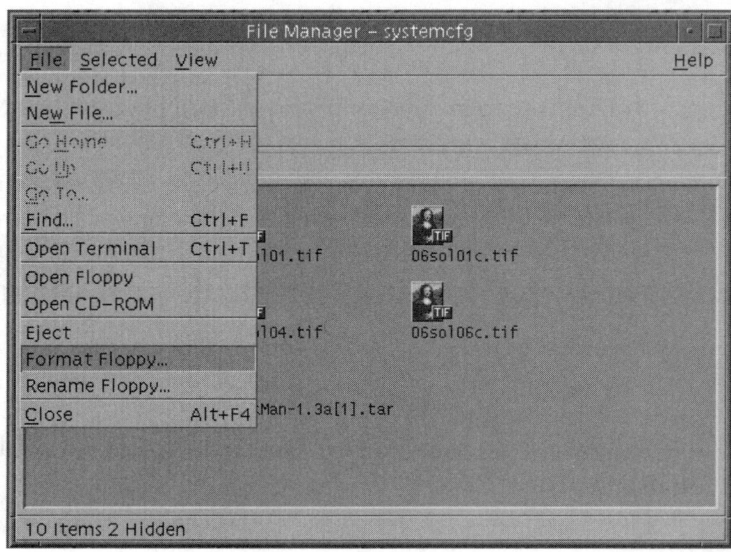

To access a diskette on another system, you will need to manually mount the file system, as follows:

1. Select a directory that will serve as the mount point of the diskette.
2. Give the `ls /remotepath/floppy` command to find the name of the diskette.
3. Log in as a superuser by entering **su**.
4. Mount the diskette by using this command:

```
# mount -F nfs <systemname>:/floppy/<diskettename> \
      <local_mountpoint>
```

5. Finally, check that the diskette was actually mounted by using the `ls /floppy` command from the mount point.

To make your local diskettes available over the network to others, you must share them by starting an NFS daemon. The procedure is as follows:

1. Log in as a superuser.
2. Enter the `ps` command to determine if the NFS daemon (`nfsd`) is running:

```
# ps -ef | grep nfsd
```

   If you see a line returned by `grep` that contains `/usr/lib/nfs/nfsd`, then this daemon is running and you can proceed to step 7.

3. If the NFS daemon isn't running, then use the `mkdir /<directoryname>` command to create a dummy directory that will be recognized by the NFS daemon.
4. Open the `/etc/dfs/dfstab` and add the line **`share -F nfs ro -d <comment> /<directoryname>`** to that file. The `-d <comment>` is optional.
5. At the command line, enter the following to start the NFS daemon:

```
# /etc/init.d/nfs.server start
```

6. Use the `ps -ef | grep nfsd` command in step 2 again to see if the NFS daemon was established.
7. Eject any diskette in the drive using the `eject floppy0` command.
8. Add root write permission to the `/etc/rmmount.conf` file by entering the following:

```
# chmod 644 /etc/rmmount.conf
```

9. Open the `rmmount.conf` file and add the following lines to share any diskette loaded into the floppy drive:

```
# File System Sharing
share floppy*
```

10. Remove the write permissions (and return to the default permissions) from the `/etc/rmmount.conf` file by entering the following:

    ```
    # chmod 444 /etc/rmmount.conf
    ```

11. Load the diskette you want to share. Your system will return these messages:

    ```
    –Insert the diskette–
    # volcheck -v
    media was found
    ```

12. Use the `share` command to determine if your diskette share has been created. You should see the following message if you were successful:

    ```
    # share
       /<directoryname> ro "<directoryname> dir to wake
       up NFS daemon"
    /<diskettename> rw ""
    ```

Ejecting a Diskette

The process for ejecting a diskette is straightforward provided that you are the only one using that diskette's content. If you have a File Manager window open for the diskette, select the Eject command from the File menu.

To eject a disk from the command line, type the following:

```
eject floppy0
```

For a SPARC system, the diskette automatically ejects. On an IA system, you will need to manually eject the diskette once you see the message telling you to do so.

WARNING Never remove a disk from an x86 system with out ejecting or umounting it first. This can cause the OS to freeze or panic.

If by chance you see the message `/vol/dev/rdiskette0/<diskettename>: Device busy`, someone else is accessing your floppy disk's content. To determine if the diskette is in use, give the `fuser -u [-k] floppy0` command; the `-u` option determines who is using the diskette, and the `-k` option kills the process of accessing the diskette.

Zip and Jaz Drives

Iomega's Zip and Jaz drives are popular on many workstations, and although they are SCSI disks, they are handled more like a large diskette than anything else. Zip and Jaz devices are sold in both parallel port and SCSI bus configurations, but Solaris works with only the SCSI drives.

NOTE For support on using Zip and Jaz drives, go to the Iomega site at `www.iomega.com/support/documents/4019.html` and `www.iomega.com/support/documents/2019.html`.

To work with a Zip or Jaz drive as a SCSI disk, you need to add format data to the disk so your system will recognize it. Solaris has built-in support for these disks as long as they are not write-protected.

To add a Zip or Jaz drive to your system, follow these steps:

1. Attach the drive to your SCSI chain and give it an unassigned SCSI ID. Make sure your system and all peripherals are powered down when you attach the device.
2. Enter the following into your `/etc/format.dat` file for a Zip drive:

```
disk_type="Zip 100"\
      :ctlr=SCSI\
      :ncyl=2406:acyl=2:pcyl=2408:nhead=2\
      :nsect=40:rpm=3600:bpt=20480\
   partition="Zip 100"\
      :disk="Zip 100":ctlr=SCSI\
      :2=0,192480
```

   For a Jaz drive, enter the following:

```
disk_type="Jaz 1GB"\
      :ctlr=SCSI\
      :ncyl=1018:acyl=2:pcyl=1020:nhead=64\
      :nsect=32:rpm=3600:bpt=16384\
   partition="Jaz 1GB"\
      :disk="Jaz 1GB":ctlr=SCSI\
      :2=0,2084864
```

3. Do a reconfiguration reboot by entering **`ok boot -r`** on a SPARC system or **`b -r`** on an IA system. (A `reboot -r` on either system when you are logged in to the shell as root will also do a reconfiguration reboot.)

   The `-r` option reconfigures the system upon reboot. Your system will query all devices on internal and external buses to see if they are operable. Then the reconfiguration dynamically rebuilds the `/devices` and `/dev` directories based on the device hierarchy it sees.

4. At the OpenBoot prompt enter the following:

   ```
   # touch /reconfiguration
   # sync; sync; init 6
   ```

5. Insert a disk into the drive, boot your computer, then enter **`format`** at the command line to format the disk.

6. Create a file system on your disk by entering the following at the command line (where *n* is the drive number for your device):

   ```
   # newfs -v/dev/sdnc
   ```

7. Make a mount point directory by entering **`mkdir /zip`** or **`mkdir /jaz`** at the command line.

8. Create a mount point by typing **`mount /dev/sdnc /zip`** or **`mount /dev/sdnc /jaz`** at the command line.

So in truth, adding a Zip or Jaz drive isn't very different than adding a hard drive to your system, as you will see in the next section. The key differences are that you need to know what to enter into the `format.dat` file, and you don't typically slice and dice a Zip or Jaz drive. You can surmount the limitation of not being able to work with read-only disks for these devices by using a program called `ziptool` (see `fy.chalmers.se/~appro/ziptool.html`.

Hard Drives

Hard drive or disk management is among the most critical tasks that you face when you administer Solaris systems. An understanding of how hard drives are configured is also essential to a number of operating system functions that you may need to perform on a day-to-day basis and is helpful to even the average Solaris user. For the following discussion on dealing with internal disks, I'll assume that you are familiar at a basic level with standard computer terms such as *tracks*, *cylinders*, *sectors*, and *partitions*.

Solaris also supports RAID (redundant array of independent disks), both as software RAID in a package like DiskSuite, which Sun sells as an add-on to Sun systems, or hardware RAID, like an external disk array such as the A1000. RAID offers redundancies, improved performance, fault tolerance, and other benefits that make it a good investment for many systems, particularly server applications. (The improved performance and fault-tolerance features are dependent upon the level of RAID you implement.) To the operating system, RAID appears as if it is a single hard drive image, and so the principles and techniques you see described in the following sections apply to RAID devices and configurations as well as to hard drives.

Slices or Partitions

When you format a disk (or hard drive) for the Solaris operating system, it is divided into a set of slices, or partitions, that contain single file systems. As you learned in Chapter 5, a file system is a group of files organized into a hierarchy and managed or tracked by an indexed table of contents. In the file system, the root (/) directory is a slice and is at the top of the hierarchy, and most of the other directories are at the top of other slices, one level down from the root. There is no particular reason why one slice contains one specific directory, but there are conventions that are almost always followed. When you install Solaris, it gives you a default configuration of directories in slices that you can, with some exceptions, change later on. Typically, most administrators or users stick with the standard directory locations because it makes it easier to work with programs and for others to understand how your system is set up.

NOTE Chapter 3, "Getting Started," included a preliminary discussion of formatting disks and creating partitions or slices. The sections that follow describe some of the standard features of partitioning disks on SPARC and IA systems.

On the SPARC platform, you use the `format` command to format the whole disk as a Solaris disk; that disk is partitioned into eight slices numbered 0 through 7. On the Intel platform, your disk is partitioned by using the `fdisk` utility, and each partition can have only one operating system on it. Using the Solaris `fdisk` utility, you can divide your disk into 4 primary partitions (more if you use extended partitions), and each Solaris partition is divided into 10 slices, numbered 0 through 9. Solaris assigns to each of the slices on SPARC and Intel systems a particular purpose. Table 6.1 lists the disk slice assignments.

TABLE 6.1: DISK SLICE ASSIGNMENTS

Slice	File System	Location	Use
0	root	Client/server	Contains operating system files and directories.
1	swap	Client/server	Contains virtual memory.
2	–	Client/server	Addresses the entire disk. The size defined by the format command should not be altered.
3	/export	Server	Contains previous or alternative versions of the OS. Clients with different architectures use these alternative versions.
4	/export/swap	Server	Contains virtual memory for clients.
5	/opt	Client/server	Contains application program files. When this slice isn't created, the /opt directory is placed in slice 0. This is the default location for local packages installed with the pkgadd command.
6	/usr	Client/server	Contains binary executable system files. System command programs, documentation, and library routines are put into this directory.
7	/home or /export/home	Client/Server	Contains user data.
8	–	Client/server	Intel system only. This is the boot slice at start of partition. Used to boot Solaris from the hard drive.
9	–	Client/server	Intel system only. This is the alternative sector slice used to store alternative disk blocks.

WARNING When working with the SunOS, keep in mind that slice 2 is an addressing scheme for the entire disk and so should not be used to store raw data created by applications. Similarly, block 0, cylinder 0 is used for the disk label. If you use this block, you may not be able to access the disk, and if you use this cylinder, you will pay a performance penalty.

In a multiple-disk system, you can split the swap slice over two or more disks. The swap slice is the only type of slice that can span multiple disks. When multiple disks are available, you can use one disk as a system disk and store the root and /user file systems on that disk. Any other disks are referred to as secondary or nonsystem disks. The advantage of using multiple disks is that it increases your storage capacity and I/O performance and makes it possible for you to alter the configuration and contents of the secondary disks offline without having to bring your system down. Multiple disks configured as a RAID drive have the same logical assignment as a single disk but typically also offer better performance.

Not all slices are required. The slices that store vital system components—slice 0 (root), slice 1 (swap), slice 2 (logical disk address), slice 5 (/opt), slice 6 (/usr), and slice 7 (/export/home)—are needed on both standalone Solaris systems and on servers. Slice 3 (/export) and slice 4 (/export/swap) are required on servers but may be left off of standalone systems and workstations. Although they are required on standalone systems and on servers, slices 5, 6, and 7 can be also be left off of workstations.

Some administrators suggest that it is a good idea to put the /var directory into its own slice, particularly on server systems and servers serving as license servers. This directory contains system logs, packages, and accounting data. When a job that fills the disk space for /var runs, you will no longer be able to write to your log files, which will start to generate large numbers of error messages. If you put the /var directory into its own slice, make your /var partition between 50MB and 150MB. (A default install of Solaris 8 with eight packages installed and the rollup patch installed has a 41MB /var.)

You may find it useful to put user home directories such as usr/home and /export/home into their own partitions, particularly on standalone workstations used by an individual; indeed, some people use an entire disk for this purpose. Other candidates to be separated are the /usr, /opt, and root partitions. When you want to export the /usr directory to another system, you will find that having a separate slice provides additional security benefits. Having /opt in its own partition enables you to resize that partition with third-party software more easily if you find yourself installing a large number of software packages; if you use /opt in a partition on a server, you can export the data in the /opt partition more easily to other systems. It's even easier to mount another disk and make it /opt if that is a possibility. Having root in its own partition makes it easier to install programs with many kernel drivers. On the Intel architecture platform, you use the Solaris fdisk utility to create up to four partitions, one of which must be a Solaris partition. That Solaris partition must be the active partition with a bootable operating system. You can create a single Solaris fdisk partition, but it is more typical to leave at least a second DOS partition on the disk; that is, the Solaris partition contains the master boot record at sector 0. Solaris fdisk partitions start at cylinder boundaries and begin at cylinder 1 rather than cylinder 0 (as SPARC systems do). Boot information like the master boot record is written to sector 0 on fdisk partitions.

NOTE Solaris 8 adds support for disks larger than 8GB on IA platforms.

Disk Management

When you install Solaris on a new SPARC system, you format your disk, create slices or partitions, and give those slices file systems. Use the Solaris `fdisk` utility to create partitions on IA systems. Each slice is a group of cylinders that contains a file system, can have an operating system installed on it, and appears logically as if it was a separate disk drive. File systems do not span slices, nor can there be more than one file system on the same slice.

WARNING The `fdisk` command wipes out all of the data that allows you to find information on your disk, so it's easy to destroy data using this command. Therefore, be especially careful when you use it, just as you would be when you use the `format` command.

To change your drive configuration after installation, rerun the Solaris installation program again, which will replace your entire system with a clean install. When you add a new disk drive or replace one that has failed, you may need to use the `format` command to format the drive; some disks are formatted at the manufacturer. The `format` command works only with disk drives; it cannot be used with CDs, diskettes, or tape. The `format` utility does more than simply format and partition your disk; it also does the following:

- Reports on mounted partitions, formatting, disk geometry, and target location
- Repairs damaged disks by marking sectors as unavailable
- Labels a disk and retrieves disk label names during analysis

On a formatted disk, the disk label or Volume Table of Contents (VTOC) stores information about the disk's controller, geometry, and slice configuration. You must label a disk after creating or modifying slices in order to have the new or modified slices recognized by your system. Part of the contents of the VTOC is the partition table, which describes the new slices. You see the disk's partition table appear when you use the `format` utility. In addition to the partition number (0–7 on SPARC), you also see tags and flags. A tag is a number used to describe the type of file system on the partition: 0=UNASSIGNED, 1=BOOT, 2=ROOT, 3=SWAP, 4=USR, 5=BACKUP, 7=VAR, and 8=HOME. Flags, or attributes, tell you whether the partition is read-only and mountable (`rm`), writeable and mountable (`wm`), or writeable and unmountable (wu rm). The swap slice is an example of `wu rm`.

To see the partition table for a disk, do this:

1. Enter the `format` command at the command line and press the Return key.

2. Specify the disk number for the label you wish to view; for example, 0 for the first disk.
3. Enter the `verify` option and press the Return key. Figure 6.12 shows an example of a disk's partition table. Note that the Cylinders column shows the start and stop cylinder for a slice, Size is in MB, and Blocks indicates the number of cylinders and sectors per slice.
4. Type **`quit`** or **`q`** to exit the format utility.

FIGURE 6.12

Use the `format` command to view a disk's partition table.

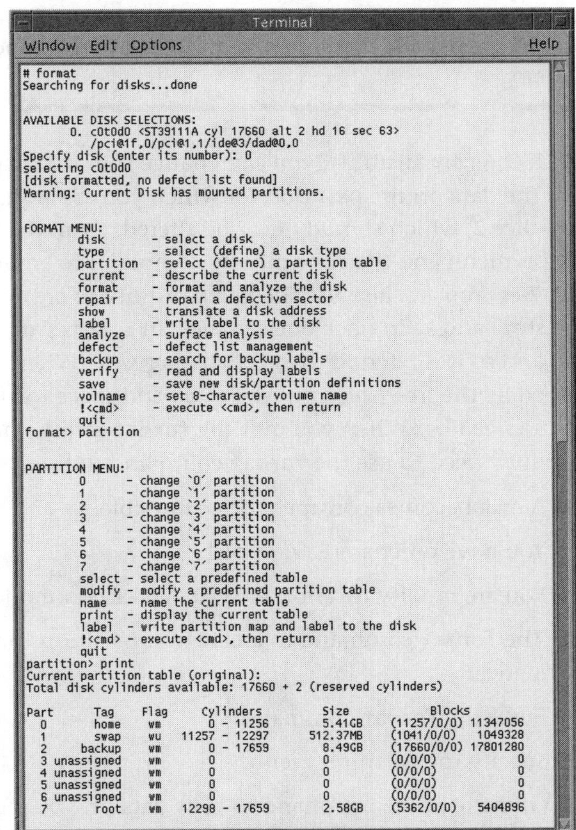

```
Terminal
Window  Edit  Options                                          Help
# format
Searching for disks...done

AVAILABLE DISK SELECTIONS:
       0. c0t0d0 <ST39111A cyl 17660 alt 2 hd 16 sec 63>
          /pci@1f,0/pci@1,1/ide@3/dad@0,0
Specify disk (enter its number): 0
selecting c0t0d0
[disk formatted, no defect list found]
Warning: Current Disk has mounted partitions.

FORMAT MENU:
        disk       - select a disk
        type       - select (define) a disk type
        partition  - select (define) a partition table
        current    - describe the current disk
        format     - format and analyze the disk
        repair     - repair a defective sector
        show       - translate a disk address
        label      - write label to the disk
        analyze    - surface analysis
        defect     - defect list management
        backup     - search for backup labels
        verify     - read and display labels
        save       - save new disk/partition definitions
        volname    - set 8-character volume name
        !<cmd>     - execute <cmd>, then return
        quit
format> partition

PARTITION MENU:
        0      - change `0' partition
        1      - change `1' partition
        2      - change `2' partition
        3      - change `3' partition
        4      - change `4' partition
        5      - change `5' partition
        6      - change `6' partition
        7      - change `7' partition
        select - select a predefined table
        modify - modify a predefined partition table
        name   - name the current table
        print  - display the current table
        label  - write partition map and label to the disk
        !<cmd> - execute <cmd>, then return
        quit
partition> print
Current partition table (original):
Total disk cylinders available: 17660 + 2 (reserved cylinders)

Part      Tag    Flag     Cylinders        Size            Blocks
  0       home    wm       0 - 11256        5.41GB    (11257/0/0) 11347056
  1       swap    wu   11257 - 12297      512.37MB    (1041/0/0)   1049328
  2     backup    wm       0 - 17659        8.49GB    (17660/0/0) 17801280
  3 unassigned    wm       0                0         (0/0/0)            0
  4 unassigned    wm       0                0         (0/0/0)            0
  5 unassigned    wm       0                0         (0/0/0)            0
  6 unassigned    wm       0                0         (0/0/0)            0
  7       root    wm   12298 - 17659        2.58GB    (5362/0/0)   5404896
```

Here are other operations you might need to do with the `format` utility:

- Print partition information, by entering **`partition`**, then **`print`**, as shown in Figure 6.12.
- Label a disk, by using the `format` command.

- Recover a corrupted disk label. In some instances, if you can't use verify to read the disk's primary label and to recover a disk label, you must supply a new label and its geometry and use the backup option to examine the disk.
- Repair a damaged sector using the analyze option on the format utility's Format menu followed by the setup and read commands.

NOTE The Print VTOC (prtvtoc) command also displays the partition table for a superuser. To use this utility, enter **prtvtoc *<diskaddress>*** (e.g., prtvtoc /dev/dsk/c?t?d?s2) at the command line. This command displays information on partitions, tags, flags, first and last sector, sector count, and the mount point directory for the file system.

With the format utility, you can change the size of slices, which will result in the loss of the data on the partition for which you are adjusting the size. The only exception is slice 2, which should never be altered. From the Format menu, select first the partition menu and then the modify command to enter the new size of the slice in megabytes. You can also use the format utility to create a temporary slice that you can use to store and keep track of free space. In Solaris parlance, this slice "hogs" the free space, and so it is referred to as the *free hog slice*. When you shrink a slice, that space is absorbed by the free hog, and when you add space to another slice, that space comes from the free hog. When you quit the format utility, the free hog disappears.

You may need to use the format command in these situations:

- A disk becomes corrupted or is unusable.
- You have purchased a new disk.
- You are modifying another system to accommodate Solaris.

Use the format command to create new partitions on a disk by entering the following sequence:

1. Enter the format command.
2. Specify the partition menu.
3. Give the print command to view data on your console.
4. Issue the modify command to select and create or alter partitions.
5. Specify the partition and the size, then enter the name of the table you desire in quotes.

6. After the format operation is complete, use the `quit` command to leave the partition menu; then enter **`verify`**, then **`quit`** again.

Once you create disk slices and label the disk, you will need to create a file system on that disk. To create a UFS file system, follow these steps:

1. Log in as superuser and give the new file system command, where `c?t?d?s?` is the raw device address for the disk:

   ```
   # newfs /dev/rdsk/c?t?d?s?
   ```

2. Enter the `mount` command at a new mount point to verify that the file system was installed, then enter the `ls` command to see the volume name, as follows:

   ```
   # mount /dev/dsk/c?t?d?s? /mnt
   # ls
   <volumename>
   ```

Adding a Disk

To add a hard drive to your system, you will need to supply a device driver and perhaps add an entry to the `/etc/format.dat` so that the `format` utility can identify the disk. The drive manufacturer should be able to provide you with both this software and the information required. Hard drives from Sun work with drivers already supplied with the operating system distribution. In some instances, third-party drives might not work with the Sun `format` utility and the manufacturer may need to supply you with its own `format` utility.

The `format` utility automatically configures SCSI drives and doesn't require a `format.dat` entry. SCSI-2 drives are all supported by Solaris since its 2.3 release.

To add a SCSI drive to a SPARC system, do the following:

1. As superuser, enter the `touch /reconfigure` command to create the `/reconfigure-` file.

2. Shut down your system using the following command:

   ```
   # shutdown -i0 -g0 -y
   ```

3. Turn off your system and peripheral devices.

4. Attach the SCSI drive to your system and set an appropriate SCSI address on the drive.

5. Turn on the drive.

6. Reboot your computer into the single-user mode by entering **`boot cdrom -s`** or **`boot net -s`** at the command line for a CD-ROM or network installation.

7. Issue the format command and the utility will automatically configure your SCSI disk drive and then use the verify command to verify that the configuration is correct when format is done. Depending upon the size of the SCSI disk, format creates an appropriate root file system and swap slice size.
8. Enter **quit** or **q** to close the format utility.

Sun doesn't provide an easy way to identify host adapters and SCSI devices from the command line. One way to find out about your SCSI subsystem is to reboot the system to the OpenBoot monitor and use the probe -scsi -all command to get a listing of all devices and controllers. Another utility you can use for this purpose is the scsiinfo utility, which can be found at ftp://ftp.cdf.Toronto.edu/pub/scsiinfo/.

When your system disk becomes damaged, you will not be able to run Solaris. A system disk contains the root (/) and/or /user file systems. To recover from this condition, you can reinstall Solaris and let the format command attempt to repair the damage, or you can install a new drive and restore your file system from a backup. After you have formatted, partitioned, and named the volume for your system disk, you will need to install the root (/) and/or /user Unix file systems. The next step is to install a boot block on a system disk to make that disk bootable, provided you are manually repairing the disk (the Solaris installer takes care of this detail for you automatically). Use the installboot command to perform this function.

Adding a disk to an Intel x86 box differs somewhat from the procedure just presented because the Solaris boot diskette is used to boot from the primary floppy drive (DOS A: drive), then after reboot, the system runs from the Solaris installation CD. When you are adding a new drive to an IA system, you should boot into the single-user mode by entering b -s when the Select the type of installation prompt appears. If you are installing a new system disk, you will need to create disk slices and label the disk during the installation.

To add a secondary disk to an Intel x86 system, the procedure is identical to the one described for the SPARC architecture earlier in this section. When you want to create a Solaris fdisk partition on an IA system, you will need to, as a superuser, give the format command and specify the disk number. At the format prompt, enter fdisk to display the fdisk menu. Options on this menu allow you to create a partition that spans an entire disk, create an fdisk partition and preserve existing non-Solaris fdisk partitions, or create a Solaris fdisk partition and add non-Solaris fdisk partitions. After you have made your selection and created or modified the partitions, use the partition menu and the modify command to create disk slices, use the label command to relabel the disk, then use quit to quit the Format menu. To add a file system to the new partitions, use the newfs command, and to add boot blocks to a system disk, use the installboot command as was described previously for SPARC systems.

Tape Drives

Sun Solaris supports many different tape drives, as was noted earlier in this chapter. Although backing up to tape does not offer immediate restoration of a system whose disk has failed (mirrored disk is a better solution for that), tape does offer the most economical means at the moment to provide an historical record of your disk's conditions. Many Solaris workstations and servers come with tape drives as standard devices. The following list includes the most common tape media you are likely to encounter:

- 1/2-inch reel tape with a capacity of 140MB
- QIC 1/4-inch tape cartridges with a capacity of 2.5GB
- DDS3 4mm cartridge tape with a storage range of 12GB, DDS2 with a 2GB or 4GB capacity
- Elliptical tape systems with capacities in the 50GB to 75GB range (such as Ecrix and OnStream drives)
- DLT 4000 and 7000 cartridge tape with storage capacities of 20GB and 35GB to 70GB, respectively, from Quantum and other OEMs.
- Linear Tape Open or LTO drives with capacities in the 50GB and greater range

Tape technology continues to advance in capacity and decrease in cost, although not quite as fast as disk, but there is still at least an order of magnitude less cost involved in committing data to tape. Given the rapidly increasing size of hard drives, there is a tendency to use tape systems with greater and greater capacity. Note also that the ranges of storage capacity represent the "native" capacity of the tape versus the capacity you achieve when you commit compressed data to tape. The compression ratio is typically in the range of 2 or 3 to 1, but it can vary considerably based on the data types you store to disk.

Remote MagTape Protocol

If you remember back to the discussion of addressing earlier in this chapter, tape drives have the device name `/dev/rmt/`*`Xabn`*, where *X* is the drive number, *a* is the optional density (`l` = low, `m` = medium, `h` = high, `u` = ultra, and `o` = compressed), *b* is the Berkeley (SunOS 4.*x*) compatibility, and *n* is the optional parameter of rewind (no letter for no rewind and *n* = rewind). The initials `rmt` are taken from the name Remote MagTape protocol. You don't have to enter optional parameters like density, but if you don't, the tape drive writes data at its default density, which is typically its highest density.

NOTE Chapter 12 describes the use of Solaris utilities and third-party applications for working with tape drives, hard drives, and Zip and Jaz drives.

A tape drive may be running on your system as you do other work, or you may want to check the status of a backup on a backup server. In any case, use the Manage Tape (`mt`) command to display information about your tape drive. The syntax for this command is `mt -f /dev/rmt/X status`. The `mt` command has a retention parameter and a rewind parameter that let you specify those operations. Many tape drive manufacturers include tape utilities and graphical user interface programs for managing their tapes, such as Veritas Netbackup, Legato Networker, CA ARCServe, and so forth. If your tape drive doesn't come with one of these programs, you can purchase them, and each program supports a very wide range of devices. Contact the tape drive manufacturer or visit the manufacturer's Web site to obtain information about programs that support their hardware.

Summary

Solaris supports devices that can be used to store data, connect to the network, or perform other important kinds of I/O. Devices are addressed as physical devices, and their characteristics are stored in physical device files. Every device has a logical device name.

Devices can access data as block, character, or raw data. Devices require device drivers to provide I/O capabilities to talk to the system kernel. When you install or remove devices and drivers, you need to perform a reconfiguration reboot.

You can partition hard drives to provide flexibility and security to your stored data. In this chapter, you learned about the configuration and contents of the standard partitions or slices that Solaris installs.

Solaris supports a very wide range of peripheral devices, including diskettes, hard drives, CD-ROM drives, tape drives, Zip and Jaz drives, and serial port devices such as terminals that can be controlled from within the operating system. These systems and their support were described in this chapter. Tape drives, which are common peripheral devices that allow you to save an historical record of your system's data, were also discussed.

CHAPTER 7

The Solaris Desktop

FEATURING:

Solaris and GUIs 224

The CDE Desktop 226

The Front Panel 253

Actions 267

Customizing the Desktop 272

OpenLook Desktop 280

The X Window System 283

In this chapter, one of the central chapters in the book, you will learn about the standard graphical interfaces used on Sun Solaris. It isn't always necessary to run a graphical desktop on a Sun workstation or, in particular, a Sun server, but for situations in which a user is interacting with applications, a desktop environment is most often used. Solaris users tend to use the Common Desktop Environment (CDE) as a standard, so this chapter describes this window manager in detail. However, Solaris is capable of running other graphical interfaces, as well as X Windows and X-terminal sessions. All of these other interfaces are briefly described in this chapter as well.

Solaris and GUIs

Until the mid-1990s, every version of Unix, including Solaris, came with a proprietary windowed graphical user interface, or GUI. There were window standards such as Motif, but they were implemented somewhat differently on each Unix version. Those differences caused developers and users considerable problems and limited the applicability of many programs to one flavor of Unix or another.

The Common Open Software Environment (COSE) led to the development of the Common Desktop Environment (CDE), which is currently the standard of choice for a GUI on many popular forms of Unix. The popularity of Linux as a desktop environment is leading Solaris to use GNOME in the future as CDE's replacement.

You select the Solaris GUI when you log in and select the Common Desktop Environment (CDE) option or the OpenWindows Desktop option from the Session submenu on the Options menu of the Login screen. Most of the windows you will see in this book are based on the CDE because OpenWindows support in Solaris will be phased out sometime in the future. A short section on OpenLook and the OpenWindows desktop is included toward the end of this chapter. Other choices on the Options menu provide for a command-line login.

Efforts to create a GUI as an alternative to the Unix command line began almost at the same time that GUIs were becoming popular in desktop systems (based on the work that had been done at Xerox PARC in the mid and late '70s). By 1984, with the appearance of the Macintosh and soon thereafter with the introduction of the Commodore Amiga, window managers began to be written for various flavors of Unix in many places. The X Windows project (described in more detail in the last few sections of the book) gave rise to an industry interface standard that is in widespread use today. There have been many window managers written for X Windows, some of which are described in the next section. Solaris's two window managers, CDE and OpenWindows, run on X Windows sessions.

Early work on Unix GUIs included systems like the Tab Window Manager (`twm`), also called Tom's Window Manager, a small and fast window system that ran on X Windows.

Although twm had no icons, and rather simple windows, it could be used on network systems with limited resources and many concurrent users. You will still find twm on Linux. The OpenLook Window Manager was another early effort that was developed by Sun Microsystems and AT&T. OpenWindows is Sun's implementation of OpenLook using the OpenLook toolkit that was the standard GUI for Sun during the late 1980s and early 1990s.

Another industry effort arose when the Motif Toolkit, which was an alternative to OpenLook, was developed by the Open Software Foundation (OSF) in the 1980s. Many of the interface features found on Motif were adopted by Microsoft Windows and vice versa. Although it was popular, Motif never achieved universal usage on Unix. Worse still, each vendor's Motif and Motif Window Manager were slightly different. This led to problems for application developers.

By 1993, several vendors got together to form the Common Open Software Environment (COSE) initiative, which aimed to create an industry-standard GUI and application programming interface, or API. The original members of the initiative included Hewlett-Packard, IBM, Novell, and SunSoft; they were joined later by Digital Equipment Corporation, Fujitsu, and Hitachi. COSE borrowed heavily from past efforts, mainly Motif, in order to create a graphical environment with more features so that it would attract Windows and Macintosh users. The result of COSE was the development of the Common Desktop Environment (CDE) version 1, which ran on Solaris 2.5. Solaris 8 runs version 1.4 of CDE. Versions of CDE run on the following systems with almost exactly the same features that CDE has on Solaris:

- IBM AIX
- Hewlett-Packard HP-UX
- Digital Unix

The majority of Unix users use Solaris and the other three vendors' Unix environments today. You will also find CDE on Linux and on FreeBSD using software offered by the third-party vendors TriTeal, X Inside, and Work Group Solutions (WGS). The TriTeal Enhanced Desktop (TED), which is the most widely used CDE on Linux and FreeBSD, offers numerous additions to the CDE standard.

Window Managers

There are many different window managers that you can run on an X Window system. The Motif Window Manager (mwm) from the Open Software Foundation (OSF) runs on X. Solaris version 2.5 and later ships with three different window managers for X—the OpenLook Window Manager (olwm), the Desktop Window Manager (dtwm), and the Virtual Tab Window Manager (vtwm)—but you can add others. The Desktop Window

Manager is part of CDE and is based on Motif, and it's responsible for the workspace and many commands.

The OpenLook Window Manager, part of Sun's proprietary OpenWindows system, was among the first window managers to run in X. OpenWindows is supported in Solaris, and you can log in to an OpenWindows session in just the same way that you log in to a CDE session. Although CDE is based on a more open standard, OpenWindows is losing popularity because it is proprietary. Future versions of Solaris will not support OpenWindows. The Virtual Tab Window Manager isn't widely used on Solaris.

There are many other window managers that run on Unix and are available for free download. Of these, Tom's Window Manager (`twm`), GNU Window Manager (`gwm`), OpenLook Virtual Window Manager (`olvwm`), Virtual Window Manager (`fvwm`), AfterStep, and xfce are popular. AfterStep is a NeXTStep clone, and xfce is a CDE clone. The *virtual* in the names of these window managers refers to the ability to create a workspace of any size (beyond the size of your monitor) as well as multiple workspaces. Two of the newest window managers that are quickly gaining popularity are GNOME and KDE. Sun recently announced that it would be aiding in the development of GNOME and would be including it as the default interface at some time in the future. GNOME has gotten strong support from IBM and HP, as well.

The CDE Desktop

The CDE is an example of a desktop manager. The desktop manager manages the use of icons or pictures to represent objects on your screen. It is responsible for giving you the ability to manipulate files and applications as icons. This is the subsystem through which you can perform actions such as delete, copy, and move. You can create symbolic links through click-drag operations on file icons as well as open executable or binary files by double-clicking them. A desktop manager works in conjunction with a window manager.

The CDE has become the standard desktop manager because it provides a common look and feel to Solaris applications, lets developers create applications and users modify the interface to support multiple languages, and provides an interapplication communications facility that allows applications running remotely or locally to work with one another.

On GUIs, objects are represented as icons and content is placed into containers called windows. Icons have pop-up menus that appear when you right-click them, and windows often show menus in a menu bar or on their title bar. You can reduce a window's representation down to an icon to conserve space and restore the icon to a window when you need to work with the contents of the window. Many icons you see on your screen represent content and are not container items. Objects like programs (executable or binary files), data files, and symbolic links that provide access to content of various types get an iconic treatment in graphical user interfaces.

NOTE Solaris uses a three-button mouse. When you left-click, you are using mouse button 1; when you right-click, you use mouse button 3. The middle button, mouse button 2, is used for copy and edit functions.

Log On

When you log in to any of the environments that Solaris offers, you use the login manager program `dtlogin`, a program that is based on an X Windows program called `xdm`. The Login Manager is a server that runs as a daemon and logs in directly to X Windows without requiring that you run a program like `xinit` or a shell script like `startx`. The Login Manager saves you from dealing with the methods used to start X Windows in the past, which involved logging in at a console, setting or checking the environment (and often setting a custom configuration), and then giving the X Windows startup command. Those tasks are now handled automatically by CDE, and a default user configuration can be established, something that helps network administrators enormously.

The Login Manager reads the settings found in the `Xresources` file (`/usr/dtconfig/<lang>/Xresources`), which controls the appearance of the login screen itself. The Login Manager can start multiple instances of both graphical and character-based environments either locally or on X-terminals or workstations remotely. The program `dtlogin` (found at `/usr/dt/bin/dtlogin`) prompts for login and password, authenticates a user, and runs a session (login shell process), which is administered by the DT Session Manager. The Login Manager runs several scripts shown in Table 7.1.

TABLE 7.1: THE LOGIN MANAGER CONFIGURATION FILES

Filename	Description
`/usr/dt/config/Xsetup`	A Korn shell script that starts the display setup
`/usr/dt/config/Xstartup`	A Korn shell script that initializes some system functions
`/usr/dt/bin/Xsession`	A Korn shell script that starts the desktop session
`/usr/dt/config/Xfailsafe`	A Bourne shell script that allows you to open a failsafe window
`/usr/dt/config/Xreset`	A Korn shell script that has a list of commands that are to be executed at session end

Because dtlogin runs as a daemon, calling the program again isn't necessary. The Login Manager is best put into the dtconfig script so that you can specify any of its options. Among the options are -d (disable autostart), -e (enable autostart), -kill (kill dtlogin), -reset (reset dtlogin), -p (update printer action), -inetd (start inet .comf /usr/dtdaemons), -inetd.ow (start inetd.conf /usr/openwin daemons). The man pages for this important system function offer over 26 pages of documentation on its actions and options.

TIP The /usr/dt/config directory contains the files that store the settings used by the Login Manager; many of these files define scripts that are run before the login screen appears and after you log off. When you upgrade your system, those files are overwritten. If you want to preserve your login behavior, copy the /usr/dt/config files over into the /etc/dt/config folder. The Login Manager uses the files and settings it finds in the /etc/dt/config folder in preference to the same files found in the /usr/dt/config folder. If you want to modify the login screen, copy the Xresources file to the /etc/dt/config/lang/Xresources file and edit that file.

When you are at the logon screen, you can choose a session type:

- The Common Desktop Environment (CDE).
- Sun's OpenWindows, part of the OpenLook window manager developed by Sun and AT&T.
- A failsafe session. Solaris runs a single version of the X-terminal (xterm) with no window manager. This session type is used to solve configuration problems and to install new hardware.
- The command line.

Although the CDE has much in common with the Unix Motif interface, it isn't actually Motif itself. Solaris comes with some Motif libraries and supports some Motif functions, but it doesn't ship with the Motif Window Manager (mwm). Therefore, if you want to use Motif, you need to install it. However, few people actually work with Motif on Solaris unless they are doing a development project that requires the developer to see how an application looks in Motif.

NOTE Chapter 3, "Getting Started," describes the options available to you as part of your login routine.

The actual application that runs the CDE desktop is the Session Manager. It is the Session Manager that is responsible for starting the desktop and saving the state of the desktop when you log out. The state of the desktop includes the condition of applications open on the desktop, the settings for desktop components, and some environmental settings like backdrop color, fonts, mouse and keyboard settings, and so on. The Session Manager runs the scripts that control the session state (see Table 7.2).

TABLE 7.2: THE SESSION MANAGER CONFIGURATION FILES

Filename	Purpose
/usr/dt/bin/dtlogin	Program that manages the login.
/usr/dt/bin/dtgreet	Program that displays the greeting and login screen.
/usr/dt/bin/dtchooser	Program that controls the host chooser screen.
/usr/dt/config/Xconfig	Data file that points to the locations of configuration files used by the login screen.
/usr/dt/config/Xservers	Data file that lists the location of X servers to be started.
/usr/dt/config/Xaccess	Data file that contains a list of computers that can access the login server. The Login Manager uses this file to determine who can log in to your local computer.
/usr/dt/config/<*lang*>/Xresources	File that contains the login screen properties.
/var/dt/Xpid	Data file that contains the process ID of the login server.
/var/dt/Xerrors	Data file with the error log of the login server.

It is possible to do many operations within the CDE, but certainly not all. For many commands, basic and most certainly advanced, you will probably find yourself working at the command line perhaps 50 percent of the time—more if you are a Solaris power user or administrator. The command line allows you to specify within a command options and settings that often aren't possible in the CDE interface. That said, it is worth noting that as Sun continues to develop the Sun desktop, it makes the CDE interface more powerful and more complete.

Figure 7.1 shows the CDE desktop after you log in, with a File Manager window open in the upper-right corner of the screen. On this system, that window shows the home directory, opened by clicking the Home Folder icon (fifth from the left) on the front panel. The Solaris CDE desktop's most prominent feature is the front panel, a launching pad shown at the bottom of the screen. Solaris stores the condition of your desktop, and if you log in with the User's Last Desktop option, you will see the windows and applications open on your screen that were open when you logged out. Here I logged in as root, and so you see the root (/) directory as the home directory. In most cases unless you log in as root to change or administer a system, you will be logging in to your home directory, which will be in another location, such as `/home/barries`.

FIGURE 7.1

The Solaris CDE desktop, showing the front panel and the File Manager window for the home directory

Most of this chapter contains information regarding the CDE desktop because it is far and away the most commonly used graphical interface in Solaris. At the end of this chapter, you'll find information about the OpenWindows interface, which, although slightly different, shares many operational features with the CDE interface. Sun will not support OpenWindows in future versions of Solaris, but OpenWindows does appear on many other versions of Unix. In truth, it is not too difficult to find your way around OpenWindows once you have learned Solaris. You will also find that most of the programs you install in the CDE interface work almost identically in OpenWindows.

Menus

Solaris offers a context-sensitive environment, with a variety of different menus that you can use to control what you see and to specify actions. When you click a window menu, the commands you see in the pull-down menu are in solid text when they are available (enabled) and grayed out when they aren't available (disabled). In many instances, menu commands may appear or disappear depending upon the current state of the desktop. There are three main types of menus that you can work with:

Pop-up menus When you right-click any interface element on the screen, you open a pop-up menu that has commands that are appropriate for the interface element you clicked: window, desktop, front panel control, and so on.

Window menus The CDE uses a window system to display program contents, and many but not all windows display menus. Dialog boxes are examples of windows without menus.

Front panel menus The drawers of the front panel offer a menu of actions that are always available on your desktop. When you click a drawer control (a front panel control with a triangle on it), you open a named menu that contains a set of controls.

Pop-up menus appear in almost any area of the screen that you right-click. The one exception to this rule is that you don't see a pop-up menu when you right-click a window frame, border, or window menu bar. When you right-click the desktop's backdrop, the Workspace menu pop-up shown in the following graphic appears (because the front panel is modifiable, what you see on the Workspace menu pop-up can change). You select a menu command by either clicking it with the mouse or using the down and up arrow keys to move to a command and then pressing the Return key. As you can see, the Workspace menu contains several commands with right-facing arrows that reveal submenus or cascading menus. When you click a command with a submenu, the submenu opens. From the keyboard, use the right arrow key to open a submenu and the left arrow or Esc key to close it. The Esc key will also close an open pop-up menu.

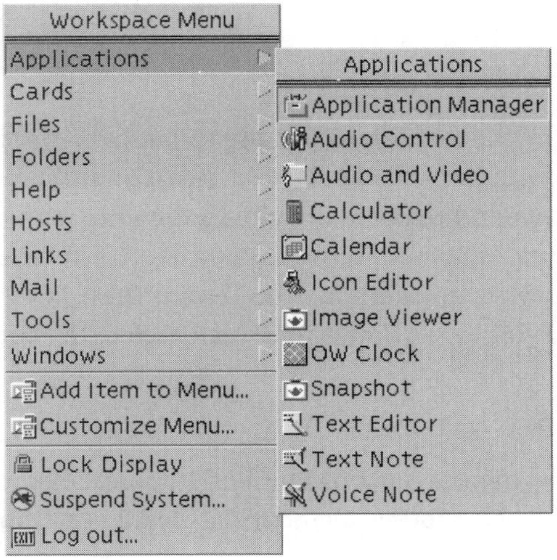

NOTE The Workspace menu changed significantly in Solaris 8, The commands Utility, Shuffle Up, Shuffle Down, Minimize/Restore Front Panel, and Restart Workspace Manager were removed from the main menu and placed onto the Windows submenu.

The following graphic shows part of a File Manager directory (or folder) window. The window includes three menus: File, Selected, and View (the File menu is showing). When a window has the input focus (a window that has the focus is the active window and has a solid dark title bar and borders), you can open a menu by pressing the Alt key at the same time you press the key that corresponds to the underlined letter in the menu name. Following that keystroke with the underlined letter of a menu command initiates the command. For example, the Close command can be initiated by using the Alt+F, C keystrokes, which are sometimes called the accelerator keys. That same Close command shows that it has a command keystroke equivalent, Alt+F4, that serves the same function.

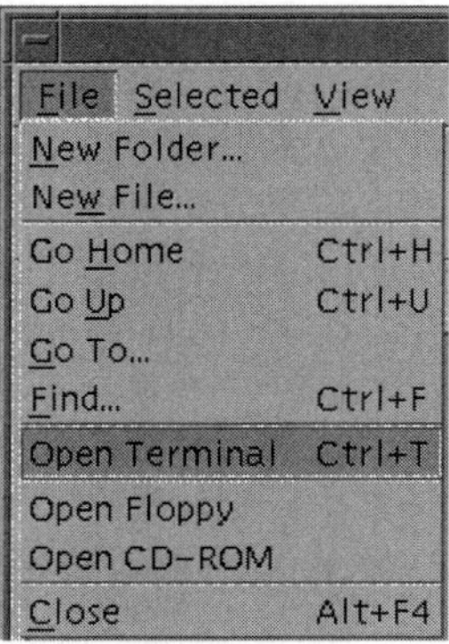

With window menus, you use the arrow keys and Esc key in exactly the same way you do with pop-up menus. Use the right and left arrow keys to move from one menu to another and to open and close submenus, the up and down arrow keys to move up and down a menu, and the Esc key to close submenus and menus. As you grow more familiar with applications, you'll learn these keystrokes and become more efficient because you won't have to manually select the commands with your mouse.

Windows

Windows are the most prominent graphical element of a GUI. Figure 7.2 shows a window with the window elements labeled. Everything you see that contains content on

your desktop is a window, including the desktop itself. A window offers you a view into the content of a file or directory, a view that can be altered by resizing the window. To resize a window, click and drag its edge or corner or use the scroll bars to move your view of the window's contents about. You can click the up arrow on the vertical scroll bar to move up a line or the down arrow to move down a line; click the scroll bar itself to move up or down a screen, and click and drag the slider (elevator) in the scroll bar to move the window up or down as far as you wish. The horizontal scroll bar performs these same actions in the right and left directions.

FIGURE 7.2

A File Manager window contains various elements you can use to control what you see in the window and the window's condition.

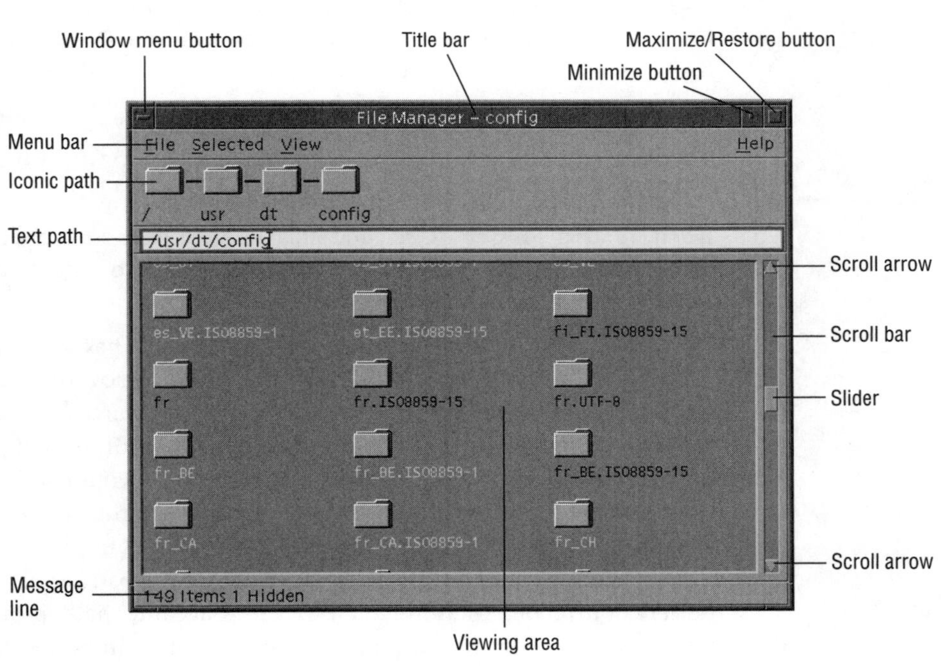

Each window and most dialog boxes contain a title bar; alert boxes do not. The difference between these types of window system elements is that the windows and dialog boxes are nonmodal and alert boxes are modal. A modal window like an alert box forces you to perform an action that removes the alert box from your screen before you can work with other screen elements. A nonmodal window can be open on your desktop and you can still work with other desktop content. Another difference between these types of windows is that alert boxes do no contain title bar elements; the title bars for windows and dialog boxes contain a Window menu button, a Minimize button, and a Maximize/Restore button, as shown in Figure 7.2.

Each part of a window contains specific elements that allow you to manipulate your view (refer to Figure 7.2):

Window menu button Click this control (or press Alt+spacebar) to open the Window menu. Double-click this button to close an application. Solaris will ask you to save any unsaved changes.

Title bar The title bar displays the name of the application and the filename. Click the title bar to drag a window to a new position. Double-click the title bar to either maximize or restore the window.

Minimize button Click the minimize button to turn the window to an icon.

Maximize/Restore button Click to fill the screen with a window or restore the window to its previous size.

Borders and corner Click and drag a border to expand or contract the window in the direction of the border. Or click a corner to resize a window in two directions at once.

A File Manager window like the one shown in Figure 7.2 has some special elements that help you determine your position in the file system. Below the menu bar is an iconic path that displays the location in the file system hierarchy of the directory or folder that you are viewing; that path is echoed as a text path in a bar just below the iconic path. If you double-click a folder in the iconic path, your window displays the contents of that folder. Some folders are in a path that contains restricted folders above them in the file system hierarchy. Solaris displays /.../ in place of the name of the restricted folder and doesn't allow you to move up the path.

At the very bottom of a window, you'll see a message line that typically describes the content of the window. For example, `9 Items 1 Hidden` indicates that there is an item not currently shown in the viewing area of the File Manager window. Hidden files are often system files or other folders, like the root (`.`). You can use the Show Hidden Objects command (Ctrl+S) on the View menu to bring these hidden objects into view.

What you see in a File Manager window can be controlled using the Set View Options command on the View menu. This command opens the Set View Options dialog box, which is shown in Figure 7.3. In the Set View Options dialog box, you can choose to view or suppress headers, change the alignment of icons in the window, show various types of icons or names, and order the appearance of objects in the window.

FIGURE 7.3

With the Set View Options dialog box, you can control how you see the elements in a File Manager window.

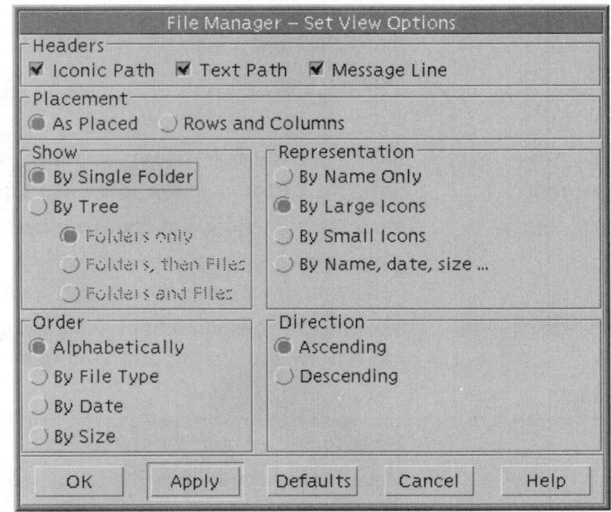

Windows and dialog boxes appear on the screen in the order they are opened; the most recently opened is always on top. The top window covers any windows below it, and you can change the order of windows on your screen by clicking the part of a window you can see to bring it to the front. Because you can work only on windows that have the current focus, the top window, indicated by an active or darkened title bar, is the one that has the focus. In most cases, you move the focus to another window and bring it to the top by clicking it. There are instances in which you only need to move your mouse over a window to give it the input focus, but those cases are not common. You can change the input focus behavior using the Windows Style Manager in the `Desktop Controls` folder. Use the Shuffle Up command on the Workspace menu's Windows submenu to bring windows that are obscured into view or the Shuffle Down command to remove them from view. Keyboard shortcuts that you can use to navigate a workspace are shown in Table 7.3.

TABLE 7.3: WORKSPACE NAVIGATION KEYSTROKES

Keystroke	Action
On Workspace	
Alt+Tab	Move to next window. This keystroke and all others like it will eventually select the front panel.
Alt+Esc	Move to next window.
Alt+Shift+Tab	Move to previous window.
Alt+Shift+Esc	Move to previous window.
Alt+up arrow	Bring the bottom window in the workspace to the front.
Alt+down arrow	Move the top window in the workspace to the back.
Alt+F6	Move to next application window, or if front panel has the focus, move between a front panel control and a subpanel.
Alt+Shift+F6	Move to previous application window, or if front panel has the focus, move between a front panel control and a subpanel.
In Window	
Tab	Move to next item in the tab group.
Alt+Tab	Move to previous item in the tab group.
Down arrow	Move to next control in a tab group.
Up arrow	Move to previous control in a tab group.
Alt+F9	Minimize window.
F10	Activate the window menu bar.
Shift+F10	Activate a window's pop-up menu.
Alt+spacebar	Activate a window's Window menu.
In Scroll Bars*	
Up arrow	Move a line up.
Down arrow	Move a line down.
Page Up	Move up a screen or page.
Page Down	Move down a screen or a page.
Home	Move to the beginning of a file or top of a page.
End	Move to the end of a file or bottom of a page.

*Note: Some scroll bars support the use of the Tab key to select the slider, the Prev and Next keys when they appear on your keyboard, and the use of the Ctrl key in conjunction with other keys to move the slider faster.

TIP Solaris has the same "cool switch" that Microsoft Windows uses. Use the Alt+Tab keystroke to cycle between windows on your desktop. If you use the Point in Window to Make Active option in the Windows Style Manager control to alter the selection method for moving the window focus, the cool switch will not work.

Many application windows and dialog boxes, such as the Print dialog box for the StarOffice 5.1 suite (see Figure 7.4), contain different kinds of controls that you can use to specify actions.

FIGURE 7.4

The Print dialog box has many of the common window controls in it.

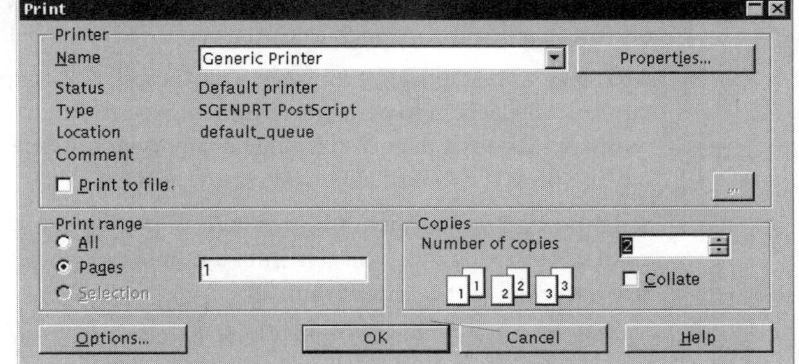

The Print dialog box contains the following types of controls:

List box The Name control is an example of a drop-down list. Click the down arrow to open the list, make a selection by clicking your choice or using the up or down arrow keys followed by the Enter key. To select an item from a list in a multiple selection list box, hold down the Shift key and click item(s) or hold down the Shift key and use the up arrow or down arrow keys to extend the range of your selection. When you double-click an item, the item is selected and the default command is initiated.

Check box The Print to File control is an example of a check box. Click a check box to put a check mark in the box and select the option; click again to remove the check mark and disable the option. Some applications (particularly database and logic programs) offer three-stage check boxes: checked, unchecked, and grayed; the grayed option generally means something specific to the application, such as "not available" or "unknown." Usually, check boxes appear as a group, but each check box works independently of the others. You can set check boxes on or off without regard to the state of the other check boxes. Use the spacebar to toggle a check box's state.

Radio buttons The All, Pages, and Selection control group are examples of radio buttons. In a group, one and only one radio button may be selected. Use the up arrow or down arrow key to move to a different radio button in a radio button group that has the focus.

Text box The box to the right of the Pages radio button is an example of a text box. In this case, the text box accepts numbers, but text boxes also accept text entry. You can perform all the actions on text in a text box that you can on text in a document, such as Cut, Copy, Paste, and Delete.

Buttons The Options, Properties, OK, Cancel, and Help controls are all action buttons. Click them to perform an immediate action. Any button with ellipsis points (...) opens a dialog box. One button (here the OK button) is the default button; press the Return key to activate that button from the keyboard.

Spin box The Number of Copies control is an example of a spin box. When you click in a spin box, you can enter a number, or you can click the up or down arrow to change the current number.

Notice that many of the control labels have underlined letters. The underlined letters indicate the existence of what Windows calls an accelerator key, which in Solaris is sometimes referred to as a mnemonic. Press the Alt key and the key that corresponds to the underlined letter to activate that specific control. Also, you will find that most dialog boxes and windows that contain controls have a tab group: use the Tab key to move forward through the tab group and the Shift+Tab keystroke to move backward in the tab group. In an option group like a set of radio buttons or check boxes, the arrow keys move you from one member of the group to another.

Text boxes are also called fields. To move about in a text box, click in a specific location or use the arrow keys. There are many shortcuts that you can use to enter and modify text in a field. You can drag+click a selection, double-click a word to select it, triple-click to select a line, and quadruple-click to select the entire box. Selected text can be cut, copied, or deleted, or it can replaced by new text you type. You can also paste into a text box. Most text boxes have pop-up menus that can offer an editing shortcut. Use the Backspace key to delete a character to the left of the cursor, the Del key to delete characters to the right of the cursor. The Ctrl+Del keystroke deletes all text to the end of the line.

Window Menu

There are some convenient shortcuts that are worth knowing about for window usage. You can open the Window menu by pressing the Alt+spacebar keystroke and issue a command by following that with the underlined letter in the menu command. Thus, pressing Alt+spacebar, n minimizes the window to an icon on your desktop. (Use the Esc key to close a menu or submenu.) The front panel, described in detail later in this chapter, is also a window with a Window menu and can be manipulated in this fashion. Next to the commands on a menu are the keyboard equivalents, which in Solaris are referred to as accelerator keys. For example, when you press the Ctrl+T keystroke with a File Manager window selected, you open a terminal window, or when you press the Alt+F4 keystroke, you close that File Manager window. You do not need to have the Window menu open on your screen to perform those actions.

NOTE In Microsoft Windows, the term *accelerator keys* is used to describe the underlined letters used as mnemonics in Solaris.

The following graphic is a close-up of a File Manager window's Window menu. The commands perform the actions described in Table 7.4.

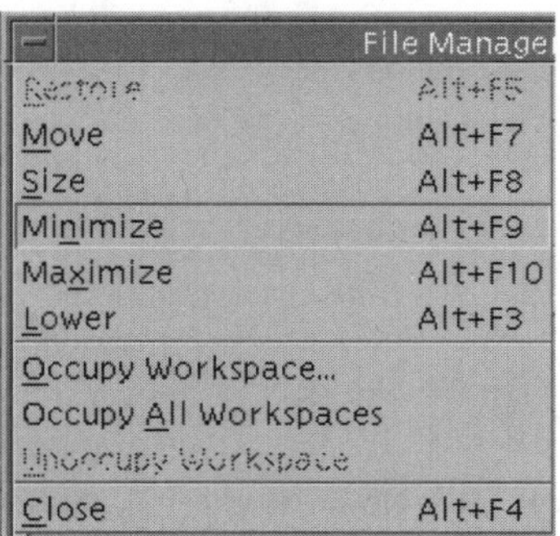

The commands you see on a Window menu vary depending upon what kind of window it is. A terminal window, for example, contains a command at the bottom of the Window menu called Toggle Menu Bar that alternately removes and adds the menu bar from the window. You can open a terminal window by selecting the Terminal command from the Tools submenu of the Workspace menu or by choosing that command from the File menu of a File Manager window (Ctrl+T). The terminal window you see in the CDE is a terminal emulator or console run from the `dtterm` program.

When you launch a terminal window, even though it appears to be a graphical application, it is interacting directly with a shell. The `dtterm` program was meant as a replacement for `xterm`. Working in a terminal window looks like a Telnet session but is more akin to working in an MS-DOS or Windows's Command Prompt window.

NOTE The terminal window is described more fully in Chapter 4, "Basic Operations."

TABLE 7.4: THE WINDOW MENU COMMANDS FOR THE FILE MANAGER

Command Name	Keystroke	Description
Restore	Alt+F5	Returns window to its expanded state. You can also perform this action by double-clicking the title bar of a maximized window.
Move	Alt+F7	Allows you to move the window by dragging it with your mouse without having to click and drag the title bar. You can also use the arrow keys to move in any direction and combine the Ctrl key with the arrow keys to move faster.
Size	Alt+F8	Lets you resize the window by dragging one side of it with your mouse.
Minimize	Alt+F9	Shrinks a window to an icon. Double-click the icon to restore it to a window, or right-click the icon and select the Restore command from the pop-up menu.
Maximize	Alt+F10	Fills the screen with the window. You can also perform this action by double-clicking the title bar of a restored window.
Lower	Alt+F3	Moves the window so it's below other windows on your screen.
Occupy Workspace	No keystroke	Brings up the Occupy Workspace dialog box, which you can use to select which workspaces you want the window to appear in.
Occupy All Workspaces	No keystroke	Puts the window in all of your defined workspaces.
Unoccupy Workspace	No keystroke	Removes the window from your current workspace.
Close	Alt+F4	Closes the window. You can also perform this action by double-clicking the Window menu button. Some applications use the Quit or Exit commands in place of the Close command.

Workspace Menu

Another place to find commands that work with windows on your screen is the Windows submenu of the Workspace menu, shown in Figure 7.5. Right-click anywhere on the desktop and select the Windows command with your mouse or the arrow keys to view this menu. The commands on the Workspace menu's Windows submenu are described in Table 7.5.

FIGURE 7.5

The Windows submenu has commands you can use to change a window's position on your screen and perform other functions.

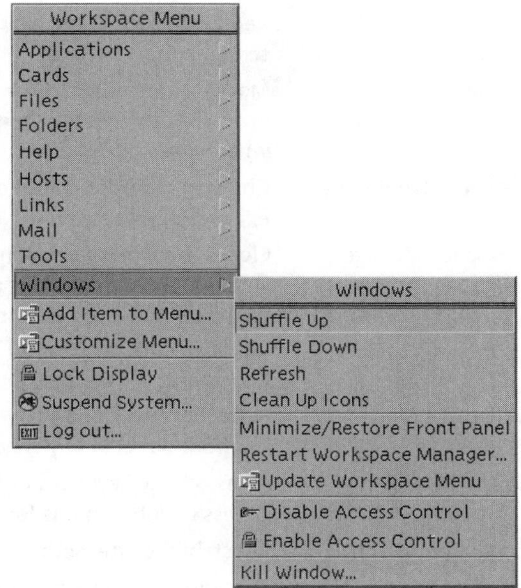

What you see in the Workspace menu can be modified using the Add Item to Menu and Customize Menu commands, as you will learn in the section "Subpanels" later in this chapter. These commands are expressions of the two controls of the same names found in the Application Manager Desktop_Controls program group. Any modifications you make to the Workspace menu appear in the Workspace menu in all of your workspaces.

One important thing to understand about windowed interface systems is that internally, Solaris has calculated and stored all of the descriptions of any windows that appear on your screen and descriptions of any windows that are specified by an application or the system software but aren't currently displayed. The CDE Window

Manager uses these internal descriptions and the current system state to display on your desktop just those elements that will fit and that aren't covered by other features as part of the screen rasterization process.

TABLE 7.5: THE WORKSPACE MENU WINDOWS SUBMENU COMMANDS

Command Name	Description
Shuffle Up	Moves a window from back to front.
Shuffle Down	Moves a window from front to back.
Refresh	Redraws your screen, which is useful if an application leaves a screen artifact behind.
Clean Up Icons	Moves your icons to a row and column display if you have the option set for window behavior to leave icons in the window where you place them.
Minimize/Restore Front Panel	Changes the front panel to an icon or restores it to its expanded size.
Restart Workspace Manager	Closes the Workspace Manager and restarts it with its last saved settings. This command is useful if you experience an application error and don't want to restart your entire system and lose unsaved work. You should also use this command if you lose the title bar off of your desktop by inadvertently repositioning it.
Update Workspace Menu	Refreshes the Workspace menu; useful if you have modified the front panel in any way.
Disable Access Control	Turns off any keyboard or beep behavior you have set in the AccessX control that is found in the `Desktop_Controls` folder.
Enable Access Control	Reestablishes the settings you have in the AccessX control.
Kill Window	Destroys a window on your screen without saving any changes.

Window managers not only control the layering of windows on your desktop, they also maintain information about window positions, the look and feel of the windows, the condition of the window, and the expression of all of the interface elements that windows contain: borders, title bars, scroll bars, and so forth. The operations you perform on windows—open a window, close a window, resize a window, move a window, and so on—are commands issued to the Window Manager's API (application programming interface). In Solaris, the Window Manager also stores session information that preserves the state of application windows and desktop conditions from one login of a user to the next.

Dialog Boxes

A dialog box is a window that identifies an error or condition that you need to know about and respond to. Some windows are modal, such as dialog boxes that display error message, and require a response before you're allowed to proceed further. Those dialog boxes are called alert boxes. Not all dialog boxes are modal. Some report conditions and allow you to continue working on your desktop while they are still open. An application's Print dialog box is one example. It asks you to select a printer and the conditions to be applied for a particular print job.

A dialog box usually contains a default action that is typically represented by a button with a double border. In Figure 7.6, which shows the File Manager's Find dialog box, the Go To button is the default (or currently selected) action. You press the Return key to initiate the action that is currently selected.

FIGURE 7.6

The Find dialog box is an example of a nonmodal dialog box that contains action buttons and options in pop-up menus.

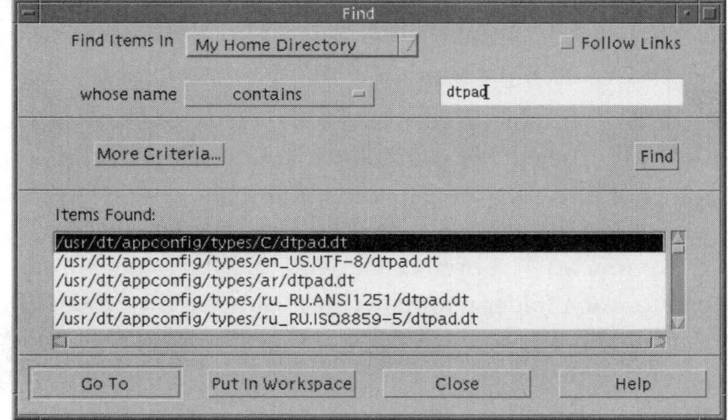

Dialog boxes also have what is commonly referred to as a tab group. As mentioned earlier, when you press the Tab key, you move between buttons, pop-up menus, text boxes, scrolling list boxes, and any other interface element that the application developer put into the tab group. The purpose of a tab group is to provide a means to use a dialog box in case your mouse heads south for the winter. You will also find the tab group a convenience because it lets you move about a dialog box with keystrokes, which are faster than mouse moves (generally speaking). You should note that not all features are put in the tab group. Typically, advanced features such as the ones contained in the More Criteria button are left out of the tab group.

The controls found in dialog boxes are described more fully in the section "Windows" earlier in this chapter.

The File Manager

The File Manager (`dtfile`) provides a graphical means of manipulating files and directories with your mouse and keyboard. The program is a file browser that is similar in function to the Macintosh Finder or the Windows Explorer. Earlier in this chapter (in the section "Windows"), the Window menu and elements of the File Manager window were described. In this section, I'll describe the File, Selected, View, and Help menus, as well as how to work with window content.

NOTE Chapter 5, "The File System," describes using the File Manager to perform numerous file management tasks. There is some overlap between the topics described in this section and that chapter; this section describes the interface features of the File Manager.

There are two ways to open the File Manager:

- Click the Home Folder icon on the front panel.
- In a terminal window, enter the command **`dtfile`**.

In both instances, you open a File Manager window with the home folder contents showing. The `dtfile` command takes numerous options you can use to specify which folder or directory to open and the size and condition of the window spawned. You should use the `-folder [`*`<foldername>`*`, `*`<foldername>`*`, …]` or `-dir [`*`<foldername>`*`, `*`<foldername>`*`, …]` option to open a specific folder window (or set of folder windows, one for each folder name specified). Among the other options are those that let you rename the title bar (`-title`), suppress the display of folders above a restricted folder (`-restricted`), turn a grid on or off (`-grid on/off`), display a file tree (`-tree_files`), and change the icon attributes (`-order`, `-view`, `-direction`, and various icon size parameters). The man `dtfile` pages contains extensive notes on this command.

Tables 7.6 through 7.9 describe the actions of each of the commands found in the Workspace menu submenus (File, Selected, View, and Help). What you see on the menus described in these tables depends upon whether the content you are looking at is from a drive, diskette, or CD-ROM and also the type of files and folders selected.

TABLE 7.6: THE FILE SUBMENU COMMANDS

Command Name	Keystroke	Description
New Folder	No keystroke	Opens the New Folder dialog box. Enter a name into the New Folder Name text box, then click the OK button to create a folder with that name within your current folder.

Continued

TABLE 7.6: THE FILE SUBMENU COMMANDS (CONTINUED)

Command Name	Keystroke	Description
New File	No keystroke	Opens the New File dialog box. Enter a name into the New File Name text box, then click the OK button to create a data file with that name within your current folder. A data file has a blank page icon.
Go Home	Ctrl+H	Opens your home directory in your current window.
Go Up	Ctrl+U	Moves your window view up one level in the file hierarchy.
Go To	No keystroke	Opens the Go To dialog box. Select a name from the System Name list box, enter a */<pathname>/<foldername>* into the Destination Folder text box, then click the OK button to move the view of your current window to the folder with that name within your current folder.
Find	Ctrl+F	Opens the Find dialog box, which you can use to search for files and folders locally, on the network, and elsewhere.
Open Terminal	Ctrl+T	Opens a terminal window so that you can execute commands from the command line.
Open Floppy	No keystroke	Opens the contents of a diskette in a window.
Open CD-ROM	No keystroke	Opens the contents of a CD-ROM in a window.
Eject	No keystroke	Ejects a diskette or CD-ROM.
Format Floppy	No keystroke	Opens the Format Floppy dialog box, which you can use to format a diskette.
Rename Floppy	No keystroke	Allows you to rename a diskette's volume label.
Close	Alt+F4	Closes the current File Manager window.

TABLE 7.7: THE SELECTED SUBMENU COMMANDS

Command Name	Keystroke	Description
Move To	No keystroke	Opens the Move Object dialog box. Enter a */<pathname>/<foldername>* into the Destination Folder text box, then click the OK button to move a selected item to that folder.
Copy To	Ctrl+C	Opens the Copy Object dialog box. Enter a */<pathname>/<foldername>* into the Destination Folder text box, a filename into the Name for Copy text box, then click the OK button to move a selected item to that folder.

Continued

TABLE 7.7: THE SELECTED SUBMENU COMMANDS (CONTINUED)

Command Name	Keystroke	Description
Copy as Link	No keystroke	Opens the Link Object dialog box. Enter a */<pathname>/<foldername>* into the Destination Folder text box, a filename into the Name for Copy text box, then click the OK button to move a selected item to that folder.
Rename	No keystroke	Places an insertion point into the selected file or folder's name. Type a new name and press the Return key to rename the object.
Put in Workspace	No keystroke	Puts a symbolic link to the selected file or folder on the desktop backdrop in the upper-right corner of your screen. You can control the default placement of the icon with the `objectPlacement` resource.
Put in Trash	No keystroke	Moves the selected file(s) or folder(s) to the Trash Can folder.
Properties	Ctrl+Backspace	Opens the Properties dialog box, which shows permissions and information for a selected file or folder.
Select All	Ctrl+/	Selects all objects in the File Manager window.
Deselect All	Ctrl+\	Deselects all objects in the File Manager window.
Open	No keystroke	Opens a selected object.
Print	No keystroke	Grayed out unless a file is selected. Opens the Print dialog box.
Open in Place	No keystroke	Opens a view containing the contents of a folder, diskette, or CD-ROM in the currently open File Manager window.
Open in New View	No keystroke	Opens a new File Manager window that contains the contents of the selected folder. (A similar command appears in the View menu for some content.)

TABLE 7.8: THE VIEW SUBMENU COMMANDS

Command Name	Keystroke	Description
Open New View	No keystroke	Opens another window showing the contents of the current folder.
Set View Options	No keystroke	Opens the Set View Options dialog box, which allows you to control what you see in a File Manager window.
Save as Default Options	No keystroke	Saves the view options you selected so that the next time you open this folder, it appears the same way.

Continued

TABLE 7.8: THE VIEW SUBMENU COMMANDS (CONTINUED)

Command Name	Keystroke	Description
Show Hidden Objects	Ctrl+S	Displays hidden objects (objects whose data types have been set to Hidden in the Set Filter Options dialog box).
Set Filter Options	No keystroke	Opens the Set Filter Options dialog box, which you can use to hide or show files of different data types.
Clean Up	No keystroke	Moves your icons to a row and column display if you have the option set for window behavior to leave icons in the window where you place them.
Update	No keystroke	Refreshes your view of a window's contents.

TABLE 7.9: THE HELP SUBMENU COMMANDS

Command Name	Description
Overview	Opens the File Manager Help window to an outline or overview of the topics.
Table of Contents	Opens the File Manager Help window to a listing of topics in the help system.
Tasks	Opens the File Manager Help window to a listing of topics about the File Manager tasks.
Reference	Opens the File Manager Help window to reference summaries about components of the CDE desktop.
On Item	Changes your cursor to a question mark. Click an object or menu for which you want information and the File Manager Help window opens to a description of that object.
Using Help	Opens the File Manager Help window to a short description of how to use the help system.
About File Manager	Displays the copyright information for the Common Desktop Environment.

There are several ways to move about the directory hierarchy. To open a folder, you can double-click it in the iconic path or you can double-click it in the File Manager window. If you click the text box to the right of the iconic path, you can enter the path to the folder you want to open and then press the Return key to view the contents of that folder in your window.

Selection

If a file or folder is selected, its name is highlighted in the File Manager window. Use one of these methods to select a file or folder:

- Single-click it.
- Press the Tab or arrow keys to move the focus to the icon and then press the spacebar.
- Drag an outline box around the icon with your mouse.

If you simply move the focus and don't press the spacebar, Solaris draws a box around the item with the focus but leaves your previously selected item selected. The following graphic shows an example of one item selected and another item with the focus. The `export` folder's name is highlighted but it isn't outlined, so it's selected but doesn't have the focus.

WARNING Selection and focus behavior can be confusing because, although you have a border around one item that has the focus, actions you specify are performed on the selected item.

To select multiple items in the File Manager window, use one of these methods:

- Hold down the Ctrl key and click additional items.
- Move the focus using the arrow keys, then press the Ctrl key and the spacebar at the same time.
- Drag an outline that touches the items of interest.

To deselect any and all selected items, click the background in the File Manager window. You can also deselect an item that is part of a group of selected items either by holding down the Ctrl key and clicking on that item or by holding down the Ctrl key, using the arrow keys to move the focus to that item, and then pressing the spacebar.

If you double-click a file, it opens within the application that is responsible for its file type. Double-click a folder to open it. Other ways to activate a file or folder is to right-click the object and select commands from the pop-up menu. The following graphic shows the pop-up menu for a folder in the File Manager window. A folder's pop-up menu offers you access to the commands shown in Table 7.7.

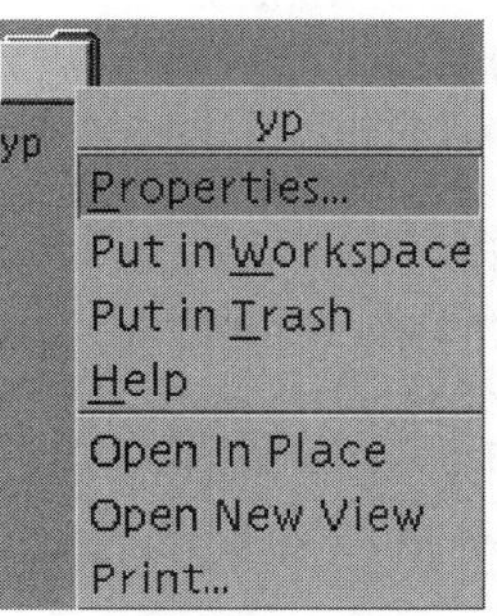

TABLE 7.7: THE COMMANDS ON THE POP-UP MENU FOR A FOLDER

Command Name	Description
Properties	Opens a dialog box that gives you permissions and information about the folder.
Put in Workspace	Puts a symbolic link on your desktop.
Put in Trash	Provides another way to delete the folder.
Help	Opens the Help system to a very brief description of the selected object.
Open in Place	Opens the folder in the same File Manager window you are viewing.
Open New View	Opens a new File Manager window with this folder open.
Print	Opens a Print dialog box you can use to print the folder's contents.

Only a subset of these commands are displayed on the pop-up menu for files in folder windows. When you create a symbolic link to a file or folder, double-clicking that link opens the original file or folder.

Moving, Copying, and Renaming Files and Folders on the Desktop

Most veteran Solaris users find that using the command line is a more powerful way to perform the actions of moving, renaming, and copying files and folders. Still, you are much less likely to make mistakes and you will require less experience when you perform these actions on your desktop using the File Manager. The easiest way to copy files and folders is to hold the Ctrl key down while performing a drag and drop of the files and folders from their current (source) window to the intended destination (target) window. The File Manager also provide a keyboard and text method for copying individual files and folders.

The easiest operation to perform on your desktop is a drag and drop. In this action, you click a file or folder, hold down the mouse button, and then drag your selection to another location and release the mouse button. To drag and drop multiple files or folders, select them, click one of them, and then hold down the mouse button and drag them to the target location. To cancel a drag and drop, either release the mouse button within the source window or location or press the Esc key. The following operations are among those you can do with drag and drop:

- Move files or folders by dragging them to another folder window.
- Move files or folders onto the Workspace, which creates a symbolic link to the files or folders you moved.
- Delete files or folders by dragging and dropping them onto the Trash Can control on the front panel. (The Del key also work for this purpose.)
- Print files by dropping them onto the Printer control on the front panel.

To copy files or folders, do this:

1. Open both the source and the destination (or target) windows.
2. In the source window, select the files or folders that you wish to copy.
3. Hold the down Ctrl key and drag and drop the items into the destination window.

You can also use this method:

1. In the source window, select the files or folders that you wish to copy.
2. Select the Copy To command (Ctrl+C) from the Selected menu. The File Manager-Copy Object dialog box (shown in Figure 7.7) appears.

FIGURE 7.7

Use the File Manager-Copy Object dialog box to enter a destination folder for a copy operation.

3. Enter the path name and folder name (*<pathname>/<foldername>*) into the Destination Folder text box and the name for the copied object into the Name for Copy text box. Then click the OK button. (If you don't enter a path name, you copy the file to the current folder, which requires a different filename.)

If you want to make a file or folder available in another location and you don't want to duplicate it, you can create a symbolic link to it. The procedure is similar to creating a copy of a file or folder, but you are essentially only creating a copy of the icon of that entity. Note that symbolic links do not have to have the same name as the object that they point to.

Follow these steps to create a symbolic link:

1. Hold down the Shift and Ctrl keys and then click on the item you want to link to.
2. Drag and drop the item to a new location, then release the mouse button. If you release the Shift and Ctrl keys before you release the mouse button, you move the file or folder instead of creating a symbolic link.

You can also create a symbolic link using your keyboard, as follows:

1. Select a file or folder using the Tab or arrow keys and then press the spacebar.
2. Choose the Copy as Link command from the Selected menu The File Manager-Link Object dialog box (shown in Figure 7.8) appears.

FIGURE 7.8

Use the File Manager-Link Object dialog box to create a symbolic link file in another location.

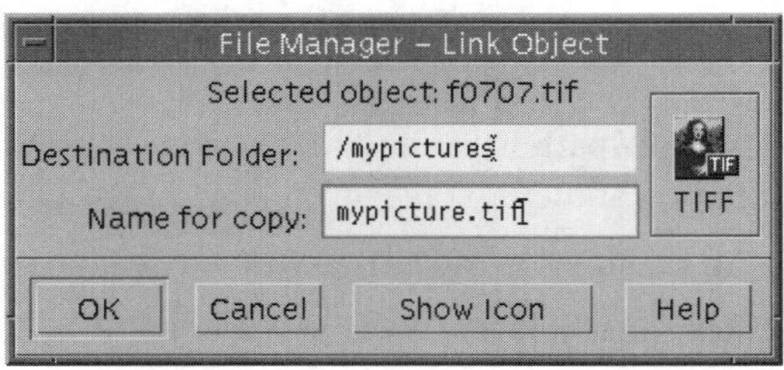

3. Enter the path name and directory name (*<pathname>/<directoryname>*) into the Destination Folder text box and the name of the symbolic link into the Name for Copy text box.
4. Click the OK button.

Moving files or folders is similar to copying them. The operation is similar to a copy operation to the destination folder followed by a deletion of the original items. The main difference is that you use the Shift key during the move operation, whereas you use the Ctrl key for the copy operation. Also, when you move a file or folder to another folder and you don't have modification privileges for the file or folder you're moving, Solaris creates a file or folder in the target folder and does not delete the original copy; an error message to that effect is posted.

To move files or folders, follow these steps:

1. Open both the source and the destination or target windows.
2. Select the files or folders in the source window that you wish to copy.
3. Hold down the Shift key and drag and drop the items into the destination window.

Or you can use this method:

1. Select the file or folder using the Tab and arrow keys and then press the spacebar.
2. Select the Move command from the Selected menu. The File Manager-Move Object dialog box shown in Figure 7.9 appears.

FIGURE 7.9

Use the File Manager-Move Object dialog box to enter a destination folder for a Move operation.

3. Enter the path name and folder name (<*pathname*>/<*foldername*>) into the Destination Folder text box of, then click the OK button.

You can rename file and folders in the File Manager window by doing the following:

1. Click the file or folder name under an icon.
2. Enter a new name from the keyboard.
3. Press the Return key.

Or you can use this method:

1. Use the Tab or arrow keys and then press the spacebar to select the file or folder.
2. Select the Rename command from the Selected menu.
3. Enter a new name from the keyboard.
4. Press the Return key.

If you want to cancel the operation, press the Esc key before you press the Return key.

The Front Panel

The front panel is the most prominent feature of the CDE desktop, as shown in Figure 7.10. It is a virtual workspace manager, giving you access to various workspaces through a central panel. The front panel includes a set of buttons or controls that allow you to perform many kinds of actions. It's more than a program launcher; it's a subprogram that runs within the Desktop Window Manager (`dtwm`).

FIGURE 7.10

The front panel is a convenient launching pad for system tools, applications, and operations.

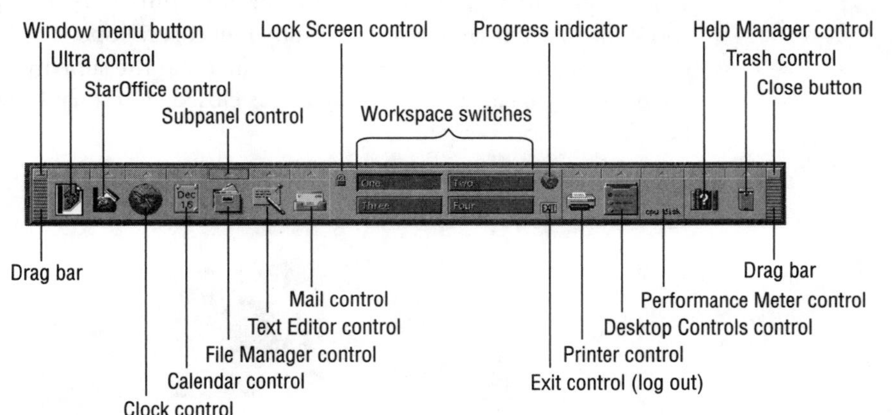

If you move your cursor over a control, Solaris shows you the name of the control in a yellow box. The buttons with small triangles on them open or close front panel drawers, called subpanels, which are configurable menus. The front panel doesn't have a title bar, but at the top left you will still find a Window menu button, and on the far top right you will see a Close button.

Under each of these two buttons is a vertical stripped rectangle called the drag bar, which you can use to click and drag the front panel about on your screen. To move the front panel, you can use the Move command on the Window menu. You can also use the arrow keys to move it in any direction and hold down the Ctrl key while using the arrow keys to move it faster in any direction. The front panel is not dockable in this version of Solaris, nor is it possible to change the orientation from horizontal to vertical. Also, you cannot resize the front panel, except by removing controls, which will make it smaller, and adding controls, which will make it bigger.

Front Panel Controls

In the default configuration of the front panel, the control are as follows (from left to right):

Ultra control The Ultra control opens a browser that describes what is installed on an Ultra workstation that you buy from Sun.

StarOffice control The StarOffice control opens the StarOffice 5.1 desktop, a file manager you can use to create text, spreadsheet, and HTML documents. You can also use it to create presentations and drawings and to open a task list, send mail, manage events, and perform other functions. The following graphic shows the StarOffice control. The subpanel control opens or closes the Star Office subpanel. An up-facing arrow means that the subpanel is open; a down-facing arrow means that the subpanel is closed. You must install StarOffice to have this option available.

Clock control The Clock control shows an icon of a globe with an analog clock. When you click this control, it opens your browser, which for Solaris 8's distribution in Q4 2000/Q1 2001 was Netscape Communicator 4.7. There was no action associated for the Clock control in Solaris 7.

Calendar control The Calendar control is an icon that shows the date. When you click on this control, you open your Calendar Manager (`dtcm`) in month view.

File Manager control This control displays the label Home Folder and opens a window for the home folder when clicked.

Text Editor control When you click this control, you open the graphical text editor utility (`dtpad`) and can create a text note. Text notes are text files that display a symbolic link on the desktop.

Mail control The Mail control opens the mail utility (`dtmail`) and lets you create new mail or read mail you have already received. From the Mail utility, you can also send and receive mail. When you have new mail, the Mail control icon changes to show an envelope in the box at an angle. Dragging a file from the desktop onto the Mail icon creates a new mail message with that file attached to it.

Lock Screen control When you click on this control, it locks your screen and displays a Password Login dialog box but leaves your session active. Enter your password to log back in to your session.

Workspace switches You can use the four Workspace controls to switch between workspaces, and so they're often called the Workspace switches (or desktop buttons) instead of controls. If you right-click the Workspace controls area, you'll get a pop-up menu that allows you to add, delete, or rename a workspace. (See the section "Workspaces" later in this chapter for more information.) These four buttons are the interface part of a set of modules in Solaris called the Graphical Workspace Manager, or GWM, which gives you access to virtual workspaces.

Progress indicator This globe icon spins when your computer is busy. It replaces a busy light from Solaris 7. If you click the Progress indicator, a Go dialog box opens. In the text box, you can enter a URL (opens your browser to that URL), directory location (opens a File Manager window with that directory open), or e-mail address (opens your mailer with a new message window addressed to that e-mail address). Figure 7.11 shows the Action: Go dialog box.

FIGURE 7.11

The Action: Go dialog box

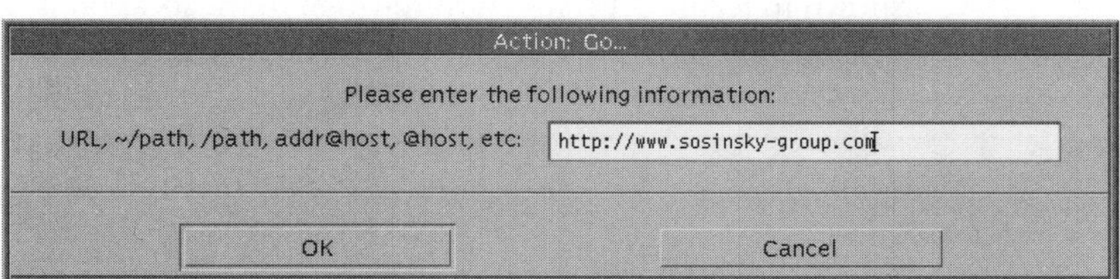

Exit control The Exit control logs you out of your current session.

Printer control When you drag and drop a file to the Default Printer icon this front panel function prints that file. If you click on the Printer control icon, you open the Printer Jobs window, which shows you the printer queue and lets you select from different installed printers.

Desktop Controls control This control opens the Application Manager window showing the `Desktop_Controls` program folder. With this directory you can modify the look and feel of your desktop. The section "Desktop Controls" later in this chapter describes the functions of these various utilities.

Performance Meter control This control shows you the CPU and disk utilization rates your system is currently experiencing. As you perform actions that spin the Progress indicator, one or both of these indictors will typically show activity bars. When you click the Performance Meter control, you open the Performance Meter utility. This utility is highly configurable, and you can use it to monitor a wide range of system functions simultaneously, as described in Chapter 15, "Memory and Process Management."

Help Manager control This control opens the Help Manager in the Help Viewer window. The various types of help available to you in Solaris 8 were described in Chapter 3.

Trash control Click on the Trash control to view the `Trash Can` folder and its contents. When you drag and drop files onto the Trash control, they are moved to the `Trash Can` folder. Items deleted to the `Trash Can` folder are not removed from your system until you use the Empty Trash Can control or the amount of files added to the Trash exceeds the allotted size of the `Trash Can` folder. Then the Trash Can shreds those files. Files in the `Trash Can` folder are deleted on a first-in-first-out (FIFO) basis. If you want to manually delete an item in the `Trash Can` folder, right-click its icon and select the Shred command. If you want to restore an object from the Trash Can, open the `Trash Can` folder, select the item (or items), then select the Put Back command from the File menu (as shown in Figure 7.12) to return the item to the location it was in before it was deleted. You can also select the Put Back command from an item's pop-up menu.

FIGURE 7.12

The Trash Can folder

Subpanels

Each of the front panel controls that aren't found in the central Workspace control portion of the panel comes with a subpanel. You click the drawer icon with an up-facing triangle to open a subpanel and click the icon again (now with a down-facing triangle) to close it. If you click and drag the title bar of a subpanel, you can place the subpanel anywhere on your desktop—panels are tear-off menus. Each subpanel has a subpanel menu that lets you restore (Alt+F5), move (Alt+F7), lower (Alt+F3), and close (Alt+F4) the subpanel. The subpanel's menu does not have to be open for these keystrokes to work (Restore, Move, Lower, and Close are options on the subpanel's menu).

The only control that doesn't have a subpanel is the Ultra control, the leftmost control on the front panel (refer back to Figure 7.10). Subpanels are menus that contain actions, and like the front panel controls themselves, they are configurable. Using the Install Icon control at the top of each subpanel, you can install additional actions.

StarOffice Subpanel

The StarOffice subpanel, shown in the following graphic, contains the StarOffice control, which starts the StarOffice desktop (the same action performed by the front panel icon itself); the SOSetup control, which opens StarOffice setup; and Printer Setup control, which opens StarOffice's Printer Installation dialog box.

Links Subpanel

The Links subpanel is shown in the following graphic. On the Links subpanel are the Web Browser control (functionally identical to the Clock control's click action); the Personal Bookmarks control, which opens the Bookmarks File Manager window (at the path `/.dt/bookmarks`); and the Find Web Page control, which goes to the site `www.sun.com/search/solaris`.

Cards Subpanel

The following graphic shows the Cards subpanel. In addition to the Install Icon control, it includes the Today control, which opens the Calendar to the current month with current date selected, and the Find Card control, which opens the Address Manager's Search dialog box.

Files Subpanel

The Files subpanel is one of the more commonly used subpanels of the front panel. It includes the Home Folder control, which opens the Home folder's window in the File Manager; the StarOffice Work Folder control, which opens the File Manager to the `/Office51/work` folder where StarOffice stores files by default; the Open Floppy and Open CD-ROM controls, which open a floppy disk and CD-ROM window, respectively; the Properties control, which opens the Properties dialog box in which you can determine the attributes of files and directories; Encryption, Compress File, and Archive controls, each of which performs the actions they are named for; and finally, the Find File control, which opens Solaris's Find utility.

Applications Subpanel

The Applications subpanel is probably the most commonly used subpanel of the front panel because it contains both applications and controls that allow you to customize and work with the CDE desktop in many ways. In addition to the Install Icon control, you will find the Text Note control, which opens a single-file text editor application that stores notes and puts a link to them on your workspace. The Text Editor control opens the text editor, which is more fully described in Chapter 16. The Voice Note control opens the CDE Audio Application, which you can use to record from a microphone or a line to a sound file.

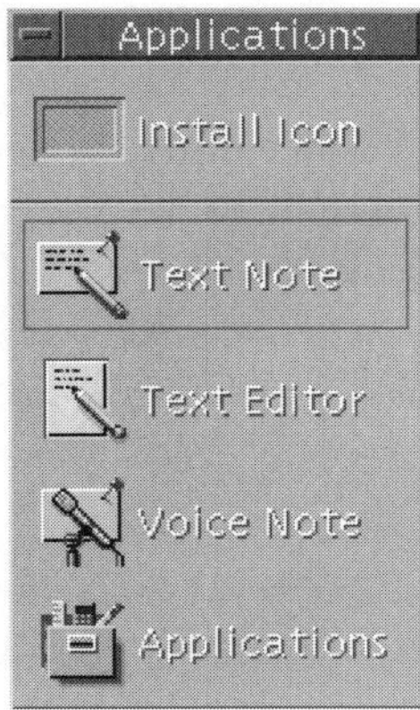

Of particular importance is the Applications control, which opens the Application Manager window shown in Figure 7.13. The reason the Applications control is important is that the Application Manager program folder window contains many desktop, system, and administrative programs and controls that you can use to modify your system behavior. Programs represented in this folder are both CDE and OpenWindows applications and actions. In fact, many of the controls on the front panel and its subpanels are found in the Application Manager folder and in the folders it contains. When you need to perform a task using a program or utility that you can't find on any of the menus, the Application Manager folder is a good place to start looking. Among the important folders you find there are the `Desktop_Apps`, `Desktop_Controls`, `Desktop_Tools`, `Information`, `OpenWindows`, and `System_Admin` folders. It's a good idea to open these folders and study their contents when familiarizing yourself with Solaris. You will also probably find a few controls therein that you may want to add to your front panel or its various subpanels. In addition to opening the Application Manager with this subpanel control, you can also use the Applications submenu of the Workspace Menu.

FIGURE 7.13

The Application Manager program folder

Mail Subpanel

The Mail subpanel is shown in the following graphic. This subpanel offers you two unique controls: the Mail control, which opens the Mail utility, and the Suggestion Box control, which creates new mail to the folks at `Solaris8_Suggestion_Box@eng.sun.com`.

Printers Subpanel

The following graphic shows the Personal Printers subpanel. This subpanel also has only two other controls besides the Install Icon control: the Default control, which opens the default printer's Printer Jobs queue, and the Print Manager control, which opens the Printer Manager dialog box.

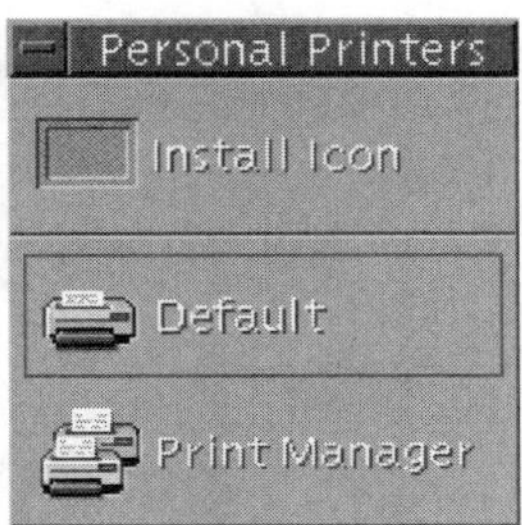

Tools Subpanel

The Tools subpanel menu opens from just above the Desktop Controls control. This subpanel has a number of different tools. Using the Desktop Controls control, you can open a folder containing tools you can use to modify the way your desktop appears. For more information, see "Desktop Controls" later in this chapter. The CDE Error Log control opens the Watch Errors window with a display of system error messages.

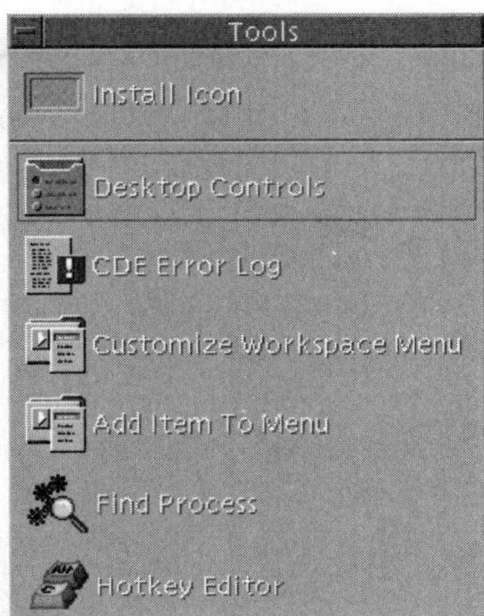

The Add Item to Menu control opens the Add Item to Workspace Menu dialog box (see Figure 7.14), through which you can add a file or folder to the `$HOME/.dt/wsmenu` directory. The Customize Workspace Menu control opens the `$HOME/.dt/wsmenu` folder, which contains symbolic links to the programs and actions that are in all of the subpanel menus, as shown in Figure 7.15. You can drag and drop additional actions and links into each of these folders and use the/wsmenu directory as a means of organizing all of your subpanels.

FIGURE 7.14

The Add Item to Workspace Menu dialog box

FIGURE 7.15

The Workspace Menu window

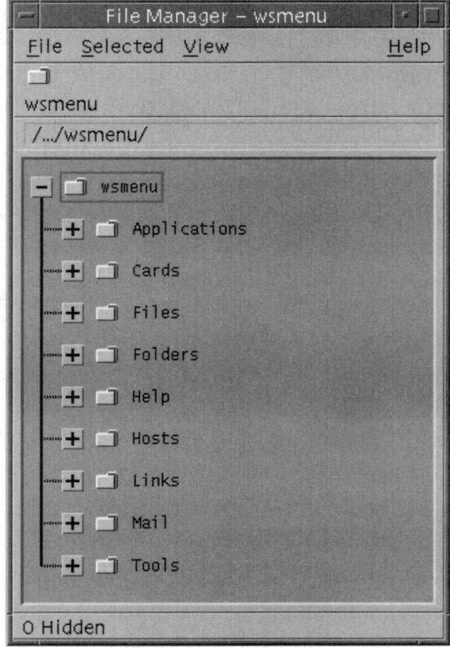

NOTE When you drag a file or directory into the wsmenu directory using the Customize Workspace Menu dialog box, that file or directory is moved (not copied) into the wsmenu directory. To create a symbolic link in the wsmenu directory, hold down the Shift and Ctrl keys before performing the drag-and-drop operation.

The Find Process control opens the Process Manager, which shows you the details of all of the processes running on your system. You can use this window to debug your system, to kill an errant process, and to perform many other tasks. Finally, the last control on the Tools subpanel is the Hotkey Editor control. It opens the Hotkey Editor, which you can use to define keystroke macros that you want to use on your system. This utility is described more fully in the section "The Hotkey Editor" later in this chapter.

Hosts Subpanel

The Hosts subpanel menu is shown in the following graphic. It contains the Performance control, which is another way to open the Performance Meter window; the This Host control, which opens a terminal window; and the System Info control, which opens the Workstation Information dialog box.

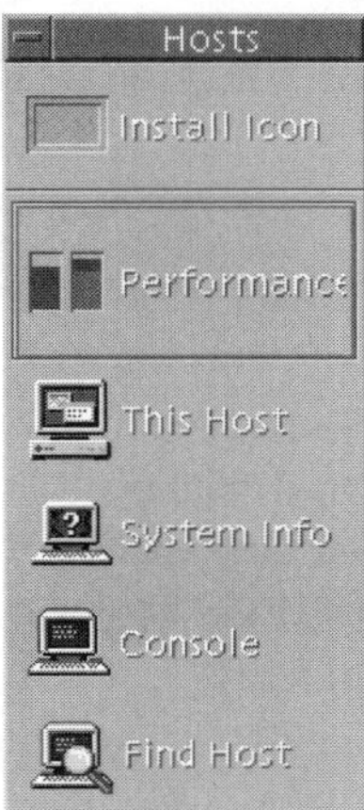

The Workstation Information dialog box, shown in Figure 7.16, shows you details about the system that you have logged in to, either the local workstation or server or a remote system. The Hosts subpanel menu also includes the Console control, which opens a console window, and the Find Host control, which opens the search utility for the Address Manager. You can use the Address Manager to find workstations and servers on the network or Internet by name or address.

FIGURE 7.16

The Workstation Information dialog box

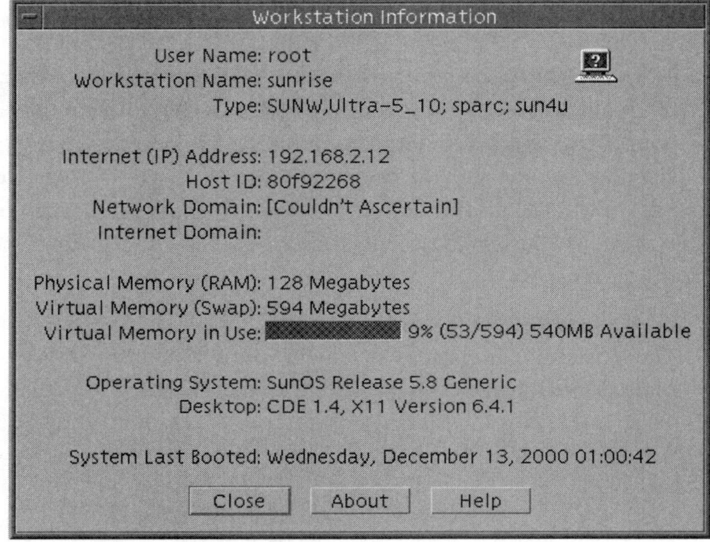

Help Subpanel

The Help Manager control opens the Help subpanel menu shown in the following graphic. This subpanel contains a number of controls for accessing the different kinds of help that is available on your system. (Chapter 3 described the various types of help in detail.) The Help Manager control duplicates the action of the front panel control by opening the Help Manager in the Help Viewer. The SunSolve Online and Solaris Support controls open your Web browser to those Sun sites. The Information control opens the Application Manager Information folder with links to the AnswerBook2 and Sample Bookmarks. Beginning users will find the Desktop Introduction and Front Panel Help controls useful; they open the Help Viewer with information on these basic tasks and with documentation of the front panel. The On Item Help control is used for context-sensitive help; when you click this control, your cursor turns into a question mark. Click on any control to open the Help Viewer to that topic.

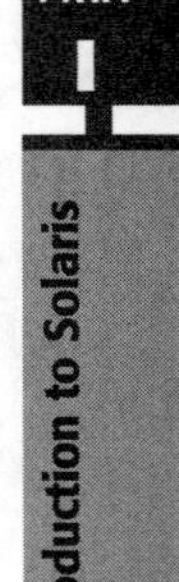

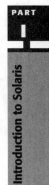

Trash Subpanel

The Trash control opens the Trash subpanel. This subpanel contains the Trash control you can use to open the `Trash Can` folder and the Empty Trash Can control for shredding all items in your `Trash Can` folder.

Modifying the Front Panel

You can add or delete a subpanel by right-clicking on a control and selecting the Add Subpanel or Delete Subpanel command from the pop-up menu. The following graphic shows the pop-up menu for the File Manager control. You'll notice that you can also use the Move Left and Move Right commands to move a control's icon around in the subpanel. Note that you can't move an icon that is at the left or right front panel border, nor can you move an icon into the Workspace panel. When you issue the Add Icon command in the pop-up menu, you add a new blank control to the front panel to the left of the pop-up menu; this control doesn't modify the icon of any of the existing controls. To provide an action to the blank control, you can drag and drop an icon from the desktop to it. The commands you see in the pop-up menus that you open on the front panel depend upon whether a menu was opened over an existing control or not.

When you add a new control to the front panel, that control is a blank embossed button, like the icon next to the Install Icon control you see at the top of every subpanel. To give that control a function, you must drag and drop an executable file (program icon), a document, or some other system content from the desktop onto the icon. If you want to delete a front panel icon by selecting the Delete Icon command from that control's pop-up menu, then Solaris will display the Workspace Manager Delete Icon dialog box. If you delete a front panel icon, you also delete any application that the control is linked to. The application may no longer exist or function. To restore your front panel to the state it was in when Solaris was first installed, double-click the Restore Front Panel application in the Desktop_Tools-Extras application group.

When you want to add an application, file, or action to the front panel, you use the Add Icon command on the pop-up men of a control or the front panel itself. That action adds the Install Icon control to the front panel. As you have already seen, each subpanel contains the Install Icon control as its top control. To enable a new control, drag and drop the following onto the Install Icon control:

- An executable file of a program
- A folder icon from a File Manager
- A file of any kind
- A script or action

Actions

An action is a scripted command that is represented by an action icon in the CDE. With an action, you can open files, launch applications, modify the file structure, print, or execute any command that you can enter from the command line. Given that only a single command-line statement can be used, actions aren't really programs, although they can certainly be program calls. The nice thing about actions is that you can create them graphically using the Create Action control found in the `Desktop_Apps` folder of the Application Manager, and the actions that you create can be added to any folder or to the front panel as a control. You can also open the Create Action window by invoking it from the command line using the `dtcreate` command.

To create an action, do the following:

1. Open the Applications subpanel on the front panel and click the Applications control. The Application Manager folder opens.
2. Double-click the `Desktop_Apps` folder, then double-click the Create Action control (shown here).

3. When the Create Action dialog box opens (shown in Figure 7.17 in Advanced mode), enter a name in the Action Name text box. That name will be attached to the icon you create for the action. No spaces are allowed in an action name.
4. Click the Find Set button to open the Find Set dialog box and select an icon for your action. Figure 7.18 shows the Find Set dialog box. You can also use the Edit Icon button to open the Icon Editor (Figure 7.19) and modify the action's icon.

   An action icon is part of a registration package that is created when the action is specified, and its integration with the desktop is managed by `dtappintegrate`. Icon image files are located in the `app_root/dt/appconfig/icons/language` folder. When specifying an action stored in this folder, you should use the base name of the action, which is the action name minus all of the suffixes that are appended to it (e.g., myaction replaces myaction.m.pm).
5. In the Command When Action Is Opened text box (in the Find Set dialog box), enter any command that you can enter from the command line or enter the full path name of any executable file or shell script.

FIGURE 7.17

The Create Action window, shown here in Advanced mode, is where you create actions and specify their properties.

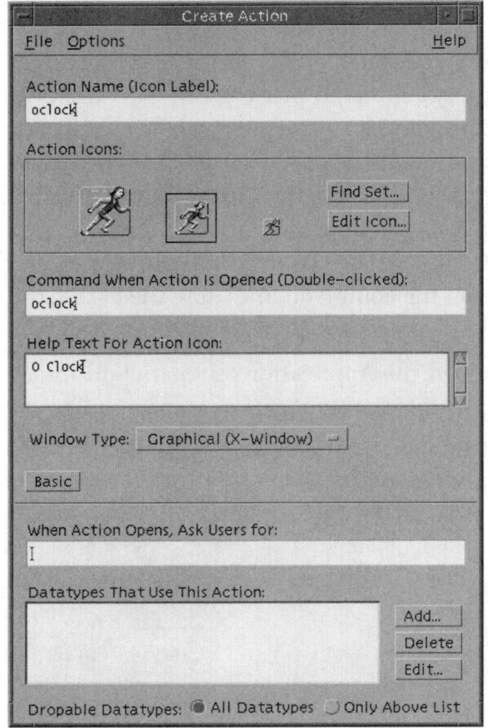

6. In the Help Text for Action Icon text box, enter the text you want to appear when a cursor is over the icon you create.
7. Select the window type from the pop-up menu: the default, Graphical (X-Window), runs an application in its own window; Terminal (Auto-Close) runs an application in a terminal window and the window closes as soon as the application completes its action; and Terminal (Manual Close) runs an application in a terminal window and requires a user to give an `exit` command to close the application.
8. If you want specific data types to work with this icon, select the Only Above List radio button in the Dropable Datatypes option group, then click the Add button to add the data types that will work with your action.
9. Select the Save command from the File menu and the action is saved to your home folder.
10. Double-click an action to test its operation (recommended).

FIGURE 7.18

Use the Find Set dialog box to specify the icon used for an action.

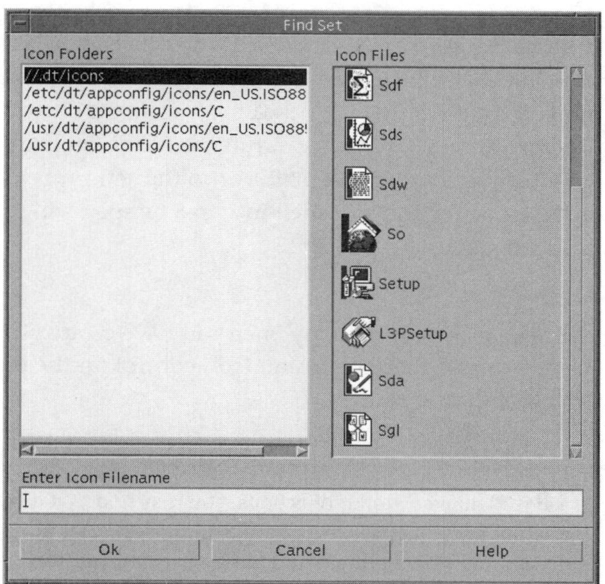

FIGURE 7.19

The Icon Editor

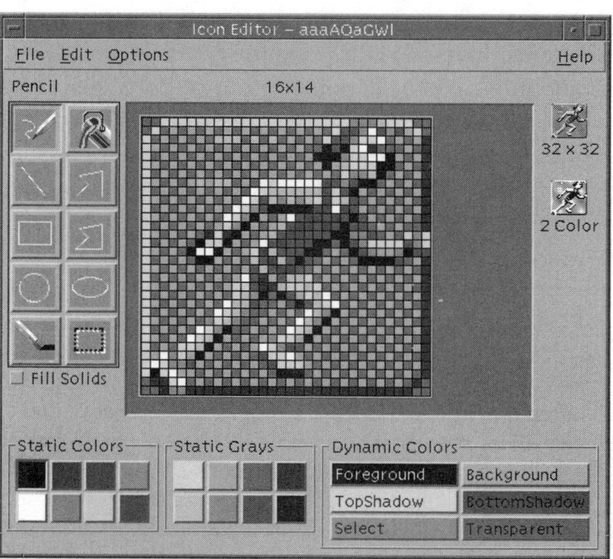

If in Step 5 you use for an action a command that requires a filename, such as `lp <filename>` or `diff <filename1> <filename2>`, then use a `<$n>` variable in place of the filename, as in `lp $1` or `diff $1 $2`. When you create an action and place in the front panel, it will then serve as a drop zone for files that you drag and drop onto it. Thus you can print the file `memo1` by dragging it onto the action specifying the line printer command, and you can run the file difference command by first dragging the `memo1` file and then the `memo2` file onto the action specifying that command. You can also pass a command to a shell in step 5 by specifying the shell and the command, as in this example:

```
/bin/sh -c 'ps | lp'
```

Installing an action is easy once you have created it. To install an action, simply click and drag it onto the Install Icon control on the menu in which you wish the action to appear.

TIP If you create a lot of actions, you may find that it makes sense to group them into a new subpanel that you create for that purpose. Create a new My Actions or Personal Applications subpanel by right-clicking the front panel and selecting the Add Icon command from the pop-up menu. Then, after you install a control (the Create Action control would be a good choice), right-click the new front panel control and select the Add Subpanel command.

Double-click the action icon on your desktop if you want to perform the action it represents. If you want to examine the code for an action, open the `/.dt/types` folder and double-click the action's definition file. The `/.dt` folder is a hidden folder in your root directory, so use the Show Hidden Objects command to view it. When you double-click an action file in the `/.dt/types` folder, you see the definition appear in the text editor, as shown in Figure 7.20. The action opened the oclock application in an X window.

TIP The Hotkey Editor contains several default hotkeys that change your current workspace. Those hotkey keystrokes include Alt+Left, which moves you to the previous workspace, and Alt+Right, which moves you to the next workspace (these two take effect everywhere, which means they work in all programs as well as on the desktop). The default hotkeys that take effect on the desktop are Left (previous workspace), Right (next workspace), SunAgain (packs icons) and SunUndo (refreshes all windows). See "The Hotkey Editor" later in this chapter for more information.

FIGURE 7.20

Shown here is the definition file for an action that opens the oclock application.

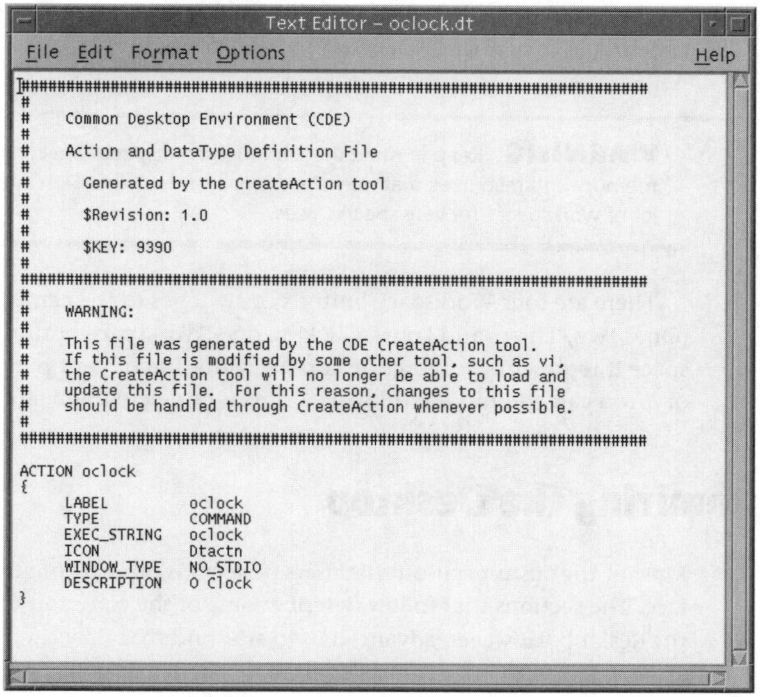

```
Text Editor – oclock.dt
File  Edit  Format  Options                                        Help
##########################################################################
#
#    Common Desktop Environment (CDE)
#
#    Action and DataType Definition File
#
#      Generated by the CreateAction tool
#
#      $Revision: 1.0
#
#      $KEY: 9390
#
##########################################################################
#
#    WARNING:
#
#    This file was generated by the CDE CreateAction tool.
#    If this file is modified by some other tool, such as vi,
#    the CreateAction tool will no longer be able to load and
#    update this file.  For this reason, changes to this file
#    should be handled through CreateAction whenever possible.
#
##########################################################################

ACTION oclock
{
     LABEL          oclock
     TYPE           COMMAND
     EXEC_STRING    oclock
     ICON           Dtactn
     WINDOW_TYPE    NO_STDIO
     DESCRIPTION    O Clock
}
```

Workspaces

Solaris offers you the ability to manage multiple desktop configurations or virtual desktops, called workspaces. You can create multiple environments to work in: one that is used to work with office applications for a productivity worker, another that includes system management functions, a third to work with the Internet, and a fourth workspace for a particular programming environment. People tend to get very creative in their use of workspaces once they become accustomed to them. Each of Solaris's four default workspaces come with very different backdrops: SunLogo, Water-Drops, Sunrise, and Dolphins. Although you can change these backdrops using the Backdrop desktop control in the Style Manager, it's a good idea to give each workspace a unique backdrop so that you can identify quickly which workspace you are currently working in.

Switching from one workspace to another is a little like logging in and out of terminal sessions, except that each set of workspaces is associated with a different password.

Because each workspace already has been set up for a particular use, they can save you a lot of setup time. The Graphical Workspace Manager is the system module that controls and manages workspaces on Solaris.

WARNING Keep in mind that although workspaces are convenient, they do consume memory and resources that may slow your system down. Don't get carried away creating a lot of workspaces for very specific uses.

There are four Workspace buttons or switches in the center of the CDE front panel (One, Two, Three, and Four). Clicking on a Workspace button moves you to the workspace it represents, leaving the current condition of your previous workspace in memory. You can add more Workspace buttons or delete them as you desire.

Customizing the Desktop

Most of the customization that users perform is done through the graphical user interface. The sections that follow describe some of the common controls for customizing the desktop. However, advanced users will find that they can directly edit CDE configuration files with finer control over their system's session characteristics. The three most important configuration files are `.dtprofile`, `sessionetc`, and `sessionexit`. The `sessionetc` file is a Bourne shell script that performs tasks like application startup. The CDE also provides a logout script in the `sessionexit` file. This script stores user-specific information on how to clean up the files in temporary folders and how to back up files that contain critical data.

When you log in to the CDE, the CDE Window Manager reads the settings stored in the `.dtprofile` file and uses those settings to establish environmental variables for your session. The `.dtprofile` file takes environmental settings in either the Bourne or Korn shell syntax. Any errors made in reading the environmental variables show up in the `startlog` (`$HOME/.dt/startlog`), as do errors generated by reading the `.login` or `.profile` files. The `.dtprofile` file is read first at session startup, and in the *<dtsourceprofile>* variable, points to the `.profile` and `.login` files to be read and executed when you start a shell. You can suppress the reading of the `.profile` and `.login` files by commenting out the line that contains the *<dtsourceprofile>* variable with a # sign.

Note that when the CDE starts up, it does not read the `.profile` file used by the Korn or Bourne shell or the `.login` file used for the C shell. The `.profile` file is ignored so that the CDE environment offers users the same look and feel. In order to use these files if you have modified your shell, you should point to them in the `$HOME/.dtprofile` file or your modifications will not appear when you escape to a shell from the CDE. Login's use of configuration files was described more fully early in this chapter.

The CDE searches in the order `$HOME/.dt, /etc/dt/config` and then `/usr/dt/config`. Thus, user customization precedes system customization, and at the very least the distribution configuration will be installed if no other configuration files can be found. All system users or system administrators wishing to customize the CDE should make changes to the `/etc/dt/config` files because upgrades to Solaris will overwrite files in the `/usr/dt` but not the `/etc/dt` directories.

The CDE maintains a session log determined by the environmental variable *<dt_sessionlogfile>*. Each session creates a log that is usually located at `$HOME/.dt/session-$$.log`.

Desktop Controls

You have control over many attributes that affect the look and feel of the Solaris desktop in the CDE through the controls found in the `Desktop_Controls` folder (Figure 7.21). To open the `Desktop_Controls` folder, click the Desktop Controls control on the front panel. Not every control you find in this window affects the desktop. Many of the controls alter input devices such as the keyboard and mouse or affect system behavior such as startup, power management, and handicapped access features. This section describes more fully the desktop-related controls. Table 7.8 gives a description of the controls, with fuller explanations of several of them offered in sections elsewhere in this book.

FIGURE 7.21

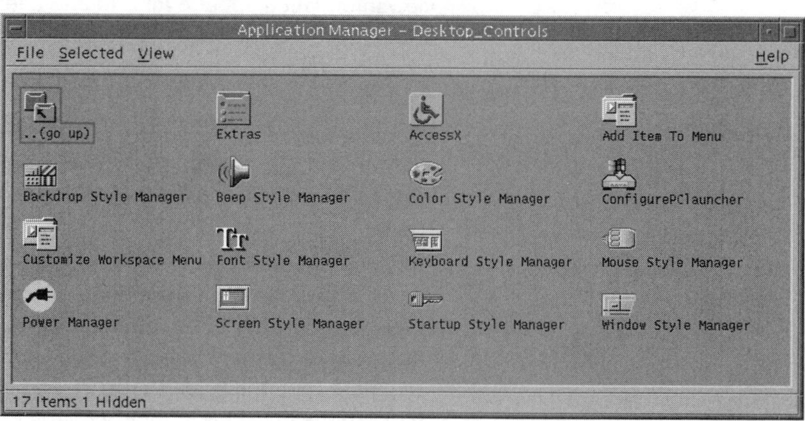

The `Desktop_Controls` folder contains controls you can use to modify the look and feel of your desktop and many other elements.

TABLE 7.8: THE `Desktop_Controls` CONTROLS

Control Name	Description
Extras	This folder icon opens the Extras application group that contains a number of useful programming and system tools. Among the useful tools in the folder are ones that work with the front panel and workspaces, window information and properties, reload actions, applications and resources, and the Style Manager.
AccessX	This control contains several keyboard and sound settings to help users with disabilities work with Solaris systems.
Add Item to Menu	This control allows you to add an application command to the Workspace menu that you see when you right-click on your desktop.
Backdrop Style Manager	This control opens the Style Manager and the Backdrop component. You can use it to modify the color and pattern of your desktop.
Beep Style Manager	Use this control to set the volume, style, and duration of system beeps.
Color Style Manager	With this control, you can use color palettes to set a color scheme for window elements like borders, title bars, and the central window section. You can also set the number of colors you see on your desktop using this control.
ConfigurePClauncher	You can use the PC Launcher to view and edit PC files by opening PC applications running in SoftWindows, Sun PC, Sun PCI, RealPC, or desk size PC or remotely over a TCP/IP network to a PC.
Customize Workspace Menu	This control opens the `wsmenu` folder you use to modify the front panel.
Font Style Manager	Use this control to alter the fonts used in windows on your desktop by applications of all types, to add and delete fonts, and to view information about a font. To add a font, click the Add button and select a font group from the System scrolling list and a font group from the User list, then click the OK button and name the new font group.
Keyboard Style Manager	With this control, you can set the Auto Repeat function that continues to enter the same character if you hold down the key on your keyboard. You can also set a click sound for key presses.
Mouse Style Manager	Use the Mouse control to change mouse button assignments, alter the double-click rate, accelerate the speed at which your cursor moves across the screen, and set a threshold for the number of pixels you must move the mouse before you get accelerated movement of your cursor. You can test your settings with a testing utility within the control window. If you are left-handed, you might want to switch the functions of mouse buttons 1 and 3.

Continued

TABLE 7.8: THE `Desktop_Controls` CONTROLS (CONTINUED)

Control Name	Description
Power Manager	Use this control to determine how long your system must be idle before monitors or disks are shut down or before an autoshutdown sequence begins. You can set a timetable for autoshutdown.
Screen Style Manager	This control sets a screen saver, both the pattern and how long your system must be idle before the screen saver comes on. You can also lock the screen when the screen saver is activated.
Startup Style Manager	This control sets the login behavior, returning you to a current or home session, and modifies the logout behavior.
Window Style Manager	The Window control alters how you activate a window and how the window behaves when selected or moved. You can also use it to adjust iconic behavior.

Whenever you open a control that alters the look of your desktop, you also open the Style Manager, shown in Figure 7.22. The icon for the Style Manager is actually installed into the Application Manager `Desktop_Apps` folder. You can think of the Style Manager as analogous to the front panel for desktop controls. Indeed, the control for the Style Manager is so useful that you might want to add it to your Tools subpanel by dragging and dropping its icon from the `Extras` folder onto the Install Icon control on the Tools submenu.

FIGURE 7.22

The Style Manager is a launching pad for nine of the controls used to alter desktop behavior.

TIP You can manually set your own backdrop using programs like `xsetroot`, `xv`, and `Esetroot` to set a color or picture. To do so, set the Backdrop setting to No Backdrops and then use one of these programs.

All of these controls contain online help that describe their features and options. Of the group of controls that affect desktop behavior, the one most likely to be confusing to new users is the Window Style Manager (shown here) because you use it to alter several key aspects of windows.

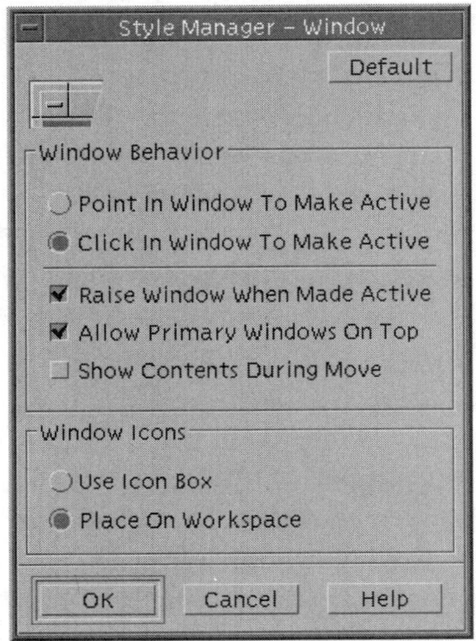

In the Window Behavior option group, you can set the method for selecting a window for the input focus. The default choice for selecting a window is to click on it. When you do that, the window is activated and becomes the topmost window on your desktop. Nearly all of the instructions in this book assume that you haven't modified this behavior. However, if you choose Point in Window to Make Active, you can make a window active by simply moving your cursor over it. You can also set the window behavior so that windows aren't raised when selected and that primary windows are always on top. The Allow Primary Windows on Top option keeps the initial window in a group above the others in its group.

A number of controls described earlier don't really modify the look of your desktop as much as they modify your workstation or your server's actions. The Startup control (shown in the following graphic), which is found on the Style Manager and in the `Desktop_Controls` folder, alters the behavior of your system's login and logout routines and thus affects your actions on the desktop. Choices you make in the At Login section affect how your next session is displayed. When you select the Resume Current Session radio button (the default), Solaris stores the state of your current processes, the nature of your displayed windows, and the condition of your workspaces and restores them when you log back in to the CDE. The Return to Home Session option starts up your desktop into what is called a home session. A home session is a special session setup that you create and store in a setup file found at `/.dt/session/home/dt.session`. A third option in the At Login section allows you to make a choice between resuming your current session or your home session when you log out.

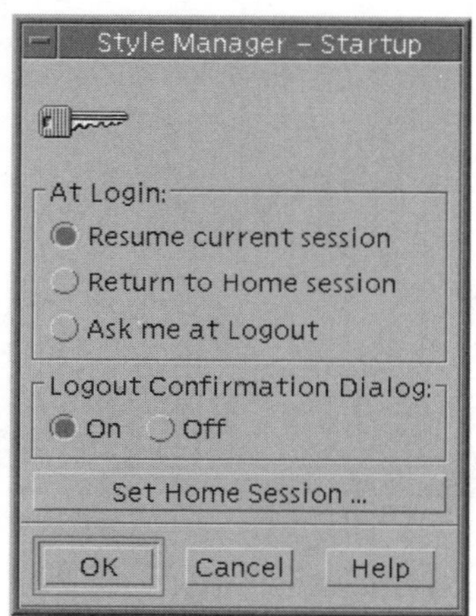

You automatically save your current session if you select the Resume Current Session option. If you want to save a session that you can return to without logging out of your system, you should save the condition of that session to your home session. To save a home session, click the Set Home Session button in the Startup dialog box, then click the OK button in the Warning dialog box that appears informing you that your action will replace the current session. You should reserve your home session for a desktop configuration that you constantly return to. For more temporary configurations, use the different workspaces to save your session states at log out.

The Hotkey Editor

The Hotkey Editor is an application that allows you to create hotkeys or keystrokes that can perform actions or run executable files and scripts. A hotkey is an accelerator key that can be defined for a workspace, the desktop, or an application. The Hotkey Editor is shown in Figure 7.23.

FIGURE 7.23

Use the Hotkey Editor to create keyboard macros.

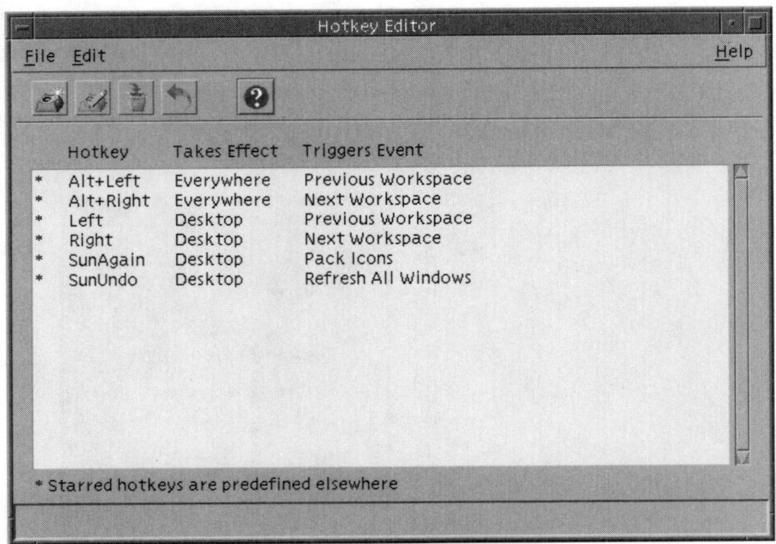

To open the Hotkey Editor, do any of the following:

- Double-click the Hotkey Editor icon in the `Desktop_Apps` folder in the Application Manager.
- Click the Hotkey Editor control on the Tools subpanel in the front panel.
- Enter **`sdthotkey`** at the command line.

Follow these steps to create a hotkey:

1. Click the New Hotkey button (the leftmost button on the Hotkey Editor's toolbar) or select the New Hotkey command from the File menu. The Edit Hotkey dialog box appears.

   The Edit Hotkey dialog box (Figure 7.24) is a graphical application for creating hotkeys. Under Step 3, the details are shown. You can hide the details by clicking the Hide Details button (which then changes to the Show Details button).

2. Select the scope of the hotkey by selecting from the target list box. Figure 7.24 shows what the dialog box looks like when you choose to create a hotkey for an application, action, or document (which you should choose for this exercise). The other choices are workspace management function or multi-monitor management function.

FIGURE 7.24

The Edit Hotkey dialog box

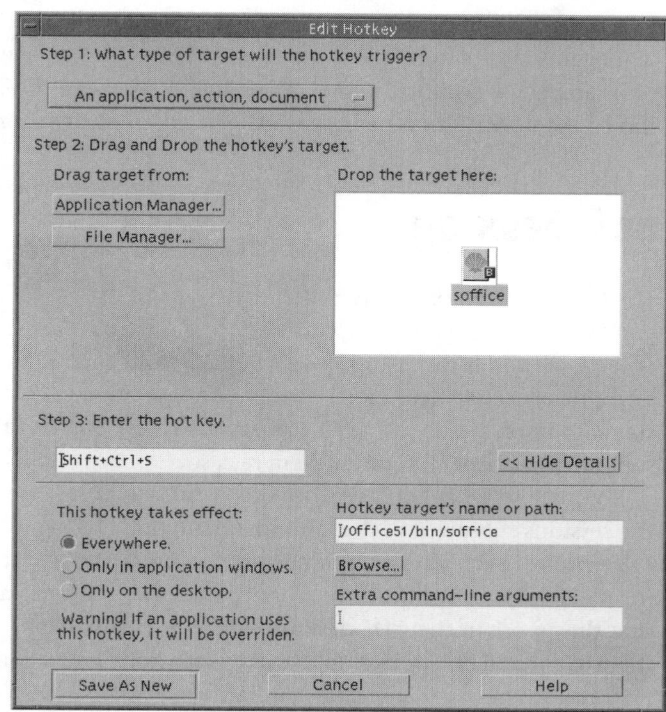

3. Click either the Application Manager or File Manager button to view the icon for the object you wish to create a hotkey for, then drag the icon onto the Drop the Target Here icon.
4. Click the Step 3 text box, then press the hotkey you are creating. You can press the Ctrl key and release it to clear the Step 3 text box.
5. In the This Hotkey Takes Effect section, click the radio button that describes the scope of the hotkey: Everywhere, Only in Application Windows, or Only on the Desktop.
6. Click in the Hotkey Target's Name or Path text box, then enter the command-line argument that will execute the action the hotkey represents.
7. If there are any options for the command line, enter them in the Extra Command-Line Arguments text box.
8. Click the Save As New button, then click Cancel to return to the Hotkey Editor.
9. In the Hotkey Editor, select the Save command from the File menu.

The Edit Hotkey dialog box will display different options depending upon the selection you make in the scope list box. For example, when you select a workspace management function, you'll see two list boxes that display different workspace functions and the workspace names. With the multi-monitor management function, you can create hotkeys that navigate between different monitors.

OpenLook Desktop

The OpenLook graphical user interface is one of the two main GUIs that Solaris offers you from the login screen. That interface is controlled by the OpenLook Window Manager (`olwm`) and is run using Sun's OpenWindows and X Window System. OpenLook is a proprietary implementation of the X Window System's guidelines, and because it isn't a standard implementation as CDE is, it is used less. Sun has also indicated that it won't support OpenLook in future system releases.

To open an OpenLook session, you must select the OpenWindows Desktop from the sessions submenu of the Options menu on your login screen. When you authenticate yourself with your username and password, the desktop opens. You will find that nearly all of your applications work in the OpenLook desktop in much the same way that they work in the CDE desktop. There are really only minor differences between the two interfaces. For example, there is no front panel equivalent in OpenLook. However, there are many more similarities. You work with menus and select objects on the OpenLook desktop using the same methods and keystrokes you do in the CDE desktop. Figure 7.25 shows the Open Windows desktop with elements labeled. The submenus of the Workspace menu are tear-off menus (the Programs submenu is shown in the figure).

When you right-click the desktop, you see the Workspace menu. This menu contains many of the commands in the CDE Workspace menu, but they're organized in a slightly different way. Use the Programs and Utilities menus to access both applications and utilities and use the Properties command to access workspace settings. The Workstation Info command is for viewing your computer's properties, the Help command opens the Help Viewer, and the Exit command logs you off. If you wish to save the OpenLook workspace in its current state, open the Workspace menu and select the Save Workspace command from the Utilities submenu.

FIGURE 7.25

The elements of the OpenLook Desktop, including the Workspace menu

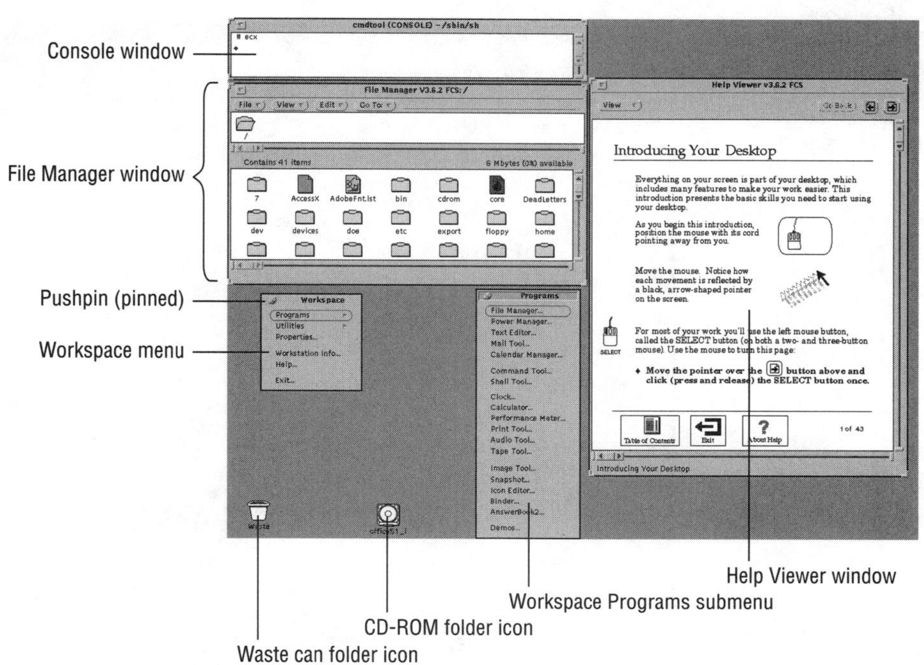

Notice that there is a pushpin in the upper-left corner of the title bar of the Workspace menu. The pushpin is a standard OpenLook interface element. When you use the pushpin, the Workspace menu stays on top of any other windows. Normal OpenLook File Manager windows don't come with pushpins. Pushpins are similar to the pushpins used in Motif tear-off menus.

The default OpenLook Workspace menu is stored in the file `/usr/openwin/lib/openwin-menu`. To modify the Workspace menu, copy that file to the home directory as the `.openwin-menu` file and modify it as you desire. Figure 7.26 shows the `/usr/lib/openwin-menu-utilities` file. Table 7.9 lists common commands in an OpenWindows menu file. Any applications that also have modifiable Preferences commands store the information used to set the preferences in the `.desksetdefaults` file in your home directory.

FIGURE 7.26

The OpenWindows Workspace Utility menu is specified by this text file during startup.

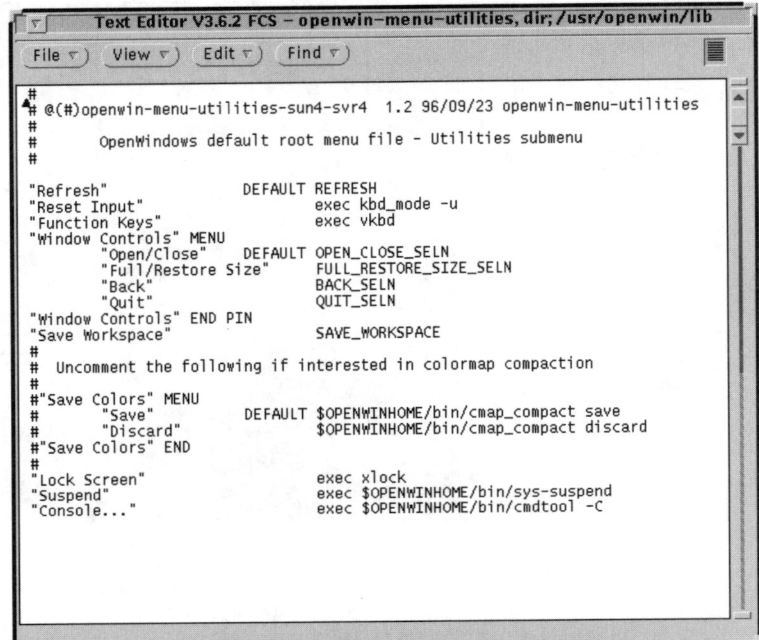

Text Editor V3.6.2 FCS – openwin-menu-utilities, dir; /usr/openwin/lib

File ▽ View ▽ Edit ▽ Find ▽

```
#
# @(#)openwin-menu-utilities-sun4-svr4  1.2 96/09/23 openwin-menu-utilities
#
#       OpenWindows default root menu file - Utilities submenu
#

"Refresh"                   DEFAULT REFRESH
"Reset Input"                       exec kbd_mode -u
"Function Keys"                     exec vkbd
"Window Controls" MENU
        "Open/Close"        DEFAULT OPEN_CLOSE_SELN
        "Full/Restore Size"         FULL_RESTORE_SIZE_SELN
        "Back"                      BACK_SELN
        "Quit"                      QUIT_SELN
"Window Controls" END PIN
"Save Workspace"                    SAVE_WORKSPACE
#
#  Uncomment the following if interested in colormap compaction
#
#"Save Colors" MENU
#       "Save"              DEFAULT $OPENWINHOME/bin/cmap_compact save
#       "Discard"                   $OPENWINHOME/bin/cmap_compact discard
#"Save Colors" END
#
"Lock Screen"                       exec xlock
"Suspend"                           exec $OPENWINHOME/bin/sys-suspend
"Console..."                        exec $OPENWINHOME/bin/cmdtool -C
```

TABLE 7.9: THE OPENLOOK MENU COMMANDS

Command	Purpose
"<*text*>"	Puts this text in the menu as a label.
DEFAULT	The default menu selection. Users press Enter to select it.
END	Ends a submenu.
exec <*program*>	Executes this program (pgm) when the "<*text*>" is selected.
EXIT	Closes the OpenLook window manager and returns to the login screen.
MENU	Starts a submenu.
PIN	Puts a pushpin on this menu.
SEPARATOR	Uses SEPARATOR to group different menu items and skips a line in the menu.
TITLE	The command name for the submenu (cascading menu).

Windows represent one area where there are differences between OpenLook and CDE. There are no accelerator keys in window menus, although there are hotkeys available once a menu is open. When you are on the OpenWindows desktop, windows have a slightly different scroll bar arrangement, as you can see in the File Manager window shown in Figure 7.27. In this window, when you click one of the bars at the end of a scroll bar, you move to that spot. The arrows on the slider move you one line in the direction that they point. To move about in the window any amount, click the drag area of the slider and drag it any amount in the direction you want to move.

FIGURE 7.27

Elements of an OpenWindows File Manager window

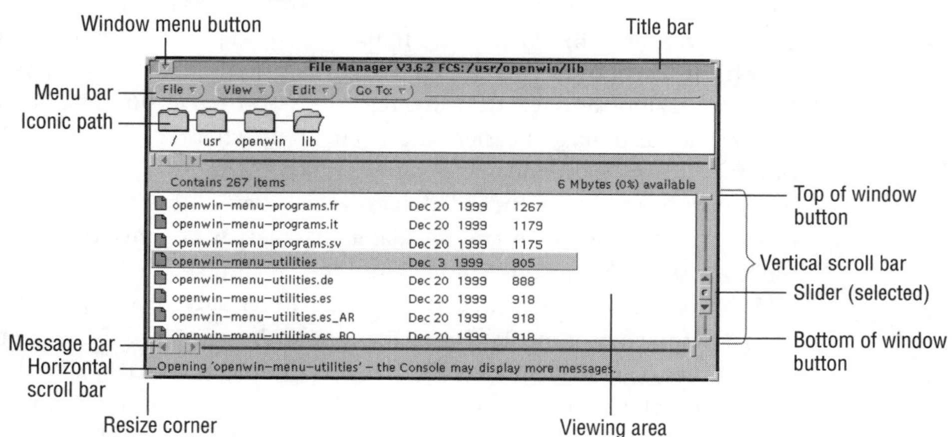

The X Window System

The X Window System is the result of work done on the Athena project at the Massachusetts Institute of Technology (MIT) in Boston, Massachusetts, in the mid-1980s. The goals of the project—which was initiated by the Laboratory of Computer Science and supported by both the Digital Equipment Corporation (DEC) and IBM—were to create a windowed interface that ran on various forms of Unix and to create a GUI that was easily portable from one version of Unix to another. The first version X (version 9) was in released 1985 as license-free software for public use. By 1988, the several companies that had combined to form the X Consortium at MIT had moved the development of this standard under the Open Group umbrella. Open Group presided over version 11, release 6.4 (X11R6.4), which was backward compatible with previous versions.

X Windows comes with the X Toolkit, a set of routines for graphics operations that developers could use with simple program calls. Within the toolkit are widget sets. Programmers can use standard toolkit routines along with the widget sets to build windowed interfaces into the applications that they create. Solaris comes with an enhanced version of the Athena widget set for 3D screen rendering (the original Athena widget set, which is widely used, is starkly ugly), as well as with the Motif and Tk widget sets. The Motif widget set makes applications run in windows that look a little like Windows 3.1. There are other widget sets that look like OpenStep and Windows 95, and toolkits like GTK have themes that emulate the look of the Macintosh, BeOS, Motif, and Windows. GIMP, a popular drawing program, uses GTK. Motif is commercial software and is used in applications like Navigator and WordPerfect; free Unix distributions like Linux tend to use other widget sets such as Lesstif.

It is the use of these toolkits and widget sets that makes X Windows–compatible applications look and feel the same regardless of what version of Unix they are run under. They also make it easier for users to apply what they know about X Windows programs running on one operating system to X Windows programs running on any other operating system. Indeed, that was the intent of the development effort. You can find X Windows emulators available for a very wide range of other operating systems, including Microsoft Windows and the Macintosh.

Some of the window managers are filled with enough features that they are referred to as desktop environments. The CDE is one such example. Other examples of desktop environments are KDE and GNOME. KDE is a semicommercial piece of software based on the qt toolkit. Version 2 has a less-restrictive license than version 1 had, but the fact that GNOME is an open-source and freeware implementation of a desktop environment has led to its adoption by many Linux vendors. GNOME is based on the GTK toolkit, and it is the standard on Linux distributions such as Red Hat Linux. GNOME comes with several full-featured applications and works with several window managers such as BlackBox, Enlightenment, SawMill, and WindowMaker. GNOME is under rather intense development in the Linux community at the moment.

Longtime Unix and Solaris users often feel that running from the command line without all of the extra resources that a GUI requires is the way to go. However, you will climb a very steep learning curve if you approach learning and using Solaris this way.

X Clients and Servers

X Window is software that runs on workstations and other clients in a client/server model typically on a network. *X Windows* defines a network protocol. Although a client/server network model is the preferred and common X Windows topology, there is no formal restriction and it is possible to have the X Window client running on the same machine as an X Window server. The concept behind the X Windows network protocol is that when X Windows is running as client and server on two different machines, the model used is somewhat different from the thin client/server model used in many applications today. X runs the application locally on a workstation (the server in X) and fetches the necessary display data from a central computer (the client in X) when required. The graphical presentation of data in windows on an X-terminal is rendered at the central computer. This is what allows you to have a single terminal, with graphical applications from multiple platforms displayed on your workstation screen. There are minimal network bandwidth requirements because the only data flowing over the wire between client and server is mouse and keyboard input on the X Window side and rasterized graphics rendered at the central computer, along with application data on both ends.

NOTE Bandwidth requirements should be minimal, but in fact with the way people are designing applications for X Windows, they are not. Running an X application over a network takes huge amounts of bandwidth. A good example of this would be to open two `xterm` sessions: one locally and one over a dial-up connection to another system. If you now telnet from the local `xterm` to the remote system, you will notice a speed difference between the local `xterm` with the telnet to the remote system and the `xterm` running from the remote system. The `xterm` running remotely will be noticeably slower. This is greatly exaggerated when you try to run a graphical application like Netscape Navigator or GIMP across a network.

X Windows was meant to work on Unix systems of all types and was most often applied to workstations. Over time, vendors created X-terminals specifically to run X Windows, which are "fat" terminals. A fat terminal has serious processing power and enough memory to store significant applications, so X-terminals are capable machines that are doing serious data processing. In many instances, X-terminals come with no diskette drive and minimal if any hard drives because the data is stored on a central computer. In the parlance of X Windows, X-terminals are *servers* and the application is the *client*. This is exactly opposite of the terminology used to describe the traditional client/server model, where the application processing occurs on a powerful central computer. This difference in the definition of the terminology of client and server causes most people a lot of confusion.

It gets worse. The term *server* is applied to the workstation or terminal in a network topology, but X Windows also calls the process running the X Window session an

X server. When you start an X Window System session, any application or utility program running on a workstation or X-terminal requesting services from the X server is a client. The window managers Desktop Window Manager (`dtwm`) and OpenLook Window Manager (`olwm`) are examples, as are applets like the X window clock (`xclock`) and the X-terminal application (`xterm`). If you open a terminal window in the CDE, you can't start another window manager because Solaris returns an X protocol error when there is already another window manager running. However, you can use `xterm` to start up an X-terminal window in your current X session, and from either the `xterm` window or the CDE terminal window, you can call up an applet like `xclock`.

X Sessions

The X Window System keeps track of displayed sessions by creating a unique ID for each X window. The global ID has the form `hostname:X-server:display-ID`, and for a local system, the `X-server:display-ID` portion is stored in the `<display>` environmental variable. The following graphic shows an `xterm` window displaying the hostname and display. When you open a window from another window, the secondary window owns the primary window. Thus the first `xterm` you open on your screen becomes the root window for the X application window opened using the first `xterm` window. In the following graphic, the `oclock` application owns the `xterm` window, and you cannot enter any other commands into the `xterm` window until you close the `oclock` application.

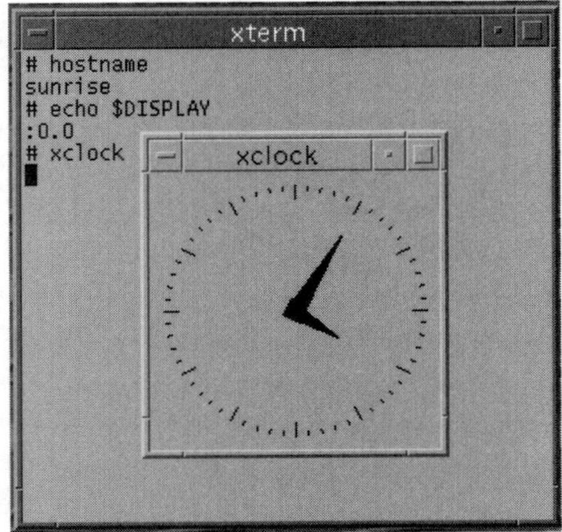

When you log in, you either log in to the CDE (dtwm) or OpenLook (olwm) window manager. If you log in to the command-line login prompt, perhaps for system maintenance, diagnostics, or some other reason, you can give either of these two commands (dtwm or olwm) to start one of these window managers. If you want to start up an X server all by itself because you have a yen to return to yesteryear or you must work with a Unix server other than Solaris, you can do so by entering the following command at the command-line login:

```
$ PATH=$PATH:/usr/openwin/bin
$ xinit
```

The X server appears as a screen without a window on your display, and it can't be modified in size or position. When you create another X-terminal window, it appears above the first one you created. You must exit from the second window to work again in the first X-terminal window. If you turn your system's power switch off, you will get a dialog box that asks if you want to either suspend your system state or shut down from X. After shutdown, Solaris returns you to the regular login screen to specify a session type.

Most of the time you use an X-terminal to access an X server, you will want to open the terminal window from within a window manager like the CDE. To do that, first open a terminal window from either the File Manager or from the This Host control on the Hosts subpanel of the front panel, then enter **xterm** at the command line. You can also open a console window using the Console command on the Hosts subpanel and enter the xterm command in that window as well.

X Windows is highly customizable and offers knowledgeable users the opportunity to work with powerful non-Sun systems in networked environments. However, most Solaris users don't spend much time using X Windows. For a full discussion of X Windows, consider reading one of the many books available on this environment.

X Applications

There are many applications that come with Solaris that run as X applications, and many more that you can obtain from a wide variety of sources. Additional X applications are found on the Solaris software disk, some are installed by your Sun hardware distributors, others are purchased from companies, and many others are downloadable from the Internet for purchase, as shareware, or free. The X Consortium is one source of X applications. It is even possible that you may obtain an X application developed in-house or eventually write one of your own. Whatever the source, you will find many of these applications useful. Table 7.10 lists some of the ones you should try and notes whether they are part of Solaris's distribution or not.

TABLE 7.10: X APPLICATIONS

Name	Solaris?	Purpose
`appres`	Y	Shows resource values of tools.
`bitmap`	Y	Creates bitmaps for icons and other purposes.
`calctool`	Y	Displays the Sun calculator.
`cm`	Y	Displays the Sun Calendar Manager.
`cmdtool`	Y	Opens the OpenLook terminal emulator or console.
`ddd`	N	Shows the `gdb` debugger window.
`dtcalc`	Y	Displays the CDE calculator.
`dtcm`	Y	Displays the CDE Calendar Manager.
`gimp`	N	GNU Image Manipulation Program for working with bitmapped images.
`gs`	N	GNU Postscript imaging engine. This program is used by ghostview and `gv`.
ImageMagick	N	Opens an image format converter.
Imagetool	Y	Displays the OpenLook image viewer for PS, GIF, TIFF, JPEG, and other image file formats.
`oclock`	Y	Displays a round analog clock.
`shelltool`	Y	Displays an OpenLook terminal emulator or console without scroll bars.
`showrgb`	Y	Displays color names in X.
`ups`	N	Opens the GUI debugger.
`wish`	N	Opens the Tcl/Tk interactive windowed shell.
`workman`	N	Plays audio CD-ROMs.
`xcalc`	Y	Displays a calculator.
`xclipboard`	Y	Provides scratch memory (a clipboard) for data transfer between applications.
`xclock`	Y	Displays an analog clock.
`Xedit`	N	Displays a text editor.
`xlsfonts`	Y	Lists all system fonts.
`xlswins`	Y	Lists the window tree for a specific window. The root window is the default.
`xmag`	Y	Magnifies an area that you select on your screen inside a window that it creates.
`xman`	Y	Opens the man pages in a text browser.
`xmodmap`	Y	Opens a utility for remapping your keyboard.
`xpdf`	N	Views Acrobat PDF files.

Continued

TABLE 7.10: X APPLICATIONS (CONTINUED)

Name	Solaris?	Purpose
`xprop`	Y	Shows window properties.
`xrdb`	Y	Loads resource settings into a database running on the system.
`xrn`	N	Opens a Usenet newsreader.
`xset`	N	Controls display, keyboard, and mouse settings.
`xsetroot`	Y	Modifies the characteristics of the root window.
`xterm`	Y	Opens a terminal window.
`xv`	N	Captures, displays, and modifies images.
`xvg/xmgr`	Y	Provide a graphing utility for Motif (`xmgr`) or OpenLook (`xvgr`).
`xwd`	Y	Captures a screen image for a window.
`xwininfo`	Y	Shows information about a window.

Summary

Solaris runs X Windows and provides two window managers called the Common Desktop Environment (CDE) and OpenWindows to provide a graphical user interface. The CDE environment is the standard Solaris desktop and window manager, and it is highly customizable. In the CDE, most applications appear in windows that contain menus for actions and commands.

In this chapter, I described the desktop, workspaces, windows, menus, and the File Manager and how to navigate and use these interface elements. The front panel is an application you can use to launch programs, utilities, and actions and modify your system in many ways. It is highly configurable. You can create actions that run scripts or provide command-line commands and install these actions in the front panel. The CDE provides a virtual graphical desktop that allows you to create and manage multiple desktops (or workspaces, as they are called).

I also discussed hotkeys, which provide a method to define actions that can be initiated with a single keystroke. You can create actions using a graphical utility and assign those actions to icons or controls on the front panel.

Finally, I included a discussion of the OpenWindows desktop, which is a part of the OpenLook initiative and is an alternative to the CDE. It is quite similar to the CDE but is a proprietary window manager. The X Window System was described along with various applications that run in X Windows and as X-terminals.

CHAPTER 8

Security

FEATURING:

Passwords and permissions **292**

Encryption **303**

E-mail security **305**

Firewalls **311**

Remote access security **315**

Login security **320**

Viruses **320**

No computer system in today's world is absolutely secure. If there are dial-in lines or if there is public access to terminals and the Internet, there are bound to be security breaches. This chapter will cover the main security issues of the day. It is impossible to cover each one in minute detail simply because every day new security issues crop up with alarming regularity. You will learn, however, to keep security a top priority when using Solaris 8.

Simple methods of establishing permissions, encrypting passwords, and restricting superuser privileges can make for a safer computing environment. How to secure your host and still get information to users, particularly those using remote access, will be discussed. E-mail security and Internet security are of paramount importance because most viruses and worms enter through those mediums. Hackers are quick to spot a weakness in a system and will use it to their advantage. How to be vigilant in spotting weaknesses will be a major point of the chapter. Physical considerations will also be discussed.

Permissions and Passwords

Security on Solaris 8 needs to be addressed on several different levels. A system connected to a network or with dial-in lines can never be completely secure. A typical user has to consider directories, login names, and passwords. A system administrator or superuser has the potential to create a quagmire if care is not taken in setting up a network and directories, handing out passwords and permissions, and dealing with the Internet. The superuser's password should be kept confidential at all times. If you are a superuser, never let anyone other than a supervisor know your password—and change it frequently.

Ordinary user passwords should also be changed frequently, and the system administrator should keep an up-to-date log of all changes. When choosing passwords, encourage users to mix cases and to use numbers as well as letters. Bear in mind that there are several programs that can crack passwords quite easily. These programs work by repeatedly encrypting words from dictionaries, names, phrases, and other sources. If the encrypted password matches the output of the program, then the program has found the password. Both `crack` and `cops` are programs that can detect passwords.

Make certain that no one except the superuser can write to files that are owned by root, which will be run in the `setuid` (set user ID) mode. It is a good practice to set the `-nosuid` flag to mount, which will cause the system to treat `setuid` programs on those file systems as regular programs. Add this option to the flags section in the `vfstab` file.

Group write permissions lower security for your files, so dole them out with caution. A free utility named `fix-modes` can be used to set all directories to more reasonable permissions. If you run this program, it will ask if you want to reset permissions.

Answer no to leave permissions in the more secure mode. If the `/etc` directory on your computer is writable by group, you will need to run `fix-modes`.

It is necessary to review your own security requirements frequently. The larger the site, the more frequent the reviews should be. There are many types of auditing mechanisms available. They are worth their weight in gold. External auditors are another option. They must have excellent references and credentials, however. Use a firewall if possible. It is one more layer of security on the Internet. The more you layer your security measures, the more difficult you make it for those with malicious intent. The risk assessment you provide for your site should clearly describe known vulnerabilities. Others may surface as time goes on. Imagine the worst-case scenario and have a disaster plan ready. Security policies will shift and change, as does technology itself, but the effort you put into it is more than worth it.

File Permissions

Files are accessible by their owner, a member of the group to which the owner belongs, and other system users. A user can access a file by reading from it, writing to it, or executing it, depending upon the permissions granted by the owner. The owner of the file has control over which users have permission to access it and how they can access it. Solaris lets you give users access to the files you want to share and yet keeps your private files confidential. You may decide to let some users only read from your files and let others write to them. You may decide that neither option is desirable and choose to protect files or entire directories from being accessed in any form.

The only exception to the access permissions you allow is that anyone who knows the root password can have full access to all files by logging in as the superuser or root. The superuser is usually the person designated as the system administrator. The superuser must have access to certain systemwide powers that the typical user never sees. The superuser is the person in charge of overall security and the administrative tasks that keep the system running at optimal performance. That person will make decisions that affect the overall system. With that responsibility comes the power to change or control some of the restrictions that apply to the general user. The system administrator or superuser can search and create directories and files as well as remove files from any directory. They automatically have read, write, and execute permission on all files, no matter who the owner is. They can change a user's password without knowing the old password. They can halt the system at any time.

TIP See the section "Access Permissions" in Chapter 5, "The File System," for a fuller discussion of the permissions the superuser has.

Because the superuser has the power to change so many things on the system, they also have the potential to do a great deal of harm if they make mistakes. A superuser should log in under their personal account name whenever they are doing routine file access tasks. This will cut down on the possibilities of erasing someone's work or inadvertently bringing down the system.

Standard Solaris file permissions are rather stringent and do not allow you to give file access to more than one group of people, nor do they allow you to give access to more than one person in a group. Access control lists (ACLs) were developed to give you control over who can access a file or directory on an individual basis. Using ACLs, you can give read, write, and execute access to as many users or groups as you wish. By default, an ACL gives everyone read access to a file. You can use the `chmod` utility to override the ACL permissions. This will be described more fully later.

TIP The options used for granting permissions are `r` for read, `w` for writes, and `x` for execute.

To designate permissions for an individual, you can use the `setfacl` utility, shown in Figure 8.1. For example, to give read and write permission to a user named Paula, you can use the following syntax. The `-m` option designates a modification of an existing ACL or creates a new one if one does not already exist:

```
$ setfacl -m o:rw- myfile
```

FIGURE 8.1

The `setfacl` *utility syntax*

Terminal

Window Edit Options Help

```
# setfacl
usage:
        setfacl [-r] -f aclfile file ...
        setfacl [-r] -d acl_entries file ...
        setfacl [-r] -m acl_entries file ...
        setfacl [-r] -s acl_entries file ...
#
```

ACLs may or may not work, depending upon your operating system, the network file system, and your remote host. ACLs work with the Network File System (NFS) on any Solaris system over 2.5. File security can be controlled by keeping a comprehensive list of ACL permissions. Be sure to record any changes made when using the chmod (change mode) utility. This utility will override ACL permissions if the chmod permissions are restrictive. For example, if you wanted to remove the write capability from the user Paula, you would use the following syntax:

```
$ setfacl -m u:paula:r myfile
```

The chmod utility is a powerful tool that changes the ways in which a file can be accessed. It uses an absolute or symbolic expression to specify the access mode. Tables 8.1 and 8.2 describe the absolute and symbolic expressions and their meanings when chmod is used to change access permissions.

TABLE 8.1: SYMBOLIC CLASSES OF USERS

Letter	Class	Meaning
u	user	Owner of the file
g	group	Group to which the owner belongs
o	others	All other users
a	all	Users and groups, replaces ugo

TABLE 8.2: SYMBOLIC OPERATORS

Symbol	Meaning
+	Add permission for the user class.
-	Remove permission for the user class.
=	Set permission for the user; reset all other permissions for the user class.
r	Set read permission.
w	Set write permission.
x	Set execute permission.
l	Enable mandatory locking.
s	Give the setuid or setgid permission to the owner of the file being executed or to the group the owner belongs to.
t	Set the sticky bit for the superuser only.
u	Match the permissions you are setting with the owners.
g	Match the permissions you are setting with the groups.
o	Match the permissions you are setting with the others.

Absolute octal numbers can also be used to represent the access permissions for a file. If you want to give full permissions to the owner, for example, you would add all the numbers for the owner to get read, write, and execute permissions (700). Table 8.3 displays the absolute numbers for changing access permissions.

TABLE 8.3: ABSOLUTE NUMBERS FOR CHANGING ACCESS PERMISSIONS

Number	Meaning
4000	`setuid` is run when program is executed.
20*n*0	`setgid` is run when program is executed with *n* when *n* is 7, 5, 3, or 1. If *n* is 6,4,2, or 0, it enables mandatory locking.
1000	Indicates a sticky bit.
0400	Owner can read the file.
0200	Owner can write to the file.
0100	Owner can execute the file.
0040	Group can read the file.
0020	Group can write to the file.
0010	Group can execute the file.
0004	Others can read the file.
0002	Others can write to the file.
0001	Others can execute the file.
7000	Sets all sticky bits or SUID/SGID depending on whether it is a directory or a file.
0700	Allow read, write, and execute (search) by owner.
0070	Allow read, write, and execute (search) by group.
0007	Allow read, write, and execute (search) by others.

TIP You can use the `ls` utility with any file to see what permissions have been granted, although you have to use `getfacl` to see the ACLs.

setuid and *setgid* Permissions

The `setuid` permission allows the executing file to take on the privileges of the file's owner. If you run a `setuid` program that removes a file in a directory, you can also remove the file in any of the owner's directories even though you do not have express permission to do so. The setgid permission acts in a similar fashion when executing the file. It will take on the privileges of the group that the file belongs to. Because of their potential to do more harm than good, it is clear that these permissions are best handled by the system administrator.

NOTE The setuid and setgid permissions were covered in more detail in Chapter 5.

Extreme caution must be taken when using the setuid and setgid programs. The ls utility will display setuid permission as an s in the owner's executable position. setgid will also display as an s in the group's executable position.

Many companies do not allow these permissions to be used at their sites because of the possibilities of inadvertent mishaps. For the really security conscious, you can remove the setuid bit from most setuid programs shipped with Solaris 8 without affecting the correct operation of the system.

WARNING Shell scripts should never be written with setuid. They can easily be subverted, so for security reasons, it is better to avoid them.

Directory Access Permissions

Access permissions are somewhat different when used with directories. Although all three types of users can read from and write to directories, a directory cannot be executed. The execute access permission has a new definition for a directory. It allows you to use the cd command on a directory to examine files if you also have read permission. Obviously, you cannot execute a directory; you can, however, use ls to list a file in the directory if you know its name. The ls command can be used with an argument to list the contents of the directory. However, if you are *in* a directory and want to see a list of its contents, a simple ls will produce the desired effect. You can view the access permissions for a directory by running ls with the -d and -l options. When you run the ls utility, the permissions will begin with a *d* on the left if a directory is accessed.

Link Permissions

Links are special pointers to files that can be shared. They are important to file security because they provide another layer of protection should a user inadvertently delete a file. When the pointer to the file is deleted, the original file is still intact, but only if you have used a hard link, not a soft link.

If you need to share information with others, you can create links to the files after first giving read and write permission to the users who will share them. If security is a problem, consider very carefully what permissions are granted. You may also have to use chmod to change permissions of the parent directory so that everyone has the access they need. Once that is done, the user can create a link to the file so that everyone has access from their separate directories. Any changes you make to the file will affect others linked to the same file. Think this through carefully.

Linking is also useful if you have a large directory hierarchy. You can link to individual files that have a common theme. Figure 8.2 shows how related files can be linked. It does not show the inode, however.

FIGURE 8.2

The long list of a set of hierarchical file links

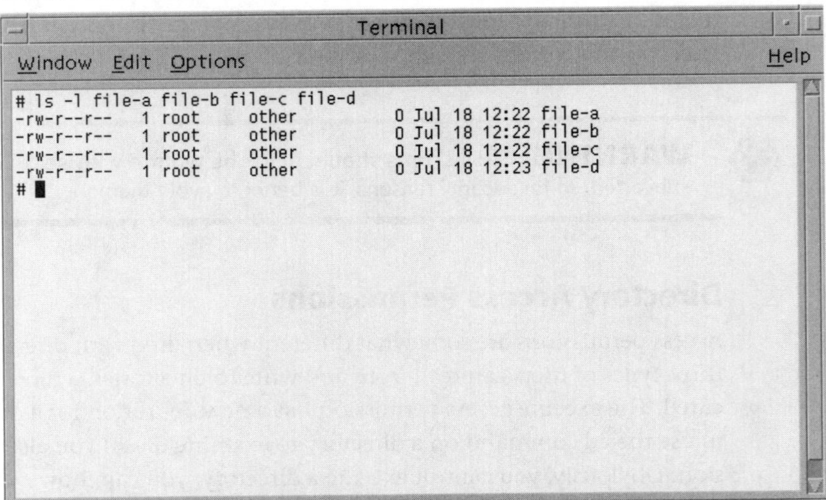

There are two distinct types of links: hard links and soft (symbolic) links. Hard links are an older, somewhat outdated method of linking. Soft links are now used more frequently. Soft links are indirect pointers to a file and contain the path name of the file to which they point. Because hard links have several limitations, soft links were developed to broaden the scope of linking. Solaris usually has several file systems in its file hierarchy and they have separate inode tables, so you cannot have hard links to files in different file systems. Hard links can be used among files in your own directories and anywhere else within the partition without creating problems.

They all have equal status. A symbolic link can point to a nonexistent file. This can be helpful if you link to a file that gets re-created and removed periodically, such as files created by the C compiler. Symbolic links have their own limitations, such as not having equal status, which will be discussed further later in this chapter. You should also note that the symbolic link does not protect against a file being deleted.

The `ln` utility is used to create a new link to an existing file. You must give a new filename to the new file if it appears in the same directory as the file it links to. The syntax for the `ln` utility is as follows:

```
ln <options> oldfile newfile
```

Figure 8.3 shows how the `ln` utility creates an additional pointer to an existing file. Keep in mind that it does not make another copy of the file, so the file status information is the same for all links. The name will be different, however. If you want to make a copy of the file, you can use the `cp` utility instead of `ln`. If you change a copy of a file, the files will be different. You can use `ls` with the `-i` option with the names of the files when you want to compare them to see if the status information is the same for linked files. It will also display differently for files that are not linked. The following example displays the syntax and output for the `-i` option:

```
$ touch file-a file-b
$ ln file-a file-c
$ ln file-a file-d
$ ls -li file*
    140443 -rw-r--r--   3 guest staff      0 Jun  5 23:48 file-a
    140471 -rw-r--r--   1 guest staff      0 Jun  5 23:48 file-b
    140443 -rw-r--r--   3 guest staff      0 Jun  5 23:48 file-c
    140443 -rw-r--r--   3 guest staff      0 Jun  5 23:48 file-d
$ chmod 0777 file-d
$ ls -li file*
    140443 -rwxrwxrwx   3 guest staff      0 Jun  5 23:48 file-a
    140471 -rw-r--r--   1 guest staff      0 Jun  5 23:48 file-b
    140443 -rwxrwxrwx   3 guest staff      0 Jun  5 23:48 file-c
    140443 -rwxrwxrwx   3 guest staff      0 Jun  5 23:48 file-d
$
```

NOTE See the section "Links" in Chapter 5 for more information on this topic.

FIGURE 8.3

The `ln` command can be used to create a pointer to an existing file.

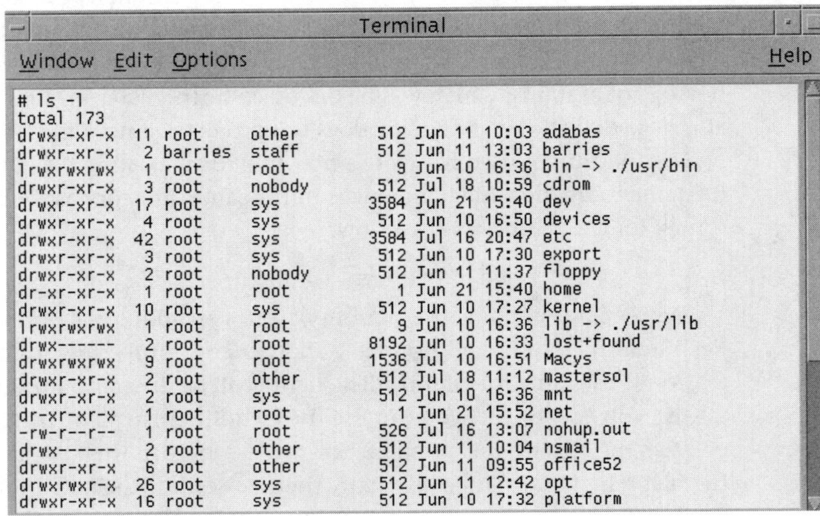

Terminal
Window Edit Options Help
ls -l
total 173
drwxr-xr-x 11 root other 512 Jun 11 10:03 adabas
drwxr-xr-x 2 barries staff 512 Jun 11 13:03 barries
lrwxrwxrwx 1 root root 9 Jun 10 16:36 bin -> ./usr/bin
drwxr-xr-x 3 root nobody 512 Jul 18 10:59 cdrom
drwxr-xr-x 17 root sys 3584 Jun 21 15:40 dev
drwxr-xr-x 4 root sys 512 Jun 10 16:50 devices
drwxr-xr-x 42 root sys 3584 Jul 16 20:47 etc
drwxr-xr-x 3 root sys 512 Jun 10 17:30 export
drwxr-xr-x 2 root nobody 512 Jun 11 11:37 floppy
dr-xr-xr-x 1 root root 1 Jun 21 15:40 home
drwxr-xr-x 10 root sys 512 Jun 10 17:27 kernel
lrwxrwxrwx 1 root root 9 Jun 10 16:36 lib -> ./usr/lib
drwx------ 2 root root 8192 Jun 10 16:33 lost+found
drwxrwxrwx 9 root root 1536 Jul 10 16:51 Macys
drwxr-xr-x 2 root other 512 Jul 18 11:12 mastersol
drwxr-xr-x 2 root sys 512 Jun 10 16:36 mnt
dr-xr-xr-x 1 root root 1 Jun 21 15:52 net
-rw-r--r-- 1 root root 526 Jul 16 13:07 nohup.out
drwx------ 2 root other 512 Jun 11 10:04 nsmail
drwxr-xr-x 6 root other 512 Jun 11 09:55 office52
drwxrwxr-x 26 root sys 512 Jun 11 12:42 opt
drwxr-xr-x 16 root sys 512 Jun 10 17:32 platform

Although `ls` by itself does not tell you exactly that files are linked to one another, using it with the `-i` option will. This option lists the inode number for each file and shows clearly that files are linked because they share the same number. If two files have the same inode number, they share the control structure and are linked to the same file. If you find that two files have different inode numbers, then they are completely different files.

The following example shows the syntax and output for the `-i` option:

```
$ ls -i file_1 file_2 file_3 file_4
4747 file_1    4747 file_2 5655 file_3 8327 file_4
```

All links to a file are of equal value. The operating system does not distinguish in what order links are created. If there is more than one hard link to a file, you can remove all but one and still be able to link through that one remaining link. The links shown in the preceding example are examples of hard links.

More About Symbolic Links

When creating symbolic links, use `ln` with the `-s` option. This will create an indirect pointer to the file you want to link to. The syntax and output for creating a typical symbolic link is shown in the following example:

```
$ ln -s myfile /tempfile/s2
$ ls -l myfile /tempfile/s2
```

```
-rw-r--r-- 1 user2  ourfiles 747 April 12 11:35 myfile
lrwxrwxrwx 1 user2  ourfiles  7 April 12 11:38 /tempfile/s2 ->
   myfile
```

As you will note, file sizes and modification dates are different for these two files. The status information is also different. The l in the line of output indicates a link.

You can use this same type of command to create a symbolic link to a directory. If you use the -s option, the system interprets it for either a file or a directory. You can change directories if you use a symbolic link as an argument to the cd utility. Be careful, however, because it is easy to get confused, especially if you do not realize you are using a symbolic link. The security of your files depends upon carefully thought-out linking because links provide access to files that you might not realize exist if you don't pay attention.

When you are in either the Bourne shell or the C shell, you can use cd to change directories to find a symbolic link to a directory. The pwd (parent working directory) command displays the name of the original directory and not the linked directory. If you use cd to change your working directory to the parent directory, you will be in the parent of the *original* directory, not the parent of the linked directory. This can create confusion if you do not understand how it works.

Korn Shell Linked Directories

The Korn shell handles symbolically linked directories differently than the Bourne and C shells handle them. It will keep track of the symbolic links when using cd to move into a linked directory and when moving back to the parent of that directory. You can tell where you really are by using /usr/bin/pwd. The pwd built-in on ksh will show you where you are according to the symbolic link:

```
$ mkdir foo; ln -s foo bar
$ ls -la foo bar
drwxr-xr-x   2 guest staff       512 Jun  6 00:03 foobar
lrwxrwxrwx   1 guest staff         6 Jun  6 00:03 nit -> foobar
$ cd bar
$ pwd
/usr/people/guest/nit
$ /usr/bin/pwd
/usr/people/guest/foobar
$
```

Because the pwd command does not identify the symbolic link, the C shell will provide the $cwd (current working directory) variable that contains the name of the symbolic link you used to access the working directory. If you did not use a symbolic link, it will provide the name of the hard link to the files. If you want to display the value of the cwd variable, use echo followed by a space and the variable name preceded by a dollar sign, as shown in the following example:

```
% pwd
/user1/tempfile/myfile
% echo $cwd
/user1/myfile
% ls -l /user1/myfile
lrwxrwxrwx  1 root root  13 Apr 12 12:14 /user1/myfile ->
  ./tempfile/myfile
```

To remove a hard link, you can delete the file or use the rm utility. Once you remove the last hard link to a file, you can no longer access that file's information. The system will free up space for other files. The space is released even though there may be other remaining symbolic links. If, however, you have more than one hard link to a file, you can remove one and still access the file from the remaining link. Once all hard links are removed, you cannot access the file through symbolic links. Table 8.4 displays the utilities commonly used with linking files.

TIP If you remove a hard link, you must remember to remove all symbolic links in the same way you remove other files.

TABLE 8.4: UTILITIES USED WITH LINKING

Utility	Function
cd	Changes working directory
chmod	Changes access permissions on a file or directory
$cwd	Contains the path name of the current working directory in C shell
ln	Links to a file in a directory
mkdir	Creates a directory
pwd	Displays the path name of the working directory
rmdir	Deletes a directory

Encryption

One level of security is encryption. It gives you the means to scramble data in your files using a key made up of a password or a certain phrase. Only those knowing the special key can decrypt the data. There are a lot of good encryption software products in today's market. They employ different encryption algorithms, some that can be broken easily and some that would take a lifetime to figure out. Developing your own encryption software is a tedious chore. Solaris has a utility named `crypt`, but it dates back to World War II technology. It is easily broken. To be absolutely certain they have top-notch security, most companies use a software program that has been tried and tested for some time. Although it is impossible to know that any algorithm is 100-percent secure, programs that have been tested for a good length of time in the public sector are a fairly safe bet.

The key to an encryption algorithm is more bits. If you keep adding bits to the length of a key, it makes it harder and harder for a malicious attacker to decrypt your algorithm. Security is not based on the length of an algorithm alone, however. Some shorter algorithms may be more secure than longer ones, depending upon the initial design. But length does matter.

There are two basic types of encryption. One is called public key encryption and the other is called private key encryption. Public key encryption is also referred to as asymmetric encryption and uses two different keys. A private key, or symmetric, encryption uses only one key known to only you and the person you are communicating with. You both keep this a secret. Public key encryption is usually in the 512-to-2048-bit range. Private key algorithms have keys typically in the 64-to-512-bit range. There is a third, not as commonly used, type of encryption called a one-time pad in which the key is the same length as the text to be encrypted. This type of encryption is very difficult to generate and distribute, hence its availability is limited. It has a random number that is mixed with the text by using an exclusive `OR`. This feature makes it virtually impossible for anyone to guess the key or short-circuit the algorithm.

You must generate two keys in order to use public key encryption. You keep one key and the other key is given to the public. If you then encrypt something with someone's public key, that person alone can decrypt it using their private key. However, when you encrypt something with your private key, anybody else can decrypt it with your public key. This feature acts as a signature. Anyone in the public knows that only you could have encrypted it with your private key. Although this may seem like an ideal situation, there are certain weak points. The algorithms designed for public key encryption are usually much slower to run than private key algorithms. Key sizes are much larger and large prime numbers need to be generated as components for the key, thereby slowing it down considerably. In addition, it is not always easy to authenticate the key. How do you prove where it came from? A 512-bit key is considered fairly weak, offering minimum protection. The 1024-bit keys are more dependable and will fend off attackers for some time yet.

The fastest way to encrypt is with secret key encryption. This occurs when you and another party agree upon the algorithm to use and create keys that you both share. This allows either of you to decrypt or encrypt a file using the same key. Secret key encryption algorithms are usually implemented as a network of black boxes. These can be hardware or software and sometimes a combination of both. Each box changes the input data to a form that can be reversed and then passes it on to the next box. It is difficult to determine which box was used and how many times the data passes through all of the boxes. Algorithms will pass data through the boxes many times without any obvious mapping from input data to output data, making it difficult to crack. The biggest problem with this method of encryption is that you must have a secure channel over which to share your key. Media such as e-mail and the telephone are surely not secure. Most people use implementations such as DES, 3DES, Blowfish, IDEA, and others. The oldest is DES, which is available only in the U.S., Canada, and Mexico. It is distributed with Solaris. Countries outside of North America have used the DES algorithm by re-implementing it with code taken from published papers. It is fairly safe to use when you e-mail or send simple correspondence. It can be broken, but at great time and expense.

Companies that make commercial software packages diligently try to use the best features of both private and public key encryption algorithms to produce products that the public will buy and use. Most use the public key algorithm first to negotiate a randomly generated secret key and to provide authenticity. They then employ a secret key algorithm such as 3DES, IDEA, or Blowfish to encrypt and decrypt the data on both ends, mainly for speed.

Some operating systems such as DOS or Microsoft Windows have virtually no file security. Solaris 8 provides some file security that is built into the operating system. Access control lists (ACLs) and commands such as `chmod` give limited access to files that you own. To provide maximum security for your files, you should have a good encryption program. It is a small price to pay for very large benefits.

One of the most popular encryption programs is PGP, or Pretty Good Privacy. It is available as a free package from Network Associates, Inc. for personal or educational use only. It has several encryption algorithms that have passed the test of time. Its default algorithm, IDEA, uses a 128-bit key and appears to be very secure. The premise of PGP is that trust is a three-way street. If you trust someone and they in turn trust someone else, the person that you trust can serve to introduce you to the third party. You perform an operation called key signing. When you sign someone else's key, you let PGP verify that person's public key and then it is safe for you to use to send them e-mail. Once you sign a key, PGP asks whether you trust this person to introduce another person's keys to you.

It is your option as to whether you assign trust to that person. The obvious cautions should be taken so that you really can "trust" that third person.

E-Mail Security

There are several tools available to help you keep your e-mail secure. Some of them are described in this section and you may find that one or more are what you have been looking for. E-mail security is a topic that requires a book in and of itself. We can touch on the highlights, but a comprehensive discussion is beyond the scope of this book.

PGP is also frequently used to help ensure e-mail security. You can also try PEM (privacy enhanced mail), which is a standard instead of software that uses an algorithm. RIPEM (Riordan's Internet Privacy Enhanced Mail) is similar to PEM and uses the RSA public key encryption toolkit (`www.rsa.com/rsalabs/index.html`). It is also available outside of the United States.

Simple Mail Transfer Protocol (SMTP), the most prominent Internet mail transfer protocol, is used to transfer electronic mail on the Internet. This protocol allows servers to exchange mail with each other on a one-to-one basis. SMTP is a communication method that enables sendmail as well as other mail transport agents such as qmail to accept connections and talk to each other in a common language. An administrator can actually test sendmail manually by telnetting to port 25 and issuing SMTP commands directly. To discourage tampering, sendmail limits the headers of each mail message to a maximum of 32 kilobytes. When a host wants to transfer a message to another server, the first server will identify the recipient of the mail to the second server and the second server will then acknowledge receipt and check to see if the user exists. If no local user matches, the acknowledgment message will say so. If the user is legitimate, the message is transmitted and the acknowledgment runs a receipt number. The first server will then request a disconnection and the second server will disconnect. There are three-digit code numbers that indicate what an acknowledgment means. For example, code 250 indicates a successful command, and code 551 indicates that a user is not local.

There are several standard SMTP commands:

DATA Precedes the body of the message

EXPN Expands local mailing lists

HELO Identifies the sending host to the receiving host

MAIL Identifies the remote user to the receiving host

RCPT Indicates the local user to whom the mail is to be delivered

QUIT Ends a session

VRFY Checks to see if the local user is known to mail system

To initiate a message transfer from a client machine to a user on another host computer, use the following:

```
Client% telnet mail.serverB.com 25
```

After connection, if you type **help**, you will receive a listing of SMTP commands that can be used to transfer mail interactively if the system administrator has not disabled this function. Use a combination of the previously listed commands to actually transmit messages successfully. A mail message contains a history of its delivery process in the headers that precede the message. Here are some common headers:

Content-Length Number of lines in the message body

Content-Type The MIME type in which the message is encoded

Date Time and date message is received

From The sender and the date and time the mail was sent

Message-ID Unique number generated by the sending host

Received How mail was received by the mail transport agent (MTA) on the server

Subject Subject of mail message

Most Content-Type listings in a header will be text. However, it is possible to send binary data by using one of the many binary encoding methods, including Multipurpose Internet Mail Extension (MIME). MIME is useful for sending multimedia files without being concerned about encoding. Because most multimedia files are binary and message bodies are transmitted as text, MIME encodes them as text and sends them as normal messages. MIME also supports the notion of multipart messages. A single e-mail message may contain more than one encoded file. You can send a number of documents to another user. And MIME supports languages that are encoded in ASCII but that need to be displayed in another language or character set. MIME will display a Content-Type header that specifies a character set or other data type for an e-mail message.

The most widely deployed MTA in use is sendmail. It is the standard and default mail transport agent supported by Solaris. It relies on a single configuration file (`sendmail.cf`). This file contains sets of rules that determine how e-mail is to be sent and which mailer is to be used for local or remote delivery. They determine the mechanism by which messages are delivered and how e-mail addresses may be rewritten to ensure accurate delivery. The sendmail MTA also ensures that the virtual envelopes that contain e-mail messages are addressed correctly. It inserts header information that identifies senders and recipients. It is difficult to configure and test sendmail because just one error in the rules can render it useless. It also has many security issues. Because of the security problems associated with sendmail, developers have tried to produce alternate systems such as qmail. Although no MTA is without problems, when a bug is discovered, a patch is usually soon available to fix it. For example, the buffer overflows have been a thorn in sendmail's side for some time. The buffer overflows allow remote users to execute arbitrary commands on a server that runs sendmail. Unix applications written in the C language have had this overflow problem whenever proper bounds checking on array sizes is not implemented. It was thought that the long MIME headers could be used to invite attacks. A patch was promptly developed that detected and denied any messages that might be associated with an outside attack.

To help configure sendmail (`sendmail.cf`), there are single-line commands, which can consist of rules and macros and/or options and headers. Rules can appear many times yet some of the commands can appear only once, particularly if they specify a directive that affects the interpretation of rules. The different commands are listed in Table 8.5; they will help you to understand how sendmail is configured.

TABLE 8.5: SENDMAIL COMMANDS

Command	Description
C	Specifies a macro, which may or may not contain more than one item
D	Specifies a macro such as `D{Domain}mail.bag.com`
E	Specifies an environmental variable set by the `sendmail.cf` file
H	Specifies a header that be simple or complex
M	Specifies the mail delivery agent
O	Specifies an option such as sending MIME error messages
P	Sets message precedence for mail with `Pfirst-class=0` as the priority
R	Specifies a rule
S	Indicates the start of a ruleset
S0	Monitors basic address parsing
S1	Processes the e-mail sender's address
S2	Processes the e-mail recipient's address
S3	Performs name canonicalization and initiates the rewriting rules
S4	Performs the final output post rewriting, including conversions
S5	Sets ruleset after all aliases are expanded

Several specifiers are user defined in rulesets from S6 and above. For example, `$-` matches a single token and `$*` matches any number of tokens, including zero. Because rule writing is a complex task, many administrators find it easy to use

Webmin, which is available at www.webmin.com/webmin/. It is a free Web-based interface for Solaris system administration. You can use any browser that supports tables and forms and employ Webmin's sendmail configuration module. It will allow you to manage sendmail aliases, masquerading, address rewriting, and other features.

Because sendmail does have security problems, you may choose to download and install the newest sendmail distribution from the Web site (www.sendmail.org). Here is the syntax for starting sendmail using its startup script (the user should read the script to see how the application is actually started):

```
/etc/init.d/sendmail start
```

And here is the syntax for stopping sendmail:

```
/etc/init.d/sendmail stop
```

A typical Solaris user will have an e-mail address. Occasionally, there are situations in which a user may not have a user account. There are also aliases that might require application programs and daemons instead of a particular individual as contacts. Typically, the programs and daemons will be forwarded to the user account of an individual who has the responsibility of being the contact at some given time. Sendmail maintains an administrative database of e-mail aliases. This allows a user to be logically different from actual Solaris users. Aliases or a package such as majordomo can be used for creating mailing lists. A user can have several aliases so that they can receive mail under several names. You should remember that you must run the `newaliases` command after making any changes to the `/etc/aliases` database (or to `/etc/mail/aliases` for newer versions of sendmail) if you want the new aliases to be up-to-date.

Local mail clients have online access to Solaris commands, which include `.forward` and `vacation`. Remote clients are GUI based and mail can be easier to use with either the POP or IMAP protocols when communicating with the user's mail spool.

The Post Office Protocol (POP) is a client/server protocol that supports offline mail delivery to remote clients when mail addressed to a user account is delivered to a centralized mail server. POP has many useful features, such as the ability to retain copies of e-mail on the server while transmitting a copy to the client. This form of reliability is advantageous when a system crashes. All the user's mail is retained as copies. A client machine makes a TCP connection to port 110. After greeting the server, the client receives an acknowledgement and then continues a session until it is terminated. The user will be authenticated and then may begin conducting transactions in the form of retrieving messages. Once the `QUIT` command is received by the server, the session is terminated. Errors are indicated by status codes. The `-ERR` code indicates negative responses and `+OK` indicates positive responses. POP is similar to SMTP in its commands and operations, giving system administrators the opportunity to use their skills in configuring the two systems. POP, however, is not noted for its security. Even though users are authenticated with their username and password on the server, the information is not encrypted. Anyone can retrieve the username and password by simply snooping around. They could then log in to the mail server as the mail user and go undetected for a good long time, in most cases. The username and password need to have an authentication wrapper such as SRP.

The Internet Message Access Protocol (IMAP) was developed to replace POP. IMAP is primarily meant for remote clients and can perform offline processing. It retains features of online processing such as `mailx` and `elm`. A remote MTA using IMAP has the capability to perform sophisticated transactions. Whereas POP retrieves all new messages on the server and passes them to the client, IMAP will take requests for just headers, or message bodies, or both. A search can be made also for messages that match certain criteria. POP can perform these operations on local copies of mail messages; IMAP, however, can perform them on a remote server. IMAP messages can also be flagged if they have not been replied to. IMAP also employs a synchronization feature that matches mailbox contents on the server. This ensures that no data corruption occurs due to errors on the client machine. IMAP offers different features than POP and may be the best choice security-wise.

There is also a supply of free mail user agents that have hooks for encryption programs. The `privtool` utility is similar to Sun's `mailtool`. It is equipped with an interface to PGP. There are also PGP-extended versions of the `elm` (e-local mail) freeware mailer. Because `elm` is a freeware package, it has become very popular to use. It supports advanced features such as MIME and DSN (Dependable Systems Networks). It can operate in beginner mode as well as intermediate and advanced modes. The interface with `elm` is very simple. You can access most commands by typing single letters from the main menu. (Table 8.6 includes some typical commands issued for `elm`.) The syntax for accessing elm is as follows:

```
client% elm
```

TABLE 8.6: TYPICAL *ELM* COMMANDS

Command	Description
|	Pipe message through user-defined command.
?	Get help for `elm`.
?<*pattern*>	Search for pattern in message.
!	Execute a shell process.
<*n*>	Set current message number to *n*.
a	Create an alias in the address book for current message sender.

Continued

TABLE 8.6: TYPICAL *ELM* COMMANDS (CONTINUED)

Command	Description
b	Bounce current message to user.
c	Change to a folder other than the inbox folder.
d	Delete the current message from inbox.
f	Forward current message to another user.
m	Create a new mail message.
p	Print current message.
q	Quit elm and save changes to inbox.
s	Save current message.
u	Undelete message marked for deletion.
x	Exit without saving changes.

The elm program uses the vi editor when editing messages. You can set the editor to emacs or pico by editing the defaults in the elmrc configuration file.

A signature is usually included at the bottom of every message that contains contact details. This is kept in ~/.signature. It enables readers to identify you and your organization. The elm program also has the ability to attach a different signature to messages addressed to either local or remote users.

PGP macros are available that allow you to send and receive encrypted email from emacs. Remote users may also use Netscape mail (www.netscape.com) or the Eudora mail client (www.eudora.com), both of which are free. Once Netscape mail software is installed, the user preferences, which impose their own security parameters, are set. In the section called Mail & Newsgroups, users need to set up contact information such as e-mail address, organization, and so on. The POP settings are then configured in the Preferences dialog box (choose Preferences from the Edit menu). The best way to learn about Netscape is to begin exploring. There are security features on the home page. The home page you are viewing with the Netscape browser is displayed in the Content area. The Menu toolbar at the top of the screen has a Help menu on the right-hand side. The thing to note about the Netscape software is that there is a security icon (looks like a lock) on the menu of the home page. This is where you establish passwords and configure the Navigator Messenger. It lets you set up certificates for yourself and other people. You can record the POP server name along with the instructions to remember the remote password and set a time for the mail to be picked up. Mail can be left on the server or stored on the local file system, depending upon your preference.

When the Netscape mail client is opened, it will display a user interface that shows the supported mailboxes on the left: the inbox, unsent mail, drafts, templates, sent mail, and a trash folder. Messages can be ordered by priority level, subject, sender, or date. Although no system can be completely secure, you can reduce the chances of malicious interference by observing common rules regarding e-mail and the Internet.

Firewalls

The use of a firewall in today's high technology environment is almost mandatory. Installing a firewall between your network and the Internet is one of the most important tasks you will perform. Firewalls help to keep problems isolated within one area. They keep them from spreading into other networks or your LAN. The actual mechanisms that are used to block traffic or allow it can be simple packet filters, which make their decisions based on the contents of the packet heard, or they can be even more complex application proxies, which stand between the client and the outside world.

Many think of a firewall as a singe device, but the firewall is actually a system of components that sit between your network and the outside world. The firewall provides a barrier, similar to a firewall in a building that prevents fire from spreading. Firewalls have changed considerably in the last five years and offer other amenities not necessarily related to security. Most are capable of caching and can store frequently accessed data locally. This saves time on the Internet. You can restrict the kinds of information that users are allowed to access on the Internet. Incoming data packets can be examined for keywords and objectionable URLs can be blocked. Most new firewalls allow address vectoring (also known as redirection), which enables the firewall to modify requests and send them to hosts using a different address than that found in the request packet. It gives the appearance of being a single host to users on the Internet and also allows servers that are using nonroutable Internet addresses to service requests from the Internet.

Even if you run a very small company, you need to establish a security policy and decide what the firewall will let through. When you decide upon a list of services that you think will benefit your company, you need to look at each service and estimate whether there is a secure form of the client or server application that is required for each service. Will the manner in which you use the service open up any possible security holes in your LAN? After you review the security issues, you can develop a firewall policy. There are two basic methods that the firewall can be used for to implement a policy:

- Permit any access unless it has specifically been denied by the rules.
- Deny any access unless it has specifically been allowed by the rules.

The best approach in most instances is to use the second method. It is always easier to specify a small list of what you will allow as opposed to a much larger list of what you will not allow. It is also easier to add new services than to take away those that employees have grown accustomed to. In this way, you'll remain secure from new developments until you've had time to review the security issues that arise.

Earlier firewalls depended upon packet filtering to protect a network from the Internet. Routers were configured to allow or deny packets from passing through based on rules created by the administrator. Routers looked only at the header information in an IP packet. A simple packet filter can be configured to allow or disallow the use of FTP but not be used to allow or disallow specific functions of FTP, such as using the PUT and GET commands.

Newer firewalls employ an application gateway or application proxy that is a software program that intercepts user requests from the local network and then makes a connection for the user to the server residing outside your LAN. The internal user never makes a connection directly to the outside service. The application proxy program is the middleman and talks to the client and server. It relays application information between them. It can be programmed to allow or deny traffic based on information contained in the payload section of the packet, not just the header information. The application proxy actually understands the fundamental communication methods used by a specific service. It can be programmed to allow or deny features of the service. It does not just block the communication based on the port, as a packet filter would do.

Whether you decide to build or buy a firewall, and whether it will be hardware or software, you need to have the protection of one in some form or another. If you want to create a secure channel that can communicate with a remote office, you may want to use a dedicated leased line or dial-up line. With the Internet already providing a quick path between most points, for a very small fee, why not consider using it? Although a dedicated leased line and a dial-up line do provide more security, the Internet provides speed. Products such as PGP (mentioned earlier) can be used to send e-mail and attachments over the Internet with protection that is tough to defeat. For Web pages, Secure Sockets Layer (SSL) can be used for exchanging confidential information. It's worth noting is that Sun provides the light version of its firewall SunScreen for free to users of Solaris 8 (x86 or SPARC) as a download from its Web site.

Security and the Superuser

Most organizations designate one person to be the system administrator. The system administrator quite naturally has access to programs and functions not required by the average user. As discussed earlier, the system administrator is also called the superuser on Solaris. Anyone can become superuser if they have access to the correct password.

Once the system is up and running in single-user mode, if you supply the correct password, you will be superuser. If the system comes up in multiuser mode, you can log in as root, and again, if you have the correct password, you can be superuser. You can also give the su command while you are logged in as yourself. If you know the appropriate password, you will have superuser privileges.

TIP If you use the official system version of su, always specify su's absolute path name, such as /usr/bin/su, when you use it.

Many of the commands used by superuser are kept in the /usr/bin directory. You can execute these commands by giving their full path names on the command line or by including the /usr/bin directory in your PATH when you are logged in as superuser.

You can also make changes to the console line in the /etc/default/login file and control where root is allowed to log directly in to. No matter what is in this file, you can log in on the machine as an ordinary user and then use su to become root. This is a good setup for computers that are accessible to the public. With no root login available on the console, it will not matter if your machine is accessible. No one will be able to log in to the root account from the console. You will have to have a valid account on the computer before you can attempt to obtain superuser privileges. Change the line that begins with CONSOLE to read as follows:

```
# root cannot login directly on any device
CONSOLE =
```

If you are going to allow root to log in directly on the console, edit the /etc/default/login file and make sure the line beginning with CONSOLE is not commented out, as in the following example:

```
# root can log in on console
# CONSOLE=/dev/console
```

If the machine is in a server room or a locked space where only trusted people have access to it, this type of access is permissible. However, even a server room should have additional physical security such as locked doors with coded key pads.

WARNING Never allow root access over the Internet. If you comment out the CONSOLE line in the /etc/default/login file, you allow root to log in on the machine directly over the network, possibly by using Telnet. Do not allow this kind of root access to any machine connected to the Internet.

If you want to limit root login to a single port, use the following example:

```
# root can login only on /dev/term/a serial port only
CONSOLE=/dev/term/a
```

Almost everyone who deals with computers on any level has heard of the Trojan horse. Briefly, it is a program that appears to be innocent but does something either disruptive or destructive to your system. As a simple example, you could store the following program in a file called `tfile`:

```
while true
do
     echo 'You look terrible today! Out late again? Shame on
   you!' > /dev/console
done
```

If you were logged on as superuser and ran this command, it would continue to write the rather amusing message to the console. A disgruntled programmer could do much worse by simply changing superuser's PATH variable to include a publicly writeable directory at the start of the PATH string. Then they would need to put the bogus file in that directory. Because the bogus version appears in a directory mentioned earlier than the real one in PATH, the shell would run it. The next time superuser tried to run `tfile`, the bogus version would run. Although this is a simple example, Trojan horses have been known to create havoc in a computer system. When you log in as root, the shell will use `/etc/default/login`, but when you use `su` to become root, the shell reads the `/etc/default/su` script. Both scripts have a line that defines the variable SUPATH, which controls the value of PATH when you become superuser. Uncomment the line that begins with `# SUPATH` and change the value assigned to SUPATH there. Do not add `.` to SUPATH because you may set up a Trojan horse as described.

The fewer directories you keep in your PATH when you are root, the less likely you will execute a bogus program as root. If possible, keep only the default `/usr/sbin` and `/usr/bin` directories. Remember, never include the working directory anywhere in the PATH string.

Leave the `/etc/hosts.equiv` and individual users' `.rhosts` files empty. You can install products such as SKIP or IPSec, but they are somewhat complicated. Easier steps like preventing remote logins go a long way in keeping your host secure. Solaris does provide a number of utilities and packages for auditing host security setup. There is a three-level package called ASET, or Automated Security Enhancement Tool, that performs security auditing and detection. Process accounting can provide a continuous record of user actions on your system, but it will slow performance somewhat. If you have a large system, you may want to send important syslog information to a secure host that stores only syslog data. There are many good, free programs available for download from the Internet. Depending upon your system size, configuration, and number of users, there will be several suited to your needs.

Remote Access Security

Like local login, remote logins need to be as secure as possible, even more secure considering the increased likelihood of illicit access. Again, you have to look at encrypted authentication clients such as STel, Kerberos, or Secure Shell (SSH), which are all discussed later in this chapter. Smart cards (discussed briefly later in this chapter) are an excellent choice for remote access login. Even if they inadvertently fall into the wrong hands, it is highly unlikely that the finder would be able to produce the correct response to a challenge.

The standard remote access tool for logging in to a Solaris computer is Telnet. A compiled client can be executed on operating systems that support the TCP/IP protocol. Any browser that runs Java natively or as a plug-in will support Telnet. Telnet is a terminal-like program that grants interactive access to a login shell of the user's choice. Most Telnet clients support VT100 or VT220 terminal emulations. This provides easy access to menu-based services. The login shell can be used to execute scripts. It can also be used to read e-mail, develop applications, or do anything a Solaris environment offers to its users. The one exception is graphics (X11, OpenWindows, CDE, and other graphical tools). A Solaris server may be located in a secure area of a site, with Telnet-only access allowed. Users never get to see the server or use CDE.

Once a request for a connection from the user to the server occurs, the server either responds or calls a timeout; if a timeout is called, a connection is either accepted or rejected. If the connection is accepted, the user is asked to enter a username followed by a password. If the username and password are valid, a shell is spawned and the user is logged in. Telnet does not encrypt your password or anything else. All data is sent as clear text across the network, making Telnet a very insecure way of logging on to a computer. This should be taken into account when logging on to Telnet. The standard port for a Telnet connection is 23. You can specify a port number on the command line.

Modems are a constant source of concern in remote security. Network lines are easily monitored. As quickly as folks come up with a new improvement to monitor security, hackers find new ways to get around it. Setting up an encrypted channel after dialing in to a modem pool is a good idea. This helps you to avoid being sniffed by the people running the dial-in pool, but it does not ensure the security of the pool.

You can do this by running SSH over PPP. Password Authentication Protocol (PAP) has stringent modem authentication policies that keep unauthorized users away from your modem. Challenge Handshake Authentication Protocol (CHAP) is also used frequently. They do not necessarily strengthen the security of the dial-in, but they make it easier to exchange data. One of the best and brightest, however, is Radius (sometimes called Steel Belted Radius). It tracks and documents all remote access activity and provides excellent authentication. Another good method of authentication is produced by Cisco and is call TACACS+. These are usually provided with Remote Access Service (RAS), which provides network access to remote users via modem.

If and when you purchase a remote access server, take a close look at what kind of security it provides and decide if that level of security is enough for your site. One technique employed by some remote access servers is callback. After you dial in, you will be prompted for a password. When you type in your password, the modem hangs up and calls you back at a phone number it has stored internally. If you have a small site with relatively few modems, this might work for you. It can be slow, however. Another technique is to use a caller ID (CLID) or automatic number identification (ANI) to decide whether or not to answer the call. You may or may not be able to use ANI, depending upon your local phone company and the type of wire it uses. ANI information is given before the call. CLID information is given along with the call.

If you have high-speed cable modem, look at security and authentication programs that are new and are compatible with the latest cable technology. The technology is changing rapidly and you'll want something with a bit of longevity.

You might consider setting up a virtual private network, or VPN. A VPN is a tunnel that shares a network infrastructure such as the Internet. It is a tunnel because the data being transferred is encrypted and then encapsulated in IP packets, protecting the sender's and recipient's identity. With today's technology, there are three principal ways to create VPNs:

Network to network This is usually with a firewall or high-end router on each end of the VPN.

Host to network A remote computer equipped with VPN client software can connect to the home office.

Dial-up ISP to network Some ISPs will provide VPN service for clients.

VPNs can be used to connect a remote host to a network across the Internet if the client host is suitably configured. The firewall on each network is responsible for encrypting and encapsulating IP traffic that is then routed to the other network. When a user on one network needs to access a server on the other network, the firewall takes the workstation's IP packets and wraps them in its own IP packets. The packets that are then transmitted through the Internet contain source and destination addresses that identify the firewalls but not the client or server on either network. VPN helps to hide the identity of your network hosts. With this method, the original IP packet travels in a compressed, encrypted format, so even if it is intercepted, the contents are useless to anyone else.

One disadvantage to this method is that the speed of the VPN is limited by the slowest link its traffic is routed through, so if there are major hardware failures at any point along the link, you can expect delays or downtime.

VPNs can be cost effective in joining offices that are geographically distance or for those who have a large need to connect remote or mobile users. Standards are being developed through Point-to-Point Tunneling Protocol (PPTP) and the IP security (IPSec) protocol. The development of standards will mean that VPNs can be created using software and hardware from multiple vendors. They will soon be commonplace features of the Internet.

Encrypted Authentication Clients

Secure Shell (SSH) is exactly that: an encrypted authentication client. SSH is a secure client and server solution that provides symmetric and asymmetric encryption of identification and authentication sequences for remote access. It was designed to replace the Telnet and rlogin applications while improving upon the functionality of `inetd`. SSH makes use of a transport layer encryption mechanism over TCP/IP by using government-endorsed triple DES algorithms or the popular Blowfish. It transmits encrypted packets with contents that can be "sniffed" on the network. The catch is that the packets appear to be random, without a key to decrypt them. This type of technology makes it very unlikely that anyone other than the client or server will be able to decipher the interactive session. Username and password combinations usually cannot be sniffed by an intruder. Another advantage to SSH is that graphics applications can also be forwarded, unlike with the older text-only Telnet.

If you want to establish a connection as an SSH client, you can connect to a server by following this sequence:

1. Connect to a server port requesting a connection on port 22.
2. Server replies with its standard public RSA host key along with an RSA server key that changes hourly.
3. Once the connection is accepted, generate a session key and choose an encryption algorithm that the server supports in 3DES or Blowfish.
4. Encrypt the session key using RSA for both the host key and server key, then return the encrypted key to the server.

5. The server decrypts the session key and enables encryption between the client and the server.
6. If the default authentication mechanism is selected, pass the username and password for the server across the secure channel.

You can configure the server to reject connections from hosts that are unknown. It will default to not accept connections from any client, however.

You can disable the username/password authentication sequence by permitting logins to clients/users that have a private RSA key as long as the server has a list of accepted public keys. If, however, the private key falls into the wrong hands, access to the server might be obtained without a valid username and password combination.

The commercial version of SSH for international users does not fall under U.S. ITAR export restrictions, which limit the export to other countries of encryption technology developed in the U.S. Both U.S. and non–U.S. users can now download and install the commercial version of SSH from `www.datafellows.com` or the freeware version from `www.ssh.fi`. If your site is amenable, you can establish a policy of using SSH remote access for all interactive logins. You can enable the SSH daemon on the server side by removing entries for the Telnet and rlogin services in `/etc/services` and `/etc/inetd.conf`. This may be too restrictive, however, because some sites don't support SSH.

Kerberos

Kerberos is a network authentication protocol designed to provide a strong authentication for client/server application. It employs secret key cryptography. The beauty of Kerberos is that a user can authenticate only once, enabling subsequent secure access to the distributed systems and services needed. Productivity increases significantly with this type of system. It is also ideal for intranet use where a central server can be installed for key management. Kerberos grew out of the Athena Project at the Massachusetts Institute of Technology. The Kerberos authentication server can provide authorization for multiple services, provided by many different servers, and can reach a large number of clients at any given time. It is designed to provide authentication to hosts on either side of a firewall, thereby circumventing any attacks from so-called "trusted" internal network users. Kerberos also introduced realms. *Realms* are external but trusted networks with authentication that extends beyond the firewall.

Kerberos Release 5 comes with the Solaris 8 operating system. It is a certificate-granting validation system (the certificates are called tickets). When you, the user on a client machine, want to make the connection with a target server, you request a ticket from an authentication server by using an additional password with your desktop password. The authentication server then authorizes an encrypted ticket that allows you to request a specific server from a specific host, usually for a specified time frame. Tickets can also be renewed with Kerberos 5. After authentication is requested from the authentication server, a session key is created. It is a random value that represents the requested service. The session key resembles a voucher that the client sends to the ticket-granting server. The ticket-granting server returns the ticket that is used to access the target server. Although this may seem to be a cumbersome route to travel, it prevents data loss by interception, a valuable commodity. Figure 8.4 shows how tickets are used in the Kerberos Release 5 security scheme. In this figure, you can see the relationship between the user, the enterprise application, and the Kerberos Key Distribution Center.

FIGURE 8.4

Kerberos uses a ticketing system to give all clients and servers secure access to network resources.

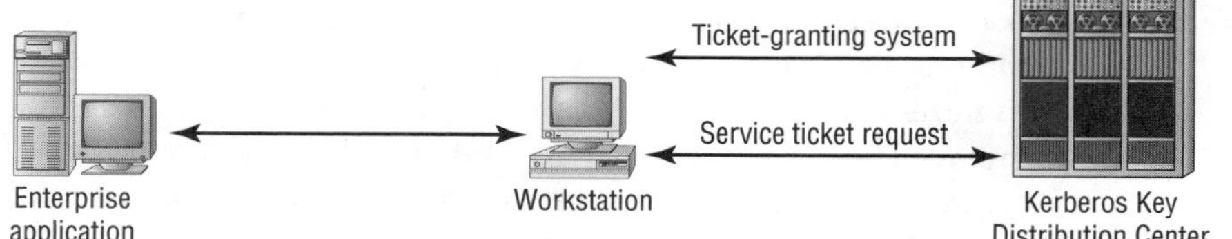

If you have the appropriate network resources, configuring Kerberos is fairly simple. A typical `/etc/krb5.conf` configuration file contains entries like this:

```
[libdefaults]
   default_realm = serv.com
[realms]
   SERV.COM = {
             kdc = kerb1.serv.com
             kdc = kerb2.serv.com
             admin_server = kerb1.serv.com
   }
```

This configuration is for a domain called serv.com that has a logical admin server called kerb1.serv.com with a backup server called kerb2.serv.com.

The downside to Kerberos is that its legal status in exporting encryption technology is still unclear. Permission has been granted for one client to export a binary version of the product on an international level. The Commerce Department currently considers each implementation on a case-by-case basis. Also, as with any security service, there are some risks that should be mentioned before you implement Kerberos. The syslog-based authentication has been found to have a bug that leads to a possible denial of service. The bug has reportedly been fixed in the latest release of Kerberos, but there is always the possibility of others yet to be found. The risk is probably small, however.

The protocol for Kerberos has been published and free implementation that includes the source code is available from MIT at `web.mit.edu/network/kerberos-form.html`. Kerberos Version 5 consists of protocol and encryption support, tools to manage TGT's, PAM modules, passwords, and system configuration. This is an ideal tool for providing a secure enterprise network.

Login Security

A host must definitely be secure or good login security will not amount to much. There are some login security tools, such as `telnetd`, `rlogind`, and `rshd`, that are not good at preserving security. A freeware program called OpenSSH is very popular at many sites and is commercially supported. Stel is also a good solution for Solaris. It has never shown a security hole as yet. Bellcore produces a system called S/Key, which employs a listing of one-time passwords. OPIE, which was developed by the U.S. Naval Research Labs, is a similar security system. A listing of one-time passwords is supplied and a different one is used each time the user logs in. A password that can be used only one time is rendered useless in the hands of a prankster. This is a good solution if you do not have software like Telnet encrypted. A better solution is to combine one-time password and encrypted logins.

More and more smart cards are appearing on the scene. These devices look like credit cards and employ a challenge/response type of authentication. They use a pass phrase or pin type to gain access to the workstation. Look to see more of these in use. A popular model called SecurID card from Security Dynamics Technologies, Inc. (now owned by RSA) is one of the forerunners.

As mentioned earlier, if you are superuser, keep a log of all user passwords in a secure place and have them changed frequently. If an employee leaves, have passwords changed immediately. A combination of letters, symbols, or numbers lessens the chance of someone easily breaking the code. Do not use initials, pet names, names spelled backwards, or other easily accessed passwords.

Viruses

Solaris and Unix are fairly safe bets when it comes to avoiding viruses over the Internet. Because of its architecture, Unix is virtually virus resistant because there is no way to infect the DOS master boot record. Unlike with MS Windows and the Macintosh, the superuser who doles out permissions in a Unix system serves as the perfect antidote to viruses and worms. If you keep your system patches up-to-date and perform periodic backups regularly, this will be the easiest part of your security to control. The first worm sent out on the Internet by an enterprising graduate student propagated itself repeatedly, causing a buffer to overflow, and once the shell took hold of it, it recompiled itself on a remote machine. It took three days and many people to disable this nasty little worm. Although it is still a remote possibility, the Unix security force has kept abreast of security holes and closes them as quickly as possible. A wide-scale disaster is highly unlikely, thanks to their efforts.

There is much software on the market for detecting viruses and worms. And you'll find a lot of information about the latest viruses on the Internet, whether they are real or just another hoax. You should be cautious about downloading attachments unless you are certain of their source. As acceptance of Linux continues to grow and as Sun reduces the cost of its hardware, we will begin to see more and more worm and virus type of attacks against Unix systems.

Physical Security

Depending upon the size of your site, physical security may be a real concern. With today's advanced technology, an unprotected server or console can be tampered with easily and quickly. If your server is in an unlocked room, you will have problems sooner or later. Anyone can walk in, remove the hard drive or copy it with a Zip drive, take it offsite, analyze it, and find out everything they need to know to access privileged information. There are ways to secure your computer from possible break-ins:

- If at all possible, keep servers in a locked room. Limit access with the use of a swipe card, a key, or a key pad combination. Keep windows locked, and if possible, install alarms.
- If you have a large system, use a fiber-optic security system. This requires that you run a fiber-optic cable through each of the machines so that the machine cannot be removed or opened without cutting through the cable. If the cable is cut, an alarm is sounded. SunSparc stations provide for this by having a screw on the back with a hard plastic cover that you can thread cable through. The cable obscures the screw, preventing anyone from opening the top of the machine. Although not foolproof, it can deter would-be pranksters on the spot. Check out other options with the vendors. They will have other means to secure the machines.
- If you use SPARC machines, use a PROM password to prevent anyone from booting the machine in a single-user mode or from the CD-ROM. Many PCs have a BIOS password as well, which allows the same functionality. You can

reset the order in which a PC searches for a boot device, thereby preventing a boot-up from a floppy disk or CD-ROM. The password will protect the BIOS from unauthorized modification.

- It is highly suggested that only fiber-optic cable be run between buildings. It is now required by building codes and is safer if lightening strikes.

Summary

In this chapter, you learned about issues involved with keeping your system secure. A system with dial-in lines can never be completely secure. Access permissions are an important part of your overall security scheme and should be distributed with great care. The root or superuser password must always be confidential because the superuser has the power to change many things on the system. Therefore, security breaches can occur easily.

Encryption is another tool you can use to keep your system secure. There are public key and private key algorithms that provides authenticity. To keep e-mail secure, e-mail headers should be kept to a maximum of 32 kilobytes. This chapter discussed the fact that there is a good supply of free mail user agents that have hooks for encryption programs. They are available to download on the Internet.

Physical security was discussed in this chapter and you learned that a fiber-optic security system can protect your computer from security breaches. Fiber-optic cable should be used to connect building to building. Keypads and swipe cards are good measures for maintaining the security of a locked area.

Finally, you learned that Solaris can use the Kerberos version 5 security scheme to provide trusted access to network resources by using a ticketing scheme.

PART II

Solaris and the Network

LEARN TO:

- *Use network services with Solaris*
- *Set up a printer and print queue*
- *Provide network resource access to users and groups*
- *Run the utilities provided with Solaris*
- *Use Solaris to work on the Internet*

CHAPTER 9

Network Services

FEATURING:

The ISO/OSI model 327

Network topologies 337

TCP/IP 343

Name services 350

DHCP 360

The Network File System (NFS) 362

Administrative tools, utilities, and commands 370

Computer networks have become commonplace in the work environment over the last 10 or 12 years, and Sun Microsystems has played an important part in that development. Networked services make good sense when you want access to resources without the cost of duplication. Devices, applications, data files, mail services, and so on can be shared items on both local area networks (LANs) and wide area networks (WANs). Solaris 8 provides you with the means to network locally or globally by configuring the most appropriate network for your environment. This chapter will give a basic overview of general networking and a more in-depth look at configuring, installing, and maintaining networks compatible with the Solaris platform. Chapter 14, "Networking and the Internet," takes up the topic of internetworking, delivering WAN services over the Internet and the World Wide Web.

Solaris network support is multifaceted. It comes with many utilities that enable users to access remote systems and many tools for administrators to use to set up and maintain network services and resources. You have the ability to send mail to users on other machines. Networking will allow you to access files on disks mounted on other computers and, similarly, to make your files available to other computers. You will be able to copy files back and forth and run programs on other machines with the results appearing on your computer.

Overview of Network Services

In order for computers to communicate with one another, both the hardware and software must follow a set of rules that determine how data is passed from one system to another. Because many different hardware and software devices have been developed over the years for network communication, designers have created conceptual frameworks that describe the different elements in a communication scheme. At the heart of data communications is the notion that there is an agreed-upon protocol that developers can use so that data is contained in a form that other developers can work with. Two different network models are described in this chapter: the well-known and established Open Systems Interconnection (OSI) networking model and the newer and more specialized model for shared network storage being developed by the Storage Networking Industry Association (SNIA). Both are layered architectures that seek to characterize different devices and data types so that their interactions with other devices, data types, and applications may be better understood.

Network services are constantly being improved. Solaris 8 adds numerous new features, including these:

- A Java-based GUI for the configuration and management of the Dynamic Host Configuration Protocol (DHCP).

- IP Security (IPSec) architecture, which adds protection for IP packets during transmission.
- The next version of the IP protocol, IPv6, which adds new features such as an extended address space to the current version IPv4.
- The Class II logical link controller driver (llc2) for interfacing between network software such as NetBIOS, SNA, and OSI.
- Network File System (NFS) transaction logging.
- A newer version of sendmail, version 8.9.3.
- The Solaris Network Cache and Accelerator for enhanced Web performance through the in-kernel caching (in the ncakmod module) of Web pages that are accessed during HTTP requests by a Web server. For this feature to be active, it must be turned on by a superuser, the interfaces must be registered, and the kernel module and NCA logging must be enabled.
- Perl 5 (Practical Extraction and Report Language), which is used in scripting. It is part of the free software included in the Solaris 8 release. Perl is popular with both Web and system administrators alike.
- The popular GNUzip utilities, which are now included as part of the Solaris install.
- The useful `traceroute` program.

The ISO/OSI Model

Network communication was designed to be very modular. To describe it, developers have modeled the process into several independent layers. The best-known model for communication is the International Standards Organization's Open Systems Interconnection (OSI) reference model. This model separates communication into a set of seven layers that is referred to as a protocol stack. Each layer describes one part of the process of both sending and receiving data from a sending and receiving host. Therefore, although the sending host's communication must travel through the seven conceptual layers of the OSI model from an application to the physical infrastructure, that same communication must also travel from the Physical layer of the receiving host's protocol stack to the Application layer where the data is processed and manipulated. The TCP/IP protocol stack is shown in Figure 9.1.

The layers of the OSI model, from top to bottom, are as follows:

Application layer (layer 7) This layer contains the applications and communication services that people use to send and receive data (browsers, mailers, FTP utilities, and so on). The Application layer is responsible for providing simple application-to-application communication mechanisms.

FIGURE 9.1

The TCP/IP protocol stack for sending and receiving hosts

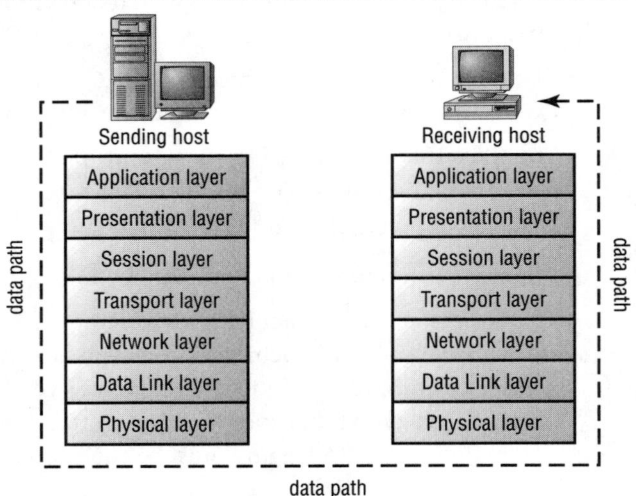

Presentation layer (layer 6) This layer manages the format of the data so that it can be used by the receiving host's application.

Session layer (layer 5) The Session layer establishes and maintains connections between computers so that there is an open channel for communications.

Transport layer (layer 4) This layer transfers data between computers and ensures the validity of the data. The Transport layer manages the assembly of data packets, for example, to determine if an entire communication data stream was successfully sent and received.

Network layer (layer 3) The Network layer ensures that data is properly addressed and delivered between networks. The Network layer is responsible for deciding the best route that data packets (messages) should follow to reach their ultimate destination.

Data Link layer (layer 2) This layer transfers the data between network media. The Data Link layer is where media access occurs and transmission mechanisms are stored.

Physical layer (layer 1) The Physical layer describes the infrastructure over which the data travels. This includes wires, interconnects, and so forth.

Each layer in the suite provides a specific set of services to other layers while abstracting the services of the layer below it in order to provide a simpler interface for the layer above it. The layers are able to intercommunicate by exchanging service primitives by means of a set of predefined addresses called *service access points*, or *ports* as they are more commonly referred to.

When a network system sends a message to a remote system, the information passes from layer to layer in a downward motion until it reaches the remote system, where it passes upward through the layers. Even though the layers assume they are communicating with their peer layer on the remote system, the information units are actually passed from one layer to a layer below. The information units contain layer-specific source and destination addresses followed by a data block. The source and destination addresses reside at the beginning, or head, of an information unit. Together they make up the section called the *header*.

Whenever an information unit is passed from one layer to the one directly below it, the lower layer adds its own header to the information unit. The new header contains layer-specific source and destination addresses. Once the remote system receives information from the local system, it passes the data back to the upper layer, which then strips off the layer-specific header. Once the top layer of the remote system receives the message, it interprets the data in the manner that the protocol dictates. Protocols are implemented as two processes: the client process and the server process. A *client process* runs on the local system and requests a particular service from a remote system on the network. The process that is running on the remote system and that answers requests for a service is called the *server process*. With Unix, the server processes are sometimes referred to as daemons because they are usually executed in the background as other Unix daemons are.

The client program for a protocol will usually have the same name as the protocol, only in lowercase letters. For example, ftp is the client name for FTP, or File Transfer Protocol. Daemon programs use names in the form *protocol*d or in.*protocol*d; *protocol* is the name of the protocol the daemon implements.

Table 9.1 shows how the different protocols use one or more of the OSI reference model layers. Many of these protocol examples are described in the next sections.

TABLE 9.1: THE TCP/IP PROTOCOL STACK

Layer #	Description	TCP/IP Layer	Protocol Examples
5, 6, 7	Session, Presentation, Application	Application	NFS, NIS+, DNS, `Telnet`, `ftp`, `rlogin`, `rsh`, RIP, RDISC, SNMP
4	Transport	Transport	TCP, UDP
3	Network	Internet	IP, ARP, ICMP
2	Data Link	Data Link	PPP, IEEE 802.2
1	Physical	Physical Network	Ethernet (IEEE 802.3), Token Ring, and RS-232 (serial)

The Application Layer

The Application layer is the first or highest layer in the model. Many of the common protocols you may be already familiar with are located at this layer. Terminal emulation (Telnet), File Transfer Protocol (FTP, see more on FTP in Chapter 14), Hypertext Transfer Protocol (HTTP), Network File System (NFS), and Simple Mail Transfer Protocol (SMTP) all reside at this layer.

The Telnet protocol allows you to create a virtual terminal connection with a remote system that acts like a direct connection to a terminal on the remote system. You can connect to a remote system using the Telnet protocol by simply executing the `telnet` command with the name of the remote host, as in this example:

```
% telnet  <hostname>
```

FTP allows you to connect to a remote system to upload files to the system or to copy or download files from the system. Use the `ftp` command with the name of the remote host to initiate an FTP session:

```
% ftp  <hostname>
```

HTTP forms the basis for the Internet's graphical World Wide Web protocol. It is discussed in more detail in Chapter 14.

The Network File System (NFS) protocol was developed by Sun. This protocol allows files to be shared seamlessly. You can make a directory tree on a remote system look like a part of your local directory tree. If programs access files stored in an NFS directory, the network request for the file is handled automatically.

SMTP handles most of the e-mail transfers on the Internet. These transfers have a different type of priority than other protocols in the Application layer. The servers that run the SMTP take care of storing, formatting, and forwarding e-mail messages correctly.

The Unix "r" commands—such as `rcp`, `rlogin`, and `rsh`—are also part of the Application layer. They allow a user to issue locally commands that are run on a remote system.

The Solaris name services—the domain name service (DNS) and the network information services (NIS and NIS+)—are also Application layer services. DNS offers host-name-to-IP-address resolution, allowing "friendly names" to be used in place of IP addresses. The DNS database is also used by sendmail for its addressing capabilities. NIS+ offers centralized management of network administration services. Using NIS+, you can map IP and Ethernet addresses, check on passwords, and perform other networking tasks. Use of DNS and NIS+ are not mutually exclusive. Both are typically used. Each name service is described in detail later in this chapter.

Additionally, the Simple Network Management Protocol (SNMP), the Router Information Protocol (RIP), and the Router Discovery Protocol (RDISC) are Application layer services. SNMP sets up trap events that provide measurements and metrics on important network parameters. Using SNMP, you can determine which computers and switches are operating on a network, get metrics on performance, analyze storage devices, and get network throughput and much more information from console management interfaces. Many networking packages are based on SNMP, including the SunNet.Manage software. The RIP and RDISC allow you to set and discover routing information contained in routing tables on servers and dedicated routing devices like Cisco routers.

The Transport Layer

Sometimes called the host-to-host layer, the Transport layer is responsible for the creation and maintenance of the network connections. Once a connection is created, the Transport layer guarantees the integrity of data exchanged across the network. The Transmission Control Protocol (TCP) and the User Datagram Protocol (UDP) are the two main transport protocols at this layer. The two major types of network communications are *connection-oriented communication* and *connectionless communication*, of which TCP and UDP are examples, respectively.

TCP is a connection-oriented protocol that guarantees delivery of packets; UDP, a connectionless protocol, does not have a guarantee of delivery. With connection-oriented communications, a logical connection is created between the two systems that need to exchange data. Data is transmitted once the connection is made. When data is received, it is acknowledged. The sender then knows that the data was received. If the sender does not receive an acknowledgement, the message will be retransmitted until it is successfully sent. Data will eventually be delivered to the remote system. Connection-oriented communications maintain information about the state of packets; hence, their protocols are often referred to as *stateful protocols*.

Connectionless communication protocols do not use a logical connection to exchange data. They send data to the remote system and anticipate that it will arrive correctly. Whether or not data arrives correctly is rather catch as catch can. In this type of communication, the state of the packets is not really maintained anywhere; each communication is separate. For this reason, connectionless protocols are called *stateless protocols*.

Network Layer

The Network layer, also called the Internet layer, is responsible for providing the transport, routing, fragmentation, and reassembly of UDP datagrams as well as the TCP segments. The two main protocols in the layer are the Internet Protocol (IP) and the Internet Control Message Protocol (ICMP). The backbone of the TCP/IP protocol suite is the Internet Protocol (IP). Both the TCP segment and the UDP datagram are transferred across the network in the form of IP datagrams. IP is a stateless, connectionless datagram delivery service between hosts on the network. It makes no guarantee that datagrams will be delivered correctly or in sequence, similar to UDP. Quite possibly, datagrams might never arrive at their intended destination. IP relies on protocols such as TCP at higher layers.

Because different hosts on the network need to exchange IP datagrams correctly, the IP protocol stipulates that every system must have an IP address that is a unique identifier. Somewhat similar to a telephone number, this address is assigned by the American Registry for Internet Numbers (ARIN); see `www.arin.net` for more information on the assignment of IP addresses. If you connect to the Internet by means of an Internet Service Provider, or ISP, then your IP addresses are supplied from a pool of addresses allotted to your ISP.

The second protocol at the Internet layer level is the Internet Control Message Protocol, or ICMP, which is used to communicate error messages and other network conditions between systems connected to the network. This protocol defines several different message types that allow systems to exchange network information efficiently. It checks to see if hosts are available and obtains routing information.

The Address Resolution Protocol, or ARP, sends and receives datagrams between the Data Link and Network layers. Datagrams are mapped to Ethernet addresses (so-called 48-bit MAC addresses) from IP addresses (32 bits long). ARP manages this process, which is called name-to-device resolution.

The Data Link Layer

The Data Link layer is the lowest layer in the model that isn't hardware specific. Also know as the Network Access layer, it is responsible for converting the data from the Network layer into a format that can be transmitted over the media that connects a system to the network by way of the system's network interface card (NIC). Although most systems contain a single NIC, some that operate on several different networks can contain two or more. Systems with more than one NIC and that operate on several different networks are referred to as *multihomed systems*.

Each NIC has a hardware or physical address associated with it; the physical address is usually referred to as the Media Access Control (MAC) address. It is made up of a unique 48-bit number hard-coded on the NIC. Some vendors, however, provide the ability to assign MAC addresses to NICs. Once the Data Link layer receives an IP datagram from the Network layer, it adds a header that contains the source and destination MAC address for the two network systems that are exchanging data.

The main protocol for this level is the Address Resolution Protocol (ARP), which handles the mapping of IP addresses for a system to the physical or hardware address of its NIC. This is a simple protocol that consists of two types of messages: the "Who is" message and the "I am" message. When the Data Link layer sends data to a system whose MAC address is unknown, it issues a "Who is" message. When a system receives this message, it will respond with the message "I am (name). My MAC address is *xx:xx:xx:xx:xx:xx*."

Solaris 8 supports several different types of physical media. Standards bodies such as the Institute of Electrical and Electronics Engineers (IEEE) have standardized the most popular physical media types. They are Ethernet, Token Ring, Fiber Distributed Data Interface (FDDI), and Asynchronous Transfer Mode (ATM).

The Physical Layer

The Physical layer can be made up of several basic types of network media configurations. Typically, the Physical layer is described in terms of topologies. You can have both physical and logical topologies. For example, the trunk (or backbone), star, and ring are examples of logical topologies. Physical topologies are particular architectures that use real equipment. Thus, Token Ring is an example of a physical network topology. In some instances, you can use the same equipment, such as hubs and routers, to implement two different logical topologies, such as backbone and stars.

Broadcast Networks

Broadcast networks, of which Ethernet is the most prevalent example, employ a network cable that can send a message at any time. It is covered in the IEEE 802.3 standard and is one of the most common physical mediums in use. Ethernet allows multiple hosts to share the same physical media for transmitting data because it is bus based: a single host can be removed from the bus without adversely affecting the overall network. Most TCP/IP traffic is sent and delivered over Ethernet networks; thus, most data communications over the Internet is Ethernet traffic. Ethernet components outsell by far all other networking topologies in use today.

Ethernet employs a transmission protocol called carrier sense multiple access with collision detection, or CSMA/CD. When a networked system is transmitting data, it listens for a carrier to determine if any other systems are transmitting. If two or more systems hear that the path is clear and begin to transmit at the same time, there will be a collision on the line. The collision will be detected by both systems. In the event of a collision, the systems will back off for a random amount of time and will then attempt to transmit again. As the number of systems increases on an Ethernet network, the frequency of collisions increases in direct proportion. The frequency of collisions and retransmissions reduces the speed of the network significantly. This type of system frequently creates an overload on the network. There are times when the collision rate gets too high and the network crashes. If a Solaris system is part of a local area network (LAN), in all probability, the LAN is an Ethernet that supports rates from 10 megabits to 1 gigabit per second with enhancements in speed occurring frequently. Due to the load on the network because of overhead and traffic, however, the transfer rates are always lower than specified.

One improvement has been a device known as an Ethernet switch. A computer that is attached to an unshared switched Ethernet segment can actually use the full 10Mbps of network bandwidth. Because each computer is isolated on its own network cable, the switch distributes data packets to those segments with the hosts that should receive them. Full-duplex Ethernet improves things further by eliminating collisions. Hosts can transmit and receive simultaneously at 10Mbps for an effective bandwidth between hosts of 20Mbps.

Ethernet technology is continuing to advance at a rapid pace, however. At the moment, 100Mbps Ethernet is the current standard for enterprise data communications over Category 5 (Cat5) cable. The older standard, 10Mbps, is in common use, and it is possible to buy auto-sensing hubs and switches that let you mix and match these older components, allowing as much throughput as is possible using the host bus adapters (HBAs) that you have. The more recently introduced standards such as "one gigabit Ethernet" (1Gbps) will replace 100Mbps as the enterprise standard within the next year or two, allowing storage traffic to be sent over Ethernet networks. By 2004–2005, we may see the introduction of a 10Gbps Ethernet standard.

The Token Ring Network

IBM made popular the network technology known as Token Ring. To avoid the collision problems inherent in the broadcast network, only one system in a token ring can send a message at any given time. The token, which is a special message, gets passed from one host to another around the ring. The host holding the token is the only one allowed to send a message until the token gets passed to the next host on the ring.

Although this method of networking does prevent collisions, it can slow things down considerably if you are waiting for the token to come your way. A break in the ring can also cause a crash in the network. For this reason, most ring-based networks are connected to a central box called a *concentrator*, which acts as a switch. When it picks up a failure on the ring, it will slice off the bad part and rejoin the rest to form another whole ring. If the token is inadvertently lost, the remaining hosts will vote upon a new token to keep the network up and running. Some Token Ring networks run with two rings, one going in a clockwise motion and one running counterclockwise. This ensures that one ring will remain running if there is a break in the other.

One of the most popular types of Token Ring networks is a network based on FDDI. It uses a bandwidth of 100Mbps and fiber-optic cable to connect to the ring. Although it became popular as a backbone for networking, it is also too expensive to be cost effective. 100BaseT Ethernet has largely overridden it, though you will still find large segments of FDDI in the field. A substitute called CDDI, or Copper Distributed Data Interface, was once thought to be a viable option for FDDI, but it never quite took hold.

Token Ring networks will be phased out over time and are largely relegated to IBM shops. Even with the more recent addition of switches and high-access speeds to

Token Ring technology, Ethernet is still the leader in installations. Figure 9.2 shows the topology of a single ring Token Ring network.

FIGURE 9.2

The Token Ring network

Fiber Distributed Data Interface

The Fiber Distributed Data Interface (FDDI) network is considered to be an enhanced version of a Token Ring network that uses a fiber-optic cabling installation to allow for transmission speeds of up to 100Mbps. Besides a better speed rate, FDDI offers extra redundancy in its ring structure. It normally uses two separate rings. One does the transmitting and one does the receiving. If either ring gets split, FDDI will employ the other ring for both transmitting and receiving. The problem with FDDI is that it is very expensive. Although it's used on high-end server systems, the overall cost makes it prohibitive for most sites. The configuration of the FDDI is shown in Figure 9.3.

Point-to-Point Networks

Another popular type of network media configuration is point-to-point. Point-to-point linking involves two endpoints. Wide area networks (WANs) use point-to-point links with wire cable, radio, or satellite links. Point-to-point networks typically have low traffic volume. The downside is that each system can service a small number of links, but it is inefficient and costly to connect each computer to all the rest. The use of serial lines, modems, and parallel ports help to make Solaris links more cost efficient. A modem with a point-to-point link can connect an isolated system into a larger network at a reasonable cost. Figure 9.4 shows a schematic of a point-to-point network configuration. FDDI has been commonly used to connect the networks of separate buildings in university and large company environments.

FIGURE 9.3

The Fiber Distributed Data Interface

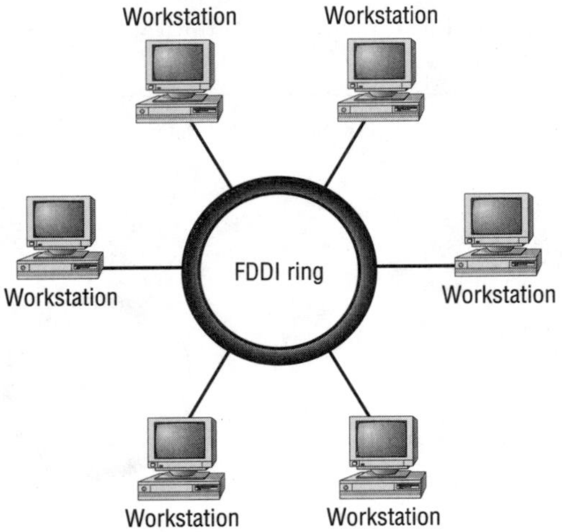

Workstation
Workstation
Workstation
FDDI ring
Workstation
Workstation
Workstation

FIGURE 9.4

The point-to-point network

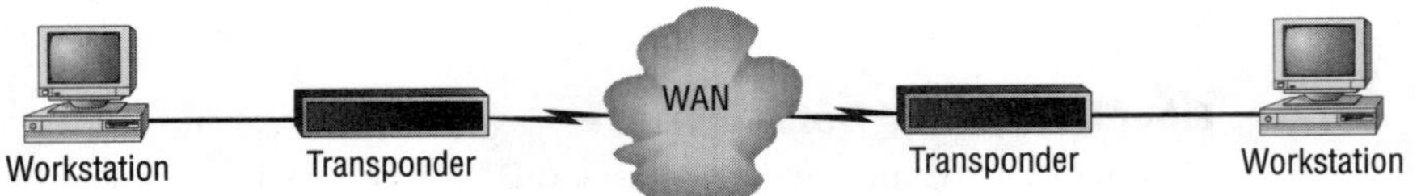

Asynchronous Transfer Mode

Asynchronous Transfer Mode (ATM) is based on the transmission of small, fixed-size frames called cells. Each cell is 53 bytes long and contains 5 bytes for a header and 48 bytes for data. ATM-built networks are connection-oriented networks. A connection is first created between the two systems that want to communicate, and then every cell that is exchanged between the hosts uses the exact same path. This allows for easy handling of constant-rate traffic like audio and video. It handles variable-rate traffic like data just as easily. The capability to handle audio and video easily has made ATM a viable option for some systems. ATM offers extremely high speeds by transmitting very small amounts of information. The standard speeds are 155Mbps and 655Mbps. Its features make it one of the most promising Link layer media technologies. ATM has been replacing FDDI on many university and large company networks to connect buildings because of its higher speed and other advantages over FDDI.

Frame Relay

Frame Relay is commonly used by ISPs to connect companies to the Internet over a T1 or Fractional T1. It is a packet-switching technology but features a smaller packet size and fewer error-checking mechanisms. It is also a Data Link layer protocol that uses frames. It supports transfer of packets only through permanent virtual circuits (PVCs) between the network's endpoint routers. The PVC's endpoints are defined by data link connection identifiers and are given a committed information rate through the Frame Relay network. The data link connection identifiers are given a minimum available quantity of bandwidth but have the option to temporarily burst beyond that limit under certain circumstances. Frame Relay contains native mechanisms for addressing. These mechanisms are somewhat primitive in comparison to other Network layer mechanisms but are generally adequate for interconnecting stub networks. A Frame Relay access device may be used to connect a LAN to a WAN. One of the primary benefits of Frame Relay is that it can reduce the cost of networking locations that are geographically far apart by minimizing the length of transmission facilities. However, there is a definite reduction in performance relative to point-to-point leased lines.

Network Topologies

There are two basic types of networks, the local area network (LAN) and the wide area network (WAN). A LAN is generally considered an intranetwork because it resides at one site, whereas a WAN can be an internetwork that can encompass two or more sites over a large geographical area.

Sharing files and utilities on a network with similar systems is called *distributed computing*. A file server can be a remote computer that houses applications or other types of documentation that can be distributed to client computers. Files can be configured in such a way that users are most often unaware that they are stored on a remote system. This type of configuration conserves valuable disk space and also allows you to update one central copy of documentation, whether it be applications or data files. This saves a lot of time because it is then unnecessary to search through all the systems on the network to update information. Shared file systems are usually stored in subdirectories under the `/export` or `usr/export` directory. A shared file system can be kept in the directory of your choice on Solaris.

Solaris 8 lends itself to distributed computing easily. The client/server model is paramount with Unix and Solaris system networking. The server system is a central resource that acts as a repository for documentation and offers services to its clients. Some servers have specific functions such as interacting with certain utilities, like Web servers or browsers. Others may support the Domain Name System or communicate with other servers, answer queries from clients, and act as a client when sending queries to other servers. This same client/server model applies to many processes that may run on one or more systems. A process may control a central database. Client processes can send queries to the server and process replies as well.

Many large enterprise-class network applications are being built around a three-tiered (or *n*-tiered) architecture. In a three-tiered architecture, the client (Presentation) layer is separated from the backend or services layer by a business logic layer. Often, *n*-tiered systems are built with a messaging service that decouples the delivery of a transaction from a client to a server. The messaging server keeps track of when transactions are sent and received and can aid in the delivery of transactions when a connection is intermittent, as would be the case in Internet connections.

The Local Area Network

A local area network is called a LAN. It is a data network that covers a small geographic area. Generally, it connects workstations, personal computers, printers, scanners, and other devices at a work site. A LAN offers computer users many advantages. They can not only share applications and devices, they can also share data files, electronic mail, and graphics. A LAN protocol will use either a CSMA/CD or a token-passing method to access the physical network medium. Sometimes called contention access, the CSMA/CD media access scheme is usually an Ethernet /IEEE 802.3 network that might include 100BaseT.

In the token-passing media access scheme, network devices access the physical medium as the token is passed, as in a Token Ring/IEEE802.5 or FDDI network.

There are three classifications that LAN data transmissions fall into (in each type of transmission, a single packet is sent to one or more nodes):

- A *unicast* transmission sends a single packet from the source to a destination on a network. The source node addresses the packet by using the address of the destination node. The package is then sent on to the network, and finally, the network passes the packet back to its destination.
- A *multicast* transmission copies a data packet and sends the copies to a specific subset of nodes on the network. The source node addresses the packet by using a multicast address. The packet is then sent on to the network, which copies the packet and sends a copy to each node that is part of the multicast address.
- A *broadcast* transmission consists of a single data packet that is copied and sent to all nodes on the network. The source node addresses the packet by using the broadcast address. The packet is then sent on to the network, which copies of the packet and sends a copy to every node on the network.

LANs may use one of four topologies: the logical ring, the star, the tree, and the bus. These topologies are logical architectures, but the actual devices need not be physically organized in these configurations. For example, logical bus and ring topologies are commonly organized physically as a star. The following list includes an explanation of each type of topology:

- A *bus* topology is a linear architecture in which transmission from network stations propagate the length of the medium and are received by all other stations. The most widely used is Ethernet/IEEE802.3.
- A *ring* topology is an architecture that consists of a series of devices connected by unidirectional transmission links to form a single closed loop. Both the Token Ring and FDDI networks implement a ring topology.
- A *star* topology is an architecture in which the endpoints on a network are connected to a common central hub or switch by dedicated links. Logical bus and ring topologies are often physically implemented in a star topology.
- A *tree* topology is an architecture that is identical to the bus topology except that it has branches with multiple nodes.

A LAN may use repeaters, extenders, or hubs to interconnect various nodes of an extended network:

- A *repeater* is a Physical layer device that is used to interconnect the media segments of an extended network. It enables a series of cable segments to be treated as a single cable, thus avoiding signal deterioration caused by long cable lengths and large numbers of connected devices.
- An *extender* is a remote access multilayered switch that connects to a host router and forwards traffic from all the standard Network layer protocols. These can be connected to the host router via a WAN.
- A *hub* is a Physical layer device that connects multiple user stations via a dedicated cable that establishes electrical interconnections inside the hub. Hubs are used to create a physical star network while still maintaining the logical bus or ring configuration of the LAN. A hub resembles a multiport repeater.

The Wide Area Network

A WAN, or wide area network, covers a broad geographical area and may use common carriers to transmit data. Telephone companies, satellites, and radio broadcast may be employed. Point-to-point networks provide a path from the initiating site through a carrier network such as a telephone company to a remote network. The point-to-point link is sometimes known as a leased line because its path is permanent and fixed for each remote network. The carrier company reserves point-to-point links for the private use of the customer. These links accommodate two different types of transmissions:

- Datagram transmissions, which are composed of individually addressed frames
- Data-stream transmissions, which are composed of a stream of data for which address checking occurs once and only once

To switch circuits, a WAN uses a method in which a dedicated physical circuit is established and maintained. It is also terminated through a carrier network for each communication session. Circuit switching accommodates two types of transmissions:

- Datagram transmissions
- Data-stream transmissions

Circuit switching operates very much like a normal telephone call operates and is used extensively in telephone company networks.

A WAN virtual circuit is a logical circuit that ensures reliable communication between two network devices. There are two types of virtual circuits:

- Switched virtual circuits (SVCs)
- Permanent virtual circuits (PVCs)

SVCs are dynamically established on demand and terminated when the transmission is complete. Communication over an SVC consists of three phases:

- Circuit establishment
- Data transfer
- Circuit termination

The first phase involves creating the virtual circuit between the source and destination devices. Data transfer involves transmitting data between the devices over the virtual circuit. The circuit termination phase involves tearing down the virtual circuit between the source and destination devices. SVCs are usually used when data transmission between devices is sporadic. SVCs increase bandwidth used due to the circuit establishment and termination phases but decrease the cost associated with constant virtual availability. (Both LANS and WANs are discussed further in Chapter 14.)

PVCs are predefined, logical connections through a switched network between two points. They are not flexible as SVCs are. Their primary benefit is the elimination of a call setup period. Typically, they are used to support communications between network devices that communicate on a routine basis. The PVC's endpoints are defined by data link connection identifiers and are given a committed information rate through the Frame Relay network. The data link connection identifiers are given a minimum available quantity of bandwidth with the option to temporarily burst beyond that limit under certain circumstances.

The SNIA Shared Storage Model

Storage networking builds on many of the principles of traditional networking but adds additional functionality and emphasizes different services. Several groups in the storage industry have begun to build shared storage models and to publish and discuss the results—predominantly the Fibre Channel Industry Alliance and the Storage Networking Industry Association (SNIA).

Creating a shared storage model serves the same purpose that creating the OSI/ISO networking model did. It allows shared storage products to be described as a set of layers and services. Using this model, it's possible to expose what services are provided and where, what future areas of interoperability need to be explored, and the pros and cons of different storage architectures. (At `www.snia.org`, you will find a glossary of storage terms that are commonly used throughout the industry.) It is also helpful in allowing vendors to better explain to their customers the differences between their products and to help customers understand the trade-offs they make by installing one type of storage system or networking component in place of another.

The shared storage model is meant to capture the functional layers and properties of networked storage systems. The model is not a specification for a "right" or "wrong" way to design a particular network architecture, nor is it an endorsement or recommendation of one vendor's product over another's or one method of installation over another.

The SNIA model breaks network storage apart into the following technologies: network and interfaces, standards, applications, file and database systems, and block storage systems. SNIA touts "open" storage, that is, storage based on industry standards that allow one vendor's product to work with another's interchangeably. From a customer's perspective, the benefits of this approach are that it increases product choice, allows for incremental component upgrade, provides protection against obsolescence, and allows customers to let their storage networks grow incrementally and to any capacity. From a vendor's point of view, the advantage of this approach is that it is easier to bring a product to market. However, standardization can tend to de-emphasize significant advantages that one vendor's product may have over the products of another group of similar vendors. So the ideal situation is to be open, but different.

To be open, storage networks rely on the following: well-defined interfaces, interface protocols, and access protocols. All of these things required published standards that are supported by real products. In creating the model, the developers broke apart networked storage into hardware, application programming interfaces (APIs), and protocols. Hardware includes Ethernet, Fibre Channel, and Infiniband; APIs are either for blocks, files, or stored objects; and protocols are FC CT (Fibre Channel Common Transport), TCP/IP, and others. Figure 9.5 shows the SNIA Shared Storage Model in block diagram form.

There are several things to notice about the shared storage model. First, the file/record subsystem provides for overlap between the file system and a database (metadata), which sits between an application on the top and data stored in blocks on devices. There are eight possible access paths from an application through the file subsystem and block aggregation layer to the storage device. The file subsystems provide access methods and packaging (naming and space allocation) as well as caching for performance and coherency in distributed systems. Most of the model is devoted to block aggregation, and this model is not device centric. That is, you don't see network-attached storage (NAS) devices, Storage Area Networks (SANs), switches, and other devices indicated as you might on a topology map.

FIGURE 9.5
The SNIA Shared Storage Network Model

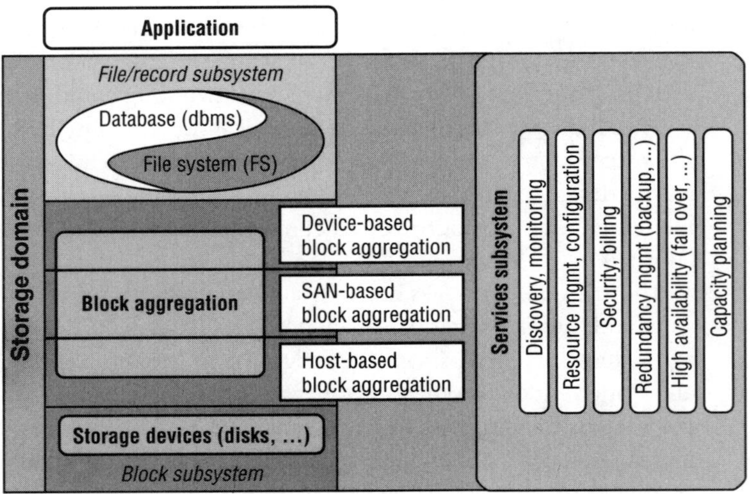

In the block subsystem are the storage devices: disks, tape drives, and solid-state devices that store data. At that level there are space management, block aggregation, striping, and redundancy (mirroring) features and address mapping. For SANs, *aggregation* means virtualization through slicing and concatenation. That includes features such as RAID, mirroring, and so forth, managed by volume managers and disk array logical unit numbers (LUNs). The block level also includes a caching function. The block subsystem determines where operations take place: on a host (logical volume, HBA, or device driver), on a storage device (array controller or disk controller), or over the SAN using an HBA or a specialized appliance. Data is moved in and out of the block system as a vector of blocks.

All of the pieces of the services subsystem remain to be more fully described and worked into this model. In truth, many of the principles of discovery and monitoring, for example, are yet to be fully worked out in the industry. Another important thing to note is that anywhere you see an interface, you are looking at the most dynamic areas of development and the places in which competing standards tend to make life difficult for storage value-added resellers (VARs) and integrators.

In drawing out an actual storage network topology, you would overlay this model with actual device types. When you go through this exercise, you'll find that a device like NAS (an OS with a file system) spans several layers, eliminating interfaces, which translates into increased reliability but decreased flexibility. To view the presentation on the SNIA Shared Storage Network model, go to `www.snia.org/English/Collaterals/Press_Releases/1999/19991021_Future.html`.

TCP/IP

A *protocol* is a formal set of rules and conventions that determine how information is passed from computer to computer. The most prominent networking protocol in use today is TCP/IP, which stands for Transmission Control Protocol/Internet Protocol. TCP/IP was developed out of the U.S. Department of Defense's Advanced Research Projects Agency (ARPA) in 1969. The original purpose for the protocol was to develop a network that could keep military sites connected even if there was considerable damage to individual sections of the network. It allowed the use of networks that could interconnect with hybrid platforms.

The predominant communications protocol suite in use today is TCP/IP. Every major computer platform in the world today supports TCP/IP; indeed connection to the Internet and the World Wide Web is impossible without having that protocol stack running on your system. Much of this chapter is devoted to working with TCP/IP on Solaris, and many different types of network technologies—from physical network transports such as Ethernet, FDDI, and Token Ring to wide area networks such as T1 (telephone lines), X.25, and ATM—all support TCP/IP. The same may be said for logical topologies: rings, hubs, stars, and so forth that you may choose to use to set up your network infrastructure. TCP/IP is as important in setting up your local area network as it is to connecting to another computer across the world.

TCP/IP uses data packets to transfer data between computers. A *packet* is a data stream of a certain length that is organized into a header and a body section. The header describes the nature of the data contained in the body of the packet so that the receiving system can interpret the data. Some of the data in a packet is compressed, and sometimes the data is encrypted. The header also describes the sender of the information, as well as the intended recipient.

Another important feature of TCP/IP is that it is used for broadcast network communication. Packets are broadcast to the network, and if the intended recipient is on the same part of the computer network (a logical address describing a subnet), that computer can receive the packet. Once the packet is received, it is acknowledged so that the sender can stop sending it. Packets meant for computers on other subnets or separate networks are routed to their intended target system by specialized network devices known as *routers*. Because data communication involves sending and delivering multiple packets for nearly every necessary communication task, the sending computer continues to send each packet until an acknowledgement arrives that the packet has been received by its target system and successfully read. Using this mechanism of repeated broadcast and acknowledgements, both the source and target systems in a network communication can indeed know that a message was successfully transmitted no matter how persistent or transient the network connection is at any particular time.

Addressing

TCP/IP has a unique IP address for each device, and that address determines what network the device resides on in the network of networks that make up the Internet. Somewhat similar to a postal address, it describes the location of a device by using a scheme that progresses from general to specific. There are two parts to an IP address:

- The network address
- The node address

The *network address* is common to all hosts and devices that are on the same physical network. The *node address*, however, is unique to a single host on that network. Both addresses are completely independent of the MAC address of the system's NIC. Because you can change both parts as needed, TCP/IP addresses are symbolic. An IP address is 32 bits (or 4 bytes) long. The numbers corresponding to the node and network parts may vary based on the IP address class to which an address belongs.

You can specify IP addresses by using a notation known as the *dotted decimal notation,* which treats the 32-bit IP address as four separate sets of bytes. Each byte is represented by its decimal equivalent. The format for this is 172.151.3.44. (See the section "Host Addresses" in Chapter 14 for more information on IP addressing.)

To create different sized network address pools, you apply a subnet mask to the IP address pool. Different subnet masks allow different possible IP address classes: A, B, C, D, and E. A Class A network can accommodate millions of nodes and is created by using the subnet mask 255.0.0.0. A Class B network can accommodate thousands of nodes and is created by applying the subnet mask 255.255.0.0. A Class C network is the most commonly used and uses three octets for network addressing and just one octet for host numbering. A typical Class C address range is from 192.0.1.0 to 223.255.254.0.

Classes D and E are reserved for specific uses. D is reserved for multicasting and E is reserved by the IEFT (Internet Engineering Task Force) for its own research.

It is virtually impossible to put all of these hosts on the same network because there are problems with limitations in the physical media, congestion due to large volumes of traffic, and wide geographic separations. To manage the hosts on a network, you have to break the network into smaller subnets. TCP/IP allows you to extend the network ID portion beyond its default boundary by using a subnet mask. This is a 32-bit number that is applied to an IP address to identify the network and node addresses. The dotted decimal notation used for subnet masks is the same as the notation used for IP addresses. You can extend the network address portion of a Class B address by reserving the three bytes for your subnet network address. If you set the subnet mask to 255.255.255.0, it appears as a Class C address. Table 9.2 illustrates subnet masks and the range of addresses that are possible.

TABLE 9.2: SUBNET MASKS FOR IPV4 ADDRESS CLASSES

Address Class	Subnet Mask	Number of Addresses	Host Address	Network Address
A	255.0.0.0	16,777,216	xxx.xxx.xxx	xxx
B	255.255.0.0	65,536	xxx.xxx	xxx.xxx
C	255.255.255.0	256	xxx	xxx.xxx.xxx

In the address space for IPv4, which is the current IP standard, you will find that the five different address classes (A, B, C, D, and E) can have a range of addresses assigned to them. Table 9.3 illustrates available numbers that can be assigned for each byte range (because Classes D and E are reserved for specific uses, they are not included in the table).

TABLE 9.3: RANGE OF ADDRESS NUMBERS

Address Class	Byte 1	Byte 2	Byte 3	Byte 4
A	0–127	1–254	1–254	1–254
B	128–191	Reserved for network address	1–254	1–254
C	192–223	Reserved for network address	Reserved for network address	1–254

The Internet is running out of address space. To solve this problem, as well as to add additional security and other functionality, eventually IPv6 will replace the current IPv4 standard. IPv6 uses a simplified header scheme, better authentication and privacy support, address autoconfiguration, and Quality of Service (QoS) functionality. IPv6 increases the IP address from 32 bits to 128 bits and allows through scoping the scaling of multicast routing to multicast addresses. Multicast support is in addition to unicast and anycast support. Unlike IPv4, IPv6 has no broadcast addresses; it uses multicast addresses instead. You will find IPv6 in Solaris 8, and the installation offers you the choice of using this networking protocol.

Adding Networks

You can use the Computers/Networks portion of the Solaris AdminSuite 3 to add a new network to your current domain. Adding a new network creates an entry in the network or netmasks table. To access this functionality in AdminSuite, follow these steps:

1. Open AdminSuite.
2. Click the Computers/Networks icon in the left (navigation) pane, as shown in Figure 9.6.

FIGURE 9.6

The Computers/Networks section of the AdminSuite

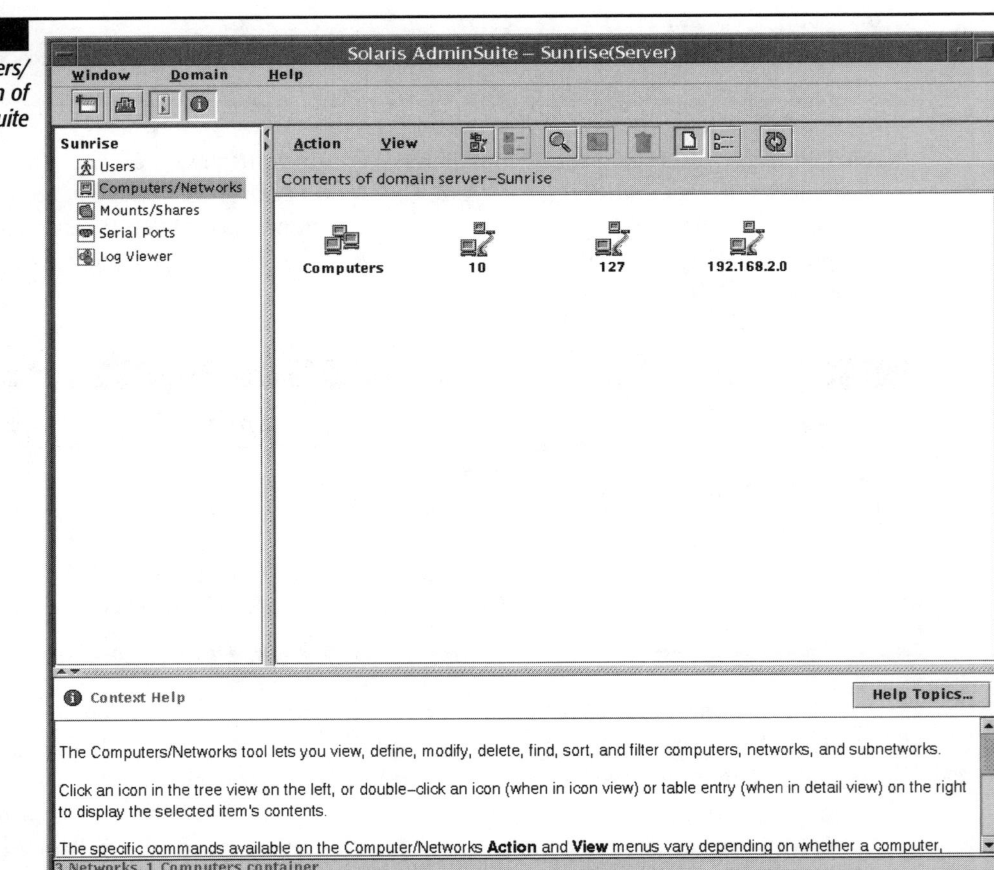

3. Select the Add Network command from the Action menu.
4. In the Add Network/Subnetwork dialog box (shown in Figure 9.7), enter the network name, IP address, and subnet mask into the Name, IP Address, and Netmask text boxes, respectively.
5. Click the OK button.

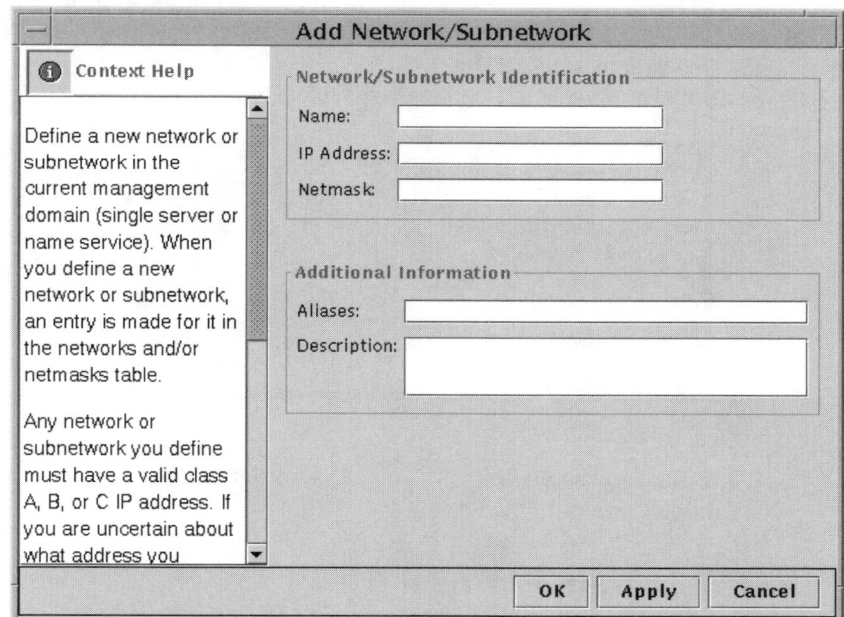

FIGURE 9.7
Use the Add Network/Subnetwork dialog box to define additional computers and their network interfaces.

You can also add a multihomed host alias for servers that contain two or more network interface cards (NICs). To define a multihomed system, perform the following procedure in AdminSuite:

1. Click the Computers/Networks icon in the left (navigation) pane.
2. Double-click the Computers icon in the right pane.
3. In the Set Initial View window, filter the information you wish to see (e.g., See All Computers) and click the OK button.
4. Select the Add Computer command from the Action menu.
5. In the Add Computer dialog box (shown in Figure 9.8), enter the name of the computer and the additional IP address(s) of the multihomed system, then click the OK button.

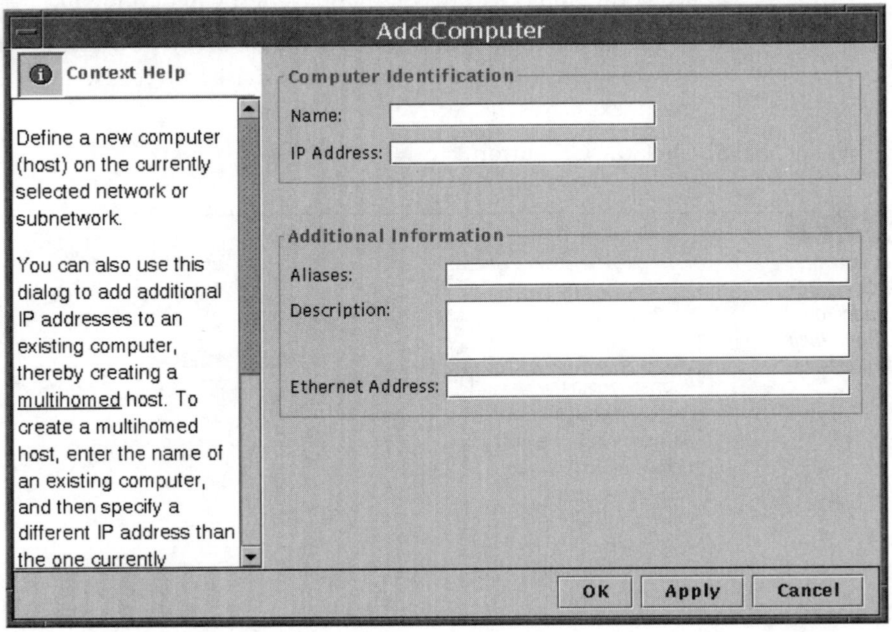

FIGURE 9.8

The Add Computer window lets you define new computers and add additional network interfaces to multihomed systems.

In the Computers window, you can also right-click a computer and either rename it, modify its settings, or delete it.

User Datagram Protocol (UDP)

The User Datagram Protocol (UDP) is a connectionless communication protocol, one of the two major network communications types (the other is connection-oriented communication). The major connection-oriented protocol is TCP, which was discussed earlier. UDP, also discussed briefly earlier, is a connectionless, unreliable transport protocol that is responsible for end-to-end transmission of data. Unlike TCP, it does not establish a connection. With little overhead, it directly transmits data needed for an application and verifies that the destination host actually receives the data. UDP adds only the source and destination port numbers, along with the checksum information for the message packet. These source and destination port numbers have the same function they do with TCP, as does the checksum, which is quite similar to the checksum in TCP. When a UDP packet with a bad checksum is received, the packet will be discarded automatically.

UDP is usually used in situations in which the size of the data being exchanged is a concern. It is best used to send small amounts of data for which guaranteed delivery is not required. For faster performance, the data should fit into a single message packet transmitted by UDP. Actually, for applications that are designed to recover from errors, the retransmission of a lost or damaged datagram will incur less overhead with a UDP connection than it would with a typical TCP connection. One of the disadvantages of UDP, however, is that the maximum packet size is 64 kilobytes of data per packet, so any protocol that uses it must be able to segment data efficiently and correctly. Like TCP, UDP is part of the Transport layer.

Hosts and Routers

Either hosts or routers handle addressing chores on a network. All networks must contain a host or hosts, but not every network has to have a router. Whether you employ a router is determined by the physical topology of your network. You use routers whenever you need to connect two or more networks together to form a larger network. Routers not only provide connection points between networks, they can also be employed to provide an alternate pathway between networks. Figure 9.9 shows how routers are used to connect networks together as well as provide alternative pathways. Having an alternative pathway helps minimize network congestion as well as provide redundancy through additional connections.

FIGURE 9.9

The use of routers to connect networks

A

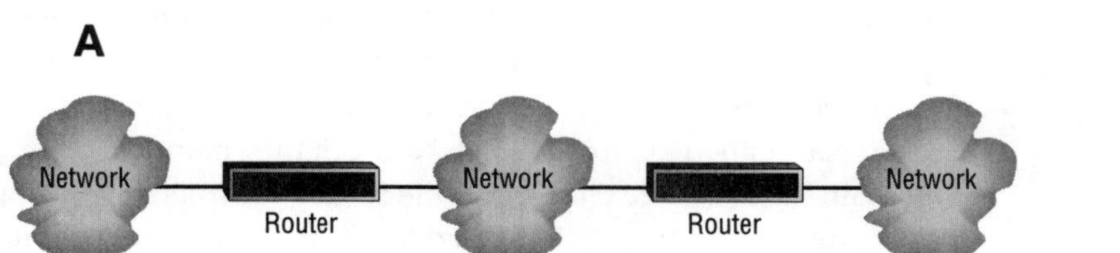

B

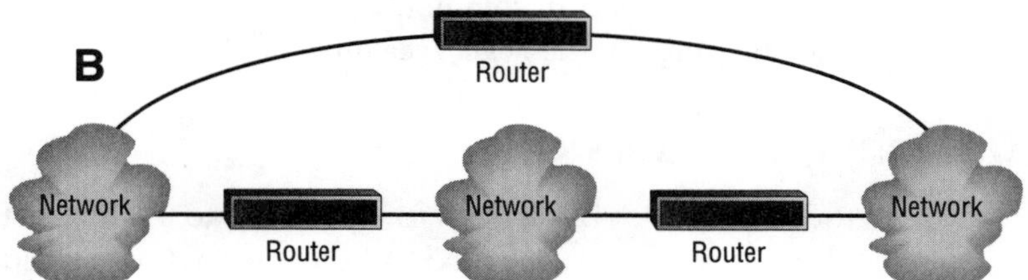

What routers do is intelligently route IP traffic based on a set of rules or algorithms. They examine the packet header, and from the address of the network in the packet, they determine the best route to use to send the packet on to the destination network. Many routers store routing tables based on historical patterns of usage and traffic as well as on historical performance. Sun and other Unix servers were widely used as routers in the early development of the Internet. These days, companies like Cisco have built router appliances that have replaced general-purpose servers for Internet routing.

Name Services

It would be tedious to have to refer to each router, computer, and NIC by its IP address, and it would be extremely hard to remember. It is harder still when each computer contains more than one NIC card because specific IP addresses are applied to NIC cards and not to computers themselves. Thus, friendly names are applied to computers and to ranges of addresses (called domains), and a mapping is done to relate the specific IP address to the friendly name. That is the purpose of DNS, which is a name service described in the following section. Each domain name must be unique on a network, and each domain name on the Internet must also be unique. If you only have an intranet (a private internetwork) set up, then your domain names can be duplicates of domain names on the Internet. It is, however, good practice not to duplicate names.

In selecting a name service, Solaris offers you the option of using local files (a manually maintained mapping table), Network Information Service (NIS), NIS+, and the domain name service (DNS). A name service maintains the mapping of host names, IP addresses, and MAC or Ethernet addresses that are related to one another.

When Solaris is installed, the host name and IP address that you specify for your system (client or server) are entered into the `hosts` and `ipnodes` network databases. These databases are used by the name services to address your system, and so deciding what name service you are going to use is an important part of your network design. The three names services in common use—NIS, NIS+, and DNS—all use local files. These files are stored in the `/var tree` directory locally.

Domain Name Service

With the initial design of ARPAnet, the precursor to the Internet, all computers on the network had a file called `hosts.txt`. All the information needed about every host on the network was contained in this file. IP address mapping was also included. At that time, the network was relatively small and the file was easily maintained. Once the network began to grow with the BSD systems, the `hosts.txt` file was adapted to support Unix and was ultimately renamed `/etc/hosts`. Administrators had to be up-to-date with a new copy of this file in order to keep their own sites current. They e-mailed their requests to the responsible party, SRI-NIC, once or twice a week. Naturally, as the network increased in size, the task for maintaining this file became monumental. SRI-NIC designed a replacement system based on a distributed database built on a hierarchical domain structure. This new system, called the domain name service, requires that every computer on the network be part of a domain and that each domain have a name server that maintains a database of the hosts for that domain. ARPAnet adopted the DNS system in September 1984 and it has remained the standard method for accessing host-name-to-IP-address mapping ever since.

Domains in DNS create a hierarchical tree structure similar to the Unix file system, with a single root domain, represented by the single period (`.`), at the top of the tree. The root domain is similar to the root directory (/) of the Unix file system. The root domain has servers that are geographically distributed. They answer queries and are maintained by SRI-NIC. Beneath the root domain are several top-level domains and their subdomains. Each system within a domain is called a *host*.

Top-level domains are located directly under the root domain and are either organizational or geographical. The organizational domains identify machines belonging to a type of organization with the United States. The geographical domains are used to identify machines that are located within a particular country. Table 9.4 describes the organizational domain types.

TABLE 9.4: ORGANIZATIONAL TOP-LEVEL DOMAINS

Domain	Description
.arpa	Used for inverse address lookups
.com	Commercial organizations and businesses
.edu	Educational organizations, universities
.gov	U.S. government agencies
.mil	U.S. military organizations
.net	Network organizations and ISPs
.org	Nonprofit organizations

Additional top-level domains have been proposed to better differentiate the types of services that are provided by the sites within a domain. Further breakdown of domain sites helps to assess which domains are associated with different commercial sites. It also allows parents to add controls for what their children view on the Internet. Table 9.5 lists the proposed domains and their descriptions.

TABLE 9.5: PROPOSED DOMAINS

Domain	Description
.aero	Air-transport businesses
.arts	Cultural or art organizations
.biz	Businesses
.coop	Cooperatives
.firm	Incorporated businesses, trades
.info	Unrestricted
.museum	Museums
.name, .nom	Personal or individual
.pro	Accountants, lawyers, physicians
.rec	Recreational, entertainment
.store	Online retailers

As with subdirectories, subdomains are created to associate hosts that are related by physical location or business function. This helps to give organization and order to the hierarchical structure. Subdomains can be created at any time without notification to the top-level domains. Just as in the Solaris parent and child relationship, when the parent top-level domain creates its child, the subdomain, it delegates authority for that subdomain to the child's name server. Although the parent knows the address of the child's name server, it doesn't know about any of the systems located in the subdomain. Subdomains are often referred to as zones. A *zone* is a piece of the naming tree that is under the administrative control of a particular name server.

Each domain within the DNS tree has a fully qualified domain name (FQDN). This is similar to a path name for a directory in the Unix directory tree. If you want to identify the FQDN, you start by getting the name of the current domain, adding the name of the parent domain, adding the name of the grandparent's domain, and so on until you reach the root of the tree.

TIP Flexibility in naming is built in to DNS, but to keep the system hearty and scalable, a few conventions are observed. Domain and hosts names must contain only lowercase letters, and uppercase letters will automatically be converted to lowercase. The hyphen character and numerals are allowed. The maximum number of characters in a domain or host name is 63. The maximum number of characters in an FQDN is 255. The maximum number of subdomains is 127. The restrictions are specifically designed to limit the DNS tree to 5 or 6 levels to keep name lookups as fast as possible.

The DNS is based on a query-and-response process. This process is called *name resolution* because it resolves the host name of a system right down to its IP address. If a DNS client wants to determine the IP address for a host, it will send a resolution request to its DNS server. That name server will then communicate with other name servers to find the information requested by the client. No single name server knows all of the information about a domain; it knows only what it needs to know at the time. When a name server does not know the address of a host, it just refers the resolver to the name servers listed in the `resolv.conf` file for a different name server that might be able to determine the address. All queries and responses are transmitted using UDP datagrams. These transmission requests are both sent and received by the DNS server on port 53.

Solaris systems by default are not configured to use DNS. However, you can enable the stub resolver to use DNS by modifying the network services configuration file, `/etc/nsswitch.conf`. To enable the DNS, edit the line

```
hosts:    files
```

to read

```
hosts:    files dns
```

You also need to configure the `/etc/resolv.conf` file, which would look like this:

```
$ cat /etc/resolv.conf
domain <domain name>
nameserver <primary name server for system>
nameserver <secondary name server for system>

$
```

You can have many name server listings, one for each system you want to use as a name server. Usually, you have only two or three.

You can configure your system to act as one of three different types of name servers if you so desire. However, most systems should just be clients or they would become overloaded with requests because no system would be caching for any others. If you do choose to configure name servers, number one is the master (or primary) name server and is the most authoritative of the three. It will have the most up-to-date records for all the hosts in its zone. In DNS, the master server is always considered to be absolutely correct. That is why the term *authoritative* is used. Number two is the slave server, which receives its updates from the master name server. It is a replica of the master name server and depends on the master to receive the zone data. The slave lists masters that it can contact to update its copy of the zone. Number three is a hint (or caching) name server and contains just a list of root name servers to resolve queries that it receives. It is not authoritative for any domain.

When a query is made to a hint server for the first time, the hint server forwards the query to an authoritative server. The hint server will then respond to further queries for that host using the IP address in its cache until the entry expires. If you are connecting to an existing network, there may be a name server already configured for it. If you are setting up a new department or a new group within an existing department, you will need to set up at least a hint name server to reduce the load on your master name server. If you are setting up a new site or a new subdomain within an existing site, you must configure a master and perhaps a slave name server.

TIP It is possible to configure a single name server to be master for one domain and slave for another and also act as a hint name server. DNS allows a single name server to have multiple roles.

A master name server responds to queries with authoritative answers for the zone in which it is located. The database file it draws on is called the *zone database file*, and it contains the host names and corresponding IP addresses for the hosts within the server's zone. The information in the zone database file is stored in the form of resource records. These records store the host name and IP address information in the database along with various other attributes. The master name server can query other name servers and maintain a cache of their responses, which reduces the time needed to resolve frequently accessed host names. It can also delegate the responsibility for subdomains to other name servers. Before the information for a domain controlled by a master name server can be changed, the zone database file must be changed. This file contains an incremental serial number that changes each time the database is altered in order to ensure that slave name servers will obtain the changes.

TIP The most common mistake that DNS administrators make is that they fail to increment the serial number. It is helpful to use a consistent serial numbering scheme, such as, for example, a date notation like 200108021 for 2001, Aug 2, revision 1.

The slave name servers act as backup name servers for the master name server if it crashes or somehow becomes inaccessible. Most domains will have at least one slave name server available. The slave name servers can also query other name servers and store a cache of responses to speed up the response time to frequently accessed host names. The slave name server will synchronize with the database on the master to update the zone information. The synchronization is based on comparing the serial numbers on both databases to make certain they match. If the serial number on the master is larger than that of the slave's, then the slave name server will perform a zone transfer, which is a procedure used by the slave name server for obtaining a new copy of the zone database from the master name server.

The hint servers do not contain authoritative information. Their only purpose is to forward queries to other name servers and cache the answer for a prescribed period of time. When a resolver queries a hint name server, that server will return the answer it has stored in its cache instead of forwarding the query to another name server. Hint name servers are used to reduce DNS traffic within large domains.

To keep your DNS server as secure as possible, you must employ two techniques. The first is to restrict responses, and the second is to restrict zone transfers. Restricting zone transfers to your slave servers is the most important consideration and will offer some security in itself. However, enterprising hackers can always find a way around the zone transfer issue.

Restricting zone transfers that contain all of the information about your zone is the number one priority in keeping your DNS server secure. Your entire zone database could be acquired through an illicit zone transfer. You need to allow queries to your primary or backup domains; otherwise, you won't be able to look up any records for the domains. But you should restrict general queries so others won't use your system as their name server. You need to specify the list of IP addresses that are allowed to initiate zone transfers with your name server. On Solaris 8 (BIND), your will need to specify an `allow-transfer` parameter for each zone directive in the name server configuration file, `/etc/named.conf`. The syntax for this parameter is as follows:

```
allow-transfer {<address1>; <address2>;…<addressN>;};
```

In this example, *<address1>* through *<addressN>* are either the IP addresses or network addresses from which you want to allow zone transfers. The `allow-transfer` is a parameter of the zone directive, which means that you need to specify it for every zone directive in order to restrict zone transfers.

The most common Solaris interface to the DNS is the Berkeley Internet Name Domain (BIND) software, which follows the client/server model. On any local network, there may be one or more systems running a name server, supporting all the local hosts as clients. If a system sends a message to another host, it queries the nearest name server to learn the remote host's IP address. The client, or resolver, may be a process running on the same computer as the name server. It may pass the request over the network to reach a server as well. To reduce network traffic and speed up the lookup process, the local name server has some knowledge of distant hosts. When a local server contacts a remote server with a request for an address, after a response, the local server adds that address to its internal table and reuses it for a while. The name server deletes the non-local information before it can become outdated.

NIS and NIS+

The Network Information Service (NIS) was developed by Sun Microsystems to simplify the task of administering common files that were controlled and maintained in a central database. Clients had to contact the database server to retrieve information. NIS was given the task of keeping system-independent configuration files such as /etc/passwd current. Many of today's networks include systems supplied by different manufacturers and may run different versions of Unix or Solaris. They do have certain commonalties, however, such as directories.

Sun had to rename the service once called Yellow Pages because another corporation owned the copyright on the name. The names of the NIS utilities still bear a resemblance to the old name because they are still prefixed with yp. For example, ypcat displays an NIS database, and ypmatch searches for matching information.

When a utility maps a number to the corresponding group name, it queries the NIS server when it sees a + sign, as in the following example:

```
$ cat /etc/group
+:*:*
$
```

You can display the group database using the ypcat utility as in the following example:

```
$ ypcat group
sos::153:barrie,kay,steve,wendel
.
.
.
```

You can also search for a particular group using the ypmatch utility:

```
$ ypmatch sos group
sos::153:barrie,kay,steve,wendel
```

Filtering the output of ypcat through grep can retrieve the same information. The most efficient way, however, is to use ypmatch simply because it uses a single process and searches the database directly. The NIS database name is the same as the simple filename. It is not the full path name of the file that it replaces. The ypmatch utility will work only on the key for the table or group name. If you must match on members of the group or other fields of the map, you must use grep with ypcat.

The system administrator sets up and maintains the NIS databases. Most users on a single-user Solaris system seldom work directly with NIS and are unaware that it manages system configuration files.

NIS+ replaces the NIS service and offers these additional features:

- A framework to set up and administer an organization in large companies
- Faster distribution of changes
- Better security

Solaris provides a name service switch file, `/etc/nsswitch.conf`, that lets you use and manage multiple network information services at the same time. Thus, DNS and NIS+ are not mutually exclusive.

NIS+ tables take the place of NIS maps. Solaris offers 16 table types: Hosts, Bootparams, Passwd, Cred, Group, Netgroup, Aliases, Timezone, Networks, Netmasks, Ethers, Services, Protocols, RPC, Auto_Home, and Auto_Master. Each table has information about different aspects of users, systems, and network parameters. Every domain keeps its own set of these tables, and you can access the information contained in them by row or by column. To work with NIS+ from the command line, use the following four commands:

`nistbladm` View and modify information in an NIS+ table.

`nisgrep` Search for data in an NIS+ table.

`nismatch` Search for data in a table.

`niscat` View the contents of an NIS+ table.

TIP It is worth mentioning that the NIS/NIS+ domain has no relation to a DNS domain, and Sun recommends that the NIS/NIS+ domain be different than your DNS domain to help keep people from confusing the two.

The Solstice Host Manager in previous versions of Solaris supports management of NIS+ tables, NIS maps, and the local `/etc` files' name services. You can use AdminSuite 3 in Solaris 8 to alter the contents of the Aliases, Auto_Home, Passwd, and Groups databases. NIS+ has a compatibility mode that allows it to pretend it's NIS, but this does negate the security features. Because only Solaris supports NIS+, it is helpful for environments in which Solaris is not the only operating system.

TCP/IP Administration

To set up a network, you will need to administer the TCP/IP settings of the various devices. This involves modifying the important network files and, when you encounter network problems, troubleshooting these files.

Local System Setup

When you have a system that is run in the local files mode, you will need to supply entries for the host name and create interface files for each NIC. During an installation, Solaris will ask you for these parameters, but should you need to change host names, modify IP addresses, or set up a router manually when you use local files, you will need to supply this new information as well. Changes made to these files must be done as a superuser.

Follow these steps to administer TCP/IP in local file mode:

1. As superuser, open the `/etc/nodename` file.
2. Enter the host name in the file and save the file.
3. Using a text editor, create a file called `/etc/hostname.interface` for each network interface or NIC.

   The network interface is typically the name of your NIC, so the filenames should be similar to `hostname.hme0`, `hostname.hme1`, and so forth.
4. Open each interface file using a text editor, enter the IP address for that interface into the file, and save the file. Also, you can enter the name for that interface as long as that name is in the `/etc/hosts` file.
5. Open the `/etc/inet/hosts` file and add the IP address of the network interface, as well as the host name for each interface.

   For a fresh hosts file, you will see entries for the primary network address as well as for the feedback loop address.
6. If the `/usr` file system is mounted by NFS, enter the IP address and name of the file server(s), then save the `hosts` file.
7. Enter the host's fully qualified domain name into the `/etc/defaultdomain` file.
8. For a network containing subnets, enter the network number and netmask into the `/etc/inet/netmasks` file, or when using NIS or NIS+, add the netmask information into the NIS database of a server on the same network.

When using router(s), perform these additional tasks:

1. Enter the router's name or IP address into the `/etc/defaultrouter` file.
2. Enter the IP address and the name of the default router into the `/etc/inet/hosts` file.

For these changes to take effect, you should reboot your computer.

The Seven Critical Network Files

Networks can be global in nature or as simple as a room with two or three computers connected together. There are two basic ways to set up the software to connect a Solaris machine to a network:

- Run the `sys-unconfig` utility and reboot the machine. After rebooting, it will ask you for system configuration information such as the host name, domain name, time zone, IP address, IP subnet mask, and root password. This is not recommended for the typical user because it can have dire effects. Only an experienced system administrator should ever attempt this, and only after doing a complete backup of the system.
- You can set up networking software by editing a few files such as `hosts`, `netmasks`, `defaultrouter`, and *<hostname>*.*<interface>*. If you change the system name, you must also edit the `/etc/net/ticlts/hosts`, `/etc/net/ticots/hosts`, and `/etc/net/ticotsord/hosts` files.

There are seven critical network files that provide TCP/IP configuration information, all of which are created by a default Solaris installation. In most instances, network problems can be resolved by examining these files, making sure the entries are correct, and/or editing the entries that are not correct.

The seven critical network files are as follows:

/etc/hostname.*<interface>* This file defines the network interface device, typically a NIC, and includes the IP address and host name. For example, in a system with two NICs (called a dual-homed system), each NIC would have a file. Dual-homed systems are often used in routers and proxy servers because they provide physical network isolation of one network (say an Internet connection) to an internal network. When you are using IPv6, the file `/etc/hostname6.`*<interface>* is used to start the network interface.

/etc/nodename This file should have only one entry in it, the host name of the local system.

/etc/defaultdomain This file should contain the fully qualified NIS domain name of the domain that the system's local host is on.

/etc/defaultrouter (optional) This file should contain the name of any router that is connected to your network in the form of the network interface name that serves as the router between networks.

hosts database The `hosts` database contains a table of IP addresses and host names for systems on your network. For any of the common name services

(DNS, NIS or NIS+), the `hosts` database is part of the database that the name service assigns for host information. The format of the entries of the `hosts` database is as follows:

<IPv4 address> <hostname> <nicknames> <#comment>

When Solaris first creates the `/etc/inet/hosts` file, it contains two entries, one for the loopback and one for the local machine. The loopback address is a private address that lets a local system send messages to itself to test its TCP/IP stack or to communicate with IP services that you don't want available on your external interfaces. If you had a dual-homed machine, you would see an entry similar to the third line below:

```
127.0.0.1     localhost     loghost
192.168.1.1     sunrise     #The local system's host name
192.168.2.1     sunrise2     #This is the interface to the
    second network for a router
```

When you are using a local file for your name service, each system looks into its `/etc/inet/hosts` file for the host names and IP addresses of the system on the network. In that case, the `hosts` file must contain at a minimum the loopback address, the IP address and host name of the local system, the IP addresses and host names of all network interfaces, the IP addresses and host names of hosts and routers on the system, and the IP address of a system that your local system wants to identify by its host name.

`ipnodes` database The `ipnodes` database contains the IPv6 addresses and host names of systems on your network. For a name service, the `ipnodes` database is managed as part of the host table in the service.

`netmask` database (optional) The `netmask` database is used only when your network contains subnets. This database is a list of networks and their associated subnet masks. Subnetting allows you to divide larger networks into smaller networks for administration and performance reasons.

Dynamic Host Configuration Protocol (DHCP)

Dynamic Host Configuration Protocol (DHCP) is used to automatically supply a TCP/IP address as a service to a system when that system boots up. DHCP servers manage addressing information, provide addresses from a pool, assign a lease or lifetime for which a system can maintain a specific address, and provide other services from the DHCP to clients. Properly configured DHCP solves two vexing problems: first, it relieves the rather onerous task of a network administrator having to assign, track, and edit addresses manually in a database or text file, and second, by doling out the addresses to systems as they appear, it helps to alleviate the problem of having limited IP addresses to assign on a network.

Solaris DHCP also offers the additional benefits of supporting BOOTP (BOOTSTRAP Protocol) clients because both BOOTP servers and DHCP servers can listen to and respond to requests from clients using the same messaging structure. DHCP can provide the IP address requested by BOOTP clients. BOOTP can send messages from one network on to another. DHCP requests, because they use the same messaging structure, can also be relayed to the router and can't be differentiated from a BOOTP request.

An additional feature that clients obtain from Solaris DHCP is the information needed to have a server boot up on the network. This can take the place of using Reverse Address Resolution Protocol (RARP) and `bootparms`. DHCP servers supply the IP address, boot server, and network configuration information that a client needs to start up correctly. DHCP is also more efficient at servicing boot requests than other systems because requests can be relayed across subnets.

DHCP is a powerful network function that can save you a lot of time and aggravation if it is set up correctly. Since it is not possible to explain every aspect of DHCP in this publication, it is strongly recommended that you purchase one of the many books that are dedicated solely to the subject of DHCP or link to a Web site such as `www.dhcp.org` for more comprehensive information.

To start and stop DHCP services on a server, you can use the DHCP Manager or a command-line utility. DHCP is typically set up to start up automatically when the server boots, and the service becomes unavailable when the server is shut down. Therefore, DHCP servers are typically left running or backed up with redundant systems.

The DHCP server stores its data in the `hdcptab` file and in a set of DHCP network tables that each has as its filename the number of the network. Thus, a network with the address 192.168.1.1 would store its DHCP information in the table with the name `192_168_1_1`.

The DHCP Manager is a GUI utility that you can use on the server to configure, start, stop, disable, and enable the DHCP service. You can also use this tool to customize your DHCP server settings. DHCP lets you choose which IP addresses will be managed, work with network configuration macros, and modify nonstandard network configuration options. You will find a thorough help system provided with the DHCP Manager.

To start the DHCP Manager, do this:

1. On a local system, log in as a superuser using the following command:

   `# xhost +<servername>`

On a remote DHCP server, enter the following:

```
# Display=localhost; export display
# /usr/sadm/admin/bin/dhcpmgr &
```

2. Make your changes in the DHCP Manager window.
3. Select the Exit command from the File menu.

Here are the four DHCP command-line utilities (each of these four commands is documented in the man pages):

in.dhcpd This command lets you control the DHCP daemon.

dhcpconfig This is a shell script that lets you configure the DHCP server using commands presented in a text-based menu system.

dhtadm This command allows you to change the configuration options and macros for DHCP clients.

pntadm This command allows you to modify DHCP network tables.

The Solaris DHCP client is the system that accepts the IP address from the server. On Solaris, it is a software program run as a daemon (dhcpagent). Solaris automatically installs the DHCP client as part of the installation of the operating system. You do not need to enable this client because it is already enabled.

The Network File System

The Network File System (NFS) allows you to work locally with files that are stored on a remote computer disk but appear as if they are present on you own computer. The remote system acts as a file server, and the local system acts as the client and queries the file server.

NOTE File systems were covered extensively in Chapter 5. You may want to refer back to that chapter for a more detailed discussion of NFS.

The system administrator configures the NFS just as they do the NIS. If you are working with a file, you will probably not be aware of where the file is physically stored. This is another perfect example of distributed computing. Because most central file servers are equipped with large-capacity disk drives and devices that make backup copies of data, some Solaris systems may be diskless. A floppy disk can be used to start Solaris and load the system software from another machine on the network. Solaris also produces a dataless system that stores only the system software and the operating system, and the applications are kept on the disk.

Use the df utility to display a list of the file systems available on your system (you can use df with the -k option to show it in kilobytes instead of blocks). It will also show you what disk space is free and how much is used. File system names that are prepended with host names are available to you.

All standard Solaris utilities work with NFS remote files in the same way that they operate on files stored locally. The physical location of the files is not important unless you lose access to the files through downtime or temporary unavailability. You will most likely get an error message if the NFS server is not able to respond. It will then give you an OK message when the files become available again.

One of the advantages of distributed computing is that you can log in on any machine on the network and all of your files will be available to you, including your startups scripts. Your home directory will always be available to you on any machine on the network.

Sharing File Systems

Sharing local files with other machines has many advantages. It saves disk space, which is a major advantage, but it also gives you a single place to change data instead of having to change it several times at different locations. Shared file systems are usually stored under the /export or /usr/export directory (though you can share any file system or directory on your system), and each subdirectory houses a shared file system. Shared files can be kept in any directory.

To share a file system, you must enable NFS by editing /etc/dfs/dfstab. This file is run by the /etc/rc3.d/S15nfs.server script once the system enters run level 3. The syntax is as follows:

```
$ cat /etc/dfs/dfstab
# place share (1M) commands here for automatic execution on
#   entering init state 3.


#Issue the command '/etc/init.d/nfs.server start' to run the
#   NFS daemon processes and the share commands, after adding
#   the very first entry to this file.

#share [-F fstype] [ -o options] [-d "<text>'] <pathname>
#   [resource] .e.g,
share -F nfs -o rw-engineering -d "home dirs" /export/home2
share -nfs -o ro-huey, rw=dewey:louie, root=dewey -d "home \
   directories" /export/home share -F
```

There are several options that specify file system properties:

- The `-F` option specifies the file system type. On a newly installed Solaris machine, NFS is the most relevant choice, although AFS (the Andrew File System) and DFS (the Distributed File System) are available as well.
- The `-o` option specifies the types of access given to the file system. It is followed by a list of arguments separated by commas. The `ro` takes zero or more values, which are separated by colons. If there are no values, read-only access is given to all users. The `rw` argument is similar to `ro` but gives read-write access. The root argument must always be followed by one or more host names, separated by colons, in a list.
- The `-d` argument is used to provide a description of a resource being shared.

A file system that is mounted on a directory within an exported file system is not exported automatically with the exported file system. It needs to be individually exported, even if it resides within an already exported file system. Most other subdirectories and files are automatically exported, however.

Sharing root files is not recommended. Files owned by root are not writeable by root from another machine. If you export the file system with read-write privileges, by default the write privileges are lost when root is exported with the file system. The `root=host` syntax allows a remote machine to create, change, and delete files owned by root. The `root` option should not be used unless it is absolutely necessary. If used, it should be removed as soon as it is no longer needed.

If you export a symbolic link, make certain that the object of the link is available on the remote machine. It must exist on a client machine; if it doesn't, you must export and mount it along with the exported link or it will not point to the file on the server.

TIP A device file refers to a kernel interface. When a device file is exported, the interface goes with it. If the remote machine does not have the same type of device, the exported device will not work. The safest way to handle devices is to disable them when mounting the file system over the network.

The NSF daemons will not be running when you first edit the `/etc/dfs/dfstab` file. Even when the `/etc/rc3.d/S15nfs.server` script runs and sees `/etc/dfs/dfstab` with comments in it, it will not start the NFS service daemons.

Once you have created the file, you can start the daemons by using one of the following procedures:

- Reboot the machine to automatically start the right services.
- Run the `/etc/rc3.d/S15nfs.server` script.

- Run the /etc/init.d/nfs.server script.
- Start the daemon scripts by hand if you are very experienced. Not recommended for the typical user.

If you want to change the /etc/dfs/dfstab file, use shareall to run it and share the file systems you specified in dfstab. Individual share commands can also be executed. Use copy and paste from the file into a window that is running a root shell.

TIP A file system cannot be unshared by deleting it from dfstab and running shareall.

Unsharing File Systems

You can remove access to a file system so that other machines cannot mount it. Use the unshare command. Here is the syntax for the unshare command:

```
$ unshare  -F nfs /export/home
```

Use unshare without arguments for all exported file systems. You should perform this just before bringing your system down if you are an administrator. When you use the unshare command on a file system others are using remotely, a message similar to the following will appear on their console:

```
Server not responding. Stale NFS file handle.
```

or something very similar.

Mounting Remote File Systems

The most advantageous way to work with the client/server distributed computing network is to mount file systems on demand. Machines mount hundreds of other machines in a large network, looking for files and/or home directories. If there is a break in the network or if machines are down for maintenance, you can have a lot of trouble accessing the information you need. Demand mounting, which is handled by the automountd daemon, is one way to alleviate this problem. If you are looking for a home directory, you can issue a command like the one in the following example:

```
ls /home/barrie
```

A command such as this will have automountd look in the auto-home map, see that barrie is a key to mount medfield:/export/home/barrie, and finally mount the remote file system. After mounting the file system, ls will display the list of files you want to see. If you then give the command ls /home, ls will show that barrie is present within the /home directory. The df utility will show that barrie is mounted from medfield. The automountd daemon will automatically unmount the file system after it has been inactive for five minutes.

The /net and /home maps are included in several other default automount maps. Use the /net mountpoint to access other hosts. If you know there are NFS servers with specific names, you can view all the file systems that are exported by each one. Use ls to display /net medfield, net medford, and so on. Once the file systems are mounted, browse through them.

NOTE You can use the AdminSuite to view and modify your shares and mounted file systems as well as to set up automounts.

Solaris has produced a very powerful automount facility. It is more powerful than that contained in other commercial versions of Unix. If you want to use a remote file system on your local machine, it needs to be mounted. The following example command will mount the file system by hand:

```
% mkdir /perhome /docs
% mount barrie:/export/home /perhome
% mount -o ro, nosuid barrie:/export/docs
% mount -o ro barrie:/export/docs/access /docs/access
```

If you use mkdir to make directories on which to mount the file systems, then you use mount to mount the file systems. The file systems will be read-write by default if the NFS server is exporting with read-write permissions. In the first line, the /export/home directory is mounted from the machine named barrie on the local directory /perhome. The second and third lines use the -o ro option to force a read-only mount. The second mount line also uses the -ro option to force a read-only mount, and in addition, it adds the -o nosuid option by using the multiple-option form of the -o option.

The nosuid option forces mounted setuid executables to run with regular Solaris permissions. Use the entries in /etc/vfstab to mount the /var/mail directory from the server whenever the machine is booted. This entry will mount the /var/mail directory from the server named mailhost whenever the machine is booted:

```
mailhost:/var/mail    -    /var/mail    nfs    -    yes \
    intr,hard,bg,noac
```

Here there is no raw device to check. The file system type is NFS and the command fsck is not run at boot. This example is designed for mounting a mail spool directory from a mail server. Table 9.6 describes the various NFS options and what they do.

TABLE 9.6: THE AUTOMOUNT OPTIONS

Option	Meaning
actimeo=*n*	Set attribute cache for files to expire in *n* seconds.
bg	After mounting failure, try again in background.
fg	After mounting failure, try again in foreground.
hard	Continue trying until server responds (use on read-write file systems; all processes that need the file system will be held until server responds).
intr(nointr)	Allow or do not allow Ctrl+C to interrupt applications waiting for mount.
noac	Do not cache file attributes for this file system.
ro	Mount file system with read-only access.
rw	Mount file system with read and write access.
soft	Give error if the server does not respond (not used on writeable file systems).
vers=*n*	Default is 3 on Solaris; force to 2 if system does not support NFSv3.

Use the automount utility to mount file systems on demand. This utility is useful when there are a large number of servers or file systems to work with. It is helpful to remove server-server dependencies. If two servers that mount file systems from each other have one of their machines down, both may hang on the way back up as each tries to mount a file system from the other when using traditional vfstab-based mounts. The automount utility circumvents this by mounting only a file system from another machine as a process tries to access it.

Automatic File System Mount

An autofs file system remains unmounted until it is needed, at which time the system will mount it automatically on demand. If it is no longer needed after the default time of five minutes, it is unmounted. The automountd daemon, which is started by the /etc/rc2d/S74autofs script when the system enters run level 2, creates autofs mount points. It appears to the user as though the autofs file system is mounted. If this feature is turned off, you must give a command such as ls /home/barrie. That command will access one of the subdirectories of the autofs mount point to create the demand that causes automountd to mount the autofs file system so it can be seen. Before you issue the ls command, /home/barrie does not appear in /home. When a process attempts to access one of the directories of the unmounted autofs file system, the file system notifies the automountd daemon, which will then mount the autofs file system.

The /etc/auto-master is the main file that has control over automountd. The +auto-master line indicates that any auto-master map in NIS or NIS+ should be automatically incorporated into the file. There are two types of maps that indicate to automountd where to look for a file system to mount on the mount point. The indirect map, the name of which does not start with a hyphen, names a file in /etc that contains names of file systems to mount under the mount point along with the remote machine and path name of the file system.

A special or built-in map deals with remote file systems in a specific manner. There are three special maps: -hosts, -xfn, and -null. The -hosts special map works by default with the /net autofs mount point. If you access /net/<*hostname*>, <*hostname*> is automatically expanded to a list of all file systems exported from server <*hostname*>. These file systems are then mounted under /net/<*hostname*>. The -xfn special map works with Sun's Federated Naming Service (FNS). These directories are mounted under /sfn. The -null map disables the entries that are inherited from NIS or NIS+. In order to be effective, any of the -null entries must precede the +auto-master entry.

TIP The /home directory is under the control of automountd. If you put a new user named Kay with a home directory in /home/kay, automounting will fail. However, putting Kay's home directory in /export/home/kay will work once you change the passwd file entry to /export/home/kay and put an entry into /etc/auto-home.

Unmounting Remote File Systems

Files that have been mounted on remote file systems will need to be unmounted at some point. The following example demonstrates how to use the umount command to unmount files from remote file systems:

```
% umount /var/mail
```

This command tells umount to check /etc/mnttab to get the information necessary to unmount the appropriate file system from the correct server.

It is also possible to unmount all remote file systems with the single command umountall. Used with the -F option, this command will unmount all NFS file systems from all remote hosts. The syntax for this command is as follows:

```
% umountall -F nfs
```

If a file system is in use when umount is trying to unmount it, a message will be displayed such as the one shown here:

```
nfs umount: /opt/reliant:  is busy
```

You can use the -k option with umountall to find processes that are using the file system that it is trying to unmount, to terminate them, and then to attempt to unmount the file system again. If that fails, ask all the users to log off the system, kill any processes that may still be using the file system you wish to unmount, and try it again. You may have to reboot the system if all else fails.

Because the -F option designates the types of file systems to unmount, you can also use umountall to unmount all file systems that were mounted by automount, UFS, or any type of file system. The following example demonstrates this:

```
# umountall -F -K nfs
# umountall -F ufs
# umountall -F lofs
# umountall -F autofs
```

The second command will unmount local UFS file systems not in use but will fail on the root file system simply because most of the system daemons are started from the root hierarchy. The third command will unmount all loopback file systems usually referred to as LOFS. A loopback file system is created by automountd when the automount map indicates that the mount point is on a local machine. If you use automount to mount a LOFS, you will not be able to unit the UFS file system that houses the mounted LOFS until the LOFS is unmounted.

Other File System Commands

You can use the dfmounts command with a host name as the argument. It will display the resources that are mounted from the server you specify. The syntax for dfmounts is displayed here:

```
dfmounts [<options>] [<hostname>]
```

If used without the host name, dfmounts will report on local file systems that are exported and can be mounted by remote hosts. If you use the host name as an argument, dfmounts will report on file systems that are local to the host name and are exported.

The automountd daemon controls a directory that has been assigned as an autofs mount point. You cannot have the same directory as an autofs mount point and as an entry that is mounted using /etc/vfstab. You should never put a /home entry in /etc/vfstab because the /etc/auto-master file also has an entry for /home. The vfstab version of /home will disappear each time you reboot the system.

You can disable automounting of /home; delete or comment out the /home entry from the /etc/auto-master file simply by starting the line with a #. If you want to disable automounting completely, use mv to rename /etc/rc2.d/S74autofs as /etc/rc2.d/.S74autofs and reboot. Giving this file an invisible filename keeps it from being seen and executed. It will still be there, however, if you want to recall it.

Network Utilities

Solaris 8 provides utilities that you should become familiar with and use when communicating with networks. If you will be using the Internet (see Chapter 14), you will use these tools often. By using a common convention for the format of network addresses, Sun has modified existing tools to use on the Internet much as you would use them on a local network. Whenever an @ sign is used, a utility such as `finger` or `talk` interprets that to mean that you are looking for a remote host computer. If the @ sign is not used, the utility assumes that you are corresponding with someone on your local host computer.

TIP The prevalence of networks has created the need for newer utilities to control and monitor their activities. The commands that are discussed in this section were created specifically for systems on a network. They will not be of use with stand-alone computers.

To display information about users on remote systems, use the `finger` utility. Although it was originally designed to use on local networks, it has been enhanced to perform with *remote* networks.

You can use the user's name or login name in front of the @ sign. This causes `finger` to retrieve the information from the remote system for that user only. If there is more than one incidence of the user's name on the remote system, `finger` will display the results for all. Figure 9.10 displays how `finger` works.

This utility works by querying a standard network service, the `fingerd` daemon that runs on the remote system. Solaris supplies this service but some sites do not run it simply to minimize the load on their system, to reduce security risks, or to maintain privacy.

TIP It is the remote `fingerd` daemon that shares information with your system and decides how much information will be shared and in what format. The `fingerd` daemon gives account information on the system that can be viewed by anyone. Many sites disable `finger` and randomize user account IDs to maintain privacy.

Reports may have a different appearance than those shown in Figure 9.10. The appearance of the information for remote `finger` is similar to the appearance of the information for local `finger` with just one difference: `finger` will report the name of the remote system before displaying the results. The name of the host that answers may not be the system name you specified on the command line, depending on how the daemon service is configured at the remote end. Several host names may be listed if the `finger` daemon needs to contact another to retrieve information.

FIGURE 9.10

Using `finger` to display users on remote systems

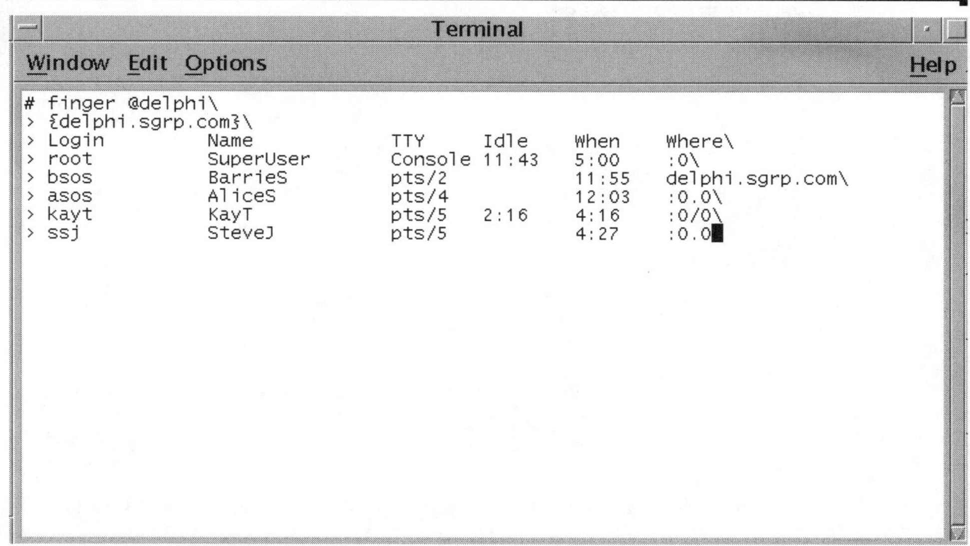

Remote Login Utilities

You can use the rlogin utility to connect and log in to an account on a remote system via the network if you want to access a special application or device available on a remote system where you have an account set up. It can be faster to take advantage of a remote system and then log out when your task has been completed. If you use a window system on your local computer, you have the ability to use many systems simultaneously by logging in to each one through a different window. To log out from a remote login, you would use the `exit` command at the command prompt.

When you log in remotely, the network can perform authentication to determine the user. Network authentication usually takes precedence over system authentication. When the remote system authenticates the user, the user is asked for a password unless the user is listed in the `/etc/hosts.equiv` or `.rhosts` file. In that case, the network can authenticate the user and no additional passwords are required.

The Telnet utility also lets you interact with a remote computer. It is similar to rlogin but will work in places where rlogin is not available. Unix supports Telnet access more heavily than it supports rlogin. Figure 9.11 shows how the remote utility logs in to a remote system using Telnet.

FIGURE 9.11

The Telnet remote utility

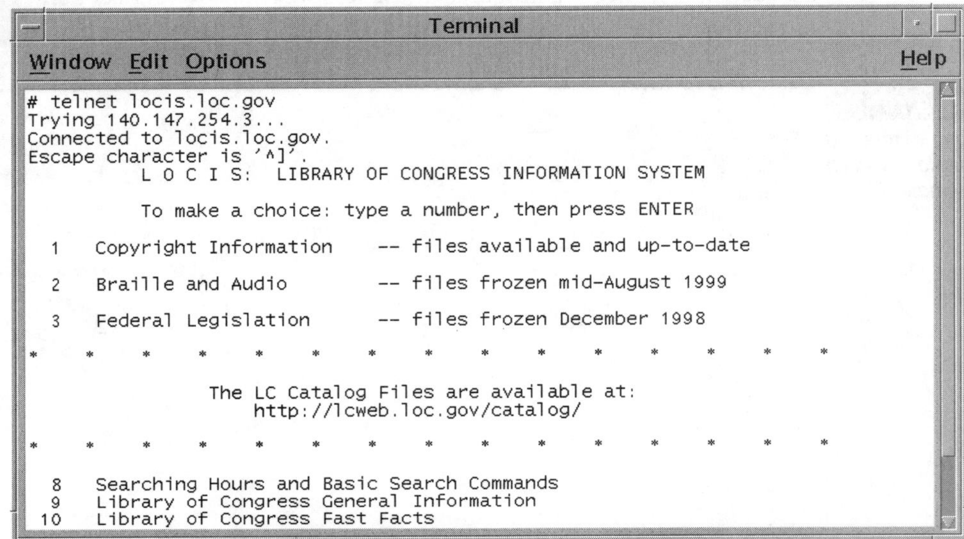
Terminal
Window Edit Options
Help
telnet locis.loc.gov
Trying 140.147.254.3...
Connected to locis.loc.gov.
Escape character is '^]'.
L O C I S: LIBRARY OF CONGRESS INFORMATION SYSTEM
To make a choice: type a number, then press ENTER
1 Copyright Information -- files available and up-to-date
2 Braille and Audio -- files frozen mid-August 1999
3 Federal Legislation -- files frozen December 1998
* * * * * * * * * * * * * * *
The LC Catalog Files are available at:
http://lcweb.loc.gov/catalog/
* * * * * * * * * * * * * * *
8 Searching Hours and Basic Search Commands
9 Library of Congress General Information
10 Library of Congress Fast Facts

If you connect to a remote Solaris system through Telnet, you will see a regular login prompt. On the other hand, rlogin naturally assumes that the login name on the remote system matches that on your local system. Because Telnet is specifically designed to work with non-Unix systems, it does not make such assumptions. To specify a different login name with rlogin, use the `-l` option.

TIP Security is an issue when you use rlogin or Telnet. Your password can be read by others who tune into the session. Refer to Chapter 8, "Security," for more information.

Telnet allows you to configure special parameters such as how returns or interrupts are processed. However, if you are using Telnet between two Unix/Solaris systems, it is rare to have to change any parameters. You should specify the name of a remote host on the command line. Telnet will run in interactive mode if you do not.

Before Telnet connects you to a remote system, it will tell you what your escape character will be. Most often it will be the Ctrl+]. If you enter a question mark in response to the `telnet>` prompt, Telnet displays a help list of the commands it recognizes. The `close` command ends the current Telnet session. To release out of Telnet's interactive mode and return to communicating with the remote system, press Return in response to a prompt.

TIP You can use remote services at special sites such as LOCIS, which is the U.S. Library of Congress Information System.

If you want to determine how long a system has been up and running, as well as the load average, use the `rup` *<systemname>* command. This command displays host name and uptime and load averages. You can also determine whether a system is connected and responding using the `ping` command, which is described in the following section. The third important command that is useful to determine system status on a network is the `rpcinfo` command. This command, typically issued in the form `rpcinfo -p` *<systemname>*, returns information about the RPC (daemon) services.

The *ping* Utility

To test a network connection or to verify that a remote system is available, the `ping` utility is used. It sends a special kind of IP data packet to the remote computer to elicit a reply. This is usually the fastest way to verify that a remote system is available and to check whether the network is operating efficiently. The `ping` utility uses a protocol called ICMP, or Internet Control Message Protocol.

The name `ping` mimics the sound of a sonar burst used by submarines to communicate with each other. Without any options, `ping` will test the connection to the remote system once and send back a reply.

TIP If you use the `-s` option and `ping` is unable to connect to the remote system, it will continue to try until you interrupt it with Ctrl+C. A failure to get a reply indicates that the system may be down or may be experiencing a software failure.

If, however, a system responds to `ping`, it does not necessarily mean that it is functional. Quite often a system will hang to the point where it no longer responds to Telnet/Web/FTP-type requests but will still respond to `ping`.

By default, the `ping` utility sends packets containing 64 bytes: 56 data bytes and 8 bytes of protocol header information. A packet sequence number called icmp_seq is also given. You can tell if a packet is dropped because a gap will occur in the sequence numbers. The round-trip time is listed in milliseconds and appears last in line. It represents the time it took for the packet to get from the local system to the remote system and for the reply to get from the remote system back to the local system. Distance between the two systems affects the time as well as other network traffic and the load on both systems.

If a host is unreachable, the `ping` utility will appear to hang because a timeout is occurring. The timeout will expire after it listens for a response from the remote system. The `ping` utility will ultimately inform you that the host is unreachable. If you try several different timeout values and you are unable to contact the remote system, try to ping other systems to determine where the problem originates. The default timeout is 20 seconds, but you can specify a different timeout. The following example displays the syntax:

```
% ping <host> <timeout>
```

In this example, *<host>* is the host name or IP address of the system you want to contact, and *<timeout>* is the timeout in seconds. On occasion, you may try to contact a host that is extremely slow. You should increase the timeout in order for your system to receive a response. Try the following example and reset the timeout to 30 seconds:

```
% ping delphi 30
```

There are times when reaching a host is a problem. Sometimes you will have periods of good connectivity and then will encounter a few intermittent instances of unreachability. To determine the problem, you can keep trying to ping a host by using the `-s` option, as in the following example:

```
% ping -s <host>
```

This causes the `ping` utility to send an ICMP echo request message to the remote system every second. Once it makes a connection, the `ping` utility will summarize the results and display how many packets were sent and received. It will display the minimum, average, and maximum round-trip delays it measured as well.

There will be times when you find that you are unable to connect to a remote system using Telnet. When you use the `ping` utility, however, you do get a response back. To debug this problem, you need to verify that the remote system is reachable for larger packets. Once you verify that you can send large packets to the remote system, you can use the `telnet` command to test whether the protocol is running on the remote system. Usually, the `ping` command sends small packets to the remote systems. If a network has heavy traffic and the systems are loaded, they can still respond to the ping. Larger packets may not reach the remote system or may be dropped in transit. You can test this by using the `ping` utility as displayed here:

```
% ping -s <host> <size>
```

In this example, *<host>* is the host name or IP address of the remote system and *<size>* is the size in bytes of the packet you wish to send. It's common to use 4,096 bytes per packet, and 512 bytes, 1,024 bytes, 4,092 bytes, and 8,096 bytes are also common packet sizes to try when testing to see if a remote system is receiving. Ethernet systems typically take the 1,024-byte packets. It is also possible to specify the number of packets that should be sent to the remote system by using the following syntax:

```
% ping -s <host> <size> <count>
```

When the number of packets has been specified, `ping` will exit and print a summary after it has finished transmitting the number you requested. You do not have to quit the program by pressing Ctrl+C. You will find this feature useful for hosts who are difficult to reach. The following example is the `ping` command requesting a try every second (`-s`) on the host Delphi, with 1,024-byte packets for 3 packets:

```
% ping -s delphi 1024 3
```

The *arp* Utility

All systems store a mapping table of IP addresses to Media Access Control (MAC) addresses for systems on their local network. This table is called the Address Resolution Protocol cache, or the ARP cache. The table is updated frequently by the Address Resolution Protocol (ARP), and the updates are based on the presence or absence of a MAC address in the broadcast traffic. Because of this, ARP is usually associated with Ethernet networks. It can be available on Token Ring and FDDI networks as well. If an address is not present in the ARP cache when it's requested by the system, ARP will create a message requesting the mapping and broadcast it on the network. When a response is received, the new mapping is added to the ARP table and any waiting messages to the remote host are forwarded. ARP will broadcast four messages before reporting a failure.

Solaris has an `arp` utility that allows you to view all of the entries in the ARP cache on your system. Figure 9.12 shows the output from the `arp` command. The syntax to use is `% arp -a`.

The first column specifies the interface that was used to learn the MAC address. The second and third columns contain the host name and network mask of the system that corresponds to the MAC address. The fourth column displays a set of flags that indicate the state of the entry. The fifth column contains the actual MAC address of the host system. If you needed to find all of the ARP entries that share a similar type of Ethernet card or are within a certain domain, you can combine the `arp` command with the `grep` command as in the following example:

```
% arp -a | grep <param>
```

In this example, the parameter you are interested in looking for is in the output. The following example shows the syntax for printing out all of the ARP cache entries for hosts in the delphi.us domain:

```
% arp -a | grep delphi.us
```

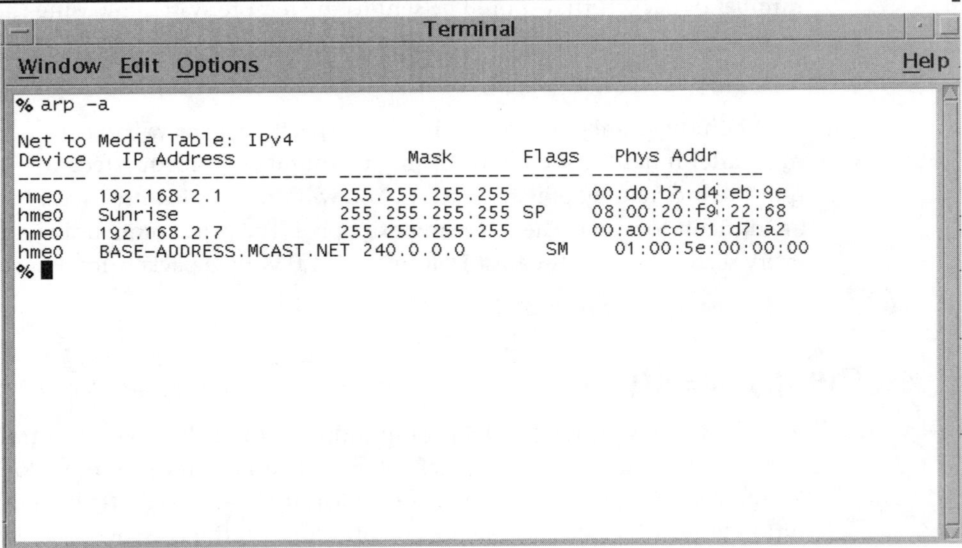

FIGURE 9.12 *You can use the `arp` utility to view the addresses of interfaces.*

The Reverse Address Resolution Protocol (RARP) does the opposite of what `arp` does. RARP is used by machines at boot time to discover their IP addresses. RARP is particularly helpful during jumpstart installations, especially with diskless clients. The `in.rarpd` daemon runs on the server and waits for RARP requests to arrive. It then utilizes the `/etc/ethers` and `/etc/hosts` databases to map the Ethernet addresses to the corresponding IP addresses. Diskless clients submit their RARP broadcast requests for an IP address to the network. At that point, the requesting machine must be defined in both the `/etc/ethers` and `/etc/hosts` databases for `in.rarpd` to respond.

The `arp` utility displays the contents of the entire ARP cache on your system. If you need to find only one host, you can display it using the following version of the command:

```
% arp <host>
```

On a rare occasion you may need to add or delete an entry from the ARP cache. It is likely that you will have more reason to delete bad entries than to add new entries, and ARP usually handles the ARP cache. However, to add an entry into the ARP cache, you can use the `arp` command as in the following example:

```
% arp -s <host> <mac> <type>
```

In this example, *<host>* is the host name or IP address of the system you wish to add, *<mac>* is the MAC address of that system, and *<type>* is an optional flag that indicates what ARP should do with this address. The two main types are `pub` and `temp`. The `pub` flag indicates that an entry should be published by ARP, and `temp` indicates that an entry is temporary and ARP can delete it as part of its normal process.

TIP To use the arp command to add or delete an entry from the ARP cache, you will need to know the MAC address of the system.

Once you have added an entry, you can verify whether it was added correctly by specifying the address, as shown in the following example:

```
% arp 10.7.12.5
10.7.12.5 (10.7.12.5) at 0.42.4.44.23.5g
```

If you need to delete an entry, you can use the arp command as follows:

```
% arp -d <host>
```

In this example, *<host>* is the host name or IP address of the system you want to delete. The following command deletes the entry for the host with the IP address 10.7.12.5:

```
% arp -d  10.7.12.5
10.7.12.5 (10.7.12.5) deleted
```

If you want to verify whether the ARP cache entry was deleted correctly, then specify the address as shown in this example:

```
% arp 10.7.12.5
10.7.12.5 (10.7.12.5) deleted
```


The *snoop* Utility

The snoop utility is a powerful debugging tool that "snoops" out networking problems. It prints out every packet that appears on the local network and shows you exactly what was transmitted and received by different protocols. It also displays only those packets sent from a particular host. The snoop utility provides an easy way of capturing communication when you are debugging problems with protocols or connectivity. When used in its simplest form, it displays a summary of information about all UDP, ICMP, and higher-level TCP protocol packets received by your system. The following is an example of the simple snoop syntax:

```
% snoop
```

TIP You must log on as root to use the snoop command. The snoop utility requires that the network interface be set in "promiscuous mode." This allows snoop to view all traffic addressed to the interface, including monocasts and broadcasts. To close out the snoop command, press the Ctrl+C keystroke.

Figure 9.13 shows some sample output from the `snoop` command. You can have the `snoop` command quit after capturing a certain number of packets if you use the `-c` option as shown in the figure.

FIGURE 9.13

The `snoop` *utility with option* `-c` *captures a certain length of packet traffic and displays it.*

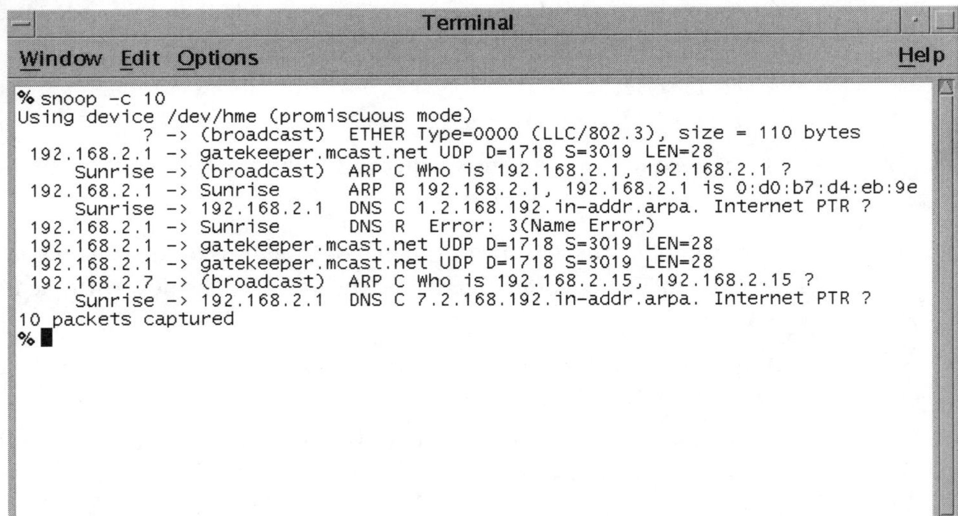
Terminal
Window Edit Options Help
% snoop -c 10
Using device /dev/hme (promiscuous mode)
? -> (broadcast) ETHER Type=0000 (LLC/802.3), size = 110 bytes
192.168.2.1 -> gatekeeper.mcast.net UDP D=1718 S=3019 LEN=28
Sunrise -> (broadcast) ARP C Who is 192.168.2.1, 192.168.2.1 ?
192.168.2.1 -> Sunrise ARP R 192.168.2.1, 192.168.2.1 is 0:d0:b7:d4:eb:9e
Sunrise -> 192.168.2.1 DNS C 1.2.168.192.in-addr.arpa. Internet PTR ?
192.168.2.1 -> Sunrise DNS R Error: 3(Name Error)
192.168.2.1 -> gatekeeper.mcast.net UDP D=1718 S=3019 LEN=28
192.168.2.1 -> gatekeeper.mcast.net UDP D=1718 S=3019 LEN=28
192.168.2.7 -> (broadcast) ARP C Who is 192.168.2.15, 192.168.2.15 ?
Sunrise -> 192.168.2.1 DNS C 7.2.168.192.in-addr.arpa. Internet PTR ?
10 packets captured
%

Usually, the summary information will give you the frequency and type of packets interchanged by the different hosts on the network. Sometimes you will want to get even more information about the packet headers at lower layers, such as the IP or TCP layers. There are two different modes that will list this information when called upon. The verbose mode and the verbose-summary mode produce two different lists. If you need a detailed breakdown of the packet contents, use the verbose mode. The output may include dozens of lines per packet and it's not always easy to read. It is best if you capture the output of `snoop` to a file. The verbose-summary mode prints out a single summary line for each layer and is easy to read in real time. The syntax for verbose mode is as follows:

```
% snoop -v.
```

The output for each packet is divided into three or possibly four sections depending upon the type of packet. The first two sections are ETHER (which contains Ethernet-specific information such as arrival time, the source and destination MAC addresses, and the packet size) and IP (which contains IP-specific information such as the header and body sizes, the source and destination IP addresses, and the IP header options).

The third and fourth sections will vary depending upon the type of packet. If there is a TCP packet, the third section is TCP and the fourth section is protocol specific. The TCP section will contain the source and destination ports plus a few lines of the protocol-specific packet headers. For UDP packets, the third section in the verbose output is UDP, which normally contains the source and destination port information. It may also contain information about the length and checksum of the UDP packet. For ICMP packets, the third section is ICMP, which contains information about the type of ICMP request and the checksum for the packet.

Each output line is labeled with the name of a layer, as in `<LAYER>: <data>`. The following example demonstrates an output line for TCP:

```
TCP: Source port = 22
```

It is easy to tell where each section of a layer starts. Figure 9.14 shows the header lines for the IP section.

FIGURE 9.14
The IP header

```
IP:
ICMP:IP:    ----- IP Header -----
ICMP:IP:
ICMP:IP:    Version = 4
ICMP:IP:    Header length = 20 bytes
ICMP:IP:    Type of service = 0x00
ICMP:IP:          xxx. .... = 0 (precedence)
ICMP:IP:          ...0 .... = normal delay
ICMP:IP:          .... 0... = normal throughput
ICMP:IP:          .... .0.. = normal reliability
ICMP:IP:    Total length = 134 bytes
ICMP:IP:    Identification = 21855
ICMP:IP:    Flags = 0x0
ICMP:IP:          .0.. .... = may fragment
ICMP:IP:          ..0. .... = last fragment
ICMP:IP:    Fragment offset = 0 bytes
ICMP:IP:    Time to live = 128 seconds/hops
ICMP:IP:    Protocol = 17 (UDP)
ICMP:IP:    Header checksum = 5f71
ICMP:IP:    Source address = 192.168.2.1, 192.168.2.1
ICMP:IP:    Destination address = 192.168.2.69, Sunrise
ICMP:IP:    No options
ICMP:IP:
```

You can filter the verbose mode with the `grep` command. If you are trying to debug a problem, you need to look at each layer in order to isolate the layer in which the problem occurs. Some of the most common problems include Ethernet frames being directed to the wrong MAC address and incorrect IP addresses. To display this type of information, you can use a command such as this:

```
% snoop - | grep <LAYER>:
```

Replace the word *LAYER* with the name of the layer you want, such as the IP layer or TCP layer.

The verbose-summary mode displays most of the same information as verbose mode but in a much shorter format. Here is the syntax for verbose-summary with snoop:

```
% snoop -V
```

In this mode, the output for each layer is displayed in a single line. For TCP packets, the output for each packet contains four lines. The first line is for Ethernet, the second line for IP, the third line for TCP, and the fourth line for the higher-level TCP protocol. The UDP and ICMP packets both have output for each packet in three lines. The first line is for Ethernet, the second line for IP, and the third line for UDP or ICMP, depending upon the packet type. The output from this mode will have the following format:

```
<source> -> <destination> <LAYER> <data>
```

<source> is the host name of the system producing the packet, *<destination>* is the remote host system, *<LAYER>* is the layer that the information corresponds to, and *<data>* is the layer-specific information. The ETHER layer data is usually the type of the frame and its size. For the IP layer, *<data>* contains the source and destination IP addresses of the packet as well as the length and ID of the packet. For TCP and UDP layers, *<data>* contains the source and destination ports. Finally, the ICMP layer data contains the type of the ICMP packet. This mode is also easy to filter using the grep or egrep command.

TIP If you are logged in to a remote system and using snoop to get information on the remote system (the interface you are connected to) or on the system you are coming from, you will get a lot of extra data. You will see all of the snoop output being displayed in the snoop log as it is sent to you. It is probably a good idea to run snoop on the console instead of being connected to the system or you will be generating traffic as well.

Capturing *snoop* Output

It is a good idea when you are debugging a network problem to capture snoop output to a file so you can analyze the contents of the file at length. There are two methods for capturing the output of snoop to a file. The first method is to use standard shell redirection:

```
% snoop <options> > <file> 2>&1
```

In this example, options for the snoop utility may be any of the options discussed in this section, and *<file>* is the path name of the file in which you want the output saved, such as /tmp/snoopy:

```
% snoop -V > /tmp/snoopy 2>&1
```

The second method for capturing the output of snoop to a file is to use the -o option:

```
% snoop -o <filename>
```

Here, <filename> is the path name of the file in which you want the output saved. Consider the following example:

```
% snoop -o /tmp/snoopy2
```

While the command is running, it will display the number of packets it is writing to the screen, as in the following example:

```
Using device /dev/be (promiscuous mode)
12
```

To terminate the capture of packets, press Ctrl+C. You can view the resulting file using the snoop command again but use the -i option this time. Direct the output of the command to a test file as in the following example:

```
% snoop -i /tmp/snoopy2>/tmp/snoopy2.txt
```

You can also capture just a certain part of a packet using the -x option. The syntax for the -x option is as follows:

```
% snoop <option> -x <offset>, <length>
```

In this example, <option> is either the -v or -V mode options and <offset> and <length> are the locations in bytes of where snoop should start and finish printing the contents of a particular packet. If you do not specify <length>, then snoop will print the contents of the entire packet from the start position. To display the entire packet, you can specify <offset> as 0 and leave off <length>, as in the following:

```
% snoop -x 0
```

The snoop utility has a powerful filtering feature that allows you to direct or deal with selective output for a single host, the source or destination host name, the network addresses, or the protocol type. The syntax for creating a filter is displayed in the following example:

```
% snoop <options> <expression>
```

<expression> is equal to any expression of a sort that can be recognized and acted upon by the snoop utility, as in `% snoop -V macys reliant`. This command will produce verbose-summary output for the two host systems.

Another type of filter that filters on the protocol type is `% snoop <type>`. <type> refers to the protocol parameter, for example, tcp, udp, or icmp. If you wanted to filter out all packets except TCP packets, you would use the following syntax: `% snoop tcp`. This command will give output on only TCP-based packets. The main snoop parameters are those that require additional arguments as described in Table 9.7.

TABLE 9.7: PARAMETERS FOR THE *SNOOP* UTILITY

Parameter	Output
`from` *<host>*	Packets coming from specified host. Argument *<host>* can be the system's host name or IP address.
`host` *<hostname>*	Packets coming from or going to the specified host name; can also be the system's IP address.
`net` *<network>*	Packets coming from or going to a network whose number is specified by *<network>*.
`port` *<num>*	Packets going to or coming from the TCP or UDP port number specified by *<num>*.
`to` *<host>*	Packets going to the specified host; argument *<host>* can be the system's host name or IP address.

The *netstat* and *ifconfig* Utilities

The `netstat` command can display important network status information. In Solaris 8, the `netstat` command supports both IPv4 and IPv6. The `netstat` command can list information such as the following:

- The condition of DHCP as applied to your network interfaces (when used with the `-i` option)
- The state of your network interfaces
- Active sockets for protocols
- Kernel routing tables (when used with the `-r` and `-n` options) and multicast routing

The `ifconfig` command is used to display detailed information about your network interfaces. You can also use it to set or reset network interfaces. When the `/etc/rc2.d/S69inet` script runs at boot-up, it runs `ifconfig` to define each network interface as it comes up. You can use `ifconfig` to display and modify network interfaces. In its common form, `ifconfig -a`, a listing of active interfaces is shown. To display information about a particular interface, use the command `ifconfig` *<interfacename>*.

The *nslookup* Utility

The `nslookup` utility is used to query the Internet domain name servers. When you give the utility a command, it will display the name and IP address of the default name server used by the system you are on. The following example shows the syntax:

```
$ nslookup


Default Server:  reliant.mfield.com
Address:    168.168.99.01
```

You can perform a specific query using the nslookup utility. Give the set query command to get nslookup to display the mail exchanger (MX) record. If present, the MX record will specify a mail address for the domain. The following example demonstrates how to set the query:

```
> set query=MX
> reliant.mfield.com

reliant.mfield.com preference = 8, mail exchanger = barrie.mfield.com

reliant.mfield.com nameserver =  barrie.mfield.com
```

You can establish different types of queries when using nslookup. If you set the query type to NS for name server, you will get three name server records. You must query a domain, however. If you query a host, the output will return start of authority (SOA) information, or you can use set query=any to get all of the information on that host.

The *whois* Utility

Use the whois utility to look for a user on the Internet (i.e., an Internet directory entry that you specify). This utility will return site contact and registry information. You will be able to track the person responsible for a site. You can search by name or by handle. You can use the handle to narrow down the search. Even though the syntax used for names and handles by different servers will differ when you use whois, you can usually distinguish a handle from a name by preceding it with an exclamation mark, as in "!xxx". You can then search for the handle.

The whois utility can also search on IP addresses. If you want to track someone who is sending spam mail, you can use whois to query the North American Internet Registry for the IP address on the header of the mail. The syntax is as follows:

```
$ whois -h whois.arin.net 195.168.xx.121
```

If the IP address is not found in the North American Internet Registry, the site will direct you to contact the European Registry for further information. You can go to the

Web site and use whois there or you can use whois locally to get the information via the command line. Try the Web page at www.ripe.net/db/whois.html. It will give you a lot of useful information and will also direct you to IANA, the Internet Assignment Number Authority, which has codes for each country outside of the United States and Europe.

File Transfer Utilities

Solaris provides utilities to transfer files over a network. You can use the rcp utility to transfer files between Unix or Solaris computers that are attached to a network. The rcp utility is similar to cp, and in like manner, you must specify the filename on the remote system or the system will use the original filename. The following example displays the syntax for using rcp to transfer a file:

```
% rcp doc.777 macys:docs/docs.423
```

You can also use the ftp utility to transfer files between systems. The difference between rcp and ftp is that ftp is interactive and will let you browse through a directory on the remote system to identify files you may want to transfer. Here is the syntax for using ftp:

```
% ftp <hostname>
```

The remote system will prompt you for a login name and password. It will default to your login name for both systems if you press Return. If you have a different login or password, enter them at the prompt. You can also give a bin (binary) command so you can transfer both ASCII and binary files. The Solaris default is ASCII, so you can transfer only ASCII files in that mode successfully.

TIP Because the Solaris default is ASCII, it is a good idea to get into the habit of using the bin command each time you transfer files using the ftp utility. It does not hurt ASCII files to transfer them in a binary format, but binary files are damaged by being transferred in ASCII format.

You can also use the ftp utility to connect to a remote site that has a distribution package of free software to download or transfer. Before downloading, determine where you are going to work. Most choose to work in the /var/tmp or /tmp directory. Log in as yourself and use cd to change to the /var/tmp directory. Then use ftp to connect to the host from which you want to download.

Daemons and the Network

On Solaris 8, the network services are initiated by daemons that either run continuously or are automatically started by the system when a request is received. The network services listed in `/etc/rpc` and `/etc/inet/services` are supported by your system. The `/etc/services` directory acts as a link to services. The executable files or daemons are usually stored in `/usr/sbin`. The names of most daemons will end with a *d* so as to distinguish them from regular utilities, and many names will have an *in.* or *rpc.* prefix.

When you run `rsh`, your local system will contact the `inetd` daemon, which will accept the connection and then hand it off to the `in.rshd` server on the remote system to establish the connection. The two systems will then negotiate the connection according to the designated protocol. The two systems will query each other and wait for replies. Each network has its own protocol. In Table 9.8, some of the daemons that support system-level network services are listed.

TABLE 9.8: NETWORK SERVICES DAEMONS

Daemon	Function
`automountd`	Automatic mounting after request from the `autofs` service
`cachefsd`	Caches network or CD-ROM file requests on local file system
`dtspcd`	Used by CDE for remote execution; provides variables for processes
`in.comsat`	Works with `biff` utility; reports new mail; launched by `inetd`
`in.dhcpd`	Assigns Internet address, subnet mask, default gateway, DNS, etc.
`inetd`	Listens for service requests on network; starts up daemon
`in.fingered`	Handles requests from the `finger` utility; launched by `inetd`
`in.ftpd`	Handles requests for Internet file transfer protocol; launched by `inetd`
`in.lpd`	Handles printing requests; launched by `inetd`
`in.rarpd`	Used for address resolution; devices use it for obtaining Internet addresses
`in.rexecd`	Allows remote users to run programs; launched by `inetd`
`in.rlogind`	Allows remote login to common domain without password
`in.rshd`	Allows commands to run on a remote machine without a password
`in.rwhod`	Shows who is logged in on other remote machines
`in.talk`	Lets you converse with another user on the same or remote machine

Continued

TABLE 9.8: NETWORK SERVICES DAEMONS (CONTINUED)

Daemon	Function
`in.telnetd`	Allows same login procedure for local login and remote
`in.tftpd`	Used to boot or get information from a network; launched by `inetd`
`in.uucpd`	Unix-to-Unix copy; launched by `inetd`
`kerbd`	MIT's Kerberos, securely authenticates local and remote users
`named`	Supports the domain name service
`nfsd`, `statd`, `lockd`, `mountd`, `rquotad`	All work together to handle NFS operations; found in `/usr/lib/fs/nfs`
`nscd`	Name service cache; requests data obtained from the `passwd`, `hosts`
`pwerd`	Manages automatic and low-power shutdowns
`rdisc`	Router discovery service that runs with one interface
`routed`	Manages the routing tables for messages for distant networks
`rpcbind`	Integral to Solaris; maps incoming requests for RPC service numbers
`rpc.bootparamd`	Used on systems with a jumpstart server for new installations
`rpc.cmsd`	Used by calendar tools for remote or central distribution of calendars
`rpc.nisd`	Runs on IIS+ masters and handles requests for NIS+ databases
`rpc.rexd`	A poor service that should be commented out; security risk high
`rpc.rstatd`	Collects info about local system
`rpc.sprayd`	Handles connections from the `spray` utility; launched by `rpc.ttdb-serverd`; used by ToolTalk services for intertool communication
`sendmail`	De facto mail transfer program on the Internet
`syslogd`	System log; transcribes important system events
`utmpd`	Keeps the `/etc/utmp` and `/var/adm/wtmp` files updated
`walld`	Sends messages to all users logged in on all machines
`Xaserver`	X Window System daemon; plays sound over the network
`Xntpd`	Network time protocol; synchronizes with network time
`ypserv`, `ypxfrd`, `ypbind`, `rpc.yppasswdd`	YP/NIS server package on Solaris operating system CD-ROM

Remote User Mail

If you know the name of the remote system or its domain and you know a user's login name, you can use an electronic mail program to send a message over the network using the @ form of addresses. For instance, you can use `dtmail` (using the syntax on the first line) or `mailtool` (using the syntax on the second line) to send a message:

```
elizabeth@delphi
elizabeth@delphiniumcorp.com
```

You can also communicate on an interactive basis with a remote user over the network by using the `talk` utility:

```
kafka% talk elizabeth@delphi
```

Although most Solaris utilities recognize the @ form of network addresses, you may find that you will do better with electronic mail than with the other networking utilities described in this chapter. Disparity occurs because the mail system can deliver a message to a remote host that does not run the IP. The message may be routed over the network until it reaches a remote system that has a point-to-point dial-up connection to the destination system. Other utilities such as `talk` must rely on the Internet Protocol and can operate only between networked hosts.

You can use a mailing list server (`listserv`) to create and manage an electronic mailing list. This type of list allows people interested in a particular topic to participate in an electronic discussion. You can then periodically disseminate information to a fairly large mailing list. You can archive e-mail postings to the list, create an index, and retrieve postings based on keywords and threads. The owner of the list can put restriction on subscribers and who can actually post messages to the list. Some popular list servers include Majordomo, Mailman, ListProc, SmartList and LISTSERV. You can use your browser to search on each of these names for further information and for types of lists they each support.

Summary

In this chapter, you learned about Solaris network services. Computer networks save money when resources are shared. Duplication is reduced while efficiency is increased. Solaris makes networking an easy task. Local area networks (LANs) and wide area networks (WANs) provide the means to network locally or globally by configuring the most appropriate network for any given site. This chapter presented a conceptual framework for network models and protocols, including a brief discussion of the various types of networks.

A protocol is a formal set of rules and conventions that determines how information is passed from computer to computer. Unix and Solaris employ the TCP/IP protocol, which stands for Transmission Control Protocol/Internet Protocol. The TCP/IP protocol is modular in design. Several layers of intercommunication form the modules. In this chapter, we showed you how to identify and assign TCP/IP addresses.

To assign friendly names to obscure TCP/IP addresses, Solaris uses name services such as DNS, NIS, and NIS+. These name services and how to access them were discussed.

Solaris relies heavily on a set of network configuration files. Seven of them are particularly important. You can solve many networking difficulties by having an understanding of these files and their contents. This chapter described these network configuration files, as well as how to set up local name services and a server-based name service.

The Network File System allows you to mount remote volumes on your system, making additional network resources available locally. In this chapter, you learned how to work with NFS to provide access to volumes and their contents over the network.

Solaris includes several utilities for accessing remote systems and for diagnosing TCP/IP configurations, traffic, and other important network activity. Several of the more important utilities were described in this chapter.

CHAPTER 10

Printing

FEATURING:

The Solaris print subsystem 390

Using the LP print system commands 398

Working with print queues and print logs 401

Adding local and network printers 407

Printing files 418

Solaris 8 provides you with a means to attach both local and network printers to print jobs. Setting up a local printer can be accomplished by using the Admintool or the command line. You can use the Solaris Print Manager as well as the command line to set up a network printer. Printers are served by print servers, and access to printers can be given to print clients. This chapter describes how to add printers, how to set their options and characteristics, how to print, and how to manage print jobs in the print queue.

The Solaris Print Subsystem

Solaris uses the SVR4 print service, which is one of the two standard Unix printing and spooling routines. (The other print subsystem used in other flavors of Unix is the BSD lpr subsystem, which can be used as part of the Solaris BSD Compatibility package.) The LP (line printer) print service provides the routines necessary to prepare print jobs; you install the printer drivers (also called print filters) as well as the printer and local or network connection. You can use the Admintool and the Solaris Print Manager (new to Solaris 8) to set up a printer. Print jobs are specified from within applications or from the command line.

The LP print service is a set of command-line utilities you can use to print files. The service consists of the print service software and a spooler. A spooler (the name is an acronym for system peripheral operation off-line) is a utility that "prints" a job as a metafile to disk so that that job may be queued and stored until the printer is able to accept it. Once the printer prints the print job, the file is deleted. In this manner, your print jobs are protected against system failures such as power outages, and you have access to the queue to alter the timing of print jobs.

The LP print service performs the following tasks:

- Initializes the printer port. The `stty` command is used for a standard printer interface routine.
- Initializes the printer. A standard printer interface program uses the `terminfo` database and the *<TERM>* environmental variable to obtain the printer control sequences that are needed.
- Prints a banner page. (You can suppress a banner page using the `-banner` option of the `lpadmin` command.)
- Prints the required copies.

The LP print service uses the `/usr/lib/lp/model` directory's standard print interface routines. Other print interface programs may be used in its place, provided that the program you use doesn't interfere with the printer connection and initialization. Table 10.1 describes the location and purpose of the important LP print service directories and files.

TABLE 10.1: LP PRINT SERVICE DIRECTORIES AND EXECUTABLE FILES

Directory	Description
`/etc/lp`	The `lp` directory contains the LP configuration files subtree.
`/etc/lp/alerts`	The `alerts` directory contains the `form`, `jobdone`, `printer`, and `sendMsg` scripts that send print alerts to users.
`/etc/lp/classes`	The `classes` directory contains the class files used by the `lpadmin -c` command.
`/etc/lp/fd`	The `fd` directory is the filter directory, with descriptions of the print filters installed.
`/etc/lp/forms`	The `forms` directory contains form descriptions.
`/etc/lp/interfaces`	The `interfaces` directory contains the printer interface binary files.
`/etc/lp/logs`	The `logs` directory is a symbolic link to the `/var/lp/logs` directory where printer log files are stored.
`/etc/lp/model`	The `model` directory is a symbolic link to the `/usr/lib/lp/model` directory, which stores the standard printer interface.
`/etc/lp/printers`	The `printers` directory stores printer setup configuration information as well as alerts generated by specific printers.
`/etc/lp/pwheels`	The `pwheels` directory stores the configuration files for the print wheel, printer disk, or print ball printers.
`/requests.`*n*	The `/requests.`*n* directories contain information about completed print requests.
`/usr/bin`	The `/usr/bin` directory contains the `lp`, `lpstat`, `enable`, and `disable` commands.
`/usr/bin/accept`	The `accept` directory contains the `accept` LP command, which accepts printer requests into the queue.
`/usr/bin/reject`	The `reject` directory contains the `reject` LP command, which rejects printer requests into the queue.
`/usr/bin/lpadmin`	The `lpadmin` command allows you to manage printers, defining them and modifying their definition. You use this command to establish printer names, print classes, print comments and options and to provide fault recovery. (Note: This and the next six items are commands in the `/usr/bin/` directory.)
`/usr/bin/lpfilter`	The `lpfilter` command adds, deletes, and lists filters.

Continued

PART II Solaris and the Network

TABLE 10.1: LP PRINT SERVICE DIRECTORIES AND EXECUTABLE FILES (CONTINUED)

Directory	Description
/usr/bin/lpforms	The lpforms command adds, deletes, and lists forms.
/usr/bin/lpmove	The lpmove command moves print requests from one print queue to another.
/usr/bin/lpshut	The lpshut command stops or shuts down the LP print service.
/usr/bin/lpsystem	The lpsystem command registers print clients and services with the LP print service.
/usr/bin/lpusers	The lpusers command establishes the queue priorities for print users.
/usr/lib/lp	The lp directory stores the LP daemons. Also contains the model directory for standard printer interface programs, the PostScript filters, and related binary files.
/usr/lib/lp/bin	The bin directory contains files for managing the print queue, generating alerts, and working with print filters.
/usr/lib/lp/local	The local directory contains the print service binaries for the local system.
/usr/lib/lp/locale	The locale directory stores locale information (language-specific files).
/usr/lib/lp/lpsched	The lpsched directory contains the daemon that manages LP print service scheduling.
/usr/lib/lp/model	In the model directory, you will find the standard printer interface program.
/usr/lib/lp/postscript	The postscript directory contains PostScript printer filters that match the description files in the /etc/lp/fd directory.
/usr/share/lib	The lib directory contains the terminfo database.
/var/lp/logs	The logs directory contains the LP print service log files.
/var/spool/lp	The lp directory stores the print queue for the spooler.
/var/spool/lp/SCHEDLOCK	The SCHEDLOCK file locks a file in the scheduler. If the scheduler stops and you can't restart it, check the contents of this file.
/var/spool/lp/admins	The admins directory is symbolically linked to the /etc/lp directory.
/var/spool/lp/bin	The bin directory is symbolically linked to the /usr/lib/lp/bin directory.
/var/spool/lp/fifos	The fifos directory contains the pipes used to communicate network print requests to the lpNet daemon.

Continued

TABLE 10.1: LP PRINT SERVICE DIRECTORIES AND EXECUTABLE FILES (CONTINUED)

Directory	Description
/var/spool/lp/logs	The logs directory is a symbolic link to the ../lp/logs directory, which contains the logs of completed print jobs.
/var/spool/lp/model	The model directory is a symbolic link to the /usr/lib/lp/model directory.
/var/spool/lp/request	The request directory is symbolically linked to the /usr/lib/lp/request directory.
/var/spool/lp/system	The system directory stores the print status file for your system.
/var/spool/lp/temp	The temp directory is a symbolic link to the /var/spool/lp/tmp/ <*printername*> directory where spooled requests are stored.
/var/spool/lp/tmp	The tmp directory has a subdirectory for each printer where print requests are logged.
/var/lp/logs/lpsched.*n*	The lpsched.*n* directory stores the daily files for the LP print log.

Printer definitions are stored in the printers directory (/etc/lp/printers), which contains several files relating to individual printers. (If you don't have any printers set up, the /etc/lp/printers directory will be empty.) The printers directory contains the following files:

alert.sh Stores the shell that is used when an alert is generated

alert.var Contains alert variables used in conjunction with the shell when an alert message is generated

comment Contains a description of the printer

configuration Contains the printer's configuration information

user.deny Stores a list of users who are prohibited from accessing this particular printer

When your system boots, the LP print service uses the terminfo database (/usr/share/lib/terminfo) to initialize local printers. The initialization procedure sends a set of control codes to the printer to set it up with the characteristics you have already specified: font, character set, form type, and so on.

The lp command takes input either as a filename or as text from standard output at the command line, then it creates a copy and places that copy in the appropriate spool directory. The lpsched daemon then schedules the print job by executing a print program or filter that formats the file and sends the appropriate control codes to the printer specified.

The spooling directory holds print jobs in the print queue and contains the print files that were created by the `lp` command prior to their being acted upon by the print filter. Typically, the spooler is located on a print server, but in situations in which the print server is not available, the print file (or files) is stored in a temporary location on the print client. When you print to a local printer, a local spooling directory is used.

A local system can print to an attached printer through a port, either a serial port or, more commonly, a parallel port. In a networked environment, you can have print clients and print servers. A print client is a system that sends a print request to another system for printing. A print server is a system that has a local printer attached to it and makes that printer available to other systems on the network.

The processing sequence for a print client's print request is as follows:

1. The print request is created on the print client.
2. A print command is created and the client searches a hierarchy of print configuration resources to locate the appropriate print server.

   The hierarchy of configuration resources includes the specified location that the atomic or Portable Operating System Interface (POSIX) format requires for the `lp -d` command, the user's *<LPDEST>* or *<PRINTER>* variables, the *<_default>* variable in the printers database of the `/etc/nssswitch.conf` file, a user's `$HOME/.printers` file, the local `/etc/printers.conf` file for NIS, the `printers.org_dir` table for NIS+, and the FNS printing contexts for NIS+ (`xfn`) nameservice, in that order.

NOTE A print job can also be filtered on the client side, and it is not uncommon to filter a text printout through a ghostscript or something similar to make it printable on a remote system.

3. The print command is transmitted to the print server, either a BSD print server or an SVR4 (LP) print server.
4. The print server sends the print job to the printer, filtering it into a form that the printer understands if necessary.
5. The print job is printed on the printer.

The Berkeley Software Distribution (BSD) print system uses the term *destination* to designate the target location of the printing process. The System V Release 4 (SVR4) print system uses the term *destination* for a print target and specifies the `-d` option for the `lp` command as a result. A destination is a name up to 14 characters long (it can be the name of a printer or a file) that is appended to the name of the print job when multiple users are printing using the LP printing system. A print job can also be sent to a class, and the `lpsched` daemon will schedule the print job to any one of the printers that are members of that class.

Print Tools

Solaris includes the following four print system components:

LP print service The print service (formerly called the LP spooler) is a set of command-line utilities such as `lp`, `lpsystem`, `lpadmin`, `lpstat`, and so on used to set up and manage printers in a nameservice environment.

Admintool The Admintool contains the functionality necessary to manage local printers.

Solaris Print Manager The Print Manager is part of the AdminSuite package and provides a superuser with a Java application as a graphical utility for managing local and networked printers. The Solaris Print Manager installs as the SUNWppm package. It is also a part of the Solaris Easy Access Server.

SunSoft Print Client software This software provides a set of administrator tools to manage printers named in a nameservice database. The client is part of the AdminSuite tools and was added to the Solaris operating system in version 2.6.

Printers are objects named and managed by the NIS+ (with and without the Federated Naming Service, `xfn`), NIS, and the `files` nameservices. The printers database in the `/etc/nsswitch.conf` nameservice switch file contains printer configuration information that clients use to print on the network.

Use Table 10.2 to determine which tool you should use to set up which kind of printer and print service.

TABLE 10.2: PRINT SUBSYSTEM FUNCTIONALITY

Printer/Print Service	Print Manager	Admintool	LP Commands
Network printers	Yes	Yes	No
Print clients and servers	Yes	Yes	Yes
NIS, NIS+, or NIS+ (`xfn`)	Yes	No	No

Local Tools

Use Admintool to install a printer on a local system, as either a print server or a print client. Admintool provides a graphical utility you can use to work with the LP print service. Admintool alters the `/etc/printers.conf` file and the `/etc/lp` directory.

When you add a printer to a network and publish it in a nameservice, the printer becomes available to other systems on the network. The procedure is simplified because all printer information is contained in that nameservice database. The Solaris print client and Solaris Print Manager are the graphical tools you can use to set up and configure printers on a network.

The LP print service provides the following functions:

- Filters the files so that they can be processed by the printer
- Schedules local and network print requests
- Provides an administrative function to manage print jobs
- Initiates the programs that provide interfaces to the printer
- Tracks the status of the jobs and their progress on the printer
- Sends and manages alerts about printing problems or progress

You can also use the `lpadmin` command if you wish to configure printers on one system at a time. The `lpadmin` command creates text files in the spooling directory that is used by the print service to add, remove, and modify printers.

The syntax for the `lpadmin` command takes one of the following forms:

```
lpadmin -p <printer><options>
lpadmin -x <destination>
lpadmin -d <destination>
lpadmin -S <print-wheel> -A <alert-type> [-W minutes] \
    [-Q <requests>]
lpadmin -M -f <formname> [-a [-o <filebreak>] \
    [-t <tray-number>]
```

Given that the Admintool and Print Manager provide graphical tools you use to add and administer a printer on Solaris and that you are less likely to make mistakes entering the data for those printers in the graphical interface, I recommend that you save the `lpadmin` command for situations in which only the command line is available to you. There are some cases in which the power of the `lpadmin` command allows you to define a printer's attributes with more granular control. If you are specifying the file contents and how alerts are generated (fault notification), printing banner pages, and limiting access to a printer, you will find that using the `lpadmin` command is helpful and exceeds what you can currently do in the Print Manager.

Here is a list of some of the many options that the `lpadmin` command takes:

-A option The `-A` (alert) option takes the form `-A` *<alert-type>* `[-W minutes]` and sets an alert action for a printer fault. You can specify a mail or console message (on the administrator's console) or use the quiet keyword to suppress error messages. You can also use `showfault` to specify a particular fault handling procedure or `none` to have no alerts generated. A shell command is one option for an alert action.

The LP print service sends alerts to the user as e-mails that specify a print request when it doesn't run correctly. Many problems, particularly print system problems, generate alerts that are sent to the administrator or superuser, typically appearing in a console window. A superuser can alter the nature of the alerts so that messages are sent either by e-mail or to a program that they specify. Alert messages can also be suppressed.

-c option The `-c` *<classname>* option specifies that the printer belongs to a particular class. If the class doesn't exist, the LP print system creates it.

-d option The `-d` *<comment>* option is used as a text description of the printer when a user requests information about that printer.

-e option The `-e` *<printername>* option copies the interface program used by an existing printer so it can be used with the printer you are adding.

-i option The `-i` *<interface>* option specifies the interface program used by the printer. Use the `-e` option when you are copying or cloning an already existing interface.

-m option The `-m` *<model>* selects a model interface program. When you select a model program, the `-e` and `-i` options do not apply.

-s option The `-s` *<systemname>* *<!printername>* option can create a remote printer using a printer server that you specify with the *<systemname>* argument. The *<printername>* is the name of the remote printer that you use to identify the printer on your computer. That printer name does not have to match the remote printer name.

-x option The `-x` *<printername>* option removes a printer from the LP printing system. For example, `lpadmin -xflash` would remove the printer named flash.

Network Tools

The `lp` command is used to set up a network print server. You will need to supply the printer name, the server name, the network printer's logical name (perhaps with a port number), an IP address for the printer, the protocol, a timeout value, the printer type, the file content type, and the fault notification policy. The print subsystem uses the BSD print protocol and TCP data to communicate, but your printer may require a different communications protocol. Refer to your printer's manual for information on its protocol support. The timeout value is the number of seconds that the system waits before trying another print attempt to a printer; the default is 10 seconds. Both printer type and file content type have as their default settings PostScript.

Follow these steps to use the `lp` command to set up a print server:

1. Attach the printer to the network.
2. Switch to a superuser using the `su` command, if needed.
3. Enter the following command at the command line to define the printer name and port:

   ```
   # lpadmin -p <printername> -v /dev/null
   ```

4. Specify the interface script with the following command:

   ```
   # lpadmin -p <printername> -i /usr/lib/lp/model/netstandard
   ```

5. Set the printer destination, protocol, and timeout by entering the following:

   ```
   # lpadmin -p <printername> \
   -o dest=<accessname>:port \
   -o protocol=<protocolname> -o timeout=<number>
   ```

6. Set the content type and printer type as follows:

   ```
   # lpadmin -p <printername> -I contenttype -T printertype
   ```

7. Set and install the filters using the following command:

   ```
   # cd /etc/lp/fd
   # for filter in *.fd;do
   >  name='basename $filter .fd'
   >  lpfilter -f $name -F $filter
   >  done
   ```

8. Enter the following command to let the printer accept requests:

   ```
   # accept <printername>
   ```

9. Enter the following command to enable the printer to print requests:

```
# enable <printername>
```

10. Verify that the printer is online and configured:

```
# lpstat -p <printername>
```

At this point, you should set up print clients to access your print server. To set up a print client, you use various `lp` commands to supply the name of the printer, server, and printer characteristics and specify the print filters. With the NIS or NIS+ nameservices on your network, you will need to enable access between systems. With no nameservice active, enter the IP address and system name for each print client in the `/etc/hosts` file on the print server.

The following sequence shows how to set up a PostScript print client. When you don't specify a printer type, the default printer is unknown. For no file content specified, either ASCII or PostScript files can be printed.

To set up a print client for a PostScript printer, follow these steps:

1. Switch to superuser using the `su` command at the command line.
2. To specify a print server as a BSD (SunOS 4.*x*) server, enter the following at the command line:

```
# lpsystem -t bsd <servername>
```

3. Register the printer and server with the client LP print service by entering this:

```
# lpadmin -p printername -s <servername>
```

4. Set the PostScript filters using the following command sequence:

```
# cd /etc/lp/fd
# lpfilter -f download -F download.fd
# lpfilter -f dpost -F dpost.fd
# lpfilter -f postio -F postio.fd
# lpfilter -f postior -F postior.fd
# lpfilter -f postprint -F postprint.fd
# lpfilter -f postreverse -F postreverse.fd
```

5. Enter the following command to let the printer accept requests:

```
# accept <printername>
```

NOTE If you enter the command in step 5 and get the response `Warning: printer is remote, accept has no meaning`, upgrade Solaris using the latest system patch. Also upgrade with the latest system patch if you enter the command in step 6 and get the response `Warning: printer is remote, enable has no meaning`.

6. Enter the following command to enable the printer to print requests:

```
# enable <printername>
```

7. Set the printer as a default (if desired) by entering this command:

```
# lpadmin -d <printername>
```

8. Verify that the printer is online and configured:

```
# lpstat -t
```

9. To determine if the PostScript print client is operational, send it a file:

```
# lp -d <printername> <filename>
```

The SunSoft print client was added to the standard Solaris distribution starting with version 2.6. The software is added to a system to allow access to remote printers on the network. You use SunSoft print client commands to locate networked printers, and these commands are sent to the print server, which then executes them.

The command sequence is as follows:

1. The print job is submitted using a SunSoft print request.
2. The print client searches the configuration resources to determine what print server to send the request to.
3. The print request is transmitted to the print server. Print servers can be running either the BSD print protocol or the SVR4 (LP) print protocol.
4. The print server sends the print job to the printer and printing is executed.

To set up network print service, you must set up local printers, print servers, and print clients. In Solaris 8, you can have the following configurations:

- A SunOS 5.8 print client with a SunOS 5.8 print server
- SunOS 5.8 and SunOS 4.1 BSD (LPD) print clients in conjunction with a SunOS 5.0 print server
- SunOS 5.8 and SunOS 4.1 print clients with a SunOS 4.1 print server
- A SunOS 5.8 and any other print server that accepts the BSD print protocol

The Java-based Solaris Print Manager is the tool that is most commonly used to manage printers in nameservice environments such as `files`, NIS, NIS+, and NIS+ with `xfn`. The Print Manager was added to Solaris 8, and it takes care of all of the details of setting up the configuration files for printers—something that is both tedious and difficult to do otherwise. Previous printer definitions do not need to be converted to work with the Print Manager.

To access the Print Manager, you need to be either a print administrator or a superuser or have a role that allows you to print conferred upon you. The Solaris Print Manager comes with a console that lets you use the `lp` command to specify print jobs or list jobs already in the print queue. The Print Manager can be run either locally or from a remote terminal.

To start the Solaris Print Manager, issue the following command:

```
# /usr/sadm/admin/bin/printmgr&
```

The Print Manager administration utility opens to allow you to add and configure printers. The Select Naming Service dialog box, shown in Figure 10.1, appears, allowing you to choose which nameservice to add a printer to or to access a printer definition in. After you click the OK button, the main Solaris Print Manager window appears.

FIGURE 10.1

The Select Naming Service dialog box

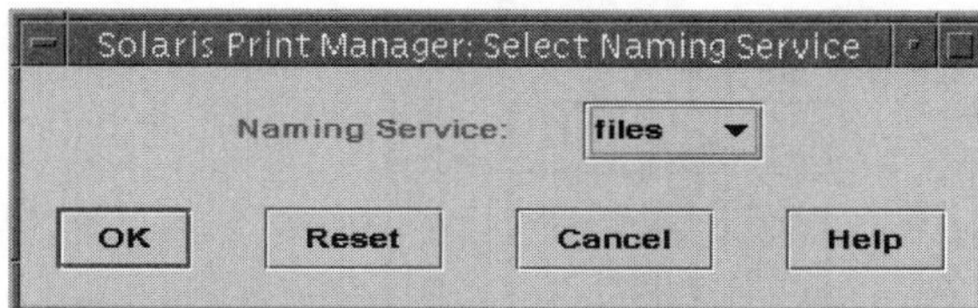

You should note that the Print Manager icon found on the Personal Printers subpanel of the front panel of the CDE does not have an administrative function. You use the Print Manager client window that appears when you click the Print Manager icon to locate and specify local printers.

Print Schedulers

The LP print service starts a scheduling daemon called the `lpsched` (print scheduler) at boot time (using the `/etc/init.d/lp` file). Each printer client and print server can have only one LP scheduler running, that is, one instance of the `lpsched` daemon. By default, your system starts the print daemon when the system boots or enters run level 2 using the `/etc/rc2.d/S80lp` control script. If you wish to stop the scheduler, use the `lpshut` command (in the `/usr/sbin/` directory). To start the daemon up again, use the `lpsched` command (in the `/usr/lib/lp/` directory). The scheduler that is local on each system is responsible for maintaining its own print requests.

The `lpsched` daemon provides the interface between the LP commands found in the `/usr/bin` directory (`enable/disable`) and commands found in the `/usr/sbin` directory (`accept/reject`, `lpadmin`, `lpfilter`, `lpforms`, `lpmove`, `lpshut`, `lpsystem`, and `lpusers`) with the LP system files located in the `/etc/lp` directory. Among the `/lp` files that the `lpsched` updates in the `/etc/lp` directory are `Systems`, `alerts`, `classes`, `fd`, `forms`, `interfaces`, `logs`, `model`, `printers`, and `pwheels`. Note that the `enable` and `disable` commands are the only commands found in the `/usr/bin` directory; they are also found in the `/usr/lib/lp/local` directory and are symbolically linked to the `accept` and `reject` commands there. Whatever means you use to print with on Solaris, be it with a graphical tool or from the command line, it is the `lpsched` that schedules your print request. Figure 10.2 shows the flow of a local print request starting with the `lpsched` daemon.

FIGURE 10.2

The `lpsched` daemon's local print routine

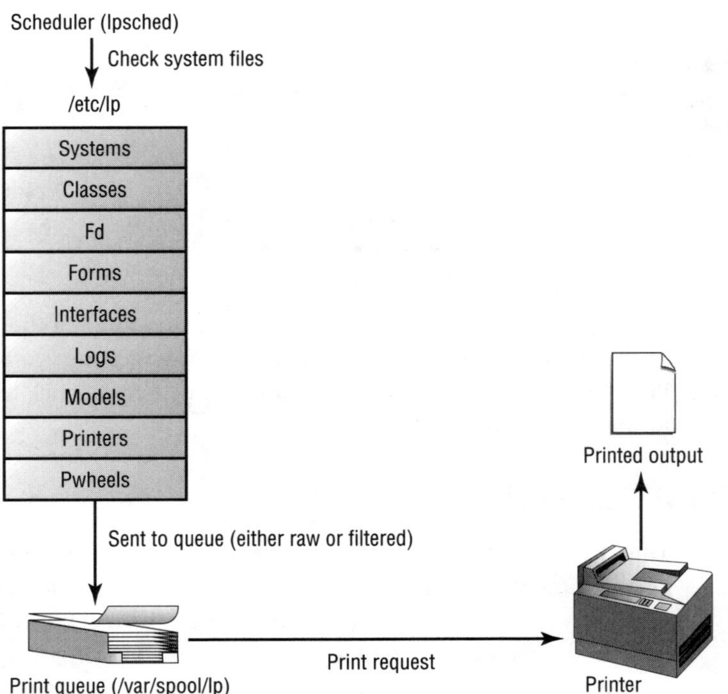

Whereas the `lpsched` daemon manages the scheduling for local print requests, it is the `lpNet` daemon that initiates network print requests. A print client and print server must have one, but can have more, `lpNet` daemon running on a system. Your system starts the `lpNet` daemon when it boots. When you use the `lpshut` command to stop the `lpsched` daemon, it also shuts down any `lpNet` daemons that are running. When you restart the `lpsched` daemon, the `lpNet` daemons also restart. The `lpNet` daemon uses the Service Access Facility—`sacadm(1M)` and `pmadm(1M)`—to work with a configured port monitor and provide the registration service so that it can listen to incoming network requests for printer services. Beginning with Solaris 2.6, it is the `inetd` Internet services super daemon that provides network print scheduling. When the daemon hears a request over the port, it starts `in.lpd`, which examines the print request and loads `bsd_lpsched`, which then has `in.lpd` pass the request through to `lpsched` for local printing.

Spooling

A spooling space is set aside on a system for a local printer and on a print server for network printing to store and process print files prior to execution. When the printer requests the next print job in the print queue, the file in the spooler directory is sent to the print filter and then the result is transmitted to the printer as a set of control codes. Files for the spooler are commonly stored in the `/var/spool/lp` directory and deleted once they are printed.

You can see what files are spooled locally in the print queue by clicking the Print Manager control on the Personal Printers subpanel of the CDE front panel. Figure 10.3 shows the queue for a local printer.

Pay attention to the amount of free space that a disk has when you designate it to be a print server. Print jobs can often be quite large, with graphics consuming a lot of disk space. It isn't uncommon to have a large spooling directory fill 600MB of disk space. You may need to make more disk space available for use in heavy print situations.

SunSoft clients do not maintain a permanent print queue, only print servers do. The client will create a temporary print queue when the print server is unavailable, but jobs in that print queue are sent to the print server's queue once the server comes back online.

If you need to move the files from one print server to another because a printer has become unavailable, you can use the `lpmove` command. The command takes the following form (this command moves the print jobs 120 and 125 to the print server of the Xerox3 printer):

```
lpmove flash-120 flash-125 xerox3
```

To move all documents from one queue to another, specify the following:

```
lpmove flash xerox3
```

FIGURE 10.3

The Printer Manager window in the CDE

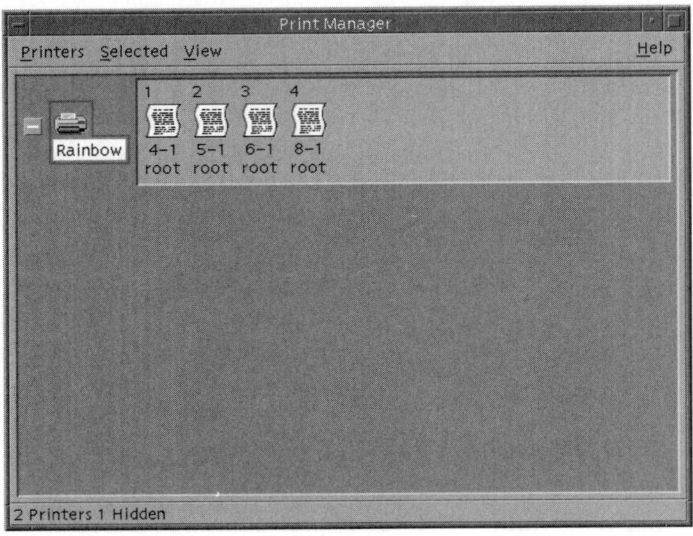

Printer Logs

One aspect of the `lpsched` daemon's function is that at `/var/lp/logs/lpsched`, it maintains a log file of print requests, of the successful execution of those requests, and of any errors relating to a print job. The `lp cron` job renames the log file every night so that you see a file `lpsched.`*n* for each day's execution. To view the last 10 print jobs run, issue the `tail /varl/lp/logs/lpsched` command. The `lpsched` log contains print execution errors and is best used when you need to troubleshoot a printer problem.

You will find a history of the print requests in the `/var/lp/logs/requests/`*<systemname>* and `/var/spool/lp/tmp/`*<systemname>* directories. For any print request, there is one file in each of these two directories. Only the user who created the print request, an `lp` user or a superuser, may view the print request log file. Log files are deleted once the print job is successfully executed and removed from the printer queue. The information in the request logs is appended to the `/var/lp/logs/requests` file. Therefore, you would use the `/var/spool/lp` log files to obtain information on pending jobs prior to their execution.

The `requests` log contains a listing of the print requests in the order in which they were executed. The log stores information about the nature of the print job, who specified it, when it was executed, and the parameters used for and by the printer. You can read the requests queue in an editor or using the Unix shell commands. Table 10.3 lists the codes used in the LP `requests` log.

TABLE 10.3: LP requests LOG FILE CODES

Code	Description
=	A separator line that is followed by the following pieces of information in a comma-delimited list: request ID, user identification (UID), group identification (GID), byte size in the unfiltered file, and the time the request was generated.
C	Number of copies printed.
D	Printer class or any printer.
f	Name of form used.
F	The print filename list in the order that it was printed.
H	Used to specify the handling characteristic: `resume`, `hold`, or `immediate`.
N	The alert used when a print request is successfully executed. `M` is used for e-mail alerts, and `W` is used when a message is sent to the console.
O	Used to specify the `-o` options used by the `lp` command.
p	A list of the pages that were printed.
P	The print request priority that was used for printing.
r	Used to specify whether the file was output as a raw file using the `-r` option of the `lp` command. Raw output is sent to the printer directly.
s	The request outcome in hexadecimal form. Among the output you see are 0x0004 (slow filtering completed), 0x0010 (printing completed), 0x0040 (print request cancelled), and 0x0100 (print request failed either conversion through the print filter or print execution from the print queue).
S	The name of the print wheel, cartridge, or character set that was used.
t	The type of content in the file(s) printed.
T	The title that is added to the banner page.
U	The name of the user who specified the print job.
x	Used to indicate that the slow filter was used for the print request.
Y	A list of the special modes that are communicated to the print filters.
z	The printer used in the request.

You would use the `/var/lp/logs` directory to read information about specific jobs that have already executed from the print queue. The `logs` directory contains `request.`*n* files that are copies of logs from previous days. The `lp cron` job stores log files from two previous days, the `.1` and `.2` file suffixes.

Print Filters

Print filters are translation routines that convert the output of a print file into the data that a printer needs to have in order to control the various printer elements. In a network print scenario, the print filters process the print client file and then send the result to the print server. Filters perform the following tasks:

- Convert a print file to a format that can control a particular printer or printer family. (Some printers' control language have become generic and are often emulated by other printers or print families.)
- Provide the means necessary to manage special features and functions of a particular printer, such as draft printing, two-side printing, printing oversized pages, and so forth.
- Monitor the printer's performance to determine if the print job has successfully executed, and if it hasn't, the filter will notify the LP print service so that the LP print service can send out an alert.

The actual set of functions that a print filter performs is specific to the printer model and to the print filter version that the manufacturer creates. A later version of the print filter often eliminates bugs and system incompatibilities while adding new features that weren't previously available.

TIP Whenever possible, try to use the most up-to-date print filter that a printer manufacturer provides. Print filters are often found posted on the vendors' Web sites.

On other systems (Windows, for example), these routines are referred to as printer drivers or print device drivers. Because each printer or printer family is unique, print manufacturers are responsible for creating and modifying these files. Many printer models have print filters that come with the standard Solaris distribution. When you purchase a new printer, you may be required to install your own print filter for it.

Solaris provides a set of PostScript print filters in the `/usr/lib/lp/postscript` directory. Any printer that can use PostScript data can use these filters. When you want to create or add a non-Postscript printer, you must add to your system a filter for that printer.

Finding Printers on the Network

The `/etc/nsswitch.conf` file contains a printers database that contains network printer information. Using the nameservice switch file, print clients can use the printer configuration information it contains without having to store a local copy of the information. In the `nsswitch` file are the following default printer entries:

- For the `files` (local) nameservice, `printers; user files`.
- For the `nis` nameservice, "`printers; user files nis`". The print client looks up information in this sequence: first for `user`, in the `$home/.printers file`;

then for files, in the /etc/printers.conf file; and finally for nis, in the printers.conf.byname table.

- For the nis+ nameservice, "printers; user nisplus files xfn". The print client looks up information in this sequence: first for user, in the $home/.printers file; then for nisplus, in the printers.org_dir table; for files, in the /etc/printers.conf file; and finally for xfn, in the FNS printer contexts.

You can use the Solaris Print Manager's Find command (not the local Print Manager) to locate printers on the network. Enter the name of the printer in the Find dialog box and the utility will search the resources in the preceding list to locate the printer.

The SunSoft print client commands are used to find printers on a network. The print command will locate a printer and determine the printer's configuration as follows:

1. Determine if the printer name or printer class is valid.
2. If the name of the printer was not a valid name or class style, then the print command examines the user's *<PRINTER>* or *<LPDEST>* environmental variable to find the default printer name.
3. If the printer name isn't found as an environmental variable, then the print command examines the .printers file in the user's home directory to determine the _default printer alias.
4. When a match isn't determined using any of the preceding three methods, the SunSoft print client examines the /etc/printers.conf file to find the printer configuration.
5. Finally, the printer will go to the nameservice such as NIS+ to see if the printer exists.

The advantage to publishing a printer in a nameservice is that any SunSoft print client can then access the printer by name and obtain its configuration information. In Solaris 8, the NIS, NIS+, and NIS+ with FNS nameservices are supported. When checking a nameservice, the SunSoft system checks atomic, POSIX, or context printers by name or class.

Adding Printers

When you add a printer locally or on the network, you need to provide some information by doing the following:

- Define the printer name, printer description, and printer port.

- Select a printer type and the file content type that it can accept.
- Define fault notification behavior and the default printer.
- Set user access to a printer.
- Set printer classes.
- Specify whether banner pages should be printed.
- Determine the fault recovery behavior.

Many of these tasks can be done inside the Solaris Print Manager for network printers or the Admintool for local printers, as you will see in the following sections. Currently, the Print Manager does not support printer classes or fault recovery; you need to use the `lpadmin` command for those settings. You will also find that, although you can use the Print Manager to specify the file contents, fault notification, banner pages, and access to a printer, the `lpadmin` command has better functionality in these areas.

The printer name must be a unique name in your domain, and it can contain up to 14 alphanumeric characters. The description is a comment field that helps people locate a printer or understand the printer type.

When you add a printer to your computer, you specify the device or printer port that the printer is attached to. You can set the printer port in the Print Manager or by using the `lpadmin` command. Typically, a system comes with two serial ports (`/dev/term/a` and `/dev/term/b`) and one parallel port. You can use any recognized port name. On an IA system, only the first port is enabled. Any other port is disabled by default. To use another port on an IA x86 system, you must edit the two port configuration files at `/platform/i86pc/kernel/drv/any.conf` and `/platform/i86pc/kernel/drv/lp.conf`.

The `lpadmin -T` command is best used for establishing printer types. The printer type is a generic name for a type of printer, most often associated with the vendor who manufactures the printer. A DECwriter printer is specified as `decwriter`. PostScript printers include Apple LaserWriter printers of various types. Information about printer types may be found in the `terminfo` database (`/usr/share/lib/terminfo`, shown in Figure 10.4). If you use the `ls` command to view that database's directory, you will see a number of single-number and -letter entries. Each single-letter entry is a subdirectory containing a number of files relating to a specific vendor's files. For example, the `e` subdirectory contains Epson printer files and the `n` directory contains NEC printer files. When possible, try to use the PostScript printer type if your printer supports it, even if you find a system file type. You can assign more than one printer type to a printer using the `lpadmin -t` option.

The second useful assignment that you should use the `lpadmin` command for is the file content type. A print filter converts the content type of a file to a content type that a printer can accept. The file content type is used by the LP print service to determine the type of file a printer can print directly without filtering. The required fonts will need to be resident in the printer or made available to the printer prior to an unfiltered file being processed. Other file types that can't be processed directly are put through the print filter first before they are handled by the printer.

FIGURE 10.4

The `terminfo` *database for printer types*

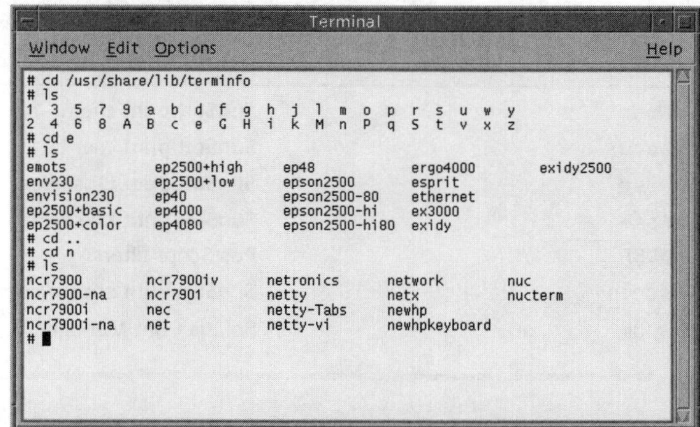

Most printers can print either the same type as the printer type (`PS` for a PostScript printer) or the type `simple` for ASCII text files. When you send a file to a printer, you can indicate the content type using the `lp -T` *<content_type>* command. When you don't specify a content type, the LP print service examines the first file in your print request to determine the file type. When a `^D%!` or `%!` symbol is the first symbol, the file is taken to be a PostScript file (those are PostScript control codes), otherwise, the file type is considered to be an ASCII text file. PostScript (`postscript`), ASCII (`simple`), or both PostScript and ASCII together (`simple,postscript`) don't require filtering. When you select None (`""`) as the file content type, any file that doesn't match the printer's type must be filtered, and when you select Any (`any`), no filtering is required. When a file content type of Any can't be processed directly, it isn't printed.

Solaris doesn't come with wide printer support built in as Windows does, but there are a number of supported printers and you can purchase third-party support for many more printers from several companies. Among the non-PostScript printers that Sun doesn't supply filters for are Daisy (`daisy`), Datagraphix (`datagraphix`), DEC LA100 (`la100`), DEC LN03 (`ln03`), DECwriter (`decwriter`), Diablo (`diablo` and `diablo-m8`), Epson 2500 (`epson2500`, `epson2500-80`, `epson-2500-hi`, and `epson25000-hi80`), Hewlett-Packard HPCL printer (`hplaser`), and the IBM Proprinter (`ibmproprinter`).

Starting with Solaris 2.6, Sun installs all print packages on a print server for both client and server. Print clients may install only their own packages. For PostScript printing, the filter software is installed as its own print package. Table 10.4 lists the current set of print packages. You will need to install the Solaris Print Manager package before you can work with network printers. Check that the Print Manager is installed by giving the following command at the command line: `pkginfo | grep SUNWppm`.

TABLE 10.4: THE PRINT PACKAGES

Package	Description
SUNWpcr	SunSoft print client
SUNWpcu	SunSoft print client
SUNWpsr	SunSoft print LP server
SUNWpsu	SunSoft print LP server
SUNWPSF	PostScript filters
SUNscplp	SunSoft print source compatibility
SUNWppm	Solaris Print Manager

Printer Status

The `lpstat` command is used to determine the status of a printer managed by the LP print service. The command gives information about print jobs in the print queue, the availability of printers, and the request IDs of specific print jobs. When `lpstat` is used without any additional options, the command returns a list of files in the print queue that you have submitted, with one line for each print job, as follows:

```
$ lpstat
flash-3    barries    1382    Dec 15    23:45    on sunrise
$
```

The display informs you about the number of the job in the flash job queue (3), the user who specified the print job, the print ID, the date and time that the job was submitted, and the system that serves as the print server or that is locally attached.

The `lpstat` takes the following options:

-a option The `-a` (accept) option specifies whether a printer destination is accepting requests.

-c option The `-c` (class) option displays print classes and members.

-d option The `-d` (destination) option shows the default destinations.

-f option The `-f` (form) option shows the forms in use.

-o option The `-o` (output) option displays the status of your output.

`-l` option The `-l` (long) option returns a long listing of the status of the LP print service when combined with other options like `-t` and `-s`. Use the `lpstat -tl` command to view a complete description of your installed printers.

`-p <list> [D] [-l]` option The `-p` (printer description) option provides the printer status for a named printer, telling you whether the printer is active or idle, enabled or disabled, and online. The `-p -l` options provide the most complete listing of a printer's characteristics, such as printer and content types, as in `lpstat -p flash -l`.

`-r` option The `-r` (request) option shows the request scheduler status.

`-s` option The `-s` (status)option tells you which printers are configured on your system. You see the status of the scheduler, the default destination, and a list of the systems and printers that are accessible.

`-S` option The `-S` (sets) option shows the character sets.

`-t` option The `-t` option returns a short list of all the status information of the LP print service, the scheduler, and the default system destination. Each printer displays a line that tells you whether or not the printer is accepting print requests and when the printer came online.

`-u` *<username>* option The `-u` *<username>* option shows the requests submitted by a user.

`-v` option The `-v` (verbose) option shows the devices that are available.

Local Printers

Use the Admintool to add local printers to your system. To access the Admintool Printers window, you must either be a superuser or a member of the sysadmin group (GID 14). When the Admintool is accessed from the Solaris Management Console, you must be logged in as a superuser because that utility also gives you access to the facility for changing the local password files.

When adding a local printer, you will be required to supply the printer's logical name, the print server, a description of the printer, the printer port, the printer type, the file contents, the fault notification type, and whether you want this to be a banner page. You will also need to specify whether this printer is the default printer. Additionally, you will need to set up user and group access rights to the local printer.

To add a local printer, follow these steps:

1. To open the Admintool, enter **`admintool&`** at a terminal window.
2. Select the Printers option from the Browse menu to view the Printers window.

3. From the Edit ➢ Add submenu, select the Local Printer command as shown in the following graphic.

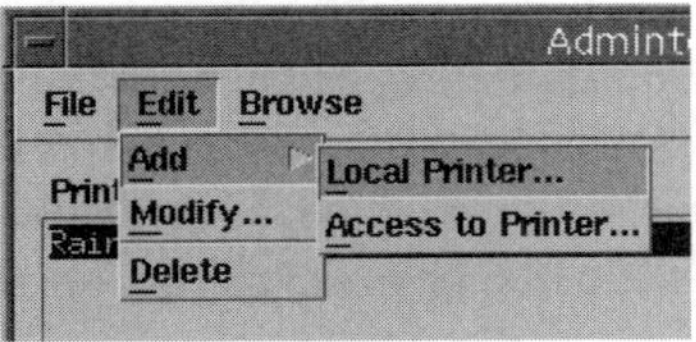

4. When the Add Local Printer dialog box shown in Figure 10.5 appears, enter the printer name and a description and select the correct settings for printer port, printer type, file contents, and fault notification.

FIGURE 10.5

The Add Local Printer dialog box

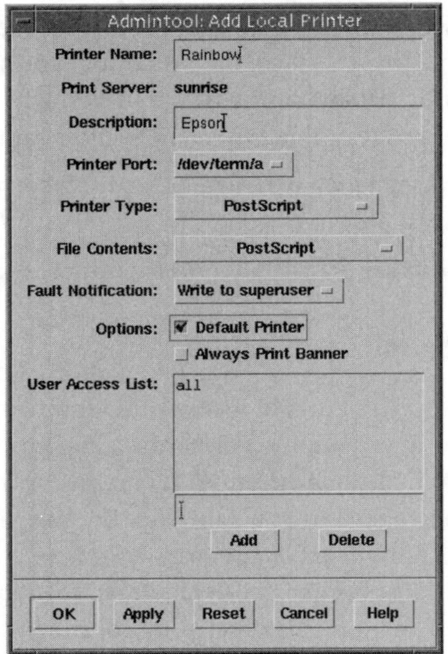

5. Select the Default Printer check box if you wish to print to this printer by default, and select the Always Print Banner check box if you want to establish that behavior.
6. In the User Access List list box, enter the name of users or groups or enter **all** for all users.

7. Click the Apply button to continue adding another local printer. Or click the OK button to return to the main Admintool Printers window. You will see the new local printer added to the Print Manager.

You can use the `lpadmin` command to add a printer to your system. As an example, the following command adds a printer named flash attached to the `tty04` device, which uses a "dumb" printer interface and is a member of the `admin` class of printers:

```
# lpadmin -pflash -v/dev/tty04 -mdumb -cadmin
```

Finally, test to make sure the printer was correctly installed by using the `lp -d` *<printername>* *<filename>* command to print a test file.

Networked Printers

Use the Solaris Print Manager to add to your system access to a networked printer. A network printer is a hardware device connected to your network that transfers data to the network. A network printer is identified by its name and its IP address, but it does require a print server to manage a queue, to schedule jobs, and to serve as the means used to communicate print jobs. You will need to know what kind of printer it is and what print server services it. Because a network can have multiple printers of the same type, it helps to know the printer's logical name and have a description of it. You will also need to know whether you want to specify that this printer is your default printer.

A network printer may use a vendor's own printing program in place of the Solaris network printer support. Whenever possible, use the vendor's routines before defaulting to Solaris's network print software. For example, the vendor may offer a SVR4 printer interface script that replaces the standard printer interface script. That script calls the vendor's printing program to print a job on a network printer.

Use the following procedure to add a printer with LP commands:

1. Connect the printer to the network.
2. Define the printer name and port device, then set the interface script using the following two commands:

```
# lpadmin -p <printername> -v /dev/null
# lpadmin -p <printername> -m netstandard
```

3. Set the printer destination, protocol, and timeout value as follows:

```
# lpadmin -p <printername> \
  -o dest=<accessname:port> \
  -o protocol=<protocol>
```

4. Then set the file content types for the printer and the printer type:

```
# lpadmin -p <printername> \
    -I <content-type> \
    -T <printer-type>
```

5. Add print filters:

```
# cd /etc/lp/fd
# for <filter> in *.fd;do
    > name='basename $<filter> .fd'
    > lpfilter -f $<name> -F $<filter>
    > done
```

6. Enable the printer to accept print jobs:

```
# accept <printername>
# enable <printername>
```

7. Verify the printer's setup using the lpstat -p <*printername*> command.
8. Add client access to the network printer as described in the next section.

Adding Printer Access

To add network printer access for a print client, follow these steps:

1. Start the Solaris Print Manager with the following command at a terminal window:

```
# /usr/sadm/admin/bin/printmgr&
```

2. In the Select Name Service dialog box, select the nameservice and click the OK button.
3. Select the Add Access to Printer command from the Printer menu. The Add Access to Printer dialog box, shown in Figure 10.6, appears.
4. Enter the printer name, the name of the print server, and a description of the printer.

FIGURE 10.6

The Add Access to Printer dialog box in Solaris Print Manager

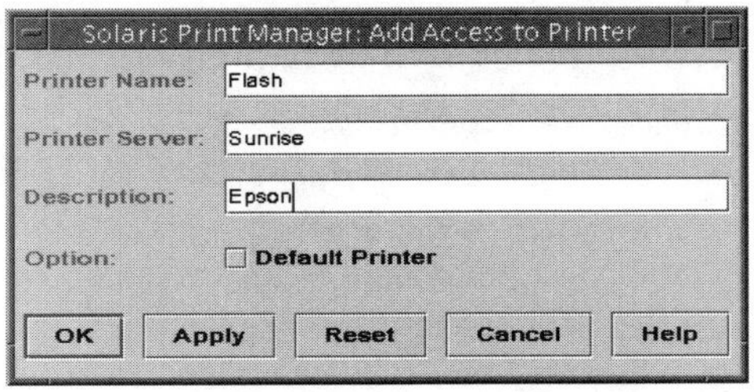

5. Select the Default Printer check box if you want all print jobs to be sent to this printer by default.
6. Click the Apply button to continue adding printers. Or click the OK button to return to the main Print Manager window.

You will see the printer added to the Print Manager, and the printer's information will be added to the appropriate nameservice configuration files.

To use the command line to add printer access with the LP commands, enter the following:

```
# lpadmin -p flash -s sunserver
# lpadmin -p flash -D "First floor laser"
# lpadmin -p flash -d flash
# lpstat -p flash
printer flash is idle. enabled since Dec 20 10:50 2001
     available.
```

The first three lines attach the printer to the print server, add a description, and set the printer as the default. The last line verifies that the printer is online.

You can also add access to networked printers using the Admintool on a local print client, as follows:

1. Open the Admintool on your screen by giving the `admintool&` command at a terminal window.
2. Select the Printers command on the Browse menu to view the Printers window.
3. Select the Access to Printer command from the Add submenu of the Edit menu. The Add Access to Printer dialog box, shown in Figure 10.7, appears.
4. Enter the name of the printer, the name of the print server, and a description, then click the Default Printer check box on or off.
5. Click the Apply button to continue adding printers. Or click the OK button to return to the main Admintool window.

You will see the printer added to the Admintool. No changes will be made to nameservices listings.

Attaching a Print Server

The process for attaching a printer to a print server is similar to the procedure just shown for a adding a networked printer. In addition to the information already requested for printer access, you will need to supply the following additional pieces of information: printer port, file contents, fault notification policy, the print policy for banners, and a user access list.

FIGURE 10.7

The Admintool's Add Access to Printer dialog box

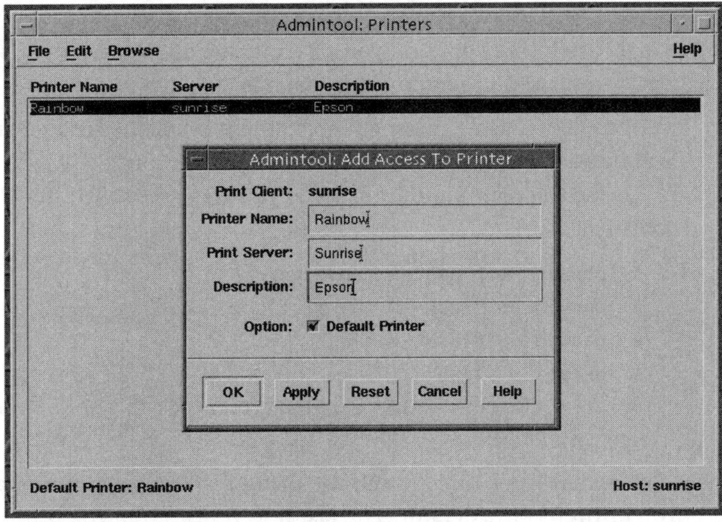

Follow these steps to add a new attached printer to a print server:

1. Start the Solaris Print Manager (see "Adding Printer Access").
2. Select the New Attached Printer command from the Printer menu. The New Attached Printer dialog box appears.
3. Enter the printer name and select the printer port, printer type, file contents, and fault notification options. Set the Default Printer and Always Print Banner options.
4. In the User Access List list box, enter the name of users or groups or enter **all** for all users.
5. Click the Apply button to continue adding additional attached printers. Or click the OK button to return to the main Print Manager window.

You will see the attached printer added to the Print Manager, and the printer's information will be added to the appropriate configuration files.

Finally, test that the network printer was correctly attached by using the `lp -d` *`<printername>`* *`<filename>`* command to print a test file.

You can enter the following sequence of commands at the command line to attach a printer and set its attributes for a print server:

```
# chown lp /dev/term/b
# chmod 600 /dev/term/b
# lpadmin -p flash -v /dev/term/b
# lpadmin -p flash -T PS
```

```
# lpadmin -p flash -I postscript
# cd /etc/lp/fd
# for <filter> in *fd;do
   > name=basename $<filter> .fd'
   > lpfilter -f $name -F $<filter>
# accept flash
destination "flash" now accepting requests
# enable flash
printer "flash" now enabled
# lpadmin -p flash -D "First floor laser"
# lpstat -p flash
printer flash is idle. enabled since Dec 20 10:50 2001.
   available.
```

In the preceding sequence, the second line gives the LP print service ownership of the port so that no other process can access it. Line 4 sets the printer type, and line 5 sets the file contents type (`PS`). Lines 7 through 9 set the print filters for the print server. The `-D` option sets the description, and the last two lines (starting with `lpstat`) show that the printer is ready to print.

Finally, you can use a very similar process to add a new network printer to a print server found elsewhere on the network (not attached). In addition to all of the parameters that were required for adding an attached printer to a print server, you will be required to specify a destination and protocol. You do not need to specify a port address for a nonattached network printer serviced by a print server.

To add a new attached printer to a print server, follow these steps:

1. Start the Solaris Print Manager.
2. Select the New Network Printer command from the Printer menu. The New Network Printer dialog box, shown in Figure 10.8, appears.
3. Enter the printer name and a description and select the correct settings for the printer type, file contents, fault notification, destination, and protocol. As before, set the Default Printer and Always Print Banner behaviors using the corresponding check boxes.
4. In the User Access List list box, enter the name of users or groups, or enter **all** for all users.
5. Click the Apply button to continue adding additional network printers. Or click the OK button to return to the main Print Manager window.

You will see the network printer added to the Print Manager, and the printer's information will be added to the appropriate configuration files.

FIGURE 10.8

The New Network Printer dialog box

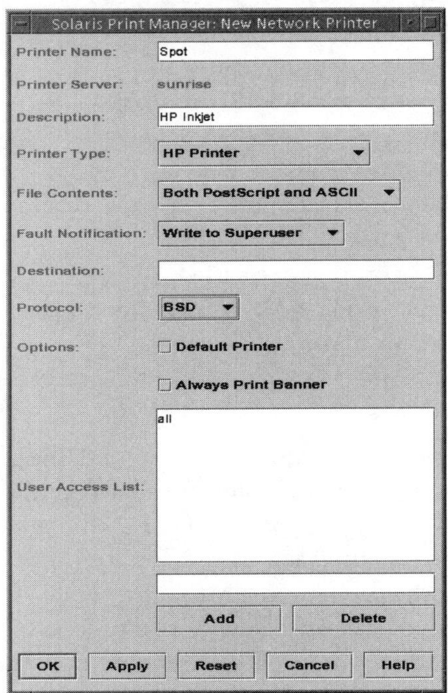

Printing a File

You can use the Default Print control on the CDE front panel to print a file on the Solaris desktop. Just drag and drop a file from one of the File Manager's windows to the Printer control on the front panel.

You use the `lp` command to print from the command line. When you specify a print job with the `lp` command, the job is placed by the LP print service into the print queue for the printer specified, the request ID number is returned, and the shell prompt is refreshed. When you don't specify a printer, the `lp` command uses the default printer. The command in that case is simply entered as `lp` *<filename>*. When a print job completes, Solaris sends an e-mail to the user who generated the print request.

When you want to specify a printer other than the default printer, use the following command:

```
$ lp -d flash /<mydirectory>/<myfilename>
```

Solaris returns output similar to the following:

```
Request id is flash-7 (1 file)
$
```

Should you print to a printer that is not available on your system, Solaris posts the following error message:

```
$ lp -d spot /<mydirectory>/<myfilename>
UX:lp: ERROR: Destination "spot" is unknown to the LP print
    service
$
```

The `lp` command takes the following options:

-c option The -c (copy) option copies a file as output to the location you specify and before your print request is printed.

-d option The -d option specifies the destination printer's name.

-h option The -h (header) option adds a header that you specify to the top of each page in your print output.

-n option Use the -n (number) option to specify the number of copies of the print job to print.

-o option The -o (no banner) option suppresses the printing of a banner page with your print job.

-t option The -t (title) option is used to print a title of the print job on the banner page. A banner page is a page printed prior to the print job that separates the print job from other jobs in the printer's output.

-w option The -w (write) option writes a message to the console of the superuser when the print job has completed printing.

As an example of a compound option, consider the following command that prints three copies and sends you e-mail when the print job completes its execution:

```
$ lp -n3 -m /<mydirectory>/<myfilename>
```

When using a SunSoft print client, you can use either the `lp` or `lpr` command to specify a print request. As part of that print request, you need to specify the target printer and the print class in any of the following styles or manner:

Atomic style The print command takes the form `lp -d` *<printername>* *<filename>*.

POSIX style The print command uses the format `lpr -P` *<servername>*: *<printername>* *<filename>*.

Context-based style Use the format `lpr -d` *<departmentname>*/ *<servicename>*/*<printername>* *<filename>*.

The LP print service manages forms printed on a printer and alerts the user when it cannot successfully print a form. You must provide the description of how to print a form, and you must also manually mount the form stock into the target printer, but the

LP print service will provide feedback as to the progress of the form's printing. Users can specify a form print job, but it takes a superuser to mount a specific form in a printer and make it available to other users.

Similar to working with forms, the LP print service can manage print wheels on impact printers such as letter-quality printers that typically use removable printer balls or daisy wheels where the ribbon is impacted by the ball or wheel to create a specific font or character set. The LP print service can detect which character set is in use and will notify the superuser when the character set the user specified isn't in the printer. The print job remains in the print queue until the correct character set in the impact printer becomes available.

The `cancel` command is use to delete a print request that is in the print queue or to terminate a print job that is currently executing. To cancel a job, you must specify the job ID as part of the command, as shown here:

```
$ cancel flash-2 flash-3
request "flash-2" cancelled
request "flash-3" cancelled
$
```

If you want to cancel the currently printing job, just give the command `cancel` *<printername>*.

Summary

The Solaris print subsystem is based on the System V printing subsystem. In this chapter, I showed you how, using the LP print system commands, you can completely set up and administer a printer and specify print jobs. Solaris maintains a print queue for each printer and a scheduler for managing print jobs. Print jobs are spooled and printed on a print server. Print logs are stored on Solaris and can be used to troubleshoot the Solaris print process.

This chapter also included a discussion of the Solaris Print Manager, which offers graphical tools for installing and managing printers, and how to use the Admintool as a graphical tool for installing and managing printers. Most of the time, you can use graphical tools to add local and network printers, but certain features require command-line modification.

Finally, you learned about the three methods you can use to print files: from within an application using the Print command, by dragging and dropping files onto the Printer control on the front panel, or by using the `lp` command.

CHAPTER 11

User Accounts and Groups

FEATURING:

Working with users and groups 422

The user database 423

Working with user accounts 428

Working with group accounts 449

Account management with AdminSuite 3 456

Administering roles 468

In this chapter, you'll learn how to create and manage user and group accounts. User accounts are used to allow access to Solaris with certain rights and privileges at login. It is also possible to assume another account during a session to get effective rights and privileges. With group accounts, you can assign to one or more users a set of rights and privileges in order to streamline security access. Users, their passwords, and groups are stored locally in a set of database files, and they're stored as part of a naming service in a networked environment. Solaris 8 also supports the creation of roles so that system tasks can be assigned to users without root privileges.

User and Groups

Users and groups are stored as named accounts in local databases, and each account has a number of important attributes. The system identifies each user account by a user identification number (UID number) and each group account by a group identification number (GID number). Accounts are stored locally in your system, and if you are on a network that uses a naming service, they're stored as part of a domain's directory.

Solaris uses three main files to store user and group accounts locally on a system (each of these three files is documented in detail in this chapter):

`/etc/passwd` file The `passwd` file stores the user database file, with a record for each user account. There is a password field that contains an `x` as a placeholder.

`/etc/shadow` file The `shadow` file stores additional information about a user account as well as the encrypted password for each account. Access to this file is by the root account only.

`/etc/group` file The `group` file stores the group database file, with a record for each group account. Users associated with each group are shown, although users may be assigned a primary group in the `passwd` file.

In networked environments, Solaris stores account information in central databases managed by name services such as NIS+ and NIS. A short introduction to the interaction of local user and group accounts with network accounts will be presented in the section "User Account Commands" later in this chapter.

It has been traditional to create, modify, and delete user accounts, group accounts, and passwords using commands at the command line. Many if not most administrators still perform these functions using the commands described in this chapter. However, Solaris 8 provides graphical tools such as the AdminSuite 3 for administering local or remote user accounts and the Admintool (part of the standard distribution) for local account management in the CDE. You can use Admintool to define users and group accounts as well as set their attributes on a local system. AdminSuite is used to work with user accounts stored on networks.

The User Database

Solaris stores data concerning a user's security access in the `/etc/passwd` file. It uses the username field to match the data found in the `/etc/passwd` file to the `/etc/shadow` file. Although many programs access the `/etc/passwd` file, to protect passwords, only logins with root privileges can access the `/etc/shadow` file, and even then, the passwords that are stored in the `/etc/shadow` file are encrypted and hidden from view. In the sections that follow, the contents of these two very important system files are described.

The *passwd* File

Although its name suggests that the `passwd` file stores the actual passwords of individual users, this is no longer the case. Passwords are stored in the `/etc/shadow` file. Figure 11.1 shows an `/etc/passwd` file. Each user's information is stored in a record, which is the information contained between two line endings. Colon characters separate fields in each user's record. The `adduser`, `usermod`, and `userdel` commands are used to add, modify, and delete user accounts in the `passwd` file, respectively.

FIGURE 11.1
The `/etc/passwd` *file*

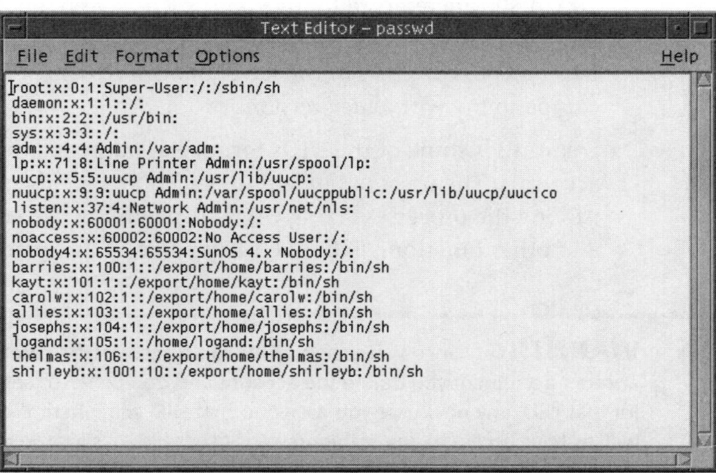

Text Editor - passwd
File Edit Format Options Help
root:x:0:1:Super-User:/:/sbin/sh
daemon:x:1:1::/:
bin:x:2:2::/usr/bin:
sys:x:3:3::/:
adm:x:4:4:Admin:/var/adm:
lp:x:71:8:Line Printer Admin:/usr/spool/lp:
uucp:x:5:5:uucp Admin:/usr/lib/uucp:
nuucp:x:9:9:uucp Admin:/var/spool/uucppublic:/usr/lib/uucp/uucico
listen:x:37:4:Network Admin:/usr/net/nls:
nobody:x:60001:60001:Nobody:/:
noaccess:x:60002:60002:No Access User:/:
nobody4:x:65534:65534:SunOS 4.x Nobody:/:
barries:x:100:1::/export/home/barries:/bin/sh
kayt:x:101:1::/export/home/kayt:/bin/sh
carolw:x:102:1::/export/home/carolw:/bin/sh
allies:x:103:1::/export/home/allies:/bin/sh
josephs:x:104:1::/export/home/josephs:/bin/sh
logand:x:105:1::/home/logand:/bin/sh
thelmas:x:106:1::/export/home/thelmas:/bin/sh
shirleyb:x:1001:10::/export/home/shirleyb:/bin/sh

The seven fields in the passwd file store the following information:

Username A username is the login name for a user account. Usernames should consist of from two to eight alphanumeric characters. The first character must be a letter, and at least one character must be a lowercase letter. No underscore or space characters are allowed in a username.

If you are using a name service such as NIS or NIS+, make sure that any username you create is different than any mail aliases used in your domain. If you create a duplicate username, mail may be delivered to the alias in place of the user. You also need to make sure that any account name you create is also not listed in the /etc/mail/aliases file, whether you use a name service or not.

Password placeholder You always see an x in this field; the x is a placeholder for the user's password. In past versions of Solaris, the encrypted password was placed in this field, and the passwd file retains this field for backward compatibility. Because many programs used the passwd file to determine permissions and needed to be able to access a readable file quickly, Solaris and other versions of Unix moved the encrypted password to the /etc/shadow file, which can be read only by users with root privileges.

User identification number The UID number is used to assign file, directory, and process ownership. The UID number is a unique number that is assigned by Solaris to a user account when the account is created. UIDs can have a value of from 0 to 2,147,483,647, with some exceptions. The UIDs from 0 to 100 and from 60,000 to 65,535 are reserved for system use. In large networks, UIDs of 100 to 500 are reserved for daemons such as Web servers or database servers. For example, the anonymous FTP server is typically assigned either UID 10,000 or UID 30,000. Use UIDs in the range of from 0 to 60,000 to preserve backward compatibility with older versions of Solaris.

Solaris uses some of the UIDs for special purposes, the so-called built-in user accounts. The users of built-in user accounts are referred to as *pseudo users*. Among the processes taking UIDs are daemons, system maintenance programs, and other functions. Table 11.1 lists some of the system UID assignments.

WARNING Once you assign a UID to an account, be careful before you reassign it to another account. If you delete the account and don't change settings such as printer access for that UID, any new user you assign to that UID will inherit the previous user's settings as well as have access to any of the previous user's files. It's a good rule of thumb never to reuse a UID. With 60,000+ numbers to choose from, you will have plenty of numbers left over.

Group identification number The GID number is used by Solaris to see if a user has group access to files, directories, and processes.

Comments The comment field contains the full name of a user. The comment field is also known as the GCOS field and has been used to store comma-delimited information such as phone numbers, department names, and so on.

Home directory The home directory of the user's account is listed in the sixth field.

User's login shell The seventh field lists the login shell that is called when the user logs in to Solaris. The three most common shells, the ones Solaris ships with, are the Bourne shell (`/bin/sh`), the Korn shell (`/bin/ksh`), and the C shell (`/bin/csh`). You may see other shells in this field if they were installed.

TABLE 11.1: SYSTEM UIDS

UID	Description
1–10	Reserved for daemons and system maintenance pseudo users.
0	Reserved for root user or superuser.
1	Used by `pseudouser` daemon for system server processes.
2	Used by username bin for ownership of user-initiated programs.
3	Used by username sys for ownership of system configuration files.
4	Used by adm for ownership of system accounting logs and files.
5	Used by username uucp for the Unix-to-Unix Copy Program (UUCP).
9	Used by username nuucp for the Unix-to-Unix Copy Program (UUCP).
11–99	Reserved for daemons.
71	Used by username lp for the line printer (`lp`) process.
100–60,000	Assignable accounts for users.
60,001	Reserved for username nobody, an account with the minimum access privileges.
60,002	Reserved for username noaccess (analogous to nobody).
60,003–2,147,483,647	Assignable accounts for users. These numbers are not generally recommended for use.
65,534	Reserved for username nobody4, as was used in the SunOS 4.*x* system. Preserved for backward compatibility.

WARNING Solaris 8 uses 64-bit data types for UID and its group equivalent GIDs. Prior to Solaris 2.5, 32-bit data types were used, which limited these ID numbers to a maximum value of 60,000. Therefore, there are interoperability issues when you use numbers greater than 60,000 with older versions of Solaris and other versions of Unix. Among the problems you may encounter are ID number truncation for a SunOS 4.*x* NFS server and client, reassignment of the UID for the `su` command to 60,001 (nobody), access denied to systems running Solaris 2.5, and incorrect UIDs and GIDs displayed in the OpenWindows File Manager when used with the extended file listing option. You will also see problems with the cpio `tar` and `ar` command utilities when you create archives, as well as problems with the `ps` command's listing when you exceed UID or GID numbers of 60,003.

The *shadow* File

Solaris stores users' passwords in the `/etc/shadow` file, which is an encrypted file that can be read only by someone with root privileges. In addition to the password, the `shadow` file stores in nine fields user account information that is protected by the operating system. Figure 11.2 shows an `/etc/shadow` file open in the text editor. You can use the `usermod` command to modify all of the account information in the `shadow` file with the exception of the password. Users can modify their password using the `passwd` command; a superuser or root account can modify all passwords using the `passwd` command.

FIGURE 11.2

The shadow *file*

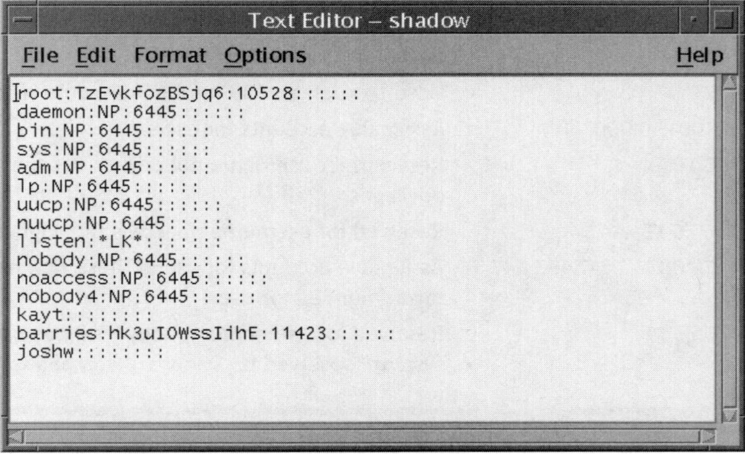
Text Editor – shadow
File Edit Format Options Help
root:TzEvkfozBSjq6:10528::::::
daemon:NP:6445::::::
bin:NP:6445::::::
sys:NP:6445::::::
adm:NP:6445::::::
lp:NP:6445::::::
uucp:NP:6445::::::
nuucp:NP:6445::::::
listen:*LK*:::::::
nobody:NP:6445::::::
noaccess:NP:6445::::::
nobody4:NP:6445::::::
kayt::::::::
barries:hk3uIOWssIihE:11423::::::
joshw::::::::

The nine fields in the shadow file store the following information:

Username The first field provides a match field for the username from the /etc/passwd file.

Password The password that corresponds to this username's account is stored in the second field as a 13-character encrypted string. When you log in, it is this field's data that is matched to the username that you enter to allow you access to a system.

In some instances, you may see other data in the password field. The string "NP" indicates that a login with this account is "Not Permitted." "LK*" indicates that this user's account is "Locked." If the password field is blank, a user could log in using this username with no password (blank).

Date last changed The third field stores the date the password for this user account was modified. The date is stored as a serial number, obtained by subtracting the serial date number of January 1, 1970, from the modification date's serial number. The number you see is the number of days between these two dates. Most spreadsheets and databases will perform this date calculation for you using functions such as DateToNum, SerialDate, and so on.

Length before change allowed The number in the fourth field indicates how many days may pass (as a minimum) before a user may change their password.

Length before change required The number in the fifth field indicates how many days may pass (as a maximum) before a user *must* change their password.

Warning The number in the sixth field indicates the number of days before a password expires or must be changed that a warning is posted indicating that the password is about to expire.

Inactivity The number in the seventh field is the number of days of inactivity a user account can have as a maximum before the user is denied access. If you leave this field blank, there is no expiration date due to inactivity.

Login expiration date The eighth field stores a date on which the user is no longer allowed access to the system. Expiration dates are stored as absolute dates and are typically used to provide users with guest or temporary access to a system.

Flag The ninth field is not used in most implementations.

Working with User Accounts

A *user account* is a named object with attributes stored in the passwd file. When you create a user account, you assign to the account a username that will be used as the account's logon name. Initially, the account is locked until you assign a password. The user account takes multiple attributes that determine what group (or groups) the account belongs to, whether the password will expire, and if so, how long it will take. Each user account is identified in the system by a UID.

After you create a user account for a user and assign the desired attributes, you still need to create the home directory, set the directory's access privileges, and create or modify the appropriate initialization files required to set the user's environment. You will find procedures for creating user accounts, setting attributes, and setting a user's environment in the sections that follow.

User Account Commands

A *root account* can use the `useradd` (add user) command to create user accounts. The `useradd` command stores a record for the username you specify in both the `passwd` and `shadow` files, along with a set of default settings.

The `useradd` command's syntax is as follows:

```
useradd <options> <username>
```

The username becomes the name of the user account and is the text that is entered at login for that account. Solaris allows usernames of from one to eight alphanumeric characters and will not create a duplicate account name for one that is already in the system. To determine if a user account was successfully added to your system, give the following command:

```
# grep <username> /etc/passwd /etc/shadow
/etc/password:username:x:101:1::/export/home/<username>:bin/sh
/etc/shadow:<username>:*LK*:::::::
```

The user account is assigned the next UID number, which in the preceding command is 101. The `useradd` command assigns a home directory, which is traditionally set at `/export/home/`*<username>*. Note that systems put the directory in `/home` if not specified. When you use the `useradd` command from the command line, you should use the `mkdir` command to create a new user's directory because the `useradd` command will not complain if the `/export/home/`*<username>* directory doesn't exist.

NOTE Name services allow you to store user account information in a central network database. This permits users to log in to the network with their user account from any location on the network. The NIS and NIS+ name services have a set of commands that create (`nistbladm`, `nisclient`, `useradd`, `make`, and `useradd`), modify (`nistbladm`, `usermod`, `make`, and `usermod`), delete (`nistbladm`, `nisclient`, `userdel`, `make`, and `userdel`), and disable (`nistbladm`, `passwd -r nis -l`, and `make`) user accounts. There are also commands to change a password (`passwd -r nisplus`, `passwd -r nis`, and `passwd -r files`), sort user accounts (`niscat`, `sort`, and `awk`), and find user accounts (`nistbladm`, `ypmatch`, and `grep`). And finally, there are commands to add groups (`nistbladm`, `groupadd`, `make`, and `groupadd`), modify groups (`nistbladm`, `groupmod`, and `make`), and delete groups (`nistbladm`, `make`, and `groupdel`). All of these commands are described in detail in the man pages. The commands `useradd`, `usermod`, `userdel`, `passwd`, `groupadd`, `groupmod`, and `groupdel` are described in this chapter, even if their use with the name services hasn't been explained. The connection between these commands and name services is described in Chapter 9, "Network Services."

PART II

Solaris and the Network

Notice that when you add a user to the system, that user has as its password in the `shadow` file `"*LK*"`, or locked. You must assign a password to each new account in order to allow the user to access it. You have fine control over each of the settings in the user database. The `useradd` command takes eight major options:

`-c` option Use the `-c` option to specify a comment for the GCOS field, which is typically a user's full name. To include spaces in the comment field, surround the text with quotation marks.

`-d` option Use the `-d` option to specify the path name for the home directory.

`-e` option The `-e` (expire) option specifies a date after which a user cannot access a user account. In the `-e` *<datenumber>* option, the date is entered as an integer number that expresses the difference between that date minus the serial date number for January 1, 1970.

`-f` option The `-f` *<number>* option specifies a number of days of inactivity after which a user cannot access a user account.

`-g` option The `-g` *<groupname>* option specifies the principal or default group name. In the form `-g GID`, it specifies the group using its group identification number.

`-m` option The `-m` option is used to specify the home directory name or to create a home directory if that directory name doesn't exist. To fully describe a path and directory name for the home directory, you would use the `-c <pathname> -d <directoryname>` combination.

-s option The `-s /<pathname>/<loginshell>` option sets the login shell for this user account. For the Bourne shell, use `/bin/sh`; for the Korn shell, use `/bin/ksh`; and for the C shell, use `/bin/csh`. If you don't enter the shell explicitly, the default, which is `/bin/sh`, is used.

-u option You can use the `-u` option to specify a UID number to assign to this user account. Solaris will not let you assign a duplicate number for a preexisting account.

All of the aforementioned options must be entered as part of the `useradd` command. An example of a compound set of options would be `useradd -c "Barrie A. Sosinsky" -d /export/home/sosinsky -m sosinsky -u 201`. The order that you enter the options doesn't matter, but make sure you use the proper syntax.

Once you have added a user account, you must use the `usermod` command to modify any of the options you specified for the `useradd` command. Here is the syntax for the `usermod` (modify user) command:

```
usermod <options> <username>
```

You can use the `usermod` command to change any option for a user account except the password. The `usermod` command takes one option: `-l`. The `-l <newusername>` option changes the name of the user account you specify in the `usermod` command.

Last, there will be times when you will want to or need to delete user accounts. It is good practice to delete accounts when a user leaves an organization. It not only lowers system overhead, it protects against future system access through that account name. Hackers typically look to assume user accounts that have been inactive for long periods of time.

The syntax for the `userdel` (user delete) command is as follows:

```
userdel <options> <username>
```

When you use the `userdel` command to delete a user account, the command leaves the user's home directory intact. In general, leaving the home directory and all its contents on the system is a good idea if there is a chance that you will reestablish that user on the system some day. However, if a user is gone and forgotten, it is better to back up that user's home directory to another medium and delete it. The `-r` option for the `userdel` command deletes the home directory as specified in the `passwd` file.

Managing User Accounts with Admintool

Solaris ships with a graphical tool called Admintool that contains a Users window listing user accounts. In the Users window, you can add, modify, and delete user accounts on a local system. You can use a similar tool called AdminSuite 3 to administer network user accounts. Figure 11.3 shows the Users window of the Admintool program. To modify local user databases, you can access Admintool using the Solaris Management console as root.

FIGURE 11.3

The Admintool: Users window

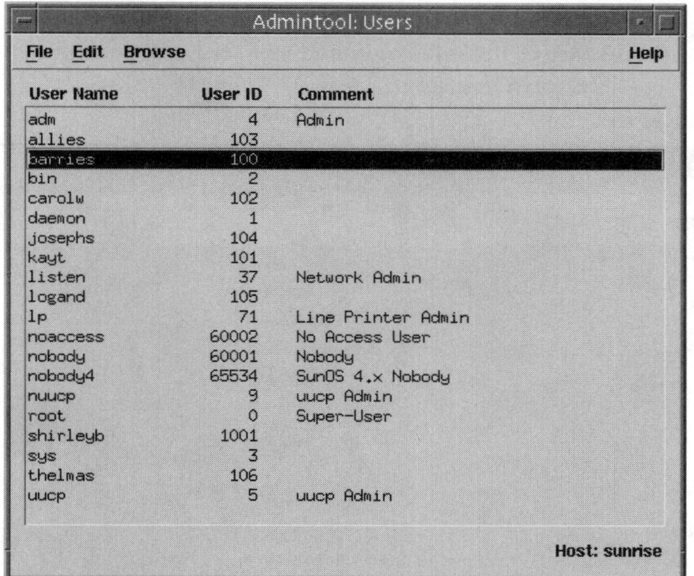

NOTE The AdminSuite 3 tool and its use for establishing user and group accounts over a network was described in Chapter 9.

To add a user account with Admintool, do the following:

1. Open a terminal window, enter the `admintool` command, and press the Return key. The command `admintool&` will display the process number and then open the Admintool window. The ampersand symbol runs the process in the background.

You can also double-click the Admintool icon found in the Application Manager's `System_Admin` folder of the CDE (the icon is shown in the following graphic). The Admintool window appears.

2. Select the Users command from the Browse menu to view the Admintool: Users window.
3. Select the Add command from the Edit menu to view the Add User dialog box, shown in Figure 11.4.

FIGURE 11.4

The Admintool: Add User dialog box

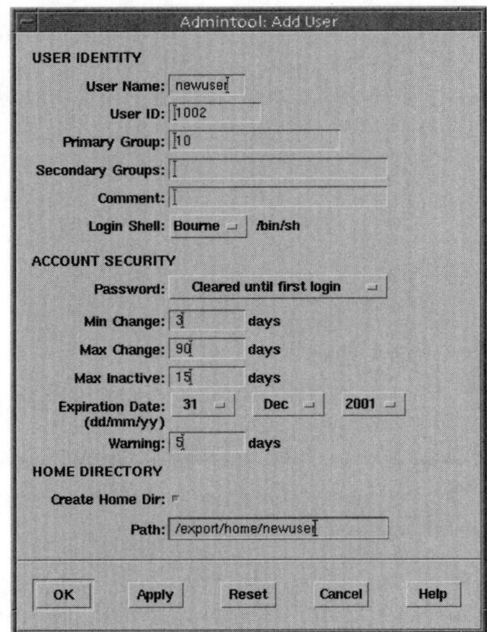

4. Enter information into the fields as follows:
   - In the User Name field, enter the login name.

- In the User ID field, enter the UID, between 100 and 60000 or (less preferably) between 60003 and 2147483647.
- In the Primary Group field, enter the GID or group name. The default 10 sets STAFF as the primary group name. It is interesting to note that the `useradd` command uses a default group of 1 (OTHER) instead of 10 (STAFF) as Admintool does.
- In the Secondary Groups field, enter a comma-delimited set of group memberships (up to 16) for this account.
- In the Comment field, enter the user's full name (optional).
- From the Login Shell pop-up list, select the desired default shell for this account (the Bourne shell is the existing default).
- From the Password pop-up, select one of the following options: Cleared Until First Login (no password set initially), Account Is Locked (account is not available), No Password, `setuid` Only (account cannot be logged in to, but the account programs can be run), Normal Password (sets a login password for the account and immediately prompts you for the password that is to be used with that account).
- In the Min Change, Max Change, Max Inactive, and Warning fields, enter the number of days desired. (Those options were explained in the section "The `shadow` File" earlier in this chapter.)
- From the Expiration Date pop-up lists, select the day, month, and year you want the password to expire.
- In the Home Directory field, enter **`/export/home/`*`<username>`*** into the text box, and click the Create Home Directory button above that text box to the In or On position if the directory doesn't exist.

NOTE You should create directories in the location `/export/home/`*`<username>`* with the owner set to the person whose home directory it is. Depending upon the privileges you wish to allow, you may want to deny access to the other members of this user's primary group and to Others.

5. Click the Apply button to create the user account and continue creating additional accounts. Or click the OK button to create the user account and dismiss the Add User dialog box. Solaris adds this information to the `/etc/passwd`, `/etc/shadow`, and `/etc/group` files.

NOTE If you specified a primary group and no secondary groups, Admintool will not modify the /etc/group file. It will not list the user on the line for their primary group because it is noted in the passwd file.

6. Set up the user initialization files, as described in the next section, "Creating User Environments."

If you want to modify a user account using the Admintool, you need to be logged in as a sysadmin (GID 14). When you want to access the Admintool in the Solaris Management Console, you must be a root user. The Modify command on the Edit menu of the Admintool: Users window opens the Admintool: Modify User dialog box. Or, you can double-click a user account name to open the Modify User dialog box.

Notice that all of the user account information is already entered for you. You can change all of the options described in the preceding steps with one exception: the home directory. If you need to change the home directory, the directory that will replace the existing directory must already exist (use mkdir from the command line or the New Folder command in the File Manager window to create the directory, if necessary).

The final basic user operation in the Admintool is the Delete command, which also requires a sysadmin group (GID 14) login. If you are deleting a user account, you should also delete the user's listing in the NIS+ Passwd database, the NIS map, or the /etc/passwd files (depending upon whether you use a name service). You should remove usernames from the NIS+ Group database, the NIS map, or /etc/group files as well. You may also want to delete a user's home directory, their mail file, and their printer access lists.

To delete a user account, follow these steps:

1. Click the account name in the Admintool: Users window to highlight it.
2. Select the Delete command from the Edit menu. The Admintool: Warning dialog box appears (shown in the following graphic).

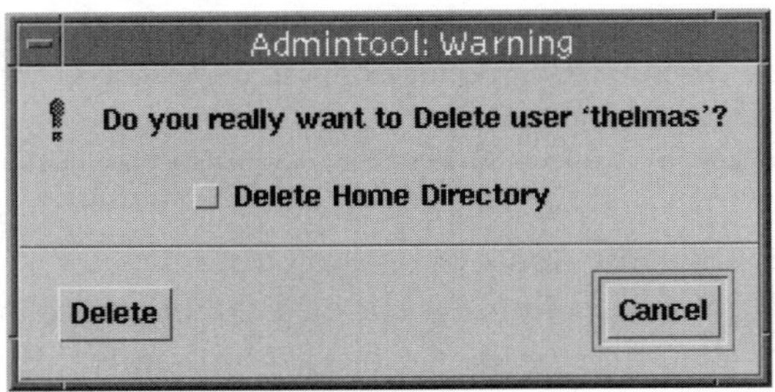

3. Click the Delete Home Directory button if you wish to delete a user account's directory.
4. Click the Delete button to delete the account. Or click the Cancel button to leave the user account intact.

Creating User Environments

When you add a user account, you still need to create a home directory for that user, automatically mount that directory, and share it with appropriate access rights. Additionally, you need to modify the initialization files to establish the settings a user needs or expects when they log in to a system. Those initialization files set various environmental variables, most particularly the default shell and path.

Creating a Home Directory

A user's home directory is stored locally at `/export/home/<username>` by default, although there is no restriction on the home directory appearing elsewhere in a local file system. Starting with Solaris 8, the user home directory is stored without the name of the server preceding home directory's path name. Wherever a user's home directory is stored, the `/home/<username>` directory is used as the mount point for that user's directory. The file system is mounted into that directory by default if the automounter tool is set up to mount that directory and is activated. The fact that a user's home directory can appear anywhere requires that scripts and programs always use `$HOME` as the pointer to the home directory and that any paths used in a user's home directory be relative paths of the type `../../../x/y/z` to keep those references valid should the home directory mount point move to another system or location in the file system.

Wherever the home directory is, you need to use the `share` command to export the file system so that a user can access their home directory from an accessible mount point. You will also need to mount the home directory automatically, by either adding an entry to the NIS+ `Auto_home` database or adding an entry to the `/etc/vfstab` file locally to allow NFS to mount the home directory.

On a network, the AutoFS service is used to make a home directory accessible to a user. An entry into the `/etc/auto_master` file lists the `/home` directory service `auto_home` with a `-nobrowse` option to automatically mount the directories in the `auto_home` database on the local `/home` directory mount point. If you look in the `auto_home` database, you will see the following mapping:

```
<username>     <systemname>/export/login/home/<username>
```

The purpose of the AutoFS service is to allow a user to log in to any system on a network and have their home directory mounted on that system's local `/home` mount point. With AutoFS active, the /home directory is left empty, and no subdirectories can be created in it.

Once you have mounted a new user's home directory, you will need to create it and assign permissions and access rights to it. Create the directory and assign permissions prior to exporting the directory or other systems' network cache will contain incorrect data. You will also need to use the `share` command for this purpose.

To create a home directory for a new user account, do the following:

1. Log in as the root on the system that will contain the user's home directory by entering the `su` command at the command line.
2. Enter **cd /*<homedirectory>***, where *<homedirectory>* is the name of the directory that will be used for the user's home directory.
3. Enter **mkdir *<username>*** and press the Return key to create a new home directory for that user.
4. Enter **chown *<username>* *<username>*** and press the Return key to change the ownership of the directory to the new user's account.
5. Enter **chgrp *<primary_GID>* *<username>*** and press the Return key to change the group ownership to the new user's primary GID.
6. Enter **chmod ### /export/*<homedirectory>*/*<username>*** and then press the Return key.

   The three numbers (###) for the `chmod` (change mode) command specify the read, write, and execute attributes, respectively. They are described in detail in Chapter 5, "The File System." For user-only access, you would specify the number 700. To give the primary group read-write access to the new user's home directory, you would specify the number 760, but this would not allow them to list the files (you need execute permission to do that), so the correct number would be 770. Finally, to offer group members read-list/execute access, you would specify the number 755 (all other people would be able to look at the listing of files in your directory as well as the contents of those files, but they would not be able to make any changes to the files).

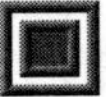

NOTE You can perform these operations in the File Manager of the CDE. Create a new folder in the `/export` directory, then right-click the folder and select the Permissions command. Owner, primary group, and directory attributes are exposed in the Properties dialog box for you to change.

To share a home directory on a Solaris server, do the following:

1. Log in as the root on the system that will contain the user's home directory by entering the su command at the command line, if necessary.
2. Enter the share command to determine if the home directory has been shared. If the home directory isn't listed, you will need to set up a share point for that user's home directory.
3. Open the /etc/dfs/dfstab file and add the line **share -F nfs /export/<*home-directory*>**.
4. At the command line, enter **shareall -F nfs**, then press the Return key.

   When you issue the shareall command, the /etc/dfs/dfstab file is run without your having to reboot the system. If you didn't issue the command, you would have to restart your system to have the shareall command run automatically.
5. Enter **ps -ef | grep mountd** and press the Return key to determine if the mountd daemon is running on your system. If the mountd daemon is running, the share is complete and established. Otherwise, perform step 6.
6. Enter **/etc/init.d/nfs.server start** and then press the Return key.

There are additional considerations that you need to account for after you share a home directory on a network. If you are running the NIS+ or NIS server, enter the server's IP address and system name into the /etc/hosts file on the user's system. This can be done conveniently in the Hosts window of the Admintool program. You might also want to create disk quotas for a user at this point to limit the size of their home directory on a server. To make the home directory available, you must add it to the Auto_home database so that AutoFS will mount it automatically (preferred in a network environment), or you can add the entry to the /etc/vfstab file so that the NFS service can mount the directory. The procedure for mounting a newly established home directory using the NFS service is very similar to procedure just described.

Follow these steps to have NFS mount a home directory:

1. As a superuser, add the entry for the user's home directory into the /etc/vfstab file; the entry will be similar to the following:

```
<systemname>:/export/home/<username> - \
    home/<username> nfs - yes, rw, intr
```

2. Then create the mount point with the mkdir /home/<*username*> command.
3. Use the chown command to assign the directory ownership to the user account.

PART II

Solaris and the Network

4. Use the chgrp command to assign the primary GID of the directory.
5. Finally, at the command line, enter the mountall command and verify that the directory was mounted by giving the mount command.

Solaris User Registration

Sun's Solaris User Registration tool gives users the option of being informed automatically when there are upgrades, new products, new information, and solutions available from a special SunSolve Online Web site. To register and access the SunSolve site, you must fill in the Solaris User Registration profile and then e-mail it to Sun. You can also send a hard copy via fax or regular mail. Once you're signed up, you create a login ID and password (six to eight alphanumeric characters, with no spaces or colons) that you can use to access the Solaris SunSolve site.

The Solaris User Registration is not available to a system administrator or superuser and does not activate when a user of that type logs in to the system. A user sees the registration introduction screen when they first log in. When you click the Register button, you are taken to the registration form. You can print and mail or fax the completed form to register.

To register, complete the form that is found at `$HOME/.solreg/uprops`. If you specify that you wish to never register, you can still start user registration by entering **`/usr/dt/bin/solreg`** at the command line or by double-clicking the Registration icon in the Application Manager `Desktop_Tools` folder in the CDE. When you register information about the user's version of Solaris, their hardware, location, system architecture, and survey type is transmitted to Sun to store in the User Registration database. Solaris User Registration is documented in the man pages at `man solregis(1)`. It's a good idea to create a user account with Solaris User Registration even if it is for some future use.

If system administrators wish to disable the Solaris User Registration feature, they can do so prior to installation by deselecting the SUNWsregu package before an interactive installation, modifying the JumpStart profile to ignore the SUNWsregu package, or creating a finish script at `/etc/default/solregis` that contains the line `DISABLE=1`. After installation, you can use the `pkgrm` command to remove the SUNWsregu package or manually add the `/etc/default/solregis` with the `DISABLE=1` line in it.

Once registered with Solaris User Registration, a user can access the Solaris SunSolve Web site. Solaris SunSolve contains information about recent Solaris upgrades, patches, and releases, as well as information about Sun contract services such as help.

Creating the User Environment

Next, you'll need to create the default user environment for your new user account. This includes defining the initialization files. Many administrators also set up the mail account, the default printer, and printer access at this stage. These additional setups are described in the chapters on printing (Chapter 10) and mail (Chapter 13). Initialization files and their effect on the system and user environment were described in Chapter 5.

As part of the login routine, Solaris first runs the `login` program, which sets several important environmental variables such as `HOME`, `LOGNAME`, and `TZ`. After `login` runs, the system profile or initialization file runs, setting the system defaults such as `PATH`, the message of the day, and `umask`. As a final step, the user profile initialization file runs and sets the environmental variables that each user specifies. A user profile can overwrite the `PATH` with its own value or any other environmental variable.

The initialization file depends upon the shell used. For the C shell, the file `/$HOME/.login` is used to define the environment at login, and the `$HOME/.cshrc` file defines the environment for any subsequent use of the C shell when the C shell is the login shell. When the C shell is not the login shell, it reads only the `.cshrc` file. The Bourne shell uses the `$HOME/.profile` to define the environment at login, as does the Korn shell. For the Korn shell, the `$/HOME/ksh-env` file sets the environment for a user account in the file that is specified in the `ksh-ENV` environmental variable.

In order to speed up the process of creating user initialization files, Solaris provides a set of skeleton user initialization files for the C, Bourne, and Korn shells that you can use in place of each of the files mentioned in the preceding paragraph. For the C shell, you can find these template files at `/etc/skel/local.login` and `/etc/skel/local.cshrc`; for the Bourne or Korn shells, the file is located at `/etc/skel/local.profile`. Figures 11.5 through 11.7 show these three files. The settings provided in these files provide minimal configuration, but they are a start. You certainly want to set the `PATH` setting in any initialization file for a user.

In a networked environment, you can create site initialization files that serve as templates for a specific language or a specific locale. The feature is new to Solaris 8. When you use a site initialization file on a local server, you set a pointer to the site initialization file in the user's initialization file. This centralization of many environmental settings enables you to change an entire site at once, a great administrative savings that makes it well worthwhile for you to consider adopting a system such as this one.

Each site initialization file must call the same shell that the user who uses it calls. For a Bourne or Korn shell user account, you would insert the following line into the user's initialization file to call the site initialization file:

```
. net/<servername>/export/<sitefiledirectory>/<sitefileinitname>
```

<servername> is the name of the server storing the site initialization file (*<sitefileinitname>*) in the directory (*<sitefiledirectory>*) reserved for these files. For a C Shell user account, that line would be as follows:

```
sourcenet/<servername>/export/<sitefiledirectory>/<sitefileinitname>
```

FIGURE 11.5
The default /etc/skel/local.login *file*

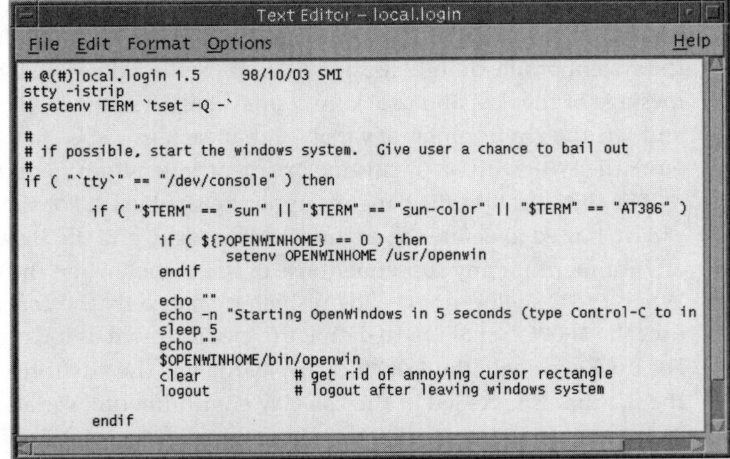

Text Editor – local.login
File Edit Format Options Help
@(#)local.login 1.5 98/10/03 SMI
stty -istrip
setenv TERM `tset -Q -`
#
if possible, start the windows system. Give user a chance to bail out
#
if ("`tty`" == "/dev/console") then
if ("$TERM" == "sun" || "$TERM" == "sun-color" || "$TERM" == "AT386")
if (${?OPENWINHOME} == 0) then
setenv OPENWINHOME /usr/openwin
endif
echo ""
echo -n "Starting OpenWindows in 5 seconds (type Control-C to in
sleep 5
echo ""
$OPENWINHOME/bin/openwin
clear # get rid of annoying cursor rectangle
logout # logout after leaving windows system
endif

FIGURE 11.6
The default /etc/skel/local.cshrc *file*

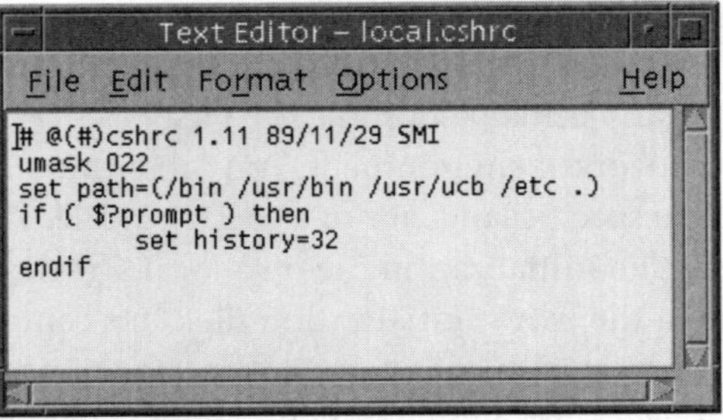

FIGURE 11.7

The default `/etc/skel/local.profile` *file*

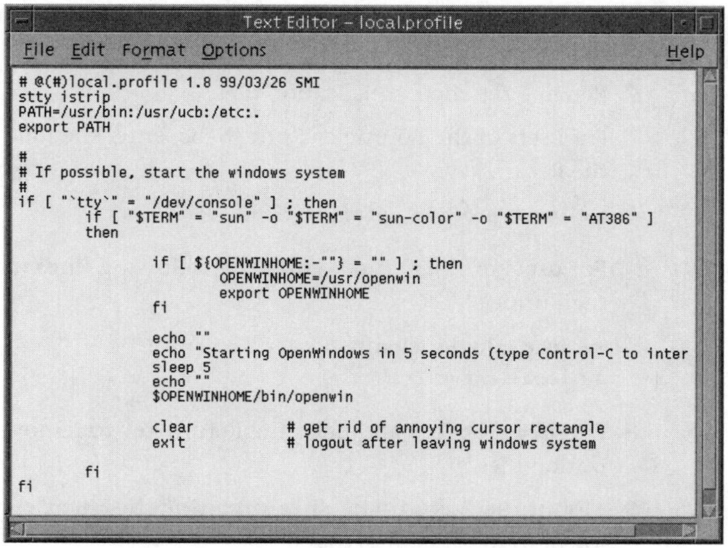

```
Text Editor - local.profile
File  Edit  Format  Options                                   Help
# @(#)local.profile 1.8 99/03/26 SMI
stty istrip
PATH=/usr/bin:/usr/ucb:/etc:.
export PATH

#
# If possible, start the windows system
#
if [ "`tty`" = "/dev/console" ] ; then
        if [ "$TERM" = "sun" -o "$TERM" = "sun-color" -o "$TERM" = "AT386" ]
        then

                if [ ${OPENWINHOME:-""} = "" ] ; then
                        OPENWINHOME=/usr/openwin
                        export OPENWINHOME
                fi

                echo ""
                echo "Starting OpenWindows in 5 seconds (type Control-C to inter
                sleep 5
                echo ""
                $OPENWINHOME/bin/openwin

                clear           # get rid of annoying cursor rectangle
                exit            # logout after leaving windows system

        fi
fi
```


Because the intent is to provide network access to a user's environment, you should avoid specifying references to a local system in the initialization file so that the user can use their account from any system they log in to. A user's home directory should always be referenced in the *$HOME* variable, and that variable should never refer to an absolute path such as */export/home/<username>/home*. The *$HOME* variable automounts the user's home directory to the local system when the user logs in to the network from another location. If you want to access files locally, you should use a global path */net/<systemname>/<directoryname>*. Therefore, any reference to */net/<systemname>* can be automatically mounted when the user logs in to a system using AutoFS.

Follow these steps to set up user initialization files:

1. Log in to the system as a superuser.
2. Enter **cd /*<pathname>*/*<username>*** to switch to the user's home directory.
3. Enter **cp /etc/skel/local.*** and press the Return key to copy all of the default user initialization files to the user's home directory.
4. Enter **chmod 744 local.*** and press the Return key to set the access rights to the initialization files, with the owner having full access.
5. Enter **chown *<username>* *** and press the Return key to have the user's account assume full ownership of the initialization files.

6. Enter **chgrp <*groupname*> local.*** and press the Return key to assign ownership of the initialization files to the primary group. You can use the GID in place of the group name.
7. Rename the shell initialization files.

   For users of the Bourne or Korn shells, enter the following line and then press the Return key:

   ```
   mv local.profile .profile
   ```

   For users of the C shell, enter the following lines (press the Return key after each line):

   ```
   mv local.login .login
   mv local.cshrc .cshrc
   ```

8. Enter **rm local.*** and press the Return key to remove the unused shell initialization files.
9. Mount the user's home directory using the `mount` command (if needed), then log in to the system as that user.
10. Use the `passwd` <*username*> command to assign a password to the user account.

With the procedure complete, you may want to open the user's initialization files to add any additional environmental variables or startup scripts that the user should have. You should also log out of the account and log back in as the user to check the environment.

The most important environmental variable you should set is the `$PATH` variable because it gives automatic access to important programs and commands. It's also not a bad idea to add the `$PATH` variable to the `skel` file. Because the `PATH` doesn't often change, this step can save an administrator valuable time when setting up multiple user accounts. In the C shell, you would edit the line `set path =(/directoryname1/directoryname2/directoryname3/…)` into the `$HOME/.cshrc` file. Once you have added this line to the C shell initialization file, you should enter **source .cshrc** at the command line to have your new path installed into the C shell. To check that your new path was set, enter **echo $PATH** and press the Return key. Solaris will display your `set path` statement. You should also add additional `setenv` statements to change the other environmental variables of interest.

For the Bourne and Korn shells, the syntax for setting environmental variables is slightly different. It takes the form `env variable=value;export variable`. An example would be `MAIL=/var/mail/username/export MAIL`.

Once you have added all of the appropriate environmental variable settings, check to see if the initiation file has its file permissions set appropriately. You can use the umask command to modify a file's permissions. The umask command takes the inverse octal values of the values you use with the chmod command. Thus, to add full permissions, you would use 000, and to remove all permissions, you would use 777. To create the permissions rwxr-xr-- (owner, group, other), you would give the command umask 723. The following is a list of octal values for umask: 0 is the value for rwx (all), 1 is the value for rw-, 2 is the value for r-x, 3 is the value for r--, 4 is the value for -wx, 5 is the value for -w-, 6 is the value for --x, and 7 is the value for --- (none).

Other settings you should check are the LANG variable and LC environmental variables. Those settings specify language- and location-specific data conventions. Among the specific settings affected by these variables are date, time, numbers, and currency formats; time zones; sort or collation orders; and data formats. The LANG variable sets all conversions and conventions and can be subdivided into parts by specifying aspects of the LANG set using the LC variable. For example, you can specify LC_COLLATE, LC_CTYPE, LC_MESSAGES, and LC_NUMERIC to control localization aspects. To set LANG for different languages, use iso_8895_1 for English, fr: for French, de: for German, it: for Italian, japanese for Japanese, korean for Korean, sv for Swedish, and tchinese for Chinese. Some of these languages, such as Korean and Japanese, require multibyte or Unicode support. Add the line sty. cs8 defeucw to either the /etc/profile file (for the Bourne and Korn shells) or the /etc/.login file (for the C shell).

Password Commands

When you first create a user account, the default password in the /etc/passwd file is set to "*LK*", or locked, and a user can't log in with that account until you change the password. A superuser or member of the sysadmin group (GID 14) can change any user account's password, but users can also change their own password as well once the initial password has been set. It's a good idea to change passwords for every account every so often to lessen the security risk of someone stealing or hacking a user's password. To change passwords, you use the passwd command.

The binary file for the passwd command is found at /usr/bin/passwd. You should use the nispasswd command when your system uses the NIS+ naming service and the yppasswd command when it uses the NIS naming service. Those command binaries are also located in the usr/bin subdirectory.

Here is the syntax for the passwd (password) command:

```
passwd <options> <username>
```

When you issue the `passwd` *<username>* command, Solaris prompts you to enter the password twice. Enter an alphanumeric string with six to eight characters for the password in the case you desire. If the two passwords match, you'll see a message informing you that the password was successfully changed. When the two passwords you enter at the New Password and Reenter New Password prompts don't match, you are notified and asked to try again. If you are changing your own password, you will be prompted for your existing password before Solaris prompts you for the new password.

NOTE Passwords are case sensitive. A common problem in logins occurs when the user has the Caps Lock key on and enters their password. When you're modifying a password, make sure the case of the string is the way you want it. The best passwords are combinations of letters and numbers that don't appear in a word or name dictionary.

There are numerous options that you can use with the `passwd` command. The following are among the most useful:

-f option Should a user forget their password, an administrator can change that user account password to some default value and then, by issuing the command `passwd -f`, the administrator can force the user to change the default when they first log in.

-l option The `-l` (lock) command prevents a user from using a password to access the system. You can use this option in place of deleting a username if you want to retain the user account for future use. For example, administrators use the `-l` *<username>* option to deny access to a user who has not paid their bill or who is temporarily being switched to a new project or department (with an option to return).

-n option The `-n` *<number_of_days>* option sets the minimum number of days that a password must be used before it can be changed.

-w option The `-w` *<number_of_days>* option sets the number of days before the password expires that Solaris warns a user that the password associated with their username is about to expire. When a user changes their password during login and then changes it back again, they change the modification date and reset the -x clock back to the full number of days. As an administrator, you might therefore want to use the `-n` option because that sets a minimum valid time that the password must be used.

-x option The -x <*number_of_days*> option sets the number of days before a password expires from the date that the password was last changed. You can change the parameter from number of days to number of weeks by entering the line MAXWEEKS=<*number_of_weeks*> into the /etc/default/passwd file.

Solaris ages passwords so that when a certain period of time expires, the password must be changed. You can use the -x option to specify how long a password is active, or you can set the -x option to a null string "" so that a password never expires. Most organizations require that a password be changed every 30, 45, 60, or 90 days.

You can use the passmgmt command to create and modify user accounts and their attributes in the passwd and shadow files. The command takes options you can use to set all of the nine fields in the passwd file associated with a user account. Among the options are -a (add a user account), -m (modify a user account), -d (delete a user account), -c (add a comment), -h (specify the home directory), -u (change the UID), -g (change the GID), -o (make a UID nonunique, when used with the -u option), -s (specify the shell), and -l (set the logname). These options are fully described in the man pages and are very similar to those described previously for the useradd command. The passmgmt command works only with local accounts and does not alter information stored by the name services.

The Root Account

The *root user*, or *superuser*, has complete access to a system's resources. You can log in as the root user or change to the root user account using the following sequence that both switches your account and changes the environment to the default environment of the root:

```
$ su - root
Password:
#
```

The display of the number symbol (or hash character symbol) indicates that you are working with root privileges. With root privileges, every action that you take has system-wide implications. A simple error that might delete a subdirectory could with root privileges delete an entire file system. Therefore, you need to exercise caution when using the root account.

You can also enter su - for the same response (because when you use su, Solaris assumes you mean root unless you define a user). Also, the - means it's a login; if you leave the - off, you get the permissions of the user you are switching to (root in this case) but you keep your environment, which is very handy at times.

TIP If you have root account access, log in as another user for your sessions and switch to the root account when you need to. It is safer to work in a less-privileged account.

As a rule, it is recommended that even if you have root privileges, you log in using another password with lower privileges. You can switch to the root account during a session as just shown; use the `exit` command to return to your previous user account as soon as you are finished making your changes. The section "Changing User Status" later in this chapter describes the `su` (switch user) command in more detail.

You need to pay particular attention to how the root account is accessed. Only knowledgeable users who require root access in order to perform system or networking functions should be given the password for the root account. It is also a good idea to change the root password often so that you minimize the chances that your system can be hacked and the root password used by another user.

Displaying Users

Root can display a list of all users defined in the system by using the `logins` command. Figure 11.8 shows the output of the `logins` command. The output shows username, UID, primary group name, GID, and comments fields.

FIGURE 11.8

All users may be displayed by a root user using the `logins` *command.*

Terminal

Window Edit Options Help

```
# logins
root        0      other      1      Super-User
daemon      1      other      1
bin         2      bin        2
sys         3      sys        3
adm         4      adm        4      Admin
uucp        5      uucp       5      uucp Admin
nuucp       9      nuucp      9      uucp Admin
listen      37     adm        4      Network Admin
lp          71     lp         8      Line Printer Admin
barries     100    other      1
kayt        101    other      1
carolw      102    other      1
allies      103    other      1
josephs     104    other      1
logand      105    other      1
thelmas     106    other      1
shirleyb    1001   staff      10
nobody      60001  nobody     60001  Nobody
noaccess    60002  noaccess   60002  No Access User
nobody4     65534  nogroup    65534  SunOS 4.x Nobody
#
```

To display only those users who are logged in to the system, use the `who` or `w` command or the `finder` command. The `who` command lists users who are logged in, what type of login device was used, the date and time of the login, and the name of the system that the user has logged in from. The output of the `who` command appears as follows:

```
# who
root        pts/1   Dec 26 18:34  (:0)
root        pts/4   Dec 28 20:04  (0:0.0)
username3   pts/7   Jan 6 08:17   (solstice.sosinsky.com)
username4   pts/6   Jan 8 23:51   (sunset.sosinsky.com)
```

The `w` *<username>* command lists information about a single user who logged in to a system. For example, the command `w barries` might return the following:

```
$ w barries
User     tty    login@   idle   JCPU    PCPU   what
barries  pts/7  Jan 6    1day   62:34    21    -sh
barries  pts/6  Jan 8    3days  1              -ksh
```


When you give the `w` command without an argument, it returns a summary of system information along with a list of the current users of the system. Figure 11.9 shows you the output of the `who` and `w` commands.

FIGURE 11.9

Output of the `who` *and* `w` *commands*

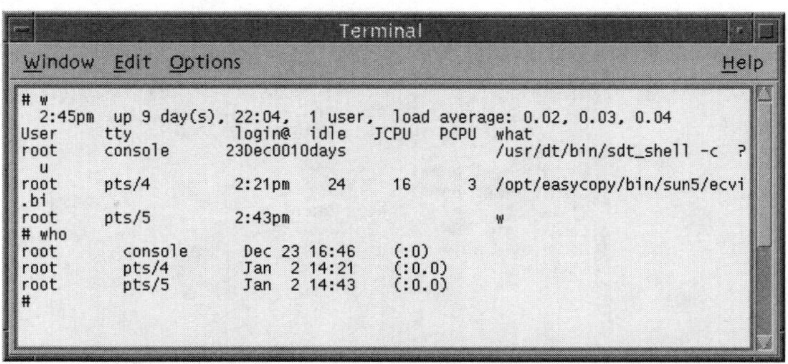

The `finger` command combines information displayed by both the `w` and `who` commands, allowing you to determine the login information for a specific login user account.

The finger command's syntax is as follows:

```
finger <option> <username>@<hostname>
```

The following options are typically added to the `finger` command:

`-l` option The `-l` (long) option gives detailed user information.

-m option The -m (<*username*> list) (match) option will display only information about users on the username list.

-p option The -p (plan) option suppresses the display of the .plan file for any user that is displayed in the username list. The .plan file contains escape sequences for modifying the display you see when it is output, and so what you see on your screen may vary from display to display. The -l option displays the .plan file unless you couple it with the -p option.

-s option The -s (short) option summarizes the information about a user login when combined with a username, as in finger -s barries. Without the -s option, finger returns a detailed listing that describes information related to the activities and current condition of a user's login, such as the home directory, shell, condition of their mail, and other details.

Figure 11.10 shows the output of the finger command in some of its various forms.

FIGURE 11.10

Output of the finger *command*

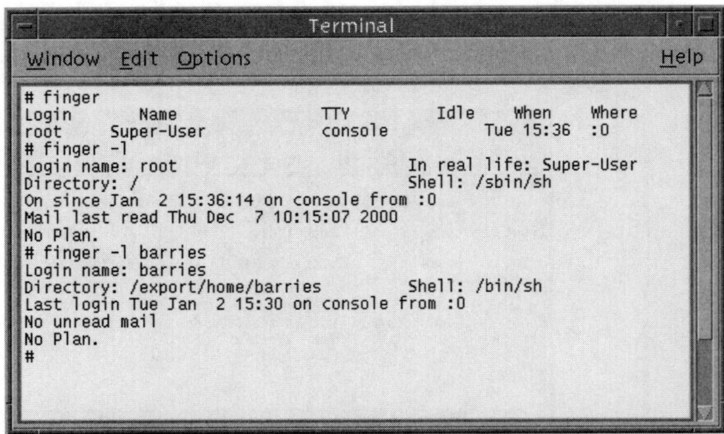

When finger is used with the @<*hostname*> argument, as in finger -s @reliant.sosinsky.com, you see a summary list of users who have logged in to a system from a particular host, which here is reliant.sosinsky.com. The host is the system from which those users connected to your system. Combining the two arguments of <*username*> and <*hostname*>, you can request information about a remote user using the command finger <*username*>@<*hostname*>.

Allowing users to run the finger command offers them a look at what could potentially be sensitive network information. You can disable finger by commenting out the command in the /etc/inetd.conf file. Place a # in front of the line containing the finger program, or simply delete the line and send a HUP (hang up) signal to the inetd process.

Another command that is very helpful is last, which is mainly a history of the results of the who command. The who command shows only those currently logged in, so it's helpful sometimes to see who has logged in previously.

Changing User Status

There may be times when you need to change your login status during a session. Most commonly, this will occur when you need to assume the role of superuser with root privileges in order to install a package, run a security program, or change a setting that is restricted to other users. You might also need to change your user account during a session to see how Solaris operates in some way for a particular user. To switch to a different user, enter the su (switch user) command. Using the command su without any options or arguments changes you to the superuser account (although it isn't, you can remember this if you think of *su* as an abbreviation for *superuser*).

Here is the syntax of the switch user command:

```
su <option> <username>
Password:
```

Solaris responds with a prompt (Password:) asking you to enter that user's password. If you change to another user account from the root account, you will not be asked to provide a password. To switch back to your original account, enter the exit command.

When you assume another user's privileges, you assume the UID of that user, obtaining all ownerships and access rights. You maintain the same shell and environment that you had before you switched unless you use the minus (-) option. The command su - *<username>* changes your environment to the default environment of the user account that you switch to. The command su - changes you to the root account and switches your environment to that account's environment; it's functionally equivalent to the command su - root.

Working with Group Accounts

A *group account* is a named object with attributes stored in the group file. When you create a group account, you assign a group name to the account. The group account is identified in the system by a group identification number, or GID number. The most important aspect of creating groups is to add the appropriate users and to assign to the group access rights to the appropriate directories and files. You will find procedures for creating group accounts in the sections that follow.

Typically, group accounts, also called Unix groups, are created as part of an overall network architecture design, so once groups are developed, they aren't deleted, and new ones aren't added very often. As an administrator, you might want to modify group access from time to time, but typically, even these changes are infrequent.

Among the group accounts you might want to create are any or all of the following (this is a partial list): ADMINS (administrative), MGT (management), EX (executives), LEGAL (law department), ACCT (accounting), IT (information technology), DEVELOPER (developer group), LOC*n* (a specific location, such as a building, city, state, or county name), PR (public relations) HR (human resources), PROJECT1 (a specific project), USER (general pool of users), STAFF (a general pool of staff members), and ANON (a group account for anonymous users).

Some applications look at a user's primary group to determine access. The File Manager, for example, considers the primary group to determine ownership of files and directories and to store accounting data into the account logs. Other applications take all group assignments, both primary and secondary, into account when determining access and privileges. The Admintool is one example of an application that considers all group memberships. You can be a member of the sysadmin group as a secondary group and the Admintool will still allow you to modify user and group accounts.

Programs and tools for older versions of Unix (such as BSD) expect to see a STAFF group with a GID of 10, so it makes sense to create this group account even if you don't populate it with users. Solaris 8 creates the STAFF group as part of its default installation. You should also definitely create a USER group and assign all users to it so that they can share files in central directories set aside for this purpose. Whereas adding all users to the USER group is straightforward and practical in smaller networks, on larger networks, it may make more sense to segregate a USER group into smaller groups that are organized around roles.

Group account information is stored locally in the `/etc/group` file. When you're operating in a networked environment using a name service, the `Group` database, NIS+ tables, and NIS maps store information that is found in the local system's `/etc/group` file. An unrelated set of groups called NIS+ groups allow access rights to NIS+ objects, but those groups are unrelated to the group account database stored by the NIS+ table. In the `Group` database, you will find four fields:

Group name Group names can have up to nine alphanumeric characters.

Group password This is a holdover from the past and is usually left blank.

GID number Group identification numbers are used by Solaris to identify group accounts (described in the section "Group Identification Numbers" later in this chapter). Solaris supports numbers from 0 to 2,137,483,647; however, in order to retain backward compatibility with previous versions of Solaris and with other Unix variants, it is recommended that you use GID numbers in the range of from 0 to 60,000.

User (or member) list A comma-delimited list of users who are members of a particular group. These names are the login names or user account login names stored in the `passwd` file. The list of users must not contain spaces after the commas. Users may belong to up to 17 group accounts: one primary group and 16 secondary groups. Not all users who have a group assignment may appear in this list in the `group` file. Users can have their primary group assignment made in the `/etc/passwd` file's GID field (the fourth field in that file as well) and not have their username appear in the `group` file's user list field.

Group Account Commands

Many of the commands that you previously saw for creating, modifying, and deleting user accounts have counterparts for working with group accounts, such as the `groupadd`, `groupmod`, and `groupdel` commands.

To add a group to your system, use the `groupadd` command. This command assigns both the group name and GID (described in the next section) to your system.

The syntax for the `groupadd` (add group) command is as follows:

```
groupadd -g <gid> <groupname>
```

To add the STAFF group described earlier, you would enter `groupadd -g 10 staff`. The safest numbers to use for GIDs are between 101 and 60,000, for reasons described in the next section.

Once you have created a group account, you can use the `groupmod` command to change the name of the group, change the group identification (GID), or add users.

Here is the syntax for the `groupmod` (modify group) command:

```
groupmod <options> <gid> <newgroupname> <oldgroupname> <username>
```

There are several options of interest for use with the `groupmod` command:

-n option The `-n` *<newgroupname> <oldgroupname>* option establishes a new group name for a preexisting group account. For example, `groupmod -n mygroup yourgroup` changes the existing group called yourgroup into a group account named mygroup.

-g option The `-g gid` *<groupname>* option changes the existing group identification number for a group to another GID number. Solaris will not let you assign a GID number to a group that has been previously assigned. You can combine the action of the -n and -g options as follows: `groupmod -g 150 -n mygroup yourgroup`. This changes the existing group account called yourgroup into a group account named mygroup and sets its GID number to 150.

-G option The `-G (`*<groupname>*` list)` *<username>* or `-G (`*<gid>*` list)` *<username>* options add a user account to a comma-separated group or set of groups specified by either their group names or their GID numbers.

The final important group account command is the `groupdel` command. It is straightforward and typically takes no options.

Here is the syntax for the `groupmod` (modify group) command:

```
groupdel <groupname>
```

The `groupmod` and `groupdel` commands require an existing group with either the group name or GID that you specify in order to function correctly.

Managing Groups Using Admintool

The Admintool: Groups window (see Figure 11.11) allows you to create new groups, modify group properties, and delete groups from within a graphical environment. You must be a member of the sysadmin group (GID 14) to work with groups or a root user to work with the Admintool from within the Solaris Management Console.

FIGURE 11.11

The Admintool: Groups window

Admintool: Groups

File Edit Browse Help

Group Name	Group ID	Members
acct	103	
adm	4	root,adm,daemon
admin	101	
bin	2	root,bin,daemon
daemon	12	root,daemon
dev	102	
lp	8	root,lp,adm
mail	6	root
noaccess	60002	
nobody	60001	
nogroup	65534	
nuucp	9	root,nuucp
other	1	
root	0	root
staff	10	
sys	3	root,bin,sys,adm
sysadmin	14	barries
tty	7	root,tty,adm
users	100	allies,barries,carolw,josephs,kayt
uucp	5	root,uucp

Host: sunrise

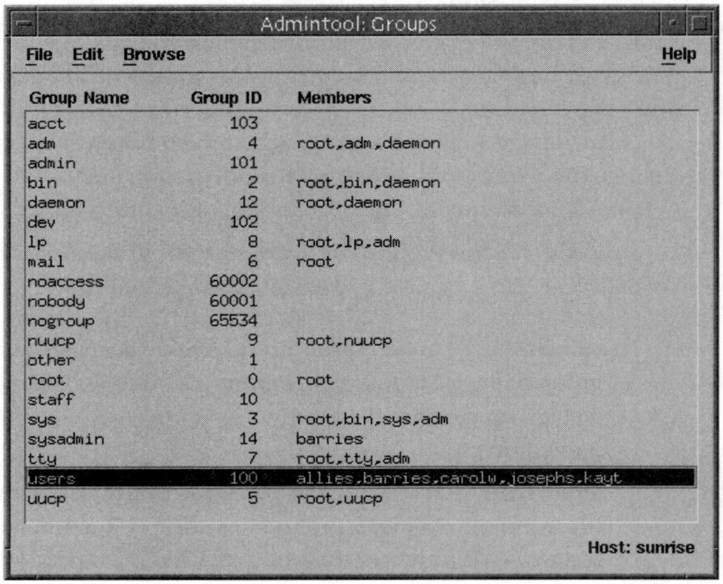

To add a group account with Admintool, do the following:

1. Open a terminal window and enter the `admintool` command followed by the Return key. Or, double-click the Admintool icon found in the Application Manager's `System_Admin` folder in the CDE. The Admintool window appears.
2. Select the Groups command from the Browse menu to view the Groups window.
3. Select the Add command from the Edit menu to view the Admintool:Add Group dialog box.

4. Enter the following information into the fields in the Admintool: Add Group dialog box:
   - In the Group Name field, enter the group account name.
   - In the Group ID field, enter the GID number.
   - In the Members List field, enter the user account names (separate them with a comma, no spaces).
5. Click the Apply button to create the group account and continue creating additional group accounts. Or click the OK button to create the group account and dismiss the Admintool: Add Group dialog box. Solaris adds this information for a new group to the `/etc/group` file.

If you want to modify a group account using the Admintool, you need to be logged in as a sysadmin (GID 14). When you want to access the Admintool in the Solaris Management Console, you must be a root user. The Modify command on the Edit menu of the Admintool: Groups window opens the Admintool: Modify Group dialog box, which is essentially identical to the Add Group dialog box shown previously. You can also double-click a group account name to open the Modify Group dialog box.

The final basic group account operation in the Admintool is the Delete command, which also requires a sysadmin group (GID 14) login.

To delete a user account, follow these steps:

1. Click the group account name in the Admintool: Groups window to highlight it.
2. Select the Delete command from the Edit menu. The Admintool: Warning dialog box appears.

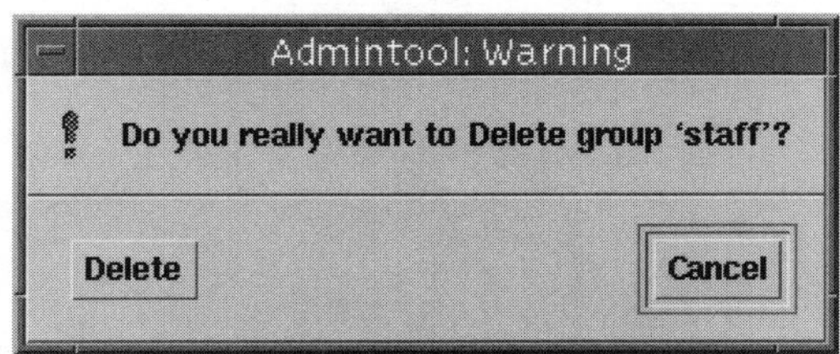

3. Click the Delete button to delete the account. Or click the Cancel button to leave the group account intact.

Group Identification Numbers

The group identification number (GID number) is used by Solaris to identify group accounts. User accounts can be assigned a GID, and that assignment gives a user access privileges to files, directories, and processes available to the group account. The `/etc/passwd` file lists as its fourth field the primary GID number for a user account (see "The `passwd` File" earlier in this chapter). GID numbers are stored in the `/etc/group` file, which is shown in Figure 11.12. The `group` file stores group records; each record is separated from the next by a line ending. You use the `groupadd`, `groupmod`, and `groupdel` commands to add, change, and delete user accounts.

Many administrators create groups that mimic the structure of an organization, such as ACCT (accounting), IT (information technology), HR (human resources), and so forth. Doing so allows a particular employee type to have access to all of the resources that other employees of that type have, thus simplifying many aspects of security design. Groups are also created to express the geographical disbursement of users in an organization. Another reason to create a group is to allow administrators to modify system files or processes. Finally, there may be special projects such as a design or development project that requires that its primary files be protected. You can protect source code by creating a group such as DEV (developers) and giving it access to the primary files, excluding everyone else except root.

You can use the `groups` command to see a list of groups. When you use the command `groups <username>`, Solaris returns a list of the groups that that username belongs to. Solaris creates some default group accounts, analogous to the system user accounts that it creates. Table 11.2 lists these groups and their GID numbers.

FIGURE 11.12

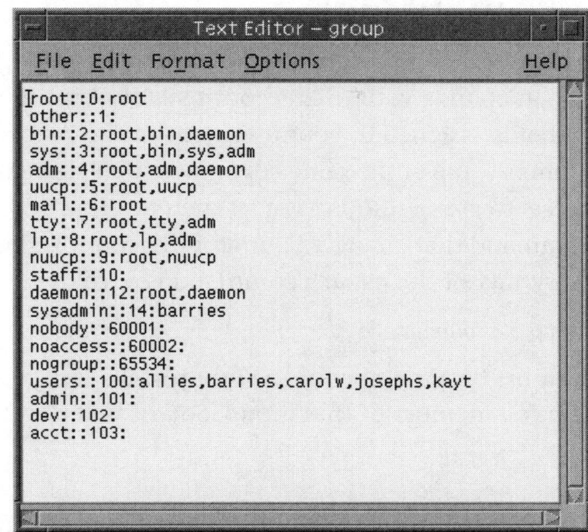

The `/etc/group` *file stores information about group accounts.*

TABLE 11.2: SYSTEM GIDS

GID	Description
1–10	Reserved for daemons and system maintenance pseudo groups
0	Root user or superuser account
1	Used by other group
2	Used by bin group
3	Used by sys group
4	Used by adm group
5	Used by uucp group (Unix-to-Unix Copy Program [UUCP])
6	Used by mail group
7	Used by tty group
8	Used by lp group
9	Used by username nuucp for the Unix-to-Unix Copy Program (UUCP)
11–99	Reserved for daemons
12	Used by daemon group
14	Used by sysadmin group
71	Used by username lp for the line printer (`lp`) process
60,001	Reserved for nobody group, an account with the minimum access privileges
60,002	Reserved for noaccess group (analogous to nobody)
65,534	Reserved for nogroup group

Changing Group Status

There may be times when you need to change your group status during a session, just as you can change your user account status. After login, your user group is the default group that is assigned to your username in the `/etc/passwd` file. Changing your group status offers some of the same advantages that changing your user account does: it gives you access to group resources or lets you test how Solaris behaves for a particular group. The command that changes your group account is the `newgrp` (new group) command.

The syntax of the `newgrp` command is as follows:

```
newgrp <groupname>
```

You must be a member of the group you specify in order to change to that group. If you aren't a member of that group, Solaris will post the error message `newgrp: Sorry`.

Using AdminSuite 3 for Account Management

You can use AdminSuite 3 to add, modify, or delete user and group accounts on a network. The software is installed on a server and typically administered from that location. This is in addition to providing domain management and acting as a console for setting security policies. In the sections that follow, you will find a description of how to use AdminSuite to manage user and group accounts.

NOTE To obtain AdminSuite 3, download it for free from `www.sun.com/bigadmin/content/adminPack`. It's included in the Solaris 8 Admin Pack. At that location you can also download the Solaris Management Console (SMC).

To open AdminSuite 3, follow these steps:

1. Double-click the Solaris Management Console (SMC) icon in the `System_Admin` folder of the Application Manager on the CDE desktop. The SMC Login dialog box appears (it's shown in Figure 11.13).
2. Enter your username and password, then click the Log In button to view the Solaris Management Console window, displayed in Figure 11.14. The Solaris Management Console window provides access to account information, system utilities, and network utilities and functions.

FIGURE 11.13

The Solaris Management Console Login dialog box

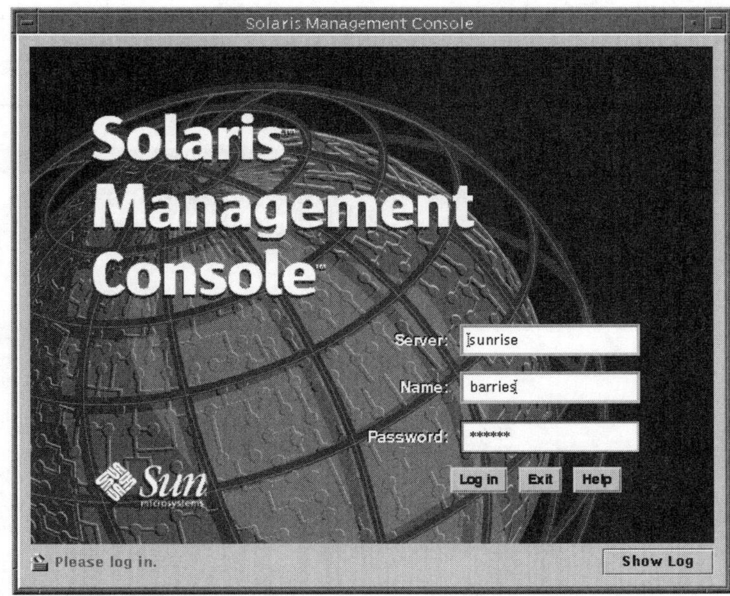

FIGURE 11.14

The Solaris Management Console window

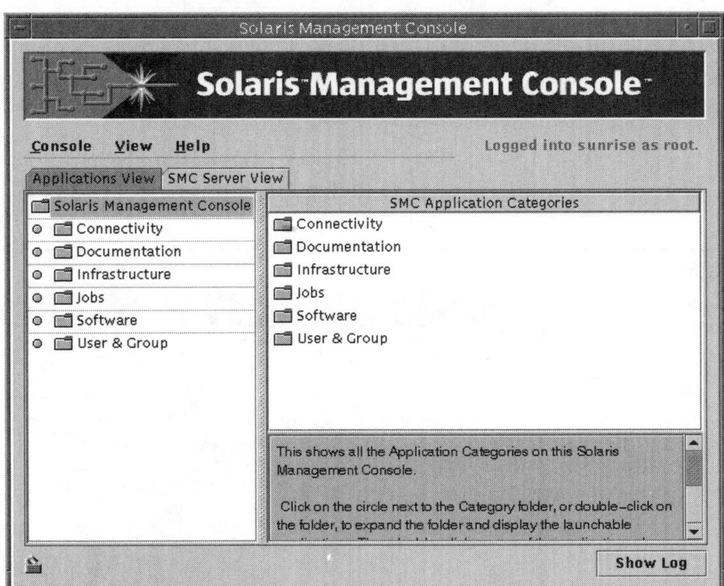

3. Click the `Infrastructure` folder in either panel. Figure 11.15 shows the contents of the Infrastructure panel, which contains the Admintool and AdminSuite utilities.

FIGURE 11.15

The Infrastructure panel

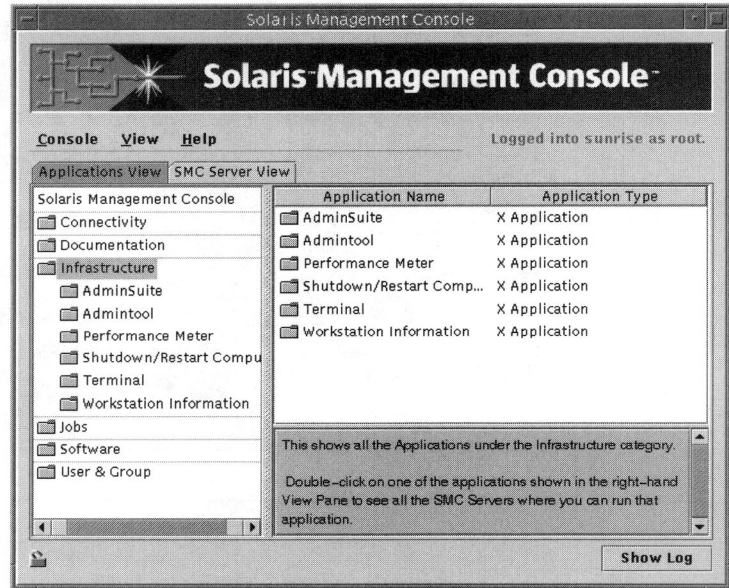

4. Double-click the `AdminSuite` folder, then double-click the AdminSuite icon. The AdminSuite Log On dialog box appears (see Figure 11.16).

FIGURE 11.16

The AdminSuite Log On dialog box

AdminSuite Log On

Context Help

Type your Solaris password.

User Name: barries

Password: ******

Domain: Sunrise (Server)

OK Cancel

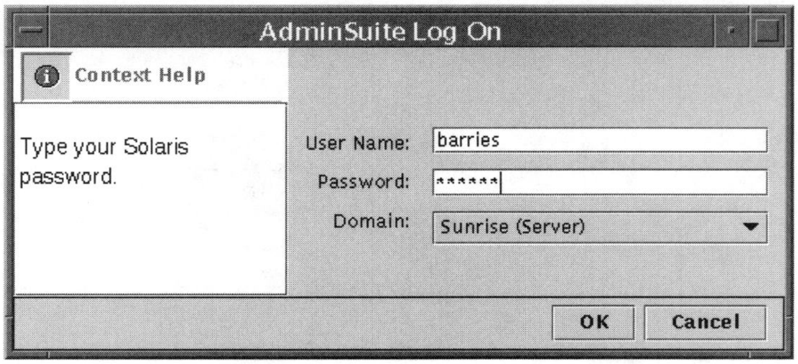

5. Enter the username and password of a user account that has superuser privileges in the AdminSuite, then click the OK button. The AdminSuite tool, shown in Figure 11.17, appears.

FIGURE 11.17

The AdminSuite tools open to the Users window

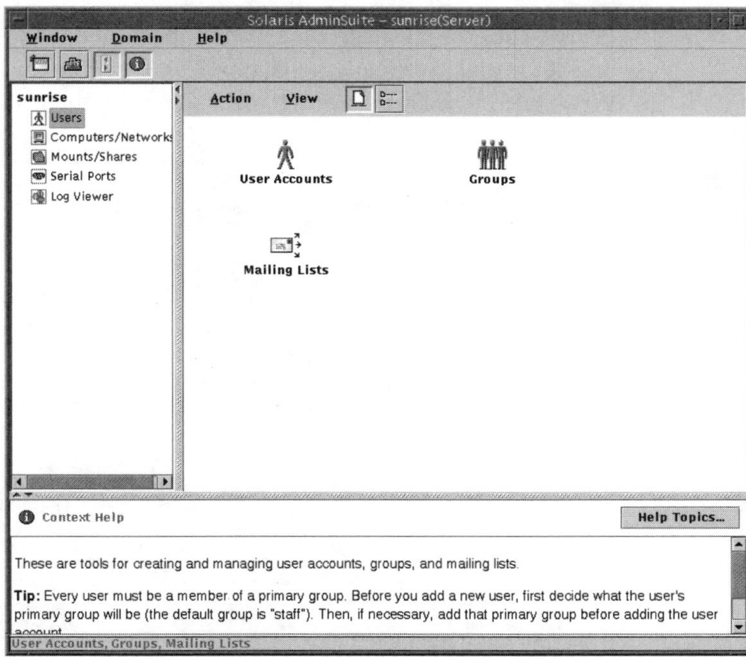

6. To close the AdminSuite tool, double-click the title bar control (the icon on the far left side of the title bar), select the Close command from the Window menu, or press Alt+F4.

Managing Network Users with AdminSuite

With AdminSuite 3 you can add, modify, and delete user accounts on a network. Using the User Accounts window, you can select a domain to modify and even add or delete domains. You can also view the attributes of an account and assign attributes within AdminSuite. Additionally, you can set up security policies and assign to users superuser rights that allow them to make changes to other user accounts from within AdminSuite.

Add a User Account

Follow these steps to add a user account in AdminSuite:

1. Click the Users icon in the left pane of the AdminSuite window. (See the preceding section for an explanation of how to open the AdminSuite tool.)
2. Double-click the User Accounts icon in the right pane of the AdminSuite window. The Set Initial View dialog box appears (shown in Figure 11.18). The Set Initial View dialog box controls which users you see in the User Accounts window.

FIGURE 11.18

The Set Initial View dialog box

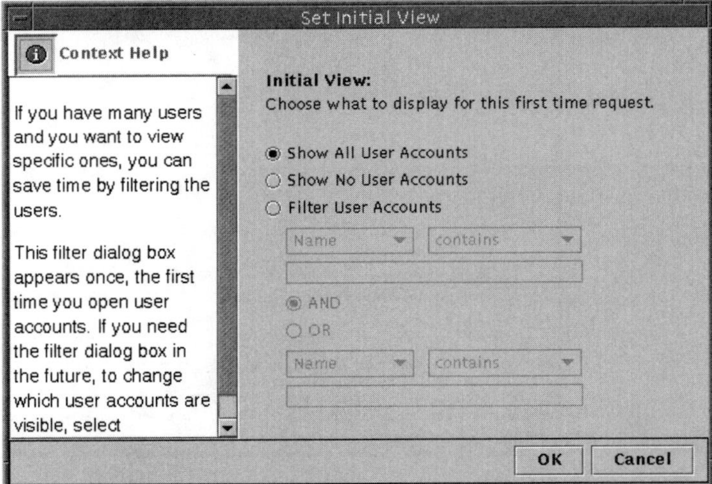

3. Click the Show All User Accounts radio button, the Show No User Accounts radio button, or the Filter User Accounts radio button. Then click the OK button.

   If you click the Filter User Accounts radio button, set the filter you desire before you click the OK button. You can alter your view of the User Accounts window by selecting commands from its View menu.
4. Select the Add User command from the Action menu to display the Add User Wizard, shown in Figure 11.19. In the first six steps of the wizard, you fill in the username, UID, password, primary group, home directory, and mail server for the new user account. The seventh step asks you to review the information before committing the new user account to the user database.

FIGURE 11.19
The Add User Wizard

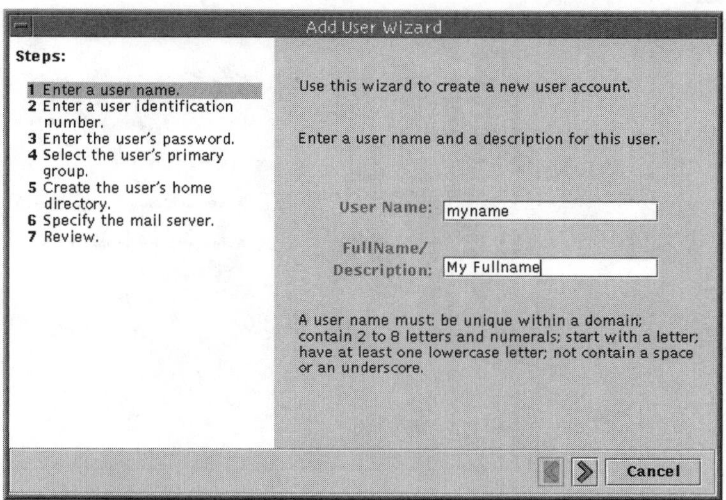

5. Enter the information requested, review the final screen, and then click the Finish button. The new user is added to the User Accounts window and selected.

Add Multiple User Accounts

Because the AdminSuite is used in network environments, administrators are often faced with the task of adding many users to the network at once. The AdminSuite has a mechanism that allows you to create many users in a single operation. You can manually enter the names one at a time from a text file, or you can create a automatically generated series of names.

Follow these steps to create multiple user accounts at once:

1. Select the Add Multiple Users command from the Action menu in the User Account window. The Add Multiple Users Wizard dialog box shown in Figure 11.20 appears.
2. Select the Specify a Text File radio button, the Type Each Name radio button, or the Automatically Generate a Series of User Names radio button.

   For the text file selection, you will need to supply the path to a file that contains names as line entries, with each name on a single line. The Automatically Generate selection adds a number to a username that you specify, creating as many user accounts as you indicate.

FIGURE 11.20

The Add Multiple Users Wizard

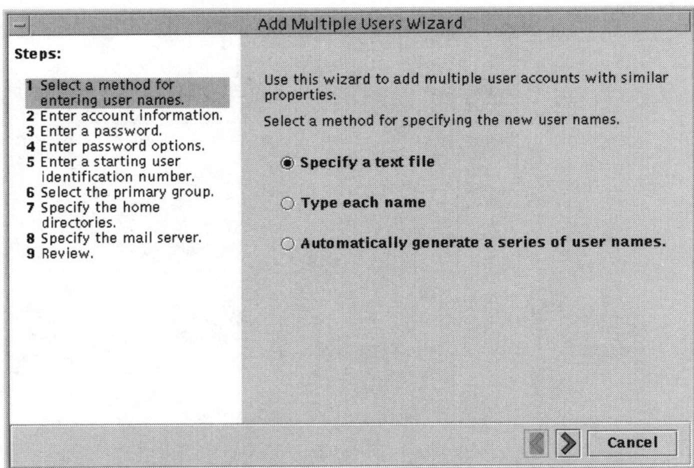

3. Complete the steps in the wizard, then review the information and click the Finish button. Solaris adds the user accounts to the home directory server you selected in the AdminSuite tool.

Modify User Accounts

You can also modify specific user accounts in the AdminSuite. To view user properties, double-click a user account of interest in the User Accounts window. The User Properties dialog box, shown in Figure 11.21, appears.

There are seven tabs in the User Properties dialog box (once you have made the changes you desire, click the OK button to put them into effect):

General On this tab you can set a name and ID number for a user. You can also specify the login shell and the duration of the account. Information about the account availability appears only if your password gives you the right to view this information.

Group Use this tab to change a user's group memberships.

Home Directory You can set the user's home directory on this tab, as well as share the directory and set all users' access.

Password On this tab, you can set or reset a user's password. An administrator can use this tab to restore a user's forgotten password or reset a password that has expired.

Password Options On this tab are settings that determine when a password expires, when to alert a user that the password is about to expire, and how long before a specific password can be used again.

Mail The Mail tab shows the name of the mail server as well as the user's mailbox.

Rights On this tab, you can view and modify the rights of a user account. You can either grant a right by checking its corresponding check box or deny a right by unchecking the check box. Categories of rights listed include Audit Management, Device Allocation, Cron and At Jobs, Login Control, Execution Profile Management, Role Management, Machine Administration, File Systems, Computers/Networks, Log Viewer, Serial Ports, and User, Groups & Mailing List Rights.

FIGURE 11.21
The User Properties dialog box

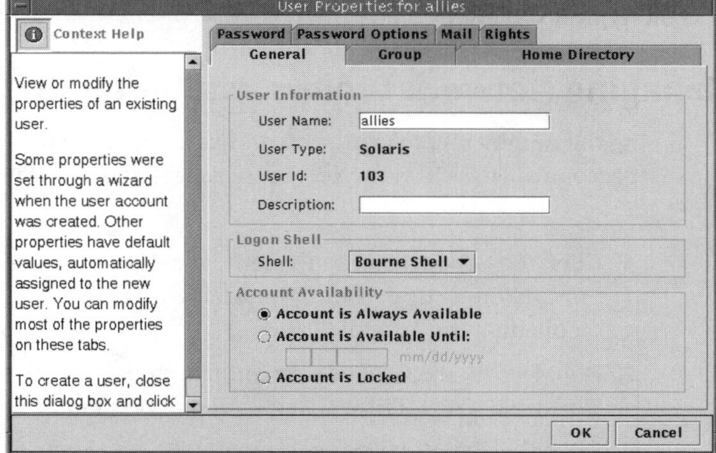

Deleting User Accounts

You can also use the AdminSuite to delete user accounts. To do so, follow these steps:

1. Click the user account you wish to delete.
2. Select the Delete command from the Action menu. The warning dialog box shown in the following graphic appears.

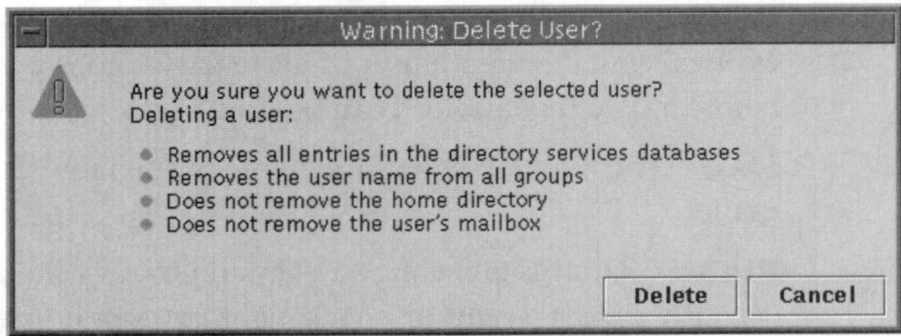

3. Click the Delete button to confirm the deletion.

Solaris deletes the user account from all entries in the directory services database and removes the user account from membership in all of the groups that it belonged to. This procedure does not delete either the home directory or a user's mailbox. You will need to manually delete those associations from the system that they are stored on (typically a server).

Managing Network Groups with AdminSuite

Using the AdminSuite to work with groups is similar to using it to create and manage user accounts. First I'll show you the steps necessary to create groups in the Admin-Suite:

1. Click the Groups icon in the left pane of the AdminSuite window. (See "Using AdminSuite 3 for Account Management" earlier in this chapter for instruction on opening the AdminSuite tool.)
2. Double-click the Groups icon in the right pane of the AdminSuite window. The Set Initial View (Filter Groups) dialog box appears (shown in Figure 11.22).
3. Click the Show All Groups radio button, the Show No Groups radio button, or the Filter Groups radio button, then click the OK button.

   For the Filter Groups selection, set the filter you desire before you click the OK button. You can alter your view of the Groups window by selecting commands from its View menu.
4. Select the Add Group command from the Action menu to display the Add Group dialog box (shown in Figure 11.23). In the Add Group dialog box, you can create a new group (either a local group or a group on a domain somewhere on the network) and assign members to it.

FIGURE 11.22
The Set Initial View (Filter Groups) dialog box

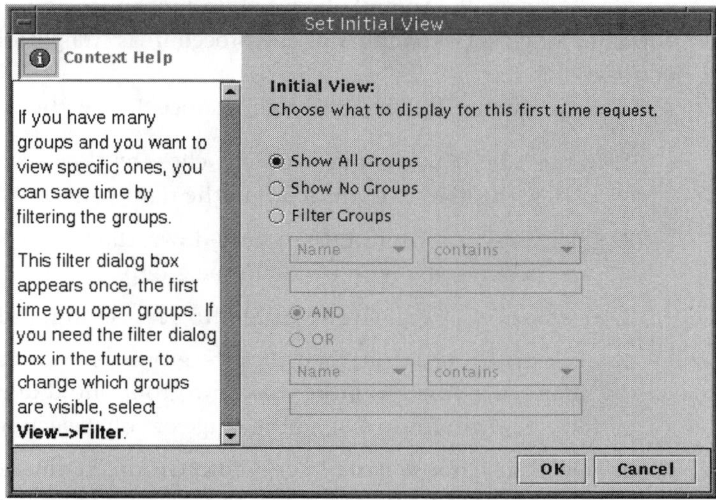

FIGURE 11.23
The Add Group dialog box

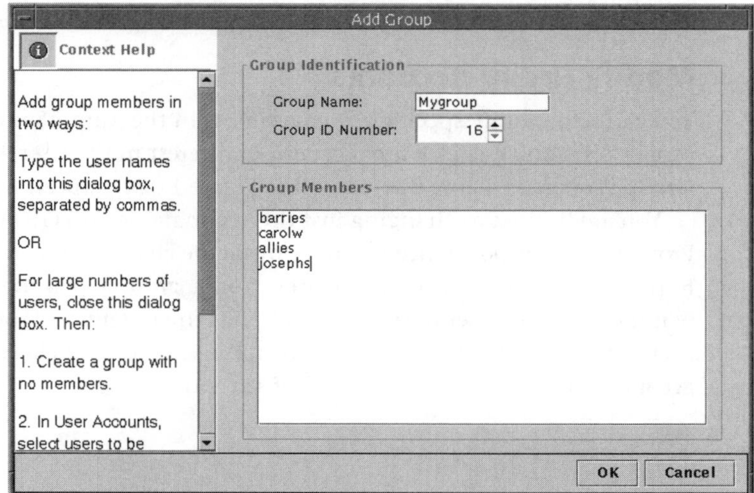

5. Enter the group name in the Group Name text box and the Group ID in the Group ID Number spin box, then click the OK button. The new group is added to the groups database along with the GID and members you assigned.

A system administrator will often have to add a number of users at a single time to a group in a domain. AdminSuite provides a means to do just that using the Copy to Group or Mailing List command. The procedure is straightforward and convenient to perform.

To add a number of users to a group at once, follow these steps:

1. In the AdminSuite window, double-click the User Accounts icon in the left pane to view the user accounts icons in the right pane.
2. Click a user of interest, then hold down the Ctrl key and click the additional user accounts you wish to add to the group.
3. Select the Copy to Group or Mailing List command from the Action menu.
4. Click the Groups icon, then click the group you want to add the users to. To add the user accounts to more than one group, hold down the Ctrl key and click additional groups to extend the range of your selection.
5. Select the Choose Paste User(s) into Group command from the Action menu. Solaris adds those user accounts to the group or groups you selected.
6. Confirm that the user accounts were added to the groups by clicking on the groups and selecting the Properties command from the Action menu. If you were successful, you will see the user accounts listed in the Group Members list box.

Modify Group Accounts

You can also modify specific group accounts in the AdminSuite. To view the group properties, double-click a user account of interest in the User Accounts window. The Group Properties dialog box, shown in Figure 11.24, appears.

You are limited to changing just the group name and GID number in the Group Properties dialog box. Once you have made the changes you desire, click the OK button to put them into effect. To delete users from a group, open the group in the Groups window, click the user to select it, and press the Delete key. You can select multiple user accounts to delete by holding down the Ctrl key and clicking on additional user accounts to add them to your range of selection.

FIGURE 11.24
The Group Properties dialog box

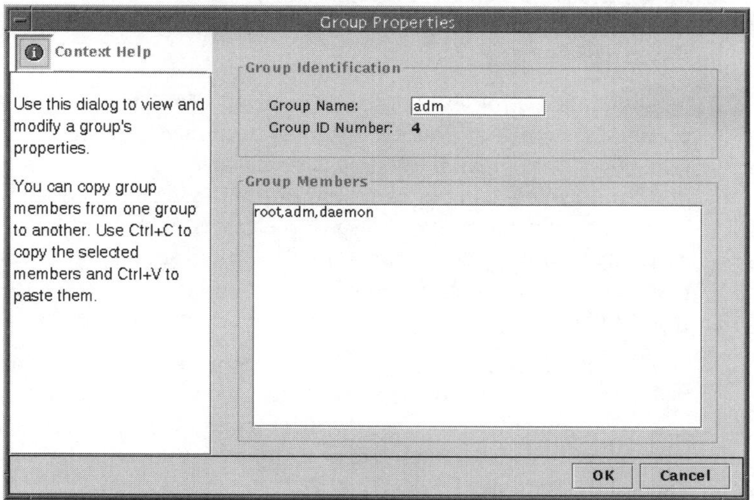

Delete Group Accounts

You can also use the AdminSuite to delete group accounts. To do so, follow these steps:

1. In the Group window, click the group account you wish to delete.
2. Select the Delete command from the Action menu. The warning dialog box shown in the following graphic appears.

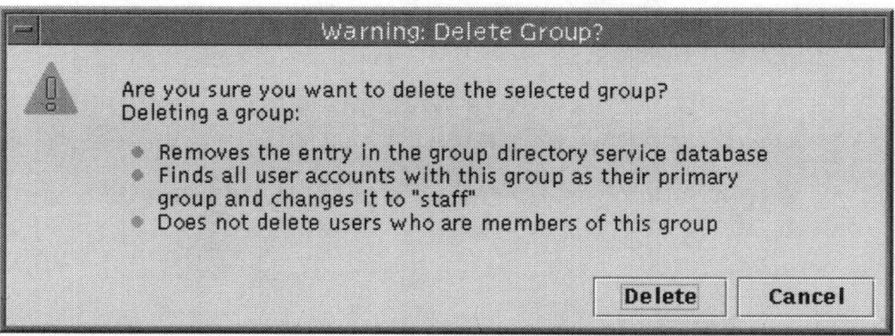

3. Click the Delete button to confirm the deletion.

Solaris deletes the group account from all entries in the group directory services database. Any user that had this group assigned as their primary group has their primary group assignment changed to the STAFF group.

Administering Roles

Solaris 8 adds a role-based access control (RBAC) feature that allows you to assign a portion of superuser privileges to user accounts for special purposes. This allows an administrator to provide the means necessary to off-load to particular types of users or groups of users a number of system responsibilities that could once only be performed by the administrators themselves. The easiest way to create authorizations for user accounts is in the AdminSuite 3, which allows access to two of the special databases that store role information: the `auth_attr` and `user_attr` databases. Authorizations are separate from roles, but roles have authorizations or access privileges assigned to them.

You can think of a role as a special user account that is used for an administrative task. You do not log in using a role; access to the role's rights and privileges are afforded you when you enter the `su` (switch user) command as `su` *<rolename>* at the command line. A role account allows a user to assume the root UID for certain commands, as defined by that role.

In the AdminSuite authentications, you can create roles that give people the ability to perform actions that would usually require root access to perform. You do this by creating the roles with the starting setting of `solaris.admin`. The true value of roles is that they allow users to perform tasks in the Admintool and AdminSuite 3 that would be difficult or impossible had those users not been granted root privileges. For example, a group's IT administrator can create and modify users and groups for that group once a role has been assigned, a situation that would have previously required that that group IT admin be given root privileges.

With RBAC, you can grant users and groups the following:

- Access rights to a superuser feature
- An execution profile in which access and commands may be grouped for use by specified UIDs and GIDs
- A role, which is a special user account that can be assumed to execute a specific job

The Role Databases

The following sections describe the four RBAC databases that store the access rights for users given superuser privileges.

/etc/user_attr

The extended user attributes database links users and their roles with their access and execution profiles. Figure 11.25 shows the default `user_attr` file.

FIGURE 11.25

The default /etc/user_attr *file*

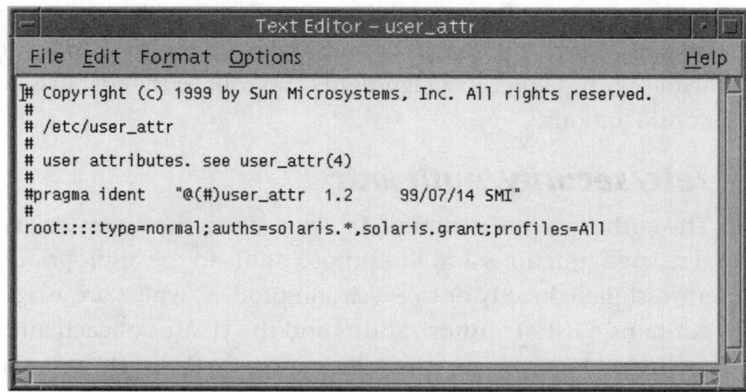

```
# Copyright (c) 1999 by Sun Microsystems, Inc. All rights reserved.
#
# /etc/user_attr
#
# user attributes. see user_attr(4)
#
#pragma ident   "@(#)user_attr  1.2     99/07/14 SMI"
#
root::::type=normal;auths=solaris.*,solaris.grant;profiles=All
```


Notice that there are five fields in the `user_attr` file; they take the form `username: qualifier:reserved1:reserved2:attribute` list. (To continue a line in this file, use the backslash symbol). The terms *qualifier*, *reserved1*, and *reserved2* are not currently assigned; they are reserved for future use as the `user_attr` file is further developed by Sun. The important variable is the attribute list, which is a semicolon-delimited list of key value pairs that apply a security level to an object when it is executed.

The four key pairs used are `auths`, a comma-delimited list of authorized object names (`solaris.printer`) that can be accessed; `profiles`, a comma-delimited list of profile names in the `prof_attr` file that a user can use to execute commands; `roles`, an optional comma-delimited list of roles taken from the user accounts database with the type field set to `role`; and finally `type`, which is either `normal` for a normal user or `role` to show that this account is used for a role.

A profile of `A11`, which is the minimum level given to a user account, indicates that a user can issue all commands but makes no additional assignments. For example, an entry in the `user_attr` file might look like this:

```
root::::type=normal;auths=solaris.*,solaris.grant;profiles=A11
```

When a role has been assigned, this entry would change to something looking like the following:

```
sysadmin::::type=role;profile=Device Management,
    Machine Administration,User Groups &  Mailing Lists,All
      sosinsky::::type=normal,auths=solaris.system.date;
      roles=sysadmin;profiles=A11.
```

You can think of the `user_attr` database as an adjunct to the passwd and shadow files. In that database file are stored extended user attributes that point to the authorizations or access rights and to execution profiles. In assigning roles, only the `user_attr` file is required, and you can assign rights and rolls in that database without any other security considerations.

/etc/security/auth_attr

The authorization attributes database stores the access rights for users and groups to restricted functions and links those rights to the appropriate help files. Authorizations are assigned directly or to execution profiles, which are assigned to users. This database contains a list of authorizations and the creator of each authorization; each set is identified by a unique string. Programs use the `auth_attr` database to determine if a user has the authorization necessary to perform an action. For example, in order for a user to modify the `crontab` file of another user, the `solaris.jobs.admin` authorization checks for this right in the `auth_attr` database. Figure 11.26 shows the default condition of the `/etc/security/auth_attr` file.

FIGURE 11.26

The default `/etc/security/auth_attr` *file*

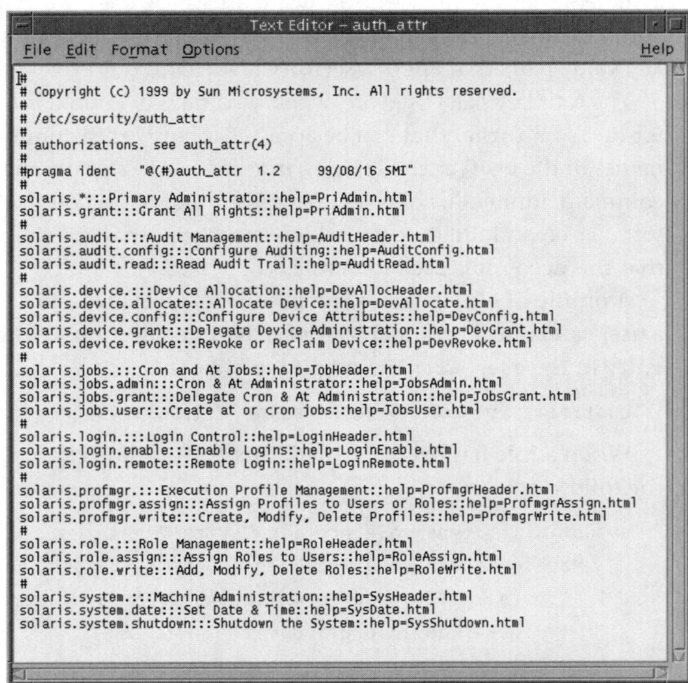


```
#
# Copyright (c) 1999 by Sun Microsystems, Inc. All rights reserved.
#
# /etc/security/auth_attr
#
# authorizations. see auth_attr(4)
#
#pragma ident   "@(#)auth_attr  1.2     99/08/16 SMI"
#
solaris.*:::Primary Administrator::help=PriAdmin.html
solaris.grant:::Grant All Rights::help=PriAdmin.html
#
solaris.audit.:::Audit Management::help=AuditHeader.html
solaris.audit.config:::Configure Auditing::help=AuditConfig.html
solaris.audit.read:::Read Audit Trail::help=AuditRead.html
#
solaris.device.:::Device Allocation::help=DevAllocHeader.html
solaris.device.allocate:::Allocate Device::help=DevAllocate.html
solaris.device.config:::Configure Device Attributes::help=DevConfig.html
solaris.device.grant:::Delegate Device Administration::help=DevGrant.html
solaris.device.revoke:::Revoke or Reclaim Device::help=DevRevoke.html
#
solaris.jobs.:::Cron and At Jobs::help=JobHeader.html
solaris.jobs.admin:::Cron & At Administrator::help=JobsAdmin.html
solaris.jobs.grant:::Delegate Cron & At Administration::help=JobsGrant.html
solaris.jobs.user:::Create at or cron jobs::help=JobsUser.html
#
solaris.login.:::Login Control::help=LoginHeader.html
solaris.login.enable:::Enable Logins::help=LoginEnable.html
solaris.login.remote:::Remote Login::help=LoginRemote.html
#
solaris.profmgr.:::Execution Profile Management::help=ProfmgrHeader.html
solaris.profmgr.assign:::Assign Profiles to Users or Roles::help=ProfmgrAssign.html
solaris.profmgr.write:::Create, Modify, Delete Profiles::help=ProfmgrWrite.html
#
solaris.role.:::Role Management::help=RoleHeader.html
solaris.role.assign:::Assign Roles to Users::help=RoleAssign.html
solaris.role.write:::Add, Modify, Delete Roles::help=RoleWrite.html
#
solaris.system.:::Machine Administration::help=SysHeader.html
solaris.system.date:::Set Date & Time::help=SysDate.html
solaris.system.shutdown:::Shutdown the System::help=SysShutdown.html
```

The addition of the AdminSuite to a system modifies the `auth_attr` database file by adding a number of administrative authorizations to it. The six field entries that you see in Figure 11.26 take the form `authname:reserved1:reserved2:short_description:long_description:attribute list` (to continue a line in this file, use the backslash symbol).

The terms *reserved1* and *reserved2* are not currently assigned; they are reserved for future use as the `auth_attr` file is further developed by Sun. The short_description field is used to store a name that is displayed in the graphical user interface, whereas the long_description provides a description of the authorization, the applications that the authorization applies to, and the type of user who might use the authorization. The important variable here (as before) is the attribute list, which is a semicolon-delimited list of key value pairs that apply a security level to an object when it is executed.

The authname field stores the name of the authentication in the format <*prefix.authname*> as a semicolon-delimited list. All Solaris authorizations use `Solaris` as the prefix and assign a suffix like `admin.usermgr.pswd` to specify the function and operation authorized. Any authorizations that aren't specific to Solaris are given in reverse Internet order, so that the prefix is in the form `com.sosinsky-group`. When <*authname*> doesn't use a suffix and the name ends with a period, as in `admin.usermgr.`, that authorization allows the use of applications in their graphical form, letting a user access the User Account Manager. If <*authname*> ends with `grant`, that indicates that the user who has been granted that authorization can use the service and can grant the authorization to other users. Thus, a user with an authorization of `solaris.usermgr.grant` can assign `solaris.usermgr.admin` to another user. You can get help for any keyword by opening the `/usr/lib/help/auths/locale/C/index.html` file with your Web browser.

For example, an entry in the `auth_attr` file might look like this:

```
Solaris.admin.usermgr.:::Users, Groups & Mailing
Lists::help=UserMgrHeader.html
```

When an authorization has been assigned, you would see the following:

```
sosinsky::::type=normal,auths=solaris.admin.usermgr;
roles=sysadmin;profiles=All
```

/etc/security/prof_attr

The profile execution attributes database stores profile definitions that identify what access rights a user or group has. It also makes available the appropriate help files. Profiles are assigned by real or session UIDs or GIDs to users or roles, with the most common assignment being the assignment of UID to root. Programs use the `prof_attr` file on a system to check for local execution profiles. Figure 11.27 shows the default condition of the `prof_attr` file.

FIGURE 11.27

The default* /etc/security/prof_attr *file

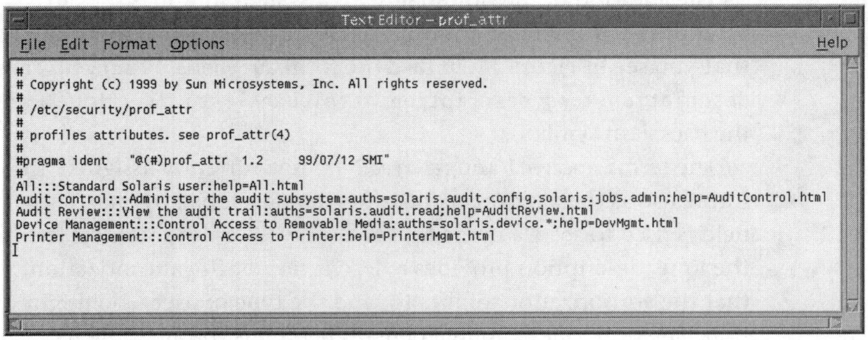

```
Text Editor – prof_attr
File  Edit  Format  Options                                        Help
#
# Copyright (c) 1999 by Sun Microsystems, Inc. All rights reserved.
#
# /etc/security/prof_attr
#
# profiles attributes. see prof_attr(4)
#
#pragma ident   "@(#)prof_attr  1.2     99/07/12 SMI"
#
All:::Standard Solaris user:help=All.html
Audit Control:::Administer the audit subsystem:auths=solaris.audit.config,solaris.jobs.admin;help=AuditControl.html
Audit Review:::View the audit trail:auths=solaris.audit.read;help=AuditReview.html
Device Management:::Control Access to Removable Media:auths=solaris.device.*;help=DevMgmt.html
Printer Management:::Control Access to Printer:help=PrinterMgmt.html
```

Profiles stored in the `prof_attr` file can contain the access granted in the `auth_attr` file as well as commands that have the attributes for the profile that are contained in the `exec_attr` file. Entries in the `prof_attr` database are named profiles, their descriptions, along with their attributes. The five fields in the `prof_attr` file take the form `profname:reseved1:reserved2:description:attribute list`. (To continue a line in this file, use the backslash symbol). The case-sensitive profname field is the name of the profile, used to identify it to programs. The terms *reserved1* and *reserved2* are not currently assigned; they are reserved for future use. The description field is used to provide a description of the profile and the type of user who might use the authorization. The important variable here (as before) is the attribute list, which is a semicolon-delimited list of key value pairs that apply a security level to an object when it is executed.

For example, an entry in the `prof_attr` file might look like this:

```
Device Management:::Control Access to Removable
Media:auths=solaris.device.*;help=DevMgmt.html
```

When the Device Management profile has been assigned to the `sysadmin` role in the `usr_attr` database, you would see the following:

```
root::::type=normal,auths=solaris.*,solaris.grant;profiles=All
advanced::::type=role;profiles=Device Management,
Printer Management
```

The profiles are read by the authorizations contained in the `auth_attr` file, where you will find named authorizations such as `solaris.device.`, `solaris.device.allocate`, `solaris.device.config`, `solaris.device.grant`, and `solaris.device.revoke`. A typical entry in the `auth_attr` file would look like the following:

```
Device Management:::Control Access to Removable
Media:auths=solaris.device.*;help=DevMgmt.html
```

/etc/security/exec_attr

The profile execution attributes database stores the information necessary to give users and groups access to those programs and operations that require superuser privileges. The security attributes that are stored in this file are UID, EUID, GID, and EGID numbers that can be assigned to a process when that process is executed by a command that the user's role allows. (The *E* in EUID and EGID refers to *effective*, which is the ID a user attains when they assume a role.) Figure 11.28 shows the default condition of the `exec_attr` file.

FIGURE 11.28

The default `/etc/security/exec_attr` *file*

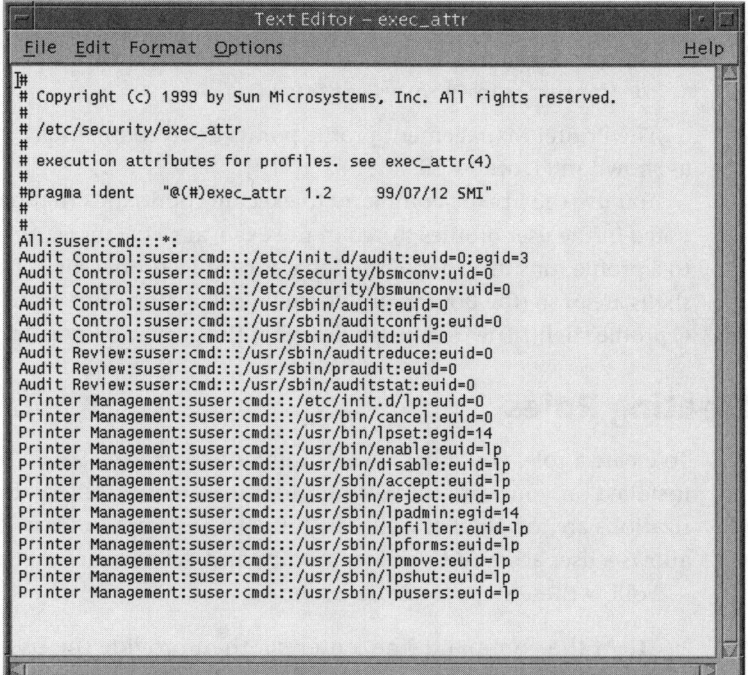


```
#
# Copyright (c) 1999 by Sun Microsystems, Inc. All rights reserved.
#
# /etc/security/exec_attr
#
# execution attributes for profiles. see exec_attr(4)
#
#pragma ident   "@(#)exec_attr  1.2     99/07/12 SMI"
#
#
All:suser:cmd:::*:
Audit Control:suser:cmd:::/etc/init.d/audit:euid=0;egid=3
Audit Control:suser:cmd:::/etc/security/bsmconv:uid=0
Audit Control:suser:cmd:::/etc/security/bsmunconv:uid=0
Audit Control:suser:cmd:::/usr/sbin/audit:euid=0
Audit Control:suser:cmd:::/usr/sbin/auditconfig:euid=0
Audit Control:suser:cmd:::/usr/sbin/auditd:uid=0
Audit Review:suser:cmd:::/usr/sbin/auditreduce:euid=0
Audit Review:suser:cmd:::/usr/sbin/praudit:euid=0
Audit Review:suser:cmd:::/usr/sbin/auditstat:euid=0
Printer Management:suser:cmd:::/etc/init.d/lp:euid=0
Printer Management:suser:cmd:::/usr/bin/cancel:euid=0
Printer Management:suser:cmd:::/usr/bin/lpset:egid=14
Printer Management:suser:cmd:::/usr/bin/enable:euid=lp
Printer Management:suser:cmd:::/usr/bin/disable:euid=lp
Printer Management:suser:cmd:::/usr/sbin/accept:euid=lp
Printer Management:suser:cmd:::/usr/sbin/reject:euid=lp
Printer Management:suser:cmd:::/usr/sbin/lpadmin:egid=14
Printer Management:suser:cmd:::/usr/sbin/lpfilter:euid=lp
Printer Management:suser:cmd:::/usr/sbin/lpforms:euid=lp
Printer Management:suser:cmd:::/usr/sbin/lpmove:euid=lp
Printer Management:suser:cmd:::/usr/sbin/lpshut:euid=lp
Printer Management:suser:cmd:::/usr/sbin/lpusers:euid=lp
```


There are seven fields in the exec_attr database that take the form `name:policy:type:reserved1:reserved2:id_string:attribute`. The name field is used to store the name of the profile, and the policy field stores the security policy model that is linked to this profile. The suser or superuser policy model is the only currently supported model. The two reserved fields have the same undefined meaning they have in the other files. For type, you will find only the `cmd` (command) attribute; no other types are currently defined. The id_string field is a description of the object specified in the security policy. A command is specified in the id_string field with its full path to the binary that executes it. When you need to pass an argument to a command, you should write a script that passes the argument to that command and point the id_string to that script file. Finally, the `exec_attr` file is a semicolon-delimited list of key value pairs that passes a security attribute such as UID, EUID, GID, or EGID to the object being executed.

When a Device Management profile has been assigned to the sysadmin role in the `usr_attr` database, you would see the following:

```
Printer Management:suser:cmd:::Control Access
to Printer:help=PrinterMgmt.html
```

The Printer Management profile points to 13 commands in the `exec_attr` database, as shown in Figure 11.28.

You use the `pfexec` command to execute commands that have the attributes designated in the user profiles stored in the `exec_attr` database. Any command that is linked to a profile runs in a special shell that is called a profile shell. The three common profile shells are `pfsh` (the Bourne profile shell), `pfksh` (the Korn profile shell), and `pfcsh` (the C profile shell). The man pages describes the `pfexec` command in detail.

Creating Roles

To create a role, you must have AdminSuite 3 and the Solaris Management Console installed on your computer. When AdminSuite is installed, the `solaris.admin` authorizations are installed as well. The following example adds a role called `usracct` that allows a user account to create, modify, and delete other user accounts.

Follow these steps to create a role:

1. At the command line, enter **su**, then provide the password for the superuser.
2. Enter **`roleadd -D`** (display default), then press the Return key. Solaris displays the default settings for the `roleadd` command.
3. Enter **`roleadd -d`** (directory) with any of the following options:
    - `-b` (base directory)
    - `-c` (comment)

- -e (expire)
- -f (inactive)
- -g (GID of primary group)
- -G (secondary group)
- -k (skeleton directory)
- -m (role home directory)
- -o (nonunique UID)
- -u (UID)

4. Use the /etc/security/auth_attr file to identify the authorizations and the /etc/security/prof_attr file to identify the profiles that you want to assign to the role you are creating.

5. Enter **roleadd -c *<comment>* -s *<pathname>*/shell -A *<authorization>* -P *<profilename>* role**, then press the Return key. Here is an example of what you might enter:

```
# roleadd -c "User Account Management" -s /bin/pfcsh -A \
solaris.admin.usermgr.pswd,solaris.admin.usermgr.write -P \
"User Account Management" usracct
```

6. Enter the line **usracct:x:1007:1:User Account Management:/home/usracct:/bin/pfcsh** into the /etc/passwd file.

7. Enter the line **usracct:*LK*::::::** into the /etc/shadow file.

8. Enter the following into the /etc/usr_attr file:

```
usracct::::type=role;auths=solaris.admin.usermgr.pswd,\
solaris.admin.usermgr.write;profiles=User Account Management
```

9. Enter **passwd**, then press the Return key. Solaris prompts you to enter the new password for the role twice. Once the password is set, a user can assume the role of user account manager provided that they know the password.

10. Enter the following line into the /etc/usr_attr file:

```
<username>::::type=role;auths=<authorization(s)>;\
roles=<rolename>;profiles=<profilename>
```

Table 11.3 lists the commands that are used to create and manage roles on Solaris. Each of these commands is detailed in the Solaris man pages.

TABLE 11.3: ROLE-BASED ACCESS COMMANDS

Command	Description
auths	Shows a user's authorizations.
makebdm	Creates a dbm file.
ncsd	Runs the Nameservice Cache Daemon, which is used to cache the user_attr, prof_attr, and exec_attr databases.
pam_roles	Alters the role account management module for Profile Account Management (PAM) and determines if a user account has the authorization for a particular role.
pfexec, pfsh, pfcsh, and pfksh	Profile shells; applied when the attributes in the exec_attr database are used to execute commands.
policy.conf	Lists granted authorizations and alters the configuration file for security policy.
profiles	Displays profile for a user.
roles	Displays roles allowed for a user.
roleadd	Adds a role to a system.
roledel	Deletes a role from a system.
rolmod	Modifies a role on a system.
useradd	Adds a user account on a system. The options -P, -R, and -A add a policy, role, and authorization, respectively.
userdel	Deletes a user account on a system.
usermod	Modifies a user account. The -P, -R, and -A modify a policy, role, and authorization, respectively.

AdminSuite and Access Rights

With AdminSuite 3, you can assign privileged rights to user accounts using the User Accounts section of the Users window. In the User Accounts section, you can grant any or all rights and deny any or all rights. When you grant a user account rights, you give the user of that user account root privileges to the commands and programs that are associated with that account.

To grant a user rights in AdminSuite 3, follow these steps:

1. Open the AdminSuite to the Users window, then double-click the User Accounts icon. The Set Initial View dialog box appears, allowing you to filter the user accounts you see in the Users window.

2. Select the user accounts you wish to see in the Set Initial View dialog box, then double-click any user account icon for which you want to grant, modify, or delete rights. The User Properties dialog box (shown in Figure 11.29) appears.

FIGURE 11.29

The Rights tab of the User Properties dialog box

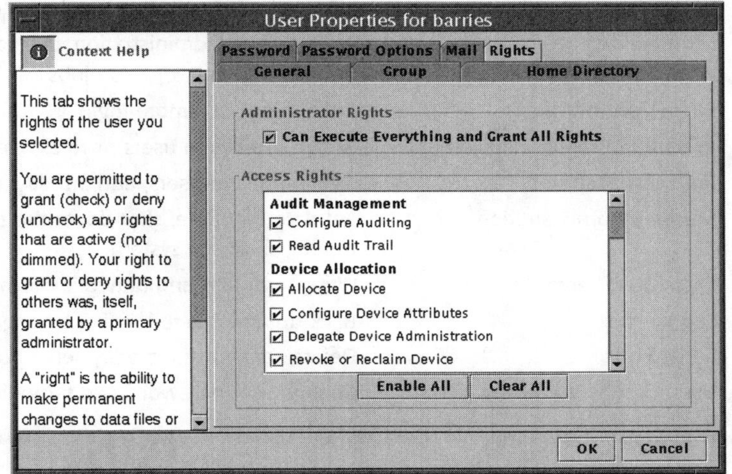

3. Click the Rights tab to display a list of rights for that account. On the Rights tab, you can assign to a particular user account rights that may be used for roles the user account may assume.
4. Select the check boxes next to the rights you wish to enable. Or, click the Enable All button to grant all rights to that user account.
5. Deselect the check boxes for the rights you wish to disable. Or, click the Clear All button to deny all rights to that user account.
6. Click the OK button to establish your selections.

Table 11.4 lists the rights that you can assign on the Rights tab of the User Properties dialog box.

TABLE 11.4: ASSIGNABLE RIGHTS FOR ROLES

Right Class	Specific Rights
Audit Management	Configure auditing, read audit trail
Device Allocation	Allocate device, configure device attributes, delegate device administration, revoke or reclaim device
Cron and At Jobs	`Cron` and `at` administration, delegate `cron` and `at` administration, create `at` or `cron` jobs
Login Control	Enable logins, remote login
Execution Profile Management	Assign profiles to users or roles; create, modify, delete profiles
Role Management	Assign roles to users; add, modify, delete roles
Machine Administration	Set date and time, shut down the systemfile systems, mount/share file system
Computer/Networks	Write computer and network information
Log Viewer	Back up and delete log files, change log settings
Serial Ports	Delete serial ports, modify serial port information
User, Groups, & Mailing Lists	Change user passwords, add, modify, and delete

Summary

In this chapter, you learned about user and group accounts. Solaris uses a system of users and groups to allow access to system and network resources. The user and group databases store information about user accounts and group accounts.

User accounts have passwords, can expire, and are linked to a primary group and up to 16 secondary groups. Group accounts allow access and rights to files, directories, and other objects for a number of user accounts. User accounts are identified by a user identification (UID) number; group accounts are identified by a group identification (GID) number.

You learned how to create and manage local group and user accounts with the graphical Admintool. After you create a new user account, you still need to specify a home directory and create a user environment for that account. This chapter also covered AdminSuite 3. As part of the Solaris Management Console, you can use AdminSuite 3 to modify user accounts and group accounts in a network environment.

CHAPTER 12

Working with File Utilities

FEATURING:

Working with archives	*480*
File compression	*486*
File encryption	*488*
Using packages for program installation	*490*
Solaris backup and restore utilities	*495*
Backup strategies	*498*

In this chapter, you'll learn about a number of file handling utilities that are important in your daily work. Archives offer you a method for combining files into a single file that can be more easily managed and handled. Archives are often used as a mechanism to transfer data between systems because they simplify the process. You'll also learn how to work with tar files. Hand in hand with archives are compression utilities. Some archival utilities, such as GNU `tar`, offer compression and some do not. However, you will certainly want to make use of utilities like the `compress` command and GNU `gzip` to compress files and archives. Compression speeds up data transfer operations.

Much of this chapter describes how to back up and restore your directories and files and why it is so important for users and administrators alike. Solaris offers several commands, such as `ufsdump` and `ufsrestore`, that allow you to back up and restore to tape drives and other devices. Unix is rich in command-line utilities for disk, directory, and file copy commands. Some of these commands are described in this chapter in the context of backing up and restoring. You will also find a discussion of backup strategies in this chapter, as well as a listing of different freeware and third-party backup programs that you might want to use with your systems.

Archives

Archives provide a method for conveniently packaging files. They can also be used to back up a small amount of files. One of the oldest utilities in Unix is the `tar` command, which writes the tar output to a single disk file. Many people use tar files as a means of distributing file trees with other users. You may encounter tar files being used on the Internet as a transfer format. The `tar` command was originally used to create a *t*ape *ar*chive, hence the name of the command. However, `tar` is often used to create a single file from a group of files and directories. Unlike utilities such as `zip`, `tar` does not offer file compression. However, tar files are often further compressed by applying commands like `compress` to archives after they are created and before they are used in file transfers.

To create a file using the `tar` command, do the following:

1. Use the `cd` (change directory) command to switch to the directory that contains the subdirectories and files you want to archive:

   ```
   # cd /usr/<directoryname>
   ```

2. Give the `du` (disk usage) command to determine the size of your archive.

   The `du -a` command returns the size of each file in blocks along with the total size of the directory. The `-k` flag will provide the output of the du command in

KB, which is easier to understand. To suppress the listing of the directory size without listing individual components, use the du -s option.

3. Create your tar archive by giving the following command:

```
# tar cvf /<pathname>/<archivename>.tar *
```

This command creates a package that includes all of the subdirectories with the filename *<archivename>*.tar in the location of the *<pathname>*. An icon of an archive is shown in the following graphic.

The tar command is one of the most useful commands you will find because it allows you to "package" files together for further manipulation. Therefore, you might want to know about some of the more common options that tar supports; some of these options are shown in the following list (note that you can use r, t, u, and x only one time for each run of tar, and they can each be augmented by f and v, as in rf and rv, tf and tv, uf and uv, and xf and xv):

c option Creates a new archive.

f *<devicename>* option The f option uses the *<devicename>* as the name of the file created. When used with a hyphen, the command writes to or reads from standard output. The tar command can be used on either side of a pipe. When f isn't specified, the command uses the device found in the TAPE environmental variable. When f is specified, the default values in the /etc/default/tar command is used.

r option Appends files to the end of an existing archive.

t option Displays a table of contents. It displays the list of files contained in the archive. The v option adds the file information to the filenames.

u option Updates the archive by adding named files to it if they aren't already contained in the archive or if they were modified since the archive was created. When you update, you also append.

v option With the verbose option, tar echoes its operations.

x *<filenames>* option Extracts or restores the files you specified from an archive to the current directory. When a filename matches a directory name, then the directory is recursively extracted. To properly place a directory, you will need to specify the directory's relative path to the current directory. You can use the x flag without *<filenames>* to extract an entire archive.

You can also archive a folder using the Archive control in the Files subpanel. When you use this control, you see the Action Archive dialog box (shown in Figure 12.1), which you can use to graphically create an archive on your desktop.

FIGURE 12.1

The Action Archive dialog box

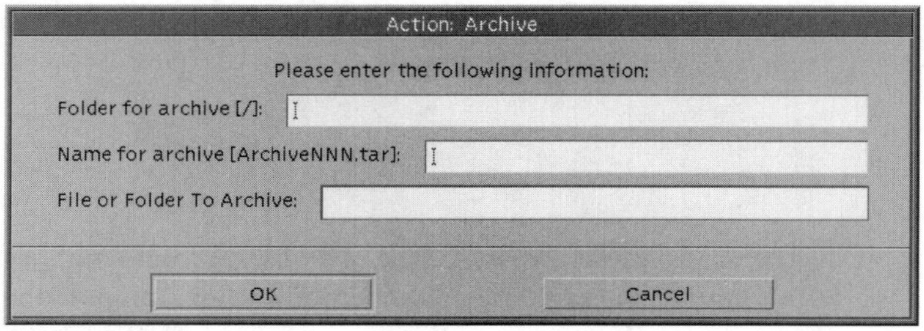

In the Action Archive dialog box, you'll need to enter information into the following fields:

Folder for Archive Enter the */<pathname>/<foldername>* into which the archive will be saved.

Name for Archive Enter the name you want to use for the archive in the format *<ArchiveNNN>*`.tar`, where *Archive* is the name of the archive and *NNN* is an identifying number such as the date.

File or Folder to Archive Enter the name of the file or folder you want to archive.

Once you click the OK button, the action creates the archive in the location you specified.

The Archive control is one of several actions (including Compress, Uncompress, Encrypt, and Decrypt) that you will find for desktop file management in the Application Manager's `Desktop_Tools` program folder. To open this folder, shown in Figure 12.2, first click the Tools subpanel, then click the Applications control, and finally, double-click the Desktop Tools icon.

FIGURE 12.2

The Application Manager `Desktop_Tools` *folder*

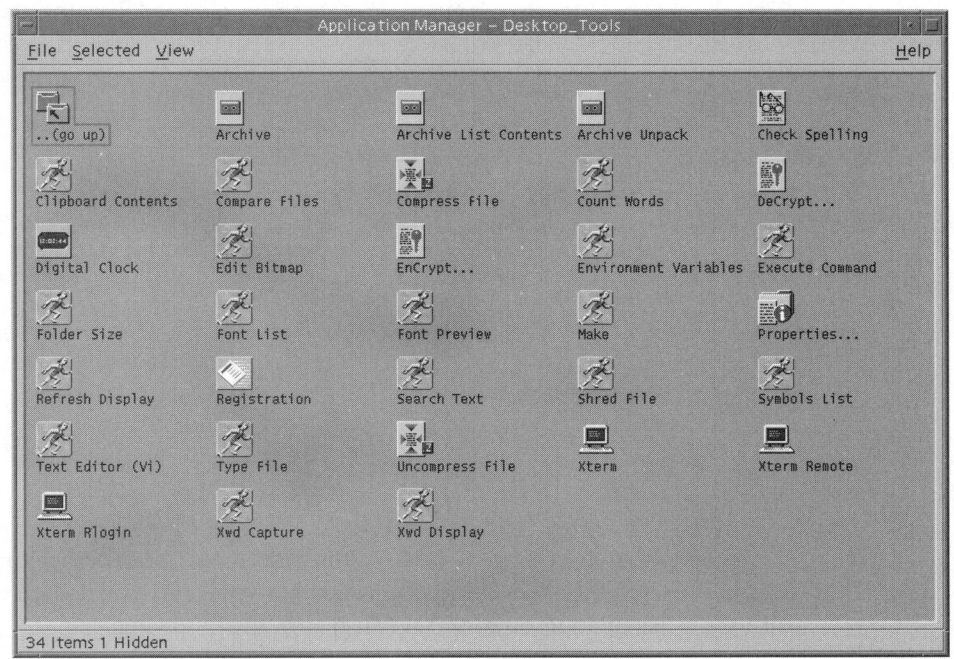

TIP Drag a file or folder onto the Archive control of the Tools subfolder to create an archive.

The second half of the `tar` command is the extraction, which is accomplished using the following two steps:

1. Use the cd (change directory) command to switch to the directory that contains the tar files you want to extract:

```
# cd /<pathname>
```

2. Extract your `tar` archive using the following command:

```
# tar xvf <archive>.tar
```

Once you have created an archive or compressed a file or folder, Solaris recognizes the file type and puts commands in the archive's pop-up menu that are appropriate to the file's condition. Thus you will find that an archive pop-up menu has a Compress File and Archive Unpack command on it, as shown in the following graphic.

The open source freeware GNU `tar` utility has more options, including a built-in compression routine. To create a compressed file with GNU `tar`, use the `gtar` command with the `z` flag in addition to the `cvf` flag, as in the following:

```
# tar zcvf file.tar *
```

When you use this option, you are using `gzip` compression. If you need to get to a file that has been compressed with the `z` flag and you need to `untar` it with a non–GNU `tar` utility, use the `gzip` utility on the tar file first to unpack it, then use `untar` as usual. Another compression flag for `gnutar`, `-I`, uses the `bzip2` compression scheme (and produces smaller archives).

The `cpio` (copy in/out) command is also used to copy archives and is particularly useful because it can span two or more volumes, placing files into a single archive file. You can use the `cpio` command to copy a directory hierarchy to another location as well as restore files in an archive. Both directory names and filenames can be input to the command to create an archive, something that `tar` can also do. When listing files and directories in the input list, use an order that allows the files to be created after the directories that contain them are created. Although Solaris will create the directories needed, if you list them, the correct time/date stamps will be used.

There are three main options for the `cpio` command:

- Copy-in mode, or `-i`, which inputs files listed in your filename specification or from the `cat` (concatenate) command.

- Copy-out mode, or -o, which takes a list of files that you specify and creates an archive of them at the path you specify.
- Copy-pass (pass-through) mode, or -p, which is similar to the copy-out command except that you simply copy the files without creating an archive.

In the copy-out mode, you create a list of files that will go into the archive, print that list as output, and then pipe the output to the cpio -o copy-out command. The find command is often used as a source of the filenames for the cpio command, and this would be a typical command syntax:

```
$ find / -depth -print | cpio -o > /<pathname>/<directoryname>
```

The -depth option forces find to search for files without changing directory modification times, which avoids some later permission problems. The -depth option in find displays the deepest files first, followed by the shallower files, which causes directories to be listed after the files in those directories. The find command does not change or even show the directory permissions to cpio. The cpio command sees the file with full path name, it creates the directory tree needed, creates the file, and then sets the permissions and other information on the file as they were set in the archive. When cpio finally gets to the directory entry, it sets the correct permissions and information for the directory.

In the cpio in mode, an archive is read and the files are extracted as follows:

```
$ cpio -i  \*.tar < /<pathname>/<archivename>
```

You extract all files that end in .tar from the archive located at /<pathname>/<archivename> either into a directory that's relative to where you are in the file structure (if you did a find) or to a fully qualified directory (if you did a find /).

In the pass-through mode, you copy files from one location to another. Effectively, the command acts as if you had created an archive using the cpio -o command and then acted on that command with the cpio -i command to extract the files to the location specified. Here's an example of the syntax of the cpio command in pass-through mode:

```
$ find . -depth - print | cpio -pdm \
    /<devicename>/<pathname>/<directoryname>
```

In this example, files from the current or working directory are input to the cpio command. The -d option tells cpio to create leading subdirectories when needed, and the -m option preserves the modification times as the files are copied. The cpio command takes many options; in addition to the options previously described, it takes options that give you control over blocks (-B) and buffer size (-C buffsize), whether the output is verbose (-v and -V), and what format to use for the input (-I) and output to files (-O). Although you can use both cpio and tar to back up files as archives to other locations, `tar` is simpler to use and somewhat more popular. The `tar` command will also do error checking for archives, which makes it safer to use with magnetic media such as tape.

Compression

The `compress` command compresses files and archives, saving you disk space and the transmission time needed to send and receive files. When you apply the `compress` command to either a file (`<filename>`) or archive (`<archive>.tar`), you obtain a compressed file or archive named `<filename>.z` or `<archive>.tar.z`, respectively. The reverse operation of the `compress` command is the `uncompress` command, which restores the file or archive to its original state. The related `zcat` command will uncompress a compressed file and send the resulting output unchanged to another command in the standard output format.

NOTE The standard output form of a command refers to the use of a single command line with a specified set of paths to the source and target.

The syntax of the `compress` command is as follows:

```
# compress -f <filename-list>
```

The `-f` option forces the `compress` command to compress a file even if the size isn't reduced. Other options include the `-c` option, which causes compress to send the compressed data to the standard output, and the `-v`, or verbose, option, which displays the name of the file and file information as well as the amount of compression that was achieved. To compress the contents of a directory, use the `cd` command to move to that directory, then use the asterisk (*) to specify all files in that directory as the `<filename-list>`.

You can also compress a file using the Compress action in the Tools subpanel or the Compress action in the Application Manager `Desktop_Tools` program folder, which was shown previously in Figure 12.2. A compressed file icon is shown in the following graphic. Once a file is compressed, an Uncompress command is shown on its pop-up menu. Archives also display the Compress File command on the pop-up menu.

TIP To compress a file or folder, drag it onto the Compress control of the Tools subfolder.

When you use the `compress` command to compress a text file, you typically reduce the size of the file by a factor of two or three. Depending upon the specific file format, graphics files can be even further compressed provided that they haven't previously been compressed by another method (many graphics file formats already include compression). A bitmapped format like uncompressed TIFF can be compressed to as little as 5 to 10 percent of its original file size. You don't get much compression if you use the `compress` command on compressed TIFF files because that file format is already compressed (typically using an LZW compression algorithm, which is a lossless algorithm) or on JPEG files (which includes lossy compression as part of the native file format).

When you use the `uncompress` command on a compressed file (`<`*`filename`*`>.z`), you return the file to its original file size. The compression routine used by this command is lossless. A *lossless* routine is one that preserves all of the data contained in the original file, whereas a *lossy* compression algorithm discards a certain amount of information in order to further compress a file. Lossy compression is never used with text, but it's commonly used with graphics such as TIFF files and with video or movie files.

The `compress` command isn't the most efficient archive and compression routine available, even though it was once the de facto standard on Solaris. The GNU `gzip` utility is known to be better for creating compressed files and is now included with Solaris 8. When you apply the `gzip` command to the `<`*`archive`*`>.tar`, you create the file `<`*`archive`*`>.tar.gz`. You uncompress a `.gz` file by using the `gunzip` utility, which is now included in Solaris 8's `uncompress` command. You will find `.gz` files widely supported on most Unix platforms.

Many free software packages you might want to download for Solaris are distributed in the Solaris software package format. You can use `gzip` to first uncompress these packages; after that you will need to extract the archive. You might want to download GNU `tar` for use in place of tar to perform the extraction. There are many locations from which you can download packages on the Internet, some of which are referenced on Sun's site. You may get good results finding sites by using Internet search engines because Solaris/Unix download sites are typically widely cited and therefore are returned at the very top of search results. For example, enter the search string "gtar and Solaris" into Google (`www.google.com`), Alta Vista (`www.altavista.com`), or Northern Lights (`www.northernlights.com`) and you will be led to several locations where the SPARC or Intel x86 version of these programs are to be found. Make sure you download the correct version for your Solaris system.

TIP One well-known site is the University of North Carolina Metalab site at `metalab.unc.edu/pub/packages/solaris/sparc/`. This address will take you to one of the mirrored sites worldwide; for example, from the Boston area, you will be taken to `www.ibiblio.org/pub/packages/solaris/`. At that site, you will find a listing of downloadable packages in different Solaris versions and for different platforms.

Encryption

Solaris has a built-in action that can encrypt your files and folders. When you encrypt an object, you rewrite the data in that object using an algorithm that requires a password to decrypt. Decryption applies a reverse algorithm to restore the file to its previous state. Although it is possible to break an encryption algorithm without the password, it is exceedingly difficult when you download something encrypted in PGP or GNU PGP. Thus, encryption provides pretty good security for your files.

Follow these steps to encrypt a file or folder:

1. Click the Encrypt control in the Tools subpanel of the front panel. The Action: Encryption dialog box appears (it is shown in Figure 12.3).
2. Enter the password into the Encryption Key text box.
3. Click the OK button.

It is even easier to encrypt a file or folder by dragging it onto the Encrypt control of the Tools subfolder. When you do that, you only need to specify the password to encrypt the file.

FIGURE 12.3

The Action: Encryption dialog box

A key is shown on a file's icon when it is encrypted. The following graphic shows an encrypted file and the DeCrypt command on its pop-up menu.

If you have encrypted a folder, Solaris writes a file called `Cryptnnnn`. If you try to open an encrypted file, Solaris posts the Action: DeCrypt dialog box, shown in Figure 12.4. To view that file or folder again, you will need to decrypt it.

FIGURE 12.4

The Action: DeCrypt dialog box

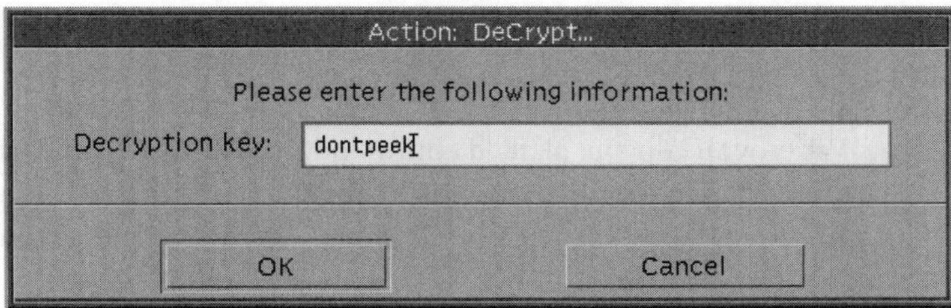

There are two methods you can use to decrypt a file or folder. The first method is as follows:

1. Double-click the file.
2. Enter the password into the Action: DeCrypt dialog box.
3. Click the OK button.

Or you can use this method:

1. Open the Application Manager `Desktop_Tools` folder.
2. Drag the encrypted file or folder onto the DeCrypt action.
3. In the Action: DeCrypt dialog box, enter the password you specified when you encrypted the object. Click the OK button and the object is decrypted.

TIP One way to make a text file harder for hackers to crack is to compress the file first and then encrypt it. Any hacker who uses a simple looping script to break into an encrypted file will find this kind of file harder to break.

Packages

Packages are the standard method used to download installable software and install them on your server or workstation. It isn't the only method used to install software; different installer programs are typically used for commercial software. However, for many third-party freeware and shareware packages, which are very common in the Unix and Solaris communities, packages are widely used.

The procedure for installing a software program from a package involves four steps:

1. Obtaining the package, typically in the form of a compressed archive from a network location or from the Internet.
2. Uncompressing the archive.
3. Extracting the files to the required location.
4. Invoking the `pkgadd` (package add) command.

When you run the `pkgadd` command, it finds the installation script and completes the installation routine. The syntax for the package add command is `pkgadd -d /` `<pathname>/<directoryname>`. The `pkgadd` utility expects to find an installable package in that location and, unless you use the `-d` option, will return an error if it doesn't find it there. Use the `-s` option to write the package to the spool directory without installing it. For example, to install a package from the Solaris installation CD-ROM, you would enter `pkgadd -d /cdrom/cdrom0/s0/Solaris_8 <packagename>` for a package that is found in the SPARC directory.

This section describes the installation of two third-party utilities to give you an idea of how this very important operation is done. First, I'll show you how to add the GNU `gtar` utility to a workstation, then you'll add the WorkMan program, which provides Unix in general and Solaris in particular with a graphical utility for playing audio CDs upon their insertion into a CD-ROM drive. WorkMan was briefly described in a sidebar in Chapter 6, "Devices."

To install GNU `gtar`:

1. Click the Links drawer on the front panel, then click the Web Browser control.

2. Connect to the Internet (if necessary) and go to a site that contains the GNU `gtar` utility. One such site is `metalab.unc.edu/pub/packages/solaris/sparc/`.

3. Download the version for either the Solaris 8 SPARC or Intel x86 platform to the `/var/spool/pkg` directory on your hard drive or diskette.

   For the SPARC version of GNU `gtar`, the file is downloaded as `GNUtar.1.13.SPARC.32bit.Solaris.8.pkg.gz` into your home directory. (Your home directory is the directory you see when you log in. Until you change directories after login, that will be your current and working directories as well.) The `/var/spool/pkg` is the `pkgadd` default directory, but you may want to download the archive into your working directory.

4. Open the File Manager window to view the `/var/spool/pkg/GNU gtar` archive.

5. Right-click the package file icon, then select the Uncompress File command to restore the compressed file to a simple archive.

   The compress command works on both `.z` and `.gz` files to remove the compression and the filename extension. When you right-click an uncompressed file or archive, you can use the Compress File command to compress it. Solaris 8 creates the zip format, placing a `.z` extension on the filename. If you want to create a `.gz` file, invoke the `gzip` command from the command line.

   Or, if you prefer to uncompress the file from the command line, use the `gunzip /var/spool/pkg/GNUtar.1.13.SPARC.32bit.Solaris.8.pkg.gz` command.

6. Next, right-click the archive and select the Archive Unpack command from the pop-up menu, shown in the following graphic.

For the GNU `gtar` utility, the `gtar` command extracts the files and creates a directory called `/GNUtar` in the same directory that contains the archive. Figure 12.5 shows the results of the unpacking action for the `GNUtar` package.

FIGURE 12.5

The results of the Archive Unpack command for the `GNUtar` package

```
Archive Unpack
x GNUtar, 0 bytes, 0 tape blocks
x GNUtar/pkgmap, 3674 bytes, 8 tape blocks
x GNUtar/pkginfo, 221 bytes, 1 tape blocks
x GNUtar/root, 0 bytes, 0 tape blocks
x GNUtar/root/usr, 0 bytes, 0 tape blocks
x GNUtar/root/usr/local, 0 bytes, 0 tape blocks
x GNUtar/root/usr/local/bin, 0 bytes, 0 tape blocks
x GNUtar/root/usr/local/bin/gtar, 759200 bytes, 1483 tape blocks
x GNUtar/root/usr/local/info, 0 bytes, 0 tape blocks
x GNUtar/root/usr/local/info/tar.info, 5082 bytes, 10 tape blocks
x GNUtar/root/usr/local/info/tar.info-1, 49886 bytes, 98 tape blocks
x GNUtar/root/usr/local/info/tar.info-2, 48095 bytes, 94 tape blocks
x GNUtar/root/usr/local/info/tar.info-3, 46870 bytes, 92 tape blocks
x GNUtar/root/usr/local/info/tar.info-4, 50628 bytes, 99 tape blocks
x GNUtar/root/usr/local/info/tar.info-5, 46417 bytes, 91 tape blocks
x GNUtar/root/usr/local/info/tar.info-6, 46857 bytes, 92 tape blocks
x GNUtar/root/usr/local/info/tar.info-7, 46626 bytes, 92 tape blocks
x GNUtar/root/usr/local/info/tar.info-8, 14724 bytes, 29 tape blocks
x GNUtar/root/usr/local/lib, 0 bytes, 0 tape blocks
x GNUtar/root/usr/local/lib/locale, 0 bytes, 0 tape blocks
x GNUtar/root/usr/local/lib/locale/cs, 0 bytes, 0 tape blocks
x GNUtar/root/usr/local/lib/locale/cs/LC_MESSAGES, 0 bytes, 0 tape blocks
x GNUtar/root/usr/local/lib/locale/cs/LC_MESSAGES/tar.mo, 35022 bytes, 69 tape blocks
x GNUtar/root/usr/local/lib/locale/de, 0 bytes, 0 tape blocks
x GNUtar/root/usr/local/lib/locale/de/LC_MESSAGES, 0 bytes, 0 tape blocks
x GNUtar/root/usr/local/lib/locale/de/LC_MESSAGES/tar.mo, 35565 bytes, 70 tape blocks
x GNUtar/root/usr/local/lib/locale/es, 0 bytes, 0 tape blocks
x GNUtar/root/usr/local/lib/locale/es/LC_MESSAGES, 0 bytes, 0 tape blocks
x GNUtar/root/usr/local/lib/locale/es/LC_MESSAGES/tar.mo, 36776 bytes, 72 tape blocks
x GNUtar/root/usr/local/lib/locale/fr, 0 bytes, 0 tape blocks
x GNUtar/root/usr/local/lib/locale/fr/LC_MESSAGES, 0 bytes, 0 tape blocks
x GNUtar/root/usr/local/lib/locale/fr/LC_MESSAGES/tar.mo, 38844 bytes, 76 tape blocks
x GNUtar/root/usr/local/lib/locale/it, 0 bytes, 0 tape blocks
x GNUtar/root/usr/local/lib/locale/it/LC_MESSAGES, 0 bytes, 0 tape blocks
x GNUtar/root/usr/local/lib/locale/it/LC_MESSAGES/tar.mo, 35217 bytes, 69 tape blocks
x GNUtar/root/usr/local/lib/locale/ko, 0 bytes, 0 tape blocks
x GNUtar/root/usr/local/lib/locale/ko/LC_MESSAGES, 0 bytes, 0 tape blocks
x GNUtar/root/usr/local/lib/locale/ko/LC_MESSAGES/tar.mo, 30592 bytes, 60 tape blocks
x GNUtar/root/usr/local/lib/locale/nl, 0 bytes, 0 tape blocks
x GNUtar/root/usr/local/lib/locale/nl/LC_MESSAGES, 0 bytes, 0 tape blocks
x GNUtar/root/usr/local/lib/locale/nl/LC_MESSAGES/tar.mo, 34735 bytes, 68 tape blocks
x GNUtar/root/usr/local/lib/locale/no, 0 bytes, 0 tape blocks
x GNUtar/root/usr/local/lib/locale/no/LC_MESSAGES, 0 bytes, 0 tape blocks
x GNUtar/root/usr/local/lib/locale/no/LC_MESSAGES/tar.mo, 34156 bytes, 67 tape blocks
x GNUtar/root/usr/local/lib/locale/pl, 0 bytes, 0 tape blocks
x GNUtar/root/usr/local/lib/locale/pl/LC_MESSAGES, 0 bytes, 0 tape blocks
x GNUtar/root/usr/local/lib/locale/pl/LC_MESSAGES/tar.mo, 34175 bytes, 67 tape blocks
x GNUtar/root/usr/local/lib/locale/pt, 0 bytes, 0 tape blocks
x GNUtar/root/usr/local/lib/locale/pt/LC_MESSAGES, 0 bytes, 0 tape blocks
x GNUtar/root/usr/local/lib/locale/pt/LC_MESSAGES/tar.mo, 34749 bytes, 68 tape blocks
x GNUtar/root/usr/local/lib/locale/ru, 0 bytes, 0 tape blocks
x GNUtar/root/usr/local/lib/locale/ru/LC_MESSAGES, 0 bytes, 0 tape blocks
x GNUtar/root/usr/local/lib/locale/ru/LC_MESSAGES/tar.mo, 35298 bytes, 69 tape blocks
x GNUtar/root/usr/local/lib/locale/sl, 0 bytes, 0 tape blocks
x GNUtar/root/usr/local/lib/locale/sl/LC_MESSAGES, 0 bytes, 0 tape blocks
x GNUtar/root/usr/local/lib/locale/sl/LC_MESSAGES/tar.mo, 34520 bytes, 68 tape blocks
x GNUtar/root/usr/local/lib/locale/sv, 0 bytes, 0 tape blocks
x GNUtar/root/usr/local/lib/locale/sv/LC_MESSAGES, 0 bytes, 0 tape blocks
x GNUtar/root/usr/local/lib/locale/sv/LC_MESSAGES/tar.mo, 34116 bytes, 67 tape blocks
x GNUtar/root/usr/local/libexec, 0 bytes, 0 tape blocks
x GNUtar/root/usr/local/libexec/rmt, 67600 bytes, 133 tape blocks
x GNUtar/install, 0 bytes, 0 tape blocks
x GNUtar/install/checkinstall, 496 bytes, 1 tape blocks

*** Select Close or Exit from the window menu to close this window ***
```

7. Log in as superuser.
8. At the command line, enter the following:

```
# cd
# pkgadd -d .
```

The first command moves you to your home directory; the second command initiates the installation. The program is installed, as shown in Figure 12.6.

9. Log out as superuser.

FIGURE 12.6

You use the pkgadd *command to install the programs distributed as packages to your system.*

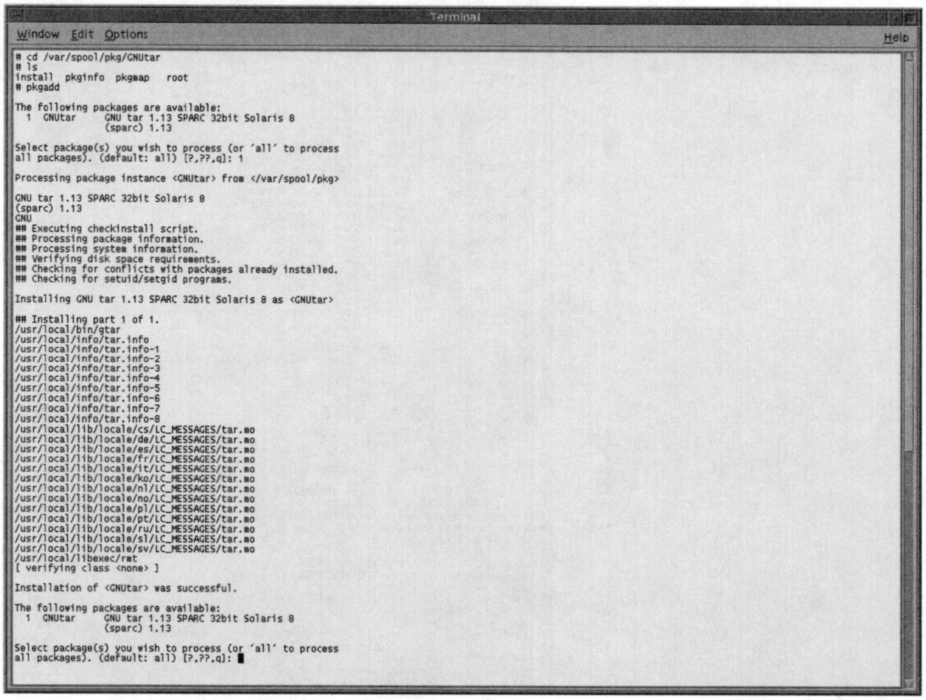

```
Window  Edit  Options                                              Help
# cd /var/spool/pkg/GNUtar
# ls
install  pkginfo  pkgmap   root
# pkgadd

The following packages are available:
  1  GNUtar     GNU tar 1.13 SPARC 32bit Solaris 8
                (sparc) 1.13

Select package(s) you wish to process (or 'all' to process
all packages). (default: all) [?,??,q]: 1

Processing package instance <GNUtar> from </var/spool/pkg>

GNU tar 1.13 SPARC 32bit Solaris 8
(sparc) 1.13
GNU
## Executing checkinstall script.
## Processing package information.
## Processing system information.
## Verifying disk space requirements.
## Checking for conflicts with packages already installed.
## Checking for setuid/setgid programs.

Installing GNU tar 1.13 SPARC 32bit Solaris 8 as <GNUtar>

## Installing part 1 of 1.
/usr/local/bin/gtar
/usr/local/info/tar.info
/usr/local/info/tar.info-1
/usr/local/info/tar.info-2
/usr/local/info/tar.info-3
/usr/local/info/tar.info-4
/usr/local/info/tar.info-5
/usr/local/info/tar.info-6
/usr/local/info/tar.info-7
/usr/local/info/tar.info-8
/usr/local/lib/locale/cs/LC_MESSAGES/tar.mo
/usr/local/lib/locale/de/LC_MESSAGES/tar.mo
/usr/local/lib/locale/es/LC_MESSAGES/tar.mo
/usr/local/lib/locale/fr/LC_MESSAGES/tar.mo
/usr/local/lib/locale/it/LC_MESSAGES/tar.mo
/usr/local/lib/locale/ko/LC_MESSAGES/tar.mo
/usr/local/lib/locale/nl/LC_MESSAGES/tar.mo
/usr/local/lib/locale/no/LC_MESSAGES/tar.mo
/usr/local/lib/locale/pl/LC_MESSAGES/tar.mo
/usr/local/lib/locale/pt/LC_MESSAGES/tar.mo
/usr/local/lib/locale/ru/LC_MESSAGES/tar.mo
/usr/local/lib/locale/sl/LC_MESSAGES/tar.mo
/usr/local/lib/locale/sv/LC_MESSAGES/tar.mo
/usr/local/libexec/rmt
[ verifying class <none> ]

Installation of <GNUtar> was successful.

The following packages are available:
  1  GNUtar     GNU tar 1.13 SPARC 32bit Solaris 8
                (sparc) 1.13

Select package(s) you wish to process (or 'all' to process
all packages). (default: all) [?,??,q]:
```

The pkgadd command makes a log entry every time it installs an application or utility. If you try to install a package that has already been installed, the utility will ask you if you want to install a previously installed package. If you answer yes, the pkgadd command will overwrite any and all of the files that are part of the installation.

The pkgrm (package remove) command returns a list of packages that are installed and can be removed. You will need to be a superuser to remove packages. For a new Ultra 5 workstation delivered from Sun with a standard SPARC Solaris 8 distribution, the pkgrm command returns a list of 1,003 files that were installed as packages. Figure 12.7 shows the routine used to remove the GNUtar program that was just installed. If you know the package that you want to remove, use the command pkgrm <*packagename*> directly.

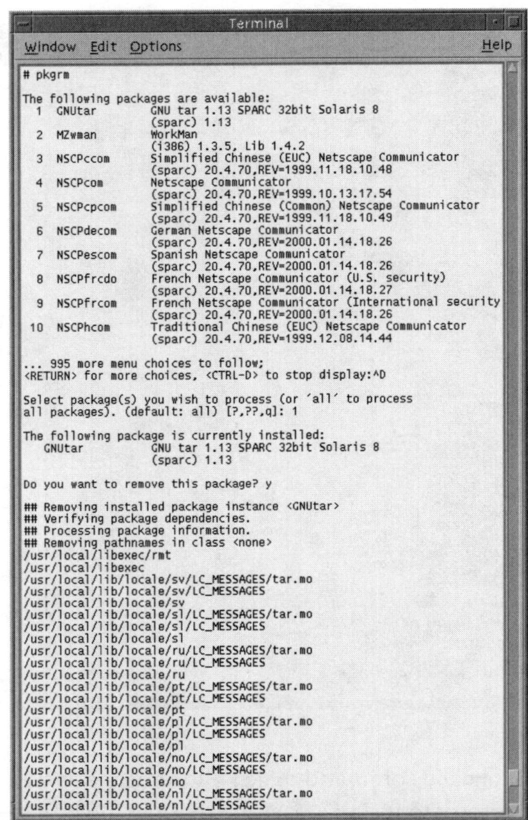

FIGURE 12.7

You use the `pkgrm` command to remove the programs installed from packages to your system.

As described in Chapter 6, the WorkMan program allows you to play music CDs. When you give the `workman` command from the command line, the WorkMan window appears with graphical controls you can use to manage the CD's playback. You install WorkMan from a package that you can download from many sites. The home page for WorkMan is `www.midwinter.com/workman/`. You can also get it at the UNC Metalab site at `http://metalab.unc.edu/pub/packages/solaris/`, where the latest versions are offered. After downloading the archive for Solaris 8 (either SPARC or Intel), place it in your home directory and do the following:

1. Right-click the `workman` archive and select the Archive Unpack command. A directory called `/<pathname>/workman` is created in the same directory that contains the archive.

2. Log in as superuser.
3. At the command line, enter the following:

```
# cd
# pkgadd -d .
```

The files from WorkMan are installed in the /usr/openwin directory and subdirectories contained therein.

4. Log out as superuser.

Backup and Restore

All hardware devices can be expected to wear out and fail after a certain amount of time. For semiconductor components, that amount of time is quite long, but for devices with moving parts, such as hard drives, failure may occur before the lifetime of the system itself ends. These days, hard drives typically have a three- to seven-year lifetime, and some high-quality drives are rated with a MTBF (Mean Time Before Failure) as high as 1,200,000 hours or 137 years. But these numbers are averages, and they are applied to normal-usage situations. The term "normal usage" might not apply in server or RAID environments where the disk runs 24/7 or in a laptop where the drive runs hot all the time. Drives do fail, and when they do, the only strategy you can use to recover your data is to restore it from a backup.

It isn't just hardware failing that makes backup so important. It is very easy to make a mistake that modifies data, deletes files, or changes the state of your system in some way that makes it necessary for you to return to a previous state of your system by using a backup. Even very simple and small changes can have profound effects. For example, if you enter the wrong string into a file that stores a password, you can make it impossible for a user to access their data. You can even render an entire system unusable by removing password access.

Think about how much time you spend on your data and how much it would cost you if you lost part of it through error or system failure. For most people, the cost of losing a couple of day's worth of data more than justifies the cost of a stand-alone tape drive or additional hard drive. Backup is like insurance: You don't need it until you need it. And when you need it you need it very badly. An investment of a few hours in a backup routine can save you many days of effort later on.

Solaris comes with system support for backup devices, including tape drives, Zip and Jaz drives, CR-RW, mirrored hard drives, and RAID. Some of this support is in the form of built-in software utilities like `ufsdump` and `ufsrestore`, which are described in this chapter. The `ufsdump` utility offers both a full backup, or "dump," and incremental backups (that is, backups that write the changed files to the backup medium). Other support requires the use of third-party software for backup and recovery. This section details some of the scenarios available to you for consideration.

In most books, a lot is written about backup technology, less about restore. Backup is difficult, but restore is a nightmare. That's why having a mirrored disk or a backup to disk is so valuable—those systems can be restored quickly. Restoration from tape is slow, and in some instances (such as when you are running mission-critical systems) tape won't be practical for you. Most stand-alone systems employ tape, and many people use tape on their workstations as their primary backup medium. One piece of practical advice about restore—do it. In a production environment, you need to know how long your restore window is, just as you need to know how long your backup window was (a backup window is the amount of time needed to perform a backup). Any backup system that is implemented needs to be tested by restoring at least part of the backup to the primary data source in order to know whether the system has worked properly. Many people who do implement backups never test them until it is too late.

The best way to think about backup is that the frequency with which you do backups is best matched to the level of availability that the data must have on your system. For immediate or near immediate availability, the best solution is to use a mirrored disk to solve a hard drive crash and back up to disk to solve an error that would be propagated to a mirrored disk. In either case, restoration involves bringing the secondary disk online in place of the primary disk , and that can happen rather quickly.

Mirrors and hard drive backups represent your most immediate solution to data or disk loss, but they aren't the entire answer because disk is still too expensive an asset to provide an historical record of your data over time. There are techniques—namely, snapshot software—that will allow the disk to provide an historical record of your data, but this software isn't in wide use at the moment. Snapshotting essentially creates and maintains a transaction log of file changes, allowing a user or administrator to go back in time to a state when the data was correct. In 2001, you will see several software/hardware solutions using snapshot technology appear for the Solaris platform from companies such as VERITAS. Snapshot software is an add-on that comes with many network-attached storage (NAS) servers today.

NAS devices represent an excellent means for adding large amounts of storage to a network quickly. NAS is primarily a client storage device; it is a server appliance that serves the role of a filer or file server. What's nice about NAS is that you plug it into a hub and turn it on. After you answer a few questions in a wizard or configure the system in a browser application, the NAS box goes out onto the network and captures a DHCP address. The system is up and running in minutes, and from the standpoint of a client, it looks like a server on the network. NAS will be very important in the next few years as a backup and restore device, and NAS devices can be bought for as little as $1,200 for an 80GB system and up to $80,000 for a multi-TB Network Appliance system. Sun sells NAS systems in various sizes as part of its StorEdge family of appliances. The StorEdge N8200 filer, which offers 200GB to 800GB of RAID 5 storage, is one example. Another nice feature of NAS is that it typically supports multiple file systems—NFS for Unix and CIFS for Windows—thus offering support for a wide range of client operating systems.

For larger, enterprise-class storage solutions, the way to go is probably constructing a Storage Area Network, or SAN. Although a discussion of SANs is beyond of the scope of this book, a SAN can be as simple as a RAID array and a switch, and both are typically connected using fibre channel. The advantage SANs offer is that they are separate high-performance networks from the LAN and thus remove the overhead of servers managing backup traffic instead of doing their primary jobs, which may be application services, network services, and so on. SANs offer the promise of "serverless backup," one of the key potential benefits of implementing this technology. SANs have a reputation for being difficult to implement, but that's only partly true. Single-vendor solutions, in which storage devices from multiple vendors don't have to interoperate, are often trouble free. SANs should become much easier to use over the next couple of years, and much more widespread.

Although NAS, which is a file-oriented transfer device, and SANs, which are block-oriented transfer architectures, appear to be mutually exclusive, they are not. You will see a merging of the two technologies over the next few years. You may choose to have NAS provide front-end and immediate non-bottlenecked file services for SANs and SANs to provide a backup to NAS.

Here's a fact that you might not be aware of—if you aren't in the business of system administration, that is. In an enterprise, particularly one with mission-critical data, it is estimated by many analysts following the storage community that nearly 15 percent of all of the servers are primarily dedicated to backing up stored data. That's an amazing figure, but it is one that indicates just how important backup is in modern computing. Companies are spending over 20 percent of their IT dollars on the insurance that backup provides.

The best historical backup medium is the one that is reliable and relatively cheap, namely, tape systems. Using single-system elliptical tape systems, it's still possible to back up 50GB to 75GB of data onto cartridges that cost $35 for roughly $0.75/GB. Compare this to the current cost of an 80GB disk at $350 and you see that it costs roughly $4/GB to back up to disk. The comparison works in favor of tape systems because you don't include the cost of a $1,000 tape drive as part of the comparison because the backup is assumed to be distributed over many, many tapes. When you look at the new Linear Tape Open (LTO) tape systems and format, the amount of data stored on tape compared to disk per unit cost is even better. There are some in the industry who feel that the cost of backing up to disk will eventually be lower than the cost of backing up to tape, but that possibility still seems several years out; at the moment, the great preponderance of backup information is written to tape drives and tape libraries.

NOTE For information about working with and installing tape drives, see Chapter 6.

Backup Strategies

Most thorough administrators use a system of rotating and saved backups. The question really isn't whether you should back up, but how often. The answer to that question is determined by variables such as these:

- The length of your backup window
- The length of your restore window
- The rate at which your data is changing
- The amount of data you can afford to lose if a critical system fails
- The amount of historical data you need to store

Before you can decide what particular type of backup strategy you need to employ, you need to know what these variables are. It's important to note that they are dependent upon hardware and software configurations, as well as on business conditions that are likely to change. For a stand-alone system, your backup strategy can be used for quite some time. In an enterprise, administrators should periodically revisit their backup strategy from time to time.

Although it might be desirable to do one or two full backups a day, it isn't often practical to do so. Most system administrators do periodic full backups with multiple incremental backups in between. When you apply that system, you need to perform a full backup and then apply all of the incremental backups that occurred since the last time you backed up fully in order to fully restore a system. The more incremental backups you do, the more time you save backing up your system but the more time you spend restoring it. It's a compromise of time versus materials.

There are actually two different types of incremental backups possible: an incremental backup to the last full backup and an incremental backup to a previous incremental backup. They each have different advantages and disadvantages. An incremental backup scheme overlaid onto a single full backup would be performed as follows:

- Sunday, full backup
- Monday, incremental backup1
- Tuesday, incremental backup1
- Wednesday, incremental backup1
- Thursday, incremental backup1
- Friday, incremental backup1
- Saturday, incremental backup1

The incremental backups you do grow throughout the week. This scheme requires more tape and longer backup times, but when you need to restore a system, you need to apply only one incremental backup to the last full backup you ran on the previous Sunday.

By comparison, progressive incremental backup scheme might work like this:

- Sunday, full backup
- Monday, incremental backup1
- Tuesday, incremental backup2
- Wednesday, incremental backup3
- Thursday, incremental backup4
- Friday, incremental backup5
- Saturday, incremental backup6

In this system, the incremental backups you do each day are limited to just the daily file changes, so they take less time and less tape to run. However, it takes longer to restore with this type of incremental backup because you must apply all of the incremental backups that have occurred since the last full backup. There is also a greater chance of something going wrong with multiple incremental backups.

Obviously, you wouldn't want to rely on a single tape because that represents a single point of failure. The idea is to have multiple backups to work with. So most backup strategies would require that you store the tape after its Saturday run and rotate in another tape. There are two strategies commonly employed in tape backup: the Grandfather-Father-Son backup rotation scheme and Tower of Hanoi backup rotation scheme.

The Grandfather-Father-Son tape rotation scheme creates 21 tapes as three generations of backup, as shown in Table 12.1. In this scheme, you recycle the daily tapes (sons) every week and use them the following week. The weekly backup tapes (fathers) are recycled so that Friday 1 becomes Friday 1 in the next month, Friday 2 becomes Friday 2 in the next month, and so on. Monthly tapes (grandfathers) are full backups, and they are recycled every year, so that Month 1 becomes Month 1 the next year. Weekly backups are first-level incremental backups, and daily backups are either first- or second-level incremental backups. Daily tapes are typically replaced after a certain life cycle because they are prone to failure through usage. Many companies retire their monthly backups in a backup library.

TABLE 12.1: GRANDFATHER-FATHER-SON BACKUP ROTATION SCHEME

	Week 1	**Week 2**	**Week 3**	**Week 4**
Daily	Monday	Monday	Monday	Monday
Daily	Tuesday	Tuesday	Tuesday	Tuesday
Daily	Wednesday	Wednesday	Wednesday	Wednesday
Daily	Thursday	Thursday	Thursday	Thursday
Weekly	Friday 1	Friday 2	Friday 3	Friday 4
Monthly			Month 1	
	Week 5	**Week 6**	**Week 7**	**Week 8**
Daily	Monday	Monday	Monday	Monday
Daily	Tuesday	Tuesday	Tuesday	Tuesday
Daily	Wednesday	Wednesday	Wednesday	Wednesday
Daily	Thursday	Thursday	Thursday	Thursday
Weekly	Friday 1	Friday 2	Friday 3	Friday 4
Monthly			Month 2	

NOTE Although this section covers tape rotations, any backup medium that can provide a cost-effective historical record is appropriate.

The Tower of Hanoi tape rotation scheme is named after a mathematical game and creates a rotating pattern of tapes. You can use as few as five tapes in this scheme, and more if you like. Each tape is used for a different period: tape A for every other day, tape B for every 4th day, tape C for every 8th day, and tape D and E for every 16th day. The pattern is shown in Table 12.2.

TABLE 12.2: TOWER OF HANOI BACKUP ROTATION

Week 1	Week 2	Week 3	Week 4
M, Tu, W, Th, F	M, Tu, W, Th, F	M, Tu, W, Th, F	M, Tu, W, Th, F
A, B, a, C, a	b, a, D, a, b	a, c, a, b, a	E, a, b, a, c
Week 5	**Week 6**	**Week 7**	**Week 8**
M, Tu, W, Th, F	M, Tu, W, Th, F	M, Tu, W, Th, F	M, Tu, W, Th, F
a, b, a, d, a	b, a, c, a, b	a, e, a, b, a	c, a, b, a, d
Week 9	**Week 10**	**Week 11**	**Week 12**
M, Tu, W, Th, F	M, Tu, W, Th, F	M, Tu, W, Th, F	M, Tu, W, Th, F
a, b, a, c, a	b, a, d, a, b	a, c, a, b, a	e, a, b, a, c

In the Tower of Hanoi scheme shown in Table 12.2, there are five tapes used and the pattern repeats every 31 days. An uppercase letter indicates the first time the tape is used for a full backup. Subsequent incremental backups are shown as lowercase letters.

In most schemes, the end-of-month tape is saved and 12 of them a year are stored, more if your system is active (if, for example, you were backing up a mission-critical system like a database with many transactions). In active systems, you may want to save weekly tapes and start to reuse them every few months. For very active systems, you might want to reuse weekly tapes after a much longer period. It is also common to provide a secondary historical backup, so you should consider backing up critical information to a CD-RW disk every week. Then, if the tape drive fails, you have your data on another medium, and even though it might not be entirely up-to-date, it will at least get you by.

Backup Tips

Whatever backup strategy you choose, there are some important things you need to remember about backups:

- Try to automate your backup routine with software so that you don't have to attend to its operation.
- When you are using a Solaris utility like `ufsdump` (described in the next section), use a scheduling utility like `cron` to run backup at predetermined times.
- Make a habit of backing up every file on every drive; you never know when it will come in handy.
- Because backup media fails, create copies of important backups—your monthly backup, for example.
- Label all your tapes because one tape or disk looks like another.
- If you aren't using a rotating backup scheme, make sure that you at least back up before any significant system change or before adding any device.
- In case of fire, keep a copy of your backup off-site.
- The most important thing to remember about backups is that you must verify a backup by testing that you can actually restore the data it contains—otherwise the backup is useless.

Backup Utilities

Solaris comes with backup tools like `tar`, `dd`, `cpio`, `ufsdump`, and `ufsrestore`. These tools can be used to back up single systems to local devices; `usfdump` can be used to back up single systems to multiple devices. This section focuses on the use of the Solaris system tools, whereas the next section concentrates on the use of third-party tools for backup/restore, both in local and networked situations.

If you simply want to make a copy of a disk or a tape, then you can use the `dd` (device to device) command for this purpose. The `dd` command copies a set of blocks, and makes an image of a partition or disk from one location you specify to another. You will find that the `dd` command works with other operating system files as well as Solaris files because the command is a block-oriented transfer. The `dd` command has several useful options, some of which you can use to set block sizes, affect character conversions, control the input file, start and stop at particular block locations, and so forth. In its default state, `dd` takes standard input and creates standard output.

Here is a common example: copying a diskette's contents to another diskette using a temp directory on your hard drive. To copy a diskette to your hard drive from the command line, follow these steps:

1. Insert the diskette.
2. Enter the following:

   ```
   # sh /etc/init.d/volmgt stop
   ```

   The `volmgt stop` command disables volume management so that you can manipulate the diskette directly.
3. Enter the following to copy the files on the diskette to disk:

   ```
   # dd if=/dev/<diskettename> of=diskette.bak
   ```

   The `if=` option specifies the input file, and the `of=` option specifies the output file. Here the contents of the diskette directory are written to the hard drive as the *<diskette>*`.bak` file in the current directory.
4. Remove the current diskette (which was the source) and replace it with the target diskette.
5. Enter the following commands (what you need to enter is in bold text):

   ```
      # dd if=diskette.bak of=/dev/<diskettename>
   3680+0 records in
   3680+0 records out
      sh /etc/init.d/volmgt start
   ```

You can also create a shell script that provides a complete device backup to a remote system by using the `rsh` utility, which runs the dd command on a remote computer, as follows:

```
# !/bin/sh
# Do a complete backup to tape on <systemname>

computer=<systemname>
<devicename>=/dev/rmt/0

echo "Backing up $<computer> to the device $<devicename>
   (proceding)…\c"
cd /
tar -cf - . | rsh -l hls $<computer> dd obs=256k of=$<devicename>
echo "Backing up $<computer> ($<devicename>) completed 'date' >
   /etc/backup.log echo "complete."
```

PART II

Solaris and the Network

Don't forget that many enterprise applications, particularly accounting programs, databases, and messaging applications, come with their own backup utility. You may find that a system such as an Oracle database offers you backup through the `exp` (for export) command.

Backup and Restore Commands

The following commands are the standard Unix backup and restore commands that you can use:

- `volcopy` and `labelit`
- `ufsdump` and `ufsrestore`

You can also use utilities such as `tar`, `cpio`, and `dd` to support backups by creating archives and duplicating disks, as you have seen previously.

The `volcopy` command takes an image of a file system in one location and writes it to another location. An image is an exact byte-for-byte copy that is transferred as blocks. Because `volcopy` needs to find as much space on the target location as it has data to write from the source, the `volcopy` command requires that you specify the size of the target media. The `volcopy` command also checks that the labels of the source and target are correct before proceeding. If the file system doesn't fit on the target media (for example, on a single tape), `volcopy` will request that a new tape be inserted when the amount of data that is transferred fills the target media you specified.

Because `volcopy` is a block-oriented transfer program, it is fast, particularly if a disk-to-disk copy is performed. One advantage of the `volcopy` utility is that it gives you a complete backup when it runs. With `volcopy`, you can run copies to two or more mounted tape drives. Another advantage of `volcopy` is that you can use it to recover lost files by copying the file system and using that copy to recover files (or an entire file system). However, `volcopy` doesn't support incremental backups.

When the `volcopy` command is interrupted, you are prompted to either quit the program or escape to the shell. You can use a volume labeling command like `labelit` to provide any missing labels to tapes before returning to finish your file system copy with `volcopy`. With the `labelit` utility, you can add a label to unmounted disk file systems or to a file system being copied to a tape. `volcopy` and other programs use the label as an identification for performing routines.

The `ufsdump` and `ufsrestore` commands are the Solaris versions of the widely used Unix dump and restore backup programs that write backup to tape drives and other devices. With `ufsdump`, you can back up an entire file system to tape or do an incremental backup of only the file changes that have occurred since your last backup (full or incremental). You can also back up individual files or a directory tree by using ufsdump. With ufsrestore, you can take the data written to a backup device and write it to your disk or another location.

NOTE Solaris has a dump command that is used to dump selected parts of object files. It is used in shell scripts. There is no restore command.

The command syntax for ufsdump is as follows (/dev/rmt/0 is the tape target and /dev/rdsk/c?t?d?1? is the address of the source disk used):

```
# usfdump 0 /dev/rmt/0 /dev/rdsk/c?t?d?s?
```

The ufsdump command is best used on a quiescent system and can back up an entire file system, a file, or a part of a file system tree. To backup an entire file system, use this command:

```
# ufsdump 0uf /dev/rmt/0 /
```

When the 0-level dump (there are levels 0 through 9) is specified, the entire file system is backed up. Level 1 backs up files that have changed since the last 0 backup; level 2 backs up files changed since the last level 1 backup, and so forth. This scheme allows you to construct scripts with very flexible backup routines. The u option updates the /etc/dumpdates file. The f option specifies that the backup is written to a file called /dev/rmt/0, which specifies a tape drive (the rmt protocol).

Therefore, to do an incremental backup that backs up data that has changed since the last full backup, enter **# ufsdump 1uf /dev/rmt/0 /**; to do an incremental backup to back up data that has changed since the last level 1 backup was done, use **# ufsdump 2uf /dev/rmt/0 /**; and so on.

The command used to restore from tape is the ufsrestore command. It creates the files and directories that are in the backup set that don't already exist on your disk, but it also overwrites any files and directories that do exist on your disk from the files and directories of the same name in your backup. Therefore, when using the ufsrestore command, you need to be very careful that you don't destroy files and directories that you intended to keep.

WARNING Be particularly careful when using the ufsrestore command because it overwrites files on disk and can destroy data that you want to keep.

To restore an entire file system from backup, follow these steps:

1. Log in as superuser.
2. Use the change directory command `cd` *<pathname>* to switch to the directory on which the file system is mounted.
3. Issue the following command:

   ```
   # ufsrestore if /dev/rmt/0
   ```

   Here the `i` option starts the `ufsrestore` command in the interactive mode, which allows you specify which files and directories should be restored. The `f` option specifies the device (`/dev/rmt/0`) that the backup tape is mounted on.

The `ufsrestore` command restores the dump with the number that is higher than the number of the dump that was restored the last time `ufsrestore` was used. If there is more than one `ufsrestore` used at the same level in the restore hierarchy, the command restores the most recent dump at that level.

The `ufsrestore r` option will restore your file system automatically without intervention, as follows:

```
# ufsrestore rf /dev/rmt/0
```

After a `ufsdump` or `ufsrestore` command is completed, tape drives typically rewind to the beginning of the tape. You can specify that the tape not rewind by appending the `n` option to the device command, as in `/dev/rmt/0n`. The `n` option is particularly useful when you're using the `ufsdump` or `ufsrestore` command to write to or read from remote tape drives in a sequential fashion, something you might do when you want to back up or restore multiple file systems to a volume.

TIP Use the `man mtio` command to view the magnetic tape I/O interface and option man page. This page documents options that help you work with tape drives.

If you wish to restore a single file on tape using `ufsrestore`, use the `x` option and input the filenames from the command line. You must be in the same working directory that you wish the restored file to appear in when you use the command, as shown here (where the /*<pathname>*/*<directoryname>*/*<filename>* argument is the file that is to be restored from tape):

```
# cd /<directoryname>
# ufsrestore xf /dev/rmt/0 /<pathname>/<directoryname>/<filename>
```

Local vs. Network Backup

For a stand-alone workstation, you will probably want to attach a tape drive or some other backup device to your system and perform a local backup. You can use `ufsdump` and `ufsrestore` to work with tape drives and other locally attached devices. Although capable, these Solaris commands are hardly what anyone would call "friendly." They have a learning curve, and it is possible to make serious mistakes using these command-line utilities. You are likely to find that the tape drive you purchase comes bundled with a backup program (make sure that that program supports Unix); if not, you may want to invest in a backup program on your own, one that provides a graphical way of automating backup functions. You can still make mistakes using a graphical tape backup program, but it's more difficult to err, and it's typically easier to learn and remember how to use backup programs of this type.

If you are a network administrator, or work in a network setup where backup is one of the network functions provided, you are probably going to be backing up your system using a network backup scheme. Although you can use `ufsdump` and `ufsrestore` to work remotely with tape drives attached to other computers across a network, there are many other programs that provide more complete functionality in this regard. Some network backups are done using a backup server that serves as an intermediary between clients and the backup device. In many instances, this backup is scripted, and an agent is placed on the client to monitor file changes.

Third-Party Backup Programs

There are many backup programs that you can purchase and install on Solaris, and a few are freeware programs. The primary distinction is between programs that do only local backup and those that do network backup as well. Commercial programs for network backup tend to contain more features, are harder to use and learn, and are more expensive than local backup programs. Unless otherwise noted, the programs described in this section don't rely on standard Solaris or Unix utilities for their data transfer engines.

If you want to use `tar` archives as output, among the programs you might want to consider are the following:

- CTAR, which provides scheduled backups with `tar` archives as its output. CTAR is a product of UniTrends Software (`www.unitrends.com/ctar.htm`).
- BRU 2000 (Backup and Restore Utility) is based on the `tar` command but with many more features. BRU is run as a daemon that provides scheduled backups. It is a product of Enhanced Software Technologies (`www.estinc.com`).

- AMANDA (Advanced Maryland Automatic Network Disk Archiver) is a freeware program that provides centralized backup of clients to a server and can restore remote machines. You can use AMANDA backup clients that support SMB, which includes Solaris, Windows NT, and Linux systems. You can obtain AMANDA from the AMANDA Web site at `www.amanda.org`; the FAQ Web site for AMANDA is located at `www.ic.unicamp.br/~oliva/snapshots/amanda/FAQ`.

AMANDA works with either a single tape drive or, less conveniently, with multiple tape drives. Currently, AMANDA will only work with a file system that is the size of the backup medium that you are using. For backup devices like DAT and DLT, that will limit you to from 18GB to 80GB (for SuperDLT), depending upon the technology used. You will not be able to use AMANDA with QIC or CD-R systems.

One nice feature of AMANDA is that it creates `tar` archives as its backup output. If AMANDA is not available on the system you are using to do a restore, you can still copy the files from the backup onto the target system. Once the files are copied, you can extract files from the archives and work with them, which is a little more trouble but provides a workaround solution. Unlike a command-line backup routine that uses the `cron` scheduling utility to create tar files, AMANDA offers a more feature-filled scheduling system, as well as a more effective tape storage management routine. AMANDA uses a dump cycle to estimate the time required for a full dump and adjusts the schedule accordingly. AMANDA also spools either full or incremental dumps to a backup server disk before that data is written up to the backup device. This is an advantage with CD-R systems because it offers a solution to buffer overrun problems where the CD-R write heads will skip tracks if data isn't available to the system quickly enough.

You can get the PerfectBACKUP+ program with both an ASCII menu and a Motif GUI interface, and you can switch between them. This program is a descendent of the Unix version of the DOS FastBack Plus that Fifth Generation created many years ago. It is offered with network support, scheduling, and `tar` and `cpio` support. The package is easy to use and fast. UniSource Systems (`www.unisrc.com`) is the supplier of this venerable backup program.

The most popular commercial network backup program for Solaris is probably VERITAS NetBackup (see `http://veritas.com`). NetBackup is an enterprise backup program that can back up data from many clients using multiple servers and backup systems. NetBackup installs client software on systems such as Windows; the client software allows people to back up their Windows-based systems to a backup Solaris server and can work with VERITAS Backup Exec clients on Windows. You can also use scripts on a server to back up clients from that server.

Many different client types and operating systems are supported by NetBackup, which makes VERITAS NetBackup running on Solaris one of the most popular backup architectures for large enterprises at the moment. Many large databases running Oracle on Unix, for example, or Web sites using Apache on Linux will back up to NetBackup on Solaris.

Legato Networker (`www.legato.com`) is another networked backup program that is often used with enterprise databases. Unlike NetBackup, which uses a distributed model for backup of clients to a server and to backup devices, Networker uses a centralized scheme (as AMANDA does) in which a single control server manages backup servers and clients. Networker has broad operating system support.

Another major network backup program is Computer Associates's ARCserve 2000 (`www.cai.com`). CA acquired ARCserve 2000 from Cheyenne Systems a few years ago and has continued to invest aggressively in its development. ARCserve 2000 has perhaps the broadest range of device support in the industry and is particularly favored in heterogeneous networking applications. You'll find that ARCserve 2000 is a feature-filled program that has grown to include many useful high-quality automation features. ARCserve is particularly well suited to working with tape libraries because it features a backup engine that is optimized for specific tape drives and includes a parallel streaming feature that supports concurrent operation to multiple tapes.

Summary

Several different utilities were described in this chapter. These utilities compress, encrypt, and package files.

An archives provide a means for packaging files together into a single file that is conveniently handled and communicated. Archives are often useful when a set of files must be used together for some purpose, such as an installation. You can use the `tar` and `cpio` commands as well as GNU `gtar` to create and work with archives. Packages provide an installation routine for the distribution of programs.

Solaris lets you compress files so that you can save on disk space, lessen the time it takes to upload and download files on the Internet, and so forth. When you compress files using utilities like `compress` and GNU `gzip`, you can reduce their file size, sometimes even greatly. There is some support in the CDE for archives and compressed files.

Solaris has built-in commands for volume and file system backup, notably `dd`, `volcopy`, and `ufsdump` and `ufsrestore`, which were described in this chapter. A backup is an important part of system maintenance and is your last line of defense when a component in your system fails or your data gets corrupted. The importance of backup, strategies for its use, and programs that provide backup were described.

CHAPTER 13

Mailer and Calendar

FEATURING:

Sending and receiving e-mail 512

Working with attachments 529

Combining Mailer and File Manager 530

Starting Calendar 535

Changing calendar views 537

The basics of Appointments and the To Do function 539

In this chapter, you'll learn about Mailer and Calendar, two applications that are included in the Common Desktop Environment (CDE). They are powerful tools that can be used together. Both support drag-and-drop functionality.

You can use the Mailer application to send and receive e-mail messages. In addition to text messages, Mailer supports a wide range of other mail features, including attached files, templates, draft copies, and drag-and-drop functionality with other desktop applications. It also has basic and advanced e-mail search tools. Mailer is a powerful yet straightforward application.

Calendar supports both an Appointments and a To Do module. Appointments produce reminders to go to meetings, hand in reports, and perform other office tasks, and a To Do list is like an agenda list with time limits.

You'll also learn how to send and receive e-mail messages, how to create and manage your To Do list, and how to schedule appointments and set alarms. You will find these functions to be very useful in your daily work.

Mailer

Mailer is a convenient front-end GUI to the e-mail system. A modern-day e-mail system uses numerous programs, files, directories, and protocols that must work together to send and receive e-mail messages. The steps necessary to transport e-mail between two different e-mail systems would be beyond the capability of a relatively simple application like Mailer. The program that actually sends and receives the e-mail messages from the workstation is called the message transfer agent (MTA). Solaris 8 comes with an MTA named `sendmail`.

The program that actually delivers the e-mail messages is the mail delivery agent (MDA). The `sendmail` utility listens to the port for mail and when it gets mail from another MTA, it then checks to see if there is a local user for which the recipient is a match. If so, the MTA then hands the message over to the MDA for local delivery, which by default is in an individual user's mail spool directory `/var/mail`. Solaris 8 uses an MDA named `mail.local`.

Neither `sendmail` nor `mail.local` has any type of user interface. They understand some very cryptic mail header files and information files. The user agent is the front-end application that communicates between the user and the MTA and MDA. This is the application that you see on your screen when you send and receive e-mail.

Mailer is only the first and last step in the e-mail chain. It is a GUI that makes the relatively cryptic mail header files needed to send and receive e-mail more easily understood by the user. Sun has provided a total of four different user agents:

- /usr/bin/mail
- /usr/bin/mailx
- /usr/openwin/bin/mailtool
- /usr/dt/bin/dtmail

The applications `mail` and `mailx` are command-line utilities; `mailtool` and `dtmail` are GUI mail tools. Any one of these applications can send e-mail files in the format the MTA and MDA need, but they also translate the files into formats that humans can easily understand and manipulate.

Starting Mailer

To start the Mailer program, click the Mail icon, which is the fifth icon on the left side of the front panel (shown in the following graphic). You can also start the Mail program by opening a console or terminal window and typing **dtmail &**. The ampersand is used in the command to make the Mailer a background process.

TIP If the Mailer program does not start, there is startup script named /etc/rc2.d/S88sendmail, which is a hard link to /etc/init.d/sendmail. It starts some of the daemons that are needed for the Mailer program to run. To start the sendmail daemons, type **/etc/rc2.d/S88sendmail start**. To stop them, type **/etc/rc2.d/ S88sendmail stop**.

When you first open Mailer, a pop-up window like the one shown in Figure 13.1 appears, asking you whether your mail account is a local account or an Internet Message Access Protocol (IMAP) account. A local account checks your local mail spool (usually /var/mail/<*username*>) for your mail. An IMAP mail setup uses a remote IMAP server that stores your mail for you on the server, including the different folders and attachments, and will usually have a username such as `john@sun.com`. If you click the wrong button or your e-mail server is changed, there is an option under the Options menu item called Move Menu Setup that you can use to change the selection you make in this pop-up window (see "Customizing Mailer" later in this chapter).

FIGURE 13.1

The e-mail setup pop-up window

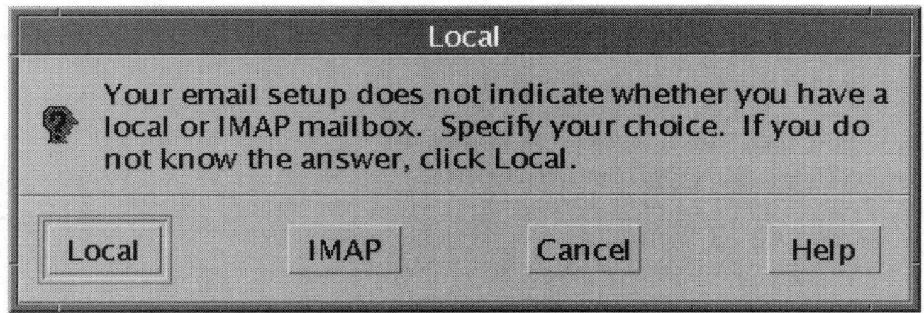

Figure 13.2 shows the dialog box that appears when you have an IMAP e-mail account. As you can see, the name of the server and a login name and password are required. The name of the server or host can be a simple name like Galaxy or a fully qualified domain name like `production.sun.com`. Contact your e-mail administrator for the name of the e-mail server you need to connect with.

FIGURE 13.2

The IMAP Login dialog box

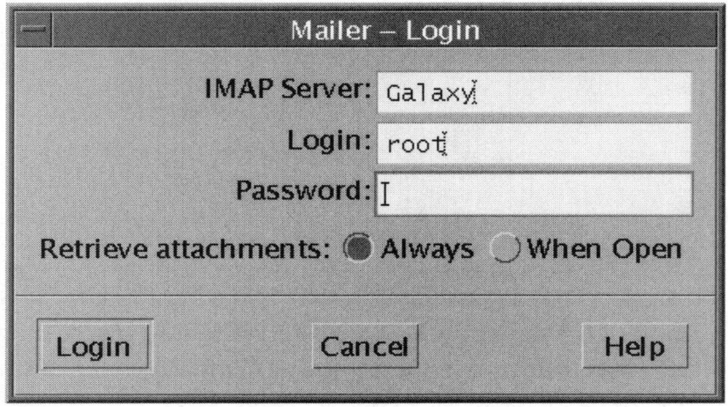

After you enter your server name, login name, and password, the main Mailer window, shown in Figure 13.3, appears. This is the window in which you can read mail, compose mail, and perform all the other mail-related tasks that will be covered in this chapter. At the top of the window is a menu bar with Mailbox, Message, Compose, View, Options, Move, and Help menus (the options on these menu will be covered later in this chapter). Under the menus is the Message Header List, which shows the following information about each message: the sender, the subject, the date and time the mail was sent, and the size. The order in which messages are displayed is controlled by the user (the numerous ways in which the Mailer interface and the messages can be manipulated are covered in "Viewing Mail Messages" later in this chapter).

There is a small icon toolbar just under the Message Header List. The icons (from left to right) are used to delete mail, view the next mail message, view the previous mail message, reply to a message, forward a message, compose a message, and print a message.

FIGURE 13.3

The main window of the Mailer application

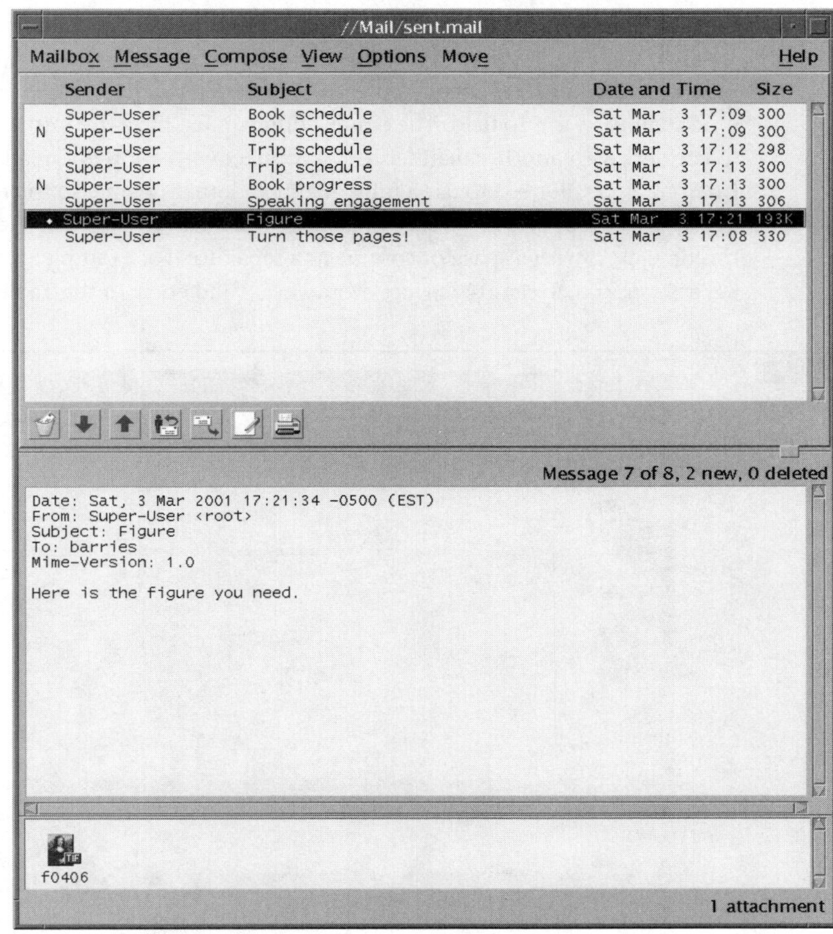

The next section of the window is the message view area, which displays the text of e-mail messages. For long messages, you can use the scroll bars on the side of the window. The attachment list is displayed in the bottom pane. If you double-click an e-mail message in the Mail Header List, only the message view area appears unless the message contains an attachment, in which case the attachment list also appears.

Creating a Mail Message

To compose an e-mail message, select the New Message command from the Compose menu. The New Message, or Compose, window appears (shown in Figure 13.4). The text fields To, Subject, and Cc are used to create the standard e-mail header information, which is passed to a mail delivery agent. In the case of Solaris, `sendmail` is the mail delivery agent used to send e-mail messages. You type in the e-mail address of the person you want to send mail to in the To field. The e-mail address must have the format *`<username>@<host>`* to connect with another mail server. To connect with another e-mail account on the Internet, you will need to use a fully qualified domain name, so the format must be *`<username>@<FullyQualifiedDomainName>`* (for example, `john@sun.com`). You can add multiple users with a space or comma as a separator. For example, `john@sun.com Karen@sun.com,Michael@msn.com` would be a valid entry in the To field.

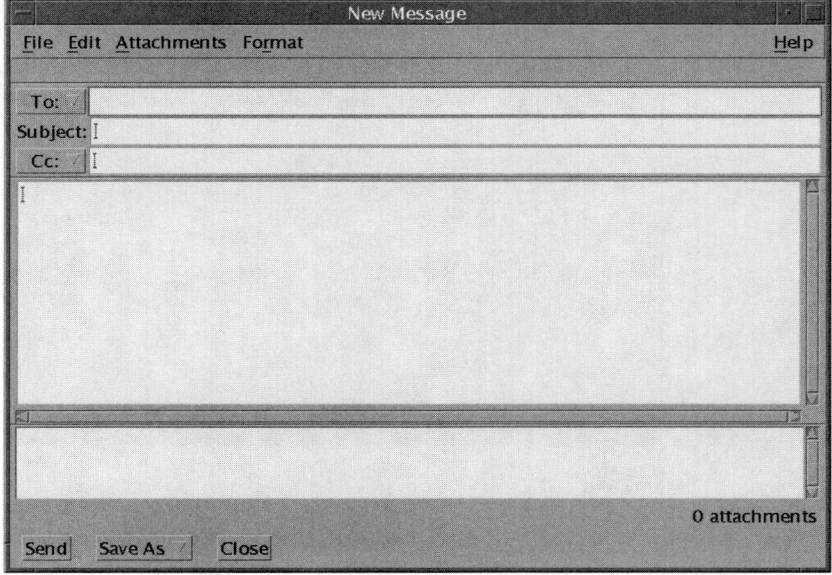

FIGURE 13.4
The Compose window

If you have aliases set up, click the To button and a small drop-down menu that includes your aliases appears. It also includes an Aliases option, which you can select to access the Aliases dialog box. Click the alias that you want and you will be returned to the Mailer Compose window. Aliases are covered in "Customizing Mailer" later in this chapter.

In the Subject text box, you enter a quick text reference to your e-mail message. The Subject line appears in almost all modern e-mail programs. You can use the Cc button to add additional recipients to your e-mail message. This button is similar to the To button: if you click it, a small drop-down menu with your aliases will appear.

The actual mail text is entered into the text area of the Compose window. You can use a template or draft or just simply type in text. Templates are basically saved e-mail messages that you can modify and send again. A draft is a message you have composed and have saved to possibly revise or double-check before you send it. When you have completed the message, click the Save As button. You can choose to save the message as a template, a draft, or text.

After you have written your e-mail message, you can choose to add a signature to it. The signature is just a simple text passage appended to the main text of the e-mail and should not be confused with a digital signature or other more advanced security signatures. When you attach a signature to an e-mail message, the `dtmail` program adds the contents of the file `$HOME/.signature` to your message. Figure 13.5 shows an e-mail ready to be sent to `john@sun.com`. The Cc box contains the aliases of some other recipients who will also get a copy of this message. This message also has an attached image file.

FIGURE 13.5
An e-mail message ready to be sent

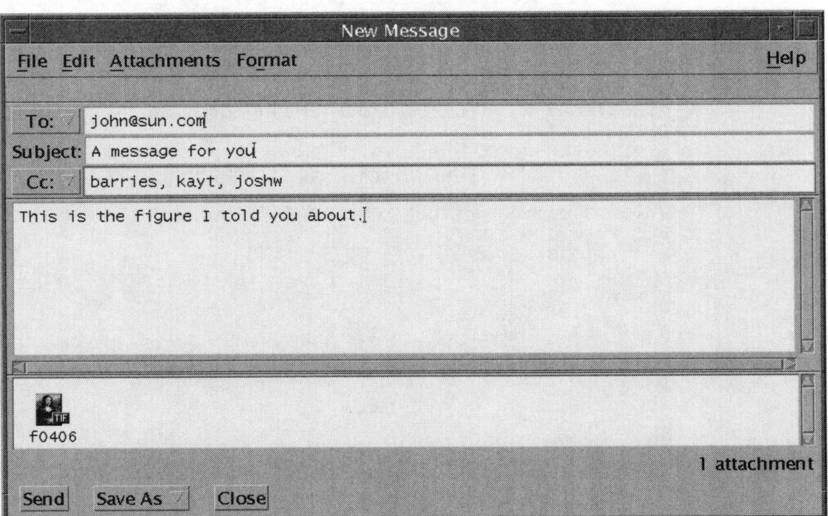

Viewing Mail Messages

Any standard e-mail server that is capable of sending messages can receive mail messages (if configured to do so). The mail message agent in Solaris 8 is `mail.local`. This software delivers mail messages to the spooler, and the Mailer checks the spooler to see if new mail has been added. When new mail arrives, the Mailer's icon will change from the standard icon to an icon that looks like the one in the following graphic.

When you open the Mailer program and log in to the IMAP server, the Mailer checks the server for new mail automatically. There are two methods you can use to check for mail yourself:

- Choose the Check for New Mail command from the Mailbox menu.
- Press the Ctrl+M keystroke.

By default, Mailer checks for new mail every 300 seconds (that is, every 5 minutes). Any new mail will be displayed in the Message Header List. Use the Next or Previous icon on the toolbar or simply double-click the message you want to open. Figure 13.6 shows what the message view area of the main Mailer window looks like when a new mail message is open. As you can see, a brief description of the e-mail is in the Subject line.

FIGURE 13.6

An open e-mail message

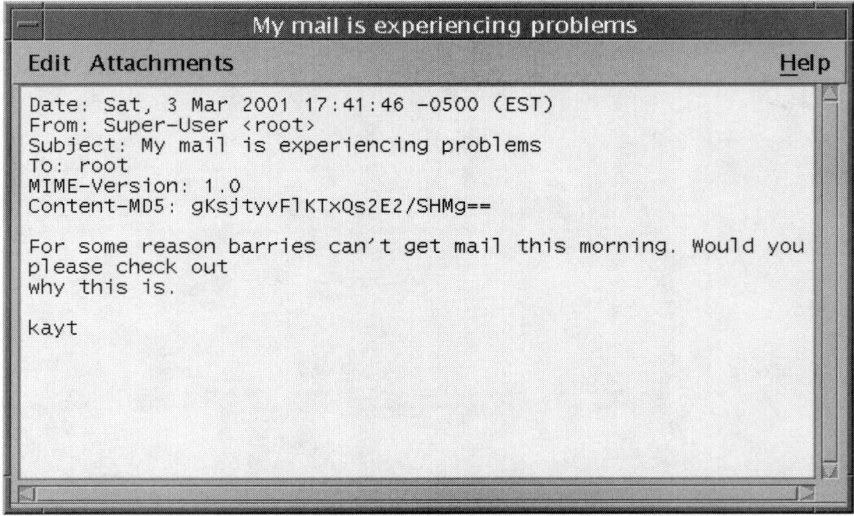

As mentioned earlier, there are seven icons just under the Message Header List that you can use to look through the e-mail messages found in the main Mailer window:

Delete Moves mail to a delete folder (doesn't permanently delete it).

Next Opens in the message view area the message that is listed next in the Message Header List.

Previous Opens in the message view area the message that appeared previously in the Message Header List.

Reply, Include Message Opens the Compose window, adds your username to the From line, and adds `Re:` and the subject of the message to which you're replying to the subject line.

Forward Opens the Compose window with mail text so that you can send the message to another recipient. You would use this feature to have another person view mail you receive.

New Message Opens the Compose window.

Print One Prints the message (requires a printer to be set up).

For users who have large quantities of e-mail coming in each day (for example, corporate managers or Unix admins often receive 100 or more messages in a day), the View menu offers some nice sorting functions in addition to commands you can use to view messages:

Next Go down the list of mail messages to the next message. This command duplicates the function of the Next button in the window.

Previous Go up the list of mail messages to the previous message. This command duplicates the function of the Previous button in the window.

Abbreviated Headers Shortens the text of the headers displayed in the Message Header List.

Change Char Set This is rarely used and changes the locale characters, the character set used by one language or locale or another. For example, Great Britain uses a slightly different character set than the U.S.

By Date/Time Sorts messages in the Message Header List by the date and time they were sent. The most recent e-mail messages appear at the bottom of the message view area. If two or more messages arrive at the same date, the earliest time is selected first.

By Sender Sorts messages in the Message Header List in alphabetical order by the name of the sender.

By Subject Sorts messages in the Message Header List in alphabetical order by subject. For example, a message with a subject line of "how are you" appears below one with a subject line of "Adam's report."

By Size Sorts message by their size, including attachments.

By Status Sorts messages by their status of read and unread.

When you receive a message, double-click its header in the Message Header List to view its contents. If you want to reply to or forward the message, you'll need to close the message view area. Once you are back to the main Mailer window, you can click the icon for the action you want to take. By default, Mailer doesn't include the original message in a reply. Click the Reply, Include Message icon to include the original message text.

When you choose to reply to a message, a Compose window similar to the one used to create new messages is displayed. The original message text is displayed at the bottom of the window with a > symbol to indicate the original text. When you are finished adding new text (and even an attachment), you can click the Send button to send the message back to the original sender. The Reply to All message window is used to send the message back to the original user and to all other users to which a copy (Cc) was sent. Open the Reply to All window by selecting the Reply to All command on the Compose menu. Your reply to the message will go to every user who received the original copy. If the original sender included an attachment, that attachment will not be sent back to the sender.

When a message is forwarded, the original recipient must enter into the To field the e-mail address of the next person to receive the message. The original text and attachment and any new text and attachments you add will be forwarded on to the new recipient.

TIP Some people reply to all of the people who received the original message even though they only need to send a reply to one person. There are also times when a message is forwarded to all the people on an e-mail distribution list when only one person needs to receive it. It is a good idea to be considerate and send messages only to the people who need to receive them. Remember, with e-mail, people don't know what your intentions are, so it's not difficult to seem rude.

You can also double-click a mail message's listing to open the message view area shown in Figure 13.6. If there is an attachment with the message, you'll see a pane under the message view area that includes the attachment list, and there are two menus, Edit and Attachments, above the message view area.

On the Edit menu, there is a Copy option and a Select All option. You must highlight the text you want to copy before you select Copy. The text you highlighted is copied into memory and you can then paste it into other applications that can receive text. The Select All option highlights all the text in the message at once.

The Attachments menu has four options: Save As, Select All, Open, and Print. Save As saves the attachment to the hard drive without opening it. The attachment's name can be changed during the save process. Select All highlights (selects) all the attachments in the attachment list. The Open option opens the attachment with the proper application (provided that your system has software installed that can read the file and open it). When you choose Print, the Print dialog box appears. It has the following features:

File Displays the name of the file.

Printer Displays the name of the printer to send the job to. Enter the name of the printer you want to use.

Copies Enter the number of copies to print.

Banner Page Title Choose this to print text at the top of each page (which isn't the same as a banner page).

Banner Page Numbers Choose this to print the page number at the bottom of each page.

One useful Mailer option is to save e-mail messages as text. To do so, open the message in the main Mailer window and choose the Save As Text command from the Message menu. Outgoing mail can be saved as text from the Save As command on the File menu (when the Compose window is open).

Mailer can also attach e-mail to the end of existing text documents. Let's say a corporate manager has a file named `johnrecords` in his home directory, and John sends a weekly status report to the manager. Each week, the manager can open the message containing the status report, choose Save As from the File menu, and click the Append button in the Save As dialog box. This will add John's e-mail message to the end of the file named `johnrecords`.

Customizing Mailer

You customize Mailer by using selections from the Options menu. In the following sections, we'll explain some of the selections in more detail.

To create an alias, which is a name that you enter that points to a valid e-mail address, do this:

1. Click the To button in the New Message dialog box and select Aliases from the drop-down menu. The Mailer–Mail Options dialog box appears.
2. Enter the alias in the Alias text box. An alias can be any valid text string.
3. Enter the valid e-mail address in the Address text box.
4. Then click the Add button.

The Basic Command

Figure 13.7 shows the Mail Options dialog box that appears when you choose the Basic command from the Options menu. You can use this dialog box to make simple configuration changes that affect the performance of Mailer. At the top of the dialog box is a section labeled Mailbox Updates. You can use it to define how often the mail server will be checked for new mail. The default time is 300 seconds (5 minutes). If, for some reason, you need to check your mail more often, you can set this time period to a lower value. The only problem with setting it to a lower value is that you will increase network traffic if you are using an IMAP server. If you are using the local mail spool instead of an IMAP server, it will increase your hard disk activity.

FIGURE 13.7

The Mail Options dialog box for the Basic command

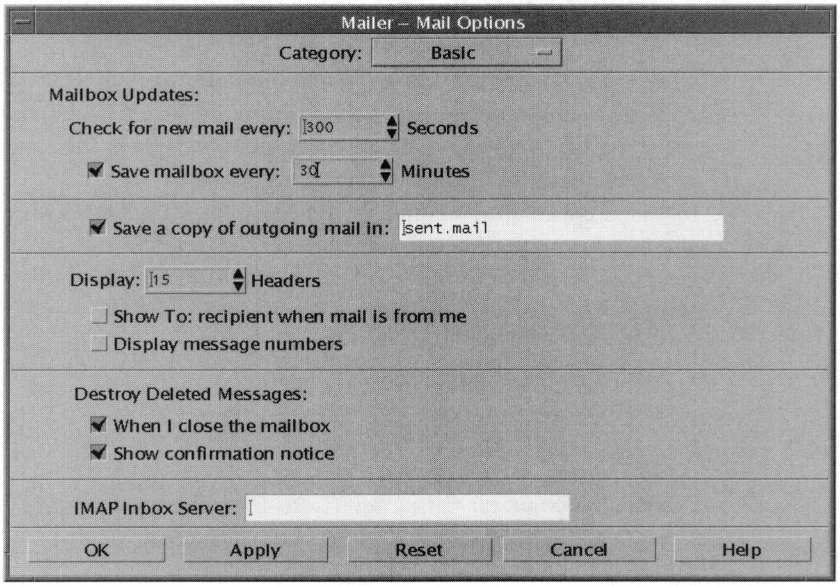

The Basic Mail Options dialog box also gives you the choice of saving copies of your sent e-mail to a file. The text box next to the Save a Copy of Outgoing Mail In check box displays the name of the backup file for your mailbox. This file is named `sent.mail`. If your company has a policy of destroying e-mail messages, you might want to edit this file on a regular basis and destroy old messages. You cannot save attachments in this file, only the text portion of your outgoing e-mails.

This file can be used by a system administrator to restore a damaged e-mail system. The default time to save the `sent.mail` file is every 30 minutes. This should be sufficient for most e-mail users. Power users might need to save this more often.

TIP Save your `sent.mail` file on a disk located on another server. Then, if your hard disk crashes and you lose your e-mail, you'll have the means to recover it. The easiest way to save `sent.mail` to another disk is to create a simple script or `cron` job that copies this file to an NFS-mounted directory. Be careful when doing this so that you don't accidentally give other users access to your mail file.

The section of the Basic Mail Options dialog box that applies to the Message Header List gives you the option to select how many e-mail headers will be shown. The next section, Destroy Deleted Messages, allows you to destroy messages that have been deleted.

One issue that comes up in the corporate world is the concept of destroying e-mail effectively. Most people think that if they delete an e-mail message, the message is gone. Wrong! Most e-mail programs have an undelete or trash directory that saves a copy of the supposedly deleted e-mail message. Mailer also has this feature. There are times when it is nice to have the ability to recover an accidentally deleted e-mail message. However, if you decide you need to destroy your e-mail messages, you can modify the default behavior of Mailer to destroy the messages you've deleted when you exit the program. This is done in the Basic Mail Options dialog box.

TIP It is fine to delete mail, but be aware that mail can be elsewhere on the server, even though you have deleted it. It can still be on backup tapes on the mail server or on the server it came from.

At the bottom of the dialog box, you can specify an IMAP e-mail server if you haven't specified one before.

The Compose Window Command

To perform more advanced customization of the Mailer program, select the Compose Window command from the Options menu. The Compose Window Mail Options dialog box (shown in Figure 13.8) has options you can use to customize the pop-up window that is shown when you compose a new message. The Compose window has a default width of 80 characters. The default size can be enlarged to take advantage of large-screen monitors. The attachment list appears with the Compose window when an attachment is added to the e-mail message, but you can choose not to show it. When you reply to a message, the standard character (called the indent character) that is used to distinguish your text from the text of the original message is the > sign. The indent character can be changed to any character that you prefer.

One of the features of Unix e-mail is the `$HOME/DeadLetters` directory. It keeps a copy of the e-mail messages you are currently working on. Usually, you will not be able to recover from this directory after a crash or you will find it empty. The `$HOME/DeadLetters` directory should have only the letters that were open for writing at the time of the crash. After a letter has been saved and closed or sent, the copy is removed from the directory.

FIGURE 13.8

The Compose Window Mail Options dialog box

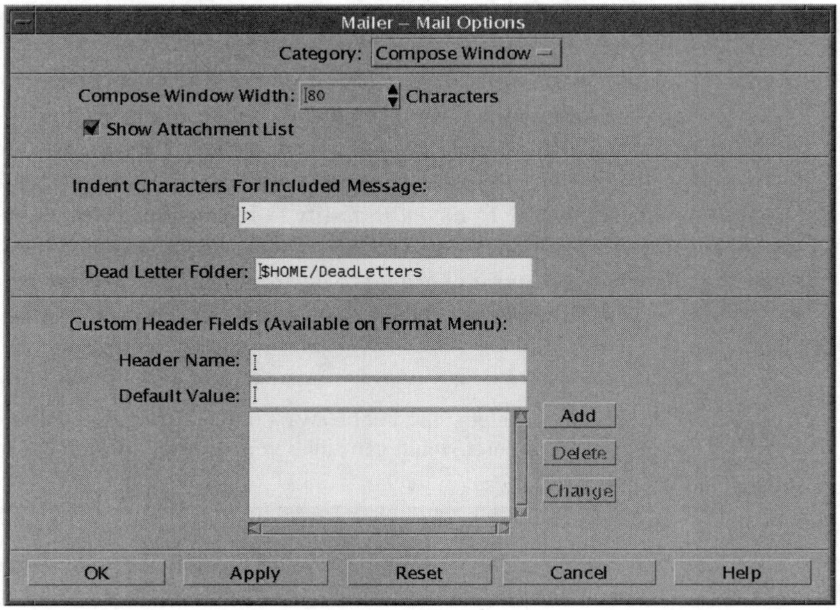

In the bottom section of the Compose Window Mail Options dialog box, you can customize the header fields in your messages. You should not use these options unless there is a strong need to do so. Incorrect header fields in an e-mail message can cause the e-mail system to crash or not work for your messages. (Manipulating the headers of e-mail messages is an advanced topic and beyond the scope of this book.)

The Advanced Command

Mailer has some more advanced configuration options. They are accessed by choosing the Advanced command from the Options menu. The Advanced Mail Options dialog box is shown in Figure 13.9.

The options in the Advanced Mail Options dialog box are as follows:

Warn if Message Exceeds 1000 Kbytes Enable this option to have a pop-up warning message displayed if you try to send an e-mail message that exceeds the size that is indicated. After the warning message is displayed, you are given three choices: Send, Cancel, and Help.

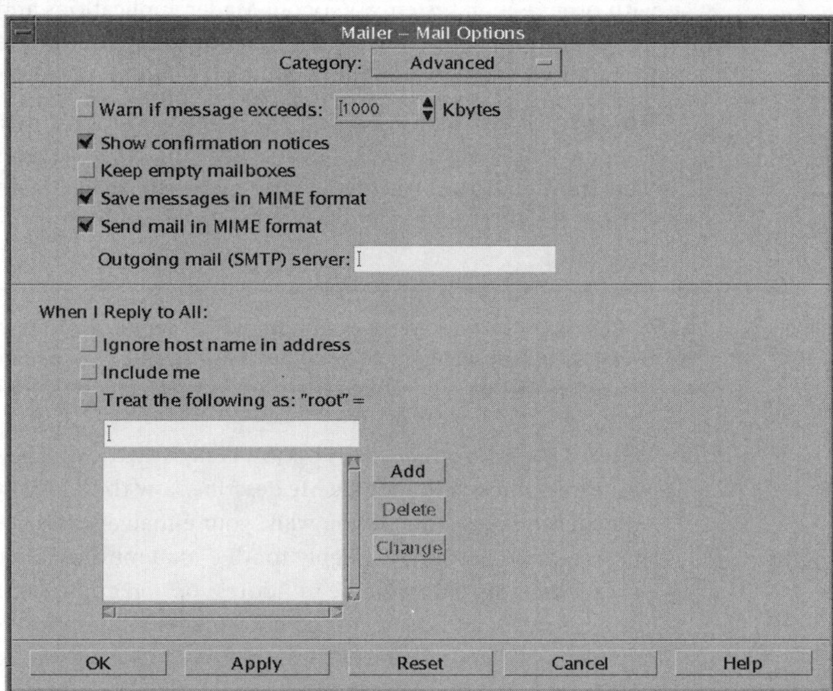

FIGURE 13.9
The Advanced Mail Options dialog box

Show Confirmation Notices This option deals with warning messages that are issued if a user tries to exit the Compose window without sending the composed mail message. If the Mail Compose window is closed, all the work performed on the e-mail message is lost. There is also another warning message that is given. When a user saves materials as a draft and then clicks the Send button, a warning message is delivered stating that the draft copy of the e-mail will be deleted. The draft copy is intended only as a temporary holding place for e-mail messages.

Keep Empty Mailboxes Mailer has a rather unpleasant feature and that is to delete mailboxes that are empty. The Keep Empty Mailboxes check box disables this feature.

Send Mail in MIME Format The Multipurpose Internet Mail Extension (MIME) format allows for a much richer set of text and characters as well as being the primary method of attaching files to an e-mail message. By default, Mailer sends and saves e-mail messages in MIME format. There is another format that mailer can use, the Sun Mail Tool format, but it's not very compatible with other e-mail systems. Very old Mailer applications and Sun applications might need this format. It is recommended that you not use the Sun Mail Tool format if you need to communicate with modern e-mail systems.

Outgoing Mail SMTP Server This option is used only in some rather rare occasions. By default, Mailer assumes that the IMAP server is the SMTP (Simple Mail Transfer Protocol) server. If your network e-mail system needs some custom settings for SMTP and POP (Post Office Protocol), use this text box for SMTP.

TIP POP is used to receive e-mail from a POP server. SMTP is used to send e-mail, either directly to a destination or to another SMTP server.

When I Reply to All This option is slightly tricky. The options Ignore Host Name in Address and Include Me describe how the To and Cc fields of Reply to All mail messages work. If you want your e-mail address `<username>@<host>` in the To and Cc portion of a Reply to All e-mail message, do not check both boxes. The Ignore Host Name in Address option applies only if the Include Me option is not selected. Treat the Following As is an option that removes the duplication of your e-mail address in Reply to All Messages. This option works only if Include Me is not set.

The Templates Command

Templates are useful for e-mail messages that are in a format that needs to be used again and again. For example, if an employee has a job that requires a weekly status report in a specific format, a template would come in handy. To create templates, choose the Templates command from the Options menu. The Templates Mail Options dialog box, shown in Figure 13.10, appears.

FIGURE 13.10

The Templates Mail Options dialog box

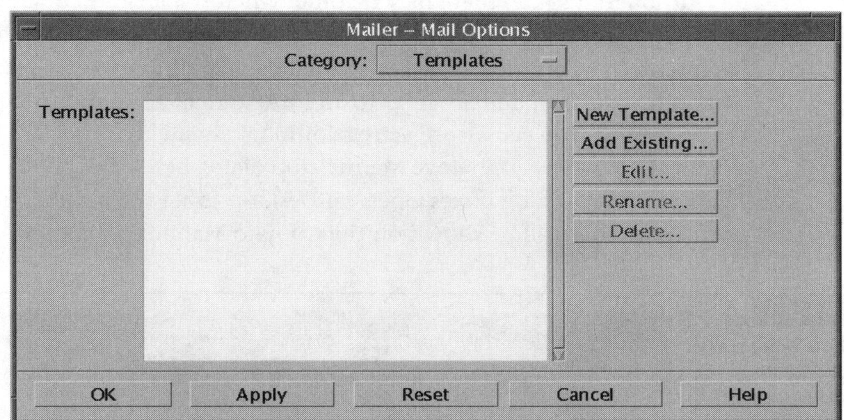

Click New Template to open a standard Compose window. From here, you can create a template message that includes recipients, text, and attachments. When you are finished, click Save As and save the message as a template. Templates are stored in the `$HOME/MailTemplates` directory.

When you close the Compose window, a warning message will appear telling you that your changes will be lost if the window is closed. As long as the template has been saved, this is not a problem. This is the default behavior of the Compose window and the message is harmless. To use the template, just select Template from the Compose menu in the main Mailer window.

TIP If you are rebuilding a workstation or transferring the e-mail system, make sure you copy the `$HOME/MailTemplates` directory to another system. Some companies also use company-wide templates.

Additional Commands

The message viewing area can also be customized, which will affect the Message Header list. Customization simply changes the height and width of the Message Header list. The option at the bottom of the screen, Abbreviated Header Will Not Include, is used only if the Abbreviated Headers option is selected. (Abbreviated Headers is a menu selection item on the View menu that is selected by default.) It defines what not to show if the header is abbreviated.

Although it's rare, there may be times when the location of an e-mail server needs to be changed. To do so, select the Move Menu Setup command from the Options menu on the Compose window. The dialog box allows you to change your e-mail server from a local e-mail server to an IMAP e-mail account by clicking the IMAP radio button. You can also specify additional e-mail accounts Mailer should check. Figure 13.11 shows the Move Menu Setup dialog box. Click the button labeled Keep Move & Copy Dialog Boxes Open on Desktop to set the number of recently opened mailboxes that will be shown on the Copy to Mailbox submenu.

FIGURE 13.11

The Move Menu Setup Mail Options dialog box

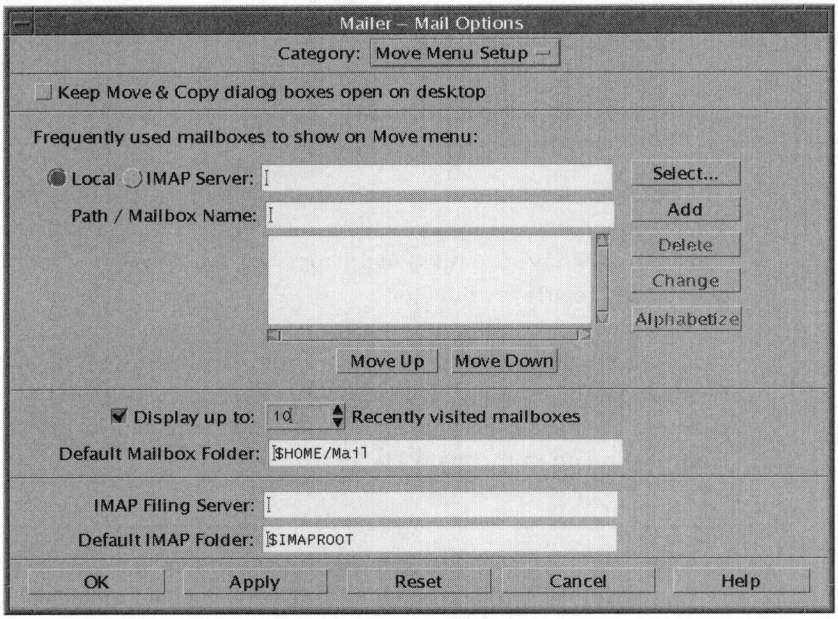

Mailer gives you the option to automatically send a vacation message response to all incoming e-mail messages. When you choose the Vacation Message command from the Options menu, the Vacation Message Mail Options dialog box appears (shown in Figure 13.12). There is an option, Interval between Replies to Repeat Senders, that limits the number of e-mail messages that are sent back to users. For example, some people might be required to send you a daily status report message. You could use this option when there is no need to reply to every status report message every day.

FIGURE 13.12

The Vacation Message Mail Options dialog box

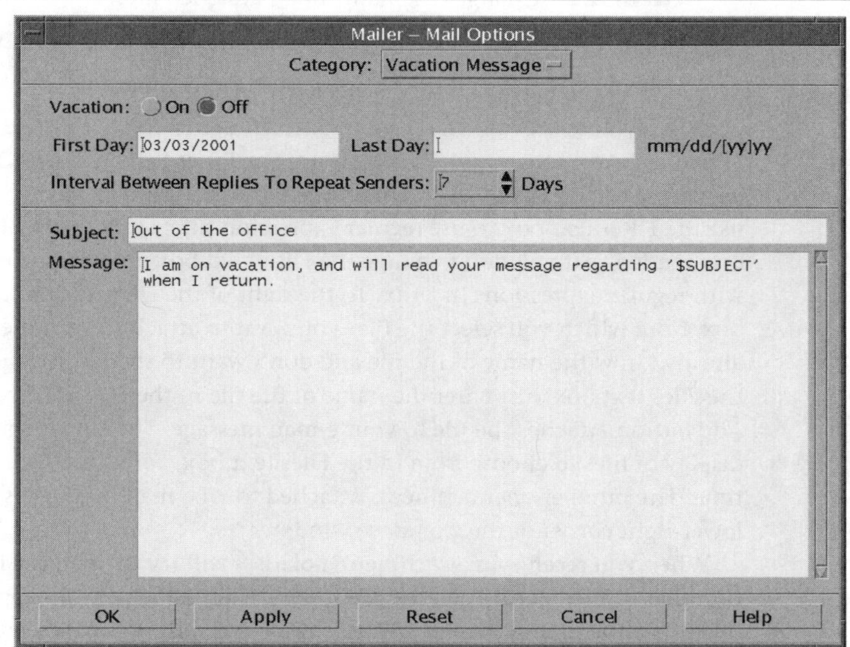

Attachments

The Mailer program can also add files to messages as attachments. Almost all modern e-mail programs will accept attachments. The lower portion of the Compose window contains the attachment list. Solaris uses a thumbnail icon of Mona Lisa to represent all image file attachments. To add an attachment, select the Add File command from the Attachments menu in the Compose window. The same menu shows up if you right-click anywhere in the lower half of the text window.

The Attachments menu has the following commands:

Add File Attaches a file to your e-mail message.

Save As Saves an attachment to your hard drive (used with incoming attachments).

Delete After selecting a file or files to attach to your message, use this menu item to delete accidentally included files. This does not delete files from your hard drive, just from the e-mail message.

Undelete Restores an attached file that was accidentally deleted from an e-mail message.

Rename Changes the name of an attached file.

Select All Selects all the files shown in the attachment list.

Show List Toggles the display of the attachment list.

When you select Add File from the Attachments menu, the Add Attachments dialog box (shown in Figure 13.13) appears. The Enter Path or Folder Name text box is used to select the directory in which the file you want to attach is located. You can use the Filter text box to use regular expression filters to locate a file. It's highly recommended that you don't change the Filter text box unless you are very comfortable with regular expressions in Unix. To the right of the Filter text box is the Files text box, from which you select the files you want to attach to your message. If you already know the name of the file and don't want to spend time browsing through the Files text box, just enter the name of the file in the Enter File Name text box. The Add button attaches the file to your e-mail message. The Update button refreshes the display of files to choose from in the Files text box. You can attach only one file at a time. The number of attachments attached to an e-mail message is shown on the lower-right corner of the Compose window.

When you receive an attachment, Solaris 8 will try to open the file with an application that can read and open the file type. If there is no desktop application that can open the attachment, Mailer will ask you if you want to save the attachment to the hard drive. If you don't want to view the attachment at this time, right-click its icon and select Save As. You can drag and drop icons used with attachments to other applications (such as File Manager, for example).

Mailer and the File Manager

The CDE environment supports drag-and-drop functionality with some applications. File Manager and Mailer can be used in coordination with each other to speed up simple tasks. One of the easiest tasks is to move e-mail attachments. If you receive an e-mail attachment and you have File Manager open, just drag the attachment's icon to the open window in File Manager and the file is moved automatically. This is a lot easier than choosing a series of menu items to transfer an attachment.

FIGURE 13.13

The Add Attachments dialog box

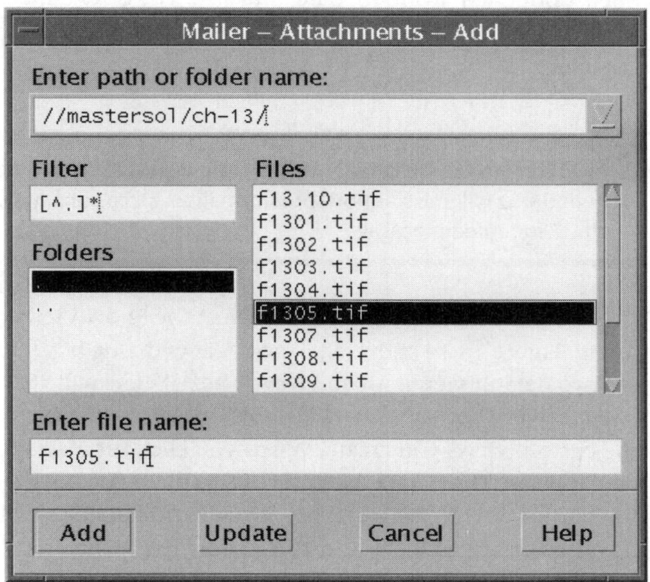

To send an attachment, just open File Manager to the directory in which the file resides and drag the file onto the attachment list within Mailer. Doing so will not remove the file from the directory; it just creates a copy and attaches it to an outgoing e-mail message.

The drag-and-drop function can be used between Mailer and other applications, too. The receiving application must understand what to do with the dragged file once it arrives. If a user drags a database file onto a graphics application, the graphics application will not understand what to do with the file and send up a warning window.

WARNING Some Internet service providers and companies limit the size of e-mail attachments. This is done to limit the amount of e-mail server resources used. Most e-mail systems also limit users' total mail capacity. If a user has a 10MB limit for e-mail messages and you send 12 messages, each with a 1MB attachment, you can accidentally disable the e-mail account. Always let the receiver know you will be sending an attachment.

Creating a Custom View

Some power e-mail users like to have a custom view of their e-mail messages. With a custom view, the power user can apply to the messages various filters such as open/unopened, from, to, date, and size. The only e-mail messages that will be displayed in the Mail Header List area are the ones that match the custom viewing criteria.

WARNING Be careful with custom views. There are times new messages will come in and you will miss important information. Occasionally switch back to the All view and check for unread messages.

To create or use a custom view, select the Show Views command from the Mailbox menu. Figure 13.14 shows the Show Views dialog box. On the top of the dialog box are two default views, All and New. The All view will show all of the messages that you receive. The New view will show only unread e-mail. The Custom Views area lists the custom views you create. When you click the New button, the View Search dialog box appears. There are two views of this dialog box, which you can access by clicking the button next to Search Type. It toggles the dialog box between Basic and Advanced. Figures 13.15 and 13.16 show the two views.

FIGURE 13.14
The Show Views dialog box

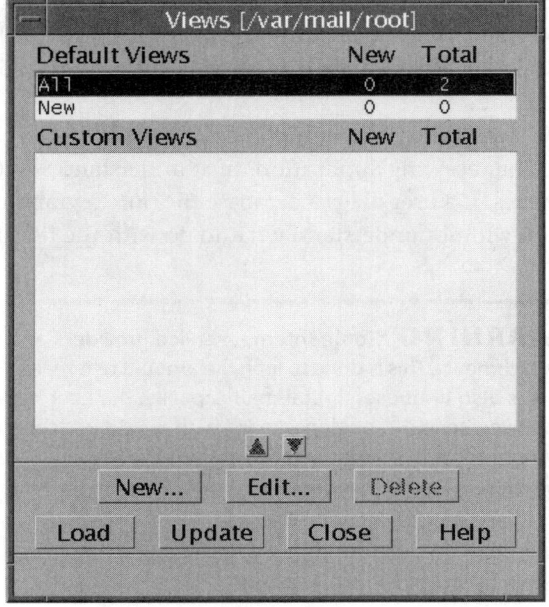

FIGURE 13.15

The View Search Basic dialog box

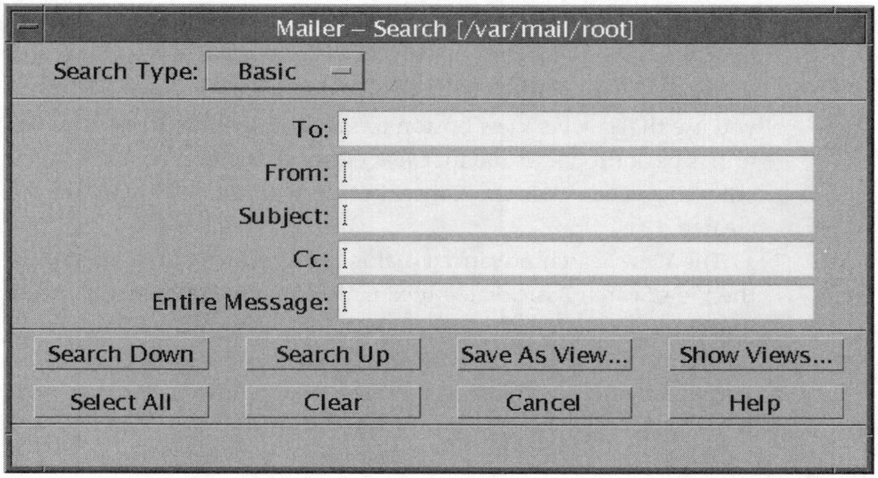

FIGURE 13.16

The View Search Advanced dialog box

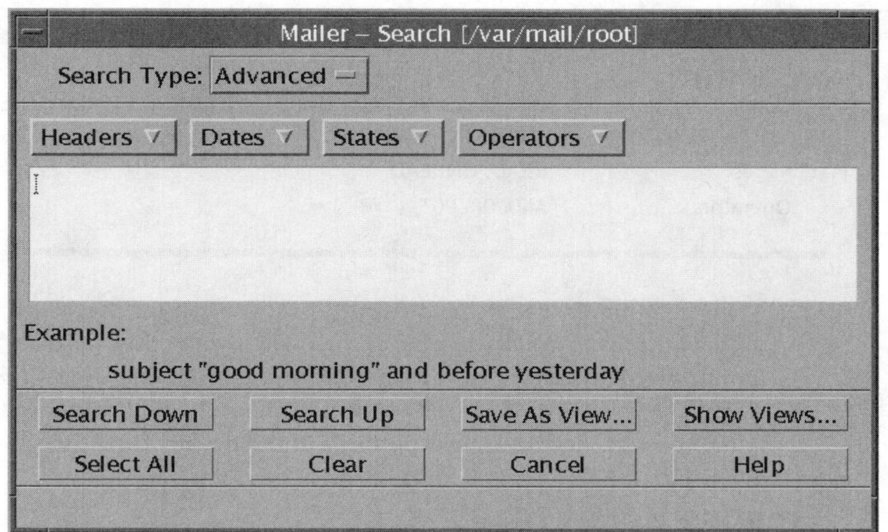

Both of these dialog boxes have two methods of operation. You can enter search criteria and search your current e-mail or you can save the search criteria as a view for repeated future use. You can use the Search Down and Search Up buttons to search the current set of e-mail messages. When a match is found, the message header is highlighted.

The View Search Basic dialog box is easy to use. It features five search text boxes: To, From, Subject, Cc, and Entire Message. Any text that is entered into these boxes is used as search criteria. The Entire Message text box is extremely useful for finding e-mail messages that have the same content. A basic search will not be saved unless you use the Save As View button to save the search criteria. The Show Views button brings back the Views menu. Clear clears all the text boxes. If you saved the search criteria, you can click the Cancel button without destroying the view you have created.

The View Search Advanced dialog box is more complex but more powerful than the View Search Basic dialog box. Unlike the five rather rigid text search boxes used in the View Search Basic dialog box, a logic keyword sentence with Boolean logic operators such as AND, OR, and NOT is used in the View Search Advanced dialog box. The search criteria offered in the View Search Advanced dialog box is listed in Table 13.1.

TABLE 13.1: ADVANCED SEARCH CRITERIA

Menu Item	Function
Header	TO, FROM, SUBJECT, CC, TEXT, BCC
Dates	BEFORE, SINCE, ON, DURING, TODAY, YESTERDAY, LASTWEEK, THISMONTH, NEXTMONTH
States	READ, UNREAD
Operators	AND, OR, NOT, ( )

As with the View Search Basic dialog box, you can use the Search Up and Search Down buttons to find the messages that match your criteria. An advanced search will not be saved unless you use the Save As View button. The Show Views button brings back the Show Views dialog box shown in Figure 13.14. If you saved the search criteria, you can click the Cancel button without destroying the view you have created.

Creating a New Mailbox

The Mailer program gives you the ability to create a new mailbox on your workstation. Most corporate networks have large-scale e-mail servers. They also tend to have policies that require the system administrator to set up an e-mail account on the server before the workstation portion of the account can be created. Remember, the Mailer is only a front-end GUI; there needs to be a valid e-mail account set up on the back end.

Calendar

Solaris comes with a desktop application named Calendar. Calendar is a utility created by Hewlett-Packard, IBM, Novell, and Sun Microsystems. It's similar to Microsoft's Schedule Plus. With Calendar, the user can save appointments and To Do lists.

Appointments have a start and finish time. The appointments are shown on all the Calendar views except the Year view. Appointment notification can be used in conjunction with e-mail, sounds, or a blinking screen. You can set your preference for how you wish to be reminded. To Do lists are basically lists of tasks that need to be completed. To Do lists don't show up on the Day, Week, Month, or Year views of Calendar. Rather, they are checklists of action items with dates and times; the action items can be checked off when they are completed. This Calendar application also has some advanced extra features, such as network calendar sharing, e-mail notification, and command-line utilities.

Starting Calendar

Use one of these methods to start Calendar:

- Click the Calendar icon on the front panel. The icon, shown in the following graphic, looks like the top sheet of a daytime appointment calendar.

- Start the Calendar Manager from a terminal or console window with the command `dtcm&`.
- Right-click the desktop to open the Workspace menu and select the Calendar command from the Applications submenu.

NOTE Any command that is typed into the terminal window or console window and ends with an ampersand runs in the background. If you type `dtcm&`, Calendar will open on the desktop and you can still use the terminal window or console window. Unfortunately, if you kill the terminal window or console window, the Calendar application also gets killed. You need to keep the terminal window or console window minimized or active to keep your calendar session alive or launch the application with the & symbol. This creates a graphical interface, which has its own session with the system.

You can only have one session of Calendar running at a time. If you click the Calendar icon on the front panel a second time, either a minimized Calendar session will be maximized or nothing will occur. The Calendar (or any other graphical application) will not be displayed over the Internet unless you have an X-terminal emulator such as an X server running on your local system.

Figure 13.17 shows the Calendar main window. The Calendar starts by default showing the username and host name on the top window title bar. Below the menu bar is a toolbar that has the icons for Appointments, To Do, Last Month, Today, Next Month, Day view, Week view, Month view, and Year view. You can set your preferences by choosing how you wish to view your Calendar. The lower part of the screen shows the Calendar view, where you see the actual appointments and To Do items.

FIGURE 13.17

The Calendar main window in Month view

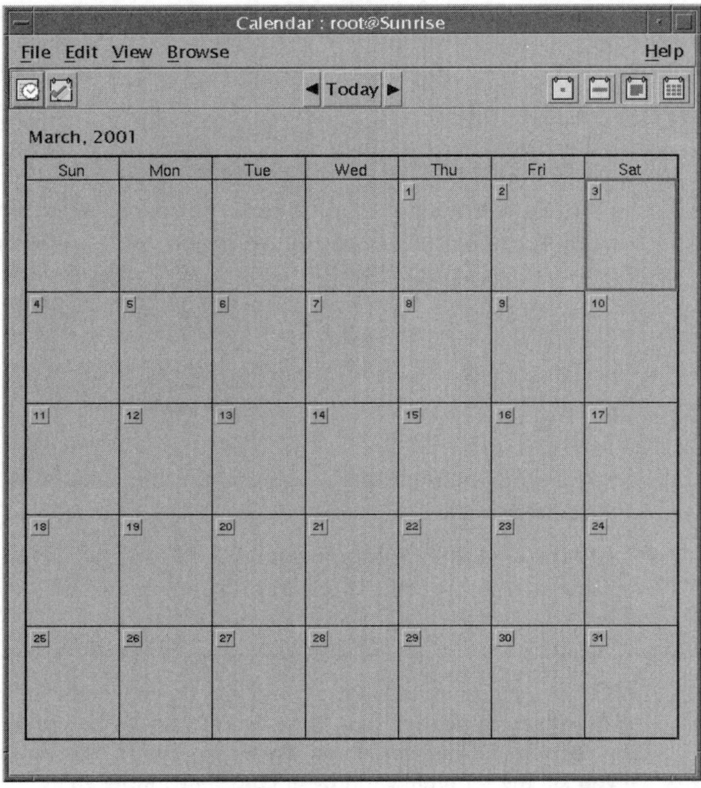

Changing Views

Calendar starts in Month view, as shown in Figure 13.17. The current day is highlighted with a thick red border. The Month view shows all the days in the month. Clicking a particular day brings up its Day view. From there you can change the view to Day view, Week view, Month view, or Year view. You can click on the Today icon to highlight the current day's box. The left and right arrows move to the next day, week, or month, depending on which view you're using. You can also move to another day by selecting Go To Date from the View menu and specifying a date in DD/MM/YY format.

The Day view has three miniature monthly calendars on the left side of the display panel and the current day's appointments and To Do items on the right side of the display. Figure 13.18 shows a Day view.

FIGURE 13.18

Calendar Day view

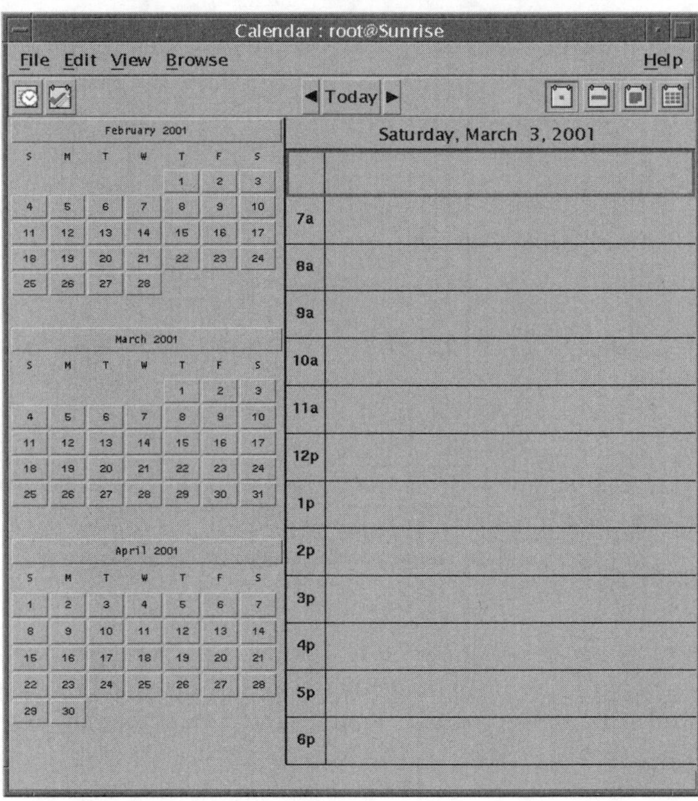

The Week view includes a week grid, with the days of the week along the top and the hours 7:00 A.M. to 7:00 P.M. along the right side. If a meeting is scheduled, the day is shaded in the week grid. On the weekly calendar, the Day boxes also have the current appointments shown. From here you can see your weekly meetings at a glance. Figure 13.19 shows the Week view.

FIGURE 13.19
Calendar Week view

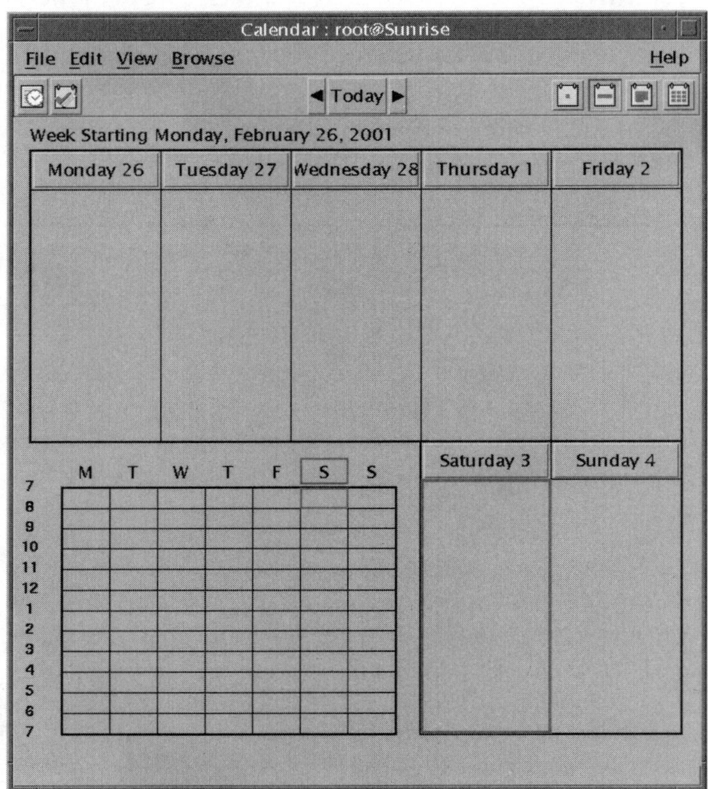

The Year view shows all 12 months of the year. This display does not show any appointments or To Do items. If you click a month title, Calendar will change views to a Month view of that month. Figure 13.20 shows the Year view.

FIGURE 13.20
The Calendar Year view

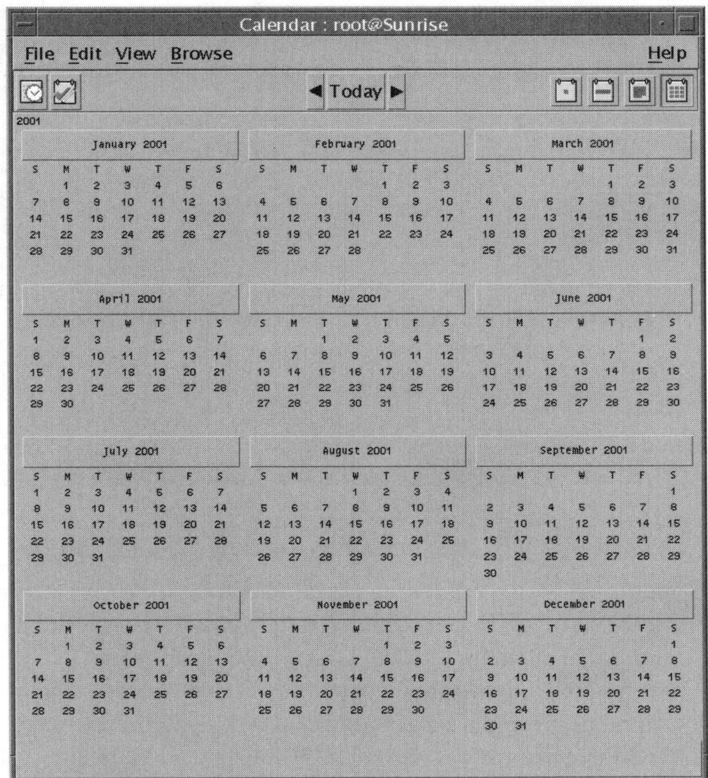

Appointments

To create an appointment, you need to open the Calendar Appointment Editor. The easiest way to access this dialog box is to click the Appointment icon on the far left side of the Calendar toolbar. Figure 13.21 shows the Appointment Editor. You can also double-click a specific day or time in any view of the Calendar except the Year view to open the Appointment Editor.

TIP The file called `callog.`<*username*>, located in `/var/spool/calendar`, is the data file with all of your appointments. You might want to copy this file to alternate locations to make sure you have a backup copy.

FIGURE 13.21

The Calendar's Appointment Editor dialog box

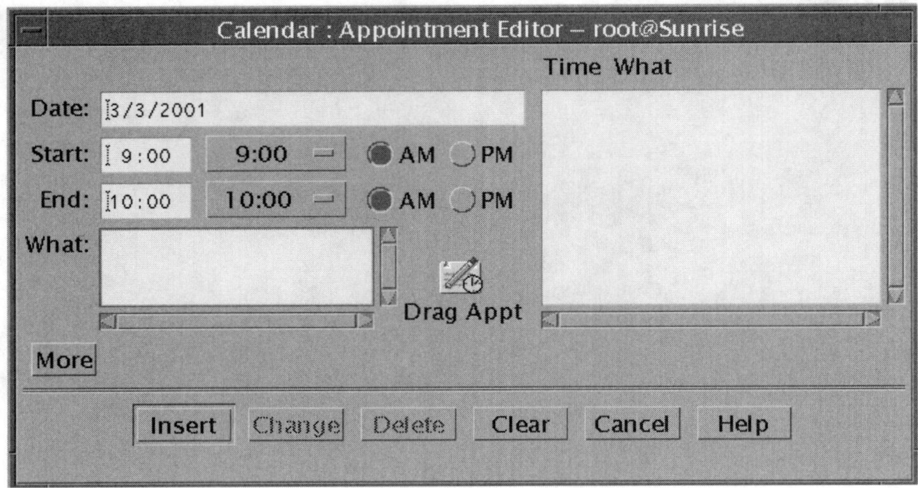

In the Appointment Editor, you can set the time for the current day's appointments or specify a different date. The default time for an appointment is 1 hour. This can be changed to a maximum of 24 hours. To save your changes, click the Insert button. If you click the Cancel button, the Appointment Editor will close, but you will not lose the appointments you inserted in an earlier session. Select the Appointment command from the Edit menu to make a new appointment or press the Ctrl+A keystroke to open the Appointment Editor.

WARNING It's rather awkward to use the Cancel button in Calendar to close windows. To make your changes stick, you usually have to click the Insert or Apply buttons and then click the Cancel button to close the window. If you make changes and click the Cancel button without clicking the Insert or Apply button, all your changes will be lost.

To Do Items

To create a To Do item, you must open the To Do Editor (shown in Figure 13.22). You can do so by using one of these methods:

- Click the To Do icon on the Calendar toolbar.

- Press the Ctrl+T keystroke.
- Select the To Do command from the Edit menu.

In the To Do Editor, enter the time, date, and a description of the task that is to be completed. If you have completed the action before the due date and time, check the Completed box. There is a toggle button, More/Less, that presents additional options. The additional options include Frequency and Reminder. The Frequency option specifies whether the To Do item you're creating is continuous. For example, a user could specify "Finish Weekly Report" and make it an action item that repeats every Friday at 5:00 P.M. The Reminder section gives you the option of having Calendar send an e-mail notifying you that a due date and time for a To Do item is approaching. To view your current To Do list, select the To Do command from the View menu.

FIGURE 13.22

The To Do Editor

Replicating Meetings

There are four different ways users can be notified of an appointment. The system can beep (on workstations only), flash the screen, display a pop-up window, or send one or more people a mail message. These warning functions are chosen in the Appointment Editor when you click the More button to display additional functionality. Figure 13.23 shows the More/Less toggle button and the options that are available when it is clicked to More.

FIGURE 13.23

The Appointment Editor with More selected

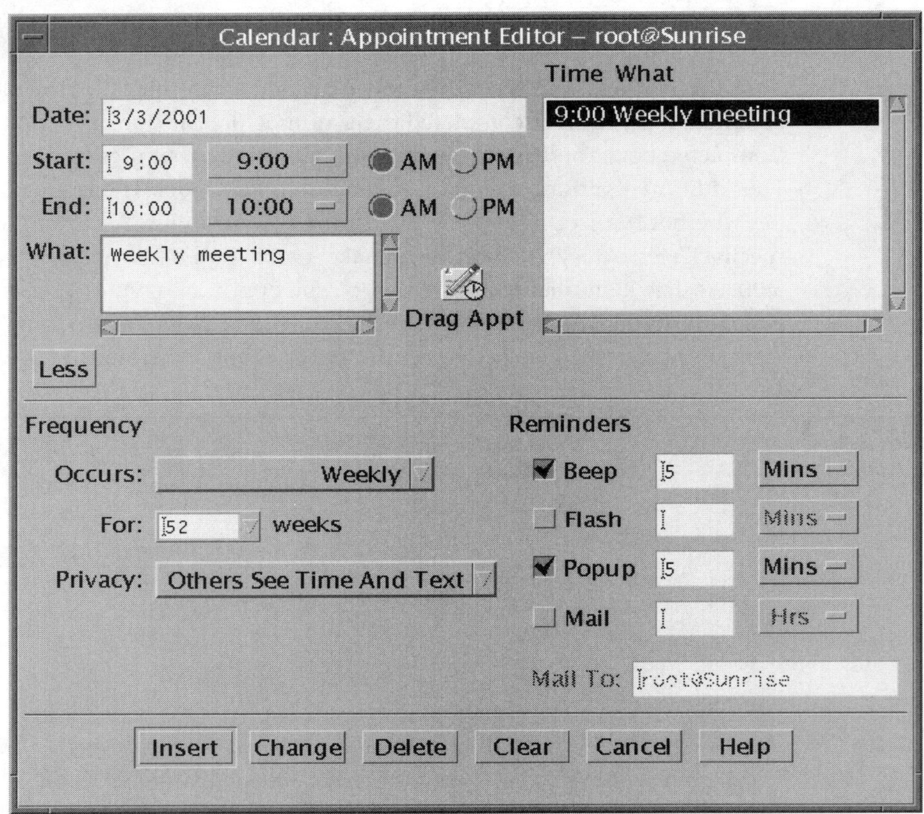

You can also have an appointment for a meeting replicate itself. For example, if you have a morning meeting each Monday for a year, the meeting can be specified as recurring. Open up the Appointment Editor to a meeting either by creating a new appointment or changing an existing appointment.

NOTE When you select the More button inside the Appointment Editor, more options are displayed in the window and the button changes to the Less button. When you select Less, the advanced portion of the window disappears and the More button is displayed.

To schedule a meeting as recurring, do this:

1. Toggle the More/Less button so that the button reads Less.

2. In the drop-down box labeled Occurs in the Frequency section, select Weekly.
3. Type in the number of weeks the meeting should occur.
4. Click the Change button to apply your selection.

Remember to click the Cancel button to close the Appointment Editor window. This is somewhat counterintuitive to Windows users who are familiar with Microsoft's OK/Cancel button combination. Just make sure you insert your changes, then click Cancel to close the window.

Searching the Calendar

You can search through your appointments with a keyword search. Select the Find command from the Calendar's View menu or use the Ctrl+F keystroke to open the Find dialog box (shown in Figure 13.24). From here, you can specify a phrase or word to search for. The default behavior of the Find feature is to search the past and future six months of your calendar. You can narrow the search down to a specific range of days. The results of the search are displayed in the Find window. This window will display numerous appointments that match the word search. Select the appointment you think is the one you are looking for and then click the Show Appointment button to highlight the appointment on your current Calendar view (Day view, Week view, or Month view only). To see details or change the appointment, double-click it.

FIGURE 13.24

The Calendar's Find dialog box

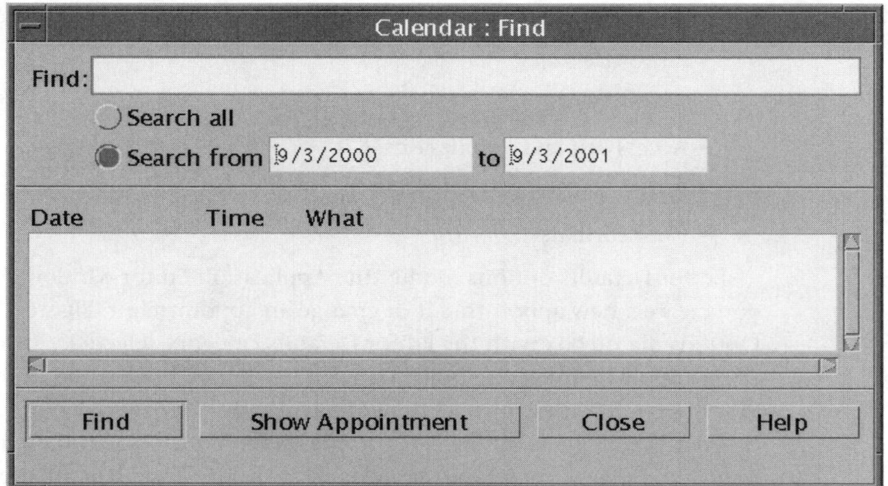

To see a list of all your current appointments, select the Appointment List command from the View menu in the Calendar main window. Your appointments will be displayed in chronological order by date and time. The appointments listed will be shown by the view you have open (Day, Week, or Month) at the moment.

Calendar has an option to print various pages and lists to your default printer. (Please refer to Chapter 10 for coverage of printer setup issues.) The Print dialog box displays various things to print, such as Day, Week, Month, Year, Appointment list, and To Do list. The user can also specify the number of copies to print, the range of days to print, and additional printer commands. The print job can be saved as a PostScript print job. A PostScript file has the `.ps` filename extension on it.

TIP To print a PostScript file, you need a PostScript-enabled printer. Solaris 8 has an application named Imagetool. This tool can view and print PostScript images, provided the printer you print to is set up to handle PostScript format.

Customizing the Calendar

Calendar users can change a wide variety of default settings using the Options dialog box. Open this dialog box by choosing the Options command from the File menu or by pressing the Ctrl+I keystroke. There are five categories of options that can be set here (they can be accessed from the Category menu at the top of the Options dialog box):

- Editor Defaults
- Display Settings
- Access List and Permissions
- Printer Settings
- Date Formats

Editor Defaults options modify the Application Editor window that pops up when you create a new appointment or change an appointment. Figure 13.25 shows the Options dialog box with the Editor Defaults category selected. The default duration of an appointment is one hour. This can be changed to a value from 15 minutes to 90 minutes. The default start time of an appointment is 9:00 A.M. There is a drop-down box that gives the user 15-minute increment slots for changing an appointment time. There are four different types of notifications for an appointment: Beep, Flash, Popup, Mail. With Mail, the *<username>@<host>* can be specified. If your workstation supports the Federated Naming System (FNS), you can use nicknames instead of `<username>@<host>`.

FIGURE 13.25

The Calendar Options dialog box showing the Editor Defaults options

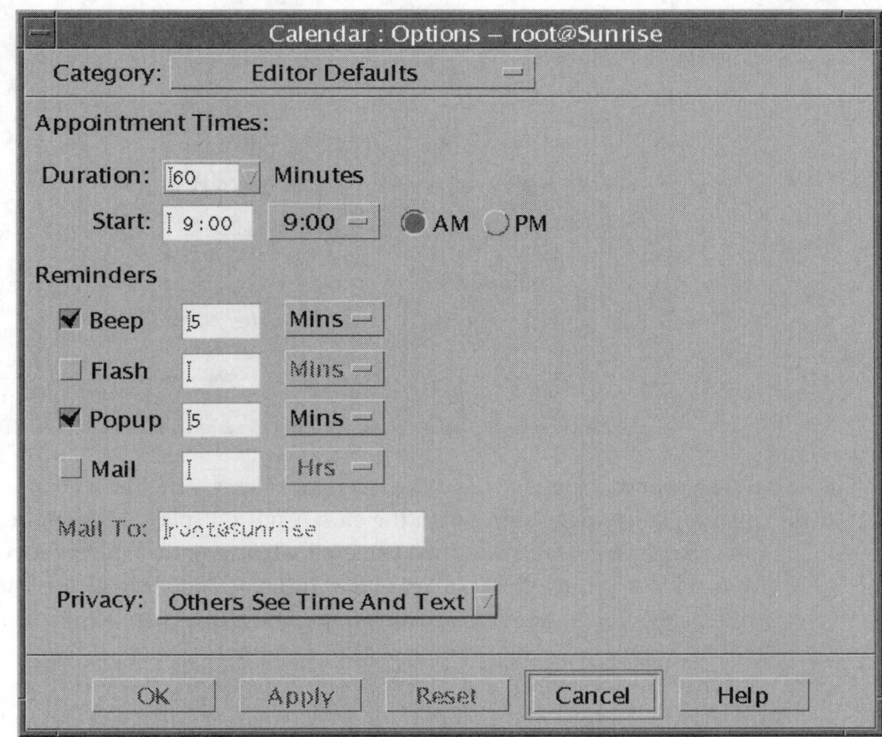

The final parameter that can be changed is the Privacy setting. This option is used primarily for group meetings. Privacy is also very useful for a manager who needs to give file-viewing permission to an administrative assistant. This option does not change edit and delete permissions; it only provides read access to others so that they can see your schedule. The Privacy setting options are as follows:

- Others See Time and Text
- Others See Time Only
- Others See Nothing

The Display Settings category deals mostly with how the viewable area of Calendar is seen by default. Figure 13.26 shows the Options dialog box with the Display Settings category selected.

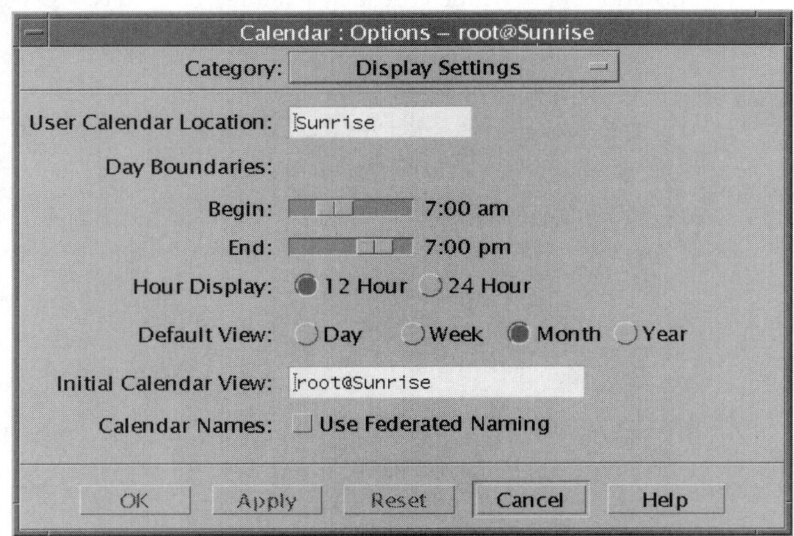

FIGURE 13.26

The Calendar Options dialog box showing the Display Settings options

The user can specify where the calendar is kept. The start and end times for meetings can be changed along with the clock's hour display (12 Hour or 24 Hour). You can change the default view of a calendar when you first start the application from Month view to Day, Week, or Year view. Initial Calendar View lets the user select which calendar is shown first. Finally, the FNS names can be selected in this window. FNS names are basically nicknames for longer names such as *<user>@<host>*.

With the Access List and Permissions options, you can give other users View, Insert, and Change permission to your calendar. Figure 13.27 shows the Options window with the Access List and Permissions category selected.

The User Name text box is where you identify who can have access to your calendar. You have the option to set an appointment time with the following privacy options: Others See Time and Text, Others See Time Only, and Others See Nothing. Table 13.2 shows the relationship between the type of appointment you make and the permissions others can have with viewing that appointment.

TABLE 13.2: ACCESS RIGHTS AND PERMISSIONS

Type of Appointment	View Permissions
Public	Others See Time and Text
Semiprivate	Others See Time Only
Private	Others See Nothing

FIGURE 13.27

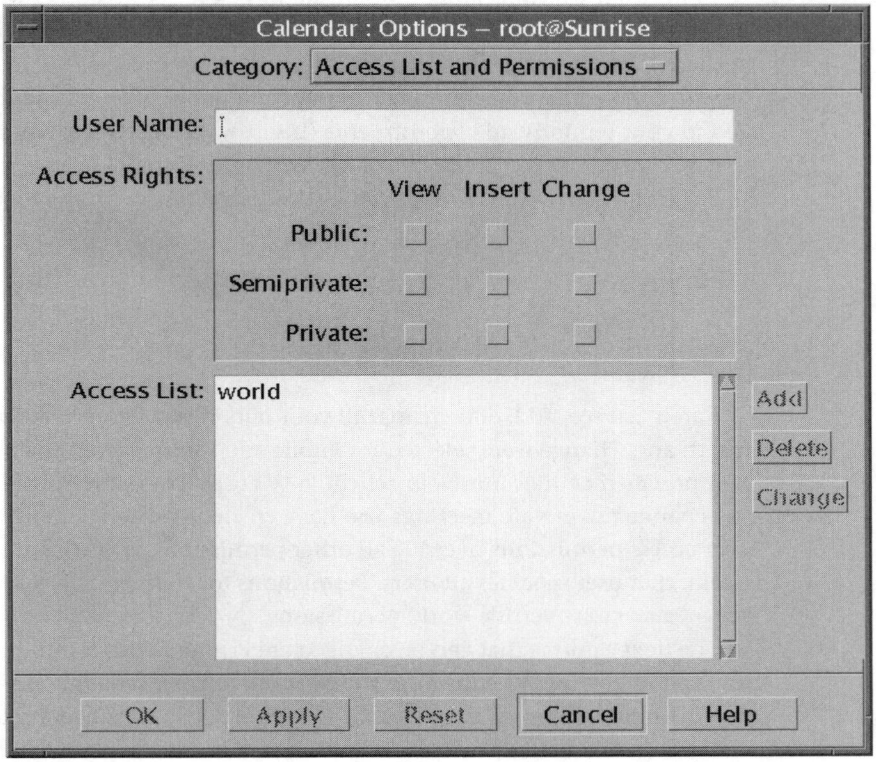

The Calendar Options dialog box showing the Access List and Permissions options

There are some appointments you make that are assigned the Public access right. Public means others can see the time and text associated with the meetings if they browse your calendar. You can also create Semiprivate appointments that allow other users to see the time of the meeting but not the accompanying text. You can also specify appointments for which nobody can see the time and text in the calendar. You can fine-tune the permissions other users have to your appointments. Suppose you want to give a user permission to view and insert meetings but you don't want that user to see or change your private meetings. With the Access Rights dialog box, you can define permissions further.

For example, let's assume that John has the following access rights:

	View	Insert	Change
Public	x	x	
Semiprivate	x		
Private			

John could see your public appointments (View permission) and insert his meetings into your schedule (Insert permission). He cannot alter the appointments you created (Change permission was not checked). John can see the times of your semiprivate appointments (semiprivate appointments show only the time), but he cannot add to your semiprivate appointments (Insert was not selected), nor can he change the appointments you created (Change was not selected).

Suppose you have an administrative assistant, Karen, with the following permissions:

	View	Insert	Change
Public	x	x	x
Semiprivate	x	x	x
Private	x	x	

Karen can see, add, and change all your public and semiprivate meetings (View, Insert, and Change were selected for Public and Semiprivate). She can view and insert new private meetings into your schedule (View and Insert were selected), but she cannot change the private meetings you have created yourself (Change was not selected). User access permissions override all other permissions. If you create a user named world, that user specifies all users. Permissions for individually named users (such as `karen@sun.com`) override world permissions.

The next options that can be changed are Printer Settings options. These permissions allow the user to customize the printout of their schedule. Figure 13.28 shows the Calendar Options window with the Printer Settings category selected.

The first text box, Printer, must contain the name of your default print command or default printer. In most cases, the `lp` command will be sufficient. In the Options text box, you can specify printer options that correspond to the print command. For example, the `lp` command has an option `-o nofilebreak` to suppress for feed signals between multiple files. You can enter **`-o nofilebreak`** in the Options text box to give this argument to your print command. Units refers to how many calendar pages you want to print. If you select 3 units, you will print the current week and the next two weeks (you can also print days or months). Copies refers to the number of printed copies. There are three check boxes at the bottom of the dialog box:

- Show Time and Text Appts
- Show Time Only Appts
- Show Nothing Appts

These listings refer to Public, Semiprivate, and Private appointments. The use of these three check boxes will limit the type of meeting list that will be printed out.

You can use the Calendar Date Format category of the Options dialog box to change the MM/DD/YYYY format.

FIGURE 13.28

The Calendar Options dialog box showing the Printer Settings options

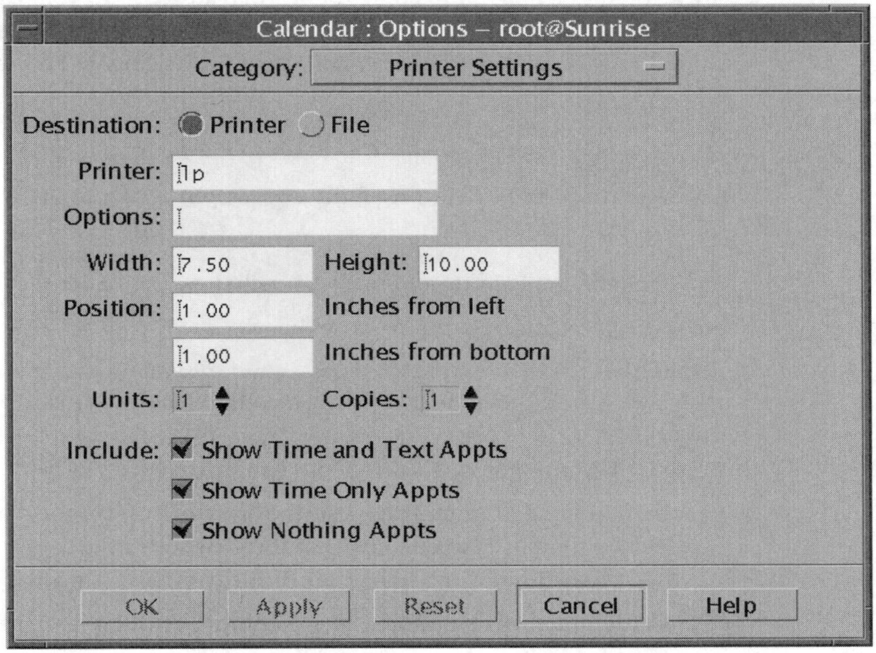

Group Meetings

One of Calendar's advanced features is the ability to view calendars from other workstations and users. To browse other people's calendars, select the Show Other Calendar command from the Browse menu on the main Calendar window. The Show Other Calendar dialog box, shown in Figure 13.29, appears. From here you can select the `<username>@<host> calendar files` that you want to browse. When you make a selection of another person's calendar, the Calendar program will append the name of the other user's calendar to the end of your Browse menu. You can then select the other user's calendars for blocks of time that are free.

FIGURE 13.29

The Show Other Calendar dialog box

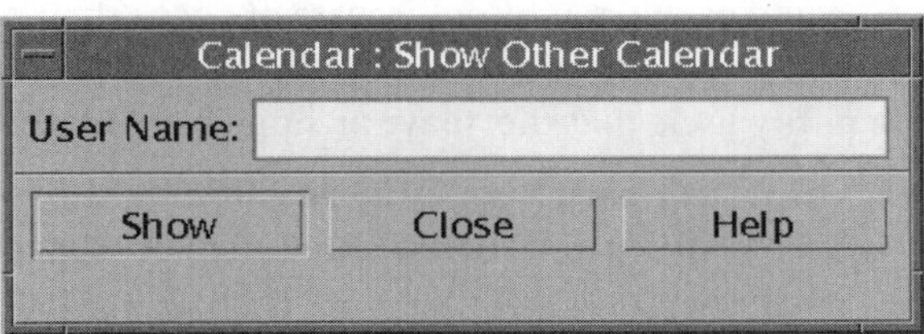

By default, Calendar allows only the world read access to your calendar. This option can be changed to let other users edit and delete items on your calendar.

To delete another user's calendar from your Browse menu, do the following:

1. Select Browse from the main menu.
2. Then choose the Compare Calendars menu item.
3. Select the Edit List button on the upper-right corner of the window.
4. Click the user's filename and then click the Remove Name button.
5. Click the Apply button to make your changes permanent.
6. Click the Cancel button to close the window.

In addition to only viewing calendars, you can set up group meetings. All of the participants have to give the host of the meeting View and Create permission on their calendars.

To set up a group meeting, do the following:

1. Highlight one or more entries on the Browse list from the main menu. This will create a composite calendar within the view section of the Calendar window. All users' busy times will be dark gray in the composite calendar.
2. Highlight an unshaded area of the composite calendar. Unshaded areas represent a free time section for all participants.
3. Click the Schedule button to open the Group Appointment Editor and make your group appointment.
4. Change the date, time, and mail options only if you need to.
5. After making the changes needed, click the Insert button and then the Cancel button.

Combining Calendar and Mail

The Calendar application and the Mailer application can be used in conjunction with each another. You can drag and drop group appointments from Calendar to Mailer and vice versa. This is a convenient way to notify other users of an appointment time—some people might not update or check their calendars on a regular basis, so it's a good reminder.

To notify users that they have an appointment, follow these steps:

1. Open the Group Appointment Editor by choosing Compare Calendars from the Browse menu and then clicking the Edit List button on the Compare Calendars screen.

2. Click the Mail button to mail an appointment attachment to selected users automatically.

3. Click Deliver in the Compose window on the Main menu.

When the users receive appointments, it's up to them to drag the appointment icon onto their calendars to make an appointment. This is necessary to keep true editing control with the original calendar's owner.

There is also an option you can use to send an e-mail message to another user and add the calendar meeting time attachment to the end of the message. This is useful if you have a lengthy proposal and you want to add a calendar attachment on the end of the proposal. The automatic mailing option described earlier sends only a calendar attachment. You cannot add extra text to the information.

To send an e-mail message and add a meeting time attachment, follow these steps:

1. Open both the Calendar and Mailer applications.

2. Open the Mailer's Compose window.

3. Drag the Drag Appt icon (refer back to Figure 13.23) from the Appointment Editor onto the Mailer's attachment list window; this will create a text attachment describing the group meeting.

4. Type all the addresses of the participants in the To text box to create a regular e-mail message.

5. Send the e-mail message.

You can also use the drag-and-drop feature to place the same text attachments into File Manager. This will place a text file into a directory for future use. When you need to schedule an appointment, just open File Manager and then drag the calendar appointment onto an e-mail attachment list window. Basically, File Manager is being used as a holding location for the calendar appointments.

There is one other method of sending calendar appointments from Mailer to Calendar. This method is completely text based and relatively cryptic. To add a calendar appointment from Mailer to Calendar, add the following lines to an e-mail message:

```
[tab]** Calendar Appointment **
[blank line]
[tab]Date:[tab]<mm/dd/yyyy>
[tab]Start:[tab]<hh:mm am>
[tab]End:[tab]<hh:mm pm>
[tab]What:[tab]<description line 1>
[tab][tab]<description line 2>
```

For example, the following hypothetical meeting is scheduled:

```
** Calendar Appointment **

 Date: 12/24/2001
 Start: 10:00 am
 End: 11:00 am
 What: Termination Meeting
  Manager and Employee Confidential
```

Now mail a message with this inside it. When the e-mail message arrives, the recipient can drag the entire e-mail message onto their Calendar application. The Calendar must be open at the time the message is dragged and dropped. Calendar will search through your e-mail for this text code so it can update your calendar at the same time. When it finds this text code in a message, it will update your Calendar to match the receiver's calendar.

This code section is not easy to read or create; the format has to be exact. There is one place where this comes in very handy. If you create a shell script that automatically mails out e-mail messages, include the calendar appointment text in the e-mail. You can then create a maintenance calendar on your desktop for your servers. If an e-mail comes in from one of your server's maintenance shell scripts and you decide to take action on the item, just drag and drop the mail message onto your calendar. This will automatically make a maintenance window visible on your calendar. Other system administrators and power users who browse your calendar can now see that you are going to work on the server performing some system maintenance. To add even more power, combine the calendar appointment text with some of Calendar's command-line options to automatically send out the e-mail message to everyone.

Calendar and Mailer have a lot more power and functionality than initially meets the eye.

Command-Line Utilities

The Calendar application is somewhat unique among calendar programs on other platforms in that it has several command-line utilities that can be run with shell scripts. These utilities can add, modify, display, and delete appointments on your schedule. If you use these shell scripts in conjunction with high-end text manipulation tools such as `sed` and `awk`, you can create very powerful calendar tools. You can also run these commands from a Telnet window or a command window.

One powerful use of these command-line utilities is that you can combine them with server maintenance. If you have a hard drive that has a constantly growing database, you can schedule maintenance times automatically on your calendar every time the hard drive's capacity reaches 95 percent. You could also create a shell script that monitors server assets other than just the hard drive. (The creation of shell scripts that monitor a server is an advanced topic and beyond the scope of this book.)

Table 13.3 shows the various command-line utilities and their general functions.

TABLE 13.3: CALENDAR COMMAND-LINE UTILITIES

Command	General Function
`sdtcm_admin`	Used to create and administer calendars.
`sdtcm_convert`	Used to prune data or convert data from older versions of Calendar. Solaris 8 comes with Calendar 4. Previous versions of Solaris came with Calendar 3.
`dtcm_editor`	Used to create appointments.
`dtcm_lookup`	Used to look up calendar appointments.
`dtcm_insert`	Used to create calendar appointments.
`dtcm_delete`	Used to remove calendar appointments.

The command `sdtcm_admin` is used to create and administer calendars. Among the various command-line arguments for `sdtcm_admin` are the following:

-a option This option adds a new calendar to a system and will automatically create *<username>@<host>*.

-c option This option adds a named calendar to a system (specify *<username>@<host>*).

-d option This option deletes a calendar from the system (the default is remove *<yourname>@<host>*).

-h option This option list calendars on other hosts.

-l option This option list calendars in a single column.

The command `sdtcm_convert` is used to prune data or convert data from older versions of Calendar. Solaris 8 comes with Calendar 4; OpenWindows comes with a slightly different version of Calendar, Calendar 3. On the rather rare chance that you will need to convert two different versions of calendar, `sctcm_convert` has been included in this text. To perform a conversion, it's a good idea to look up the `sdtcm_convert` man page.

The command `dtcm_editor` is not really a true command-line utility. It does bring up an appointment editor that is similar to the Appointment Editor but tends to be slightly more limited in functionality (see Figure 13.30). The Date text box shows the current date by default and can be changed to show another date. The What text box is used to give a text description of the appointment. The Frequency section is used to indicate if an appointment is reoccurring and how long an appointment will continue. Click the Save button to apply your changes.

FIGURE 13.30

The `dtcm_editor` *for setting Calendar appointments*

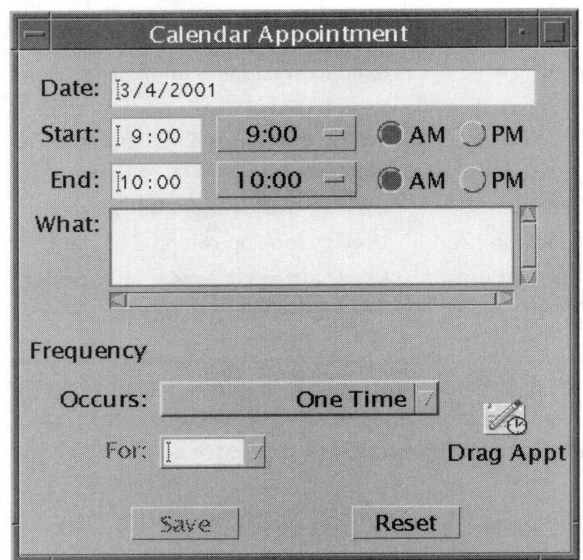

The following arguments are used most commonly with `dtcm_editor` when setting appointments:

-v option Specifies the version of data (3 indicates OpenWindows Calendar, 4 indicates Extensible Data Format).

-c option Specifies a locale (`ja`, `us`, and so on).

-s option Removes appointments before a specific date.

-d option Specifies a save directory. Calendar's data is saved in a file called `callog.`*<username>* (in the default directory `/var/spool/calendar`).

The Drag Appt button is used to drag and drop an appointment onto the Mailer and File Manager applications. To use this button with Mailer, first have the Mailer application running. Open a Compose e-mail window and type in the recipient's e-mail name. Add some text to the body of the e-mail (if desired). Now drag the icon onto the Attachment List section of the Compose window.

The commands dtcm_lookup, dtcm_delete, and dtcm_insert are extremely useful commands. They provide a method for looking up and changing your appointments inside a terminal window or console window. This function comes in handy if you need to check your appointments and can't open a GUI interface, such as if you were in a Telnet session connected over a slow modem. The command dtcm_lookup shows the current date and all appointments within the date are shown by default. Figure 13.31 shows the output from the command dtcm_lookup.

FIGURE 13.31

The output for the dtcm_lookup *command*

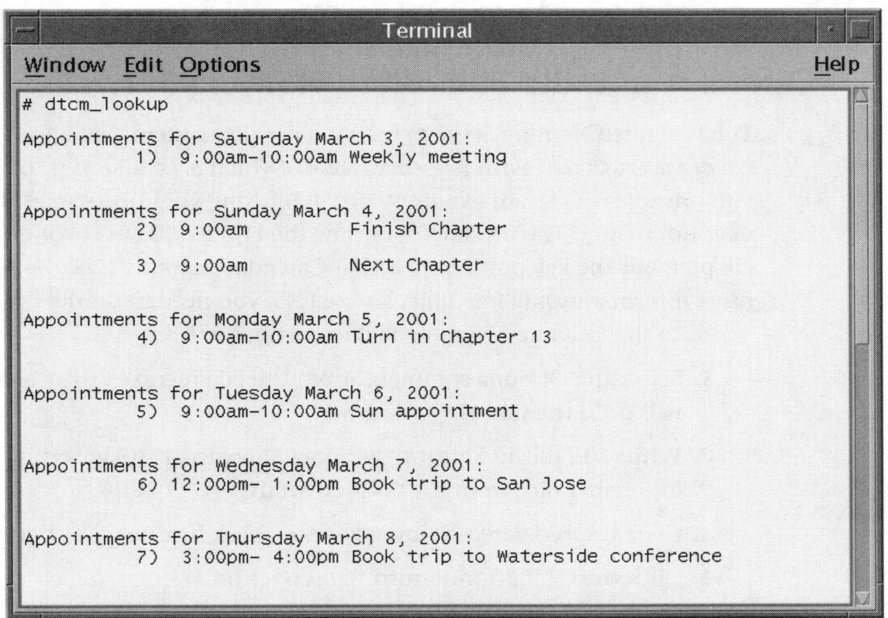

Terminal
Window Edit Options Help
dtcm_lookup
Appointments for Saturday March 3, 2001:
1) 9:00am-10:00am Weekly meeting
Appointments for Sunday March 4, 2001:
2) 9:00am Finish Chapter
3) 9:00am Next Chapter
Appointments for Monday March 5, 2001:
4) 9:00am-10:00am Turn in Chapter 13
Appointments for Tuesday March 6, 2001:
5) 9:00am-10:00am Sun appointment
Appointments for Wednesday March 7, 2001:
6) 12:00pm- 1:00pm Book trip to San Jose
Appointments for Thursday March 8, 2001:
7) 3:00pm- 4:00pm Book trip to Waterside conference

The following arguments are used most commonly with dtcm_lookup:

-c option Returns the name of the Calendar

-d option Returns the date of the Calendar

-v option Sets the view (Day, Week, Month)

The commands dtcm_insert and dtcm_delete are used in the same context as dtcm_lookup. These commands allow the user to add and remove appointments from the command line.

For the `dtcm_delete` command, the most significant option is the `-d` option, which specifies a date to delete from the calendar. The following arguments are used most commonly with `dtcm_insert`:

-d option Sets the date of appointment

-e option Shows appointment end time (HH:MMam or HH:MMpm)

-s option Shows appointment start time (HH:MMam or HH:MMpm)

-w option Adds text that describes the appointment. This is the same text that is found in the What text box.

Calendar and the Federated Naming Service

The Federated Naming Service (FNS) is a naming system that allows you to replace *<username>@<host>* with just *<username>* (which is an alias type of name that allows you privacy to a certain extent by not publishing your hostname). The host location does not matter. The mechanics of how the FNS works are beyond the scope of this chapter, but the key point here is that Calendar supports FNS (see AnswerBook2 for more information). Before you can use FNS, you need to set the `useFNS` resource.

To set the Federated Naming Service to on, do this:

1. Select the Options command from the File menu in the Calendar program. You will be in the Category window.
2. While still in the Category window, show the Display Settings options by selecting that choice from the drop-down list.
3. Click the Federated Naming Service check box near the bottom of the window.
4. Click the OK button to turn the service on.

Other calendar users can use your FNS name or they can still use your *<username>@<host>* name.

TIP One key point: Other users may not have registered their FNS names. Calendar has no search or lookup feature. You need to talk with other calendar users to get their calendar names. For example, one user's calendar name could be jsmith and another's could be jkaren@sun.com. The administrators of your site should establish conventions for naming calendars.

If you change your username or host name, make sure you update your FNS name. This can be done inside the Calendar Options dialog box with the Display Settings category selected. There is a text box labeled Calendar Location. After you click the OK button, Calendar will automatically try to register your username and host location with the FNS server. Calendar requires that the system restart before the changes can take effect. If the other calendar users in your area use FNS, they will not need to be notified of your new host's name or location.

Summary

This chapter covered Mailer and Calendar, two powerful tools that come with Solaris 8 to help you with your work.

Mailer supports a wide range of mail features including attached files, templates, draft copies, and drag-and-drop functionality. You can also use attachments with Mailer, and it includes basic and advanced e-mail search tools.

This chapter also covered Calendar, which is another desktop application that comes with the CDE. It supports two main notification features: appointments and To Do lists. Appointments are reminders to yourself to go to meetings, turn in reports, and perform other similar office tasks. Appointments can also be managed in a group environment. To Do lists are like agenda lists with time limits.

One of the most important features of Mailer and Calendar is that they support drag-and-drop functionality and so they can be used together. For example, if you have a group meeting in Calendar, you can drag the meeting into Mailer and Mailer will automatically send the meeting information via e-mail to all the participants.

CHAPTER 14

Networking and the Internet

FEATURING:

Internetworking overview 560

DNS and the Internet 565

The Internet and the World Wide Web 567

Browsers 573

Electronic mail 579

The Apache Web server 587

Solaris is built from the ground up to support connections to the Internet. As communications technology rapidly improves on a global level, the Internet has become a major force in information technology, networking, and daily life. Solaris comes with domain support, Internet naming conventions, tools like the Netscape browser to view content, and a variety of FTP utilities for transferring files.

Solaris is widely used in Internet deployments, and this is one of Sun's primary focuses. Many of the world's largest Web sites run on Sun Solaris, and this chapter gives a brief overview of the Apache Web server, which is part of the standard distribution for Solaris 8. Automating Web servers with CGI scripts is also discussed in this chapter, as are Usenet groups, electronic mail, and the `pine` utility.

Internetworking Overview

An *internetwork* is a large collection of individual networks that are connected by intermediate network devices. It functions as a single large network. An *intranet* is a network that resides within an organization, connecting computers internally but restricting access to their information to in-house users. Although similar to a LAN, intranets are based on Internet technology. They provide services such as databases, e-mail, and Web pages to limited users in the group. The beauty of intranets is that they are configured to connect different types of systems and computers via their IP addresses, much as the Internet does. Intranets take the technology one step further, however.

While the Internet uses one common protocol suite, an intranet can be configured to use a number of different protocols, such as Internet Protocol (IP), AppleTalk, DECnet, IPX, Extensible Name Service (XNS), or others that have been developed more recently. To communicate across networks that use different protocols, you can set up special gateways in remote sites. The gateways allow you to tunnel or encapsulate the protocols as IP packets so they can be used on the public network. More and more vendors with proprietary networking protocols like AppleTalk (Apple) and IPX (Novell) are supporting them as legacy protocols and adopting and recommending TCP/IP in their place.

An intranet can work in tandem with the Internet and still keep privileged information secure within a site. A TCP/IP network that contains an internal intranet component and an external connection to the Internet (which clients or vendors can access) is called an *extranet*.

Implementing a functional internetwork has its challenges. Because the speed of different networks and their connections varies, bandwidth issues often require a precise choreography of services, media, configurations, performance, and security. One of the major concerns is flexibility so that expansion with new applications and services can take place without undue strain on the internetwork. Because individual users and organizations have come to depend on ready, consistent access to network resources, reliability must be maintained at all costs. Internetwork management must provide both troubleshooting capabilities and centralized support in a rapidly growing environment. It is truly a daunting task. However, it is one that is being accomplished at an astonishing pace.

Network Communications

There are three basic types of network configurations:

- Broadcast network
- Token Ring network
- Point-to-point network

The Internet is based on point-to-point technology. It is also the largest wide area network (WAN) in existence. The Internet's WAN is built largely over dedicated data lines leased from a telephone company. Radio or satellites transmit the data over this large-scale network.

A local area network (LAN) uses a gateway to connect to a (WAN). *Gateway* is a common term that is used to describe a computer or other special device with multiple network connections. Its purpose is to convert the data traffic from the format used on a LAN to that of a WAN. In other words, the data is translated into a format that the communications equipment can read. Once the data reaches its destination, another gateway converts it to the format appropriate for the receiving network. The end user is rarely aware of how the data is transformed and how the transformation is carried out.

The most common form of a gateway is a *router*. A router acts as a mapping device and chooses the routes over which the message will travel, passing through intermediary systems and networks. Routers can communicate with each other dynamically. Unix and Solaris servers used to be widely used on the Internet as routers, and that function is still contained in Solaris (as you saw in Chapter 9, "Network Services"). However, today specialized router appliances like Cisco routers are in much wider use for Internet applications.

Figure 14.1 illustrates the use of routers on the Internet. Local area networks are set up at different sites but are all routed through the Internet. Ethernet LANs are shown as straight-line connections and ring networks are illustrated as such. The routers relay messages between the LAN and the Internet.

FIGURE 14.1
Solaris and the Internet

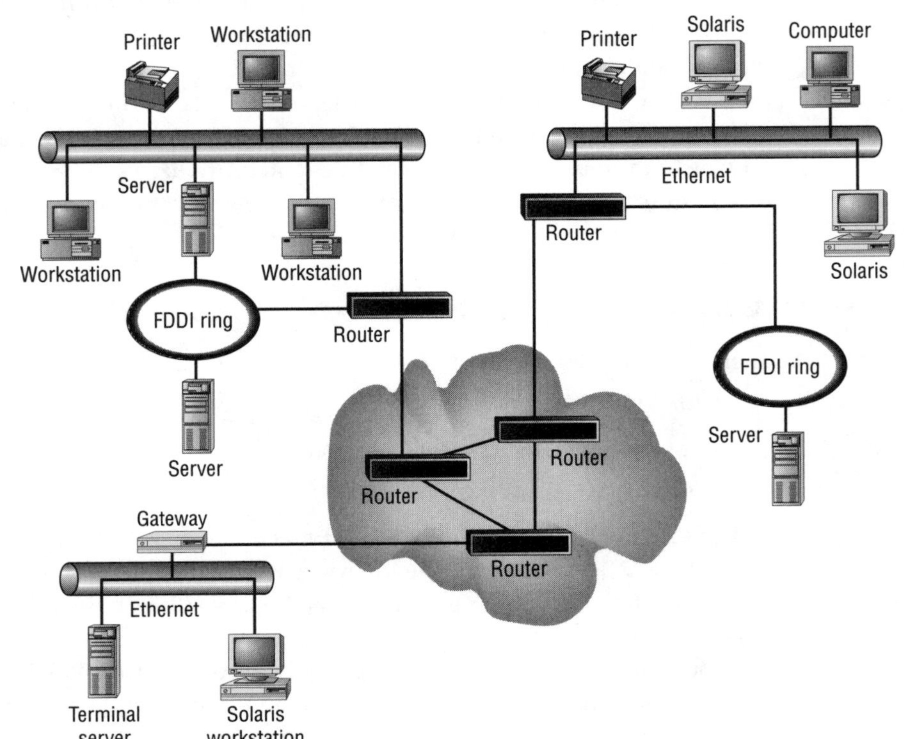

The Open Systems Interconnection (OSI) reference model provides a conceptual framework for the communication that takes place between computers. As was presented in Chapter 9, the OSI is composed of seven layers, each specifying different specific network functions. The model divides the steps involved in moving information between networked computers into smaller, manageable tasks. Because each layer is fairly self-contained, each task can be implemented independently, enabling the solutions offered by one layer to be updated without affecting the other layers.

Each layer uses various forms of control information to communicate with its peers in other computer systems. This may include specific requests and instructions exchanged between peer OSI layers. Control information has two forms: headers and trailers. Headers are prepended to data coming down from upper layers. Trailers are appended to data that has come down from upper layers. Although the data requires neither a header nor a trailer, they may appear depending upon the layer that analyses the information unit. The data portion of an information unit at any OSI layer can potentially contain headers, trailers, and data from higher layers. This is known as *encapsulation*.

The seven OSI layers, which were introduced in Chapter 9, are as follows:

Application layer (layer 7) The Application layer is the OSI layer that is closest to the user. This means that both the Application layer and the user interact on a direct basis with the software applications that implement a communicating component. The functions for this layer usually include the identification of communication partners, the determination of resource availability, and the synchronization of communication. An application like the Netscape browser works principally at the Application layer.

Presentation layer (layer 6) The Presentation layer provides coding and conversion functions that apply to Application layer data. They ensure that information sent from the Application layer of one system will be readable by the next layer. Common data representation formats, character conversion, data compression, and data encryption are some of the schemes present in this layer. Conversion schemes are used to exchange information with systems that use different text and data representations, such as ASCII. Standard data compression schemes enable data to be properly decompressed at the destination. Conversely, data encryption schemes enable data encrypted at the source to be deciphered at the destination. Developing standards like XML work at the Presentation layer.

Session layer (layer 5) The Session layer initiates, manages, and then ends communication sessions between presentation layer functions. These sessions consist of service requests and responses between applications located in different devices. Session-layer implementations include Zone Information Protocol (ZIP), the AppleTalk protocol that coordinates the name-binding process, and the Session Control Protocol (SCP) that is the DECnet Phase IV protocol.

Transport layer (layer 4) The Transport layer implements reliable internetwork data transport services. These services are transparent to upper layers and have functions that include flow control, multiplexing, and virtual circuit management. They also include error checking and recovery. This layer manages both data transmission between devices and flow control to ensure that no more data is sent than the receiving device can process. Virtual circuits are established and maintained. Multiplexing enables data from several applications to be transmitted onto a physical link while error checking creates various mechanisms for detecting transmission error. Error recovery resolves any errors that occur. A few of the Transport layer implementations that are important on the Internet include Transmission Control Protocol (TCP), Name Binding Protocol (NBP) and OSI transport protocols. TCP is the protocol that provides reliable transmission of data and NBP is the protocol that relates AppleTalk names to addresses. OSI transport protocols are a series in the OSI protocol suite.

Network layer (layer 3) The Network layer is responsible for routing and related functions that combine multiple data links in an internetwork. Logical addressing of devices results. This layer supports both connection-oriented and connectionless service protocols. Other types of protocols are implemented at the Network layer. Common routing protocols include Border Gateway Protocol (BGP) and Internet inter-domain routing protocol; Open Shortest Path First (OSPF), a link-state interior gateway protocol developed for use in TCP/IP networks; and Router Information Protocol (RIP), an Internet routing protocol that uses hop count as its metric.

Data Link layer (layer 2) This layer provides a reliable form of transit of data across the physical network. Specifications for physical addressing, network topology, flow control, frame sequencing, and error notification define the different network and protocol characteristics. Specifications for physical addressing define the way devices are addressed. Network topology consists of specifications that define the way devices are to be physically connected. Upper-layer protocols are notified when a transmission error has occurred, and data frames that are transmitted out of sequence are reordered (frame sequencing).

Physical layer (layer 1) The Physical layer consists of the wiring and connections that are common to any type of network. This layer includes all the electrical, mechanical, functional, and procedural specifications for the physical link between network systems. They are activated, maintained, and deactivated through this level. Specifications define certain characteristics, such as voltage levels, voltage changes, physical data rates, maximum transmission distances, and physical connectors. This layer can implement as either a LAN or a WAN.

The terms used to describe the format in which internetworks transmit data and control information vary, but the action is the same. They are commonly called packets, datagrams, segments, messages, and data units. For consistency, they will be referred to as packets in this chapter. A *packet* is an information unit that is composed of the Network layer header and possible trailer and upper-layer data. The header and trailer contain control information intended for the Data Link layer of the destination system. The data from upper-layer entities is also encapsulated in the header and trailer.

Computers communicate using a common language, which is called a protocol. A *protocol*, which is a formal set of rules and conventions, determines the format of the message packet. As discussed in Chapter 9, the most prominent protocol used by Unix and Solaris 8 is TCP/IP, the Transmission Control Protocol/Internet Protocol.

A simpler protocol is UDP, which is utilized for some system services. (UDP is covered in more depth in Chapter 9.) A network service such as `rwho` works very well with UDP, which is an unreliable connection. Network services such as rlogin and `rcp` need very reliable connections. TCP/IP fits the bill because it has a mechanism for determining if and when packets that were sent are received.

Solaris also uses protocols such as Serial Line Internet Protocol (SLIP) and Point-to-Point Protocol (PPP). They both provide serial line connections that support the standard IP protocol and are in common use for dial-up connections to the Internet. Both are designed to work efficiently over serial lines. Because of their compatibility, any IP-based service will run successfully over these connections. There are two protocols that run over serial lines and speed things up considerably. They are Xremote and LBX (low bandwidth X). Xremote functions by compressing the X Window System protocol and makes it more efficient over slow serial lines. LBX is based on the same technology and is a part of the X Window System.

DNS and the Internet

As discussed in Chapter 9, the domain name service (DNS) is a distributed service that is housed in a database. The DNS database is stored in a set of name servers that manage the root domains of the Internet. Thousands of machines cooperate on a global level in keeping the database up-to-date and replicate the information for fault tolerance and performance. These name servers translate the names of network nodes as friendly names into network or IP addresses.

The Internet's DNS database contains information that maps literally hundreds of thousand of alphanumeric host names into numeric IP addresses. It is so huge that it is not contained in one place but exists on several hosts that are local to the calling site. DNS is organized in a hierarchical structure. Each country uses its International Standards Organization (ISO) country code as its domain name. The United States, however, is an exception and uses six standard (.) addresses: .com (commercial); .edu (educational), .gov (government), .mil (military), .net (network), and .org (organization). Many new extensions have been proposed and are about to be added to the pool of possible addresses. Each primary DNS domain is serviced by a set of servers. (DNS names and conventions were discussed in greater detail in Chapter 9.)

Domain names are assigned by Network Solutions (which used to be a part of InterNIC) and other, similar companies. A system's full DNS name is completely unambiguous. In the U.S., the domain name tells you something about where the system is located but adds enough diversity to the name to avoid any confusion if different sites happen to choose a similar name for their system. The top-level domain name in the U.S. appears last and is not case sensitive on the Internet. The following example illustrates a typical U.S. domain:

```
locis.loc.gov
```

This is the address to connect to the U.S. Library of Congress Information System (LOCIS). Once a domain has been assigned to a host, the local site can extend the hierarchy to meet its needs. Functional subdomains often spring from these needs.

On most Unix systems, the common interface to the DNS is Berkeley Internet Name Domain (BIND) software, which follows the client/server model. On a local network, there may be several systems running a name server and supporting all the local hosts as clients. If a system wants to send a message to another host, it asks the nearest name server to learn the remote host's IP address. The client (resolver) may be a process running on the name server computer, or it may pass the request over the network to reach another server. If it gets a response, the local server will add that address it its internal table and reuse it. The name server will delete the nonlocal information before it can become outdated or obsolete.

Host Addresses

Just as each computer has its own unique address, each interface has a unique address or host number. If a system is attached to multiple networks, it has multiple interfaces, each with an address of its own for each network. Similarly, each packet of information that is broadcast over the network has a destination address. All hosts on the network process each packet to see if it is addressed to that host. If it is, the host will process the message. If it is not, the host ignores it. One exception is that the Ethernet hardware filters out unicast packets that are not addressed to a particular machine. The operating system on that machine will never get to see them.

On Solaris systems, the address you see will be an IP address, which is a number broken into four segments with a period between each segment: 198.198.162.1 is a good example.

The American Registry for Internet Numbers (ARIN) is the authority that assigns a block of IP addresses to an organization to use on hosts. InterNIC, now known as Network Solutions, is in the business of maintaining some of the master databases described in the preceding section and some of the name servers that provide DNS to servers on the Internet. Before it became known as the for-profit company Network Solutions, InterNIC was the nonprofit company in charge of all domain names in the U.S. When the Internet changed from a government network to a public/corporate network, InterNIC had to start sharing control of the name servers, so it changed its identity to Network Solutions and became a true business to compete with the other new name services.

The service provider more often uses DHCP to assign IP addresses dynamically and on an as-needed basis to individuals connecting to the server, just as DHCP is used to dole out IP addresses to systems on a network. This allows inactive addresses to be recycled. The network administrator at any given site will usually determine how a company will use its assigned IP addresses. Each operating system converts the address to a binary equivalent.

For many systems, such as those staging Web sites or running mail servers, dynamically assigned IP addresses are not sufficient. In order for these services to be reliably discovered and have message routed correctly to them, static IP addresses are required. Many networks circumvent these issues by using one static IP address to service an entire network, say, on a router or proxy server, and having that device route traffic to Web servers and other application services on hosts from there. Even in these cases, the servers have static IP addresses.

The Internet and the World Wide Web

Originally, the Internet was called ARPAnet. The brainchild of the Department of Defense, it was intended to allow government engineers and scientists to share the government's computing resources. ARPAnet was expanded in the early 1980s when two major networking developments were initiated. The first was the development of the Transmission Control Protocol and the Internet Protocol (TCP/IP). This standardized the communications protocol used by computers on the ARPAnet. The ARPAnet would become a backbone of the entire network called the Internet. In 1988, however, the government stopped funding the ARPAnet project. The National Science Foundation (NSF) supported the Internet for a time until, in 1995, private companies such as Sprint, MCI, and BBNPlanet took over the backbone.

The World Wide Web appeared on the scene with the development of the Uniform Resource Locator, which everyone knows as the URL. It began with a system for sharing results of physics experiments in a high-energy particles field. The system, developed by Tim Berners-Lee, could link documents located on one server to documents on several other servers. The documents could be accessed from any machine by means of a "browser." Once graphics were added along with a Web browser called Mosaic, which introduced users to a point-and-click interface to the Web, the Web exploded into a huge global network that is still growing at a rapid pace.

The main server, Apache, which handles more than half of all the world's Web sites, uses the Hypertext Transfer Protocol (HTTP), which allows text files embedded with URLs to be transferred from the server to a client machine that requests them. These text files are what is known as *Web pages*. Web pages are written in a language called the Hypertext Markup Language (HTML). It controls how different resources referred to in the page can be retrieved. It also allows you to link to other pages by means of embedded URLs.

When you search on the Web, you can use a keyword search or a URL. The URL tells you what machine your information is located on and the path name to the document on that machine. A URL can also contain a protocol that identifies the method you want to use to access the page. Machines on which Web pages live are called *Web servers*. A *Web client* is the machine that requests pages from a server.

HTTP

The communication between the server and the client requires the use of HTTP. When a client requests a document, it issues an HTTP request to the machine specified in the URL. When the server receives the request, it looks for the page requested by the client. If the server finds the correct page, it responds with the contents of the page. This is called an *HTTP transaction*.

A client machine needs to have a Web browser that can make HTTP requests. Some of the more popular browsers are Microsoft Internet Explorer and Netscape Navigator. Many e-mail programs such as Microsoft Outlook, Qualcomm's Eudora, and others also can place HTTP requests and process HTML pages. Machines that receive HTTP requests must have a Web server program that understands them.

An HTTP request is a single line of text that provides information to the server about the client, its capabilities, and the page being requested. There are five specific parts to an HTTP request:

- Type of request
- A general header
- A request header
- An entity header
- The entity body

The first line of the HTTP request is the request type, which tells the server how to retrieve the page the client is requesting. This is a required parameter for all HTTP requests. The other four parts are optional. The general headers can be used to send information to the server detailing the type of connection or the current time. Request headers describe the client and its capabilities. They can also include information about the name of the machine the client is running, the client's name, and the type of information the client understands. The entity head and body are used to send documents to the server and employ tools that allow you to create and publish Web pages to a server or submit a form.

The HTTP request type tells the server the way your request is being made and specifies several different methods by which a client can request information from the server. The usual syntax for a request type is as follows:

```
<method> <pathname> HTTP/<version>
```

<method> is usually GET, POST, or HEAD. *<pathname>* is the part of the URL that contains the pathway to the file on the server. *<version>* indicates what version of HTTP you are using; the server will respond in that particular version.

Because versions of HTTP will be updated periodically, Web browsers and Web servers support all versions. Earlier versions of HTTP were simple in nature and defined only one method for requesting pages. They did not support images, applets, compressed files, or binary files. They only supported the GET method, whereby the client could ask the server to get a particular document. Since then, the HEAD and POST methods have been added as well as PUT, DELETE, and TRACE. Upgraded versions, of course, add on more and more capabilities, allowing servers to return tailor-made responses:

- The HEAD method resembles the GET method except that the server returns information about the requested document in place of the document itself. This method is often used by browsers to determine the size of a document, the type of data it contains, and the type of server it employs.
- The POST method lets the client send data to special data processing programs that live on the server. The URL that is specified is usually the path to a special program on the server that knows how to handle the data.
- POST is also used in the handling of forms. The user is allowed to input information into text fields or check boxes. Each input field on a form is associated with a name and a value (the value is usually the user's input). The browser will gather all of the names and their corresponding values, place them into the entity body of the form, and then send the request to the server.
- The PUT method transfers files from the client machine to the server.
- The DELETE method can be used by a client to delete files on the server.
- The TRACE method can be used to determine how the request traveled through the Internet.

The HTTP server responds to requests from clients. As in the request, there are five parts to an HTTP response:

- The response status
- General headers

- Response headers
- The entity headers
- The entity body

The response status consists of a single line with the following syntax:

```
HTTP/<version><status_code> <reason_phrase>
```

<version> corresponds to the version of HTTP that the server is using to respond. <status_code> is a number from 100 to 599, which indicates whether the request was successful or not. The response codes are categorized in Table 14.1.

TABLE 14.1: RESPONSE CODES

Range	Explanation
100–199	Information from the server
200–299	Successful requests
300–399	Redirected requests
400–499	Incomplete or failed requests
500–599	Server errors

The two most common status codes are 301 and 302. Status code 301 indicates that a URL has been relocated permanently, and status code 302 indicates that a URL has been relocated temporarily. Clients that receive a status code from 300 through 399 make a new request to the new URL automatically. The error codes 400 through 499 and 500 through 599 indicate client or server errors, respectively. The client has requested a page that it does not have permission to access or the page does not exist or has been removed.

<reason_phrase> is a readable description of the status code and is usually OK to indicate a successful request. ERR indicates a failed request.

The general headers, as in the request, include information such as the type of connection and the time the server began its task. The response header contains information about the server. It may also indicate which HTTP methods the general headers and response headers support.

The entity header and body are returned by the server if the client's request was successful. The entity header contains information about the type of data that is being returned, including the size of the requested document and the time the file was last modified.

The Common Gateway Interface

The Common Gateway Interface (CGI) is a standard that defines the interface between the Web server and an external program. It has been around for quite awhile and is still widely used on the World Wide Web. As the Web server receives a request for a CGI program, it executes it and returns the output of the program as its response to the client. CGI programs present dynamic information to users of a Web site, such as providing access to search engines or databases. Because they are executed by the Web server, they can get easily overloaded. In an effort to avoid this problem, you should make sure CGI programs are short and execute quickly. Most CGI programs are written in the Perl language, so they execute quickly, in addition to being powerful. Some programs may be written in C/C++, TCL (which is easy to use), and the Bourne shell (for the sake of compatibility with operating systems). The basic requirement for a CGI program is that it is executable by the user who executes the Web server.

Most executable programs are stored in a special directory such as `/cgi-bin`. Apache and other Web servers are capable of executing programs stored in other directories if they end with the `.cgi` suffix, and Apache will execute programs with any suffix as long as it's specified in the `httpd.conf` file. Use of the `.cgi` suffix is discouraged because it can create security problems. Malicious users can install into their Web directories programs that will give them access as a privileged user just by adding `.cgi` to their files. The programs can then be executed from the Web. It is a good idea to do regular checks of the `.cgi` files, but it is easy for someone to change the name of the file and avoid detection. If you use a server that limits itself to running programs from a single directory, it is easier to control the programs that are placed in the directory. Security problems can be kept to a minimum.

The HTTP request for a CGI program is exactly the same as it is for any other type of page. Consider the following request:

```
http://kafka/cgi-bin/formtwo
```

The client wants to retrieve the page `/cgi-bin/formtwo`. The Web server sees that the requested file resides in the `/cgi-bin` directory and proceeds to execute the program `formtwo`. If any output is produced, the Web server puts it into the entity body of its response.

It is sometimes necessary to send information to a CGI program so that it can be processed on the server, typically with programs used for search engines and database access. In a `GET` request, the information that needs to be processed by the CGI program is appended to the path name of the URL:

```
GET /cgi-bin/find.pl?dir=docs HTTP/1.0
```

In this example, `name=value` corresponds to `dir=docs`. When the CGI program is called by the Web server, the list of name value pairs sent by the client is provided in a single environmental variable named QUERY_STRING. The CGI programs will usually convert the name value pairs stored in this environmental variable into separate variables. This adds overhead to CGIs that respond to GET requests. Another drawback is that some clients limit the maximum length of the request to about 1KB. This is a problem if you need to send a large amount of data to a CGI program.

To circumvent this problem, many CGI programs use the POST method instead of GET. If the POST method is used, the variable definitions are placed into the entity body instead of being appended to the path name of the URL. This is a good remedy for complicated HTML forms. The amount of information transmitted in a POST request is not subject to the limitations that the GET method is. Client forms can then transmit as much information as required to a CGI program. Online shopping sites and many of the e-commerce sites use the POST request simply for this reason.

The CGI programs do put a large load on the Web server. Each client that submits a form or requests a CGI-based page causes a process to be created on the machine on which the Web server is running. If you have heavy traffic on the server, you can translate this to thousands of processes demanding resources concurrently. If the CGI programs need to create databases or network connections, the problems are compounded. When the system is overloaded, this can take inordinate amounts of time, which is unacceptable to the client. An application called FastCGI is available and runs in separate processes. They are very persistent and are reused for multiple requests, over and over. This is a more efficient way to handle requests without overloading the server. A FastGCI application library was designed to allow for the migration of existing CGI applications. The good thing is that applications built with the library can also run as CGI programs for backward compatibility with old Web servers. The FastCGI library is available for all major Web servers from www.fastcgi.com. Documentation for its use is available as well. There are other options, including the modPerl for Apache, which allows Perl code to keep running instead of having to be launched each time it is called.

The servlet standard is intended as a replacement for CGI. It was developed by Sun Microsystems from Java programs that load and execute inside the Web server. *Servlets* are Java programs that execute on the Web server in a fashion similar to how CGIs execute. They are called from HTML pages, using GET or POST requests. They can interpret CGI parameters and are able to generate HTML code that is then piped back to the client application. The major difference between CGI (and FastCGI) and servlets is that servlets execute on a servlet runner, which is a single-process, multithreaded Java server that is supported by most Web servers and provides the interface between the server and the Java Virtual Machine. When a servlet is invoked by a client, it runs rapidly on the single process. Servlets easily support large numbers of concurrent users. They also boast the object-oriented characteristics of Java. Because of the persistence of variables on the server, there is no need for cookies. References to distributed objects can be created and maintained throughout the life cycle of the servlet. This is very useful when performing queries against legacy database systems.

Servlets are loaded only once at invocation, thus they minimize the effect of initializing resources. Database and network connections can also be pooled, reducing overhead. To develop servlets, you can download and install a Java Development Kit from Sun. There are several servlet engines available for the Apache Web server. JServ from the Apache Project is a free download.

Browsers

The first graphical user interface for the Web was a browser called Mosaic. Designed and implemented in 1993 at the University of Illinois, it was instrumental in the huge increase in the number of World Wide Web users. One of the initial developers of Mosaic, Marc Andreessen, joined with the founder of Silicon Graphics, Jim Clark, and together they founded Netscape and created Netscape Navigator. Netscape Navigator is a bigger and better Web browser that supports many more features than Mosaic ever could. It has proven to be one of the most popular browsers for those using the World Wide Web.

Netscape is the browser that is included with Solaris 8, and it has far and away the largest browser market share on Solaris. Sun maintains packages of various versions of Netscape Communicator (4.75 and 4.76) as well as Netscape 6.01a (at the time this was written) at `www.sun.com/software/solaris/netscape/` (see Figure 14.2). On Netscape's own Web site, you will find additional versions of Netscape's browser, but whenever possible you should use the versions on Sun's Web site (which are free downloads). Those Sun packages install easier, and the XPInstaller allows someone without root privileges to install the browser package.

NOTE Solaris 8 ships with Netscape version 4.75 as part of its default installation. If you wish to use Netscape 6.01a (the current version at the time this book was written), you can install it and have both versions available to you. It is recommended that you install both versions instead of replacing 4.75 with version 6.01a.

Netscape provides a multipurpose graphical user interface. You can display pictures and text, view live news reports, listen to music and sounds, watch Web events, or follow a sporting event, all with access to hypermedia. All underlined and highlighted words or phrases on a Web page are links to more detailed information. Similarly, images with colored borders are hypertext links.

FIGURE 14.2

The download page on Sun's site for Netscape

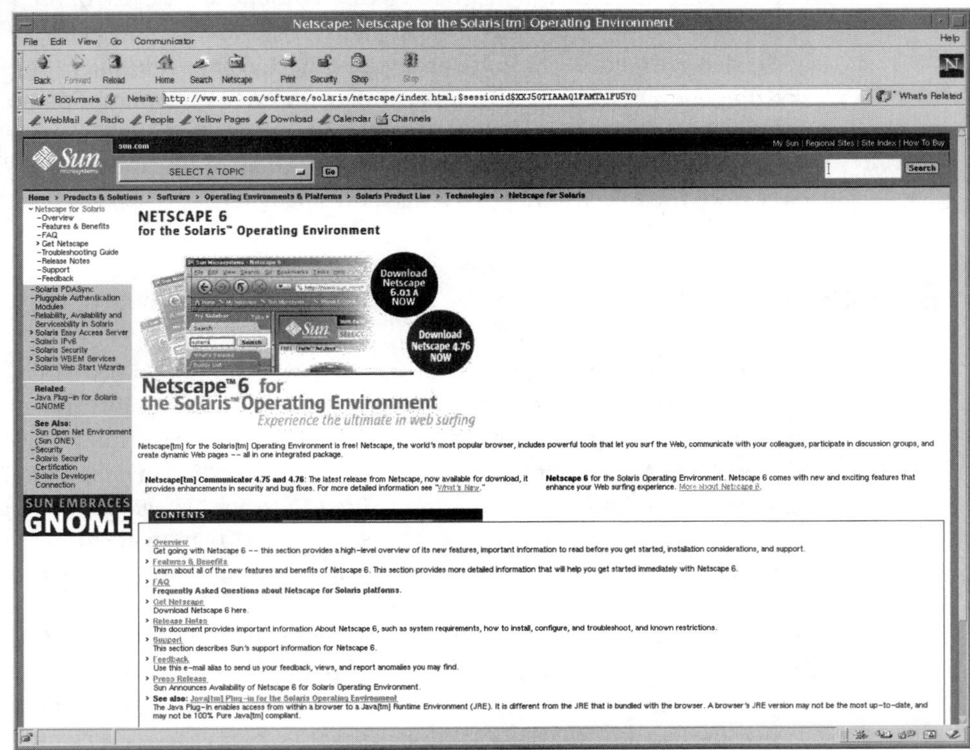

Microsoft's Internet Explorer is the most popular browser worldwide. A version of Internet Explorer exists for Solaris and can be downloaded from the Microsoft Web site. At the time this book was written, you could obtain Internet Explorer 5 Service Pack 1 for Solaris (SPARC) Public Beta at `www.microsoft.com/windows/ie/download/`.

Netscape and Microsoft Internet Explorer run only on a graphical user interface. If you want to use a popular text-based browser, use Lynx to access the Internet. Lynx is particularly useful when you are working on a character-based terminal; it looks like many of the microbrowsers that are bundled with early versions of wireless phones. To get Lynx, go to the Web site `http://lynx.browser.org`.

Many sites will identify their WWW servers by adding the prefix *www* to the host or domain name. For example, you can reach the Web server at the Massachusetts Institute of Technology at `www.mit.edu`. With the use of a browser, you may never need to use a URL directly. As the World Wide Web continues to expand, you may find URLs just about everywhere. Even television newscasters and popular programs refer to them on a regular basis. You can also do a keyword search and usually find the appropriate URL for what you are looking for.

There may be a time when you want to create your own Web page. It is useful to learn HTML for this purpose. Many browsers, however, including Netscape, allow you to construct a Web page by following easy directions and guidelines. HTML editors are fairly easy to use, and you can get started creating HTML files with a standard text editor such as `vi` or `dtpad`. StarOffice also includes templates for making HTML pages and can export standard documents to HTML files.

Netscape

When you start Netscape, the browser opens to your home page. In the default installation, Solaris sets Sun's home page (`www.sun.com`) as the home page, as shown in Figure 14.3. Click an underlined topic of interest and the link takes you to the destination specified. When a new page is transferred to your browser, the Content area changes to show the structure and content of the new page. The status indicator in the upper-right portion of the screen moves while the information is in transit. The progress bar and the Status Message field, in the lower-left portion of the Netscape window, provide details about the transfer's progress.

The information you are viewing with the Netscape browser is displayed in the content area, the large frame in the center of the screen.

At the right side of the menu bar is a Help menu. If you click the word *Help*, a pop-up menu of items that will take you to Netscape resources will appear. These resources can help you become familiar with the features of Netscape. You can view the interactive Netscape documentation by selecting Help Contents from this menu.

Netscape offers you three toolbars below the menu bar:

Navigation toolbar Use the Back and Forward buttons to move through your previously viewed Web pages. The Reload button refreshes your Web page, and the Stop button ends your request for information transfer from a Web server. Use the Home button to return to your home page and the Print button to print the current Web page.

Location toolbar The Location toolbar includes the Goto text box (labeled Netsite in Figure 14.3), in which you can enter a URL. Press the Enter key to go to the location specified by the URL. The Location toolbar gives you access to more information about Netscape and several other useful directories. If you click a link and display a page in the content area, the URL for that page will appear in the Goto text box. The Location toolbar also includes your bookmarks.

Personal toolbar This location contains buttons that are links to your favorite sites. You can add and delete buttons on this toolbar.

FIGURE 14.3

Elements of the Netscape browser screen

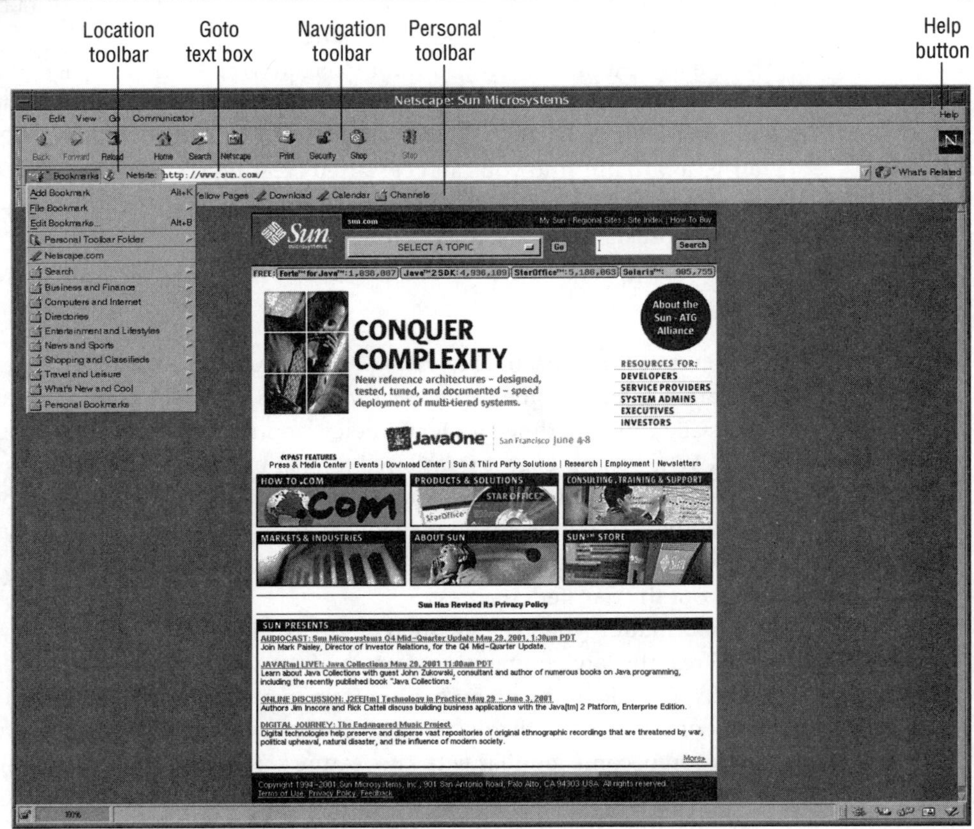

The pointer changes shape when it is over a hyperlink. The Status Message box at the bottom of the screen displays the link's URL.

You can also use a search engine to navigate the Web. A search engine is an interface to a large database of resources. Some search sites, like Yahoo!, are built around a search engine that returns directory listings; others, like Google, are built around an engine that returns listings according to relevance, which is determined by the number of other Web sites that link to a Web site. A search engine will rely on its own database, which is spread out on the Web. It can pull back information from indexes it has built over a measure of time.

Most users are familiar with Yahoo! (`www.yahoo.com`). If you click the Search button on the Navigation toolbar, you will see a list of search engines. Click the name of a search engine, enter the string you want to search for in the small query window, and press the Return key. The search engine will then search extensively through its database of URLs for the words you specified. It will display a list of sites that contain the words. Each name in this list is a hypertext link. Simply click the name to visit the site.

There are many different types of search engines on the Internet, some good and some fairly mediocre. The following are among the better ones:

- Yahoo! (`www.yahoo.com`)
- Google (`www.google.com`)
- AltaVista (`www.altavista.com`)
- Lycos (`www.lycos.com`)
- Northern Light (`www.northernlight.com`)
- WebCrawler (`www.webcrawler.com`)

Downloading Files

Giving you the ability to download files is an important function of a browser like Netscape. You can download files from either FTP or HTML sites. To download a file, follow these steps:

1. Enter an FTP address in the Goto Field of the Location toolbar and press the Return key.
2. When the initial set of directories is displayed, click one you wish to download.
3. Netscape will open a window asking you where to put the file on your system. Give it an address such as `/tmp` or `/var/tmp`.
4. Change the Selection window so that the file is stored in `/var/tmp`.
5. Click OK.

While downloading, Netscape will display a Download window that shows you the progress of the file transfer. Once the Download window closes, the file is ready for you to view. Exit from Netscape or choose another window.

The file you download is archived with `tar` and compressed with the `gzip`, as indicated by the `.tgz` or `tar.gz` filename extension. To open the archive, follow these steps:

1. Use `cd` to change to the `/var/tmp` directory.
2. Set the `umask` so that file permissions are correct.

3. Decompress the archive and extract with the following commands (in the last line, *<filename>* will no longer have the "gz" attached to it):

```
$ cd /var/tmp
$ umask 0
$ gunzip <filename>
$ tar -xvf <filename>
```

Netscape Bookmarks

The bookmark feature enables you to save the names and URLs of Web pages that are of special interest to you. This feature saves you the task of trying to remember the long complicated URLs. There are several ways you can use the bookmark feature:

- To create a bookmark, click the Bookmarks button on the Location toolbar. A list of bookmarks is displayed; the first three items on the list are Bookmark menu options, as shown in Figure 14.3.
- Click a bookmark to go to the site it points to.
- Select Add Bookmark to add the URL you are currently viewing as a bookmark.
- Choose File Bookmark to file it in a folder.
- Choose Edit Bookmarks to change the properties of bookmarks or move or delete them.
- You can also choose Bookmarks from the Communicator menu on the menu bar to browse through the list of bookmarks.

The first component in the URL points to the type of resource the page contains, such as HTTP, FTP, or Gopher. The *http*, colon, and double slash that follow act as identifiers to the Web, but they may be omitted from a URL in print. You usually do not have to enter them to get to the site the URL points to; they are implied. The full name of the host acting as the server for the information follows this. The rest of the URL is a relative path name to the file that contains information you are looking for.

Customizing Netscape

Netscape has a set of preferences that you can use to customize the program's behavior. To open these preferences, select the Preferences command from the Edit menu.

Figure 14.4 shows the Navigator section of the Preferences dialog box. You can choose the home page, which is the page that appears when you first open Netscape, by choosing the Home Page radio button under the Browser Starts With area and entering the URL into the Location text box under Home Page.

FIGURE 14.4

The Navigator section of the Netscape Preferences dialog box

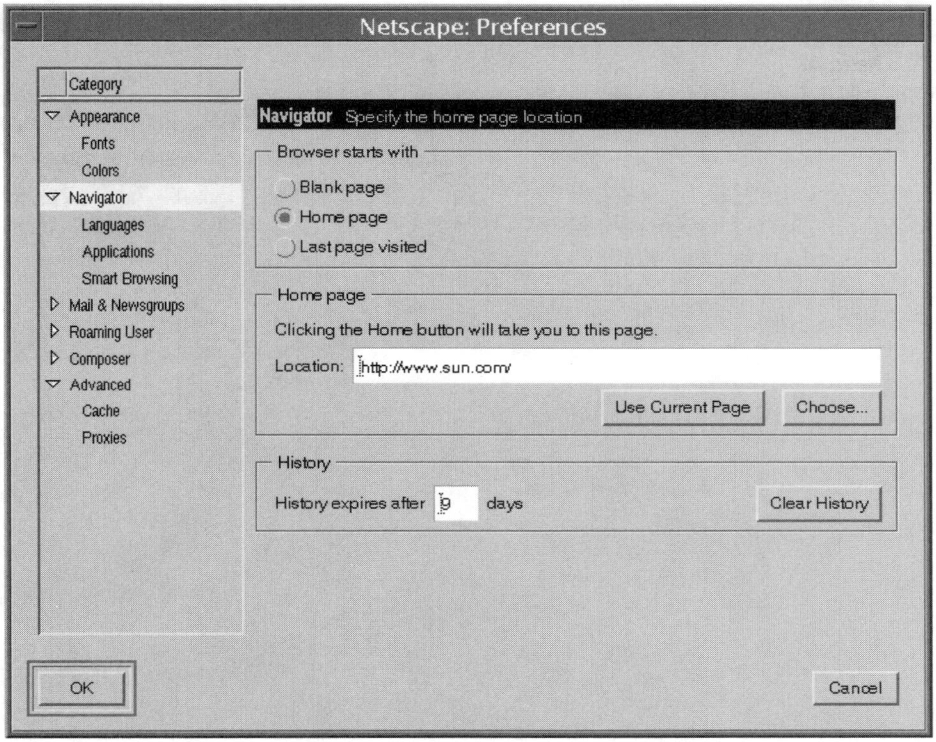

There are two additional pages that you will want to visit. The first is the Netscape Advanced Cache Preference page, on which you can set the size and behavior of the cache. The second important page is the Advanced Proxies page, shown in Figure 14.5. On that page, you can configure how Navigator connects to the Internet: directly, through a proxy server, or using a configuration script. Click the View button to manually set different protocols and their servers and ports, as shown in Figure 14.6, but only if recommended by the system's administrator. Incorrect settings will cause the browser to stop working. It will load but you won't be able to view any Web pages.

Electronic Mail

Electronic mail (or e-mail, as it is commonly known) is probably the most popular feature of the Internet. It's quick and you can use it to send invitations, memos, letters, pictures, and so on, and you never need a stamp! One advantage of e-mail is that you

FIGURE 14.5

The Advanced Proxies page of the Netscape Preferences dialog box

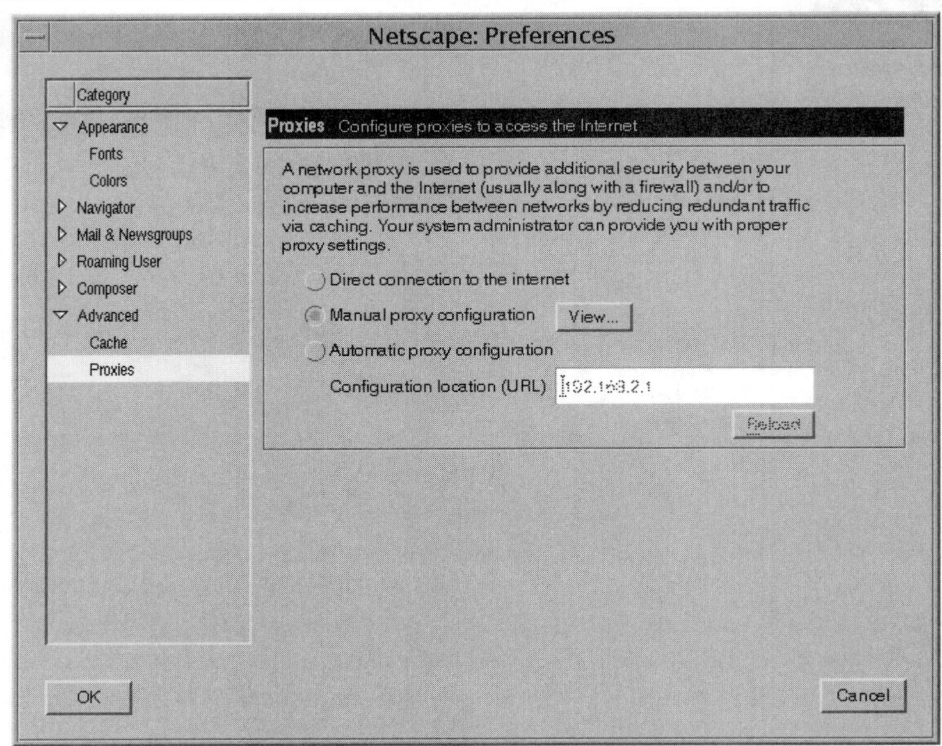

can attach other documents to it, like a resume, for example. Attachments are opened by programs or browsers that are called by your mail program.

E-mail can be used to communicate with users on a local system, with users on a wide area network system, and with other users on the Internet. On a LAN or WAN, you can send messages to users who are logged on and are willing to receive them. E-mail utilities, however, allow you to send messages to parties not logged on as well as those who are. You can also send a message to several parties at one time. You can reply to an incoming message instantaneously. You can also delete messages you do not want to read.

Solaris has several utilities for receiving and sending e-mail. The `dtmail`, `mailtool`, `mail`, and `mailx` utilities are some of the many mail programs available for Solaris 8 users in addition to Netscape, `pine`, `emacs`, and `xmh` (`xmh` is a graphical interface to the MH Message Handling System).

FIGURE 14.6
The View Manual Proxy Configuration dialog box

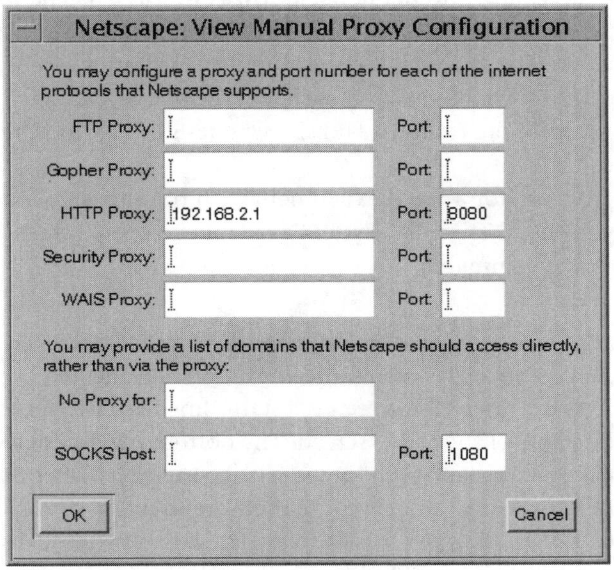

In many ways, the `dtmail` and `mailtool` programs are similar. They are both graphical interfaces to mail programs. Although either program can be run from the Common Desktop Environment (CDE) or OpenWindows, each program runs better on the window manager it was designed for. If either program is represented by an icon, the icon will indicate whether or not you have mail waiting to be read (the program does not have to be open). The `mailtool` program icon will show you if you have new mail or mail that has already been read. Both programs open with a list of messages; new messages are marked, and you can read, reply to, and dispose of messages as you choose. The difference is that `dtmail` uses an *N* for new mail and `mailtool` uses a *U* for unread mail. Each program then allows you to sort messages and store them in folders for easy retrieval. You can compose and send new messages to users on your system or on any system on the network you are connected to.

Using *pine* for Electronic Mail

There is a Unix mailer called `pine` (Program for Internet News & Email) that, at its inception, was particularly easy for beginners to learn. This mail utility is user friendly and has capabilities that attract many users. It now has advanced capabilities for accessing Internet newsgroups, as well as a mechanism for transmitting files containing any kind of data. There are ways to customize pine according to individual preferences. Sun does not supply pine, but it can be obtained by contacting ftp://ftp.cac.washington.edu/pine or www.cac.washington.edu/pine. As you will note from the URLs, it was designed by the University of Washington for Unix.

Again, you should experiment with the various features until you feel comfortable with them. There is help text available for every screen. To get started, type in the following command:

```
$ pine
```

You will see a pine main menu screen that has seven commands in the middle. Each command is represented by a letter on the left.

At the top of the screen is a status line with the version of pine you are using and the name of the active screen. The bottom two lines give all the commands for the main menu, each highlighted with a single character that is displayed to the left of the command name. Because there are so many commands, you must enter O (other) to view another two-line display. These two two-line displays comprise the full set of commands for the Main menu; another O command takes you back to the original two-line display.

To execute a pine command, you can do either of the following:

- Press the key that corresponds to the character to the left of the command you want to execute.
- Use the arrow keys for Next and Previous to position the cursor over the command you want and then press the Return key.

The main menu has additional commands than don't fit in the display at the bottom of the screen. With the O command, you can view other commands. There is also help text available. You can use the M command to get back to the main menu and the Q command to quit pine. Experimentation is the key to learning pine or any mail system.

If you want to send mail from pine, try sending it to yourself first by following these steps:

1. Type **pine** in a terminal window to bring up main menu.
2. Choose the command Compose Message (Figure 14.7 shows the pine Compose Message window).

FIGURE 14.7

The `pine` *Compose Message window*

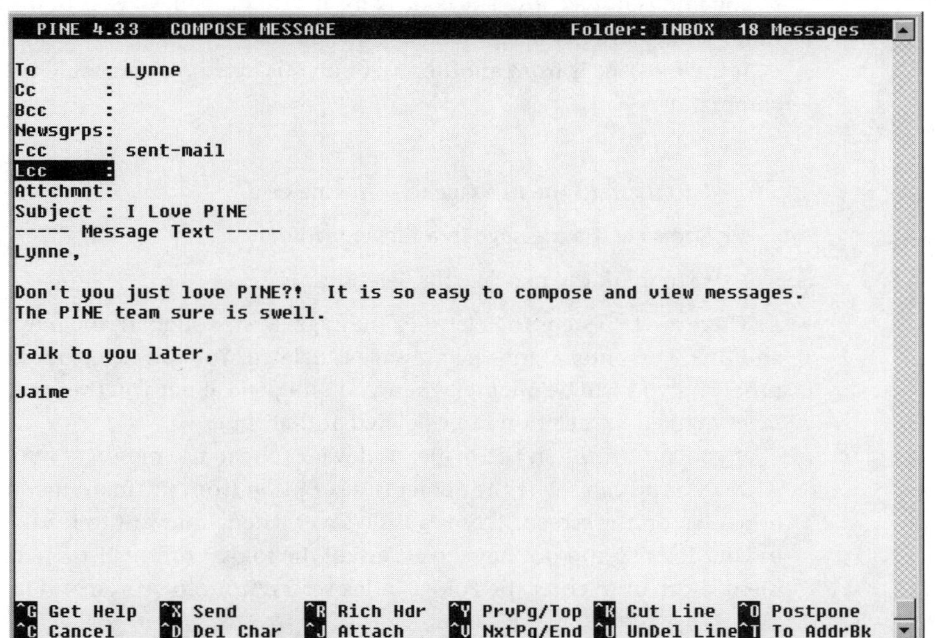
PINE 4.33 COMPOSE MESSAGE Folder: INBOX 18 Messages
To : Lynne
Cc :
Bcc :
Newsgrps:
Fcc : sent-mail
Lcc :
Attchmnt:
Subject : I Love PINE
----- Message Text -----
Lynne,
Don't you just love PINE?! It is so easy to compose and view messages.
The PINE team sure is swell.
Talk to you later,
Jaime
^G Get Help ^X Send ^R Rich Hdr ^Y PrvPg/Top ^K Cut Line ^O Postpone
^C Cancel ^D Del Char ^J Attach ^V NxtPg/End ^U UnDel Line ^T To AddrBk

3. In the To field, type in your own login name and then type your message. Use the Ctrl key to type in commands (the display commands at the bottom of the screen). You can use Enter or the arrow keys to move down through the fields.
4. Use the Cc portion of the header to send copies. (To find other users' addresses, press Ctrl+G.)
5. Press Ctrl+X to transmit the message. You will be asked if you are ready to send it. Answer with a yes or a no.
6. Press the Q key to return to the shell.

The first time you use `pine`, it will create a link to the user's mail spool called INBOX. Folders called `sent-mail` and `saved-messages` are created and are put in the `${HOME}/mail` folder by default. The INBOX will link to your unread messages, and the `sent-mail` folder will hold copies of mail already sent out. The `saved-messages` folder will hold messages that you want to save. You can create more folders in `pine`; you can also delete messages or transfer them from one folder to another. You can organize folders into collections of topics as you prefer. When you receive a message, you will see codes listed on the left. A code + means that the message was sent directly to you and is not a copy. The code N means that the message is new. Code D means that the message has been marked for deletion.

If the message is from another user on your network, you could use the following commands:

- R to reply
- F to forward the message to someone else
- S to save the message in a message folder
- D to mark the message for deletion

There are two steps to deleting a message. First, you mark the message for deletion, and then you enter Y and the message is deleted. You can delete messages at any time, and you will be queried when you quit `pine` about whether you want the messages marked for deletion to be deleted at that time.

If you are already in the mailer and want to read the messages in the default folder (INBOX), you can select the Folder Index option from the main menu and bypass the folder list on the screen. This is a time-saver when you want to read just the messages in your INBOX and not have to access all the folders on the list. There is also a convenient shortcut to enter the Folder Index screen from the command line:

```
$ pine -i
```

Again, you can send mail such as a memo to more than one person at a time. You can access the message composer directly by typing the following command at the shell prompt (this will send messages to all three users):

```
$ pine al dave jim
```

You will be able to send messages to users on other systems if your system is a part of a network. You need to know their login name and a machine name and type both separated by the @ character, such as in the following example:

```
$ pine barrie@reliable
```

To send a message over the Internet, you would also have to know the domain name but not necessarily the machine name, such as in this example:

```
$ pine barrie@sosinsky-group
```

The *pine* Newsreader

There is also a news interface called `pine`, which is related to the `pine` mail interface. There is consistency between commands, screen displays, and folder organization, which makes the newsreader easy to use. If you use the Netscape browser, you can use Netscape News as well. However, you have the option of using `pine` as a newsreader. You must have access to Usenet news for pine to function as a newsreader. If your site has no news server, you will not be able to read the news, so you should request a server from the system administrator.

If pine is installed on your system, you can start it as a newsreader by following these steps:

1. Enter **pine** at the command line to start pine.
2. Select Setup from the Main menu and wait until pine prompts you for the setup task on the bottom lines.
3. Enter **C** (Config) to ask pine to display the Setup Configuration screen.
4. View and modify any aspects of the configuration you wish to change.
5. Highlight the pine variable nntp-server and select A if it's not already set.
6. Enter the name of the news server.

This is usually all you need to do to start pine as a nåewsreader. Each time you run pine, it will automatically contact the news server as you enter commands to read and post the news. If you are already accustomed to seeing the Folder List screen containing the INBOX and sent-mail and saved-messages folders, you will be familiar with the way pine displays individual folders within a collection when you select Folder List. Once the news is enabled, an additional collection called, appropriately, the news-collection is automatically defined, and the Folder List screen changes to display a list of the two folder collections (mail and news) instead. You will see a name identifying each collection. Highlight the line that says Select Here to See Expanded List. This will make the corresponding collection current. Highlight the line for the news-collection to let pine know that you plan to use the news feature. The command lines at the bottom of the screen will show that the label for command D has changed from Delete to Unsubscribe and that the label for command A has changed from Add to Subscribe.

Sharing Information

Information regarding Solaris 8 can be found in several ways. One of the most widely used services is Usenet.

Usenet is an informal information service somewhat like an electronic bulletin board that allows users with common interests to exchange information and news items. Usenet has been around since the early 1980s when the IT community decided to share information on topics of common interest. Information was passed along over dial-up telephone lines using Unix's uucp utility. Because of its popularity, major changes in uucp were needed to handle the volume of messages and sites. Today, the news travels over network links using a sophisticated protocol specifically designed for this purpose. It is called Network News Transfer Protocol (NNTP). Messages are stored in a standard format and are read by one of many public domain programs available. One of the older interfaces is called readnews. You can use others such as rn and its X Window System release, xrn, to browse through the articles that are available and reply or create articles of your own. In addition to rn and xrn, popular interfaces are tin, nn, and xvnews. You can also read Usenet news in CDE by using the Netscape Message Center.

Usenet software has been ported to non-Unix systems, so the community of netnews users has grown considerably. Netscape includes as part of its Web browser a graphical interface called Netscape News that you can use to read news. As is the Unix tradition, categories of netnews groups are structured hierarchically. At the top level are designations such as comp, misc, rec, sci, soc, and talk. These abbreviations stand for computer, miscellaneous, recreational, science, social issues, and talk discussions, respectively.

There is usually one regional category at the top level that includes information about local events. New categories are always being added. Newsgroup names resemble domain names but are read from left to right like Solaris filenames. For example, talk.politics, soc.singles, rec.racing, and so on are just a few of the newsgroups.

Using Usenet requires patience and perseverance, but you will certainly get to what you need and meet some interesting people along the way. There are netnews archives where you can most likely find an answer to almost any question because others have probably had the same question at one time or another. You can read Usenet news to find out about new tools and services. The comp.os.Unix hierarchy is always of interest to Unix users. People will announce the availability of free software there and give instructions on how to get a copy for your own use.

There are some great resources for questions and answers about Solaris 8 on the World Wide Web. The comp.unix.solaris forum is a Usenet group for Solaris 8 information and discussion. It also allows you to contribute your knowledge to assist others who have questions. You may be able to provide them with an answer or two.

In addition to Usenet, there are other ways to find and share information about Solaris on the Internet. The Solaris 8 FAQ, which is maintained by Casper Dik, is a wonderful source of general information. The latest version is at www.wins.uva.nl/pub/solaris/solaris2/.

For Intel users, there is a forum site called alt.solaris.x86 forum, which is informative and kind to the neophyte. No question is considered too unimportant to answer. Both the SPARC and Intel platforms have an available FAQ site, which can be accessed at www.sunhelp.org/faq/sunadm.html.

For the latest Solaris 2 FAQs including an HTML version and other interesting goodies, contact `ftp://ftp.wins.uva.nl/pub/solaris`.

Another option for asking questions and finding answers is to use mailing lists. The Sun Manager's List is a famous list and contains questions, answers, and summaries of previous queries. Just about all Solaris-related topics are covered. There is also an x86 mailing list that has great tips, tricks, and advice for those who are relatively new to Solaris 8. This is a good resource if you have difficulties with specific hardware configurations.

For more information about Solaris help resources, refer to Chapter 1, "The Solaris 8 Operating System."

Apache

The Apache Project is a software development project that is managed jointly by a group of volunteers. Located all around the world, and using the Internet and the World Wide Web to communicate, this a core group that created a commercial, free source code implementation of an HTTP Web server with related documentation. Based on the NCSA httpd server, Apache is now a completely rewritten server with a good measure of security.

Solaris 8's distribution contains a version of the Apache Web server for your use. If you don't have the operating system's distribution or if you decide you need the latest version, the Apache Web server may be obtained free of charge from the Apache Group (`www.apache.org`). This will get you all the latest bug fixes and current security features. The prerelease of version 2 is now on the Internet for download for developers. One of the major reasons that Apache is free is that users often contribute by suggesting feature enhancements and bug fixes and by actively supporting others in public newsgroups. Individual effort is usually minimal, but the combination of everyone's input has resulted in a very strong product. Although users will still be using 1.3.20, it will not be long before version 2 is ready for the public. Version 2 has many new enhancements that make it even more robust.

If you decide to download Apache, be sure to do the following:

1. Obtain a valid IP address.
2. Obtain a host name to use for your Web server.
3. Have your Web server added to domain name server.
4. Use a separate machine as a Web server if you plan to support CGI or servlets.
5. Check your system to make sure it has required components for compiling Apache.

6. Decide which directory Apache should be installed in after compiling.
7. Decide which modules should be compiled into Apache.

It is important to configure your Apache Web server after checking to make certain it has all the required components for compiling. Apache handles this automatically when you use the `configure` command:

```
$ ./configure --prefix=[install_dir] --enable-module=
   <module-name>
```

If you prefer to enable more than one module, enter multiple `enable-module` statements as in the following example:

```
$ ./configure --enable-module=<module-name> --enable-
   module=<module-name> --enable-module=<module-name> ...
```

If you do not need any extra modules and use only the defaults, you can use the `configure` command with the `--prefix` option.

To compile Apache after the `configure` command is finished, use the following command:

```
$ make
```

Be sure you're in the directory in which the distribution is decompressed when you type the `make` command. You may have to use the full path if you are using the Sun `make` utility, as in the following example:

```
$ /usr/ccs/bin/make
```

This command will cause Apache to compile with all its default modules. After completion, there will be a single file named `httpd` in the `src` directory.

You can now install Apache by using the following command:

```
$ make install
```

This copies the httpd, the executable, and the configuration files into an installation directory. If error messages occur, your permissions may not be adequate. If so, execute the command as root:

```
$ su root -c '/usr/ccs/bin/make install'
```

Once this command is completed, you will have Apache installed on your system. At this point, you should test it thoroughly to make sure it is working. You should consider having Apache start running with the system startup. There is a subdirectory named `bin` that contains a script named `apachectl`. This script can be used to start and stop Apache. Place a copy of the `apachectl` script in the directory `/etc/init.d`. This will integrate Apache into the startup procedure. Use the following command as root:

```
# cp /hm/httpd/bin/apachectl /etc/init.d
```

If you installed into a different directory, then change the command to read with the correct path name.

After you have copied the apachectl script, change the directory to /etc/rc3.d, then issue the following root command:

```
#ln  -s ../init.d/apachectl S85apachectl
```

This link will automatically start Apache during the boot-up when it reaches run level 3.

If you want to have Apache automatically shut down, you can create another link by issuing the following root command:

```
# ln -s ../init.d/apachectl K15apachectl
```

Because you are still in /etc/rc3.d, Apache will be stopped and then started when the system reaches level 3. You need to put the kill in rc0.d, rc1.d, rc2.d, and rcS.d.

At this point it is wise to test the Apache Web server startup by issuing the following root command:

```
# /etc/init.d/apachectl start
```

If the script fails, check to make sure the executable bit has been set to the apachectl file. You may have forgotten to copy the startup file to /etc/init.d. If this is the case, change to the directory in which Apache is installed and issue the following root command:

```
# ./bin/apachectl start
```

This will start the Web server. You can test it out with the telnet command:

```
$ telnet localhost 80
```

You will see the following output:

```
Trying 127.0.01
Connected to localhost.
Escape character is '^]'.
```

Although you will not receive a prompt, your terminal's cursor will be at the beginning of a blank line. This indicates that you are connected to the Web server. However, if you receive a message saying connection refused, check the process list to make sure Apache started properly.

The following example can be used to test the Web server:

```
GET / HTTP/1.0
```

After you input this line, press Return twice. After the second Return, you will see an HTML page scroll across the screen. The HTTP response headers and start of the page will look like this:

```
HTTP/1.1 200 OK
Date: Wed, 9 May 2001 09:35:46 EST
```

```
Server: Apache/1.2.1 (Unix) mod-fastcgi/2.2/1
Last-Modified: Tue, 17 May 2001 05:14:12 EST
Etag:  "800f-312-363ee09f"
Accept-Ranges:  bytes
Content-Length:  807
Connection:  close
Content-Type: text/html
<HTML>
  <HEAD>
   <TITLE>Test Page for Apache Installation on Web Site
   </TITLE>
```

You are now ready to configure Apache for your Web site.

Configuring Apache

Once you have tested the installation and find it is successful, you can begin to configure Apache to use it to serve Web pages to your clients. For versions 1.3.4 and higher, all of the configuration information is stored in a file named `httpd.conf`. You may find that in the directory tree where you installed Apache, you have two additional configuration files named `access.conf` and `srm.conf`. These are outdated files used by previous versions of Apache and should be ignored.

The `httpd.conf` file has three sets of "directives" that let the Apache Web server know how it should configure itself and its modules. All lines in the file except the blank lines or lines starting with the # character are treated as part of a directive. The three sections are as follows:

- Global configuration
- Server configuration
- Virtual hosts configuration

Global Configuration

The overall operation of Apache is affected by the global configuration directives. The following list includes some of the key points defined in global configuration section:

- The location of directories and files that Apache uses for finding configuration files, storing process information, and internal statistics
- How network connection parameters such as timeouts and persistent connections are handled
- How Apache behaves when it needs to service multiple requests

Directives for Directories and Files

To define files and directories, use the following directives:

```
ServerType  standalone
ServerRoot  "/hm/httpd"
LockFile  /var/log/httpd/httpd.lock
PidFile  /var/log/httpd.pid
ScoreBoardFile  /var/log/httpd/httpd.scoreboard
ExtendedStatus  On
```

The `ServerType` directive controls how Apache is started. The two modes are `standalone` and `inetd`. Apache has a much faster response time and utilizes the resources of your machine more effectively in `standalone`, which is the default mode. The `inetd` mode is provided for backward compatibility. It should be used only by small sites that are not subject to a lot of hits.

The `ServerRoot` directive defines the top directory under which all of Apache's log file, error files, and configuration files will be stored. If you choose a different directory, you will need to make certain that `ServerRoot` is set to that directory.

WARNING Do not store the `httpd` executable file or the configuration files in the `DocumentRoot` directory or any of its subdirectories. The files in those directories are accessible to anyone using a Web client. It is a great security risk!

The `PidFile` and `LockFile` directives define the location of files that Apache uses to prevent startup collisions. These directives are helpful because if you start Apache and then try to start it again later, the second instance of Apache will look at these files and discover the first instance. It is a good way to prevent conflicts from occurring between two versions of Apache. You should not change the default locations for these two files.

The `ScoreBoardFile` directive defines the location of the file in which the internal statistics are stored. The information such as the number of requests that were handled, the origin of some of the recent requests, and the average time it took to handle a request are all stored in this file. It is permissible to relocate this file to another location if you prefer to change it. The `ExtendedStatus` directive is related to the `ScoreBoardFile` directive. If the value is `On`, you will be able to browse the statistics of your Web server by requesting the page or server status from it.

WARNING Web server statistics can provide information to malicious users or hackers. If your Web server will be on the Internet, the `ExtendedStatus` directive should be set to `Off`. If your intranet site is secure, you can set the directive to `On`.

Controlling Network Connections

The settings of the following directives determine how Apache handles network connections:

```
Timeout  300
KeepAlive  On
MaxKeepAliveRequests  100
KeepAliveTimeout  15
```

The `Timeout` directive controls the number of seconds that Apache waits for a request before timing out the connection to the client. The default number is 300 seconds. Although this is reasonable for installations, you may want to increase the number if you find that your site is receiving requests from clients that are very slow. If you are working with Web-based applications that require user authentication, then after the timeout expires, your users may have to reauthenticate themselves to the Web servers. If you want to decrease the frequency of reauthentication, you may need to set the `Timeout` directive to a higher number, such as 600 or 1,200 seconds.

The HTTP version 1.1's persistent connections feature allows clients to open a single connection to the Web server and use this connection for more than one query. The `KeepAlive`, `MaxKeepAliveRequests`, and `KeepAliveTimeout` directives control the behavior of persistent connections. The `KeepAlive` directive is used to activate persistent connections and should be set to `On`, which is the default. Apache allows clients to use this feature. Using persistent connections increases the efficiency of a Web server and the performance of browsers connecting to your site, so there is no reason to turn this off.

The `MaxKeepAliveRequests` directive limits the number of requests a client can make using the same connection. The default number is 100 requests. If clients are reconnecting multiple times, you may want to increase this number. Although it's not recommended, it is possible to allow clients to reuse a single connection as many times as needed by setting this directive to 0.

The `KeepAliveTimeout` directive is similar to the `Timeout` directive. Its value will determine how long Apache will wait before it closes a connection to a client. The default value is 15 seconds, but if your site is accessed by slow clients, you can increase the value to 20 or 30 seconds.

Controlling the Server Pool

When it is starting up, Apache creates several copies of itself to be used to handle incoming requests in a reasonable amount of time. When a request is received, the first idle copy of Apache will start to respond to the request. If another request comes in before Apache has finished responding to the first, another copy of Apache will answer the second request. This will go on for as many copies as necessary and the cycle will restart. This reduces the overall waiting time for clients. Depending upon the frequency of requests received by a site, you will want to tailor the number of servers available. The directives listed here will allow you to do that:

```
StartServers  5
MinSpareServers  5
MaxSpareServers  10
MaxClients  150
MaxRequestPerChild  30
```

The `StartServers` directive is used to tailor the number of copies Apache makes of itself on startup. The default value is 5, a reasonable number for small or medium sites. If you run your department's intranet web site or a Web site on the Internet, you should increase this number. Most sites work well with 10 to 20 initial servers. If you get complaints that your server is unavailable, try increasing the number by increments of 5 until you hit upon a number that is good for you. Make certain, however, that the number is not too high because it will put an unreasonable load on your system. It is not an easy task to determine the exact number of Web servers you need to have running at any given time. To simplify the task, Apache allows you to set both the minimum and maximum number of idle servers that should be present. By resetting these parameters, you can be certain that during periods of high traffic, your system will be able to handle requests in a reasonable amount of time. If things are slow, you can terminate any extra server to reduce the overall load on your machine.

The minimum number of idle servers is controlled by the `MinSpareServers` directive. The default value for this directive is 5. If the number of idle servers drops below 5, Apache will compensate by creating more, allowing you to keep a good response time. If you have a small site, this default will be fine. However, if you run a larger site, you may need to boost this directive to 10 or 15. Similarly, the maximum number of idle servers is 10. If Apache detects that there are more than 10 idle servers, it will terminate the extra ones to reduce the system load.

The `MaxClients` directive is intended to limit the number of simultaneous clients your Web server can handle because trying to handle thousand of simultaneous requests can bring a system to its proverbial knees. The default value of 150 is reasonable for most systems. If your Web server ever receives more than this number of simultaneous requests, the extra clients will be locked out until a copy of Apache becomes available. It is not a good idea to lock out too many clients, so do not set this value too low, especially under 50.

The `MaxRequestPerChild` directive is designed to avoid problems with running Apache for extended periods of time. On some operating systems, the networking libraries are heavily used. By limiting the number of requests that Apache handles, these problems can be kept to a minimum. The default value for this directive is 30. You should not change this number.

Server Configuration

The server configuration section includes server-specific configuration directives that are used to control the various aspects of Apache's responses to client requests:

```
Port  80
User  nobody
Group  nobody
ServerName  www.reliable.us
UseCanonicalName  On
ServerAdmin  root@barrie.reliable.us
```

The `Port` directive defines the port on which Apache listens for requests; the default is the HTTP port of 80. If you want to use a port other than 80, remind your clients that they will have to modify their URLS to access your Web server. The new port number must be identified in client URLs.

TIP If a non-root user is going to be starting Apache, the port number has to be over 1024 because any port below 1024 is called a reserved port and you have to be root to attach to it.

The `User` and `Group` directives should be used to run each instance or copy of Apache. The default is `nobody`. The user nobody has the lowest set of privileges on your system. On some versions of Unix, Apache cannot be run as nobody because that user does not have enough permissions to create network connections. To circumvent these problems, Apache must run as a different user, such as www, web, or httpd. This is not a problem on Solaris 8, but the option is available anyway.

The `ServerName` directive lets you set a host name that is sent out to clients for your server if it is different that the one the program would usually receive. You must define a host name with a valid DNS name. If your host runs on multiple networks, you may have to use an IP address so that clients can access it correctly.

The `UseCanonicalName` directive is related to the `ServerName` directive. It controls how Apache constructs the absolute URL on your server. If this directive is set to `On`, Apache will use the value of `ServerName` to construct the URLs. Optionally, it will rely on information provided by the client. This option should always be set to `On`.

The `ServerAdmin` directive defines the e-mail address of the system administrator. This e-mail address appears on pages generated by the server and should be set to the e-mail address of the person who will maintain the server on a daily basis. This person is usually the system administrator but may be someone else. Be sure that this e-mail address is fully qualified and not an address that only local users can get to.

Directory Directives

The directory directives control access to different directories where the HTML files are stored. The document root of the Web server is the main directory. All your HTML documents are stored in DocumentRoot. After receiving a request for a document, Apache searches for it relative to this directory. The document root is defined using the following directive:

```
DocumentRoot "/home/httpd/htdocs"
```

Once the root directory for your Web server as been defined, you should define the access permissions for that directory by using the Directory directive:

```
<Directory />
    Options FollowSymLinks
    AllowOverride None
</Directory>

<Directory "/home/httpd/htdocs">
    Options Indexes FollowSymLinks Multiviews
    AllowOverride None
    Order allow,deny
    Allow from all
</Directory>
```

The first Directory setting for root / is to let Apache know that the entire system only allows FollowSymLinks but not indexes or other information. The second Directory setting for "/home/httpd/htdocs" changes those permissions to allow the information to be visible to the client. The Options directive controls what types of actions Apache takes when in the DocumentRoot directory. Available options include Indexes, Includes, FollowSymLinks, ExecCGI, and MultiViews. When you use the Indexes option, Apache generates a directory listing if a client requests a directory rather than a document and there is no default HTML file for the directory. The Includes option filters the contents of documents before sending them to clients. The FollowSymLinks option translates symbolic links into files and directories but must be used with caution because it can allow users to link to other parts of the system that you won't want to be visible. The ExecCGI option tells Apache that documents in one directory should be treated as programs and then executed.

The AllowOverride directive has control over whether or not special.htaccess files can override the Options settings. Because extra options can be enabled from this file, you may want to prevent them from being enabled in the root directory for your HTML documents. You can also control access to your Web server using the Order directive, which allows you to define the hosts for which you want to permit access and those that you want to deny. Once the root directory has been defined, you can define the names for special files used by Apache: the directory index file, access control files, and the MIME types file. Apache uses the directory index file to handle client requests for a directory. When a client requests a directory, Apache will list its contents. If this is not what the client wants, you can use the DirectoryIndex directive to specify the name of an HTML file to use. Use the following syntax, and if the file exists, it will be returned to the client:

```
DirectoryIndex  index.html
```

The access control files are used to allow access to certain directories whose names have been defined using the AccessFileName directive.

```
AccessFileName  .htaccess
<Files  .htaccess>
    Order   allow, deny
    Deny  from all
</Files>
```

TIP Access files can contain privileged or sensitive information. In the interest of security, you may want to define a Files directive that prevents clients from accessing these files. By default, Apache has code protecting these files from being viewed or downloaded by Web clients.

The MIME types file is used to determine the correct MIME type for a specific file. You can control the location of this file by using the TypesConfig directive as in the following example:

```
TypesConfig /home/httpd/conf/mime.types
```

This location does not have to be changed because it is part of the standard configuration files and is installed along with the httpd.conf file.

The DefaultType directive defines the default MIME type for documents on the Web server. It is related to the MIME types file:

```
DefaultType  text/plain
```

If your server contains mostly text or HTML documents, then text/plain is the best value to use. However, if most of the content is binary, you can use the value application/octet-stream instead. The browsers will then not try to display binary files as though they were text.

CGI Scripts

CGI scripts give you the ability to execute commands on the server and return the output to clients. Because CGI scripts carry information about your server, access permissions should be more stringent for them than for the root directory.

If you want safe CGI scripts, you should use the ScriptAlias directive in combination with a Directory directive. The ScriptAlias directive lets Apache know that the files stored in a directory are scripts and should be executed. This directive acts as an alternative to ExecCGI, which allows you to mark a directory and all its subdirectories as those that contain only CGI programs. To enable CGI programs, use the following:

```
ScriptAlias /cgi-bin/ "/home/httpd/cgi-bin"
<Directory "/home/httpd/cgi-bin">
   AllowOverride  None
   Options  None
     Order allow, deny
     Allow from all
</Directory>
```

TIP After defining ScriptAlias, define a Directory directive for the CGI directory that disallows all options and prevents any overriding. This prevents visitors to the Web site with malicious intent from finding out which CGI programs you have.

Directory Listings

If Apache receives a request for a directory instead of a file, it tries to find the index file for that directory. If the file doesn't exist, Apache will respond with a listing of the contents of the directory. The IndexOptions directive controls the style of the listing. If you want a simple directory list, you simply set this option to Standard:

```
IndexOptions  Standard
```

If you prefer a description to be returned for each file in a directory, use this:

```
IndexOptions  FancyIndexing
```

You can also add descriptions for files when you use FancyIndexing. The syntax for this directive is as follows:

```
AddDescription  "description" .file-extension
```

Logging Directives

Apache controls log information about requests with the use of the logging directives:

```
HostnameLookups  Off
ErrorLog  /var/log/httpd/error-log
```

```
LogLevel  warn
LogFormat "%h %l %u %t \"%r\" %>s %b \"%{referer}I\"
   \"%{User-\Agent}I\""combine
LogFormat "%h %l %u %t \"%r\" %>s %b" common
LogFormat "%{referer}i -> %U referer
Logformat  "%{User-agent}i" agent
#CustomLog /var/log/httpd/access-log common
#CustomLog /var/log/httpd/referer-log referrer
#CustomLog /var/log/httpd/agent-log agent
#CustomLog /var/log/httpd/access-log  combined
```

The `HostnameLookups` directive controls whether or not the host name is logged on instead of the IP address of the client. Because resolving the host name of a client requires at least one DNS query, you should turn this option off to reduce the amount of network traffic generated by each request. Apache comes with a script for looking up the host names at a later time.

The `ErrorLog` directive defines the location of the error log, which stores information about request errors and response errors. It is useful when debugging CGI programs. Although you can store this anywhere you wish, the default is used most often by most sites.

The `LogLevel` and `LogFormat` directives define the Syslog level and format used for logging information. It is possible to define your own formats providing the defaults do not have enough information for you. The `CustomLog` directive uses requests, client's type, and the referring page.

BrowserMatch Directives

The `BrowserMatch` directives are used to modify the normal HTTP response behavior. Here is the standard set:

```
BrowserMatch "Mozilla/2"  nokeepalive
Force-response-1.0
BrowserMatch "RealPlayer 4\.0" force-response-1.0
BrowserMatch "Java/1\.0" force-response-1.0
BrowserMatch "JDL/1\.0: force-response-1.0
```

The first directive disables keepalive for I2.*x*. This version has problems dealing with persistent connections. The rest of the directives force RealPlayer and Java to use HTTP version 1 because they do not support HTTP version 1.1.

Virtual Hosts Configuration

There may be times when you need to host the Web sites of different organizations, particularly if you have departmental Web servers that have Web sites for different groups. It makes it easier for each group if users can access their Web pages using a simple URL such as www-res or www-docs rather than having to know the name of the server and the full path on that server. Apache provides a simple way of serving multiple Web sites from the same Web server by using an idea called virtual hosts. A *virtual host* uses the DNS feature of creating aliases to simulate multiple Web servers. For example, if you want to host the www-eng on your Web server, you would have to have www-eng added to DNS as an alias for your Web server.

There are several steps you must follow to configure virtual hosting:

1. The first step is to add aliases to DNS for the Web server. (See Chapter 9, which covers DNS in detail.)
2. The second step is to let Apache know about these different virtual hosts by using the VirtualHost directive. The following example shows how this is done:

```
NameVirtualHost 192.168.1.13

<VirtualHost www-eng.reliant.us>
      ServerAdmin root@www-eng.reliant.us
      DocumentRoot /home/httpd/eng-docs
      ServerName www-eng.reliant.us
      ErrorLog /var/log/httpd/eng-error_log
      TransferLog /var/log/httpd/eng-access_log
</VirtualHost>
```

3. The third step is to monitor the traffic by using the ErrorLog and TransferLog directives.

The virtual host configuration is somewhat like a miniature version of the full Web server configuration. Apache will invoke this directive when it detects that an incoming request was made using the name www-eng instead of the regular server's name. In the preceding example, the document root was set to a directory that is not stored in the DocumentRoot directory of the normal Web site. This allows other groups to maintain their Web sites independently. When you must make a change to one Web site, you won't affect other sites as long as the document root settings are completely different for the two sites. You can have hundreds of VitualHost entries all attached to the same IP address.

Other directives, such as ServerAdmin, ErrorLog, and TransferLog, are useful for accounting purposes. You can use the ServerAdmin directive to redirect support e-mail messages to whomever is in charge of the content for a Web site. The ErrorLog and TransferLog directives will allow you to log the traffic received by a Web site separately from the other Web sites, allowing you to monitor the traffic fairly easily.

TIP Older versions of AOL's browser are not able to handle virtual hosting. If you have a large number of users with such browsers, you may need to set up separate Web servers for each virtual site. If, however, your main traffic is from users with Netscape 3 or higher and Microsoft Internet Explorer 3 or higher, you can stick with virtual hosting.

Summary

This chapter discussed how you can use Solaris to support connections to the Internet, which has become a major force in global communications, and to intranets, which are networks that resides locally within an organization.

You learned that WANs operate over large geographical areas using dedicated data lines, radio, or satellites that transmit data, and that they connect LANs to the Internet on a global level. LANs use a gateway to connect to a WAN. A gateway is a computer or other special device with multiple network connections. Another gateway converts data to the appropriate format for the receiving network. Routers act as mapping devices and choose the routes that can dynamically communicate with each other.

This chapter also covered the domain name service (DNS), which translates the names of network nodes into network addresses. The database is updated on a global level by cooperating systems. It is too large to be housed at one site but is contained in several different databases, which are mapped to alphanumeric host names.

You learned that the American Registry for Internet Numbers (ARIN) manages the IP address assignments. Refinement of the IP addressing plan is being implemented as deficiencies are discovered. It will offer support for security, performance, and control features.

The Hypertext Transfer Protocol (HTTP) allows for text files embedded with Uniform Resource Locators (URLs) to be transferred from a server to a client machine requesting a file. Apache, a server that handles more than half of all the world's Web sites, uses this protocol. The Apache Project developed software for an HTTP server that is free of charge and available for download on the Internet. It has many enhancements and is supported by many users as well as network developers.

This chapter also discussed URLs, which can contain a protocol identifying the method you want to use to access a Web page. Web pages are text files written in a language called the Hypertext Markup Language (HTML). This language controls the way different resources on the page can be retrieved on the Internet. The Common Gateway Interface (CGI) is a standard that defines the interface between the Web server and an external program. CGI programs can put a large burden on a Web server but are used widely on networks.

CHAPTER 15

Memory and Process Management

FEATURING:

Viewing processes 606

The process file system 618

Controlling processes 622

Running jobs 627

Memory, real and virtual 630

The Solaris operating system consists of a set of software modules you can use to manage the way users interact with programs and hardware. The central module, the Unix kernel, controls memory, system input/output (I/O), files, and process management. In this chapter, I'll describe how Solaris initiates a process, how you can determine what processes are running, and how you can use Solaris commands and utilities to interact with processes.

Anything running on your system runs as a process and is both named and identified. Processes are system services, applications, routines, and jobs that consume processor cycles. Understanding processes and how to identify and manage them is at the heart of system optimization, debugging, and fault isolation. Although the terminology may seem somewhat technical or arcane, the information presented in this chapter will help you out when you need it most, when your system is malfunctioning or hung and when performance is an issue. Solaris 8 offers you many different commands to help you discover what processes are running on your system, adjust their priorities, and even terminate or kill them when they fail.

Processes are related to memory and require memory to run. Solaris provides several commands you can use to look at your system's memory configuration and alter memory contents. Just as Solaris creates and manages a virtual process file system, the operating system creates and manages a temporary file system to map memory contents to disk. A system of physical RAM with a swap file for paging program segments and code to and from disk is used to extend your system's resources.

System Process Overview

When executable programs run, they are made up of five parts: text, data, backing storage section (BSS), the stack, and the user area. The text part contains shareable program code in machine language. The data portion stores initialized program variables, and the BSS portion stores uninitialized program variables. The stack is an area of dynamic memory that stores local variables and parameters used for system and function calls. Finally, the user area stores Unix kernel process information.

The first program that runs on your computer that a user interacts directly with is the shell itself. The shell can spawn other shells and programs, and each instance of a shell or program is a separate set of processes that are identified and associated with the application and user that spawned or executed them. Thus, multiple instances of a program or process may be running, but as far as the system is concerned, each is unique.

Every process that is created has a unique identification number called its process ID, or PID, assigned to it. Your system uses the PID to recognize the process it represents. The PID number is identified with the user who executed or spawned the process through their user ID (UID) and with the user's group through the group ID (GID). The UID can be either the real UID of the user or the effective UID that was assumed by the user during a session in which they switched to a different user account. The GID can also be the real or effective GID. When the effective UID and GID are used, the user executes the application using the `setuid` and `setgid` commands, respectively.

Process 0 is the process created when your system initializes. A program or a shell can spawn another shell or program using the `system()` call in a C program. More often, new programs and all other processes are spawned or created from Process 1. Process 1, `init`, is spawned by the system scheduler (Process 0). That is why many of the system processes you launch show a PPID of 1. For application processes, you will see a PPID of `dtwm` if you launch them by using a button click from the GUI; you'll see the PPID of the shell you launched them from if you launched them from the command line. The set of `fork()`, `vfork()`, or `exec()` system calls don't spawn a new shell. These aforementioned calls have the following functions:

- `fork()` creates a new duplicate child process that is combined with processes created by `exec()` system calls.
- `vfork()` creates a new process without duplicating the parent process, but `vfork()` allows for sharing the data of the parent process, thus conserving memory.
- `exec()` overlays a process's current state with a new process image or executable. There are six forms of Unix `exec()` system calls: `execl()`, `execv()`, `execle()`, `execve()`, `execlp()`, and `execvp()`.

As a process runs, it exists in a certain state in your system. Solaris maintains a process queue to determine what processes are running, what their state is, and which process to run first or with higher priority (meaning the process can command system resources more often than a process with a lower priority). You have some control over the Solaris process queue. Unix creates process structure information using the instructions contained in the `/usr/include/sys/proc.h` and `/usr/include/sys/user.h` files. The `.h` file extension indicates that the file contains header information that contains instructions used to compile a program. To get a sense of how a process is structured, take a look at the `proc.h` file, a portion of which is shown in Figure 15.1. The directives contained in the `proc.h` header file direct the kernel to follow and maintain various structures and flags once a process is initiated.

TIP The various header files (`*.h`) in the `/usr/include` directory contain system documentation that describes how Solaris operates internally. You may find it useful to examine those files. Additionally, Unix stores a list of standard errors with some documentation in the `errno.h` file. For unknown system errors, check this file for its contents.

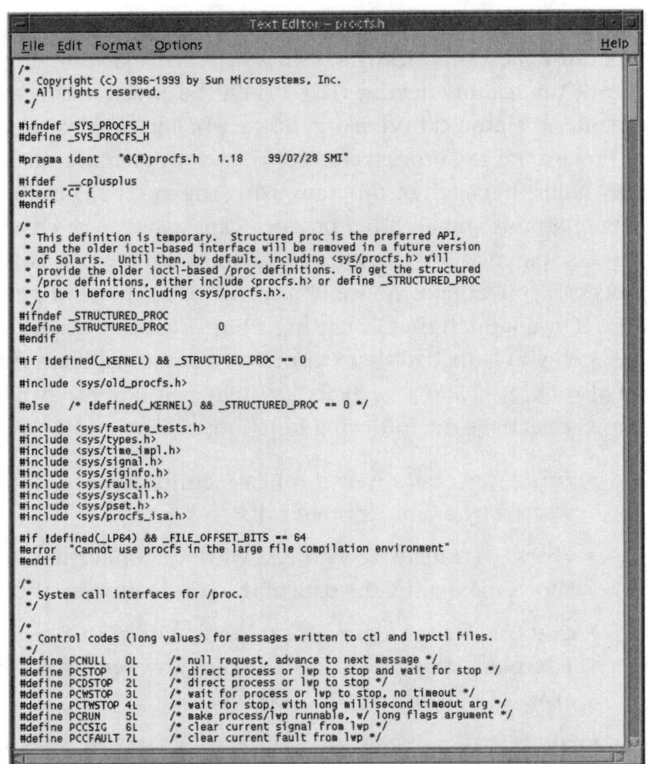


```
/*
 * Copyright (c) 1996-1999 by Sun Microsystems, Inc.
 * All rights reserved.
 */

#ifndef _SYS_PROCFS_H
#define _SYS_PROCFS_H

#pragma ident   "@(#)procfs.h   1.18    99/07/28 SMI"

#ifdef  __cplusplus
extern "C" {
#endif

/*
 * This definition is temporary.  Structured proc is the preferred API,
 * and the older ioctl-based interface will be removed in a future version
 * of Solaris.  Until then, by default, including <sys/procfs.h> will
 * provide the older ioctl-based /proc definitions.  To get the structured
 * /proc definitions, either include <procfs.h> or define _STRUCTURED_PROC
 * to be 1 before including <sys/procfs.h>.
 */
#ifndef _STRUCTURED_PROC
#define _STRUCTURED_PROC        0
#endif

#if !defined(_KERNEL) && _STRUCTURED_PROC == 0

#include <sys/old_procfs.h>

#else   /* !defined(_KERNEL) && _STRUCTURED_PROC == 0 */

#include <sys/feature_tests.h>
#include <sys/types.h>
#include <sys/time_impl.h>
#include <sys/signal.h>
#include <sys/siginfo.h>
#include <sys/fault.h>
#include <sys/syscall.h>
#include <sys/pset.h>
#include <sys/procfs_isa.h>

#if !defined(_LP64) && _FILE_OFFSET_BITS == 64
#error  "Cannot use procfs in the large file compilation environment"
#endif

/*
 * System call interfaces for /proc.
 */

/*
 * Control codes (long values) for messages written to ctl and lwpctl files.
 */
#define PCNULL    0L    /* null request, advance to next message */
#define PCSTOP    1L    /* direct process or lwp to stop and wait for stop */
#define PCDSTOP   2L    /* direct process or lwp to stop */
#define PCWSTOP   3L    /* wait for process or lwp to stop, no timeout */
#define PCTWSTOP  4L    /* wait for stop, with long millisecond timeout arg */
#define PCRUN     5L    /* make process/lwp runnable, w/ long flags argument */
#define PCCSIG    6L    /* clear current signal from lwp */
#define PCCFAULT  7L    /* clear current fault from lwp */
```

FIGURE 15.1

The `/usr/include/sys/procfs.h` *file contains instructions for initiating system processes.*

A process exists in any one of five possible states:

`SIDL` (idle) The process is defined and is listed by the scheduler to run.

`SRUN` (run) The process is in the run queue.

`SSLEEP` (sleep) The process is temporarily suspended in the run queue. Typically, a process is in the sleep state when a system resource that it depends upon for execution is not available, such as data requiring I/O from disk.

`SSTOP` (stopped) An executing process is stopped. The parent process can stop a child process, or the process could be stopped by a signal from another process. To continue a stopped process, the system must receive a `SIGCONT` signal.

SZOMB (zombie) A zombie process is a process that has terminated (exited) and no longer exists in the system but is still referenced in the system as existing, typically as an association with the parent process. That is, the parent process, having issued a wait() system call to determine when the child process terminates, will store a zombie when the child process doesn't issue a SIGCLD (child death) signal when it terminates.

The job scheduler module determines which process has access to the CPU at any moment. A process runs either in real time or as a time-share (the default) in a round-robin schedule. Processes that run in a round-robin schedule are assigned priorities and their access time to the microprocessor is measured. When an appropriate time slice has occurred, the scheduler interrupts or preempts the execution of the process after the completion of a thread and moves the focus of program execution to another process. The system stores process-specific information and performs a context switch to the next process in the run queue. In an attempt to balance system resources, the algorithms used to assign the access to the processor take into account the amount of time that the process has already had access.

The terms *foreground process* and *background process* are often used to describe the priority that is assigned to a certain process. A foreground process is one that has a high priority and is executed in preference to another process. A background process has a lower priority, receives less processor attention, and executes more slowly. Typically, transaction processing and screen redraws are foreground processes, and printing and I/O to serial devices like modems are executed as background processes.

You can modify a process from time-share to real time by using the priocntl system call. In normal operations, although it is somewhat uncommon to adjust a program's or subsystem's priority in the time-share mode, changing something to real time is almost never done. When a process runs real time, its priority is set to infinity and the system must start the process and then complete it before returning the system focus to another process. Thus, real-time processes are usually reserved for system functions, and unless designed to run as real-time processes, there is a much higher likelihood that they will hang the system if switched into the time-share mode. Additionally, denying access to a real-time process like a kernel system process will also likely crash the system.

You can use the priocntl (priority control) command to view or modify the job queue, altering the scheduling priorities of a process. You can also use the command to change a time-shared process into a real-time process. Solaris returns the output shown in Figure 15.2 when you issue the priocntl -l command. On Solaris, there is a class called IA, or interactive, that offers interactive users enhanced performance. SYS indicates a system or kernel process, and TS is a time-sharing process.

FIGURE 15.2

The `priocntl -l` *command shows the CPU scheduler settings.*

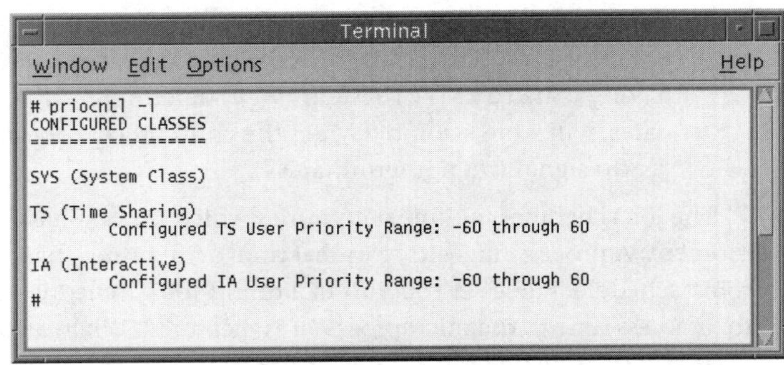
Terminal
Window Edit Options Help
priocntl -l
CONFIGURED CLASSES
==================
SYS (System Class)
TS (Time Sharing)
Configured TS User Priority Range: -60 through 60
IA (Interactive)
Configured IA User Priority Range: -60 through 60
#

Viewing Processes

Solaris offers you a number of commands to view processes running on your system. They provide detailed information about processes and their states, and each command is useful in a different way. Additionally, you can use the Process Manager in the CDE to monitor active processes. The sections that follow show you how to use these utilities and tools.

The *ps* Command

The ps (process) command is used to determine the status of processes currently running on your system. This command is a diagnostic utility that every Solaris and Unix user should have in their bag of tricks. When you give the ps command by itself, it returns just those processes that were executed by the user who issued it. The ps command returns a display similar to the following:

```
$ ps
PID     TTY     TIME    CMD
11530   pts/6   0:00    sh
```

The output identifies the PID of the process, the TTY (terminal) that it was executed from, the time the process consumed, and the command that was executed. Typically, the ps command is coupled with one or more of its many options, of which the following are a useful selection:

-a option Reports all processes, including some system processes.

-c option Displays the class of the process.

-e (or -A) option The -e option reports on everything, including all system processes.

-d option Lists all processes.

-f option Generates a full listing.

-g (or -G) option The -g option lists process information for a single group, and the -G option lists the processes for a list of groups.

-j option Displays the session identifier (SID).

-l *<format>* option Generates a long listing with detailed information.

-L *<format>* option The -L option outputs a list of lightweight processes (LWPs) that are running on your system. LWPs are virtual CPU or execution resources that are designed to optimize the use of CPU resources based on priority and scheduling class.

-o *<format>* option Outputs the results of ps command according to the format you specify. The ps man pages have a description of these formats in the "Display Formats" section.

-p *<PID>* list option Displays the processes belonging to the PID number(s) specified in the comma- or space-delimited list.

-P option Lists the CPU ID that a process is bound to.

-u *<UID>* list option Displays the processes belonging to the username that has the UID(s) specified as a comma- or space-delimited list.

Figure 15.3 shows the output of the ps -ef command on a system running several programs. The command returns a list of the active processes or jobs running on your system. The display for a workstation running only a screen capture utility runs about two screenfuls worth of information. When you use the -c option to display process classes, the kernel processes are the ones in the SYS class. Figure 15.4 shows the output for the ps command used with the -efc options; notice that the third column displays the class.

FIGURE 15.3

The `ps -ef` *command returns a list of the processes running on your system.*

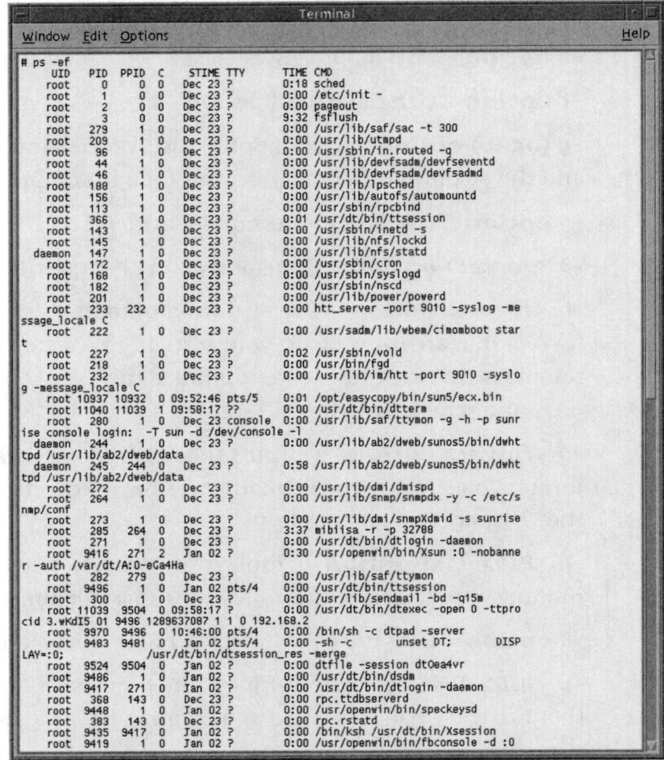

Table 15.1 includes descriptions of the columns you see in the various output displays of the ps command.

WARNING When the -c option is used, the higher the PRI listing, the higher the priority. If you don't use the -c option, the higher the PRI, the lower the priority. This can sometimes cause much confusion.

FIGURE 15.4

The ps command with the -efc option returns the classification that the processes belong to as well.

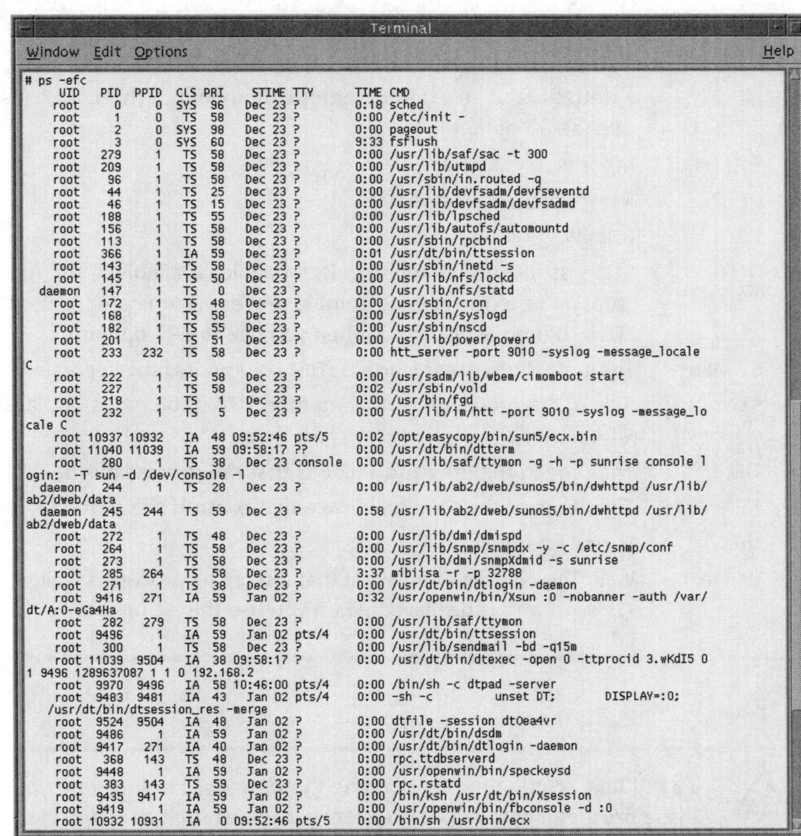

TABLE 15.1: THE OUTPUT COLUMNS OF THE ps COMMAND

Title	Description
ADDR	Memory address in hexadecimal format.
C	Processor utilization.
CLS	Class of process: SYS is a kernel process, TS is a terminal state, and IA is interactive. (This column is displayed when you use the -c option.)
CMD	The command line that initiated the process, truncated so that it fits on a single line.
F	Flags belonging to the process, used for compatibility with previous versions of Solaris. (This column is displayed when you use the -l option.)

Continued

PART II

Solaris and the Network

TABLE 15.1: THE OUTPUT COLUMNS OF THE ps COMMAND (CONTINUED)

Title	Description
NI	Niceness value, used to determine the priority. (This column is displayed when you use the `-l` option.)
PID	Process ID number.
PPID	Parent process ID number.
PRI	Priority.
S	State, as follows: O, running; R, runnable (available in the run queue); S, sleeping; T, stopped or terminated; Z, zombie process (terminated without informing parent). (This column is displayed when you use the `-l` option.)
STIME	The time the process started. (This column is displayed when you use the `-f` option.)
SZ	Size of the process in virtual memory. (This column is displayed when you use the `-l` option.)
TIME	The time in minutes and seconds that the process has been running.
TTY	The name of the terminal device that controls the process.
UID	User ID number.
WCHAN	Wait. The address of an event that a sleeping process is waiting for in order to execute. (This column is displayed when you use the `-l` option.)

TIP Take a little time to examine the processes that run on your system, particularly those processes that are core system processes such as `init`, the scheduler, the logging system, the NIS cache, and so on. When you have a feeling for how many CPU cycles they consume normally, you can better understand what might be making your system malfunction when you see abnormal results.

As you can see in Figures 15.3 and 15.4, the `ps` command overwhelms you with information about running processes. As a system administrator, you typically want to know about the "top" processes running on a system (the processes that consume the most CPU time) that you are trying to diagnose. That's what the `top` command is designed to do. The `top` command samples your system at specific intervals and returns the topmost 10 or 20 processes to the terminal windows, allowing you to monitor a system. You have control over the sampling period as well as the number of processes that are returned.

The top command is not a native Solaris command. To obtain this utility, download it from ftp://ftp.groupsys.com/pub/top. There are several different downloadable versions of the program at that site. Once you install top, you can call the top command from the command line.

The top command generates process statistics by reading the proc file system as a setuid process. You can run the program as root, but to allow other users and groups to run top, you need to reset the read and execute permissions. You may want to be careful about allowing nonprivileged users to run top because a setuid process allows users to make changes and presents a security risk. When compiling top for Solaris 8, make sure that the GNU gcc compiler is the right version or top will report incorrect results. Download the top program from ftp://sunsite.unc.edu/pub/solairs/sparc/ as a package called top* (recommended) and save yourself the trouble of compiling it.

The *truss* Command

Another useful diagnostic command is the truss (trace a process) command. This command returns a list of the system calls executed by a program, the signals that that program receives from the system, and any faults that were encountered. Figure 15.5 shows the output of the truss date command. You might recall that the date command returns the system date. Just this one very simple system command returns 43 lines from the truss command. Not all Unix systems support the truss command, but Solaris 8 does.

Here are a list of the most commonly used options that the truss command offers:

-a option Reports all arguments passed to an exec() call after a fork.

-c option Counts system calls, faults, and signals and outputs a summary report.

-e option Shows all environmental variables that existed when exec() was called.

-f (fork) option Traces all child processes.

-o *<outputfile>* option Outputs the results to an output file.

-r *<fd>* option Shows the contents of buffers for read calls as file descriptor *<fd>*. Shows calls to other file descriptor and writes calls as *<fd>*.

-s [!]*<signal>* list option The option -s displays signals from a comma-delimited list.

-t [!]*<call>* list option The option -t displays system calls from a comma-delimited list.

-v option Shows a verbose display.

`-x [!]`*`<call>`* `list` option The option `-x` displays data passed to the system calls as hexadecimal values in a comma-delimited list.

`-w` *`<fd>`* option Shows the contents of buffers for write calls as file descriptor *<fd>*. Shows calls to other file descriptor and reads calls as *<fd>*.

FIGURE 15.5

The output of the `truss date` *command*

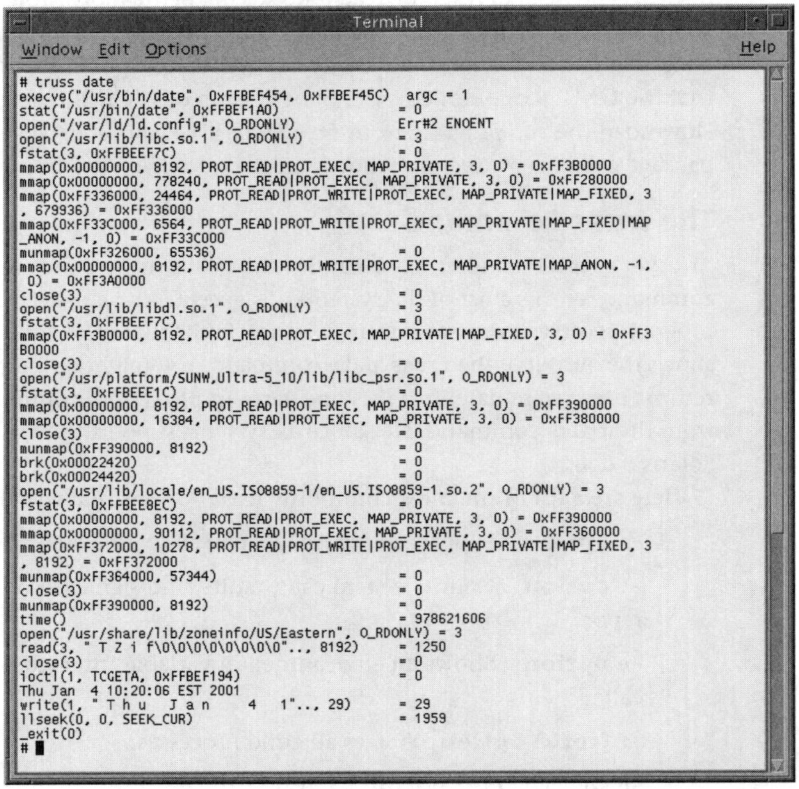

```
Terminal
Window  Edit  Options                                                    Help
# truss date
execve("/usr/bin/date", 0xFFBEF454, 0xFFBEF45C)  argc = 1
stat("/usr/bin/date", 0xFFBEF1A0)               = 0
open("/var/ld/ld.config", O_RDONLY)             Err#2 ENOENT
open("/usr/lib/libc.so.1", O_RDONLY)            = 3
fstat(3, 0xFFBEEF7C)                            = 0
mmap(0x00000000, 8192, PROT_READ|PROT_EXEC, MAP_PRIVATE, 3, 0) = 0xFF3B0000
mmap(0x00000000, 778240, PROT_READ|PROT_EXEC, MAP_PRIVATE, 3, 0) = 0xFF280000
mmap(0xFF336000, 24464, PROT_READ|PROT_WRITE|PROT_EXEC, MAP_PRIVATE|MAP_FIXED, 3
, 679936) = 0xFF336000
mmap(0xFF33C000, 6564, PROT_READ|PROT_WRITE|PROT_EXEC, MAP_PRIVATE|MAP_FIXED|MAP
_ANON, -1, 0) = 0xFF33C000
munmap(0xFF326000, 65536)                       = 0
mmap(0x00000000, 8192, PROT_READ|PROT_WRITE|PROT_EXEC, MAP_PRIVATE|MAP_ANON, -1,
 0) = 0xFF3A0000
close(3)                                        = 0
open("/usr/lib/libdl.so.1", O_RDONLY)           = 3
fstat(3, 0xFFBEEF7C)                            = 0
mmap(0xFF3B0000, 8192, PROT_READ|PROT_EXEC, MAP_PRIVATE|MAP_FIXED, 3, 0) = 0xFF3
B0000
close(3)                                        = 0
open("/usr/platform/SUNW,Ultra-5_10/lib/libc_psr.so.1", O_RDONLY) = 3
fstat(3, 0xFFBEEE1C)                            = 0
mmap(0x00000000, 8192, PROT_READ|PROT_EXEC, MAP_PRIVATE, 3, 0) = 0xFF390000
mmap(0x00000000, 16384, PROT_READ|PROT_EXEC, MAP_PRIVATE, 3, 0) = 0xFF380000
close(3)                                        = 0
munmap(0xFF390000, 8192)                        = 0
brk(0x00022420)                                 = 0
brk(0x00024420)                                 = 0
open("/usr/lib/locale/en_US.ISO8859-1/en_US.ISO8859-1.so.2", O_RDONLY) = 3
fstat(3, 0xFFBEE8EC)                            = 0
mmap(0x00000000, 8192, PROT_READ|PROT_EXEC, MAP_PRIVATE, 3, 0) = 0xFF390000
mmap(0x00000000, 90112, PROT_READ|PROT_EXEC, MAP_PRIVATE, 3, 0) = 0xFF360000
mmap(0xFF372000, 10278, PROT_READ|PROT_WRITE|PROT_EXEC, MAP_PRIVATE|MAP_FIXED, 3
, 8192) = 0xFF372000
munmap(0xFF364000, 57344)                       = 0
close(3)                                        = 0
munmap(0xFF390000, 8192)                        = 0
time()                                          = 978621606
open("/usr/share/lib/zoneinfo/US/Eastern", O_RDONLY) = 3
read(3, " T Z i f\0\0\0\0\0\0\0\0".., 8192)     = 1250
close(3)                                        = 0
ioctl(1, TCGETA, 0xFFBEF194)                    = 0
Thu Jan  4 10:20:06 EST 2001
write(1, " T h u   J a n     4   1".., 29)       = 29
llseek(0, 0, SEEK_CUR)                          = 1959
_exit(0)
# 
```

When you know the PID number of the process you want to monitor, you can use the `truss -p` *<PIDnumber>* command to follow the trace of the process and watch it run if you are a root user or the user who owns the program. If you want to monitor other people's processes, you will need root privileges. You can get the PID number from the `ps -ef` command. The `truss` command is particularly useful in tracking down client/server problems. If a process is hung, you can use the `truss` command on either the client or the server to see if the process is sleeping or has terminated.

You can also observe whether there are signals being returned to the process (and what signals they might be) and whether there were any faults associated with the process. For example, you can use the `truss ping` command or the Oracle database equivalent `truss tnsping` (ping against an Oracle database) to determine how a network responds.

Here's something else that is very useful. If you want to capture the entire session (that is, if the program you are running `truss` on is interactive and you want to capture your input as well as the output from `truss`), you can use the `script` command. You first run `script` *<filename>*, replacing *<filename>* with what you want the log of the session to be called, then run the `truss` command. After you have completed the interactive session with `truss` and the program you are testing, press the Ctrl+D keystroke and the script will exit. You now have a file with a full log of your interaction.

The Process Manager

Solaris provides a graphical utility called the Process Manager, which not only is visually more appealing than the `ps` command, it offers an interactive real-time display of processes executing on a system. To open the Process Manager, double-click the Process Manager icon (shown in the following graphic) in the Desktop_Apps window of the Application Manager. The Application Manager is accessible from the Applications control on the Applications subpanel of the front panel of the CDE.

In the Process Manager window shown in Figure 15.6, you see a list of processes with the following information included (from left to right):

- PID
- Name of the process
- Owner of the process; that is, the person who executed the process
- CPU%, which measures the percentage of microprocessor cycles that the process is consuming
- RAM, amount of memory that the process occupies
- Swap, how much virtual memory is consumed by the process
- Started, when the process was initiated
- Parent, the PID of the process that spawned or created the processes
- Command, the *<pathname>*/*<filename>* of the program that created the process

FIGURE 15.6

The Process Manager

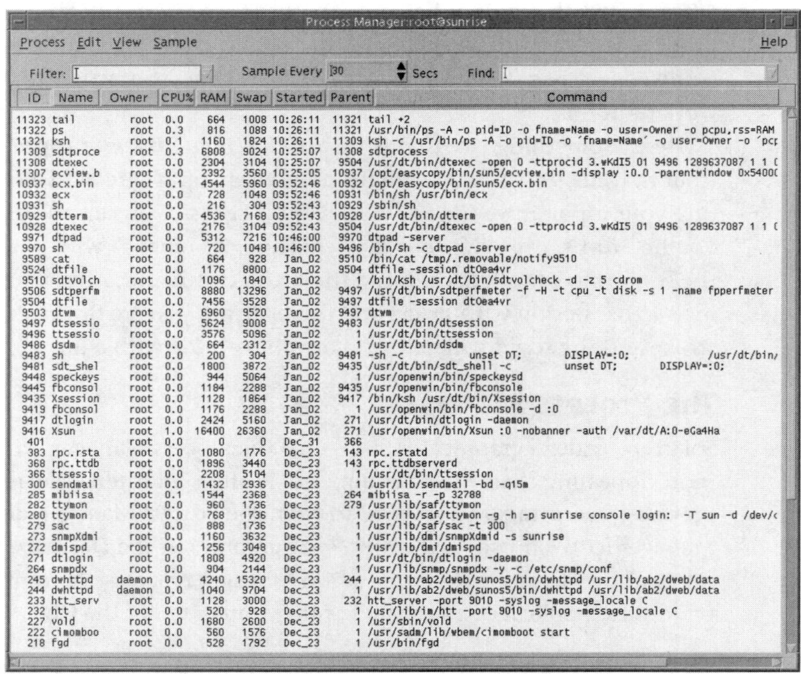

Although the top command is a more powerful tool, the Process Manager is easier to work with and learn. There are a number of useful functions in the Process Manager for debugging and tracing processes as well as for identifying the owner. The Kill command (Ctrl+C) that allows you to terminate an errant process is found on the Process menu, which is shown in the following graphic.

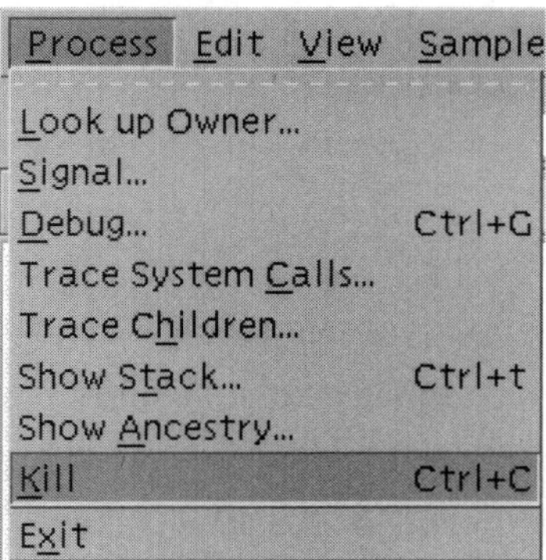

When you're using the Process Manager to troubleshoot a system, the telltale sign of a runaway process is the existence of several identical jobs all owned by the same user. An example would be an errant script that initiates processes without checking to see if the previous processes complete themselves first. Also, if a process is using a considerable percentage of CPU time, that might indicate that the process is in an endless loop. Other telltale signs are processes that execute with high nice numbers (see the next section) or processes that are using more and more CPU time as they execute.

Process Priorities

Solaris and Unix provide commands you can use to alter the scheduling priority under which a process runs. To view the default scheduling policies of the process scheduler, use the `dispadmin` command.

WARNING If you are going to change process priorities, be aware that you could cause your system to crash if you make a mistake. Take extra caution when adjusting priorities, and if possible, try your changes on a non-production system.

The `nice` command allows you to change a scheduling priority, whereas the `priocntl` command provides a general interface to the Unix scheduler. The `nice` command runs as a shell command, and not every process supports it. You can control what shell is used to execute the `nice` command; otherwise, it uses your default shell during execution. The `nice` command sets a priority (the so-called nice number) from 0 to 39 (or a range of 40), where 0 is the best and 39 is the worst. Processes inherit their nice number from their parent, and the `ps -el` lists the number in the NI column. Mostly, `nice` is supported for backward compatibility, and you should spend your time mastering the `priocntl` (priority control) command.

Processes are assigned a user execution level of from 1 to 19, and it is assumed that 10 is the default increment. A higher priority than 19 is run as 19. If a superuser enters a negative increment, the commands issued by the superuser with a negative increment are run with a higher priority than normal. Priority 1 is the highest level, 19 the lowest. The `nice` command's syntax allows you to specify the command as well as an argument used by that command.

You can adjust the nice number to a lower priority by raising it (either with a `nice -n` *<positivenumber>* or `nice` *<negativenumber>*) from 1 to 19 points, where 19 points (either `nice -n 19` or `nice -19`) will result in the maximum nice number of 39. You can raise the priority by lowing the nice number (using `nice -n` *<negativenumber>*) to a nice total of 0 by using the smallest number, –20 (that is, `nice -n -20`). The default nice level is 20 (or `nice -n 0` from the command line). For the programmer, this scheme is different, because they can use the `nice()` function to set the nice level directly to 0 through 39.

TIP If you have a large compile you need to run but still need to use the system as your desktop, you may run the compile at a higher nice level so that your other applications will have more time at the CPU.

WARNING Inappropriate use of the `nice` command, and in particular the `priocntl` command, can cause your system to respond sluggishly and malfunction and possibly cause you to have to reboot your system should you alter the priority of an essential system function. Changing process priorities isn't something end users typically do, and it's rarely done in system administration.

The `priocntl` (priority control) command allows you to display (as you have seen previously with the `-l` option) or set the scheduling parameters of specific processes. The priority range for both time-sharing and interactive processes can range from –60 to +60; real-time processes have a maximum configured priority of 59. System functions like the scheduler and the paging mechanism (pageout) are assigned higher priorities, typically in the high 90s so that they execute with strong preference. You can use the `ps -ecl` command to display the global priority of a process. That priority is shown in the seventh (PRI) column. Figure 15.7 shows the output of the `ps -ecl` command.

Using the `priocntl` command, you can alter the performance of the scheduler, allowing you access to the real-time, time-sharing, and interactive classes of processes. The `priocntl` man pages go into great detail about the options of this command.

To use the `priocntl` command to designate a process priority, do the following:

1. Switch to a superuser with the `su` command.
2. Start a process with a designated priority using the following command:

   ```
   # priocntl -e -c <class> -m <userlimit> -p <pri> <commandname>
   ```

   `-e` executes the command; `-c` *<class>* specifies the class, which is typically `TS` for time-sharing or `RT` for real time; `-m` *<userlimit>* is the maximum amount that you change your priority when `-p` is used; and `-p pri` *<commandname>* is the relative priority for the RT thread. When you use `-p`, you can change a user-designated priority by –20 to +20.

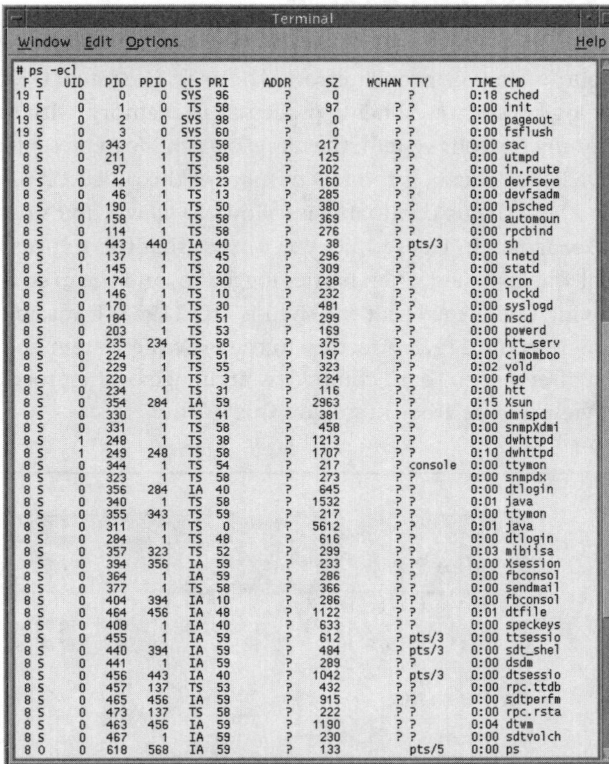

Terminal
Window Edit Options Help
ps -ecl
 F S   UID   PID PPID CLS PRI   ADDR   SZ   WCHAN TTY   TIME CMD
19 T   0   0   0 SYS 96   ?   0   ?   0:18 sched
 8 S   0   1   0   TS 58   ?   97   ? ?   0:00 init
19 S   0   2   0 SYS 98   ?   0   ? ?   0:00 pageout
19 S   0   3   0 SYS 60   ?   0   ? ?   0:00 fsflush
 8 S   0   343   1   TS 58   ?   217   ? ?   0:00 sac
 8 S   0   211   1   TS 58   ?   125   ? ?   0:00 utmpd
 8 S   0   97   1   TS 58   ?   202   ? ?   0:00 in.route
 8 S   0   44   1   TS 23   ?   160   ? ?   0:00 devfseve
 8 S   0   46   1   TS 13   ?   285   ? ?   0:00 devfsadm
 8 S   0   190   1   TS 50   ?   380   ? ?   0:00 lpsched
 8 S   0   158   1   TS 58   ?   369   ? ?   0:00 automoun
 8 S   0   114   1   TS 58   ?   276   ? ?   0:00 rpcbind
 8 S   0   443   440   IA 40   ?   38   ? pts/3   0:00 sh
 8 S   0   137   1   TS 45   ?   296   ? ?   0:00 inetd
 8 S   1   145   1   TS 20   ?   309   ? ?   0:00 statd
 8 S   0   174   1   TS 30   ?   238   ? ?   0:00 cron
 8 S   0   146   1   TS 10   ?   232   ? ?   0:00 lockd
 8 S   0   170   1   TS 30   ?   481   ? ?   0:00 syslogd
 8 S   0   184   1   TS 51   ?   299   ? ?   0:00 nscd
 8 S   0   203   1   TS 53   ?   169   ? ?   0:00 powerd
 8 S   0   235   234   TS 58   ?   375   ? ?   0:00 htt_serv
 8 S   0   224   1   TS 51   ?   197   ? ?   0:00 cimomboo
 8 S   0   229   1   TS 55   ?   323   ? ?   0:02 vold
 8 S   0   220   1   TS   3   ?   224   ? ?   0:00 fgd
 8 S   0   234   1   TS 31   ?   116   ? ?   0:00 htt
 8 S   0   354   284   IA 59   ?   2963   ? ?   0:15 Xsun
 8 S   0   330   1   TS 41   ?   381   ? ?   0:00 dmispd
 8 S   0   331   1   TS 58   ?   458   ? ?   0:00 snmpXdmi
 8 S   1   248   1   TS 38   ?   1213   ? ?   0:00 dwhttpd
 8 S   1   249   248   TS 58   ?   1707   ? ?   0:10 dwhttpd
 8 S   0   344   1   TS 54   ?   217   ? console   0:00 ttymon
 8 S   0   323   1   TS 58   ?   273   ? ?   0:00 snmpdx
 8 S   0   356   284   IA 40   ?   645   ? ?   0:00 dtlogin
 8 S   0   340   1   TS 58   ?   1532   ? ?   0:01 java
 8 S   0   355   343   TS 59   ?   217   ? ?   0:00 ttymon
 8 S   0   311   1   TS   0   ?   5612   ? ?   0:01 java
 8 S   0   284   1   TS 48   ?   616   ? ?   0:00 dtlogin
 8 S   0   357   323   TS 52   ?   299   ? ?   0:03 mibiisa
 8 S   0   394   356   IA 59   ?   233   ? ?   0:00 Xsession
 8 S   0   364   1   IA 59   ?   286   ? ?   0:00 fbconsol
 8 S   0   377   1   TS 58   ?   366   ? ?   0:00 sendmail
 8 S   0   404   394   IA 10   ?   286   ? ?   0:00 fbconsol
 8 S   0   464   456   IA 48   ?   1122   ? ?   0:01 dtfile
 8 S   0   408   1   IA 40   ?   633   ? ?   0:00 speckeys
 8 S   0   455   1   IA 59   ?   612   ? pts/3   0:00 ttsessio
 8 S   0   440   394   IA 59   ?   484   ? pts/3   0:00 sdt_shel
 8 S   0   441   1   IA 59   ?   289   ? ?   0:00 dsdm
 8 S   0   456   443   IA 40   ?   1042   ? pts/3   0:00 dtsessio
 8 S   0   457   137   TS 53   ?   432   ? ?   0:00 rpc.ttdb
 8 S   0   465   456   IA 59   ?   915   ? ?   0:00 sdtperfm
 8 S   0   473   137   TS 58   ?   222   ? ?   0:00 rpc.rsta
 8 S   0   463   456   IA 59   ?   1190   ? ?   0:04 dtwm
 8 S   0   467   1   IA 59   ?   230   ? ?   0:00 sdtvolch
 8 O   0   618   568   IA 59   ?   133   pts/5   0:00 ps

FIGURE 15.7

The output of the `ps -ecl` *command*

3. Use `ps -ecl | grep` *<commandname>* to make sure the process priority was actually changed.

You can also use the `priocntl` command to alter the scheduling parameters of a time-share process. The procedure is identical to the preceding one; the command syntax is as follows:

```
# priocntl -s -m  <userlimit> -p <userpriority> -i \
     <idtype> <idlist>
```

Here the options take on the following meanings: `-s` sets the upper limit on the user priority range and changes the priority; `-m` *<userlimit>* sets the maximum amount that you change your priority when `-p` is used; `-p` *<userpriority>* assigns a priority; and finally, `-i` *<idtype>* *<idlist>* uses these two parameters to identify a particular process. The *<idtype>* is the PID or UID. You can also change the class of a process using `priocntl`.

The Process File System

In Chapter 5, "The File System," you were introduced to the virtual file system mounted in the /proc directory. The proc file system (PROCFS) stores pointers to objects (or logical addresses) being processed in memory, with one file for each active process running on your system; the name of each file (represented as a folder or container in the CDE File Manager) is the PID number of the process it represents. To see how this might work, use the ps command as follows to view a user's running process: `ps -eaf | grep <username>`. In Figure 15.8, you can see that this returns two lines, the (Bourne) shell that was spawned when barries logged in, and the grep command that was just issued. Having established that the shell is PID 11978, I was able to use the cd command to switch to the 11978 directory in the proc file system and `ls -l` to list the contents of the directory so that I could view an image of the process with all of its child processes in view. Figure 15.8 shows you this listing.

FIGURE 15.8

An image of the child processes running under a process

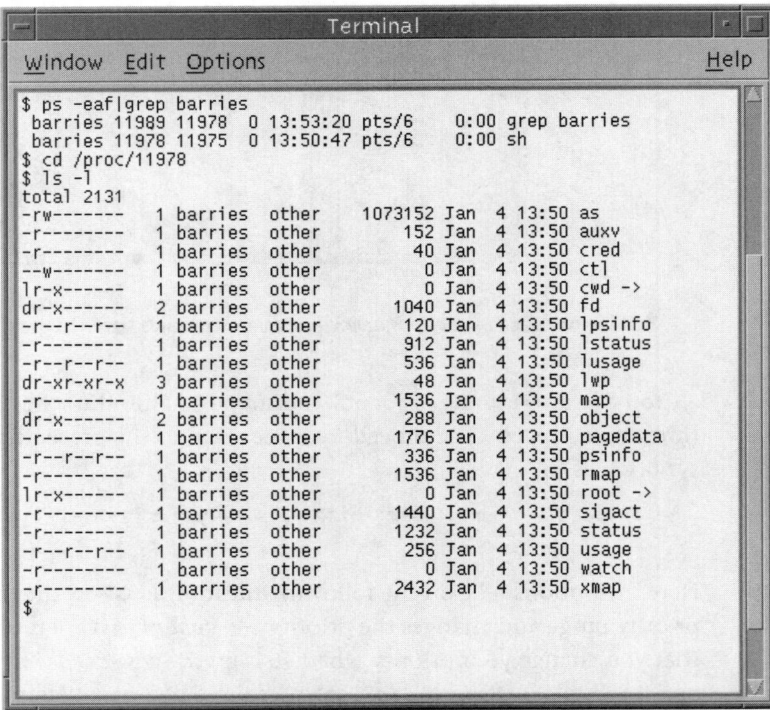

NOTE Sometimes the grep command does not show itself in the process command's listing. That is done to keep people from wondering why grep shows up when it is initiated from another system.

Notice that, as all other processes do, the shell process has a number of subdirectories (indicated by the first letter *d* in the attributes listing) that store state information and control functions related to the state of the shell process. Each directory and subdirectory also has a watch-point access that is used to control memory access of the process.

Although the proc file system is represented as if it were a real file system, it cannot be viewed or modified with standard commands such as cat, file, rm, pg, commands that you would use to manipulate standard files. Solaris provides some commands that you can use to display information about the proc file system, the so-called proc tools. One command that accesses the proc file system you are already familiar with, the ps (process) command. The ps command returns system information to you quickly because it only has to read the information and attributes of the objects in the proc file system to respond. Other programs can read the proc file system, but only one program, referred to as the controlling process, can write to it. Figure 15.9 shows the output of several of the proc commands for the shell process shown previously in Figure 15.8.

Here is a list of some of the commands that display information from the process file system:

pfiles When you give the pfiles *<PIDnumber>* command, Solaris returns the status and control information for any open files relating to the process you specify. The pfiles command is one of the more commonly used proc tools because it exposes all of the operational dependencies between applications and their data files.

pflags Use the pflags *<PIDnumber>* command to display signal and flag information for a process.

pcred The pcred *<PIDnumber>* command prints the effective, real, and saved UIDs and GIDs associated with a process. Those numbers are owner and group identification numbers of the person who executed the process.

pldd The pldd *<PIDnumber>* command displays the dynamically linked libraries called by a process.

pmap The pmap *<PIDnumber>* command prints an address map for each process. Figure 15.10 shows the pmap 1 command exposing the memory assignment of the initialization process.

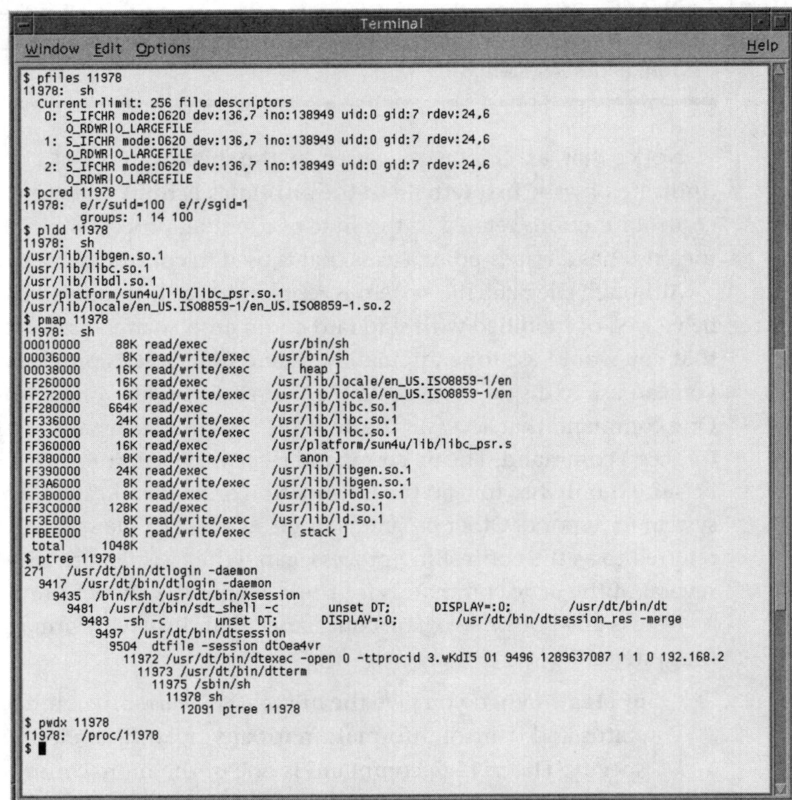

FIGURE 15.9

The output of various `proc` *commands*

psig Use the `psig` *<PIDnumber>* command to display process signal actions.

pstack The `pstack` *<PIDnumber>* command performs a stack trace (similar to an LWP) and outputs the results in hexadecimal form.

ptree The `ptree` *<PIDnumber>* command outputs the hierarchical tree representation of a process and its subprocesses. Figure 15.9 shows an example. Again, the `ptree` command is very useful for exposing operational dependencies.

pwait Use the `pwait` command to display the status of a process after it terminates.

pwdx Use the `pwdx` *<PIDnumber>* command to display a process's current working directory.

FIGURE 15.10

The pmap *command for the* init *process*

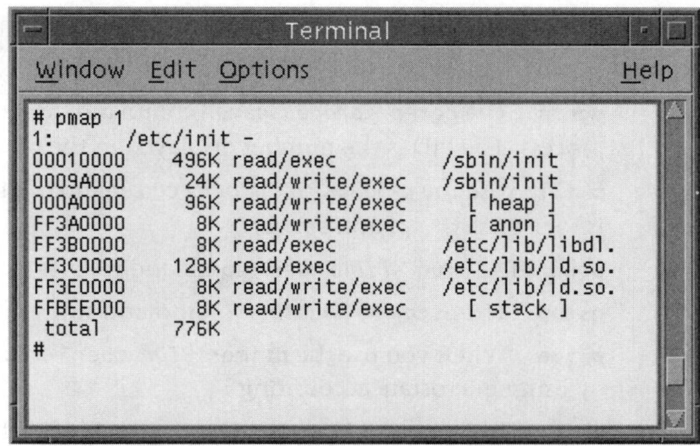
Terminal
Window Edit Options Help
pmap 1
1: /etc/init -
00010000 496K read/exec /sbin/init
0009A000 24K read/write/exec /sbin/init
000A0000 96K read/write/exec [heap]
FF3A0000 8K read/write/exec [anon]
FF3B0000 8K read/exec /etc/lib/libdl.
FF3C0000 128K read/exec /etc/lib/ld.so.
FF3E0000 8K read/write/exec /etc/lib/ld.so.
FFBEE000 8K read/write/exec [stack]
total 776K
#

To execute these commands, you need to specify them as follows:

```
# /usr/proc/bin/pcommand <PIDnumber>
```

If the `/usr/proc/bin` directory is in your `PATH` environment, you need to specify only the command itself.

The `lsof` (list open file) command is another command that isn't included in Solaris 8 but that you might find useful to download and install. The program lists information about open files used by active processes. Using `lsof`, you can identify which process gave rise to a file in the `tmp` directory by specifying that file as an argument to the command. You can also identify processes that continue to write to unlinked files and consume space, something that isn't easily tracked with other commands. The `lsof` command is useful when you want to unmount a file system that has open system files on it, something Unix doesn't allow you to do. You can use `lsof` to determine which file is open and kill the process associated with that file. You can download the `lsof` program from `ftp://vic.cc.purdue.edu/pub/tools/unix/lsof`.

Although `lsof` isn't included with Solaris, the `fuser` command is, and it performs a similar function. The `fuser` command identifies processes using a file or file structure and will display the PIDs of the processes that are using the files specified in the command as arguments. Each PID is identified by a letter code, as follows: `c`, the process is using a file in the current directory; `m`, the process is using a mapped file; `o`, the process is using the file as an open file; `r`, the process is using the file as its root directory; `t`, the process is using the file as a text file; and `y`, the process is using the file as its controlling terminal.

Controlling Processes

Several of the proc tools can be used to control processes. The following are among the more useful:

pgrep The `pgrep` *<processname>* command displays information about the process. The PID is the number displayed in the first column.

pkill Use the `pkill` *<PIDnumber>* command to kill a process. An alternative is to use `pkill` *<processname>*.

prun The `prun` *<PIDnumber>* command restarts a process.

pstop The `pstop` *<PIDnumber>* command stops a process.

ptime When you use the `ptime` *<PIDnumber>* command, it times the process by using microstate accounting.

psig This command lists the signal actions of each process.

pwait The `pwait -v` *<PIDnumber>* command waits for a process(s) to terminate prior to execution.

As before, to execute these commands, you need to specify them as follows:

```
# /usr/proc/bin/pcommand <PID>
```

If the `/usr/proc/bin directory` is in your `PATH` environment, you need to specify only the command itself.

You can control processes through the use of signals, using commands that mirror many of the commands that were just described. Processes use signals to communicate with one another. Signals are created from the `signal()` call inside a C program, or they can be sent directly to a program from a shell. There are several different signal types, each providing a way for applications to communicate with one another and to call for application and system services, something that is commonly referred to as *interapplication communications*.

When you issue some keyboard commands, especially simple ones like Ctrl+C, you are issuing a signal to the foreground program to terminate or kill the current process. The `kill` command at the command line also terminates a process. A Ctrl+Z keystroke is the signal to suspend a foreground process but not kill it.

The `kill` command is a good example of a command that issues some simple signals. The syntax of the `kill` command is as follows:

```
kill <option> <PID> list
```

The only significant options are the signal type followed by a process or job list. A root user can kill any process, but other users can terminate only processes that they own. If you don't specify the signal type, then the `kill` command uses the software termination signal, `SIGTERM` or signal 15. All three of Solaris's shells—the Bourne, Korn, and C shells—have built-in commands that emulate the kill command. As an alternative to using the PID list, you can use the option %<*job*> list.

Although processes can choose to ignore commands, the kill command is the one command that must be obeyed. Try using signal 9 when the default signal 15 doesn't work. When the signal type 0 is used, the command specifies that all processes associated with the currently logged-in username should be killed. If that user is a root user, your current session is toast and you must reboot your system. Use kill -KILL 0 to forcibly terminate all processes for your user session.

WARNING The command kill -s 9 0 or kill -9 0 terminates all current processes for a user. When root issues this command, the system will shut down.

Table 15.2 includes a short list of signal numbers. You can access a more complete listing at /usr/include/sys/signal.h or by issuing the kill -l command. There are 45 signal types listed.

TABLE 15.2: SIGNAL DESCRIPTIONS

Number	Name	Description
0	N/A	Exit command. (Not a signal, but used in program traps.)
1	SIGHUP	Hang up or disconnect line.
2	SIGINT	Terminal interrupt. You can perform the same action by pressing the interrupt keystroke (Ctrl+C).
3	SIGQUIT	Quit. You can perform the same action by using the quit keystroke (Ctrl+Shift+| or Ctrl+Shift+\).
4	SIGILL	Illegal instruction.
5	SIGTRAP	Used for program tracing.
6	SIGABRT	Abort.
7	SIGEMT	Emulation trap.
8	SIGFPE	Provides an arithmetic exception.
9	SIGKILL	Kill. The kill -9 command terminates a process.
10	SIGBUS	Signals a bus error.
11	SIGSEGV	Segmentation fault.
12	SIGSYS	Bad system call.
13	SIGPIPE	Broken pipe.
14	SIGALRM	Alarm clock.
15	SIGTERM	Software termination. This is the default kill signal.
24	SIGTSTP	Stop. The job control stop key is the equivalent of the Ctrl+Z keystroke.

Notice that several of the signals used with the `kill` command don't simply terminate processes. Some are useful to suspend a process, and others provide a necessary trap that can be used to debug programs while they run.

There are many other signals you can use to change the behavior of running applications. For example, when you suspend an application with Ctrl+z and then type `bg` and press the Return key, you send the current foreground application into the background and assign a background job number to that application. Type **`fg #`** with the assigned background number to bring that process back to the foreground. These operations are examples of signals that you send to active processes.

Of course, processes are sending signals to one another all the time without your manual intervention. One particularly interesting command is the `psig` command. It exposes which processes are communicating with the process you specify by listing the signals that these processes send to one another. Figure 15.11 shows you a list of the signals associated with the shell process you saw in the previous figures.

FIGURE 15.11

The `psig` command's output shows what signals have been sent.

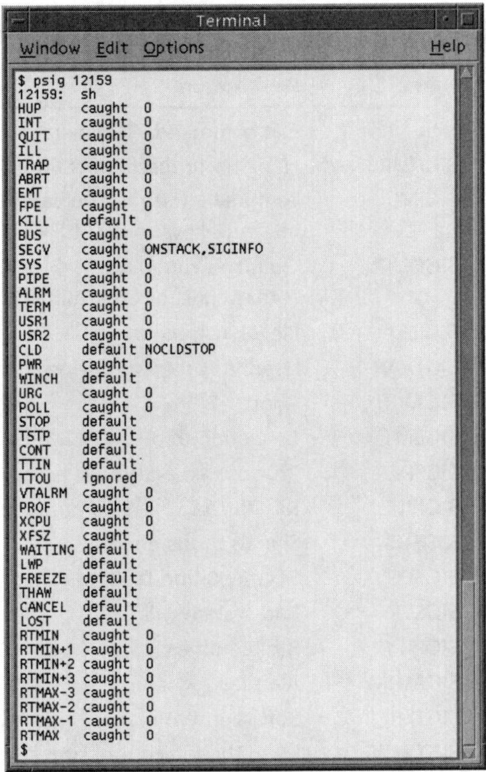

Performance Meter

The Solaris CDE comes with a graphical utility you can use to observe a number of system functions. In its default state, the Performance Meter shows you CPU access as a bar chart on the CDE icon and as a strip chart in the graphical window. However, you can add a number of other parameters to observe, and some of them are significant from the standpoint of memory.

To display the Performance Meter with additional options, follow these steps:

1. Click the Performance Meter control on the front panel (the Performance Meter control is shown in the following graphic).

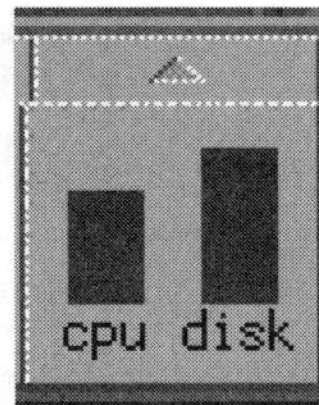

The default Performance Meter, shown here, appears.

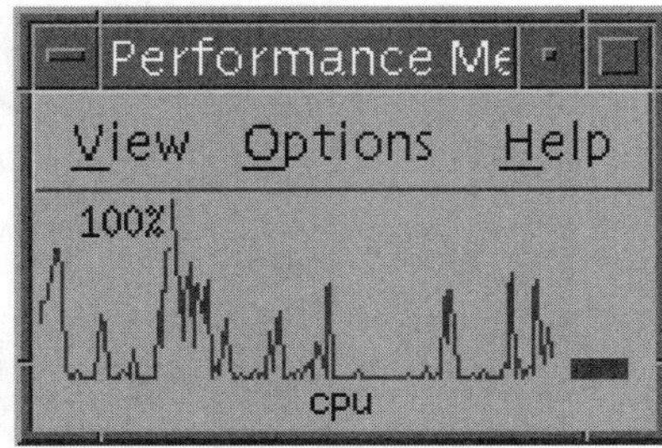

2. Right-click the Performance Meter to view the pop-up menu, shown in the following graphic, then make the selections that you desire. Alternatively, click the View menu and make the appropriate menu selections.

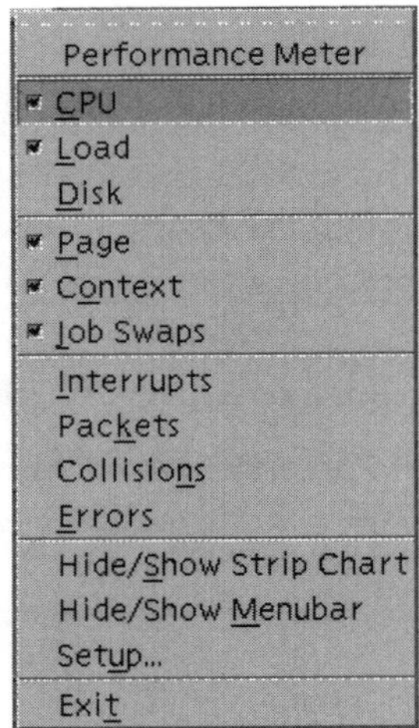

Figure 15.12 shows you the Performance Meter with views into the cpu, load, page, context, and swap events.

FIGURE 15.12

The Performance Meter with several counters showing

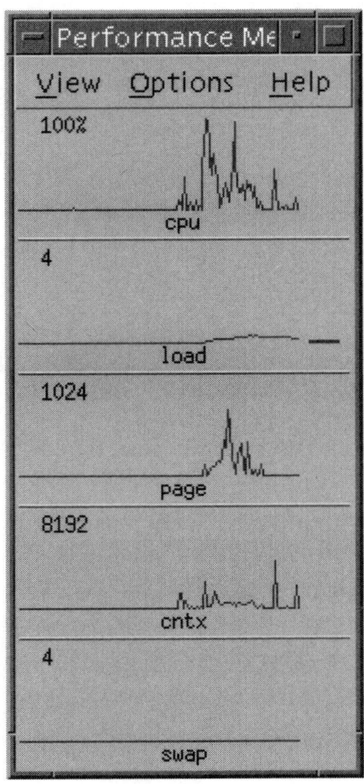

Managing Jobs

Part of a system administrator's task is to set up jobs to perform system functions at regular intervals. Solaris provides utilities for scheduling jobs, running scripts, or starting applications. Among the tasks commonly automated are backup routines, automated log file captures, disk management functions, sending mail, and so forth. The two commands most often associated with scheduling jobs are the `at` command and the `cron` command.

The *at* Command

The `at` (execute at) command is used to schedule a job to run at a particular time as part of a shell script in the working directory at the date and time you specify. Jobs are stored in `/var/spool/cron/atjobs`, and `atjobs` is read by the program found at `/usr/sbin/cron`. A job can be a command or a script that contains one or more commands. When you specify a job, the `at` command saves the environmental variables and the current working directory so that they can be used when the job executes. Unless you specify a shell type, the `at` command uses the one specified in the `SHELL` environmental variable.

The time and date specify when the job executes. For the time, you can use a one-, two-, or four-digit number to specify the hour, or you can specify the time in hh:mm format. Unless you add `am`, `pm`, `midnight`, or `noon` to the time, the `at` command assumes you are using a 24-hour clock. Use `now` in place of the time to run the job immediately. The date is the day of the week or day of the month. If no date is specified, the `at` command use the next available time that matches the time you entered. Dates can be a full day name, a three-letter abbreviation, or the word `today` or `tomorrow`. Use the `increment` option to enter a number of minutes, hours, days, or weeks to add to the time you have specified so that after that specified increment, the job executes. If you enter a date, you cannot use the `increment` option.

The `at` command has the following syntax:

```
at <options> <time> <date> <increment>
```

Here are the important options for the `at` command:

`-c` option Runs commands by using the C shell.

`-f` option The `-f` (file) option provides the name of a file containing a list of commands to be executed when the `at` job runs.

`-k` option Runs commands by using the C shell.

`-l` option The `-l` *<job>* `list` option displays information about the jobs you specify that are in the queue. If no job is listed, the `-l` option outputs information on all of the jobs in the queue, which is equivalent to using the `atq` command. This option is not used to execute a job.

-m option The -m option sends a mail message as confirmation when the job completes execution. Note there if there is output from your job, it will be e-mailed to you as well unless you set the output to go to /dev/null.

-r option Use the -r *<job>* list option to remove or delete jobs in the at queue. When used without a job list, the command is equivalent to the atrm command. You can use the -l option to obtain the job number and specify it in the job list for removal. This option is not used to execute a job.

-s option Runs commands by using the Bourne shell.

-t option Use the -t (time) option to submit a job at the time specified in a format similar to the format for the touch command for submitting a job.

You can use the atq command to display a list of jobs in the at job queue. Use the atrm command to remove all at jobs that are in the job queue; the atrm command removes jobs placed in the at queue by all users. You can use atrm to remove all of the jobs of a specific user if you are root. In fact, if you are root, you can flush the entire queue. If you are a regular user, you can use the tool to flush all of your queue. You can even put atrm in interactive mode (as you can with the rm command), where it will ask you about removal for each job in the queue.

If the at.allow (/usr/lib/cron/at.allow) and at.deny (/usr/lib/cron/at.deny) files do not exist, only root and people who have the solaris.jobs.user authorization can use at. If at.allow exists, only people on the allow list can use at; the at.deny file is ignored. If there is only an at.deny, anyone except those listed in at.deny can use at. If at.deny if empty, everyone can use at. The default configuration of Solaris is an at.deny file with a few system accounts in it so that all regular users can use at.

As an example of the at command, the following sequence prints a file called myfile at 7 A.M. on Monday:

```
$ at 7am mon
at> pr myfile | lp
at> Ctrl+D
at> <EOT>
commands will be executed using /bin/sh
job 987436228.a at Mon Dec 3 07:00:00 2001
```

The *cron* Command

The cron (command run on) utility allows you to run a command at a specified time more than once and is more generally useful to system administrators for regular system maintenance than it is for regular users. For example, you can use the cron command to store in a crontab file commands that will back up a system (either local or remote), such as the `ufsdump` command. Unless there is a command in the `crontab` file that redirects output, `cron` also mails you notification that it ran and indicates any errors. A very common use of the `cron` command is to launch a script every night or week that will roll over all of your log files, keeping any individual one from becoming too large.

A job can be a command or a script that contains one or more commands. The program's configuration files can be found at `/etc/cron.d`, and when it runs, it checks to see if there is a `cron.deny` file that specifies whether or not a user can run the command. A blank `cron.deny` file allows all users to run a `cron` job. The `cron` command also checks for a `cron.allow` file, and if one exists, `cron` will allow only users specified in the file to run a `cron` job. If the `cron.allow` file exists and no users are specified, only a superuser can run the `cron` job.

The `cron` command has the following two types of syntax:

```
crontab <time> <date> <pathname>/<filename>
crontab <time> <date> <options> (<username> list)
```


Use the first version of the command to specify the file that contains the `cron` commands and the second version of the command to allow a superuser to modify the file for a user using the default file location.

There are three main options that you can use with version number 2 of the `cron` utility:

`-e` option The `-e` (edit) option opens your text editor so that you can create or edit the specified user's or your commands prior to their being run.

`-l` option The `-l` (list) option displays the jobs listed in the specified user's or your `crontab` file.

`-r` option The `-r` (remove) option deletes the `crontab` file that you specify.

WARNING Be careful when you use the `-r` option. If you are root and you type `crontab -r` with no username, the root's `crontab` file will be deleted without a dialog box appearing to ask you if you are sure. Then all you can do is go to your backup to retrieve it.

The time and date are required options that tell `cron` when to execute the command file. There are five fields that precede a `crontab` entry in a file:

- Minutes from 0 to 59
- Hours from 0 to 23
- Day of the month from 1 to 31

- Month of the year from 1 to 12
- Day of the week from 0 to 6, where 0 is Sunday

To specify a repeating value, use an asterisk in place of one of the five fields. For example, a file containing the `ufsdump` command that would execute every day at 3 A.M. would be entered by the root user at the console in the following way:

```
# crontab
0 3 * * * /usr/opt/dumproutine
Ctrl+D
```

However, if you perform the preceding operation, your `crontab` file will be deleted and replaced by your new entry. Unless you want to do that and you are willing to lose anything you had in the `crontab` file, use the `crontab -e` command to change your `crontab` files.

When you gave the `crontab -l` command, you'll see the entry `0 3 * * * /usr/opt/dumproutine` in your file. To take a look at the standard system `crontab`, use the `crontab -l root` command. Figure 15.13 shows the default entries. Notice that `crontab` runs a check to see if the `cron` log file is at its limit at 3:10 A.M. every Sunday and Thursday. `cron` also creates a new system log at 3:10 on Sunday and adjusts any time differences it finds with the computer's system clock at 2:01 every day (line 4).

FIGURE 15.13

The default `crontab` *file for a root user*

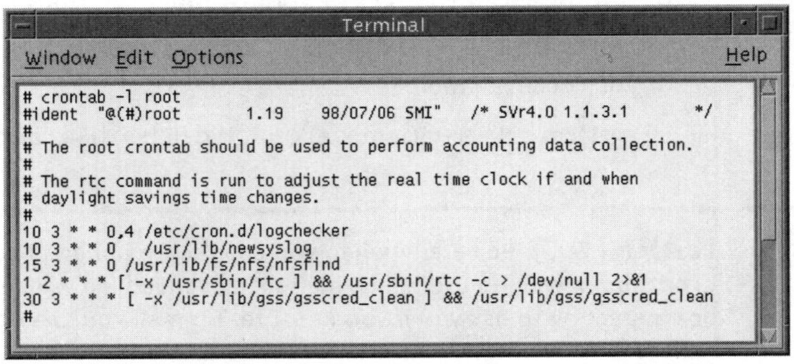

```
Terminal
Window  Edit  Options                                          Help
# crontab -l root
#ident  "@(#)root       1.19    98/07/06 SMI"   /* SVr4.0 1.1.3.1       */
#
# The root crontab should be used to perform accounting data collection.
#
# The rtc command is run to adjust the real time clock if and when
# daylight savings time changes.
#
10 3 * * 0,4 /etc/cron.d/logchecker
10 3 * * 0   /usr/lib/newsyslog
15 3 * * 0 /usr/lib/fs/nfs/nfsfind
1 2 * * * [ -x /usr/sbin/rtc ] && /usr/sbin/rtc -c > /dev/null 2>&1
30 3 * * * [ -x /usr/lib/gss/gsscred_clean ] && /usr/lib/gss/gsscred_clean
#
```

Memory

In order to better understand the way processes work, it is valuable to know how they use memory. By examining the consumption of memory, you can diagnose a malfunctioning system and optimize a system for performance.

As described in Chapter 5, Solaris creates a memory-based file system called the temporary file system (TMPFS) to track the physical and virtual memory in your system. Some of the TMPFS is stored on disk as virtual memory, and some of the data for the TMPFS is stored in physical memory. The TMPFS describes the combination of the two types of memory and was created to improve performance for processes that create temporary files that will be used later for additional work. Program compilations, for example, are programs that create and use `tmp` files. You'll find the temporary file system mounted by default by the automounter (`vfstab`) at the `/tmp` mount point. The contents of the TMPFS is volatile and is lost when you reboot your system.

When you store files in the `tmp` folder, you are essentially using up system memory. Storing large files in the `tmp` folder can have an impact on the amount of system memory that other programs have available to run. Additionally, when a large program or group of programs consuming a lot of RAM is resident in memory, the amount of space available in the `tmp` folder and that the TMPFS can use is reduced by a like amount. The TMPFS is also limited in terms of the number of files that it can hold by the amount of physical memory installed in your system, and that limitation is not altered by the size of virtual memory on disk that you create. The TMPFS is created and deleted using the `swap` command, but it is otherwise handled in a manner entirely analogous to using the `mount` command on other file systems.

Physical Memory

Solaris 8 stores an image of the physical memory of the system in a special file called `/dev/mem` and an image of the kernel virtual memory at `/dev/kmem`. These files can be used to examine a system's memory or to patch the system for an upgrade. Entries in the `mem` file are byte addresses in memory interpreted as memory addresses. Byte addresses in the `kmem` file are references to kernel virtual memory addresses. Any nonexistent locations are stored as errors in these files.

The `kmem` file can access up to 4GB of kernel virtual memory. Because the `mem` file references real physical memory, it is the same size as the installed RAM. When RAM is greater than 4GB, Solaris uses special techniques to access the additional information on disk.

You can use the `sar` (system activities resources) command to monitor various system activities. What you see with the `sar` command depends upon the option you use. In particular, for memory, you would use this command with the `-g`, `-k`, `-p`, `-r`, and `-w` options. The `sar` options are as follows:

-a option Displays file access operation statistics.

-A option Displays overall system performance.

-b option Displays buffer activity statistics for caching metadata.

-c option Displays system call statistics.

-d option Displays disk activity statistics.

-g option Displays page-out and memory-freeing activity averages.

-k option Displays a report on the Kernel Memory Allocator (KMA). The KMA is a kernel subsystem used to allocate and free memory as required.

-m option Displays a report on interprocess communications activities.

-p option Reports the page-in activity for protection and translation faults.

-q option Determines the average queue length when the queue is occupied, as well as the percentage of time that the queue is occupied.

-r option Displays a report on the number of memory pages and swap file blocks that are free.

-u option Creates a report to display CPU utilization.

-v option Checks on the status of the process table, inode table, file table, and shared memory record table.

-w option Displays swapping and switching activity.

-y option Monitors terminal devices.

You can use the sadc, sa1, and sa2 commands to periodically collect the data on system activity and save it into a binary file. Each day's results are stored as a separate file. The sadc is typically run once an hour or whenever a system boots into the multiuser mode. The syntax for the sadc command is as follows (the *<time>* variable refers to the time interval between data collection):

```
/usr/lib/sa/sadc <time> <number> <outputfile>
```

WARNING Be careful when using the sar command because it logs all events over a 31+ day period. It can create data files that are quite large. Even medium-size servers can run out of space over a weekend if you are not attentive and don't realize that, although sar reports only the specific things you asked it for, it logs all events.

Virtual Memory

The virtual memory system extends physical memory by allowing programs and data segments to be swapped or paged to disk as needed. When a segment isn't accessed in a while, it is overwritten with newer information. The paging algorithm is optimized to maintain on disk segments that are the most likely to be recalled by active processes.

Virtual memory is a benefit in that it trades the lower performance of disk access for the lower cost of disk space to extend a system's apparent memory allocation. However, there is a limit to how much virtual memory can be used before a system becomes sluggish due to constant reads and writes—a problem that is referred to as *disk thrashing*. Typically, systems set a limit so that the ratio of virtual memory to real memory is no more than 3:1; 2:1 is more common. Thus, a Sun Ultra 5 workstation with 256MB of RAM might use a swap file of 512MB on disk. For a Sun server running Solaris 7 and 8, for which you need significant performance from your 32-bit OS, the maximum swap size is 2GB. A good-sized swap space in a server would be on the order of 512MB to 1GB in size. To extend this limit, you can use multiple swap partitions, although Sun doesn't recommend this because you can use more than 2GB of swap space only if you are running 64-bit Solaris.

WARNING If you are running a server that requires very large swap spaces, you are going to encounter performance problems reading and writing to disk. It is generally advised that you upgrade your physical memory in those instances.

Solaris and Unix provide the `vmstat` command to view the condition of a system's virtual memory allocation. The command returns statistics about disk usage, memory, and CPU utilization. You can specify options that provide information about specific disks at specified time intervals.

The syntax for the `vmstat` command is as follows:

```
vmstat <options> (<diskname> list) <interval> <count>
```

Without options, `vmstat` returns a one-line summary of how virtual memory was used since your system was last booted up. You can specify up to four disks that fit on a summary line. The `<count>` variable determines how often the command is repeated and how many lines of data you will eventually see. The `<interval>` option specifies the time in seconds before the count is incremented, and the `vmstat` command outputs another summary line. The `<count>` and `<interval>` options do not apply to the `-i` and `-s` options described in the list that follows.

Here are the important options available for the `vmstat` command:

-c option The `-c` option returns disk cache flushing statistics as a report.

-i option The `-i` option returns the statistics associated with device interrupts as a report.

-p option Use the `-p` option with the following parameters to view paging activity: `epi` (executable page-ins), `epo` (executable page-outs), `epf` (executable page-frees), `api` (anonymous page-ins), `apo` (anonymous page-outs), `apf` (anonymous page-frees), `fpi` (file system page-ins), `fpo` (file system page-outs), and `fpf` (file system page-frees).

-s option This option displays the total number of system events since boot-up.

-S option The `-S` option provides a report on swapping rather than on paging activity.

Figure 15.14 shows the output of several versions of the `vmstat` command. The procs columns indicate the number of processes, the number of processes in the run queue are under r, the number of processes that are blocked for resources such as I/O or paging are under b, and the number of processes that are run using swap data are under w. The memory columns report on the amount of swap space available (given in kilobytes) and the amount free and the size in kilobytes of the free list. The page columns return information about page faults and paging: re (page reclaims), mf (minor faults), pi (KB paged in), po (KB paged out), fr (KB freed), de (anticipated short-term memory shortfall in KB), and sr (pages scanned by the clock algorithm). The disk column reports the number of disk operations per second for the up to four disks you can specify. Faults reports on the trap/interrupt rates (number per second): in (non-clock device interrupts), sy (system calls), and cs (CPU context switches). Finally, the cpu column gives you a breakdown of the usage of CPU time: us (user time), sy (system time), id (idle time).

The `crash` command (found in `/usr/sbin/crash`) returns a map of your system memory output as a crash file and is useful for examining the memory image of either a running system or a system that has malfunctioned. The memory table shows the allocation of processes by PID to memory blocks. The `crash` command must be run by a root user, and it offers you a valuable diagnostic snapshot of your system's processes in memory. There are three arguments for the `crash` command: `-d` specifies the dumpfile, `-n` specifies a text file namelist, and `-w` specifies the output file. Additionally, you can use the following options: `-e` displays every entry in the table, `-f` displays the full structure, `-p` interprets all address arguments in the command line as physical addresses, `-s` *<PIDnumber>* (process) specifies a process slot, and `-w` *<filename>* redirects output to a file of that name. The `crash` command takes many options and provides fine control over the output you see. There is a note in the `crash` man pages that says after Solaris 8, Sun may no longer support the `crash` command.

FIGURE 15.14

The `vmstat` *command is used to determine the state of virtual memory.*

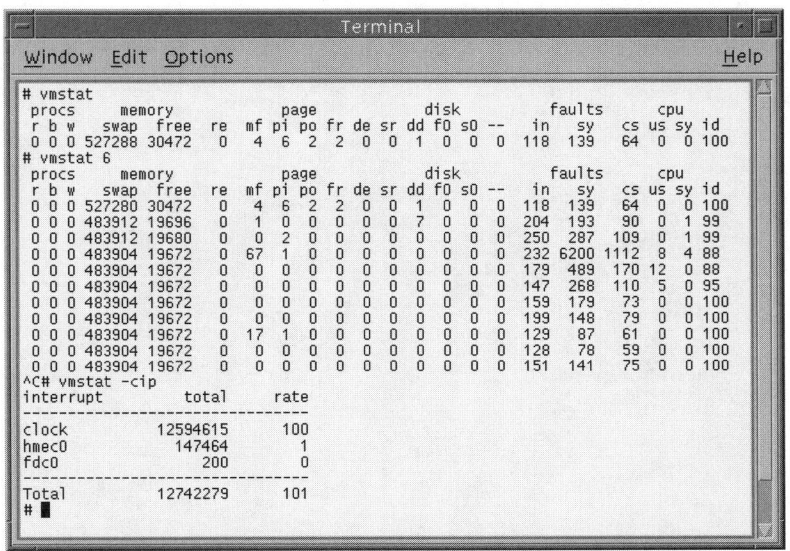

Summary

In this chapter, you learned that Solaris creates and runs the operating system and all programs as a set of processes. By understanding how processes are run and how to display process information, you can diagnose your system. You can use the `ps` command or Process Manager to view and control processes. Processes run with priorities that you can view and alter.

You also saw how processes use memory. Memory is apportioned by using a combination of real physical RAM and virtual memory. A swap file on your hard drive is used to store recently used processes and data so that they can be returned to memory quickly.

You learned that the process file system stores references to processes running in memory. That file system looks like a normal file system but contains references to processes instead. The temporary file system (TMPFS) stores data that programs have used and might use again.

I also described how you can use certain utilities to automate processes. You can use the `at` command and the `cron` command to automate jobs as commands or scripts containing commands.

PART III

Working with Shells in Solaris

LEARN TO:

- ***Understand how Solaris uses shells***
- ***Use text editors to create and modify text, programs, and scripts***
- ***Work with the three major Solaris shells***
- ***Understand scripting***

CHAPTER 16

Using the *vi* and Text Editor

FEATURING:

The vi *modes* 645

Navigating in the vi *editor* 650

Editing in the vi *editor* 653

Setting parameters 660

Unix editors 664

The visual display (vi) editor is an interactive text editor in Solaris that is used to both create and modify text files. You can invoke vi from the terminal window and from the command line of many terminals. The vi editor is of particular importance because you can use it to modify system files in Solaris without being concerned about embedding invalid characters into the files. In addition, the vi editor can be used when the graphical user interface is not available and you have access to only a keyboard as an entry device.

In this chapter, you'll learn about this powerful yet cryptic program that contains many features for navigating, editing, searching, modifying, and outputting files. It isn't really possible to learn vi well without extensive practice, so most people start by learning a subset of the editor's features and adding to that knowledge over time. This chapter will help you get started with vi and will tell you where you need to go to learn more about it.

This chapter also covers the CDE Text Editor. When the CDE is active, you will probably find that the less-powerful but much easier to learn Text Editor is a friendly alternative to the vi editor. Text Editor is easily accessed from the CDE front panel or from a terminal window, and it contains a fully documented online help system. Although you lose significant editing functionality when you use Text Editor, most people will find that Text Editor will suffice for 90 percent of the tasks involving editing text.

Finally, you'll learn about the word processor available to you if you have StarOffice installed on your computer. It is a straightforward task to create, modify, and save text files using StarOffice's word processor. StarOffice offers you many additional tools to aid you in your work: spell checkers, a thesaurus, advanced editing capabilities, and the ability to incorporate data from different data files.

About the *vi* Editor

The original text editor that came with standard Unix distributions were line editors, such as ed, which was replaced with an expanded version called ex. In ex, it was possible to turn on a full-screen, visual-editing mode of the program using the vi command. Most people preferred the visual-editing display, so a better editor was needed for BSD Unix. ex was rewritten and the new program defaulted to the visual-editing mode. This new program was named vi. vi is a superset of ex, and you can switch back and forth between the visual (vi) and line-based (ex) interfaces while using the vi program.

If you come to learn vi from a user's perspective, having worked primarily with a word processor, then you will find it somewhat challenging to get used to the interface.

vi allows only keyboard entry and provides few visual clues on its current state. When you use vi, you can use only the letter, number, and punctuation keys and the Esc key. The intent of vi's designers was to make keystrokes correspond to actions so that people could remember them mnemonically.

Although the arrow keys are often supported (depending upon the type of terminal you are working at), the F1 through F12 function keys and many other additional keys on the keyboard are not. It is this modest reliance on your keyboard's input capabilities that makes the vi editor (and other system editors in common use) so helpful when your graphical user interface (the CDE) hangs or when something else goes wrong on your system. Administrators often rely on vi when they are using Telnet or rlogin to remotely edit files over the network.

Furthermore, vi is modal in its operation. In vi, you give commands in the Command mode, enter text in the Insert, Input, and other modes, and work with data in areas of memory referred to as buffers. You will need to get familiar with vi's modes (described in the next section) in order to begin working with this program.

It's worth learning to use the vi editor at a level that is sufficient enough for you to function successfully in it if for no other reason than this: the skills will help you when you work on terminals or in other variants of Unix or when all else fails and your desktop is not available to you.

An Overview of the *vi* Editor

Perhaps the best way to get a feeling for using the vi editor is to open it and create a simple text document. In the example shown in this section, you will get a sense for how the vi editor is displayed in the terminal window and how to move between modes.

TIP To get help with the vi editor while in a terminal window or at the command line, type **man vi** and then press the Return key to view the vi's man pages.

To open the vi editor from the desktop, follow these steps:

1. Right-click the desktop to open the Workspace menu and then select the Terminal command from the Tools submenu, shown in Figure 16.1. (You can also click the home folder icon in the front panel to open the File Manager and then press Ctrl+T to open the terminal window.)
2. Type the command **vi** ***<pathname>/<filename>*** to start vi in the terminal window and enter the Command mode.

FIGURE 16.1

Opening a terminal window from the Workspace menu

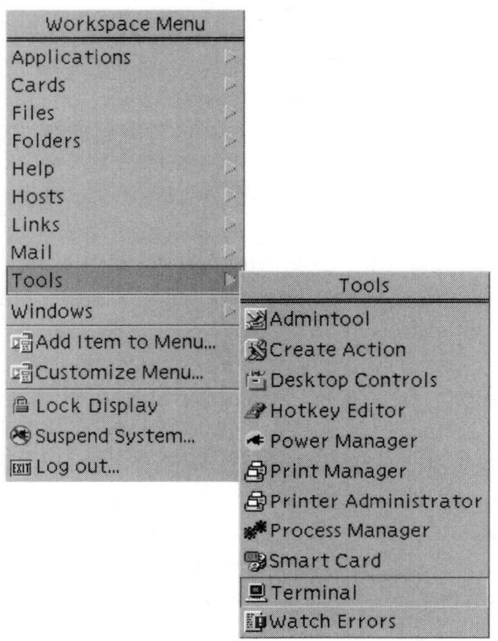

Unfortunately, the `vi` editor window does not change in its appearance when you are in the Command mode. However, you will not be able to enter text in that mode. Figure 16.2 shows the `vi` editor with a new file open. Note the use of tilde (~) characters that appear on the left side of each line, indicating that the line is past the end-of-file; that is, that the editor is showing additional lines that aren't part of the text (they are line placeholders).

3. Press the i key to enter the Insert submode of the Input mode; there is no visual change, but you can now enter text into the editor.
4. Type your text and press Enter to begin a new line.
5. To save your work and exit the `vi` editor, press Esc followed by ZZ to save the file to disk. As an alternative, you can use the Esc followed by the w and q keys (for "Write-Quit") to save your file's contents and exit the editor.

   It's important to use the uppercase ZZ because the lowercase zz does not work. Figure 16.3 shows the state of the terminal window after the ZZ command is issued and the file is saved to disk.

FIGURE 16.2

A new file opened in the `vi` editor

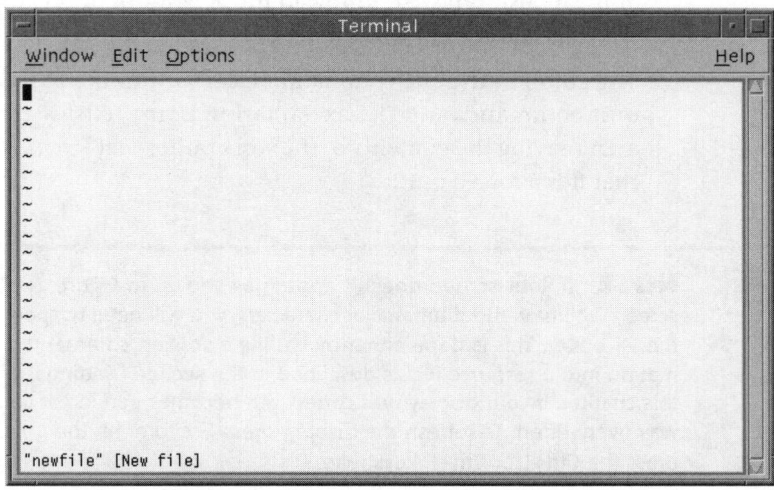

FIGURE 16.3

The terminal window after a file is saved to disk from the `vi` editor

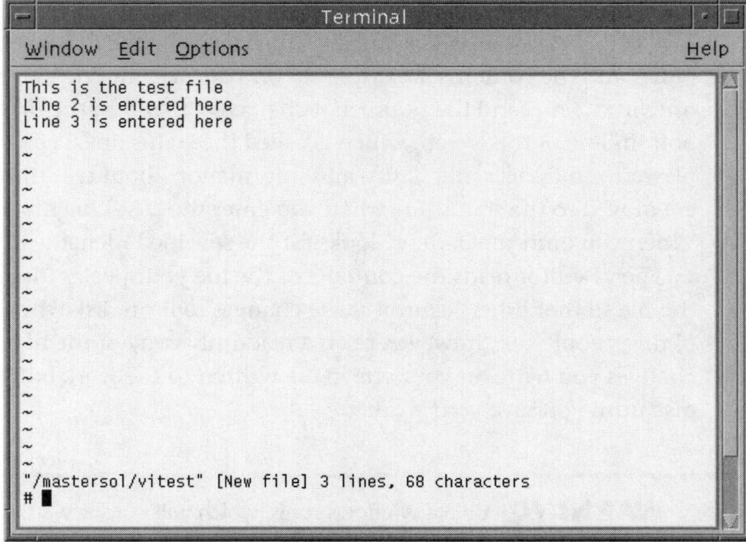

You can also type **ESC** followed by **`:q!`** and then press the Return key to quit without saving your work.

The colon in the `:q!` command places `vi` into the Last-Line mode, the `q` is the quit command, and the exclamation point tells `vi` that you know that you aren't saving the contents of the work buffer that stores what's on your screen or that it is a forced quit.

NOTE If your screen doesn't appear as shown in Figure 16.3 or you see a garbled screen with or without unfamiliar characters, you will need to specify your terminal type to the `vi` editor. This is done either by issuing a session command or by entering the information into a resource file as described in the section "Setting the Terminal Type" later in this chapter. If your display was correct but becomes garbled, it could be that your screen was overwritten. To refresh the display, press Esc to enter the Command mode and then press the Ctrl+L or Ctrl+R keystroke.

In the command you entered in step 2, the path name and filename are optional. If you omit the filename, then `vi` opens with a blank screen in Command mode with the message `new file` displayed on the status line. If you enter a path name and filename that doesn't exist, `vi` names the file on your screen and will create that file when you save your work. When you specify a filename, the file (if it exists) is read into the work buffer and the contents are displayed on your screen. The filename, the number of lines in the file, and the number of characters found in the file are displayed in the bottom line of the screen, which is called the status line. (The status line is used to display error messages, file status, and information about text that you add or delete. You are moved to the status line when you enter the Last-Line mode to enter commands.) When you omit the path, `vi` looks for the specified filename in your current directory.

The `vi` editor reads the contents of the file you specify into a work buffer and locks the file so that others cannot make changes to it on disk when you are editing it. (Other people can, however, open a read-only copy of the file you are editing.) Any changes you write on your screen are written to the work buffer but aren't written to disk until you save your work.

WARNING Unlike Windows tools, which will quickly warn you if a file is larger than they can handle, `vi` will start loading the file and continue loading it until it runs out of memory or it fits it all in. If you are looking at a large firewall or Web server log file, for example, loading can take a very long time.

If you don't specify a file, any input you enter is stored into the work buffer until you save it to a file. Because vi works entirely in memory, the program is very fast and doesn't suffer from traditional file-size limitations. The work buffer can read any file format written to disk. Within the size of the memory available to vi, the editor can read any line size. One newline or linefeed character delimits a line. The size of the file you can create in vi is limited only by available disk space.

WARNING If you open a file that contains a variety of characters beyond simple alphanumeric and punctuation characters, you have either opened an application document or a binary executable file. In either case, you can easily do serious damage to that file if you remove any of those characters. You should close the file immediately by issuing the `:q!` command.

vi Modes

The vi editor is modal, which means you can perform certain actions only when you are in a particular state of the editor. There are several main modes of operation in **vi**:

Command mode When you first open a file using the vi editor, you will already be in Command mode. In Command mode, you can create and open files, specify cursor positioning and editing commands, save your work to a file, and so forth. Keystrokes you enter in Command mode aren't shown on your screen but are acted upon immediately. You can return to the Command mode at any time by pressing the Esc key.

Entry mode In Entry mode, you can enter text into the display on your screen. To enter Entry mode, you must first type an input command, such as i (inserts text), o (overwrites text), or a (appends text) to enter a submode of the Entry mode. These different submodes allow you to add and edit text and differ primarily in the manner in which text is added and removed from your display.

Last-Line mode When in Command mode, you can type a colon (**:**) to move to the end of the file on your display, which is called the Last-Line mode. In Last-Line mode, you enter into a single-line command processor in which you can issue commands before you press the Return (or Enter) key to enter the Input state of the Entry mode.

Figure 16.4 shows how you move between the main vi modes and some of the primary submodes. Mostly, you will be working in the Command mode specifying actions and in the various Entry submodes (such as Insert or Overwrite) entering and editing text. In the Open submode, vi starts up with a new line in which you can add text. You can also open a file in the Read-Only mode by using the -R option with the vi command. You can also open a file in the Read-Only mode by using the view command, which is the same as running vi -R.

FIGURE 16.4

These keystrokes move you between the three main vi modes.

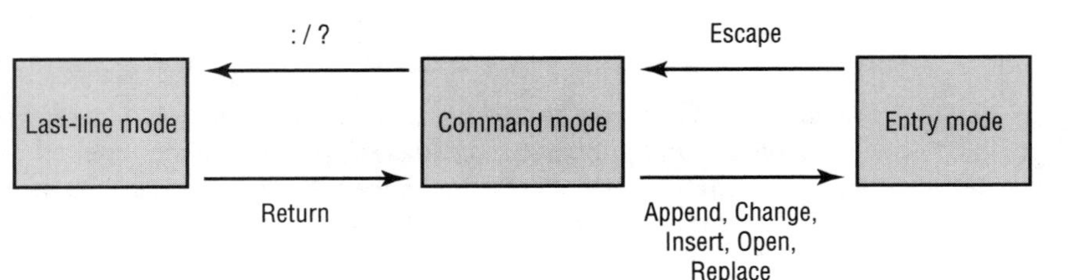

When you are in vi and need to perform system functions, you can use a mode called the Shell Escape mode, in which you can spawn a shell. When you're working in the Shell Escape mode, you can perform actions such as creating directories, renaming files, and so forth. While you are in the new shell, vi is left running as a process, and when you exit the shell, you are returned to the vi editor.

Remember, the vi editor, as with all Unix programs, is case sensitive. For example, when you use i in the Command mode to go to the Insert submode, characters you enter are added to the right of your cursor. When you enter I in the Command mode, the characters you enter are placed to the left of the cursor (at the beginning of the current line). Similarly, using a in the Command mode puts you into the Append submode, where characters are added to a line after your text ends (to the right of the cursor). With the A command, characters are appended to the end of the current line. (For a list of the vi editing commands, see Table 16.4 later in this chapter.)

WARNING If you find that the vi editor is acting strangely, make sure you haven't accidentally turned the Caps Lock or Shift Lock key on. The vi editor will cause your workstation or terminal to beep (if it supports sound) or flash when you enter an inappropriate keystroke.

The vi editor offers two additional commands that allow you to modify your text:

Change command When you use the Change command, you delete the text you want to change (putting the deleted text into a buffer) and enter the Entry or Input mode.

Replace command The Replace command deletes any characters you overwrite and inserts the new characters you enter.

The vi editor is a superset of the ex editor, and it is possible to return to the ex Command mode and the ex Input mode from vi and vice versa, but it isn't something you are likely to want to do because vi offers you expanded capabilities that most people miss in the ex editor.

TIP If you are confused about what mode you are in, press the Esc key twice to return to the Command mode (pressing the Esc key twice ensures that you will be in the Command mode from wherever you are). You can also use the `:set showmode` command to have vi display the current mode on the status line (last line).

Therefore, vi offers you the following six modes:

- vi Command mode
- ex Command mode
- vi Entry or Input mode
- ex Input mode
- vi Last-Line mode
- vi Shell Escape mode

Invoking *vi*

There are several commands that you can use to summon the vi editor:

```
/usr/bin/vi <options> <files>
/usr/bin/view <options> <files>
/usr/bin/vedit <options> <files>
/usr/xpg4/bin/vi <options> <files>
```

In most instances, your path will be automatically set, so you can simply omit the path to the binary executable file and give the command in this form:

```
vi <options> <files>
```

When you use the view form of the command, you cause the text file to be displayed on your screen in Read-Only mode. The vedit form of vi is a beginner's mode that offers additional help working with the program. Table 16.1 lists the options that the vi command allows.

TABLE 16.1: THE `vi` COMMAND OPTIONS

Option	Effect
+ *<command>*	Executes the + (plus) command when `vi` starts.
`-c`	Opens `vi` in the Encryption submode. This is the same as `-x`, but it assumes that all the text read is encrypted.
`-l`	Opens `vi` in the LISP editing submode. LISP is short for List Processing, a programming language.
`-L`	Reports any files that were saved after `vi` was improperly shut down.
`-R`	Opens `vi` in Read-Only submode.
`-r` *<filename>*	Recovers a file after a system crash. This is a particularly useful option to remember.
`-s`	Runs `vi` in the noninteractive mode and suppresses feedback.
`-t` *<tag>*	Edits the file with a tag and moves the cursor to the position where the tag was placed.
`-v`	Opens `vi` in Input mode instead of in Command mode.
`-V`	Opens `vi` in the Verbose submode. Output is sent to standard error statements. Programmers can use `-v` with the `-s` mode.
`-w` *n*	Sets the window size to *n* columns.
`-x`	Opens `vi` in Encryption submode. You are prompted for a key to both encrypt and decrypt the file. The temporary buffer is also encrypted.

Working with Files

It is a good idea to save your work from time to time because the `vi` editor's display only exists in the work buffer's memory. Here are the various methods for saving your work:

- Enter **ESC:w** (write command) to save your work to the original file without quitting `vi`.
- Enter **ESC ZZ** or **:wq** to save your work and quit `vi`.
- Enter **ESC:q!** to quit *without* saving your work.

TIP Saving your work at short regular intervals is the best defense against loss of text during a system crash. It seems that it is inevitable that the time will come when your system crashes while you are working in `vi`. This is often true because `vi` is called upon to perform maintenance when your system has become unstable. When your system comes back, you may find that `vi` sent you e-mail telling you that it had saved the contents of its work buffer. You can also use the `vi -r` *<filename>* command to see if the work buffer can be restored. Peruse that display and, after any required editing, save the results back to disk.

If you want to edit another file in `vi` without quitting the program, save your work using the `:w` command and then use the `:e` *<filename>* command. If the file exists, it will be read into the work buffer; if not, a new file will be created. You can also concatenate a file into the one you are working with (similar to using the `cat` command) by using the `:r` *<filename>* command. The file you specify will be added to your display after the current line.

Table 16.2 lists the different file manipulation commands.

TABLE 16.2: THE vi FILE MANIPULATION COMMANDS

Command	Action
`:!` *<command>*	Gives the Run command and returns you to `vi` (but this doesn't affect your document).
`!!` *<command>*	Gives the Run command and replaces the current line with the output from the command (can be more than one line).
`:e` *<filename>*	Opens the specified file for editing. You may need the path for that file as part of the filename.
`:e!`	Reopens a file for editing (refresh from disk) without saving changes first.
`:f` or Ctrl+G	Gives the File command or the Status command.
^G	Reports on the current filename and line.
`:n`	Specifies a new arguments list.
`:q`	Quits `vi` without saving changes.
`:sh`	Spawns a shell. Use the Exit command to return to `vi` when you are through.
`:ta` *<tag>*	Positions the cursor at the specified tag.
`:w` *<filename>*	Saves to the specified file.
`:w`	Writes out (saves) changes without exiting.
`:w!` *<filename>*	Saves the file and overwrites the original file if one exists. The exclamation point indicates a forced save, which is used to save changes to a read-only file.
ZZ	Saves any changes made and exits `vi`.

If you find that you can't write the file back to the original filename, you may have opened a file that you do not have write permission for. In that instance, save the file to a different filename using the Write command.

The File command displays the same information as the Status command: the name of the file being edited, the file's state, and the position of the cursor in the file are displayed on the status line. For example, you may see something like the following displayed:

```
"vitest" [Modified] line 3 of 5 --60%--
```

Navigating in the *vi* Editor

The `vi` editor has numerous keystrokes that help you move the position of the cursor. All of these keystrokes will work on a standard Sun keyboard, but at least one set will work with most terminal keyboards. From a keyboard supporting the arrow keys, you can move the cursor in the direction of the arrows in any mode.

Not all terminals have arrow keys and some that do have arrow keys aren't necessarily compatible with Sun systems, and so in Command mode, the `vi` editor uses the h, j, k, and l keys to move left one character, down one line, up one line, and right one character, respectively. These keys are found under the right hand on the same middle row of a standard QWERTY keyboard. To move several lines or characters in a direction at once, you precede these four keys with a number, such as 4l to move four characters to the right.

Table 16.3 shows the most widely used navigation keystrokes, most of which are used in the Command mode.

TABLE 16.3: THE vi NAVIGATION KEYSTROKES

Keystroke	Action
$	Go to the end of the line.
%	Find pairs of brackets or parentheses.
(	Go to the beginning of the current sentence.
)	Go to the end of the current sentence.
/<*pattern*>	Go to the next occurrence of the specified pattern, a forward search.
/<*pattern*>/+*n*	Go to the *n*th line after the specified pattern.
/<*pattern*>/-*n*	Go to the *n*th line before the specified pattern.
:$	Go to the end of the file.

Continued

TABLE 16.3: THE vi NAVIGATION KEYSTROKES (CONTINUED)

Keystroke	Action
`:1`	Go to the beginning of the file.
;	Repeat the last `f`, `F`, `t`, or `T` command that was issued.
?<*pattern*>	Go to the last occurrence of the specified pattern, a backward search.
[[	Go to the previous section.
]]	Go to the next section.
{	Go to the beginning of the paragraph.
}	Go to the end of the paragraph.
Arrows	Move one character or line in the direction of the arrow.
B	Go back one space-delimited word. This movement ignores punctuation.
b	Go back one word.
Carat (^)	Go to the first nonblank character on the current line.
Ctrl+B	Go back one screen.
Ctrl+D	Move down one-half screen.
Ctrl+F	Go forward one screen.
Ctrl+U	Move up one-half screen.
e	Go to the end of a word.
E	Go to the last character of a space-delimited word.
Enter or plus (+)	Go to the first nonblank character on the next line.
F*x*	Find the next occurrence of *x*.
F*x*	Find the previous *x*.
h or Ctrl+H	Move left or back one character.
H	Go to the top or head of the screen.
j or v	Go down one line, but in the same column.
k	Go up one line, but in the same column.
l or spacebar	Move right one character.
L	Go to the bottom (last line) of the screen.
Minus (-)	Go to the first nonblank character on the previous line.
n	Repeat the last ? or / search.
N	Reverse the last / or ? search.
n|	Move to the *n*th column.
*n*G	Go to the beginning of the line numbered *n*.
T*x*	Move to the character following the next *x*.

Continued

TABLE 16.3: THE vi NAVIGATION KEYSTROKES (CONTINUED)

Keystroke	Action
t*x*	Move to the character just before the next *x*.
W	Go forward one space-delimited word.
w	Go forward one word.
Zero (0)	Go to the beginning of the current line.

Figures 16.5 and 16.6 show the most commonly used navigation keystrokes.

FIGURE 16.5

Moving the cursor by character, words, and lines

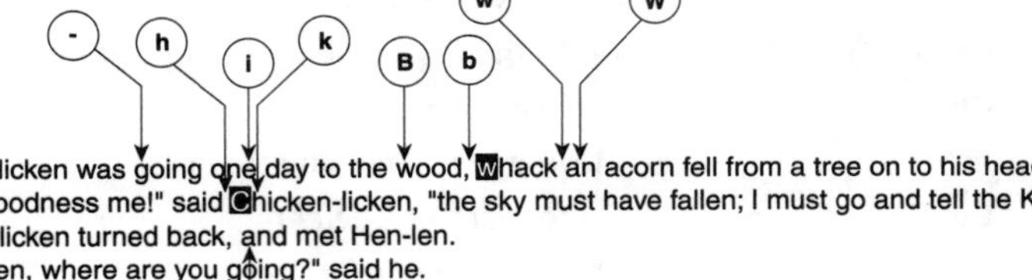

FIGURE 16.6

Moving the cursor about the screen

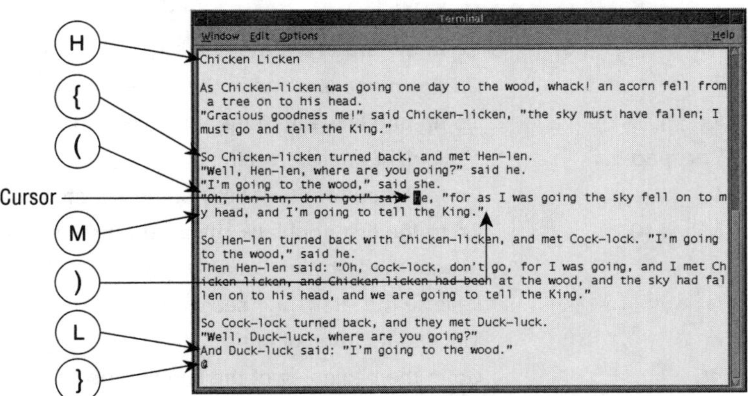

It is worth noting that vi specifies a word as a sequence of characters without spaces, punctuation (, . " " ? -), or digits. Therefore, *9 th* is two words; *9* is the first word and *th* is the second. Similarly, *99?* would be two words: *99* and *?*. vi makes provisions for the standard space-delimited words by providing the navigation commands W, B, and E.

A line is a string of characters separated by the newline character or by a return. Paragraphs are considered to be lines separated by one or more blank lines on each side.

Although you don't see line numbers in vi unless you specify that you want to see them, the program keeps track of the number of lines in your text file. You can use the *n*G keystroke to jump to the line numbered *n*. To see the line numbers in your display, use the :set nu command (which stands for "set number of"). You turn off numbering by issuing the :set nonu command.

One rarely used feature of vi is the use of markers to mark positions in your file. Markers exist only during a session, but they serve the same role as bookmarks, providing a position in the file that you can jump to during your work. To set a marker, move to the start of the line you wish to mark and give the ma command. This creates the a marker for that line. Unless you delete the line or specify the marker again at a different line beginning, the a marker stays with that line.

Markers serve as positions that you can use in ranges with other commands. For example, use the d'a command to delete everything from the cursor's current position to the beginning of the a marker line.

Editing in the *vi* Editor

The most commonly used editing commands are those that put you into the Input submodes. These are i (insert before the current character) and a (append text right after the cursor position). You can also use the I and A commands to enter text at the beginning of the current line or enter text at the end of the line, respectively. I and A save you from having to reposition the cursor prior to text entry.

As you are entering text, you can correct the mistakes you make by using the same commands that you would at the shell, including the Erase (Ctrl+H), Line Kill (Ctrl+U), and Word Kill (Ctrl+W) keystrokes. As you move the cursor backward in the Insert mode, vi doesn't remove text. However, as you enter new text or press Return, the old text is moved down the document to make room for the new text.

Two other common commands are the o and O commands, which are used to create open lines. The o command opens a new line directly below the current line, and the O command opens a new line directly above the current line. In both instances, your cursor is moved to this new line, which saves you from having to reposition the cursor for input.

You don't have to enter additional lines to force a page break in `vi`, even though the editor doesn't support formatting. As part of the command set, Ctrl+L commands a printer to add a page break. When you press Ctrl+L, you should see `^L` appear on your display. If you don't see that symbol, then press Ctrl+V before you press Ctrl+L. The Quote character, inserted by using the Ctrl+V keystroke, works in the Input mode to remove any special meaning from characters used for actions in `vi`.

Joining and splitting lines is very straightforward. To join two lines, go to the line to which you will join the second line and in Command mode, enter the `J` command. To split lines, go to the character to the right of the line ending and press Enter in the Input mode (this doesn't work in the Command mode).

One advanced feature that you may find useful in your work is the use of macros and shortcuts. You can create these key sequences using the `:map` command. The syntax of the command is as follows:

```
:map <keystroke> <action>
```

You can use the Esc and Ctrl keys with keystrokes, but you should avoid any commonly used command key in `vi`. To see current macros, use the `:map` command by itself. Using the `:abbrev` command, you can substitute keystrokes in the Input mode with any set of characters. Here is the syntax:

```
:abbrev <keystroke(s)> <text>
```

Deleting and Undoing

You delete text in the Command mode. `vi` provides you with commands you can use to delete characters, words, text to the end of a line, or even an entire line. Use the `x` command to delete a single character covered by the cursor; use `4x` to delete a single character and three more to the right of the cursor. Other commonly used deletion commands include the `dw` command to delete a word and the `dd` command to delete a line. You can delete a specific line in Last-Line mode by using a numeric prefix before the `:d` command, such as `:10d` or the range `:1, 10d` to delete the first 10 lines of a file. You can even use a relative line address for deletions, so that if you are on line 5 and you want to delete the first 10 lines of the file, you can enter `:.-5,.+5d` as the command. Table 16.4 contains a summary of editing commands.

TABLE 16.4: THE vi EDITING COMMANDS

Command	Action
^D	Tabs one character left and resets left margin in Edit mode. In Command mode, this keystroke moves you down half a screen.
^H or erase character	Deletes previous character (backspace) in Edit mode. In Command mode, this moves the cursor back (backspace) with no changes to the document.
^V	Uses the following nonprintable character in Edit mode. No action in Command mode.
^W	Deletes the preceding word in Edit mode. No action in Command mode.
0^D	Tabs to the beginning of the line and resets the left margin in Edit mode. In Command mode, it moves you to the beginning of a line and then down one-half page.
<	Shifts left in Edit mode. No action in Command mode.
>	Shifts right in Edit mode. No action in Command mode.
\	Displays the current kill and erase characters in Edit mode. No action in Command mode.
!	Filters the text with a command in Edit mode. No action in Command mode.
~	Changes the case of the selected character(s) in Command mode and moves the cursor to the next character on the right. In Edit mode, it inserts a tilde character into the text.
Ctrl+D	Tabs to the beginning of the line without resetting the left margin.
a	Appends text after the cursor in Command mode.
A	Appends text to the end of the line in Command mode.
c	Changes selection.
C	Changes a line of text from current point to the end of the line.
d	Deletes a word in Command mode.
D	Deletes a line of text in Command mode.
dd or kill character	Deletes the current line in Command mode.
i	Inserts text before the character under the cursor in Entry mode.
I	Inserts text before the first nonblank character or at the beginning of the line in Command mode.
J	Joins lines in Command mode.
p	Puts yanked lines before cursor.
P	Puts yanked lines after cursor.

Continued

TABLE 16.4: THE vi EDITING COMMANDS (CONTINUED)

Command	Action
r<*char*>	Replaces a character with the char string in Command mode.
R<*chars*>+Esc	Replaces multiple characters specified by <*chars*>, and when you press the Esc key it ends the replace operation.
s	Substitutes characters by replacing the characters under the cursor and putting vi into the Insert submode.
S	Substitutes (deletes) the entire current line, leaving the cursor in the first column in the Insert mode.
u	Undoes the last change.
x	Deletes character under cursor.
X	Deletes character to the left of cursor.
y	Yank or copy selected lines to buffer. (To yank text is to copy it into the unnamed buffer without deleting it.)
Y	Yank or copy lines.

You can use the u and U commands to undo changes you've made to your text. The u command will undo the most recent change. The U command undoes all recent changes to the current line. If you use multiples of commands, such as 6d, the u command will restore the entire action.

The Change command is very similar to the Delete command. When you specify the Change command along with a measure of length, vi deletes that amount of text (or for *C*, or some number of, lines of text) and puts the program into the Input mode. For example, c5w would remove five words, including the word that the cursor is on; c$ would remove text from the current cursor position to the end of the current line. To complete the change, enter new text and press Esc to return to the Command mode.

The Substitute command offers another text replacement method. Use the s command to delete the character the cursor is on and put vi into the Input mode. After you have entered text and pressed Esc, the net effect will have been to replace the character with your entry. The S command replaces the current line.

To change the case of a character or set of characters, use the Case command, ~. With this command, the case of the character under the cursor will be changed from lowercase to uppercase or vice versa. When you combine the ~ with a number, such as 3~, you perform this action for the character under the cursor and the next two characters.

Copying and Pasting

When you delete or cut text, you place the text you deleted into a buffer, called the unnamed or general purpose buffer. You can use the `p` command, the Put command, to insert the contents of the unnamed buffer into your text to the right of the cursor; the `P` command inserts the data to the left of the cursor. The Put command can be used as many times as you wish to place the text in the buffer in multiple locations in your text file.

You can copy text into the unnamed buffer without deleting it, a process that the `vi` editor calls a *yank*. You use the `y` or `Y` command to place text in the buffer. For example, `yw` puts the current word in the buffer, and `6yw` puts the current word and the next five words into the buffer. The `Y` command yanks text from the current cursor position to the left, a reverse yank. Use the `yy` command to yank a sentence and the `y$` command to yank text from the current cursor position to the end of the line.

TIP You can repeat the last command by pressing the period (`.`) key.

You can use the delete character and delete line keys in combination with the Put command to exchange characters or lines that are out of order. To exchange characters, move the cursor to the first character and then give the `xp` command. To exchange lines, move the cursor to the first line and give the `ddp` command.

Searching and Replacing

In any long text file, it can become difficult to locate particular strings of characters. The `vi` editor offers a search and replace function you can use to find words, phrases, or numbers as well as do wildcard searches. Searching and replacing involves a combination of the Command and Input modes.

There are several ways you can find a character:

- To find the next occurrence of the *x* character (moving forward), press the `fx` keystroke on the current line.
- To find the last occurrence of the *x* character (moving backward), press the `Fx` keystroke on the current line.
- To repeat the last find command in either direction, press the `;` keystroke on the current line.
- To repeat the last find command in the opposite direction, press the `,` keystroke on the current line.

NOTE The `f`, or find, keystroke finds characters only on the current line.

To do a pattern search, follow these steps:

1. Press the / keystroke. This has the effect of moving you to the Last-Line mode and searching forward in the file. You can also press the ? key to search backwards toward the beginning of the file.
2. Enter a character or string and then press the Return key.
3. Press the `n` keystroke to move to the next occurrence following the first match. Or press the `N` keystroke to move to the previous occurrence of the pattern.

NOTE Remember that `vi` is case sensitive and that your search pattern or character must be in the exact case you wish to search for.

You will find the special characters in Table 16.5 useful in search strings.

TABLE 16.5: SEARCH STRING CHARACTERS

Character	Purpose
^	Specifies the beginning of a line.
$	Specifies the end of a line.
Period (.)	Acts as the wildcard symbol for any character, which may be substituted in place of the wildcard.
\>	Specifies the end of word indicator. Use this character to specify a match using the end of a word.
\<	Specifies the beginning of word indicator. Use this character to specify a match using the beginning of a word.
\(...\)	Saves the search pattern into a buffer. You can call back the search pattern and place it into one of the numbered buffers (\1 through \9). The ellipsis points are the search pattern in this case.
*	Matches 0 or more occurrences of the character that precedes the asterisk. For example, /tal*e would find the string "tal" and match it to "tal", "tale", "talee", and so forth.
[ ]	Provides matches to any character contained within the square brackets. For example, use "tal[ek]" to find occurrences of "tale" and "talk" in your file.

WARNING Be careful when you use characters such as *, [, ^, $, \, and the period (.) in your search pattern. These characters are used by `vi` for other purposes. For example, to search for "end of file.", you must use the backslash symbol to turn the period into simple text, as in "`/end of file.\`". Otherwise, the period is used as a wildcard to locate any string starting with file, such as files, filename, and so forth.

The search and replace (substitute) function is very similar to the search function with the addition of another option. Here's the search and replace command syntax:

```
:[range]s/<pattern>/<newpattern>/[g]
```

The range parameter specifies the beginning and ending lines of the search and replace and is optional. If you don't specify a range, only the current line will be replaced. To search an entire file, use the `1,$` range parameter, to search from your current position to the 20th line, use `.,20`, and to search from line 10 to 20, use the `10,20` parameter.

The pattern you use can be a fixed string or an expression containing wildcards. The new pattern must be a fixed string and cannot contain wildcards. If you include the optional `g` parameter at the end of the search and replace expression, the `vi` editor knows to do a global search and replace on the line or range of lines that you specified. If you omit the `g` parameter, `vi` goes to the first match in the range, replaces it, and stops.

Working with Buffers

One of the more advanced topics with `vi` is the use of its buffers. In addition to the work buffer, which displays your file and changes on the screen, and the general purpose, or unnamed, buffer that is used as scratch memory for the Put command, the `vi` editor offers you 26 named buffers, each designated by a letter of the alphabet, in addition to 9 named buffers designated by the numbers 1 through 9. You can store yanked material in any of these named buffers and the `vi` editor will maintain the contents of the buffers during your editing session.

To place text into a named buffer, use a command like `"m3yy`, which places the current line and the next two lines into the m buffer, overwriting the current contents. If you use the command `"M2yy`, then those three lines are appended to contents of the m buffer. To put the contents of the m buffer back into your text at any location, use the `"mp` command in the Insert mode.

The nine numbered buffers are essentially read-only buffers containing the nine most recent deletions. `vi` uses a last-in, first-out system to fill the 1 buffer, moving that content to the 2 buffer when the next deletion is specified. The most useful action you can use with numbered buffers is to restore former deletions. You can use the `"1p` command to put the contents of the 1 buffer into your text. If you don't see what you want to restore, give the `u` command to undo the put and then use the period (`.`) command to repeat your previous action. `vi` puts the contents of the numbered buffers into your file starting with the 2 buffer and proceeding to the 9 buffer.

Setting Parameters

There are numerous parameters or options that you can set to modify the behavior and appearance of the `vi` editor. Some of these options are set in system resource files that require the root privileges of a system administrator. Other options are ones you set in user preference and in the `vi` editor application startup or resource files.

The following are methods you can use to set parameters:

- Use the `:set` command with a parameter to establish a session setting.
- Enter your parameters into the `.profile` file in either the Bourne or Korn shell or the `.login` file in the C shell.
- Enter your parameters into a startup file that `vi` uses, such as the `.exrc` file.

In the latter two cases, the parameters you set will always be available to you whenever you work in `vi`.

vi Options

To set options from within `vi`, you use the `set` command. The `set` command has the following syntax:

```
:set <option1> <option2> <option3> …
```

Press the Return key to establish the options. Some of these options are turned on and off, while others offer several conditions set by variables. The ones set by variables require that you enter the variable, such as `option = n`, where *n* is a number. Table 16.6 includes some of the common options you may want to set within `vi`; the two-letter option is the terse command name. To view all the options available in `vi`, give the `:set all` command. To see which parameters you have set that are different than the default parameters, give the `:set` command.

When you want to add statements to your `.profile` or `.login` file in your home directory, they should have the following syntax (EXINT is a shell variable that `vi` reads upon loading):

```
EXINT='set <option1> <option2>…
export EXINT
```

TABLE 16.6: THE OPTION PARAMETERS

Option	Modification
autoindent (ai)	Sets each newly appended line to the same white space as the preceding line. The default is noautoindent (noic).
beautify (bf)	Tells vi to ignore control characters with the exception of newline, tab, and formfeed. The nobeautify (nobf) option is the default.
errorbells (eb)	Rings the terminal bell when an error is made. The default is noerror-bells (noeb).
flash (fl)	Causes the terminal to flash instead of beep. This command is useful for hearing-impaired readers. The default is noflash (nofl).
ignorecase (ic)	Forces vi to ignore case in search and replace operations. The default is noignorecase (noic).
list (li)	When on, displays tabs and end-of-line markers. Tabs appear as ^I, and eol markers appear as $. The default is nolist (noli).
magic	Gives special meaning to characters for searches. The nomagic parameter removes the special meaning.
number (nu)	Turns on line numbering. The nonumber (nonu) option is the default.
report=*n*	Tells vi to issue a message whenever more than *n* lines are modified. The default is 5.
shell (sh)	Specifies the shell type that is used when the :! and :sh commands are used. To set the shell, enter shell=<*pathname*>, where the <*pathname*> is the location of the shell.
shiftwidth (sw)	Sets the software tab setting used when the autoindent option is on. The default is 8.
showmatch (sm)	Used by programmers to move to braces or parentheses in programs. The noshowmatch (nosm) is the default.
showmode	Displays the mode on the status line. The default is noshowmode. (This is a very useful setting.)
term=<*name*>	Specifies the terminal type.
warn	Tells vi to warn you if you issue a :! shell command that would move you to the shell without saving the contents of your work buffer first. The default is warn.
wrapmargin (wm)	Specifies the number of columns before vi moves text to the next line. A line break is automatically inserted after the last word that will fit in the margin. The default is 0, with wm turned off.
wrapscan (ws)	Allows vi to search past the beginning or end of the buffer. The nowrap-scan (nows) stops a search at the buffer boundary.

Setting the Terminal Type

In most instances, the `vi` editor will function properly when you first attempt to use it. This is particularly true when you use a Solaris workstation like Sun Ultra, where the display is full featured and properly specified in system configuration. In certain situations, you may find that `vi` doesn't display or update on a terminal correctly. Different terminals use different control codes and `vi` needs to know which terminal it is working with in order to know what codes are appropriate. Typically, an administrator will set up this parameter for you, but it is relatively straightforward to set the parameter yourself.

You can enter the terminal type from within `vi` and that terminal type will be used for the terminal session, or you can specify the terminal type parameter using the `$TERM` variable as part of a shell's login script. Many terminals will prompt you to confirm the terminal type during login, as in `TERM = (vt100)`, or allow you to change the terminal type at login.

To see what your system thinks is the current terminal, follow these steps:

1. Type **echo $TERM** at the system prompt.
2. Press the Return key.

If you don't get the answer you expect or if you are using the Bourne or Korn shell, you can use the `TERM=`*<name>* command followed by the export name command to replace the terminal type. When you use one terminal type consistently, put these commands in your `.profile` file. For the C shell, you will need to use the `setenv TERM` *<name>* command. The *<name>* variable is replaced with the name of your terminal, and the command line for the console in the CDE using the C shell would be `% sentenv TERM dtterm`. You can also put this command into your `.login` file.

Solaris supports both `terminfo` and `termcap` name styles that are part of System V or BSD. The following terminals are in common use:

- `dtterm` (CDE from the console)
- `sun-cmd` (OpenLook from the console)
- VT100, using a terminal emulator
- `xterm` or VS100 (when you are on an X-terminal)

If you are unsure of what terminal to use, try the VT100 because most displays will support this emulation. For PCs and Macs, you may find that you can run applications using either the VT100 or VT220 terminal emulation.

Spawning a Shell

You can spawn a shell from within a `vi` editing session if you need to check your e-mail, do housekeeping on files, set system parameters, or execute a particular command from within your shell. When you escape to the shell, you leave the `vi` editor suspended, but the process will continue to run in the background.

There are two methods you can use to spawn a Solaris shell:

- Use the `:!` command followed by the Solaris command you want to execute. This method is particularly useful for executing a single Solaris command.
- Use the `:!sh` command to start a new shell that can be used for any number of commands. To return to your `vi` session, issue an exit command in the shell or press the Ctrl+D keystroke.

WARNING When users issue the `:!sh` command within the `vi` editor to spawn a shell and forget that the `vi` editor is still running, there is a tendency to not issue the exit command and to use the `vi` command again to start a second `vi` session. When you create a second session of `vi`, you overwrite the work buffer and can loose your previous work. If you want to know if `vi` is running, use the `ps` (process) command in the shell to get a list of running processes.

TIP It's a good idea to always save your work to disk before you spawn a shell or execute a command using the `! pass through` command. If your command hangs, you can loose all of your changes.

Other Editors

PART
III
Working with
Shells in Solaris

Although the `vi` editor is the text editor that most experienced people with years of working in Solaris use, it isn't your only choice for editing text files, nor is it in many cases your best choice. There are other text editors that you can download and install, some equally powerful and many, if not most, free.

NOTE It is important that you have at least a basic understanding of how to work with the `vi` editor because there will come a time when the system will crash and the only editor you can use is `vi` (such as when you're in single user mode). It is important not to become too dependent on the graphical user environment.

There are instances when a visual editor such as the `vi` editor makes sense; in fact, it may be your only choice on a system that has processes that are hung. But if you're working on a healthy system in the graphical user interface of the Common Desktop Environment (CDE) and you can access the CDE Text Editor, you may be much less likely to suffer catastrophic damage to a text file by making mistakes. You may be faster and more efficient and there may be less of a learning curve when you use Text Editor. And if Text Editor isn't powerful enough for your editing needs, you may find that working with StarOffice's word processor provides the features that you need in an almost equally easy-to-use environment. These additional choices and the provisos that you must be aware of are presented to you in the sections that follow.

Unix Editors

It is highly unlikely that you will want to substitute a single line text processor for the visual display that the `vi` editor offers because `vi` has so much more additional editing functionality that you will miss the conveniences. However, you can do that if you wish within the `vi` editor by returning to the `ex` editor, a subset of `vi`.

There are many Unix text editors, and many have a similar syntax, sharing as they do a common Unix heritage. Here is a list of some other Unix text editors:

`emacs` A macro editor (*e*ditor *mac*ro*s*).

TECO Text Editor and Corrector; originally called Tape Editor and Corrector.

`vim` A `vi` replacement that extends the power of `vi` to support things like color screens, multiple levels of undo, and a graphical interface. Fully compatible with `vi`.

The `emacs` program is widely distributed and favored by many people, with the freeware version GNU `emacs` in common use. Unlike `vi`, `emacs` is modeless. When you enter the editor, it saves all entries in the file buffer. `emacs` also offers online help.

Two other text editors in use are `pico` and `joe`. The `pico` editor, from the *pi*ne *co*mposer, can be used as either a stand-alone editor or as part of an e-mail system. `pico` was developed at the University of Washington. `joe`, developed by Joe Allen, is a freeware ASCII-text screen editor. Both programs are editors that are typically used for mailing applications but could be used for file editing.

The `vi` editor is probably the most widely used editor in Unix. Versions of `vi` appear on all versions of Unix, with the exception of Linux. Because Linux ships as an open source code distribution and the `vi` editor contains code that is proprietary to AT&T, clones of `vi`—such as `elvis`, `nvi`, `ni`, `vine`, and `vile`—are sometimes used. You should note that Linux does have a `vi` command, but that command refers to the `vim` clone of `vi`. As it turns out, the `vi` editor has been ported to several other operating systems beyond Unix, including MS-DOS, Windows, and DEC VMS.

Using Text Editor

While in the CDE, Text Editor (dtpad) offers an easier-to-use alternative to the vi editor and should be sufficient for most of your text-editing needs. With Text Editor, you give up some of the power of vi, but you also eliminate some of the risks involved with manipulating vi. Using Text Editor also allows you to partake of some of the economies of a windowed environment and use of the mouse and keyboard together.

TIP Use the mnemonic keystrokes to speed command selection by pressing Alt+underscore (Alt+_) to activate the menu bar. Then you can press Alt+F to open the File menu and Alt+S to save your work.

To open Text Editor, click the text note icon in the front panel. Text Editor is a WYSIWYG text editor, and if you have used a word processor before, Text Editor's functions will be familiar to you. You can enter text directly into the window in Insert mode, edit text as you go, and use your mouse for movement and selection. There are few options in Text Editor, but one of them is to shift to Overstrike mode using the Overstrike command on the Options menu. You have very minor control over the appearance of the window, primarily to affect text justification in the Settings dialog box accessed from the Format menu and word wrap using the Wrap to Fit command on the Options menu. You can also turn on a status line using that command on the Options menu. Figure 16.7 shows the Text Editor window with the status line and some text entered into it.

FIGURE 16.7

Text entered into the Text Editor window

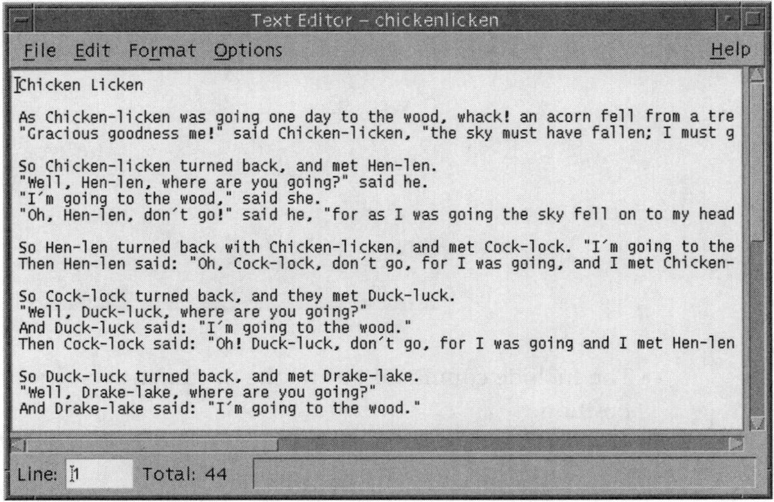

Most of the file manipulation commands are on the File menu:

- Use the New command to create a new document; Text Editor will prompt you to save any changes to your current document before opening a new one.

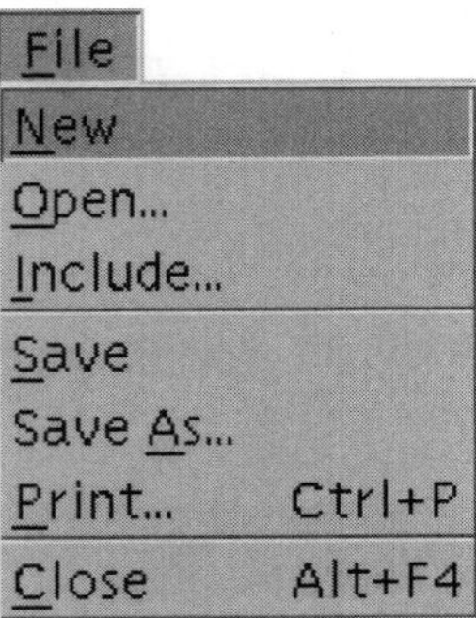

- Use the Open command to open a preexisting document. The following graphic shows the Open dialog box.

- The Include command inserts the document you specify at the current cursor position.

- The Save command writes your changes back to disk. Text Editor indicates when you need to save by placing (`needed`) in the command.
- Use Save As to create a new document with a different name. The following graphic shows the Save As dialog box.

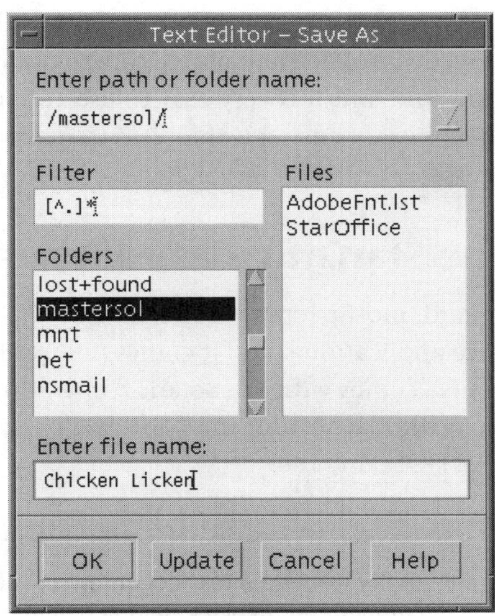

The File menu also includes a Print command (Ctrl+P) as well as the Close (Alt+F4) command.

There are a number of methods you can use to select text with the mouse:

- Single-click to place an insertion point.
- Double-click to select a word.
- Triple-click to select a line.
- Quadruple-click to select the entire document.
- Click and drag to select any continuous block of text.
- Use the Shift key to extend your range of selection.

Selected text can be replaced by typing in new text or by using the keyboard to paste text.

Text Editor offers a standard clipboard function, with Cut (Ctrl+X), Copy (Ctrl+C), and Paste (Ctrl+V) as well as an Undo command (Ctrl+U). Clear removes selected text and replaces it with spaces, and Delete removes selected text without putting it on the clipboard. One feature that Text Editor offers you that isn't in `vi` is the Spelling command. You will find that the Find/Change command (Ctrl+F) offers basic search-and-replace functionality with only a search forward capability. All of these functions are on the Edit menu.

Text Editor is also nice because it contains online help, accessed through the Help menu or by clicking the Help buttons in any of the program's dialog boxes. Text Editor isn't powerful, but it is very easy to use and understand, and it is much more difficult to make mistakes using it than it is to make mistakes using `vi` or the StarOffice word processor.

Text and the StarOffice Word Processor

Going forward, most people who run the Solaris operating system will use the StarOffice office application suite. It comes preinstalled with new Sun workstations, a StarOffice disk comes with the Solaris 8 operating system distribution package, and the suite is downloadable for Intel and SPARC architectures from the Sun Web site (`www.sun.com/staroffice`).

NOTE If you try to open a text document in the StarOffice word processor, Solaris will open that document in the Solaris default text editor.

The advantage the StarOffice word processor offers is that it has more extensive utilities than Text Editor. Figure 16.8 shows a text document open in the word processor. StarOffice comes with its own document desktop, and the word processor integrates with other functions, such as the database for data exchange. Using the word processor for simple text editing is a little like cracking a walnut with a hammer, but it gets the job done. StarOffice offers substantial online help, and you can also find many books explaining how to use this program; this is just a brief introduction.

The main thing to know about working with text documents in the word processor is that StarOffice (as do all other standard applications) makes use of higher ASCII characters in its native file format to preserve your formatting information. To work with text documents, you must be certain that you save your text file out as text only, which you can do by choosing Text from the File Type drop-down menu in the Save As dialog box (Figure 16.9 shows the Save As dialog box).

FIGURE 16.8

A document in the StarOffice word processor

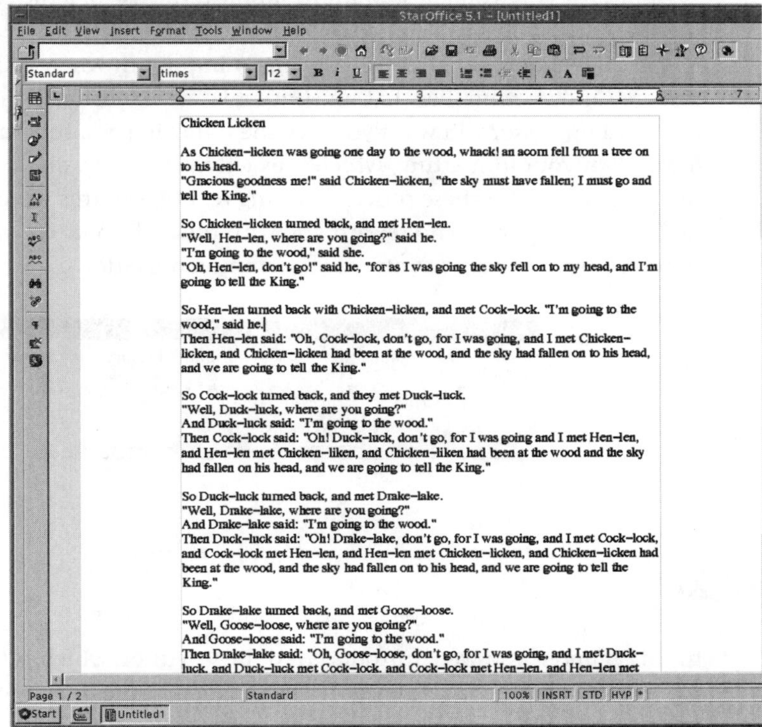

FIGURE 16.9

The word processor Save As dialog box

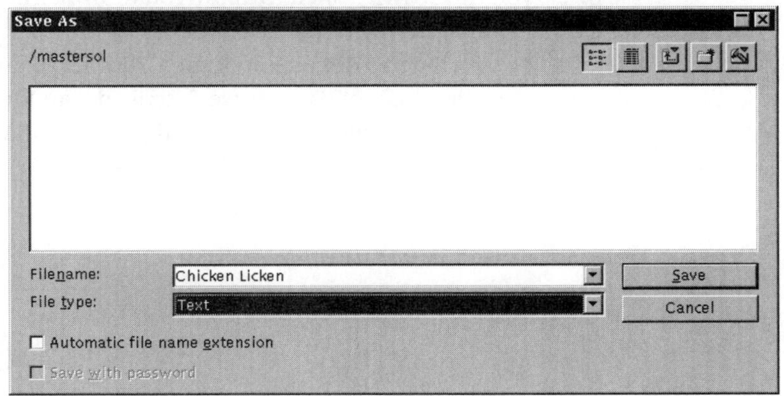

Typically, you would also want to suppress the use of a file extension by deselecting the Automatic File Name Extension check box; otherwise your file will have the name `<filename>.txt`. This is particularly important when you are working with resource and start-up files that must not take an extension. Before you save a text file, the word processor will warn you (see the following graphic) that you are about to loose all of your formatting, which is exactly what you want to do when you are saving a text file. With these provisos, saving text files in this word processor will present no further difficulties and reward you with the additional conveniences of not having to remember command syntaxes for common operations.

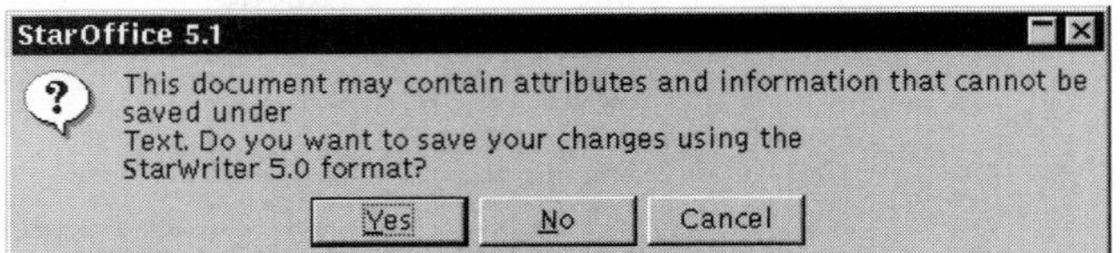

Summary

In this chapter, you were introduced to the `vi` editor, which is the tool of choice for editing text and resource files from the command line or a terminal window in Solaris. With the `vi` editor, you can open, modify, create, and save text files.

The `vi` editor is a modal editor, which means it separates commands you enter from text you input. The `vi` editor has a very extensive editing command set, with many capabilities that were described in this chapter.

While in `vi`, you can spawn a shell to allow you to work interactively with the Solaris operating system from within the editor.

This chapter also included a discussion of the CDE's Text Editor, which is an easier-to-use alternative to the `vi` editor. Finally, we described StarOffice's word processor; if you have StarOffice installed you can use its word processor to create, modify, and save text files.

CHAPTER 17

Understanding Shells

FEATURING:

The background of the shell 672

Creating scripts 674

Job control 675

Separate and group commands 676

Parameters and variables 679

Built-ins 686

Shell compatibilities 690

In this chapter, the history and background of the shells shipped with Solaris are described. Solaris uses several shells, which are high-level programming languages that allow you to write programs or scripts to simplify complex tasks. When you log in and enter a command, the designated shell interprets the command and acts upon it. This chapter is meant to be an introduction to the three chapters that follow, in which Solaris shells will be discussed individually and in detail. Among the topics described in this chapter are how to create shell scripts (which can execute specific commands) and job control (which is a pipe command and can be run in the foreground or, to allow the user to continue working on the desktop, can be run in the background).

The "parent" and "child" hierarchy and how Solaris "forks" a process will be explained. Parameters and variables describe how user-defined shell parameters are used. Keyword variables, global and local variables, and positional parameters are all covered in this chapter.

The Background of the Shell

Shells are high-level programming languages that double as command interpreters. When you respond to a prompt on the command line, the shell will interpret your response and act upon it. A shell acts as an interface between the user and the kernel of the system.

Shells originated with the Unix system when it was first developed at Bell Laboratories in the late 1960s. The objective with Unix was to create a simple modifiable system with a third-generation programming language. Unix was developed with a core kernel that ultimately implemented a high-level language called C in 1973. At that time, AT&T, the owners of Unix, licensed the source code to educational institutions. Because there was no technical support and no way to fix bugs, a group of students at the University of California, Berkeley (the group was known as the Berkeley Software Distribution, or BSD) fine-tuned the operating system and developed applications software, such as `vi`, the visual editor described in Chapter 16, "Using the `vi` and Text Editor."

Sun Microsystems was also formed by former graduate students from Stanford and Berkeley. They developed the workstation market to successfully compete with mainframe companies. They also transformed BSD into a commercial product. Solaris was originally derived from the BSD distribution from Berkeley. A major plus is that the BSD group started a community-oriented free software movement, making BSD software available and entirely free. Sun eventually changed from a BSD-based Unix (SunOS 1–4.1.4, or Solaris 1.*x*) to the AT&T System V–based system it currently uses (SunOS 5.0–5.8) for Solaris, versions 2–8.

Sun has enhanced its hardware so that workstations and servers are fast and efficient. Their emphasis on innovative hardware allows them to freely give away the Solaris 8 operating system.

Solaris 8 supports several different cross-platform modes of interoperability; one such mode is Lxrun, which allows the execution of SPARC Linux binaries under Solaris. The Solaris 1.*x* application may also be run without modification. Sun also promotes a free version of Solaris 8 for the SPARC and Intel hardware platforms. Binary compatibility has been a problem, but with Java programming, there is an attempt to make that a thing of the past. Development in Java is becoming easier and promises to make complete binary compatibility between operating systems and architectures a reality.

Solaris features three primary shells:

Bourne shell (`sh`) The Bourne shell, which is the root shell for single-user mode and the Solaris default shell, was written by Steve Bourne of AT&T's Bell Laboratories. It was originally written for Unix in 1969. It is used for formulating shell scripts and processing groups of commands. It is the interface, if you will, between the user and the kernel, and it has many features but does not have history or aliasing capabilities. The Bourne shell is the subject of Chapter 18.

Korn shell (`ksh`) The Korn shell is very similar to the Bourne shell but adds features such as history and aliasing capabilities while retaining most of the Bourne shell attributes. You can think of the Korn shell as a superset of the Bourne shell. The Korn shell is covered in Chapter 19.

C shell (`csh`) The C shell grew out of the C programming language. The C shell originated at Berkeley for Unix also. It can be customized for easier use and is familiar to most users who understand the C programming language. Its conventions vary slightly between the Bourne and the Korn shells. The C shell is covered in Chapter 20.

There are many other shells that Solaris users adopt: one is the Job shell (`jsh`) and another is the Bourne Again shell (`bash`), while yet another is `tcsh` (the extension of `csh`), which is currently a very popular shell. These last three examples are not as prominent as the first three, but they are important in their own right. Each shell is capable of spawning its own subshells.

You can switch back and forth between the three bundled Solaris shells by giving a brief command. The Bourne shell is run by using `sh` as a shortcut (default sign is `$`), the Korn shell by `ksh` (default sign is `$`), and the C shell by `csh` (default sign is `%`). To change to the shell you wish to use, type the appropriate command and press the Return key.

These simple commands allow you to switch back and forth between shells whenever you need to. If you start a new shell, you can exit it and press Return to return to the previous shell prompt. These shortcut commands are actually nested one on top of the other just as the shells are. By using and repeating the `exit` command, you will return to the original shell. If you want to replace your current shell with a new shell, you can use the `exec` command to start the new shell (for example, `exec ksh`). The new shell will then become your primary shell for the current session and typing `exit` will not return you to your old shell.

NOTE The administrator determines which shell will be the login shell. This becomes the default shell. If you have been switching shells, you must keep giving the `exit` command to get back to the default shell to log out, or you can use the `exec` command to change shells.

Creating Scripts

Groups of commands stored in files are called scripts or shell scripts. The Bourne shell is statically linked and therefore all system scripts are written in this shell. Scripts may be short commands on one line or they may be long with complex instructions that may repeat when encountering certain parameters.

Scripts are actually mini-programs that help you customize the tasks you want Solaris to perform. The following set of instructions demonstrates how to run a simple script:

1. To run a script, give its filename on the command line (in this example, the filename is `barriers`):

   ```
   $ barriers
   ```

   The shell will then interpret and execute the script command if it is in your path. To execute the script, you must have permission to access the file that contains it. If the shell does not recognize the filename as executable, you will get an error message as in this example:

   ```
   $ barriers
   barriers:  execute permission denied
   ```

2. Use `chmod` to change access privileges. The `chmod` command uses an argument to give the owner permission to execute a file (Chapter 5, "The File System," explains this in detail). If all else fails, try placing a `./` in front of the filename:

   ```
   $ ./barriers
   ```

3. Precede the filename with `sh` so the shell will take this as an argument and execute the command (you can also try this in `ksh` or `csh`):

   ```
   $ sh barriers
   ```

4. Use the `file` command to find out what kind of shell script you're accessing. If the type of script is unknown, the file command will report that it's an ASCII file, which is usually what a Bourne shell script is.

Job Control

Job control enables you to move jobs to the background, bring them to the foreground, or stop them. This function gives the user greater flexibility and efficiency while working. Jobs may be running behind the scenes while the desktop is active. A command pipeline or multiple commands on a single command line are good examples of jobs. The names of individual jobs are followed by the &. If the & is trailing the command, it signals to the shell to run the job in the background. The shell will display information about background jobs. It will provide a job number in brackets and the process identification (PID) number of the final process in the job. There is a specific shell aptly named the Job shell (`jsh`); the Bourne shell does not support job control. In addition to having all the capabilities and built-ins of the Bourne shell, the Job shell fully supports job control. The Korn shell and C shell both support job control as well.

Solaris also has a utility named `jobs` in the Bourne shell. It lists all background jobs. Even though Bourne does not support job control, it will not generate an error message if you give the `jobs` command. It will allow you to enter the `sleep` command, which will create a background job that the utility can report on. The `jsh` command will then invoke the Job shell while the `jobs` utility displays job information.

Before issuing a prompt, the Job shell will issue a list of the job numbers and PID numbers of any jobs running in the background. One or more of these jobs may be moved into the foreground by using the `fg` built-in with a % sign preceding the job number. If there is only one job running in the background or it is listed with a + sign, you can use `fg` without arguments.

Conversely, if you want to send a foreground job to the background, you must press Ctrl+z or Ctrl+y. This will suspend the job immediately (Ctrl+z) or after it tries to read input from the terminal (Ctrl+y). You need to use the `bg` built-in because Ctrl+y or Ctrl+z puts the commands into a suspended mode and you have to tell them to reactivate in the background. When a background job reads from the terminal, the shell will put it to sleep until you give further input. Move the job into the foreground so it can read from the terminal. The command line will be displayed. The shell will let you know about the status of a job. It will tell you step-by-step when the job begins, ends, or is waiting for further input. The shell will delay disrupting your work, however, until it's ready to display the next prompt. It will not allow you to exit if any job has stopped. Use `jobs` to review what is left or to leave the shell. The shell will then allow you to exit but will terminate any stopped jobs. Background jobs will continue to run.

Solaris 8 allows you to schedule jobs that must be run on a one-time basis for a specific time by using the `at` command, as described in Chapter 15, "Memory and Process Management." Jobs can consist of a single command or a script with a set of commands. The jobs are specified by files in `/var/spool/cron/atjobs` and configuration is managed by the file `/etc/cron.d/at.deny`. The following example demonstrates how to use the `at` command:

```
$ at 0900
at> /usr/lib/phnlist -bd
at>  <Ctrl-D>
commands will be executed using /bin/sh
job 879764542 at Fri Feb 3 09:00:00 2001
```

Because the `at` job executes only once and some system events need to be repeated on a regular schedule, the `cron` command is extremely useful (for a more detailed discussion of the `cron` command, see Chapter 15). Users on the system may have a `crontab`, allowing them to schedule events to occur at different times and dates. The jobs are specified by files in `/var/spool/cron/cronjobs`, and the configuration files are `/etc/cron.d/cron.allow` and `/etc/cron.d/cron.deny`. This is a standard `crontab` generated by Solaris:

```
$ crontab -1 root
10 2 * * 0,4 /etc/cron.d/logchecker
10 3 * * 0  /usr/lib/newsyslog
15 3 * * 0 /usr/lib/fsnfs/nfsfind
1 2 * * * [ -x /user/sbin/rtc/ ]  & & /usr/sbin/rtc -c
    /dev/null 2 >&1
30 3 * * * [ -x /usr/lib/gss/gsscred_clean ] &&
    /usr/lib/gss/gsscred_clean
```

The six leading fields represent minutes, hours, days of the months, months of the year, days of the week, and the command to execute. You can add or delete entries from your `crontab` with the `-e` command. This will invoke your text editor. All you need to do is edit and save your changes.

Separate and Group Commands

When you write a shell script or give shell commands, the commands must be separate from one another. A semicolon (;) may be used to keep commands separate without initiating their execution. Enter the commands on a single line (as in the following example) and press the Return key:

```
$ l;m;n &
```

The preceding example would first run `l`, then `m`, and then put `n` in the background. To put all of the jobs in the command line in the background, you would type this:

```
$ ( l;m;n ) &
```

The Return initiates the execution of the commands. You do not need to use spaces after the semicolon; you may string the entire command together in one line. If you want to continue a long command line onto the next line, you can use a backslash (\ ) immediately followed by Enter to tell the computer to continue typing without terminating.

The pipe symbol (|) and the ampersand (&) are also command separators. The pipe symbol alters the standard input and the destination of standard output. The pipe symbol must always have a command in front of it and one behind it. It signifies that each group of commands separated by the pipe symbol is a different job. The ampersand tells the computer to run the job in the background so that you can continue to work on the desktop. The following example demonstrates a typical pipe command:

```
$ /usr/barriers |grep `$0`
$ /usr/barriers/tester &
```

You can group commands within parentheses. This induces the shell to create a copy of itself (subshell) for each group of commands, thereby creating a new process to execute each command. Subshells have their own environment, sets of variables, and values that may be different from those in other subshells. Commands may be executed sequentially, as in the following example:

```
$ (l ; m) & n &
10021
10022
```

This sample command line will cause commands `l` and `m` to execute sequentially in the background while `n` is also executing in the background. The prompt will appear immediately.

The following example demonstrates how the command line causes `l` and `m` to execute sequentially in the background while also executing `n` and `o` sequentially in the background. The subshells running `l` and `m` and `n` and `o` run concurrently:

```
$(l;m) & (n;o) &
10022
10023
```

Command-line expansion is the transformation of the command line by the shell. The shell processes a command after it parses the command line into token or words; that is, it isolates strings of characters. The shell then scans each token for special character references so that it can take certain actions. It will substitute filenames for a symbol, if found. It will separate the following example into three tokens, scan them, and then perform command-line expansion. The asterisk and the question mark perform in a similar manner except that the asterisk will match any number of characters, including zero characters, in a filename, as shown in the following example:

```
$ cp `$MAIL/*     .`
```

Command substitution permits you to use the standard output of a command within a shell script. This is similar to command expansion in that it occurs after the tokens on the command line have been identified. If the shell runs a command successfully, it will recognize a token in the following form:

```
touch newfile-`date +%d%m%y`.txt
```

The notation marks tell the shell to replace the token with standard output of command.

Path-name expansion is performed by a shell if it finds an unreadable file reference. Special or ambiguous characters such as *, ?, and so on will be left alone if the shell does not find a string match. An error message will be displayed, as in the following example:

```
$ls
dept101 dept102 dept103
$echo dept*
dept101 dept102 dept103
    demonstrating no match!
$ rm dept*
$ echo dept*
dept*
$ csh
% echo tmp*
echo:  no match
```

Putting single quotation marks around an argument will suppress expansion. Double quotation marks will cause the shell to suppress path name but not parameter and variable expansion as shown in the following example:

```
$ wordproc=currier; export wordproc
$ echo dept* $wordproc
dept101 dept102 dept103 currier
```

```
$ echo "dept* $wordproc"
 dept* currier
$ echo `dept* $wordproc`
 dept* $wordproc
```

Parameters and Variables

Shell parameters are values that are accessible to the owner. Shell parameters may consist of letters, digits, and underscores. Variables may not start with a number or contain hyphens. User-created variables are shell variables that you name and assign values to. To set a variable in sh or ksh, you would not precede or follow the equal sign with a space or tab, as shown in the following example:

```
$ car=van
$ echo car
car
```

To bring the value of the variable to output, you must place another dollar sign in front of the value:

```
$ echo $car
van
```

This dollar sign causes the shell to pass the value of the variable to echo, which displays it on the screen. You may also use quotation marks to deal with variables. For example, you may place double or single quotes around a variable to control the output. The following example shows what the output will be if you use double or single quotes:

```
$ echo $car
van
$ echo "$car"
van
$ echo `$car`
$car
$ echo \$car
$car
```

Quotation marks are good to use if you need to maintain spacing in the output. The following example shows what the output will look like if you need a literal space or tab:

```
$ car="Dodge Van Sport Model"
$ echo $car
Dodge Van Sport Model
```

Always use quotes when you need literal spaces or tabs, or output will be sent to the screen with a single space.

It's also important to use quotes when you use a special character such as *. Depending upon which one you are in, the shell may expand a variable that has a special character added to it. The asterisk as shown here is a good example:

```
$ car=van*
$ echo "$car"
van*
```

If you do not quote the variable, the shell may expand the value of the variable as an object found in the directory, such as in the following example:

```
$ car=van*
$ echo $car
van.report   van.summary
```

Solaris uses special one-character parameters to interact with shells. These parameters are absolute and are preceded by a dollar sign. Each argument on the command line becomes the value of a positional parameter, which enables you to access command-line arguments. Special parameters such as $1, $#, and $? indicate certain interactions with the shell. You cannot assign values to these parameters.

Positional parameters allow you to access command-line arguments. Each argument you type on the command line becomes the value of a positional parameter. Table 17.1 lists the special characters and their meanings, and Table 17.2 lists the variables and their purposes.

TABLE 17.1: SPECIAL CHARACTERS

<table>
<tr><th>Character</th><th>Meaning</th></tr>
<tr><td>Newline</td><td>Initiates the execution of a command</td></tr>
<tr><td>;</td><td>Separates commands</td></tr>
<tr><td>:</td><td>Null, returns true exit status</td></tr>
<tr><td>&</td><td>Executes a command in the background</td></tr>
<tr><td>&&</td><td>Executes command on the right if the command on left succeeds</td></tr>
<tr><td>()</td><td>Groups commands or identifies a function</td></tr>
<tr><td>|</td><td>Separates commands in a pipe</td></tr>
<tr><td>></td><td>Redirects standard output</td></tr>
<tr><td>>></td><td>Appends standard output</td></tr>
<tr><td><</td><td>Redirects standard input</td></tr>
</table>

Continued

TABLE 17.1: SPECIAL CHARACTERS (CONTINUED)

<table>
<tr><th>Character</th><th>Meaning</th></tr>
<tr><td><<</td><td>Identifies here document</td></tr>
<tr><td>*</td><td>Identifies a string of characters in an ambiguous file reference</td></tr>
<tr><td>?</td><td>Identifies a single character in an ambiguous file reference</td></tr>
<tr><td>\</td><td>Quotes the following character</td></tr>
<tr><td>'</td><td>Quotes a string; no substitutions allowed</td></tr>
<tr><td>"</td><td>Quotes a string; allows variable, command substitution</td></tr>
<tr><td>`...`</td><td>Performs command substitution</td></tr>
<tr><td>[ ]</td><td>Identifies a character class in an ambiguous file reference</td></tr>
<tr><td>.</td><td>Built-in; executes command or script in current shell instead of spawning a new shell</td></tr>
<tr><td>||</td><td>Logical OR; executes command on right if command on left fails</td></tr>
<tr><td>!</td><td>Logical NOT; reverses exit status</td></tr>
</table>

TABLE 17.2: VARIABLES/PARAMETERS

Variable	Purpose
$0	Gives the name of the script being called. However, in the shell, it would report the shell you are in.
$*n*	Gives the value of the *n*th command argument.
$*	Gives all command-line arguments.
$#	Gives a count of the command-line arguments.
$$	Gives the PID number of the current process.
$!	Gives the PID number of the most recent background task.
$?	Gives exit status of last task.

Local Variables

Basic conventions for assigning values to variables are the same in the Bourne and Korn shells. There is no white space in a variable; it should be one word as in the following example:

```
$ bsos=1mn
```

You may also use the variable name preceded by a dollar sign to produce the value of a variable:

```
$ echo $bsos
lmn
```

It should be noted that it is usually unnecessary to change the value of variables that are initialized in `/etc/profile`. If you must change the value of a variable, do so in the home directory under `.profile` in the Bourne or Korn shell. You will use `.login` in the C shell. Keyword variables may be local or global and can be user defined or built in. To make a local variable available in all shells, it must be exported via the command line or by adding it to the initialization file.

To set a local variable, refer to this example:

```
$ MN=/adm/manu
$ echo $MN
/adm/manu
$ cd $MN
$ pwd
/adm/manu

$ unset MN
$ echo $MN

$ cd
$ pwd
/home/admin
```

To display local variables, type **`$ set`** on the command line.

Global Variables

Different conventions are used to differentiate global variables from local variables. Uppercase letters are used for global variables, and mixed or lowercase letters are used for others. Global variables are not available to all shells and other programs forked from the original shell unless you make them available. The `export` built-in may be used in `sh` and `ksh` to make a variable available in a child process. If you are in the C shell, you will use `setenv` before you use `export`. The following example shows how you can export a variable to child processes without changing the parent process in any way:

```
$ cat dealers1
van=dodge
echo "dealer1 1: $van"
dealers2
```

```
echo "dealers1 2: $van"
$cat dealers2
echo "dealers2 1: $van"
van=sport
echo "dealers2 2: $van"
$ dealers1
dealers1 1: dodge
dealers2 1:
dealers2 2: sport
dealers1 2: dodge
```

This example will display nothing for `dealers2 1` because it is an undeclared variable in that subshell.

Variable expansion occurs when a shell encounters a token consisting of a dollar sign followed by a variable name. The shell will replace the token with the value of the variable. The `$VARIABLE` differs from the more general `${VARIABLE}` in that the braces insulate the variable name from what is around it. The following examples demonstrate the differences in the output:

```
$ PREF=window
$ KIND=$PREFpane
$ TYPE=$PREFglass
$ echo $KIND $TYPE
$
```

Because `PREFpane` and `PREFglass` are valid variable names, this script will not work because the names were not set. Depending upon the shell you are in, you will get a blank line or an error message on the output line. If, however, you use braces around the `PREF` variable, the results will be as follows:

```
$ PREF=window
$ KIND=${PREF}pane
$ TYPE=${PREF}glass
$ echo $KIND $TYPE
windowpane windowglass
```

The use of braces adds to the readability of code, even if they are not needed. Their use can keep mistakes at a minimum.

Exporting Variables

Exporting variables at the command line will make them available to the current shell and all of its child processes. If a variable is set in a subshell, it will not be exported to a parent shell. It will, however, be available to any shell opened after the subshell.

To export variables at the command line, refer to the following example:

```
VAR=val;export VAR
(or export VAR=val)
```

TIP The Bourne shell does not allow you to define and export a variable at the same time. It has to be done in two separate steps.

This example demonstrates the export process:

```
$ cat dealers2
export dodge
dodge=dayton
echo "dealers 2 1: $dodge"
anyone
echo "dealers 2 2: $dodge"
$ cat anyone
echo "anyone 1: $dodge"
dodge=silver
echo "anyone 2: $dodge"
$ dealers2
dealers 2  1: dayton
anyone 1: dayton
anyone 2: silver
dealers 2 2: dayton
```

In this example, the parent process retains its value of dodge while dayton is passed down to the child process, which changes it to `silver`, but because it was a child process, the change to dodge is not passed back to its parent.

The read command is used frequently with user-created variables. This is helpful when you must enter a response to a prompt on the desktop. This command allows you to accept input from the user and store it in variables for further use:

```
$ cat read8
echo "catalog pages: \c"
read answerline
echo "Enter Please: $answerline"
$ read8
catalog pages: annual sale
Enter Please: annual sale
```

This example shows how the echo command prompts the user to respond. Quotes are used in the response line because the user response may be varied.

You may also make your variables read-only, which means their value cannot be changed. The readonly built-in allows you to make a variable permanent. If you try to change a read-only built-in after you change its value, you will receive an error message. If used without an argument, readonly will display a list of read-only variables.

TIP You can't unset a read-only variable once it has been set.

Environmental Variables

When you log in, the shell (Bourne or Korn) receives shell keyword variables from the environment. Key environmental variables are usually short words that describe directories to search or paths to follow to locate a command. When you log in, the shell will initiate default variables. You will be able to change the values of most of these variables. The following example shows a simple keyword variable; this command will list all the environmental variables:

```
$ set
```

There are several other environmental variables, such as HOME, PATH, SHELL, MAIL, LOGNAME, and so on, that fulfill special environmental functions. The values of these may be temporarily changed at the command line. The change would affect only the current shell. They will default back to their original value when you change shells or exit. HOME refers to your home directory unless your home directory is temporarily changed with a cd command. Your home directory is stored in the /etc/passwd file.

The PATH variable is used to locate commands in directories in a specified direction. Here is an example of how to set the PATH variable:

```
$ PATH=/usr/bin:/usr/mail/bsp:/etc:.
$ export PATH
$ echo $PATH
/usr/bso:/usr/mail/bso:/etc:.
```

The SHELL variable invokes the name of the shell, and LOGNAME is a variable that holds the user's session login name.

The MAIL variable contains the path name of your mail file. It is usually accessed with /var/mail/<*username*> or /var/spool/mail/<*username*> (where <*username*> is your login name). The MAILCHECK variable tells you how often the shell checks for new mail. You may set this variable to zero and the shell will check before each

prompt. The default time is 600 seconds (10 minutes). If MAILCHECK is not set, the shell will not check for mail at all.

The Prompt the User (primary), or PS1, variable (a $ prompt in the csh shell) tells you that the shell is waiting for you to give it a command. A $ followed by a space is the usual prompt. It is stored as a string in the PS1 variable. If you want to change the appearance of your prompt, you may change the value of the variable.

The Prompt the User (secondary) variable is stored in a string in PS2. This variable is used with unclosed quotes on the first line. Unclosed quotes tell the shell that the command is not finished. The shell will then respond with the default prompt (>), which indicates that the shell is waiting for the user to complete the response. The shell will wait for the closing quotation marks before it executes the command.

The IFS variable is used to specify what characters you use to separate arguments on the command line. It has a default value of SPACE TAB NEWLINE, which means that you may use a space or tab on the command line if these characters are not quoted. IFS can have an impact on the interpretation of a command line by means of word splitting. The following example demonstrates how:

```
$ barries=l:m:n:o
$ cat $barries
cat: cannot open l:m:n:o
$IFS=":"
$ cat $barriers
cat: cannot open l
cat: cannot open m
cat: cannot open n
cat: cannot open o
```

WARNING The IFS variable should be used sparingly. It is usually reserved for use with shell scripts, where it will not affect the parent. You should have a complete understanding of how it works in relation to the parent/child process.

Built-Ins

Built-ins are commands that are built in to the shell and are always available, making a directory search redundant. The shells recognize built-ins and execute them without spawning a new process. If a command is not recognized as a built-in, then the shell will search the directory for the correct program.

All control structure keywords—such as `for in`, `do`, `done`, `while`, `until`, and so on—are built-ins. Table 17.3 lists many of the built-ins used by different shells. Although most may be used in all three shells, some may be shell dependent.

TABLE 17.3: BUILT-INS

Built-In	Shell	Purpose
`%job`<*number*>	csh, jsh, ksh	Brings job number to the foreground. A synonym for the `fg` built-in.
`%job`<*number*> `&`	csh, jsh, ksh	Places job number in the background. A synonym for the `bg` built-in.
`@`	csh	Evaluates numeric expressions.
`alias`	csh, ksh	Creates aliases.
`bg`	csh, jsh, ksh	Moves jobs into the background.
`cd`	csh, ksh, sh	Changes working directory.
`chdir`	csh, sh	Changes working directory.
`dirs`	csh	Displays directory stack.
`echo`	csh, ksh, sh	Displays text on the screen.
`eval`	csh, ksh, sh	Scans command line.
`exec`	csh, ksh, sh	Executes a command.
`exit`	csh, ksh, sh	Exits and returns status to parent process.
`fg`	csh, jsh, ksh	Moves jobs into foreground.
`glob`	csh	Performs as `echo` does, but without spaces.
`hashstat`	csh	Reports status of C shell's hash mechanism.
`history`	csh	Displays history of commands in a list.
`jobs`	csh, ksh, sh	Lists current jobs or commands.
`kill`	csh, ksh, sh	Ends job or process.
`limit`	csh	Creates limits on computer resources.
`login`	csh, ksh, sh	Permits user to log on to the system.
`logout`	csh, ksh, sh	Permits user to leave the system.
`nice`	csh	Reduces priority of a command.
`nohup`	csh	Allows log out while processes continue.
`notify`	csh	Notifies user if job status changes.
`onintr`	csh	Controls interrupt actions.
`popd`	csh	Removes a directory.
`pushd`	csh	Places working directory on top.

Continued

TABLE 17.3: BUILT-INS (CONTINUED)

Built-In	Shell	Purpose
rehash	csh	Re-creates sorted list of all commands.
repeat	csh	Repeats simple specified arguments.
set	csh, ksh, sh	Sets the values of local variables.
setenv	csh	Sets the values of environmental variables.
shift	csh, ksh, sh	Promotes the indexes of argv array.
source	csh	Executes shell script as argument.
stop	csh, jsh, ksh	Accepts multiple arguments.
suspend	csh, jsh, ksh	Stops the current shell.
time	csh	Displays time-related information.
umask	csh, ksh, sh	Assigns access permissions.
unalias	csh, ksh	Removes an alias.
unhash	csh	Closes the hash mechanism.
unlimit	csh	Removes limits on current process.
unset	csh, ksh, sh	Removes a declared variable.
unsetenv	csh	Removes an environmental variable.
wait	csh, ksh, sh	Causes the shell to wait for all child processes to terminate.

Another type of built-in is the . or Dot built-in. If you change the values of keyword variables after you edit your .profile, you may put the changes into effect immediately by using the . in front of .profile. The . literally means to run the job in the current shell instead of spawning a child shell to run it:

```
$ cat .profile
PS1="fineline $"
.
.
$ . .profile
fineline $
```

With the CDPATH variable, you can use a simple filename to change your working directory to a directory that isn't spawned from your working directory. This variable is a time-saver when you want to work out of more than one directory and you don't want to use cd with long path names over and over. When CDPATH is set, cd will search for a subdirectory in the directories in the CDPATH list. The one it finds then becomes the working directory. The CDPATH variable allows you to use cd and a simple filename to change the working directory to a child of any directories in the stored list.

The following example illustrates CDPATH:

```
CDPATH=$HOME:$HOME/saleslog
Export CDPATH
```

This will cause cd to search the home directory first and then the saleslog directory. Then, if the search of all other directories fails, cd searches the working directory. You can force cd to search the working directory first by including a null string as in the following example.

```
CDPATH=::$HOME:$HOME/saleslog
Export CDPATH
```

Because it is first on the argument command line, the $0 parameter is the parameter in which the shell stores the name of the command you used to call a program. The echo command is used to verify the name of the script:

```
$ cat pogen
echo "command name"
echo "shell script execution $0"
$ ./pogen
command name
shell script execution ./pogen
$
```

Each argument on a command line is represented by parameters consisting of dollar signs in front of a number from 1 through 9. The shift built-in promotes, or shifts up, arguments beyond number 9 by discarding the first and changing number 10 to number 9. Discarded arguments cannot be retrieved. Arguments will continue to shift upward until all are completed:

```
$ cat gearbox
echo "first1= $1  first2= $2  first3= $3"
shift
echo "first1= $1  first2= $2  first3= $3"
shift
echo "first1= $1  first2= $2  first3= $3"

$ gearbox first second third
first1= first    first2= second    first3= third
first1= second   first2= third    first3=
first1= third    first2=        first3=
$
```

Shell Compatibilities

The Solaris 8 operating system employs several shells for use as command interpreters. As discussed earlier, the three primary shells are the Bourne shell (`sh`), which is used most often by system administrators; the Korn shell (`ksh`), which is used heavily by developers and advanced users; and the C shell (`csh`), which is favored by the typical user. There are three freeware shells shipped with Solaris 8: the Bourne Again Shell (`bash`), the Z Shell (`zsh`), and the TC Shell (`tcsh`).

NOTE Only the three primary shells will be described in this section. There may be a brief reference to other shells when necessary.

Certain features are common to the three primary shells. The administrator defines the default shell for the user, but you can change the shell from the command line. The main reasons to change a shell are that one may have more capabilities than another and you may be more familiar with the commands and language in one. Table 17.4 describes some features found in all three of the primary shells.

TABLE 17.4: COMMON FEATURES OF PRIMARY SHELLS

Feature	Bourne	Korn	C
Aliases	No	Yes	Yes
Command-line editing	No	Yes	Yes
History list	No	Yes	Yes
Ignore Ctrl+D	No	Yes	Yes
Separate from `.profile`	No	No	Yes
Job control or (`jsh`)	Yes	Yes	Yes
Logout file	No	Yes	Yes
Overwrite protection	No	Yes	Yes
Bourne syntax compatible	Yes	Yes	No

Summary

This chapter gave you an overview of the shell, which is a dual-purpose tool you can use as both a command interpreter and a programming language. The three main shells in Solaris 8—the Bourne shell, the Korn shell, and the C shell—are similar in some respects, yet they have different capabilities. For example, you can declare single numeric variables with @ in the C shell only. The Bourne shell is the default shell for Solaris 8. The Job shell is exactly like the Bourne shell but has an added feature called job control. A job is one or more commands connected by pipes and may be run in the background or in the foreground. With the help of the `bg` or `fg` built-in, jobs can be switched from front to back as needed.

This chapter also covered scripts. You learned that you can write scripts in all of the shells; however, system scripts are written in the Bourne shell. Scripts are actually mini-programs that execute from the command line. You can run a shell script by giving its name on the command line. The shell will check to see if you have the appropriate permissions and will then execute the script. You can execute the script in a different shell by entering `sh`, `csh`, `ksh`, or `jsh`, depending upon which shell you want to use.

You learned how to define variables and set values for them. Variables can be exported by using the `export` built-in in the Bourne and Korn shells or `setenv` in the C shell. You learned about the special rules that govern the assignment of values to variables, such as do not use a `$` when assigning a value to a variable and use `set` to declare nonnumeric variables. There are also positional and special parameters that are preceded with a dollar sign. You cannot assign values to them.

Finally, you learned about the different types of command-line expansion, many invoked by special characters within a word. Expansion takes place in a specific order: parameter expansion, variable expansion, command substitution, and path-name expansion. Use `set` to declare nonnumeric expressions. You can suppress all but parameter and variable expansion by using double quotation marks around a word. The use of single quotation marks suppresses all types of expansion.

CHAPTER 18

The Bourne Shell

FEATURING:

Control structures 695

The `here` *script* 714

Bourne built-in commands 716

Functions 717

The `.profile` *file* 718

This chapter delves more deeply into Bourne shell programming and how to work with it in Solaris 8. The Bourne shell is a high-powered programming language and command interpreter. It is the default shell for Solaris 8.

This chapter will discuss control structures, which allow you to write looped command-line arguments that make a decision based on true or false results and then execute a command based on those results. These control flow commands work with the `break` and `continue` statements to alter the order of execution within the shell script. You will learn how to test and verify arguments in a script. The null string or unset variables may be expanded, and you will learn to set a default value.

More sophisticated built-ins—such as the `exec` and `trap` built-ins—will be discussed. They allow you to execute a command by replacing a process and to detect and respond to operating system signals, respectively. Functions will also be demonstrated, and examples will display how the commands interact and how you can solve more complex problems.

We'll also discuss how you can store functions to be used at a later time. More work with the `.profile` file will also be addressed.

Because the Bourne shell is the heartbeat of Solaris 8, it is wise to become familiar with its capabilities. It shares many similarities with the Korn shell and the C shell, and although it lacks a few of the features they provide, it is nevertheless a powerful shell in its interaction with the Solaris kernel.

About the Bourne Shell

The Bourne shell is the default shell of Solaris 8. Programs written in this shell are called shell scripts. They are capable of providing control structures that allow easy access to user programs and utilities. Scripts provide an easy way to modify and simplify complex functions. The Bourne shell control structures use decisions to select alternatives by means of `if` statements (`if…then`, `if…then…else`, and `if…then…elif…else`). The `case` control structure allows branching by matching string patterns in commands. Other control structures that play a major part in writing scripts are the looping control structures such as `for…in`, `for`, `until`, and `while`. These allow structures to perform tasks repeatedly until certain conditions are met. Special built-ins can evaluate expressions in a script or offer a comparison or inquiry of files. The `trap` built-in traps a signal sent by the system to the process running the script and lets you specify actions to be taken upon receipt of that signal. The `exec` built-in executes a command that replaces the current process while assuming the same environment and PID number for that process. The `exec` built-in executes user programs as well as commands when it is not necessary to return control to the calling process.

A *here document* allows you to script the interaction of a program from within another script. It is called a here document because it is immediately accessible in the shell script. A *function* is a group of commands that are parsed before storage into main memory. Faster than shell scripts, functions may be used over and over. There are several ways to define functions. You may use the command line or place one within a script, or if you want to retain a function for more than one login session, you can define it in your `.profile` file. It can then be called by giving its name along with other arguments.

Solaris utilities are important in the Bourne shell. The `find` utility performs both simple and complex tasks. It is most often used to find files in the system, but it has many other uses. Shortcuts (like using brackets around arguments to call up the `test` built-in, which automatically tests the arguments) make routine tasks easier to remember and carry out. Square brackets are synonymous with the `test` built-in and make a script easier to follow. However, because `test` is rarely used anymore, it is recommended that you use the brackets surrounding the arguments instead.

Standard techniques are part of a shell script. To be well written, a script needs to adhere to techniques that verify, report command errors, and redirect informational messages to standard error.

The Bourne shell, although not the most voluminous of the three shells, has some sophisticated capabilities for getting the job done. A little practice with writing shell scripts and using control structures will fine-tune a program as well as a user's skills. There is a `sh`-compatible shell in every distribution of Unix, so familiarity with the Bourne shell is the first step in becoming proficient with all of the Unix systems as well as Solaris 8.

Control Structures

The execution of commands with a shell script can be altered by the use of what are called *control flow commands,* or *control flow structures*. Based on Boolean logic, these structures consist of statements that test a condition. The following sections discuss the control flow structures that are used most often in the Bourne shell.

The *if…then* structure

The `if…then` statement is a common example of a control flow structure:

```
If test-case; then
    commands
```

```
fi
```

Figure 18.1 illustrates the flow of the `if` command. The `fi` command is simply *if* spelled backwards; it marks the end of the `if` structure.

FIGURE 18.1

An `if...then` *flowchart*

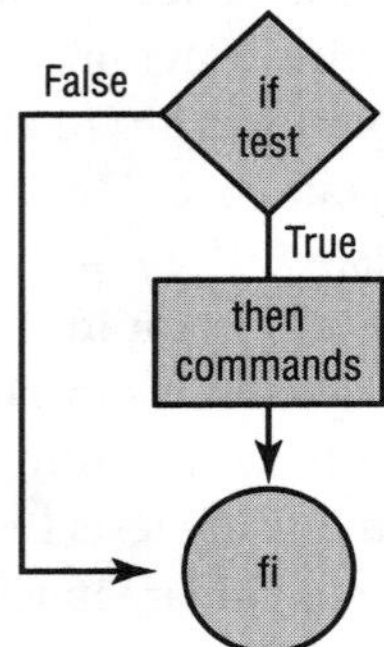

The shell will take this statement and, if the first argument is true, pass it on to the `then` statement and execute the command. If the statement is false, the control structure will end.

WARNING The `test` built-in returns the results in the `if...then` statement. You should not use the word *test* as a script name. Solaris will treat it as a utility and your results will not be dependable

In the following script, follow the flow of the `if` statement and check your results. You will be prompted for two words, which will be read in. The shell will use the `if` structure to evaluate the result returned by `testcase`. If `testcase` is true, then the command will be executed. Placing double quotes around each of the arguments ensures that the `test` utility works correctly in the event that you enter a space or special character:

```
$ cat ify
echo "testcase 1: \c"
read testcase1
echo "testcase 2: \c"
read testcase2
if [ "$testcase1" = "$testcase2" ]
```

```
then
    echo "Same"
fi
echo "The End!"
$ ify
testcase 1:  testcase 1
testcase 2:  testcase 1
Same
The end!
```

In this example, the `test` built-in returns a true status if the first and third arguments are matched strings. The shell would then execute the commands between the `then` and `fi`. If a false status is returned, the shell passes control to the statement after `fi` and does not execute the statements between `then` and `fi`. In this case, that means that if both words are the same, the script will display `Same`.

The following example shows the same program with different input. It goes directly to `The end!`, skipping `Same` because the two did not match:

```
$ ify
testcase 1:  testcase 1
testcase 2:  testcase 2
The end!
$
```

The `test` built-in is also a utility in the Bourne shell. It may stand alone and be kept in `/usr/bin/test`. In place of the word *test*, you can use square brackets [ ], which results in less confusion when writing scripts. You can use the built-in version if available or the utility if it is not. You can use the `type` built-in to determine whether you are using a built-in or standalone utility:

```
$ type test cat echo read
test is a shell builtin
cat is hashed (/bin/cat)
echo is a shell builtin
read is a shell builtin
```

You can get more information by using the `man` command before the name of the utility. Type **man** followed by the name of the shell and the shell will look up the built-ins. Table 18.1 lists the built-ins that are available in the Bourne shell. Chapter 19 includes a list of built-ins for the Korn shell and Chapter 20 includes a list of built-ins for the C shell.

TABLE 18.1: BOURNE SHELL BUILT-INS

Built-In	Description
`alias` (`unalias`)	Creates or removes a pseudonym or shorthand for a command or series of commands.
`bg`	Background; controls process execution.
`break`	Used to exit from a `for` or enclosing `while` loop, if one is executing. If you specify *n* (a number), then that many levels of looping is terminated.
`case`	Allows user a choice from a list of actions by evaluating a series of true and false statements. The first true response is executed, ending the `case` statement.
`cd`	Changes the working directory.
`chdir`	Same as `cd`.
`continue`	Allows escape from or advance within an enclosing `while`, `for`, `foreach`, or `until` loop.
`echo`	Causes arguments to be separated by blanks and terminated by a newline to standard output.
`eval`	Allows arguments to the `eval` command to be read as input to the shell and executes the resulting commands.
`exec`	Specified by arguments; executes in place of the shell without creating a new process. Input/output arguments may appear and, if no other arguments are given, cause the shell input/output to be modified.
`exit`	Causes the calling shell or shell script to exit.
`export`	Sends the variable and its value to the shell environment, causing its value to be set and used by all other commands until the `unset` command is used.
[...]	When used in a loop or as a control, it is a shortcut for the `test` built-in.
[...]	When used in file access, it can be used to match one of a set (abc) or a range (a-c) of characters. (i.e., `` `ls [cb]at` ``, which would find *cat* and *bat* but not *nat*).
`fg`	Foreground; controls process execution. Also brings a job to the foreground.
`for`	Repeatedly executes an action a specified number of times.
`getopts`	Retrieves options and option arguments from a list of parameters.
`hash`	Recalculates the internal hash table of the contents of the directories listed in the path environmental variable to account for new commands added.

Continued

TABLE 18.1: BOURNE SHELL BUILT-INS (CONTINUED)

Built-In	Description
`if`	Control structure; a test statement that evaluates to true or false and then either executes an action or exits if the test condition is false. Also used with `then`, `else`, or `elif` to evaluate statements true or false.
`jobs`	Reports all jobs that are stopped or executing in the background.
`kill`	Terminates a process that you specify as an argument using the PID number or job ID.
`login`	Establishes the user and their associated group and environment based on a name and password given; the same as the command `su -` *<username>*.
`logout`	Used to exit from a login session.
`newgrp`	Used to log in to a new group. Changes your real and effective group ID; user stays logged in but a new shell is spawned.
`pwd`	Returns the present working directory.
`read`	Reads a line from standard output.
`readonly`	Shell built-in that protects the value of a given variable from reassignment.
`return`	Enables the execution of the shell to advance beyond its current sequence of steps. Designed for functions; as if called from the main body of the script, it causes the script to exit.
`set`	Used to determine the value of environmental variables of the current shell and its descendents.
`shift`	Used to traverse a shell's argument list or a list of field-separated words.
`stop`	Stops a specified job.
`suspend`	Halts the current shell.
`test`	Synonymous with square brackets `[…]`; evaluates a condition, and if the condition is true, executes an action.
`times`	Prints the total user and system times for processes running from the shell.
`trap`	Responds to hardware signals.
`type`	Writes a description of a command type.
`typeset`	Sets or gets attributes and values for shell variables and functions.
`ulimit`	Sets or gets limitations on the system resources available to the current shell and its descendents.
`umask`	Sets or gets the file mode creation mask.

Continued

TABLE 18.1: BOURNE SHELL BUILT-INS (CONTINUED)

Built-In	Description
`unset`	Changes an environmental variable for the current shell and its descendents back to the default.
`until`	Repetitively executives a series of actions.
`wait`	Used to await process completion until conditions are evaluated to true.
`while`	Repetitively executes a series of commands while conditions are evaluated as true.

When using control structures, you must supply at least one argument or your output will be garbled. The `test` utility will check to see that you have at least one argument in a script. It may also ask a question about the status of a file argument, and it will test the argument to see if it is the name of a regular file and not a directory. The `test` utility has several options that may be used to test the characteristics of a file. They are listed in Table 18.2.

TABLE 18.2: TEST OPTIONS

Option	Test
`-d`	Existing directory file
`-f`	Existing regular file
`-r`	Existing readable file
`-s`	Existing file with length greater than 0
`-w`	Existing writeable file
`-x`	Existing executable file

Use the options to test arguments as in the following example:

```
$ cat checker
#!/bin/sh
# checker - checks to see if there are arguments to checker
if [ $# -gt 0 ]
then
    echo "You put $# arguments on my command line."
    exit 1
fi
echo "You did not put any arguments on my command line."
```

```
$ ./checker
You did not put any arguments on my command line.
$ ./checker foo bar bat
You put 3 arguments on my command line.
$
```

It is a good idea to try all of the options until you are familiar with them. You will find it easier to debug your scripts and your arguments will be verified routinely.

The `test` utility can check two files to see what the relationship is and whether one is more recent than the other. As mentioned earlier, you also have the option of putting arguments in square brackets, which is synonymous with using `test`. There must be spaces or tabs after and before the brackets as in the following example (in this script, `-eq` is equal to 0):

```
$ cat checker
if [ $# -eq 0 ]
then
    echo "usage: checker args" 1>&2
    exit 1
fi
echo "aokay"
$ checker
usage: checker args
$ checker abc
aokay
```

The usage message displays and uses the `1>&2` notation to redirect its output to standard error. Many Solaris utilities give usage messages similar to the one in `checker`. If you call a program or utility with the wrong arguments or numbers, you will see a usage message.

The other component to the `if…then` statement is `…else`. By adding `…else` to the control structure, you cause the structure to branch into two segments. If the `if` condition is true, then the commands are executed; if false, then a different set of commands are executed. Figure 18.2 shows an `if…then…else` flowchart.

The proper syntax for the `if…then…else` control structure is as follows:

```
If <test-command>
then
    commands
else
    commands
fi
```

FIGURE 18.2

An `if...then...else` *flowchart*

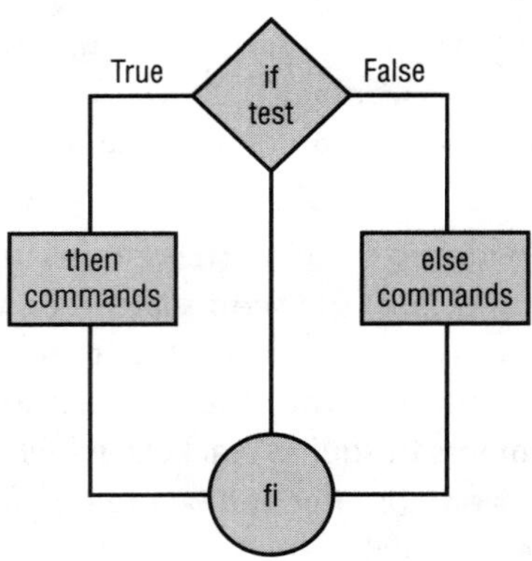

To save space, you can put `then` on the same line as `if` by preceding it with a semicolon. Because they are separate built-ins, they require a semicolon if the newline character is not used:

```
if <test-command>; then
    commands
else
    commands
fi
```

You can display files on the terminal by running the `out` command with arguments that are filenames. When the first argument is a `-v` (or option), `out` uses `pg` (similar to `more`) to display the files. The `out` command tests the first argument to see if it is `-v`. If true, the `out` command shifts the arguments to delete the `-v` and displays the files using `pg`. You can view a new page by pressing Return after each page. Here is the script:

```
$ cat out
if [ $# -eq 0 ]
then
    echo "usage: out [-v]  file ..." 1>&2
    exit 1
fi
if [ "$1" = "-v" ]
then
    shift
    pg -- $@
else
    cat -- $@
fi
```

The -- argument to cat and pg informs the utility that no more options follow. The utility will not consider the leading hyphens as options, so you may see a filename with a leading hyphen. You may also create such a file by using the command `cat > -fname`. The -- argument will not work with more, but it does work with other Solaris utilities. Use the double dash with the rm command to remove an unwanted file that begins with a hyphen.

The *if...then...elif* structure

Adding another parameter to the `if...then` statement allows a "nested" set of control structures to be built. By replacing `else` with `elif` (meaning else if), you can construct a command line with multiple nested statements that require a single `fi` to close. This statement tests for two conditions and then falls through to the `else` if neither of the two conditions are met. The following example displays the `elif` *<test-command>* syntax:

```
if <test-command>
    then
    commands
elif <test-command>
then
    commands
    .
    .
    .
else
    commands
fi
```

The following example demonstrates the `elif` command structure and its output:

```
$ cat ify3
echo "case 1: \c"
read case1
echo "case 2: \c"
read case2
echo "case 3: \c"
read case3
if [ "$case1" =  "$case2" -a "$case2" = "$case3" ]
then
    echo "Same: case 1 & 2 & 3"
```

```
elif  [ "$case1" = "$case2" ]
then
    echo  "Same: case 1 & 2"
elif  [ "$case1" = "$case3" ]
then
    echo "Same: case 1 & 3"
elif  [ "$case2" = "$case3" ]
then
    echo "Same: case 2 & 3"
else
    echo "nada"
fi
$ ify3
case 1:  letter
case 2:  number
case 3:  symbol
nada
$ ify3
case 1:     letter
case 2:     number
case 3:  letter
Same: case 1 & 3
$ ify3
case 1:  letter
case 2:  letter
case 3:  letter
Same: case 1 & 2 & 3
```

If the three cases are not the same, the first `elif` tests to see whether any pair of words are the same. If any of the `if` statements are true, then the structure passes control to the next…then statement and finally to `fi`. The double quotes in the `ify3` arguments tell the shell not to interpret special characters literally. Figure 18.3 shows an `if...then...elif` flowchart.

The *for…in* structure

The for…in structure has two other components, do and done. Here is the syntax:

```
for <loop-var> in <args-list>
do
    <commands>
done
```

FIGURE 18.3

An `if...then...elif` *flowchart*

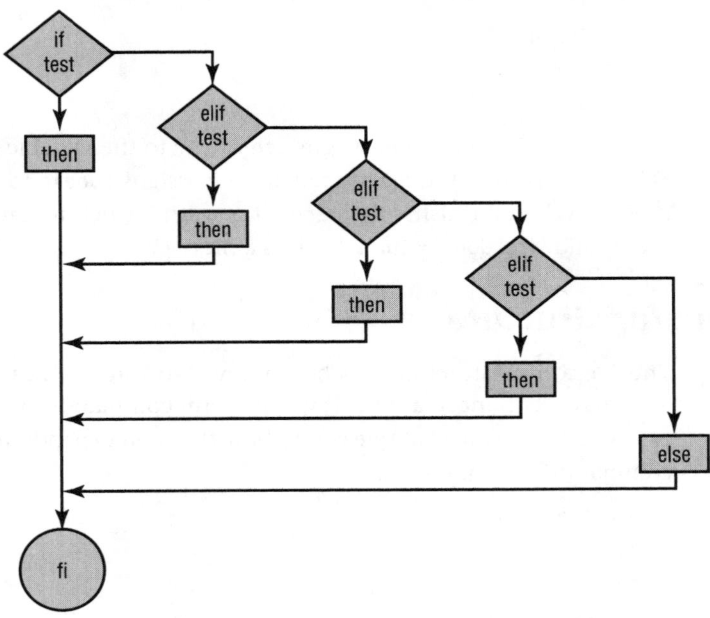

The value of the first argument is given to the `loop-var` and executes the commands between the do and done statements. The do and done mark the beginning and end of the `for` loop. After passing control to the done statement, the structure assigns the value of the second argument in the `args-list` to the `loop-index` and repeats the commands. It will repeat the commands between the do and done statements for each argument on the *<args-list>*.

The following example displays the sequence initiated by the `for...in` control structure:

```
$ cat dogs
for dogs in schnauzer poodle dachshund spaniel
do
    echo "$dogs"
done
echo "Finished."
$ dogs
schnauzer
```

```
poodle
dachshund
spaniel
Finished.
```

The preceding example assigns schnauzer to the variable dogs, then displays the value of dogs, which is schnauzer. It then assigns poodle to dogs and repeats the process. When it finishes the *<args-list>*, the structure transfers control to the statement following done, which displays a message.

The *for* structure

The for control structure may be employed to automatically take on the value of each argument one at a time. It will perform commands involving each argument in turn. The following example shows how the shell expands an implied **$@** into a list of command-line arguments:

```
$ cat args_list
for args
do
    echo "$args"
done
$ args_list china plastic stoneware china
china
plastic
stoneware
china
```

The *while* Structure

The while control structure has the following syntax:

```
while <test-com>
do
    commands
done
```

The structure will execute commands as long as the *<test-com>* returns a true status. If the status is false, then it will exit via the done command and pass control on to the next command in the script. Figure 18.4 shows a while flowchart.

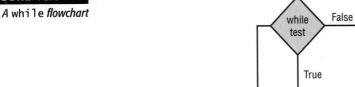

FIGURE 18.4
A `while` *flowchart*

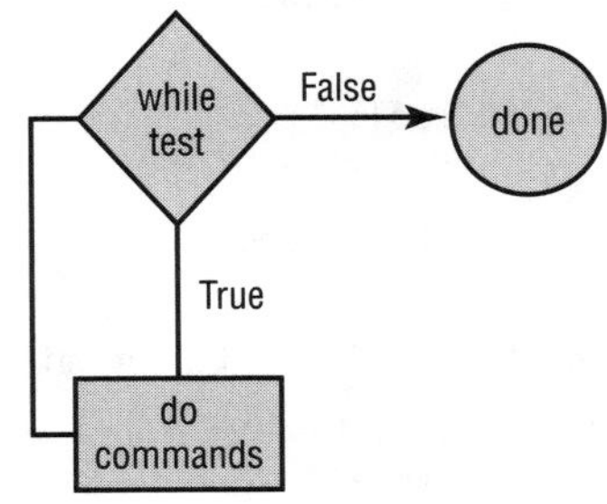

The *until* Structure

The `until` structure is similar to the `while` structure in that `until` continues to loop until the *<test-com>* returns a true condition. The `while` structure loops while the *<test-com>* continues to return a true condition. If the results are false, then control will pass to the do commands. Figure 18.5 shows an `until` flowchart, and the following example demonstrates the syntax for the `until` structure:

```
until <test-com>
do
    commands
done
```

FIGURE 18.5
An `until` *flowchart*

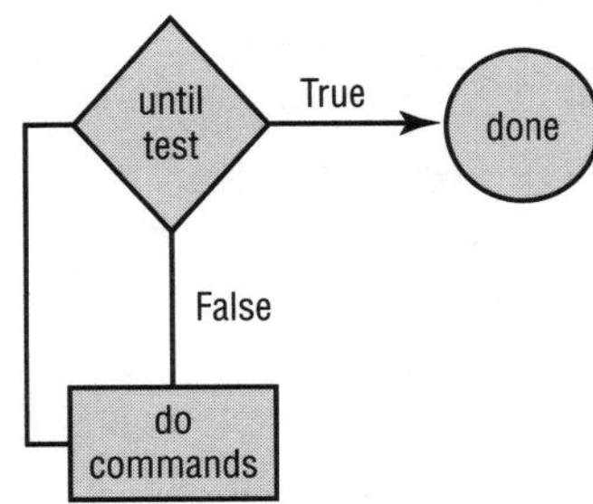

Working with Shells in Solaris

The following script uses the `until` structure:

```
$ cat toolcrib
toolname=pliers
tool=" "
echo "Guess the missing tool:"
echo
```

```
until [ "$tool" = "$toolname" ]
do
    echo " which tool: \c"
    read tool
    echo "Looking for: $tool"
done
echo "That's it! The $tool is the missing tool!"
$./toolcrib
Guess the missing tool:

 which tool: wrench
Looking for: wrench
 which tool: hammer
Looking for: hammer
 which tool: pliers
Looking for: pliers
That's it! The pliers is the missing tool!
$
```

A for…while or until structure can be interrupted with a break or continue statement. The break statement terminates execution of the loop by transferring control to the statement after the done statement. The continue command continues the execution of the loop by transferring control to the done statement.

The following script illustrates how break and continue can be used:

```
$ cat filedrawers
for file in 1 2 3 4 5 6 7 8
do
    if [ $file -lt  4 ] ; then
        echo "continue"
        continue
    fi
#
    echo $file
#
    if [ $file -ge 6 ] ; then
        echo "break"
        break
    fi
done
$ filedrawers
```

```
continue
continue
continue
4
5
6
break
```

Numerical arguments in a script are stated as `-ne` (not equal),`-eq` (equal), `-gt` (greater than or equal to), `-lt` (less than) or `-le` (less than or equal to) for comparisons, and = (equal) or != (not equal).

The *case* Structure

The `case` structure looks for strings of characters (stringsearch) that the user enters after a prompt. This is a sophisticated command that makes multiple decisions before executing other commands. This structure is used in creating menus because it relies upon user input. The following example demonstrates how `case` works:

```
$ cat testpattern
echo "Enter YES, NO or MAYBE: \c"
read answer
case "$answer" in
    "YES")
        echo "You answered YES"
        ;;
    "NO")
        echo "You answered NO"
        ;;
    "MAYBE")
        echo "You answered MAYBE"
        ;;
    *)
        echo "You did not answer YES, NO or MAYBE"
        ;;
esac
$ testpattern
Enter YES, NO, or MAYBE:  NO
You entered NO
$ testpattern
Enter YES, NO, or MAYBE:  no
You did not enter YES, NO, or MAYBE
```

The flowchart in Figure 18.6 illustrates the use of the case command.

FIGURE 18.6
A case *command flowchart*

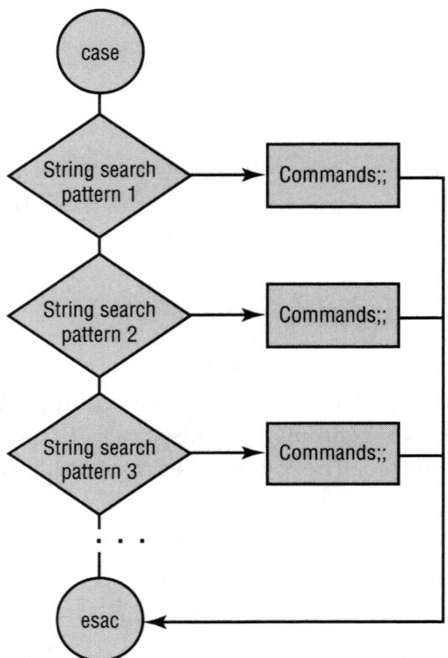

The * denotes a wildcard in a string pattern. It can indicate any string of characters and serves as a catchall in case of no match. If no string is found that matches the test pattern, then control passes to the command following the esac statement without the case structure taking action.

To have the script accept either upper- or lowercase responses, you need to list the arguments, such as a|A, b|B, and so on.

String search patterns include the following:

- * matches any string, default case.
- ? matches any single character.
- | separates alternative choices.
- [ ] tries enclosed characters one at a time, looking for a match.

The case structure is used to create menus. The following is an example of a simple menu:

```
$ cat <magic-menu>
#!/bin/sh
# menu commands
echo "\n    MAGIC MENU \n"
echo "  a. Current date and time"
echo "  b. Department number"
echo "  c. Department name"
echo "  d. Department Budget
echo "Enter a, b, c, or d: \c"
read answer
echo
case "$answer" in
    a)
        date
    ;;
    b)
        dnum
    ;;
    c)
        dname
    ;;
    d)
        dbud
    ;;
    *)
        echo "Nothing selected: $answer"
   ;;
 esac
 $ magic-menu

    MAGIC MENU

  a. Current date and time
  b. Department number
  c. Department name
  d. Department budget
 Enter a, b, c, or d:  a
 Fri Feb 05 12:17:07 EST 2001
```

The \n string in the first echo statement is interpreted as newline characters. This is one of the formatting characters you have available to you. To make the menu more readable, it helps to include formatting characters. Other characters that may be useful in creating menus are \b (backspace), \c (suppresses trailing newline), \f (formfeed), \n (newline), \r (return), \t (horizontal tab), and \v (vertical tab).

The case control structure will branch to different actions depending upon the number of arguments on the command line. The following example demonstrates how case treats a vi editor file while branching several arguments:

```
$cat filedit2
#!/bin/sh
# Patterned after filedit by S. King edited by J. Newbury
# Hobgoblins, VIII:2 p 233, summary

PATH=/bin:/usr/bin
Script=`basename $0`

case $# in
    0)
        vi
        exit 0
    ;;
    1)
        if [ ! -f "$1" ]
        then
            vi "$1"
        elif [ ! -r "$1" -o ! -w "$1" ]
        then
            echo "$Script: check permissions " \
                "on $1" 1>&2
            exit 1
        elif [ ! -w "." ]
        then
            echo "$Script: backup cannot be " \
                "created in the working " \
                "directory" 1>&2
            exit 1
        else
            editfile=$1
```

```
                tfile=/tmp/$$.$Script

                cp $editfile $tfile
                if vi $editfile
                then
                    mv $tfile bak.`basename $editfile`
                    echo "$Script: backup file created"
                else
                    mv $tfile ederror
                    echo "$Script: edit error-copy of " \
                        "original is in ederror" 1>&2
                fi
            fi
        ;;
        *)
            echo "$Script: please do not specify more " \
                "than one file."
            exit 1
        ;;
esac
```

When called without arguments, filedit2 relies on the case structure to execute the first branch and summon vi without an argument. The filedit2 script does not create the backup file because an existing file is not edited. If vi does not let you exit, then you can use the write command (:w) to name the file and write it to disk. (:w *<fname>*) by typing the name of the file in *<fname>* and pressing the Return key. You can then use :q to quit vi. If you have not made any changes, you do not need to use the exclamation point.

In the preceding example, case branches down the arguments, checks to see that the user has write permissions, then goes on to present a usage message and exit. The PATH variable is set to search /bin and then /usr/bin, which stores standard utilities. Problems may be avoided by setting PATH inside a script. Name mix-ups between the user's directories and utilities will be prevented.

TIP PATH determines what directories the shell will search and in which order. By setting the PATH variable to search /bin and /usr/bin from within the script, you ensure that the utility searches the user's directories first and will not get mixed up with scripts or programs with the same names the script uses.

The basename utility relies on command substitution and sends the filename component to standard output. It takes a full or partial path from its argument list and prints out the rightmost name (it changes /bin/sh to sh and /var/log/ to log). The $Script variable is used in place of the filename (the name you used to start the script) in the usage message. With this variable name, you can create links to the script or rename it and the usage and error messages will still be accurate.

The $$ read-only variable stores the PID of the current process. This variable, which is stored in the /tmp directory, begins with the PID number so that it remains unique, is not overwritten, and cannot be truncated incorrectly. If you launch the same program more than once, each launch will have its own PID.

The *here* Script

There are times when the Bourne shell allows you to redirect input to a script from a script. This feature is called the here document simply because it is "here" already in the script. To indicate a here statement, use two less than symbols (<<). Two delimiting characters must be used to indicate to the script that the here document is embedded within it. They need to be the same characters (the first shows the system what to use for the end marker):

```
$ cat grad
grep -i $1" <<+ <<EOF
John Fine         June
Mary Gregory      December
Kevin Hinds       June
Alice Johnson     December
Peter Klein       December
Alfred Marks      June
EOF
$ grad Peter Klein
Peter Klein       December
$ grad            June
John Fine         June
Kevin Hinds       June
Alfred Marks      June
```

The text between the opening delimiter and the closing delimiter, which must be placed on a line by itself, is sent to the process as standard input. When you run grad, it displays Peter Klein and December because you called for Peter Klein's graduation month. The second call displays all the graduates for the month of June. You can use the here document to create scripts that have several files embedded in them.

Variables

The Bourne shell provides variable expansion when the shell processes a token consisting of a dollar sign ($) followed by a user-defined name or keyword, such as `$newname`. The shell will replace the token with the value of the variable. The use of braces { } around the variable name—as in `${`*<newname>*`}`—isolates the variable from what surrounds it, but they do not replace the dollar sign. Braces are necessary when concatenating a variable value with a string. Be certain to set the variable names. The Bourne shell by default will evaluate an unset variable as an empty string and display it as a blank. The alternatives are to use a default value for the variable, use a default value and assign that value to the variable, or display an error. Use a modifier with the variable name when making a choice.

The `:-` modifier replaces a null with a default value. It will allow a non-null variable to represent itself, as in `${name:-default}`. The literal interpretation by the shell is this: "For unset or null variable *<newname>*, expand default and use the expanded value in place of *<newname>* or else use *<newname>*." The `:-` modifier does not change the value of the variable *<newname>*. You can change the value of a null or unset variable in a script by using the `:=` modifier, as in `${`*<newname>*`:=default}`. The shell expands the expression `${newname:=default}` and also sets the value of *<newname>* to the expanded value of `default`.

The `unset` command is used to clear the value of the variables. If you leave out the colon from the `:=`, `sh` will assign values for the unset variables but not for null ones. Many Bourne shell scripts begin with the colon (`:`) built-in followed by a space and the expansion modifier to set null or unset variables. The `:` built-in looks at each token in the remainder of the command line but does not execute any commands. If there is no leading colon, the shell will look at and attempt to execute the command that results from the evaluation. If the variable is a command and you give it a name, it will be executed. When the `:` is at the beginning of the command line, leave a space after it, as in the following:

```
: ${newfile : =/tmp}
```

You can display an error message when you have not set a default when you write a script. If the variable is null or unset, you can use the modifier `:?` and the script can terminate with an exit status of 1 and display an error message:

```
cd ${GAMFILE:?message}
```

The shell will display the expanded value of `message` on standard error and end the script. Use quotes if `message` contains blanks. `Parameter not set` will be displayed if you omit the `:` (colon).

Bourne Built-Ins

Built-ins do not cause a shell to fork a new process when executed. The `trap` built-in catches a signal, which in turn reports to a process about a certain interrupt condition Solaris uses signals to report an interrupt by the user or system. Interrupts may be caused by hitting the interrupt or Esc key or by a broken pipe line, illegal instructions, bad system calls, and other problems that periodically occur. By using `trap`, you can direct the actions a signal gives a script. There are six signals you can use in the Bourne shell when you work with scripts. (Signals were discussed in more detail in Chapter 15, "Memory and Process Management.") Table 18.3 describes the `exit` command signal and the six system signals used in the Bourne shell.

TABLE 18.3: SIGNALS USED IN THE BOURNE SHELL

Signal	No.	Description
No signal	0	Exit command given or end of program
SIGHUP	1	Indicates a hang up or disconnected line
SIGINT	2	Terminal interrupt, Ctrl+C
SIGQUIT	3	Quit, the quit key was pressed
SIGKILL	9	The kill command with the -9 option was given
SIGTERM	15	The default of the kill command
SIGSTP	24	Press the job-control stop key

The numbers are the signals that `trap` catches. The command part is optional. The `trap` command resets the trap to its earlier condition, which is usually an `exit` command. When the commands part is present, the shell will execute the commands as it catches one of the signals. After it does so, the shell will resume executing from where it left off. If you use `trap` with a null or empty built-in, you can get `trap` to prevent a script from exiting and running any commands. An example of `trap` is `trap 9`. If trap is called without arguments, a list of commands will be displayed and an exit status of 1 will be given. The following example illustrates the `trap` built-in:

```
$ cat <trapper>
#1/bin/sh
trap `echo PROGRAM INTERRUPT; exit 1` 2
while true
do
    echo "Program up."
```

```
done

$ trapper
Program up.
Program up.
Program up.
^C PROGRAM INTERRUPT
$
```

On the second line of the trapper script, a trap is set for signal number 2. After catching the signal, the shell executes two commands between the single quote marks. The echo built-in displays the message PROGRAM INTERRUPT. Then exit terminates this shell. The parent shell displays a prompt. The while loop repeats until the script receives a signal. When a script terminates prematurely, temporary files will be cleaned up by a function that you created earlier that performs the cleanup and then exits.

Functions

A shell function stores a series of commands for execution at a later time. Because a function is stored in main memory, you can access it more quickly than you can access a script. The Bourne shell parses a function so it can start up quickly. The shell will execute a function in the same shell that called it. The syntax for a shell function is as follows:

```
<functionname> ()
{
    commands
}
```

You call the function by using the function name. The function executes a list of commands when you call it. The commands can be anything you might include in a shell script. The following example displays a simple function:

```
$ whodo ()
{
    date
    echo "Users logged on"
    who
}
$ whodo
Mon Feb 5 08:23:10 EST 2001    Reliant
Users Logged on
```

```
Hls  console  Feb 5  08:14  (:0)
JC   del/2    Feb 5  08:16  (0.0)
CT   del/3    Feb 5  08:24  (ind.liv.com)
CW   del/1    Feb 5  08:31  (ind.liv2.com)
```

You can use the whodo command to find out what users on a system are doing. The whodo command will produce formatted and dated output by using information from the /var/adm/utmpx and /tmp/ps-datam abd .proc/pid files. The display is headed by the date, time, and machine name.

The *.profile* file

When you log in to your system, the Bourne shell looks for a file named /etc/profile that contains the systemwide startup commands. Once it executes the commands in /etc/profile, the shell looks for a file named .profile in the home directory. If .profile is found, the shell executes the command after those in /etc/profile. If .profile is not found, the shell just goes on. You can use .profile to override any systemwide commands given in /etc/profile. The following example sets the TERM, PATH, PS1, and CDPATH keyword variables in .profile:

```
$ cat .profile
TERM=vt100
PATH=/usr/uc/:/usr/bin:/usr/sbin:/home/alex/bin:
PS1="barrie: "
CDPATH=:$HOME
export TERM PATH PS1 CDPATH
TERM=vt100
PATH=/usr/ucb:/usr/bin:/usr/sbin:/home/alex/bin:
PS1="barrie: "
CDPATH=:$HOME
export TERM PATH PS1 CDPATH
```

Keyword variables can be inherited or declared and initialized by the shell when it is started. You can use .profile to assign values to these variables from the command line. If you want these variables to apply to any other shells or subshells, as well as to the Bourne shell, you must use export to make them available to the other shells, either before or after they are set, as in the preceding example.

After editing your .profile file to change the values of keyword variables, it is not necessary to wait until the next login to put the changes into effect. You can run .profile with the . (dot) built-in in the Bourne shell. Here is the syntax:

```
. ./.profile
```

In the Bourne shell, you can use `function` to define aliases in the `.profile` file. The syntax for creating an `alias` function is as follows:

```
<alias-name> () (
    <command-sequence>
)
```

If you frequently use the `ftp` command to send batches of files and do not want to be prompted for each file, you can create an alias for the `ftp -I` command to turn off interactive prompting. When you add the following line to your `.profile` file, `ftp` is started with interactive prompting turned off:

```
ftp()  {
    ftp -i
}
```

The changes will be recognized after you type `. ./.profile` or after you log off and log in again.

TIP Remember that, when you are removing shell variable names, the shell accepts the `unset` command. However, if you use `unset` a second time with the same name, it will remove a function with that name.

The *spell* Utility

The `spell` utility checks a file for misspelled words. Input originates from a file named on the command line or from standard input. Misspelled words are displayed on standard output. Use the following syntax for the spell utility:

```
$ spell < letter.txt
```

NOTE The `spell` utility works with all shells and is included in this chapter on the Bourne shell because it is often used with the `while` structure.

You can use a `while` structure when you're using `spell` to check for misspelled words in a file. The `while` structure enables you to specify a list of correct words and removes these words from the output of `spell`. You can remove words that you use frequently but that do not appear in a standard dictionary.

You can duplicate the functionality of the script by using `spell` with the + option. This designates a personal dictionary file. Create your personal file by adding as many words as you can think of. For example, you can add names of businesses, Internet terminology, and names of friends or business associates.

Shell Script Debugging

Debugging is necessary when you begin writing more involved scripts. It is easy to overlook a simple point and wonder why the script is not working. You can use the -x option, which causes the shell to display each command before running it. It traces the execution of each command and can give you information about where a bug may be lurking. You have the option of running option -x in just one script or in all of them. Each command that the script executes is preceded by a plus sign (+), so it is easy to distinguish the output of the trace from what the script produces. You can also use `set -x` at the top of the script. The debug option is turned off by `set +x`. It is also helpful to use the `script` command to log your interaction with the debugging session because the information can scroll past your window too rapidly for you to catch everything, particularly if you `cat` a file that has captured a `vi` session. By default, `script` captures the session in a file named <*typescript*>. The syntax for the `script` command is as follows:

```
$ script
Script started, file is typescript
```

You can change the filename by following the `script` command with a space and typing the name of the file you want to use, as in the following example:

```
$ script payrolldb
```

Bourne Again

Although this chapter deals with the Bourne shell, mention must be made of the Bourne Again shell (`bash-2.03$`) because of its obvious similarity to the Bourne shell. Bourne Again is a GNU-developed shell written by Richard Stallman, who intended GNU to be a free replacement for Unix. Bourne Again has many more features than the original Bourne shell and is a favored shell of many Unix programmers. To obtain the Bourne Again shell, go to `www.gnu.org/software/bash/bash.html`.

Summary

In this chapter, you learned that the Bourne shell is the default shell of Solaris 8. Programs written in this shell are called shell scripts. Shell scripts provide an easy way to modify, as well as simplify, complex functions. A function is a group of commands that are parsed before storage into main memory. You learned that you must use caution when naming functions.

You also learned that if you have shell variables with the same name, `unset` will first remove the variable and then remove the function if called again. The greatest advantage to functions is that they can be used over and over and they run faster than scripts.

The Bourne shell employs control structures that use decisions to select alternatives by means of `if` statements, for example, `if…then`, `if…then…else`, and `if…then…elif`. The `case` control structure provides a means to express alternatives using a simple pattern-matching syntax. When you use special built-ins, you can use looping control structures that perform one or more tasks repetitively.

You learned that commands are an integral part of the Bourne shell. For example, you can give the command `kill -1` for a list of signal names or for a list complete with names and numbers. Commands like `exec`, which do not cause a shell to create a new process, run very quickly.

The here document allows input to a command in the shell script to actually come from within the script itself. The here document is identified with the use of an opening and closing delimiter, and the shell sends everything between the two delimiters to the process as standard input.

Finally, this chapter covered some of the utilities found in the Bourne shell. The Bourne shell utilities perform a wide range of tasks, some simple, some complex. For example, the `find` utility searches for files in the system hierarchy and then performs various tasks. To be well written, a script will use the standard techniques outlined in the Bourne shell. The user will treat the Bourne shell not only as a means for becoming familiar with its own capabilities, but as a precursor to using the other shells. Mastering the Korn and C shells, as well as the Job shell, will be easier once you're familiar and comfortable with using the Bourne shell.

CHAPTER 19

The Korn Shell

FEATURING:

Korn shell variables 727

Control structures 735

Processing options 737

Korn shell special characters 738

Redirecting input and output 743

Functions 748

History files 755

The Korn shell (`ksh`) has a larger number of features than either the Bourne shell or the C shell. Although it includes many of their features and configurations, it also has many new ones. The Korn shell is an extension of the Bourne shell and was developed at AT&T labs.

Because the shells have so many of the same capabilities, you'll find that some of the information in this chapter was presented in other chapters. Chapters 17 ("Understanding Shells"), 18 ("The Bourne Shell"), and 20 ("The C Shell") also discuss the shells and provide background information. In this chapter, you'll learn how to customize `ksh` to suit your preferences.

This chapter covers some basic Korn shell features, such as command-line editing and programming and running scripts. A discussion of the built-ins and variables, as well as Korn shell options, will follow along with some valuable tips on command processing. Because there are so many Korn shell features, it is not possible to present all of them. You should experiment with the Korn shell only after you become familiar with the material presented in this chapter.

Korn Shell Basics

The Korn shell is the largest of the three main shells supported by Solaris 8. It can be set up by the administrator (superuser) in the `/etc/passwd` file as the login shell, if you prefer. Basically, it is similar to the other shells but has more features and can be helpful for advanced programming. The Korn shell has many advantages as a programming shell. It is interactive, has history and aliasing capabilities, and has excellent editing mechanisms. It also contains features not available in the other shells. The shell provides programming structures used in procedural languages such as C or Pascal. It provides string variables, string operators, and integer variables with a comprehensive set of arithmetic operators. The `select` control structure provides a simple method for creating menus in scripts and prompting the user for responses. The `repeat` statement provides a way to repeat a sequence of commands over and over.

The capability to break down large problems into smaller ones by creating subprograms is a productive tool. Creating functions and calling scripts from other scripts (recursively) allows you to solve problems quite easily. A recursive construct is one that has a special case that is not self-referential. It is defined in terms of itself. The `read` and `print` built-ins give you the ability to manipulate file descriptors, thereby giving shell scripts control over input and output programs written in lower-level languages.

When it's executing statements, the Korn shell allows conditional statements such as `if`. It also allows iterative execution of the `while` and `for` statements. It has the capability to transfer data to and from a program as needed. It makes problem solving an easier task because of its programming flexibility. Another important feature of the

Korn shell is its unique capability to launch a coprocess alongside the initial process. The initial process, executed in tandem with the parent shell, connects standard input and output via a two-way pipe to and from the parent shell. The use of functions is also a powerful feature. For example, the `autoload` built-in can load a function efficiently when needed.

As do the other shells, the Korn shell allows jobs to be run in the background and foreground. It also has editing capabilities (`vi` and `emacs`) that provide an environment geared to producing excellent programs, whether simple or complex.

In addition to the ones discussed in the preceding paragraphs, the Korn shell has the following features:

- You can use history editing to modify command lines.
- You can evaluate variables, search for aliases or functions, and expand ambiguous file references.
- You can redirect before executing a command.
- You can use `ksh` to execute a Korn shell script as an argument.

Start Files

To start the Korn shell from another shell, type **ksh** and press the Return key. The default Korn shell prompt is a dollar sign ($). If you are logged in as a superuser to the Korn shell, you will see a number sign prompt (#). Also, if you start a script with `#!` on the first line followed by the path of `ksh`, the Korn shell will run the script no matter which shell you call the script from. To set your environment in the Korn shell, the shell looks at two initialization files in the user's home directory: the `.profile` and the `ksh-env`. The latter is a file that you create and choose a name for and that will control your user environment. This file is similar to the C shell `.cshrc` file. For the purpose of uniformity, you could call it `.kshrc`, but any name you choose is correct. When you log in, the `.profile` file is read followed by the `.ksh-env` file. You can use the `.ksh-env` file to configure the session to your needs. Because many of the commands you place in the `.ksh-env` file can be executed only by the Korn shell, they cannot be placed in the `.profile` file.

The syntax for setting the environment variables in the Korn shell is as follows:

```
export <VARIABLE>=value
```

You must export the variable to make it available to the shell. You can also set the environment in the Korn shell the same way you do in the Bourne shell. The following example shows this:

```
ENV=$home/.kshrc; export ENV
```

The Korn shell uses options that control the execution of commands while also specifying the user environment. To see the list of current option settings, you can type **set -o** and press the Return key. Table 19.1 displays the default options employed by the Korn shell.

To enable any of the options listed in Table 19.1, type **set -o *<option>*** and press the Return key. To disable any of the options, type **set +o *<option>***.

TABLE 19.1: KORN SHELL DEFAULT OPTIONS

Option	Default	Shell Function
allexport	Off	Automatically exports defined variables.
bgnice	On	Lowers priority to background and executes job.
emacs	Off	Sets emacs as the inline editor.
errexit	Off	When command value is False, executes the ERR trap and exits.
gmacs	Off	Sets gmacs an the inline editor.
ignoreeof	Off	Prevents the shell from exiting when you give an EOF (Ctrl+D). Type **exit** to quit.
interactive	On	Prompts the user to reply in interactive mode.
keyword	Off	Places words that are variables in a variable assignment list.
markdirs	Off	Displays a / after names of expanded pathway directories.
monitor	On	Enables job control.
noclobber	Off	Specifies that an existing file is not overwritten if (>)is used.
noexec	Off	Specifies that commands are read but not executed. Debugging tool.
noglovb	Off	Disables filename expansion.
nolog	Off	Specifies that function definitions are not stored in the history file.
nounset	Off	Displays error message when variable expansion is not set.
privileged	Off	Uses the UID and GID. If privileged is on, they are set to prior values.
restricted	Off	Sets a restricted shell.
trackall	Off	Makes command-tracked aliases.
verbose	Off	Displays the input as it is read.
vi	Off	Sets vi as the inline editor.
viraw	Off	Specifies input from vi one character at a time.
xtrace	Off	Displays commands and/or arguments as executed.

Just as with the other shells, the Korn shell performs an evaluation of the variables on the command line. A closer look at the steps the Korn shell takes when using functions, aliases, input/output redirection, variable expansion, tilde expansion, and substitutions should make the ksh capabilities clearer. You can execute a script by using the script name as an argument. The following example demonstrates this:

```
$ ksh <scriptname>
```

This will call ksh even if you are in a Bourne or C Shell mode. If you want to execute the file containing the script, you can, with the correct permission, use the filename as a command, as in the following:

```
$ <filename>
```

If you use the symbols #! and follow that with the ksh path, the shell will run the script no matter what shell you call it from, as in the following example (unless you specify a different script):

```
#!/bin/ksh
```

Korn Shell Variables

The Korn shell allows you to assign values to variables much like the Bourne shell does. Here is the syntax:

```
<VARIABLE>=value
```

TIP When assigning values to variables, do not leave space on either side of the equal sign. If you want to have spaces in your command, put quotes around the value or the space.

The conventions for referencing the value of a variable in the Korn shell are the same as they are in sh and csh. Precede the variable name with a dollar sign and enclose it in braces. The Korn shell refers to arguments on the command line by their position. It uses special variables such as $1, $2, and so on up to $9. Arguments past the ninth must have braces, as in ${10}.

In the Korn shell, the typeset built-in sets attributes. By using typeset, you can set for a variable attributes that control its value, such as readonly. To unset the value, you can use the unset built-in, which removes the variable's value and attributes. The following example demonstrates how to assign a lowercase attribute:

```
$ typeset -l <TEXT>
$ <TEXT>="DEPARTMENT STORE"
```

```
$ ECHO $ <TEXT>
department store
```

The `typeset -l` assigns a lowercase attribute to the variable *<TEXT>*. You could do the opposite by assigning the `typeset -u` attribute to lowercase variables to produce output with uppercase letters.

Another useful feature of the Korn shell is that it gives you the ability to assign integer attributes when you want to do mathematical calculations on a variable. The shell will take a string variable, convert it internally to a number, work calculations on it, then convert it back into a string. The variable is stored as an integer, which makes calculations much quicker. Refer to the following example:

```
$ typeset -i COUNT
```

Because the `integer` built-in in `ksh` is so close in identity to `typeset -i`, you can use the following command:

```
$ integer COUNT
```

The Korn shell allows you to assign a base other than 10 to an integer variable. It will then display the variable. Here is the syntax:

```
typeset -I <base variable>
```

The *`<base variable>`* is the base you want to use in the calculation. If it's more than 10, the value is displayed as `base # value`.

If a variable is given the `export` attribute, a copy of it is sent to all child processes. The Korn shell supports the `export` built-in and also provides `typeset -x` to set the `export` attribute. The `export` attribute may be set for functions as well as variables and will be available in subshells. All Korn shell variables that you create and use in a shell script are global once exported; therefore, they will be available in the current shell and in subshells as well. You may create variables that are local to a function, but they will be recognized only within that function.

TIP When a function has a local variable with the same name as a global variable, all references within the function refer to the local variable. References outside the function refer to the global variable.

Caution should be used when naming variables. Because local variables may be used in a general way, and because scripts may be written by several different people, it is better to have unique names for variables within a function. To avoid naming confusion, you can use the `typeset` built-in to declare that a variable be local to the function it is defined in.

Keyword Variables

Like the Bourne shell and the C shell, the Korn shell has inherited a set of keyword variables. Some have values that are set and can be changed by you. Others are absolute and cannot be changed. Some may have special meaning to the shell. Table 19.2 lists the keyword variables available to the Korn shell with brief descriptions of their functions or their use. Several will be new to you since they are available only in `ksh`. All are preceded by the $ symbol when used in script writing.

TABLE 19.2: KEYWORD VARIABLES IN THE KORN SHELL

Keyword	Description
#	Denotes number of command-line arguments
*	Makes all command-line arguments single arguments
@	Makes all command-line arguments individual arguments
_	Denotes last argument of previous command
`CDPATH`	Produces a list of absolute path names of directories searched by `cd` if set
`FCEDIT`	Names the editor that the `fc` built-in uses
`FPATH`	Lists files that contain functions
`HISTFILE`	Stores history of filenames
`HISTFILESIZE`	Indicates the number of lines of history stored in `HISTFILE`
`HISTSIZE`	Indicates the number of events stored in the history list during a session
`HOME`	Gives the path name of your home directory
`IFS`	Denotes an Internal Field Separator
`LINENO`	Sets the value to the line number of the command it executes
`MAIL`	Denotes the file where your mail is stored
`OPTARG`	Denotes a variable set by the `getopts` built-in
`OPTIND`	Denotes a variable set by the `getopts` built-in
`PATH`	Denotes a list of directories searched for commands
`PPID`	Indicates the value of the PID (parent process)
`PS1`	Denotes a shell prompt string
`PS2`	Denotes a shell secondary prompt string
`LINES`, `COLUMNS`, and `PS3`	Control the format of output
`PS4`	Denotes a prompt string used in debugging; used with `set -x`
`OLDPWD`	Denotes an old, previous working directory
`PWD`	Denotes a previous working directory; may be toggled back with `OLDPWD`
`RANDOM`	Assigns a random integer value for testing, dummy data, etc.
`SECONDS`	Denotes an integer variable of number of seconds since start of shell session
`TMOUT`	Sets a time to exit shell after elapsed seconds

The Korn shell uses the underscore (_) to refer to specific arguments and not the symbols on the command line. This example demonstrates how the underscore is used:

```
$ cat      box1     box2     box3 > all3boxes
$ echo $_
box3
```

The Korn shell refers to the last argument of the previous simple command, which is box3 in the output.

Built-In Variables

The Korn shell allows you to use a larger set of built-ins than do the Bourne and C shells. These built-in variables include sets for option processing, input/output, control flow, and control of the user's environment. Korn shell built-in commands are shown in Table 19.3. Most of the keyword variables will be discussed further later in this chapter. Examples will be given so that you may try out the scripts while you become more familiar with keyword variables.

TABLE 19.3: KORN SHELL BUILT-IN COMMANDS

Command	Description
( )	Subshell, creates a copy of itself
$( )	Command substitution, a command executed from within a subshell
(( ))	Assignment operator (used with an enclosed equal sign)
$(( ))	Expression evaluation, not used with an equal sign
[ ]	Test command
[[ ]]	String comparisons, adds strings that match

As discussed in Chapter 18, parentheses are used to group commands. The Korn shell will create a copy of itself (a subshell) for each group of commands and a new process to execute each command. Each subshell will have its own set of variables with values that may or may not be different from the values of the variables in other subshells. The following example demonstrates how a subshell is created and executed:

```
#! (six ; ten) & d &
```

Tasks six and ten will be executed sequentially in the background, and task d will be run in the background at the same time.

The Korn shell performs command substitution by using a string within parentheses. The string is treated as a command and is executed within a subshell. The text and parentheses will be replaced by standard output of the command. Here is an example of command substitution:

```
#! ls -1 $(find . -name README -print)
```

When double sets of parentheses are used together, `ksh` treats them as enclosures for arithmetic expressions. You can use an arithmetic expression enclosed between `(( ))` and preceded by `$` in place of any numeric value. See the following example:

```
#! echo "There are $((52*7)) days in the year."
```

The Korn shell does not expand the filename within the `$(( ))`, so it is easy to use operators such as the asterisk for mathematical expressions. Because these operators signify an arithmetic expression, if you want to use a parenthesized subshell within `$( )`, you must place a space between the `$(` and the next `(`.

The enclosed brackets `[ ]` are used synonymously with the `test` built-in or utility.

TIP To find out whether a command is a built-in or a system utility in `ksh`, use the built-in `type` <*command*>.

The Korn shell has more built-ins than either the Bourne or C shell, and most were covered in the two previous chapters. In this chapter, built-ins that were not covered previously will be discussed. The Korn shell includes built-ins for option processing, control flow, input/output, and control of the user's environment.

The Korn shell commands that are not simple are referred to as control structures or control flow commands. Control flow commands are used for shell programming and may be useful in interactive work. Korn shell control structures that control the process flow are `if…then`, `for…in`, `while`, `case`, `until`, and `select`. You can use the same syntax you use in the Bourne shell for these test commands. You can also use the `test` built-in, the `[[` built-in, or any other command as the test command. The syntax for the `[[` built-in is as follows:

```
[[ <conditions> ]]
```

The result for this built-in is a return status, just like the results for the `test` built-in. The Bourne shell uses `-a` as a logical `AND` with two expressions, whereas the Korn shell uses && for the same effect. The `sh` also uses `-o` for logical `OR` for two expressions while the Korn shell uses `||`. Table 19.4 lists more Korn shell test options.

TABLE 19.4: KORN SHELL TEST OPTIONS

Test	Result
`-o <option>`	True if the option named *<option>* is set or on
`(<expression>)`	True if *<expression>* is true
`! <expression>`	True if *<expression>* is false
`<expression1> && <expression2>`	True if *<expression1>* and *<expression2>* are both true
`<expression1> || <expression2>`	True if either *<expression1>* or *<expression2>* is true

The `[[` will probably be used the most as the test command for control structures. It also allows an arithmetic test when inside double parentheses instead of square brackets. The double parentheses are not preceded by a $ sign. This test yields only a true or false. All of the logical Korn arithmetic operators may be used. Consider the following examples:

```
if [[ $(( ${#FORM} + 21 )) -lt $ {#PWD} ]]
then
   …
fi

or

if (( $(( ${#FORM} + 21 )) < ${#PWD} ))
then
   …
fi

or
if (( ${#FORM} + 21 < ${#PWD} ))
    then
   …
fi
```

The comparison operators that are similar to arithmetic operators may be familiar to you. The Korn shell treats the tokens `[[` and `((` as special symbols instead of commands. You do not need to follow them with a SPACE.

Shell Variable Expansion

The Korn shell expands all the shell variables used by the Bourne shell and adds its own to the mix. You may want to review the discussion of variable expansion in the previous two chapters. Many of the conventions will be the same. The Korn shell expands an unset name to a null string just as the Bourne shell (sh) does.

The same modifiers (:=, :, :?) are used to assign default values. The Korn shell makes use of a set of pattern-matching string operators used to manipulate path names and other strings. You can delete prefixes or suffixes that match patterns from strings. Table 19.5 displays these pattern-matching operators.

TABLE 19.5: STRING OPERATORS

String Operator	Description
#	Removes minimal matching prefixes
##	Removes maximal matching prefixes
%	Removes minimal matching suffixes
%%	Removes maximal matching suffixes

Here is the syntax for string operators:

```
${<variable> op string}
```

The abbreviation <op> can be used for any one of the operators listed in Table 19.5 and <string> is a matching pattern of characters used for filenames. Use these operators to extract components, remove patterns, or change suffixes. The following example demonstrates how this is done:

```
$ STOREFILE=/usr/local/src/dept.c
$ echo ${STOREFILE#/*/}
local/src/dept.c
$ echo ${STOREFILE##/*/}
dept.c
$ echo ${STOREFILE%/*}
/usr/local/src
$ echo ${STOREFILE%%/*}

$ echo ${STOREFILE%/C}
/usr/local/src/dept.c
$ CUTFIRST=${SOURCEFILE#/*/}
```

```
$echo $CUTFIRST
local/src/dept.c
$ NEXT=${CUTFIRST%%/*}`
$ echo $NEXT
local
```

Array Variables

The Korn shell allows you to assign an array of values to a variable by using the `set` built-in. The syntax for an array variable is as follows:

```
set -A <name> factor1 factor2
```

The following example demonstrates how you would use an array variable. The first element of the array is the subscript 0:

```
$ set -A NAMES    barrie kay rose peter joe
$ echo $NAMES
barrie
$ echo ${NAMES[2]}
rose
```

TIP Because the subscripting is zero based, the subscript 2 displays the third element of the array.

You can display all the elements by using an asterisk, as in this example:

```
$ echo ${NAMES[*]}
barrie kay rose peter joe
```

The use of double quotation marks changes the outcome of the array. If quotation marks are used with subscripts `[*]` and `[@]`, the shell will extract the array differently. The `@` will cause the array to duplicate itself. The * will produce a single element that holds all of the other elements of the array separated by an internal field separator, which is usually a space.

The following example illustrates that * is used to fill array A with elements of the NAMES variable and @ is used to fill array B. The `set` built-in displays the values of the A and B arrays without using an argument:

```
$ set -A A "${NAMES[*]}"
$ set -A B "${NAMES[@]}"
$ set | head -5
```

```
A='barry kay rose peter joe'
B[0]=barry
B[1]=kay
B[2]=rose
B[3]=peter
```

Korn Shell Control Structures

Control structures are sophisticated commands that control the flow of processes throughout the program. Many employ a form of Boolean logic to test a condition and, after determining whether the condition is true or false, produce a result to output. The use of if…then statements, while…do statements, and so on provide a means of control that is very specific. These statements create an internal looping mechanism until the appropriate condition is met, thereby breaking the loop and returning control of the function to the program that called it. Control structures are powerful tools for building a program or script that needs to conform to certain conditions.

The Select Control Structure

The Korn shell uses the select control structure to display a menu, assign a value to a variable, and execute a series of commands. The syntax for the select structure is as follows:

```
select <variable> [in args..]
do
    commands
done
A menu of the args items is displayed. The menu is
    formatted with preceding numbers.
```

The args list can be very long or it can be short. The select structure uses the values of the LINES (default 24) and COLUMNS (default 80) variables to determine the size of the display. Ordinarily, a page of the green barred computer output paper can support 24 lines and 80 columns, hence the default numbers. The select structure will then display the value of PS3 (default ?#), which is the special select prompt. You can set the value to something more meaningful to you.

If the user selects a valid number from the menu, then the select structure sets the value of <*variable*> to the argument with the number the user entered and executes the commands between do and done. The select structure will then reissue the PS3 prompt and wait for the user's response. It will repeat this sequence until it is forced to exit between the do and the done. This is most often caused by a user-given break (which causes the select structure to exit from the loop), by a return from within a function, or by the user giving the exit command, which causes the select structure to exit from the current shell.

The following example demonstrates the select structure:

```
$ cat cakes
#!/bin/ksh
PS3="Which flavor of cake do you purchase most often?"
select CAKE chocolate white yellow confetti STOP
do
   if [[ $CAKE = STOP ]]; then
      echo "Thank you for your answer!"
      break
   fi
   echo "You prefer $CAKE ."
   echo "That is choice number $REPLY."
   echo
done
$cake
1) chocolate
2) white
3) yellow
4) confetti
5) STOP
Which flavor of cake do you purchase most often?:  4
You prefer confetti.
That is choice number 4.

Which flavor of cake do you purchase most often?:
```

A null string will be assigned to the variable if the menu choice is ambiguous. If the user inadvertently presses Return without entering a choice, the menu will redisplay along with the prompt. The user's response is stored in the keyword variable REPLY.

If an invalid menu choice causes ksh to assign a null string to a variable and to execute the commands between do and done, or if the user presses Return without entering a choice, the Korn shell will redisplay the menu and the PS3 prompt. The Korn shell stores the user's response in the keyword variable *<REPLY>* even if the answer is invalid.

Processing Options

A specific utility will interpret its command line based upon its own conventions. Solaris has its own convention; it recognizes a letter preceded by a hyphen as a command-line option. It is a good idea to become familiar with processing options and to follow the accepted conventions when programming scripts. Options always precede other arguments. Most utilities let you combine options behind a single hyphen. An option command may be written in other ways, such as the following examples:

```
$ ls -1 -r -t
$ ls -lrt
```

Other utilities, such as `cc` and `gcc`, have options that themselves require arguments. These `cc` and `gcc` utilities have for the output file the `-o` option, which must be followed by the name you want to give the executable file that is being generated by the user. Use a space to separate the option from the argument, as in the following example:

```
$ cc -o obtr obtr.c
```

Not all utilities work with filenames that start with a hyphen. If you have filenames that start with hyphens, your command could be ambiguous. The system could interpret it as an option. If you do not want a long list of files that have names that begin with a hyphen in the working directory, it is better to use another naming system. If you absolutely have to have filenames beginning with hyphens, there are many utilities for which a double hyphen indicates the end of options. For example, consider the following examples (the second example demonstrates the use of the path):

```
$ ls -- -1
$ ls ./-1
```

Using Solaris 8 conventions will make it easier to find your files and read your programs. It is best to write shell programs using the Solaris option conventions.

Parse Option *getopts*

The `getopts` command is a Korn shell built-in. It can also be a utility (`/usr/bin/getopts`), which helps make it easier for you to write programs that follow Unix/Solaris argument conventions. The syntax is as follows:

```
getopts optstring <variable>[args]
```

The `opstring` command is a list of valid option letters that can be used in an argument. The use of a colon following the corresponding letter tells the shell that it should search for options. The getopts built-in checks an argument list for options in optstring. It then stores the option letters it finds in <*variable*>. The getopts command will default to the command-line arguments unless you supply a list of arguments after <*variable*>.

The getopts built-in uses <*OPTIND*> and <*OPTARG*> variables to store option-related values. At the beginning of a shell script, the value of <*OPTIND*> is 1 until getopts locates an argument. It then increments <*OPTIND*> to be the index of the next argument to be processed. If the option takes an argument, then the Korn shell assigns the value of the argument to <*OPTARG*>.

Using getopts does not make your program shorter, but it will help you keep a uniform programming style that is easy to follow, and it enforces standard option handling. It is beneficial to experiment with the getopts built-in until you are familiar with its capabilities. Here is the syntax for getopts:

```
getopts optstring <name> [arg]
```

Korn Shell Special Characters

Certain characters—such as the question mark (?), the asterisk (*), the brackets ([])—have special meaning to the shells. The Korn shell treats these special characters in much the same way the other shells do. (A comprehensive description of special characters and their use was given in Chapter 17.)

When using the Korn shell, you can put quotes around special characters when you want to use them in scripts and the shell will treat them as regular characters. It is recommended that you avoid using them in filenames, however, simply to reduce confusion. They are used with the arguments to print and echo. Also, if you precede a special character with a backslash, the Korn shell will interpret it as a regular character. For example, the backslash character is used before print escape commands such as \n, which signifies a NEWLINE, and allows a single call to print to multiple lines. Without double quotes, the script will interpret this and display it as n. If you place double quotes around the argument, the display would be NEWLINE. This has a very different meaning in a script. To avoid programming errors, use special characters discreetly.

One use of special characters is to generate filenames with matching patterns of characters, as discussed in the next section.

Generating Filenames

Filename generation is an important feature of the shells. They are capable of referring to files by matching patterns in filenames. When you give a shell abbreviated filenames containing special characters (metacharacters), the shell generates filenames that match the names of existing files. Referred to as *wildcards*, these special characters appear in an argument on the command line. The shell then expands the argument and passes the list to the program that the command line calls. These special wildcard characters are called *ambiguous file references* because they do not refer to a specific file. This action is called *globbing*. Globbing is used for identifying files with a single pattern or long filenames with a short string. The Korn shell supports the `noglob` option (`set -0 noglob`), which turns off all pattern matching so that you have to give exact filenames.

The ? Special Character

The question mark (?) is used to match any character in the name of an existing file. When the shell encounters this character at the command line, it expands the argument preceding it and generates a list of the files in the working directory that have the same beginning characters followed by any single character. The following example displays this:

```
$ lp letter?
```

The shell would then pass the list to the `lp` utility. If no filename matches the file reference, the shell will pass the string (`letter?`) to `lp` or it will display an error message. Use `ls` to display a list of all files in the working directory. It will also find any match with the string `letter?`. Here is an example:

```
$ ls
letter+     letter11  letterDev  letterpress letters
letter1     letter21  letterG    lettera     letters99
$ ls letter?
letter+     letter1   letterG    lettera    letters
```

You can also place the question mark in the middle of the file reference:

```
$ ls  letter?May
letter6May  letter8May  letter.May  letter5May  letter1May
```

You can use the echo command to generate filenames. It displays the arguments that the shell passes to it. The following example demonstrates how:

```
$ echo my?report
my.report      my1report      mynreport      my$report
```

The shell expands the ambiguous file reference into a list of files in the working directory that have names that match the string. It then gives the list to echo, which responds in turn by displaying the list of filenames.

TIP A period before a filename indicates a hidden file. If you want to match filenames beginning with a period, you must include the period in the ambiguous file reference.

The * Special Character

An asterisk special character, quite similar to the ? character, can match any number of characters in a filename. This includes zero characters. The following example displays how the asterisk special character operates in finding character strings:

```
$ ls
letter  letters  letter.my 168  letterbarrie  user.letter
let  letter.0212  letterx.save  kayletter  lettera
letalx    lettA    letterfile    lettersave
$ echo letter*
letter letter.0212  lettera  letteralx  letterfile  letterbarrie
$ echo *my
letter.my
$ echo *ers*
letters    lettersave
```

The -a option permits `ls` to display invisible filenames. The command `echo *` does not display the working directory (signified by `.`), the parent working directory (signified by `..`), or `.profile`. It will display filenames that have a period within the name. The command `echo .*` will display all files whose names are preceded by periods.

TIP It is a good idea to establish naming conventions so that you can take advantage of string searching with special characters. Many companies use `.txt` or `.mem` to distinguish documents. Some use dates or special symbols. If uniform conventions are established early, finding the appropriate document becomes an easy task.

The *[ ]* Special Characters

Brackets on either side of a list of characters or strings will cause the shell to match filenames containing those characters or strings. The brackets define a character class that includes all the characters within them; for example, `[ 1 2 3 4 ].txt`.

The shell handles the brackets by expanding an argument that includes a character class definition. It will replace each set of brackets and its contents with the character class. The shell will then pass a list of matching filenames to the program being called. The brackets act as a question mark that replaces just the members of the character class, as in the following examples. The first example lists the names of files in the working directory that begin with *a*, *b*, *c*, *d*, or *e*:

```
$ echo [abcde]*
american babies children dogs eagles
.
.
```

The second example displays the contents of files named `doc1.txt`, `doc2.txt`, `doc3.txt`, and `doc4.txt`:

```
$ cat doc[1234].txt
doc1.txt doc2.txt doc3.txt doc4.txt
.
.
```

You can use a hyphen to define a range of characters within a character class in square brackets, for example, `[a-e]` or `[1-4]`.

Korn Shell Arithmetic

The Korn shell performs assignments and evaluations of different types of mathematical expressions. Arithmetic is done using integers. Numbers may be represented in a base from 2 to 36 using the *<base>#<VALUE>* syntax. The `let` built-in in `ksh` allows the shell to perform some arithmetic assignments as in the following example:

```
$ let "<VALUE>=VALUE *20 + INT"
```

Both `VALUE` and `INT` should contain integer values. Double quotes enclose the arguments and prevent the shell from expanding the asterisk as an operator that matches file patterns. Arguments containing `spaces` also must have quotes. The Korn shell will accept `((expression))` as a synonym for `let "expression"`. Either form is allowed on the command line.

Korn shell expressions are virtually the same as C language expressions, with a few exceptions. The Korn shell does not support the ++, `--`, `?:`, and `,` operators. Table 19.6 lists the accepted operators for the Korn shell.

TABLE 19.6: KORN SHELL OPERATORS

Operator	Description
+	Unary plus
-	Unary minus
!	Logical NOT
~	Complement
&	Bitwise AND
^	Bitwise XOR
|	Bitwise OR
*	Multiplication
/	Division
%	Remainder
+	Addition
-	Subtraction
<<	Left shift
>>	Right shift
<	Less than
>	Greater than
<=	Less than or equal to
>=	Greater than or equal to
==	Equality
!=	Inequality
&&	Logical AND
||	Logical OR
=, +=, -+, *=, /=, %=, &=, ^=, I=	Assignments

You can use arithmetic expressions as arguments. You can also use an arithmetic expression and enclose it between `$(( ))` in place of numeric values. Because the Korn shell does not perform filename expansion within the `$(( ))`, you do not need to enclose it within quotation marks. You may use the `(*)` for multiplication.

The operators && and `||` are used for "short circuiting," meaning that if the results of one of these operators can be decided by looking at the left operand, then the right operand is not evaluated. The following example illustrates how this works:

```
$ ((N=10))
$ ((Z=0))
```

```
$ echo $ ((N || ((Z+=1)) ))
1
$ echo $Z
0
```

Because the value of *N* is not a zero, the result of the `||(OR)` operation is `1(true)`. The value of the right side is not evaluated. *Z* keeps its original value. Here are three rules for using arithmetic expressions in the Korn shell:

- Assignment operators act as shorthand notations: `((T+=3))` is the same as `((T=T+3))`.
- A remainder operator (`%`) gives the remainder when its first operand is divided by its second. A logical operation always has a value of either 0 for false or 1 for true.
- An exclamation point, if enclosed in double parentheses `((!))`, will not be interpreted as a history by the Korn shell.

Input and Output

The Korn shell command (or built-in) for input is `read` and the output command is `print`. The Korn shell's `read` provides more functionality than the Bourne shell's `read`. It will read an entire input line from standard input and place it into the variable `REPLY`. If you supply arguments on the command line, `read` treats them as variable names and splits the input line by using the characters in IFS as separators. Each word is sequentially assigned to a variable argument. If there are not enough variables, a string equal to the remainder of the input line will be assigned to the last variable. If there are not enough words, the leftover variables are set to null. You may specify an input prompt by using `variable? prompt` for the first input variable name.

The `read` built-in supports the following options:

`-p option` Specifies a coprocess; gets input from the input pipe of the shell using `|&`

`-r option` Specifies raw input

`-s option` Specifies a save in the history file

`-un option` Specifies a read to integer *n*, a one-digit file descriptor

The `read` built-in has an exit status of 0 if it reads any data. It has a nonzero exit status when it reaches the end of file:

```
$ cat clients
```

```
Mary James
Ken Smith
Gary Knox
Paul Johnson
$ while read First Rest
> do
>     print $Rest, $First
> done <clients
James, Mary
Smith, Ken
Knox, Gary
Johnson, Paul
```

Redirecting I/O and the Coprocess

Most commands you enter from the keyboard (with the exception of built-ins) are executed in a new process. Input/output (I/O) redirection is performed on the new process before the command is run. The Korn shell arranges for redirection to apply to a built-in alone, even though the built-in executes in the same process as the shell. Although they have their own sets of parameters, options, or traps, shell functions execute in the current process as well.

The Korn shell has a feature known as the *coprocess*. The coprocess allows you to start a process that runs in the background while it is communicating with its parent shell. You can invoke a process as the coprocess by ending the command line with `|&`. The coprocess is very useful if you are working in a client/server environment. The coprocess command is a filter that reads from standard input and writes to standard output. It will flush its output when it has accumulated a line rather than waiting for successive lines. The diagram in Figure 19.1 shows that the coprocess is connected to the current shell. A two-way pipe is used to read and write standard output (read with <&p, write with >&p). You can write new scripts that act as an interface on an interactive program by using the `coprocess` command. The following script invokes `to_roof` as the coprocess:

```
$ cat to_roof
#!/bin/ksh
while read to_roof; do
echo "$to_roof" | tr '1-26' '[1-26]'
done
```

FIGURE 19.1

A coprocess's connection to the current shell

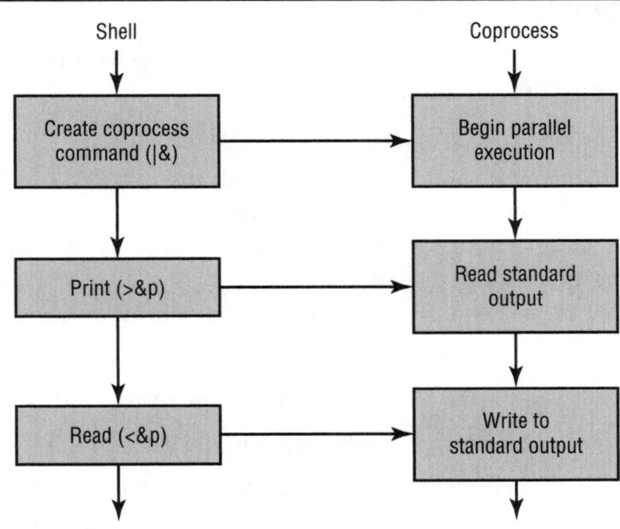

Raw Input

If the input line ends in a backslash (\), the backslash and the newline character that should follow it are discarded. The next line is treated as the continuation of the same line of input. The trailing backslash is treated as a regular character. This is beneficial for reading an input file that is itself a shell script containing backslashes.

The -s option saves input as a command in the history file, while the -u*n* option uses the *n* integer as a file descriptor that read takes its input from. Consider the following examples, which are both correct and will produce the same result:

```
read -u4 argsone  argstwo
read argsone argstwo <&4
```

Each time you redirect input, the shell opens the file and places the read pointer at the beginning. If you are using a while structure with the redirection symbol (<), it is very important that you place it at the done statement and not at the call to read. Consider the following examples, paying attention to where the redirect symbol is placed. In the first example, the pointer is repositioned at the start of the file:

```
$ read line1 < pnames; print $line1; read line 2 < pnames;
    print $line2
Andrea Jenkins
Andrea Jenkins
$ (read line 1; print $line1; read line2; print $line2) < pnames
Andrea Jenkins
Diane Smith
```

PART III

Working with Shells in Solaris

Output Display

The `print` built-in is a replacement for the `echo` command. You use the following syntax for the print built-in:

```
print [-nRrps] [-un] [<string...>]
```

The `print` built-in recognizes both the `\c` and the `-n` options for suppressing the trailing newline character and writes the strings to standard output. You must always use double quotation marks around the arguments to `print` and `echo`. If you forget, the `\n` would be displayed as `n`.

The `read` command has the following print options:

-p option Directs the output line to standard input of the coprocess.

-s option Directs output to the history file.

-un option Sends output to file descriptor *n*.

-n option Suppresses trailing newline characters.

-r option Tells the shell to ignore the special meaning of the escape characters and displays them as ordinary characters. Treats fields that follow escape characters as string arguments, even if they start with a hyphen (unless they begin with `-n`).

The following example displays how the print escapes work:

```
$ print "We are interested in three vehicles:\
 \nThe Caravan\nThe Explorer\nthe Sable"
We are interested in three vehicles:
The Caravan
The Explorer
The Sable
```

Table 19.7 lists some of the escapes used with the `print` built-in.

TABLE 19.7: ESCAPE OPTIONS FOR THE `print` BUILT-IN

Escape	Description
\a	Alert character; makes a flash or display beep
\b	Backspace character
\c	Does not print output and suppresses trailing newline character
\e	Escape character
\f	Formfeed character; puts a Ctrl+L character in the output

Continued

TABLE 19.7: ESCAPE OPTIONS FOR THE print BUILT-IN (CONTINUED)

Escape	Description
`\n`	Newline character; allows multiple lines from a single call to print
`\r`	Return character; puts a Ctrl+M character in the output
`\t`	Tab character
`\v`	Vertical tab character
`\\`	Backslash character
`\0`	ASCII character with octal value of *nnn* (you can omit leading zeros)
`\x`*nnn*	ASCII character with hexadecimal value of *nnn*

TIP The backslash (\) character is special to the shell. To use it in any of the print escapes, it must be quoted or escaped.

When a process opens a file, a file descriptor number is associated with the file. Each process opens its own set of files and file descriptors. After a process opens a file, it reads from and writes to that file by referring to it with the file descriptor. When the process is done, it closes the file and frees the file descriptor. Solaris is typical in starting with three open files: standard input, which uses the file descriptor 0; standard output, with the file descriptor 1; and standard error, with the file descriptor 2. Usually these are all the file needs. The Korn shell allows you to redirect any of the commands you call, just as the Bourne shell does. You can redirect standard output with the symbol > or the symbol `1>`, and you can redirect standard error with the symbol 2>. Both the Bourne and Korn shells allow you to open files using the `exec` built-in and redirect other file descriptors you may have written yourself. This is rarely necessary.

The token <& duplicates both input and output file descriptors. File descriptors may be duplicated by making <& refer to the same file another open file descriptor refers to, such as standard input or output. The following example redirects file descriptor `n` as a duplicate of file descriptor `n`:

```
n<&n
```

Once the file is opened, you can use it for input or output. I/O redirection on any command line is allowed. You can redirect standard output to a file descriptor with `>&n` or redirect standard input from a file descriptor with `<&n`. You can also use the `read` and `print` built-ins. Other commands, including functions, also use the open files and descriptors. You can close a file with this command:

```
exec n<&-
```

Functions

The Korn shell accepts two formats for functions: The syntax for the first format is as follows:

```
<func_name>()
{
   commands
}
```

Here is the syntax for the second format:

```
func <func_name>
{
   commands
}
```

If aliases are included in the functions, they are expanded when the function is read, before it is executed. The `break` built-in inside a function can terminate its execution. The Korn `functions` built-in lists all of the defined functions.

There is no `setenv` built-in in the Korn shell, so the following example shows how to mimic it:

```
$ setenv()
{
   if [ $# -eq 2]; then
      eval $1="$2"
      export $1
   else
      echo "Usage: setenv NAME VALUE" >&2
   fi
}
```

The `sentenv` function displays a usage message if it does not find two arguments. If it does find two, it assigns the value of the second argument to the name of the first and then exports the first.

The `unfunction` built-in deletes a function definition as shown in this example:

```
unfunction <func_name>
```

All functions are stored in memory so that the Korn shell can make the most efficient use of them. The source for the function is loaded into memory each time a shell or subshell is started. The downside to this is, if you define too many functions, the memory is sluggish when you run your scripts. It is wise to use functions sparingly or to use the autoload built-in, which is available only in the Korn shell.

You can store functions in files and make them available to memory the first time they are called. The autoload built-in notifies the shell that a function is stored in a file. The autoload function executes usually at the beginning of a new shell. The shell does not load the function into memory but remembers the name. When a script calls for an autoload function, the Korn shell searches through the directories listed in FPATH for a file with the same name. It then loads the function into memory and leaves it there. Here is the syntax for autoload:

```
autoload <func_name>
```

Make certain that the function definition and the file you store it in have the same name. Confusion will arise if you store it in a different file.

Function Commands

The job control command under the Korn shell is similar to that of the C shell and Job shell. You can move commands between the foreground and background, suspend jobs temporarily, and produce a list of current jobs. The percent (%) sign references a job when followed by a job number or a string prefix.

The alias built-in in the Korn shell does not accept arguments as such. Use a shell function (as discussed earlier) with the alias command if you need to use an argument. This will disguise the argument. Here is the syntax for the alias built-in:

```
alias [-tx] [<name>[=command]]
```

The <*name*> argument is the name of the alias and <*command*> is the command line the alias is replaced with when it is called. If you want to track an alias, use the -t option. The -x option will export the alias. If you establish aliases in your .profile file, they will be available every time you log in.

The Korn shell has some built-in aliases that can be unset or redefined:

```
autoload='typeset -fu'
functions='typeset -f'
history='fc -l'
integer='typeset -i'
local=typeset
r='fc -e -'
stop='kill -STOP'
suspend='kill -STOP $$'
```

The `kill` built-in sends a termination signal to a process or job. It sends the number 15 signal (termination) as mentioned in Chapter 18. The signals are the same for all three shells. The following two examples give the syntax for the `kill` built-in:

```
[$ kill <signal> PID
$ kill -TERM %1
```

Either line will terminate a process. Remember that when you kill a process, unfinished work may be left in temporary files or permissions may be changed. A well-written program will detect and trap the arrival of signals and will clean up the tasks before exiting. Well-written applications trap the `INT`, `QUIT`, and `TERM` signals. Try `INT` with Ctrl+C. If the `INT` signal is ignored, then use `KILL` because it cannot be trapped or ignored.

The Korn shell has a `whence` built-in that tells you the absolute path name of a utility. The following shows its usage:

```
$ whence grep
/bin/grep
```

The `whence` command reports only the path names of utilities that have a path name but does not give you correct information about aliases, functions, or built-ins. If you use the `-v` option, it will report the type of commands or reserved words that you can use in the Korn shell. It supplies more descriptive and accurate information than `whence` alone. The `whence` built-in serves the same function as the `type` built-in in the Bourne and Korn shells.

The `trap` built-in executes a command when it receives an error or signal or upon exiting from a script or function. The syntax for `trap` is as follows:

```
trap '<command>' event
```

The command must be quoted because it must be passed to `trap` as a single argument. The event arguments are names of signals (`INT`, `TERM`) or signal numbers. This list that follows includes event arguments other than the ones mentioned in the example:

DEBUG Occurs after every simple command. Causes your script to append the line number and the path name of the working directory to `/temp/dir_trace`.

ERR Occurs if a command exits with a nonzero status. Causes your script to execute cleanup and then exit with a status of 1.

HUP, INT Occurs when the signal (or SIG) is received.

EXIT or 0 Occurs whenever the script exits.

As discussed in Chapter 18, you will speed up your script writing by becoming familiar with the Korn shell's collection of built-ins. The unique built-ins will help you solve problems not easily remedied in the other shells.

Command-Line Editing

If you make a mistake on the current command line, the Korn shell allows you to edit the line or press the line kill key (Ctrl+K) and begin again. You can use one of the command-line editors to modify the command line. It is also possible to access and edit previous command lines stored in the history file. The Korn shell has two command-line editors. One is similar to vi and the other is similar to emacs. If you are not certain whether your Korn shell employs one or both of these, editors use one of the following four commands to check:

```
$ <visual>=vi
$ set -o vi
$ <visual>=emacs
$ set -0 emacs
```

Using *vi* in the Korn Shell

You are in the Input mode when you type commands using `vi` as your command-line editor. If the visual variable is not set, the shell looks at the `<editor>` variable and selects an editor to use. Be sure to set the `<visual>` variable if you want to use `vi` in the Korn shell. If you discover an error in your command before you hit Return, you can switch to the `vi` Command mode by pressing the Esc key.

You can then use many of the `vi` commands to edit the command line. You can also edit previous command lines. Use the arrow keys to position the cursor if you are on a terminal that supports arrow keys. The `vi` editor's positioning commands like `h` and `l` (for letters) and `w` and `b` (for words) may be preceded by a repeat factor that moves the cursor at a specified rate. (For example, `5w` will move the cursor forward 5 words, and `50w` will move it forward 50 words. You can specify exactly how many by putting a number before the `w`.) You can use the search forward or search backward commands. Use the `x` to delete characters or the `r` to replace them. The ~ will change case and `.` will repeat the last change. You will execute the command when you press Return. This will take effect even if you are in the middle of the command line.

When you want to edit the command line by using the full power of `vi`, press Esc and type **v**. The Korn shell will call the `vi` editor, but it won't be the Korn shell's command-line `vi`; it will be the full editor as described in the preceding paragraphs. When you exit with ZZ after editing with `vi`, the Korn shell will execute the commands you edited. In this way, you can create multiple lines of commands.

While in Command mode, you can also use several commands not found in the stand-alone `vi` editor. You have to set up your environment first (`$ <visual>=vi`) and then you can use path-name listing, path-name completion, and path-name expansion facilities to manipulate filenames.

To find a path name listing, enter Command mode and type an equal sign (=). The vi editor will respond by listing all the path names matching the current word as if an * were appended to it. The following example shows how vi reacts if you have a directory called Music and you want to use cat to display one of its files but you can't remember the full name:

```
$ cat music/Bri
```

Before you press the Return key, you press the Esc key and then =. The vi command-line editor will list files and then re-echo the partial command. An example follows:

```
1) British Marching Band
2) Britney Spears
3) Brittany Travis and Company
```

The cursor is still on the *t* and you are in Command mode. Type **a** to append the name you are looking for.

The path-name completion facility will allow you to type a portion of a path name and vi will supply the rest. If you press the Esc key and follow it with a backslash (\), the portion of the path name that you have typed thus far may be unique enough to have vi finish it for you. If not, vi will finish it as far as it can until there are choices to be made. The vi editor will leave you in Input mode so that you can type more. When there is no further ambiguity, the shell will append a space and leave you in Input mode.

The path-name expansion facility is much like an interactive version of file generation. To summon path-name expansion, you type a pattern followed by pressing the Esc key and an asterisk (*). This will cause the pattern to be replaced by all path names that match. The following example demonstrates how this works:

```
$ cat music/Brit
```

Press Esc*.

```
$ cat music/BritneySpears
```

If no filenames match, your terminal will flash or beep.

If Britney Spears and Brittany Travis spelled their first names alike, then path-name expansion would have listed them both. After filling in the filenames, vi will leave you in Input mode. You can continue editing or press the Return key to execute the command.

When editing, you may use the arrow keys to move about. Arrow keys work no matter which mode you are in. Table 19.8 shows the keystroke commands supported by the Korn shell.

TABLE 19.8: THE vi COMMANDS SUPPORTED BY THE KORN SHELL

Cursor Movement Commands	Action
h	Moves the cursor one character to the left
l or spacebar	Moves the cursor one character to the right
w	Moves the cursor one word to the right
b	Moves the cursor one word to the left
W	Moves the cursor one space-delimited word to the right
B	Moves the cursor one space-delimited word to the left
0	Moves the cursor to beginning of line
$	Moves the cursor to end of line
e	Moves the cursor to end of word
E	Moves the cursor to end of space-delimited word
^	Moves the cursor to first nonblank position on line
f*x*	Moves the cursor to next occurrence of *x* (to the right)
F*x*	Moves the cursor to previous occurrence of *x* (to the left)
:	Repeats last f or F command
,	Repeats last f or F command in opposite direction
*n*l	Moves the cursor to column *n*
Text Editing Commands	**Action**
i	Causes text editor to enter Insert mode before current character
a	Causes text editor to enter Insert mode after current character
I	Causes text editor to enter Insert mode before first nonblank character
A	Causes text editor to enter Insert mode at end of line
r*x*	Replaces current character with *x*
R	Overwrites text, starting at current character, until Esc is pressed
*n*x	Deletes *n* characters, starting at current character
*n*X	Deletes *n* characters, starting just past current character
D	Deletes from current character to end of line
dd	Deletes entire command
C	Moves the cursor from current character to end of line

Continued

TABLE 19.8: THE vi COMMANDS SUPPORTED BY THE KORN SHELL (CONTINUED)

History Editing Commands	Action
j	Moves cursor forward one command in the history list of commands
k	Moves cursor backward one command in the history lists of commands
/<*string*>+Return	Searches backward for a command with a string
?<*string*>+Return	Searches forward for a command with a string
n	Repeats previous search
N	Repeats previous search in opposite direction
*n*v	Enters full-screen vi to edit command number *n*
#	Inserts current command as a comment in history file
Miscellaneous Commands	**Action**
Escape+=	Lists path names that match current word
Escape+\	Completes current word to a partial or unique path name
Escape+*	Expands current word to all matching path names
u	Undoes previous change
~	Changes case of character
n.	Repeats *n* times the most recent command that caused change

TIP Pressing the Return key will execute the command no matter where you are on the command line or what mode you are in. The prompt that appears after the command is executed will put you back in Input mode.

Using *emacs* in the Korn Shell

The Korn shell also offers the emacs editor, which does not depend on modes. When you use the emacs editor, you will not switch between Command mode and Input mode; you'll move around the command line to modify text. The emacs editor provides a command history as well as path-name listing, path-name completion, and path-name expansion, as vi does. Control characters are widely used in emacs, which dispenses the need for switching between modes.

The Korn shell emacs differs somewhat from emacs in other shells. Cursor movement is performed by using both Ctrl and Esc commands. For example, to move the cursor one character forward, press Ctrl+F; to move it one character backward, press Ctrl+B. You can precede these movements with counts, just as you can in vi. You must, however, press the Esc key first, then follow it with a number. If you type the numbers first without pressing Esc, the numbers will appear on the command line.

You can also perform word motions and line motions in emacs. Press Esc+B to move backward one word, and press Esc+f to move forward one word. To move several words, count them and press Esc and then enter the number that corresponds to the number of words you want to move. If you want to get to the beginning of the line, press Ctrl+A. To get to the end of the line, press Ctrl+E. To reach the next instance of the character *c*, press Ctrl+XC and then Ctrl+F followed by the *c*.

Adding text to the command line is simple. Just move the cursor to the correct place and type. Deleting is just as simple. Move the cursor to the right of the characters you want to delete and press the Delete key once for each character. The line kill character is used to delete the entire command line. Delete from the cursor to the end of the line by using Ctrl+K.

TIP The emacs path name commands are the same as those in vi except that you type **escape escape** for path-name completion.

History Files

The Korn shell stores a history of executed commands in a file. You can use this file from one session to the next to edit and reexecute any command line in it. This is very helpful if you write scripts or programs that are similar in content and capabilities. Many times, portions or modules of the program will be exactly the same with only different paragraphs here and there. Often different modules may be used for completely different programs. You can save a lot of time by referring to the history files. The Korn shell history records multiline commands completely and allows you to edit them. The Korn shell also stores two variables that can be used to track the size and the place where the history file is stored.

The *<HISTSIZE>* variable determines the number of commands in a history list. The *<HISTFILE>* variable saves commands and, when *<HISTFILE>* is invoked, allows the Korn shell to read the commands back in when the system is later restarted. They become part of the history for the current session. When you want to access any of the commands in the history file, you can do so with `vi`, `emacs`, or the `fc` built-in.

If you are using the `vi` command-line editor in Command mode (don't forget to press the Esc key first), you can access previous commands. The `vi` commands move the cursor up and down just as though you were editing a copy of the history file. When you press the `k` command to move up one line, you will access the previous command. You would use the `j` command to get back to the original line. You can string search while in the Command mode by pressing the ? key followed by a string. The shell will look through your history list for the most recent command containing that string. You can move ahead to string search by using the forward slash (/). The use of the caret (^) will force the Korn shell to locate only those commands that start with the search string. To repeat the search for the next string occurrence, use the `n`. Event numbers are also available in the history list. If you are in the Command mode, enter the event number followed by a G to go to that numbered event. Because you are in the Command mode, you can edit the command or execute it with a Return.

The *<HISTFILE>* and *<HISTSIZE>* variables work the same way in `emacs` as in `vi`. access and edit any of the commands in the history file, you can use the `emacs` command-line editor, the `vi` command-line editor, or the `fc` built-in when in the Korn shell.

The Korn shell fix command (`fc`) allows you to display the history file for editing and reexecuting previous commands. Although unique to `ksh`, it provides many of the command-line editing features `vi` and `emacs` provide. When used with the `-l` option, `fc` displays the commands from the history file on standard output. If no argument is used, the 16 most recent commands will be displayed in a numbered list. The Korn shell creates an alias called `history` for the `fc -l` command. This can be used to display the history list. The oldest events will be at the top but you can reverse the order by using the `-r` option.

The `fc` built-in has several features that you will find useful in editing commands. It can take zero, one, or two arguments with the `-l` option. The following example displays the syntax:

```
fc -l [<firstarg>[<lastarg>]]
```

Using this command will call a list beginning with the most recent event matching the first argument. You can use the event number, the first few characters of the command, or a negative number. If there is no second argument, `fc` will display the command line from the first through the most recent event. If you use two arguments, `fc` will display all commands from the most recent event that matches the first argument through the most recent event that matches the second argument.

TIP If you call `fc` with the `-e` option followed by the name of one of the editors, `fc` calls the editor with an event in the work buffer. If there are no arguments, `fc` defaults to the most recent event. If there is an argument, `fc` will start the editor with an event number. If you leave anything in the editor work buffer, it will get executed when you exit from the editor unless you delete it first!

You can re-execute previous commands without going into an editor. Call `fc` with the `-e` option and an argument of `-`. The `fc` will skip the editing phase and re-execute the command. The following example shows the syntax for that command:

```
$ fc -e -
```

Processing Commands

The Korn shell will recognize commands that cover more than one line. In an interactive session, the shell will prompt you with the PS2 prompt after it sees the first line of a multiline command. The default value of PS2 is the same one you see in the Bourne shell.

The Korn shell carries out several steps when processing a command. The order in which the steps are carried out affects the way your commands are carried out. The shell will evaluate your commands and carry out the execution in its logical order. The basic order for command execution is as follows:

1. Token splitting. The stream of input characters are divided into words and I/O redirection is recognized.
2. Alias substitution. Aliases are recognized and expanded.
3. Filename expansion. Words that begin with a hyphen are replaced with expanded values.
4. Parameter expansion. Variable expressions that are not quoted are expanded.
5. Command substitution. Commands inside back quotes or brackets are evaluated.
6. Arithmetic expansion. Arithmetic expressions are replaced with values.
7. Filename generation. Path names that contain filename-matching patterns are replaced with expanded lists of path names.
8. Removal of quotation mark. Most quotation marks from the command-line processing are removed.

9. I/O redirection. Standard input, output, error, and file descriptors are redirected.
10. Command execution. The resulting command line is executed.

The Korn shell also supports the following redirection operators:

`>|filename` Forces standard output to filename, even if the file exists

`<&n` Duplicates standard input from file descriptor *n*

`>&n` Duplicates standard output from file descriptor *n*

`[n]<&-` Closes standard input or file descriptor *n* when specified

`[n]>&-` Closes standard output or file descriptor *n* when specified

`[n]<&p` Transfers the input from the coprocess to standard input or file descriptor *n* if specified

`[n]>&p` Transfers the output to the coprocess to standard output or file descriptor *n* if specified

The following rules must be observed when you program multiline code in the Korn shell:

- If you want the Korn shell to interpret compound commands in a different order than the order in which they appear, use parentheses when you write them.
- You must put variable assignments at the beginning of a command line.
- The first expansion is alias substitution where the shell determines whether the first token is an alias and replaces it if it is. An alias will not be replaced when it is being processed. This prevents infinite recursion.
- The Korn shell tilde (~) expansion feature replaces a ~ by itself with the name of your home directory and replaces a ~ followed by a user's login name with the name of that user's home directory.
- The Korn shell uses the `find` command to find files that are named `README` in the working directory.
- The Korn shell treats the `$ ( (` and `$ (` symbols as separate tokens. They are used to introduce an arithmetic expression, not a command substitution. You must have a space between the `$(` and the next `(` if you want a parenthesized subshell.
- The Korn shell treats any string within double quotation marks as a single command-line argument. Variables that are expanded within double quotation marks are still treated as part of a single argument.

- The Korn shell does not allow arithmetic expansion if the argument is enclosed within single quotation marks.
- If you have not set the noglob option, the Korn shell uses patterns to generate filenames for use as arguments to the command. If no filenames match the pattern, the shell displays an error message.
- The Korn shell removes all single and double quotation marks except for escaped quotation marks and ones that are the result of expanding variables.

Summary

In this chapter, you learned about the Korn shell, which is the largest and most commonly used shell for Sun Solaris. It has many additional features and expanded capabilities not found in the other shells. You learned how to write scripts using variables and Korn shell built-ins.

You also learned how to configure startup files to modify the way the Korn shell behaves, and how the Korn shell allows the use of variables in expressions, provides for variable expansion, and can assign variables to arrays. The use of control structures was discussed along with the fact that you can embed programming logic in Korn shell scripts. Processing always proceeds according to a set of rules based on the syntax of programming statements. Using symbols such as parentheses, you can affect the order in which elements of a statement are processed. You learned that the Korn shell uses special characters such as ?, *, and [ ] as placeholders in expressions and that the shell performs assignments and evaluations of different types of mathematical expressions.

The Korn shell command for input is `read` and the output command is `print`; using those commands, you can redirect input and output. Korn shell command-line editing may be done using the `vi` and `emacs` editors.

The Korn shell stores a history of executed commands in a file. You can use this file from one session to the next to edit and re-execute any command line in the history file from the `vi` command line, the `emacs` command line, or the `fc` built-in.

The Korn shell will recognize commands that cover more than one line. The rules for processing multiline commands were covered.

CHAPTER 20

The C Shell

FEATURING:

Starting in the C shell 762

The `history` *built-in* 764

The `alias` *built-in* 766

Command-line expansion 767

Directory stacks 768

Variables: types, substitution, and structure 771

Creating scripts 777

The C shell has special meaning for Solaris 8 because the operating system (kernel) is written mostly in the C programming language and is emulated by the shell. It is also a command interpreter. Written by Bill Joy of the University of California, Berkeley, for Unix, the C shell has its own syntax that is quite different from the syntax of either the Bourne or Korn shell. It comes with Solaris 8 and provides a useful interface with the kernel or core program. It is accessed by `csh`. It has some useful features, such as command history, which stores the most recent commands you have given so you may reuse them. It also has command editing for changing commands as necessary. You can run it simultaneously with the other shells showing in different windows. The `alias` feature lets you assign short names for frequently used commands or sequences of commands. While sharing some of the features of both the Bourne and Korn shells, the C shell has other features uniquely its own.

The C shell can be customized to make it easier to use. You can set shell variables so the shell will warn you of impending errors or file write-overs. Using spaces on either side of the equal sign in commands is optional. You will be able to write scripts in a comfortable, and perhaps familiar, environment. Lowercase letters are used in the C shell to name variables by accepted conventions. This chapter will cover most of the primary features of the C shell.

Starting in the C Shell

To enter the C shell from the command line, give the command `csh`. You can use the `ps` utility to find out which shell you are in if you are not certain. It will show whether you are using `csh`, `ksh`, or `sh`. Chapter 17, "Understanding Shells," included an explanation of how to change shells as needed. If you prefer to change your login shell to the C shell, you can change it in `/etc/passwd`. Briefly, if you start from another shell, you can change to the C shell by typing `csh` and pressing the Return key. The default C shell prompt is the system name followed by a percent (%) sign.

TIP When you invoke another shell, the original shell does not terminate. It is there in the background. When you exit the current shell, you will be returned to the shell under which you logged in. It is possible to have several shells running without being aware of it. You can change this by running `exec csh`, which will terminate the current shell and replace it with the new one.

A login directly to the C shell causes an automatic execution of several files. The first file is the system file, `/etc/.login`, which contains systemwide configuration information such as the default path. The `/etc/.login` file tests to see if the term variable is set, and if not, it sets it. Also, it tests for the `.hushlogin` file, and if that does not exist, it runs the mail app to see if you have mail. After executing these files, `csh` reads and executes commands from the files in your home directory. These files are as follows:

`.cshrc` When a `csh` process begins running, it executes this file from your home directory. Use the `.cshrc` file to establish variables and parameters that are local to a specific shell. Every time you create a new shell, `csh` reinitializes these same variables for the new shell. The following example demonstrates how to set variables with `.cshrc`:

```
% cat ~/.cshrc
set noclobber
set ignoreeof
set history=250
set path = (~/bin/ $path /usr/vids)
```

`.history` If you are running `csh` as your login shell, after processing `.cshrc`, `csh` will rebuild the history list from the contents of the `.history` file in your home directory, providing it exists.

`.login` If you are running `csh` as a login shell, it will read and execute the commands in `.login` in your home directory. This file should contain the commands you want to execute only once, at the beginning of each session. You can declare environment variables with the `setenv`. The syntax is `setenv` `<variable> value`, then press Return.

`.logout` The C shell runs this file in your home directory when you exit from the login shell, but it is not required. The following example demonstrates a typical `.logout` message:

```
% cat ~/.logout
date `+logout on %A %B %d at %I:%M %p`
sleep 4
```

The `sleep` command gives `echo` enough time to display the message before the system logs you out.

PART III Working with Shells in Solaris

TIP If you try to use your Backspace or Delete key and you see characters appear on the screen when you mean to erase them, you can fix it by typing **`stty erase`** followed by Ctrl+V and the key you want to use for erasing and then pressing Return.

The *history* Built-In in the C Shell

One of the best features of the C shell is the ability to maintain a complete history of command lines in your program. The C shell `history` built-in displays your history list of commands or events. The built-in also provides an abbreviated form of your recent commands, which enables you to execute or reuse their arguments. You can also make minor variations to your previous commands and use them again. The `history` built-in provides you with a reference of the series of complicated commands, which can be replicated or changed slightly. The built-in works by saving the most recently used commands in the `~/.history` file (if `savehist` has been set) and initializing the file when you restart the shell. The C shell will then assign an event number to each command line in sequential order. These numbers can be displayed as part of the `csh` prompt, and you can use them to easily track commands. For example, if you want to see the first 50 lines of your source code, you can use the `set` command with `history` as in the following example:

```
% set history = 50
```

This command will save the first 50 lines of commands, even through more than one login if `savehist` has been set, as shown here:

```
% set savehist = 50
```

You would then use `% set savehist = 50` and could log in and out several times. The 50 most recent events from these sessions would be found in your history file. To keep them in your event list indefinitely, set them in your `.cshrc` file. The oldest event will be at the top of the list and the most recent at the bottom, just before the `history` command. When your history list becomes too long and unwieldy, you can use a pipe to send output through `pg` or you can reduce it by changing the number 50 to something more manageable, perhaps 10 or 20.

TIP It is a good idea to keep the history list of commands below the 100 count to keep the list manageable and to keep it from slowing down the shell as it tries to start.

You can edit commands from the history list by using this syntax:

`s/`*<oldcommand>*`/`*<newcommand>*`/`

It is easy to re-execute any event in the list by using an exclamation point (!) before it to let the shell know that you want to re-execute it. You will save a lot of time by using this list over and over. Reference the event by either its event number or its number relative to the current event or by the text it contains preceded by an `!`. If you want to re-execute just the previous event, use two exclamation points (`!!`). The C shell will display the command it is re-executing. You can repeat the last word in the previous command in a C shell by typing `!$` and then pressing the Return key.

You will get an error message if the number is not on the event list. If you remember that it is four events before the current event, you can use a negative number (`!-4`) and the event will be re-executed. Also, you can follow the exclamation point with a string of text. The C shell will look for that string in the list of events and execute the event that begins with a matching string.

You can select any word from an event. You can also select one from a previous event. Because the words are numbered starting with 0 as the first word on the line and 1 as the first word after the command, you can count words to *n*, which would be the last word. To specify the exact word, use the `!n` with a colon and the number of the word in the previous event. Here is the syntax:

```
% !12:7
```

You can also use a hyphen to specify a range of words:

```
% !12:0-4
```

If you want to modify a previous event before re-executing it, you can add a colon and a modifier after the event or word that you want to modify, as in this example:

```
%  cat /busyness/dept/number/locker
file not found
% !!:s/busyness/business
cat /business/dept/number/locker
```

You can also do a quick substitution by using the caret symbol. It allows you to change some of the event text before re-executing the event:

```
% ^busyness^business
```

The C shell will display the command line after the substitution just as any other command-line substitutions appear.

If you want to change some aspect of an event you are re-executing, you can modify it by following the event or word specifier with a colon and a modifier. The following syntax shows how:

```
% !!:s/bird/dog
```

Table 20.1 shows event modifiers and explains how they might be used.

TABLE 20.1: EVENT MODIFIERS IN THE C SHELL

Event Modifier	Explanation
e	Extension remover, removes all but the filename
gs/<*old*>/<*new*>	Globally substitutes <*new*> for the first occurrence of <*old*>
h	Head, removes the last word of a path name
p	Prints the modified event but does not execute it
r	Root, removes the filename extension
t	Tail, removes all elements of a path name except the last

TIP The s modifier substitutes the first occurrence of the old string with the new one. If you place a g before the s, a global substitution takes place and all occurrences of the old string will be replaced with the new one.

The C Shell *alias* Built-In

You can define new commands in the C shell by substituting any string for any command with the alias built-in. It is the same as in the Korn shell. The syntax for the alias built-in is as follows:

```
alias [<name>[<value>]]
```

Quotation marks must be used if <*value*> must contain spaces or tabs. You must be careful to not place the name of the alias either within the value or in the value of another alias.

The alias built-in is a powerful tool, but care must be taken with its conventions. The use of single and double quotes should be handled with caution. If value is enclosed in double quotes, then any other variables in <value> are expanded when you create the alias. If you use single quotes around <value>, then variables are not expanded until you use the alias. You should experiment with both sets of quotation marks and observe what happens to your variables when they are employed. Both the alias and history built-ins work hand in hand. You can substitute arguments on the command line with the history built-in and by using a single exclamation point to represent the input line containing the alias. The same modifiers are used by both the history and alias built-ins. To avoid incorrect results, you should quote the exclamation points so the shell does not mistakenly interpret them.

You can create short names for often used commands. This saves a lot of time when you're programming scripts that use the same types of commands repeatedly. Numbers are allowed as aliases. If an alias is not defined, it will report nothing. If you give the alias built-in without arguments, you will get a list of all the defined aliases.

You can protect yourself from making mistakes when deleting files by using the alias mechanism. In the following example, the interactive version of rm is replaced by the command rid. The -i option causes rm to query you on each file to be deleted so that you do not accidentally delete the wrong files:

```
% alias rid 'rm -i'
% rid t*
rm: remove 'timetable.trn'? n
rm: remove 'tina.txt'? n
rm: remove 'tipa.mem'? n
```

An alias can be removed with the unalias built-in. Here is the syntax for the unalias built-in:

```
% unalias rid
```

The C Shell and Command-Line Expansion

Unlike the history and alias built-in expansions, which are available only in interactive shells such as the C shell, command-line expansion is available in shell scripts. When the shell looks at a command, it first parses the command into tokens or words. It then scans each token for special characters and patterns, which might instruct the shell to take certain actions. Before executing the command, the shell will perform expansion on the tokens wherever necessary. Ambiguous characters such as [ ], *, and ? may end up with an actual filename.

Brace expansion is used to specify filenames and can be used to generate arbitrary strings as well. Comma-separated strings enclosed in braces { } are usually prepended with an optional identifier and appended with an optional string. Left-to-right order is preserved. Brace expansions may be nested. You can create directories with related names using brace expansion with no spaces between the braces and words. A simple example of brace expansion follows:

```
% echo chap_{ten,eleven,twelve}.txt
chap_ten.txt chap_eleven.txt chap_twelve.txt
```

Tilde (~) expansion occurs when the shell finds a token that begins with one as a special character. The shell then looks at a string of characters up to the first / or to the end of the word when there is no /. It determines whether it is a login name or not. If not, the shell substitutes (expands) the value of the variable for the tilde. The following example shows how this occurs:

```
% echo $POSTBOX
/postbox/barrie
% echo ~
/postbox/barrie
% echo ~/mail
/postbox/barrie/mail
% cp ~/mail .
```

If a string of characters forms a login name, the path of the home directory associated with that login name will be substituted for the tilde and name. If it is not null nor a valid login, no substitution will be made:

```
% echo $HOME
/home/username
% echo ~
/home/username
% echo ~/memo
/home/username/memo
% cp ~/memo .
```

TIP **Parameter expansion, variable expansion, and `cmd` command substitution are the same in the C shell as they are in the Bourne and Korn shells.**

Job control in the C shell is much the same as it is in the other shells. There is a minor difference between `jsh` and `csh` when a multiple-process command line is run in the background. The C shell displays all the numbers for processes, whereas `jsh` displays the PID number of the last job in the background.

Directory Stacks

The C shell allows you to store a list of working directories for easy access. This is commonly referred to as a *stack*. A `dirs` built-in is used to display the directory stack. Figure 20.1 shows a typical directory structure. You can change directories, add new directories, and remove directories with the help of some additional built-ins. Picture your directories as you would a stack of CDs. The structure of the stack can be changed many times while you move directories to the top or bottom or push them into the middle. Figure 20.2 shows the structure of the stacks. The syntax for the `dirs` built-in is as follows (a tilde is used to represent your home directory):

```
46 % dirs
~/music
```

FIGURE 20.1

Typical directory structure for `dirs` built-in

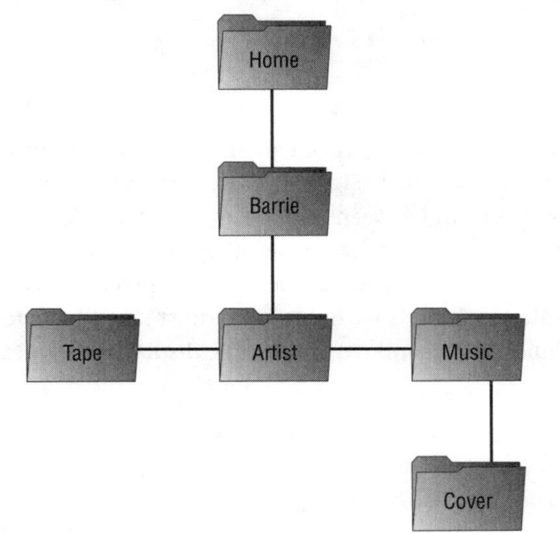

FIGURE 20.2

The directory stack

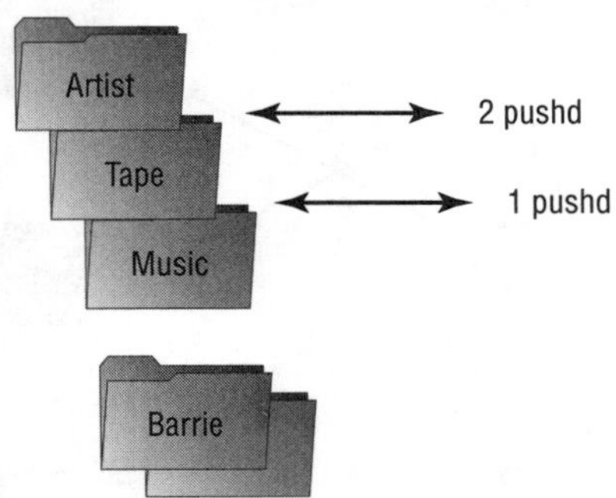

The pushd built-in allows you to add a new directory to the top of the stack while changing directories. Just as the dirs built-in does, pushd will display a list of the contents. The following example demonstrates the pushd built-in:

```
23 % pushd  ~/tape
~/tape ~/music
24 % pwd
/home/barrie/tape
25 % pushd ~/artist
~/artist/ ~/tape ~/music
26 % pwd
/home/barrie/artist
```

If you use pushd without an argument, it will swap the top two directories, making the second one first (Figure 20.3 illustrates the pushd command). You can then move back and forth between directories, using one for the working directory whenever necessary. If you need to access another directory in the stack, you can use a numeric argument with pushd. The number must be preceded by a + sign. Because the name of the top directory starts with zero, you must take that into account when calling a directory by number. The following example displays the syntax for numbered directories:

```
27 > pushd +2
-/music -/artist -/tape
28 > pwd
/home/barrie/music
```

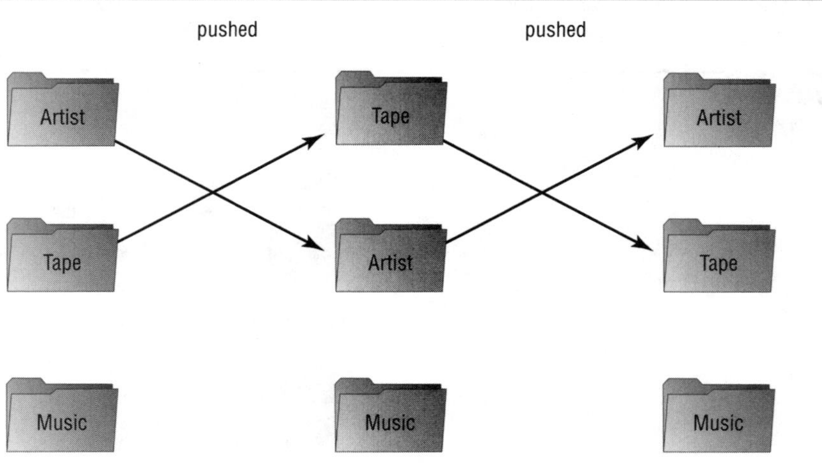

FIGURE 20.3

Changing working directories with the pushd *command*

If you want to remove a directory from the stack, you can use the popd built-in provided by the C shell. If popd is used without an argument, it will remove the top directory from the stack. The working directory would then become the top directory. Figure 20.4 illustrates how popd removes a directory from the stack. If you want to remove a directory from somewhere else in the stack, you can use a numeric argument, just as you did with pushd. Keep in mind that the top directory is always zero, so begin counting with 0 and precede the number with a + sign as in the following example:

```
% popd +1
~/music ~/tape
% pwd
/home/barrie/music
```

FIGURE 20.4

Removing a directory from the stack with the popd *command*

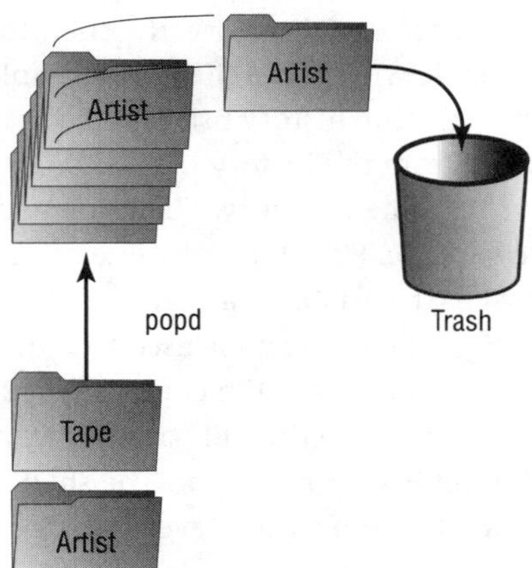

The use of these built-ins will aide you in manipulating your directory stacks with ease. You will save time by getting accustomed to their use.

C Shell Variables

The C shell sets some variables, retains some that are inherent in the environment, and uses some that are set by the user. Most of the variables listed in this section belong uniquely to the C shell, though a few may be used by other shells. Some shell variables have significant values such as the PID number. Some shell variables act as on switches when declared and off switches when not declared. Most can be set within the shell's `.login` or `.cshrc` startup files.

Several shell variables are available for working with arrays. The `argv` array variable contains positional parameters from the command that initiated the shell. Because this array's index starts at 1, the `argv[1]` variable contains the first command-line argument. Any element of this array can be changed. You can use `argv[*]` to refer to all the arguments. If you want to abbreviate references, use `$*` and `$n`. Reference the name of the calling program with `$0`.

The shell uses the `$#argv` to set the number of elements in the `argv` array. The `cdpath` variable takes on an array of absolute path names after being set in the `.login` file. If you call `cd` with a filename, it will search the working directory for a subdirectory. If the subdirectory of that name is not found, `cd` goes on to search `cdpath` for the file.

The C shell sets the variable `cwd` to the name of the working directory. If you use a symbolic link to access a directory, the shell sets `cwd` to the name of the symbolic link. The `filec` variable will enable filename completion when set. The `history` variable controls the size of the history list. The `savehist` specifies the number of commands you want saved from the history list. These are events that are saved in a file named `.history` in the home directory. The home local variable is initialized by the environmental `HOME` variable. `HOME` has the value of the path name of the user's home directory. The local `path` variable is an array set by the C shell. The `PATH` environmental variable is part of the shell and is used to initialize the `path` local variable. The shell will search the directories in the `path` array for executable commands. If <PATH> is unset, then you must use the full path name to execute commands. The `prompt` variable when not set is `%`, or `#` for root. The shell will expand an exclamation point in the prompt string to the current event number. Here is the syntax for setting the value of `prompt`:

```
set prompt = ' ! % '
```

The `shell` variable contains the path name of the shell you are currently using, and the `status` variable contains the exit status returned by the last command.

The `time` variable has two distinct functions: first, it automatically times commands that use the `time` built-in. Second, it sets the format used by <time>. The first is the automatic timing of commands that use the `time` built-in. And the second is the format used by `time`. The variable can be set to a single numeric value or an array holding a numeric value and a string. The numeric values control automatic timing. The string is used to control the formatting of statistics. Special formatting sequences are listed in Table 20.2.

TABLE 20.2: C SHELL TIME VARIABLE FORMATTING SEQUENCES

Sequence	Result
%U	Time spent by the command running user code, by CPU seconds in the user mode
%S	Time spent by the command running system code, by CPU seconds in the kernel mode
%E	Elapsed wall clock time
%P	Percent of CPU time spent
%D	Average data memory used in kilobytes
%F	Major faults per pay of memory
%I	Number of input operations
%O	Number of output operations
%K	Total memory used in kilobytes
%W	Number of times processes were swapped to disk
%X	Average amount of shared code memory in kilobytes

Time commands can be used when you want to monitor system performance. Page faults and swaps can indicate memory deficiencies and the time reports can be used for comparisons of performance. It is a handy diagnostic tool! The following example shows how the `time` built-in generates output. The default string is `"%Uu %Ss %E %P% %X+%DK`, which produces the following output:

```
% time
0.0u 1.0s 3:32:52 0% 0+0k 0+0io 0pf+0w
```

The user variable is set to your login name. The $ contains the PID number, just as it does in the Bourne and Korn shells.

Environmental Variables, Variables and Substitution

The C shell allows you to work with string variables as numeric expressions. A special character `@` built-in tells the shell to evaluate arithmetic expressions yet works only with integers. A numeric value is a string variable that contains a number that the shell sees as a logical or arithmetic computation, but it is not a true numeric value. The `@` built-in allows letters, digits, and even underscores in the value or in its name. The first character, however, cannot be a digit. To substitute variables, the C shell employs the `set`, `@`, and `setenv` built-ins. Both the `set` and `setenv` built-ins allow numeric strings but treat them as text strings, and the @ built-in works with numeric variables. The C shell recognizes the $ as a variable when it precedes a word but will not substitute if the $ is preceded by a \. If, however, you put a variable within double quotation marks, a substitution will occur even with a quoted dollar sign.

TIP Using the `setenv` built-in is similar to using the `export` built-in in the Bourne shell. It assigns a value to a variable and places it in the calling environment of the child processes.

Once the C shell identifies the value of a variable, it substitutes the value when it finds the variable on a command line or in a script.

String Variables

The C shell declares and assigns string variables somewhat differently than the Bourne or Korn shell does. String variables in the C shell are set by the `set` or `setenv` built-in. Unlike the other shells, the C shell allows space around the equal signs (=). The following example displays the use of the `set` built-in:

```
% set file = Tanya
% echo $file
Tanya
% set
argv            ( )
cwd             /home/barrie
file            Tanya
path            (/usr/bin)
prompt          %
shell           /bin/csh
status          0
term            vx400
user            barrie
```

The variable `file` is declared on the first line. It is then displayed on the second line. The `set` command, without arguments, displays a list of the shell's local variables and their values. If you give a `set` command and the name of a variable that has no value, the variable will assume a null string. You can use the `unset` built-in to remove a declared variable in the same way. The `setenv` built-in separates the variable name from the string by one or more spaces and does not use an equal sign (=).

Numeric Variables

In the C shell, the @ built-in assigns a value to a numeric variable. The @ built-in and the set built-in are used similarly, although the @ built-in must have a numeric argument. Use of the @ command without arguments produces a list of all shell variables, just as the set command does.

TIP If you give a nonnumeric value to the @ built-in, you will get an error message!

The @ built-in evaluates most of the operators found in the C programming language. Table 20.3 includes a list of expressions evaluated by the @ built-in.

TABLE 20.3: NUMERIC EXPRESSIONS

<table>
<tr><th>Expression</th><th>Function</th></tr>
<tr><td>+</td><td>Add</td></tr>
<tr><td>-</td><td>Subtract</td></tr>
<tr><td>*</td><td>Multiply</td></tr>
<tr><td>/</td><td>Divide</td></tr>
<tr><td>%</td><td>Remainder</td></tr>
<tr><td>( )</td><td>Change evaluation order</td></tr>
<tr><td>~</td><td>One's complement</td></tr>
<tr><td>!</td><td>Logical negation</td></tr>
<tr><td>++</td><td>Postfix increment</td></tr>
<tr><td>--</td><td>Postfix decrement</td></tr>
<tr><td>>></td><td>Shift right</td></tr>
<tr><td><<</td><td>Shift left</td></tr>
<tr><td>&&</td><td>Logical AND</td></tr>
<tr><td>||</td><td>Logical OR</td></tr>
<tr><td>&</td><td>AND</td></tr>
<tr><td>^</td><td>OR exclusive</td></tr>
<tr><td>|</td><td>OR inclusive</td></tr>
<tr><td>></td><td>Greater than</td></tr>
<tr><td><</td><td>Less than</td></tr>
<tr><td>>=</td><td>Greater than or equal to</td></tr>
<tr><td><=</td><td>Less than or equal to</td></tr>
<tr><td>!=</td><td>Not equal to, compare</td></tr>
<tr><td>==</td><td>Equal to, compare</td></tr>
</table>

There are some simple rules in the use of expressions. The C shell will evaluate a missing argument as 0. All results will be decimal numbers. Each element of an expression must be separated from others with a space with the exception of &, (or), < or >, and |. Operators act on numeric arguments except for != and ==. The postfix increment (++) and decrement (--) can be used only in an expression that contains a single variable name.

Numeric Arrays

The `set` built-in is used to declare an array of numeric variables before using the `@` command to assign values. When you're working with arrays, you can use the `set` built-in to assign values to their elements as simply as you can assign a value to a single numeric value. You must, however, specify the element or index of the array. Here is the syntax:

```
@ <variable-name>[index]operator expression
```

The index must be either a numeric constant or a variable, not an expression. The first element has the index of 1.

If your specified index is too large for the array, you will get the error message `@: Subscript out of range`. Even though a numeric array behaves as simple numeric variables, you must use `set` to declare it. This brief example shows how to set the array:

```
% set speeds = (0 0 0 0 0)
% @ speeds[2] = 15
% @ speeds[3] = ($speeds[2] + 4)
% echo $speeds[3]
19
```

Switch Variables

The C shell has variables that act as switches with no significant values. A declared variable causes the shell to take action and an undeclared variable does not. The variables can be set in the `.cshrc` file, on a command line, or in a script. The `echo` variable can be set, or if you call `csh` with the `-x` option, `csh` sets the variable.

Once `echo` is declared, the shell will display each command before it executes them. The `ignoreeof` variable is a special tool that keeps you from exiting the shell accidentally with Ctrl+D. Once this variable is set, you must use `exit` or `logout` to exit the shell.

The `noclobber` variable is another safeguard that prevents you from accidentally overwriting a file when you redirect output, although you can still append to it. It will not let you create a file when you append output to a nonexistent file. If you want to override `noclobber`, you can append an exclamation point to the symbol used for redirecting the output (`>!` and `>>!`).

The `x>opfile` command redirects standard output from `x` to `opfile` and will overwrite a file called `opfile` if it exists, but only if you do not declare the `noclobber` variable. If you do declare the `noclobber` variable, the `x>opfile` command redirects standard output from process `x` to `opfile`. It will display an error message if `opfile` exists and it will not overwrite the file.

By the same token, if the `x>>opfile` command is given and not declared, it will redirect standard output from process `x` to `opfile`. It will append new output to the end of `opfile` if it exists, or it will create `opfile` if it does not. If the `x>>noclobber` is declared, it will redirect standard output from process `x` to `opfile` and append new output to the end if the file exists. The shell will give an error message if `opfile` does not exist and will not create the file.

The variable `noglob`, when declared, does not expand ambiguous filenames. It allows you to use *, ?, ~, and `[ ]` in a script or on the command line without quoting. The `nonomatch` variable, when set, causes the shell to pass an ambiguous reference that doesn't match a filename to the command being called. The C shell will not expand the file reference. If not set, `nonomatch` causes the shell to generate a `No match error` message and the command is not executed.

The `notify` variable, when set, causes the shell to send a message to your terminal letting you know that a background job has finished. Finally, the `verbose` variable is declared by the C shell when you call the shell with the `-v` option. You can also declare it by using the `set` command. The verbose argument will display each command after a history substitution.

Creating Scripts

Writing and executing scripts in the C shell is similar to the same activities in both the Bourne and Korn shells. The differences lie in the methods of declaring values and assigning them to variables. The syntax for this is as follows (unlike in `sh`, spaces on either side of the equal sign are optional in `csh`):

```
set <variable>=value
```

Many of the control structures have a different syntax. You can run scripts while using any one of the shells, but the first line must read `#!/bin/csh`. If the first character is anything other than `#`, `csh` will call `sh` to execute the script.

You should give yourself execution permission with the `chmod u+x` *<filename>* command. The script file can contain any commands that can be typed in. You can type in the filename as if it were a regular command. When a shell script is written, it creates a special array variable, argv, that contains the elements of its arguments.

Command-Line Shortcuts

The C shell provides some shortcuts by means of the keyboard. If you type the Esc key preceded by a partial command or filename, the C shell will attempt to complete the filename. However, if you have more than one filename that matches, the common letters are completed and the C shell will beep a signal. In the C shell, you need to run the command `set filec` to enable file-name completion. The Ctrl+W key will erase the previous word.

Variable Control Structures

The C shell uses most of the control structures found in the Bourne shell but the syntax is somewhat different. The effects, however, are the same. Refer to Chapter 18, "The Bourne Shell," and Chapter 19, "The Korn Shell," for more comprehensive descriptions of the control structures.

The syntax for the `if` control structure is as follows:

```
If (expression) simple-command
```

Because the `if` structure works only with simple commands, do not use lists of commands or pipes. Those require the `if…then` control structure to execute.

The goto built-in transfers control to the statement that begins with `label`. Here is an example of a goto statement:

```
$ cat goto_1
#!/bin/csh
#
# test for 2 args
#
if ($#argv == 2) goto myargs
echo "Usage: goto_1 arg1 arg2"
exit 1
myargs
```

The `if…then…else` control structure has three separate forms:

```
Form 1
if (expression) then
    commands
endif
Form 2
```

```
if (expression) then
    commands
else
    new-commands
endif
Form 3
if (expression) then
    commands
else if (expression) then
    new commands
    .
    .
    .
else
    more commands
endif
```

All three forms of the `if…then…else` control structure check to see if certain conditions return a true. If false, they move on to the next set of instructions and again look for true. If the true condition is encountered, then the appropriate commands are executed. If no true conditions exist, then the program exits.

The `foreach` built-in is similar to the `for…in` structure of the Bourne shell. The syntax is as follows:

```
foreach loop-index (<arguments>)
   <commands>
end
```

This `foreach` structure loops through the commands after assigning the value of the first argument to the loop index. Once the control is passed to the `end` statement, it goes back to the next argument and executes the commands until all arguments are exhausted.

The `while` built-in is a control structure that continues to loop through commands while the expression remains true. When it encounters a false expression, the structure does not execute the commands. Use this syntax for the `while` structure:

```
while (<expression>)
   <commands>
end
```

Both the `foreach` and `while` control structures may employ the use of the `break` and `continue` statements. These statements will execute the remaining commands on the command line before they transfer control. The break statement will pass control to the statement after the end statement, thereby terminating the execution of the loop. The continue statement passes control to the end statement, which continues the execution of the loop.

The switch control structure is similar to the case structure of the Bourne shell. The syntax for the switch structure is as follows:

```
switch (<string-test>)
    case pattern:
        commands
    break
    case pattern:
        commands
    break
    .
    .
    default:
        commands
    break
end
```

C Shell Built-Ins

Like the other shells, the C shell has a comprehensive list of built-in commands. If you give a filename as a command, the C shell will look to see if it is a built-in. If so, it will be executed as part of the calling process. A new process will not be forked to execute the built-in. It doesn't look in the directory structure because the program is available to the shell. When the filename is not a built-in, the shell must search the directory structure for your program. The shell will use PATH as a guide and will fork a new process to execute the program. All control structure keywords described in the preceding section are built-ins. Table 20.4 lists the built-ins included in the C shell.

TABLE 20.4: C SHELL BUILT-INS

Built-In	Purpose
%Job	Specifies the job number of the job you will bring into the foreground.
%Job&	Specifies the job number of the job you want to put into the background.
@	Evaluates numeric expressions, similar to set built-in.
alias	Creates aliases, same as in the Korn shell.

Continued

TABLE 20.4: C SHELL BUILT-INS (CONTINUED)

Built-In	Purpose
`bg`	Indicates background, moves jobs into background.
`cd/chdir`	Changes working directories.
`dirs`	Displays the directory stack.
`echo`	Displays its (`echo`'s) arguments.
`eval`	Evaluates the command line once before it is passed to the shell to evaluate.
`exec`	Permanently replaces the current program with a new one.
`exit`	Causes exit from the C shell.
`fg`	Moves a job to the foreground.
`glob`	Similar to `echo` but does not display spaces between arguments, no newline is used.
`hashstat`	Reports on `csh`'s hash mechanism.
`history`	Displays the history list of commands.
`jobs`	Identifies the current jobs or commands.
`kill`	Terminates a process or job.
`limit`	Limits resources that the current process can use, such as CPYU time.
`login`	Logs in the user.
`logout`	Ends a login session from the login shell.
`nice`	Lowers or raises the processing priority of a command or shell.
`nohup`	Allows logout while background processes are still running without terminating the processes. Jobs run in the background with & under `csh` are implicitly run with nohup.
`notify`	Sends notification from shell when job status changes.
`onintr`	Controls an interrupt action for scripts.
`popd`	Removes a directory from the stack.
`pushd`	Changes working directory and puts new directory at top of stack.
`rehash`	Re-creates internal tables used by hash mechanism.
`repeat`	Takes a count and simple command and repeats the command according to the count number.
`set`	Declares, initializes, and displays the values of local variables.
`setenv`	Declares and initializes the values of environmental variables.
`shift`	Promotes the indexes of the `argv` array or `with` argument on another array.

Continued

TABLE 20.4: C SHELL BUILT-INS (CONTINUED)

Built-In	Purpose
`source`	Executes the shell script given as argument, similar to the `.` built-in in Bourne.
`stop`	Stops jobs or processes running in background, accepts multiple arguments.
`suspend`	Stops the current shell, similar to Ctrl+Z.
`time`	Accepts arguments, then executes them for the current shell.
`umask`	Identifies or changes access permissions assigned to files.
`unalias`	Removes an alias.
`unhash`	Turns off the hash mechanism.
`unlimit`	Removes limits on the current process.
`unset`	Removes a variable declaration.
`unsetenv`	Removes an environmental variable declaration.
`wait`	Forces the shell to wait for child processes to terminate.

Most of the built-ins have been discussed in detail either in this chapter or in the chapters on the Bourne and Korn shells (Chapters 18 and 19, respectively). It is recommended that you experiment with each one until you're familiar with its operation and see what results it produces in different scripts.

The Rehash Command

The C shell generates an internal table of commands called the hash table, which is named with the `$PATH` variable. If you add a new command to the directory file, the shell does not execute it because it cannot be found. To tell the shell that you have added it to the path, use the `rehash` command (described in Table 20.4) and press Return. The new command will be incorporated into the command search path. The following example demonstrates this:

```
% <new-command>
"<new-command>:command not found"
% rehash
% <new-command>
```

Process Control

The C shell has several commands to help in controlling processes. A number of them actually start the process and several report on the status of jobs being run. They can be used with the `at` utility, which is found in all the shells.

Once a job has been successfully run, you will receive a status message similar to the following:

```
Commands will be executed using /usr/sbin/csh
Job 47180555.a at Fri Feb 23 10:13:43 2001
```

The following options may be used with the `at` command:

`-c` option Indicates that a command should run with `csh`

`-f <filename>` option Tells `at` to use the file and not standard input as the job

`-k` option Indicates that a command should run with `ksh`

`-l` option Lists all scheduled jobs

`-m` option Notifies the user's mail when job completes

`-q` option Lets you specify a queue to put the job in

`-r id` option Removes a job with the ID specified by `id`

`-s` option Indicates that the job should run with `sh`

`time` option Runs the job at time specified

The following arguments can also be used with the `at` command options and are allowed by the C shell:

`atq` argument When used with the `-c` option, will list jobs according to queue order, creation date, and time. If used with the `-n` option, will display the number of jobs in the queue.

`atrm` argument Removes jobs already in queue. If used with option `-a`, will remove all jobs from queue. If used with option `-f` (force), will suppress all informational messages, and if used with `-I`, will interactively inquire about each job before it is removed.

`job id` argument Reports job IDs when jobs are originally scheduled by the `at` command.

`jobs` argument When used with option `-l`, lists the process IDs of each job.

`kill` argument Terminates a process or sends special signals to processes. If used with the `-l` option, lists all signals. If `stat` has specified an exit status, the terminating signal will be displayed. If used with the `-s` signal option, specifies the signal to send to the process.

`nice` argument Runs a command with modified scheduling for better CPU usage. If used with the `-n` option, it sets priority to *n*, where *n* is 1 through 19; 1 is the highest priority, 19 the lowest, and the default is 10.

pgrep argument Reports PIDs that match a regular expression. If used with -d delimiter, it specifies the delimiter you should place between PIDs; the default is newline. If used with the -f option, it matches patterns against arguments rather than names. If used with the -g option, will process only in specified process groups. If used with the -G gids option, will process with real group IDs matching those in gids. If used with -l option, gives verbose output. If used with -n option, it will return on the most recent process that matches the pattern. If used with the -p ppids option, it only processes with the parent process IDs specified in ppids. If used with -s sids, shows processes with the specified session IDs. If used with -t terminals, shows only those processes associated with the specified terminal. If used with -u euids, only processes IDs matching those specified. If used with the -v option, inverts the matching pattern and shows only those that do not match. If used with the -x option, processes with executable names that match the one on the command line are reported. If used with the -signal option, specifies a signal to send to each process reported.

pkill argument Kills or terminates processes matching a specified pattern. If used with the -f option, matches patterns against the full process argument instead of the name. If used with the -g groups option, processes in the process groups specified by groups. If used with the -G gids option, only processes with real group IDs matching those in gids. If used with the -n option, returns only the most recent process matching the pattern. If used with the -ppids option, only processes with the parent process IDs specified by ppids are shown. If used with the -s sids option, only processes with the specified session IDs are shown. If used with the -t terminals option, only processes that show specified terminals are shown. If used with the -u euids, shows only processes with effective IDs matching those specified. If used with the -U uids option, only processes with user IDs matching those specified are shown. If used with the -v option, inverts the pattern matching and shows only those not matching. If used with the -x option, only processes with executable names matching the ones specified on the command line are shown. If used with the -signal option, specifies a signal to send to each process shown. Default signal is SIGKILL.

pr stat argument Reports statistics on the current active processes. The default action is to display statistics on all processes. The output can be limited by adding options to the command line. If the -c option is not used, then the statistics are updated in place rather than by scrolling. The update period can be specified in seconds on the command line. If used with the -a option, adds user statistics to the default output mode and includes the number of processes and the username, virtual memory size, memory resident set size, percent usage, cumulative execution time, and percent of CPU usage. If used with the -c option, prints new statistics below the current screen. If used with the -c list option, reports only those processes that are bound to the processor designated in list and expressed as integers. If used with the -l option, reports lightweight process statistics. If used with the -m option, reports microstate process statistics. If used with the -n option, limits the number of output lines to the number of processes specified. If used with the -p pids option, reports only those process ID numbers specified in pids. If used with the -p cpus option, reports only those processes that have been executed by the processor specified by cpus. If used with the -s criterion option, sorts output by the specified criterion in descending order by one of the following: cpu, time, size, rss, pri. If used with the -S option, sorts in ascending order. If used with the -t option, show user statistics only, including number of processes, username, total virtual memory size, memory resident set size, percent usage, cumulative execution time, and percent CPU usage. If used with the -u euids option , reports processes with user ID numbers matching those in euids. If used with -U uids, reports processes with real user ID numbers matching those specified in uids. If used with -v option, verbose output shows all statistics for processes.

ps (UCB) argument Displays process information. If used with the -a option, lists all processes, excluding process group leaders. If used with the -c option, lists processes with more reliable command name information. If used with the -g option, lists all processes including process group leaders. If used with the -l option, formats a long listing. If used with the -n option, replaces USER field with UID. If used with -r option, lists running processes. If used with -s option, displays total CPU time for processes, including child processes. If used with the -t term option, lists processes controlled by the terminal. If used with the -u option, formats running processes as a user listing. If used with the -U option, updates ps database. If used with the -v option, displays virtual memory. If used with the -w option, gives wide output format using 132 characters. If used with the -x option, lists processes that have no controlling terminal. If used with the -ww option, puts no limits on output width.

ps argument Displays information about processes currently running. If used with the -a option, lists all processes that are not group leaders. If used with the -A option, lists all processes. If used with the -c option, formats output as described in priocntl. If used with the -d option, lists all processes except session leaders. If used with the -e option, lists all processes that are currently active. If used with the `-f` option, formats output as a full list. If used with `-g grouplist`, lists process for listed group leaders. If used with `-G gidlist`, lists processes with realgroup ID listed in `gidlist`. If used with `-j`, lists processes including session ID and group ID. If used with the `-l` option, formats output as a long list. If used with `-o format`, formats output as specified. If used by `-p proclist`, lists processes for all sessions leaders listed in `sidlist`. If used with `-t term`, lists all processes connected to the terminal specified by `term`. If used with the `-u uidlist`, lists all processes with the same UID as those in `uidlist`. If used with the `-U uidlist`, lists all processes with the same real UID as those listed in `uidlist`.

Input/Output Redirection

When a program types something to your terminal, it is performing *standard output* operations. When you type something into your terminal, usually in response to a prompt, it is called *standard input*. These operations make your terminal "interactive." They make programming an easier task because the C shell can read your commands from standard input and write responses to standard output. A *standard error* will occur if a running program encounters an inaccurate response, such as a typo or a misspelling. The program can send error messages to standard error, keeping it from getting mixed in with standard output. If you do not redirect one or the other, you may not understand the difference between the output the command sends to standard output and the output it sends to standard error.

Standard input, output, and error messages are usually attached to the terminal. It is possible to reassign their connections to something else quite easily. The input and output of commands can be redirected by using the < > tokens in shell scripts. Output from the file `datasafe` can be redirected as in the following example:

```
cat datasafe  > databank
```

If you want to do a sort on the output, you can give the `sort` command as shown in the following example:

```
sort datasafe >>  databank
```

WARNING If you want to add output to the end of the output file, use >> instead of >. Otherwise, normal output redirect can overwrite the output file completely and without warning.

The `sort` command will return its output and append it to the file `databank`. If you add an ampersand (&) to the end of an output redirection command, it will combine both the standard error and the standard output and place the output into the specified file. You can send the output of one command to the input of another command by using a pipe to separate the commands, as in the following example:

```
ls -1 | sort -m -n
```

You can append an ampersand (&) after the pipe, which will combine the standard error and standard output and send it to the standard input of the program receiving the piped output.

You can redirect standard input just as you can redirect its standard output. The redirect input symbol (<) instructs the C shell to connect the command's standard input to a specified file. The format of a command line redirecting standard input is as follows:

```
<command> [<arguments>] < <filename>
```

<command> may be any command or executable script, with or without arguments. *<filename>* is the name of the file from which the shell redirects the input. Spaces around the redirect symbol (<) are optional. Each I/O connection is identified by a positive integer number called a *file descriptor*. When the program wants to read or write to a file, it must first open the file. It opens it with the file descriptor assigned to that file. When the program no longer needs the file, it closes it and frees up the file descriptor for new use whenever necessary.

TIP A running program opens three file descriptors: 0 for standard input, 1 for standard output, 2 for standard error. The redirect input symbol < is shorthand for <0, and the redirect output symbol > is short for 1>. Therefore, 2> is used to redirect standard error. By default, these three standard files are connected to your terminal.

Although different from I/O redirection, the C shell uses a pipe to connect standard output of one command directly to standard input of another command. It obviates the need for an intermediate file and separate commands. Here is the syntax for the pipe:

```
<command> [<arguments>] | <command> [<arguments>]
```

You can also use pipes and I/O redirection on the same command line. The following example demonstrates how this is done:

```
ls -1 | sort > list.sort.wd
```

Because there is no limit to the number of pipes you can use on one line, you will save time and space by using the pipes with redirection.

Summary

This chapter covered the C shell, which is based on the high-level C programming language. Although different from both the Bourne and Korn shells, it has many capabilities and can be customized for easier use. Script writing is simple, particularly for those with C language experience. Login to the C shell causes automatic execution of several files or directories such as the system file (`/etc/.login`) and your mail application. It permits you to set the environmental variables as commands.

The C shell provides a `history` built-in, which maintains a complete history of command lines in a program. Beneficial for debugging, the `history` built-in also provides an abbreviated form of recent commands that enables re-execution of commands. The `alias` built-in allows the creations of short names for often used commands. This saves time in scripting when you use the same type of commands repeatedly.

Command-line expansion, which is available in the C shell, was also covered. The shell parses a command into tokens or words and expands them whenever necessary. Tilde (~) expansion occurs if the shell finds a token that begins with one as a special character.

You learned that a list of working directories can be stored as a stack by means of the `dirs` built-in command. It allows you to change directories, add new directories, and remove other directories as needed. Several related built-ins that allow manipulation of the stacks were also covered.

The C shell sets some variables, retains environmental variables inherent in the shell, and lets the user set others. Some variables act as switches and, when declared, cause the shell to take action, whereas an undeclared variable does not.

Environmental variables such as `PATH` and `HOME` are inherent to the C shell. The `PATH` environmental variable is used to initialize the `path` local variable. `HOME` is used to initialize the local variable `home`.

Writing scripts in the C shell is similar to writing them in both the Bourne and Korn shells, although many of the control structures have a different syntax. The use of the `break` and `continue` statements creates an easy flow of control from the beginning to the `end` command. As it is with the C programming language, writing scripts in the C shell is enhanced by the use of a comprehensive list of built-in commands.

Finally, this chapter covered several commands that help in controlling processes, both in startup and status reporting. Several options can be used with arguments. Both input and output of commands can be redirected by use of tokens in shell scripts. The `sort` command will return output and append it to the file `databank`. Pipes can be used to separate commands on the same command line.

PART IV

Troubleshooting

LEARN TO:

- ***Diagnose and fix operating system and application probelms***
- ***Recognize specific hardware errors***
- ***Plan for trouble***
- ***Use troubleshooting resources***

CHAPTER 21

Troubleshooting

FEATURING:

Planning for trouble	793
The psychology of troubleshooting	796
Resources	797
Troubleshooting SPARC and Intel hardware	805
Troubleshooting the file system	816
Troubleshooting the operating system	818
Troubleshooting applications	824

No one wants to see trouble appear on their computer system. It is usually not something we plan for. However, no matter how efficient the operating system or the hardware is, at some point there will be a problem. You can count on it.

This chapter describes some of the problems that may arise and how to resolve them. Successful troubleshooting is really a consequence of experience with a particular system. The more experience you have, the easier it is to figure out what went wrong and why. More important, experience tells you what should be done to anticipate problems and to correct them when they occur.

Solaris has several useful utilities and tools to help you troubleshoot. You will learn how to use them by troubleshooting the three layers of failure described in this chapter.

The Three Layers of Failure

There is a hierarchy of troubleshooting steps that seasoned administrators use when something goes wrong with a Sun Solaris server or workstation. The steps are closely related to the three layers of failure:

- The hardware
- The operating system
- Applications

The first level of troubleshooting deals with the hardware, and so the procedures are specific to the Intel- and the SPARC-based architectures. This chapter describes some of these specific procedures.

The hardware on Sun servers varies depending on the type of server purchased, but Sun Microsystems does keep a fairly uniform naming convention and interface for its hardware. For lower-level servers, desktop machines, and mid-level servers, the hardware is uniform. For high-end servers, such as an E-5500 or an E-10K, there is a wider variety of issues and interfaces to deal with. The main diagnostics tool for Sun hardware is the Sun Validation Test Suite (SunVTS). It performs a series of diagnostic tests on the hardware. Within the nonvolatile random access memory (NVRAM), there is a hardware application named OBDiag. It provides chip-level system diagnostic testing and validation. The operating system also has a series of commands that can be used to identify the devices the kernel "sees." Sun servers based on the Intel architecture have a much wider variety of hardware components and interfaces. This is because there is a wider variety of manufacturers, whereas Sun Microsystems is the only manufacturer of the SPARC-based architecture systems. Unfortunately, Sun does not have any diagnostics tools that reside within the firmware of Intel-based servers. The manufacturer

of the motherboard will in most cases have diagnostics tools within the BIOS. These tools tend to be very limited. Most of them find only IDE hard drives and change BIOS chip default options.

If the hardware on the server is working properly, the server's operating system is the next layer of failure. For an operating system to work, it must have the following hardware:

- A system disk or CD-ROM drive (diskless workstations are not covered here)
- A CPU
- The minimum required memory
- A functional system board
- A keyboard or terminal (required in most cases)

Other optional components, such as a printer or a modem, will not cause the operating system to fail to boot up. These devices add extra functionality to the server but are not required for the minimum operation of a server or workstation. Sun Microsystems provides a wide range of built-in tools for diagnosing operating system problems. The operating system also includes some detailed tracking logs that can indicate when and where a problem has occurred. Most of these logs are in the `/var/adm` directory. Boot information can be reviewed with the command `dmesg`. There are cases in which the operating system will save a copy of the system's memory to a file before a system crash. The core dump file can then be sent to Sun support engineers for troubleshooting, provided the warranty or service-level agreement covers the computer.

The final layer of troubleshooting consists of the applications themselves. The applications can be the applications bundled with the operating system (such as FTP or NFS), or they can be applications purchased separately (such as Netscape's Web server). It is extremely difficult to troubleshoot software errors because they can be confused with or intermingled with operating system errors. Most software developers provide troubleshooting tools and troubleshooting logs to track error messages that relate directly to their software. Sun's bundled applications are covered in the docs.sun.com Web page. Third-party vendors' applications are usually covered by some type of support Web page on their respective sites.

Planning Ahead

There are many situations in which troubleshooting is aided by the system administrator's documentation and by a backup that was performed before a crash or emergency happened. The two key items that must be present before a backup can take place are system documentation and a previous system backup.

Documentation

System documentation answers the basic question, What is on the computer? The documentation can be in the form of a notebook, a Web page, or a text document. No matter where the documentation is or what form it's in, it must be readily accessible during the troubleshooting process. The system's documentation should never reside only on the system itself. Ask yourself if you will be able to access the documentation if the system goes down. Most large companies put their servers' documentation on secure Web pages. This allows any member of the team to access the information from any location (even at home late at night). This Web page should have all the servers' critical information, such as the host name, IP address, disk labels, and so on. Critical pieces of information not directly related to the server should also be saved:

- The IT manager's home and office telephone numbers
- The in-house software developer's home and office telephone numbers
- The security guard's contact information, to gain access to remote facilities if needed
- Contact information of others who are directly related to the server, such as the system administrator, the computer operator, or anyone with superuser status
- Sun telephone support numbers and/or the names of Sun engineers who have worked with the server before
- The location and schedule of backup tapes or the backup server
- Previous notes on past emergency and repair work
- The terminal server's IP address and access information
- The actual location of the server

This information is critical to the fast recovery of a server. Most network teams will hire a junior system administrator to maintain this type of documentation because it tends to be rather boring work.

The Web page should also have some form of username/password security. Hackers will take any piece of information they can in order to compromise a network's security. Ideally, the Web site should be replicated to another offsite server. This eliminates a sitewide location fault.

Backups

A complete backup is paramount in maintaining an efficient and ongoing system. Backups should be performed on a regular basis and tested to make sure they will restore when needed. Some sites are backed up completely each week and then a copy of the backup is made in case of failure with the first copy. Establish a policy concerning backups and follow it faithfully. It can mean the difference between success and failure when something goes wrong with your system.

A full system backup is sometimes the only thing that will bring a server or workstation back to life. All hardware—particularly computer chips, disks, and cables—have a useful service life; some components have longer MTBF (Mean Time Before Failure) intervals than others. It is therefore inevitable that a backup will be needed at some time in the future, especially if you have numerous servers. The question is not *if* it will be needed; it's *when* it will be needed.

Mirrored disks and clustered servers can lead some system administrators to develop a false sense of security. Although these concepts do help with system uptime, there are times when corrupt data is introduced to the system. There is also the human factor—accidentally deleting the wrong file or directory, for example. Solaris does not have a file undelete option that is native to the operating system.

There is a wide variety of backup solutions available. Most backup solutions eventually end up with a tape somewhere in the loop. Tape media is the least expensive backup solution to date. Tape also tends to be the slowest media to read and write to. In any case, you need to have a complete backup of the data on your system. It can be either a full backup or an older full backup and any up-to-date incremental changes to the file system since the last full backup. Partial backups of changes occur frequently (sometimes daily). A full backup is done usually on a monthly basis. It includes all the programs and software. Incremental backups include only the changes or additions made since the last full backup.

If a full backup is not available at the time of a system crash, try to perform a full backup as soon as possible. There are situations in which the system will have limited functionality. Perhaps the server cannot communicate over the network but the hard drives and tape drive are still accessible through the terminal server. In these cases, it might be possible to do a full backup before continuing on with the troubleshooting. The main point is that it's important to have a full backup or to make a full backup of the system before troubleshooting. Once a file or directory is deleted in Solaris, it cannot be recovered.

TIP When working on a critical system text file, make a backup copy before editing it even if the file exists on tape. Some partitions are several terabytes in size. It can be extremely time consuming to try to recover a single file. Also, Solaris is very sensitive to hidden characters and incorrect spaces in some files. It isn't too difficult to make tar archives of the `/etc` directory before troubleshooting.

The Psychology of Troubleshooting

This section is without a doubt the most important section in this chapter. Being in the right frame of mind during an emergency troubleshooting situation is 90 percent of the battle. A frantic "poke around–change something–try something else" method is the worst possible method in a troubleshooting situation. When an individual becomes panicked, compounded errors can make a problem situation worse. It can become impossible to retrace one's steps.

TIP One of the most important steps in troubleshooting is to try to relax, collect your thoughts, and formulate a recovery plan.

Frantically editing files and making changes can make the situation worse. Although there may be times this technique will bring a server back to life very quickly, in most cases, unfortunately, it only produces a false sense of security and accomplishment. An emergency situation can be a learning process that can highlight weaknesses in documentation and backups. The quick-and-dirty session may be regarded as a victory while critical documentation and backup problems are allowed to persist and may lead to future problems such as an unrecoverable system crash. If the backup system, for whatever reason, failed to produce a useable backup, the server's data may never be retrieved.

TIP Test your backups frequently to see if you can actually use them to restore data. Make sure your backup media contains the data you think it contains.

When troubleshooting, try to avoid taking any irreversible steps. Most changes to the system can be reversed if documented. Copy a file before making changes. Instead of deleting a file, change its name or location to nullify the file's function (provided disk space exists). Make a copy of a disk before you change the size of the slices. Don't throw away a component before the new component is proven to work. There are countless examples of situations that can't be reversed.

Don't guess. Guessing rarely works, and it can take more time to repair damage done by guessing than to repair the original problem. The chance of your Sun workstation or server and the Solaris operating system having a unique problem that has not been encountered and solved before is rare. If you become skilled at using SunSolve Online (sunsolve.sun.com), you will be able to remedy even the toughest of all situations quickly.

TIP One common question fielded at Sun Microsystems is, How can I get a SunSolve account? Sun will not sell a subscription to SunSolve alone. SunSolve comes with a service-level contract. The most economical way to get a SunSolve account is to get a software maintenance contract. This costs about $21.00 per month. For independent consultants, it's the only practical way of ensuring SunSolve access for your clients.

Provide step-by-step documentation of what you have done. If you need to ask for help, the first step is to explain the problem succinctly and outline what steps you have already taken to correct the problem. One suggestion is to keep a file of your Telnet session. You can do this with the `tee` command. Don't shut down the Telnet session and try to recall what commands you typed. Most terminal window programs will have a scroll back history. Make this history as large as possible so that in the worst-case scenario, others will be able to scroll back and look at the changes you made. Keep notes in a notebook beside your computer.

Resources

As a Solaris administrator, you have a wide variety of tools available from Sun Microsystems other than the applications within the operating system. Most of this information can be obtained from the Web page docs.sun.com and from the private section of SunSolve Online. (Sun Microsystems's main Web page, www.sun.com, is filled mostly with marketing and sales information. The documentation found on these Web pages is generally of little value to a system administrator.) There are also searchable databases, support accounts, and educational resources.

Web Sites

The docs.sun.com site has all the AnswerBooks online. From here, you can read an almost endless amount of technical white papers on the Solaris operating system, Sun hardware, system administration, and Sun's proprietary applications. One of the important features of docs.sun.com that isn't part of the AnswerBooks' server or workstation installation is that the site comes with a search engine you can use to search across all of the manuals. This search feature alone makes the online implementation vastly superior to working with the AnswerBook version locally or on a LAN.

There are Web pages that are extremely useful. A new site that Sun recently unveiled is aimed directly at the Unix system administrator: `www.sun.com/bigadmin/`. The BigAdmin site is a free site supported by Sun with links to large amounts of general Unix and Solaris-specific technical information and discussion forums.

The AnswerBooks' documents can be read online or downloaded in Adobe Acrobat PDF (Portable Document Format). Once they're downloaded, you must have Adobe Acrobat Reader installed to view and print them. The key strength to the Web page docs.sun.com is the documentation on hardware. Figure 21.1 shows the docs.sun.com home page.

FIGURE 21.1

The home page of docs.sun.com, an online version of the AnswerBooks

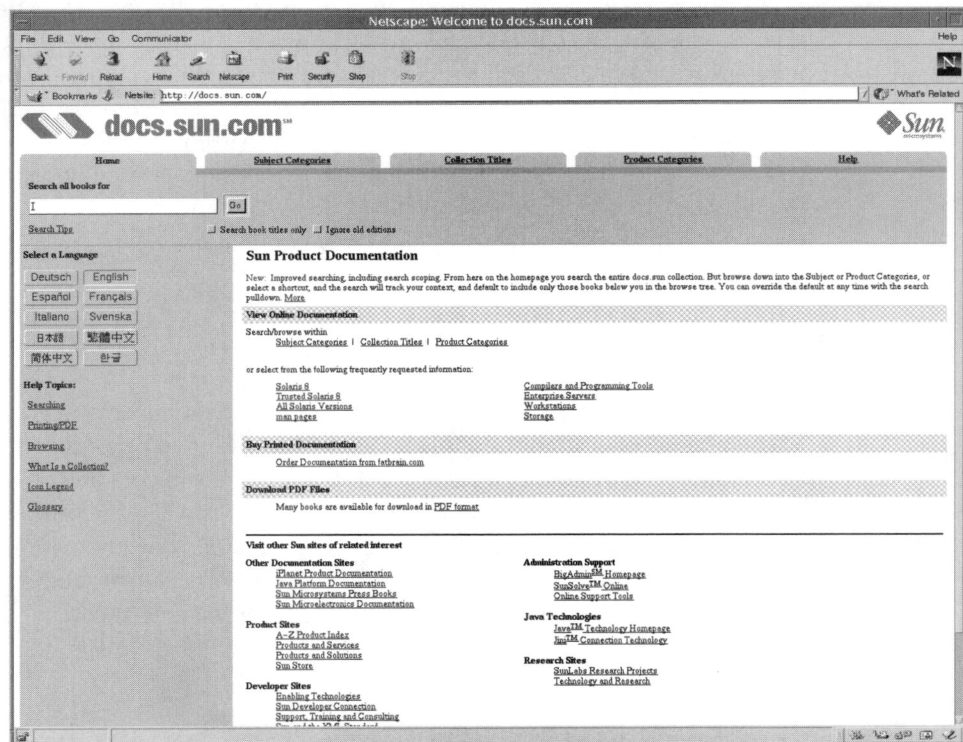

Another useful tool is SunSolve Online (`http://sunsolve.sun.com`). There are two versions of this Web site: a public version and a paid account version. The public section offers patches, security information, and a rather limited searchable collection of patch and security bulletins. You can also download the Explorer Data Collector, which collects a wide variety of system information about your server. During a service call, you can use this utility to send system information to the Sun service engineers. There are also some useful articles that Sun puts out from time to time. Figure 21.2 shows the SunSolve public Web page.

The paid version of SunSolve Online includes an account section that has a much wider variety of knowledge-based articles, patches, and technical white papers. To access this section, you need a username and password for a paid account. Once the username and password are entered, more SunSolve content can be accessed. The section on patches alone is about the same size as the entire public section. Almost all other sections have increased content.

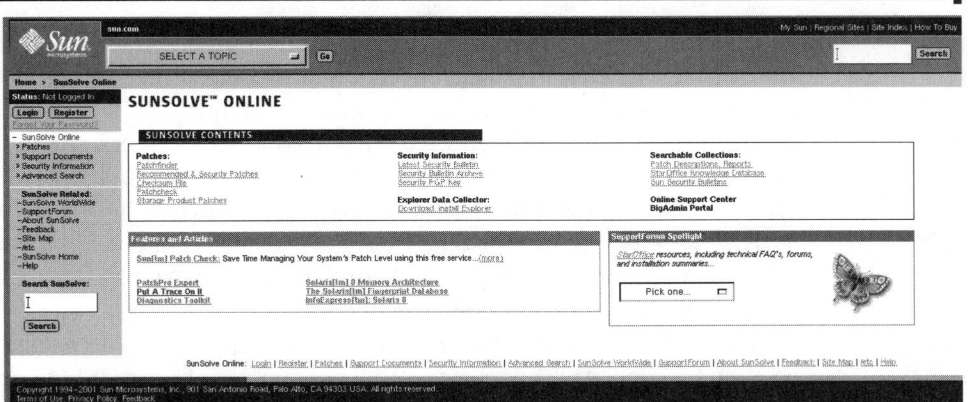

FIGURE 21.2
The public SunSolve Web page

Searchable Collections

Within the private SunSolve Web page, the most useful resources are the knowledge-based files known as the Searchable Collections. The search engine gives the user the ability to look at all documented known problems and their possible solutions. The Web pages in the Searchable Collections are produced by the Sun support engineers and Sun developers when they encounter and solve problems. It is rather rare for a system administrator to have a Sun hardware or operating system problem that has never been seen before. When you access SunSolve Online, click Sun Security Bulletins and then click SupportForum on the menu on the left side of the screen. Just specify the databases you wish to search and try a keyword search.

You can select from the following collections:

- StarOffice Support
- SunCobalt Support
- iPlanet Support
- Free Solaris Support
- SunCluster 3.0 Support
- Sun Alerts and Security Bulletins
- Sun Grid Engine Support
- HighGround SRM
- Other Resources

The most useful collection for system administrators is the Big Admin for SAs, which is in the Other Resources collection. It includes a site map and feedback help/FAQs as well as shell commands, scripts, and links.

Each category provides pertinent FAQs, feedback from users, and information. Bug information and patches are available in most of the categories. StarOffice Support provides StarOffice bug fixes, a handy section for solving the "bug" problems that arise. Sun Alerts and Security is an excellent category. It provides information on the top 10 alerts, along with security bulletins and security patches. Discussion forums let you interact with other users and share information.

It is a good idea to select only the section that applies to your needs; otherwise, you will be flooded with Web pages that contain your keywords but not the correct information. The knowledge base has grown to a point where it takes a good deal of time to find a solution to your problem. Keyword searches tend to bring up numerous Web pages that may have your keyword but do not contain the information you are looking for. When you do find an article that applies to what you are looking for, there will be an option for a printer-friendly page. Select this option. The printer friendly page has larger, easier-to-read fonts and the lines wrap correctly.

Sun's site includes less information on problems relating to Intel-based architectures than it does information on the SPARC systems. There are more manufacturers for the Intel-based architecture, which can lead to even more unsolved problems.

The SunSolve account can also be ordered with a CD-ROM subscription. The CD-ROM has most of the same tools and databases as the Web page. The main difference is that the Web page is current and the CD-ROMs are published about once a month. This can lead to a situation in which a new patch is released on the Web page but is not available on the CD-ROM. Most system administrators will use the SunSolve Web pages and will burn a CD-ROM with the latest patches available.

Support Accounts

If Sun's documentation does not help, you can purchase service-level agreements with Sun. These agreements provide for telephone assistance and onsite support with Sun engineers. The service Web site, `www.sun.com/service/support/sunspectrum`, has detailed information on the support available from Sun Microsystems. The SunSpectrum program provides comprehensive Sun hardware and software support—from proactive, mission-critical service to complete self-maintenance support. For one monthly price, you receive support for all Sun system components including hardware and the Solaris operating environment, and you also receive Solaris software upgrades at no additional cost. There are four levels of SunSpectrum, from Bronze to Platinum. Figure 21.3 shows the home page for SunSpectrum.

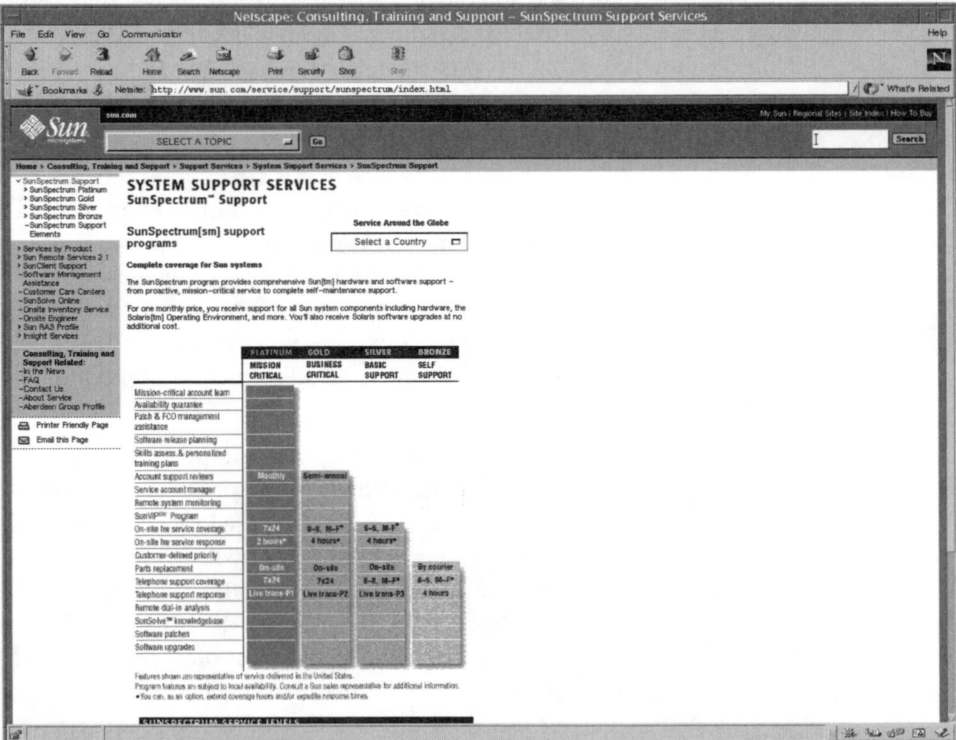

FIGURE 21.3
The SunSpectrum home page

The telephone support Sun offers is mostly for problems with the operating system and official Sun applications. The support personnel range from first-level engineers to the developers. The first-level engineers are highly trained, each with expertise in a very small area. If the first-level engineers can't help with a problem, they will forward calls to higher-level engineers. If a problem cannot be solved with the engineers, the developers will assist. In some cases, the developers will set up a test server with the exact same hardware, firmware upgrades, operating system, and patches your system has to troubleshoot the problem. Sun Microsystems's support has an excellent reputation for speed and efficiency.

The onsite support personnel deal primarily with Sun hardware and are known as Sun field engineers. In most cases, the account management team calls the field engineers and directs them to replace parts or make other configuration changes. Most onsite employees have only rudimentary knowledge of the Solaris operating system.

The SunSpectrum accounts are negotiated with Sun Microsystems for assistance with your server and networked workstations. These service-level agreements are not included with the purchase of the server or workstations alone. Sun systems do come with a one- to three-year warranty on the hardware (depending on the server purchased).

To give you an idea of the range of support offered, here is a list of the current set of SunSpectrum accounts:

Platinum Support Provides telephone support and onsite support. The telephone support is with a hardware-specific service account management team. This support is available 24 hours a day, 7 days a week. The onsite support is also 24 hours a day, 7 days a week. The price of this support agreement varies depending on how many times you call. Most large-scale corporations have Platinum Support contracts on all of their production-level servers, for example.

Gold Support Also provides telephone support 24 hours a day, 7 days a week. The onsite support is available only from 8:00 A.M. to 8:00 P.M. Monday through Friday, however. Gold Support is used mostly with test-level servers, which replicate the problem encountered by the production-level servers (customers). They are usually not mission critical, nor are they used in a production environment. Test servers give the Sun developers a platform on which to try different programs and replicate different problems. When it has been determined that the program, operating system and hardware work well together, the test server's setup is replicated to the production-level servers to try to determine where the problem lies and to come up with a solution.

Silver Support Features telephone support from 8:00 A.M. to 8:00 P.M. Onsite support is limited to from 8:00 A.M. to 5:00 P.M. This is a slightly more economical support option for test servers than the Gold Support. The main disadvantage of this option is the limited telephone support hours, which can be a problem if a server is down and evening support is needed.

Bronze Support The lowest level of support from Sun. The only feature of Bronze Support is telephone coverage from 8:00 A.M. to 5:00 P.M., Monday through Friday. There is no field support offered with this service contract. You can still have onsite support for warranty-related hardware issues. If the issue is not an onsite hardware issue, support can be obtained on a time-and-material basis. At the time of this book's publication, Sun is charging $175.00 an hour with a 2-hour minimum for onsite support without a contract. Your telephone support is still available at no cost.

The Silver, Gold, and Platinum contacts all come with a SunSolve Online account. For software developers, there is a separate type of support called Developer Access. It covers the most common programming languages, such as C, C++, Java, and so on. The support personnel for this type of contract understand both the Sun Solaris operating system and its software coding. They are not skilled system administrators and most likely cannot solve higher-level hardware or operating system problems. If they do run across a difficult problem with the operating system, they will contact the Sun support engineers for help.

To place a service call to Sun, call Professional Services at 888-980-7263.

Educational Resources

The Sun Certification training material is an excellent troubleshooting tool. The material it contains is written by Sun Microsystems. It covers both the Solaris operating system and general concepts about Sun SPARC hardware. To obtain this material, however, you need to take the certification training.

In addition to the training material, Sun has Web pages and support agreements and also features a wide variety of education classes, mainly directed toward those desiring certification or those who have certification and want to take it to another level. They are primarily for system administrators and software developers. The Web site for Sun Educational Services (`http://suned.sun.com`, shown in Figure 21.4) has a full listing of the classes available from Sun. The classes are taught by Sun certified instructors in Sun Authorized Education Centers and can be found in several locations around the United States and worldwide. The instructors have passed the latest certification exams from Sun and have received additional training. The classes are rather expensive, depending on the instructor, dates, and facilities.

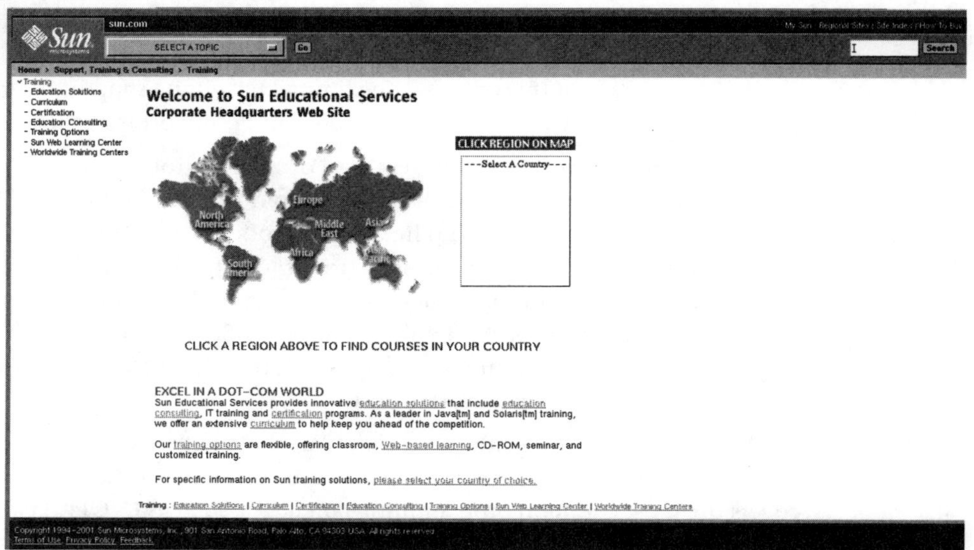

FIGURE 21.4

The Sun Educational Services home page

TIP Sun certification books can sometimes be found at Internet auction sites such as www.ebay.com. They are books that students who have taken the class are selling. (As mentioned, Sun doesn't sell the books directly to the public.) The books can be expensive when they are sold by students. Sun Microsystems owns the copyrights and therefore the books cannot be legally reproduced.

There are other training materials and books that can be used for additional information. The general public can purchase computer-based training (CBT) CD-ROMs from Sun. The CD-ROMs have pictures, moving text, and practice test questions and answers. They cover the certification material very accurately and are easy to use. They vary in cost. Unfortunately, the information is hard to use in a troubleshooting situation when you need to retrieve answers quickly.

Another possible source for material from Sun is Web-based training. This training tool gives a user the option of accessing the certification material online, from anywhere, day or night. The only drawback is that the Web-based training has a time limitation. The Web-based training material serves as an excellent reference for troubleshooting. You can access these materials by linking to `www.getsolariscertified.com`.

Sun Press publishes some books that are available to the public. These books are similar to the certification material and the material on docs.sun.com. They cover a more limited range of topics but are good for general reference for problems with isolated servers.

Within the Solaris 8 operating system there are various README files. They provide some basic guidelines on the installation and use of the software. Also, there are information paragraphs within some of the configuration files. These paragraphs are usually commented with the # symbol so they are not interpreted by the shell. The README files can be found somewhere on the distribution CD-ROM (varies depending on the CD-ROM and software).

The AnswerBook server and documentation come with the Solaris 8 distribution CD-ROMs. Before you can view the AnswerBook documentation, you need to install the AnswerBook. The software package SUNWabs contains the AnswerBook Server. The AnswerBook Server is a crude Web server and thus can be opened by the browser in StarOffice should you wish to do so or if Netscape Navigator fails to work for some reason. There is also the HotJava Web browser that ships with Solaris. If you are having problems with a server that has the AnswerBook on it, the pages to the AnswerBook can be read on another workstation with a browser. This is good for systems that do not have Internet access. If your location does have reliable Internet access, it is advised that you don't set up an AnswerBook Server. The same documentation can be found at docs.sun.com.

Troubleshooting Hardware

Before the operating system and applications can work properly, the Intel or SPARC hardware must be in good working order. Some devices are controlled by software and require the operating system to be running before they will run. The hardware diagnostics covered in this section deal with the most rudimentary tests at the chip level.

Before the operating system boots up, a series of diagnostic tests called the POST (power-on self test) runs automatically. The POST runs through some chip diagnostic routines on the server before the server boots the system disk. During the POST, the system's LEDs will blink in a prearranged pattern for each successful POST test. For example, if there is a hardware error before the operating system starts, the service LED will flash while the power LED and cycling LED will remain on. The actual LEDs used for each piece of equipment vary depending on the hardware. You need to obtain the system board and power supply LED status tables for your particular system. The tables tell you what each series of blinking lights means. This information is available in the AnswerBook documentation.

If all goes well and you do not have a bootable OS loaded on the system, the OK prompt should be seen through the terminal session connected to the serial port A or to the graphical console. If the OK prompt does not appear through the terminal session, double-check your terminal emulator settings and the LED blinking lights.

WARNING Sometimes when the settings on a terminal server have not been configured correctly, a system administrator will incorrectly assume that the Sun server went down and power-cycle it. Basically, the system administrator is hard-crashing a perfectly good server. Try other communication channels, such as a Telnet session through the Ethernet card or connecting through a modem. Also check to see if the "Activity Light" is blinking for the server.

If you are absolutely sure the operating system has not started, power-cycle the server and check the LEDs. A service call must be put in for hardware that is still covered by the warranty or that is covered by a service-level agreement. Most Sun servers come with warranties and service agreements that can become void if non-Sun technicians work on the hardware. This is especially true with the high-end servers, such as the E-10K. No keyboard command can correct a hardware failure, so broken hardware must be fixed. On mission-critical servers, some noncritical hardware (printers, modem, etc.) may be bypassed to bring the server up, but eventually, the broken hardware should be repaired or replaced.

The OpenBoot Prompt

Once the system POST has completed and the OK prompt is visible in a terminal session, a series of commands called the OpenBoot Prompt (OBP) diagnostics commands can be run. If your system has a bootable install of Solaris on it, you will not be shown the OK prompt; the system will start loading the OS automatically. You can stop this by pressing Stop+A during the memory test or kernel load phase. Do not do that after the system has started booting, though, or you can cause corruption (just as you can if you shut down the system by pulling the power plug). These commands provide the system administrator with direct command-line manipulation and testing of the server's hardware.

During the boot sequence, the system's memory is tested and system information is presented. The system information includes the host ID, Ethernet address, memory, CPU type, system architecture, and so on. At any time in the OBP, you can type the banner command to display the same information again, unless the banner information has been replaced by a system notice as it is in many government offices.

There are various OBP commands you can type to interact directly with the hardware. The banner command, mentioned in the preceding paragraph, is an OBP command.

One of the most often used commands is printenv, which will show the system administrator the various system parameters.

There are 44 standard OBP variables that come with OBP 3.*x*; Table 21.1 lists three of them as an example of how the values and default values appear. The OBP variables cover a wide variety of system configurations. There are some differences in the OBP variables depending on the age of the system board and the type of server specified. For example, older Sunstation 5s have an SBUS architecture, whereas most of Sun's newest hardware tends to use the PCI bus architecture. The Sunstation 5 has the OBP command sbus-probe-list, and newer machines have the OBP command pci-probe-list (some have both because it is possible to have both on higher-end Enterprise servers). There are Internet firmware downloads available from Sun that can update the system's chips.

TABLE 21.1: SAMPLE OBP VARIABLES

Variable Name	Value	Default Value
initiator-id	7	7
tpe-link-test	true	true
dkeyboard-click?	true	false

The following list includes some of the OBP variables:

initiator-id Defines the ID of the SCSI controller itself. If you have a SCSI device that needs SCSI ID #7 for some reason, you can change the value of this variable to reassign the controller's ID. If two servers are sharing a disk array, this variable often has to be reset to a new value.

diag-level Defines how detailed the POST should be. Always have this variable set to max.

output-device Defines where the system output is sent. The default value is the screen. You should not have to change this value. The terminal port always works. If a video card is not present, the terminal session will still work by default.

input-device Defines the system's input. The default value is the keyboard. If a keyboard is not present, the output will default to terminal port A. This is another variable that should not be changed.

boot-device Defines the primary and secondary boot devices for the server. On most systems, this is the device alias disk. This device alias represents the physical device path to the controller, disk, and slice c0t0d0s0. This is the first controller, first disk, and first slice. On this slice is the boot sector. The default boot device can be changed to another properly defined device alias. The device alias must point to a boot sector on a boot device. For example, you could not boot to c0t0d0s4 because there is no boot sector in that location.

auto-boot? Determines if the server should boot the default boot device on power up. If `auto-boot?` is false, the system will not automatically start the operating system. The boot process will stop at the OK prompt. If the `auto-boot?` variable is set to true, the device specified with the variable `boot-device` is booted. During hardware troubleshooting and initial server setup, having the `auto-boot?` set to false is helpful. Otherwise, you will have to halt the operating system each time you power-cycle the server to return to the OK prompt.

security-passwd Most companies leave this variable blank. Once you set a security password, the system can never go back to a blank password. If the password is forgotten, the NVRAM chip on the motherboard must be sent into Sun to have the password cleared.

The commands `oem-logo`, `oem-logo?`, `oem-banner`, and `oem-banner?` are rather useless commands that determine the initial logo and banner that are displayed when the system boots up. These banners and logos do not affect the system's operation. The only real use for any of these commands is to issue an `unauthorized use of this system is prohibited` type message at the OK prompt.

Here are some other useful OBP commands:

devalias Aliases are used to make the system administrator's life easier. The alias disk is actually represented by the following line:

```
/sbus@1,f8000000/esp@0,800000/sd@0,0:a
```

Obviously, the process of typing in this line repeatedly can be rather tedious and prone to errors. If you type the command `devalias` by itself, you will see the aliases that are on your particular system. You can create your own device aliases with this command:

```
devalias alias physical-device-path
```

To make an alias permanent, the variable `use-nvramrc?` must be set to true and the command `nvstore` must be run to enter the variable into non-volatile RAM.

`.enet-addr` Displays the Ethernet address. Do not confuse the Ethernet address with the IP address. The Ethernet address is burned in to the hardware and takes the form 03:2a:13:04:2b:3c, whereas the IP address is a numeric network identifier such as 136.23.18.203.

`led-off` and `led-on` Turns the system LEDs on and off. The best recommendation is to not use these commands because they can mislead other system administrators when it comes to troubleshooting. For hardware configuration and diagnostics, Sun provides the `probe-xxxn` series of commands, where *xxxn* is a device category (such as ide, SCSI, pci, and so on). These `probe` commands show you what devices are configured for a category. For example, if you type the command `probe-SCSI`, you will see all the SCSI devices on the system. If you type the command `probe-pci-all`, you will see all the PCI devices on the system.

`probe-SCSI` or `probe-ide` These commands will show you the hard drives at the hardware level. If the hardware does not recognize the disks, either there is a hardware fault or the disks are not compatible with Sun's hardware. Most Sun vendors have enough experience to sell hardware that is compatible with Sun servers. You can still check the hardware at docs.sun.com. If the hardware is compatible, either there is a configuration problem (wrong jumper set) or the hardware is broken. `probe-SCSI-all` and `probe-ide-all` will scan the entire system for all SCSI devices or IDE devices.

`probe-pci` and `probe-sbus` Probe all the PCI and SBUS ports for devices and errors.

WARNING Be careful with `probe-pci`. Some devices, when probed by the system, can become confused and not reset properly until the system is power-cycled.

There is another set of diagnostic commands called the `show` commands. The `show-devs` command shows the various devices on the server, and the others give a more limited view than `show-devs`:

`show-devs` Shows all devices on the server. The output from this command is verbose and confusing. About the only people who can understand and use this command are Sun field engineers and members of Sun support teams. If you are lucky, you can pick out some devices from the output.

`show-disks` Shows the physical device paths of the disks that are recognized within the server. This command is very useful when it's used to define a new device alias. For example, if you have a nonstandard configuration on your server and you need to define a new device alias, this command will show you the physical device path to your disks. You can then copy and paste the output to make a new device alias.

show-displays Shows the physical device path to the frame buffer. The frame buffer is what puts out the graphical display on a Sun server. Most likely, this command will be used only by Sun field engineers and Sun support teams.

show-nets Shows the physical path to network devices. The network devices are one or more network cards.

show-post-results Shows some detailed output of the POST test. The output can be seen only if critical hardware is still available. If a simple device such as a modem goes out, it will be indicated in the output. If a critical piece of hardware such the CPU goes out, the only way of detecting it is with the system LEDs.

show-sbus This command works only on older systems that have the SBUS architectures. Newer systems don't even have this command in the NVRAM chip.

show-tapes This is just like the other `show` commands. This command might not pick-up on third-party solutions that do not use the interface.

There is another command called `test`. It will run diagnostics on devices that have hardware-level diagnostic test routines built in. If a device is driven by software device drivers for hardware operations (such as moving the disk heads), this command might not work or it might produce limited results. Most Sun peripheral equipment will respond to the `test` command. The format is `test device-alias`. You can also use `test-all` to test everything. It is fun the first time and can be useful if the system is acting flaky.

If you have to contact Sun for hardware support, the support team member will most likely ask you to run the OK command `.version`. This command displays the OBP and POST firmware versions for your server. The most common OBP versions are 2.*x* and 3.*x*. OBP version 1.0 was in use around the early 1980s and is extremely rare if it can be found at all. Most current servers support firmware upgrades from software. The support representative might ask you to download the latest hardware firmware for your server and upgrade the firmware before continuing with the hardware troubleshooting session.

There are some `probe` and `show` commands that require the system to be reset before they can be used:

1. First have the system at the OK prompt.
2. Then use the command `setenv` to set the variable `auto-boot?` to false.
3. Now type the command **`reset-all`**.

4. Once the tests have been conducted, make sure you reset the OBP variable `auto-boot?` back to true. If you don't reset this variable, future power-up will only go as far as the OK prompt and no further and could be misunderstood as a hardware error.
5. Once the system has gone through the POST again and has returned to the OK prompt, you can run the `probe` and `show` commands.

The first command, `auto-boot?`, will disable an automatic boot-up of the operating system. The second command, `reset-all`, clears the memory and starts the boot process from the beginning. Don't confuse the command `reset-all` with the command `set-default`. The command `reset-all` will not change the values of the OBP variables. The command `set-defaults` will change all the variables back to the factory default values.

At any point, if you make a very bad mistake with the OBP variables, there are two ways to reset them back to the default settings. If the OK prompt is still visible, you can type the command `set-default <variable>`. This will reset a variable back to its factory default value. There is another command, `set-defaults`, which will reset *all* the OBP variables back to their default values. The `set-defaults` command is a strong and somewhat dangerous command to use, especially if you have a high-end power server such as an E-4500 or an E-10K. Using `set-defaults` will cause all the OBP configurations to be lost, and that can be catastrophic to some servers.

There is also a way to clear the OBP variables with hardware. If the server will not boot or the OK prompt cannot be seen, you can attach a Sun keyboard to the server and then shut off the server. Power on the server and hold down the Stop and N keys simultaneously during power-up. This will reset all the OBP variables back to their factory default values. From here, you will have to go into the server through the terminal port and reset all the OBP variables back to your custom configurations.

You can run the diagnostic tests by using the OK commands `setenv diag-switch? true` and `setenv diag-level` [`max` or `min`] followed by a reboot. Another method is to press the Stop key and the D key simultaneously just after the power is started. There are other computer systems on which you can bypass the diagnostic tests by holding down the Stop key while the system powers on. This is not recommended because problems can be overlooked.

There is a very powerful OK prompt application named `obdiag`. This program actually allows the system administrator to send signals to the hardware and perform almost chip-level diagnostics on a system. If you decide to use this program, use it with extreme care. You can cause damage to your system if you are not careful. In order for `obdiag` to function, you must use `set mfg-mode on` before the `reset-all`.

The OpenBoot diagnostic (OBDiag) is a menu item tool that can be used to gather information on the following hardware:

- I/O systems
- Ethernet cards
- The keyboard
- The mouse
- Disk drives
- Parallel ports and serial ports
- The NVRAM itself
- Audio devices
- The video card

The following menu structure illustrates what you see for the `obdiag` command:

```
OBDiag Menu
0..... PCI/Cheerio
1..... EBUS DMA/TCR Registers
2..... Ethernet
3..... Keyboard
4..... Mouse
5..... Floppy
6..... Parallel Port
7..... Serial Port A
8..... Serial Port B
9..... NVRAM
10..... Audio
11..... EIDE
12..... Video
13..... All Above
14..... Quit
15..... Display this Menu
16..... Toggle script-debug
17..... Enable External Loopback Tests
18..... Disable External Loopback Tests
Enter (0-13 tests, 14 -Quit, 15 -Menu) ===>
```

From here you can perform diagnostics clear down to the chip or pin level. For example, if you were to select option 0, PCI/Cheerio, you would then be able to select, for example, the `-pin_test` option, which will verify that the interrupt pin is at 1 after a reset. If you select option 4, you could, for example, force the Ethernet card into twisted-pair loopback mode for network diagnostics with the `-100_mb_twister_loopback_test` option. The type of tests available with each menu option depends on the hardware on your server or workstation. The examples above only illustrate the types of tests possible.

There are two methods of receiving diagnostic messages from your server using hardware. On some Sun servers, there is a regular start and a diagnostics mode start. The start modes are determined by a key switch that is found on mid-range and high-range servers. This feature is not found on desktop machines and low-end servers. A great deal of information is displayed about a server when it is started in diagnostics mode.

The diagnostics start can also be run from the OK prompt by typing in the following command:

```
boot -d or boot <device> -d
```

TIP The diagnostic information from the diagnostic mode start scrolls past the terminal session very quickly. Most likely you will need to save a copy of your terminal session and review it after the server has been started.

The diagnostics level that is used is determined by the OBP variable `diag-level`. If the variable is set to `max`, it could take up to 30 minutes to boot up some of the higher-level Sun servers.

When you have completed all your hardware diagnostic tests, you need to type the following commands to reset the server so it can boot normally:

```
setenv diag-switch? false
 setenv auto-boot? true
  reset-all
```

The first command turns off the diagnostics mode. The second command tells the server to boot automatically when the power is applied. And the third command resets the server and clears the memory. This command will turn off the manufacturer mode:

```
setenv mfg-mode off
```

The best place to gather information on hardware troubleshooting is from docs.sun.com; look up your particular server. There is a section, "Hardware Troubleshooting," that will cover the `obdiag` tests available for your particular hardware.

Hardware Troubleshooting within the Operating System

Even though `obdiag` and the OK prompt have some very powerful hardware diagnostics tools, there are some servers and workstations that can not be taken down for hardware diagnostics. Fortunately, the Solaris operating system does have some nice utilities that allow the system administrator to understand what the operating system "sees." This level of diagnostics is generally not as strong as the `obdiag` diagnostics, but it is still useful.

When it comes to building a new server or workstation, there is a hardware-stressing tool named SunVTS. This program validates and tests Sun hardware platforms and peripherals. It allows users to access the system device connection status and isolate system faults. SunVTS supports a wide range of interfaces, such as CDE, OpenLook, and TTY. These tests can be run in real time or at scheduled test times. There are different versions of SunVTS (link to `www.sun.com/microelectronics/vts/`):

- SunVTS 4.1 (Requires patch 1103553; Solaris 8 10/00 Release)
- SunVTS 4.0 (Solaris 8)

Each hardware device that Sun supports has a built-in hardware test. The SunVTS uses system calls and driver interfaces for its testing. The actual tests for fault isolation are slightly limited. Error messages point toward the Field Replacement Unit (FRU) that might have problems. The SunVTS sends a status message to the SunVTS kernel. The SunVTS kernel then probes the operating system kernel for installed hardware devices. After these devices have been found, the SunVTS presents tests and test options for the found devices.

The SunVTS tests can be run in three different modes:

Connectivity mode A low-stress quick testing mode that tests only the availability and connectivity of a device.

Online mode A slightly more thorough, nonintrusive test mode. Does not affect applications running at the same time.

Offline mode Requires that no other applications are running at the same time. A test run in this mode can use any resource or system call it wants.

Sun's support for SunVTS will be available only for Sun customers who purchased the Sun SPARC board-level products during the board warranty period.

The SunVTS Toolkit provides developers with tools to integrate the SunVTS tools into their applications. The toolkit has 32-bit and 64-bit test libraries, utilities, sample development files, SunVTS kernel monitoring tools, and the SunVTS Developer's

Guide. Unfortunately, the toolkit is a freeware utility that does not have any technical support.

Here are some problems you can run into and what may cause them:

Bus errors Bus errors occur when the CPU cannot reference a physical location or virtual location due to hardware error. The physical location can be a memory location, a CPU location, a device's memory location, and so on. Basically, the error is a bus error when the CPU wants to put or pull information from a physical location and it receives an error message or bad data.

Illegal address If you have a program that requests information from a memory location that does not exist (the location is not physically there), an illegal address error message will occur.

Interrupts Most devices attached to a Sun server have what is known as an "interrupt" to the CPU. When an interrupt is given, the CPU is notified that a device needs its attention. If a modem needs the CPU's attention, it will send out an interrupt. If you see an interrupt error, it is referencing a device that is trying to communicate with the CPU.

System panics Most of the time, these occur because of software-related issues. Key phrases to look for are "Asynchronous Memory Error" and "Asynchronous Memory Fault." These are rather rare system panics that relate to memory problems.

Watchdog resets A watchdog reset occurs when there is an error condition so severe that the system resets itself. This is analogous to a pilot making an emergency forced landing of his airplane before a major system fault causes the plane to crash uncontrollably. The watchdog reset is caused and controlled by the SPARC hardware itself. This can be controlled by the SPARC architecture and can be enabled or disabled with the NVRAM variable. During a watchdog reset, no core dump is taken (a core dump is a snapshot of the memory of the system at the time of a crash). There are two major types of watchdog resets:

CPU watchdog reset Happens with a single machine when a trap occurs when it should not (a CPU error). The CPU reverts to protected memory and brings the system reset down immediately.

System watchdog reset Occurs with multiprocessor machines. There is some type of major system fault that causes the system to be reset. Typically, the current memory is not affected, but the latest system read/writes might be lost. This could cause data inconsistencies with database applications like Oracle.

Once the operating systems starts, you can press the Stop key plus A and bring the system down to the OK prompt. It is highly recommended that you don't try any hardware diagnostics or troubleshooting by breaking out of the operating system and using the previously mentioned diagnostic techniques. A problem comes from the fact that the operating system is stopped. During this process, the memory is basically "frozen." If you test some devices and perform other tests and then restart the operating system, the operating system could be confused when it "unfreezes." The best technique is to bring the system down to the OK prompt using the regular shutdown procedure and then perform diagnostic tests. The NVRAM variables can be reset safely with the `eeprom` command without damaging the operating system. Just understand that the NVRAM variables will not affect the operating system until the server is rebooted. If you do stop the system, the command to return to the OS is `go`.

File System Problems

Before you can diagnose operating system problems, you must be able to mount a file system and execute files. The file system that is used within a Sun server is the Unix file system (UFS). A file system that is mounted over a network is referred to a network file system (NFS). The operating system can be on either a Unix file system or a network file system. Diskless workstations and other NFS-based operating systems will not be covered in this troubleshooting section.

To check the UFS, start with the `format` command. If the `format` command cannot "see" the hard drive that the UFS should be on, no further file system functions can be performed. When you type the `format` command, you are presented with a list of hard drives that are found and you need to select a hard drive to work on. The hard drive should be listed within the initial hard drive selection list. If it cannot be found there, check to see if the device is visible with the `prtconf -v` command. If the kernel does not "see" the hard drive, there is a `disk` command that might be able to make the hard drive visible. Check to see that the hard drive is connected with both the data cable (IDE or SCSI) and the power supply connector. The last possible solution is to bring the operating system down to the OK prompt and perform some `obdiag` tests.

TIP If it is a newly attached drive, you need to be sure you had the system scan its devices on boot. You do this either with a `boot -r` at the OK prompt or with `reboot -- -r` in the OS. As explained in an earlier chapter, you need to use the double-dash to tell reboot that there are no more arguments so it will pass the `-r` on to the PROM for the reboot.

If the hard drive is "seen" from the format command but there is a corrupt disk label (a partition table), you should be able to "relabel" the hard drive without any problems, although any data that may have been on the disk from before will be completely lost. If the file system seems to be corrupt, use the fsck command to check it. When the fsck utility checks the file system, the file system cannot be mounted. If you encounter a file system that cannot be unmounted, such as the / file system, you will have to reboot the server from the CD-ROM or another operating system partition to check the partition with fsck. In the worst-case scenario, the disk will need to be reformatted and labeled and a new file system will need to be created and mounted. Once the file system is rebuilt, the files and directories will need to be restored from tape or some other backup solution. You should double-check the file and directory permissions. With time-sensitive databases, it is a good idea to talk with the database administrators for consistency checks.

In a situation in which the format command and operating system absolutely cannot "see" the hard drive, bring the system down to the OK prompt, and from there, use the probe SCSI or probe-ide command, depending on the hardware that exists on the system.

If the hard drive cannot be "seen" from either of the probe commands, double-check the hard drive settings. For a SCSI drive, double-check the SCSI ID of each disk and the SCSI ID of the disk controller itself. Then double-check the hardware connection, cables, and power to the disks and check to make sure the SCSI chain is properly terminated. One easy test is to connect only the system disk (c0t0d0s0) and then add more disks onto the system. Each time, power up the system and type the appropriate probe command. The SCSI ID is incorrect, the cables or power supply is bad, or the disk is bad. With enough time and patience, it starts to become clear which component does not work. Most Sun systems (and all older ones) actually use the SCSI ID of 3 (which is readdressed in Solaris to c0t0d0s0) to boot. It can be quite confusing.

The most common problem with IDE hard drives is that one or both try to identify themselves as both the master and slave drive on the same cable. Double-check the hard drive's jumper settings. If that does not resolve the problem, connect only the master hard drive and set the jumper settings to single hard drive only. If the system cannot "see" the hard drive, double-check the cables and power supply. Once the system disk is recognized, reset the jumper settings for the appropriate master/slave relationship. Eventually, the failed component (hard drive, disk power supply, cable, or disk controller) will be found.

If the format command now recognizes the hard drive, boot the server to a different partition and use the fsck command. The fsck command will test a file system for errors. This is critical because further file system corruption could occur if you try to mount a corrupted file system. The slice that fsck is checking cannot be mounted during the test.

Once it has been established that the hard drive is visible and the file system is okay, you need to try to mount the hard drive. The `mount` command, if typed without any arguments, will display all the mounted slices. The next step is to create a test mount point and then try to mount the slice. The final step would be to try to copy to the mount point a directory tree with files within it. One common problem is a file system that is not mounted automatically when the server is rebooted. The most common problem is an error in the `/etc/vfstab` file. Either the mount point is not in the `/etc/vfstab` file or there is a typo in the `vfstab` file system.

If a file system has no files on it, just reformat the slice and try mounting it again. Don't waste time trying to fix an unoccupied file system. If there is a problem with the hardware, an error message should pop up some time within the rebuild steps.

Another simple problem could be that the user does not have the proper permissions to the directory. Use the command `ls -l` to view the directories' permissions. As the root user, you can access any directory or file. Be aware that Sun Solaris does have another command named `setfacl`. This command sets a file access control list on a file. Check the file or directory for an access control list using the `getfacl` command.

There are some other useful file manipulation commands. The command `fstyp` displays extensive file system parameters for a given file system. The `fsdb` command is also a high-level file system debugger. The utility `aset` is used to check the security permissions within a file system. The command `df -k` will give you the free and used space in a file system. The next useful command, `dfmounts`, displays information on remotely mounted file systems. For your shared files, use the command `dfshares`. The command `disks` is used to create symbolic links in `/dev/dsk` and `/dev/rdsk` to create a block-special file or character-special file within the `/dev` directory.

The best place to find out what is wrong with your system is from the private section of SunSolve Online. That site goes into detail about file system problems. There is a rather generic document from Sun named "Solaris Common Error Messages and Troubleshooting Guide." It gives only very generic error messages and possible solutions. It is valuable when you are in a situation in which Internet access is not available. Most file system error messages can be found within this document at `www.ebsinc.com/solaris/common_err.html`.

Operating System Problems

After the hardware is shown to be reliable and working, the next level of troubleshooting is the operating system. The theoretical line between the application and the operating system tends to be a blurry one. For example, Solaris 8 comes with the Apache Web Server. The Apache Web Server is included with the installation CD, so it could be considered part of the operating system. The Apache Web Server is also a third-party application. In this chapter, the operating system problems will be defined as the lowest-level processes or functions (Solaris users, kernel processes, file systems, etc.).

When the operating system first starts, a series of messages is displayed while the run control scripts are being executed. The command dmesg will display the messages that are displayed during the system startup. After a longer period of uptime, the usual boot information reported by dmesg will be replaced by messages from the standard operation of the system.

If the operating system experiences some critical startup problems, it will revert to run level S. There are two common reasons for operating system startup problems: a corrupt file system or a bad run control script. At the S run level, only the / file system is mounted and the only user who can log on is the root user. From here, the root user can try to fix the problems encountered and continue the boot process.

Some useful log files are shown in Table 21.2.

TABLE 21.2: SYSTEM LOG FILES USED FOR TROUBLESHOOTING

Log File	Purpose
/etc/default/cron	Specifies cron log files from the cronlog variable.
/etc/default/su	Specifies su log files from the sulog variable.
/etc/mnttab	Displays lists of currently mounted file systems.
/etc/netconfig	Displays the network configuration database read during network use and initialization.
/etc/protocols	Lists the known protocols that are used for network connections.
/etc/rmtab	Lists the file systems that are currently mounted remotely. The mount command uses this file.
/etc/rpc	This file has the known rpc services available for use.
/var/adm/messages	Lists the latest console and startup messages. The command dmesg uses this file. Use the command tail /var/adm/messages to look at the last couple of messages that were displayed in the console window. The file gets quite large and is rolled over once a week.
/var/adm/sulog	Displays the previous usage of the su command.
/var/lp/log	Stores printer log files.
/var/sadm/install/contents	Lists all software packages installed on the system. This is also a very large file.

Working with Patches

Patches are software upgrades that you run to add functionality or fix bugs in either the operating system or applications. Applying a patch can change the version number (point release .#) of the Solaris operating system. Sun releases patches to the operating system regularly, typically every quarter. With the release of a new version of the operating system, the patch upgrades begin again.

To view the current revision level for hardware and software, give the following command:

```
/usr/bin/showrev [-p] [-w] [-a] [-c command] [-s system]
```

When you type the command `showrev -p`, you will be given a long list of patches currently on the system.

Software developers will sometimes require that a specific patch be installed on the Solaris operating system. To check if your system has a desired patch, type this command:

```
showrev -p | grep <patchname>
```

This will show you if the patch is applied to the system. If a patch is not on your system, go to SunSolve Online and click the Patchfinder hyperlink.

There is a utility program available on SunSolve Online named PatchDiag (version 1.0.4). This tool searches for the following types of patches:

- Latest revisions to the operating system
- Recommended patches
- Security patches
- Year 2000 patches
- Patches that are relevant to the system's software environment

You will need a private SunSolve account to retrieve the PatchDiag software. Once you've logged on to SunSolve Online, click the hyperlink PatchDiag Tool under the patch section. You will then need to download the following files:

- PatchDiag tool (in a `tar.Z` file format)
- PatchDiag tool User's Guide
- PatchDiag `README` (included in the PatchDiag tool `tar.Z` file)
- `patchdiag.xref/`

The `patchdiag.xref` file has an up-to-date list of patches that have been produced by Sun. The `README` instructions and User's Guide are rather easy to understand and use. There is also a sample PatchDiag tool output report on SunSolve Online.

After installing the PatchDiag tool, run the script. The script produces a text file that will show you the patches that are not current on the server.

To download a specific patch, go to the SunSolve Online home page (`http://sunsolve.sun.com`) and click the link Solaris Patches under the Patches section. To find the patches that you need to download, select the operating system and hardware that applies to your server or workstation.

For example, if you chose "Solaris 8.0 (SunOS 5.8) SPARC," the next Web page would show the current patches for the Solaris 8 operating system and the SPARC architecture. You can select an HTTP or FTP download. The Web page also includes a `README` file that details exactly what the patch fixes. In some cases, you might have no need to update a patch on a server. For example, Patch 110932-01 is a fix for a DHCP agent's use of the CPU when the lease exceeds 48 days. If your network or your server does not use DHCP, there is no need to use this patch.

A recommended Patch Cluster is an accumulation of all released patches for an operating system and hardware architecture. These patches fix operating system problems and the latest security problems. Maintenance Updates are patches that have been tested to work together, whereas the Patch Cluster just includes the latest patches all together. Sometimes the `patchdiag` tool will report that you need a patch that is newer than one of the patches in a Patch Cluster. It will have to be downloaded and patched by itself because the Patch Clusters are not built regularly.

Useful Diagnostics Commands

To view detailed system configuration information, give the following command:

```
prtdiag - v ->
```

The main use of this command is to show you what the kernel "sees." For example, if an Ethernet card's device driver is not shown with this command, higher-level functions such as TCP/IP will not be possible.

To view current system information, use the following command (the command is similar to the `prtdiag` command but not as detailed):

```
/usr/sbin/prtconf
```

Another useful command is the `psrinfo` command, which shows the CPU and clock speed. You can call this command from the shell as follows:

```
/usr/sbin/psrinfo -v
```

For TCP/IP troubleshooting, use the `arp` command. This command shows the Address Resolution Protocol (ARP) table, which in turn shows how the system resolves IP addresses to host names.

When you type the command `ping server1`, the Sun server will look into the ARP table for the host name `server1` and the IP address that it represents. The `ping` command uses the actual IP address that relates to `server1`.

The following list includes some other utilities you will find useful as diagnostic commands:

`crash` A utility that diagnoses core crash dumps.

`iscda script` A script that is available with a private SunSolve account. The Sun Solution Center support engineers will often request that this script be run for analysis. This script gives the output of the `adb` and `crash` utilities in a convenient format that can be used for quick diagnostics.

`devlinks` A utility that re-creates in the `/dev` directory symbolic links from the `/devices` directory.

`eeprom` A command you can use to view the NVRAM variables from within the operating system. You can also change the value of the variables. The effects of the changes will not be seen until the system is rebooted.

`grpck` and `pwck` Two very useful utilities that check the `passwd` and `group` files for problems.

`ifconfig` Command that gives the status of the network interface. It will indicate whether the interface is up and running and give the IP address, subnet mask, and other status information on the network interface.

`iostat` Command that gives the performance of various I/O parameters. It works with the CPU, hard drive, and network card.

`perfmeter` A GUI utility that gives several parameters that are similar to the parameters given by `iostat`. This utility does require X server software on the server to monitor the utility and an X display on the client to view the results.

Many of these utilities are documented in the Solaris man pages or can be found in AnswerBook2.

System Communication

There are four primary means of communication with a Sun server or workstation:

- A keyboard, mouse, and monitor directly connected to the server
- A terminal server connected to serial port A
- A network connection through a network card
- A PPP or SLIP connection through a modem

A network connection is typically through an Ethernet card. The first step in troubleshooting network problems is to use the command `ping 127.0.0.1` and look for a `<servername> is alive` response. The IP address 127.0.0.1 is a local loopback address used for testing and internal TCP/IP operations. If you cannot ping 127.0.0.1, double-check the `/etc/hosts` file for typing errors.

Ping the address of the local Ethernet card to see if it is up. Then try pinging the default router's IP address. When a Sun server does not know where an IP packet should be sent, it will send the packet to the default router. The default router is the first router the server is capable of contacting. Any further IP resolution is performed by the default router and is of no further concern to the server. If you cannot contact your default router, you will have no further communications to the network through that particular network interface. To test the default router, ping its IP address, as in the following command (where `###.###.###.###` is the IP address of the default router):

```
ping ###.###.###.###
```

The default router is defined by the file `/etc/defaultrouter`.

TIP Solaris sends only packets that are not destined for computers on its local network to the router. If the Sun workstation believes that the IP address it is trying to reach is part of its local network, then it will attempt to send the packets directly to the system and ignore the router.

If you still can't ping the router, make sure the router itself is up and running. Try pinging the router from another server and see if that server has a ping response from the default router's IP address. The next step would be to double-check the Ethernet cable between the network interface and the default router's Ethernet port. Before trying to go to another system to ping the router, you should attempt to ping one other system on the same subnet. You should then check the cable from the workstation to the network.

If you cannot reach this Ethernet IP address, double-check three files: `/etc/hosts`, `/etc/netmask`, and `/etc/defaultrouter`. These three files define the IP address, the subnet mask, and the default router.

There is another command that is useful for diagnosing the Ethernet card itself, the `ifconfig` command. There are actually two different versions of `ifconfig`: `/usr/sbin/ifconfig` and `/sbin/ifconfig`. The `/sbin/ifconfig` is used by the Solaris operating system itself to configure the network interfaces during the system boot-up. The `/usr/sbin/ifconfig` is affected by a file named `/etc/nsswitch.conf`. The file `/etc/nsswitch.conf` determines if a Sun server will receive its configuration information locally or from a remote source like an NIS server or a DNS server. So, the

/sbin/ifconfig command works only with local files, whereas the /usr/sbin/ifconfig command will work with network information sources like NIS or DNS if that option is specified in /etc/nsswitch.conf. The command ifconfig -a shows the output from all the network cards.

NOTE The output of ifconfig and its use are covered in Chapter 9, "Network Services."

Applications and Scripts

The Solaris operating system runs a series of startup scripts from the directories /etc/rc2.d and /etc/rc3.d. These are Bourne shell scripts that set up environmental variables, initialize hardware, and configure the operating system. They can be modified to customize the server for a particular environment. Unfortunately, sometimes these run control scripts can have typos or other problems that prevent their successful execution. During the startup process, it is possible to press Ctrl+C to skip the execution of a faulty script. This could cause some problems, though, because some variables won't be set properly or some executable files won't be run. You can manually run these scripts by hand to check their operations. For example, you can run the script /etc/rc3.d/S15NFS.server. To disable a particular script (to prevent it from running), change the first letter of the script from an uppercase *S* or *K* to a different letter or number.

Another check for run control scripts is to copy the lines out of the script and run them on the command line. You could, for example, run the line /opt/SUNWvm/vm on the command line to see if the process is running. Basically you are executing particular statements manually and seeing the results of these actions.

Most of the Sun Solaris scripts have been thoroughly tested by Sun. Check the file's last modification time (using the ls, or list, command) to see if anyone has modified the file since the original installation date. If the file still has the same install creation date, open the file with the vi command and make sure it has valid text lines. The script should be executable by root only, so double-check this permission.

All the scripts should have roughly the same date and time, and they should correspond to the initial installation date. If a run control script is very badly damaged or corrupted for some reason, you might be able to copy the script from the install CD-ROM or a from another well-functioning Sun computer of the same system type.

During the startup process, a series of text messages is displayed. The dmesg command displays the initial startup messages. You can also check these messages by viewing the text file /var/adm/messages.

If you type the name of an application and it does not run, it may be that the application is not in the user's path. If a command or shell script is not in a user's path, the command will not be recognized (which is a common problem). To run an application outside the path type, use this command:

```
./<application>
```

This will run the command from the current working directory. To view the path variable, type the following command:

```
echo $PATH
```

Sometimes there are multiple copies of a command. For example, as mentioned earlier, there are two versions of ifconfig. There is an /sbin/ifconfig and a /usr/sbin/ifconfig. To know which version of a command you are running, type this command (this shows the path to the command being selected):

```
which command
```

You could also have a problem with file and directory permissions. The user needs to have executable permissions to a command. The executable permission can be a user, group, or other executable permission. The command ls -l will show all the permissions on the command.

The command id *<username>* will show the user ID and group ID of a user. Once you know who the file belongs to, the final step is to make sure the file is not corrupt. The command file will run a series of tests on a file. Check the file's size, and if it is unusually small (say, 0MB) or unusually large (like 3MB), the file could be corrupt.

If none of these commands work, try reloading the software package or just the executable file itself. The only other option is to check the operating system version and patch level. Often developers will compile an executable on a specific Sun version and patch level. Later patches and operating systems may not be compatible with the compiled executable. You can either recompile the code yourself (if you have the source code) or change the patch level to match the executable's patch level. The command showrev -p shows all the patches on the system.

Following Program Execution

If an executable will run but something goes wrong during its execution, you can try the truss command to follow the program's execution. The truss command will show all the flags and routines called by the executable. The output from `truss` will be a rather cryptic series of text messages:

```
exec (" /usr/bin/ls", 0xEFFFF510, 0xEffff513 )
open ("/opt/SUNWvm/vm, O_RDONLY )
admin
core
```

Most developers can read through this series of system calls with practice. For a system administrator without previous experience developing and debugging code, the `truss` command can still provide clues as to why an application is not running. This is particularly true if you understand the five primary system calls: `exec()`, `open()`, `mmap()`, `munmap()`, and `brk()`. A short explanation of some of the important system calls follows:

exec() Opens an executable program. For example, `exec("/usr/bin/ls", 0xEFFFF510, 0xEffff513)` opens the `ls` command. You most likely will not have to worry about the memory locations that are shown with the executable command. Basically, the `exec()` system call shows you what executable programs are being loaded into memory.

open() Opens a standard library archive file. You will see a line like `open("/usr/lib/Sunap32.so.1" , O_RDONLY)`. This is basically opening a standard library subroutine. If there is an error message similar to `Err#2 ENOENT` after you try to open a library, this would indicate that the file does not exist. The `open()` system call will tell you where an executable command is looking for a standard library archive. You are looking for an error message. The next step would be to go to a directory indicated by the error message and look at the library file. Is the file there? Is the file corrupt or does it have zero bytes? What is the latest file modification date and time compared to the other files in the directory?

mmap() Maps an image to memory. After a program is opened or executed—`open()` `orexec()`—you should see some `mmap()` system calls. Look for error messages or unusual attributes.

munmap() Unmaps an image from memory. Look for error messages.

brk() Requests a memory location.

All of these system calls are somewhat cryptic and hard to understand. You can use them to look for red flags, such as error messages or unusual terminations of a program.

One power technique that is useful with the `truss` command is to pick through its output and look through the source code of an application. Even if you are not a developer, it's not too hard to understand what a program is doing (source code) and what the results or output will be (truss output).

Debugging Shell Scripts

Shell scripts are a lot easier to debug than compiled executable programs. Most shell scripts have commands and lines of text that a typical system administrator should understand. When it comes to troubleshooting shell scripts, the first step is to check the permissions on the shell script itself. A user needs to have some type of executable permission on a shell script to run the script. The most important things to find out are whether the user can get to the script (directory permissions) and whether the user can execute the script (script executable permission).

When you want to debug a script, you can use the shell's -x option in the Bourne shell or the Korn shell. This option causes the shell to display each command before it runs the command. This trace of a script's execution can give you information about where the bugs are. You can set the -x option for the current shell so that all scripts display commands as they are run or you can use the -x option to affect only the script you are currently debugging. Use the set command at the top of the script:

```
set -x
```

Once this option is set, each command that the script executes will be preceded by a plus sign so that you can distinguish the output of the trace from any output that your script produces. To turn off the debug option, set the +x option:

```
set +x
```

If the user can execute the shell script but problems occur, the easiest troubleshooting technique is to look for obvious typos. Look for long lines that don't have the proper line wrap character for the particular shell. In most cases, the line wrap character at the end of the line should be the backslash character.

Also look for commands and text files that are not in the correct directory. For example, suppose you are troubleshooting a shell script with the line /etc/ls in it. That line executes the command ls from the /etc directory. Because ls does not reside in the /etc directory, that line could be one source of the problem. Use the find / -name ls command to find the proper location of ls and repair the incorrect line.

When it comes to small scripts, comment out everything with a # sign before each line of code. Remember, any line in a shell script with the # sign and a space as the first two characters is only a comment. Now slowly uncomment each logical section of code until the problem is found. Add the echo $VARIABLE lines into the code to see what is happening with any variable. It's easy enough to comment out the echo $VARIABLE lines when they are not needed.

The easiest way to troubleshoot logical control statements (`if`, `which`, `while`, and so on) inside scripts is to uncomment them out (as shown in the following example) so the lines of script inside their control will execute automatically:

```
if (dog = 2)
{
    echo "the value of dog is two"
}
fi
now to debug this change the code to the following,
# if (dog = 2)
# {
    echo "the value of dog is two"
# }
# fi
```

With larger shell scripts, selective commenting and uncommenting will be needed. It would be rather tedious to comment out five thousand lines of code and then uncomment the same lines of code when you are finished. So clearly, this power technique of selectively commenting out blocks of code to see what happens is really only practical with smaller scripts.

Another common problem with a shell script is when the shell script either tries to call a nonexistent command or tries to call a command in a directory without the user's permissions. Check to make sure the called files exist and are accessible from the script.

The developers of professionally produced software will give system administrators the names of the processes that are associated with their applications. You can use the `line ps -ef | grep` command to show if a process is running.

Developers typically also include log files with their programs. These text files have various error messages that relate to the running of the application. Another common technique is to include a `README` file with the program. The `README` file will have information that did not make it into the user's guide and the system administrator's guide.

Summary

This chapter explained some of the methods that you can use to troubleshoot a Solaris workstation or server. You can make the process easier to deal with by documenting your equipment and software prior to encountering difficulties. An essential practice in escaping problems that can't be solved is to make sure that you have a qualified backup (and sometimes a copy of that backup) and that you have tested that backup by doing a restoration.

You can also make your troubleshooting work more successful by approaching the task with patience and giving yourself the time to solve the problem logically. Also introduced in this chapter was a hierarchy of troubleshooting steps that you should follow: first troubleshooting the hardware, then the operating system, and finally the applications.

You learned about several resources that Sun maintains on its Web site. Of particular note are docs.sun.com, where you can find the AnswerBook2 documentation set, and SunSolve Online, which contains both a public portion and a paid or subscription portion. You will find numerous searchable databases, articles, tools, and patches that can aid you in your troubleshooting work on that site. Sun also sells support accounts, which were described in this chapter.

This chapter presented techniques and utilities that allow you to diagnose problems with SPARC and Intel hardware. For SPARC hardware, you will find the OpenBoot Prompt useful. The SunVTS Toolkit was also described. This chapter also summarized many utilities that were more fully described in other chapters and placed them in a troubleshooting context. Operating system problems often show up in the numerous log files that Solaris maintains. Those log files were also highlighted.

One method for eliminating problems with Solaris is to apply system and application patches. You can find information on determining the current state of your system with respect to patches, where to find patches, and how to apply patches once you download them. Routines for communicating with your workstation or server were also described.

To diagnose application and script errors, you can use the `truss` command to follow program execution. This will give you an output of system calls that were made. You can debug scripts by using a technique of commenting out and then uncommenting lines in the script and determining the effect.

INDEX

Note to the Reader: Throughout this index **boldfaced** page references indicate main discussions of a topic and definitions. *Italicized* page references indicate illustrations.

Symbols

@ sign|@, **370**
(*) asterisk special character, **740**
:! command, **663**
:-modifier, **715**
:q! command, 644, 645, **663**
$HOME/DeadLetters directory, **523**

A

absolute numbers, *296*
absolute path name, defined, **126**
accelerator key, **238**
access control lists (ACLs)
  defined, **132**
  encryption and, 304
  file permissions and, 294, 295
access permissions. *See also* permissions and passwords
  of Calendar, *546*, **546–548**
  defined, **131–132**
  directory, 297
  file system problems and, 818
  users, operators, and numbers and, *295–296*
access rights. *See also* security
  AdminSuite and, **476–478**
  Apache Server configuration and, 595–596
  of Calendar, *546*, **546–548**
  modifying, **135–137**
  viewing, **132–133**
account management. *See* AdminSuite 3
ACLs. *See* access control lists (ACLs)
Action Archive dialog box, *481*, 481
actions
  of CDE desktop, **267–271**
  Create Action window, *268*
  Icon Editor and Find Set dialog box, *269*
  oclock operation, *271*
Adabas D installation, 87
Add Item to Menu control, 261–262, *262*
Add Local Printer dialog box, *412*
address. *See also* Internet Protocol (IP) address
  arp utility and, 375–377
  of devices, **186–187**
  Ethernet, 809, 823
  host, **566–567**
  illegal, **815**
  numbers, *345*
  Remote MagTap protocol and, 221
  service, **69**
  space, 33, **52**, 53
  TCP/IP and, **344–346**
  vectoring, **311**
Address Manager, 264
Address Resolution Protocol (ARP)
  diagnostic commands and, 821–822
  TCP/IP and, 332
  utility of, **375–377**, *376*
administration, name services and, **357–358**
AdminSuite 3, **456–478**
  access rights and, **476–478**
  Add Group dialog box, *465*
  Add Multiple Users Wizard of, *462*
  Add User Wizard of, **461**
  delete command of, *467*
  in general, **456–459**
  Group Properties dialog box, *466*
  Log on dialog box, *458*
  network groups, managing with, **464–468**
  network users, managing with, **459**
  networks, adding with, *346*, **346–348**, *347*, *348*
  role databases and, **468–474**
  roles, creating, **474–476**
  Set Initial View dialog box, *460*, *465*
  tools opens to the Users window, *459*
  user account, adding, **460–464**
  User Properties dialog box, *463*
Admintool
  Add Access to Printer dialog box, *416*
  Add User dialog box, *432*
  defined, **395**
  group accounts and, 450, *452*, **452–454**
  printers and, **395**, **396**, 411–413
  serial ports and, 192–193
  user accounts, managing with, **431–435**
  Users window of, *431*
Advanced command, Mailer, *525*, **525–526**
AGP video cards, 71

alerts, of LP print service, **397**
algorithms, 59, **303–304**, **487**
alias built-in, C shell, **766–767**
alias built-in, Korn shell, **749**
aliases, **517**, **522**, 808
Allen, Joe, 664
AllowOverride directive, **595**
AMANDA (Advanced Maryland Automatic Network Disk Archiver) program, **508**
American Registry for Internet Numbers (ARIN), **332**, 566
Andreessen, Marc, **573**
anon layer, 54–55
anonymous memory, **51**, **54–58**
AnswerBook server, 805
AnswerBook2, **15–17**, *16*
AnswerBooks, troubleshooting and, 797, 798
AOL browser, 600
Apache Web Server, **587–600**
  configuration of, **590–600**
    global, **590–593**
    server, **594–598**
    virtual hosts, **598–600**
  in general, **587–590**
  troubleshooting and, 818–819
  World Wide Web and, 567
Apple Computer, OS X, 7–8
AppleTalk, 560
Application layer, OSI, **327**, **330–331**, **563**
Application Manager
  archives and, *482*, **482–486**
  CDE desktop and, *106*
  program folder, *260*
application proxy program, **312**
applications
  in general, 793
  troubleshooting and, **824–828**
    program execution, following, **825–827**
    shell scripts, debugging, **827–828**
Applications control, 260
Applications subpanel, *259*, 259–260
applications, X, 287, *288–289*
Appointment Editor, Calendar, **539–540**, **541–543**
appointments, Calendar and
  creating, **539–540**
  customizations and, 544–549
  getting started, 535–536
  Mailer, combining with, 550–552
  meetings and, 541–543
  searching Calendar and, 543–544
  views for, 537–539
Archive Unpack command, 491, *492*
archives, **480–486**
  Action Archive dialog box, *481*
  Application Manager, *482*
  pop-up menu of, *484*
ARCserve 2000, **509**
argv array variable, **772**
ARIN (American Registry for Internet Numbers), **332**, 566
arithmetic expressions, 731–732, **741–743**, *742*
ARP. *See* Address Resolution Protocol (ARP)
arp -a command, **115**
arp utility, **375–377**, *376*
ARPAnet, 350, **567**
array variable, **734–735**, **772**
arrays, numeric, **776**
ASCII files, 384, 409, 668
ASET (Automated Security Enhancement Tool), **314–315**
asterisk (*) special character, **740**
asymmetric encryption, **303–304**
asynchronous signals, defined, **35**
Asynchronous Transfer Mode (ATM), **336**
at command, **627–628**, 676, **783–786**
AT&T Bell Laboratories, 24, 26, 672
Athena project, 283, 318
Athena widget set, 284
ATM (Asynchronous Transfer Mode), **336**
atq argument, **783**
atq command, 628
atrm argument, **783**
atrm command, 628
attachments
  e-mail and, 580–581
  Mailer and, **521**, **529–530**, *531*
authentication clients, encrypted, **317–318**
authorizations, **468–474**
auto boot? command, 811
auto-boot? variable, **808**
autoconfiguration, defined, **189–190**
AutoFS service, **435–438**
Automated Security Enhancement Tool (ASET), **314–315**
automatic file system mount, **367–368**
automount utility, Solaris, **366–367**, *367*
availrmem (system global variable), 56

B

Backdrop desktop control, 271
backdrop, setting, 275
background process, defined, **605**
backslash character, 745, 747
backup and restore, **495–509**
  commands for, **504–506**
  in general, **495–498**

local vs. network backup, **507**
strategies for, **498–502**
tape drives and, 221–222
third-party backup programs, **507–509**
utilities for, **502–504**
backups, troubleshooting and, **794–795**, 796
bandwidth requirements, 285
banner command, 807
basename utility, 714
Basic command, Mailer, *522*, **522–523**
Berkeley Fast File System, 161
Berkeley Internet Name Domain (BIND) software, **355**, 566
Berkeley Software Distribution (BSD), 672
Berkeley System Distribution, 161
Berners-Lee, Tim, 567
BigAdmin site, **798**, **800**
/bin directory, **140**
binary kernel modules, **48–49**
BIND (Berkeley Internet Name Domain) software, **355**, 566
BIOS interface, startup and, **92–93**
block device, defined, **185**
block-special file, defined, **128**
blocks, **165–168**
Blowfish, **304**
bookmarks, Netscape, **578**
books, Sun Press, **805**
boot block, defined, **166**
boot device, 85, **808**
boot process
mounting file systems and, 169
OpenBoot Prompt and, **806–816**
startup and, **95–97**
BOOTSTRAP Protocol (BOOTP), **361**
borders and corners, **234**
Bourne Again shell, **673**, **720**
Bourne shell, **694–721**
compatibility of, 690
control structures of, **695–714**
built-ins of, *698–700*
case structure, **709–714**, *710*
for...in structure, **704–706**
here script, **714**
if...then structure, **695–697**, *696*, **700–703**
if...then...elif structure, **703–704**, *705*
for structure, **706**
test utility options, *700*
until structure, *707*, **707–709**
while structure, **706–707**
defined, **673**
desktop customization and, 272–273
in general, **694–695**
scripts of, **99**
shell scripts, debugging in, 827–828
symbolic links and, 301
user environment and, 439, 442
variables and, **715–720**
built-ins of, *716*, **716–717**
environmental, 685
exporting, 684
functions and, **717–720**
in general, **715**
local, 681–682
Bourne, Steve, 673
brace expansion, **767**
braces, variables and, 715
bracket [ ] special character, **740–741**
brk ( ) system call, **826**
broadcast networks, **333–334**, 343–344
broadcast transmission, defined, **338**
Bronze Support, SunSpectrum, **803**
BrowserMatch directives, **598**
browsers, **573–579**
Internet Explorer, **574–575**
Java and, **6–7**
Mosaic, **573**
Netscape, *574*, **575–579**, *576*, *579*
BRU 2000 (Backup and Restore Utility), **507**
BSD (Berkeley Software Distribution), 672
buffer overflows, 307
buffers, in vi editor, 657, **659–660**
bugs, 319, 800. *See also* debug; troubleshooting
built-ins
of Bourne shell, **694**, *698–700*, *716*, **716–717**
@ built-in, **773–774**, 775, 776
of C shell, **780–787**
for input/output redirection, **786–787**
list of, *780–782*
for process control, **782–786**
rehash command, **782**
variable control structures, **778–780**
of Korn shell, **730–732**, *732*
shells and, **686–689**, *687–688*, **690**
bus architecture, Intel hardware compatibility, 70
bus errors, **815**
bus topology, defined, **339**
buses, hierarchy of, 27
buttons, **238**

C

C programming language, 24
C shell (csh), **762–788**
compatibility of, 690
creating scripts in, **777–787**
command-line shortcuts, **778**
variable control structures, **780–787**

defined, **673**
starting in, **762–777**
alias built-in of, **766–767**
command-line expansion and, **767–768**
directory stacks and, **768–771**, *769*, *770*, *771*
environmental variables of, **773–777**
in general, **762–763**
history built-in of, **764–766**
variables of, **771–773**, *773*
symbolic links and, 301, 302
terminal type, vi editor and, 662
user environment and, 439–440, 442
variables and, 682–683
Cache File System (CacheFS), 162
cache, pages and, 59
Calendar, **535–557**
appointments and, **539–540**, *540*
changing views in, **537–539**
Day view, *537*
Week view, *538*
Year view, *539*
command-line utilities and, **552–556**, *554*, *555*
customizing, **544–549**
access rights and permissions, *546*
Calendar Options dialog box, *545*, *546*, *547*, *549*
To Do items, **540–541**, *541*
Federated Naming Service and, **556–557**
functions of, 512
group meetings, **549–550**
Mailer, combining with, **550–552**
meetings, replicating, **541–543**, *542*
searching the, *543*, **543–544**
starting, **535–536**, *536*
caller ID (CLID), **316**
callog. <username> file, 539
cancel command, 420
Cards subpanel, *258*, 258
carrier sense multiple access with collision detection (CSMA/CD), **333**
case command, 656, **709–710**
case control structure, **694**
case sensitivity, 444, 646
case structure, **709–714**, *710*
cat command, **115**
cd command, 154–155
CD-ROMS, **197–204**
contents of, *198*
educational, 804
ejecting, **202–204**, *203*
file system hierarchy and, 36–37
file systems for, 161
files and directories, working with, **200**
Intel hardware compatibility and, 70
Intel installation and, 83
mount points and symbolic links and, 194–195
mounting, **197–200**
mounting CDs and, **195–196**
startup and, 93
volume management and, 193–194
WorkMan and, *201*
CDE desktop. *See* Common Desktop Environment (CDE)
CDPATH variable, **688–689**
CDs, **195–196**, *201*, 494–495
cfgadm command, **188**
CGI (Common Gateway Interface), **571–573**, **597**
Challenge Handshake Authentication Protocol (CHAP), **316**
Change command, vi editor, **646**, 656
character device, defined, **185–186**
character-special file, **129**
characters, special, **738–743**
arithmetic expressions, **741–743**, *742*
filename generation and, **738–741**
check box, **237–238**
chgrp command, **136–137**
child processes, 618, 684
chmod command, 436
chmod utility, *295*, 295
chown command, **135–136**
circuit switching, **340**
Clark, Jim, **573**
CLID (caller ID), **316**
client/server model, 337–338
clients
Apache Web Server and, 592–594
CGI and, 572–573
Hypertext Transfer Protocol and, 568–570
spooling and, 403
X Windows, 284–286
collisions, 333–334
command interpreters, **690**
command-line. *See also* LP print service
C shell history built-in and, 764–766
commands of, **110–111**
editing, in Korn shell, **751–755**
emacs editor, using in, **754–755**
vi editor, using in, **751–752**, *753–754*
expansion, in C shell, **767–768**
Session Manager and, 228
shell scripts and, 677–678
shortcuts, in C shell, **778**
utilities, Calendar, **552–556**, *554*, *555*
Command mode, vi editor, 641–642, **645**, 646–647, 751–752
command substitution, 731
Command tool, **107**, 109

commands. *See also* Bourne shell; built-ins; C shell; shell scripts, creating
  for access rights modification, 135–137
  for Apache, 588–589
  backup and restore, 504–506
  Bourne shell functions and, 717–720
  for Calendar, 552–556
  compress command, 486–487
  copy, **154**, 157–158, 207–208
  diagnostic, 190–192, 821–822
  for disk quotas, 176–177
  for disk repair, 177–179
  for disk utilization, 172–175
  for editing in vi editor, 653–654, *655–656*
  elm (e-local mail) freeware and, 309–310
  file, 115–117
  of File Manager, *244–247*
  file manipulation, in vi editor, *649*
  find, 111–114
  for finding system information, 114–115
  GNU tar command, 484–486
  for group accounts, 451–452
  for GUI Login screen, 102
  of Korn shell, 737–738, 749–750, 757–759
  Korn shell built-ins, *730*, 730–732
  for links, 159–160
  for Mailer, 522–529
  in man and xman pages, *11–13*
  for managing jobs, 627–630
  mount, 169–170
  for navigating directories, 154–155
  of Network File System, 369
  of OpenBoot Prompt, 808–811, 813
  of OpenLook Desktop, *282*
  for packages, 490–495
  password, for user accounts, 443–445
  pine, 582–584
  print, 407
  of process file system, 618–621
  for process priorities, 615–617
  of role-based access, *476*
  sar command, 631–632
  of sendmail, *307*
  for shell scripts, 676–679
  shutdown, 101
  SMTP, 305–306
  tar command, 480–483
  unmount, 171–172
  of user accounts, 428–430
  of vi editor, 645–647, *648*, *655–656*, *753–754*
  for viewing processes, 606–613
  in Window menu, 239–240
  of Workspace menu, 241–242
comments, **425**
commercial license, for Solaris, 63
Common Desktop Environment (CDE), **226–272**. *See also* Calendar; Mailer; text editors
  actions of, **267–271**
  customizing, **105–106**
  exiting, **117–118**
  File Manager of, **244–252**
  front panel of, **253–266**
  GUIs and, **105–106**, 224–225
  invisible filenames in, 126
  log on of, **227–230**
  login screen of, 104
  menus of, **230–232**
  new directory, creating in, 153–154
  startup resource files and, 152
  terminal and console windows and, **108–109**
  windows of, **232–243**
  workspaces of, **271–272**
Common Gateway Interface (CGI), **571–573**, **597**
Common Open Software Environment (COSE), **224–225**
Compaq Storage Array servers, 93
compatibility, Solaris, **5–6**, **65**, **70–71**
Compose Window command, Mailer, **524–525**
Compose window, Mailer, *516*, 519–520, *524*
compress command, **486–487**
compression, 480, 484, **486–488**, 491
Computer Associate, **509**
concentrator, defined, **334**
configuration files, *38–39*
Confirm Information screen, 78
confirmation notice, e-mail, **526**
Connectionless communication protocols, **331**
connectivity mode, SunVTS, 814
console port, startup and, **93–95**
console session, **94–95**
Console window, **108**, **109**
continue command, **708–709**
control scripts
  instructions of, *100*
  startup and, **98–100**
  subdirectories of, *99*
  troubleshooting, 824–825
control structures
  of Bourne shell, **695–714**
    built-ins of, *698–700*
    case structure, **709–714**, *710*
    for...in structure, **704–706**
    function of, 694
    here script, **714**
    if...then structure, **695–697**, *696*, **700–703**
    if...then...elif structure, **703–704**, *705*
    for structure, **706**
    test utility options, *700*

until structure, *707*, **707–709**
while structure, **706–707**
of C shell, **778–780**
of Korn shell, **735–736**
controller numbers, **187**
controls, Desktop, **273–277**
coprocess, **744–748**, *745*
copy command
defined, **154**
for diskettes, 207–208
for files and directories, 157–158
links and, 159
in vi editor, **657**
Copy Object dialog box, *250*
COSE (Common Open Software Environment), **224–225**
cpio command, **484–486**
CPU
errors, troubleshooting, 815
Performance Meter and, 625–626
pr stat argument and, 785
Process Manager and, 615
watchdog reset, 815
crash command, **634**
crash, system, 649, 793, 795
crash utility, **822**
Create Action window, 267–268, *268*
cron command, **628–630**, 676
csh. *See* C shell (csh)
.cshrc variable, **763**
CSMA/CD (carrier sense multiple access with collision detection), **333**
CTAR program, **507**
cursor, vi editor and, *652*
customization
of Calendar, **544–549**
access rights and permissions, *546*
Calendar Options dialog box, *545*, *546*, *547*, *549*
of desktop controls, **273–277**
with Hotkey Editor, **277–280**
of Mailer, **521–529**
additional commands, **528–529**
Advanced command and, *525*, **525–526**
Basic command and, *522*, **522–523**
Compose window and, *524*, **524–525**
custom view, creating, **531–534**
Move Menu Setup Mail Options dialog box, *528*
Templates command and, **527**, *527*
Vacation Message Mail Options dialog box, *529*
of Netscape browser, 578–579
of Solaris desktop, **272–280**
cwd variable, **772**

D

daemons, 364–365, **385–386**
data, 45–46, 185–186
Data Link layer, OSI, **328**, **332–333**, **564**
Data Link Provider Interfaces (DLPIs), 27
data locks, 26
data packets, **343**
data-stream transmissions, **339**, 340
datagram transmissions, **339**, 340
date
at command and, 627
cron command and, 629–630
network addressing and, 69
DCA (Device Configuration Assistant), **83–85**
dd command, **502–503**
DDI (device driver interface), **42**
deadlocks, virtual memory and, 34
debug, **377–382**, **720**, 827–828
decryption, **488**, 489
default mount points, *164–165*
default router, 823
DELETE method, **569**
deleting and undoing, in vi editor, **654**, **656**
demand paging, **26–27**, 34
DES algorithm, **304**
desktop, Solaris, **224–289**
CDE desktop, **226–272**
actions of, **267–271**
File Manager of, **244–252**
front panel of, **253–266**
log on and, **227–230**
menus of, **230–232**
windows of, **232–243**
workspaces of, **271–272**
customizing, **272–280**
desktop controls, **273–277**
with Hotkey Editor, **277–280**
graphical user interface and, **224–226**
OpenLook desktop, **280–283**
X Window System, **283–289**
X applications, **287–289**
X clients and servers, **284–286**
X sessions, **286–287**
destination, defined, **394–395**
/dev directory, *39*, **140–141**, 183–184
devalias command, **808**
Device Configuration Assistant (DCA), **83–85**
device directories, *39*
device driver interface (DDI), **42**
device drivers, **189–193**
diagnostic utilities of, **190–191**
functions of, 41–42

serial ports, **192–193**
in Solaris, 27
device file, defined, **364**
device to device command, **502–503**
device tree, *41*
devices, **182–222**
addresses of, **186–187**
CD-ROMS, **197–204**
ejecting, **202–204**, *203*
files and directories, working with, **200**
mounting, **197–200**
WorkMan and, *201*
device drivers, **189–193**
diagnostic utilities of, **190–191**
serial ports, **192–193**
diskettes, **204–210**
ejecting, **210**
files and directories, working with, **207–210**
formatting, **205–207**
mounting, **205**
file system structure and, 122
in general, **182–183**
hard drives, **212–220**
adding a disk, **219–220**
disk management and, **216–219**
partitions of, **213–215**
installation and removal of, **187–189**
interrupts and, 815
mappings of, **183–184**
mount points and symbolic links and, **194–195**
mounting file systems and, 169–171
OpenBoot Prompt and, 807–810
removable media, mounting, **195–196**
tape drives, **221–222**
troubleshooting and, 793
types of, **184–186**
unmounting file systems and, 171–172
volume management for, **193–194**
zip and jaz drives, **211–212**
/devices directory, **141**
devlinks utility, **822**
df command, **172–173**
df utility, 363
DHCP. *See* Dynamic Host Configuration Protocol (DHCP)
diag-level variable, **807**
diagnostic
commands, **808–811**, **813**, **821–822**
OpenBoot Prompt and, **807–813**
tests, POST, **805–806**
utilities, device, **190–192**
dialog boxes, 235–238, **243**
directives, for Apache, **591–599**
directories, **137–160**. *See also* home directory
access permissions for, **297**
on CDs, working with, 200–204
configuring, *39*
copying and moving, **157–158**
creating, **152–154**
defined, **138**
defining in Apache, 591
deleting, **156–157**
device, *39*
on diskettes, 207–210
links and, **158–160**
list of, **138–150**
navigating, **154–155**
program, *40*
startup resource files, **151–152**
temporary, *40–41*
user accounts and, 433
working and home directories, **151**
Directory directives, **595–596**
directory file, defined, **129**
directory hierarchy, **48–49**
directory listings, Apache, **597**
directory stacks, C shell, **768–771**, *769*, *770*, *771*
directory tree, **122–124**, *123*
dirs built-in, C shell, **768–771**, *769*, *770*, *771*
Disk Selection screen, 80–81, *81*
disk storage, **160–179**
disk structures, **165–166**
disk utilization, **172–179**
commands for, **172–175**
disk quotas, **176–177**
disk repair, **177–179**
file systems
adding new, **168–169**
in general, **161–162**
mounting, **169–171**
unmounting, **171–172**
virtual, **162–165**
superblocks and inode tables, **166–168**
disk thrashing, defined, **633**
diskettes, **204–210**
copying from, 503
ejecting, **210**
files and directories, working with, **207–210**
formatting, *205*, **205–207**
mounting, **195–196**, **205**
volume management and, 193
distributed computing, defined, **337**
DLPIs (Data Link Provider Interfaces), 27
dmesg command, **191–192**, 819, 825
docs.sun.com site, **797**, *798*, 813
documentation, troubleshooting and, **794**, 797

dollar sign ($)
  Korn shell variables and, 727
  shells and, 679, 682, 683, 689
  variables and, 715
Domain Name Screen, **75–76**
Domain Name Service (DNS), **350–355**
  domains, proposed, *352*
  domains, top-level, *351*
  installation and, **76–77**
  internetworking and, **565–566**
  OSI Application layer and, 330
doors, **34–35**, 185
dotted decimal notation, **344**
double indirection, **54–55**
download
  of AdminSuite 3, 456
  of Apache, 587–588
  of backup programs, 507–509
  of Bourne Again shell, 720
  of compression programs, 487–488
  of FastCGI, 572
  of files, FTP site, 577–578
  of Internet Explorer, 574
  of Netscape, 573
  packages and, 490–495
  of patches, 88, 821
  of Secure Shell, 318
  of servlets, 573
  software, compatibility and, 10
  of Solaris, 64
  of StarOffice suite, 85
  of StarOffice Word Processor, 668
  of top command, 611
  of WorkMan program, 495
drag and drop action, **250–251**, 530–531
drivers, 52. *See also* device drivers
drives
  hard drives, **212–220**
    adding a disk, **219–220**
    disk management and, **216–219**
    file system problems and, 816–817
    Intel hardware compatibility and, 70
    life span of, 495
    OpenBoot Prompt and, 809
    slices or partitions of, **213–215**
  tape, **187**, **221–222**
  zip and jaz, **211–212**
drvconfig command, **184**
dtcm_delete command, 555, **556**
dtcm_editor command, **553–554**, *554*
dtcm_insert command, **555**
dtcm_lookup command, **555**
dtfile. *See* File Manager
dtlogin GUI, **103–107**
  CDE desktop, **105–106**
  in general, **103–104**
  Open Windows, customize, **106–107**
dtlogin manager, **227–228**
dtmail agent, **513**, 517
dtmail program, 580–581
.dtprofile file, **272–273**
du command, **174–175**
dump command, **505**. *See also* ufsdump utility
DVD, format for, 161, 162
Dynamic Host Configuration Protocol (DHCP), **360–369**
  in general, **360–362**
  host addresses and, 566–567
  installation and, 75
  Network File System and, **362–369**
  screen of, 75
dynamic linking, 27

E

e-local mail (elm) freeware, **309–310**
e-mail, **579–585**. *See also* Mailer
  address, 516
  Apache server configuration and, 594
  Calendar and, 550–552
  in general, **579–581**
  message, open, *518*
  message, ready, *517*
  pine newsreader, **584–585**
  pine, using for, **581–584**
  posting, 387
  security of, **305–311**
  setup pop-up window, *514*
eBay, 18
echo command, 684–685
echo statement, 711–713
echo variable, 776
Edit Defaults option, Calendar, **544–545**, *545*
Edit Hotkey dialog box, *279*, 280
editors. *See* text editors
edquota command, **176–177**
educational resources, **803–805**, *804*. *See also* resources
eeprom command, **822**
EEPROM (Electrically Erasable Programmable Read Only Memory), **49**
eject command, 202, *203*
electronic mail. *See* e-mail; Mailer
elm (e-local mail) freeware, **309–310**
emacs editor, **664**, **754–755**
encapsulation, **562**
encrypted authentication clients, **317–318**
encrypting program, 292
encryption
  The Action: DeCrypt dialog box, *489*

The Action: Encryption dialog box, *488*
file utility for, **488–490**
secret key, **304**, **318**
symmetric and asymmetric, **303–305**
.enet-addr command, **809**
Enhanced Software Technologies, **507**
enterprise servers, 112
Entry mode, vi editor, **645**
env command, **114**
environmental variables, **685–686**, 725–726, **773–777**
ErrorLog directive, **598**
errors, 715, 786, 815. *See also* bugs; troubleshooting
Esc key, vi editor, 647, 648
escape options, print built-in, *746–747*
/etc/defaultdomain file, **359**
/etc/defaultrouter file, **359**
/etc directory, *38–39*, **115**, **141–143**
/etc/group file, *455*
/etc/hostname.<interface> file, **359**
/etc/inittab file, **100**
/etc/nodename file, **359**
/etc/nsswitch.conf file, **406–407**
/etc/security/auth_attr, *470*, **470–471**
/etc/security/exec_attr, *473*, **473–474**
/etc/security/prof_attr, **471–472**
/etc/skel/local.cshrc file, *440*
/etc/skel/local.login file, *440*
/etc/skel/local.profile file, *441*
/etc/user_attr, **468–470**
/etc/vfstab file, *170*
Ethernet address, 809, 823
Ethernet network, **333–334**, 375
Ethernet switch, **334**
Eudora mail client, **310**
event modifiers, C shell, *766*
events, history built-in and, 764–766
ex line editor, 640
exec built-in, Bourne shell, **694**
exec ( ) system call, **603**, **826**
executable files, **133–134**, *391–393*
executable programs
CGI, 571
system process and, **602–605**
troubleshooting, **825–827**
execute access, **131**
<execute command>, **113–114**
exit command signal, *716*
expansion
command-line, C shell and, **767–768**
shell scripts and, **678–679**
shell variable, **733–734**
Explorer Data Collector, 799
/export directory, **143**
<expression> parameter, 112–113
expressions, numeric, *775*, 776
ExtendedStatus directive, **591**
extender, **339**
extensions, file, **125–126**, 670
extranet, defined, **560**

F

FAQs, resource for Solaris 8, **18–21**
FastCGI, 572
Fatbrain.com, 15
fc command, 756–757
FDFS (file descriptor file system), **164**
fdisk, 69
fdisk command, 216
Federated Naming Service (FNS), **556–557**
Fiber Distributed Data Interface (FDDI), **335**, *336*
fiber-optic cabling, 335
fiber-optic security system, 321
FIFOS (first-in-first-out file system), **164**
file command, **115–117**
file descriptor file system (FDFS), **164**
File Manager, **244–252**
commands and, *240*, **244–247**
diskettes and, 207–208
files, moving, copying, and renaming in, **249–252**
group accounts and, 450
log on and, 228–229
Mailer and, **530–531**
menus and, 232
new directory, creating with, 153–154
selection in, **248–249**
user home directory and, 436
windows and, 234–235
file manipulation commands, *649*, 818
file permissions, **293–297**
directory access permissions, **297**
in general, **293–296**
setuid, setgid permissions, **296–297**
file system, **122–180**. *See also* Network File System (NFS); Unix file system (UFS)
directories, **137–160**
copying and moving, **157–158**
creating, **152–154**
deleting, **156–157**
links and, **158–160**
list of, **138–150**
navigating, **154–155**
startup resource files, **151–152**
working and home directories, **151**
disk storage, **160–179**
disk structures, **165–166**
disk utilization and, **172–179**

file systems, adding new, **168–169**
file systems and, **161–162**
file systems, mounting, **169–171**
file systems, unmounting, **171–172**
superblocks and inode tables, **166–168**
virtual file systems and, **162–165**
files, working with, **124–137**
attributes and properties of, **127–137**
filenames, **125–127**
structure of, **122–124**
troubleshooting, **816–818**
file system, hierarchical, **35–41**, *164–165*
File Transfer Protocol (FTP)
defined, **330**
ftp command, 719
site, downloading from, **577–578**
utility for, 384
file transfer utilities, **384**
file utilities, **480–509**
archives, **480–486**
backup and restore, **495–509**
backup strategies, **498–502**
backup utilities, **502–504**
commands for, **504–506**
in general, **495–498**
local vs. network backup, **507**
third-party backup programs, **507–509**
compression, **486–488**
encryption, **488–490**
packages, **490–495**
filec variable, **772**
fileedit2 script, 713
filenames, **125–127**, **738–741**
Files subpanel, 258, *259*
files, working with, **124–137**
attributes and properties of, **127–137**
access permissions, **131–132**
access rights, modifying, **135–137**
access rights, viewing, **132–133**
file types, **127–131**
SUID and SGID permissions, **133–134**
on CDs, 200–204
copying and moving, **157–158**
deleting, **156–157**
on diskettes, 207–210
filenames, **125–127**
extensions, **125–126**
invisible, **126**
path name, **126–127**
linking, *302*
moving, copying, renaming, **249–252**
filters, print, **405–406**
find command, **111–114**
Find dialog box, *243*, *543*, **543–544**
Find Process control, 263
Find Set dialog box, *269*
find utility, Bourne shell, **695**
finger command, **447–449**, *448*
finger utility, **370**, *371*
firewalls, 77–78, **311–312**
first-in-first-out file system (FIFOS), **164**
fix-modes utility, **292–293**
floating point exceptions, **43**
floppy disks, 161, 193. *See also* diskettes
FNS (Federated Naming Service), **556–557**
folder
defined, **138**
moving, copying, renaming, **249–252**
selection of, **248–249**
for...in structure, **704–706**
foreach built-in, C shell, **778–779**
foreground process, defined, **605**
fork ( ) system call, **603**
format command, **216–220**, *217*
format utility, **216–220**
FQDN (fully qualified domain name), **352**
fragmentation, 169, 178
Frame Relay, **336–337**
free hog slice, **218**
"Free Solaris Binary License Program", 62
front panel, **253–266**
controls of, **254–256**
menus, **231**
modifying, **265–266**
subpanels of, **257–265**
fsck command, **177–179**, 817
FTP. *See* File Transfer Protocol (FTP)
fully qualified domain name (FQDN), **352**
function, defined, **695**
functions
Bourne shell and, **717–720**
Bourne Again shell, **720**
.profile file, **718–719**
shell script debugging, **720**
spell utility, **719–720**
Korn shell and, **748–750**
fuser command, **202**, **621**

G

gateway, **561**, *562*
GET request, 571–572
getopts command, **737–738**
GID number. *See* group identification number (GID number)
GNOME, 7, 226, 284
GNU gtar utility, **490–492**

GNU tar command, **484**
Gold Support, SunSpectrum, **802**
goto built-in, C shell, **778**
Grandfather-Father-Son backup rotation scheme, **499–500**, *500*
graphical user interface (GUI), **102–103**, **224–226**, **280–283**
Graphical Workspace Manager, 272
group account, defined, **449**
group accounts. *See* user accounts and groups
group database, **450–451**
group file, **422**
group identification number (GID number)
  data types and, 426
  defined, **422**
  explained, **454–455**
  passwd file and, **425**
  role databases and, 471–474
  system process and, 603
groupadd command, **451**
groupdel command, **452**
groupmod command, **451–452**
grpck utility, **822**
gtar command, **490–492**
GTK toolkit, 284
GUI. *See* graphical user interface (GUI)
gzip compression, **484**, **487**

H

hackers, 102, 794
hard drives, **212–220**
  adding a disk, **219–220**
  disk management and, **216–219**
  file system problems and, 816–817
  Intel hardware compatibility and, 70
  life span of, 495
  OpenBoot Prompt and, 809
  partitions of, **213–215**
hard link
  defined, **158–159**
  link permissions and, **298**, **300**
  removal of, 302
hardware
  backup and restore and, 495
  Intel, compatibility of, **70–71**
  resources for, 18
  troubleshooting, **805–816**
    backups and, 795
    in general, 792–793, **805–806**
    OpenBoot prompt and, **806–813**
    within operating system, **814–816**
Hardware Address Translation (HAT) layer, 33–34, **51–52**, **53**
HEAD method, **569**
headers
  defined, **329**
  OSI model and, **562**, 564
  request, HTTP, **568–570**
Help Manager, 264
Help menu, Netscape, 575
Help subpanel, 264, *264*
here script, **695**, **714**
hidden files, **126**
hierarchical file system, **35–41**, *164–165*
High Sierra file system (HSFS), **36–37**, 161
hint (caching) server, **353–355**
<HISTFILE> variable, **755–756**
history built-in, C shell, **764–766**
history files, Korn shell, **755–757**
.history variable, C shell, **763**
<HISTSIZE> variable, **755–756**
home directory
  automatic file system mount and, 368
  creating a, **435–438**
  defined, **143**
  partition for, 215
  in passwd file, 425
  working directory and, **151**
/home partition, **68**
HOME variable, **772**
host
  addresses, **566–567**
  addressing and, 344–345
  Apache server configuration and, 594
  arp utility and, 375–377
  database file of, **359–360**
  finger utility and, 370–371
  ping utility and, 373–375
  snoop utility and, 377–382
  TCP/IP and, 332, **349–350**
  virtual hosts, Apache, **598–600**
host name, defined, **69**
hostid command, **114**
HostNameLookups directive, **598**
hot-plugging, **188**
Hotkey Editor
  actions and, 270
  customization with, **277–280**
  defined, **263**
  for keyboard macros, *278*
HSFS (High Sierra file system), **36–37**, 161
HTML editors, 575
HTML files, 595–596
HTML site, downloading from, **577–578**
httpd.conf file, **590**
hub, **339**
HyperTerminal software, 94

Hypertext Transfer Protocol (HTTP)
- BrowserMatch directives and, **598**
- OSI Application layer and, **330**
- World Wide Web, the Internet and, **568–570**

I

I/O architecture, **41–50**
- directory hierarchy, **48–49**
- linking, **49–50**
- Solaris kernel and, **42–44**
- synchronization and, **45–47**
- system clock and, **44–45**

IBM, Token Ring network, 334
ICMP. *See* Internet Control Message Protocol (ICMP)
Icon Editor, *269*
icons, **226–227**, 266, 519–520
IDE hard drive, 817
IDEA algorithm, **304**
if control structure, C shell, **778**
if...then structure, **695–697**, *696*, **700–703**
if...then...elif structure, **703–704**, *705*
ifconfig -a command, **115**
ifconfig command, **822**
ifconfig utility, **382**
IFS variable, **686**
IMAP (Internet Message Access Protocol), **309**, 513–514, 528
INBOX, pine, **583–584**
incremental backup, **498–501**, 504–505
infinite loop symbolic directory, 113
information sharing, **585–587**
init process, **101**
initiator-id variable, **807**
inode numbers, 300
inode tables, **166–168**, *167*
input and output, Korn shell, **743–750**
- coprocess, redirecting I/O, **744–748**, *745*
- functions and, **748–750**

input-device variable, **808**
input/output redirection, **744–748**, **786–787**
install server, 82
installation of Solaris 8, **62–89**
- distributions of Solaris and, **62–65**
- installing, **65–71**
  - installation types and, **65–66**
  - Intel hardware compatibility and, **70–71**
  - network addressing and, **69–70**
  - partitioning schemes and, **66–69**
- patches and, **87–88**
- procedure for, **71–87**
  - Intel installation, **83–85**
  - preboot process, **72–74**
  - on SPARC, **71–83**
  - StarOffice installation, **85–87**
  - system configuration, **74–78**
  - Web Start, **78–83**

instructions trap, **43**
integer attributes, Korn shell, 728
Intel
- adding a disk, 220
- hardware, compatibility of, 65, **70–71**
- installation of Solaris and, **83–85**
- newsgroup for, 586
- startup and, **92–93**

Interactive (IA) class, 32
interactive installation, **66**
interchange format, **126**
International Standards Organization (ISO), 565
Internet and networking
- Apache, **587–600**
  - configuration of, **590–600**
  - in general, **587–590**
- browsers, **573–579**, *574*
  - Netscape, **575–579**, *576*, *579*
- e-mail and, **579–585**
  - pine newsreader, **548–585**
  - pine, using for, **581–584**
- information sharing, **585–587**
- internetworking, **560–567**
  - domain name service and Internet, **565–566**
  - host addresses and, **566–567**
  - network communications and, **561–565**, *562*
- security and, 313
- whois utility and, 383–384
- World Wide Web and, **567–573**
  - Common Gateway Interface and, **571–573**
  - HTTP and, **568–570**

Internet Control Message Protocol (ICMP), 331, 332, 373, 374
Internet Explorer, Microsoft, **574–575**
Internet Message Access Protocol (IMAP), **309**, 513–514, 528
Internet Protocol (IP) address
- defined, **69**
- DHCP screen and, 75
- domain name service and, 565–566
- host addresses and, 566–567
- network files and, 359–360
- system communication and, 823
- TCP/IP and, 344
- whois utility and, 383–384

Internet Protocol (IP), defined, **331–332**
internetworking, **560–567**
- domain name service and, **565–566**
- host addresses and, **566–567**
- network communications and, **561–565**, *562*

InterNIC. *See* Network Solutions
interprocess communication (IPC), **34–35**
interprocessor interrupts, 43
interrupts, **42–43**, 815
intranet, **560**
invisible filenames, **126**
Iomega, zip and jaz drives, 211
iostat command, **822**
IP. *See* Internet Protocol (IP)
IP packets, **316–317**
ipnodes database, **360**
IPV4 address classes, *345*
IPX (Novell), 560
iscda script, **822**
ISO (International Standards Organization), 565
ISO/OSI model, **327–337**

J

Java applet, **7**
Java programming language, **6–7**
Java Runtime Environment, 86–87, *87*
jaz drives, **211–212**
job control
    in C shell, 768, **782–786**
    in Korn shell, 749–750
    shell scripts and, **675–676**
job id argument, **783**
job scheduler, 605
Job shell, **673**, **675–676**
jobs argument, **783**
jobs, managing, **627–630**
    att command and, **627–628**
    cron command and, **628–630**
joe text editor, **664**
Joy, Bill, 762
JPEG file, 487
JumpStart server, **66**, 82

K

KDE toolkit, 284
KeepAlive directive, **592**
KeepAliveTimeout directive, **592**
Kerberos, security and, **318–320**
kernel
    defined, **27**
    directory hierarchy and, 48–49
    functions in Solaris, 27
    platform specific, 189
    Solaris, explained, **42–44**
    synchronization and, 46
    system clock and, **44–45**
kernel architecture, **27–35**
    in general, **27–30**
    interprocess communication and, **34–35**
    linking and, 49–50
    signals and, **35**
    threads and, **31–32**
    virtual memory and, **33–34**
/kernel directory, **144**
kernel dispatcher, 31–32
kernel mode, **42**
kernel process execution, *29*
key signing, **304–305**
keyboard commands, 622
keyboard shortcuts. *See also* commands
    in C shell, 778
    HotkeyEditor and, **277–280**
    for shells, 673–674
    in Window menu, 239, *240*
keyboards, vi editor and, 650
keystrokes
    in CDE Text Editor, 665
    HotkeyEditor and, **277–280**
    in vi editor, 641, *645*, *650–652*, 653–654
    workspace navigation, *236*
keyword variables, 718–719, *729*, **729–730**
kill argument, **783**
kill built-in, Korn shell, **750**
kill command, **622–623**, 624
Kill command, Process Manager, **614**, *614*
kill scripts, **100**
kmem files, **631**
Korn shell (ksh), **724–759**
    basics of, **724–727**
        default options of, *726*
        start files of, **725–726**, **727**
    command-line editing in, **751–755**
        emacs editor, using in, **754–755**
        vi editor, using in, **751–752**, *753–754*
    compatibility of, 690
    control structures of, **735–736**
    defined, **673**
    desktop customization and, 272–273
    directory navigation in, 155
    history files of, **755–757**
    input and output of, **743–750**
        coprocess, redirecting I/O, **744–748**, *745*
        functions and, **748–750**
    linked directories, *301*
    processing commands and, **757–759**
    processing options of, **737–738**
    shell scripts, debugging in, 827
    special characters of, **738–743**
        arithmetic expressions, **741–743**, *742*
        filename generation and, **738–741**

user environment and, 439, 442
variables and, 681–682, 685
variables of, **727–735**
array, **734–735**
built-in, **730–732**, *732*
in general, **727–728**
keyword, *729*, **729–730**
shell variable expansion, **733–734**
ksh. *See* Korn shell (ksh)

L

LAN. *See* local area network (LAN)
laptop, 94
Last-Line mode, vi editor, **645**
Lay Out File Systems screen, 81–82, *82*
LBX (low bandwidth X), 565
lebelit utility, **504**
LEDs, **805–806**, 809
Legate Networker program, **509**
/lib directory, **144**
line, defined, **653**
line editors, 640
Linear Tape Open (LTO) tape systems, **497–498**
lines, in vi editor, 653–654
link command, defined, **159**
link permissions, **297–300**
linking, 27, **49–50**
links, **158–160**, *298*, **302**
Links subpanel, 257, *258*
Linux, **7**
list box, **237**
list command, 198–199
ln utility, **299**, *300*
local area network (LAN)
defined, **337**
explained, **338–339**
network communications and, 561, *562*
local backup, 507
local printers, **411–413**, *412*
local socket, defined, **34**
Location toolbar, Netscape, **575**
LockFile directive, **591**
locks, **46–47**
LOFS (loopback file system), **164**
logging directives, Apache, **597–598**
logical device name, **168**
login
of CDE desktop, **227–230**
dtlogin manager and, **103–107**
group accounts and, 451
IMAP login dialog box, *514*
remote access and, 315
remote login utilities, **371–373**
root, 313–314
security of, **320**
user environment and, 439
user home directory and, 435–436
to X Windows, 287
Login Manager, **227–228**
login screen, GUI, **102–103**
login shell, user, **425**
.login variable, C shell, **763**
logins command, 446, *446*
LogLevel directive, **598**
.logout variable, C shell, **763**
logs, printer, **404–405**, *405*
loopback file system (LOFS), **164**
looping control structures
defined, **694**
for...in structure, **704–706**
for structure, **706**
until structure, **707–709**
while structure, **706–707**
lossless compression, **487**
lossy compression, **487**
low bandwidth X (LBX), 565
lp command
Calendar and, 548
network tools and, **398–401**
networked printers and, 413–414
for printing a file, 418–420
spooling and, 393–394
LP print service
directories and executable files of, *391–393*
in general, **390–391**, **393–395**
print schedulers of, **401–406**
printing a file with, 418–420
lp utility, 739
lpadmin command, **396–397**, 408–409, 413, 415
lpsched daemon, *402*, **402–403**, **404**
lpstat command, **410–411**
ls command, 297, 299–300
lsof command, **621**
Lynx, **574**

M

MAC (Media Access Control) address, **332–333**, 375
macros, HotkeyEditor and, **277–280**. *See also* keyboard shortcuts
magic files, **116**
mail agent, **513**
mail delivery agent (MDA), **512**
Mail subpanel, *260*, 260
MAIL variable, **685**
MAILCHECK variable, **685–686**

Mailer, **512–534**
attachments and, **529–530**, *531*
Calendar, combining with, **550–552**
custom view, creating a, **531–534**, *532*, *533*
customization of, **521–529**
Advanced command and, *525*, **525–526**
Basic command and, *522*, **522–523**
commands for, **528–529**
Compose Window command and, *524*, **524–525**
Move Menu Setup Mail Options dialog box, *528*
Templates command and, *527*, **527**
Vacation Message Mail Options dialog box, *529*
File Manager and, **530–531**
in general, **512–513**
mail message, creating a, *516*, **516–517**, *517*, *518*
mail message, viewing, **518–521**
mailbox, creating a new, **534**
starting the, **513–516**, *514*, *515*
mailing list server, 387
mailing lists
defined, **20**
as resource, **18–21**
for Solaris, 587
mail.local MDA, **512**, 518
mailtool agent, **513**
mailtool program, 580–581
mailx agent, **513**
man command, 697
man pages, **10–13**, *11*
Management Console, Solaris, 456, *457–458*
mapping, 53, *54*
mappings, device, *183*, **183–184**
masking, defined, **35**
Massachusetts Institute of Technology (MIT), 283, 318
master server, **353–354**
MaxClients directive, **593**
maximize button, **234**
MaxKeepAliveRequests directive, **592**
MaxRequestPerChild directive, **593**
MaxSpareServers directive, **593**
MDA (mail delivery agent), **512**
Media Access Control (MAC) address, **332–333**, 375
meetings, Calendar and, **541–543**, *542*, **549–550**
mem file, **631**
memory
frozen, 816
Intel hardware compatibility and, 70
interprocess communication and, 35
Korn shell functions and, 749
memory architecture, **50–59**
anonymous memory, **51**, **54–58**
in general, 50–53
pages, **58–59**
process management and, **630–635**
physical memory, **631–632**
relationship to, 602
virtual memory, **632–635**
system calls and, 826
virtual file systems and, 162–163
virtual memory, 33–34
memory management trap, **43**
memory management unit (MMU), 33–34, **51**, 59
menus
case structure and, 711–713
of CDE desktop, **230–232**
OBDiag tool and, **811–813**
select control structure and, 735–736
message transfer agent (MTA), **512–513**
metacharacters. *See* characters, special
Microsoft Internet Explorer, **574–575**
Microsoft, Solaris and, 6
MIME. *See* Multipurpose Internet Mail Extension (MIME)
minimize button, **234**
MinSpareServers directive, **593**
mirrored disk, **496**, 795
mkdir command, **152–153**
mmap ( ) system call, **826**
MMU. *See* memory management unit (MMU)
/mnt directory, **144**
modems, 189, **315–316**
modules, 48–50
more pager, *13*
Mosaic browser, **573**
Motif Window Manager, 228
MotifToolkit, **225**
mount command, **169–170**, 817
mount points, *164–165*, **194–195**
mouse, 227
Move Menu Setup Mail Options dialog box, *528*
move operation, *252*
MS-DOS file system, 161
mt command, **221**
MTA (message transfer agent), **512–513**
multicast transmission, **338**
multihomed systems, **332**
Multipurpose Internet Mail Extension (MIME)
Apache Web server and, 596
e-mail security and, **306**, 307
send mail in, 526
munmap ( ) system call, **826**
mutex lock, **47**

N

name file system (NAMEFS), **164**
name resolution, defined, **353**

name service, defined, **69**
Name Service Screen, **75–76**
name services
  Domain Name Service, **76–77**, 330, **350–355**, **565–566**
  network files, critical, **359–360**
  NIS and NIS+, **356–357**
  TCP/IP administration and, **357–358**
  user accounts and, 429
named pipe file, **130**
NAMEFS (name file system), **164**
NAS (network-attached storage) devices, **496–497**
navigation, in vi editor, **650–653**
Navigation toolbar, Netscape, **575**
nested traps, **43–44**
netmask database, 360
Netscape browser, **575–580**
  Advanced Proxies page of, *580*
  bookmarks and, **578**
  customization of, **578–579**
  downloading files with, **577–578**
  introduction of, **573**
  Navigator section, *579*
  screen elements of, *576*
  toolbars of, **575–577**
  View Manual Proxy Configuration dialog box of, *581*
Netscape Communicator, **573**
Netscape mail, **310–311**
Netscape Navigator, **573**
netstat utility, **382**
network
  address, **69–70**, **344**
  authentication, **318–320**, **371–373**
  backup of, 507
  communications, **561–565**, *562*
  connections, Apache and, 592
  installation of, **66**
  printer, adding to, 396
  printer, finding on, **406–407**
  problems, troubleshooting, 823–824
  protocol, 284–285
Network Access layer. *See* Data Link layer, OSI
network-attached storage (NAS) devices, **496–497**
Network Cache, Solaris, **327**
Network Connectivity dialog box, *75*, 75
Network File System (NFS)
  access control lists and, 295
  automatic file system mount, **367–368**
  commands of, **369**
  file system hierarchy and, 36
  file system structure and, 124
  in general, **362–363**
  mounting remote file systems in, **365–367**
  OSI Application layer and, 330
  sharing file systems and, **363–365**
  unmounting remote file systems in, **368–369**
  unsharing file systems and, **365**
Network Information Service (NIS), 330, **356–357**, 429, 450
network interface card (NIC), **332**, 347–348
Network layer, OSI, **328**, **331–332**, **564**
Network News Transfer Protocol (NNTP), **586**
network services, **326–388**
  daemons and, **385–386**, *385–386*
  Dynamic Host Configuration Protocol, **360–369**
    in general, **360–362**
    Network File System and, **362–369**
  name services, **350–360**
    Domain Name Services, **350–355**
    network files, critical, **359–360**
    NIS and NIS+, **356–357**
    TCP/IP administration and, **357–358**
  network utilities, **370–384**
    arp, **375–377**
    for file transfer, **384**
    in general, **370–371**
    netstat and ifconfig, **382**
    nslookup, **382–383**
    ping, **373–375**
    remote login, **371–373**
    snoop, **377–382**
    whois, **383–384**
  overview of, **326–343**
    ISO/OSI model, **327–337**
    network topologies, **337–340**
    SNIA shared storage model, **340–343**
  remote user mail, **386–387**
  TCP/IP, **343–350**
    adding networks, **346–348**
    addressing, **344–346**
    hosts and routers and, **349–350**
    User Datagram Protocol, **348–349**
Network Solutions, 565, **566**
network topologies, **337–340**
networked printers, **413–417**
networking and the Internet, **560–600**
  Apache, **587–600**
    configuration of, **590–600**
    in general, **587–590**
  browsers, **573–579**, *574*
    Netscape, **575–579**, *576*, *579*
  e-mail and, **579–585**, *580*
    pine newsreader, **548–585**
    pine, using for, **581–584**
  information sharing, **585–587**
  Internet and World Wide Web, **567–573**
    Common Gateway Interface and, **571–573**
    HTTP and, **568–570**

internetworking, **560–567**
domain name service and Internet, **565–566**
host addresses, **566–567**
network communications, **561–565**, *562*
newfs command, **168–169**
newgrp command, **456**
newsgroups, **18–21**, **584–587**
newsreader, pine as a, **584–585**
NFS. *See* Network File System (NFS)
NFS daemon, 209–210
NIC (network interface card), **332**, 347–348
nice argument, **783**
nice command, **615–616**
NIS (Network Information Service), 330, **356–357**, 429, 450
NNTP (Network News Transfer Protocol), **586**
noclobber variable, **776–777**
noglob variable, **777**
notify variable, **777**
Novell, 25
nslookup utility, **382–383**
null modem cable, 93–94
null string, 736
numeric arrays, **776**
numeric variables, *775*, **775–776**

O

O command, 653–654
OBDiag tool, **792**, **811–813**
OBP. *See* OpenBoot Prompt (OBP)
oclock application, *271*, 286
octal method, access rights and, **135**
Offline mode, SunVTS, 814
OK prompt
freezing operating system with, 97
hardware troubleshooting and, 806
OpenBoot Prompt and, 810–811
shutdown commands and, 101
startup and, **93–95**
Online mode, SunVTS, 814
"open architecture", of Solaris, **5**
Open Group, 25, 283
open ( ) system call, **826**
Open Systems Interconnection (OSI) networking model, **327–337**
Application layer of, **330–331**
Data Link layer of, **332–333**
defined, **326**
network communications and, **562–565**
Network layer of, **331–332**
Physical layer of, **333–337**
Asynchronous Transfer Mode, **336**
broadcast networks, **333–334**
Fiber Distributed Data Interface and, **335**
Frame Relay and, **336–337**
Point-to-Point networks and, **335–336**
Token Ring network and, **334–335**
Transport layer of, **331**
OpenBoot Prompt (OBP), **806–816**
OpenLook Desktop, **280–283**, *281*
OpenLook Window Manager, 225, **226**
OpenOffice, 8
OpenSSH program, **320**
OpenWindows
customizing, **106–107**
exiting, 118
File Manager window, *283*
front panel and, 105
introduction of, 225
opening Command and Shell tool in, 109–110
removal of, 105
startup resource files and, 152
operating environment, defined, **4**
operating system
defined, **4**
freezing, 97
troubleshooting, **818–822**
in general, 793
hardware within, 805–806, **814–816**
patches and, **820–821**
system log files for, *819*
operations, basic, **92–119**
dtlogin GUI, **103–107**
CDE desktop, **105–106**
in general, **103–104**
Open Windows, customize, **106–107**
exiting CDE, **117–118**
exiting OpenWindows, **118**
GUI Login screen, **102–103**
startup, **92–101**
boot options, **95–97**
console port and OK prompt, **93–95**
control scripts, **98–100**
freezing operating system, **97**
init process, **101**
kill scripts, **100**
run levels, **97–98**
shutdown commands, **101**
terminal and console windows, **107–117**
command-line commands, **110–111**
file command, **115–117**
find command, **111–114**
opening command or shell tool, **109–110**
opening in CDE, **108–109**
system information, finding, **114–115**
operators, Korn shell, *742*

operators, symbolic, *295*
OPIE program, **320**
/opt directory, **144**
/opt partition, **68**
optical disks, 165
OSI. *See* Open Systems Interconnection (OSI) networking model
out command, Bourne shell, 702
output-device variable, 807
output display, Korn shell, **746–748**
output/input redirection, **786–787**
output, snoop, 380–382

P

packages, **490–495**
packet filtering, 311–312
packets
  defined, **343**, **564**
  host addresses and, 566–567
  IP, 316–317
  ping utility and, 373–375
  snoop utility and, 377–382
page break, in vi editor, 654
pages, memory architecture, **58–59**
PAP (Password Authentication Protocol), **316**
parameters, in vi editor, **660–662**
parameters, shell, 679, *680–681*
parent process, 28, 684
parent working directory (pwd), 301, 302
parse option, getopts, **737–738**
Partition Magic, 69, 83
partitions
  disk management and, **216–219**
  disk utilization and, 172–175
  hard drive and, **213–215**
  installation of Solaris 8 and, **66–69**
  Intel installation and, 83
  Web Start and, 80–82
passmgmt command, **445**
passwd command, **443–445**
passwd file, user database and, **422**, *423*, **423–426**
password
  commands for user accounts, 429, **443–445**
  encryption and, 303
  login security and, 320
  permissions and, **292–302**
    file permissions, **293–297**
    link permissions, **297–300**
    symbolic links and, **300–302**
  PROM and BIOS, 321–322
  root account and, 446
  root password, **69**, 293
  security-passwd variable, 808
  shadow file and, **426–427**
  SUID flag and, 133
  superuser and, 312–313
  user, 102
Password Authentication Protocol (PAP), **316**
password placeholder, **424**
Patch Cluster, **821**
patchadd command, 88
PatchDiag program, **820–821**
patches, **87–88**, 798–799, **820–821**
path name
  defined, **123**
  filenames and, **126–127**
  Korn shell and, 752
PATH variable, **442**, 685, 713
PC cards, 70–71
PC file system (PCFS), **36–37**, **161–162**
PCMCIA card, 196
pcred command, **619**
PDF (Portable Document Format), 15
PEM (privacy enhanced mail), **305**
PerfectBACKUP+ program, **508**
perfmeter utility, **822**
Performance Meter, *625–626*, **625–626**
peripherals, **140–141**, **187–189**. *See also* devices
permanent virtual circuits (PVCs), **337**, **340**
permissions, access
  of Calendar, *546*, **546–548**
  defined, **131–132**
  directory, 297
  file system problems and, 818
  users, operators, and numbers and, *295–296*
permissions and passwords, **292–302**
  file permissions, **293–297**, 825
  link permissions, **297–300**
  symbolic links, **300–302**
permissions, SUID and SGID, **133–134**
Personal toolbar, Netscape, **575–576**
pfiles command, **619**
pflags command, **619**
PGP (Pretty Good Privacy) encryption program, **304–305**, 310
pgrep argument, **784**
pgrep command, **622**
physical device, defined, **186**
Physical layer, OSI, **333–337**
  Asynchronous Transfer Mode, **336**
  broadcast networks, **333–334**
  defined, **328**, **564**
  Fiber Distributed Data Interface (FDDI), **335**
  Frame Relay, **336–337**
  Point-to-Point networks, **335–336**
  Token Ring network, **334–335**
physical memory, **631–632**
physical security, **321–322**

pico text editor, **664**
PID. *See* process ID (PID)
PidFile directive, **591**
PILs (Process Interrupt Levels), **42**
pine newsreader, **548–585**
pine (Program for Internet News & Email), **581–584**, *583*
ping command, 822, 823
ping utility, **373–375**
pipe
  command, **677**
  defined, **130**
  input/output redirection and, 787
  interprocess communication and, **34**
pkgadd command, **490**, **493**, *493*
pkgrm command, **493**, *494*
pkill argument, **784**
pkill command, **622**
/platform directory, **144–145**
Platinum Support, SunSpectrum, **802**
pldd command, **619**
pmap command, **619**, *621*
Point-to-Point networks, **335–336**, *336*, 339
Point-to-Point Protocol (PPP), **565**
pointers, **166–168**, *300*
POP (Post Office Protocol), **308–309**, 310
pop-up menus, **231–232**, 248–249
popd built-in, C shell, **771**, *771*
Port directive, **594**
Portable CD-ROM File System (iso9660), **36**
Portable Document Format (PDF), 15
Portable Operating System Interface for Computer Environments (POSIX), **4–5**, 35, **59–60**
ports, **192–193**, **328–329**, 594
Post Office Protocol (POP), **308–309**, 310
POST (power-on self test), **569**, 572, **805–806**
PostScript (PS), **126**, 399, 409
power management, installation and, **70**
Power Management screen, *77*
power-on self test (POST), **569**, 572, **805–806**
PPP (Point-to-Point Protocol), **565**
pr stat argument, **784–785**
preboot process, **72–74**
Presentation layer, OSI, **328**, **563**
Pretty Good Privacy (PGP) encryption program, **304–305**, 310
print built-in, Korn shell, *746–747*, **746–748**
print client
  add network access for, **414–415**
  defined, **394**
  setting up a, **399–400**
Print Client software, SunSoft, **395**, **400**, 407
Print dialog box, **237–238**
print filters, **405–406**
Print Manager, Solaris
  adding a printer with, **408–410**
  defined, **395**
  find command of, 407
  in general, 401
  networked printers and, **413–417**, *414*
  print server, attaching with, **415–417**
  window of, *404*
print schedulers. *See* printing, Solaris print subsystem
print server, attaching, **415–417**
Print VTOC command, 218
printenv command, **95**, *96*
Printer Settings option, Calendar, **548–549**
Printers subpanel, 261, *261*
printing, Solaris print subsystem, **390–420**
  add printers, **407–417**
    in general, **407–410**
    local printers, **411–413**
    networked printers, **413–417**
    printer status, **410–411**
  find printer on network, **406–407**
  in general, **390**
  LP print service, **390–391**, *391–393*, **393–395**
  print a file, **418–420**
  print filters, **405–406**
  print schedulers, **401–405**
    in general, **401–403**
    printer logs, **404–405**
    spooling, **403**
  print tools, **395–401**
    local tools, **396–397**
    network tools, **398–401**
priocntl command, **605**, *606*, **616–617**
privacy enhanced mail (PEM), **305**
Privacy setting, Calendar, **545–548**
private key encryption, **303–304**, 317–318
privtool utility, **309**
probe-ide command, **809**
probe-pci command, **809**
probe-sbus command, **809**
probe-SCSI command, **809**
/proc directory, **145**
proc file system. *See* process file system (PROCFS)
/proc folder, *163*
proc tools, **619–621**, **622–624**
process control, C shell and, **782–786**
process execution, *29*
process file system (PROCFS), **618–621**
  child processes and, *618*
  file system hierarchy and, 36–37
  kernel architecture and, 28
  origin of, **37**
  pmap command and, *621*
  proc commands, output of, *620*

process files and directories in, *37*
as virtual file system, 162
process ID (PID)
C shell and, 784
case structure and, 714
defined, **602–603**
kernel and, 28
truss command and, 612
Process Interrupt Levels (PILs), **42**
process management, **602–635**
in general, **602–606**
kernel architecture and, 28
managing jobs, **627–630**
at command and, **627–628**
cron command and, **628–630**
memory and, **630–635**
physical memory, **631–632**
virtual memory, **632–635**
Performance Meter, *625–626*, **625–626**
Process File System, *618*, **618–621**, *620*, *621*
processes, controlling, **622–624**, *623*, *624*
processes, viewing, **606–617**
Process Manager and, **613–615**, *614*
process priorities and, **615–617**, *617*
ps command and, **606–611**, *608*, *609–610*
truss command and, **611–613**, *612*
Process Manager, 263, **613–615**, *614*
processes
commands for, **757–759**
defined, **28**
hierarchical file system and, 36–37
interprocess communication and, 34–35
threads and, 31–32
processing options, Korn shell, **737–738**
processor, 31–32, 70
processor resets trap, **43**
PROCFS. *See* process file system (PROCFS)
proc.h file, 603, *604*
.profile file, **719**
profiles, role databases and, **468–474**
program directories, *40*
program folder, Application Manager, *260*
programmable read-only memory (PROM). *See* OK prompt
prompt variable, **772**
Properties dialog box, *137*
protocol. *See also* Transmission Control Protocol/Internet Protocol (TCP/IP)
BOOTSTRAP, **361**
Challenge Handshake Authentication Protocol (CHAP), **316**
defined, **343**, **564**
Dynamic Host Configuration Protocol (DHCP), **360–369**
intranet and, **560**
network protocol, **284–285**
OSI networking model and, **563–565**
Remote MagTap protocol, **221–222**
Router Information Protocol, 330–331
Telnet protocol, **330**
Proxy Server Configuration Screen, 77–78, *78*
proxy server, installation and, **69**
prtconf command, **115**, 190, *191*
prun command, **622**
PS. *See* PostScript (PS)
ps argument, **785–786**
ps command, **606–611**, *608*, *609–610*, 618
ps -ef command, **607**, *608*
ps (UCB) argument, **785**
PS1 variable, **686**
psig command, **620**, **622**, *624*
pstack command, **620**
pstop command, **622**
ptime command, **622**
ptree command, **620**
public access right, Calendar, **547–548**
public key encryption, **303–304**
pushd built-in, C shell, **770**, *770*
Put command, vi editor, 657
PUT method, **569**
PVCs (permanent virtual circuits), **337**, **340**
pwait command, **620**, **622**
pwck utility, **822**
pwd (parent working directory), 301, 302
pwdx command, **620**

Q

query, nslookup utility and, 382–383
question mark (?) special character, **739**
queue, job, **628**
quotation marks, shell and, 679–680, 766

R

radio buttons, **238**
Radius, **316**
RAID (redundant array of independent disks), **213**
RAM, 162–163, 631
RARP (Reverse Address Resolution Protocol), **376**
raw device, **185**
raw input, **745**
RBAC databases. *See* role databases
RDISC (Router Discovery Protocol), 330–331
read access, **131**
read built-in, Korn shell, **743**, 745
read/write locks, **47**

README files, **805**, 827
Real-time (RT) class, 32–33
realms, defined, **318**
reboot, 188–189
recursive construct, defined, **724**
redirection, defined, **311**
registration, User Registration package, **105**
regular file, defined, **128**
relative path name, defined, **126–127**
remote access, security of, **315–320**
  encrypted authentication clients, **317–318**
  in general, **315–317**
  Kerberos and, **318–320**
remote file systems
  file transfer utilities and, 384
  finger utility and, 370–*371*
  mounting, **365–367**
  snoop utility and, 380
  unmounting, **368–369**
remote login utilities, **371–373**
Remote MagTap protocol, **221–222**
remote user mail, **386–387**
removable media, mounting, **195–196**
repeater, defined, **339**
Replace command, **647**
replace, in vi editor, **657–659**
Reply to All window, Mailer, 520
requests, **404**, *405*, 568–570, **592–599**
reserved swap space, **55**
resources, for Solaris 8, **10–21**
  AnswerBook2, **15–17**
  man and xman pages, **10–13**
  newsgroups, mailing lists, and FAQs, **18–21**
  Sun Microsystems, **14–15**
  third-party Web sites, **18**
  web searches, **21**
resources, for troubleshooting, **797–805**
  educational, **803–805**, *804*
  searchable collections, **799–800**
  support accounts, **801–803**
  web sites, **797–799**, *798*, *799*
response codes, *570*
response, HTTP, **569–570**
restore. *See* backup and restore
Reverse Address Resolution Protocol (RARP), **376**
Rich Text Format (RTF), **126**
rights, for roles, *478*
Rights tab, *477*
ring topology, defined, **339**
RIP (Router Information Protocol), 330–331
RIPEM (Riordan's Internet Privacy Enhanced Mail), **305**
Ritchie, Dennis, 24
rm command, **160**
rmdir command, **156**
Rock-Ridge extensions, 36–37
rogue daemon, **67**
role databases, **468–474**
  /etc/security/auth_attr, **470–471**
  /etc/security/exec_attr, **473–474**
  /etc/security/prof_attr, **471–472**
  /etc/user_attr, **468–470**
roles
  administering, *468*
  creating, **474–476**, *476*
  rights for, *478*
root account, 428, **445–449**
root directory
  of Apache Web server, 595–596
  file system structure and, **122–124**
  in Solaris 8, **138–140**, *139*
root domain, **351**
root files, sharing, 364
root login, 313–314
/ (root) partition, **68**, **69**
root password, **69**, 293
round-robin schedule, 605
Router Discovery Protocol (RDISC), 330–331
Router Information Protocol (RIP), 330–331
routers
  to connect networks, *349*
  defined, **343–344**
  network communications and, **561–562**
  system communication and, 823
  TCP/IP and, **349–350**
rsh utility, **503**
RTF (Rich Text Format), **126**
run control script, 824–825
run levels, **97–98**, *98*
runtime linker, 50
rup <systemname> command, **373**

S

SAN (Storage Area Network), 342, **497**
Santa Cruz Operation (SCO), 25
sar command, **631–632**
savehist variable, **772**
/sbin directory, **145**
schedulers
  classes of, 32
  job, **627–630**, **676**
  kernel architecture and, 28
  print
    in general, 401–403
    printer logs, 404–405
    spooling, 403
  process priorities and, 615–616
  in Solaris, 27

SCO (Santa Cruz Operation), 25
ScoreBoard directive, **591**
scripts. *See also* shell scripts
  control, defined, **98–100**
  creating, in C shell, **777–787**
  kill, **100**
  troubleshooting, 824–828
SCSI devices
  adding a drive, **219–220**
  CD-ROMS, 197
  installation and removal of, 187
  LEDs and, 809
  OBP variable and, 807
  zip and jaz drives, 211
SCSI drive, 817
sdtcm_admin command, **553**
search
  the Calendar, *543*, **543–544**
  find command and, **111–114**
  in vi editor, **657–659**
  View Search Advanced dialog box, Mailer, **534**
search engine, **576–577**
search string characters, *658*, 659
searchable collections, for troubleshooting, **799–800**
secret key encryption, **304**, 318
Secure Shell (SSH), **317–318**
secure sockets, defined, **131**
SecurID, **320**
security, **292–322**
  of documentation, 794
  of e-mail, **305–311**
  encryption, **303–305**
  firewalls, **311–312**
  login, **320**
  permissions and passwords, **292–302**
    file permissions, **293–297**
    link permissions, **297–300**
    symbolic links, **300–302**
  physical, **321–322**
  remote access, **315–320**
    encrypted authentication clients, **317–318**
    in general, **315–317**
    Kerberos and, **318–320**
  role databases and, 468–474
  superuser and, **312–315**
  user access and, 102
  for viruses, **320–321**
security-passwd variable, **808**
segment driver, **52–53**, *52–53*
seg_vn driver, **53**
select control structure, 724, **735–736**
Select Installation Type screen, *86*
Select Type of Install screen, 79–80
selection, in File Manager, **248–249**
semaphore, defined, **47**
sendmail
  commands, *307*
  e-mail security and, **305–306**
  explained, **512–513**
  mail message creation and, 516
  MTA, **306–308**
sentenv function, 748
sent.mail file, **523**
Serial Line Internet Protocol (SLIP), **565**
serial ports, **192–193**
server pool, Apache, **592–593**
server process, defined, **329**
ServerAdmin directive, **594**
ServerName directive, **594**
ServerRoot directive, **591**
servers. *See also* Apache Web server; network services; troubleshooting
  advantages of Solaris and, **6–7**
  Domain Name Service and, 350–355
  encrypted authentication clients and, 317–318
  enterprise, 112
  home directory, sharing on, 437
  Hypertext Transfer Protocol and, 568–570
  physical security of, 321–322
  power-cycle and, 806
  Solaris, new features of, 10
  X Windows, 284–286
ServerType directive, **591**
service access point, defined, **328–329**
service call, **803**
servlet, 7, **572–573**
Session layer, OSI, **328**, **563**
Session Manager, 118, **228–229**
sessionetc file, 272
sessionexit file, 272
sessions, X Windows, 286–287
set built-in, C shell, **774**, 776
set command, vi editor, 660
Set Group ID (SGID) permission, **133–134**, **296–297**
Set User ID (SUID) permission, **133–134**, **296–297**
Set View Options dialog box, **234–235**, *235*
setenv built-in, C shell, **774**
setfacl utility, *294*, **294–295**
SGID (Set Group ID) permission, **133–134**, **296–297**
shadow file, **422**, **426–427**
share command, 435, 436
shared storage model (SNIA), **340–343**, *342*
shell
  defined, **602**
  interpreters, **107–108**
  redirection, **380**
  spawning in vi editor, **662–663**
Shell Escape mode, vi editor, **646**

shell scripts
  Bourne shell and, 694
  debugging, **827–828**
  security and, 297
shell scripts, creating
  in C shell, **777–787**
    built-ins of, *780–782*
    command-line shortcuts for, **778**
    input/output redirection and, **786–787**
    process control and, **782–786**
    rehash command and, **782**
    variable control structures and, **778–780**
  commands for, separate and group, **676–679**
  in general, **674–675**
  job control and, **675–676**
  parameters and variables for, **679–686**, *680–681*
Shell tool, **108**, **110**
shell variable, 685, **772**
shells, **672–691**. *See also* Bourne shell; C shell; Korn shell; vi editor
  background of, **672–674**
  built-ins and, **686–689**, *687–688*, **690**
  shell scripts, creating, **674–686**
    commands for, separate and group, **676–679**
    in general, **674–675**
    job control and, **675–676**
    parameters and variables for, **679–686**, *680–681*
shift built-in, 689
show-devs command, **809**
show-disks command, **809**
show-displays command, **814**
show-nets command, **814**
show-post-results command, **814**
show-sbus command, **814**
show-tapes command, **814**
Show Views dialog box, **532**, *532*
showrev -p command, **820**
shutdown commands, **101**
signals
  in Bourne shell, *716*
  descriptions, *623*
  kernel architecture and, 28, **35**
  processes, controlling with, **622–624**, *623*
  truss command and, 613
signature, e-mail message, 517
Silver Support, SunSpectrum, **803**
Simple Mail Transfer Protocol (SMTP)
  e-mail security and, **305–306**
  OSI Application layer and, 330–331
  outgoing mail in, 526
slab allocator, 34
slave server, **353–354**
sleep command, 763
slices
  assignments of, *214*
  defined, **186–187**
  disk management and, **216–219**
  hard drive and, **213–215**
SLIP (Serial Line Internet Protocol), **565**
smart cards, 315, **320**
SMTP. *See* Simple Mail Transfer Protocol (SMTP)
snapshotting, **496**
SNIA shared storage model, **340–343**, *342*
SNIA (Storage Networking Industry Association), **326**
snoop utility, **377–382**
  in general, **377–380**
  IP header of, *379*
  with option -c, *378*
  parameters for, *382*
  snoop output, capturing, **380–382**
socket file, defined, **130–131**
sockets, 185
soft links. *See* symbolic link (SYLK)
software traps, **43**, **44**
software, troubleshooting, 793
Solaris
  development of, **25–27**, *26*
  information sharing and, 585–587
  the Internet and, *562*
  User Registration tool of, 438
Solaris 1.x, 189
Solaris 2.x, 189
Solaris 8. *See also* installation of Solaris 8
  Domain Name Service and, 353
  file system format of, 161–162
  introduction to, **4–9**
    advantages of, **6–9**
    Solaris and Unix, **4–6**
  new features of, **9–10**, 26–27, 326–327
  operating system, diagram of, *45*
  resources for, **10–21**
    AnswerBook2, **15–17**
    man and xman pages, **10–13**
    newsgroups, mailing lists, and FAQs, **18–21**, **586**
    Sun Microsystems, **14–15**
    third-party Web sites, **18**
    web searches, **21**
  shells, compatible, 673, **690**
Solaris, about, 24–60
  hierarchical file system, **35–41**
    file system layout, **38–41**
    in general, 35–38
  I/O architecture, **41–50**
    directory hierarchy, **48–49**
    linking, **49–50**
    Solaris kernel, **42–44**

synchronization and, **45–47**
system clock, **44–45**
kernel architecture, **27–35**
in general, **27–30**
interprocess communication, **34–35**
signals, **35**
threads, **31–32**
virtual memory, **33–34**
memory architecture, **50–59**
anonymous memory, **54–58**
in general, 50–53
pages, **58–59**
POSIX, **59–60**
Unix history, **24–27**
Solaris, development of, **25–27**
Solaris desktop. *See* desktop, Solaris
Solaris Developer Connection, 17
Solaris Installation Guide, 72
Solaris kernel, **42–44**
Solaris Support controls, 264
Solstice Host Manager, **357**
sort command, 786–787
SPARC
adding a drive to, **219–220**
disk management for, 216
ejecting diskette on, 210
freezing operating system on, 97
GNU gtar utility and, 491
installation of Solaris 8 on
preboot process, **72–74**
procedure, **71–83**
system configuration, **74–78**
Web Start, **78–83**
partitions on, 213
processors, 46
security for, 321–322
startup and, 93
special file system (SPECFS), **164**
spell utility, **719–720**
spin box, **238**
SSH (Secure Shell), **317–318**
stack, defined, **602**, **768**
STAFF group, 450, 451
Stallman, Richard, 720
standard error, **786**
standard input operation, defined, **786–787**
standard output operation, defined, **786–787**
standards, of Unix, 4–5
star topology, defined, **339**
StarOffice installation, **85–87**
StarOffice subpanel, *257*, 257
StarOffice suite, 8–9
StarOffice Support, **800**
StarOffice Word Processor, **668–670**, *669*, *670*
StartServers directive, **593**
startup, **92–101**
boot options and, **95–97**
console port and OK prompt and, **93–95**
control scripts and, **98–100**
freezing operating system and, **97**
init process and, **101**
kill scripts and, **100**
problems, troubleshooting and, **819**, 824–825
resource files for, **151–152**
run levels and, **97–98**
shutdown commands and, **101**
Startup control, **276–277**, *277*
stateful protocols, defined, **331**
status codes, response, 570
Stel program, **320**
sticky bit (SGID flag), **134**
Storage Area Network (SAN), 342, **497**
Storage Networking Industry Association (SNIA), **326**
string operators, *733*, 733–734
string variables, **774**
structure, **706**
Style Manager, **275–277**
su command, 449
subdirectories, **123**
subdomains, DNS, **352**
Subject text box, 517
subnet mask, **69**, *345*
subpanels, of front panel, **257–266**
Substitute command, vi editor, 656
SUID (Set User ID) permission, **133–134**, **296–297**
Sun Certification training material, 803
Sun Educational Services web site, **803–804**, *804*
Sun field engineers, 802
Sun Freeware site, 18
Sun Managers List, **20**, **587**
Sun Microsystems
advantages of Solaris and, 6–9
distributions of Solaris, 62–65
explained, **4**
Netscape and, 573, *574*
network-attached storage devices of, 497
Network Information Service of, 356
printers and, 409–410
resources of, **14–15**, **797–805**
shells and, 672–673
Solaris development and, **25–27**
troubleshooting and, 792, 793
web site of, *14*, 14–15, 63–64
Sun Press, **805**
Sun Solaris AnswerBook2, **15–17**, *16*, *17*
Sun Ultra Enterprise (UE) 10000, 4
Sun VTS (Sun Validation Test Suite), **814–815**
SunHELP site, 18

SunOS 4.1.2 operating system, 4
SunOS 5.x, 189
SunSoft Print Client software, **395**, **400**, 407, 419
SunSolve account, 797, **800**, 803
SunSolve Online
  file system problems and, 818
  Help subpanel and, 264
  patches and, 88, 820–821
  as resource, **797–799**
  searchable collections of, **799–800**
  user registration and, 438
SunSpectrum program, *801*, **801–803**
Sunstation 5, 807
SunSunSun hardware site, 18
superblocks, disk storage and, **166–168**
superuser. *See also* system administrator
  administering roles of, *468*
  file permissions and, **293–294**
  LP print service and, **397**
  password of, 292
  root account and, 445–446
  security and, **312–315**
support accounts, **801–803**
swap allocations, *57*
SWAP file system (SWAPFS), **54–56**, 57, **162–163**
swap partition, **68**
swap slice, 214
swap space
  anonymous memory and, *55*, **55–57**, *56*
  installation of Solaris 8 and, 73–74
  virtual memory and, 633
switch control, **779**
switch variables, **776–777**
switched virtual circuits (SVCs), **340**
symbolic link (SYLK)
  creating, 251
  defined, **158**
  devices and, 194–195
  export of, 364
  features of, 160
  file, **129–130**
  filename extensions and, 126
  link permissions and, **298–299**
  working with, **300–302**
symbolic operators, *295*
symmetric encryption, **303–304**
synchronization, **45–47**
synchronous signals, **35**
sysdef command, 190
system accounting, **175**
system administrator. *See also* superuser
  backup and, 498, 795
  BigAdmin site and, 800
  file permissions and, **293–294**
  security and, **312–315**
  shells and, 674
  terminal server settings and, 806
  truss command and, 826
system calls, **44**, 611–613, 826–827
system clock, **44–45**
system communication, troubleshooting, **822–828**
system configuration, **74–78**
system crash, 649, 793, 795
system disk, damaged, 220
system documentation, **794**
system files, locked, 124
system information, finding, **114–115**
system log files, *819*
system panic, **188**, 815
System (SYS) class, 32
System V IPC facilities, 35
System V Release 4 (SVR4), 26
system watchdog reset, **815**
System_Admin window, 202–204

T

tab group, defined, **243**
Tab Window Manager (twm), **224–225**
Table Base Address (TBA), **43**
tag, defined, **216**
talk utility, **387**
tape drives, 187, **221–222**
tape systems, backup
  backup strategies and, **498–502**
  commands and, 504–506
  in general, 795
  local vs. network backup and, 507
  reason for use of, **497–498**
tar archives, **507–509**
tar command, **480–483**
TCP. *See* Transmission Control Protocol (TCP)
tear-off menu, defined, **109**
technical support. *See* resources, for troubleshooting; support accounts
TECO (Text Editor and Corrector) program, **664**
telephone support, 802–803
Telnet
  GUI Login screen and, 102
  protocol, **330**
  remote access security and, **315**
  remote utility, **371–373**, *372*
  troubleshooting and, 797
Templates command, Mailer, *527*, **527**
temporary file system (TMPFS)
  characteristics of, **631**
  defined, **37**
  directories of, *40–41*

Solaris and, 36
as virtual file system, **162–163**
term session, **95**
terminal and console windows, **107–117**
command-line commands, **110–111**
file command, **115–117**
find command, **111–114**
opening command or shell tool, **109–110**
opening in CDE, **108–109**
system information, finding, **114–115**
terminal, serial ports and, 192–193
terminal server, defined, **95**
terminal type, setting in vi editor, **662**
terminal window
Calendar and, 535
opening in CDE, **108–109**
in vi editor, *642*, *643*
Window menu and, 239–240
in X Windows, 287
terminfo database, *409*
test built-in, Bourne shell, **695**, **696–697**, *700*, 700–701
test command, **814**
test options, Korn shell, 731–732, *732*
test utility options, *700*
text box, **238**
text editors, **663–670**. *See also* vi editor
emacs editor, **664**, **754–755**
StarOffice Word Processor, **668–670**, *669*, *670*
Text Editor, CDE, 640, *665*, **665–668**, *666*, *667*
Unix editors, **664**
text file, **487**, 521
third-party Web sites, **18**
Thompson, Ken, 24
threads
kernel architecture and, 28, **31–32**
processes and, *31*
Solaris development and, 26
Solaris kernel and, 42
tickets, Kerberos, **318–319**, *319*
TIFF file, 487
Tilde (~) expansion, **768**
time, network addressing and, 69
Time-share (TS) scheduling class, 32
time variable, **772–773**
timeout, **374**
Timeout directive, **592**
title bar, **233–234**
title character, **127**
/tmp directory, defined, **145**
TMPFS. *See* temporary file system (TMPFS)
To Do Editor, Calendar, **540–541**
To Do items, Calendar, **535**, **540–541**, *541*
Token Ring network, **334–335**
Tom's Window Manager, **224–225**
Tools subpanel, 261
top command, **611**
Tower of Hanoi backup rotation scheme, **501**
TRACE method, **569**
trailers, **562**, 564
Transmission Control Protocol/Internet Protocol (TCP/IP), **343–350**
adding networks, **346–348**
addressing, **344–346**
administration of, **357–358**
hosts and routers and, **349–350**
protocol stack, *328*, *329*
User Datagram Protocol, **348–349**
Transmission Control Protocol (TCP), 331, 379–380
Transport layer, OSI, **328**, **331**, **563–564**
trap built-in, **694**, 716–717, **750**
trap handler, **44**
traps, **43–44**, 58
Trash subpanel, 265
tree topology, defined, **339**
Trojan horse program, **314**
troubleshooting, **792–829**
diagnostic commands for, **821–822**
file system problems, **816–818**
hardware, **805–816**
in general, **805–806**
OpenBoot prompt and, **806–813**
within operating system, **814–816**
operating system problems, **818–822**
patches and, **820–821**
system log files for, *819*
planning ahead, **793–795**
backups and, **794–795**
documentation and, **794**
psychology of, **796–797**
resources for, **797–805**
educational, **803–805**, *804*
searchable collections, **799–800**
support accounts, **801–803**
web sites, **797–799**, *798*, *799*
system communication, **822–828**
applications and scripts, **824–828**
three layers of failure, the, **792–793**
truss command, **611–613**, *612*, 825–826
type arguments, **113**

U

UDF (Universal Disk Format) file system, **161**
UDP. *See* User Datagram Protocol (UDP)
ufrestores utility, **505–506**
UFS. *See* Unix file system (UFS)

ufsdump utility, **495–496**, **504–506**
UID number. *See* user identification number (UID number)
UltraSPARC, **43–44**
uname command, **114**
underscore character, 125
unicast transmission, defined, **338**
Uniform Resource Locator (URL)
  bookmarks and, **578**
  browsers and, 574–575
  HTTP and, 569, 570
  World Wide Web and, **567–568**
Unisource Systems, **508**
UniTrends Software, **507**
Universal Disk Format (UDF) file system, **161**
University of California, Berkeley, 24
University of North Carolina Metalab site, 488, 495
Unix
  editors, **664**
  history of, **24–27**
  shells and, 672
  Solaris and, **4–6**
  text editors and, 640
  top-level overview of, *25*
Unix file system (UFS)
  decision to keep, 161
  diskette format of, 206–207
  new file systems and, 168–169
  problems and troubleshooting, 816–818
  structure of, **122–124**
  superblocks and, **166–168**
  viruses and, 320–321
  X Windows and, 285
UNIX Systems Laboratories (USL), 24–25
unmount command, **171–172**, **368–369**
unset command, **715**
unshare command, **365**
until structure, *707*, **707–709**
URL. *See* Uniform Resource Locator (URL)
UseCanonicalName directive, **594**
Usenet, **585–586**
user access, GUI Login screen and, 102–103
user account, defined, **428**
user accounts and groups, **422–478**
  AdminSuite 3, using, **456–478**
    access rights and, **476–478**
    in general, **456–459**
    network groups, managing with, **464–468**
    network users, managing with, **459**
    role databases and, **468–474**
    roles, creating, **474–476**
    user account, adding, **460–464**
  group accounts, working with, **449–456**
    Admintool, managing with, **452–454**
    commands for, **451–452**
    in general, **449–451**
    group identification numbers and, **454–455**
    group status, changing, **456**
  user accounts, working with, **428–449**
    Admintool, managing with, **431–435**
    commands of, **428–430**
    password commands of, **443–445**
    root account and, **445–449**
    user environments, creating, **435–443**
    user status, changing, **449**
  user database, **423–427**
    passwd file, **423–426**
    shadow file, **426–427**
  users and groups, **422–423**
user database. *See* user accounts and groups
User Datagram Protocol (UDP)
  explained, **348–349**
  Network layer and, 331–332
  OSI model and, 564–565
  Transport layer and, 331
USER group, 450
user identification number (UID number)
  data types and, 426
  defined, **424**
  role databases and, 471–474
  system, *425*
  system process and, 603
  use of, 422
user initialization files, **441–443**
user mode, Solaris kernel and, **42**
user password, 102. *See also* password
User Registration package, **105**
User Registration tool, Solaris, 438
user status, changing, **449**
user threads, 31–32
useradd command, **428–430**
userdel command, **430**
usermod command, **430**
username
  Calendar and, 556–557
  defined, **424**
  in shadow file, 427
  user account commands and, 428–430
users
  partitions and, 67
  symbolic classes of, *295*
  whois utility and, 383–384
USL (UNIX Systems Laboratories), 24–25
/usr directory, *40*, **145–148**, *146*
/usr/dt/config directory, **228**
/usr file system, 169
/usr partition, **68**
utilities. *See also* file utilities
  backup, 502–504
  in Bourne shell, 695, **719–720**

of DHCP, 362
diagnostic, 822
e-mail, 581–585
of Korn shell, 737–738
for linking, *302*
utilities, network, **370–384**
arp, **375–377**
for file transfer, **384**
in general, **370–371**
netstat and ifconfig, **382**
nslookup, **382–383**
ping, **373–375**
remote login, **371–373**
snoop, **377–382**
whois, **383–384**

V

Vacation Message Mail Options dialog box, *529*, **529**
/var directory, *40–41*, *149*, **149–150**, 215
/var partition, **68**
variable control structures, **778–780**
variables
Bourne shell, **715–720**
built-ins of, *716*, **716–717**
functions and, **717–720**
in general, **715**
C shell, **771–773**, *773*
Korn shell, **727–735**
array, **734–735**
built-in, **730–732**, *732*
in general, **727–728**
keyword, *729*, **729–730**
shell variable expansion, **733–734**
of OpenBoot Prompt, **807–808**
shell, **679–686**
environmental, **685–686**
exporting, **683–685**
global, **682–683**
local, **681–682**
special characters, *680–681*
VERITAS NetBackup program, **508–509**
vfork ( ) system call, **603**
VFS. *See* Virtual File System (VFS)
vfstab file, 170–171
vi editor, **640–670**
about, **640–641**
case structure and, 712–713
editing in, **653–663**
buffers, working with, **659–660**
commands for, *655–656*
copying and pasting, **657**
deleting and undoing, **654**, **656**
parameters, setting, **660–662**
searching and replacing, **657–659**, *658*
spawning a shell, **662–663**
terminal window, *642*, *643*
Korn shell and, **751–752**, *753–754*
navigating in, *650–652*, **650–653**
other editors and, **663–670**
StarOffice Word Processor, text and, **668–670**, *669*, *670*
Text Editor, using, *665*, **665–668**, *666*, *667*
Unix editors, **664**
overview of, **641–650**
in general, **641–645**
invoking vi, **647–648**, *648*
vi modes and, **645–647**
working with files in, **648–650**, *649*
video cards, AGP, 71
View Search dialog box, *533*, **534**
views, in Calendar, **537–539**
vim program, **664**
Virtual File System (VFS)
disk storage and, **162–165**
feature of, 27
file system hierarchy and, 36
virtual nodes of, 168
virtual hosts, **598–600**
virtual memory (VM)
address space, segments, and pages of, *33*
kernel architecture and, **33–34**
kmem file and, 631
memory architecture and, **50–51**
process management and, **632–635**
virtual nodes, defined, **168**
virtual private network (VPN), **316–317**
virtual swap space, **55**, 56–57
viruses, security and, **320–321**
visual display editor. *See* vi editor
vmstat command, **633–634**, *635*
vnode, defined, **36**, **168**
vnode driver, **52–53**
vnode/offset pair, 58–59
volcopy command, **504**
volume management, **193–194**
Volume Manager, 205
Volume Table of Contents (VTOC), **216**
VPN (virtual private network), **316–317**
VTOC (Volume Table of Contents), **216**

W

w <username> command, **447**, *447*
WAN. *See* wide area network (WAN)
watchdog resets, **815**
watchpoints, **57–58**
Web-based training, Sun, **804**

web pages
 defined, **567–568**
 HTTP and, 568–570
 system documentation on, 794
web searches, **21**
web servers, **571–573**, **587–600**
web sites. *See also* resources; SunSolve Online
 for Solaris 8, *19–20*
 Sun Educational Services web site, **803–804**, *804*
 third-party, 18
 for troubleshooting resources, **797–799**, *798*, *799*
Web Start Installation Kiosk, **65–66**, **78–83**, *79*
Webmin, 308
Welcome screen, *74*
Welcome screen, StarOffice installation, *85*
whence built-in, Korn shell, **750**
while built-in, C shell, **778–779**
while structure, **706–707**
who command, **446–447**
whodocommand, **718**
whois utility, **383–384**
wide area network (WAN)
 defined, **337**
 explained, **339–340**
 network communications and, 561, *562*
 point-to-point networks and, 335
widget sets, X Toolkit, 284
Window Behavior option group, 276
window managers, **225–226**, 242, 284. *See also* Common Desktop Environment (CDE)
Window menu, **239–240**
Window menu button, **234**
window menus, defined, **231–232**
windows, of CDE desktop, **232–243**
 File Manager and, *233*
 in general, **232–238**
 Window menu, **239–240**
 Workspace menu, **241–242**
windows, terminal. *See also* terminal and console windows
work buffer, 644–645
working directory, **151**
WorkMan program, *201*, **494–495**
Workspace menu, *231*, 231–232, **241–242**
Workspace menu, OpenLook Desktop, **280–282**, *281*, *282*
Workspace menu window, *262*, 263
workspace navigation keystrokes, *236*
workspaces, of CDE desktop, **271–272**
Workstation Information dialog box, 263–264, *264*
World Wide Web, **567–573**
 Common Gateway Interface and, **571–573**
 HTTP and, **568–570**
worm, 321
WORM disks (Write Once Read Many optical disks), 165
write access, **131**
write permissions, 292

X

x command, 654
X Toolkit, 284
X Window System, **283–289**
 X applications, **287–289**
 X clients and servers, **284–286**
 X sessions, **286–287**
 xman pages and, **10–13**
X Windows project, 224–225
xman pages, **10–13**, *11*, *12*
x>opfile command, **777**
xterm window, *286*

Y

Y command, vi editor, 657
Yahoo!, **576–577**

Z

zip drives, **211–212**
zombie process, **605**
zone, **352**, 353
zone database file, **354**
zone transfers, **355**